D1706255

COOS BAY OREGON FHC   037-008

In Memory of
Billy Morgan
wife of
Elmer Morgan
January 1997

EARLY OHIO SETTLERS

(Prepared by: Land Office of the Auditor of State, Columbus, Ohio)

MAP OF PRESENT STATE OF OHIO SHOWING AREA OF SOUTHWESTERN OHIO AND A PORTION OF SOUTHEASTERN INDIANA COVERED BY THE INDEX.

(A) MIAMI RIVER SURVEY   (B) THE "GORE" OF INDIANA
(C) BETWEEN THE MIAMIS SURVEY   (D) SYMMES PURCHASE
(E) EAST AND NORTH OF THE 2ND PRINCIPAL MERIDIAN SURVEY

EARLY OHIO SETTLERS

Purchasers of Land in Southwestern Ohio, 1800–1840

Compiled by

Ellen T. Berry & David A. Berry

Copyright © 1986
Genealogical Publishing Co., Inc.
Baltimore, Maryland
All Rights Reserved
Second printing, 1993
Library of Congress Catalogue Card Number 86-81332
International Standard Book Number 0-8063-1162-2
Made in the United States of America

This book is an alphabetized listing of the original purchasers of federal land sold under the U. S. Land Act of 10 May 1800 by or from the Cincinnati Land Office, Cincinnati, Hamilton County, Ohio, and provides genealogists with a means of tracing the movements of ancestors who came to the newly-opened territory of southwestern Ohio between the years 1800 and 1840. Over 25,000 purchasers are listed. The names are of those persons who agreed to pay from $1.25 to $4.00 per acre for the land and who, upon completion of the total payment, received from the land office a certificate which listed the completed payments and a final certificate number. This final certificate was then forwarded to the U. S. Government in Washington, D. C. which issued a deed (or patent). In addition to the purchaser's name, the date of purchase, place of residence at the time of purchase, and the range, township and section are listed. In the many instances where the parcel of land purchased may have spread over more than one township or section, or even into another range, only the first location is given. However, purchases made on different dates by a buyer are listed, even though the range, township and section numbers may be duplicated. Most of the land was sold in 40 to 160-acre parcels but not included in the description of the land are fractions of a section, e.g. the "SW 1/4 of the NE 1/4 of Section 10." With the data contained herein, it is possible to secure additional information either by writing to the Land Office of the State Auditor, 88 East Broad Street, P. O. Box 1140, Columbus, Ohio 43216, or to the U. S. Dept. of the Interior, Bureau of Land Management, Eastern States Office, 350 S. Pickett Street, Alexandria, Virginia 22304.

Cincinnati was the terminus of several migration trails and the federal land office there served southwestern Ohio and eastern Indiana. The records, therefore, are particularly valuable to researchers. In the late eighteenth and early nineteenth centuries, the Ohio River was used by pioneers pushing westward across Pennsylvania into the new Northwest Territory. Later, the Ohio River became the dividing line between slavery and non-slavery states. Anti-slavery settlers from the Carolinas and from Tennessee crossed the Ohio River at several points, but Cincinnati was a major gateway to lands guaranteed free from slavery by the Ordinance of 1787. In fact, the Cincinnati area represents a microcosm of history, a history so complex that a brief discussion of the situation is necessary to enable the researcher to use these records to the best advantage.

The first effort to survey and settle Ohio lands resulted from the Ordinance of 20 May 1785. Congress specifically designed this law for "ascertaining the mode of disposing of lands in the Western Territory." This Ordinance, which completely changed surveying methods, specified the use of the newly-developed rectangular grid system. Since the new Republic desperately needed money, and land was a commodity of which it had plenty, this Ordinance was soon applied to eastern Ohio - the first public land in the United States to be subdivided. The Northwest Territory was ceded by Great Britain to the infant nation by the 1783 Treaty of Paris and was its first possession. It was only natural to sell this to settlers who were moving westward from the populous eastern areas. The development of the grid system was destined to influence the parceling of federally-owned land as the boundaries of the country expanded westward. Considering the amount of land west of Ohio yet to be surveyed and subdivided, this Ordinance was truly a major act of legislation. Ohio was, therefore, the experimental area in changing from the old indiscriminate system of "metes and bounds" to a rectangular grid system where each parcel, no matter how small, could be located precisely. This grid system facilitated the selling process and, although not an anticipated advantage at the time, has allowed genealogists to determine the exact locations of ancestors' lands. Ohio was the divider between the indiscriminate surveys of the eastern states and the national rectangular system to the west. It was the testing ground for the new system, with seven different survey methods being used across the present State of Ohio. Today genealogists benefit from its orderly land descriptions.

The surveyors were instructed to divide the territory into townships six miles square by running lines due north and south, with other lines crossing these at right angles. The first north-south line was to begin at the Ohio River, at a point due north from the western terminus of a line which was the southern boundary of the State of Pennsylvania; the first line running east and west started at the same point and extended throughout the entire territory. The north-south lines, six miles apart, separated the land from east to west into "ranges," a term still in use. The lines running at right angles separated the ranges into "townships" (not to be confused with political townships carrying names). These numerical "townships" were also six miles in length and were numbered from the Ohio River northward, wherever the vagaries of the twisting river allowed. Inward from the Ohio River this resulted in townships each containing thirty-six square miles. It was natural to further subdivide these into one-square mile parcels called "sections," each section containing 640 acres. Thus, the first survey known as the "Old Seven Ranges" was made, the surveyed area extending westward into the present State of Ohio a distance of forty-two miles from the Ohio-Pennsylvania border.

Several additional Congressional acts were passed during the period 1785-1800 but the next major one was the Act of 10 May 1800, which called for the establishment of four land offices throughout Ohio for the auction and private sale of public lands. The cities chosen for these offices were Chillicothe, Cincinnati, Marietta and Steubenville. The sales from the Cincinnati office are the subject of this book. The land is in the southwestern portion of Ohio and in parts of eastern Indiana.

Of the four land offices first established, the business of the Cincinnati office was the most complex. The land to be sold in the Cincinnati District was covered by five different surveys, two of which were for land in the eastern and southeastern part of the present State of Indiana (frontispiece map). As a result, these individual surveys must be identified for each purchase since similar range and township numbers are used in each survey. The researcher would be hopelessly frustrated in trying to establish an exact location for any given land parcel if the survey name and area were unknown. In addition, these survey names must be given, together with the range, township and section numbers, date of purchase, and the purchaser's name, if additional information is desired. Thus, the five surveys which encompass land sold by the Cincinnati office are of primary importance.

The limits of authority for each of the four offices were established by the Act of 1800. These are well-defined for all except Cincinnati. In this case, the Act simply defines the area under the Cincinnati office as being "lands below the Little Miami, which have not heretofore been granted." This statement is full of ambiguities. For instance, "below the Little Miami" means downstream from the point where the Little Miami enters the Ohio River until it reaches a point across from Carrollton, Kentucky, at the mouth of the Kentucky River, the point designated by the Act of 1800 as the boundary for the sale of these lands - but it does not say this precisely. Some of Ohio's western lands had already been granted to the Indians under several treaties, and such land came under the phrase "not heretofore ....granted."

One of the principal surveys begins at the state line between Ohio and Indiana beginning at the mouth of the Great Miami River and running northward. Later, the Ohio-Indiana border was designated by the surveyors as the First Principal Meridian. This is an arbitrary north-south line and the name has nothing in common with the Greenwich meridians used for navigation. The survey of land between this line and the Great Miami River is known as the "Miami River Survey" or "West of the Miamis Survey."

The Greenville Treaty Line was drawn in 1795 after the Battle of Fallen Timbers (which took place near the present town of Maumee, Ohio). This Treaty line came across central Ohio to Fort Recovery (map, MIAMI RIVER SURVEY), then dropped sharply southwesterly to the Ohio River, meeting it at the point across from where the Kentucky River empties into the Ohio River. This resulted in a pie-shaped wedge known as "the Gore" (map, MIAMI RIVER SURVEY) and included several Indiana counties. This survey is known as the "West of the First Principal Meridian Survey."

Another survey is known as the "Between the Miamis Survey." The land lies between the Little Miami and the Great Miami Rivers, the latter reaching the Ohio at the present Indiana state line. It reaches from the Ohio River northward approximately ninety to one hundred miles to the Greenville Treaty Line and includes the cities of Cincinnati, Dayton and Springfield. For reasons unknown, the ranges were numbered north from the Ohio River, contrary to the established practice of numbering the ranges east to west. To make matters worse, two partial ranges touching the Ohio River are called Fractional Ranges I and II. From the northern boundary of Fractional Range II, proceeding northward, the numbering starts over, finally ending at Range XV at the Greenville Treaty Line. As far as this book is concerned, this is another survey and is so designated, otherwise the researcher could not be certain in what part of the "Between the Miamis Survey" an ancestor's land was located if it were simply designated as Range I or II. The map, BETWEEN THE MIAMIS SURVEY, shows this area and the fractional ranges in some detail.

The Symmes Purchase is an integral part of the land purchases in this region. John Cleves Symmes held certificates of indebtedness for aiding General Washington in New Jersey in 1776 and applied for 1,000,000 acres between the Miami Rivers. His original intent was to pay for the land by enlisting the interest of others, and he formally petitioned Congress for the land in 1787. The arrangements were much the same as those used by the Ohio Company of New England which settled part of the Marietta, Ohio area. However, Symmes and his associates were unable to pay for even the 311,682 acres finally granted him. Symmes' land was located between the Ohio River and the northern boundary of the entire Range III of the "Between the Miami Rivers Survey." The Symmes Purchase is shown on the map, BETWEEN THE MIAMIS SURVEY, and also on the outline map of the State of Ohio prepared by the Land Office of the State Auditor, Columbus, Ohio. The complete history of the Symmes Purchase does not fall within the scope of this book but the reader is reminded that within the Symmes Purchase Sections 8, 11 and 26 were reserved for use by the federal government and were later sold out of the Cincinnati Land Office. Purchases in these "reserved" sections will have a special designation in this book.

Another north-south line in Indiana is known as the "Second Principal Meridian," again arbitrarily chosen by the surveyors. It runs from an east-west base line fifty to seventy-five miles north of the Ohio River to Lake Erie, not far from Gary, Indiana. Land in this region sold from the Cincinnati office is designated as being "North and East of the Second Principal Meridian." It is therefore apparent that land sold from the Cincinnati Land Office covered an extremely large area and its sale benefited families from many states.

The original records of the Cincinnati Land Office are in the State Archives at the Ohio Historical Center, Columbus, Ohio. Thirteen volumes out of a total of one hundred fifty-one volumes were used in compiling this work. Twelve volumes, labeled Series 395, cover the years 1800 through 1819 and are the original Books of Entries showing the sales of land under the credit system; the thirteenth original volume, Series 409, covers the years 1820 through 1840 and is the Book of Entries for the cash sales of these years. The remaining volumes in the Cincinnati Land Office group are ledgers and journals, account and sales books, and receipt and survey records, along with relinquishments, letters of inquiry and other extraneous material. A few of the Books of Entries contain partial indexes, but the collection is virtually unusable unless an exact purchase date is known. It is the purpose of this book to make these valuable records available to researchers everywhere.

Some words of caution. First, every effort has been made to record the names of purchasers in exactly the form found in the original books. Even in those instances where there seemed to be obvious errors in spelling, the names have been copied exactly as originally entered. Often the handwriting was difficult to decipher. In such instances the names are recorded under two spellings. All possible variations in spelling should be checked before a search is discontinued. The volume containing the last three months of 1819 was water-damaged to such an extent that only the names could be read, and at times even these were difficult to read. The names were therefore recorded by the best spelling decipherable. However, these comprise only between four and five hundred of approximately 26,000 names. Since there are no other data, these names are found in an **Appendix** in the back of the book.

Second, capital letters (A, B, C, D, E) have been placed after the name of every purchaser and are enclosed within parentheses. This is not an initial. The letter designates the survey under which the land was sold. Without this important data each parcel of land sold cannot be located within its proper survey. This survey information is needed if the researcher plans to obtain additional information either from the State Auditor's Office in Columbus, Ohio, or from the Bureau of Land Management in Alexandria, Virginia. In the absence of correct survey designations, the land could be mistakenly identified as much as one hundred miles from its actual location. The five surveys are listed below, along with the present counties covered by each.

(A) Miami River Survey, Ranges I-VIII: Land lying east of a meridian drawn from the mouth of the Great Miami River. Hamilton, Butler, Shelby, Warren, Montgomery, Miami, Preble, Logan and Darke Counties (may be all or only a part of each county) - all in Ohio.

(B) Indiana Survey: Land lying west of a meridian drawn west of the Great Miami River (known as the "Gore"). Switzerland, Dearborn, Franklin, Ohio, Union and Randolph Counties (all or only a part of each county) - all in Indiana.

(C) Between the Miamis, Ranges IV-XV: Lands lying north of the northern boundary of Range III. Greene, Clark, Champion, Shelby and Logan Counties (all or a part of each county) - all in Ohio.

(D) Symmes Purchase, Ranges I, II and III and Fractional Ranges I and II: Actually the southern tip of the Between the Miamis Survey. Warren, Butler and Hamilton Counties (all or only a part) - all in Ohio.

(E) East and North of the Second Principal Meridian, Ranges XI-XV, Townships 10-23: Lands lying entirely in the present State of Indiana. Jefferson, Jackson, Lawrence, Ripley, Jennings, Monroe, Brown, Bartholomew, Decatur, Franklin, Fayette, Rush, Shelby, Johnson, Morgan, Marion, Hancock, Henry, Hamilton, Wayne and Randolph Counties (all or a part of each) - all in Indiana.

These survey areas are shown on the maps and the reader is advised to use these at all times.

Third, there are multiple purchases shown in the index where the same name is given many times. This is not a duplication of the name. The years covered by this work were a time of speculation in land and, although no claim is made by the authors that these men were speculators, the theory is at least plausible. Buying land at extremely low prices, sometimes as low as $1.25 per acre, must have been attractive for anyone with sufficient funds to engage in such speculation. On the other hand, these multiple purchases might have been made by wealthy men with a strong desire to own land. Also, many entries contain more than one name on the purchase. Each name is listed separately in the index but we have not indicated such partnerships.

Fourth, a purchaser of land did not have to pay taxes for five years. Any reader who plans to search tax records should keep this fact in mind.

The following abbreviations have been used for the places of residence. All residence names not listed below are either Ohio counties or towns:

ABBREVIATIONS OF COUNTIES AND CITIES:

Abbreviation	Present State
Aken	– probably South Carolina
Alabama	– Alabama
BeaverCo.Pa	– Pennsylvania
BooneCo.Ky	– Kentucky
BrookeCoVir	– Virginia
BrownsvillePa	– Pennsylvania
CampbellCo,Ky	– Kentucky
CecilCo.,Md	– Maryland
Cincinati(FR)	– Cincinnati (Symmes)
	FR = fractional range
Connecticut	– Connecticut
Dearborn(Ind	– Indiana
Decatur(Ind	– Indiana
DelawareCoPa	– Pennsylvania
Detroit Dist.	– Michigan
DistColumbia	– District of Columbia
East Tennessee	– Tennessee
Fayette	– Ohio or Indiana,
	depending upon survey
Fayette(Ind)	– Indiana
FlemingCo.Ky	– Kentucky
FortWayneInd	– Fort Wayne, Indiana
Fountain(Ind)	– Indiana
Franklinton	– Ohio
Frankfort,Ky	– Kentucky
Franklin(Ind	– Indiana
Franklin	– Ohio
GallatinCoKy	– Kentucky
GeorgiaCo	– may be State of Georgia
GreeneCoPa	– Pennsylvania
Hancock(Ind)	– Indiana
HendricksInd	– Indiana
HenryCo.,Ind	– Indiana
HenryCo.,Ky	– Kentucky
Indiana	– Indiana
Indian Creek	– location unknown
Ind.Territory	– unsurveyed territory
Jackson	– probably Ohio
Jay Co.,Ind	– Indiana
JeffersonInd	– Indiana
Laurancebrgh	– Lawrenceburg, Indiana
LouisvilleKy	– Kentucky
Madison	– Ohio or Indiana
Marion(Ind)	– Indiana
MasonCo.,Ky	– Kentucky
Massachusett	– Massachusetts
Mississippi	– Mississippi
MissTerritory	– Mississippi

MtvilleConn	-	Montville, Connecticut Abbreviation as in original record
New Hampshire	-	New Hampshire
New Jersey	-	New Jersey
Nor.Carolina	-	North Carolina
NWTerrWashtn	-	Washington County, Ohio
OldhamCo.,Ky	-	Kentucky
OrangeCo.Ind	-	Indiana
Piqua	-	Ohio
Philadelphia	-	Pennsylvania
Pittsburgh	-	Pennsylvania
Randolph(Ind	-	Indiana
RipleyCo.Ind	-	Indiana
Rush(Ind)	-	Indiana
Shelby	-	Ohio or Kentucky
ShelbyCo.Ind	-	Indiana
So. Carolina	-	South Carolina
Union(Ind)	-	Indiana
U. S. Army		
Vevay(Ind)	-	Indiana
WashCo.Penn	-	Washington County, Pennsylvania
Wayne(Ind)	-	Indiana
Waynesville	-	probably Ohio

A task of this magnitude cannot be accomplished without the assistance of many able persons. We particularly desire to thank Messrs. Thomas Aquinas Burke and Richard H. Schorr of the Land Office of the State Auditor, Columbus, Ohio. The book simply would not have been possible without their fine cooperation. The same is true of the staff of The Ohio Historical Society, with particular thanks to Mr. Thomas Rieder and Mrs. Arlene J. Peterson. We owe all of them our most sincere gratitude. Last, but not least, we include our gratitude to Messrs. James Edgar and Harvey G. Shulman, without whose special talents in the technical area this work would not have been completed.

Ellen Thomas Berry, M.A., C.G.
David A. Berry, B.S.

Columbus, Ohio
2 April 1986

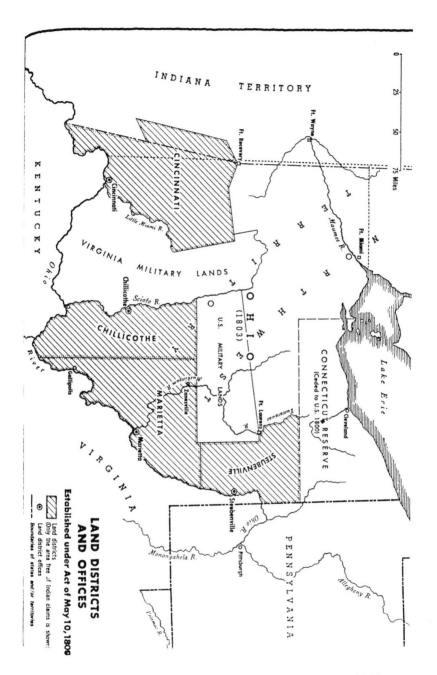

BOUNDARIES OF FOUR LAND OFFICES ESTABLISHED IN OHIO.
From Malcomb J. Rohrbough, *The Land Office Business* (New York: Oxford University Press, 1968), p. 24.

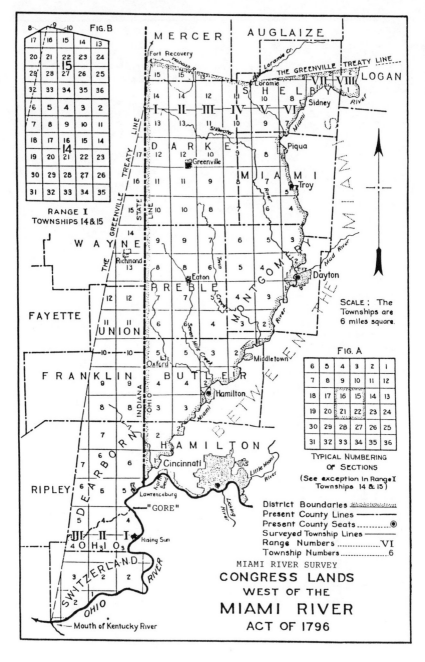

MIAMI RIVER SURVEY, INCLUDING THE GORE AREA, COVERED IN
RECORDS OF THE CINCINNATI LAND OFFICE, CINCINNATI, OHIO.

From C. E. Sherman, *Original Ohio Land Subdivisions,* Vol. III of the Final Report
(1925; repr. Columbus, Ohio, State of Ohio, Dept. of Natural Resources, Division of
Geological Survey, 1976), p. 121.

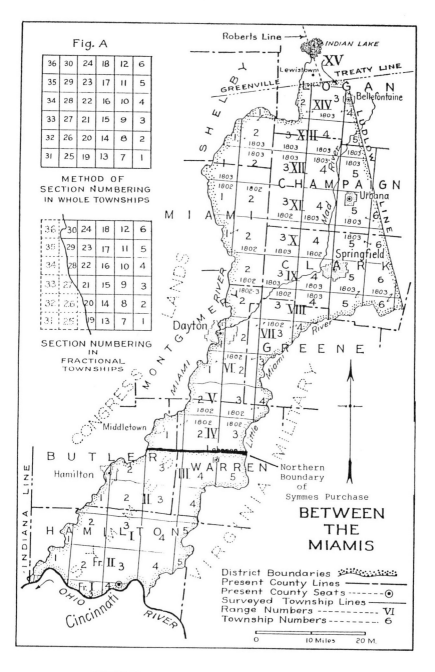

BETWEEN THE MIAMIS SURVEY, INCLUDING
THE SYMMES PURCHASE, COVERED IN RECORDS OF
THE CINCINNATI LAND OFFICE, CINCINNATI, OHIO.

Original Ohio Land Subdivisions, III, p. 71.

PURCHASER	YEAR	DATE	RESIDENCE	R	T	S
Abbett, Samuel(A)	1825	Feb. 22	Hamilton	01	01	06
Abbitt, Amstead(B)	1836	Nov. 07	Dearborn(Ind	03	06	34
Abbitt, James(A)	1815	Feb. 10	Preble	03	07	11
Abborcrombie, Hugh(B)	1824	June 09	Fayette	01	07	03
Abbot, Elihu(E)	1812	April 04	Hamilton	12	14	25
Abbot, James(A)	1805	Nov. 05	Montgomery	03	07	13
Abbot, Jeremiah(B)	1814	Sept. 05	Butler	01	09	02
Abbot, Joseph(A)	1814	Sept. 05	Butler	01	03	03
Abbot, William(B)	1817	Oct. 25	Hamilton	02	04	18
Abbot, William(B)	1835	April 14	Dearborn(Ind	02	04	07
Abbott, David(B)	1832	Oct. 11	Hamilton	02	04	17
Abdon, James(B)	1837	June 23	Dearborn(Ind	03	05	25
Abel, Henry(C)	1824	June 07	Clark	10	02	08
Abercrombee, John(E)	1816	Oct. 16	Montgomery	15	21	07
Abercrombie, Alexander(B)	1816	May 13	Franklin(Ind	01	04	27
Abercrombie, Alexander(B)	1817	Nov. 20	Franklin(Ind	01	08	33
Abernathey, Robt.(E)	1829	Dec. 10	Union(Ind)	14	14	31
Abernathy, Abel(E)	1829	Dec. 14	Union(Ind)	14	14	31
Abernathy, Hugh(E)	1813	June 21	Franklin(Ind	13	13	32
Abernathy, Robert(E)	1814	March 10	Franklin(Ind	13	14	35
Abernathy, Robert(E)	1814	Nov. 26	Franklin(Ind	13	14	35
Abernathy, Wm.(B)	1825	June 17	Franklin(Ind	02	10	22
Abfal, Henry(A)	1806	Nov. 13	Montgomery	05	05	20
Abfel, Henry(A)	1813	Dec. 28	Montgomery	04	04	15
Abicht, John Hy.(E)	1838	Aug. 09	Butler	14	22	34
Abornath, Hugh(B)	1809	April 19	Dearborn(Ind	02	10	21
Abornathy, William(B)	1815	Feb. 17	Franklin(Ind	02	10	10
Abraham, Benj'm.(B)	1811	Dec. 13	Franklin(Ind	01	08	01
Abraham, Benjamin(B)	1813	Dec. 15	Franklin(Ind	01	09	36
Abraham, Benjamin(E)	1836	Feb. 22	Franklin(Ind	12	11	29
Abraham, Benjamin(E)	1837	Jan. 05	Franklin(Ind	12	11	19
Abraham, Enoch(E)	1836	Aug. 04	Franklin(Ind	11	10	10
Abraham, George(B)	1818	June 03	Hamilton	03	05	11
Abraham, James(E)	1836	March 24	Franklin(Ind	12	11	29
Abraham, James(E)	1836	Sept. 06	Franklin(Ind	12	11	29
Abraham, James(E)	1837	Jan. 05	Franklin(Ind	12	11	29
Abraham, Lott(A)	1806	Nov. 22	Clermont	01	04	32
Abraham, Lott(B)	1812	April 15	Butler	01	04	32
Abrahams, Benjamin(B)	1808	Nov. 11	Kentucky	01	09	36
Abrahams, George(B)	1817	Sept. 22	Hamilton	03	05	13
Abshier, James(E)	1819	June 30	Preble	14	19	33
Abshire, Isaac(A)	1815	Sept. 13	Preble	01	09	04
Abshire, James(E)	1827	Jan. 13	Randolph(Ind	14	19	28
Abshire, James(E)	1826	Jan. 13	Randolph(Ind	14	19	29
Abshire, James(E)	1835	Jan. 28	Randolph(Ind	14	19	15
Abshire, James(E)	1836	March 17	Randolph(Ind	14	19	15
Ackerman, Jno. Hy.(A)	1837	Dec. 09	Hamilton	04	11	32
Ackerman, John Henry(A)	1835	Aug. 11	Hamilton	03	12	14
Ackermon, Abraham(E)	1837	May 29	Richland	15	22	31
Acree, Abner(B)	1815	April 01	Wayne(Ind)	01	13	32
Acton, John(A)	1824	June 08	Preble	02	07	15
Acton, John(A)	1824	June 08	Preble	02	07	15
Acton, John(A)	1824	June 08	Preble	02	07	15
Adair, George Ross(E)	1811	Dec. 23	Franklin(Ind	13	14	30
Adair, James Junr.(E)	1811	Oct. 23	Franklin(Ind	12	14	25
Adair, James Senr.(B)	1805	March 21	DistColumbia	02	08	03
Adair, James Sr.(B)	1803	April 21	So. Carolina	01	07	04
Adams, David(A)	1816	Dec. 03	Preble	01	09	32
Adams, David(A)	1819	Oct. 08	Miami	05	07	01
Adams, Demas(A)	1836	Feb. 10	Franklin	08	02	33
Adams, Demas(C)	1836	Feb. 10	Franklin	13	03	33

PURCHASER	YEAR	DATE	RESIDENCE	R	T	S
Adams, Edmond(E)	1817	July 12	Franklin(Ind	13	11	15
Adams, Edmund(E)	1817	Sept. 08	Franklin(Ind	11	11	24
Adams, George(A)	1814	Sept. 07	Montgomery	03	10	27
Adams, George(A)	1815	Oct. 07	Montgomery	03	10	33
Adams, George(A)	1815	Dec. 13	Montgomery	03	10	28
Adams, George(A)	1820	Nov. 27	Darke	03	09	18
Adams, George(C)	1801	Dec. 28	Hamilton	06	01	21
Adams, George(E)	1811	Oct. 21	Ind.Territry	12	12	35
Adams, Isaiah(A)	1819	Feb. 06	Preble	02	09	17
Adams, Isaiah(A)	1819	Feb. 06	Preble	02	09	17
Adams, Isaiah(A)	1819	July 09	Preble	02	09	17
Adams, James(A)	1832	April 19	Preble	01	12	30
Adams, James(A)	1837	Feb. 24	Hamilton	02	14	20
Adams, Joseph(A)	1811	Jan. 05	Miami	05	09	35
Adams, Joseph(B)	1816	May 01	Hamilton	02	07	25
Adams, Joseph(B)	1816	May 09	Hamilton	02	07	14
Adams, Nathaniel(B)	1835	Dec. 26	Randolph(Ind	01	17	26
Adams, Patrick(E)	1835	Oct. 24	Franklin(Ind	12	12	33
Adams, Philip(A)	1831	Nov. 03	Miami	05	08	15
Adams, Philip(A)	1831	Nov. 03	Miami	05	08	27
Adams, Robert(B)	1832	April 19	Preble	01	17	36
Adams, Sarles T.(A)	1838	Jan. 24	Miami	02	14	13
Adams, Seleucus(A)	1836	May 09	LouisvilleKy	02	13	12
Adams, Seleucus(A)	1836	May 09	LouisvilleKy	03	11	01
Adams, William(E)	1813	Aug. 24	Franklin(Ind	13	13	21
Adams, William(E)	1814	July 30	Franklin(Ind	12	12	35
Adamson, Abraham(E)	1837	March 01	Randolph(Ind	13	18	04
Adamson, Elisha(C)	1804	Sept. 04	Greene	11	05	32
Adamson, John(E)	1820	Dec. 09	Clinton	13	19	15
Adcock, Francis(E)	1814	Oct. 19	Wayne(Ind)	14	18	10
Addington, Henry(A)	1816	Sept. 21	Butler	04	07	08
Addington, Henry(A)	1824	Aug. 31	Butler	04	07	15
Addington, James Jr.(E)	1835	April 25	Randolph(Ind	13	21	34
Addington, James(A)	1830	Jan. 20	Darke	04	07	07
Addington, James(A)	1831	Feb. 18	Darke	04	07	07
Addington, Jesse(E)	1834	June 25	Randolph(Ind	13	21	22
Addington, John(B)	1806	Nov. 03	Dearborn(Ind	01	14	17
Addington, John(B)	1806	Nov. 03	Dearborn(Ind	01	14	20
Addington, John(B)	1806	Dec. 04	Dearborn(Ind	01	14	08
Addington, John(B)	1806	Dec. 04	Dearborn(Ind	01	14	09
Addington, John(B)	1807	May 11	Dearborn(Ind	01	14	09
Addington, John(B)	1808	May 13	Dearborn(Ind	01	14	17
Addington, John(B)	1813	April 14	Wayne(Ind)	01	14	04
Addington, John(B)	1829	Jan. 05	Wayne(Ind)	01	17	35
Addington, Joseph(B)	1807	May 11	Dearborn(Ind	01	14	04
Addington, Joseph(E)	1835	Aug. 19	Randolph(Ind	13	21	34
Addington, Thomas(B)	1807	May 11	So. Carolina	01	14	08
Addington, Thomas(E)	1834	May 27	Randolph(Ind	13	21	26
Addington, Thomas(E)	1837	March 25	Randolph(Ind	13	21	26
Addington, Thomas(E)	1835	Aug. 19	Randolph(Ind	13	21	35
Addington, Thomas(E)	1836	Nov. 24	Randolph(Ind	13	21	23
Addleman, John M.(B)	1827	Aug. 10	Wayne(Ind)	01	15	15
Addleman, Jos.(B)	1827	June 25	Wayne(Ind)	01	15	15
Addleman, Joseph(B)	1827	Nov. 15	Wayne(Ind)	01	15	34
Addleman, William(B)	1818	Dec. 30	Wayne(Ind)	01	15	22
Adkins, Parker(C)	1804	Dec. 24	Montgomery	09	02	03
Adkinson, Abraham(B)	1833	Aug. 26	Switzerland	02	03	35
Adkinson, Samuel(B)	1833	June 22	Cincinnati	02	03	35
Adkinson, Samuel(B)	1833	Dec. 11	Cincinnati	02	03	35
Adney, Charles Thomas(B)	1832	Oct. 03	Dearborn(Ind	03	05	36
Adney, John(C)	1808	Jan. 12	Virginia	12	02	31
Adney, John(C)	1813	May 05	Miami	11	02	34
Adney, John(C)	1813	Oct. 18	Miami	11	02	35
Aerl, Isaac(A)	1814	Jan. 05	Adams	08	01	12
Aerl, Rebecca(A)	1811	Dec. 11	Miami	06	07	07
Aerl, Thomas(C)	1801	Dec. 09	Hamilton	04	03	07
Aert, Thomas(A)	1806	Oct. 23	Warren	06	07	07
Agins, James(E)	1811	Oct. 21	Ind.Territry	12	12	09
Agins, William(E)	1811	Oct. 22	Ind.Territry	12	13	14

PURCHASER	YEAR	DATE	RESIDENCE	R	T	S
Ahlers, Jno. Frederick(B)	1836	Aug. 25	Hamilton	03	09	01
Aid, Jacob(A)	1816	Feb. 20	Ross	01	07	26
Aikelberger, John(A)	1814	June 17	Montgomery	03	05	13
Aikenberry, Henry(A)	1805	Nov. 01	Montgomery	03	05	31
Aikenberry, Henry(A)	1805	Nov. 01	Montgomery	03	05	29
Aikins, Israel(A)	1831	Oct. 28	Warren	05	10	33
Aikman, John(A)	1812	Oct. 22	Preble	03	07	23
Ailes, Aaron(E)	1836	Feb. 12	Franklin(Ind	11	11	01
Ailes,William Dela Fletcher(E)	1836	Feb. 22	Franklin(Ind	12	11	06
Aker, Michael(E)	1837	Feb. 06	Randolph(Ind	13	20	36
Aker, Michael(E)	1838	Feb. 06	Randolph(Ind	13	20	12
Aker, Michael(E)	1838	Sept. 10	Randolph(Ind	14	21	36
Aker, Samuel(A)	1831	July 13	Preble	01	10	12
Aker, Thomas(E)	1833	May 20	Preble	14	20	27
Akin, James(A)	1832	Feb. 24	Shelby	05	09	02
Akin, James(C)	1804	Sept. 24	Montgomery	06	01	08
Akin, John J.(B)	1837	Aug. 21	Dearborn(Ind	03	05	03
Akin, Joseph(E)	1814	July 11	Warren	14	16	32
Akins, Benjamin(A)	1817	May 30	Montgomery	01	11	27
Akins, James(C)	1801	Dec. 29	Hamilton	05	02	12
Akright, Rachel(E)	1836	April 21	Franklin(Ind	12	11	03
Albaugh, Jacob(A)	1831	Dec. 02	Montgomery	04	09	19
Albaugh, Jacob(A)	1832	March 19	Montgomery	04	09	19
Albaugh, Sam'l.(A)	1829	June 24	Montgomery	04	07	26
Albaugh, Samuel(A)	1812	Aug. 25	Maryland	03	04	05
Albaugh, Stephen(E)	1838	Nov. 16	Preble	14	20	12
Albein, Samuel(C)	1814	Nov. 14	Greene	09	04	26
Alben, Gabriel(C)	1824	June 07	Clark	08	04	11
Alben, Samuel(C)	1824	June 07	Clark	09	04	26
Alber, Frederick William(A)	1832	Sept. 10	Warren	03	10	08
Albers, Christopher(E)	1836	Oct. 21	Cincinnati	11	10	12
Albers, Christopher(E)	1836	Nov. 21	Cincinnati	11	10	13
Albertson, Joshua(E)	1815	Jan. 07	Wayne(Ind)	13	17	11
Albin, Gabriel(C)	1814	Jan. 18	Champaign	08	04	11
Albin, Sam'l.(C)	1828	Feb. 18	Clark	09	04	07
Albin, William(C)	1813	Dec. 28	Greene	08	04	11
Albough, David(A)	1816	Dec. 09	Preble	02	12	36
Albough, Jacob(A)	1816	May 06	Montgomery	05	05	06
Albough, Jacob(A)	1816	Aug. 15	Montgomery	05	05	06
Albrecht, John(A)	1818	Nov. 10	Dearborn(Ind	01	11	27
Albright, Jonas(A)	1824	July 17	Preble	03	08	35
Albright, William(A)	1819	Sept. 23	Preble	03	07	05
Alden, Isaac(B)	1831	Oct. 13	Dearborn(Ind	03	08	26
Alden, Isaac(B)	1835	April 01	Dearborn(Ind	03	08	14
Aldman, Matthew(B)	1814	Jan. 31	Wayne(Ind)	01	15	29
Aldrich, Collin(A)	1829	Dec. 31	Cincinnati	06	08	33
Aldrich, Paris(A)	1819	Sept. 06	Cincinnati	06	08	08
Aldrich, Paris(A)	1819	Sept. 06	Cincinnati	06	08	33
Aldrich, Robert(A)	1819	Sept. 06	Cincinnati	06	08	08
Aldrich, Robert(A)	1819	Sept. 06	Cincinnati	06	08	33
Aldrich, Robert(C)	1819	Sept. 28	Hamilton	13	02	23
Aldrich, Robert(C)	1819	Sept. 28	Hamilton	13	02	23
Aldrich, Robt.(C)	1819	Sept. 28	Hamilton	13	02	33
Aldrich, Robt.(C)	1819	Sept. 28	Hamilton	13	02	33
Aldrich, Wailes Jr.(C)	1831	April 09	Clarke	12	02	27
Aldrich, Wailes(C)	1813	Aug. 30	Champaign	09	06	18
Aldrick, Wailes(C)	1812	Oct. 28	Champaign	09	06	33
Aldridge, Nathan(E)	1813	Aug. 21	Franklin(Ind	12	13	01
Alexander, Amos(A)	1832	June 08	Miami	04	07	10
Alexander, Andrew(C)	1802	Dec. 24	Hamilton	05	03	31
Alexander, Carnes(C)	1817	Sept. 02	Fairfield	12	03	17
Alexander, Daniel(E)	1815	Dec. 07	Warren	14	15	20
Alexander, Gabriel(B)	1832	Aug. 06	Randolph(Ind	01	16	01
Alexander, Gabriel(B)	1836	Sept. 08	Randolph(Ind	01	16	12
Alexander, Henry(A)	1832	June 09	Darke	04	07	15
Alexander, Hugh(B)	1831	Oct. 27	Dearborn(Ind	02	05	06
Alexander, James(A)	1811	Dec. 23	Ind.Territry	01	09	07
Alexander, James(A)	1811	Dec. 23	Ind.Territry	01	10	28
Alexander, James(A)	1816	May 22	Wayne(Ind)	01	09	18

3

PURCHASER	YEAR	DATE	RESIDENCE	R	T	S
Alexander, James(B)	1805	Sept. 23	Nor.Carolina	01	14	36
Alexander, James(E)	1814	May 03	Franklin(Ind	12	14	28
Alexander, Jno.(B)	1832	Aug. 06	Randolph(Ind	01	16	01
Alexander, John A.(C)	1817	Sept. 02	Greene	12	03	25
Alexander, John A.(C)	1817	Sept. 02	Greene	12	03	27
Alexander, John Mc.(C)	1829	Oct. 07	Champaign	12	03	18
Alexander, John(A)	1835	Nov. 09	Butler	08	02	33
Alexander, John(B)	1807	Sept. 16	Nor.Carolina	01	14	24
Alexander, John(B)	1818	Jan. 31	Dearborn(Ind	02	04	32
Alexander, John(B)	1836	June 07	Dearborn(Ind	03	06	12
Alexander, John(B)	1836	Aug. 24	Randolph(Ind	01	16	01
Alexander, John(E)	1832	Aug. 28	Preble	14	21	11
Alexander, John(E)	1836	June 18	Preble	14	21	01
Alexander, John(E)	1836	Oct. 18	Preble	14	21	01
Alexander, Joseph(C)	1816	Aug. 22	Butler	09	02	29
Alexander, Joseph(C)	1824	Dec. 17	Logan	13	03	26
Alexander, Robert(C)	1824	Sept. 09	Warren	12	02	01
Alexander, Thomas(E)	1834	Feb. 25	Preble	15	21	19
Alexander, Thornton Jr.(B)	1834	Jan. 27	Randolph(Ind	01	17	35
Alexander, Thornton Jr.(B)	1834	May 27	Randolph(Ind	01	16	12
Alexander, Thornton(B)	1822	Aug. 23	Darke	01	16	01
Alexander, Thornton(B)	1832	Aug. 06	Randolph(Ind	01	16	01
Alexander, Thornton(B)	1833	Sept. 25	Randolph(Ind	01	16	01
Alexander, Thornton(B)	1835	March 11	Randolph(Ind	01	16	01
Alexander, William(A)	1828	May 03	Preble	02	11	21
Alexander, William(A)	1828	Dec. 01	Preble	02	11	21
Alexander, William(B)	1811	Dec. 23	Ind.Territry	01	14	13
Alexander, William(B)	1814	July 06	Pennsylvania	02	04	36
Alexander, Wm. Mc.(C)	1831	Feb. 26	Champaign	12	03	11
Alfred, Harrison(B)	1836	Sept. 01	Hamilton	03	05	01
Alfred, Harrison(B)	1837	Oct. 16	Dearborn(Ind	02	04	06
Alfred, Harrison(B)	1837	Oct. 20	Dearborn(Ind	03	06	36
Allaire, Andrew B.(B)	1818	April 13	Dearborn(Ind	02	07	27
Allaire, Samuel Y.(B)	1817	Sept. 29	New York	02	07	31
Allaire, Samuel Y.(B)	1817	Oct. 03	New York	03	08	36
Allaire, Samuel Y.(B)	1817	Oct. 03	New York	03	08	36
Allaire, Samuel Y.(B)	1817	Oct. 03	New York	02	06	06
Allbaugh, John(E)	1837	May 12	Montgomery	15	20	05
Allbaugh, Stephen(E)	1836	May 30	Preble	14	20	07
Allbaugh, Stephen(E)	1836	May 30	Preble	14	20	34
Allbaugh, Stephen(E)	1836	Aug. 27	Preble	15	20	21
Allbright, Adam(A)	1829	May 01	Darke	03	08	26
Allen, Bethuel(A)	1815	May 26	Warren	02	11	34
Allen, Clabourn(B)	1813	Feb. 16	Dearborn(Ind	01	04	33
Allen, Claiborn(B)	1817	Aug. 20	Dearborn(Ind	02	05	31
Allen, Claiborne(B)	1817	July 07	Dearborn(Ind	02	04	04
Allen, Claiborne(B)	1817	July 07	Dearborn(Ind	03	06	36
Allen, David(B)	1832	Nov. 08	Hamilton	02	02	31
Allen, David(B)	1833	Oct. 25	Switzerland	02	02	31
Allen, David(E)	1837	May 31	Athens	14	20	03
Allen, David(E)	1837	May 31	Athens	14	20	11
Allen, Eli(E)	1811	Dec. 16	Pennsylvania	12	11	09
Allen, Eli(E)	1815	July 29	Pennsylvania	12	11	08
Allen, Elijah(E)	1816	Sept. 28	Butler	12	13	28
Allen, George(E)	1837	May 31	Athens	14	20	04
Allen, Hugh(E)	1818	June 05	Montgomery	13	17	30
Allen, Isaac(B)	1809	Aug. 16	Dearborn(Ind	02	05	33
Allen, Isaac(B)	1818	Jan. 09	Dearborn(Ind	02	05	33
Allen, James(A)	1808	Jan. 14	Butler	01	06	10
Allen, James(A)	1824	June 08	Butler	03	04	22
Allen, James(A)	1824	June 08	Butler	02	06	22
Allen, James(B)	1816	March 15	Dearborn(Ind	02	04	24
Allen, James(B)	1816	Dec. 13	Dearborn(Ind	02	04	24
Allen, Jeremiah Jr.(C)	1832	April 20	Montgomery	12	02	21
Allen, Jeremiah(E)	1814	Nov. 19	Wayne(Ind)	14	15	19
Allen, Jeremiah(E)	1816	Oct. 15	Wayne(Ind)	14	15	20
Allen, Jno. S.(B)	1813	March 02	Dearborn(Ind	01	08	11
Allen, John Jnr.(E)	1813	Aug. 26	Franklin(Ind	13	12	04
Allen, John Milton(E)	1836	Feb. 13	Franklin(Ind	11	11	01

4

PURCHASER	YEAR	DATE	RESIDENCE	R	T	S
Allen, John(A)	1808	Jan. 14	Butler	01	06	10
Allen, John(B)	1805	July 06	Hamilton	02	09	29
Allen, John(B)	1805	Aug. 06	Dearborn(Ind	01	07	25
Allen, John(B)	1806	June 14	Dearborn(Ind	01	08	29
Allen, John(B)	1811	Dec. 31	Dearborn(Ind	01	08	01
Allen, John(B)	1811	Dec. 31	Dearborn(Ind	01	08	02
Allen, John(B)	1814	Dec. 05	Franklin(Ind	02	09	14
Allen, John(B)	1814	Dec. 16	Franklin(Ind	02	09	15
Allen, John(B)	1814	Dec. 16	Franklin(Ind	02	09	14
Allen, John(B)	1815	Feb. 02	Preble	01	11	36
Allen, John(C)	1813	Dec. 28	Greene	09	04	07
Allen, Jonathan(E)	1814	Jan. 28	Franklin(Ind	13	11	18
Allen, Joseph White(B)	1831	Aug. 20	Dearborn(Ind	01	06	04
Allen, Josiah(E)	1813	Aug. 26	Franklin(Ind	13	12	04
Allen, Peter(B)	1811	July 16	Dearborn(Ind	02	04	13
Allen, Peter(B)	1814	Aug. 30	Dearborn(Ind	02	04	13
Allen, Scott(C)	1831	Sept. 06	Montgomery	12	03	32
Allen, Solomon(B)	1816	Oct. 21	Franklin(Ind	02	08	05
Allen, Solomon(B)	1834	March 08	Franklin(Ind	02	08	35
Allen, Wm. B.(B)	1813	March 02	Dearborn(Ind	01	08	11
Allen, Wm.(C)	1815	Sept. 30	Hamilton	09	06	28
Allensworth, William(B)	1801	Dec. 09	Hamilton	01	07	13
Allensworth, William(B)	1806	Feb. 01	Dearborn(Ind	01	08	11
Allensworth, William(B)	1806	Feb. 01	Dearborn(Ind	01	08	24
Allerman, Gerhard Hy.(B)	1836	Sept. 08	Cincinnati	03	09	01
Alley, Andrew(E)	1836	Sept. 07	Hancock(Ind)	12	10	02
Alley, Cyrus(E)	1814	Oct. 12	Franklin(Ind	13	11	18
Alley, David Jr.(E)	1836	Dec. 07	Franklin(Ind	12	11	13
Alley, David(E)	1812	Sept. 25	Franklin(Ind	13	11	18
Alley, David(E)	1833	March 02	Franklin(Ind	12	11	24
Alley, David(E)	1836	Feb. 20	Franklin(Ind	13	11	19
Alley, David(E)	1836	Oct. 10	Franklin(Ind	12	11	35
Alley, James Mitchell(E)	1836	Jan. 11	Franklin(Ind	13	11	18
Alley, James(E)	1812	Oct. 29	Franklin(Ind	13	11	19
Alley, James(E)	1833	March 25	Franklin(Ind	13	11	31
Alley, James(E)	1836	Oct. 10	Franklin(Ind	13	11	30
Alley, John Senr.(E)	1836	Sept. 07	Franklin(Ind	12	11	24
Alley, John(E)	1817	Sept. 30	Franklin(Ind	12	11	25
Alley, Jonathan(E)	1831	Oct. 01	Franklin(Ind	12	11	35
Alley, Jonathan(E)	1836	Feb. 10	Franklin(Ind	13	11	08
Alley, Jonathan(E)	1836	Oct. 07	Franklin(Ind	13	11	08
Alley, Peter(E)	1814	Aug. 29	Franklin(Ind	13	11	30
Alley, Samuel(E)	1811	Nov. 07	Franklin(Ind	13	11	07
Alley, Samuel(E)	1812	Oct. 05	Franklin(Ind	13	11	07
Alley, Thomas W.(E)	1836	Dec. 01	Franklin(Ind	12	11	13
Alley, William(E)	1832	June 06	Franklin(Ind	12	11	25
Alley, William(E)	1836	Feb. 16	Franklin(Ind	12	11	25
Allison, Asberry(E)	1832	Jan. 17	Fayette	12	12	05
Allison, James(E)	1836	Nov. 17	Franklin(Ind	12	12	06
Allison, Timothy(E)	1829	Oct. 13	Franklin(Ind	11	12	01
Alloway, Thomas(B)	1818	Jan. 05	Kentucky	02	06	31
Allred, James(A)	1816	Feb. 02	Preble	02	06	10
Almonrod, David(E)	1837	May 13	Preble	14	20	01
Almonrod, Margaret(E)	1837	May 13	Preble	14	20	01
Alms, George Hy.(A)	1837	July 15	Cincinnati	03	13	26
Alter, David(A)	1837	Oct. 16	Butler	01	14	04
Alter, David(A)	1838	Feb. 19	Butler	01	14	05
Althiser, Peter(B)	1833	April 22	Switzerland	03	04	36
Altick, Christian(A)	1836	Sept. 01	Montgomery	03	12	11
Altick, John(A)	1818	Nov. 05	Montgomery	04	05	23
Amack, William Jr.(E)	1837	Jan. 07	Franklin(Ind	12	11	20
Aman, John Junr.(A)	1833	Feb. 16	Hamilton	02	12	25
Aman, John(A)	1833	Feb. 13	Hamilton	02	12	25
Aman, John(A)	1833	Dec. 23	Hamilton	03	10	19
Ambler, John(C)	1808	Jan. 19	Greene	08	04	24
Ambler, John(C)	1813	April 14	Champaign	08	04	24
Ambrose, Peter(A)	1813	Oct. 12	Pennsylvania	01	04	29
Ambrose, Peter(A)	1813	Oct. 12	Pennsylvania	01	04	33
Ambrose, Peter(A)	1813	Oct. 12	Pennsylvania	01	04	31

PURCHASER	YEAR	DATE	RESIDENCE	R	T	S
Ambrose, Peter(B)	1814	Sept. 30	Pennsylvania	02	09	12
Ames, Austin(B)	1818	Nov. 09	Hamilton	01	02	15
Ames, Rich'd.(A)	1837	Jan. 23	Montgomery	03	13	36
Ames, Richard(A)	1834	Oct. 06	Montgomery	07	02	28
Ames, Richard(A)	1834	Oct. 28	Montgomery	08	01	05
Ames, Richard(A)	1834	Nov. 28	Montgomery	08	02	31
Amidion, Abner(A)	1804	Sept. 15	Cincinnati	01	02	18
Ammen, David(C)	1814	Nov. 30	Champaign	12	05	35
Ammen, David(C)	1814	Nov. 30	Champaign	14	04	32
Ammerman, Philip(A)	1815	Nov. 02	Kentucky	01	07	29
Amthauer, Henry(E)	1836	Sept. 19	Cincinnati	12	11	22
Andayon, George(A)	1821	Oct. 15	Warren	04	05	25
Anderson, Abner(E)	1835	June 10	Wayne(Ind)	15	19	17
Anderson, Andrew(C)	1811	Dec. 16	Kentucky	14	03	21
Anderson, Benj'n.(A)	1837	Dec. 15	Montgomery	01	13	02
Anderson, Branson(B)	1835	Oct. 14	Randolph(Ind	01	17	23
Anderson, Branson(B)	1836	Dec. 21	Randolph(Ind	01	17	23
Anderson, Chas. B.(A)	1827	Oct. 03	Warren	06	03	05
Anderson, Dan'l. H.(C)	1830	Sept. 25	Pennsylvania	12	02	10
Anderson, David(B)	1831	Aug. 17	Wayne(Ind)	01	15	11
Anderson, David(C)	1830	Aug. 02	Miami	12	03	26
Anderson, David(C)	1830	Aug. 02	Miami	12	02	15
Anderson, Fergus(A)	1827	Aug. 20	Butler	02	03	22
Anderson, George(B)	1836	Sept. 15	Butler	01	16	13
Anderson, Henry(B)	1814	April 20	Butler	02	04	24
Anderson, Isaac(A)	1813	June 14	Butler	02	06	22
Anderson, James C.(C)	1812	Jan. 31	Montgomery	06	01	14
Anderson, James Jr.(A)	1828	March 20	Montgomery	06	03	08
Anderson, James(A)	1811	Dec. 21	Butler	02	06	19
Anderson, James(A)	1819	Feb. 02	Miami	04	08	25
Anderson, James(B)	1818	Feb. 13	Hamilton	03	06	10
Anderson, James(B)	1832	March 30	Hamilton	01	07	22
Anderson, Jane D.(C)	1830	Sept. 25	Miami	12	02	10
Anderson, Jane(C)	1814	Dec. 23	Champaign	10	04	24
Anderson, John B.(A)	1836	Aug. 13	Montgomery	01	14	22
Anderson, John(B)	1807	July 09	Greene	08	05	28
Anderson, John(B)	1827	Aug. 21	Wayne(Ind)	01	15	11
Anderson, John(B)	1827	Dec. 22	Wayne(Ind)	01	15	11
Anderson, John(C)	1824	June 07	Clark	11	04	07
Anderson, Joseph(E)	1836	July 07	Wayne(Ind)	15	21	09
Anderson, Julius(A)	1801	June 13	Pennsylvania	02	04	25
Anderson, Sam'l. S.(C)	1828	Feb. 11	Hamilton	11	02	03
Anderson, Samuel(B)	1818	Jan. 12	Cincinnati	02	06	08
Anderson, Samuel(C)	1813	April 05	Champaign	10	05	23
Anderson, Silas(E)	1814	July 22	Butler	13	13	12
Anderson, Thomas(A)	1837	May 08	Warren	01	13	10
Anderson, Thomas(B)	1817	Sept. 05	Warren	03	08	25
Anderson, Thomas(B)	1817	Sept. 05	Warren	03	08	24
Anderson, Thomas(C)	1804	Nov. 12	Greene	11	04	05
Anderson, Thomas(C)	1813	June 25	Champaign	11	03	28
Anderson, Will'm. H.(C)	1830	Sept. 25	Warren	12	02	15
Anderson, Will'm.(A)	1827	Sept. 22	Montgomery	06	03	08
Anderson, William Alfred(E)	1836	Jan. 26	Franklin(Ind	12	12	07
Anderson, William(A)	1817	Oct. 01	Miami	05	09	28
Anderson, William(A)	1828	March 20	Montgomery	06	03	08
Anderson, William(B)	1816	Nov. 01	Maryland	02	02	07
Anderson, William(B)	1827	Aug. 21	Wayne(Ind)	01	15	11
Anderson, William(B)	1838	Sept. 28	Wayne(Ind)	01	17	11
Anderson, William(C)	1804	Dec. 17	Greene	08	04	31
Anderson, William(C)	1813	Aug. 10	Greene	08	05	35
Anderson, William(E)	1836	Oct. 08	Wayne(Ind)	15	21	10
Anderson,William(B)	1831	July 07	Wayne(Ind)	01	15	11
Andrew, Adam(A)	1805	March 19	Butler	03	03	23
Andrew, James(B)	1817	June 10	Hamilton	02	08	09
Andrew, James(C)	1805	Dec. 03	Greene	07	04	36
Andrew, James(C)	1805	Dec. 03	Greene	07	04	35
Andrew, James(C))	1813	April 08	Greene	07	04	36
Andrew, John(B)	1817	June 10	Hamilton	02	08	09
Andrew, Joseph(B)	1818	June 23	Hamilton	03	07	23

6

PURCHASER	YEAR	DATE	RESIDENCE	R	T	S
Andrew, Samuel(A)	1818	June 27	Montgomery	04	06	12
Andrews, Arthur(B)	1818	Sept. 17	Butler	03	03	04
Andrews, Barton(E)	1833	Nov. 18	Randolph(Ind	13	19	32
Andrews, Hugh(A)	1816	May 21	Preble	01	09	25
Andrews, James(A)	1814	June 06	Butler	01	04	17
Andrews, Jno.(A)	1813	July 30	Cincinnati	09	04	05
Andrews, John	1808	March 01	?	?	?	?
Andrews, John	1808	March 01	?	?	?	?
Andrews, John	1808	March 02	Cincinnati	?	?	?
Andrews, John	1808	March 02	Cincinnati	?	?	?
Andrews, John	1808	June 15	?	?	?	?
Andrews, John	1813	Aug. 10	Cincinnati	?	?	?
Andrews, John(A)	1804	Oct. 13	Hamilton	02	03	32
Andrews, John(A)	1807	June 27	Cincinnati	06	05	33
Andrews, John(A)	1808	Dec. 15	Cincinnati	02	03	05
Andrews, John(A)	1809	Dec. 13	Cincinnati	05	03	31
Andrews, John(A)	1810	Dec. 14	?	04	02	03
Andrews, John(A)	1815	April 11	Cincinnati	05	03	31
Andrews, John(A)	1817	July 30	Cincinnati	04	03	09
Andrews, John(B)	1812	Nov. 25	Cincinnati	01	09	29
Andrews, John(B)	1814	Sept. 30	Franklin(Ind	02	11	03
Andrews, John(C)	1808	Jan. 28	Cincinnati	05	03	28
Andrews, John(C)	1808	Nov. 02	Cincinnati	12	01	29
Andrews, John(C)	1808	April 21	Cincinnati	09	01	03
Andrews, John(C)	1812	Dec. 04	Cincinnati	09	03	07
Andrews, John(C)	1813	April 01	Cincinnati	10	02	24
Andrews, John(C)	1814	Feb. 11	Cincinnati	12	04	10
Andrews, John(D)	1809	July 24	Cincinati(Fr	01	01	18
Andrews, John(E)	1811	Dec. 10	?	13	15	07
Andrews, John(E)	1817	July 30	Cincinnati	13	15	07
Andrews, Peter(A)	1814	Jan. 22	Montgomery	04	04	09
Andrews, Robert R.(B)	1817	Sept. 08	Switzerland	03	03	02
Andrews, William(B)	1836	June 13	Switzerland	03	04	27
Andrieus, John(A)	1809	Dec. 13	Cincinnati	05	03	31
Angel, Benjamin D.(E)	1817	Sept. 15	Wayne(Ind)	13	18	10
Angel, Benjamin D.(E)	1817	Sept. 15	Wayne(Ind)	13	18	10
Angel, Jacob(A)	1815	Oct. 06	Maryland	05	07	09
Angevine, James(B)	1817	July 25	New York	02	06	05
Angevine, James(B)	1817	July 31	New York	02	06	02
Angle, Michael(A)	1809	Oct. 24	Miami	05	08	20
Angle, Michael(C)	1801	Dec. 15	Hamilton	04	03	23
Annis, Thomas(B)	1831	June 30	Dearborn(Ind	01	06	31
Ansley, Daniel(B)	1818	Feb. 28	Pennsylvania	03	06	36
Ansley, Thomas(B)	1818	Feb. 18	Pennsylvania	03	05	02
Anspach, Michael(A)	1814	June 24	Butler	01	08	32
Anthony, George(B)	1811	Sept. 27	Ross	02	09	35
Anthony, John(A)	1818	Feb. 05	Hamilton	04	07	11
Anthony, William(A)	1809	Aug. 23	Butler	01	04	18
Antram, Adin(A)	1813	Aug. 10	Butler	02	05	01
Antrim, Charles W.(E)	1837	Jan. 21	Butler	14	19	01
Antrum, Daniel(C)	1801	Dec. 17	Hamilton	04	04	15
Apple, Adam(C)	1826	Aug. 14	Montgomery	11	03	05
Apple, Christopher Jr.(A)	1829	Oct. 10	Clermont	04	06	09
Apple, George(C)	1826	Aug. 14	Montgomery	11	03	10
Apple, Solomon(C)	1826	Aug. 14	Montgomery	11	03	10
Apple, Solomon(C)	1828	May 16	Montgomery	11	03	10
Appleton, Abel(A)	1807	Sept. 19	Hamilton	01	03	26
Appleton, Thomas(A)	1807	Aug. 26	Hamilton	01	03	26
Appleton, Thomas(A)	1813	April 14	Butler	01	03	26
Arbocosh, Peter(C)	1812	Jan. 30	Champaign	10	06	19
Arbocost, Michael(C)	1813	Jan. 28	Champaign	10	05	20
Arbogast, Michael(C)	1813	Nov. 30	Champaign	10	05	21
Arbogast, Silas(A)	1835	Jan. 28	Clark	08	02	32
Archer, Benjamin(C)	1801	Dec. 29	Hamilton	06	02	19
Archer, David(B)	1815	May 24	Montgomery	02	10	02
Archer, David(C)	1818	Oct. 07	Logan	13	03	11
Archer, John(C)	1829	Oct. 05	Logan	13	03	17
Archibald, David(C)	1814	Sept. 27	Montgomery	08	02	11
Archibald, Robert(B)	1816	Sept. 10	Cincinnati	02	09	06

7

PURCHASER	YEAR	DATE	RESIDENCE	R	T	S
Archibald, Robert(C)	1814	Sept. 27	Montgomery	08	02	11
Arderey, William(B)	1811	Nov. 02	Kentucky	01	09	14
Ardery, William(B)	1811	Nov. 21	Kentucky	01	09	23
Arehart, Andrew(B)	1818	June 26	Butler	01	16	36
Arehart, Michael(B)	1818	June 26	Butler	01	16	36
Arhard, Michael(A)	1816	March 06	Butler	02	04	22
Armacost, Christophel Murray(E	1835	Oct. 28	Maryland	15	19	29
Armacost, John Murray(E)	1835	Oct. 28	Maryland	15	19	04
Armagost, John(E)	1837	Dec. 13	Maryland	15	19	30
Armantrout, Charles(A)	1818	Sept. 30	Preble	02	09	20
Armentrout, Chas.(A)	1828	Nov. 28	Preble	02	09	21
Armetrout, Charles(A)	1806	Nov. 26	Montgomery	02	08	23
Armstrong, Archibald(A)	1802	July 27	Hamilton	02	05	09
Armstrong, Cyrus(C)	1831	Aug. 08	Clark	08	06	30
Armstrong, Edward(C)	1806	April 26	Champaign	09	05	05
Armstrong, Edward(C)	1811	Aug. 13	Champaign	09	05	05
Armstrong, Edward(C)	1811	Dec. 11	Champaign	09	05	05
Armstrong, Edward(C)	1816	Dec. 02	Champaign	09	05	05
Armstrong, Ephraim(B)	1808	July 04	Ind.Territory	01	11	02
Armstrong, Henry(E)	1836	Jan. 27	Franklin(Ind	13	12	29
Armstrong, James	1808	March 02	Hamilton	?	?	?
Armstrong, James S.(A)	1837	Feb. 22	Cincinnati	02	14	29
Armstrong, James S.(A)	1837	Feb. 22	Cincinnati	02	14	29
Armstrong, James S.(A)	1837	Feb. 22	Cincinnati	02	14	28
Armstrong, James S.(A)	1837	Feb. 22	Cincinnati	02	14	33
Armstrong, James S.(A)	1837	Feb. 22	Cincinnati	02	14	34
Armstrong, James S.(A)	1837	Feb. 22	Cincinnati	03	12	24
Armstrong, James S.(A)	1837	Feb. 22	Cincinnati	03	13	32
Armstrong, James S.(A)	1837	Feb. 22	Cincinnati	02	15	21
Armstrong, James S.(A)	1837	Feb. 22	Cincinnati	01	13	02
Armstrong, James S.(A)	1837	Feb. 22	Cincinnati	01	13	03
Armstrong, James S.(A)	1838	May 21	Cincinnati	01	14	11
Armstrong, James S.(A)	1838	May 21	Cincinnati	01	14	20
Armstrong, James S.(A)	1838	May 21	Cincinnati	02	14	34
Armstrong, James S.(A)	1838	May 21	Cincinnati	02	15	28
Armstrong, James S.(A)	1838	May 21	Cincinnati	03	11	17
Armstrong, James S.(A)	1838	May 21	Cincinnati	03	12	27
Armstrong, James S.(A)	1838	May 21	Cincinnati	03	12	27
Armstrong, James S.(A)	1840	April 01	Cincinnati	02	14	22
Armstrong, James S.(A)	1840	April 01	Cincinnati	02	14	22
Armstrong, James S.(A)	1840	April 01	Cincinnati	01	13	09
Armstrong, James S.(A)	1840	April 01	Cincinnati	02	14	26
Armstrong, James S.(E)	1838	May 21	Cincinnati	13	21	13
Armstrong, James S.(E)	1838	May 21	Cincinnati	13	21	13
Armstrong, James S.(E)	1838	May 21	Cincinnati	13	21	25
Armstrong, James S.(E)	1838	May 21	Cincinnati	14	19	04
Armstrong, James S.(E)	1838	May 21	Cincinnati	15	20	31
Armstrong, James S.(E)	1838	May 21	Cincinnati	15	20	32
Armstrong, James(A)	1835	May 18	Hamilton	02	12	21
Armstrong, James(B)	1814	Nov. 15	Hamilton	02	11	12
Armstrong, Job(A)	1836	Nov. 30	Morgan	03	11	05
Armstrong, John	1808	March 02	Hamilton	?	?	?
Armstrong, John(A)	1834	March 22	Darke	01	13	35
Armstrong, John(B)	1817	Nov. 15	Indiana	02	03	26
Armstrong, John(B)	1818	June 16	Cincinnati	01	06	21
Armstrong, John(C)	1807	Jan. 01	Cincinnati	05	04	30
Armstrong, John(C)	1807	Jan. 01	Cincinnati	10	02	36
Armstrong, John(E)	1818	June 29	Cincinnati	13	21	11
Armstrong, Nathaniel	1808	March 02	Hamilton	?	?	?
Armstrong, Rachel(A)	1811	July 06	Darke	04	09	02
Armstrong, Rachel(A)	1811	July 08	Darke	02	12	35
Armstrong, Rachel(A)	1811	Dec. 12	Darke	02	12	26
Armstrong, Richard(A)	1818	Aug. 03	Miami	05	08	26
Armstrong, Robert(A)	1837	Dec. 23	Cincinnati	01	13	28
Armstrong, Robert(E)	1839	Feb. 09	Cincinnati	14	21	30
Armstrong, Robt.(E)	1839	June 06	Cincinnati	15	22	01
Armstrong, Samuel(A)	1835	May 18	Hamilton	02	12	21
Armstrong, Thomas	1808	March 01	Hamilton	?	?	?
Armstrong, Thomas(C)	1813	April 15	Champaign	09	05	25

PURCHASER	YEAR	DATE	RESIDENCE	R	T	S
Armstrong, Walter(B)	1814	April 14	Dearborn(Ind	01	06	33
Armstrong, Walter(B)	1835	Oct. 26	Dearborn(Ind	02	02	29
Armstrong, Walter(B)	1835	Oct. 26	Dearborn(Ind	03	03	23
Armstrong, Walter(B)	1835	Oct. 26	Dearborn(Ind	02	02	20
Armstrong, Walter(B)	1835	Oct. 26	Dearborn(Ind	02	02	17
Armstrong, Walter(B)	1835	Oct. 26	Dearborn(Ind	02	02	19
Armstrong, Walter(B)	1835	Oct. 26	Dearborn(Ind	02	02	30
Armstrong, Walter(B)	1835	Oct. 26	Dearborn(Ind	02	02	31
Armstrong, William(B)	1812	Aug. 07	Butler	01	09	09
Armstrong, William(B)	1836	July 29	Dearborn(Ind	03	04	27
Armstrong, Wm.(B)	1837	Dec. 15	Switzerland	03	04	21
Arnd, David(A)	1829	Dec. 01	Miami	04	07	22
Arnd, David(A)	1831	April 15	Miami	04	07	22
Arnd, Henry(A)	1829	June 30	Montgomery	04	07	27
Arneet, George(A)	1823	Dec. 10	Montgomery	04	06	01
Arnet, William(E)	1811	Oct. 23	Franklin(Ind	13	11	04
Arnett, Asbury(E)	1835	Sept. 14	Greene	13	18	26
Arnett, Jesse(E)	1837	Feb. 02	Wayne(Ind)	13	21	36
Arnett, Samuel(B)	1805	July 11	Ind.Territry	01	13	18
Arnett, Samuel(B)	1805	July 24	Ind.Territry	02	09	32
Arnett, William(B)	1804	Dec. 26	Ind.Territry	02	08	04
Arnett, William(E)	1811	Oct. 23	Franklin(Ind	13	11	05
Arnett, Willis(E)	1837	Feb. 02	Wayne(Ind)	13	21	36
Arnett, Willis(E)	1837	March 22	Wayne(Ind)	13	21	26
Arney, Jacob(C)	1811	May 01	Champaign	11	05	12
Arney, Jacob(C)	1813	April 06	Champaign	11	05	06
Arnold, Benj'n.(B)	1831	Nov. 16	Wayne(Ind)	01	16	15
Arnold, Charles(C)	1806	Nov. 10	Kentucky	11	04	21
Arnold, David(A)	1814	Sept. 24	Miami	04	09	13
Arnold, David(A)	1821	Aug. 02	Darke	02	11	24
Arnold, David(A)	1831	Dec. 01	Miami	04	09	34
Arnold, Elijah(E)	1833	June 04	Randolph(Ind	13	18	04
Arnold, Elijah(E)	1833	June 04	Randolph(Ind	13	18	05
Arnold, George(A)	1830	Dec. 30	Darke	02	11	13
Arnold, George(B)	1816	Sept. 05	Hamilton	03	03	14
Arnold, Jacob Jr.(A)	1827	April 23	Montgomery	04	07	34
Arnold, Jacob(A)	1816	Nov. 23	Montgomery	04	06	12
Arnold, Jacob(C)	1804	Dec. 31	Greene	07	03	22
Arnold, Jacob(C)	1806	March 24	Montgomery	08	02	18
Arnold, Jeremiah(B)	1831	Sept. 14	Randolph(Ind	01	16	34
Arnold, John R.(B)	1818	March 19	Hamilton	02	05	08
Arnold, John(A)	1805	July 04	Montgomery	04	05	01
Arnold, John(E)	1811	Oct. 21	Butler	12	12	10
Arnold, John(E)	1816	Dec. 02	Franklin(Ind	12	12	10
Arnold, Moses(A)	1816	Oct. 12	Warren	02	11	13
Arnold, Richard(B)	1814	Feb. 12	Hamilton	01	11	06
Arnold, William(A)	1815	Aug. 23	Warren	02	11	11
Arnold, William(A)	1826	Jan. 16	Darke	03	09	03
Arnold, William(B)	1818	March 19	Hamilton	02	05	17
Arnold, William(B)	1830	April 10	Randolph(Ind	01	16	26
Arnold, William(B)	1832	March 13	Wayne(Ind)	01	15	03
Arnt, Bartholomew(A)	1813	June 05	Montgomery	04	06	35
Arnt, David(A)	1818	June 04	Montgomery	04	06	12
Arnt, Jacob(A)	1828	Aug. 14	Montgomery	04	07	33
Arnt, John(A)	1830	Aug. 27	Montgomery	04	07	33
Arrowsmith, Ezekiel(C)	1804	Sept. 26	Greene	11	04	12
Arrowsmith, Ezekiel(C)	1816	Nov. 04	Champaign	11	03	22
Arstingstall, Barnard(A)	1820	April 24	Hamilton	05	10	23
Ascue, Amos(E)	1814	April 11	Franklin(Ind	12	15	20
Ashbaugh, Jacob(A)	1833	May 28	Logan	08	01	02
Ashbey, Bladen(B)	1806	Oct. 28	Butler	01	14	12
Ashbrook, Aaron(?)	1811	Dec. 16	Fairfield	14	14	18
Ashbrook, William(A)	1831	Nov. 16	Logan	08	02	27
Ashby, Abraham(A)	1817	July 11	Wayne(Ind)	01	11	29
Ashby, Abraham(A)	1817	July 11	Wayne(Ind)	01	11	29
Ashby, Bayliss(B)	1801	Sept. 16	Kentucky	01	07	14
Ashby, Bladen(A)	1802	March 23	Hamilton	04	02	18
Ashby, Bladen(B)	1807	Jan. 29	Butler	01	14	12
Ashby, Bladen(B)	1812	April 15	Wayne(Ind)	01	14	12

PURCHASER	YEAR	DATE	RESIDENCE	R	T	S
Ashby, David(E)	1834	Oct. 13	Clinton	13	19	22
Ashby, Hankerson(A)	1817	Aug. 15	Wayne(Ind)	01	11	32
Ashcraft, Felix(A)	1807	Jan. 14	Dearborn(Ind	01	04	32
Ashcraft, Felix(A)	1812	April 15	Butler	01	04	32
Ashcraft, Felix(A)	1814	Jan. 15	Butler	01	04	33
Ashcraft, Felix(A)	1814	Jan. 26	Butler	01	03	04
Ashford, William(B)	1832	Oct. 29	Dearborn(Ind	02	07	27
Ashley, Alanson(A)	1831	Dec. 19	Darke	03	11	32
Ashley, William(B)	1819	Nov. 26	Dearborn(Ind	02	07	12
Ashton, William(B)	1834	June 11	England	01	08	05
Ashton, William(B)	1834	July 21	England	01	08	08
Askew, Amos(E)	1815	May 26	Franklin(Ind	12	13	25
Askren, David(C)	1809	Nov. 15	Champaign	13	04	23
Asmann, Herman Hy.(E)	1836	Nov. 11	Cincinnati	12	10	10
Asmann, John Bernard Hy.(E)	1837	May 15	Cincinnati	12	11	15
Aston, John(A)	1837	Feb. 22	Hamilton	02	14	28
Aston, John(B)	1818	March 28	Hamilton	03	04	14
Aston, Samuel(B)	1818	March 28	Butler	03	04	20
Atchison, Silas(A)	1815	Nov. 30	Montgomery	04	10	19
Atchison, Silas(A)	1818	May 05	Ohio	03	10	30
Atchison, Silas(A)	1818	May 26	Darke	03	10	30
Atchison, Silas(A)	1818	July 18	Montgomery	03	10	30
Aten, Adrain(A)	1814	Dec. 20	Kentucky	03	06	35
Aten, Adrian(A)	1814	Oct. 19	Kentucky	03	06	13
Athearn, Prince(B)	1814	Dec. 27	Hamilton	02	03	13
Atherton, Amos(B)	1812	Aug. 25	Butler	01	09	27
Atherton, Elijah(B)	1813	Sept. 11	Hamilton	01	09	15
Atherton, James(A)	1831	Dec. 10	Guernsey	08	02	34
Atherton, James(A)	1831	Dec. 10	Guernsey	08	02	33
Atherton, Peter(A)	1802	Jan. 04	Hamilton	01	02	02
Atkins, Chauncey(C)	1813	Aug. 11	Champaign	09	06	25
Atkins, William(A)	1836	Nov. 05	Cincinnati	01	15	28
Atkins, William(B)	1836	Dec. 13	Cincinnati	01	16	12
Atkins, William(B)	1836	Dec. 13	Cincinnati	01	16	13
Atkins, William(B)	1836	Dec. 13	Cincinnati	01	16	25
Atkins, William(B)	1836	Dec. 26	Cincinnati	01	16	12
Atkinson, John(B)	1818	Jan. 02	Cincinnati	02	08	28
Atkinson, Robt.(E)	1819	Jan. 12	Clinton	13	20	14
Atkinson, William(B)	1832	July 02	Switzerland	02	02	29
Atkinson, William(B)	1836	Feb. 25	Switzerland	02	02	29
Atkinson, Wm.(B)	1824	Sept. 23	Switzerland	02	02	29
Atwood, James(A)	1813	Sept. 01	Kentucky	01	07	01
Auchinbaugh, Peter(A)	1834	Nov. 18	Montgomery	02	15	18
Aughe, John(C)	1805	Feb. 25	Warren	05	02	08
Aughenbaugh, Peter(A)	1840	Aug. 01	Montgomery	02	15	21
Aughinbaugh, Peter(A)	1834	Nov. 18	Montgomery	02	15	17
Aughinbaugh, Peter(A)	1834	Nov. 18	Montgomery	02	15	19
Augur, William(E)	1836	Dec. 19	Cincinnati	11	11	11
Aukeney, Henry(A)	1804	Dec. 10	Maryland	02	05	26
Aukerman, John(A)	1806	Feb. 01	Montgomery	02	08	35
Aungst, Christian(B)	1837	May 24	Richland	01	18	35
Austin, Josiah(A)	1836	Nov. 05	Logan	02	14	02
Austin, Josiah(A)	1836	Nov. 05	Logan	02	14	11
Austin, Josiah(A)	1836	Nov. 05	Logan	02	14	23
Austin, Josiah(A)	1836	Nov. 05	Logan	02	14	26
Austin, William(B)	1835	Jan. 20	Switzerland	03	04	32
Austin, William(B)	1835	Jan. 20	Switzerland	03	04	29
Auter, Thomas(A)	1805	Aug. 09	Hamilton	03	02	18
Auter, Thomas(A)	1806	Feb. 18	Butler	02	04	23
Avery, Charles(A)	1815	June 08	Cincinnati	01	02	26
Avery, Simon H.(A)	1815	May 24	Cincinnati	01	02	26
Ayres, Ebenezer B.(A)	1815	Feb. 13	Warren	03	04	29
Ayres, James(A)	1806	Aug. 08	Tennessee	01	09	09
Ayres, John(C)	1813	June 17	Champaign	10	05	21
Ayres, Samuel(A)	1810	Dec. 12	Butler	02	04	09
Ayres, Samuel(B)	1808	Sept. 03	Cincinnati	01	10	19
Babbs, Noah(B)	1814	Aug. 24	Hamilton	01	04	32
Babcock, Thomas(C)	1807	April 06	Warren	08	03	23
Babcock, Thomas(C)	1813	Feb. 19	Greene	08	03	30

PURCHASER	YEAR	DATE	RESIDENCE	R	T	S
Bachus, Marous(B)	1816	Aug. 28	Switzerland	03	02	04
Bachus, Marvin(B)	1816	Oct. 01	Switzerland	02	02	07
Backer, Malyne(C)	1804	Dec. 22	Butler	09	04	25
Aydelott, John(A)	1829	April 30	Butler	04	06	31
Ayer, William(B)	1819	May 15	Dearborn(Ind	02	04	06
Ayers, Alexander H.(A)	1837	April 01	Shelby	03	12	26
Ayers, Alfred(B)	1837	Jan. 27	Darke	01	18	35
Ayers, Amsey(A)	1819	Dec. 08	Warren	04	05	19
Ayers, Ansey(A)	1820	March 03	Warren	04	05	19
Ayers, William C.(A)	1837	April 01	Shelby	03	12	25
Ayres, Caleb(C)	1827	Aug. 23	Hamilton	10	03	28
Ayres, John B.(A)	1817	Aug. 14	Preble	03	06	24
Ayres, John(B)	1817	July 21	Franklin(Ind	02	08	24
Babbitt, Edwin Burr(E)	1832	June 19	Franklin(Ind	12	12	14
Babbs, William(B)	1818	Feb. 26	Hamilton	02	04	33
Babcock, Jacob(C)	1827	March 02	Clark	10	03	15
Babcock, James(B)	1818	March 18	Hamilton	03	07	11
Babcock, William(A)	1832	Aug. 15	Clark	08	01	15
Babinger, Abraham(B)	1817	Sept. 09	Cincinnati	02	07	30
Babst, Anthony(E)	1836	Oct. 03	Pennsylvania	12	10	09
Bachman, Enoch(A)	1830	March 23	Butler	04	06	20
Bachmann, John Henry(A)	1836	April 09	Hamilton	02	13	25
Bachus, John(E)	1836	Oct. 03	Pennsylvania	12	10	09
Backhouse, Allen(B)	1832	Jan. 12	Franklin(Ind	02	08	13
Backhouse, Allen(B)	1836	Jan. 23	Franklin(Ind	02	08	24
Backhouse, James(B)	1811	Dec. 11	Dearborn(Ind	01	07	02
Backhouse, James(B)	1828	Sept. 11	Hamilton	01	07	36
Backus, Marvin(B)	1816	Oct. 01	Switzerland	02	02	07
Bacome, William(C)	1810	April 10	Champaign	11	04	17
Bacon, Henry(C)	1812	Feb. 29	Champaign	11	05	27
Bacon, Henry(C)	1815	March 10	Champaign	12	04	25
Bacon, Henry(C)	1817	Aug. 01	Montgomery	11	05	27
Bacon, Joseph Y.(A)	1816	Aug. 20	Warren	01	07	27
Bacorn, George(C)	1815	Jan. 31	Champaign	12	04	20
Badgley, Joseph Abbot(E)	1833	Jan. 03	Hamilton	14	20	28
Badgley, Robt.(E)	1823	Dec. 18	Hamilton	12	16	01
Baechus, Marvin(A)	1805	Jan. 31	Hamilton	01	02	12
Baeley, Andrew(B)	1814	Dec. 28	Cincinnati	03	04	10
Baeley, Andrew(C)	1815	May 15	Cincinnati	10	04	12
Baggs, Joseph(C)	1828	Nov. 13	Champaign	12	04	11
Baggs, Thomas(B)	1825	July 25	Dearborn(Ind	03	06	14
Bailey, And'w.(A)	1814	Aug. 24	Cincinnati	04	05	12
Bailey, And'w.(B)	1815	Sept. 23	Cincinnati	01	04	21
Bailey, And'w.(E)	1815	Sept. 25	Cincinnati	12	14	23
Bailey, And.(A)	1814	Nov. 24	Cincinnati	01	03	13
Bailey, Andrew(A)	1814	Aug. 20	Cincinnati	01	06	02
Bailey, Andrew(A)	1815	Jan. 07	Cincinnati	04	03	30
Bailey, Andrew(A)	1815	April 01	Cincinnati	02	08	11
Bailey, Andrew(A)	1815	April 01	Cincinnati	01	07	07
Bailey, Andrew(A)	1815	April 01	Cincinnati	03	04	26
Bailey, Andrew(A)	1815	Nov. 01	Cincinnati	02	08	11
Bailey, Andrew(B)	1814	Aug. 04	Cincinnati	03	04	10
Bailey, Andrew(B)	1814	Sept. 15	Cincinnati	01	14	25
Bailey, Andrew(B)	1814	Dec. 31	Cincinnati	02	09	14
Bailey, Andrew(B)	1814	Dec. 08	Cincinnati	03	03	36
Bailey, Andrew(B)	1815	March 25	Cincinnati	01	08	17
Bailey, Andrew(C)	1815	March 20	Cincinnati	10	01	06
Bailey, Andrew(C)	1815	April 10	Cincinnati	11	02	07
Bailey, Andrew(E)	1814	Aug. 09	Cincinnati	13	13	03
Bailey, Andrew(E)	1814	Aug. 20	Cincinnati	13	15	01
Bailey, Andw.(C)	1815	May 04	Cincinnati	11	04	07
Bailey, Andw.(C)	1815	May 04	Cincinnati	11	04	07
Bailey, Andw.(C)	1815	May 04	Cincinnati	12	05	34
Bailey, Andw.(C)	1815	June 03	Cincinnati	10	03	33
Bailey, Andw.(E)	1815	June 19	Cincinnati	12	11	20
Bailey, Andw.(E)	1815	June 19	Cincinnati	12	11	20
Bailey, Daniel(A)	1812	May 09	Hamilton	01	02	08
Bailey, David(B)	1807	June 23	Dearborn(Ind	01	13	23
Bailey, David(B)	1813	April 14	Wayne(Ind)	01	13	23

11

PURCHASER	YEAR	DATE	RESIDENCE	R	T	S
Bailey, David(E)	1813	Dec. 21	Wayne(Ind)	14	17	31
Bailey, George(E)	1836	Sept. 24	Randolph(Ind	13	19	23
Bailey, George(E)	1837	Feb. 18	Randolph(Ind	13	18	09
Bailey, Henry(B)	1817	Aug. 14	Wayne(Ind)	01	16	34
Bailey, Henry(B)	1831	Nov. 04	Randolph(Ind	01	16	12
Bailey, Henry(B)	1831	Nov. 10	Randolph(Ind	01	16	15
Bailey, Henry(E)	1814	March 01	Wayne(Ind)	14	16	06
Bailey, Henry(E)	1815	May 09	Wayne(Ind)	14	16	07
Bailey, Henry(E)	1836	Sept. 13	Montgomery	15	21	21
Bailey, Hiram(E)	1829	Nov. 12	Warren	14	18	24
Bailey, James E.(A)	1831	Aug. 17	Miami	05	07	26
Bailey, James W.(A)	1813	Sept. 02	Franklin(Ind	01	03	07
Bailey, James W.(A)	1813	Sept. 04	Franklin(Ind	01	03	07
Bailey, James(A)	1837	March 28	Preble	01	13	12
Bailey, Job(A)	1835	Dec. 15	Mercer	01	15	17
Bailey, John L.(B)	1837	Feb. 22	Dearborn(Ind	02	04	06
Bailey, John(A)	1832	June 02	Preble	01	09	02
Bailey, John(A)	1835	April 14	Darke	02	13	30
Bailey, John(C)	1801	Dec. 30	Hamilton	06	02	25
Bailey, John(E)	1814	April 15	Wayne(Ind)	13	18	28
Bailey, John(E)	1815	July 25	Wayne(Ind)	13	17	03
Bailey, John(E)	1817	Sept. 01	Wayne(Ind)	13	17	03
Bailey, John(E)	1829	Dec. 10	Wayne(Ind)	13	17	03
Bailey, Leonard(B)	1837	Sept. 30	Switzerland	02	03	06
Bailey, Lewis(C)	1814	Oct. 20	Hamilton	09	06	25
Bailey, Mary(E)	1838	April 26	Randolph(Ind	15	20	20
Bailey, Richard(B)	1814	Aug. 15	Hamilton	01	04	18
Bailey, Stanton Jr.(E)	1833	Sept. 16	Wayne(Ind)	15	19	08
Bailey, Stanton(B)	1820	Oct. 21	Wayne(Ind)	01	16	14
Bailey, Stanton(B)	1823	May 12	Randolph(Ind	01	16	14
Bailey, Stanton(E)	1831	Oct. 04	Wayne(Ind)	15	19	09
Bailey, Thomas(A)	1831	June 23	Montgomery	01	09	13
Bailey, Timothy(C)	1815	May 01	Hamilton	09	06	25
Bailey, William(A)	1814	Dec. 26	Pennsylvania	02	07	32
Bailey, William(A)	1832	Aug. 29	Preble	02	13	32
Bailey, William(A)	1836	April 08	Preble	02	13	32
Bailey, William(A)	1837	March 28	Preble	01	13	01
Baily, Henry(C)	1809	Aug. 01	Champaign	09	04	22
Baily, Henry(C)	1809	Aug. 01	Champaign	09	04	27
Baily, Henry(E)	1811	Oct. 25	Warren	14	16	05
Baily, James W.(E)	1811	Oct. 28	Dearborn(Ind	12	12	27
Baily, John(C)	1816	March 15	Montgomery	10	04	33
Bainter, Dan'l.(A)	1831	Dec. 05	Darke	04	09	07
Baird, James(A)	1815	Oct. 03	Preble	01	06	15
Baird, James(B)	1831	Sept. 06	Switzerland	03	02	04
Baird, John	1808	March 01	Virginia	?	?	?
Baird, John	1808	March 01	Virginia	?	?	?
Baird, John	1808	March 01	Virginia	?	?	?
Baird, John	1808	March 02	Virginia	?	?	?
Baird, John	1808	March 02	Virginia	?	?	?
Baird, John(A)	1816	Oct. 02	Pickaway	02	10	09
Baird, John(A)	1816	Nov. 12	Pickaway	08	10	08
Baird, John(A)	1836	May 16	Darke	02	13	29
Baird, Joseph(A)	1805	June 11	Butler	03	03	12
Baird, Thomas(C)	1815	Nov. 29	Greene	09	04	29
Baird, Thomas(E)	1811	Oct. 24	Wayne(Ind)	13	15	19
Baird, William(C)	1818	July 14	Clark	09	06	29
Baird, Zebulon(C)	1808	Sept. 06	Nor.Carolina	09	04	18
Baird, Zebulon(C)	1813	Dec. 15	Champaign	09	04	18
Bake, Jacob(B)	1806	Nov. 10	Dearborn(Ind	01	10	13
Bake, John(B)	1824	June 09	Franklin(Ind	01	10	21
Bake, William(B)	1827	Oct. 18	Union(Ind)	01	10	22
Baker, Aaron(C)	1812	Feb. 13	Montgomery	07	02	30
Baker, Abraham S.(C)	1827	Aug. 23	Champaign	11	03	15
Baker, Benj'n.(A)	1830	Feb. 01	Montgomery	04	06	17
Baker, Benjamin(A)	1837	June 16	Montgomery	01	14	04
Baker, Christopher(E)	1819	May 17	Ross	15	20	20
Baker, Clark(A)	1831	Oct. 18	Butler	03	08	18
Baker, Dan'l.(C)	1828	May 05	Champaign	11	03	13

12

PURCHASER	YEAR	DATE	RESIDENCE	R	T	S
Baker, Daniel(C)	1813	April 14	Champaign	11	06	25
Baker, David Clark(A)	1834	Oct. 06	Montgomery	08	01	05
Baker, David Clark(A)	1834	Oct. 06	Montgomery	08	01	08
Baker, David Clark(A)	1834	Oct. 23	Montgomery	08	01	14
Baker, Enoch(E)	1837	May 16	Clark	14	20	06
Baker, Enoch(E)	1837	May 16	Clark	14	21	19
Baker, Enos(A)	1831	April 18	Montgomery	03	07	01
Baker, Evan(A)	1832	April 03	Darke	03	08	30
Baker, Frederick(A)	1815	Dec. 21	Montgomery	04	04	21
Baker, Fredrick(A)	1805	May 14	Montgomery	05	03	30
Baker, George(A)	1831	Nov. 07	Preble	02	09	04
Baker, Henry(A)	1836	Oct. 25	Warren	03	12	09
Baker, Henry(C)	1811	Dec. 11	Champaign	10	04	20
Baker, Jacob(A)	1815	Dec. 30	Warren	04	04	15
Baker, Jacob(A)	1829	July 02	Montgomery	04	06	08
Baker, Jacob(C)	1813	June 24	Champaign	10	04	14
Baker, Jacob(C)	1824	Dec. 17	Clark	10	03	14
Baker, James(A)	1829	Feb. 27	Preble	01	10	31
Baker, John(A)	1803	June 23	Butler	03	03	25
Baker, John(A)	1818	Jan. 05	Montgomery	04	06	28
Baker, John(A)	1818	June 27	Butler	01	02	31
Baker, John(A)	1831	Dec. 05	Shelby	07	01	05
Baker, John(E)	1813	Sept. 10	Franklin(Ind	12	15	26
Baker, John(E)	1813	Oct. 14	Franklin(Ind	12	13	24
Baker, John(E)	1836	Sept. 03	Butler	14	21	19
Baker, Jonathan(A)	1831	June 11	Preble	02	11	25
Baker, Jonathan(E)	1817	Nov. 03	Montgomery	12	11	33
Baker, Joseph E.(B)	1836	May 02	Dearborn(Ind	02	05	07
Baker, Joseph(A)	1830	April 23	Montgomery	04	06	19
Baker, Joshua(B)	1834	Jan. 15	Franklin(Ind	02	08	20
Baker, Mark(B)	1818	Nov. 16	Hamilton	03	06	33
Baker, Martin(B)	1836	March 22	Franklin(Ind	02	08	29
Baker, Matthias(C)	1828	Dec. 09	Shelby	10	03	29
Baker, Melyn(C)	1806	Feb. 11	Champaign	09	04	25
Baker, Melyn(C)	1806	Feb. 11	Champaign	09	04	25
Baker, Melyn(C)	1806	Feb. 11	Champaign	09	04	25
Baker, Melyn(C)	1806	Feb. 11	Champaign	09	04	25
Baker, Michael(A)	1805	Oct. 19	Montgomery	04	06	26
Baker, Michael(A)	1813	Aug. 11	Montgomery	04	06	27
Baker, Michael(A)	1814	Dec. 08	Montgomery	04	06	27
Baker, Michael(A)	1837	June 16	Montgomery	01	14	04
Baker, Moses(E)	1811	Oct. 22	Ind.Territory	12	13	12
Baker, Philip(C)	1813	May 10	Virginia	10	04	08
Baker, Richard(B)	1825	April 04	Switzerland	02	02	09
Baker, Richard(B)	1825	April 04	Switzerland	02	02	07
Baker, Rudolph(C)	1824	Oct. 23	Clark	10	04	26
Baker, Rudolph(C)	1824	Oct. 23	Clark	10	03	08
Baker, Sam'l.(C)	1824	Oct. 25	Clark	10	04	29
Baker, Samuel(C)	1814	Aug. 20	Champaign	10	04	15
Baker, Shelby(B)	1833	Nov. 25	Franklin(Ind	03	09	24
Baker, Shelby(B)	1836	Feb. 27	Franklin(Ind	03	09	24
Baker, Thomas Senr.(E)	1835	Oct. 02	Randolph(Ind	14	21	30
Baker, Thomas(A)	1803	May 18	Hamilton	03	03	25
Baker, Thomas(A)	1817	Dec. 01	Butler	01	09	26
Baker, William(B)	1836	Oct. 07	Franklin(Ind	03	09	13
Baker, William(E)	1814	Feb. 16	Butler	12	15	32
Bakes, Robert(B)	1814	Jan. 07	Ind.Territory	03	02	17
Bakes, Robert(B)	1816	Dec. 11	Switzerland	03	02	17
Bakes, Robert(B)	1817	Dec. 17	Switzerland	03	02	08
Baldridge, Samuel(D)	1812	Aug. 10	Hamilton(Fr	02	01	08
Baldridge, Samuel(E)	1816	Dec. 02	Wayne(Ind)	13	17	30
Baldwin, Amos(B)	1814	Aug. 18	Franklin(Ind	02	09	25
Baldwin, Charles(B)	1813	Dec. 11	Wayne(Ind)	01	15	30
Baldwin, Daniel Jnr.(E)	1818	March 14	Wayne(Ind)	14	18	22
Baldwin, Daniel(B)	1815	Oct. 30	Ohio	01	07	08
Baldwin, Daniel(B)	1815	Oct. 31	Ohio	01	07	08
Baldwin, Daniel(E)	1813	Sept. 22	Wayne(Ind)	14	17	11
Baldwin, Edward(A)	1805	Sept. 16	Montgomery	03	06	20
Baldwin, Elias(A)	1805	Dec. 03	Butler	02	03	06

PURCHASER	YEAR	DATE	RESIDENCE	R	T	S
Baldwin, Elias(B)	1814	Dec. 12	Butler	02	09	02
Baldwin, Enos(C)	1814	Feb. 14	Champaign	12	04	06
Baldwin, Enos(C)	1814	Feb. 14	Champaign	13	04	01
Baldwin, Isaac(E)	1827	Nov. 14	Wayne(Ind)	13	17	14
Baldwin, James R.(C)	1811	Sept. 23	Champaign	10	06	33
Baldwin, James R.(C)	1829	Dec. 12	Logan	13	03	23
Baldwin, James(C)	1806	July 10	Champaign	12	05	19
Baldwin, James(C)	1806	July 10	Champaign	10	06	33
Baldwin, James(C)	1808	June 06	Champaign	10	06	34
Baldwin, James(C)	1811	Aug. 13	Champaign	10	06	33
Baldwin, James(C)	1812	April 14	Champaign	10	05	06
Baldwin, Jesse(E)	1819	Jan. 23	Wayne(Ind)	13	18	26
Baldwin, Jesse(E)	1819	May 22	Wayne(Ind)	13	18	26
Baldwin, John Senr.(E)	1826	March 16	Wayne(Ind)	13	17	14
Baldwin, John(E)	1811	Nov. 18	Wayne(Ind)	14	17	14
Baldwin, John(E)	1814	June 10	Wayne(Ind)	14	17	14
Baldwin, John(E)	1817	Dec. 20	Wayne(Ind)	14	18	33
Baldwin, Jonah(C)	1813	April 14	Champaign	10	05	04
Baldwin, Jonah(C)	1813	Sept. 27	Champaign	10	05	10
Baldwin, Jonas(B)	1815	Sept. 11	Warren	03	03	25
Baldwin, Joshua(C)	1806	May 12	Champaign	10	05	09
Baldwin, Joshua(C)	1806	May 12	Champaign	10	05	02
Baldwin, Joshua(C)	1806	May 21	Champaign	10	05	05
Baldwin, Joshua(C)	1806	May 21	Champaign	10	05	05
Baldwin, Joshua(C)	1806	July 10	Champaign	12	05	19
Baldwin, Joshua(C)	1806	July 10	Champaign	10	06	33
Baldwin, Joshua(C)	1811	Aug. 13	Champaign	10	06	33
Baldwin, Joshua(C)	1811	Aug. 13	Champaign	10	05	05
Baldwin, Joshua(C)	1811	Aug. 13	Champaign	10	05	05
Baldwin, Joshua(C)	1811	Sept. 23	Champaign	10	06	33
Baldwin, Joshua(C)	1811	Sept. 23	Champaign	10	05	05
Baldwin, Joshua(C)	1812	April 14	Champaign	10	05	06
Baldwin, Joshua(C)	1817	Aug. 01	Virginia	10	05	06
Baldwin, Lucas(A)	1814	Oct. 10	Butler	01	07	05
Baldwin, Lucas(A)	1814	Nov. 26	Butler	02	06	17
Baldwin, Thomas(B)	1815	Jan. 02	Champaign	02	09	13
Baldwin, Thomas(E)	1812	Nov. 11	Wayne(Ind)	14	17	14
Baldwin, William(A)	1805	Aug. 14	Montgomery	03	06	06
Baldwin, William(A)	1805	Aug. 14	Montgomery	03	06	05
Balenger, Isaac(A)	1805	Aug. 21	Montgomery	05	07	29
Balenger, Jonathan(A)	1805	July 25	Montgomery	05	06	04
Balentine, Robt.(E)	1838	Oct. 02	Clark	14	21	34
Bales, Clark(B)	1811	Dec. 11	Hamilton	02	10	13
Bales, Dilevin(E)	1815	Dec. 05	Wayne(Ind)	13	17	07
Bales, Dilwin(E)	1816	May 29	Wayne(Ind)	13	17	06
Balinger, Daniel(A)	1815	Jan. 21	Miami	04	09	14
Balinger, Isaac(A)	1815	Jan. 21	Miami	04	09	23
Ball, Abener(E)	1813	Nov. 10	Butler	12	14	27
Ball, Calvin(C)	1801	Dec. 05	Hamilton	04	04	30
Ball, Chester(E)	1836	Aug. 18	Warren	14	19	23
Ball, Ezekiel(C)	1822	Oct. 31	Butler	12	02	09
Ball, James(A)	1804	Sept. 15	Hamilton	01	02	14
Ball, James(C)	1812	Dec. 30	Greene	09	03	13
Ball, Nelson Smith(E)	1835	March 30	Randolph(Ind	13	19	04
Ballard, Anderson S.(A)	1819	July 05	Montgomery	02	10	17
Ballenger, Benj'n.(E)	1826	Feb. 27	Ross	13	17	11
Ballenger, David(E)	1835	March 18	Franklin(Ind	11	12	12
Ballenger, Evan(A)	1818	March 31	Miami	04	09	03
Ballenger, James(E)	1826	Dec. 23	Wayne(Ind)	13	17	11
Ballenger, Joshua(E)	1815	Nov. 07	Ross	13	17	02
Ballenger, William(E)	1816	Oct. 24	Kentucky	13	17	01
Ballinger, Isaac(A)	1813	April 23	Miami	05	07	29
Ballinger, James(E)	1835	May 27	Randolph(Ind	13	18	01
Ballinger, James(E)	1836	April 21	Randolph(Ind	13	18	02
Ballinger, Jess(E)	1817	June 04	Wayne(Ind)	13	20	34
Ballinger, John(E)	1816	Dec. 05	Clinton	13	20	27
Bals, William(B)	1836	Sept. 26	Franklin(Ind	03	09	36
Balser, Abraham(E)	1837	Nov. 13	Butler	14	21	32
Baltimore, Philip(C)	1801	Nov. 25	?	05	03	24

14

PURCHASER	YEAR	DATE	RESIDENCE	R	T	S
Baltimore, Philip(E)	1816	Oct. 31	Montgomery	12	17	24
Bambarger, William(A)	1806	Nov. 06	Montgomery	06	02	03
Band, Edward(E)	1811	Nov. 09	Wayne(Ind)	14	17	22
Band, Joseph(E)	1811	Nov. 09	Wayne(Ind)	14	17	15
Banebrak, Jacob(A)	1814	Dec. 29	Preble	01	08	24
Banes, Evan & Co.(C)	1804	Dec. 31	Warren	05	03	22
Banes, Evan(C)	1804	Dec. 24	Warren	05	04	28
Banes, Evan(C)	1804	Dec. 24	Warren	05	03	15
Banes, Horatio(C)	1813	Oct. 25	Champaign	10	05	22
Banes, Sarah(C)	1812	June 27	Champaign	10	05	22
Banfield, Enoch(A)	1814	Dec. 17	Preble	02	08	14
Banfill, Enoch(A)	1813	July 16	Preble	03	07	10
Banfill, John(A)	1813	April 14	Preble	02	08	25
Banfill, John(A)	1814	Nov. 03	Preble	02	08	23
Banfill, John(A)	1814	Oct. 01	Preble	02	08	23
Banfill, Thomas(A)	1814	Oct. 01	Preble	02	08	23
Banker, Jos.(A)	1813	Sept. 21	Butler	04	03	34
Banks, Adam(E)	1813	Oct. 01	Wayne(Ind)	12	15	27
Banks, Thomas S.(E)	1836	Nov. 28	Cincinnati	12	12	31
Banner, Jacob(A)	1814	Nov. 14	Montgomery	01	08	11
Banta, Albert(A)	1837	Feb. 16	Randolph(Ind	01	13	28
Banta, Albert(E)	1818	Feb. 06	Preble	14	20	26
Banta, Albert(E)	1818	Feb. 07	Preble	14	20	26
Banta, Albert(E)	1818	Feb. 07	Preble	13	20	23
Banta, Albert(E)	1818	March 09	Preble	14	20	23
Banta, Albert(E)	1818	March 20	Preble	14	19	10
Banta, Albert(E)	1818	April 21	Preble	14	19	03
Banta, Albert(E)	1818	April 27	Randolph(Ind	14	19	02
Banta, Benj'n.(A)	1831	Jan. 27	Preble	02	09	02
Banta, Daniel(A)	1815	Aug. 25	Warren	02	09	13
Banta, Isaac(B)	1832	Sept. 03	Switzerland	03	02	19
Banta, Peter(A)	1831	Aug. 09	Preble	03	06	19
Banta, Peter(A)	1831	Aug. 09	Preble	03	06	19
Banter, Adam(C)	1816	Oct. 29	Virginia	12	03	10
Bantz, Ezra(A)	1831	Aug. 19	Montgomery	03	96	97
Bantz, John(A)	1817	Dec. 05	Preble	03	06	07
Barbae, William(A)	1805	Dec. 04	Montgomery	06	05	07
Barbe, William(A)	1805	Sept. 05	Ohio	06	05	28
Barbee, Elias(C)	1831	Sept. 13	Butler	13	02	02
Barbee, William(A)	1803	Dec. 22	Kentucky	06	05	08
Barbee, William(A)	1803	Dec. 22	Kentucky	06	05	17
Barber, Hallett(A)	1836	Sept. 24	Delaware	02	13	21
Barber, Hallett(A)	1836	Oct. 29	Darke	02	13	21
Barber, Isaac(E)	1817	June 04	Wayne(Ind)	13	20	23
Barber, James(A)	1809	July 01	Kentucky	01	04	19
Barber, James(A)	1809	July 01	Kentucky	01	04	31
Barber, John(A)	1816	Aug. 19	Butler	05	08	08
Barber, John(B)	1816	Aug. 01	Dearborn(Ind	01	07	05
Barber, John(B)	1834	Oct. 21	Dearborn(Ind	01	07	05
Barber, John(C)	1830	Nov. 01	New Jersey	13	01	01
Barbour, Thos.(A)	1831	Aug. 17	Miami	05	07	12
Barcalow, Jno. Marshall(A)	1835	Oct. 20	Montgomery	01	14	09
Barcalow, William Francis(A)	1835	Oct. 20	Montgomery	01	14	09
Barcalow, Wm. Francis(A)	1831	Sept. 09	Montgomery	05	09	21
Bard, Samuel(A)	1813	Sept. 01	Butler	02	05	18
Bardleman, Henry Jos.(E)	1837	April 28	Cincinnati	11	11	25
Bardleman, Jno. Hy. Jos.(E)	1838	May 07	Cincinnati	11	11	35
Bardwell, Simeon(C)	1807	Feb. 24	Champaign	09	06	24
Bare, David(C)	1807	April 13	Champaign	09	06	35
Bare, Jacob(A)	1812	Aug. 20	Warren	03	05	26
Bare, Jacob(A)	1817	Aug. 22	Warren	03	06	25
Barekman, Jacob(B)	1811	April 15	Kentucky	02	09	10
Barger, Jacob(C)	1832	March 02	Champaign	12	04	21
Baricklow, Farrington(B)	1813	Nov. 12	Pennsylvania	01	04	19
Baricklow, John(B)	1813	Nov. 12	Pennsylvania	01	04	19
Baricklow, John(B)	1815	Oct. 03	Dearborn(Ind	01	03	06
Barkalaw, William(A)	1801	Aug. 17	Kentucky	05	02	33
Barkalaw, William(A)	1801	Aug. 17	Kentucky	05	01	03
Barkalow, Derrick(A)	1836	Nov. 12	Warren	03	11	03

15

PURCHASER	YEAR	DATE	RESIDENCE	R	T	S
Barkalow, William P.(C)	1816	Aug. 26	Warren	12	01	18
Barkalow, William P.(C)	1818	April 08	Warren	13	01	07
Barkalow, William(A)	1836	Dec. 01	Butler	02	14	09
Barker, Austin(C)	1826	Nov. 04	Shelby	14	01	19
Barker, Edwin(A)	1819	Sept. 03	Shelby	06	08	07
Barker, Hiram(B)	1839	Feb. 22	Dearborn(Ind	02	03	06
Barker, Hiram(B)	1839	Feb..22	Dearborn(Ind	03	04	15
Barker, Isaac(A)	1831	Oct. 22	Hamilton	01	09	13
Barker, Isaac(A)	1831	Oct. 22	Hamilton	01	09	14
Barker, Isaac(B)	1808	Aug. 11	Dearborn(Ind	01	14	08
Barker, Jacob(D)	1813	Dec. 15	Hamilton(Fr)	02	04	11
Barker, Joseph(B)	1818	May 26	Dearborn(Ind	02	03	04
Barkhurst, George(A)	1819	Aug. 07	Warren	02	08	15
Barkhurst, Isaac(B)	1835	May 06	Dearborn(Ind	01	07	07
Barkley, Edward(C)	1808	Oct. 20	Warren	10	06	25
Barkley, John(C)	1814	Dec. 08	Warren	08	06	04
Barkshire, Dickey(B)	1804	Nov. 15	Kentucky	02	04	31
Barkuloo, John(B)	1814	Aug. 26	Butler	01	06	12
Barkuloo, John(B)	1818	July 09	Dearborn(Ind	01	07	08
Barkuloo, John(B)	1818	Aug. 01	Dearborn(Ind	01	07	07
Barley, James(B)	1807	March 23	Dearborn(Ind	02	11	26
Barlow, Joseph(C)	1804	Dec. 28	Greene	09	03	30
Barn, Michael(A)	1816	March 26	Miami	05	08	20
Barnard, George(B)	1814	Aug. 15	Hamilton	02	02	03
Barnard, James(A)	1808	June 14	Montgomery	06	03	28
Barnard, Saml.(A)	1813	Aug. 10	Montgomery	06	03	28
Barner, John(C)	1807	Feb. 05	Hamilton	08	05	28
Barner, John(E)	1820	Feb. 08	Wayne(Ind)	14	18	30
Barnes, Absalom(A)	1814	Sept. 09	Hamilton	01	02	04
Barnes, Benoni(C)	1824	June 28	Champaign	11	04	26
Barnes, Isaac(E)	1815	July 06	Wayne(Ind)	13	18	07
Barnes, Jared(A)	1817	Aug. 05	Darke	02	12	18
Barnes, John(A)	1831	March 29	Darke	01	13	33
Barnes, John(A)	1831	June 25	Darke	01	13	33
Barnes, John(C)	1812	April 15	Champaign	08	05	28
Barnes, John(E)	1820	Sept. 06	Wayne(Ind)	14	18	24
Barnes, Stephen(B)	1833	Oct. 22	Randolph(Ind	01	16	25
Barnes, Thomas E. F.(E)	1836	Dec. 05	Montgomery	15	20	17
Barnes, Thomas(A)	1830	Oct. 28	Darke	01	12	05
Barnes, Thomas(A)	1835	Aug. 24	Darke	01	12	04
Barnes, William(C)	1813	June 16	Champaign	13	04	13
Barnes, William(E)	1814	May 17	Ross	13	18	20
Barnes, William(E)	1836	Oct. 11	Randolph(Ind	14	19	23
Barnet, Abraham(C)	1804	Dec. 31	Montgomery	07	03	32
Barnet, John(C)	1801	Dec. 31	Hamilton	07	01	07
Barnet, John(C)	1802	Dec. 31	Hamilton	05	02	19
Barnet, John(C)	1804	Sept. 04	Montgomery	06	01	11
Barnet, Philip(B)	1818	July 29	Hamilton	01	07	35
Barnett, James(C)	1806	Nov. 01	Montgomery	06	01	12
Barnett, Joseph(A)	1836	Aug. 18	Montgomery	02	15	20
Barnhart, Jacob(A)	1815	Nov. 20	Maryland	02	06	14
Barnhart, Jacob(C)	1829	June 18	Champaign	11	03	24
Barnhill, Robert(A)	1805	Sept. 23	Kentucky	02	05	11
Barns, Blackslee(B)	1815	Nov. 29	Pennsylvania	02	09	09
Barns, James(C)	1802	Dec. 31	Hamilton	06	03	31
Barns, Robert(A)	1808	Jan. 12	Miami	06	06	31
Barnum, Daniel Jr.(A)	1836	Aug. 03	New York	03	12	36
Barr, Alexander(A)	1815	June 14	Preble	01	09	26
Barr, James(C)	1815	Aug. 21	Champaign	10	05	24
Barr, John(C)	1829	Dec. 12	Logan	13	03	11
Barr, Robert(C)	1831	Aug. 08	Champaign	14	03	08
Barr, Robert(C)	1831	Aug. 08	Champaign	13	05	29
Barr, Robert(C)	1831	Aug. 08	Champaign	14	03	08
Barr, Robert(C)	1831	Aug. 08	Champaign	13	05	29
Barr, Robert(C)	1831	Aug. 08	Champaign	14	04	33
Barr, Robert(C)	1831	Aug. 08	Champaign	14	04	33
Barr, Robert(C)	1831	Aug. 09	Champaign	12	04	05
Barr, William(A)	1818	April 20	Hamilton	01	02	08
Barr, William(B)	1811	April 12	Cincinnati	02	09	17

PURCHASER	YEAR	DATE	RESIDENCE	R	T	S
Barr, William(B)	1818	Feb. 26	Cincinnati	03	04	14
Barr, William(B)	1818	Feb. 26	Cincinnati	03	03	02
Barr, William(B)	1818	Feb. 26	Cincinnati	03	04	28
Barr, William(B)	1818	Feb. 26	Cincinnati	03	04	27
Barr, William(B)	1818	April 22	Hamilton	01	06	06
Barr, William(B)	1818	April 22	Hamilton	01	06	06
Barr, William(B)	1818	April 22	Hamilton	01	06	06
Barr, William(B)	1818	April 22	Hamilton	01	06	06
Barr, William(B)	1818	April 22	Hamilton	01	06	05
Barr, William(B)	1818	April 22	Hamilton	01	06	05
Barr, William(B)	1818	April 22	Hamilton	01	06	05
Barr, William(B)	1818	April 22	Hamilton	01	06	05
Barr, William(B)	1818	April 25	Hamilton	02	06	23
Barr, William(B)	1818	April 25	Hamilton	02	06	23
Barr, William(B)	1818	April 25	Hamilton	02	06	14
Barr, William(B)	1818	April 25	Hamilton	03	07	24
Barr, William(B)	1818	April 25	Hamilton	02	02	17
Barr, William(B)	1818	April 25	Hamilton	03	04	29
Barr, William(B)	1818	April 25	Hamilton	02	07	27
Barr, William(C)	1816	July 06	Cincinnati	13	02	35
Barr, William(E)	1818	April 09	Cincinnati	14	16	33
Barr, William(E)	1818	April 09	Cincinnati	14	16	33
Barr, Wm.(B)	1818	April 22	Hamilton	01	06	30
Barr, Wm.(B)	1818	April 22	Hamilton	01	06	30
Barrekman, Jacob(B)	1811	March 28	Kentucky	02	10	34
Barret, James(C)	1801	Dec. 08	Hamilton	06	02	09
Barret, William(A)	1831	Feb. 03	Warren	02	12	15
Barrett, Abner(A)	1816	March 15	Miami	04	07	13
Barrett, Caleb(E)	1816	Aug. 15	Montgomery	12	17	25
Barricklow, Farrington(B)	1813	Nov. 06	Pennsylvania	01	04	30
Barricklow, Farrington(B)	1813	Nov. 12	Pennsylvania	01	04	30
Barricklow, Farrington(B)	1816	July 15	Dearborn(Ind	01	04	19
Barricklow, John(B)	1813	Nov. 06	Pennsylvania	01	04	30
Barricklow, John(B)	1813	Nov. 12	Pennsylvania	01	04	30
Barricklow, John(B)	1814	March 14	Dearborn(Ind	02	04	36
Barricklow, John(B)	1815	Sept. 25	Dearborn(Ind	01	03	07
Barricklow, John(B)	1815	Sept. 25	Dearborn(Ind	01	04	21
Barrickman, Jacob(E)	1814	July 25	Franklin(Ind	13	13	20
Barry, James(A)	1813	March 20	Preble	02	06	20
Bart, Casper(A)	1806	Nov. 06	Virginia	02	07	26
Bartel, Jno. Fred'k.(B)	1838	May 14	Cincinnati	03	05	35
Bartel, John Frederick(E)	1837	March 01	Cincinnati	11	10	11
Bartho, William(C)	1807	Feb. 06	Warren	11	02	23
Bartho, Wm.(C)	1812	April 15	Miami	11	02	23
Barton, Levin(A)	1826	Aug. 11	Wayne(Ind)	01	10	21
Barton, Robert(A)	1813	Aug. 23	Warren	01	09	28
Barton, Volentine(B)	1813	May 03	Kentucky	01	04	06
Barton, William Jr.(B)	1836	March 19	Dearborn(Ind	02	06	31
Barton, William(B)	1818	May 11	Hamilton	02	06	31
Barwick,Rawzel Pitt Chandler(E	1836	May 19	Franklin(Ind	12	12	29
Bascom, Erastus Cylvester(B)	1834	July 08	Switzerland	02	03	30
Bascom, Linus(A)	1813	Sept. 01	Montgomery	06	03	35
Bascom, Silas(B)	1817	Nov. 03	Hamilton	03	03	28
Bascum, Isaac Gibson(B)	1833	Sept. 03	Hamilton	03	04	22
Bascum, Linus(A)	1813	July 21	Montgomery	06	02	03
Baskerville,JasMshl.Pnkatham(A	1835	June 10	Darke	03	10	30
Baskerville,JasMshl.Pnkatham(A	1835	June 10	Darke	02	12	21
Baskerville,JasMshl.Pnkatham(A	1835	June 10	Darke	03	10	30
Bass, James(A)	1828	Dec. 12	Darke	01	11	08
Bass, John(A)	1830	Feb. 13	Darke	01	11	08
Bassett, Elisha(A)	1810	Dec. 08	Hamilton	01	04	06
Bassett, Jonathan(B)	1818	April 16	Hamilton	02	10	27
Basye, Lesmund(B)	1812	Feb. 08	Franklin(Ind	02	09	03
Basye, Lesmund(B)	1813	Aug. 20	Franklin(Ind	02	09	08
Bateman, Jeremiah(C)	1814	Sept. 12	Champaign	08	03	03
Bates, Clark(B)	1814	Jan. 11	Hamilton	02	10	13
Bates, Harvey(B)	1816	May 03	Franklin(Ind	02	08	08
Bates, Hervey(A)	1836	Aug. 03	Miami	03	12	25
Bates, Isaac(B)	1817	Oct. 20	Cincinnati	02	02	11

17

PURCHASER	YEAR	DATE	RESIDENCE	R	T	S
Bates, Isaac(C)	1812	Dec. 21	Hamilton	09	05	30
Bates, Isaac(C)	1812	Dec. 21	Hamilton	09	05	30
Bates, Isaac(C)	1813	April 17	Hamilton	09	05	36
Bates, Isaac(C)	1813	May 29	Hamilton	09	05	32
Bates, Isaac(C)	1813	Sept. 14	Hamilton	09	05	32
Bates, James Sr.(B)	1812	Nov. 19	Jefferson	02	02	31
Bates, John(B)	1832	Feb. 22	Wayne(Ind)	01	16	25
Bates, Samuel(C)	1830	April 01	Champaign	12	05	35
Bates, Seth H.(B)	1815	Jan. 30	Butler	02	10	03
Bates, Willis(B)	1816	May 16	Dearborn(Ind	01	03	19
Batterel, John(C)	1804	Dec. 31	Montgomery	09	02	36
Batterell, John(C)	1809	Nov. 13	Miami	11	02	07
Batterell, John(C)	1817	Sept. 23	Champaign	11	03	25
Batterell, John(C)	1828	Sept. 29	Miami	11	03	26
Baty, William(E)	1836	Nov. 08	Franklin(Ind	12	11	19
Bauder, John(A)	1822	April 26	Shelby	05	10	29
Bauer, Alvis(B)	1833	Oct. 28	Germany	02	08	30
Bauer, John(B)	1836	Feb. 22	Franklin(Ind	03	09	24
Baugh, John(E)	1836	Dec. 15	Randolph(Ind	14	21	12
Baugher, Isaac(C)	1813	Dec. 13	Pennsylvania	09	04	08
Baughman, Geo.(A)	1831	April 06	Montgomery	04	06	08
Bauldridge, Samuel(E)	1814	Aug. 04	Wayne(Ind)	13	18	21
Baum, Martin	1808	March 02	Cincinnati	?	?	?
Baum, Martin	1808	March 02	Cincinnati	?	?	?
Baum, Martin	1808	March 02	Cincinnati	?	?	?
Baum, Martin	1808	March 03	Cincinnati	?	?	?
Baum, Martin(A)	1803	April 23	Cincinnati	03	02	13
Baum, Martin(A)	1805	July 05	Cincinnati	01	04	27
Baum, Martin(A)	1810	April 11	Cincinnati	02	05	26
Baum, Martin(A)	1810	April 11	Cincinnati	02	05	26
Baum, Martin(B)	1804	Sept. 18	Cincinnati	01	02	34
Baum, Martin(B)	1804	Nov. 27	Cincinnati	02	04	24
Baum, Martin(B)	1805	Oct. 09	Cincinnati	01	10	08
Baum, Martin(B)	1805	Oct. 09	Cincinnati	01	10	07
Baum, Martin(B)	1805	Oct. 09	Cincinnati	01	10	07
Baum, Martin(B)	1805	Oct. 09	Cincinnati	01	10	08
Baum, Martin(B)	1805	Oct. 09	Cincinnati	02	10	12
Baum, Martin(B)	1805	Oct. 09	Cincinnati	01	10	26
Baum, Martin(B)	1805	Oct. 09	Cincinnati	01	10	02
Baum, Martin(B)	1805	Oct. 09	Cincinnati	01	10	11
Baum, Martin(B)	1805	Oct. 09	Cincinnati	01	10	07
Baum, Martin(B)	1805	Oct. 19	Cincinnati	02	11	33
Baum, Martin(B)	1809	Dec. 12	Cincinnati	01	03	31
Baum, Martin(B)	1810	April 12	?	01	03	31
Baum, Martin(B)	1815	Aug. 09	Cincinnati	01	03	31
Baum, Martin(C)	1804	Sept. 13	Cincinnati	04	04	26
Baum, Martin(C)	1804	Sept. 13	Cincinnati	04	04	26
Baum, Martin(C)	1804	Sept. 13	Cincinnati	05	02	08
Baum, Martin(C)	1804	Sept. 13	Cincinnati	05	02	08
Baum, Martin(C)	1804	Sept. 13	Cincinnati	06	01	26
Baum, Martin(C)	1804	Sept. 13	Cincinnati	07	03	26
Baum, Martin(C)	1804	Sept. 13	Cincinnati	07	03	26
Baum, Martin(C)	1804	Sept. 13	Cincinnati	07	03	26
Baum, Martin(C)	1804	Sept. 13	Cincinnati	07	03	26
Baum, Martin(C)	1804	Nov. 27	Cincinnati	06	01	20
Baum, Martin(C)	1804	Dec. 27	Cincinnati	07	03	32
Baum, Martin(C)	1804	Dec. 31	Cincinnati	08	04	07
Baum, Martin(C)	1804	Dec. 31	Cincinnati	08	04	03
Baum, Martin(C)	1804	Dec. 31	Cincinnati	07	02	05
Baum, Martin(C)	1804	Dec. 31	Cincinnati	07	03	23
Baum, Martin(C)	1804	Dec. 31	Cincinnati	08	03	01
Baum, Martin(C)	1804	Dec. 31	Cincinnati	08	04	13
Baum, Martin(C)	1804	Dec. 31	Cincinnati	08	04	01
Baum, Martin(C)	1804	Dec. 31	Cincinnati	07	02	03
Baum, Martin(C)	1804	Dec. 31	Cincinnati	08	04	27
Baum, Martin(C)	1804	Dec. 31	Cincinnati	08	04	15
Baum, Martin(C)	1804	Dec. 31	Cincinnati	08	03	22
Baum, Martin(C)	1804	Dec. 31	Cincinnati	09	04	01
Baum, Martin(C)	1804	Dec. 31	Cincinnati	09	02	06

18

PURCHASER	YEAR	DATE	RESIDENCE	R	T	S
Baum, Martin(C)	1804	Dec. 31	Cincinnati	07	03	27
Baum, Martin(C)	1806	March 12	Cincinnati	08	05	35
Baum, Martin(C)	1806	Aug. 26	Cincinnati	02	03	08
Baum, Martin(C)	1813	April 14	Cincinnati	09	04	07
Baum, Martin(C)	1813	April 14	Cincinnati	09	04	07
Baum, Martin(C)	1813	April 14	Cincinnati	08	04	07
Baum, Martin(C)	1813	April 14	Cincinnati	08	04	21
Baum, Martin(C)	1813	April 14	Cincinnati	08	04	21
Baum, Martin(C)	1813	April 15	Cincinnati	08	04	28
Baum, Martin(D)	1811	Dec. 11	Cincinnati	02	03	08
Bausman, Laurence(C)	1813	Nov. 18	Champaign	10	02	26
Baxter, James(B)	1809	Nov. 18	Hamilton	01	10	26
Baxter, James(B)	1809	Nov. 18	Hamilton	01	10	23
Baxter, James(B)	1811	Feb. 02	Hamilton	01	10	25
Baxter, James(C)	1804	Dec. 31	Montgomery	07	02	25
Baxter, James(D)	1814	Oct. 01	Hamilton	02	04	26
Baxter, John(E)	1831	July 01	Randolph(Ind	14	19	34
Baxter, William D.(A)	1836	Sept. 02	Hamilton	03	12	10
Bay, James(C)	1804	Sept. 24	Montgomery	06	01	08
Bayles, Benjamin(C)	1808	Jan. 12	Kentucky	13	02	20
Bayles, Daniel Jr.(E)	1814	Sept. 22	Adams	13	14	26
Bayles, Daniel Jr.(E)	1814	Sept. 22	Adams	13	14	26
Bayles, David(C)	1813	April 14	Champaign	11	03	01
Bayles, David(C)	1813	April 14	Champaign	11	03	01
Bayles, John(C)	1813	April 14	Champaign	11	03	07
Baylis, William(B)	1811	Dec. 11	Wayne(Ind)	01	13	07
Bayman, Charles(A)	1817	Sept. 01	Miami	05	07	13
Bayman, Thomas(A)	1817	June 20	Miami	04	10	19
Baymiller, Jacob(B)	1818	Aug. 17	Cincinnati	02	04	30
Baymiller, Jacob(B)	1818	Aug. 17	Cincinnati	03	05	08
Baymiller, Jacob(B)	1818	Aug. 19	Cincinnati	02	08	15
Baymiller, Jacob(B)	1818	Nov. 16	Cincinnati	02	04	30
Baymiller, Jacob(C)	1818	July 21	Cincinnati	09	06	08
Bays, Thos. Jefferson(B)	1833	Jan. 23	Switzerland	02	02	31
Baysinger, Peter Jr.(C)	1828	Nov. 11	Clark	10	03	28
Baysinger, Peter(C)	1813	May 03	Champaign	10	03	02
Beach, Benj'n. Senr.(B)	1821	Jan. 23	New Jersey	03	07	26
Beach, Benjamin Senr.(B)	1819	Aug. 18	New Jersey	03	07	23
Beach, Comfort R.(C)	1814	April 08	Cincinnati	09	06	31
Beach, Dwight(E)	1835	Jan. 24	Warren	13	19	34
Beach, Jesse(E)	1834	Jan. 01	Darke	15	21	03
Beach, Jesse(E)	1834	Jan. 01	Darke	15	21	04
Beach, Jesse(E)	1834	Sept. 22	Randolph(Ind	15	21	03
Beach, Job A.(B)	1817	Sept. 02	Butler	02	07	30
Beach, Job A.(B)	1817	Sept. 02	Butler	02	07	30
Beach, Milton(E)	1835	Oct. 16	Randolph(Ind	15	21	04
Beach, Nathan(E)	1838	May 21	Randolph(Ind	15	22	27
Beach, Nathan(E)	1837	Oct. 16	Randolph(Ind	15	22	27
Beach, Solomon(B)	1814	Sept. 02	Hamilton	02	11	36
Beach, Solomon(B)	1816	Oct. 22	So. Carolina	01	11	30
Beach, Timothy Clark(E)	1834	Oct. 14	Warren	13	19	14
Beach, Timothy Clark(E)	1835	Jan. 06	Warren	13	19	14
Beacom, Henry(C)	1809	Oct. 27	Champaign	12	04	36
Beacome, Henry(C)	1807	July 27	Champaign	12	04	35
Beacome, Henry(C)	1810	July 21	Champaign	12	04	14
Beadle, Joseph(A)	1805	March 15	Warren	06	06	32
Beadle, Joseph(A)	1805	March 28	Warren	06	05	05
Beaird, James(E)	1831	March 26	Union(Ind)	13	14	01
Beakley, Samuel(A)	1806	Nov. 19	Montgomery	05	08	31
Beal, Aaron(C)	1810	Aug. 14	Greene	07	03	10
Beal, Aaron(C)	1815	Dec. 12	Greene	07	03	10
Beal, Isaac(C)	1805	June 25	Pennsylvania	07	03	10
Beal, Isaac(C)	1805	Oct. 31	Pennsylvania	06	03	25
Beal, Isaac(C)	1810	Aug. 14	Greene	07	03	10
Beal, Jacob(C)	1805	Nov. 08	Pennsylvania	08	03	02
Beal, Jonathan(A)	1812	April 07	Butler	02	03	02
Beal, Jonathan(A)	1814	Aug. 16	Butler	01	03	12
Beal, Jonathan(A)	1816	May 09	Butler	01	03	02
Beal, Jonathan(C)	1813	March 13	Greene	07	03	10

19

PURCHASER	YEAR	DATE	RESIDENCE	R	T	S
Beal, Jonathan(C)	1819	March 01	Greene	13	04	30
Beal, Josiah(B)	1811	Dec. 28	Franklin(Ind	01	09	24
Bealar, Samuel(E)	1814	Feb. 05	Wayne(Ind)	12	14	25
Beale, James E.(C)	1814	Feb. 07	Hamilton	08	04	11
Beale, William(E)	1816	Oct. 28	Kentucky	14	16	28
Bealer, Frederick(B)	1833	July 18	Cincinnati	03	08	26
Beall, Archibald(C)	1814	Feb. 10	Kentucky	14	17	31
Beall, Archibald(C)	1814	Feb. 10	Kentucky	14	17	31
Beall, Archibald(E)	1814	March 21	Kentucky	13	17	15
Beall, Archibald(E)	1816	Jan. 13	Kentucky	14	17	31
Beall, Archibald(E)	1816	Oct. 08	Kentucky	14	16	08
Beall, Charles(A)	1815	Jan. 23	Preble	02	06	04
Beall, William(E)	1816	Nov. 23	Kentucky	14	16	09
Bealor, Samuel(E)	1814	March 01	Wayne(Ind)	13	15	08
Beals, Curtis(E)	1831	Dec. 22	Randolph(Ind	14	19	29
Beals, John(E)	1836	June 11	Randolph(Ind	14	19	20
Beals, Pleasant(E)	1836	Jan. 18	Randolph(Ind	14	19	20
Beals, Pleasant(E)	1836	Aug. 23	Randolph(Ind	14	19	20
Beam, Adam(A)	1831	Feb. 24	Darke	03	11	31
Beam, George(A)	1813	Aug. 14	Montgomery	04	06	35
Beam, Jacob(A)	1831	Sept. 26	Darke	02	13	36
Beam, John(A)	1835	March 25	Montgomery	02	13	35
Beamer, Henry(B)	1816	May 01	Pennsylvania	02	07	14
Bean, William(B)	1818	Oct. 05	Dearborn(Ind	02	06	13
Beanblossom, Abraham(A)	1816	June 19	Montgomery	04	09	08
Beanblossom, Christian(A)	1817	May 27	Montgomery	02	12	01
Beanblossom, Christian(A)	1829	July 24	Darke	02	12	01
Beanblossom, Geo.(A)	1824	July 08	Darke	02	12	01
Beanblossom, John(A)	1817	May 27	Montgomery	02	12	01
Bear, Ezra G.(B)	1836	Sept. 05	Dearborn(Ind	03	04	15
Bear, Isaac(A)	1808	Oct. 05	Montgomery	04	04	31
Bear, Isaac(A)	1808	Oct. 05	Montgomery	04	03	07
Bear, Isaac(A)	1811	April 29	Montgomery	04	03	06
Bear, Michael(A)	1836	Oct. 27	Montgomery	01	13	27
Bear, Peter(B)	1818	July 07	Switzerland	03	04	24
Beard, Enoch(E)	1832	April 16	Randolph(Ind	14	18	01
Beard, George(A)	1806	June 03	Montgomery	05	05	08
Beard, James(A)	1807	Feb. 19	Kentucky	01	04	30
Beard, James(A)	1812	April 15	Butler	01	04	30
Beard, Jesse(E)	1811	Oct. 23	Ind.Territry	12	16	24
Beard, John(A)	1811	Dec. 10	Preble	01	06	09
Beard, John(A)	1818	Aug. 31	Warren	04	04	06
Beard, John(A)	1824	June 08	Montgomery	01	10	22
Beard, John(A)	1836	May 28	Montgomery	03	12	13
Beard, John(B)	1806	Nov. 29	Dearborn(Ind	01	12	18
Beard, John(E)	1811	Oct. 24	Wayne(Ind)	13	15	31
Beard, Paul(E)	1815	Aug. 09	Nor.Carolina	14	18	10
Beard, Paul(E)	1815	Aug. 09	Nor.Carolina	14	18	11
Beard, Paul(E)	1830	Sept. 03	Randolph(Ind	14	18	02
Beard, Paul(E)	1836	July 07	Randolph(Ind	14	18	03
Beard, Philip(A)	1818	Nov. 16	Preble	02	09	22
Beard, Thomas Senr.(C)	1816	March 06	Greene	10	03	08
Beard, Thomas(E)	1811	Oct. 22	Ind.Territry	12	15	25
Beard, Thomas(E)	1811	Oct. 22	Ind.Territry	12	15	12
Beard, Thomas(E)	1811	Dec. 12	Wayne(Ind)	13	15	20
Beard, Thomas(E)	1812	March 05	Wayne(Ind)	13	15	21
Beard, William(B)	1815	Oct. 21	Nor.Carolina	01	11	28
Beard, William(B)	1817	Aug. 02	Franklin(Ind	01	11	35
Beard, William(B)	1817	Aug. 02	Nor.Carolina	01	11	21
Beard, William(B)	1817	Aug. 04	Nor.Carolina	01	11	35
Beard, William(C)	1807	March 14	Kentucky	09	06	30
Beard, William(E)	1835	Jan. 17	Randolph(Ind	14	18	03
Beard, William(E)	1836	Dec. 12	Randolph(Ind	14	18	03
Beardshear, Isaac(E)	1838	May 18	Montgomery	15	22	15
Beardshear, John(E)	1838	May 21	Montgomery	15	22	14
Beardslee, David(A)	1833	Sept. 05	Mercer	01	15	17
Bearly, Henry(A)	1822	Nov. 21	Montgomery	03	07	12
Beatty, Charles(B)	1816	Nov. 02	Hamilton	02	02	35
Beatty, Jeremiah(A)	1801	April 27	Hamilton	02	04	24

PURCHASER	YEAR	DATE	RESIDENCE	R	T	S
Beatty, William(C)	1829	Dec. 12	Shelby	13	01	07
Beaty, David Junr.(D)	1808	Nov. 01	Butler	03	02	26
Beaty, David S.(E)	1834	April 10	Franklin(Ind	13	12	05
Beaty, Elizabeth S.(E)	1834	April 10	Franklin(Ind	13	12	05
Beaty, Hugh(B)	1815	May 17	Dearborn(Ind	01	03	06
Beaty, James(C)	1801	Dec. 25	Hamilton	05	03	12
Beaty, Jno. R.(D)	1813	Sept. 30	Butler	03	03	08
Beaty, John R.(E)	1814	May 27	Franklin(Ind	13	12	05
Beaty, John R.(E)	1814	May 27	Franklin(Ind	13	12	05
Beaty, John R.(E)	1814	May 27	Franklin(Ind	13	12	05
Beaty, John(C)	1812	Sept. 18	Champaign	11	03	09
Beaty, John(C)	1814	Sept. 15	Champaign	11	03	09
Beaty, John(C)	1831	Oct. 29	Champaign	11	03	21
Beaty, Samuel(C)	1812	Sept. 18	Champaign	11	03	09
Beaty, William(C)	1812	Sept. 18	Champaign	11	03	09
Beaty, William(C)	1814	Sept. 15	Champaign	11	03	09
Beauchamp, Jesse(A)	1801	Nov. 26	Kentucky	02	04	02
Beauchamp, Noah(E)	1812	Dec. 14	Montgomery	12	14	24
Bebb, Edward(A)	1801	June 29	Hamilton	01	03	27
Bechel, Sebastian(E)	1836	Oct. 03	Pennsylvania	12	11	27
Bechtle, Henry(C)	1807	Sept. 22	Cincinnati	09	06	35
Bechtle, Henry(C)	1813	April 14	Cincinnati	08	03	18
Bechtle, Henry(C)	1813	April 16	Cincinnati	08	04	36
Bechtle, Henry(C)	1814	Aug. 24	Cincinnati	07	03	24
Bechtle, Henry(C)	1827	Aug. 22	Clark	09	04	11
Beck, Arthur Dillahunt(A)	1831	Sept. 03	Miami	05	10	24
Beck, Edward(A)	1831	Oct. 19	Miami	06	08	19
Beck, Henry(B)	1813	Dec. 02	Clermont	02	12	26
Beck, Henry(B)	1814	Jan. 26	Wayne(Ind)	02	11	02
Beck, John(C)	1801	Dec. 29	Hamilton	06	02	19
Beck, John(E)	1811	Oct. 24	Greene	13	16	22
Beck, John(E)	1835	July 01	Hamilton	13	18	04
Beck, Samuel(C)	1801	Dec. 29	Hamilton	06	02	13
Beck, Samuel(C)	1802	Dec. 18	Hamilton	07	02	07
Beck, Samuel(C)	1815	Jan. 24	Greene	11	02	24
Beck, Samuel(C)	1815	Feb. 15	Greene	11	02	27
Beck, Samuel(E)	1817	July 11	Greene	13	15	03
Beck, Solomon(B)	1813	Dec. 02	Clermont	02	12	36
Beck, Wright Anderson(B)	1825	Nov. 03	Wayne(Ind)	01	13	36
Beckett, Benjamin(B)	1814	Dec. 01	Ohio	02	02	33
Beckett, William(E)	1814	Dec. 10	Butler	13	13	23
Beckford, Moses(B)	1818	May 09	Hamilton	02	05	04
Beckman, Henry(B)	1834	Oct. 23	Hamilton	02	08	21
Beckman, John Hy.(A)	1839	Jan. 21	Cincinnati	02	15	26
Beckmann, Henry(A)	1837	Dec. 21	Cincinnati	02	14	01
Beckworth, Samuel(B)	1816	Jan. 30	Dearborn(Ind	02	03	03
Bedford, Elias(B)	1819	Nov. 08	Canada	02	05	22
Bedwell, James(B)	1812	June 06	Clermont	01	12	14
Beechingham, Enoch(B)	1815	Jan. 02	Hamilton	02	09	24
Beeden, Benj'n.(C)	1825	March 30	Shelby	14	01	19
Beeden, Benjamin(A)	1819	June 30	Montgomery	07	01	04
Beedle, Dan'l.(A)	1831	Aug. 01	Miami	06	05	07
Beeks, William T.(E)	1836	Jan. 26	Franklin(Ind	13	11	15
Beel, James(E)	1836	Sept. 12	Hamilton	12	12	32
Beeler, John(C)	1831	Dec. 01	Hamilton	12	02	11
Beeler, John(C)	1831	Dec. 01	Hamilton	12	02	17
Beeler, Samuel(A)	1803	March 04	Kentucky	01	05	25
Beeler, Samuel(A)	1805	Aug. 02	Butler	02	05	19
Beeler, Samuel(E)	1811	Oct. 23	Butler	12	16	36
Beeler, Samuel(E)	1811	Oct. 24	Butler	13	16	31
Beeler, Samuel(E)	1811	Oct. 24	Butler	13	16	31
Beer, Alexander(C)	1832	Feb. 01	Shelby	13	02	04
Beers, John(A)	1831	April 25	Darke	02	12	22
Beers, John(A)	1831	May 28	Darke	02	12	22
Beers, John(A)	1835	Nov. 12	Darke	02	12	03
Beers, John(A)	1836	Feb. 02	Darke	02	12	04
Beery, John(E)	1836	Oct. 25	Clark	14	21	33
Beery, Joseph(E)	1837	March 01	Clark	14	21	33
Beesley, Isaac(B)	1832	Aug. 10	Franklin(Ind	01	08	08

```
PURCHASER                        YEAR  DATE       RESIDENCE       R  T  S

Beesley, John(B)                 1836  Feb. 15    Hamilton        01 08 07
Beesley, Thomas(B)               1835  Sept. 04   Darke           01 17 02
Beeson, Amos(B)                  1818  May 04     Hamilton        01 06 10
Beeson, Benjamin(E)              1812  July 30    Nor.Carolina    12 15 24
Beeson, Isaac(B)                 1806  Sept. 10   Nor.Carolina    01 13 29
Beeson, Isaac(E)                 1821  Nov. 05    Nor.Carolina    14 18 06
Beeson, Richard(E)               1818  Oct. 05    Greene          14 21 21
Beeson, William(E)               1811  Nov. 02    Wayne(Ind)      13 15 10
Beezley, John(C)                 1812  April 13   Hamilton        10 05 19
Beezley, Joseph(C)               1817  Aug. 01    Champaign       10 05 19
Beezley, Thomas(A)               1831  July 25    Darke           01 12 09
Beezley, Thomas(B)               1835  Sept. 04   Darke           01 17 01
Behrens, John Bernard(A)         1837  July 13    Mercer          03 13 25
Behrins, Bernard(A)              1837  Sept. 30   Cincinnati      03 13 33
Belcher, Loring(A)               1804  Aug. 28    Butler          04 03 33
Belk, Joel(B)                    1814  Dec. 02    Franklin(Ind    02 10 29
Bell, Benjamin(A)                1803  Dec. 07    Pennsylvania    03 03 11
Bell, Darius(C)                  1831  April 09   Clark           12 02 28
Bell, David(A)                   1809  March 13   Cincinnati      01 03 10
Bell, David(A)                   1809  Dec. 21    Cincinnati      01 03 10
Bell, David(A)                   1810  Nov. 30    ?               01 03 09
Bell, David(B)                   1806  Oct. 22    Dearborn(Ind    02 09 08
Bell, David(B)                   1834  Nov. 07    Preble          01 16 09
Bell, Elijah(C)                  1808  March 15   Kentucky        11 04 14
Bell, Henry(A)                   1816  Sept. 24   Butler          01 09 02
Bell, Henry(A)                   1816  Sept. 24   Butler          01 09 10
Bell, Hiram(A)                   1836  Oct. 31    Darke           02 14 35
Bell, Hiram(A)                   1838  Aug. 24    Darke           02 13 04
Bell, Hugh(E)                    1814  April 01   Kentucky        13 14 36
Bell, Jacob(B)                   1813  Jan. 22    Butler          01 10 23
Bell, Jacob(B)                   1814  Oct. 27    Butler          01 10 22
Bell, James(C)                   1814  Dec. 30    Greene          10 03 22
Bell, John(C)                    1806  Nov. 10    Kentucky        11 05 34
Bell, John(E)                    1812  Aug. 21    Nor.Carolina    14 16 17
Bell, John(E)                    1815  June 05    Nor.Carolina    12 15 11
Bell, John(E)                    1817  June 30    Wayne(Ind)      12 15 10
Bell, John(E)                    1817  June 30    Wayne(Ind)      12 15 09
Bell, Joseph Senr.(C)            1817  Aug. 01    Virginia        10 06 36
Bell, Joseph(B)                  1817  July 02    ?               02 03 28
Bell, Josiah(B)                  1834  Nov. 07    Preble          01 16 09
Bell, Nathaniel(A)               1802  Feb. 02    Hamilton        03 03 01
Bell, Robert(C)                  1807  Jan. 30    Butler          08 03 33
Bell, Robert(C)                  1812  April 15   Greene          08 03 33
Bell, Samuel Senr.(E)            1815  Jan. 06    Kentucky        13 14 33
Bell, Samuel(A)                  1838  May 01     Fairfield       01 14 05
Bell, Samuel(B)                  1814  Aug. 17    So. Carolina    01 11 24
Bell, Samuel(E)                  1813  Oct. 12    Kentucky        13 14 33
Bell, Samuel(E)                  1814  Jan. 07    Kentucky        13 14 33
Bell, William(A)                 1814  Aug. 17    So. Carolina    01 06 27
Bell, William(A)                 1832  Jan. 11    Greene          06 08 15
Bell, William(B)                 1818  March 28   Hamilton        03 04 25
Bell, William(E)                 1814  Dec. 14    Franklin(Ind    12 14 10
Bellas, Thomas(A)                1831  Aug. 06    Miami           05 08 15
Belt, John(A)                    1808  Jan. 13    Warren          01 03 11
Belville, Jacob(E)               1837  March 27   Montgomery      15 20 07
Benbridge, Thomas T.(C)          1818  July 21    Cincinnati      09 06 08
Benbridge, Thos. T.(B)           1818  Aug. 17    Cincinnati      02 04 30
Benbridge, Thos. T.(B)           1818  Aug. 17    Cincinnati      03 05 08
Benbridge, Thos. T.(B)           1818  Aug. 19    Cincinnati      02 08 15
Benbridge, Thos. T.(B)           1818  Nov. 16    Cincinnati      02 04 30
Benefiel, John(E)                1814  April 12   Hamilton        13 15 23
Benefiel, Robert(E)              1814  April 12   Hamilton        13 15 26
Benefiel, Robert(E)              1814  April 15   Hamilton        13 15 25
Benge, Alfred(E)                 1833  Sept. 26   Wayne(Ind)      14 19 03
Benge, Alfred(E)                 1836  Feb. 15    Randolph(Ind    14 19 14
Benham, Robert(C)                1805  Oct. 22    Warren          03 04 11
Benham, Robert(C)                1806  April 01   Warren          03 04 08
Benham, Robert(C)                1808  Nov. 07    Warren          03 04 08
Benjamin, Nathaniel(A)           1818  April 18   Cincinnati      02 08 13
```

22

PURCHASER	YEAR	DATE	RESIDENCE	R	T	S
Bennet, David(A)	1817	Oct. 06	Warren	04	04	04
Bennet, Isaac(A)	1817	Oct. 06	Warren	04	04	03
Bennet, James(A)	1807	Feb. 05	Greene	01	06	10
Bennet, James(B)	1806	March 12	Ind.Territry	01	06	23
Bennet, John(A)	1818	Aug. 03	Miami	05	08	35
Bennet, Jonathan(B)	1817	May 28	Hamilton	02	06	26
Bennet, Jos.(B)	1831	Sept. 01	Franklin(Ind	01	08	18
Bennet, Joseph(A)	1817	July 03	Miami	05	08	25
Bennet, Robert(B)	1808	Oct. 20	Butler	01	12	20
Bennet, Samuel(E)	1836	Feb. 09	Franklin(Ind	13	11	28
Bennet, Thomas(B)	1834	Dec. 15	Franklin(Ind	02	08	23
Bennet, William(B)	1818	Jan. 09	Cincinnati	03	05	02
Bennet, William(E)	1813	Aug. 05	Kentucky	12	14	21
Bennett, Abraham(B)	1816	May 31	Cincinnati	01	02	01
Bennett, Amos Smith(A)	1836	Sept. 16	Warren	02	12	04
Bennett, David Presson(A)	1835	June 23	Warren	02	12	03
Bennett, Ebenezer(C)	1815	Dec. 14	Champaign	09	06	20
Bennett, James(B)	1806	April 02	Ind.Territry	01	06	23
Bennett, James(B)	1811	Aug. 13	Ind.Territry	01	06	23
Bennett, John(B)	1818	June 17	Dearborn(Ind	02	06	08
Bennett, John(B)	1828	April 22	Dearborn(Ind	02	06	18
Bennett, Joseph(B)	1833	March 02	Franklin(Ind	01	08	30
Bennett, Titus(C)	1804	Sept. 05	Greene	12	05	21
Benney, Joshua(E)	1816	Feb. 01	Wayne(Ind)	13	17	22
Benson, Andrew(C)	1806	Dec. 04	Virginia	09	05	12
Benson, Andrew(C)	1812	April 15	Champaign	09	05	12
Benson, Andrew(C)	1814	July 30	Champaign	09	05	12
Benson, Andrew(C)	1817	Aug. 01	Champaign	09	05	12
Benson, Arthur(C)	1829	Jan. 29	Warren	11	03	13
Benson, George H.(C)	1817	Aug. 01	Champaign	09	05	12
Benson, Henry(E)	1831	June 30	Randolph(Ind	14	19	36
Benson, Mich'l.(Black)(E)	1836	Sept. 19	Wayne(Ind)	14	19	28
Benson, Thomas G.(B)	1836	Aug. 30	Dearborn(Ind	03	06	36
Benson, William(B)	1818	Feb. 23	Hamilton	03	07	35
Benson, William(C)	1829	Sept. 24	Champaign	11	03	13
Benson, William(E)	1830	Feb. 19	Warren	14	19	35
Benson, Wm.(Black)(E)	1836	Sept. 19	Wayne(Ind)	14	19	28
Bentley, Joseph(B)	1818	July 20	Switzerland	02	02	31
Bentley, Joseph(B)	1818	Aug. 07	Vevay, Ind.	02	02	29
Benton, Joshua(B)	1828	Sept. 25	Wayne(Ind)	01	13	36
Benton, Oliver(B)	1816	Oct. 12	Franklin(Ind	01	08	18
Benton, Thos.(B)	1829	June 18	Wayne(Ind)	01	13	25
Benton, Wm. H.(B)	1815	Sept. 23	Cincinnati	01	04	21
Berger, John Baptist(A)	1836	March 21	Stark	03	11	11
Berger, John Peter(A)	1836	March 21	Stark	03	11	11
Berger, Joseph(A)	1836	March 21	Stark	03	11	11
Berket, David(A)	1806	Oct. 10	Montgomery	05	06	14
Berket, David(A)	1806	Oct. 10	Montgomery	05	06	23
Berkheimer, Isaac(E)	1836	Nov. 07	Muskingum	15	22	35
Berkit, Thomas(A)	1806	Sept. 27	Kentucky	01	08	17
Bernard, Peter(A)	1837	April 03	Stark	03	12	25
Berns, Bernard(E)	1836	Nov. 12	Cincinnati	12	11	33
Berns, Joseph(E)	1836	Nov. 12	Cincinnati	12	11	33
Berons, Benjamin(A)	1806	March 21	Butler	01	09	29
Berry, Achary(C)	1805	April 15	Champaign	12	03	01
Berry, Achory(C)	1813	June 04	Champaign	12	03	01
Berry, David(A)	1828	Feb. 01	Montgomery	02	11	31
Berry, James(B)	1806	Sept. 13	Hamilton	01	10	19
Berry, John W.(E)	1817	Sept. 02	Hamilton	13	17	04
Berry, John W.(E)	1817	Sept. 02	Hamilton	12	17	36
Berry, John(C)	1816	July 05	Greene	08	05	34
Berry, Joseph(A)	1815	June 02	Montgomery	01	08	17
Berry, Samuel(A)	1806	March 24	BrownsvllePa	05	07	08
Berry, William(C)	1808	March 05	Kentucky	12	01	23
Berryhill, Elizabeth(C)	1831	June 10	Greene	12	03	26
Berte, John Hy.(E)	1836	Nov. 11	Cincinnati	12	10	09
Bertin, Joseph(A)	1836	July 18	Hamilton	03	11	02
Best, Francis(C)	1806	Jan. 10	Champaign	09	04	04
Best, Samuel(C)	1811	Aug. 14	Cincinnati	10	04	23

23

PURCHASER	YEAR	DATE	RESIDENCE	R	T	S
Betts, William(A)	1804	Sept. 28	Cincinnati	02	04	34
Betts, William(A)	1805	June 19	Cincinnati	02	03	05
Beudel, Philip(E)	1835	March 07	Wayne(Ind)	14	19	10
Beudel, Philip(E)	1835	Oct. 17	Wayne(Ind)	14	19	10
Bevan, Owen(E)	1836	Nov. 16	Clinton	13	19	02
Bevens, David(B)	1819	April 10	Dearborn(Ind	02	04	30
Beverlin, John(E)	1815	Dec. 28	Hamilton	14	17	17
Bevis, David(A)	1831	Nov. 29	Hamilton	05	07	11
Bevis, James(A)	1831	Nov. 29	Hamilton	05	07	14
Bevis, Jesse Jr.(A)	1831	Nov. 29	Hamilton	05	07	14
Bevis, Martin(A)	1831	Nov. 29	Hamilton	05	07	14
Bickel, Andrew Jr.(A)	1830	Aug. 05	Montgomery	01	12	15
Bickel, Jacob Jr.(A)	1825	Sept. 28	Preble	02	09	26
Bicket, William(A)	1812	Nov. 16	Butler	02	04	15
Bickham, William(A)	1836	July 08	Hamilton	03	11	24
Bickham, William(A)	1836	July 08	Hamilton	03	12	23
Bickle, Jacob(A)	1823	Jan. 03	Preble	03	06	07
Biddle, Bouldin(A)	1816	Sept. 18	Hamilton	02	11	28
Bigger, John Junr.(C)	1801	Dec. 31	Hamilton	07	03	25
Bigger, John(C)	1801	Dec. 16	Hamilton	05	03	06
Bigger, John(C)	1801	Dec. 16	Hamilton	05	04	36
Bigger, John(C)	1801	Dec. 24	Kentucky	06	02	15
Bigger, John(C)	1801	Dec. 24	Hamilton	04	03	31
Bigger, John(C)	1804	Sept. 03	Warren	04	03	25
Bigger, John(C)	1804	Nov. 13	Kentucky	06	02	21
Bigger, Joseph(C)	1801	Dec. 30	Hamilton	05	02	12
Biggers, Robert(C)	1817	Oct. 21	Pennsylvania	12	01	10
Biggs, Aaron(A)	1804	Nov. 03	Warren	02	06	32
Biggs, Aaron(A)	1815	Feb. 14	Preble	02	06	06
Biggs, Horace P.(A)	1837	Jan. 07	Butler	02	15	19
Biggs, John S.(E)	1836	Oct. 10	Cincinnati	13	10	06
Biggs, John S.(E)	1836	Oct. 11	Cincinnati	14	19	09
Biggs, John S.(E)	1836	Oct. 25	Cincinnati	12	11	11
Biggs, John S.(E)	1836	Oct. 25	Cincinnati	14	19	08
Biggs, John S.(E)	1836	Oct. 26	Cincinnati	12	11	12
Biggs, John S.(E)	1836	Nov. 17	Cincinnati	12	11	12
Biggs, John S.(E)	1836	Nov. 18	Cincinnati	13	11	18
Biggs, John S.(E)	1836	Nov. 18	Cincinnati	12	11	13
Biggs, John S.(E)	1836	Dec. 06	Cincinnati	12	11	13
Biggs, John S.(E)	1836	Dec. 20	Cincinnati	13	11	08
Biggs, John(B)	1814	Feb. 02	Wayne(Ind)	01	12	29
Biggs, Thomas(E)	1815	Oct. 10	Kentucky	13	17	27
Biggs, Thomas(E)	1817	Nov. 20	Kentucky	13	18	10
Biggs, Thomas(E)	1836	Nov. 17	Cincinnati	12	11	13
Bilbee, Joseph(A)	1830	Jan. 22	Preble	01	09	13
Bilderback, Gabriel(A)	1807	April 25	Greene	06	07	01
Bilderback, Gabriel(C)	1814	June 01	Champaign	09	04	08
Billing, John(A)	1816	Sept. 16	Pickaway	04	10	19
Billingsley, Charles(A)	1831	Oct. 24	Butler	05	08	28
Bills, Abraham(A)	1814	June 24	Dearborn(Ind	03	04	03
Bills, William(B)	1816	March 30	Dearborn(Ind	01	04	27
Bills, William(B)	1816	July 01	Dearborn(Ind	01	04	27
Bingham, Daniel B.(E)	1838	May 21	Randolph(Ind	15	22	23
Binkley, Samuel H.(A)	1837	Aug. 30	Montgomery	01	14	03
Binninger, Martin(B)	1818	Nov. 03	Hamilton	02	07	11
Birch, Charles(A)	1807	Aug. 25	Hamilton	02	03	19
Birdzell, William C.(B)	1836	Sept. 16	Dearborn(Ind	02	04	06
Birney, James G.(A)	1836	Aug. 30	Hamilton	01	14	22
Birney, James G.(A)	1836	Nov. 26	Hamilton	01	14	33
Birney, James G.(A)	1836	Nov. 26	Hamilton	01	14	22
Birney, James G.(A)	1836	Nov. 26	Hamilton	01	14	21
Birney, James G.(A)	1836	Nov. 26	Hamilton	01	15	23
Birney, James G.(A)	1836	Nov. 26	Hamilton	01	15	24
Birney, James G.(A)	1836	Dec. 31	Cincinnati	01	14	34
Birney, James G.(A)	1837	Jan. 19	Cincinnati	01	15	21
Birney, James G.(A)	1837	Jan. 19	Cincinnati	01	15	34
Birney, James G.(A)	1837	March 01	Cincinnati	01	14	27
Birney, James G.(A)	1837	March 01	Cincinnati	01	13	03
Birney, James G.(A)	1837	April 01	Cincinnati	01	14	32

24

PURCHASER	YEAR	DATE	RESIDENCE	R	T	S
Birney, James G.(A)	1837	April 08	Cincinnati	01	13	10
Birney, James G.(A)	1837	April 08	Cincinnati	01	13	03
Birney, James G.(E)	1836	July 29	Hamilton	14	20	08
Birney, James G.(E)	1836	Aug. 15	Hamilton	14	20	08
Birney, James G.(E)	1836	Aug. 30	Hamilton	14	20	07
Birney, James G.(E)	1836	Aug. 30	Hamilton	14	21	33
Birney, James G.(E)	1836	Sept. 05	Hamilton	15	21	08
Birney, James G.(E)	1836	Nov. 26	Hamilton	14	21	29
Birney, James G.(E)	1836	Nov. 26	Hamilton	14	21	32
Birney, James G.(E)	1836	Nov. 26	Hamilton	14	20	04
Birney, James G.(E)	1836	Nov. 26	Hamilton	14	20	09
Birney, James G.(E)	1836	Nov. 26	Hamilton	15	21	15
Birney, James G.(E)	1836	Nov. 26	Hamilton	15	21	22
Birney, James G.(E)	1836	Nov. 28	Hamilton	15	21	17
Birney, James G.(E)	1837	Jan. 23	Cincinnati	15	20	18
Birney, James G.(E)	1837	Jan. 23	Cincinnati	15	21	15
Birney, James G.(E)	1837	Jan. 23	Cincinnati	15	22	17
Birney, James G.(E)	1837	April 08	Cincinnati	15	22	17
Birney, James G.(E)	1837	April 21	Cincinnati	15	22	17
Birney, James G.(E)	1837	April 22	Cincinnati	15	22	17
Birney, James G.(E)	1837	Sept. 18	Cincinnati	15	21	14
Birney, James G.(E)	1837	Sept. 18	Cincinnati	15	22	17
Birt, William(C)	1808	Sept. 29	Warren	09	06	02
Birum, Wm.(E)	1838	Feb. 02	Preble	15	21	17
Bisbee, Isaiah(B)	1817	Aug. 18	Cincinnati	03	09	01
Bisbee, Isaiah(E)	1817	Aug. 27	Indiana	12	12	08
Bisecher, David(A)	1826	Oct. 06	Montgomery	04	06	22
Bisecher, David(A)	1827	Sept. 11	Montgomery	04	06	21
Bisecher, David(A)	1828	June 10	Montgomery	04	06	22
Bisecher, Nicholas(A)	1829	Feb. 12	Montgomery	04	06	20
Bishop, Amos J.(E)	1837	Feb. 21	Wayne(Ind)	14	20	25
Bishop, Aquila(C)	1827	Aug. 22	Clark	10	05	08
Bishop, Aquila(C)	1828	Dec. 01	Champaign	11	05	08
Bishop, Benjamin(A)	1806	Oct. 20	Hamilton	02	06	25
Bishop, James(C)	1806	May 13	Champaign	10	05	03
Bishop, James(C)	1806	Nov. 01	Champaign	10	06	32
Bishop, James(C)	1807	Jan. 17	Champaign	10	06	31
Bishop, James(C)	1809	June 02	Champaign	10	05	07
Bishop, James(C)	1813	Feb. 06	Champaign	10	05	20
Bishop, James(C)	1813	Feb. 06	Champaign	10	05	07
Bishop, James(C)	1813	Oct. 06	Champaign	10	05	08
Bishop, Joel(B)	1819	June 03	Cincinnati	02	05	04
Bishop, John(A)	1805	Sept. 19	Butler	01	06	04
Bishop, John(B)	1831	Sept. 19	Wayne(Ind)	01	15	26
Bishop, John(B)	1831	Oct. 19	Wayne(Ind)	01	15	26
Bishop, John(C)	1808	Nov. 04	Ross	14	02	03
Bishop, John(C)	1810	Jan. 13	Champaign	10	05	02
Bishop, John(E)	1834	March 17	Franklin(Ind	11	12	24
Bishop, Lewis(B)	1816	May 08	Franklin(Ind	02	09	15
Bishop, Lewis(E)	1816	Oct. 26	Franklin(Ind	12	13	29
Bishop, Lewis(E)	1816	Nov. 12	Franklin(Ind	12	13	07
Bishop, Robert(A)	1805	Aug. 19	Butler	01	06	05
Bishop, Robert(A)	1813	Feb. 24	Preble	01	07	31
Bishop, Robert(A)	1816	Aug. 08	Preble	01	07	32
Bishop, Thomas(B)	1816	Aug. 22	Hamilton	02	03	27
Bittle, Richard(E)	1836	May 23	Preble	14	19	11
Bittle, Richard(E)	1836	June 08	Preble	14	19	04
Bittle, William(E)	1836	June 08	Preble	14	19	10
Bixby, Perry(B)	1837	Jan. 10	Dearborn(Ind	03	06	36
Bixby, Perry(B)	1837	Jan. 18	Dearborn(Ind	03	06	36
Bixler, John(A)	1834	Dec. 03	Darke	03	10	01
Black, Alex'r. C.(E)	1826	Jan. 12	Wayne(Ind)	14	15	18
Black, Alexander C.(E)	1816	Jan. 20	Kentucky	14	15	06
Black, Alexander(C)	1809	July 24	Champaign	12	05	23
Black, Alexander(C)	1811	Dec. 11	Champaign	13	05	19
Black, Alexander(C)	1812	April 15	Champaign	13	05	25
Black, Alexander(C)	1814	May 31	Champaign	13	05	13
Black, Alexr.(C)	1813	March 15	Champaign	13	05	25
Black, Andrew(A)	1818	July 06	Miami	05	09	18

PURCHASER	YEAR	DATE	RESIDENCE	R	T	S
Black, Andrew(C)	1806	July 15	Montgomery	10	03	25
Black, Andrew(C)	1813	April 14	Miami	09	02	02
Black, David(B)	1814	July 30	Hamilton	02	09	23
Black, David(B)	1814	Aug. 29	Hamilton	01	10	11
Black, Elwell(E)	1833	Aug. 13	Clinton	13	19	10
Black, Elwell(E)	1837	Jan. 18	Brown	13	19	12
Black, Elwell(E)	1837	Jan. 18	Brown	13	19	10
Black, Frederick(A)	1811	Jan. 28	Preble	03	07	18
Black, Frederick(A)	1811	Jan. 28	Preble	03	07	19
Black, Frederick(A)	1814	May 04	Preble	03	07	15
Black, Frederick(A)	1818	Jan. 24	Preble	03	08	34
Black, George(C)	1812	Feb. 25	Kentucky	14	03	28
Black, Jacob(A)	1818	July 11	Miami	04	10	13
Black, Jacob(A)	1830	March 26	Shelby	04	10	13
Black, James Jr.(E)	1814	March 08	Wayne(Ind)	14	16	29
Black, James(A)	1814	Nov. 21	Preble	02	06	09
Black, James(C)	1809	Aug. 02	Champaign	11	03	03
Black, James(C)	1811	Sept. 25	Montgomery	08	02	24
Black, James(C)	1813	April 14	Montgomery	08	02	29
Black, James(C)	1813	May 06	Champaign	10	03	22
Black, James(C)	1813	May 25	Champaign	10	03	32
Black, James(C)	1814	July 25	Montgomery	08	02	29
Black, James(E)	1813	Dec. 10	Wayne(Ind)	14	16	10
Black, James(E)	1815	July 15	Wayne(Ind)	14	16	09
Black, Janus(A)	1814	Dec. 29	Preble	02	06	04
Black, Jeremiah(B)	1813	July 29	Kentucky	01	09	05
Black, John(A)	1818	June 16	Preble	03	08	34
Black, John(A)	1822	Jan. 10	Preble	03	08	34
Black, John(E)	1814	March 29	Kentucky	13	13	11
Black, Robert(E)	1813	Dec. 10	Wayne(Ind)	13	16	36
Black, Samuel(C)	1806	June 30	Montgomery	10	03	25
Black, Samuel(C)	1806	July 15	Montgomery	10	03	25
Black, Samuel(C)	1806	July 15	Montgomery	10	03	19
Black, Samuel(C)	1806	July 15	Montgomery	10	03	19
Black, Samuel(C)	1810	April 09	Champaign	13	03	03
Black, Samuel(E)	1811	Oct. 24	Kentucky	13	15	05
Black, Samuel(E)	1811	Oct. 24	Kentucky	13	15	05
Black, William(C)	1813	Aug. 12	Virginia	10	03	23
Black, William(C)	1815	July 10	Champaign	10	03	30
Black, William(C)	1815	July 10	Champaign	11	03	19
Black, William(C)	1816	July 01	Virginia	10	03	20
Black, William(C)	1819	Aug. 19	Clark	11	03	25
Black, William(C)	1828	Oct. 23	Champaign	12	05	29
Black, William(E)	1816	Feb. 02	Wayne(Ind)	13	15	12
Blackburn, Bryson(B)	1813	Nov. 02	Butler	01	09	11
Blackburn, David(A)	1805	July 15	Butler	02	04	07
Blackburn, David(C)	1802	Dec. 28	Hamilton	06	01	19
Blackburn, Edward(B)	1819	Sept. 20	Cincinnati	02	08	31
Blackburn, James(C)	1801	Dec. 09	Hamilton	04	03	07
Blackburn, John(B)	1818	Feb. 17	Cincinnati	02	06	07
Blackburn, Robert(A)	1806	Jan. 30	Hamilton	01	02	13
Blackburn, Robert(A)	1806	Sept. 04	Hamilton	01	02	12
Blackburn, William(A)	1803	Nov. 30	Butler	01	03	36
Blacker, Edward(A)	1813	April 06	Butler	01	04	30
Blacker, Robert(B)	1817	Sept. 04	Butler	02	02	01
Blackford, Ephraim(C)	1804	Dec. 24	Warren	05	03	27
Blackford, Ephraim(C))	1801	Dec. 29	Hamilton	05	03	31
Blackford, Jeremiah K.(A)	1817	Sept. 04	Warren	02	09	33
Blackford, Jeremiah(A)	1825	May 04	Warren	02	09	34
Blackford, Jeremiah(C)	1804	Dec. 28	Warren	05	03	14
Blackford, John(C)	1801	Dec. 30	Hamilton	05	03	19
Blackford, John(C)	1804	Dec. 27	Warren	05	03	19
Blackford, John(C)	1808	Jan. 11	Champaign	09	06	01
Blackford, John(C)	1811	Sept. 23	Champaign	09	06	14
Blackford, Levi(A)	1822	Aug. 23	Warren	02	09	27
Blackford, Nathaniel(C)	1801	Dec. 30	Hamilton	04	04	36
Blackford, Nathaniel(C)	1804	Dec. 24	Warren	05	03	19
Blackford, William(A)	1826	Oct. 10	Preble	02	09	21
Blackford, Wm.(A)	1830	Jan. 09	Preble	02	09	19

PURCHASER	YEAR	DATE	RESIDENCE	R	T	S
Blackhouse, James(B)	1806	Nov. 07	Hamilton	01	07	02
Blackleach, Hudson(A)	1836	Nov. 09	Butler	02	14	31
Blackleach, Hudson(A)	1836	Nov. 09	Butler	02	13	27
Blacklidge, Harvey(E)	1835	July 20	Franklin(Ind	13	12	30
Blacklidge, Harvey(E)	1835	Nov. 02	Franklin(Ind	13	12	30
Blacklidge, Jacob(E)	1811	Nov. 13	Franklin(Ind	13	12	19
Blacklidge, Jacob(E)	1813	Nov. 08	Franklin(Ind	13	12	23
Blacklidge, Jacob(E)	1814	July 21	Franklin(Ind	12	13	24
Blacklidge, Jacob(E)	1833	May 25	Franklin(Ind	13	12	18
Blacklidge, Jacob(E)	1833	May 25	Franklin(Ind	13	12	19
Blacklidge, James(E)	1832	March 10	Franklin(Ind	13	12	26
Blacklidge, James(E)	1835	Dec. 19	Franklin(Ind	13	12	26
Blacklidge, James(E)	1836	July 02	Franklin(Ind	13	12	27
Blackmon, James(A)	1837	Jan. 19	Cincinnati	01	15	32
Blackmon, James(A)	1837	Jan. 19	Cincinnati	01	15	33
Blackmore, James(A)	1819	May 25	Warren	06	05	31
Blackwood, Joseph(A)	1819	Nov. 20	Shelby	05	09	23
Blackwood, Joseph(A)	1825	Nov. 04	Miami	05	09	22
Blain, Adam(C)	1801	Dec. 22	Hamilton	04	03	05
Blair, Robert	1808	March 02	Cincinnati	?	?	?
Blair, Robert(B)	1814	April 18	Hamilton	01	09	35
Blair, Robert(E)	1812	July 01	Hamilton	13	16	25
Blair, Samuel(A)	1821	Sept. 06	Montgomery	04	06	30
Blair, Thomas(A)	1807	June 18	Butler	02	04	14
Blair, Thomas(A)	1814	Sept. 10	Butler	02	03	05
Blake, John(A)	1819	Dec. 28	Miami	06	08	14
Blake, John(A)	1819	Dec. 28	Miami	06	08	23
Blake, John(A)	1819	Dec. 28	Miami	06	08	23
Blake, John(A)	1819	Dec. 28	Miami	05	08	23
Blake, John(A)	1819	Dec. 28	Miami	05	08	23
Blake, John(A)	1819	Dec. 28	Miami	06	08	23
Blake, Thomas C.(B)	1819	April 19	Highland	02	05	03
Blakely, Robert(A)	1819	Sept. 14	Franklin	06	08	12
Blaney, John(B)	1814	Jan. 15	Hamilton	03	02	10
Blaney, John(B)	1815	July 20	Switzerland	02	01	05
Blankinship, Benjamin(C)	1818	May 16	Virginia	13	02	06
Blasdel, Jacob(B)	1804	Aug. 06	Hamilton	01	06	28
Blasdel, Jacob(B)	1804	Sept. 17	Hamilton	01	06	29
Blattner, John(B)	1831	Aug. 29	Cincinnati	02	07	27
Blazer, David(E)	1836	Jan. 28	Franklin(Ind	12	12	13
Bleakenstaff, Christian(A)	1808	May 18	Pennsylvania	06	04	27
Bleakley, Achison(A)	1818	Feb. 03	Miami	05	09	13
Bledsoe, Abraham(B)	1806	Aug. 01	Kentucky	01	08	02
Bledsoe, Abraham(B)	1815	July 29	Kentucky	01	02	21
Bliss, Asa(A)	1832	Aug. 14	Warren	02	10	13
Bliss, Jacob(A)	1831	Sept. 12	Warren	02	10	13
Bliss, Nathaniel(A)	1831	Sept. 12	Warren	02	10	13
Blocher, Joseph(A)	1831	Oct. 04	Darke	02	10	05
Blocker, Joseph(A)	1832	Jan. 06	Darke	02	10	05
Blodget, Dan'l.(B)	1832	Feb. 20	Switzerland	03	03	17
Blodget, Daniel(B)	1833	July 20	Switzerland	03	03	17
Blodget, Joseph(B)	1833	Jan. 31	Switzerland	03	03	20
Blodget, Nathan(B)	1818	Oct. 26	Hamilton	02	07	14
Blodget, Ora(B)	1836	Oct. 18	Switzerland	03	03	17
Blodget, Samuel(B)	1831	July 09	Switzerland	03	03	28
Bloom, Joseph(A)	1831	Oct. 24	Darke	01	10	36
Bloom, William(B)	1815	Feb. 14	Dearborn(Ind	01	07	08
Bloomfield, John(A)	1813	Dec. 18	Preble	02	08	30
Bloomfield, Lot(E)	1832	May 14	Wayne(Ind)	14	16	33
Bloomfield, Nathaniel(A)	1815	Aug. 25	Preble	02	07	08
Bloomfield, Samuel(A)	1815	Jan. 07	Preble	02	08	32
Blount, Eli(E)	1819	Oct. 12	Highland	14	21	12
Blount, William(E)	1815	April 10	Wayne(Ind)	13	18	08
Bloyd, Jacob(A)	1814	Aug. 02	Franklin(Ind	12	15	22
Bloyd, Jacob(B)	1806	Sept. 12	Dearborn(Ind	02	10	17
Blucker, Robert(A)	1810	Dec. 17	Hamilton	01	04	30
Blue, Barnabas(A)	1831	March 11	Shelby	06	08	21
Blue, Barnabas(C)	1804	Dec. 25	Montgomery	10	01	12
Blue, Barnabas(C)	1805	Dec. 26	Montgomery	11	02	28

27

PURCHASER	YEAR	DATE	RESIDENCE	R	T	S
Blue, Benjamin(B)	1807	Feb. 19	Kentucky	01	09	25
Blue, Cornelius(C)	1810	Dec. 10	Virginia	11	04	33
Blue, David(B)	1809	March 22	Butler	02	05	01
Blue, David(B)	1812	Oct. 30	Dearborn(Ind	02	04	27
Blue, David(B)	1817	June 11	Dearborn(Ind	02	04	27
Blue, Frederick(C)	1813	April 19	Miami	11	02	21
Blue, John(C)	1804	Dec. 28	Greene	08	04	32
Blue, John(C)	1815	Feb. 02	Champaign	11	04	32
Blue, Michael(C)	1804	Dec. 26	Montgomery	11	01	07
Blue, Samuel(C)	1814	Oct. 08	Champaign	11	04	21
Blue, Uriah Junr.(C)	1806	Aug. 19	Montgomery	11	01	02
Blue, Uriah(A)	1831	Nov. 24	Miami	07	01	05
Blue, Uriah(C)	1802	Dec. 31	Hamilton	10	01	18
Blue, Uriah(C)	1807	Aug. 26	Miami	11	01	23
Blue, William(B)	1807	Feb. 19	Ind.Territry	01	09	25
Blue, William(B)	1811	Nov. 26	Dearborn(Ind	02	04	22
Blue, William(B)	1815	April 25	Dearborn(Ind	02	04	27
Blunt, Will'm.(E)	1814	April 15	Wayne(Ind)	13	18	32
Blunt, William(E)	1814	March 03	Wayne(Ind)	13	18	29
Boady, Lewis(C)	1817	Oct. 31	Champaign	12	03	03
Boady, Susan(C)	1828	March 27	?	12	03	11
Boal, Robert Junr.(A)	1819	Oct. 27	Hamilton	03	06	06
Boal, Robert(A)	1831	June 29	Cincinnati	03	06	06
Boals, Francis(A)	1815	July 03	Pennsylvania	01	03	21
Board, James(C)	1804	Dec. 31	New Jersey	06	02	22
Boardman, Amos(B)	1809	Nov. 25	Dearborn(Ind	02	05	25
Boardman, David G.(B)	1809	Nov. 25	Dearborn(Ind	02	05	25
Boardman, David G.(B)	1814	Aug. 24	Dearborn(Ind	02	05	14
Boardman, David G.(B)	1817	Dec. 30	Dearborn(Ind	03	07	36
Boardman, John C.(C)	1809	March 28	New York	09	05	27
Boardman, Simeon(C)	1810	Feb. 23	Cincinnati	09	05	21
Boardwell, Simeon(C)	1813	April 14	Champaign	09	06	24
Boas, Peter(B)	1818	April 10	Switzerland	01	02	23
Boase, Jacob(A)	1837	March 28	Montgomery	01	13	03
Boblets, Jacob(A)	1812	Feb. 22	Preble	03	05	01
Bobo, Garner(C)	1807	Jan. 03	Greene	12	01	21
Bock, Nicholas(A)	1814	Oct. 26	Montgomery	04	04	08
Bockus, Isaac(B)	1818	May 06	Hamilton	03	03	09
Bocock, Lewis(B)	1817	July 08	Switzerland	02	02	11
Bocock, Lewis(B)	1833	Jan. 07	Switzerland	02	02	11
Bocock, Louis(B)	1832	Feb. 14	Switzerland	02	02	11
Bodeker, John Herman(E)	1836	Nov. 11	Cincinnati	12	10	06
Bodeker, John Herman(E)	1837	July 06	Cincinnati	12	11	13
Boden, Samuel Jr.(A)	1831	Nov. 07	Belmont	04	10	11
Bodine, William Alworth(B)	1835	Sept. 29	Dearborn(Ind	01	07	21
Bodkin, Charles(C)	1817	July 10	Champaign	12	02	18
Bodkin, Jeremiah(C)	1813	March 25	Champaign	08	07	36
Bodkin, John Junr.(C)	1813	Feb. 08	Champaign	09	03	18
Bodkin, William(E)	1831	Sept. 21	Shelby	05	09	02
Bodle, Hugh(B)	1830	May 24	Dearborn(Ind	02	03	12
Bodt, Adam(A)	1825	April 11	Montgomery	04	06	22
Body, Christian(C)	1817	Oct. 23	Champaign	12	03	04
Boes, John(A)	1812	March 31	Butler	02	03	17
Bogart, William(A)	1818	Oct. 27	Pickaway	06	08	20
Bogert, Ruliff(B)	1815	Dec. 09	Cincinnati	02	06	03
Bogert, Ruliff(B)	1817	Aug. 12	Cincinnati	01	06	08
Bogert, Ruliff(B)	1817	Aug. 12	Cincinnati	02	06	12
Bogert, Ruliff(B)	1818	Jan. 06	Cincinnati	01	06	09
Bogert, Ruliff(B)	1818	Jan. 06	Cincinnati	02	07	34
Boggett, Joseph(A)	1811	May 01	Butler	01	03	33
Boggs, John(C)	1806	Jan. 08	Ross	13	03	12
Boggs, John(C)	1811	April 09	Pickaway	13	03	12
Boggs, John(C)	1829	Dec. 11	Pickaway	13	03	06
Bogue, Stephen(A)	1812	Aug. 07	Preble	02	06	17
Bohl, Adam(B)	1833	March 15	Cincinnati	02	07	03
Bohl, Peter(E)	1836	Sept. 19	Cincinnati	12	11	23
Bohli, Andrew(B)	1835	Jan. 16	Hamilton	02	07	05
Bohman, Joseph(A)	1839	Jan. 21	Cincinnati	02	15	27
Bohrer, Christian(B)	1835	Nov. 23	Hamilton	03	09	25

PURCHASER	YEAR	DATE	RESIDENCE	R	T	S
Bohrer, George(B)	1835	Nov. 23	Hamilton	03	09	24
Bohrer, Sebastian(B)	1831	Aug. 01	Cincinnati	02	07	20
Boiles, John(B)	1806	July 30	Kentucky	01	13	07
Boils, Martin(C)	1817	Aug. 16	Miami	13	02	13
Boisseau, Jacob(B)	1833	Aug. 07	Switzerland	02	02	29
Boisseau, John(B)	1814	May 27	Jefferson	02	01	05
Boisseau, John(B)	1817	June 06	Switzerland	02	02	28
Bolar, Jno. Gerhard(A)	1839	Jan. 21	Cincinnati	02	15	36
Bolay, David(B)	1834	Jan. 23	Cincinnati	02	07	07
Bolender, John(E)	1836	Nov. 01	Wayne(Ind)	14	20	31
Bolin, John(A)	1832	April 07	Darke	03	08	06
Bolinger, David(A)	1830	June 12	Montgomery	04	07	24
Bolinger, David(A)	1831	May 30	Montgomery	04	07	24
Bolinger, Jacob(E)	1837	July 13	Cincinnati	14	20	12
Bolinger, Stephen(E)	1837	April 13	Dearborn(Ind	12	11	28
Bolsel, Peter(C)	1811	Aug. 05	Hamilton	12	01	14
Bolser, John H.(A)	1817	Oct. 28	Butler	02	10	34
Bolser, Samuel(B)	1833	June 03	Cincinnati	02	06	12
Boltin, William(A)	1816	Oct. 24	Montgomery	03	10	26
Bolton, James Alexr.(E)	1831	Nov. 18	Fayette	13	13	15
Bolton, James(C)	1814	Oct. 20	Wayne(Ind)	14	14	08
Bolton, William Price(E)	1831	Nov. 18	Fayette	13	13	15
Boltsel, George(C)	1824	June 07	Miami	12	01	08
Boltz, John(B)	1831	July 05	Dearborn(Ind	03	08	34
Bolun, Enoch(A)	1838	April 20	Greene	02	14	24
Boman, Joseph(A)	1837	Dec. 11	Miami	03	13	29
Bonbrake, Devalt(A)	1808	March 01	Montgomery	02	08	18
Bond, Benj'n.(E)	1836	Nov. 29	Wayne(Ind)	14	19	28
Bond, Edward(E)	1817	Nov. 15	Wayne(Ind)	14	17	17
Bond, Exum S.(A)	1813	Dec. 08	Preble	02	06	12
Bond, Jesse(B)	1813	April 14	Wayne(Ind)	01	14	31
Bond, Jesse(E)	1814	June 10	Wayne(Ind)	13	17	35
Bond, Jno.(E)	1831	March 26	Union(Ind)	13	14	01
Bond, Joseph(E)	1816	Oct. 30	Wayne(Ind)	14	17	15
Bond, Lewis(B)	1814	May 26	Butler	01	09	13
Bond, Lewis(B)	1814	June 21	?	01	09	17
Bond, Nathaniel(C)	1802	Dec. 23	Hamilton	04	02	10
Bond, Nathaniel(C)	1806	April 08	Warren	08	02	24
Bond, Samuel(A)	1832	Feb. 03	Hamilton	01	01	06
Bond, Samuel(B)	1808	Aug. 27	Virginia	01	05	19
Bond, Samuel(B)	1808	Aug. 27	Virginia	01	05	09
Bond, Samuel(B)	1808	Aug. 27	Virginia	01	05	09
Bond, Samuel(B)	1808	Aug. 27	Virginia	01	05	05
Bond, Samuel(B)	1809	Nov. 13	Virginia	01	05	04
Bond, Samuel(E)	1814	May 21	Highland	14	17	22
Bond, Thomas(B)	1815	June 26	Virginia	01	09	12
Bond, William(B)	1816	Sept. 24	Wayne(Ind)	01	14	15
Bonebrake, Conrad(A)	1816	Feb. 15	Preble	02	08	19
Bonebrake, Fredrick(A)	1815	Jan. 05	Preble	02	08	19
Bonebrake, George(A)	1817	July 02	Maryland	01	10	24
Bonebrake, Jacob(A)	1813	July 30	Preble	02	08	19
Boner, Elisha(E)	1838	Feb. 08	Preble	15	21	18
Bonham, Aaron R.(B)	1814	Oct. 05	Hamilton	01	07	33
Bonham, Aaron R.(B)	1817	July 05	Dearborn(Ind	01	06	10
Bonham, Benj'n. B.(B)	1825	April 22	Dearborn(Ind	02	07	22
Bonham, Israel W.(B)	1819	March 05	Dearborn(Ind	01	07	30
Bonham, James Hervey(B)	1835	Oct. 07	Dearborn(Ind	01	07	17
Bonham, James Hervey(B)	1836	May 02	Dearborn(Ind	01	07	17
Bonham, Zedekiah(B)	1815	Oct. 24	Hamilton	01	07	30
Bonine, David(B)	1825	March 09	Wayne(Ind)	01	13	21
Bonnel, Aaron(A)	1807	May 08	Hamilton	01	02	18
Bonnell, Samuel(A)	1836	Nov. 21	Butler	02	14	15
Bonner, David(A)	1807	June 17	Butler	01	06	14
Bonner, David(B)	1813	Dec. 07	Franklin(Ind	01	11	33
Bonner, John(A)	1837	May 09	Montgomery	02	13	32
Bonner, Nathaniel(A)	1806	Sept. 08	Greene	03	10	34
Bonner, Nathaniel(A)	1806	Sept. 08	Greene	03	10	27
Bonner, Samuel(B)	1813	Aug. 18	So. Carolina	01	11	33
Bonta, Aalbert(A)	1804	Dec. 07	Montgomery	03	05	01

PURCHASER	YEAR	DATE	RESIDENCE	R	T	S
Bonta, Abraham(A)	1805	Aug. 19	Montgomery	03	05	08
Bonta, Abraham(A)	1814	Dec. 07	Preble	02	09	25
Bonta, Abraham(A)	1815	Nov. 28	Preble	03	06	13
Bonta, Abraham(A)	1816	April 17	Preble	03	05	11
Bonta, Albert(A)	1805	June 27	Warren	04	03	31
Bonta, Albert(A)	1805	July 16	Montgomery	04	03	31
Bonta, Albert(A)	1805	Aug. 02	Montgomery	03	06	30
Bonta, Albert(A)	1805	July 30	Warren	04	03	31
Bonta, Albert(C)	1801	Dec. 11	Hamilton	05	02	36
Bonta, Albert(E)	1818	March 20	Preble	14	19	15
Bonta, Daniel(C)	1801	Dec. 31	Hamilton	04	04	19
Bonta, David(B)	1805	Aug. 07	Kentucky	02	05	35
Bonta, Henry(B)	1806	Aug. 15	Dearborn(Ind	02	04	02
Bonta, Isaac(A)	1804	Dec. 07	Montgomery	03	05	12
Bonta, Jane(B)	1815	Dec. 21	Hamilton	02	06	03
Bonta, John(B)	1816	Dec. 11	Warren	02	02	36
Bonta, Peter A.(A)	1804	Nov. 30	Montgomery	03	05	14
Bonta, Peter J.(B)	1816	Jan. 05	Cincinnati	02	06	03
Bonta, Peter(A)	1803	Oct. 14	Montgomery	03	05	09
Bonta, Peter(A)	1803	Oct. 14	Montgomery	03	05	10
Bonta, Peter(A)	1804	Oct. 26	Montgomery	03	05	04
Bonta, Peter(A)	1805	Jan. 15	Montgomery	03	05	01
Bonta, Peter(A)	1805	Feb. 21	Montgomery	03	05	01
Bonta, Peter(C)	1804	Sept. 03	Montgomery	06	01	19
Bonta, Peter(C)	1804	Sept. 24	Montgomery	06	01	20
Bonta, Peter(C)	1809	Dec. 12	Montgomery	05	02	11
Bonta, Peter(C)	1809	Dec. 12	Montgomery	05	02	11
Bonta, Peter(E)	1816	Dec. 02	Montgomery	13	15	02
Bonte, Peter J.(B)	1817	Dec. 06	Dearborn(Ind	02	07	34
Bonte, Peter J.(B)	1819	Jan. 11	Dearborn(Ind	02	07	25
Bonte, Peter J.(B)	1834	June 16	Cincinnati	02	06	07
Bonwill, Henry M.(E)	1825	Nov. 01	Franklin(Ind	13	12	26
Boogher, John(A)	1813	Sept. 29	Montgomery	05	05	18
Booher, Daniel(E)	1838	May 18	Montgomery	15	22	15
Booher, John(A)	1818	Sept. 03	Montgomery	05	09	05
Booher, John(A)	1818	Sept. 11	Montgomery	05	09	05
Booher, Susanna(E)	1824	Oct. 28	Wayne(Ind)	13	16	35
Booing, Herman Hy.(E)	1836	Nov. 11	Cincinnati	12	10	05
Booling, Enoch(B)	1814	Nov. 28	Warren	01	12	35
Boomershein, Abraham(A)	1823	June 18	Montgomery	04	06	10
Boomershine, Henry(A)	1804	Aug. 10	Montgomery	04	03	03
Boomershine, Henry(C)	1801	Dec. 15	Hamilton	04	03	23
Boomershine, Peter(A)	1826	Aug. 17	Montgomery	04	05	22
Boomershire, Henry(A)	1809	Dec. 12	Montgomery	04	03	03
Boon, Daniel(A)	1805	Aug. 12	Kentucky	03	04	11
Boon, Daniel(A)	1810	Dec. 12	Kentucky	03	04	11
Boon, Daniel(A)	1814	Nov. 12	Preble	03	04	10
Boon, John Jr.(E)	1828	April 10	Randolph(Ind	14	18	12
Boon, John(E)	1836	Jan. 28	Randolph(Ind	14	19	35
Boon, Joseph(E)	1828	Aug. 29	Hamilton	13	17	01
Boone, Benjamin(B)	1808	April 25	Nor.Carolina	02	12	13
Boone, Thomas(A)	1806	Aug. 01	Hamilton	01	04	04
Boorom, Jonathan(C)	1832	March 16	Hamilton	13	03	03
Boots, Martin(E)	1820	March 28	Ross	14	21	20
Borchelt, John Hy. Wm.(E)	1836	Oct. 17	Cincinnati	11	10	13
Borders, Peter(C)	1807	March 11	Greene	13	01	14
Borders, Peter(C)	1812	April 15	Greene	13	01	14
Borders, William Blizzard(B)	1834	Sept. 25	Darke	01	16	15
Boreing, Ephraim(E)	1814	April 02	Clermont	13	13	10
Borgchas, Hy. Wm.(A)	1839	Jan. 21	Cincinnati	02	15	35
Borket, John Hy.(B)	1838	April 25	Cincinnati	03	05	24
Born, Henry Jnr.(A)	1818	March 17	Miami	03	10	03
Born, Henry Senr.(A)	1818	March 17	Miami	03	10	11
Bort, George(A)	1811	Oct. 10	Montgomery	03	07	20
Bortorf, Casper(A)	1808	March 12	Preble	02	07	34
Bosche, John Frederick(A)	1837	Sept. 15	Cincinnati	03	13	34
Bosche, John Frederick(A)	1837	Sept. 16	Cincinnati	03	13	27
Bosler, Henry(A)	1831	March 12	Miami	06	07	07
Bosow, John Senr.(B)	1818	Sept. 25	Switzerland	02	02	30

PURCHASER	YEAR	DATE	RESIDENCE	R	T	S
Bosseau, Jno. B.(B)	1831	Feb. 26	Switzerland	02	01	06
Bostick, Enoch(B)	1837	March 27	Dearborn(Ind	03	05	21
Boswell, Isom(E)	1836	April 21	Randolph(Ind	14	21	04
Boswell, Jacob(B)	1814	Dec. 09	Wayne(Ind)	01	14	02
Boswell, Jason(B)	1836	June 20	Wayne(Ind)	01	17	34
Boswell, Mariam(B)	1818	Jan. 24	Wayne(Ind)	01	14	11
Bothel, William(C)	1815	March 22	Ross	12	02	06
Botkin, Hugh(E)	1817	Sept. 29	Wayne(Ind)	13	18	03
Botkin, Hugh(E)	1831	July 04	Randolph(Ind	13	18	03
Botkin, James(E)	1833	Oct. 19	Randolph(Ind	13	19	28
Botkin, John(C)	1812	Jan. 04	Champaign	10	03	13
Botkin, John(C)	1812	Jan. 04	Champaign	10	03	19
Botkin, Peter(E)	1831	Dec. 01	Randolph(Ind	13	19	34
Botkin, Peter(E)	1835	Feb. 16	Randolph(Ind	13	19	34
Botkin, Peter(E)	1836	July 12	Randolph(Ind	13	19	34
Botkin, William(A)	1807	June 03	Kentucky	05	08	13
Botkin, William(B)	1804	Dec. 18	Kentucky	02	11	21
Bottorf, Casper(A)	1804	Oct. 27	Virginia	02	07	27
Bottorf, Casper(A)	1804	Oct. 27	Virginia	02	07	23
Bottorf, Casper(A)	1804	Oct. 27	Virginia	02	07	26
Bottorf, Casper(A)	1810	Oct. 19	Preble	02	07	34
Bottorf, Casper(A)	1810	Dec. 12	Preble	03	05	08
Bottorff, David(A)	1831	Nov. 08	Montgomery	04	09	30
Bottorff, David(A)	1832	May 01	Darke	04	09	21
Bottorff, David(A)	1832	May 30	Montgomery	04	09	30
Bouce, Amen(B)	1814	June 28	Dearborn(Ind	01	05	18
Boucher, Joshua(A)	1831	June 28	Miami	05	08	26
Boudenot, Elias(C)	1802	Nov. 25	Philadelphia	05	02	20
Bouge, Josiah(A)	1812	March 04	Preble	02	06	18
Bouge, William(A)	1812	March 04	Preble	02	06	18
Boulden, William L.(A)	1817	Dec. 16	Miami	05	08	04
Bounne, Ezra L.((B)	1814	Nov. 18	Ind.Territry	01	09	01
Bourn, Henry(A)	1815	May 23	Miami	07	05	07
Bourn, Henry(A)	1815	May 23	Miami	05	07	17
Bourne, Prince(A)	1812	Nov. 24	Butler	01	04	04
Bourne, Prince(A)	1815	Feb. 13	Butler	02	06	27
Bourne, Samuel(B)	1814	Aug. 08	Cincinnati	03	04	01
Bourne, Samuel(B)	1814	Aug. 24	Hamilton	01	09	01
Bousman, Adam(E)	1837	May 13	Preble	15	21	29
Bousman, Adam(E)	1838	May 21	Preble	14	20	01
Bousman, Noah(E)	1837	May 13	Preble	14	21	23
Bousman, Washington(E)	1837	May 13	Preble	14	20	01
Boutcher, Samuel(B)	1832	Aug. 22	Franklin(Ind	01	08	33
Bovard, Robert(B)	1817	Sept. 29	Hamilton	02	02	09
Bovard, Robert(B)	1817	Dec. 02	Hamilton	02	02	17
Bovard, Robert(B)	1817	Dec. 16	Hamilton	02	03	22
Bovard, Robert(B)	1817	Dec. 02	Hamilton	02	02	18
Bove, Benjamin(E)	1813	May 04	Franklin(Ind	12	14	21
Bovee, John(B)	1815	Dec. 21	Hamilton	02	06	10
Bowen, David(A)	1810	Sept. 12	Greene	05	04	29
Bowen, Enoch(A)	1817	Aug. 01	Montgomery	05	04	31
Bowen, Ephraim L.(B)	1831	Dec. 28	Randolph(Ind	01	17	34
Bowen, Ephraim(B)	1814	April 30	Greene	01	16	28
Bowen, Ephraim(B)	1818	Feb. 07	Wayne(Ind)	01	16	02
Bowen, James Collier(B)	1833	April 11	Randolph(Ind	01	16	21
Bowen, Jeremiah(E)	1834	March 25	Wayne(Ind)	13	17	07
Bowen, Joseph P.(A)	1811	Nov. 28	Pennsylvania	05	04	21
Bowen, Joseph(E)	1834	March 01	Wayne(Ind)	12	17	24
Bowen, William(A)	1817	Oct. 21	Pickaway	06	08	07
Bowen, William(A)	1818	Aug. 25	Piqua	06	08	07
Bower, Henry(A)	1836	June 02	Montgomery	01	13	04
Bower, John(A)	1813	Aug. 24	Montgomery	04	06	35
Bower, John(A)	1816	Oct. 26	Montgomery	04	06	11
Bower, John(A)	1828	April 18	Montgomery	04	06	09
Bowers, David(B)	1815	Aug. 05	Warren(Ind)	02	04	15
Bowers, Edward Eugene(B)	1836	Sept. 29	Kentucky	03	05	02
Bowers, James W.(A)	1836	July 08	Kentucky	01	15	10
Bowers, James W.(A)	1836	Oct. 15	Kentucky	01	15	15
Bowers, James W.(A)	1836	Oct. 15	Kentucky	01	15	15

PURCHASER	YEAR	DATE	RESIDENCE	R	T	S
Bowers, James W.(A)	1836	Dec. 01	Kentucky	01	15	25
Bowers, James W.(A)	1836	Oct. 15	Kentucky	03	12	05
Bowers, James W.(E)	1836	July 23	Kentucky	14	21	10
Bowers, John D.(A)	1814	Nov. 03	Hamilton	01	03	32
Bowers, Joseph(A)	1835	Jan. 30	Darke	01	13	23
Bowers, Joseph(A)	1836	Nov. 19	Darke	01	13	23
Bowersock, David(C)	1816	May 01	Warren	12	02	19
Bowersock, Samuel(C)	1831	Dec. 26	Miami	13	03	31
Bowin, John Dunkin(B)	1835	Oct. 14	Dearborn(Ind	02	05	07
Bowles, David(B)	1817	Aug. 29	Maryland	01	06	04
Bowles, David(E)	1817	Aug. 29	Maryland	14	17	03
Bowles, George F.(B)	1831	May 06	Randolph(Ind	01	16	11
Bowls, George Fox(E)	1836	Oct. 03	Wayne(Ind)	14	19	36
Bowls, Robert(C)	1806	May 28	Kentucky	09	03	09
Bowlsby, Enos(B)	1814	Aug. 15	Butler	02	11	36
Bowman, Benjamin(A)	1816	Sept. 10	Montgomery	04	09	15
Bowman, David(A)	1805	Oct. 28	Montgomery	04	05	35
Bowman, David(A)	1817	June 10	Montgomery	03	10	12
Bowman, Henry(A)	1805	July 02	Maryland	05	05	30
Bowman, Henry(A)	1805	July 02	Maryland	05	05	28
Bowman, Jacob Henry(C)	1818	Oct. 01	Cincinnati	13	02	13
Bowman, Jacob(A)	1805	Oct. 14	Montgomery	05	04	13
Bowman, Jacob(A)	1815	March 16	Montgomery	04	09	03
Bowman, Jacob(E)	1826	Aug. 31	Montgomery	14	15	29
Bowman, James(B)	1824	Aug. 30	Switzerland	03	03	18
Bowman, Jane(A)	1837	Jan. 05	Butler	01	13	35
Bowman, John(A)	1805	July 01	Montgomery	04	06	25
Bowman, John(A)	1806	March 06	Montgomery	05	05	08
Bowman, Richard E.(A)	1817	Oct. 27	Butler	05	09	32
Bowman, Thomas(B)	1816	Aug. 23	Dearborn(Ind	02	07	09
Bowman, Thomas(B)	1833	Sept. 20	Dearborn(Ind	01	08	33
Bowser, Catharine(A)	1814	July 25	Montgomery	04	09	27
Bowser, Daniel(A)	1801	Aug. 03	Hamilton	05	03	26
Bowser, Daniel(A)	1804	Oct. 09	Montgomery	05	03	30
Bowser, Daniel(A)	1804	Oct. 15	Montgomery	06	02	19
Bowser, Daniel(A)	1814	July 25	Montgomery	04	09	27
Bowser, David(A)	1814	July 25	Montgomery	04	09	27
Bowser, George(A)	1828	Dec. 03	Montgomery	04	05	21
Bowser, Henry(A)	1814	July 25	Montgomery	04	09	27
Bowser, Jacob(A)	1806	Dec. 26	Montgomery	06	02	17
Bowser, Philip(A)	1804	Oct. 25	Montgomery	05	04	13
Bowser, Philip(A)	1804	Oct. 25	Montgomery	05	03	30
Bowser, Sarah(A)	1814	July 25	Montgomery	04	09	27
Bowser, William(A)	1805	Oct. 16	Montgomery	05	04	10
Bowsman, Lawrence(C)	1810	Oct. 13	Virginia	12	04	21
Bowyer, John(A)	1831	Sept. 19	Warren	03	08	33
Bowyer, John(A)	1831	Sept. 27	Warren	03	08	32
Bowyer, John(A)	1832	Aug. 03	Warren	03	08	07
Boyd, Alexander(B)	1835	Oct. 09	Hamilton	01	08	08
Boyd, And'w.(A)	1828	Nov. 14	Darke	04	08	03
Boyd, Andrew(A)	1817	Aug. 22	Miami	03	11	35
Boyd, Andrew(A)	1831	Dec. 08	Miami	04	08	02
Boyd, Andrew(A)	1832	Jan. 16	Miami	04	09	35
Boyd, Elijah Lindsay(B)	1832	Feb. 10	Switzerland	02	02	21
Boyd, Elizabeth K.(A)	1828	Oct. 11	?	08	01	21
Boyd, Henry(B)	1833	March 02	Switzerland	02	02	29
Boyd, Jacob(B)	1838	Dec. 07	Switzerland	03	04	19
Boyd, James(B)	1819	Jan. 14	Kentucky	02	02	21
Boyd, James(B)	1832	Sept. 24	Switzerland	02	02	21
Boyd, James(E)	1811	Oct. 24	Preble	13	16	09
Boyd, James(E)	1817	Aug. 18	Wayne(Ind)	13	16	09
Boyd, James(E)	1832	June 21	Wayne(Ind)	13	16	09
Boyd, John J.(C)	1831	July 05	Champaign	12	03	31
Boyd, John(A)	1810	March 16	Kentucky	08	01	13
Boyd, John(B)	1836	Feb. 25	Switzerland	02	02	29
Boyd, Levi(B)	1836	Jan. 01	RipleyCo.Ind	03	06	15
Boyd, Melinda J.(A)	1828	Oct. 11	?	08	01	21
Boyd, Samuel(A)	1818	March 12	Darke	03	10	27
Boyd, Samuel(C)	1804	Dec. 21	Warren	05	03	21

PURCHASER	YEAR	DATE	RESIDENCE	R	T	S
Boyd, Samuel(E)	1811	Oct. 24	Preble	13	16	06
Boyd, Samuel(E)	1811	Oct. 24	Preble	13	16	22
Boyd, William(A)	1836	July 26	Miami	03	12	32
Boyd, William(C)	1801	Dec. 30	Hamilton	05	03	19
Boyd, William(C)	1812	Nov. 23	Champaign	12	04	06
Boyde, James(A)	1812	Oct. 03	Preble	01	06	07
Boyer, Benjamin(E)	1834	April 11	Franklin(Ind	11	10	02
Boyland, Nicholas(B)	1818	June 16	Butler	02	02	06
Boyle, James(B)	1818	Dec. 28	Dearborn(Ind	02	04	33
Boyle, James(B)	1831	Aug. 09	Dearborn(Ind	02	03	12
Boyle, John(E)	1836	Oct. 14	Cincinnati	11	10	27
Boyn, Christopher(A)	1830	March 03	Montgomery	06	07	04
Boyr, Christopher(A)	1830	March 03	Montgomery	06	07	04
Boyse, Dennis(A)	1807	Sept. 01	Pennsylvania	02	05	18
Boyse, James(A)	1807	Aug. 08	So. Carolina	01	06	08
Boyse, James(A)	1807	Aug. 08	So. Carolina	01	06	07
Boyse, James(A)	1807	Aug. 08	So. Carolina	01	06	17
Boyse, James(A)	1814	March 26	Preble	01	06	04
Boyse, Robert(A)	1808	Jan. 14	Butler	01	06	03
Boysworth, Henry(A)	1805	Dec. 16	Montgomery	01	08	19
Boze, Jacob(A)	1830	Sept. 17	Montgomery	03	08	36
Bracken, Jesse(C)	1804	Dec. 28	Greene	09	03	07
Bracken, Jesse(C)	1829	Sept. 28	Champaign	11	03	20
Bracken, Levi(B)	1816	June 10	Hamilton	01	06	09
Bracken, Mathew(C)	1811	Nov. 25	Greene	11	05	05
Bracken, Thomas(B)	1816	June 10	Hamilton	01	06	09
Brackenridge, Thomas(B)	1818	June 10	Dearborn(Ind	01	07	23
Brackenridge, Thos.McElrath(B)	1833	Feb. 20	Dearborn(Ind	01	07	23
Brackin, Jesse(C)	1825	June 17	Clark	10	03	29
Bradberry, Dan'l.(E)	1828	Dec. 31	Wayne(Ind)	13	17	09
Bradberry, Dan'l.(E)	1828	Dec. 31	Wayne(Ind)	13	17	09
Bradberry, David(E)	1814	March 23	Butler	13	17	21
Bradberry, Josiah(E)	1814	July 09	Champaign	13	17	21
Bradbery, David(A)	1809	Dec. 15	Butler	03	06	36
Bradburn, John(B)	1827	Dec. 04	Franklin(Ind	02	08	05
Bradburn, John(B)	1828	Nov. 12	Franklin(Ind	02	08	19
Bradburn, John(E)	1812	Oct. 08	Franklin(Ind	12	14	11
Bradbury, Ezekiel(E)	1828	Jan. 05	Wayne(Ind)	13	17	28
Bradbury, Gibens(B)	1814	April 12	Clermont	02	06	35
Bradbury, Thomas(B)	1814	May 17	Wayne(Ind)	01	12	17
Bradfield, Cary(E)	1836	Oct. 18	Wayne(Ind)	14	19	20
Bradfield, Elias(E)	1830	Dec. 15	Highland	13	17	15
Bradford, David(B)	1816	Jan. 15	Franklin(Ind	02	09	35
Bradford, Jesse(B)	1833	Oct. 16	Switzerland	02	02	01
Bradford, Joel(B)	1818	Aug. 13	Hamilton	01	02	15
Bradford, John Senr.(A)	1816	May 04	Montgomery	06	03	21
Bradford, John(A)	1816	May 04	Montgomery	06	03	22
Bradford, John(A)	1824	Aug. 07	Montgomery	06	03	22
Bradford, John(C)	1801	Dec. 14	Hamilton	07	02	19
Bradford, John(C)	1802	Nov. 29	Hamilton	07	02	15
Bradford, John(C)	1802	Dec. 28	Hamilton	06	02	28
Bradford, John(C)	1804	Sept. 24	Montgomery	07	02	26
Bradford, Samuel D.(A)	1819	Oct. 11	Montgomery	06	08	14
Bradford, William(A)	1819	Oct. 18	Montgomery	06	08	13
Bradford, Wm.(A)	1824	Aug. 07	Montgomery	06	03	22
Bradford, Wm.(E)	1837	Nov. 24	Montgomery	15	20	05
Bradin, Robert(C)	1826	May 02	Logan	13	04	11
Brading, James(C)	1831	Sept. 22	Shelby	12	01	10
Bradley, Edw'd.(C)	1815	Sept. 30	Hamilton	09	06	28
Bradley, John(E)	1811	Oct. 23	Ind.Territry	13	11	03
Bradley, Turpin K.(B)	1837	April 08	Clermont	03	05	35
Bradrick, Isaiah(A)	1831	Oct. 11	Greene	01	11	33
Bradshaw, Robt.(B)	1824	June 28	Dearborn(Ind	01	07	21
Bradway, Josiah(B)	1814	Sept. 27	Warren	01	12	32
Bradwell, Simeon(C)	1806	Nov. 08	Champaign	10	06	19
Bradwell, Simeon(C)	1807	Feb. 24	Champaign	09	06	24
Bradwell, Simeon(C)	1811	Dec. 11	Champaign	10	06	19
Brady, Asenath(A)	1818	Sept. 18	Darke	01	11	02
Brady, James(A)	1816	Aug. 31	Greene	01	12	26

33

COOS BAY OREGON FHC   037-008

PURCHASER	YEAR	DATE	RESIDENCE	R	T	S
Brady, James(A)	1817	Aug. 06	Dearborn(Ind	01	12	34
Brady, William(A)	1829	Oct. 15	Darke	01	11	20
Braffet, Alfred(A)	1831	Nov. 21	Darke	01	10	27
Braffet, Silas(A)	1818	Dec. 19	Warren	01	10	36
Bragg, Ephraim(E)	1837	Jan. 20	Randolph(Ind	14	21	14
Brake, George(C)	1816	Aug. 01	Greene	08	03	34
Brake, George(C)	1826	Nov. 29	Greene	08	03	29
Brake, John(A)	1816	Dec. 21	Greene	01	12	35
Brake, John(C)	1818	Feb. 03	Greene	08	03	34
Bramble, Ayers L.(B)	1836	April 02	Hamilton	03	05	09
Bramble, Laban(B)	1818	April 21	Hamilton	03	05	10
Bramble, Laban(B)	1834	May 01	Dearborn(Ind	03	05	09
Bramkamp, Diederich(A)	1834	Sept. 25	Montgomery	03	11	04
Brand, John(C)	1817	Nov. 03	Fairfield	12	03	25
Brandenburg, Henry(A)	1812	March 02	Warren	01	03	35
Brandenburg, Henry(B)	1813	Sept. 28	Warren	01	11	26
Brandenburg, Henry(C)	1809	July 27	Champaign	10	03	13
Brandenburg, Samuel(C)	1813	Aug. 06	Champaign	10	03	22
Brandenburg, Samuel(C)	1814	June 03	Champaign	09	03	30
Brandenburgh, Jacob(A)	1830	Oct. 13	Warren	03	08	31
Brandingburgh, Henry(C)	1804	Dec. 31	Warren	04	04	22
Brandom, John(B)	1832	Dec. 15	Switzerland	03	03	33
Brandon, Abel(A)	1814	April 14	Miami	05	08	05
Brandon, Abel(A)	1814	June 28	Miami	05	08	06
Brandon, Alexander B.(A)	1818	April 22	Warren	04	10	08
Brandon, Armstrong(A)	1808	July 07	Miami	05	08	24
Brandon, Armstrong(A)	1813	Dec. 18	Miami	05	08	24
Brandon, Benjamin(A)	1808	Jan. 12	Miami	05	08	13
Brandon, Benjamin(A)	1813	April 14	Miami	05	08	13
Brandon, David(A)	1820	Jan. 04	Warren	04	10	09
Brandon, Jesse(A)	1819	Sept. 28	Miami	06	08	26
Brandon, John(A)	1817	Sept. 26	Warren	04	10	05
Brandon, Moses R.(B)	1836	May 30	Switzerland	03	03	29
Brandon, Richard Jun.(A)	1817	Sept. 26	Warren	04	10	20
Brandon, Richard(A)	1817	Sept. 26	Warren	04	10	18
Brandon, Squire M.(A)	1831	Sept. 17	Darke	04	10	07
Brandon, Walter(A)	1817	Sept. 26	Kentucky	04	10	07
Brandt, Felix(B)	1818	April 13	Hamilton	02	03	14
Brandt, Felix(B)	1818	April 13	Hamilton	03	05	20
Brandt, Felix(B)	1818	April 13	Cincinnati	03	05	33
Brandt, Felix(B)	1818	April 13	Cincinnati	03	05	33
Brandt, Felix(B)	1818	April 15	Cincinnati	03	04	01
Brandt, Felix(B)	1818	June 18	Hamilton	03	05	34
Braner, Lewis(C)	1811	Dec. 30	Montgomery	08	02	17
Branett, Felix(B)	1817	Nov. 07	Cincinnati	03	02	20
Brann, Jeremiah(A)	1815	June 12	Hamilton	02	03	18
Brann, Matthew(A)	1813	Dec. 01	Warren	02	03	07
Brannan, James(A)	1806	Feb. 07	Hamilton	02	08	35
Brannen, Thomas(B)	1831	June 22	Dearborn(Ind	01	06	25
Brannon, Lawrence H.(E)	1818	March 21	Wayne(Ind)	14	15	08
Brannon, Lawrence H.(E)	1818	March 21	Wayne(Ind)	14	16	33
Brasher, Charles(B)	1812	April 09	Dearborn(Ind	03	04	02
Brasher, Jacob(B)	1812	March 16	Dearborn(Ind	03	04	04
Brasher, Jacob(B)	1812	April 09	Dearborn(Ind	03	04	02
Brasher, Jacob(B)	1815	March 16	Dearborn(Ind	01	05	06
Bratton, George(A)	1806	Oct. 18	Butler	06	06	30
Bray, Henry(E)	1814	Feb. 07	Hamilton	13	13	11
Bray, John((E)	1814	Jan. 28	Hamilton	13	13	10
Bray, John(B)	1816	March 05	Franklin(Ind	04	02	25
Bray, Thomas(E)	1814	Aug. 27	Hamilton	13	13	06
Breckenridge, Robert(B)	1817	June 30	Cincinnati	03	09	01
Brees, Henry(E)	1835	July 14	Franklin(Ind	12	10	02
Brelsford, James(C)	1821	Dec. 24	Greene	11	02	06
Brelsford, James(C)	1824	June 07	Greene	12	02	02
Brelsford, James(C)	1825	April 14	Greene	12	02	08
Brelsford, Sam'l.(C)	1829	Oct. 31	Montgomery	12	02	14
Brelsford, Sam'l.(C)	1830	Dec. 01	Montgomery	12	02	14
Brennaman, John(E)	1837	April 25	Butler	14	21	02
Bretney, Tobias(D)	1814	March 26	Warren	03	05	11

PURCHASER	YEAR	DATE	RESIDENCE	R	T	S
Brewater, Henry(E)	1836	Oct. 21	Cincinnati	11	10	12
Brewater, John Hy.(E)	1837	Jan. 12	Cincinnati	11	10	15
Brewer, Abram(A)	1837	Feb. 01	Warren	02	15	33
Brewer, Charles(B)	1815	Sept. 22	Warren	03	03	08
Brewer, Jesse(E)	1818	March 23	Wayne(Ind)	14	19	03
Brewer, Jesse(E)	1818	March 23	Wayne(Ind)	14	20	25
Brewer, Peter(A)	1818	May 26	Montgomery	03	11	33
Brewer, Stephen(E)	1831	Jan. 17	Randolph(Ind	13	18	03
Brewer, Stephen(E)	1834	Feb. 26	Randolph(Ind	13	18	02
Brewington, Benj'n.(B)	1835	Dec. 31	Dearborn(Ind	02	05	29
Brewington, Chas.(B)	1831	Sept. 03	Dearborn(Ind	03	06	13
Brewington, John(B)	1827	Nov. 12	Dearborn(Ind	03	06	13
Brewster, Samuel(C)	1801	Dec. 31	Hamilton	06	02	01
Brewster, Samuel(C)	1805	Aug. 28	Greene	06	02	01
Brian, Benj'n. Jr.(B)	1826	July 17	Dearborn(Ind	03	06	24
Brian, James(C)	1816	Jan. 08	Montgomery	13	01	03
Brian, John(C)	1816	Jan. 08	Montgomery	13	01	03
Brick, John(D)	1809	Oct. 23	Hamilton	01	01	08
Bridge, John(A)	1806	April 05	Butler	02	07	01
Bridge, John(A)	1811	Aug. 13	Preble	02	07	01
Bridged, George(B)	1813	Sept. 21	Butler	01	11	02
Bridges, John(B)	1814	Jan. 22	Clermont	02	10	03
Bridges, John(E)	1813	Dec. 21	Clermont	12	13	20
Bridges, William(E)	1816	Oct. 12	Greene	12	14	32
Brier, Andrew D.(C)	1805	Aug. 28	Montgomery	11	03	28
Brier, Andrew D.(C)	1806	April 12	Montgomery	11	03	35
Brier, Andrew D.(C)	1812	Nov. 13	?	09	02	11
Brier, George(C)	1812	Nov. 13	?	09	02	11
Brier, George(C)	1816	Dec. 19	Miami	10	03	26
Brier, George(C)	1824	June 25	Clark	10	03	26
Brier, James(C)	1807	June 17	Pennsylvania	11	03	27
Brier, John(C)	1806	Feb. 06	Montgomery	11	03	28
Brier, John(C)	1811	July 16	Montgomery	11	03	28
Brier, William(C)	1807	June 17	Pennsylvania	11	03	27
Brierton, Henry(B)	1836	April 14	Hamilton	02	03	20
Briggs, Ab'm.(B)	1827	Aug. 21	Dearborn(Ind	01	07	15
Briggs, Abel(E)	1835	Jan. 08	Warren	13	19	33
Briggs, Abm.(B)	1829	Dec. 08	Dearborn(Ind	01	07	20
Briggs, David(A)	1812	April 27	Darke	02	12	36
Briggs, William Smith(A)	1804	Oct. 09	Hamilton	01	02	01
Bright, Benjamin(E)	1834	June 02	Randolph(Ind	15	19	08
Bright, Benjamin(E)	1837	Jan. 05	Randolph(Ind	15	19	08
Bright, Goodone(C)	1804	Dec. 24	Warren	05	04	34
Bright, Henry(C)	1829	Dec. 11	Miami	11	02	08
Bright, Jesse(B)	1834	June 02	Preble	01	17	35
Bright, Jesse(B)	1836	June 20	Preble	01	17	35
Bright, Samuel(C)	1827	Dec. 03	Clark	10	03	29
Bright, William(B)	1832	June 13	Switzerland	03	03	29
Brill, Henry(A)	1805	June 19	Greene	02	08	02
Brill, John(A)	1804	Dec. 24	Warren	02	08	01
Brill, John(A)	1804	Dec. 24	Warren	02	09	36
Brindle, William(B)	1817	Oct. 29	Pennsylvania	02	03	26
Brindle, William(B)	1817	Oct. 29	Pennsylvania	02	03	21
Brindle, William(B)	1830	Feb. 25	Pennsylvania	02	03	27
Brindle, William(B)	1831	July 05	Pennsylvania	02	03	27
Brindley, Jonathan(A)	1814	June 22	Montgomery	04	06	28
Briney, Christopher(B)	1825	May 04	Dearborn(Ind	02	04	08
Briney, Daniel(A)	1817	Sept. 16	Warren	03	08	20
Briney, David(A)	1816	March 19	Butler	03	08	29
Briney, Frederick W.(A)	1831	May 28	Darke	03	08	07
Briney, John D.(A)	1828	April 01	Darke	03	08	19
Brinkman, Jno. Anthony(E)	1837	July 11	Kentucky	12	11	20
Brinkman, John(B)	1838	Dec. 20	Cincinnati	03	05	23
Brinley, John(A)	1825	Dec. 07	Butler	01	09	11
Brisbee, Isaiah(E)	1817	Aug. 01	Franklin(Ind	13	11	31
Brisbin, Robert(B)	1814	Oct. 24	Hamilton	01	10	29
Brison, Hugh(B)	1808	Dec. 14	Dearborn(Ind	01	07	05
Brison, Hugh(E)	1811	Oct. 21	Ind.Territory	12	12	22
Brison, Hugh(E)	1817	Sept. 11	Franklin(Ind	12	12	30

PURCHASER	YEAR	DATE	RESIDENCE	R	T	S
Brison, John(E)	1811	Oct. 22	Ind.Territry	12	13	02
Brison, John(E)	1812	March 13	Franklin(Ind	12	12	28
Bristow, Henry(A)	1812	Aug. 22	Preble	01	07	13
Bristow, Henry(A)	1814	Aug. 02	Preble	01	07	02
Bristow, Nero(B)	1835	Jan. 17	Preble	01	16	25
Bristow, Peyton(A)	1814	April 08	Preble	01	07	13
Bristow, Peyton(A)	1815	Jan. 26	Preble	01	07	02
Bristow, Thomas(A)	1814	Jan. 22	Preble	01	07	01
Brittain, Benj'n.(E)	1828	Aug. 16	Wayne(Ind)	14	18	29
Brittain, George(E)	1835	Feb. 24	Wayne(Ind)	13	18	13
Brittain, James(A)	1816	July 01	Preble	02	06	04
Brittain, James(E)	1826	Oct. 28	Wayne(Ind)	14	18	33
Britton, Henry(B)	1818	Feb. 03	Dearborn(Ind	02	04	19
Britton, Henry(B)	1818	March 18	Dearborn(Ind	02	04	19
Britton, Henry(B)	1827	Aug. 21	Dearborn(Ind	02	04	19
Britton, James(E)	1829	April 29	Wayne(Ind)	14	18	27
Broadbery, David(A)	1804	Nov. 03	Butler	04	04	08
Broadbury, David(A)	1804	Nov. 03	Butler	03	06	36
Broadbury, David(C)	1804	Sept. 03	Butler	04	02	11
Broadbury, Hezekiah(A)	1803	Nov. 16	Butler	02	05	34
Broadbury, Simeon(E)	1836	Oct. 07	Butler	13	12	18
Broadstone, Christian(A)	1814	Dec. 24	Montgomery	04	06	34
Broadstone, Christian(A)	1822	May 29	Montgomery	04	06	32
Broadstreet, Daniel(C)	1802	Nov. 17	Hamilton	05	03	33
Broadwell, Jacob	1808	March 02	Hamilton	?	?	?
Broadwell, Josiah(A)	1824	July 07	Montgomery	05	05	21
Broadwell, Josiah(A)	1824	July 07	Montgomery	05	05	21
Brocaw, Benjamin(A)	1817	Nov. 13	Miami	05	07	25
Brocaw, Henry(B)	1817	Dec. 09	Hamilton	03	05	02
Brock, Elijah(E)	1818	April 29	Wayne(Ind)	14	18	20
Brock, Frederick(A)	1815	June 07	Preble	03	07	23
Brock, Richard(E)	1814	Nov. 05	Wayne(Ind)	14	14	18
Brockamp, Henry(E)	1836	Nov. 11	Cincinnati	12	10	05
Brodberry, Simeon(A)	1806	Jan. 30	Butler	02	05	27
Broderick, John(A)	1827	June 30	Montgomery	04	07	35
Brodrick, Anthony(B)	1816	May 31	Hamilton	02	06	20
Brodrick, Anthony(B)	1828	Sept. 01	Hamilton	01	07	21
Brodrick, David(C)	1808	Dec. 27	Ohio	15	03	31
Brodrick, David(C)	1808	Dec. 27	Ohio	14	04	36
Brodrick, Patrick(A)	1812	Oct. 14	Montgomery	06	03	04
Brodrick, Solomon(A)	1815	Sept. 09	Butler	01	10	28
Bromagem, Elias(A)	1831	April 14	Darke	01	10	04
Brondon, Abel(A)	1818	Feb. 06	Miami	05	08	24
Bronius, Peter(A)	1811	June 03	Butler	02	04	20
Brook, Elias(B)	1829	Dec. 17	Franklin(Ind	02	09	10
Brook, Elias(E)	1836	Oct. 12	Franklin(Ind	12	11	02
Brookbank, Thomas H.(E)	1836	Oct. 11	Franklin(Ind	11	10	26
Brooks, Daniel(E)	1817	Dec. 27	Cincinnati	13	11	09
Brooks, Daniel(E)	1817	Dec. 27	Cincinnati	13	11	22
Brooks, Daniel(E)	1818	March 31	Hamilton	13	11	09
Brooks, Daniel(E)	1818	March 31	Hamilton	13	11	22
Brooks, Eli(B)	1816	Aug. 22	?	02	08	27
Brooks, Joab(B)	1813	Nov. 18	Warren	01	11	09
Brooks, Michael(E)	1837	Nov. 04	Richland	15	21	19
Brooks, Moses(B)	1817	July 12	Cincinnati	02	03	07
Brooks, Moses(B)	1818	Jan. 19	Cincinnati	02	03	20
Brooks, Moses(B)	1818	Jan. 19	Cincinnati	03	04	26
Brooks, Moses(B)	1818	Jan. 19	Cincinnati	02	03	29
Brooks, Moses(B)	1818	Jan. 19	Cincinnati	03	04	26
Brooks, Moses(B)	1818	Jan. 19	Cincinnati	03	04	26
Brooks, Moses(B)	1818	Nov. 23	Hamilton	03	04	34
Brooks, Moses(B)	1818	Dec. 28	Hamilton	03	03	09
Brooks, Moses(B)	1819	Feb. 15	Cincinnati	03	04	34
Brooks, Moses(E)	1818	Jan. 21	Cincinnati	14	20	26
Brooks, Moses(E)	1818	Jan. 21	Cincinnati	14	20	23
Brooks, Moses(E)	1818	Jan. 21	Cincinnati	14	20	34
Brooks, Moses(E)	1818	Jan. 21	Cincinnati	14	20	35
Brooks, Moses(E)	1818	Jan. 21	Cincinnati	14	20	33
Brooks, Moses(E)	1818	Jan. 31	Cincinnati	11	10	15

PURCHASER	YEAR	DATE	RESIDENCE	R	T	S
Brooks, Moses(E)	1818	Jan. 31	Cincinnati	11	10	25
Brooks, Moses(E)	1818	Jan. 31	Cincinnati	13	12	21
Brooks, Moses(E)	1818	Jan. 31	Cincinnati	11	10	10
Brooks, Moses(E)	1818	Jan. 31	Cincinnati	11	10	27
Brooks, Moses(E)	1818	April 06	Hamilton	14	20	30
Brooks, Moses(E)	1818	May 20	Hamilton	14	20	30
Brooks, Moses(E)	1818	June 08	Cincinnati	14	20	30
Brooks, Moses(E)	1818	June 08	Cincinnati	14	20	30
Brooks, Moses(E)	1818	July 15	Cincinnati	14	19	10
Brooks, Moses(E)	1818	July 30	Cincinnati	14	19	05
Brooks, Moses(E)	1818	July 30	Cincinnati	14	20	19
Brooks, Moses(E)	1818	July 30	Cincinnati	14	19	05
Brooks, Moses(E)	1818	July 30	Cincinnati	14	20	19
Brooks, Nimrod(A)	1817	Aug. 22	Montgomery	04	06	01
Broombaugh, Henry(A)	1811	Aug. 17	Montgomery	05	05	07
Bross, John E.(E)	1838	May 21	Preble	15	22	09
Brower, Christian(A)	1806	April 04	Montgomery	02	08	29
Brower, George(A)	1831	July 06	Montgomery	01	11	26
Brower, Henry(A)	1814	Dec. 31	Montgomery	02	08	30
Brower, Henry(A)	1816	July 24	Preble	03	05	22
Brower, Jacob(A)	1815	April 26	Montgomery	04	04	22
Brower, Jacob(A)	1825	Nov. 02	Preble	01	07	07
Brown, Aaron(A)	1837	March 01	Clark	01	13	17
Brown, Aaron(B)	1822	Feb. 22	Butler	03	03	02
Brown, Abraham(A)	1815	Nov. 27	Warren	01	06	13
Brown, Alex'r.(C)	1813	April 14	Champaign	11	04	31
Brown, Alexander(A)	1824	July 27	Miami	04	07	09
Brown, Alexander(C)	1815	March 22	Madison	12	03	12
Brown, Amos A.(B)	1824	Oct. 08	Switzerland	01	02	21
Brown, Amos A.(B)	1824	Oct. 08	Switzerland	01	02	15
Brown, Amos(B)	1814	Aug. 22	Dearborn(Ind	02	11	20
Brown, Amos(B)	1814	Feb. 18	Dearborn(Ind	01	02	27
Brown, Andrew(A)	1805	April 27	Hamilton	02	05	12
Brown, Ashur(C)	1804	Dec. 13	Warren	05	03	20
Brown, Benj'n.(B)	1820	Oct. 13	Cincinnati	02	07	05
Brown, Benjamin(B)	1813	June 07	Wayne(Ind)	01	13	32
Brown, Charles(C)	1801	Dec. 26	Hamilton	04	03	24
Brown, Clayton(A)	1815	Nov. 27	Warren	01	06	02
Brown, Clayton(E)	1837	March 24	Preble	13	21	25
Brown, Conrad(A)	1814	April 25	Preble	02	09	01
Brown, Daniel(C)	1829	Dec. 25	Clark	10	03	05
Brown, David(B)	1817	May 31	Cincinnati	01	12	12
Brown, David(B)	1817	Aug. 19	Cincinnati	03	08	26
Brown, David(B)	1817	Sept. 10	Cincinnati	03	09	13
Brown, David(B)	1818	June 05	Hamilton	03	06	23
Brown, David(B)	1834	Aug. 20	Switzerland	03	04	27
Brown, David(B)	1837	Feb. 28	Switzerland	03	04	23
Brown, David(C)	1814	Aug. 23	Champaign	11	04	27
Brown, David(C)	1816	Dec. 06	Cincinnati	13	03	09
Brown, David(C)	1816	Dec. 06	Cincinnati	13	03	09
Brown, David(C)	1816	Dec. 06	Cincinnati	13	03	15
Brown, David(C)	1817	Aug. 01	Wayne(Ind)	14	03	23
Brown, David(C)	1817	Aug. 01	Cincinnati	10	05	15
Brown, David(D)	1817	Aug. 01	Cincinnati	03	04	08
Brown, Eli(E)	1816	May 16	Wayne(Ind)	13	16	01
Brown, Elias(A)	1831	July 09	Darke	01	10	17
Brown, Ephraim(A)	1805	Feb. 23	Hamilton	01	06	17
Brown, Ephraim(B)	1813	Oct. 20	Hamilton	01	11	02
Brown, Ephraim(E)	1814	July 02	Hamilton	13	15	25
Brown, Ephraim(E)	1814	Nov. 05	Hamilton	12	15	26
Brown, Ethan A.(A)	1818	Jan. 20	Cincinnati	07	01	11
Brown, Ethan A.(A)	1818	April 13	Cincinnati	02	05	07
Brown, Ethan A.(B)	1818	Jan. 31	Cincinnati	02	03	18
Brown, Ethan A.(B)	1818	April 04	Cincinnati	01	02	01
Brown, Ethan A.(B)	1818	April 04	Cincinnati	03	03	17
Brown, Ethan A.(B)	1818	April 04	Cincinnati	03	03	04
Brown, Ethan A.(B)	1818	April 04	Cincinnati	03	04	32
Brown, Ethan A.(E)	1818	Jan. 20	Cincinnati	14	20	28
Brown, Ethan A.(E)	1818	Jan. 20	Cincinnati	14	20	28

PURCHASER	YEAR	DATE	RESIDENCE	R	T	S
Brown, Ethan A.(E)	1818	Jan. 20	Cincinnati	14	20	27
Brown, Ethan A.(E)	1818	Jan. 20	Cincinnati	14	20	27
Brown, Ethan A.(E)	1818	Jan. 20	Cincinnati	13	16	23
Brown, Ethan A.(E)	1818	May 02	Cincinnati	12	16	01
Brown, George M.(A)	1836	Oct. 27	Montgomery	01	13	27
Brown, George M.(A)	1838	Aug. 20	Greene	01	13	23
Brown, George M.(B)	1817	Aug. 04	Cincinnati	01	08	30
Brown, George M.(B)	1817	Aug. 04	Cincinnati	01	08	30
Brown, George(A)	1814	Dec. 21	Preble	01	06	15
Brown, George(B)	1836	April 07	Preble	01	17	14
Brown, George(E)	1815	Aug. 25	Highland	13	16	22
Brown, Harvey(E)	1811	Oct. 31	Franklin(Ind	13	11	04
Brown, Henderson S.(E)	1837	March 01	Preble	13	21	24
Brown, Henderson S.(E)	1837	March 27	Preble	13	21	24
Brown, Henderson Smiley(E)	1836	Feb. 20	Preble	11	11	02
Brown, Henry(A)	1803	April 04	Hamilton	02	04	36
Brown, Henry(A)	1806	Nov. 06	Montgomery	06	02	03
Brown, Henry(A)	1803	April 04	Hamilton	03	02	31
Brown, Henry(A)	1808	April 09	Butler	06	02	03
Brown, Henry(A)	1810	April 11	?	05	05	14
Brown, Henry(E)	1811	Oct. 23	Kentucky	12	16	24
Brown, Henry(E)	1811	Oct. 24	Kentucky	13	16	07
Brown, Henry(E)	1811	Oct. 31	Kentucky	13	16	07
Brown, Jacob(A)	1814	Nov. 10	Montgomery	02	07	24
Brown, Jacob(C)	1804	Dec. 31	Pennsylvania	06	01	05
Brown, Jacob(D)	1811	Sept. 02	Hamilton	01	03	08
Brown, James E.(B)	1817	Sept. 04	Hamilton	03	03	12
Brown, James Junr.(A)	1805	June 15	Butler	03	02	18
Brown, James Senr.(A)	1830	Jan. 05	Montgomery	01	11	32
Brown, James(A)	1805	June 13	Butler	03	02	17
Brown, James(A)	1805	June 13	Butler	01	04	01
Brown, James(A)	1805	June 15	Butler	03	02	18
Brown, James(A)	1805	Aug. 29	Butler	02	04	13
Brown, James(A)	1805	Sept. 27	Kentucky	06	04	31
Brown, James(A)	1807	Jan. 15	Butler	01	06	23
Brown, James(A)	1807	Feb. 27	Butler	01	06	24
Brown, James(A)	1807	Feb. 27	Butler	01	06	23
Brown, James(A)	1808	May 31	Kentucky	01	09	28
Brown, James(A)	1813	Aug. 10	Wayne(Ind)	01	09	28
Brown, James(A)	1813	Dec. 31	Preble	01	06	22
Brown, James(A)	1814	March 26	Butler	01	06	18
Brown, James(A)	1814	Sept. 02	Butler	01	06	19
Brown, James(A)	1817	June 07	Montgomery	02	09	29
Brown, James(C)	1807	March 14	Montgomery	09	02	31
Brown, James(C)	1808	April 12	Champaign	12	05	20
Brown, James(C)	1808	April 30	Champaign	12	05	13
Brown, James(C)	1808	April 30	Champaign	12	05	07
Brown, James(C)	1813	Aug. 10	Champaign	12	05	20
Brown, James(E)	1811	Oct. 24	Wayne(Ind)	13	16	08
Brown, John Campbell(B)	1836	March 03	Switzerland	02	02	29
Brown, John Jr.(A)	1818	Nov. 23	Maryland	01	10	18
Brown, John Jr.(A)	1818	Nov. 23	Maryland	01	10	08
Brown, John Junr.(B)	1807	June 18	Dearborn(Ind	02	11	25
Brown, John Junr.(B)	1813	April 14	Franklin(Ind	02	11	25
Brown, John Newell(A)	1831	Nov. 14	Miami	05	07	03
Brown, John P.(B)	1825	June 13	Dearborn(Ind	03	07	11
Brown, John Senr.(B)	1807	June 18	Dearborn(Ind	02	11	35
Brown, John Sr.(B)	1813	April 14	Franklin(Ind	02	11	35
Brown, John(A)	1805	Sept. 18	Dearborn(Ind	02	03	32
Brown, John(A)	1810	March 08	Miami	02	12	25
Brown, John(A)	1815	Nov. 27	Warren	01	06	12
Brown, John(A)	1816	Oct. 12	?	06	05	30
Brown, John(A)	1818	May 27	Preble	03	07	10
Brown, John(A)	1819	March 04	Miami	05	06	01
Brown, John(A)	1828	Feb. 04	Darke	01	10	18
Brown, John(A)	1829	Feb. 10	Warren	02	10	36
Brown, John(A)	1831	July 25	Miami	05	08	23
Brown, John(A)	1831	Aug. 09	Darke	01	10	08
Brown, John(A)	1831	Aug. 12	Miami	02	13	15

PURCHASER	YEAR	DATE	RESIDENCE	R	T	S
Brown, John(B)	1801	Aug. 13	Kentucky	01	07	09
Brown, John(B)	1801	Aug. 29	Kentucky	01	07	11
Brown, John(B)	1805	July 22	Dearborn(Ind	02	09	33
Brown, John(B)	1806	Dec. 03	Kentucky	01	05	10
Brown, John(B)	1814	Oct. 04	Butler	01	11	24
Brown, John(C)	1813	April 14	Champaign	11	04	31
Brown, John(E)	1811	Oct. 25	Ind.Territory	13	11	03
Brown, John(E)	1814	Oct. 17	Franklin(Ind	13	12	01
Brown, Jonathan(A)	1836	Aug. 12	Montgomery	02	12	05
Brown, Joseph Jnr.(A)	1816	Jan. 05	Warren	02	06	08
Brown, Joseph Jnr.(A)	1816	Jan. 20	Warren	02	07	29
Brown, Joseph(A)	1815	April 20	Butler	02	03	32
Brown, Joseph(A)	1830	Oct. 19	Warren	04	07	32
Brown, Joseph(B)	1816	April 30	Nor.Carolina	03	02	30
Brown, Joseph(B)	1818	Jan. 16	Wayne(Ind)	01	15	34
Brown, Joseph(B)	1818	Jan. 16	Wayne(Ind)	01	15	35
Brown, Joseph(C)	1807	Aug. 27	Clermont	12	01	22
Brown, Joseph(E)	1827	Sept. 24	Wayne(Ind)	14	16	03
Brown, Loyd(E)	1836	Oct. 11	Maryland	15	19	18
Brown, Martin(A)	1831	June 03	Stark	08	02	34
Brown, Matthew(A)	1803	July 02	Ohio	01	02	17
Brown, Matthew(A)	1836	Nov. 26	Butler	02	13	33
Brown, Matthew(B)	1806	Aug. 22	Kentucky	02	11	35
Brown, Matthew(B)	1806	Aug. 22	Kentucky	02	11	24
Brown, Matthew(B)	1816	Sept. 02	Franklin(Ind	02	10	17
Brown, Mercer(A)	1804	Nov. 10	Butler	03	04	25
Brown, Mercer(A)	1805	Nov. 19	Butler	03	04	11
Brown, Michael(A)	1810	Nov. 03	Preble	03	07	21
Brown, Michael(A)	1815	Aug. 24	Preble	02	09	12
Brown, Michael(E)	1814	June 07	Virginia	13	14	27
Brown, Michael(E)	1814	June 07	Virginia	13	13	02
Brown, Paul(B)	1815	Sept. 30	Hamilton	02	07	36
Brown, Paul(B)	1816	April 06	Hamilton	02	07	36
Brown, Paul(B)	1817	Nov. 19	Dearborn(Ind	02	06	01
Brown, Philip(A)	1827	Aug. 06	Darke	02	11	36
Brown, Philip(E)	1836	May 26	Preble	14	19	23
Brown, Philip(E)	1836	June 27	Preble	14	19	13
Brown, Philip(E)	1836	July 09	Preble	14	19	22
Brown, Richard(A)	1804	Nov. 06	Butler	04	03	26
Brown, Richard(A)	1805	June 07	Butler	04	03	18
Brown, Richard(A)	1805	June 07	Butler	04	03	19
Brown, Richard(A)	1809	Dec. 12	Montgomery	04	03	26
Brown, Richard(A)	1815	Jan. 03	Montgomery	03	04	20
Brown, Richard(A)	1815	Jan. 03	Montgomery	03	04	20
Brown, Richard(A)	1815	Feb. 18	Montgomery	03	04	20
Brown, Richard(A)	1815	Aug. 08	Preble	03	04	22
Brown, Richard(A)	1831	Aug. 09	Darke	01	10	08
Brown, Robert(A)	1806	Dec. 31	Butler	06	05	31
Brown, Robert(A)	1829	Oct. 03	Darke	04	07	09
Brown, Robert(E)	1811	Oct. 23	Butler	13	14	30
Brown, Robert(E)	1811	Oct. 31	Butler	13	14	19
Brown, Robert(E)	1813	Oct. 25	Butler	13	14	20
Brown, Robert(E)	1816	Nov. 30	Franklin(Ind	13	14	28
Brown, Robt.(A)	1829	June 24	Hamilton	04	06	21
Brown, Sam'l. H.(A)	1828	Jan. 28	Preble	01	09	21
Brown, Samuel Junr.(A)	1807	July 08	Miami	05	08	19
Brown, Samuel(A)	1808	March 29	Butler	02	06	07
Brown, Samuel(A)	1808	March 29	Butler	02	06	06
Brown, Samuel(A)	1812	Oct. 05	Butler	02	03	21
Brown, Samuel(A)	1813	Dec. 15	Preble	01	06	01
Brown, Samuel(A)	1816	Dec. 18	Warren	01	07	27
Brown, Samuel(A)	1817	June 17	Warren	01	07	20
Brown, Samuel(E)	1811	Oct. 23	Franklin(Ind	13	11	11
Brown, Samuel(E)	1813	Sept. 13	Franklin(Ind	13	15	18
Brown, Simon(E)	1836	May 09	Preble	11	12	36
Brown, Thomas(A)	1811	Dec. 20	Preble	02	06	07
Brown, Thomas(A)	1815	Aug. 08	Preble	01	06	27
Brown, Thomas(A)	1816	Feb. 01	Miami	05	06	08
Brown, Thomas(B)	1806	Nov. 14	Ind.Territory	02	11	26

PURCHASER	YEAR	DATE	RESIDENCE	R	T	S
Brown, Thomas(B)	1810	Sept. 06	Dearborn(Ind	01	11	30
Brown, Thomas(B)	1815	Aug. 29	Franklin(Ind	01	11	19
Brown, Thomas(B)	1817	Aug. 30	Cincinnati	01	11	19
Brown, Thomas(B)	1833	Sept. 06	Darke	01	16	25
Brown, Thos.(B)	1813	Aug. 31	Franklin(Ind	01	11	19
Brown, Timothy(A)	1812	Sept. 15	Warren	02	03	11
Brown, Timothy(E)	1835	Dec. 30	Franklin(Ind	12	11	01
Brown, Turner(E)	1838	Feb. 09	Darke	15	22	21
Brown, William(A)	1817	Sept. 05	Montgomery	02	09	29
Brown, William(A)	1822	Jan. 30	Darke	04	07	17
Brown, William(A)	1832	April 19	Greene	03	10	18
Brown, William(B)	1805	Dec. 18	Butler	01	11	24
Brown, William(B)	1808	Jan. 13	Butler	01	12	10
Brown, William(B)	1808	Jan. 13	Butler	01	12	11
Brown, William(B)	1817	Aug. 23	Tennessee	01	14	21
Brown, William(B)	1831	Oct. 06	Miami	01	16	36
Brown, William(B)	1832	June 11	Switzerland	03	03	14
Brown, William(B)	1838	Dec. 07	Switzerland	03	04	20
Brown, William(C)	1806	Aug. 25	Warren	11	02	22
Brown, William(C)	1807	Feb. 05	Warren	11	02	22
Brown, William(C)	1811	Dec. 11	Miami	11	02	22
Brown, William(C)	1828	Oct. 23	Miami	12	02	26
Brown, William(E)	1812	Oct. 16	Kentucky	12	16	13
Brown, William(E)	1836	Feb. 08	Wayne(Ind)	13	17	18
Brown, William(E)	1836	Feb. 08	Wayne(Ind)	13	17	18
Brown, William(E)	1836	Feb. 27	Wayne(Ind)	13	17	07
Brown, William(E)	1836	June 04	Randolph(Ind	14	20	07
Browning, Hiram(A)	1836	Nov. 04	Darke	02	13	21
Brownlee, Hugh(B)	1806	Jan. 16	Ind.Territory	01	07	24
Brownlee, James(E)	1813	Aug. 05	Franklin(Ind	12	13	13
Brownlee, James(E)	1813	Oct. 26	Franklin(Ind	12	14	34
Brownson, Asa(C)	1804	Dec. 31	Cincinnati	10	02	31
Brownson, Asa(C)	1804	Dec. 31	Cincinnati	10	02	31
Brownson, John(A)	1806	Dec. 29	Ind.Territory	06	07	28
Brownson, John(B)	1803	Jan. 24	Ind.Territory	02	04	23
Brownson, John(B)	1803	Jan. 24	Ind.Territry	02	04	13
Brownson, John(B)	1804	Nov. 27	Ind.Territry	02	04	13
Brownson, John(C)	1804	Dec. 31	Cincinnati	08	04	03
Brownson, John(C)	1804	Dec. 31	Cincinnati	07	02	05
Brownson, John(C)	1804	Dec. 31	Cincinnati	07	03	23
Brownson, John(C)	1804	Dec. 31	Cincinnati	08	03	01
Brownson, John(C)	1804	Dec. 31	Cincinnati	07	02	03
Brownson, John(C)	1804	Dec. 31	Cincinnati	08	04	27
Brownson, John(C)	1804	Dec. 31	Cincinnati	09	04	01
Brownson, John(C)	1804	Dec. 31	Cincinnati	06	01	07
Brownson, John(C)	1804	Dec. 31	Cincinnati	10	02	31
Brownson, John(C)	1804	Dec. 31	Cincinnati	09	02	06
Brownson, John(C)	1804	Dec. 31	Cincinnati	08	03	18
Brownson, John(C)	1807	Jan. 13	FortWayneInd	11	01	02
Brownson, John(C)	1807	Jan. 13	FortWayneInd	11	01	04
Brownson, Reuben(E)	1814	April 02	Butler	12	15	10
Brubaker, Barbara(C)	1828	May 23	Champaign	12	03	09
Brubaker, Dan'l.(A)	1825	June 17	Preble	01	08	26
Brubaker, Sam'l.(A)	1828	April 23	Preble	01	07	13
Bruce, Aman(B)	1817	Aug. 06	Dearborn(Ind	03	06	12
Bruce, Amer(B)	1813	Dec. 21	Dearborn(Ind	02	05	01
Bruce, Amer(B)	1817	Nov. 22	Dearborn(Ind	03	06	01
Bruce, Amer(B)	1827	Aug. 21	Dearborn(Ind	02	05	22
Bruce, Amor(B)	1806	Jan. 07	Ind.Territory	02	05	23
Bruce, Charles(A)	1804	July 23	Butler	05	04	26
Bruce, Harden(A)	1816	Feb. 01	Preble	04	09	05
Bruce, Henry(B)	1829	May 06	Dearborn(Ind	02	05	22
Bruce, Henry(E)	1815	Sept. 11	Dearborn(Ind	13	12	23
Bruce, James(B)	1807	Jan. 07	Ind.Territry	02	05	23
Bruce, James(B)	1811	Dec. 12	Dearborn(Ind	02	05	24
Bruce, John Jr.(B)	1833	April 17	Dearborn(Ind	02	05	22
Bruce, John(B)	1836	May 31	Dearborn(Ind	02	05	22
Bruce, Stephen(B)	1836	May 31	Dearborn(Ind	02	05	22
Bruce, William(A)	1804	Aug. 27	Butler	04	03	23

PURCHASER	YEAR	DATE	RESIDENCE	R	T	S
Bruce, William(A)	1804	Sept. 01	Butler	02	07	03
Bruce, William(A)	1804	Sept. 01	Butler	05	04	29
Bruce, William(A)	1804	Sept. 13	Butler	02	07	04
Bruce, William(A)	1804	Sept. 13	Butler	05	04	18
Bruce, William(A)	1804	Sept. 25	Butler	06	06	07
Bruce, William(A)	1804	Sept. 25	Ohio	06	02	01
Bruce, William(A)	1806	March 03	Butler	02	07	02
Bruce, William(A)	1806	May 24	Montgomery	02	08	36
Bruce, William(A)	1806	June 30	Montgomery	02	07	04
Bruce, William(A)	1806	July 22	Montgomery	02	07	11
Bruce, William(A)	1806	Dec. 31	Montgomery	02	07	04
Bruce, William(A)	1806	Dec. 31	Montgomery	02	07	11
Bruce, William(A)	1807	May 07	Montgomery	02	07	11
Bruce, William(A)	1807	May 07	Montgomery	02	08	29
Bruce, William(A)	1813	Oct. 13	Preble	02	07	04
Bruen, Luther(A)	1807	Jan. 15	Dayton	05	07	25
Bruengart, Sebastian(E)	1833	May 13	Randolph(Ind	13	21	12
Brumback, John(A)	1815	Oct. 10	Pennsylvania	04	09	10
Brumback, John(A)	1815	Oct. 10	Pennsylvania	04	09	11
Brumback, John(A)	1815	Oct. 10	Pennsylvania	04	09	14
Brumbaugh, David(A)	1830	April 10	Montgomery	04	07	25
Brumbaugh, George(A)	1815	Aug. 19	Montgomery	04	09	11
Brumbaugh, Henry(A)	1827	May 18	Montgomery	04	06	01
Brumbaugh, Henry(A)	1830	April 10	Montgomery	04	07	36
Brumbaugh, Jacob(A)	1828	Oct. 07	Montgomery	04	07	36
Brumbaugh, John(A)	1818	Nov. 19	Miami	04	10	32
Brumbaugh, John(A)	1818	Nov. 19	Miami	04	10	33
Brumbaugh, William(A)	1805	Oct. 24	Pennsylvania	05	04	30
Brumbaugh, William(A)	1814	June 17	Montgomery	05	05	06
Brumbaugh, William(A)	1817	Aug. 26	Montgomery	04	09	02
Brumblay, John(B)	1817	Nov. 17	Cincinnati	03	06	11
Brumfield, Jesse(E)	1836	Aug. 24	Ross	14	19	30
Brumfield, John(A)	1806	Oct. 20	Pennsylvania	01	04	04
Brumfield, John(A)	1818	Dec. 08	Butler	13	12	21
Brumfield, Thos.(E)	1827	Oct. 18	Wayne(Ind)	13	16	30
Brumlu, Saml.(B)	1815	Oct. 17	Dearborn(Ind	03	05	01
Brummit, Spencer(A)	1832	Oct. 02	Darke	01	10	08
Brummitt, Peter(E)	1837	Feb. 16	Preble	15	21	15
Brummitt, Spencer(E)	1836	Jan. 27	Darke	15	21	15
Brummitt, Spencer(E)	1836	Nov. 12	Darke	15	21	15
Bruner, Simon(C)	1810	June 12	Montgomery	08	02	17
Bruner, Simon(C)	1810	June 12	Montgomery	08	02	12
Brunner, John(B)	1832	Dec. 28	Cincinnati	02	07	19
Brunson, John(C)	1832	March 29	Logan	14	02	06
Brush, Edward(E)	1815	May 27	Franklin(Ind	12	12	14
Brush, Edward(E)	1815	June 05	Cincinnati	12	12	14
Brush, Edward(E)	1816	March 22	Franklin(Ind	12	12	15
Brush, Jared(B)	1837	June 07	Clermont	03	05	35
Bryan, Abram(C)	1831	Jan. 31	Champaign	12	04	15
Bryan, Abram(C)	1831	Feb. 10	Champaign	12	04	15
Bryan, Henry(E)	1811	Oct. 22	Butler	12	13	34
Bryan, Henry(E)	1811	Oct. 24	Wayne(Ind)	13	15	01
Bryan, Henry(E)	1811	Oct. 24	Ind.Territry	13	16	36
Bryan, Henry(E)	1811	Oct. 24	Ind.Territry	13	16	36
Bryan, Henry(E)	1811	Oct. 28	Wayne(Ind)	13	16	33
Bryan, Henry(E)	1812	Feb. 14	Wayne(Ind)	13	15	29
Bryan, Henry(E)	1816	Dec. 02	Wayne(Ind)	13	16	33
Bryan, Henry(E)	1828	Oct. 13	Wayne(Ind)	14	16	28
Bryan, James(A)	1819	Oct. 08	Shelby	06	08	13
Bryan, John(C)	1816	Sept. 03	Miami	13	01	03
Bryant, Joseph(B)	1819	March 26	Switzerland	03	03	19
Bryant, Joseph(B)	1833	Dec. 28	BrookeCo.Vir	03	03	19
Bryant, Joseph(B)	1836	Feb. 26	Belmont	03	03	19
Bryant, Thomas C.(B)	1837	Aug. 25	Belmont	03	03	19
Bryson, Archibald(A)	1815	Aug. 25	Darke	02	11	06
Bryson, James F.(E)	1836	July 22	Butler	14	21	04
Bryson, James(A)	1818	Feb. 03	Darke	02	11	05
Bryson, James(A)	1818	June 29	Montgomery	02	11	05
Buchanan, James(E)	1814	Oct. 22	Franklin(Ind	12	13	17

PURCHASER	YEAR	DATE	RESIDENCE	R	T	S
Buchanan, John(A)	1803	July 09	Warren	03	03	35
Buchannon, John(A)	1807	July 04	Virginia	05	06	14
Buchannon, John(A)	1812	March 13	Butler	01	04	09
Buchannon, John(C)	1801	Dec. 28	Hamilton	04	04	27
Buchter, Frederick(A)	1827	Dec. 07	Montgomery	04	06	21
Buck, Abiathar O.(C)	1817	Sept. 18	Champaign	12	03	04
Buck, Conrod(B)	1815	Feb. 24	Hamilton	01	03	30
Buck, Conrod(B)	1815	Aug. 16	Switzerland	01	03	31
Buck, David(A)	1832	March 10	Preble	03	08	22
Buck, John(A)	1815	Oct. 24	Preble	01	06	18
Buck, John(A)	1818	Feb. 12	Preble	01	06	29
Buck, John(A)	1821	March 27	Warren	04	05	17
Buck, Nicholas(A)	1805	Sept. 19	Montgomery	03	07	28
Buck, Nicholas(A)	1814	June 16	Montgomery	04	04	20
Buck, Sherman A.(B)	1824	Aug. 07	Franklin(Ind	01	08	21
Buck, Warren(E)	1817	July 11	Warren	13	12	20
Buck, William Sherman(B)	1818	Sept. 14	Hamilton	01	02	22
Buckannon, Robert-Heirs(C)	1802	Dec. 28	Hamilton	04	03	21
Buckel, David(B)	1834	April 04	Hamilton	02	06	08
Buckel, Matthias(B)	1834	April 04	Hamilton	02	06	15
Buckengham, Enoch(B)	1815	Jan. 02	Hamilton	02	09	11
Buckhannan, John(B)	1804	Sept. 18	Dearborn(Ind	01	01	05
Buckhannon, Eleanor(C)	1801	Dec. 30	Hamilton	04	03	21
Buckhannon, James(A)	1813	Dec. 23	Miami	06	07	20
Buckhanon, James(B)	1814	Aug. 18	Hamilton	01	04	31
Buckingham, Enoch(B)	1815	Jan. 18	Hamilton	01	09	21
Buckingham, Enoch(B)	1815	Jan. 18	Hamilton	02	09	03
Buckingham, Enoch(B)	1815	Jan. 18	Hamilton	01	09	15
Buckingham, Joshua(E)	1831	June 04	Randolph(Ind	15	19	06
Buckingham, Joshua(E)	1826	Aug. 11	Randolph(Ind	15	19	06
Buckingham, Thomas(E)	1836	June 13	Randolph(Ind	15	19	06
Buckler, Joel Jackson(E)	1836	Feb. 04	Franklin(Ind	12	12	32
Buckles, Abraham(B)	1815	Aug. 28	Montgomery	02	11	34
Buckles, John(C)	1801	Dec. 31	Hamilton	05	02	05
Buckles, John(C)	1802	Dec. 28	Hamilton	05	03	34
Buckles, John(C)	1802	Dec. 31	Hamilton	05	04	27
Buckles, Robert(C)	1802	Dec. 28	Hamilton	05	04	28
Buckles, William(C)	1801	Dec. 31	Hamilton	05	04	34
Buckles, William(C)	1817	May 31	Montgomery	11	02	30
Buckly, William(C)	1814	Nov. 29	Champaign	09	04	30
Buckly, William(C)	1826	Sept. 12	Greene	11	03	30
Buckman, John Hy.(E)	1836	Oct. 21	Cincinnati	12	10	08
Buckman, John Hy.(E)	1837	Jan. 12	Cincinnati	11	10	15
Bucknall, John(A)	1801	July 02	Cincinnati	01	01	21
Budd, John(C)	1828	March 19	Clark	08	05	29
Buel, Walter(E)	1811	Oct. 24	Preble	13	16	06
Buell, George Pearson(B)	1835	Nov. 07	Dearborn(Ind	02	07	05
Buell, George Pearson(B)	1836	Feb. 01	Dearborn(Ind	02	07	05
Buell, George Pearson(B)	1836	Feb. 01	Dearborn(Ind	02	08	32
Buff, John(A)	1837	Oct. 17	Clermont	01	14	31
Buffenbeger, George(C)	1806	Nov. 26	Greene	08	06	35
Buffenberger, Peter(C)	1811	Nov. 18	Virginia	08	05	05
Buffington, Benjamin(A)	1836	July 13	Butler	01	13	35
Buffington, Jacob H.(E)	1836	Dec. 15	Warren	15	22	14
Buffington, Jahiel(B)	1814	May 05	Dearborn(Ind	02	04	09
Buffington, Jahiel(B)	1814	June 28	Dearborn(Ind	01	05	18
Buffington, Johiel(B)	1815	Feb. 10	Dearborn(Ind	02	04	03
Buffington, John(B)	1811	Jan. 28	Dearborn(Ind	02	04	02
Buffington, John(B)	1811	Feb. 15	Dearborn(Ind	01	05	30
Buffington, Jonathan(B)	1814	Sept. 12	Dearborn(Ind	02	04	04
Buffum, John(B)	1818	July 21	Hamilton	01	07	33
Buhler, Augustin(A)	1834	April 14	Montgomery	03	10	19
Buhler, Augustin(A)	1834	May 12	Montgomery	03	10	30
Bulkley, Anson(E)	1836	Nov. 26	Franklin(Ind	11	10	14
Bulkley, Isaac(B)	1816	Sept. 04	Franklin(Ind	02	10	29
Bull, Nathan(C)	1814	Oct. 26	Greene	12	02	35
Bull, Nathan(C)	1814	Dec. 22	?	12	02	35
Bulla, Isaac(A)	1824	June 08	Wayne(Ind)	01	08	21
Bulla, Thomas(A)	1824	June 21	Wayne(Ind)	01	08	21

PURCHASER	YEAR	DATE	RESIDENCE	R	T	S
Bulla, Thomas(A)	1825	Feb. 09	Wayne(Ind)	01	08	21
Bulla, Thomas(B)	1806	March 07	Montgomery	01	13	13
Bulla, Thomas(B)	1814	Nov. 05	Wayne(Ind)	01	13	14
Bulla, Thomas(B)	1824	June 21	Wayne(Ind)	01	13	22
Bulla, William(E)	1815	Feb. 03	Wayne(Ind)	13	17	23
Bulla, William(E)	1815	Feb. 03	Wayne(Ind)	13	17	28
Bullock, Stephen(E)	1814	Aug. 24	Franklin(Ind	12	12	30
Bumgarner, Andrew(C)	1811	April 19	Clinton	10	06	20
Bunce, Richard(B)	1834	April 18	Franklin(Ind	01	08	31
Bunch, Nazareth(A)	1824	July 10	Wayne(Ind)	01	10	19
Bundy, Josiah(B)	1833	April 24	Randolph(Ind	01	16	35
Bundy, Josiah(B)	1833	Sept. 30	Randolph(Ind	01	16	35
Bundy, Josiah(E)	1815	May 18	Nor.Carolina	13	16	11
Bundy, Josiah(E)	1815	Oct. 28	Wayne(Ind)	13	16	20
Bundy, Samuel(E)	1834	Oct. 09	Wayne(Ind)	13	17	19
Bundy, William H.(E)	1831	July 05	Wayne(Ind)	14	16	33
Bunger, George(A)	1817	June 13	Butler	03	07	25
Bunger, George(A)	1824	Sept. 28	Preble	02	09	22
Bunger, John(A)	1818	June 25	Ohio	03	07	25
Bunker, Freeman(C)	1832	March 10	Logan	14	03	21
Bunnel, James(A)	1805	Nov. 07	Warren	04	04	08
Bunnel, James(C)	1804	Dec. 28	Warren	05	03	14
Bunnell, Jonas(C)	1815	July 06	Madison	11	02	17
Bunnell, Jonas(C)	1815	July 06	Madison	11	02	17
Burbidge, Elijah(B)	1814	Sept. 30	Franklin(Ind	02	11	03
Burbidge, Robert(B)	1814	Sept. 30	Franklin(Ind	02	11	03
Burbow, Edward(E)	1814	July 20	Warren	14	17	31
Burch, Arnold(B)	1818	July 13	Hamilton	03	06	22
Burch, Charles(A)	1805	Sept. 02	Hamilton	02	02	06
Burch, Charles(B)	1812	Aug. 24	Hamilton	01	09	02
Burch, Daniel(A)	1805	Oct. 24	Kentucky	02	05	19
Burch, Daniel(A)	1807	Sept. 02	Hamilton	02	05	17
Burch, Henry(B)	1818	March 06	Butler	03	03	08
Burcham, Dan'l.(B)	1824	Feb. 12	Switzerland	03	03	29
Burcham, Daniel(B)	1834	April 19	Switzerland	03	03	28
Burdg, Anthony(A)	1807	June 01	Butler	02	06	05
Burditt, Booth(C)	1818	April 30	Miami	13	02	05
Buren, Daniel(B)	1817	Oct. 23	Switzerland	03	02	29
Burges, John(B)	1806	Aug. 27	Warren	01	13	05
Burgess, Dyer(A)	1817	Oct. 27	Miami	06	05	18
Burgess, Dyer(A)	1817	Oct. 27	Miami	06	05	18
Burgess, Nelson(B)	1817	July 12	Dearborn(Ind	02	05	30
Burgess, Nelson(B)	1817	Dec. 22	Dearborn(Ind	02	05	29
Burgess, Walter S.(B)	1811	Oct. 09	Kentucky	01	12	08
Burgess, Wert(C)	1812	June 22	Maryland	08	03	17
Burgess, West(C)	1812	July 28	Maryland	08	03	15
Burget, Emanuel(A)	1806	April 08	Butler	01	04	35
Burget, Emanuel(A)	1807	Jan. 21	Montgomery	01	04	09
Burget, Emanuel(A)	1812	April 15	Butler	01	04	09
Burget, George(A)	1804	June 29	Butler	02	04	34
Burget, Henry(B)	1812	Aug. 24	Butler	01	09	03
Burget, Jacob(B)	1824	Oct. 20	Cincinnati	02	07	22
Burgoine, Wm.(B)	1833	Aug. 06	Cincinnati	01	07	18
Burgoine, Wm.(B)	1834	May 09	Cincinnati	01	07	18
Burgoyne, Horatio Nelson(E)	1832	Feb. 01	Franklin(Ind	12	13	17
Burgoyne, Horatio Nelson(E)	1832	Feb. 21	Franklin(Ind	12	13	19
Burk, Elisha(B)	1817	Oct. 18	Hamilton	04	02	25
Burk, Elisha(B)	1818	Aug. 05	Hamilton	01	07	25
Burk, Hansberry(E)	1833	Oct. 01	Rush(Ind)	11	12	24
Burk, Hardin(E)	1833	Oct. 01	Rush(Ind)	11	12	24
Burk, James(B)	1813	Nov. 04	Kentucky	01	04	19
Burk, James(B)	1816	Oct. 29	Dearborn(Ind	03	05	36
Burk, John(A)	1809	Dec. 21	Butler	01	04	22
Burk, John(A)	1814	May 17	Butler	01	04	15
Burk, Thomas(A)	1804	Dec. 24	Butler	01	04	26
Burk, Thomas(A)	1810	July 09	Butler	01	04	22
Burk, Thomas(A)	1813	July 22	Butler	01	04	26
Burk, Thomas(B)	1806	April 08	Butler	01	10	26
Burk, Thomas(B)	1806	July 23	Butler	01	12	08

43

PURCHASER	YEAR	DATE	RESIDENCE	R	T	S
Burk, Thomas(B)	1806	July 23	Butler	01	12	05
Burk, Thomas(B)	1806	July 28	Butler	01	12	07
Burk, Ulick(B)	1832	May 24	Hamilton	01	07	25
Burk, Ullick(B)	1818	Aug. 05	Hamilton	01	07	25
Burkdol, Abraham(B)	1816	Feb. 14	Hamilton	02	02	23
Burke, Elisha(B)	1832	March 07	Hamilton	01	07	36
Burke, James(B)	1814	July 14	Dearborn(Ind	02	01	06
Burke, John(B)	1818	Jan. 16	Dearborn(Ind	01	06	07
Burke, Stephen(B)	1832	March 07	Hamilton	01	07	36
Burket, Catharine(A)	1831	Sept. 26	Montgomery	03	10	02
Burket, David Junr.(A)	1808	July 23	Miami	04	09	14
Burket, Jacob(A)	1827	Aug. 08	Miami	06	04	18
Burket, Joseph Jr.(A)	1826	June 26	Miami	05	07	18
Burket, Solomon(A)	1831	Sept. 20	Miami	05	06	02
Burket, Solomon(A)	1831	Oct. 15	Miami	05	06	01
Burkett, John(A)	1818	May 26	Montgomery	03	11	20
Burkhalter, Abraham(B)	1810	Dec. 29	Dearborn(Ind	02	11	11
Burkhart, Joseph(A)	1811	Sept. 26	Miami	05	06	14
Burley, John(A)	1837	May 12	Butler	01	12	02
Burn, Daniel(A)	1826	July 28	Miami	05	08	31
Burn, Michael(A)	1811	Aug. 27	Montgomery	05	07	08
Burn, Michael(A)	1831	June 17	Miami	04	09	21
Burn, Michael(A)	1831	June 17	Miami	04	09	28
Burn, Michael(A)	1831	Oct. 06	Darke	04	09	28
Burnan, Thomas G.(A)	1826	March 09	Preble	01	09	21
Burnberger, William(C)	1807	March 14	Montgomery	09	02	31
Burnes, Henry(A)	1814	Dec. 07	Ohio	05	07	17
Burnes, James(C)	1816	Oct. 09	Madison	08	07	36
Burnet, Jac.(E)	1811	Nov. 16	?	13	17	13
Burnet, Jacob(A)	1815	April 01	Cincinnati	02	08	11
Burnet, Jacob(A)	1815	April 01	Cincinnati	01	07	07
Burnet, Jacob(A)	1815	April 01	Cincinnati	03	04	26
Burnet, Jacob(A)	1815	April 24	Cincinnati	01	02	25
Burnet, Jacob(A)	1815	Nov. 01	Cincinnati	02	08	11
Burnet, Jacob(A)	1816	Aug. 01	Cincinnati	08	01	01
Burnet, Jacob(A)	1819	May 18	Cincinnati	08	01	10
Burnet, Jacob(B)	1815	March 18	Ohio	03	03	02
Burnet, Jacob(B)	1815	March 18	Ohio	03	03	11
Burnet, Jacob(B)	1815	March 18	Cincinnati	03	03	11
Burnet, Jacob(B)	1815	May 04	Cincinnati	02	07	24
Burnet, Jacob(B)	1815	Nov. 01	Cincinnati	03	02	03
Burnet, Jacob(C)	1804	Dec. 31	Cincinnati	09	03	07
Burnet, Jacob(C)	1804	Dec. 31	Cincinnati	08	05	34
Burnet, Jacob(C)	1804	Dec. 31	Cincinnati	08	05	34
Burnet, Jacob(C)	1804	Dec. 31	Cincinnati	08	05	34
Burnet, Jacob(C)	1804	Dec. 31	Cincinnati	09	02	06
Burnet, Jacob(C)	1804	Dec. 31	Cincinnati	09	04	20
Burnet, Jacob(C)	1810	Dec. 12	Cincinnati	09	05	21
Burnet, Jacob(C)	1812	April 15	Cincinnati	10	05	28
Burnet, Jacob(C)	1812	April 15	Cincinnati	10	05	35
Burnet, Jacob(C)	1812	April 15	Cincinnati	10	05	35
Burnet, Jacob(C)	1812	April 15	Cincinnati	10	05	34
Burnet, Jacob(C)	1812	April 15	Cincinnati	10	05	35
Burnet, Jacob(C)	1812	April 15	Cincinnati	10	05	34
Burnet, Jacob(C)	1812	April 15	Cincinnati	10	05	34
Burnet, Jacob(C)	1812	April 15	Cincinnati	10	05	34
Burnet, Jacob(C)	1812	April 15	Cincinnati	10	05	36
Burnet, Jacob(C)	1812	April 15	Cincinnati	10	05	36
Burnet, Jacob(C)	1812	April 15	Cincinnati	10	05	36
Burnet, Jacob(C)	1812	April 15	Cincinnati	10	05	28
Burnet, Jacob(C)	1812	April 15	Cincinnati	10	05	28
Burnet, Jacob(C)	1812	April 15	Cincinnati	10	05	35
Burnet, Jacob(C)	1812	April 15	Cincinnati	10	04	05
Burnet, Jacob(C)	1812	April 15	Cincinnati	10	04	04
Burnet, Jacob(C)	1812	April 15	Cincinnati	10	04	03
Burnet, Jacob(C)	1813	June 29	Cincinnati	02	02	26
Burnet, Jacob(C)	1813	Oct. 09	Cincinnati	08	03	09
Burnet, Jacob(C)	1815	April 10	Cincinnati	11	02	07
Burnet, Jacob(C)	1815	April 22	Cincinnati	09	04	36

PURCHASER	YEAR	DATE	RESIDENCE	R	T	S
Burnet, Jacob(C)	1815	May 04	Cincinnati	11	04	07
Burnet, Jacob(C)	1815	May 04	Cincinnati	11	04	07
Burnet, Jacob(C)	1815	May 04	Cincinnati	12	05	34
Burnet, Jacob(C)	1815	May 08	Cincinnati	13	04	35
Burnet, Jacob(C)	1815	May 08	Cincinnati	13	04	35
Burnet, Jacob(C)	1815	May 08	Cincinnati	13	04	34
Burnet, Jacob(C)	1815	May 08	Cincinnati	13	04	34
Burnet, Jacob(C)	1815	May 08	Cincinnati	13	03	04
Burnet, Jacob(C)	1815	May 08	Cincinnati	14	03	28
Burnet, Jacob(C)	1815	May 08	Cincinnati	14	03	34
Burnet, Jacob(C)	1915	May 08	Cincinnati	14	03	34
Burnet, Jacob(C)	1815	May 08	Cincinnati	14	03	33
Burnet, Jacob(C)	1815	May 08	Cincinnati	14	02	09
Burnet, Jacob(C)	1815	May 08	Cincinnati	14	03	10
Burnet, Jacob(C)	1815	May 08	Cincinnati	14	03	09
Burnet, Jacob(C)	1815	May 08	Cincinnati	14	03	09
Burnet, Jacob(C)	1815	May 08	Cincinnati	14	03	09
Burnet, Jacob(C)	1815	May 08	Cincinnati	14	03	03
Burnet, Jacob(C)	1815	May 08	Cincinnati	14	03	03
Burnet, Jacob(C)	1815	May 08	Cincinnati	14	03	10
Burnet, Jacob(C)	1815	May 08	Cincinnati	14	03	03
Burnet, Jacob(C)	1815	May 08	Cincinnati	14	03	02
Burnet, Jacob(C)	1815	May 08	Cincinnati	14	03	02
Burnet, Jacob(C)	1815	May 08	Cincinnati	14	03	02
Burnet, Jacob(C)	1815	May 08	Cincinnati	14	03	02
Burnet, Jacob(C)	1815	May 08	Cincinnati	14	04	32
Burnet, Jacob(C)	1815	May 08	Cincinnati	14	04	32
Burnet, Jacob(C)	1815	May 08	Cincinnati	14	04	32
Burnet, Jacob(C)	1815	May 08	Cincinnati	14	02	17
Burnet, Jacob(C)	1815	May 09	Cincinnati	14	03	15
Burnet, Jacob(C)	1815	May 09		14	03	15
Burnet, Jacob(C)	1815	May 09		14	03	10
Burnet, Jacob(C)	1815	May 09		14	03	10
Burnet, Jacob(C)	1815	May 09		14	03	14
Burnet, Jacob(C)	1815	May 09		14	03	14
Burnet, Jacob(C)	1815	May 09		14	03	14
Burnet, Jacob(C)	1815	May 09		14	03	14
Burnet, Jacob(C)	1815	May 09		14	03	15
Burnet, Jacob(C)	1815	May 09		14	03	15
Burnet, Jacob(C)	1815	May 09		14	03	17
Burnet, Jacob(C)	1815	May 09		14	03	17
Burnet, Jacob(C)	1815	May 09		14	02	03
Burnet, Jacob(C)	1815	May 09		14	02	34
Burnet, Jacob(C)	1815	May 09		14	02	34
Burnet, Jacob(C)	1815	May 15	Cincinnati	10	04	12
Burnet, Jacob(C)	1815	May 18		15	03	31
Burnet, Jacob(C)	1815	May 18		14	03	06
Burnet, Jacob(C)	1815	May 18		14	03	17
Burnet, Jacob(C)	1815	May 18		14	03	18
Burnet, Jacob(C)	1815	May 19	Cincinnati	14	03	18
Burnet, Jacob(C)	1815	May 19		14	03	06
Burnet, Jacob(C)	1815	May 19		14	03	18
Burnet, Jacob(C)	1815	May 19		14	03	06
Burnet, Jacob(C)	1815	June 03	Cincinnati	10	03	33
Burnet, Jacob(C)	1815	May 18		14	04	36
Burnet, Jacob(C)	1831	Aug. 08	Cincinnati	14	03	11
Burnet, Jacob(C)	1831	Aug. 08	Cincinnati	14	03	11
Burnet, Jacob(C)	1831	Aug. 08	Cincinnati	14	03	11
Burnet, Jacob(E)	1811	Oct. 28	Cincinnati	12	15	01
Burnet, Jacob(E)	1811	Oct. 28	Cincinnati	14	16	20
Burnet, Jacob(E)	1811	Oct. 28	Cincinnati	14	16	20
Burnet, Jacob(E)	1811	Oct. 28	Cincinnati	12	13	35
Burnet, Jacob(E)	1815	June 19	Cincinnati	12	11	20
Burnet, Jacob(E)	1815	June 19	Cincinnati	12	11	20
Burnet, Ralph(A)	1830	Feb. 16	Miami	06	07	09
Burnet, Robert(B)	1814	Nov. 15	Wayne(Ind)	01	12	20
Burnett, Jacob(C)	1815	May 08	Cincinnati	13	04	36
Burnett, Jacob(C)	1815	May 08	Cincinnati	14	03	04
Burns, Anthony(A)	1811	Aug. 12	Butler	03	03	07

45

PURCHASER	YEAR	DATE	RESIDENCE	R	T	S
Burns, Archibold(A)	1805	Aug. 06	Hamilton	01	04	28
Burns, Barnabas(A)	1814	March 14	Darke	02	11	04
Burns, James(C)	1806	July 24	Champaign	10	04	36
Burns, James(C)	1806	Nov. 28	Champaign	09	06	13
Burns, James(C)	1810	Oct. 26	Champaign	08	06	06
Burns, James(C)	1814	July 18	Madison	08	07	36
Burns, James(C)	1815	Dec. 12	Champaign	08	06	06
Burns, James(E)	1817	Sept. 15	Warren	13	18	12
Burns, Jeremiah(A)	1819	Dec. 14	Warren	04	05	18
Burns, John(A)	1805	Aug. 06	Hamilton	01	04	28
Burns, John(B)	1815	Feb. 03	Clermont	02	11	35
Burns, Joseph(C)	1828	April 16	Logan	14	03	36
Burns, Michael(A)	1805	June 18	Montgomery	05	05	29
Burns, Michael(C)	1805	Nov. 01	Montgomery	07	03	12
Burns, Robert(A)	1810	Oct. 13	Miami	06	06	31
Burns, Robert(C)	1804	Sept. 03	Warren	05	04	26
Burns, Robert(E)	1835	Jan. 23	Wayne(Ind)	13	18	22
Burns, Thomas(B)	1818	Jan. 24	Hamilton	01	04	17
Burns, Thomas(C)	1817	Aug. 22	Hamilton	12	01	03
Burntrager, David(A)	1802	Dec. 29	Hamilton	05	02	08
Burntrager, David(A)	1806	July 21	Montgomery	05	08	19
Burntrager, David(A)	1806	Aug. 06	Montgomery	05	07	06
Burr, Charlotte(E)	1833	May 31	Cincinnati	13	11	09
Burr, Charlotte(E)	1817	Dec. 27	Cincinnati	13	11	22
Burr, Edwd. W.(E)	1817	Dec. 27	Cincinnati	13	11	22
Burroughs, Elhanan(B)	1836	May 12	RipleyCo.Ind	03	06	33
Burroughs, Ephraim(B)	1819	Jan. 22	Dearborn(Ind	03	05	12
Burroughs, Ephraim(B)	1835	May 09	Dearborn(Ind	03	05	12
Burroughs, James L.(B)	1837	Jan. 28	Hamilton	03	04	27
Burroughs, James(B)	1836	Sept. 27	Hamilton	03	04	27
Burroughs, William(E)	1816	Aug. 06	Miami	13	18	26
Burroughs, William(E)	1816	Aug. 06	Miami	13	17	14
Burrows, Aaron(B)	1816	Dec. 18	Hamilton	01	06	31
Burrows, Stephen(B)	1817	Dec. 01	Cincinnati	03	06	25
Burrows, Stephen(B)	1818	Feb. 28	Hamilton	02	03	06
Burrows, Stephen(B)	1818	Feb. 28	Hamilton	02	03	06
Burrows, Stephen(B)	1818	Feb. 28	Hamilton	03	04	23
Burrows, Stephen(B)	1818	Feb. 28	Hamilton	03	04	27
Burrows, Stephen(B)	1818	Feb. 28	Hamilton	02	03	08
Burrows, Stephen(B)	1818	March 11	Cincinnati	03	04	28
Burt, Andrew(A)	1838	Jan. 31	Greene	02	14	24
Burt, Andrew(C)	1813	April 14	Cincinnati	09	05	32
Burt, William(C)	1801	Dec. 30	Hamilton	05	04	21
Burt, William(C)	1801	Dec. 31	Hamilton	05	04	21
Burt, Zephaniah(B)	1814	June 17	Pennsylvania	01	11	08
Burtis, Jesse(B)	1818	Jan. 15	Cincinnati	02	06	08
Burton, Allen(B)	1815	Oct. 28	Hamilton	03	03	25
Burton, Bazel(A)	1816	March 26	Miami	06	08	19
Busch, John Fred'k.(E)	1836	Oct. 17	Cincinnati	11	10	13
Busch, John Fred'k.(E)	1836	Oct. 18	Cincinnati	11	10	13
Bush, John Henry(B)	1832	Aug. 14	Germany	02	07	34
Bush, Martin D.(B)	1817	Oct. 09	Cincinnati	03	04	14
Bush, William(A)	1811	Jan. 29	Miami	06	08	30
Bushnell, Chauncey K.(A)	1837	Sept. 13	Cincinnati	01	13	02
Buson, Hugh(E)	1816	Sept. 16	Franklin(Ind	12	12	21
Buster, William(B)	1813	May 22	Franklin(Ind	01	08	10
Butcher, George(B)	1817	Dec. 08	Hamilton	03	03	20
Butcher, Joseph(C)	1811	Feb. 04	Champaign	09	03	17
Butler, Amos(A)	1806	April 04	Pennsylvania	01	01	18
Butler, Amos(A)	1807	Jan. 05	Dearborn(Ind	01	06	35
Butler, Amos(B)	1804	Dec. 04	Pennsylvania	02	09	20
Butler, Amos(B)	1805	July 11	Dearborn(Ind	02	09	29
Butler, Amos(B)	1806	March 18	Pennsylvania	02	09	29
Butler, Amos(B)	1806	March 18	Pennsylvania	02	09	20
Butler, Amos(B)	1806	April 04	Pennsylvania	02	09	20
Butler, Amos(B)	1806	Oct. 01	Pennsylvania	02	09	29
Butler, Amos(B)	1808	Aug. 22	Dearborn(Ind	02	09	20
Butler, Amos(B)	1811	Dec. 05	Franklin(Ind	02	09	21
Butler, Beal(E)	1816	Sept. 28	Wayne(Ind)	14	16	15

PURCHASER	YEAR	DATE	RESIDENCE	R	T	S
Butler, Beale(B)	1806	July 23	Dearborn(Ind	01	12	18
Butler, Beale(B)	1806	July 29	Warren	02	13	23
Butler, Chas. E.(A)	1838	May 21	New York	02	13	02
Butler, Chas. E.(A)	1838	May 21	New York	02	13	01
Butler, Eli(E)	1814	Jan. 31	Wayne(Ind)	14	16	21
Butler, Elias P.(B)	1817	Dec. 18	Cincinnati	02	05	32
Butler, Enos(E)	1816	Sept. 17	Wayne(Ind)	14	16	31
Butler, Enos(E)	1816	Sept. 17	Wayne(Ind)	14	16	32
Butler, Hiram(E)	1816	Sept. 28	Wayne(Ind)	14	16	32
Butler, Hiram(E)	1816	Sept. 28	Wayne(Ind)	14	16	15
Butler, Ira(C)	1814	May 14	Champaign	09	06	25
Butler, Ira(C)	1816	May 09	Champaign	09	06	31
Butler, Isaac(E)	1838	May 21	Jay Co.,Ind.	15	22	02
Butler, James(A)	1817	Nov. 24	Greene	04	08	18
Butler, James(B)	1815	Nov. 09	Dearborn(Ind	01	03	35
Butler, James(C)	1815	Sept. 08	Champaign	09	06	26
Butler, James(E)	1837	Jan. 09	Randolph(Ind	13	19	13
Butler, Joseph(B)	1832	March 16	Dearborn(Ind	02	07	13
Butler, Joshua(B)	1814	Jan. 20	Butler	02	10	26
Butler, Nathan(E)	1836	Oct. 05	Highland	14	19	21
Butler, Nathan(E)	1836	Oct. 11	Highland	14	19	21
Butler, Noble(B)	1804	Oct. 22	Pennsylvania	01	06	11
Butler, Stephen(B)	1817	Dec. 18	Cincinnati	03	06	13
Butler, Stephen(B)	1817	Dec. 18	Cincinnati	03	06	34
Butler, Stephen(E)	1817	Dec. 05	Cincinnati	13	11	15
Butler, Susannah(B)	1806	Aug. 01	Dearborn(Ind	02	13	12
Butler, Susannah(B)	1806	Aug. 01	Dearborn(Ind	01	14	17
Butler, Thomas(C)	1804	Oct. 11	Warren	05	03	14
Butler, William(B)	1814	Nov. 23	Franklin(Ind	02	09	21
Butler, William(C)	1809	April 08	Cincinnati	02	04	26
Butler, William(E)	1817	Sept. 01	Wayne(Ind)	14	15	05
Butnet, Jacob(C)	1812	April 15	Cincinnati	10	05	36
Butt, Adam(A)	1812	Nov. 21	Montgomery	04	04	17
Butt, Henry Jr.(E)	1836	May 23	Preble	11	10	14
Butt, Henry Jr.(E)	1836	July 28	Preble	11	10	14
Butt, Henry Senr.(E)	1836	July 28	Preble	11	10	23
Butt, Henry(A)	1814	March 18	Montgomery	04	04	08
Butt, Henry(A)	1814	Sept. 20	Montgomery	02	07	13
Butt, Henry(A)	1818	Oct. 21	Montgomery	04	05	20
Butt, Henry(A)	1828	April 09	Montgomery	04	05	15
Butt, Jacob(A)	1824	Jan. 29	Montgomery	04	05	30
Butt, John(A)	1828	Oct. 15	Montgomery	04	05	15
Butt, John(E)	1836	May 23	Preble	11	10	11
Butt, Thomas(A)	1815	March 07	Pickaway	05	10	32
Butter, Stephen(B)	1817	Dec. 05	Cincinnati	02	08	07
Butterfield, Warren W. S.(B)	1837	Feb. 04	Darke	01	18	35
Button, James(A)	1824	June 08	Preble	02	07	21
Buxton, Brook(A)	1810	Jan. 02	Butler	04	03	26
Buxton, Moses(A)	1836	Dec. 16	Hamilton	02	15	32
Buzzard, Henry(C)	1813	Jan. 01	Champaign	10	05	21
Buzzard, Samuel(B)	1835	Dec. 26	Randolph(Ind	01	16	14
Byard, David(A)	1832	Aug. 14	Darke	02	13	35
Byerly, William(C)	1818	Feb. 28	Butler	13	01	01
Byers, Elizabeth(A)	1816	Nov. 13	?	02	13	24
Byers, Isaac(E)	1835	March 09	Preble	14	21	29
Byers, James(B)	1834	June 24	Dearborn(Ind	02	05	07
Byers, Samuel(A)	1831	July 08	Shelby	06	08	34
Byers, William(A)	1815	March 15	Preble	03	07	04
Byram, Benjamin(A)	1807	June 01	Montgomery	01	09	32
Byram, David C.(A)	1836	Aug. 19	Butler	01	12	06
Byram, Ebenezer(A)	1816	Sept. 03	Warren	03	10	26
Byram, Ebenezer(A)	1816	Sept. 03	Warren	02	12	29
Byram, Ebenezer(A)	1816	Sept. 30	Warren	02	12	20
Byres, David(C)	1812	July 13	Champaign	11	05	06
Byrkit, Solomon(A)	1831	June 30	Miami	05	07	36
Byrkit, Solomon(E)	1815	Nov. 11	Wayne(Ind)	12	15	22
Byrne, Charles(A)	1817	Oct. 23	Cincinnati	02	08	22
Byrne, Charles(A)	1817	Oct. 23	Cincinnati	02	09	26
Byrne, Charles(A)	1818	Jan. 03	Cincinnati	02	09	29

PURCHASER	YEAR	DATE	RESIDENCE	R	T	S
CXonwell, Francis A.(E)	1836	June 16	Franklin(Ind	12	12	07
Cabe, Elias(B)	1822	Feb. 05	Warren	01	15	31
Cable, John(A)	1815	Aug. 19	Montgomery	05	08	18
Cable, John(A)	1817	July 14	?	04	09	08
Cable, Martin(A)	1810	March 05	Montgomery	04	05	26
Cable, Martin(A)	1824	June 08	Darke	04	09	15
Cadbury, Henry(B)	1801	Dec. 17	Hamilton	01	03	09
Cadbury, Henry(C)	1804	Dec. 31	Philadelphia	09	05	23
Cadbury, Henry(C)	1804	Dec. 31	Philadelphia	09	05	17
Cadbury, Henry(C)	1804	Dec. 31	Philadelphia	09	05	18
Cadbury, Henry(C)	1804	Dec. 31	Philadelphia	09	05	24
Cadbury, Henry(C)	1804	Dec. 31	Philadelphia	09	05	23
Cadbury, Henry(C)	1804	Dec. 31	Philadelphia	09	05	24
Caderman, Michael(A)	1805	Nov. 25	Montgomery	04	05	13
Cadwalader, Abner(E)	1831	Jan. 20	Wayne(Ind)	14	18	13
Cadwalader, Amos(B)	1818	March 21	Wayne(Ind)	01	15	02
Cadwalader, Thomas Jr.(E)	1837	April 15	Wayne(Ind)	14	19	36
Cady, David(B)	1818	March 12	Hamilton	02	03	08
Cahill, William(E)	1835	July 21	Franklin(Ind	12	12	18
Cahill, William(E)	1836	Jan. 25	Franklin(Ind	12	12	18
Cain, Abijah(B)	1813	April 14	Wayne(Ind)	01	14	20
Cain, Abijah(C)	1804	Dec. 29	Warren	05	04	33
Cain, Abner(B)	1807	June 26	Warren	01	14	20
Cain, David(B)	1831	Aug. 11	Switzerland	04	02	35
Cain, David(B)	1836	Sept. 10	Switzerland	03	03	09
Cain, Hardy(B)	1814	Sept. 22	Montgomery	01	14	19
Cain, Humphrey(B)	1837	April 05	Dearborn(Ind	03	05	02
Cain, John(E)	1814	Aug. 02	Wayne(Ind)	13	17	10
Cain, Joseph(B)	1814	Sept. 22	Montgomery	01	14	19
Cain, Joshua(B)	1827	Sept. 07	Switzerland	04	02	35
Cain, Samuel(E)	1818	Oct. 26	Greene	14	21	21
Cain, Samuel(E)	1836	March 11	Randolph(Ind	14	21	28
Cairnes, Mary(A)	1830	July 31	Shelby	06	08	21
Cairns, William(B)	1817	July 25	Dearborn(Ind	02	07	31
Caldwell, Bartholomew(B)	1824	June 09	Dearborn(Ind	02	05	15
Caldwell, Bartholomew(B)	1832	April 23	Dearborn(Ind	02	05	15
Caldwell, James Junr.(B)	1812	Dec. 10	Dearborn(Ind	01	08	02
Caldwell, James(A)	1805	Sept. 04	Butler	01	06	09
Caldwell, James(A)	1805	Sept. 19	Butler	01	06	09
Caldwell, James(A)	1810	Dec. 12	Butler	01	06	09
Caldwell, James(A)	1814	July 26	Miami	05	08	07
Caldwell, James(A)	1814	July 26	Miami	06	08	01
Caldwell, James(E)	1811	Oct. 22	Preble	12	14	03
Caldwell, James(E)	1814	Aug. 18	Dearborn(Ind	12	14	03
Caldwell, Jno.(B)	1812	Dec. 10	Dearborn(Ind	01	08	02
Caldwell, Jno.(B)	1824	June 09	Dearborn(Ind	02	05	15
Caldwell, John(E)	1814	March 04	Preble	12	15	28
Caldwell, Joseph(A)	1805	Sept. 19	Butler	01	06	05
Caldwell, Joseph(A)	1810	Dec. 12	Butler	01	06	05
Caldwell, Joseph(E)	1811	Oct. 22	Preble	12	15	33
Caldwell, Joseph(E)	1813	Dec. 11	Franklin(Ind	12	14	04
Caldwell, Manlove(E)	1814	April 23	Wayne(Ind)	12	15	28
Caldwell, Matthew(A)	1804	Sept. 25	Kentucky	06	06	19
Caldwell, Matthew(A)	1805	Sept. 27	Kentucky	06	06	19
Caldwell, Matthew(A)	1805	Oct. 26	Kentucky	06	06	19
Caldwell, Matthew(A)	1804	Sept. 24	Kentucky	06	06	19
Caldwell, Matthew(A)	1804	Sept. 24	Kentucky	06	06	30
Caldwell, Robert(A)	1817	Oct. 14	Pennsylvania	07	01	18
Caldwell, Robert(A)	1817	Oct. 14	Pennsylvania	07	01	18
Caldwell, Robert(C)	1816	Jan. 15	Hamilton	11	05	08
Caldwell, Samuel(B)	1824	Aug. 16	Dearborn(Ind	02	07	13
Caldwell, Train(E)	1811	Oct. 22	Preble	12	15	34
Caldwell, Wesley(B)	1836	Jan. 29	Dearborn(Ind	02	05	04
Caldwell, William(A)	1813	April 14	Preble	01	06	36
Caldwell, William(A)	1814	Nov. 25	Butler	01	06	35
Caldwell, William(B)	1812	Dec. 07	Dearborn(Ind	01	05	04
Calfee, James(E)	1835	Aug. 08	Franklin(Ind	13	11	09
Calfer, Henry(E)	1811	Oct. 23	Franklin(Ind	13	11	10
Calland, William(C)	1831	Oct. 05	Champaign	13	03	08

PURCHASER	YEAR	DATE	RESIDENCE	R	T	S
Callaway, Jacob(C)	1812	Jan. 18	Hamilton	09	05	07
Callaway, John(A)	1805	July 13	Warren	04	04	17
Callaway, John(C)	1806	Feb. 06	Greene	08	05	10
Callaway, John(C)	1806	Feb. 06	Greene	08	05	23
Callaway, John(C)	1814	Feb. 21	Greene	09	05	07
Callaway, Thomas(C)	1812	Jan. 18	Hamilton	09	05	07
Callen, William(C)	1829	Nov. 09	Ohio	13	03	14
Calleson, John(C)	1812	July 13	Champaign	09	04	24
Calver, Samuel(C)	1810	Dec. 12	Champaign	11	06	32
Calwell, Abraham R.(C)	1817	May 27	?	13	04	01
Calwell, John(B)	1808	Jan. 13	Dearborn(Ind	01	08	01
Calwell, Matthew(C)	1808	March 03	Miami	12	01	05
Camblin, George(D)	1812	Feb. 24	Warren	03	04	26
Cambridge, Levine(E)	1815	Aug. 25	Franklin(Ind	13	13	17
Camell, Stephen(C)	1817	Aug. 01	Champaign	09	05	15
Cammack, James(B)	1814	Jan. 21	Montgomery	01	16	33
Cammons, Nathan(E)	1817	Dec. 11	Wayne(Ind)	13	16	23
Camp, Aaron(A)	1832	March 26	Darke	02	10	15
Camp, David N.(E)	1818	Aug. 05	Connecticut	12	12	05
Camp, David N.(E)	1818	Aug. 05	Connecticut	12	12	11
Campbell, Abraham(A)	1831	Oct. 28	Miami	08	01	08
Campbell, Abraham(C)	1811	Nov. 27	Champaign	11	04	34
Campbell, Alexander(A)	1814	March 11	Preble	03	04	23
Campbell, Alexander(A)	1818	April 18	Preble	03	05	12
Campbell, Alexander(A)	1818	April 20	Preble	03	05	12
Campbell, Colin(C)	1802	Dec. 29	Hamilton	04	02	06
Campbell, Daniel(C)	1830	Dec. 28	Miami	08	01	08
Campbell, Ebenezer G.(E)	1837	May 19	Greene	15	22	34
Campbell, Ephraim Cole(C)	1831	Sept. 06	Montgomery	12	03	32
Campbell, Howell(E)	1817	Oct. 23	Warren	12	17	24
Campbell, James G.(E)	1837	May 19	Greene	15	22	34
Campbell, Jno. P.(E)	1837	Sept. 13	Greene	15	22	34
Campbell, John P.(E)	1837	May 19	Greene	15	22	34
Campbell, John(A)	1814	Oct. 14	Butler	01	07	34
Campbell, John(A)	1816	July 30	Nor.Carolina	01	08	21
Campbell, John(A)	1816	July 30	Nor.Carolina	01	08	22
Campbell, John(A)	1831	Aug. 23	Miami	06	08	30
Campbell, John(B)	1814	June 28	Franklin(Ind	02	11	15
Campbell, John(B)	1817	Dec. 16	Franklin(Ind	02	11	10
Campbell, John(C)	1826	Jan. 17	Champaign	11	03	17
Campbell, John(E)	1814	Aug. 19	Warren	12	11	08
Campbell, John(E)	1815	Oct. 27	Dearborn(Ind	13	13	25
Campbell, Joseph W.(A)	1828	March 08	Darke	01	10	17
Campbell, Joseph(E)	1838	Oct. 30	Clark	13	21	25
Campbell, Joshia(A)	1826	Nov. 02	Preble	02	08	22
Campbell, Moses(A)	1812	June 09	Butler	02	05	15
Campbell, Philip(E)	1836	Sept. 14	Warren	13	19	26
Campbell, Robert(A)	1813	Oct. 30	Butler	02	08	36
Campbell, Robert(A)	1816	June 25	Wayne(Ind)	01	09	06
Campbell, Robert(A)	1826	Feb. 14	Preble	01	10	29
Campbell, Robert(D)	1818	April 23	Hamilton	01	02	26
Campbell, Robert(D)	1818	April 23	Hamilton	01	02	26
Campbell, Robert(D)	1818	April 23	Hamilton	01	02	26
Campbell, Robert(D)	1818	April 25	Hamilton	01	02	26
Campbell, Stephen(C)	1816	Sept. 14	Champaign	09	05	10
Campbell, William(A)	1814	April 18	Preble	03	05	11
Campbell, William(A)	1818	April 18	Preble	03	05	12
Campbell, William(A)	1818	April 20	Preble	03	05	12
Campbell, William(B)	1814	May 31	Dearborn(Ind	01	02	32
Campbell, William(B)	1814	June 07	Dearborn(Ind	01	02	32
Campbell, William(B)	1814	June 07	Dearborn(Ind	01	03	25
Campbell, William(B)	1817	Sept. 06	Switzerland	01	02	30
Campbell, William(B)	1817	Sept. 06	Switzerland	02	02	20
Campbell, William(B)	1817	Oct. 08	?	01	02	02
Campbell, William(B)	1831	Aug. 09	Switzerland	01	03	32
Campbell, William(B)	1831	Aug. 09	Switzerland	01	03	32
Campbell, William(C)	1808	Jan. 20	Greene	09	06	19
Campbell, William(E)	1811	Oct. 24	Kentucky	13	16	33
Campbell, Wm. L.(E)	1837	Sept. 13	Greene	15	22	34

PURCHASER	YEAR	DATE	RESIDENCE	R	T	S
Campbell, Wm. L.(E)	1837	Sept. 13	Greene	15	21	05
Campbell, Wm. L.(E)	1837	Sept. 21	Greene	15	21	02
Campbell, Wm.(C)	1824	July 16	Logan	13	03	17
Campbill, Wm. L.(E)	1837	Sept. 21	Greene	14	20	01
Campion, Kyren(B)	1806	Nov. 10	Cincinnati	01	10	30
Camron, Joseph(B)	1835	Jan. 05	Dearborn(Ind	02	07	08
Canaday, David(B)	1815	Dec. 15	Wayne(Ind)	02	12	26
Canaday, John(E)	1816	Nov. 15	Wayne(Ind)	13	18	33
Canaday, Robert(E)	1815	Oct. 28	Wayne(Ind)	13	18	29
Canaday, Robert(E)	1826	Dec. 19	Wayne(Ind)	13	18	29
Canady, Joel(E)	1817	June 10	Butler	14	21	09
Canby, Joseph(A)	1831	Jan. 24	Logan	08	01	22
Canby, Joseph(C)	1831	Jan. 31	Logan	13	04	36
Canby, Joseph(E)	1818	May 20	Warren	14	17	35
Canby, Richard S.(C)	1825	Feb. 08	Logan	13	03	06
Canby, Sarah(C)	1827	Aug. 22	JeffersonInd	09	05	26
Canfelt, Augustin(C)	1812	Oct. 12	Champaign	10	04	21
Canfield, Edwin(B)	1836	April 04	Dearborn(Ind	02	06	31
Canfield, Noyes(B)	1828	Nov. 26	Dearborn(Ind	02	05	06
Canfield, Noyes(B)	1828	Nov. 26	Dearborn(Ind	02	06	31
Cannada, Samuel H.(C)	1813	July 24	Champaign	09	05	01
Cannon, James(A)	1813	Dec. 03	Miami	06	08	28
Cannon, James(A)	1813	Dec. 03	Miami	06	08	29
Cannon, James(C)	1801	Dec. 30	Hamilton	05	02	27
Cannon, James(C)	1804	Dec. 31	Montgomery	11	01	21
Cansley, Thomas(B)	1807	Jan. 17	Kentucky	01	13	19
Cantley, James(B)	1818	June 02	Franklin(Ind	02	08	31
Cantrell, Joshua(C)	1812	April 02	Champaign	10	05	11
Cantrell, Joshua(C)	1812	April 02	Champaign	10	05	05
Cantrell, Joshua(C)	1829	Sept. 14	Clark	10	05	29
Cantrell, Zebulon G.(C)	1812	April 02	Champaign	10	05	11
Cantrell, Zebulon G.(C)	1829	Sept. 14	Clark	10	05	29
Cantrell, Zebulon(C)	1829	Sept. 14	Clark	12	04	17
Capehart, George(A)	1816	May 16	Montgomery	03	07	08
Capehart, Henry(A)	1806	April 11	Montgomery	06	02	18
Capehart, Henry(A)	1806	April 11	Montgomery	06	02	19
Capehart, John(A)	1811	Aug. 13	Butler	04	02	09
Capeheart, John(A)	1806	June 12	Butler	04	02	09
Capler, Lewis(C)	1806	Aug. 28	Greene	09	03	18
Capper, Samuel(C)	1806	Dec. 02	Champaign	09	03	24
Capper, Samuel(C)	1814	April 23	Miami	11	02	10
Capper, Thomas(B)	1825	Feb. 18	Franklin(Ind	01	10	21
Capron, Welcome Metcalf(A)	1832	July 05	Miami	04	07	10
Capron, Welcome(A)	1831	Aug. 23	Miami	04	07	02
Caraway, John(C)	1812	March 09	Champaign	10	05	18
Caraway, John(C)	1817	Aug. 01	Champaign	10	05	18
Caraway, John(C)	1831	Dec. 22	Champaign	12	04	08
Caraway, Joseph(C)	1812	March 09	Champaign	10	05	18
Carbough, Abraham(B)	1813	May 22	Dearborn(Ind	02	04	12
Carey, Cephas(A)	1811	Jan. 29	Miami	06	08	30
Carey, Daniel(C)	1816	Aug. 01	Champaign	14	03	23
Carey, David(C)	1815	Feb. 15	Miami	12	01	02
Carey, Leah(C)	1801	Dec. 30	Hamilton	04	02	17
Carey, Thos. McClish(A)	1831	Nov. 25	Shelby	06	08	19
Carleck, Jacob(A)	1814	Nov. 09	Miami	04	10	32
Carleton, Charlotte(E)	1833	May 31	Cincinnati	13	11	09
Carleton, Charlotte(E)	1818	March 27	Cincinnati	13	11	22
Carleton, Jonathan(C)	1817	July 02	Cincinnati	12	03	19
Carleton, Jonathan(E)	1817	Dec. 27	Cincinnati	13	11	09
Carleton, Jonathan(E)	1817	Dec. 27	Cincinnati	13	11	22
Carleton, Jonathan(E)	1818	March 31	Hamilton	13	11	09
Carleton, Jonathan(E)	1818	March 31	Hamilton	13	11	22
Carley, Jestus(B)	1816	April 04	Butler	02	03	33
Carlock, Duke A. N.(A)	1831	Jan. 15	Darke	04	10	17
Carlock, Jacob(A)	1814	Nov. 09	Miami	04	10	31
Carlough, Abraham(B)	1812	Jan. 31	Dearborn(Ind	01	05	31
Carlton, Isaac(B)	1814	March 25	Kentucky	02	04	24
Carman, Joshua(C)	1801	Dec. 31	Hamilton	05	03	09
Carmichael, David(C)	1831	June 06	Logan	13	02	04

PURCHASER	YEAR	DATE	RESIDENCE	R	T	S
Carmichael, John Hanley(E)	1835	Jan. 19	Fayette	13	13	31
Carmin, Benjamin(C)	1813	Dec. 23	Miami	10	03	35
Carmin, Lewis(C)	1824	July 02	Clark	10	03	29
Carmony, Jacob(C)	1818	June 03	Montgomery	11	03	35
Carmony, Joseph(C)	1831	July 05	Warren	12	03	31
Carnahan, Abraham P.(A)	1836	Dec. 03	Butler	01	14	11
Carnahan, Elias L.(A)	1828	Sept. 13	Darke	03	09	06
Carnahan, James A. Jr.(A)	1836	Oct. 21	Hamilton	01	14	15
Carnahan, John P.(A)	1836	Oct. 21	Hamilton	01	14	15
Carnahan, Robert A.(A)	1836	Oct. 21	Hamilton	01	14	09
Carnahan, Will'm. T.(A)	1815	Oct. 10	Preble	03	09	06
Carnahan, William S.(A)	1836	Nov. 29	Hamilton	01	14	09
Carnahan, William T.(A)	1814	March 15	Butler	01	08	25
Carnahan, William(A)	1811	Nov. 20	Pennsylvania	02	12	12
Carnahan, William(A)	1811	Nov. 20	Pennsylvania	02	12	11
Carnan, John(B)	1836	Aug. 22	Cecil Co.,Md	01	16	24
Carneal, Thomas D.(C)	1817	Sept. 17	Kentucky	13	03	23
Carneal, Thomas Davis(C)	1832	April 28	Ohio	13	03	18
Carnell, Thomas(E)	1816	Feb. 20	Butler	14	15	04
Carney, David L.(C)	1804	Dec. 31	Kentucky	07	02	31
Carney, Edward(B)	1814	Nov. 22	Franklin(Ind	02	08	26
Carney, Edward(E)	1814	Dec. 05	Franklin(Ind	13	13	35
Caron, Charles(A)	1833	March 21	Cincinnati	02	12	24
Carothers, John(A)	1837	March 01	Butler	01	12	02
Carpenter, Calvin(E)	1836	Dec. 10	Cincinnati	12	12	06
Carpenter, George(B)	1837	May 29	Dearborn(Ind	03	04	14
Carpenter, Ira(A)	1836	Oct. 31	Darke	02	13	13
Carpenter, Ira(A)	1836	Oct. 31	Darke	02	14	26
Carpenter, Ira(A)	1836	Oct. 31	Darke	02	13	13
Carpenter, John(C)	1811	Dec. 11	Greene	08	03	09
Carpenter, Joseph(B)	1806	Aug. 08	?	02	10	13
Carpenter, Joseph(B)	1832	Aug. 22	Dearborn(Ind	02	05	30
Carr, Jacob(A)	1814	Nov. 25	Butler	02	04	21
Carr, John(A)	1812	March 07	Kentucky	01	10	23
Carr, John(B)	1813	April 16	Kentucky	01	10	33
Carrell, John(A)	1832	Jan. 11	Darke	04	08	33
Carrick, Robert(C)	1801	Dec. 31	Hamilton	05	02	14
Carrick, Robert(C)	1802	Dec. 30	Hamilton	04	02	19
Carson, Aaron(A)	1818	Oct. 27	Miami	05	09	31
Carson, Adam(B)	1812	Aug. 07	Butler	01	09	11
Carson, Benjamin(A)	1818	June 29	Miami	05	09	31
Carson, David(B)	1807	May 28	Dearborn(Ind	02	13	26
Carson, Elijah(B)	1816	May 17	Franklin(Ind	02	11	03
Carson, John Jr.(B)	1828	Dec. 19	Franklin(Ind	03	09	36
Carson, John(A)	1814	Oct. 27	Delaware	05	08	09
Carson, John(A)	1814	Oct. 27	Delaware	05	08	09
Carson, John(A)	1814	Oct. 27	Delaware	02	08	36
Carson, John(B)	1813	April 14	Franklin(Ind	02	09	23
Carson, John(C)	1801	Dec. 30	Hamilton	04	02	25
Carson, John(C)	1813	Sept. 21	Montgomery	09	02	29
Carson, Joseph L.(B)	1807	Sept. 14	Warren	01	09	30
Carson, Joseph L.(B)	1813	April 14	Warren	01	09	30
Carson, Robert(A)	1806	May 16	Hamilton	03	03	03
Carson, Robert(B)	1833	Sept. 06	Cincinnati	02	06	14
Carson, Thomas Jr.(E)	1816	Feb. 29	Franklin(Ind	14	17	30
Carson, Thomas(A)	1817	June 16	Montgomery	01	10	14
Cart, George(C)	1817	June 17	Champaign	10	04	20
Carter, Caleb(C)	1804	Dec. 29	Greene	11	04	30
Carter, Caleb(C)	1807	March 19	Champaign	09	06	36
Carter, Caleb(C)	1807	March 19	Champaign	09	06	20
Carter, Caleb(C)	1807	April 02	Champaign	09	05	06
Carter, Caleb(C)	1813	April 14	Champaign	09	06	36
Carter, Caleb(C)	1813	April 14	Champaign	09	05	06
Carter, Cornelius(C)	1806	Aug. 20	Champaign	09	05	05
Carter, Elisha(A)	1814	Nov. 21	Preble	02	06	09
Carter, Freeman(B)	1804	Sept. 20	Dearborn(Ind	02	04	29
Carter, John(B)	1816	Oct. 16	Switzerland	02	02	07
Carter, Joseph(C)	1801	Dec. 30	Hamilton	04	04	34
Carter, Mordecai(B)	1806	Aug. 01	Warren	01	14	14

PURCHASER	YEAR	DATE	RESIDENCE	R	T	S
Carter, Robert(A)	1816	Sept. 30	Butler	05	08	05
Carter, Samuel C.(A)	1837	May 22	Hamilton	01	14	32
Carter, Samuel C.(E)	1837	April 05	Hamilton	15	22	20
Carter, Samuel C.(E)	1837	April 08	Hamilton	15	22	20
Carter, Samuel L.(A)	1838	Sept. 18	Hamilton	01	14	28
Carter, Samuel(A)	1837	Feb. 22	Hamilton	02	14	28
Carter, Thomas(B)	1836	April 12	Switzerland	01	02	19
Carter, Thomas(E)	1811	Oct. 28	Franklin(Ind	12	15	36
Carter, Thomas(E)	1836	Feb. 13	Randolph(Ind	14	19	03
Carter, William(B)	1802	Aug. 17	Hamilton	02	04	28
Carter, William(B)	1807	May 09	Dearborn(Ind	02	10	03
Carter, William(B)	1808	April 13	Dearborn(Ind	02	04	28
Cartmell, John H.(C)	1831	Aug. 08	Clark	10	06	17
Cartmell, William(C)	1813	June 10	Champaign	13	04	10
Cartmill, Nathaniel(C)	1808	Nov. 02	Champaign	10	06	29
Cartmill, Nathaniel(C)	1808	Nov. 07	Champaign	10	06	29
Cartmill, Nathaniel(C)	1811	Dec. 10	Champaign	10	06	21
Cartmill, Nathaniel(C)	1814	June 15	Champaign	10	06	29
Cartmill, Nathaniel(C)	1814	Dec. 08	Champaign	10	06	27
Cartmill, Nathanl.(C)	1813	Dec. 28	Champaign	10	06	29
Cartmill, Thomas(C)	1811	Dec. 10	Champaign	10	06	23
Cartwright, Ahaz(B)	1833	Nov. 08	Randolph(Ind	01	16	10
Cartwright, Ahaz(B)	1836	Aug. 09	Randolph(Ind	01	16	03
Cartwright, Ahaz(E)	1836	Aug. 09	Randolph(Ind	15	19	08
Cartwright, John(B)	1806	Dec. 02	Warren	01	12	34
Cartwright, William(B)	1815	Oct. 27	Hamilton	01	11	10
Carver, Christian(B)	1813	June 11	Dearborn(Ind	01	02	28
Carver, Christian(C)	1806	Dec. 08	Montgomery	08	02	18
Carver, Jacob(C)	1813	Dec. 02	Dearborn(Ind	08	02	12
Carver, Michael(C)	1804	Dec. 21	Montgomery	10	02	27
Carver, William(B)	1815	July 28	Switzerland	01	02	20
Cary, Calvin Senr.(C)	1816	March 07	Madison	12	03	23
Cary, Calvin(C)	1815	Aug. 10	Madison	12	03	29
Cary, Cephas(A)	1814	Jan. 25	Miami	06	08	19
Cary, Christopher(C)	1806	Feb. 13	Cincinnati	04	02	17
Cary, Christopher(D)	1809	Sept. 16	Hamilton	01	03	26
Cary, Colwin(C)	1815	March 22	Madison	12	03	29
Cary, Elias(A)	1813	June 24	Miami	06	07	03
Cary, Ephraim(A)	1829	Feb. 18	Shelby	06	08	33
Cary, Ephraim(A)	1830	Nov. 05	Shelby	06	08	33
Cary, George(Black)(E)	1836	Oct. 12	Cincinnati	12	11	29
Cary, Rufus(A)	1811	Dec. 10	Miami	06	07	10
Cary, Thomas(C)	1815	Sept. 21	Miami	12	01	03
Cary, William(A)	1808	Jan. 20	Hamilton	01	02	33
Casad, Aaron(C)	1818	Aug. 27	Greene	10	03	15
Casad, Aaron(C)	1818	Aug. 27	Greene	10	03	15
Casad, Abner S.(C)	1818	Jan. 30	Greene	10	03	28
Casady, Wear(E)	1816	Dec. 02	Wayne(Ind)	12	14	02
Case, Aaron(E)	1836	Feb. 01	Union(Ind)	11	10	01
Case, Aaron(E)	1836	Feb. 01	Union(Ind)	12	10	07
Case, Aaron(E)	1836	Feb. 10	Franklin(Ind	11	10	12
Case, Henry(B)	1813	July 17	Hamilton	02	08	02
Case, Isaiah(E)	1819	March 13	Wayne(Ind)	14	18	29
Case, Isaih(E)	1811	Nov. 04	Nor.Carolina	14	18	29
Case, Jacob(A)	1801	July 27	Hamilton	03	03	27
Case, Jacob(B)	1813	April 14	Franklin(Ind	02	11	34
Case, Jacob(E)	1811	Nov. 11	Butler	13	14	19
Case, Jacob(E)	1811	Nov. 11	Butler	12	14	24
Case, Joseph(A)	1806	Feb. 08	Warren	06	04	08
Case, Nancy(B)	1832	Jan. 02	Dearborn(Ind	02	08	28
Case, Nathaniel(E)	1818	Jan. 06	Wayne(Ind)	14	18	07
Case, Peter(E)	1836	March 30	Preble	11	10	12
Case, Samuel(A)	1803	March 05	Kentucky	03	03	12
Case, Samuel(B)	1813	Aug. 06	Franklin(Ind	02	08	10
Case, William(B)	1807	Feb. 05	Butler	01	07	04
Casebolt, Robert(C)	1831	Aug. 08	Logan	14	03	17
Casey, William(A)	1818	Oct. 02	Warren	04	07	05
Cason, Thomas Jnr.(E)	1816	March 14	Franklin(Ind	14	17	28
Cason, William(B)	1814	June 24	Greene	02	11	01

52

PURCHASER	YEAR	DATE	RESIDENCE	R	T	S
Cason, William(B)	1814	Aug. 16	Greene	02	11	02
Cassaday, John(B)	1832	Feb. 15	Dearborn(Ind	01	07	21
Cassaday, Levi(A)	1828	Sept. 08	Butler	02	10	20
Cassaday, Levi(B)	1828	March 14	Butler	01	15	03
Cassaday, Wear(A)	1804	Oct. 12	Montgomery	03	04	01
Cassaday, Weir(E)	1811	Oct. 23	Preble	13	14	06
Cassaday, William(B)	1835	Sept. 29	Dearborn(Ind	01	07	21
Cassady, Robert(B)	1835	Oct. 22	Dearborn(Ind	01	07	26
Cassady, Thomas(A)	1803	March 05	Hamilton	03	05	35
Cassady, Wear(A)	1804	Sept. 25	Montgomery	03	04	01
Cassady, Weire(A)	1806	July 30	Montgomery	03	05	23
Cassady, Weire(A)	1806	July 30	Montgomery	03	05	26
Cassait, Francis(C)	1801	Dec. 30	Hamilton	04	04	20
Cassart, Jacob(C)	1804	Dec. 22	Virginia	08	03	20
Casseday, James(C)	1805	Nov. 04	Virginia	03	04	26
Cassel, Henry(A)	1814	Dec. 03	Butler	03	07	13
Cassett, Albert(C)	1801	Dec. 30	Hamilton	04	04	14
Cassiday, Sarah(A)	1816	Oct. 12	Butler	02	09	23
Cassiday, Sarah(A)	1816	Oct. 12	Butler	02	09	23
Cassidy, Patrick(A)	1837	May 16	Cincinnati	02	14	20
Cassler, Lewis(C)	1812	June 18	Greene	08	04	29
Casson, John(B)	1814	Sept. 17	Franklin(Ind	01	09	20
Caster, Benjamin(A)	1818	May 21	Montgomery	03	10	23
Caster, Cornelius(C)	1811	Sept. 14	Champaign	09	06	34
Caster, William(A)	1811	Dec. 11	Preble	02	08	20
Castle, John H. P.(C)	1816	Jan. 19	Hamilton	12	01	14
Castrow, Charles(A)	1803	Nov. 28	Butler	04	03	25
Castrow, Peter(A)	1803	Nov. 28	Butler	04	03	25
Cater, Henry(E)	1836	July 05	Hamilton	13	12	27
Catey, Henry(E)	1821	Aug. 25	New Jersey	14	17	09
Catey, William(E)	1833	Dec. 13	Randolph(Ind	13	18	10
Cathcart, John(A)	1815	Sept. 30	So. Carolina	01	06	35
Cathcart, William(A)	1831	Oct. 22	Pennsylvania	05	10	36
Cather, Robert Jnr.(E)	1818	March 24	Butler	13	12	06
Cather, Robert Senr.(E)	1818	March 24	Butler	13	12	06
Catlin, Horace R.(B)	1818	April 08	Switzerland	02	03	30
Catlin, James(E)	1836	July 30	Fayette	12	12	29
Catro, Joseph(A)	1810	Feb. 23	Butler	04	03	33
Catron, Joseph(A)	1804	Sept. 24	Butler	04	02	03
Catterlin, John D.(B)	1815	July 27	Butler	02	12	34
Caughfield, Augustine(C)	1817	Dec. 02	Champaign	10	04	21
Cave, Jacob(E)	1811	Nov. 02	Butler	12	14	13
Caven, George M.(C)	1808	Nov. 29	Miami	12	01	01
Caven, George(C)	1813	Nov. 05	Miami	12	01	02
Caven, John A.(C)	1812	Nov. 26	Miami	12	02	31
Cavenaugh, James(C)	1817	May 30	Champaign	13	04	01
Cavender, Robert(A)	1836	Sept. 03	Miami	03	12	32
Cavender, Samuel(A)	1836	Sept. 03	Miami	03	12	32
Cavender, Samuel(C)	1804	Sept. 24	Greene	05	03	11
Cavender, Thomas(C)	1815	Jan. 21	Montgomery	11	01	02
Cavileer, Edmund Burke(C)	1831	Aug. 08	Champaign	13	05	13
Cawley, John(A)	1818	Jan. 09	Cincinnati	04	05	31
Cecil, Aaron(A)	1816	June 06	Miami	06	07	17
Cecil, Elizabeth(E)	1837	April 10	Warren	15	21	32
Cecil, Jacob(E)	1837	April 10	Warren	15	21	32
Cecil, James B.(A)	1830	Nov. 10	Warren	03	07	01
Cecil, James B.(E)	1837	April 10	Warren	05	21	32
Cecil, John(E)	1837	April 10	Warren	15	21	32
Cecil, Magdalena(A)	1830	Nov. 10	Warren	03	07	01
Cecil, Magdalena(E)	1837	April 10	Warren	15	21	32
Cecil, Sarah(E)	1837	April 10	Warren	15	21	32
Cecill, Thomas(C)	1814	May 28	Miami	10	02	26
Cecill, Thomas(C)	1814	June 13	?	10	02	26
Cetrow, Thomas(A)	1837	Aug. 21	Montgomery	01	14	03
Chadwick, Sam'l. Richard(A)	1833	July 03	Preble	01	09	01
Chadwick, Sam'l. Richard(A)	1833	July 03	Preble	01	09	12
Chadwick, Samuel Richards(E)	1835	March 10	Preble	14	19	29
Chadwick, William(A)	1818	Jan. 08	Cincinnati	04	05	33
Chamberlain, Aaron(B)	1818	Jan. 27	Hamilton	02	02	08

PURCHASER	YEAR	DATE	RESIDENCE	R	T	S
Chamberlain, John(A)	1803	June 23	Butler	05	02	32
Chamberlain, Joseph(A)	1803	July 08	Montgomery	05	02	17
Chamberlain, William(B)	1814	June 28	Dearborn(Ind	02	05	35
Chamberlin, Horton(B)	1831	Aug. 09	Switzerland	03	03	01
Chamberlin, Horton(B)	1831	Aug. 09	Switzerland	03	03	01
Chamberlin, Tylee(A)	1836	Oct. 27	Hamilton	02	15	33
Chamberlin, William B.(B)	1817	July 26	Hamilton	02	06	34
Chamberlin, Wm. B.(B)	1827	Aug. 21	GallatinCoKy	01	02	14
Chamberlin, Wm. B.(B)	1827	Aug. 21	GallatinCoKy	01	02	22
Chamberlin, Wm. Brattle(B)	1831	Aug. 09	Kentucky	01	02	05
Chamberlin, Wm. Brattle(B)	1831	Nov. 26	Kentucky	02	02	15
Chambers, Absalom(C)	1832	Feb. 01	Logan	13	03	28
Chambers, Alen(A)	1802	March 23	Hamilton	04	02	18
Chambers, Benjamin(B)	1802	Sept. 21	Hamilton	02	04	13
Chambers, Benjamin(B)	1802	Sept. 21	Hamilton	02	04	23
Chambers, Benjamin(B)	1804	Sept. 29	Ind.Territory	01	03	31
Chambers, Benjamin(B)	1804	Oct. 03	Ind.Territory	01	03	28
Chambers, Benjamin(B)	1806	Dec. 03	Ind.Territory	01	05	15
Chambers, Benjamin(C)	1801	Dec. 31	Hamilton	07	02	28
Chambers, Benjamin(C)	1801	Dec. 31	Hamilton	08	02	07
Chambers, Benjamin(C)	1801	Dec. 31	Hamilton	07	02	28
Chambers, Benjamin(C)	1802	Dec. 31	Hamilton	08	04	14
Chambers, James N.(A)	1811	Dec. 13	Ross	13	15	08
Chambers, James N.(E)	1815	Nov. 02	Wayne(Ind)	13	14	02
Chambers, John(A)	1814	Nov. 07	Greene	01	07	02
Chambers, Manuel(B)	1816	Feb. 20	Hamilton	01	08	17
Chambers, Minor(B)	1816	July 05	?	03	03	13
Chambers, Minor(B)	1832	Sept. 25	Switzerland	03	03	03
Chambers, Samuel(E)	1837	May 12	Preble	15	21	19
Chamnys, Anthony(E)	1811	Nov. 02	Greene	14	17	07
Champion, Thomas(B)	1835	Dec. 25	Hamilton	02	02	14
Chance, James(C)	1820	Feb. 09	Champaign	10	03	15
Chance, James(E)	1830	Jan. 26	Franklin(Ind	12	12	15
Chance, James(E)	1835	Oct. 26	Franklin(Ind	12	12	24
Chance, John(B)	1818	March 07	Hamilton	03	06	14
Chance, John(E)	1833	March 02	Franklin(Ind	12	12	23
Chance, John(E)	1835	Jan. 01	Franklin(Ind	12	12	23
Chance, John(E)	1836	Feb. 04	Franklin(Ind	12	12	23
Chandler, Henry(E)	1836	Oct. 17	Randolph(Ind	15	21	04
Chandler, Henry(E)	1836	Oct. 17	Randolph(Ind	15	22	33
Chandler, Robert(B)	1832	Aug. 14	Switzerland	02	02	13
Chandler, Robert(B)	1833	Dec. 13	Switzerland	02	02	13
Chandler, Shadrach(E)	1837	June 26	Wayne(Ind)	15	22	30
Chaney, John(C)	1826	Nov. 18	Clark	13	03	11
Chanslor, John(C)	1806	Aug. 19	Kentucky	10	04	15
Chapman, David(A)	1817	June 09	Miami	05	09	25
Chapman, Elijah(C)	1804	Dec. 31	Greene	10	05	09
Chapman, Elijah(C)	1806	Feb. 10	Champaign	10	05	09
Chapman, Elijah(C)	1806	Feb. 11	Champaign	10	05	14
Chapman, Elijah(C)	1806	July 31	Champaign	10	05	08
Chapman, Elijah(C)	1806	Feb. 18	Champaign	10	05	09
Chapman, Enoch(B)	1815	July 12	Franklin(Ind	08	01	11
Chapman, Jonathan(E)	1817	July 14	Franklin(Ind	13	12	30
Chapman, William(C)	1804	Dec. 31	Greene	10	04	03
Chapman, William(C)	1804	Dec. 31	Greene	10	04	10
Chapman, William(C)	1805	Oct. 16	Champaign	10	04	23
Chapman, William(C)	1805	Oct. 16	Champaign	10	04	22
Chapman, William(C)	1805	Nov. 25	Champaign	10	05	15
Chapman, William(E)	1831	July 05	Franklin(Ind	13	12	28
Chapman, William(E)	1832	May 29	Franklin(Ind	13	12	28
Chapman, Wm.(A)	1828	Jan. 11	Darke	02	11	21
Chappel, Silas(A)	1838	Feb. 06	Clark	01	13	02
Chappelow, William(B)	1835	Dec. 02	Dearborn(Ind	01	07	05
Charles, Daniel(E)	1837	March 01	Wayne(Ind)	14	20	03
Charles, Daniel(E)	1837	March 01	Wayne(Ind)	15	20	20
Charles, Sam'l. Senr.(A)	1830	Jan. 04	Wayne(Ind)	01	11	30
Charles, Samuel(B)	1815	Jan. 03	Wayne(Ind)	01	14	08
Charles, Samuel(E)	1813	Sept. 30	Wayne(Ind)	14	18	28
Charles, Samuel(E)	1818	April 15	Wayne(Ind)	14	20	15

PURCHASER	YEAR	DATE	RESIDENCE	R	T	S
Charles, Smith(A)	1805	Dec. 14	Warren	01	06	09
Charles, Smith(A)	1806	Dec. 30	Montgomery	01	07	28
Charlton, James(A)	1813	Jan. 06	Butler	01	03	32
Charters, George(A)	1818	Dec. 04	Hamilton	01	06	21
Chase, Abraham Jr.(A)	1814	April 23	Hamilton	01	02	22
Chase, Abraham(A)	1806	Dec. 03	Hamilton	01	04	05
Chase, Abraham(A)	1806	Dec. 03	Hamilton	01	04	05
Chase, Abraham(A)	1806	Dec. 03	Hamilton	01	04	06
Chase, Leonard(B)	1815	May 15	Ind.Territry	01	05	06
Chase, Salmon P.(B)	1836	Feb. 29	Hamilton	03	08	35
Chattam, John(A)	1818	Aug. 03	Hamilton	05	08	10
Cheek, Francis(B)	1812	Feb. 07	Dearborn(Ind	01	05	19
Cheek, Page(B)	1811	April 09	Dearborn(Ind	01	05	20
Cheek, William(B)	1802	Aug. 17	Hamilton	02	04	28
Cheeseman, Richard W.(E)	1811	Dec. 16	Warren	14	17	29
Cheevers, John M.(A)	1818	Oct. 01	Cincinnati	05	09	20
Cheevers, John Mann(A)	1831	Dec. 24	Piqua	05	10	28
Chenault, Abner(B)	1813	Sept. 17	Wayne(Ind)	02	12	27
Cheney, Robert(A)	1837	Feb. 17	Clermont	01	15	32
Cheney, Robert(A)	1837	Feb. 27	Clermont	01	15	32
Chenoeth, Abraham(B)	1817	Sept. 24	Pike	01	17	26
Chenoweth, Abraham(B)	1834	April 14	Pike	01	17	23
Chenoweth, Jacob(B)	1834	Jan. 15	Darke	01	17	23
Chenoweth, Jacob(B)	1834	April 14	Darke	01	17	24
Chenoweth, Jacob(B)	1836	Jan. 29	Darke	01	17	25
Chenoweth, John B.(E)	1837	Oct. 14	Maryland	15	19	30
Chenoweth, John B.(E)	1837	Oct. 14	Maryland	15	19	18
Chenoweth, John B.(E)	1837	Oct. 14	Maryland	14	19	13
Chenoweth, John(A)	1817	Sept. 02	Franklin(Ind	01	12	32
Chenoweth, John(A)	1818	Dec. 10	Darke	01	12	32
Chenoweth, John(A)	1826	May 12	Pike	01	12	17
Chenoweth, John(A)	1828	Feb. 04	Pike	01	12	17
Chenoweth, John(A)	1831	July 23	Darke	01	12	17
Chenoweth, Joseph(C)	1817	Oct. 24	Warren	11	03	29
Chenoweth, Thomas(C)	1804	Dec. 24	Warren	05	04	33
Chenoweth, Thomas(C)	1812	Jan. 24	Warren	09	07	32
Chenoweth, Thomas(C)	1812	Jan. 24	Warren	09	06	07
Chenoweth, William(B)	1834	Nov. 07	Maryland	01	16	09
Chenoweth, William(E)	1834	Nov. 07	Maryland	15	19	20
Chenowith, Abraham(B)	1817	Sept. 24	Pike	01	17	26
Chenowith, Jacob(A)	1817	Sept. 24	Pike	01	12	19
Chenowith, Thomas(C)	1811	Aug. 19	Warren	09	06	01
Chenowith, William(B)	1817	Sept. 24	Ross	01	17	25
Chenowith, William(B)	1817	Sept. 24	Ross	01	17	24
Chenowith, William(C)	1810	Oct. 29	Champaign	10	05	10
Cherrey, Benjamin(C)	1806	Sept. 20	Champaign	12	05	35
Cherry, Isaac(E)	1836	Oct. 08	Randolph(Ind	14	21	04
Cherry, John(A)	1804	Sept. 24	Hamilton	01	02	13
Chesnut, Joseph(C)	1812	June 20	Champaign	09	03	24
Chess, Robert(C)	1817	June 16	Champaign	09	06	10
Chevaleer, Antony(C)	1802	Dec. 29	Hamilton	06	01	32
Cheyney, Benjamin(A)	1805	Dec. 02	Virginia	06	04	05
Chidester, Dan'l. Landen(B)	1832	Oct. 01	Dearborn(Ind	02	06	13
Childre, Thomas(A)	1814	March 11	Preble	01	08	29
Childres, Benj'n.(B)	1825	May 17	Franklin(Ind	03	09	36
Childress, Henry(A)	1827	Aug. 23	Preble	02	09	23
Childress, Henry(A)	1831	April 16	Montgomery	04	09	01
Childress, John(C)	1813	June 26	Miami	12	01	07
Childress, Thomas(C)	1813	June 26	Miami	12	01	07
Childs, George(C)	1814	April 05	Champaign	13	02	21
Chiles, Geo.(C)	1831	Jan. 03	Shelby	13	02	15
Chiles, William(C)	1831	Jan. 03	Shelby	13	02	15
Chinoueth, Thomas(C)	1804	Sept. 03	Warren	05	03	08
Chittenden, John H.(B)	1836	Oct. 19	Switzerland	03	04	28
Chivington, John(B)	1814	Oct. 22	Hamilton	01	10	29
Choat, Cautious J.(B)	1829	Dec. 08	Switzerland	01	02	11
Choat, Seth Storer(B)	1832	March 28	Switzerland	01	02	23
Chribe, Daniel Junr.(A)	1809	June 26	Montgomery	04	05	12
Chribe, Daniel(A)	1802	Jan. 26	Hamilton	05	03	17

PURCHASER	YEAR	DATE	RESIDENCE	R	T	S
Chribe, Daniel(A)	1803	Nov. 05	Montgomery	05	04	35
Chribe, Daniel(A)	1805	Nov. 16	Montgomery	04	06	34
Chribe, Daniel(A)	1805	Nov. 16	Montgomery	04	06	34
Chribe, Daniel(A)	1805	Nov. 16	Montgomery	04	06	34
Chribe, Daniel(A)	1805	Nov. 16	Montgomery	04	05	03
Chribe, John(A)	1804	May 07	Pennsylvania	05	04	35
Chribe, Samuel(A)	1804	May 07	Ohio	05	04	35
Chrisley, Aaron(A)	1816	Dec. 13	Preble	02	09	26
Chrisman, Daniel(A)	1805	April 22	Montgomery	03	04	11
Chrismer, Jacob(E)	1838	Sept. 15	Montgomery	15	22	19
Chrissman, Lewis(A)	1828	April 11	Preble	02	08	24
Chrissman, Peter(A)	1804	Sept. 11	Warren	03	06	30
Chrissman, Peter(A)	1804	Sept. 11	Warren	03	06	31
Chrissman, Peter(A)	1804	Sept. 13	Warren	02	08	25
Christ, George(A)	1801	April 27	Hamilton	01	05	02
Christian, John(A)	1831	May 02	Darke	04	09	22
Christian, Joseph(A)	1818	Nov. 07	Pennsylvania	04	09	20
Christian, Joseph(A)	1818	Nov. 07	Pennsylvania	04	09	20
Christian, Joseph(A)	1822	Oct. 08	Pennsylvania	04	07	36
Christian, Joseph(A)	1822	Oct. 08	Pennsylvania	04	06	01
Christian, Joseph(A)	1828	Oct. 18	Miami	04	07	36
Christian, Joseph(A)	1834	July 09	Darke	04	11	31
Christian, Ludwick(A)	1814	Dec. 09	Montgomery	04	09	05
Christian, Solomon(A)	1814	Nov. 10	Pennsylvania	04	09	09
Christian, Solomon(A)	1835	July 08	Montgomery	03	12	27
Christian, Solomon(A)	1836	Nov. 25	Darke	03	12	26
Christian, Solomon(A)	1836	Nov. 25	Darke	03	12	27
Christian, Solomon(A)	1836	Nov. 25	Darke	04	11	30
Christman, Jacob(A)	1803	Feb. 22	Nor.Carolina	03	05	36
Christopher, Cornelius(A)	1820	May 17	Warren	04	06	32
Christopher, John(A)	1816	Jan. 19	Warren	01	09	35
Christy, Andrew(C)	1813	April 14	Butler	03	02	11
Christy, James(C)	1808	Feb. 09	Butler	03	02	11
Christy, John(B)	1837	Nov. 06	Dearborn(Ind	02	05	30
Church, John Alvah(E)	1836	June 17	Franklin(Ind	11	10	13
Churchel, Asahel(E)	1811	Nov. 23	Franklin(Ind	12	12	26
Churchill, Joseph Junr.(B)	1817	Dec. 17	Cincinnati	03	06	13
Churchill, Lorenzo(A)	1837	April 03	Knox	02	13	17
Churchill, Simeon(A)	1818	July 23	Cincinnati	05	10	07
Cilley, Henry(A)	1837	Feb. 13	Hamilton	01	13	14
Cilley, Henry(A)	1837	Feb. 13	Hamilton	01	13	23
Cilley, Henry(A)	1837	Feb. 13	Hamilton	02	13	12
Cilley, Henry(A)	1837	Nov. 06	Hamilton	01	13	14
Cilley, Joseph(B)	1812	April 15	Hamilton	01	09	26
Cilley, Joseph(B)	1812	April 16	Hamilton	01	09	23
Circle, Emanual(C)	1825	Aug. 13	Clark	10	04	02
Circle, Emanuel(C)	1811	Nov. 11	Champaign	10	04	02
Circle, Emanuel(C)	1826	Aug. 28	Clark	10	04	01
Circle, Lewis(A)	1809	Oct. 09	Virginia	04	06	23
Cisco, Henry(C)	1831	Aug. 26	Butler	13	02	15
Ciser, John(C)	1814	March 30	Miami	12	02	25
Clabough, Henry(A)	1817	Nov. 15	Pennsylvania	01	11	34
Clammer, Andrew(A)	1815	May 29	Montgomery	04	05	32
Clammer, John(A)	1814	Nov. 16	Virginia	04	05	29
Clancey, George(A)	1831	Sept. 29	Greene	06	08	10
Clancey, William(A)	1831	Sept. 29	Greene	06	08	10
Clansey, James(C)	1802	Dec. 30	Hamilton	06	03	32
Clansey, Jam's.(C)	1802	Dec. 30	Hamilton	06	03	31
Clanton, Edward(B)	1812	April 25	Wayne(Ind)	01	12	05
Clap, Lodawick(A)	1818	Oct. 28	Darke	01	11	17
Clap, Ludawick(A)	1827	Dec. 21	Darke	01	11	15
Clap, Tobias(A)	1815	Jan. 05	Preble	03	06	26
Clapp, John B.(E)	1836	Aug. 23	Randolph(Ind	14	21	17
Clapp, John(A)	1834	March 07	Darke	01	12	17
Clapp, Lodowick(A)	1824	Oct. 11	Darke	01	11	15
Clark, Abraham(A)	1813	Aug. 16	Hamilton	02	05	18
Clark, Abraham(A)	1813	Aug. 16	Hamilton	02	05	18
Clark, Abraham(D)	1809	April 05	Hamilton	01	03	08
Clark, Alexander P.(A)	1837	Feb. 06	Montgomery	02	15	21

PURCHASER	YEAR	DATE	RESIDENCE	R	T	S
Clark, Barzilla(B)	1815	Oct. 23	Indiana	02	02	33
Clark, Benjamin(B)	1818	June 26	Butler	01	07	36
Clark, Benjamin(E)	1819	Aug. 05	Butler	14	15	31
Clark, Carlton(B)	1815	Oct. 23	Dearborn(Ind	01	07	08
Clark, Chauncy(C)	1815	Oct. 19	Ross	12	03	05
Clark, Daniel(A)	1804	Jan. 18	Maryland	05	02	30
Clark, Daniel(B)	1815	Jan. 30	Wayne(Ind)	01	13	22
Clark, Daniel(E)	1811	Oct. 24	Wayne(Ind)	13	17	13
Clark, David(A)	1818	March 26	Hamilton	05	09	32
Clark, David(A)	1821	Jan. 01	Shelby	05	09	19
Clark, David(C)	1816	March 05	Miami	05	08	03
Clark, Dennis(A)	1806	March 18	Hamilton	01	01	10
Clark, Dennis(A)	1811	Aug. 13	Hamilton	01	01	10
Clark, Dennis(B)	1814	Oct. 22	Ind.Territry	01	07	21
Clark, Ephraim(A)	1815	Dec. 12	Pennsylvania	05	09	23
Clark, Ephraim(E)	1812	Oct. 16	Kentucky	13	17	32
Clark, George Washington(B)	1836	Jan. 23	Dearborn(Ind	02	05	04
Clark, George Washington(B)	1836	Feb. 17	Dearborn(Ind	02	05	05
Clark, George(A)	1836	Nov. 28	Darke	01	15	29
Clark, George(B)	1824	June 09	Dearborn(Ind	02	05	15
Clark, George(B)	1830	March 18	Dearborn(Ind	02	06	27
Clark, George(B)	1832	Sept. 25	Switzerland	03	03	03
Clark, Hugh(A)	1814	Jan. 25	Pennsylvania	05	08	08
Clark, Hugh(A)	1814	Jan. 25	Pennsylvania	05	08	08
Clark, James(A)	1816	April 24	Butler	02	11	01
Clark, James(A)	1816	Oct. 22	Butler	02	11	15
Clark, James(A)	1834	Sept. 18	Darke	02	11	30
Clark, James(C)	1808	Nov. 10	Butler	03	03	11
Clark, James(C)	1831	May 19	Hamilton	13	02	15
Clark, James(E)	1818	June 30	Wayne(Ind)	14	19	15
Clark, James(E)	1831	Sept. 08	Randolph(Ind	15	18	07
Clark, Jedde(B)	1832	Oct. 01	Dearborn(Ind	02	05	09
Clark, Jedde(B)	1836	Jan. 27	Dearborn(Ind	02	05	09
Clark, Jesse(B)	1813	Sept. 30	Wayne(Ind)	01	14	22
Clark, Jesse(B)	1813	Dec. 28	Wayne(Ind)	01	14	22
Clark, Jesse(B)	1814	Jan. 14	Wayne(Ind)	01	14	22
Clark, John Bliven(B)	1832	May 22	Dearborn(Ind	02	06	32
Clark, John(A)	1810	Aug. 14	Butler	03	03	26
Clark, John(A)	1814	Jan. 25	Pennsylvania	05	08	07
Clark, John(A)	1814	March 28	Hamilton	01	04	21
Clark, John(A)	1814	April 01	Hamilton	01	04	28
Clark, John(A)	1818	June 20	Hamilton	05	09	28
Clark, John(A)	1827	Nov. 20	Miami	06	04	33
Clark, John(A)	1831	Oct. 21	Warren	02	10	24
Clark, John(B)	1827	Aug. 21	Dearborn(Ind	03	04	23
Clark, John(B)	1838	Dec. 22	Dearborn(Ind	03	04	24
Clark, John(C)	1802	Dec. 28	Hamilton	05	01	07
Clark, John(C)	1804	Sept. 07	Warren	04	02	08
Clark, John(C)	1804	Sept. 24	Warren	04	02	11
Clark, John(C)	1804	Dec. 28	Greene	11	05	33
Clark, John(C)	1806	March 11	Champaign	10	06	14
Clark, John(C)	1811	Jan. 14	Hamilton	01	04	26
Clark, John(C)	1812	April 01	Champaign	11	06	33
Clark, John(C)	1812	May 01	Champaign	11	05	10
Clark, John(C)	1816	June 05	Greene	13	02	07
Clark, John(C)	1817	Aug. 01	Champaign	11	05	10
Clark, John(C)	1817	Nov. 04	Miami	12	02	32
Clark, John(E)	1816	March 08	Montgomery	13	20	13
Clark, Louis Morgan(E)	1836	Nov. 14	Franklin(Ind	13	11	08
Clark, Louis Morgan(E)	1836	Jan. 11	Franklin(Ind	13	11	08
Clark, Louis Morgan(E)	1836	Jan. 11	Franklin(Ind	13	11	09
Clark, Marcus(C)	1806	Oct. 29	Virginia	12	04	23
Clark, Nelson(E)	1836	Dec. 14	Montgomery	13	20	02
Clark, Nelson(E)	1836	Dec. 14	Montgomery	13	20	12
Clark, Olive(E)	1817	June 10	Franklin(Ind	12	13	36
Clark, Patrick(A)	1831	Nov. 01	New York	05	07	11
Clark, Pharaoh(E)	1831	Jan. 19	Randolph(Ind	14	18	13
Clark, Rhoda(A)	1816	April 01	Butler	03	09	04
Clark, Richard(C)	1807	Feb. 16	Kentucky	12	05	35

PURCHASER	YEAR	DATE	RESIDENCE	R	T	S
Clark, Richard(C)	1807	Aug. 05	Kentucky	12	05	35
Clark, Richard(C)	1811	June 27	Champaign	13	05	25
Clark, Richd.(C)	1813	March 15	Champaign	13	05	25
Clark, Robert(A)	1817	Nov. 15	Pennsylvania	05	09	33
Clark, Robert(C)	1814	March 02	Champaign	12	04	06
Clark, Robt.(C)	1829	June 20	Logan	13	04	24
Clark, Robt.(C)	1831	Nov. 23	Logan	13	04	23
Clark, Robt.(C)	1831	Nov. 23	Logan	13	04	30
Clark, Sam'l.(C)	1829	Feb. 17	Champaign	11	03	25
Clark, Samuel(E)	1836	Sept. 02	Franklin(Ind	12	11	01
Clark, Stephanus(A)	1814	Jan. 28	Warren	03	05	06
Clark, Stephen(A)	1806	March 22	Butler	03	03	26
Clark, Thomas(A)	1818	Nov. 02	Hamilton	05	09	31
Clark, Thomas(B)	1811	Dec. 11	Franklin(Ind	02	08	13
Clark, Thomas(B)	1816	Aug. 01	Franklin(Ind	01	08	20
Clark, Thomas(C)	1811	June 27	Champaign	13	05	25
Clark, Thomas(C)	1817	Aug. 01	?	13	05	32
Clark, Thomas(E)	1813	Aug. 04	Hamilton	13	13	04
Clark, Thomas(E)	1813	Aug. 12	Wayne(Ind)	13	15	28
Clark, Thomas(E)	1832	Oct. 02	Franklin(Ind	12	12	32
Clark, Thomas(E)	1836	Feb. 06	Franklin(Ind	13	11	07
Clark, Thomas(E)	1836	Feb. 12	Franklin(Ind	12	11	12
Clark, William Jr.(A)	1818	Aug. 31	Darke	03	09	06
Clark, William Senr.(A)	1818	Oct. 24	Darke	03	10	28
Clark, William(A)	1801	Sept. 19	Franklin(Ind	04	03	14
Clark, William(A)	1805	Aug. 30	Hamilton	01	02	23
Clark, William(A)	1811	Aug. 13	Hamilton	01	01	10
Clark, William(A)	1819	July 28	Darke	03	10	28
Clark, William(B)	1813	Aug. 31	Franklin(Ind	01	09	19
Clark, Wm. S.(B)	1824	June 09	Union(Ind)	01	11	22
Clark, Wm.(A)	1814	July 13	Hamilton	01	02	27
Clarke, John(C)	1801	Dec. 28	Hamilton	04	02	06
Clarke, John(C)	1804	Dec. 28	Greene	11	05	27
Clarke, Lewis A.(B)	1836	Oct. 13	Switzerland	03	04	28
Clarkson, Abner(C)	1818	July 02	Switzerland	12	05	31
Clary, Deaveirn(A)	1815	Oct. 16	Adams	03	09	08
Clary, William(E)	1814	July 07	Kentucky	13	13	24
Clauson, Peter(C)	1801	Dec. 25	Hamilton	06	01	03
Clawson, Abner(B)	1817	Sept. 17	Wayne(Ind)	01	14	21
Clawson, Abner(B)	1833	Feb. 07	Wayne(Ind)	01	15	22
Clawson, Abner(B)	1833	Feb. 28	Wayne(Ind)	01	15	26
Clawson, Josiah(B)	1813	Oct. 09	Wayne(Ind)	01	14	21
Clawson, Josiah(C)	1801	Dec. 31	Hamilton	06	02	31
Clawson, Mahlon(B)	1833	June 27	Wayne(Ind)	01	17	34
Clawson, Thomas(C)	1801	Dec. 29	Hamilton	06	03	31
Clawson, Will'm.(B)	1815	Oct. 09	Wayne(Ind)	01	14	21
Clawson, William(E)	1811	Oct. 24	Wayne(Ind)	13	17	12
Clawson, William(E)	1811	Nov. 02	Wayne(Ind)	13	17	23
Clayton, John(A)	1824	Aug. 12	Montgomery	04	05	15
Clayton, John(A)	1826	Aug. 26	Montgomery	04	05	15
Clayton, Jonathan(C)	1810	Sept. 05	Greene	08	02	07
Clayton, Rich'd.(A)	1828	Aug. 05	Montgomery	04	05	22
Clayton, Richard(A)	1824	Dec. 06	Montgomery	04	05	22
Clayton, Thomas(C)	1801	Dec. 31	Hamilton	04	04	31
Clear, Philip(A)	1829	Jan. 02	Darke	01	11	09
Clearwater, Jacob(B)	1815	Oct. 19	Franklin(Ind	02	09	10
Clearwaters, David(B)	1814	Sept. 21	Franklin(Ind	02	09	34
Cleaver, John(A)	1814	Oct. 13	Hamilton	01	03	30
Clem, John(A)	1806	March 28	Kentucky	01	04	01
Clemans, John Burrow(C)	1831	Aug. 08	Logan	14	03	23
Clemens, Adam(B)	1833	Dec. 06	Cincinnati	02	07	06
Clemens, Jacob(B)	1834	March 08	Pennsylvania	02	07	06
Clemens, Jacob(B)	1834	Sept. 02	Pennsylvania	02	07	06
Clemens, Jacob(B)	1835	Jan. 03	Hamilton	02	07	06
Clemens, Jacob(B)	1835	July 17	Hamilton	02	07	06
Clemens, Jacob(B)	1835	July 17	Hamilton	02	07	06
Clemens, Saml.(C)	1815	Aug. 09	Champaign	13	03	04
Clement, John(B)	1817	Aug. 13	Dearborn(Ind	02	04	31
Clements, Caleb B.(C)	1814	June 23	Warren	13	12	08

PURCHASER	YEAR	DATE	RESIDENCE	R	T	S
Clements, Isaac(E)	1827	Oct. 22	Warren	14	17	04
Clements, John(A)	1829	Oct. 13	Warren	03	08	31
Clements, John(A)	1830	Feb. 08	Warren	03	08	31
Clements, Richard(E)	1814	Aug. 02	Warren	13	12	17
Clemmens, James(Black)(A)	1818	Oct. 16	Warren	01	11	05
Clemmens, James(Black)(A)	1818	Oct. 16	Warren	01	11	05
Clemmens, John(Black)(A)	1821	Sept. 13	Ross	01	11	08
Clemons, John(E)	1832	May 28	Montgomery	12	17	36
Clemons, William W.(A)	1817	June 07	Pennsylvania	01	01	06
Clencey, James(C)	1804	Sept. 03	Greene	06	03	32
Clency, Daniel(B)	1833	July 03	Cincinnati	02	07	21
Clendining, John(B)	1807	July 23	Dearborn(Ind	01	09	33
Clenny, Curtis(E)	1815	Jan. 07	Preble	14	18	11
Clenny, Curtis(E)	1835	Jan. 23	Randolph(Ind	15	19	31
Clensy, James(C)	1810	Dec. 12	Greene	06	03	25
Cleveland, Luther(B)	1836	March 10	Hamilton	03	07	22
Cleveland, Luther(B)	1836	April 06	Hamilton	03	07	22
Clevenger, Daniel(E)	1816	Feb. 10	Warren	14	15	19
Clevenger, Sylvester(A)	1818	Sept. 04	Warren	04	07	07
Clevenger, Thomas(E)	1836	May 13	Randolph(Ind	14	19	36
Clevenger, Thos.(E)	1823	Nov. 25	Warren	14	18	01
Clevinger, Zachariah(C)	1801	Dec. 30	Hamilton	04	03	04
Click, Joel(C)	1826	Nov. 22	Clark	10	03	14
Cliffin, Benjamin(B)	1819	March 11	Dearborn(Ind	01	07	06
Clifton, Henry(C)	1826	Jan. 21	Clark	10	04	35
Clifton, Henry(C)	1826	April 28	Clark	11	04	01
Clifton, Henry(C)	1826	Nov. 21	Clark	11	03	14
Clifton, Henry(C)	1827	May 23	Champaign	11	03	14
Clifton, John(B)	1818	July 21	Dearborn(Ind	01	07	06
Clifton, John(B)	1831	Oct. 19	Dearborn(Ind	01	07	06
Clifton, John(B)	1819	March 11	Dearborn(Ind	01	07	06
Clindinin, Evert(B)	1829	March 31	Hamilton	02	05	10
Cline, Ann(A)	1831	Nov. 01	Warren	02	10	13
Cline, Frederick(A)	1831	Nov. 01	Warren	02	10	12
Cline, Jacob(A)	1831	Nov. 01	Warren	02	10	11
Clingan, Edw. Heirs(C)	1828	Oct. 13	Miami	10	03	11
Clingan, Edw.(C)	1828	Oct. 13	Miami	10	03	11
Clingan, James(A)	1836	June 03	Miami	04	11	18
Clingan, James(C)	1828	Oct. 13	Miami	10	02	11
Clingan, James(C)	1828	Oct. 13	Miami	10	03	17
Clingan, James(C)	1829	Feb. 27	Clark	10	03	17
Clingan, John Heirs(C)	1828	Oct. 13	Miami	10	03	17
Clingan, John(C)	1804	Dec. 28	Montgomery	09	02	23
Clingen, John(C)	1806	Oct. 25	Montgomery	09	02	23
Clinger, John(C)	1811	Dec. 11	Miami	09	02	23
Close, David B.(B)	1809	March 27	New York	01	04	34
Close, David B.(B)	1812	Feb. 11	New York	01	03	04
Close, David(B)	1814	Sept. 05	Dearborn(Ind	01	03	04
Close, David(B)	1815	June 19	Dearborn(Ind	01	04	34
Close, David(B)	1819	May 11	Dearborn(Ind	01	03	34
Cloud, Baylis(B)	1811	Nov. 29	Kentucky	01	07	28
Cloud, Henry(B)	1803	Aug. 23	Ind.Territry	02	04	11
Cloud, Henry(B)	1804	Nov. 27	Ind.Territry	01	04	07
Cloud, Henry(B)	1812	Aug. 18	Dearborn(Ind	02	04	22
Cloud, James(B)	1806	July 09	Dearborn(Ind	01	08	12
Cloud, James(B)	1811	Aug. 13	Dearborn(Ind	01	08	12
Cloud, James(B)	1812	Oct. 06	Dearborn(Ind	01	07	27
Cloud, James(B)	1816	Nov. 25	Dearborn(Ind	01	07	14
Cloud, James(B)	1817	June 11	Dearborn(Ind	01	07	34
Cloud, James(B)	1831	June 06	Dearborn(Ind	01	07	14
Cloud, John S.(E)	1836	Oct. 17	Randolph(Ind	13	20	36
Cloud, Jonathan(E)	1814	Sept. 03	Wayne(Ind)	13	16	01
Cloud, Ramey Scandlin(B)	1832	March 15	Franklin(Ind	01	07	26
Cloud, William(B)	1806	July 28	Kentucky	01	09	31
Cloud, William(B)	1814	May 21	Kentucky	01	07	19
Cloud, William(B)	1816	March 06	Dearborn(Ind	02	07	25
Cloud, William(E)	1814	April 01	Kentucky	12	14	10
Clough, Ezekiel C.(E)	1837	April 24	Hamilton	15	22	28
Clough, Moses(E)	1836	Oct. 31	Cincinnati	15	22	32

PURCHASER	YEAR	DATE	RESIDENCE	R	T	S
Clough, Timothy(E)	1836	Oct. 31	Cincinnati	15	22	32
Cloyd, James(A)	1810	April 11	Montgomery	03	05	01
Cloyd, James(A)	1811	April 09	Preble	03	05	26
Cloyd, James(A)	1811	Nov. 25	Preble	03	05	02
Cloyd, James(A)	1814	April 11	Darke	01	11	12
Cloyd, James(A)	1815	Jan. 14	Darke	01	11	26
Cloyd, James(A)	1816	March 26	Preble	01	11	35
Cloyd, James(A)	1824	Sept. 20	Darke	01	11	22
Cloyd, James(A)	1824	Sept. 20	Darke	01	11	15
Cloyd, James(A)	1829	March 31	Darke	01	11	22
Cloyd, James(A)	1832	March 01	Darke	01	11	15
Cloyd, Joshua(A)	1816	Sept. 17	Preble	01	11	26
Cloyd, Stephen(A)	1828	Dec. 15	Preble	04	05	19
Clyne, Jacob(C)	1830	Sept. 10	Miami	13	04	29
Clyne, John(C)	1825	Aug. 08	Miami	11	02	08
Clyne, John(C)	1827	Aug. 20	Miami	11	02	08
Clyne, Peter(C)	1829	June 22	Logan	14	03	26
Coapland, John(E)	1814	June 28	Wayne(Ind)	14	16	05
Coapstick, Samuel(C)	1801	Dec. 30	Hamilton	04	02	13
Coat, Henry(A)	1806	Oct. 24	Montgomery	04	07	01
Coat, Henry(A)	1819	June 08	Miami	05	06	06
Coat, James(A)	1806	July 19	Montgomery	05	07	32
Coat, Jesse(A)	1806	Nov. 13	So. Carolina	04	08	03
Coat, Marmaduke(A)	1804	Nov. 05	Warren	05	07	32
Coat, Moses(A)	1804	Sept. 25	Montgomery	05	06	05
Coat, Samuel(A)	1804	Nov. 05	Warren	05	06	05
Coate, Henry(A)	1805	Aug. 08	Montgomery	05	06	06
Coate, Henry(A)	1816	Nov. 13	Miami	05	06	18
Coate, Henry(A)	1816	Nov. 13	Miami	04	08	36
Coate, Henry(A)	1831	Jan. 10	Miami	04	08	26
Coate, James(A)	1831	July 05	Miami	05	07	23
Coate, John Jr.(A)	1830	Aug. 16	Miami	04	08	25
Coate, John(A)	1831	April 21	Miami	04	08	35
Coate, John(A)	1831	April 21	Miami	05	07	21
Coate, Moses(A)	1819	May 17	Miami	04	07	01
Coate, William(A)	1806	July 23	Montgomery	05	06	07
Coates, Thomas(B)	1820	Oct. 13	Cincinnati	02	07	05
Coats, George(A)	1831	Oct. 21	Miami	04	09	29
Coats, Isaac(E)	1832	Feb. 25	Randolph(Ind	14	20	24
Coats, James(E)	1837	June 30	Randolph(Ind	14	20	01
Coats, John(E)	1827	Aug. 22	Randolph(Ind	14	20	23
Coats, John(E)	1837	March 01	Randolph(Ind	14	20	13
Coats, Joseph(A)	1818	Nov. 19	Miami	04	09	04
Coats, Joseph(A)	1818	Nov. 19	Miami	04	10	34
Coats, Thomas W.(E)	1831	July 05	Randolph(Ind	14	20	23
Coats, Thomas W.(E)	1837	June 30	Randolph(Ind	14	20	23
Coats, Thos. W.(E)	1838	Nov. 02	Randolph(Ind	14	20	23
Coats, William(A)	1807	July 10	Miami	06	04	19
Coats, William(A)	1811	Jan. 28	Miami	05	08	30
Coats, William(A)	1815	Jan. 14	Miami	04	09	11
Coats, William(E)	1836	Dec. 15	Randolph(Ind	14	20	23
Coats, William(E)	1837	March 01	Randolph(Ind	14	20	03
Cobel, Anthony(A)	1806	March 27	Montgomery	05	05	01
Coblance, Adam(C)	1806	June 09	Maryland	06	01	06
Coble, Anthony(A)	1806	Aug. 06	Montgomery	06	03	18
Coble, Anthony(A)	1836	Sept. 20	Montgomery	04	11	07
Coble, John(A)	1815	Dec. 09	Preble	03	05	02
Coble, John(A)	1818	Oct. 28	Darke	01	11	08
Coble, John(A)	1819	June 17	Preble	01	11	17
Coburn, Joseph H.(B)	1819	Jan. 21	Dearborn(Ind	02	04	28
Cochran, Enoch(B)	1836	Jan. 21	Dearborn(Ind	02	03	18
Cochran, John(B)	1816	Oct. 25	Adams	03	03	25
Cochran, William(C)	1817	Aug. 22	Hamilton	11	01	11
Cochran, William(D)	1816	Dec. 04	Hamilton	02	04	26
Cochren, James(A)	1837	Oct. 19	Preble	02	14	32
Cochron, Aaron F.(B)	1836	June 15	Dearborn(Ind	02	02	01
Cochrun, John(C)	1817	June 05	Champaign	13	04	28
Cockey, Richand(B)	1814	Nov. 19	Franklin(Ind	02	09	11
Cockey, Richard(B)	1814	Aug. 08	Franklin(Ind	01	09	20

PURCHASER	YEAR	DATE	RESIDENCE	R	T	S
Cockrem, Philip(C)	1824	Aug. 26	Miami	10	02	08
Codrington, William(E)	1817	Aug. 15	Montgomery	12	17	25
Coe, Joseph(C)	1802	Dec. 31	Hamilton	11	01	19
Coe, Joseph(C)	1815	April 17	Kentucky	12	05	24
Coe, William(B)	1814	Jan. 13	Hamilton	01	10	07
Coem, Edward(B)	1814	June 15	Butler	03	03	27
Coen, Josiah(E)	1835	Sept. 17	Franklin(Ind	13	11	20
Coen, Josiah(E)	1836	Sept. 14	Franklin(Ind	13	11	20
Coen, Thomas(E)	1832	May 29	Franklin(Ind	13	11	20
Coffelt, Augustus(C)	1817	Dec. 23	Champaign	10	04	35
Coffey, Spencer(E)	1836	Sept. 07	Kentucky	12	11	03
Coffin, Adam(A)	1807	Sept. 30	Montgomery	06	03	28
Coffin, Andrew(B)	1817	May 27	Switzerland	02	02	12
Coffin, Duncan Cameron(E)	1833	May 06	Randolph(Ind	14	21	15
Coffin, Hervey(E)	1831	Nov. 19	Wayne(Ind)	13	18	27
Coffin, Hezekiah(B)	1819	Oct. 18	Hamilton	02	07	01
Coffin, Levi(E)	1836	Nov. 28	Wayne(Ind)	14	19	31
Coffin, Levi(E)	1838	Jan. 30	Wayne(Ind)	14	20	12
Coffin, Stephen(E)	1837	Jan. 30	Randolph(Ind	14	20	23
Coffman, David(A)	1814	Dec. 21	Montgomery	05	05	32
Coffman, John(E)	1836	Oct. 21	Montgomery	15	21	32
Cohee, Benjamin(C)	1816	Sept. 18	Butler	12	04	21
Cohee, Vincent Dill(C)	1816	Sept. 18	Butler	12	04	21
Cohee, Vincent Dill(C)	1816	Oct. 17	Butler	12	04	15
Cohoon, Robert(A)	1836	July 08	Hamilton	03	11	24
Cohoon, Robert(A)	1836	July 08	Hamilton	03	12	15
Colbert, Jesse(C)	1813	June 10	Champaign	11	03	17
Colby, Hiram(A)	1837	May 22	Shelby	02	14	06
Colby, Isaac(A)	1836	Nov. 26	Butler	02	14	35
Colby, Joseph(A)	1806	April 14	Hamilton	03	03	07
Colby, Joseph(A)	1806	May 09	Hamilton	03	03	17
Colclesser, Jacob(A)	1829	June 12	Montgomery	04	07	35
Coldman, Rolland(B)	1815	April 24	Hamilton	01	11	21
Coldwell, Abraham R.(C)	1817	May 27	Champaign	13	04	02
Coldwell, Joseph(A)	1806	Sept. 13	Butler	01	06	05
Cole, Adam(B)	1817	June 10	Hamilton	03	03	28
Cole, David(A)	1821	Jan. 24	Darke	01	12	32
Cole, Eleazer(B)	1816	Nov. 08	Virginia	03	04	14
Cole, Hartshorn(E)	1836	Feb. 01	Franklin(Ind	12	11	23
Cole, Harvey(B)	1838	Sept. 04	Dearborn(Ind	03	05	33
Cole, Hugh(B)	1836	Oct. 27	Switzerland	03	04	15
Cole, James(B)	1815	Aug. 07	Dearborn(Ind	01	07	33
Cole, James(E)	1818	Sept. 03	Dearborn(Ind	12	12	24
Cole, Jas.(A)	1828	Nov. 19	Darke	01	12	21
Cole, John Jr.(B)	1831	June 20	Switzerland	03	04	32
Cole, John(B)	1817	Dec. 17	Dearborn(Ind	03	05	32
Cole, Jos.(A)	1828	Nov. 19	Darke	01	12	21
Cole, Joseph Allen(B)	1832	June 08	Switzerland	03	03	09
Cole, Joseph Junr.(B)	1835	Dec. 30	Switzerland	03	03	22
Cole, Joseph(A)	1824	Jan. 20	Clermont	01	12	20
Cole, Joseph(A)	1824	Sept. 10	Clermont	01	12	21
Cole, Joseph(A)	1827	Oct. 05	Darke	01	12	21
Cole, Joseph(B)	1817	June 24	Hamilton	03	03	21
Cole, Joshua(A)	1818	Aug. 25	Piqua	06	08	06
Cole, Joshua(A)	1831	Nov. 28	Shelby	06	08	05
Cole, Martin R.(B)	1836	March 21	Switzerland	03	03	21
Cole, Richard(A)	1829	Sept. 21	Pickaway	06	08	22
Cole, Samuel Junr.(A)	1816	Dec. 21	Greene	01	12	27
Cole, Samuel(A)	1819	Dec. 22	Darke	01	12	28
Cole, Samuel(A)	1831	April 13	Montgomery	06	08	22
Cole, Samuel(B)	1817	Dec. 17	Dearborn(Ind	03	05	32
Cole, Samuel(B)	1837	May 20	Montgomery	01	18	36
Cole, Samuel(E)	1837	May 10	Montgomery	15	20	04
Cole, Samuel(E)	1837	June 14	Montgomery	15	21	32
Cole, Shadrack(A)	1811	Sept. 10	Pickaway	06	07	20
Cole, Shadrack(A)	1816	Dec. 02	Pickaway	06	07	20
Cole, Silas S.(B)	1836	March 15	Switzerland	03	03	21
Cole, Solomon(E)	1818	Sept. 03	Dearborn(Ind	12	12	24
Cole, Thomas(B)	1831	Aug. 09	Switzerland	02	03	34

PURCHASER	YEAR	DATE	RESIDENCE	R	T	S
Coledin, Caleb(B)	1833	Sept. 05	Dearborn(Ind	02	05	22
Coledin, Caleb(B)	1834	Jan. 01	Darke	02	05	22
Coleman, Asa(A)	1815	April 11	Miami	06	04	15
Coleman, Benjamin(C)	1807	March 19	Kentucky	10	02	17
Coleman, Elias(B)	1828	Oct. 22	Randolph(Ind	01	16	22
Coleman, Jacob(A)	1805	April 25	Montgomery	04	04	19
Coleman, Jonathan(E)	1813	Dec. 06	Butler	13	15	33
Coleman, Joseph(C)	1810	Dec. 12	Montgomery	06	02	35
Coleman, Joseph(C)	1810	Dec. 12	Montgomery	06	01	05
Coleman, Joseph(C)	1810	Dec. 12	Montgomery	06	02	36
Coleman, Nicholas(A)	1805	Nov. 25	Montgomery	03	07	33
Coleman, Nicholas(A)	1809	July 24	Montgomery	03	06	04
Coleman, Nicholas(A)	1810	May 22	Pennsylvania	03	06	15
Coleman, Philip(A)	1806	Nov. 13	Pennsylvania	05	08	18
Coleman, Philip(A)	1814	Oct. 10	Warren	06	08	01
Coles, Thomas K.(B)	1817	Oct. 28	Dearborn(Ind	02	04	26
Colescott, Thomas W.(B)	1816	May 03	Franklin(Ind	02	08	08
Colgrove, Samuel(C)	1811	July 02	New York	08	03	29
Colgrove, Samuel(C)	1811	July 02	New York	08	03	34
Coller, Jacob(A)	1830	Nov. 10	Warren	03	07	01
Coller, Jacob(dec'd.)(E)	1837	April 10	Warren	15	21	32
Collett, Charles(E)	1814	Jan. 05	Franklin(Ind	13	14	10
Collett, Isaac(E)	1831	Sept. 13	Clinton	14	20	13
Collett, Williamson(E)	1813	Feb. 23	Franklin(Ind	13	12	34
Collingsworth, Ezekiel(B)	1817	Dec. 02	Franklin(Ind	01	11	17
Collingsworth, John(A)	1812	April 15	Preble	03	05	19
Collins, Amos W.(E)	1840	Jan. 14	Jay Co.,Ind.	14	22	27
Collins, Henry(B)	1831	Sept. 21	Dearborn(Ind	01	04	29
Collins, Henry(B)	1833	Jan. 28	Dearborn(Ind	01	04	29
Collins, Hugh T.(B)	1837	April 13	Dearborn(Ind	02	03	04
Collins, Humphry(C)	1831	March 07	Champaign	11	03	04
Collins, John(A)	1814	Feb. 05	Preble	02	07	13
Collins, John(A)	1818	Jan. 02	Preble	01	07	17
Collins, John(A)	1818	Jan. 10	Baltimore	04	05	33
Collins, John(A)	1830	Oct. 26	Warren	02	09	03
Collins, John(B)	1808	Jan. 13	Dearborn(Ind	01	13	19
Collins, John(B)	1811	Nov. 28	Franklin(Ind	02	09	34
Collins, John(B)	1814	Sept. 29	Franklin(Ind	02	09	35
Collins, John(E)	1815	Nov. 25	Franklin(Ind	12	12	08
Collit, Charles(E)	1813	June 10	Franklin(Ind	13	12	34
Colliver, Richard(B)	1812	Feb. 20	Kentucky	01	09	10
Colliver, Richard(E)	1814	Sept. 08	Kentucky	13	14	34
Collwell, Abm. R.(C)	1817	May 27	Champaign	12	05	36
Collyer, Thomas(E)	1830	Feb. 18	Franklin(Ind	13	12	17
Colman, Joseph(C)	1805	July 20	Montgomery	06	02	36
Colthoff, Frederick(E)	1836	Oct. 21	Cincinnati	12	10	07
Columbia, John(B)	1831	Sept. 22	Dearborn(Ind	02	05	32
Colver, Samuel(C)	1805	Sept. 30	Champaign	11	06	32
Colvill, John(A)	1831	May 17	Darke	03	08	21
Colvin, John(A)	1836	June 06	Kentucky	03	09	36
Colwell, Abram R.(C)	1817	May 27	?	13	04	02
Colwell, James(B)	1816	May 07	Warren	02	06	10
Colwell, James(B)	1816	May 10	Warren	02	07	23
Colwell, James(B)	1816	Aug. 06	Warren	02	07	23
Combs, Job(A)	1814	Nov. 30	Preble	01	08	08
Combs, John(A)	1811	April 17	New Jersey	02	04	13
Combs, Joseph(E)	1837	Jan. 07	Montgomery	15	20	17
Combs, Manuel(C)	1814	Feb. 08	Miami	09	02	12
Combs, Micajah(E)	1837	Jan. 07	Montgomery	15	20	17
Comelison, Andrew(A)	1808	Jan. 13	Butler	02	06	01
Comer, Joseph(B)	1807	July 01	Dearborn(Ind	01	14	34
Comer, Philip(C)	1809	March 16	Champaign	12	03	08
Comer, Philip(C)	1815	Nov. 15	Champaign	12	03	09
Comer, Rebecca(A)	1816	June 07	Preble	01	06	12
Comer, Rebecca(A)	1816	June 10	Preble	01	06	12
Comer, Robert(B)	1807	July 01	Dearborn(Ind	01	14	35
Comer, Stephen(E)	1813	Sept. 08	Wayne(Ind)	14	17	27
Comes, Philip(C)	1811	May 20	Champaign	12	03	08
Commings, Isaac(B)	1808	June 15	Dearborn(Ind	01	14	01

PURCHASER	YEAR	DATE	RESIDENCE	R	T	S
Commons, Ezekiel(E)	1814	Aug. 12	Wayne(Ind)	13	16	22
Commons, William(E)	1814	Oct. 22	Franklin(Ind	14	17	29
Compstock, Joab(A)	1805	July 26	Hamilton	02	03	19
Compton, Amos(A)	1829	Feb. 16	Darke	03	09	30
Compton, Eli(A)	1827	Aug. 20	Montgomery	06	03	15
Compton, Henry R.(B)	1816	Nov. 18	Hamilton	01	09	32
Compton, Isaac(B)	1827	Dec. 05	Wayne(Ind)	01	15	12
Compton, Jacob R.(B)	1806	March 10	Hamilton	01	06	02
Compton, Jacob R.(D)	1813	June 04	Hamilton	01	02	08
Compton, James(B)	1817	June 20	Wayne(Ind)	01	15	01
Compton, John(A)	1804	Oct. 12	Montgomery	05	06	07
Compton, John(A)	1804	Oct. 12	Montgomery	05	06	08
Compton, John(C)	1805	April 04	Montgomery	05	04	30
Compton, Joseph(A)	1805	June 11	Butler	03	03	13
Compton, Rebecea(A)	1806	May 19	Butler	03	04	30
Compton, William(A)	1805	Aug. 05	Montgomery	06	03	14
Comstock, Joab(A)	1801	July 23	Hamilton	02	03	28
Comstock, Joab(A)	1801	June 22	Hamilton	02	02	08
Conarroe, Rich'd.(A)	1832	July 05	Butler	01	09	11
Conarroe, Rich'd.(A)	1832	July 05	Butler	01	09	12
Conarroe, Richard(E)	1836	Oct. 15	Butler	14	19	29
Conarroe, Richard(E)	1837	Jan. 21	Butler	15	19	06
Conaway, Cornelius(A)	1832	Jan. 12	Miami	04	08	12
Conaway, Daniel(B)	1812	Sept. 25	Dearborn(Ind	02	04	14
Conaway, Daniel(B)	1836	Feb. 25	Dearborn(Ind	02	03	06
Conaway, Hezekiah(A)	1836	Oct. 27	Montgomery	01	13	29
Conaway, James(B)	1804	Sept. 20	Dearborn(Ind	02	04	29
Conaway, James(B)	1816	Aug. 26	Dearborn(Ind	02	04	33
Conaway, James(E)	1815	Aug. 29	Wayne(Ind)	13	14	24
Conaway, James(E)	1815	Aug. 29	Wayne(Ind)	13	14	25
Conaway, John(B)	1832	Oct. 06	Dearborn(Ind	02	04	32
Conaway, Robert(B)	1813	Nov. 04	Dearborn(Ind	02	04	32
Conaway, Robert(B)	1836	March 01	Dearborn(Ind	02	03	04
Conaway, Simon(B)	1828	Sept. 05	Dearborn(Ind	03	02	06
Conaway, Simon(B)	1833	May 29	Dearborn(Ind	02	03	06
Conaway, Simon(B)	1833	May 29	Dearborn(Ind	02	03	06
Concannon, William(C)	1802	Dec. 28	Hamilton	06	02	28
Concannon, William(C)	1806	Jan. 27	Montgomery	11	02	36
Condon, Curtis(E)	1836	Oct. 05	Butler	12	12	32
Cone, Charles(B)	1813	Aug. 23	Hamilton	01	09	12
Cone, Gustavus A.(B)	1818	July 29	Hamilton	01	07	35
Cone, Lucius(A)	1831	Sept. 13	Miami	05	08	11
Conely, John(E)	1812	April 02	Virginia	13	15	14
Cones, John(E)	1836	Aug. 23	Franklin(Ind	12	12	18
Congar, David(B)	1818	Jan. 16	Dearborn(Ind	03	07	14
Congar, Moses(B)	1813	Feb. 22	Hamilton	02	08	12
Conger, Enoch(B)	1818	April 25	Dearborn(Ind	03	07	02
Conger, Enoch(B)	1818	Sept. 14	Dearborn(Ind	03	07	01
Conger, Enoch(B)	1827	May 26	Dearborn(Ind	03	07	14
Conger, Enoch(B)	1832	Jan. 27	Dearborn(Ind	03	07	14
Conger, Enoch(B)	1832	Sept. 22	Dearborn(Ind	03	07	02
Conger, Josiah(A)	1812	April 03	Preble	01	07	23
Conger, Josiah(E)	1835	Dec. 17	Preble	14	19	18
Conger, Zachariah S.(B)	1816	Sept. 07	Dearborn(Ind	03	07	02
Conkle, Elizabeth(E)	1833	July 06	Randolph(Ind	15	19	05
Conkle, Michael(A)	1817	Nov. 15	Pennsylvania	01	11	36
Conklin, Abner(A)	1814	Dec. 21	Cincinnati	01	04	28
Conkling, Joseph(A)	1806	Aug. 09	Hamilton	01	04	14
Conkling, Joseph(A)	1812	Oct. 24	Hamilton	01	04	14
Conklyn, Samuel(E)	1836	Sept. 05	Montgomery	15	20	09
Conklyn, Samuel(E)	1836	Sept. 05	Montgomery	15	20	09
Conklyn, Samuel(E)	1837	Feb. 13	Montgomery	15	20	09
Conlan, Hugh(B)	1830	Jan. 09	Dearborn(Ind	02	07	22
Conley, Isaac(B)	1816	Oct. 09	Wayne(Ind)	01	12	02
Conley, Samuel(B)	1818	Aug. 28	Dearborn(Ind	02	04	33
Conly, James(B)	1817	June 19	Pennsylvania	02	03	04
Conn, James(B)	1801	Dec. 19	Cincinnati	01	05	29
Conn, William(E)	1815	Dec. 01	Franklin(Ind	13	11	30
Connel, Jonathan(C)	1807	Jan. 01	Champaign	08	06	18

PURCHASER	YEAR	DATE	RESIDENCE	R	T	S
Connel, William(C)	1814	March 23	Champaign	13	04	09
Connel, William(C)	1831	March 21	Champaign	13	04	21
Connell, William(C)	1816	Sept. 10	Champaign	13	04	21
Connell, William(C)	1827	June 30	Champaign	13	04	21
Connell, Zachariah(A)	1836	Oct. 19	Clermont	01	15	17
Connell, Zachariah(A)	1836	Oct. 20	Clermont	01	15	22
Connell, Zachariah(A)	1837	Dec. 02	Hamilton	01	15	17
Connell, Zachariah(A)	1838	May 10	Hamilton	01	15	28
Connelly, Lemuel(B)	1832	Oct. 03	Dearborn(Ind	03	08	23
Conner, Abner(B)	1814	Dec. 14	Dearborn(Ind	01	08	34
Conner, Daniel(B)	1804	Sept. 18	Cincinnati	01	04	04
Conner, Daniel(B)	1833	Dec. 17	Dearborn(Ind	02	03	35
Conner, Daniel(B)	1835	Jan. 02	Switzerland	02	03	35
Conner, Daniel(E)	1813	June 07	Franklin(Ind	13	14	28
Conner, David(A)	1815	April 20	Darke	02	12	34
Conner, David(A)	1818	June 12	Darke	01	15	09
Conner, David(E)	1814	July 30	Franklin(Ind	13	14	32
Conner, David(E)	1817	July 10	Darke	14	21	09
Conner, Edward O.(B)	1818	April 07	Dearborn(Ind	02	05	29
Conner, Isaac(B)	1815	Feb. 07	Dearborn(Ind	01	04	06
Conner, James(A)	1815	Oct. 18	Butler	02	04	21
Conner, James(A)	1818	Oct. 20	Kentucky	08	02	35
Conner, James(B)	1817	Sept. 16	Hamilton	01	06	31
Conner, John(B)	1805	April 16	Dearborn(Ind	02	08	14
Conner, John(B)	1805	July 11	Ind.Territory	02	08	11
Conner, John(B)	1810	Aug. 14	Dearborn(Ind	02	08	14
Conner, John(B)	1810	Aug. 14	Dearborn(Ind	02	08	13
Conner, John(B)	1810	Aug. 14	Dearborn(Ind	02	08	11
Conner, John(B)	1815	Aug. 10	Montgomery	01	04	18
Conner, John(E)	1811	Oct. 21	Dearborn(Ind	12	12	27
Conner, John(E)	1811	Oct. 23	Wayne(Ind)	12	16	35
Conner, John(E)	1812	Nov. 13	Franklin(Ind	12	14	25
Conner, John(E)	1812	Nov. 13	Franklin(Ind	12	14	23
Conner, John(E)	1814	Dec. 15	Franklin(Ind	12	13	22
Conner, Reuben(E)	1813	Nov. 17	Kentucky	12	13	22
Conner, Richard(B)	1806	March 20	Ind.Territory	01	08	18
Conner, Timothy(B)	1833	Dec. 17	Dearborn(Ind	02	03	35
Conner, William(E)	1813	Dec. 23	Kentucky	12	13	04
Conner, William(E)	1814	June 17	Kentucky	12	13	15
Conner, Wm.(E)	1814	Oct. 15	Franklin(Ind	12	13	27
Conrad, Christian(B)	1835	Sept. 14	Hamilton	02	07	04
Conrey, Jonathan F.(A)	1836	Oct. 11	Butler	01	13	34
Conrey, Stephen F.(A)	1836	Oct. 11	Butler	01	13	34
Conroy, Edward(C)	1818	June 08	Champaign	12	02	10
Conroy, Edward(C)	1831	Jan. 27	Miami	12	02	10
Conroy, Isaac(C)	1827	Dec. 20	Shelby	13	02	08
Constable, Mary(E)	1837	Jan. 23	Miami	14	21	01
Constable, Thomas J.(E)	1837	April 12	Miami	14	21	01
Conway, Charles(E)	1817	July 10	Tennessee	14	20	20
Conway, Charles(E)	1832	Feb. 06	Randolph(Ind	14	20	08
Conway, Daniel(B)	1815	May 09	Dearborn(Ind	02	04	12
Conway, Robert(B)	1811	Jan. 21	Dearborn(Ind	02	04	29
Conway, Simon(B)	1817	Nov. 15	Dearborn(Ind	02	04	31
Conwell, Elias(B)	1829	Dec. 10	Dearborn(Ind	02	05	21
Conwell, Francis A.(E)	1836	Nov. 17	Franklin(Ind	12	13	32
Conwell, Francis A.(E)	1836	Dec. 10	Franklin(Ind	12	12	06
Conwell, Francis A.(E)	1836	Dec. 10	Franklin(Ind	12	12	12
Conwell, James(E)	1829	March 18	Franklin(Ind	12	12	04
Conwell, James(E)	1831	Jan. 01	Franklin(Ind	12	13	35
Conwell, James(E)	1831	Dec. 16	Franklin(Ind	12	13	33
Conwell, James(E)	1831	Dec. 16	Franklin(Ind	12	13	21
Conwell, James(E)	1831	Dec. 16	Franklin(Ind	12	12	15
Conwell, James(E)	1831	Dec. 22	Franklin(Ind	12	12	11
Conwell, James(E)	1831	Dec. 22	Franklin(Ind	12	12	02
Conwell, James(E)	1832	May 23	Franklin(Ind	12	12	05
Conwell, James(E)	1832	Nov. 28	Franklin(Ind	12	12	02
Conwell, James(E)	1832	Nov. 28	Franklin(Ind	12	12	15
Conwell, James(E)	1832	Nov. 28	Franklin(Ind	12	12	15
Conwell, James(E)	1833	Jan. 03	Franklin(Ind	12	12	05

PURCHASER	YEAR	DATE	RESIDENCE	R	T	S
Conwell, James(E)	1833	March 15	Franklin(Ind	12	13	35
Conwell, James(E)	1834	Sept. 19	Franklin(Ind	11	13	36
Conwell, James(E)	1834	Sept. 19	Franklin(Ind	11	13	36
Conwell, James(E)	1834	Oct. 11	Franklin(Ind	12	12	08
Conwell, James(E)	1834	Oct. 31	Franklin(Ind	12	12	08
Conwell, James(E)	1834	Oct. 31	Franklin(Ind	12	13	35
Conwell, James(E)	1834	Oct. 31	Franklin(Ind	12	12	04
Conwell, James(E)	1834	Oct. 31	Franklin(Ind	12	12	05
Conwell, James(E)	1834	Oct. 31	Franklin(Ind	12	12	17
Conwell, James(E)	1834	Oct. 31	Franklin(Ind	12	12	23
Conwell, James(E)	1834	Oct. 31	Franklin(Ind	12	12	15
Conwell, James(E)	1834	Oct. 31	Franklin(Ind	12	12	14
Conwell, James(E)	1834	Oct. 31	Franklin(Ind	12	12	08
Conwell, James(E)	1834	Oct. 31	Franklin(Ind	12	12	08
Conwell, James(E)	1834	Oct. 31	Franklin(Ind	12	12	14
Conwell, James(E)	1834	Nov. 24	Franklin(Ind	12	13	21
Conwell, James(E)	1834	Nov. 27	Franklin(Ind	12	13	36
Conwell, James(E)	1834	Nov. 27	Franklin(Ind	12	13	30
Conwell, James(E)	1835	March 02	Franklin(Ind	12	13	19
Conwell, James(E)	1835	March 02	Franklin(Ind	12	13	17
Conwell, James(E)	1835	Dec. 10	Franklin(Ind	12	13	30
Conwell, James(E)	1836	March 31	Franklin(Ind	12	12	22
Conwell, Jeremiah(E)	1833	March 15	Franklin(Ind	12	13	35
Cooch, Thomas(A)	1802	Aug. 07	Hamilton	02	05	29
Cooch, Thomas(A)	1802	Aug. 20	Hamilton	02	05	32
Cook, Andrew(B)	1815	Oct. 28	Hamilton	02	05	11
Cook, Charity(B)	1807	Jan. 14	Butler	01	14	31
Cook, Christian(A)	1830	Jan. 28	Montgomery	04	06	10
Cook, Cornelius(E)	1828	May 20	Wayne(Ind)	13	18	25
Cook, Cornelius(E)	1831	Sept. 15	Wayne(Ind)	13	18	25
Cook, Eli(A)	1805	May 31	Butler	03	04	32
Cook, Eli(A)	1805	May 31	Butler	03	03	05
Cook, George(B)	1836	Feb. 01	Dearborn(Ind	01	06	05
Cook, Isaac(A)	1805	July 27	Butler	02	05	11
Cook, Isaac(A)	1806	Aug. 28	Warren	05	06	03
Cook, Isaac(B)	1814	April 12	Clinton	02	11	13
Cook, Isaac(B)	1814	Dec. 13	Wayne(Ind)	01	14	18
Cook, Isaac(E)	1816	Oct. 08	Warren	14	18	09
Cook, Jacob C.(A)	1805	Aug. 01	Virginia	02	09	35
Cook, Jacob C.(A)	1805	Aug. 01	Virginia	03	06	08
Cook, Jacob C.(A)	1805	Aug. 01	Virginia	03	06	09
Cook, Jacob(B)	1817	Aug. 13	Butler	01	02	18
Cook, Jacob(B)	1833	July 05	Cincinnati	02	07	27
Cook, Jacob(E)	1817	Nov. 21	Nor.Carolina	14	18	34
Cook, James(A)	1805	July 15	Butler	03	03	05
Cook, James(E)	1828	March 28	Wayne(Ind)	13	18	24
Cook, John(A)	1806	May 13	Montgomery	06	02	04
Cook, John(C)	1806	March 27	Virginia	11	02	14
Cook, John(C)	1806	March 27	Virginia	11	02	19
Cook, John(E)	1836	Sept. 01	Dearborn(Ind	12	12	32
Cook, Joshua(B)	1814	Dec. 01	Ohio	02	02	33
Cook, Mary(B)	1807	Jan. 14	Butler	01	14	31
Cook, Michael(A)	1819	Sept. 04	Preble	02	09	08
Cook, Nathan(E)	1816	July 18	Wayne(Ind)	13	16	13
Cook, Nathan(E)	1836	April 06	Wayne(Ind)	13	19	01
Cook, Samuel(B)	1834	May 22	Philadelphia	02	07	01
Cook, Seth(E)	1816	Oct. 08	Warren	14	18	15
Cook, Thomas Bishop(B)	1836	May 26	Dearborn(Ind	02	05	17
Cook, Thomas(B)	1807	Sept. 01	Warren	02	11	13
Cook, Thomas(B)	1813	April 14	Franklin(Ind	02	11	13
Cook, Thomas(B)	1814	Dec. 12	Franklin(Ind	02	11	13
Cook, Thos. Bishop(B)	1832	Aug. 03	Dearborn(Ind	02	05	17
Cook, William(A)	1806	Aug. 28	Warren	05	06	10
Cook, William(B)	1813	Oct. 06	Wayne(Ind)	01	14	24
Cook, William(E)	1817	Aug. 11	Wayne(Ind)	13	18	25
Cook, Wright(B)	1813	Dec. 18	Warren	02	11	12
Cooke, Christian(A)	1821	Sept. 03	Montgomery	04	06	10
Cooksey, Jonathan G.(E)	1837	March 01	Franklin(Ind	12	11	20
Cooksey, Thomas(E)	1833	Nov. 25	Franklin(Ind	12	11	20

PURCHASER	YEAR	DATE	RESIDENCE	R	T	S
Cooksey, Thomas(E)	1836	Sept. 07	Franklin(Ind	11	10	23
Cooksey, Zachariah(E)	1815	Aug. 21	Franklin(Ind	13	13	17
Cooley, Isaac(E)	1836	Oct. 19	Franklin(Ind	13	11	17
Cooley, Thadeus(B)	1804	Sept. 18	Dearborn(Ind	01	06	27
Cooley, William(A)	1803	Sept. 02	Hamilton	02	05	33
Cooley, William(A)	1804	Sept. 13	Butler	02	04	03
Cooley, William(A)	1805	July 09	Butler	02	04	04
Cooley, William(A)	1805	Oct. 07	Butler	02	04	10
Cooley, William(A)	1805	Dec. 19	Butler	02	04	09
Coolman, Henry(A)	1829	Jan. 22	Darke	01	10	34
Cooly, James(C)	1818	April 06	Champaign	14	03	07
Cooly, James(C)	1818	June 24	Champaign	14	03	07
Coombs, Edward(B)	1832	Sept. 04	Switzerland	04	02	36
Coombs, John(B)	1818	June 02	Cincinnati	03	03	13
Coombs, John(E)	1822	Jan. 25	?	12	13	19
Cooms, William Jr.(A)	1814	July 27	Franklin(Ind	02	10	12
Coon, David(A)	1828	Dec. 18	Shelby	06	08	19
Coon, Isaac(B)	1810	Sept. 22	Dearborn(Ind	01	10	14
Coon, Jacob(A)	1805	Oct. 05	Kentucky	03	06	24
Coon, Jacob(A)	1806	Oct. 15	Kentucky	02	08	26
Coons, Henry(A)	1813	Dec. 06	Hamilton	01	04	11
Cooper, Alexander(A)	1832	Nov. 15	Preble	02	09	04
Cooper, Christian(B)	1814	Dec. 31	Kentucky	01	02	30
Cooper, Christian(B)	1832	Aug. 11	Switzerland	03	04	22
Cooper, Christian(B)	1832	Oct. 13	Switzerland	03	04	22
Cooper, Daniel C.(C)	1801	Dec. 31	Hamilton	07	02	23
Cooper, Daniel C.(C)	1801	Dec. 31	Hamilton	07	01	13
Cooper, Daniel C.(C)	1801	Dec. 31	Hamilton	07	01	03
Cooper, Daniel C.(C)	1801	Dec. 31	Hamilton	07	01	02
Cooper, Daniel C.(C)	1801	Dec. 31	Hamilton	07	01	09
Cooper, Daniel C.(C)	1801	Dec. 31	Hamilton	07	02	34
Cooper, Daniel C.(C)	1801	Dec. 31	Hamilton	07	01	10
Cooper, Daniel C.(C)	1801	Dec. 31	Hamilton	07	02	35
Cooper, Daniel C.(C)	1801	Dec. 31	Hamilton	07	04	04
Cooper, Daniel C.(C)	1802	Nov. 12	Hamilton	07	02	27
Cooper, Daniel C.(C)	1802	Nov. 12	Hamilton	04	03	06
Cooper, Daniel C.(C)	1802	Nov. 12	Hamilton	07	02	32
Cooper, Daniel C.(C)	1802	Dec. 30	Hamilton	05	02	28
Cooper, Daniel C.(C)	1802	Dec. 30	Hamilton	07	02	32
Cooper, Daniel C.(C)	1802	Dec. 31	Hamilton	08	04	14
Cooper, Daniel C.(C)	1804	Sept. 05	Montgomery	07	01	11
Cooper, Daniel C.(C)	1804	Sept. 05	Montgomery	07	02	11
Cooper, Daniel C.(C)	1804	Sept. 05	Montgomery	07	02	29
Cooper, Daniel C.(C)	1804	Sept. 05	Montgomery	06	01	06
Cooper, Daniel C.(C)	1804	Sept. 06	Montgomery	07	01	08
Cooper, Daniel C.(C)	1804	Sept. 06	Montgomery	07	02	11
Cooper, Daniel C.(C)	1804	Dec. 31	Montgomery	08	04	28
Cooper, Daniel C.(C)	1804	Dec. 31	Montgomery	09	04	07
Cooper, Daniel C.(C)	1804	Dec. 31	Montgomery	07	03	24
Cooper, Daniel C.(C)	1804	Dec. 31	Montgomery	08	04	17
Cooper, Daniel C.(C)	1804	Dec. 31	Montgomery	07	04	23
Cooper, Daniel C.(C)	1804	Dec. 31	Montgomery	08	04	14
Cooper, Daniel C.(C)	1804	Dec. 31	Montgomery	07	03	13
Cooper, Daniel C.(C)	1804	Dec. 31	Montgomery	08	03	14
Cooper, Daniel C.(C)	1804	Dec. 31	Montgomery	07	02	07
Cooper, Daniel C.(C)	1804	Dec. 31	Montgomery	07	02	33
Cooper, Eli(B)	1836	Sept. 05	Dearborn(Ind	03	04	22
Cooper, Ezekel(E)	1837	Aug. 05	Greene	15	21	19
Cooper, Isaac(A)	1811	Dec. 11	Montgomery	05	05	34
Cooper, Isaac(B)	1834	Dec. 15	Preble	01	16	25
Cooper, Isaac(B)	1834	Dec. 15	Preble	01	16	26
Cooper, Isaac(D)	1811	Dec. 30	Hamilton	02	01	26
Cooper, Jacob(A)	1815	Nov. 08	Kentucky	01	07	18
Cooper, John Wayne(B)	1836	July 13	Hamilton	01	17	01
Cooper, John(A)	1817	Nov. 05	Virginia	01	06	06
Cooper, John(C)	1818	July 22	Butler	11	02	29
Cooper, John(E)	1836	July 02	Preble	14	20	26
Cooper, Jonathan(A)	1807	June 04	So. Carolina	02	05	02
Cooper, Joseph(A)	1804	Sept. 24	Warren	05	05	23

PURCHASER	YEAR	DATE	RESIDENCE	R	T	S
Cooper, Joseph(A)	1804	Dec. 10	Warren	05	05	36
Cooper, Joseph(A)	1806	Feb. 28	Montgomery	06	03	32
Cooper, Joseph(A)	1810	Dec. 12	Warren	05	05	23
Cooper, Joseph(A)	1811	Nov. 26	Montgomery	05	05	27
Cooper, Thomas(B)	1818	Jan. 12	Hamilton	02	02	08
Cooper, Thomas(B)	1818	Jan. 12	Hamilton	02	02	08
Cooper, Thomas(C)	1817	Sept. 02	Hamilton	11	02	01
Cooper, Thomas(C)	1817	Sept. 02	Hamilton	11	02	01
Cooper, Thomas(C)	1818	July 22	Butler	11	02	29
Cooper, Thomas(E)	1815	May 31	Hamilton	13	14	14
Cooper, Thomas(E)	1835	Dec. 10	Franklin(Ind	12	12	18
Cooper, William	1808	March 02	Hamilton	?	?	?
Cooper, William	1808	March 02	Hamilton	?	?	?
Cooper, William(A)	1807	May 21	So. Carolina	02	05	02
Cooper, William(A)	1808	Jan. 11	Butler	01	08	34
Cooper, William(A)	1808	Jan. 11	Butler	01	07	04
Cooper, William(A)	1808	Jan. 19	Butler	01	08	34
Cooper, William(A)	1808	March 03	Butler	01	08	34
Cooper, William(A)	1808	March 09	Butler	01	07	09
Cooper, William(A)	1808	March 09	Butler	01	07	27
Cooper, William(A)	1814	March 29	Butler	02	06	35
Cooper, William(A)	1815	Jan. 30	Butler	02	05	02
Cooper, William(B)	1804	Oct. 09	Dearborn(Ind	01	07	04
Coover, Michael(A)	1836	Nov. 07	Montgomery	03	12	04
Copeland, Samuel(E)	1835	Jan. 01	Wayne(Ind)	14	20	27
Copen, James(C)	1802	Dec. 31	Hamilton	06	02	03
Copland, Jonathan(B)	1806	Sept. 13	Hamilton	01	10	19
Coppess, Adam Jr.(A)	1836	Oct. 18	Darke	03	11	20
Coppiss, Adam(A)	1819	June 17	Greene	03	10	04
Coppock, Aaron(A)	1829	July 30	Miami	04	08	36
Coppock, Benjamin(A)	1805	Oct. 31	So. Carolina	04	07	01
Coppock, Benjamin(A)	1831	Oct. 21	Miami	04	07	02
Coppock, Catharine(A)	1828	Sept. 17	Miami	04	08	03
Coppock, Isaiah(A)	1831	April 20	Miami	04	08	34
Coppock, James(A)	1810	Aug. 22	Miami	06	04	29
Coppock, Jesse(A)	1824	March 01	Miami	04	08	12
Coppock, John(A)	1804	Sept. 25	Montgomery	05	06	05
Coppock, John(A)	1805	Aug. 13	Warren	05	06	07
Coppock, John(A)	1831	Nov. 05	Miami	04	08	24
Coppock, Joseph R.(A)	1829	June 02	Miami	05	06	06
Coppock, Joseph(A)	1805	July 31	So. Carolina	05	06	04
Coppock, Joseph(A)	1806	Aug. 26	So. Carolina	05	06	08
Coppock, Joseph(A)	1812	Nov. 06	Miami	04	07	01
Coppock, Joseph(A)	1831	May 09	Miami	04	08	33
Coppock, Matilda(A)	1828	Sept. 17	Miami	04	08	03
Coppock, Moses(A)	1809	Oct. 26	Montgomery	06	04	32
Coppock, Sam'l.(A)	1824	June 08	Miami	04	08	36
Coppock, Samuel(A)	1807	June 29	Miami	05	06	08
Coppock, Samuel(A)	1825	Sept. 02	Miami	04	08	36
Coppock, Thomas(A)	1804	Sept. 25	Montgomery	05	06	04
Coppock, Thomas(A)	1831	April 20	Miami	04	08	34
Coppock, Wright(A)	1831	Sept. 24	Miami	04	08	26
Copse, William(C)	1811	Dec. 14	Muskingum	12	05	22
Copse, William(C)	1813	Feb. 15	Champaign	12	05	08
Corbet, Jeremiah(B)	1833	Jan. 09	Randolph(Ind	01	16	25
Corbin, Elijah(E)	1814	April 02	Kentucky	13	13	22
Corbitt, Rich'd.(B)	1836	Feb. 20	Randolph(Ind	01	16	21
Corbly, Isaiah M.(A)	1836	Nov. 22	Warren	02	14	09
Corbly, John(C)	1807	Sept. 30	Hamilton	11	01	23
Corbly, Justice(C)	1817	June 05	Hamilton	11	03	30
Corbly, Paul(C)	1817	May 30	Hamilton	11	02	05
Corcoran, John(A)	1830	Oct. 13	Cincinnati	04	06	17
Corcoran, John(A)	1830	Oct. 13	Cincinnati	04	06	19
Corcoran, John(A)	1830	Oct. 19	Cincinnati	04	06	18
Cord, Caspar(A)	1839	Jan. 22	Cincinnati	02	15	27
Cordengly, William W.(A)	1815	June 23	Kentucky	06	08	18
Corey, Daniel(C)	1801	Dec. 30	Hamilton	04	03	07
Corey, Elnathan(C)	1804	Nov. 17	Greene	09	02	04
Corey, Elnathan(C)	1804	Nov. 17	Greene	09	02	03

PURCHASER	YEAR	DATE	RESIDENCE	R	T	S
Corey, Elnathan(C)	1804	Nov. 17	Greene	09	02	24
Corey, Elnathan(C)	1806	June 28	Champaign	09	03	33
Corey, Elnathan(C)	1806	Aug. 04	Champaign	10	02	23
Corey, Elnathan(C)	1806	Sept. 13	Montgomery	09	03	30
Corey, Elnathan(C)	1818	March 30	Clark	10	02	04
Corey, James(C)	1804	Nov. 17	Montgomery	09	02	04
Corey, James(C)	1804	Nov. 17	Montgomery	09	02	03
Corey, Thomas(C)	1804	Nov. 17	Montgomery	09	02	03
Cormany, Henry(A)	1815	Oct. 02	Warren	03	07	14
Corn, Nancy(C)	1813	June 18	Scioto	11	04	19
Cornelison, Andrew(B)	1810	Jan. 19	Butler	01	10	32
Cornelius, Absalom(B)	1817	Dec. 29	Kentucky	01	07	26
Cornelius, Andrew(A)	1804	June 04	Butler	03	03	13
Cornelius, George(B)	1837	March 01	Dearborn(Ind	02	05	30
Cornelius, Greenburg(E)	1813	Dec. 11	Wayne(Ind)	13	16	24
Cornell, Benj'n. H.(C)	1825	Jan. 10	Clark	13	03	11
Cornell, Benjamin(C)	1812	April 16	Champaign	10	05	14
Cornell, Benjamin(C)	1812	April 16	Champaign	10	05	07
Cornell, Benjamin(C)	1812	April 17	Champaign	10	05	15
Cornell, Benjamin(C)	1817	Aug. 01	Champaign	10	05	14
Cornell, Sylvanus(A)	1818	Dec. 01	Warren	02	10	01
Cornick, Samuel(A)	1836	Oct. 25	Hamilton	01	15	23
Cornthwait, Edward(A)	1814	Sept. 07	Butler	03	03	21
Cornwell, John(B)	1806	Dec. 01	Kentucky	02	12	36
Cornwell, Sam'l.(A)	1828	Oct. 09	Preble	02	06	15
Cornwell, Samuel(A)	1818	Dec. 03	Preble	02	06	15
Cornwell, Samuel(A)	1818	Dec. 03	Preble	02	06	15
Cornwell, Samuel(E)	1837	March 24	Preble	14	21	29
Cornwell, Samuel(E)	1837	April 05	Preble	14	21	29
Corrimore, Joseph(C)	1801	Dec. 02	Hamilton	04	02	14
Corrington, William(A)	1811	Jan. 28	Butler	04	05	02
Corson, Aquilla(B)	1832	March 27	Dearborn(Ind	02	03	05
Corson, Ithamar(A)	1837	March 01	Hamilton	02	13	01
Corson, Parmenas(A)	1837	March 01	Hamilton	02	13	01
Corwin, Ichabod(A)	1831	Aug. 30	Warren	02	10	36
Corwin, Ichabod(C)	1801	Dec. 31	Hamilton	04	04	25
Corwin, Ichabod(C)	1804	Sept. 03	Warren	04	04	11
Corwin, Ichabod(C)	1804	Sept. 03	Warren	04	04	26
Corwin, Ichabod(C)	1814	June 08	?	11	04	24
Corwin, Ichabod(C)	1814	Aug. 31	Warren	11	04	24
Corwin, Ichabod(C)	1814	Nov. 26	Warren	12	04	19
Corwin, Matthias H.(A)	1831	Aug. 22	Preble	03	07	06
Corwin, William(A)	1831	Aug. 22	Warren	03	07	06
Cory, David(C)	1828	Sept. 27	Warren	10	03	30
Cory, Elnathan(C)	1812	April 15	Champaign	09	03	33
Cory, Elnathan(C)	1812	April 15	Champaign	11	02	10
Cory, Elnathan(C)	1812	April 15	Champaign	11	02	10
Cory, Elnathan(C)	1813	Jan. 22	Champaign	12	05	19
Cory, Elnathan(C)	1814	Dec. 08	Champaign	09	02	09
Cory, Elnathan(C)	1817	Dec. 02	Champaign	09	02	36
Cory, Elnathan(C)	1817	Dec. 02	Champaign	10	02	03
Cory, Elnathan(C)	1824	June 07	Clark	09	02	11
Cory, Elnathan(C)	1824	June 07	Clark	09	02	11
Cory, Elnathan(C)	1827	Aug. 23	Clark	09	02	08
Cory, Elnathan(C)	1827	Aug. 23	Clark	09	02	08
Cory, Elnathan(C)	1829	May 20	Clark	08	02	02
Cory, Elnathan(C)	1829	May 20	Clark	08	02	02
Cory, Elnathan(C)	1829	Dec. 11	Miami	08	05	29
Cory, Jeremiah(C)	1828	Aug. 22	Warren	10	03	30
Cory, John D.(C)	1818	Sept. 23	Butler	12	02	03
Cory, John D.(C)	1818	Sept. 23	Butler	12	02	03
Cory, John D.(C)	1825	Nov. 25	Miami	12	02	02
Cory, John(C)	1813	April 06	Miami	11	02	17
Cory, John(C)	1828	Oct. 14	Miami	12	02	26
Cory, John(E)	1838	May 12	Shelby	15	20	18
Cory, Nathan(C)	1826	Aug. 24	Warren	10	03	28
Cory, Thomas(C)	1818	April 14	Clark	10	03	32
Cossairt, Albert(B)	1816	Dec. 11	Warren	01	02	31
Cossairt, Francis(A)	1827	Oct. 01	Warren	02	09	12

PURCHASER	YEAR	DATE	RESIDENCE	R	T	S
Cossairt, Jacob(A)	1830	May 08	Preble	02	10	26
Cossairt, Peter(E)	1812	Feb. 06	Warren	13	17	31
Cossart, Jacob(C)	1805	May 20	Greene	08	03	34
Cossins, Joseph(B)	1836	Feb. 26	Dearborn(Ind	03	05	21
Cossurd, Anthony W.(C)	1815	April 14	Greene	09	04	30
Cost, Philip Francis(A)	1834	May 19	Greene	08	02	30
Cost, Philip Francis(A)	1834	May 19	Greene	08	02	30
Cothran, Alexander(A)	1810	Sept. 21	Miami	05	07	32
Cotter, Nodiah(C)	1802	Dec. 23	Hamilton	04	02	25
Cotton, Isaac(E)	1837	Jan. 28	Randolph(Ind	14	21	31
Cotton, John F.(B)	1836	Sept. 14	Switzerland	03	03	09
Cotton, Nathaniel(B)	1812	Nov. 02	Jefferson	03	02	01
Cotton, Ralph Jr.(B)	1812	Nov. 02	Jefferson	03	02	01
Cotton, Ralph(B)	1815	Nov. 01	Switzerland	03	03	09
Cotton, Robert(B)	1812	Jan. 09	Ind.Territory	03	04	02
Cotton, Robert(B)	1816	Oct. 07	Indiana	03	03	34
Cotton, William(B)	1805	June 10	Ind.Territry	03	03	34
Cotton, William(B)	1814	Dec. 08	Switzerland	03	03	27
Cotton, William(B)	1815	March 18	Ind.Territory	03	03	14
Cotton, William(B)	1815	March 18	Indiana	03	03	02
Cotton, William(B)	1815	March 18	Indiana	03	03	11
Cotton, William(B)	1815	March 18	Cincinnati	03	03	11
Cotton, William(B)	1815	Nov. 01	Cincinnati	03	02	03
Cotton, Zachariah(B)	1818	Jan. 31	Switzerland	03	02	20
Cottrell, Bradbury(B)	1818	June 26	Indiana	02	08	28
Cottrell, Joseph(A)	1836	Feb. 05	Montgomery	03	11	23
Couald, Jonathan(A)	1806	Sept. 08	Hamilton	01	04	03
Couble, Anthony(A)	1813	March 12	Maryland	06	03	07
Coulter, David(C)	1813	Sept. 15	Champaign	10	05	26
Coulter, John(B)	1806	Sept. 19	Hamilton	01	09	33
Counover, John(E)	1815	Feb. 28	Wayne(Ind)	13	16	32
Counts, Adam(A)	1818	Jan. 12	Miami	07	01	03
Counts, Joseph(C)	1815	March 16	Kentucky	11	01	03
Courcier, John Mary(B)	1833	May 10	Franklin(Ind	01	08	08
Courtney, John(B)	1818	May 11	Hamilton	02	03	36
Covalt, Ephraim(C)	1812	May 22	Montgomery	06	01	08
Covalt, Timothy(A)	1811	April 06	Montgomery	06	01	14
Covenhoven, Dennis(A)	1821	Oct. 15	Hamilton	04	05	09
Coverdale, Jacob(B)	1818	Sept. 07	Kentucky	01	07	07
Coverdale, Perry(B)	1834	Oct. 29	Dearborn(Ind	02	07	05
Coverdale, Perry(B)	1835	Dec. 09	Dearborn(Ind	02	08	29
Coverstone, Jacob(C)	1829	March 27	Ohio	12	03	29
Covington, Edward(C)	1804	Sept. 03	Hamilton	05	03	11
Covington, Edward(C)	1804	Sept. 10	Hamilton	05	03	11
Covington, Henry(C)	1813	March 15	Champaign	09	05	11
Covington, Henry(C)	1813	June 23	Champaign	10	05	27
Covington, Henry(C)	1817	May 30	Champaign	13	04	01
Covington, Henry(C)	1824	Oct. 14	Logan	13	04	01
Covington, Henry(C)	1831	July 05	Champaign	13	04	01
Covington, Samuel(C)	1813	March 15	Champaign	10	05	21
Cowan, David(C)	1813	Nov. 03	Champaign	09	05	19
Cowan, John Steele(A)	1831	Nov. 25	Shelby	06	08	21
Cowan, John(C)	1813	March 15	Champaign	13	02	28
Cowgill, Caleb(E)	1827	Sept. 18	Wayne(Ind)	14	18	35
Cowgill, Caleb(E)	1832	Jan. 30	Wayne(Ind)	13	18	33
Cowhick, Thomas(C)	1804	Dec. 28	Greene	11	05	34
Cowhick, Thomas(C)	1805	Sept. 14	Champaign	11	03	28
Cowhick, Thomas(C)	1810	Dec. 12	Champaign	11	03	28
Cowles, Rice(B)	1838	Jan. 12	Dearborn(Ind	03	05	22
Cownover, James(E)	1811	Nov. 09	Kentucky	12	15	01
Cownover, John(E)	1811	Nov. 09	Kentucky	12	15	01
Cox, Amy(E)	1824	Sept. 24	Randolph(Ind	15	20	29
Cox, Benj'n. Senr.(E)	1836	Dec. 06	Randolph(Ind	14	20	23
Cox, Benj'n.(C)	1828	Dec. 09	Miami	13	03	29
Cox, Benj'n.(E)	1829	Feb. 02	Randolph(Ind	13	18	03
Cox, Benjamin Senr.(E)	1837	March 10	Randolph(Ind	14	20	26
Cox, Benjamin(A)	1805	Aug. 02	Kentucky	06	02	17
Cox, Benjamin(B)	1806	June 23	Nor.Carolina	01	14	05
Cox, Benjamin(E)	1817	Sept. 11	Ross	14	20	15

PURCHASER	YEAR	DATE	RESIDENCE	R	T	S
Cox, Benjamin(E)	1817	Nov. 19	Wayne(Ind)	14	20	14
Cox, Benjamin(E)	1818	Feb. 06	Wayne(Ind)	14	20	25
Cox, Benjamin(E)	1835	Feb. 17	Randolph(Ind	13	18	04
Cox, Benjamin(E)	1835	Oct. 07	Randolph(Ind	14	20	25
Cox, Daniel-Heirs(C)	1804	Dec. 25	Montgomery	11	01	20
Cox, David A.(E)	1836	Nov. 18	Union(Ind)	14	21	34
Cox, David A.(E)	1837	Jan. 30	Union(Ind)	14	21	27
Cox, David(A)	1805	July 20	Montgomery	05	05	35
Cox, David(A)	1831	May 21	Montgomery	04	06	03
Cox, David(A)	1831	May 21	Montgomery	04	06	04
Cox, Gabriel(C)	1807	March 19	Champaign	09	06	33
Cox, Gabriel(C)	1808	Nov. 02	Champaign	09	06	11
Cox, George(C)	1805	Sept. 20	Champaign	14	02	01
Cox, George(C)	1821	Sept. 22	Hamilton	11	02	04
Cox, George(C)	1823	June 11	Hamilton	11	02	04
Cox, Henry(A)	1825	March 17	Darke	01	11	04
Cox, Jacob Junr.(A)	1816	Oct. 11	Darke	01	12	23
Cox, Jacob(A)	1814	Oct. 14	Pennsylvania	01	12	14
Cox, Jacob(A)	1814	Oct. 14	Pennsylvania	01	11	01
Cox, Jacob(A)	1814	Oct. 14	Pennsylvania	01	11	12
Cox, Jacob(A)	1815	June 05	Pennsylvania	01	12	13
Cox, Jacob(A)	1816	Oct. 25	Darke	01	12	11
Cox, Jacob(A)	1816	Oct. 25	Darke	01	11	01
Cox, Jacob(A)	1819	June 09	Darke	02	12	06
Cox, James(B)	1818	Jan. 29	Hamilton	02	06	26
Cox, Jeremiah(B)	1806	June 25	Dearborn(Ind	01	13	05
Cox, Jeremiah(B)	1807	Jan. 10	Dearborn(Ind	01	14	33
Cox, Jeremiah(B)	1808	April 07	Dearborn(Ind	01	14	12
Cox, Jeremiah(E)	1811	Oct. 24	Wayne(Ind)	13	17	29
Cox, Jeremiah(E)	1818	Feb. 06	Wayne(Ind)	14	20	35
Cox, Jeremiah(E)	1818	Feb. 06	Wayne(Ind)	15	20	19
Cox, Jeremiah(E)	1818	May 29	Wayne(Ind)	15	20	18
Cox, Jesse(E)	1817	Oct. 16	Montgomery	13	18	02
Cox, Jesse(E)	1817	Oct. 16	Montgomery	13	18	15
Cox, John C.(E)	1817	Sept. 11	Ross	14	20	14
Cox, John(A)	1802	June 11	Hamilton	06	02	32
Cox, John(A)	1806	Aug. 12	Montgomery	06	03	19
Cox, John(A)	1812	Feb. 14	Montgomery	06	03	20
Cox, John(A)	1814	Oct. 14	Pennsylvania	02	12	31
Cox, John(A)	1816	Oct. 11	Dearborn(Ind	01	12	36
Cox, John(A)	1818	April 22	Warren	04	11	32
Cox, John(A)	1836	Nov. 12	Warren	03	12	06
Cox, John(B)	1806	July 30	Dearborn(Ind	02	13	24
Cox, John(C)	1802	Dec. 31	Hamilton	08	03	28
Cox, John(C)	1806	March 07	Greene	08	03	23
Cox, John(C)	1832	June 26	Greene	08	03	28
Cox, John(E)	1818	Sept. 14	Montgomery	13	18	09
Cox, John(E)	1820	Jan. 07	Indiana	14	20	14
Cox, John(E)	1836	Dec. 05	Franklin(Ind	12	12	29
Cox, John(E)	1836	Dec. 15	Randolph(Ind	14	20	24
Cox, Jonathan(A)	1805	April 26	Montgomery	06	02	06
Cox, Jonathan(A)	1805	April 26	Montgomery	05	04	01
Cox, Jonathan(E)	1817	Oct. 16	Montgomery	13	18	15
Cox, Jonathan(E)	1817	Nov. 05	Montgomery	13	18	15
Cox, Joseph B.(A)	1837	May 09	Montgomery	01	13	22
Cox, Joseph(B)	1806	Aug. 25	Dearborn(Ind	02	12	15
Cox, Joseph(B)	1806	Oct. 02	Dearborn(Ind	02	12	02
Cox, Joseph(C)	1807	March 19	Champaign	09	06	15
Cox, Joseph(C)	1807	July 27	Champaign	13	05	17
Cox, Joseph(C)	1813	April 14	Champaign	13	05	23
Cox, Joseph(E)	1814	Sept. 20	Nor.Carolina	13	16	12
Cox, Joseph(E)	1816	June 27	Wayne(Ind)	15	18	19
Cox, Joshua(E)	1817	Nov. 19	Wayne(Ind)	14	20	15
Cox, Joshua(E)	1822	Dec. 10	Randolph(Ind	15	20	30
Cox, Joshua(E)	1836	Nov. 04	Randolph(Ind	14	20	09
Cox, Joshua(E)	1838	Nov. 16	Randolph(Ind	14	20	13
Cox, Levi(E)	1831	June 10	Wayne(Ind)	13	17	08
Cox, Martin(A)	1816	Oct. 25	Darke	01	12	11
Cox, Martin(A)	1825	March 17	Darke	01	12	03

PURCHASER	YEAR	DATE	RESIDENCE	R	T	S
Cox, Martin(B)	1835	Sept. 19	Darke	01	17	13
Cox, Martin(B)	1835	Sept. 19	Darke	01	17	14
Cox, Martin(B)	1836	June 07	Darke	01	17	13
Cox, Martin(B)	1836	Aug. 15	Darke	01	17	23
Cox, Peter(A)	1831	April 29	Preble	03	07	05
Cox, Samuel(A)	1819	June 09	Darke	02	13	29
Cox, Simon(E)	1831	April 08	Randolph(Ind	14	20	14
Cox, Solomon(E)	1826	May 16	Randolph(Ind	15	20	29
Cox, Stephen(E)	1831	June 10	Wayne(Ind)	13	17	09
Cox, Thomas(E)	1829	Feb. 02	Randolph(Ind	13	18	03
Cox, Thomas(E)	1836	Feb. 20	Franklin(Ind	12	12	06
Cox, Thomas(E)	1836	Dec. 07	Franklin(Ind	12	12	07
Cox, Watten(A)	1803	Jan. 19	Hamilton	04	03	36
Cox, William(B)	1808	Nov. 08	Dearborn(Ind	02	14	13
Cox, William(C)	1808	Jan. 13	Champaign	12	05	07
Cox, William(C)	1808	April 12	Champaign	12	05	13
Cox, William(C)	1816	Aug. 21	Warren	12	02	01
Cox, William(E)	1817	Sept. 13	Franklin(Ind	12	12	06
Cox, William(E)	1829	Nov. 05	Wayne(Ind)	13	18	22
Cox, William(E)	1832	Jan. 04	Randolph(Ind	13	18	15
Cox, William(E)	1833	June 06	Randolph(Ind	13	18	15
Coxe, John(B)	1811	Dec. 11	Wayne(Ind)	02	12	02
Coxe, Joseph(B)	1811	Dec. 11	Wayne(Ind)	02	12	02
Coy, Elnathan(C)	1802	Dec. 31	Hamilton	08	03	06
Coy, Elnathan(C)	1802	Dec. 31	Hamilton	09	03	34
Coy, Jacob(C)	1801	Dec. 31	Hamilton	07	02	09
Coy, Jacob(C)	1802	Dec. 10	Hamilton	06	03	36
Coy, Jacob(C)	1802	Dec. 27	Hamilton	06	02	06
Coy, Jacob(C)	1804	Sept. 05	Montgomery	07	02	08
Coy, Jacob(C)	1804	Sept. 05	Montgomery	07	02	08
Coy, Jacob(C)	1804	Sept. 05	Montgomery	07	02	08
Coy, Jacob(C)	1804	Sept. 05	Montgomery	07	02	08
Coy, Jacob(C)	1804	Oct. 06	Greene	07	03	25
Coy, Jacob(C)	1804	Nov. 06	Greene	06	02	05
Coy, Jacob(C)	1805	March 22	Greene	06	02	05
Coy, Jacob(C)	1809	Aug. 28	Greene	06	02	11
Cozad, John(C)	1813	April 14	Greene	07	03	30
Cozad, Wm. V.(A)	1838	May 09	Greene	02	13	11
Cozine, Martin(B)	1810	Oct. 23	Cincinnati	01	05	31
Cozine, Martin(B)	1815	Dec. 12	Dearborn(Ind	01	05	31
Cozine, Martin(B)	1829	June 03	Dearborn(Ind	02	05	28
Crabb, James S.(E)	1828	Jan. 28	Wayne(Ind)	14	16	33
Crabb, Jeremiah(C)	1819	Feb. 26	Pickaway	11	03	27
Cracken, Mark W.(B)	1815	July 28	New Jersey	02	06	33
Cracken, Robert(B)	1815	July 28	New Jersey	02	06	33
Cracken, Sarah(B)	1815	July 28	New Jersey	02	06	33
Craft, Caleb A.(B)	1818	March 10	Dearborn(Ind	02	03	11
Craft, Caleb A.(B)	1818	March 16	Dearborn(Ind	02	03	34
Craft, Caleb A.(B)	1818	March 16	Dearborn(Ind	02	03	35
Craft, Jacob(C)	1831	Nov. 23	Champaign	13	04	15
Cragun, Caleb(E)	1819	March 02	Dearborn(Ind	13	11	30
Cragun, Caleb(E)	1836	Feb. 20	Franklin(Ind	12	11	35
Craig, Ann(C)	1813	Dec. 29	Champaign	08	05	06
Craig, George(B)	1804	Oct. 09	Kentucky	03	02	02
Craig, George(B)	1804	Oct. 25	Kentucky	03	02	32
Craig, George(B)	1804	Oct. 09	Kentucky	03	02	02
Craig, George(B)	1809	Dec. 12	Ind.Territory	03	02	32
Craig, George(B)	1814	Nov. 29	Switzerland	03	02	30
Craig, George(B)	1815	Dec. 16	Switzerland	03	02	09
Craig, George(B)	1816	Dec. 09	Switzerland	03	02	06
Craig, George(B)	1818	March 03	Switzerland	03	02	20
Craig, George(B)	1832	April 19	Switzerland	03	02	31
Craig, Jacob(B)	1811	April 15	Kentucky	02	09	11
Craig, James(C)	1813	March 10	Franklin(Ind	13	13	33
Craig, James(C)	1814	Aug. 15	Champaign	09	05	01
Craig, John Junr.(C)	1807	Aug. 13	Hamilton	09	06	33
Craig, John(A)	1805	June 11	Butler	03	03	11
Craig, John(C)	1807	Aug. 13	Hamilton	09	06	32
Craig, John(C)	1813	April 14	Champaign	09	06	32

PURCHASER	YEAR	DATE	RESIDENCE	R	T	S
Craig, Robert(B)	1832	Oct. 01	Switzerland	01	02	06
Craig, Stephen(B)	1817	Nov. 29	Hamilton	01	09	22
Craig, Stephen(B)	1818	April 21	Hamilton	01	08	05
Craigg, James(A)	1817	Dec. 16	Darke	02	12	29
Craigg, James(A)	1817	Dec. 16	Darke	02	12	24
Crain, Joseph(C)	1801	Dec. 17	Hamilton	05	02	28
Cramer, Richard(C)	1816	Sept. 23	Madison	08	07	30
Crandall, Robt.(C)	1830	Jan. 28	Clark	10	03	11
Crandel, Elihu(E)	1815	Jan. 19	Butler	13	13	14
Crane, Abner(C)	1801	Dec. 30	Hamilton	04	03	15
Crane, Andrew(C)	1801	Dec. 16	Hamilton	04	03	24
Crane, Esther(A)	1814	Sept. 06	Preble	01	07	27
Crane, George(A)	1813	July 30	Butler	02	07	17
Crane, James P.(E)	1838	Oct. 24	Champaign	15	20	30
Crane, James(B)	1814	July 04	Cincinnati	02	04	35
Crane, James(B)	1814	July 18	Cincinnati	02	03	02
Crane, John R.(A)	1818	June 29	Butler	02	06	22
Crane, Jonas(B)	1815	Feb. 15	Hamilton	01	07	25
Crane, Jonathan(B)	1807	April 17	Warren	01	11	08
Crane, Jonathan(C)	1801	Dec. 26	Hamilton	04	03	15
Crane, Jonathan(C)	1804	Sept. 03	Warren	04	03	08
Crane, Jonathan(C)	1804	Sept. 04	Warren	04	03	08
Crane, Joseph H.(A)	1818	Feb. 16	Ohio	06	04	15
Crane, Joseph H.(A)	1818	Feb. 16	Ohio	05	07	25
Crane, Joseph(C)	1802	Dec. 31	Hamilton	05	02	28
Crane, Moses(C)	1801	Dec. 26	Hamilton	04	03	15
Crane, Ruth(B)	1807	April 17	Warren	01	11	08
Crane, William(C)	1802	Dec. 31	Hamilton	05	02	19
Craner, Joshua(E)	1815	May 25	Wayne(Ind)	14	17	08
Craner, Thomas(E)	1813	Sept. 13	Wayne(Ind)	14	17	06
Craner, Thomas(E)	1833	Aug. 27	Randolph(Ind	13	18	02
Cranor, Thomas Washington(E)	1836	Feb. 06	Randolph(Ind	13	18	04
Cranor, Washington(E)	1835	Dec. 01	Randolph(Ind	13	18	04
Crapper, Bela Walker(E)	1833	May 17	Warren	13	19	21
Crapper, Joseph Yates(E)	1833	Sept. 11	Clinton	13	19	21
Crapper, Silas A.(E)	1837	Jan. 09	Randolph(Ind	13	19	14
Crary, Wm.(C)	1811	Dec. 14	Hamilton	01	03	26
Craven, Thomas(?)	1813	Nov. 03	Franklin(Ind	01	09	02
Cravens, Joseph(E)	1819	May 11	Wayne(Ind)	14	21	14
Craw, Jonathan(B)	1824	Nov. 09	Hamilton	02	06	36
Crawford, Abel(A)	1802	June 11	Hamilton	06	02	32
Crawford, Abel(C)	1812	March 10	Champaign	10	04	32
Crawford, Alexander(A)	1831	Oct. 06	Warren	02	10	13
Crawford, Alexander(B)	1834	March 31	Franklin(Ind	02	08	15
Crawford, David(E)	1838	May 21	Randolph(Ind	13	21	25
Crawford, James Lee(C)	1802	Dec. 31	Hamilton	09	02	04
Crawford, James(A)	1805	July 24	Kentucky	02	07	14
Crawford, James(A)	1824	June 08	Preble	02	07	22
Crawford, John(A)	1807	Sept. 10	Miami	06	05	30
Crawford, Norman B.(A)	1830	Nov. 12	Warren	04	07	31
Crawford, Robert C.(C)	1802	Dec. 31	Hamilton	08	02	25
Crawford, Robert C.(C)	1810	Dec. 12	Champaign	09	02	22
Crawford, Robert C.(C)	1818	June 08	Miami	09	02	11
Crawford, Robert(C)	1802	Dec. 31	Hamilton	08	02	06
Crawford, Robert(C)	1802	Dec. 31	Hamilton	09	02	04
Crawford, Robt. C.(C)	1828	Nov. 04	Miami	10	03	17
Crawford, Samuel(E)	1816	Nov. 29	Virginia	13	16	35
Crawford, Thomas(E)	1815	Sept. 25	Wayne(Ind)	13	18	21
Crawford, William(B)	1806	Oct. 28	Butler	01	10	13
Crawl, David(A)	1816	Oct. 23	Montgomery	04	09	24
Crawley, James(E)	1832	Sept. 12	Fayette	12	12	12
Crawley, James(E)	1832	May 28	Fayette	12	12	12
Crawley, Joseph(E)	1832	May 28	Fayette	12	13	36
Crawley, Milton Ladd(E)	1834	Aug. 28	Fayette	12	12	01
Crawley, Milton Ladd(E)	1835	Nov. 13	Franklin(Ind	12	12	01
Creagmile, Alexander(A)	1810	Aug. 04	Hamilton	01	04	18
Creagmiles, Alexander(A)	1813	Aug. 31	Hamilton	01	04	20
Creagmiles, Alexander(A)	1814	Feb. 17	Butler	01	04	08
Creamer, Jacob(A)	1816	July 06	Pennsylvania	04	05	06

PURCHASER	YEAR	DATE	RESIDENCE	R	T	S
Creegan, James(C)	1806	Aug. 05	New York	12	01	21
Creek, John(B)	1808	Feb. 13	Highland	01	11	31
Creek, John(B)	1808	Feb. 13	Highland	01	11	32
Creek, John(B)	1810	Aug. 20	Dearborn(Ind	01	11	31
Creek, John(B)	1810	Aug. 20	Dearborn(Ind	01	11	32
Creek, John(B)	1814	June 23	Franklin(Ind	01	11	31
Creek, John(B)	1814	Dec. 12	Franklin(Ind	01	11	30
Creek, John(B)	1814	Dec. 12	Franklin(Ind	01	11	30
Creek, John(B)	1815	Jan. 07	Franklin(Ind	02	11	25
Creek, John(E)	1814	Dec. 12	Franklin(Ind	13	14	24
Creekmore, William(E)	1834	Oct. 04	Franklin(Ind	12	12	08
Crehfield, Arthur(C)	1806	Nov. 17	Warren	11	02	09
Crehfield, John(C)	1806	Nov. 17	Warren	11	02	09
Crekfield, John(C)	1806	July 30	Warren	11	05	17
Creson, James(A)	1812	May 04	Preble	01	07	24
Cress, Jacob(A)	1809	Oct. 23	Montgomery	05	05	12
Cressman, Daniel(A)	1810	Aug. 14	Preble	02	08	28
Cretcher, Jabez(C)	1826	Jan. 18	Logan	13	04	35
Cretcher, Jabez(C)	1828	April 23	Logan	13	04	34
Cretcher, Matthew(A)	1836	Feb. 04	Champaign	08	02	32
Cretcher, Matthew(C)	1814	Nov. 26	Kentucky	13	03	07
Creviston, Henry(A)	1815	May 15	Darke	02	12	20
Creviston, Joseph(C)	1815	April 04	Champaign	14	04	19
Crew, Joseph(E)	1819	April 15	Nor.Carolina	13	20	36
Crew, Josiah(E)	1835	June 25	Randolph(Ind	14	19	36
Crews, David Jr.(B)	1813	Nov. 06	Franklin(Ind	02	11	15
Cribe, Daniel(A)	1806	April 07	Montgomery	04	05	03
Crichfield, Arthur(A)	1806	Oct. 25	Warren	06	04	19
Crichfield, John(A)	1818	April 28	Greene	05	10	18
Cricket, John(C)	1801	Dec. 30	Hamilton	04	03	10
Crihfield, John(C)	1806	Oct. 25	Warren	12	05	34
Crikfield, Arthur(A)	1805	Aug. 24	Warren	06	04	17
Crikfield, John(A)	1805	Aug. 24	Warren	06	04	08
Cripe, Abraham(E)	1831	March 19	Wayne(Ind)	12	16	01
Cripe, Abraham(E)	1831	March 19	Wayne(Ind)	12	16	01
Crisler, Allen(A)	1830	July 27	Preble	02	09	15
Crisler, Allen(E)	1813	Nov. 17	Kentucky	12	13	27
Crisler, Allen(E)	1818	April 07	Franklin(Ind	12	13	27
Crisler, Thos. Jefferson(E)	1831	Dec. 05	Fayette	12	13	26
Crisler, William(A)	1829	Jan. 20	Preble	02	09	03
Crisman, Jacob(A)	1813	Nov. 17	Preble	02	08	23
Crisman, Jacob(A)	1817	Sept. 08	Preble	02	08	15
Crissman, Daniel(A)	1805	July 17	Montgomery	03	05	04
Crissman, John(A)	1804	Dec. 05	Nor.Carolina	02	08	13
Crissman, John(A)	1804	Dec. 05	Nor.Carolina	02	08	24
Crissman, John(A)	1832	Feb. 21	Preble	05	09	07
Crist, George W.(B)	1814	Sept. 17	Hamilton	01	11	07
Crist, George W.(B)	1814	Sept. 19	Hamilton	02	11	12
Crist, George(E)	1811	Oct. 21	Ind.Territry	12	12	27
Crist, Henry(A)	1805	Nov. 11	Butler	03	05	14
Crist, Henry(A)	1816	Oct. 28	Montgomery	01	11	13
Crist, John(E)	1811	Oct. 28	Franklin(Ind	12	13	27
Crist, John(E)	1811	Dec. 11	Wayne(Ind)	12	13	27
Crist, John(E)	1812	Feb. 29	Franklin(Ind	12	12	21
Crist, John(E)	1834	June 12	Franklin(Ind	12	12	29
Cristopher, John(A)	1837	April 10	Montgomery	01	12	01
Critz, Conrad(C)	1812	March 11	Champaign	08	06	17
Critz, Conrad(C)	1813	Aug. 23	Madison	08	06	11
Critz, Conrad(C)	1813	Dec. 18	Montgomery	08	06	17
Critzer, Andrew(A)	1816	Jan. 29	Montgomery	06	03	08
Critzer, Andrew(A)	1817	Nov. 06	Montgomery	02	11	35
Critzer, John(C)	1815	Jan. 31	Ohio	09	03	05
Croall, Joseph(B)	1817	June 04	Pennsylvania	02	02	30
Crocker, Benjamin(B)	1814	Aug. 24	Hamilton	01	09	01
Crockett, Cartmill(C)	1829	Dec. 12	Logan	13	04	04
Crockett, James Senr.(C)	1810	Nov. 23	Kentucky	13	05	19
Crockett, Robert(C)	1811	Nov. 19	Kentucky	13	04	04
Crockett, Robt. Heirs(C)	1829	Dec. 12	Logan	13	04	04
Croford, Thomas(E)	1816	Sept. 30	Wayne(Ind)	13	18	08

PURCHASER	YEAR	DATE	RESIDENCE	R	T	S
Croft, George(C)	1806	June 23	Champaign	09	03	12
Croggeshale, Tristam(E)	1815	Nov. 25	Nor.Carolina	14	17	10
Crogins, Elisha(E)	1814	Sept. 05	Franklin(Ind	13	11	19
Croker, John(E)	1817	Oct. 16	Dearborn(Ind	02	06	28
Croll, John(A)	1804	Nov. 16	Pennsylvania	05	03	05
Cromas, William(E)	1838	Oct. 04	Montgomery	15	21	29
Cromwell, Vincent(B)	1808	Jan. 11	Kentucky	01	11	04
Crook, John(A)	1836	Aug. 13	Warren	01	14	22
Crookham, George L.(C)	1807	April 22	Ross	09	06	27
Crookham, George L.(C)	1807	June 04	Ross	08	06	18
Crookham, George(C)	1807	April 21	Ross	08	06	17
Crooks, James(B)	1806	Jan. 28	Butler	01	10	24
Crooks, Samuel(A)	1811	April 09	Butler	01	04	05
Crooks, Samuel(B)	1806	Jan. 28	Butler	01	04	05
Crooks, William(B)	1814	Dec. 31	Butler	02	09	12
Crookshank, Nathaniel(A)	1814	July 27	Hamilton	01	02	35
Crookshank, Nathaniel(B)	1818	March 05	Hamilton	01	07	24
Crookshank, Nathaniel(E)	1815	Oct. 28	Hamilton	13	13	12
Crosley, Moses Senr.(A)	1821	Jan. 31	Warren	03	10	17
Cross, Aquila(E)	1814	Dec. 17	Franklin(Ind	12	11	29
Cross, Aquilla(B)	1815	Dec. 14	Franklin(Ind	01	07	30
Cross, Aquilla(B)	1818	Jan. 22	Dearborn(Ind	01	07	32
Cross, Aquilla(B)	1818	Jan. 22	Dearborn(Ind	01	07	31
Cross, Cyrus(B)	1828	March 26	Dearborn(Ind	03	07	35
Crothers, James(C)	1828	Sept. 05	Montgomery	11	01	06
Crouch, Andrew(E)	1811	Oct. 30	Ross	13	15	07
Crouch, Benjamin(B)	1832	March 19	Dearborn(Ind	02	06	15
Crow, Jacob(C)	1815	Jan. 17	Miami	11	01	18
Crow, Joseph(C)	1814	March 08	Champaign	13	04	13
Crow, Mathias(C)	1806	Feb. 19	Hamilton	09	02	32
Crowel, Henry(A)	1828	Nov. 05	Montgomery	05	08	32
Crowel, John(B)	1807	July 23	Hamilton	01	09	32
Crowel, John(E)	1836	Oct. 29	Franklin(Ind	13	12	07
Crowel, John(E)	1836	Nov. 25	Franklin(Ind	13	12	07
Crowell, Devault(A)	1808	May 19	Virginia	01	08	12
Crowell, Henry(A)	1806	Oct. 17	Montgomery	05	05	12
Crowell, Henry(A)	1806	Oct. 18	Montgomery	05	07	05
Crowell, Henry(A)	1806	Oct. 18	Montgomery	05	07	05
Crowell, Henry(A)	1811	Dec. 11	Montgomery	05	05	12
Crowell, Jac.(A)	1814	Nov. 11	Montgomery	03	06	29
Crowell, Michael(A)	1828	Sept. 13	Miami	05	08	31
Crowford, Jas.(A)	1811	Dec. 11	Preble	02	07	14
Croy, John(C)	1805	Feb. 11	Montgomery	06	02	35
Crull, Jacob(A)	1807	Jan. 07	Montgomery	06	04	28
Crum, Abraham(E)	1815	April 05	Hamilton	12	16	14
Crumbaugh, Jno.(C)	1831	Jan. 11	Shelby	13	02	27
Crume, Daniel(A)	1805	March 30	Butler	03	03	08
Crume, Daniel(A)	1805	June 12	Kentucky	03	03	26
Crume, Daniel(A)	1810	Aug. 14	Butler	03	03	26
Crume, Daniel(B)	1809	Dec. 12	Butler	02	04	29
Crume, Daniel(B)	1810	Sept. 25	Dearborn(Ind	02	04	21
Crume, Daniel(B)	1812	June 26	Dearborn(Ind	02	02	35
Crume, Daniel(B)	1817	Nov. 28	Dearborn(Ind	02	04	20
Crume, Daniel(B)	1818	May 12	Dearborn(Ind	02	04	15
Crummel, John Senr.(A)	1818	Jan. 24	Hamilton	01	09	25
Crump, Rhoda(E)	1814	Nov. 05	Dearborn(Ind	13	12	05
Crumrin, Michael(A)	1816	March 11	Darke	02	11	18
Crumrine, Dan'l.(A)	1828	Oct. 09	Darke	01	11	11
Crumrine, John(A)	1835	Sept. 21	Darke	01	13	28
Crumrine, John(A)	1836	June 22	Darke	01	13	33
Crumrine, John(B)	1836	Feb. 01	Darke	01	18	25
Crumrine, John(B)	1836	June 22	Darke	01	18	25
Crumrine, Peter(A)	1817	May 28	Montgomery	01	11	12
Crumrine, Peter(A)	1817	Dec. 12	Montgomery	01	11	13
Crumrine, Peter(A)	1823	May 06	Darke	01	11	11
Crumrine, Peter(A)	1824	Sept. 18	Darke	01	11	14
Crumrine, Peter(A)	1825	Dec. 07	Darke	01	12	22
Crumrine, Peter(B)	1819	May 26	Preble	01	16	01
Crunkleton, Joseph Senr.(C)	1817	Aug. 06	Delaware	12	03	12

74

PURCHASER	YEAR	DATE	RESIDENCE	R	T	S
Cruse, Henry(A)	1805	Nov. 11	Butler	03	01	07
Cruwell, Martin(B)	1815	Jan. 14	Hamilton	02	02	23
Culbertson, Francis(E)	1814	March 21	Kentucky	14	16	08
Culbertson, John B.(C)	1814	July 08	Champaign	12	05	12
Culbertson, Robert(E)	1814	Jan. 17	Kentucky	14	16	30
Culbertson, Robert(E)	1814	March 21	Kentucky	14	17	32
Culbertson, Sam'l. C.(A)	1828	Dec. 30	Darke	03	09	09
Culbertson, Sam'l. C.(A)	1830	Oct. 01	Darke	03	09	09
Cull, Hugh(B)	1806	Oct. 09	Dearborn(Ind	01	13	29
Cullom, William T.(B)	1818	May 02	Hamilton	03	04	30
Cullver, Michael(B)	1813	Dec. 28	Butler	01	12	31
Cully, Thomas(B)	1814	Nov. 14	Greene	02	11	02
Cully, Thomas(B)	1814	Nov. 30	Greene	02	11	03
Cully, Thomas(B)	1814	Nov. 30	Greene	02	11	03
Cully, Thomas(E)	1814	Oct. 21	Greene	12	13	04
Culp, Cornelius(B)	1817	July 26	Switzerland	02	03	19
Culp, John(E)	1835	Oct. 05	Randolph(Ind	13	21	24
Culp, John(E)	1837	Oct. 05	Randolph(Ind	14	21	30
Culp, Joseph(B)	1831	July 11	Cincinnati	02	03	30
Culp, Joseph(B)	1834	June 11	Dearborn(Ind	03	04	22
Culver, Aaron(B)	1818	Jan. 28	Switzerland	03	02	31
Culver, Jonathan(A)	1832	Aug. 13	Hamilton	04	07	33
Culver, Michael(B)	1813	Dec. 28	?	02	12	35
Culver, Samuel(C)	1817	Aug. 01	Madison	11	06	33
Cumins, James(A)	1836	June 18	Darke	01	15	29
Cumins, James(A)	1836	Dec. 17	Darke	01	15	29
Cumins, James(E)	1836	Dec. 17	Darke	15	22	12
Cumins, William(C)	1811	Aug. 15	Champaign	13	04	32
Cumming, Alexander(A)	1819	March 13	Warren	02	09	28
Cumming, Alexander(A)	1833	Oct. 28	Warren	03	10	18
Cumming, Alexander(B)	1816	April 20	Warren	02	09	14
Cumming, James(A)	1806	Nov. 18	Butler	02	05	01
Cummings, Cornelius(E)	1815	April 25	Kentucky	13	13	05
Cummings, Joseph(C)	1815	Dec. 25	Madison	08	06	30
Cummings, Lyman(C)	1814	Oct. 12	New York	08	06	12
Cummings, William(B)	1818	Oct. 26	Cincinnati	02	08	27
Cummings, William(E)	1834	Jan. 16	Darke	15	22	11
Cummins, David(B)	1817	Aug. 22	Hamilton	02	03	36
Cummins, David(B)	1817	Aug. 22	Hamilton	02	03	36
Cummins, David(B)	1817	Sept. 08	Hamilton	02	03	35
Cummins, David(B)	1817	Sept. 08	Hamilton	02	03	34
Cummins, David(B)	1818	May 19	Hamilton	02	03	26
Cummins, David(B)	1818	June 22	Hamilton	01	02	18
Cummins, David(B)	1818	June 22	Hamilton	01	02	19
Cummins, David(B)	1818	July 07	Hamilton	02	06	32
Cummins, David(B)	1818	July 13	Hamilton	02	06	12
Cummins, David(B)	1818	July 13	Hamilton	02	06	24
Cummins, David(B)	1818	July 13	Hamilton	03	03	23
Cummins, David(B)	1818	July 20	Hamilton	01	06	10
Cummins, Isaac(B)	1813	Aug. 10	Wayne(Ind)	01	14	01
Cummins, James(A)	1805	Sept. 02	Pennsylvania	02	06	36
Cummins, James(A)	1806	June 05	Pennsylvania	01	06	25
Cummins, William H.(E)	1837	Jan. 09	Clermont	13	19	24
Cummins, William(E)	1811	Dec. 11	Wayne(Ind)	13	16	13
Cummins, William(E)	1835	Sept. 21	Randolph(Ind	15	22	11
Cummins, Wm. H.(E)	1836	Sept. 20	Clermont	13	19	24
Cummins, Wm.(E)	1814	Feb. 01	Wayne(Ind)	13	15	08
Cumpton, Samuel(A)	1806	Aug. 16	Greene	06	03	10
Cundale, John(B)	1824	June 09	Dearborn(Ind	02	05	10
Cunningham, Francis A.(B)	1838	May 14	Preble	01	17	02
Cunningham, James(B)	1818	March 26	Hamilton	02	02	24
Cunningham, James(C)	1801	Dec. 30	Hamilton	05	04	24
Cunningham, John(B)	1815	Nov. 27	Hamilton	02	06	30
Cunningham, John(B)	1833	Jan. 30	Switzerland	03	03	02
Cunningham, John(B)	1834	Feb. 22	Switzerland	03	04	35
Cunningham, Matthew(A)	1831	April 13	Preble	01	10	25
Cunningham, Nancy(A)	1818	Feb. 28	Butler	01	11	02
Cunningham, Robert(B)	1818	March 26	Hamilton	02	02	13
Cunningham, Samuel(B)	1814	July 13	Butler	02	06	24

PURCHASER	YEAR	DATE	RESIDENCE	R	T	S
Cunningham, William(B)	1804	Oct. 31	Ind.Territry	02	11	33
Cunningham, Wm.(A)	1831	April 22	Virginia	02	10	30
Cunningham, Wm.(A)	1831	Oct. 26	Darke	03	10	26
Cupp, Philip(E)	1836	Aug. 20	Kentucky	11	11	02
Curby, James(E)	1836	Aug. 12	Kentucky	12	11	18
Curby, James(E)	1836	Oct. 28	Franklin(Ind	12	11	18
Cure, James(B)	1831	June 30	Dearborn(Ind	02	05	33
Cure, James(B)	1836	May 30	Dearborn(Ind	02	05	33
Curl, Isaac(C)	1825	June 17	Clark	13	03	17
Curl, William Junr.(B)	1814	Nov. 26	Champaign	10	06	14
Curl, William(C)	1808	Dec. 30	Warren	10	06	25
Curl, William(C)	1809	July 01	Warren	10	06	19
Currey, John(E)	1833	June 07	Franklin(Ind	12	12	25
Currey, John(E)	1836	Jan. 22	Franklin(Ind	12	12	13
Currie, Daniel(B)	1811	July 22	Butler	01	09	04
Currie, James(B)	1813	Aug. 16	Butler	01	10	10
Currie, Jas.(E)	1813	Sept. 14	Hamilton	13	12	15
Curry, David(C)	1801	Dec. 29	Hamilton	05	04	36
Curry, David(C)	1814	Oct. 26	Greene	12	03	24
Curry, Henry(E)	1837	Jan. 07	Cincinnati	12	11	31
Curry, James(A)	1810	Jan. 20	Dearborn(Ind	02	03	02
Curry, James(B)	1812	Jan. 23	Dearborn(Ind	01	03	28
Curry, John Jnr.(A)	1815	Nov. 08	Preble	02	09	30
Curry, John(A)	1814	Dec. 22	Preble	01	09	26
Curry, John(A)	1814	Dec. 22	Preble	01	09	35
Curry, Moses(C)	1814	Aug. 23	Greene	12	03	30
Curry, Robert(C)	1825	Sept. 01	Hamilton	10	02	08
Curry, Samuel(C)	1814	Aug. 23	Greene	13	03	13
Curry, Thomas(E)	1811	Nov. 04	Franklin(Ind	12	12	25
Curry, William(A)	1805	April 12	Butler	03	02	18
Curry, William(A)	1805	Aug. 23	Butler	01	04	03
Curry, William(A)	1810	Dec. 12	Butler	01	04	03
Curry, William(A)	1818	Sept. 09	Preble	01	10	21
Cursley, James(C)	1801	Dec. 31	Hamilton	05	02	23
Curtis, George(A)	1816	June 15	Butler	03	10	34
Curtis, James(A)	1806	June 04	Montgomery	05	06	26
Curtis, James(A)	1811	Aug. 13	Montgomery	05	06	26
Curtis, John(A)	1806	June 04	Montgomery	05	05	11
Curtis, John(A)	1811	Aug. 13	Montgomery	05	05	11
Curtis, Spencer(Black)(B)	1824	June 09	Dearborn(Ind	02	06	07
Curtis, William(C)	1814	Dec. 23	Greene	10	06	27
Curtner, Daniel(A)	1832	Jan. 25	Miami	03	08	05
Curtner, George(A)	1816	Aug. 29	Montgomery	03	10	09
Curtner, Peter(A)	1832	Jan. 13	Montgomery	07	02	30
Curtner, William(A)	1816	Aug. 03	Ind.Territry	03	08	17
Cushman, Joshua(A)	1817	Nov. 29	Clermont	06	03	05
Cusmiercik, Albert(B)	1838	April 30	Dearborn(Ind	03	04	25
Custard, Abraham(C)	1818	July 08	Champaign	11	02	04
Custard, William(C)	1805	July 24	Kentucky	11	04	05
Custer, William(C)	1810	Dec. 12	Champaign	11	04	05
Custor, Arnold(C)	1810	May 23	Champaign	11	04	05
Cutter, Cyrus(B)	1815	Dec. 12	Cincinnati	02	07	35
Cutter, Cyrus(B)	1817	Aug. 16	Cincinnati	02	03	25
Cutter, Cyrus(B)	1817	Aug. 19	Cincinnati	02	03	21
Dagger, John(C)	1829	Jan. 29	Champaign	12	04	15
Dagger, John(C)	1831	Sept. 08	Champaign	12	04	17
Daggett, Henry(B)	1818	July 20	Hamilton	01	07	26
Dahavan, Samuel(E)	1812	Oct. 07	Kentucky	12	14	11
Dailey, Edmund P.(B)	1836	Jan. 13	Preble	01	17	22
Dailey, Edmund P.(B)	1836	Sept. 21	Preble	01	17	22
Dailey, James(B)	1828	Jan. 11	Franklin(Ind	01	10	33
Dailey, Jesse Vanmeter(B)	1835	March 20	Switzerland	02	02	23
Daily, William(A)	1825	Dec. 12	Preble	02	08	24
Daines, Hiram(E)	1832	Aug. 28	Preble	14	21	11
Daines, Hiram(E)	1836	May 27	Randolph(Ind	14	21	01
Dale, Alexander(E)	1811	Oct. 28	Kentucky	12	14	04
Dale, Alexander(E)	1814	Sept. 09	Franklin(Ind	12	14	09
Dale, Joseph(E)	1814	March 09	Franklin(Ind	12	14	04
Dallas, James(C)	1812	July 14	Champaign	11	05	26

PURCHASER	YEAR	DATE	RESIDENCE	R	T	S
Dallas, James(C)	1813	March 31	Champaign	11	05	32
Dalmazza, James(B)	1816	June 01	Switzerland	03	03	23
Dalmazzo, James(B)	1836	Aug. 13	Switzerland	03	02	20
Dalton, Josiah Bailey(A)	1831	July 15	Butler	05	09	13
Daly, Geo. Washington(E)	1836	Sept. 17	Preble	14	19	21
Daly, George Washington(E)	1836	Jan. 26	Preble	14	19	21
Dana, Micajah(B)	1814	Feb. 18	Hamilton	01	06	19
Danby, Thomas(A)	1814	Aug. 20	Cincinnati	01	06	02
Danby, Thomas(A)	1814	Nov. 24	Cincinnati	01	03	13
Danby, Thomas(A)	1815	Sept. 16	Cincinnati	03	06	26
Danby, Thomas(A)	1815	Sept. 16	Cincinnati	03	06	26
Danby, Thomas(A)	1815	Sept. 16	Cincinnati	02	08	03
Danby, Thomas(A)	1815	Sept. 16	Cincinnati	02	08	36
Danby, Thomas(B)	1814	Aug. 04	Cincinnati	03	04	10
Danby, Thomas(B)	1815	Jan. 17	Cincinnati	02	07	24
Danby, Thomas(E)	1814	Aug. 20	Cincinnati	13	15	01
Daniel, Moses(B)	1815	Dec. 26	Cincinnati	02	03	10
Daniel, Samuel(C)	1806	July 30	Virginia	10	05	14
Daniel, Thomas(A)	1809	Sept. 15	Fairfield	13	04	19
Daniel, Thomas(C)	1817	Sept. 04	Champaign	12	03	04
Danner, Jacob(E)	1838	Aug. 09	Butler	14	22	34
Danner, Joseph(A)	1830	March 27	Preble	02	10	26
Danner, Joseph(E)	1837	July 13	Montgomery	15	22	29
Darby, Henry(B)	1837	March 25	Hamilton	02	04	19
Darby, Hy.(B)	1837	March 25	Hamilton	02	04	20
Darby, James(A)	1825	March 12	Darke	02	11	05
Dare, Abiel(B)	1812	Jan. 03	Warren	01	10	29
Dare, Robert(B)	1816	July 08	Cincinnati	01	04	27
Darland, Isaac(A)	1810	Dec. 08	Dearborn(Ind	01	09	30
Darling, David(A)	1819	Nov. 29	Montgomery	02	13	23
Darling, Jacob(B)	1816	Nov. 26	Cincinnati	02	06	25
Darling, Jno.(B)	1832	May 25	Dearborn(Ind	02	06	23
Darling, John(B)	1832	March 05	Dearborn(Ind	02	06	27
Darling, Thomas(B)	1816	Nov. 26	Cincinnati	01	06	30
Darling, Thos. Jefferson(B)	1834	March 07	Dearborn(Ind	02	06	15
Darlington, Joseph(C)	1815	Aug. 09	Adams	14	01	08
Darlinton, Joseph(C)	1814	Sept. 24	Adams	14	01	13
Darnald, Nathan(C)	1813	April 14	Champaign	11	04	31
Darnall, Abimelech(C)	1825	Oct. 21	Champaign	11	03	08
Darnall, Joshua(C)	1813	Dec. 27	Champaign	11	04	20
Darnell, Isaac(C)	1807	July 08	Kentucky	11	04	33
Darnes, Alex'r. W.(Black)(E)	1836	Oct. 25	Cincinnati	13	12	29
Darnold, Nathan(C)	1806	Jan. 08	Kentucky	11	04	25
Darr, Conrod(A)	1807	June 08	Butler	02	04	05
Darst, Isaac(C)	1813	Sept. 13	Montgomery	09	02	26
Darst, Jacob(A)	1836	Oct. 27	Montgomery	01	13	26
Darst, Jacob(B)	1807	May 04	Greene	01	10	02
Darst, John(C)	1813	Sept. 13	Montgomery	09	02	26
Darst, John(C)	1817	Sept. 20	Miami	11	02	14
Dart, Amor(B)	1831	Sept. 17	Dearborn(Ind	02	08	28
Dart, Diodat(B)	1837	Dec. 08	Hamilton	02	03	04
Dart, George(B)	1819	June 10	Hamilton	02	04	30
Dart, Joseph(B)	1831	Oct. 19	Dearborn(Ind	02	08	32
Dart, Moses(B)	1831	Sept. 17	Dearborn(Ind	02	08	28
Dart, William S.(B)	1818	Aug. 10	Cincinnati	03	05	25
Dart, William S.(B)	1819	June 10	Hamilton	02	04	30
Dartengton, Joseph(C)	1814	Nov. 09	Adams	14	01	13
Dartengton, Joseph(C)	1814	Nov. 09	Adams	13	02	12
Dartengton, Joseph(C)	1814	Nov. 09	Adams	13	03	30
Dartinton, Joseph(C)	1815	June 03	Miami	13	02	18
Dashiell, Charles(B)	1817	Nov. 01	Greene	03	06	10
Dashiell, Charles(E)	1816	Oct. 26	Greene	15	21	07
Dashiell, John(B)	1818	June 12	Dearborn(Ind	03	06	03
Dashiell, John(B)	1818	June 27	Dearborn(Ind	02	05	07
Dashiell, John(B)	1818	Sept. 04	Dearborn(Ind	03	05	07
Daubenheyer, Peter Gorden(B)	1836	Jan. 20	Dearborn(Ind	03	04	22
Daubenheyer, Peter Gordon(B)	1834	May 13	Dearborn(Ind	03	04	22
Daugherty, Dan'l.(A)	1831	Jan. 13	Hamilton	01	10	35
Daugherty, Dan'l.(A)	1832	Jan. 03	Darke	01	10	36

PURCHASER	YEAR	DATE	RESIDENCE	R	T	S
Daugherty, Daniel(A)	1832	May 11	Darke	02	10	31
Daugherty, James(B)	1831	Sept. 03	Dearborn(Ind	03	06	13
Daugherty, John(C)	1806	July 22	Champaign	09	05	27
Daughters, Sarah(B)	1824	Aug. 04	Dearborn(Ind	03	06	22
Daus, Anthony(E)	1837	March 27	Cincinnati	12	11	21
Davee, Zachariah(E)	1816	Oct. 25	Franklin(Ind	13	14	27
Davenport, Martin(B)	1824	Oct. 07	Wayne(Ind)	01	12	15
Davenport, Noah(A)	1822	June 24	Miami	04	09	35
David, Bartley(A)	1828	Sept. 17	Preble	02	09	15
David, Carpenter(B)	1811	Aug. 14	Ind.Territory	01	08	14
David, James(B)	1811	Aug. 14	Ind.Territory	01	08	14
Davidson, Hezekiah(C)	1811	Jan. 21	Champaign	08	06	05
Davidson, Isaac(C)	1810	Dec. 24	Champaign	12	05	33
Davidson, Isaac(C)	1811	Jan. 21	Champaign	08	06	05
Davidson, James(A)	1834	May 09	Darke	04	11	32
Davidson, John(B)	1807	Feb. 09	Kentucky	01	13	08
Davidson, John(B)	1824	June 09	Wayne(Ind)	01	13	15
Davidson, Robert(B)	1818	May 22	Dearborn(Ind	02	07	10
Davidson, Robert(B)	1825	Jan. 04	Dearborn(Ind	01	07	07
Davidson, Robert(B)	1834	Dec. 23	Dearborn(Ind	02	07	07
Davidson, Wm.(E)	1830	July 13	Randolph(Ind	13	18	14
Davies, William(B)	1833	Dec. 16	Dearborn(Ind	02	06	14
Davies, William(B)	1836	Jan. 11	Dearborn(Ind	02	06	14
Davis, Abiather(A)	1804	Aug. 06	Montgomery	05	06	17
Davis, Agness(A)	1813	Sept. 13	Butler	01	02	23
Davis, Allen(B)	1835	Jan. 03	Randolph(Ind	01	16	02
Davis, Amos(A)	1805	May 31	Butler	04	03	28
Davis, Amos(A)	1805	June 25	Butler	02	08	28
Davis, Amos(A)	1805	June 25	Butler	02	08	28
Davis, Amos(A)	1810	Aug. 14	Butler	04	03	28
Davis, Amos(A)	1832	Feb. 13	Fayette	04	06	05
Davis, Andrew(C)	1807	Jan. 08	Champaign	11	04	32
Davis, Andrew(C)	1807	Jan. 12	Champaign	11	04	32
Davis, Andrew(C)	1812	April 15	Champaign	11	04	32
Davis, Andrew(C)	1812	April 15	Champaign	11	04	32
Davis, Andrew(C)	1817	Sept. 15	Champaign	10	03	06
Davis, Benj'n.(C)	1829	Dec. 12	Champaign	13	04	20
Davis, Benjamin Carson(B)	1836	Feb. 22	Darke	01	16	24
Davis, Benjamin D.(B)	1816	Dec. 04	Butler	03	02	06
Davis, Charles(E)	1812	Jan. 16	Kentucky	12	15	35
Davis, Dan'l. Richison(A)	1835	Oct. 10	Darke	03	11	23
Davis, Daniel R.(A)	1836	Dec. 12	Darke	03	11	26
Davis, Daniel(A)	1819	June 08	Warren	03	10	20
Davis, Daniel(C)	1831	Nov. 07	Champaign	11	03	14
Davis, David D.(B)	1833	Jan. 21	Dearborn(Ind	02	07	36
Davis, David(A)	1810	Dec. 12	Preble	03	05	31
Davis, David(A)	1812	June 29	Greene	05	04	32
Davis, David(E)	1815	Dec. 14	Butler	14	16	10
Davis, Drewry(B)	1818	Feb. 12	Wayne(Ind)	01	16	02
Davis, Dunham(B)	1818	April 23	Butler	02	04	07
Davis, Elijah T.(C)	1808	Dec. 26	Champaign	13	04	35
Davis, Elijah T.(C)	1810	March 19	Champaign	13	04	19
Davis, Elijah T.(C)	1818	Aug. 03	Champaign	13	04	20
Davis, Elisha(E)	1836	Feb. 01	Franklin(Ind	11	10	01
Davis, Elisha(E)	1836	March 28	Union(Ind)	11	10	01
Davis, Elisha(E)	1836	March 28	Union(Ind)	12	10	06
Davis, Elnathan(A)	1819	Oct. 23	Butler	07	01	05
Davis, Enoch(E)	1831	Nov. 07	Randolph(Ind	14	20	23
Davis, Enoch(E)	1837	March 01	Randolph(Ind	14	20	11
Davis, George W.(A)	1812	June 29	Pennsylvania	05	04	30
Davis, George W.(A)	1812	June 29	Pennsylvania	05	04	31
Davis, George(A)	1811	Jan. 23	Preble	02	06	01
Davis, George(A)	1814	Dec. 05	Preble	02	06	12
Davis, George(A)	1816	Aug. 01	Preble	02	06	01
Davis, George(A)	1828	Nov. 07	Preble	02	09	15
Davis, Giles(A)	1804	May 12	Kentucky	02	06	01
Davis, Giles(A)	1804	Sept. 13	Butler	02	06	12
Davis, Giles(A)	1804	Oct. 31	Kentucky	02	06	12
Davis, Giles(B)	1806	July 19	Dearborn(Ind	01	10	07

PURCHASER	YEAR	DATE	RESIDENCE	R	T	S
Davis, Giles(E)	1836	July 28	Preble	11	10	14
Davis, Henry(B)	1834	Jan. 21	Randolph(Ind	01	16	11
Davis, Henry(E)	1828	April 28	Franklin(Ind	12	11	17
Davis, Henry(E)	1835	Sept. 19	Randolph(Ind	15	19	05
Davis, Israel(B)	1813	April 05	Franklin(Ind	01	08	35
Davis, Israel(B)	1815	Sept. 09	Franklin(Ind	01	08	23
Davis, Isreal(B)	1813	Nov. 17	Franklin(Ind	01	08	35
Davis, Jacob(C)	1812	Dec. 21	Greene	08	03	24
Davis, Jacob(C)	1821	Feb. 20	Clark	09	03	27
Davis, Jacob(C)	1821	March 22	Clark	09	03	27
Davis, Jacob(C)	1827	Dec. 08	Champaign	12	04	10
Davis, James K.(E)	1836	March 30	Preble	11	10	13
Davis, James(A)	1810	June 02	Ind.Territry	01	04	14
Davis, James(A)	1832	July 17	Darke	02	11	08
Davis, James(B)	1806	Sept. 09	Butler	01	10	06
Davis, James(B)	1806	Sept. 09	Butler	01	10	06
Davis, James(B)	1811	Dec. 11	Franklin(Ind	01	10	06
Davis, James(B)	1814	Nov. 28	Franklin(Ind	01	12	23
Davis, James(C)	1829	Dec. 09	Champaign	13	03	20
Davis, Job(A)	1832	April 20	Warren	02	10	24
Davis, John(A)	1804	Nov. 03	Warren	02	05	06
Davis, John(A)	1814	April 22	Greene	01	08	27
Davis, John(A)	1814	April 22	Greene	01	08	32
Davis, John(A)	1814	Nov. 14	Butler	02	07	31
Davis, John(A)	1831	Nov. 02	Miami	04	08	34
Davis, John(B)	1813	Dec. 24	Clermont	02	04	25
Davis, John(B)	1818	April 23	Butler	02	04	07
Davis, John(B)	1818	Aug. 19	Cincinnati	02	08	29
Davis, John(B)	1819	July 31	Cincinnati	02	05	33
Davis, John(B)	1831	June 22	Dearborn(Ind	01	06	25
Davis, John(C)	1831	Dec. 15	Clark	13	04	15
Davis, John(E)	1817	Aug. 13	Montgomery	13	18	34
Davis, Jonathan S.(E)	1816	April 11	Hamilton	13	16	19
Davis, Joseph W.(E)	1836	Aug. 29	Indiana	14	20	26
Davis, Joseph(A)	1806	March 29	Warren	01	07	33
Davis, Joseph(A)	1812	Oct. 31	Preble	01	07	32
Davis, Leroy(A)	1826	March 17	Preble	02	07	33
Davis, Leroy(E)	1834	Nov. 11	Preble	14	19	14
Davis, Lewis	1808	March 02	Greene	?	?	?
Davis, Lewis	1808	March 03	Greene	?	?	?
Davis, Lewis	1808	March 03	Greene	?	?	?
Davis, Lewis A.(C)	1828	June 19	Virginia	10	03	17
Davis, Lewis(A)	1807	July 04	Butler	02	05	06
Davis, Lewis(A)	1814	Jan. 27	Greene	08	01	24
Davis, Lewis(A)	1815	Aug. 09	Champaign	08	01	13
Davis, Lewis(C)	1802	Nov. 19	Hamilton	08	04	14
Davis, Lewis(C)	1802	Dec. 31	Hamilton	08	04	20
Davis, Lewis(C)	1802	Dec. 31	Hamilton	08	04	14
Davis, Lewis(C)	1802	Dec. 31	Hamilton	08	05	32
Davis, Lewis(C)	1804	Dec. 27	Greene	08	04	20
Davis, Lewis(C)	1804	Dec. 31	Greene	07	03	04
Davis, Lewis(C)	1805	Nov. 21	Greene	07	03	09
Davis, Lewis(C)	1805	Dec. 16	Greene	08	05	18
Davis, Lewis(C)	1805	Dec. 16	Greene	08	05	18
Davis, Lewis(C)	1805	Dec. 16	Greene	08	05	18
Davis, Lewis(C)	1805	Dec. 16	Greene	08	05	18
Davis, Lewis(C)	1806	Jan. 04	Greene	08	04	08
Davis, Lewis(C)	1806	Jan. 06	Greene	08	04	26
Davis, Lewis(C)	1806	Jan. 27	Greene	08	04	08
Davis, Lewis(C)	1806	Jan. 27	Greene	08	04	08
Davis, Lewis(C)	1806	Jan. 29	Greene	09	06	17
Davis, Lewis(C)	1806	Jan. 29	Greene	09	06	17
Davis, Lewis(C)	1806	Sept. 17	Greene	08	05	18
Davis, Lewis(C)	1806	Sept. 17	Greene	09	06	05
Davis, Lewis(C)	1807	Jan. 01	Ohio	11	05	28
Davis, Lewis(C)	1807	Jan. 31	Greene	12	03	28
Davis, Lewis(C)	1807	Jan. 31	Greene	12	03	22
Davis, Lewis(C)	1807	March 11	Greene	09	04	02
Davis, Lewis(C)	1807	April 17	Greene	13	02	21

PURCHASER	YEAR	DATE	RESIDENCE	R	T	S
Davis, Lewis(C)	1807	April 17	Greene	08	05	27
Davis, Lewis(C)	1807	April 17	Greene	08	05	24
Davis, Lewis(C)	1808	Jan. 13	Greene	08	05	24
Davis, Lewis(C)	1808	June 22	Greene	08	05	24
Davis, Lewis(C)	1809	June 20	Greene	08	04	19
Davis, Lewis(C)	1811	Dec. 11	Greene	09	06	05
Davis, Lewis(C)	1812	April 15	Ind.Territry	11	05	28
Davis, Lewis(C)	1812	April 15	Greene	12	03	22
Davis, Lewis(C)	1812	April 15	Greene	12	03	28
Davis, Lewis(C)	1812	April 15	Greene	09	04	02
Davis, Lewis(C)	1812	April 16	Greene	10	04	06
Davis, Lewis(C)	1812	April 16	Greene	10	04	06
Davis, Lewis(C)	1812	April 21	Greene	10	05	33
Davis, Lewis(C)	1814	Jan. 07	Greene	09	04	02
Davis, Lewis(C)	1814	Jan. 07	Greene	09	04	07
Davis, Lewis(C)	1814	Jan. 15	Greene	08	04	29
Davis, Lewis(C)	1814	Jan. 27	Greene	13	03	18
Davis, Lewis(C)	1814	Jan. 27	Greene	13	03	24
Davis, Lewis(C)	1814	Jan. 28	Greene	13	03	05
Davis, Lewis(C)	1814	Feb. 10	Greene	13	03	06
Davis, Lewis(C)	1814	Feb. 10	Greene	13	03	06
Davis, Lewis(C)	1814	Feb. 10	Greene	13	03	06
Davis, Lewis(C)	1814	Feb. 10	Greene	13	03	06
Davis, Lewis(C)	1814	Feb. 10	Greene	14	02	01
Davis, Lewis(C)	1814	Feb. 10	Greene	14	02	01
Davis, Lewis(C)	1814	Feb. 10	Greene	14	02	01
Davis, Lewis(C)	1814	Feb. 10	Greene	13	03	10
Davis, Lewis(C)	1814	Feb. 10	Greene	13	03	04
Davis, Lewis(C)	1814	Feb. 10	Greene	13	03	17
Davis, Lewis(C)	1814	Feb. 10	Greene	14	03	31
Davis, Lewis(C)	1814	Feb. 10	Greene	13	04	36
Davis, Lewis(C)	1814	Feb. 10	Greene	13	04	36
Davis, Lewis(C)	1814	Feb. 10	Greene	13	03	11
Davis, Lewis(C)	1814	Feb. 10	Greene	13	03	11
Davis, Lewis(C)	1814	Feb. 10	Cincinnati	09	05	20
Davis, Lewis(C)	1814	Feb. 10	Cincinnati	09	05	20
Davis, Lewis(C)	1814	Feb. 10	Cincinnati	09	05	26
Davis, Lewis(C)	1814	Feb. 10	Cincinnati	09	05	26
Davis, Lewis(C)	1814	Feb. 11	Cincinnati	12	03	28
Davis, Lewis(C)	1815	May 08	Cincinnati	13	04	36
Davis, Lewis(C)	1815	May 08	Cincinnati	13	04	35
Davis, Lewis(C)	1815	May 08	Cincinnati	13	04	35
Davis, Lewis(C)	1815	May 08	Cincinnati	13	04	34
Davis, Lewis(C)	1815	May 08	Cincinnati	13	04	34
Davis, Lewis(C)	1815	May 08	Cincinnati	13	03	04
Davis, Lewis(C)	1815	May 08	Cincinnati	14	03	28
Davis, Lewis(C)	1815	May 08	Cincinnati	14	03	34
Davis, Lewis(C)	1815	May 08	Cincinnati	14	03	34
Davis, Lewis(C)	1815	May 08	Cincinnati	14	03	33
Davis, Lewis(C)	1815	May 08	Cincinnati	14	02	09
Davis, Lewis(C)	1815	May 08	Cincinnati	14	03	04
Davis, Lewis(C)	1815	May 08	Cincinnati	14	03	10
Davis, Lewis(C)	1815	May 08	Cincinnati	14	03	09
Davis, Lewis(C)	1815	May 08	Cincinnati	14	03	09
Davis, Lewis(C)	1815	May 08	Cincinnati	14	03	09
Davis, Lewis(C)	1815	May 08	Cincinnati	14	03	03
Davis, Lewis(C)	1815	May 08	Cincinnati	14	03	03
Davis, Lewis(C)	1815	May 08	Cincinnati	14	03	10
Davis, Lewis(C)	1815	May 08	Cincinnati	14	03	03
Davis, Lewis(C)	1815	May 08	Cincinnati	14	03	02
Davis, Lewis(C)	1815	May 08	Cincinnati	14	03	02
Davis, Lewis(C)	1815	May 08	Cincinnati	14	03	02
Davis, Lewis(C)	1815	May 08	Cincinnati	14	03	02
Davis, Lewis(C)	1815	May 08	Cincinnati	14	04	32
Davis, Lewis(C)	1815	May 08	Cincinnati	14	04	32
Davis, Lewis(C)	1815	May 08	Cincinnati	14	04	32
Davis, Lewis(C)	1815	May 08	Cincinnati	14	02	17
Davis, Lewis(C)	1815	May 08	Cincinnati	14	02	02
Davis, Lewis(C)	1815	May 09	Cincinnati	14	03	15

PURCHASER	YEAR	DATE	RESIDENCE	R	T	S
Davis, Lewis(C)	1815	May 09		14	03	15
Davis, Lewis(C)	1815	May 09		14	03	10
Davis, Lewis(C)	1815	May 09		14	03	10
Davis, Lewis(C)	1815	May 09		14	03	14
Davis, Lewis(C)	1815	May 09		14	03	14
Davis, Lewis(C)	1815	May 09		14	03	14
Davis, Lewis(C)	1815	May 09		14	03	14
Davis, Lewis(C)	1815	May 09		14	03	15
Davis, Lewis(C)	1815	May 09		14	03	15
Davis, Lewis(C)	1815	May 09		14	03	17
Davis, Lewis(C)	1815	May 09		14	03	17
Davis, Lewis(C)	1815	May 09		14	02	03
Davis, Lewis(C)	1815	May 09		14	02	34
Davis, Lewis(C)	1815	May 09		14	02	34
Davis, Lewis(C)	1815	May 18		15	03	31
Davis, Lewis(C)	1815	May 18		14	03	06
Davis, Lewis(C)	1815	May 18		14	03	17
Davis, Lewis(C)	1815	May 18		14	03	18
Davis, Lewis(C)	1815	May 19	Cincinnati	14	03	18
Davis, Lewis(C)	1815	May 19		14	03	06
Davis, Lewis(C)	1815	May 19		14	03	18
Davis, Lewis(C)	1815	May 19		14	03	06
Davis, Lewis(C)	1816	Dec. 02	Cincinnati	14	03	01
Davis, Lewis(C)	1816	Dec. 03	Cincinnati	13	04	02
Davis, Lewis(C)	1816	Dec. 03	Cincinnati	13	04	03
Davis, Lewis(C)	1816	Dec. 03	Cincinnati	13	04	03
Davis, Lewis(C)	1816	Dec. 03	Cincinnati	13	04	03
Davis, Lewis(C)	1816	Dec. 03	Cincinnati	13	04	02
Davis, Lewis(C)	1816	Dec. 03	Cincinnati	13	04	02
Davis, Lewis(C)	1816	Dec. 06	Cincinnati	13	03	03
Davis, Lewis(C)	1816	Dec. 06	Cincinnati	13	03	03
Davis, Lewis(C)	1816	Dec. 06	Cincinnati	13	03	09
Davis, Lewis(C)	1816	Dec. 06	Cincinnati	13	03	09
Davis, Lewis(C)	1816	Dec. 06	Cincinnati	13	03	15
Davis, Lewis(C)	1816	Dec. 09	Cincinnati	08	05	29
Davis, Lewis(C)	1816	Dec. 09	Cincinnati	08	05	29
Davis, Lewis(C)	1816	Dec. 09	Cincinnati	08	05	30
Davis, Lewis(C)	1816	Dec. 09	Cincinnati	08	05	24
Davis, Lewis(C)	1815	May 18		14	04	36
Davis, Lewis(C)	1817	Aug. 01	Cincinnati	14	03	28
Davis, Lewis(C)	1829	July 21	Hamilton	14	02	03
Davis, Lorenzo(A)	1819	Oct. 23	Montgomery	07	01	07
Davis, Martha(A)	1801	Aug. 03	Hamilton	03	03	34
Davis, Martha(A)	1804	Sept. 24	Butler	02	05	13
Davis, Martha(A)	1804	Sept. 24	Butler	02	05	13
Davis, Mary(?)	1813	April 14	Montgomery	07	01	01
Davis, Mary(A)	1815	June 23	Kentucky	06	08	30
Davis, Matthias(E)	1833	Sept. 16	Franklin(Ind	11	11	14
Davis, Miles(E)	1834	Dec. 19	Randolph(Ind	15	18	06
Davis, Moses(A)	1814	June 14	Preble	02	06	01
Davis, Moses(A)	1836	Nov. 21	Miami	03	12	27
Davis, Moses(E)	1831	June 27	Randolph(Ind	14	18	29
Davis, Nancy(B)	1818	June 12	Cincinnati	03	06	02
Davis, Nicholas(?)	1816	Dec. 04	Butler	03	03	33
Davis, Nicholas(B)	1815	Aug. 28	Butler	03	02	05
Davis, Nicholas(B)	1816	Nov. 08	Butler	03	02	07
Davis, Oowen(C)	1804	Dec. 24	Greene	08	05	32
Davis, Owen(?)	1813	April 14	Montgomery	07	01	01
Davis, Owen(A)	1817	June 23	Greene	04	09	31
Davis, Owen(C)	1801	Dec. 22	Hamilton	07	03	19
Davis, Owen(C)	1801	Dec. 22	Hamilton	07	03	25
Davis, Paul(E)	1813	July 17	Dearborn(Ind	12	14	21
Davis, Peter(B)	1806	July 19	Dearborn(Ind	01	10	07
Davis, Peter(B)	1806	July 19	Dearborn(Ind	01	10	08
Davis, Reason(E)	1812	Jan. 16	Kentucky	12	15	35
Davis, Reuben(A)	1831	Jan. 03	Clark	03	09	19
Davis, Robert(A)	1811	June 28	Greene	02	05	07
Davis, Samuel Jr.(A)	1832	Jan. 19	Miami	04	08	34
Davis, Samuel(A)	1801	July 27	Hamilton	03	03	19

PURCHASER	YEAR	DATE	RESIDENCE	R	T	S
Davis, Samuel(A)	1806	March 14	Clermont	01	04	02
Davis, Samuel(A)	1811	Dec. 12	Butler	02	04	06
Davis, Spencer(B)	1817	Nov. 17	Cincinnati	03	06	14
Davis, Spencer(B)	1818	Feb. 03	Dearborn(Ind	03	06	11
Davis, Stephen(A)	1836	June 11	Miami	03	11	07
Davis, Stephen(A)	1838	April 10	Miami	02	13	20
Davis, Stephen(B)	1815	March 08	Kentucky	01	09	29
Davis, Stephen(B)	1831	Sept. 10	Wayne(Ind)	01	16	02
Davis, Stephen(C)	1804	Dec. 24	Montgomery	10	02	07
Davis, Thomas M.(E)	1837	Jan. 21	Randolph(Ind	14	20	10
Davis, Thomas(B)	1814	March 12	?	03	02	30
Davis, Thomas(B)	1818	March 18	Franklin(Ind	03	03	28
Davis, Thomas(B)	1834	April 02	Switzerland	03	04	26
Davis, Thomas(C)	1801	Dec. 31	Hamilton	07	01	01
Davis, Thomas(C)	1802	Dec. 30	Hamilton	07	01	01
Davis, Thomas(C)	1812	Jan. 02	Fairfield	12	05	01
Davis, Thomas(C)	1830	Jan. 11	Clark	11	03	21
Davis, Thomas(C)	1832	Feb. 06	Clark	11	03	21
Davis, Thos. Jones(B)	1832	Dec. 05	Dearborn(Ind	03	04	32
Davis, Timothy(B)	1815	Jan. 18	Dearborn(Ind	01	05	04
Davis, Vincent(B)	1814	Sept. 20	Butler	02	10	23
Davis, Ward(B)	1834	Nov. 13	Franklin(Ind	02	08	15
Davis, Ward(B)	1835	May 12	Franklin(Ind	02	08	15
Davis, Waymouth(E)	1834	Feb. 05	Randolph(Ind	15	18	06
Davis, William(A)	1835	April 17	Clark	08	01	03
Davis, William(B)	1819	Sept. 15	Hamilton	02	08	32
Davis, William(B)	1833	Feb. 06	Dearborn(Ind	02	07	26
Davis, William(B)	1835	Jan. 03	Dearborn(Ind	01	07	32
Davis, William(B)	1836	Jan. 11	Dearborn(Ind	02	06	14
Davis, William(C)	1809	Sept. 09	Hamilton	10	03	36
Davis, William(C)	1814	Dec. 30	Hamilton	10	03	24
Davis, William(E)	1817	July 08	Butler	14	16	03
Davis, William(E)	1817	July 08	Butler	14	16	10
Davis, Wm. Forrest Ray Jr.(A)	1832	Jan. 11	Greene	06	08	10
Davis, Zachariah(B)	1814	Oct. 08	Butler	01	10	32
Davison, Alexander(E)	1832	Oct. 01	Franklin(Ind	12	11	04
Davison, Alexander(E)	1833	Jan. 07	Franklin(Ind	11	11	01
Davison, John(B)	1817	July 31	Dearborn(Ind	02	07	31
Davison, John(B)	1817	July 31	Dearborn(Ind	02	06	02
Davison, Jonah(A)	1815	Aug. 25	Warren	02	09	14
Davison, Jonah(A)	1815	Aug. 25	Warren	02	10	34
Davison, Samuel(E)	1836	Sept. 12	Franklin(Ind	12	11	04
Davison, Thos.(A)	1830	Jan. 09	Montgomery	04	06	07
Davison, William(A)	1836	Oct. 10	Montgomery	01	13	15
Daviss, Samuel(A)	1802	March 19	Hamilton	03	03	18
Davisson, David(A)	1837	Feb. 25	Virginia	02	14	02
Davisson, David(A)	1837	Feb. 27	Virginia	02	14	03
Davisson, Devecmon D.(A)	1837	Feb. 27	Virginia	02	14	03
Davisson, Elias(E)	1835	Oct. 08	Randolph(Ind	13	18	14
Davisson, Moses(E)	1836	Dec. 12	Wayne(Ind)	13	18	14
Davisson, Samuel(A)	1814	July 11	Preble	01	09	33
Davisson, Silvanus(E)	1836	Dec. 03	Randolph(Ind	13	18	14
Davisson, Silvanus(E)	1838	Oct. 26	Randolph(Ind	13	18	14
Davisson, Wm. A.(A)	1836	Sept. 20	Mercer	02	14	11
Dawson, Charles(B)	1804	Aug. 23	Dearborn(Ind	01	06	26
Dawson, Charles(B)	1804	Sept. 18	Dearborn(Ind	01	06	23
Dawson, Charles(B)	1815	Feb. 09	Dearborn(Ind	01	05	07
Dawson, Charles(B)	1816	April 11	Dearborn(Ind	02	06	19
Dawson, George(C)	1806	May 30	Champaign	10	06	21
Dawson, George(C)	1811	Aug. 13	Champaign	10	06	21
Dawson, James H.(E)	1833	Feb. 05	Wayne(Ind)	13	17	06
Dawson, Jesse(E)	1814	Aug. 29	Franklin(Ind	13	14	10
Dawson, John(B)	1806	Dec. 17	Dearborn(Ind	01	06	20
Dawson, John(B)	1813	Sept. 01	Dearborn(Ind	01	06	08
Dawson, John(B)	1814	Nov. 22	Dearborn(Ind	01	06	20
Dawson, John(B)	1814	Nov. 22	Dearborn(Ind	01	06	29
Dawson, John(B)	1817	May 28	?	01	06	20
Dawson, John(B)	1817	Oct. 30	Dearborn(Ind	02	06	23
Dawson, John(C)	1813	April 14	Champaign	11	05	15

PURCHASER	YEAR	DATE	RESIDENCE	R	T	S
Dawson, Mathias(E)	1811	Oct. 24	Wayne(Ind)	13	15	32
Dawson, Matthias(E)	1815	June 23	Wayne(Ind)	13	14	04
Dawson, Thomas(E)	1813	Aug. 02	Butler	13	14	15
Day, Bryan(A)	1829	Jan. 20	Miami	04	08	24
Day, David(E)	1815	Aug. 26	Clermont	13	15	13
Day, Henry(A)	1829	Sept. 29	Belmont	05	09	08
Day, Henry(A)	1829	Oct. 09	Belmont	05	09	05
Day, Henry(A)	1829	Dec. 11	Belmont	05	09	05
Day, Henry(A)	1831	May 09	Shelby	05	09	07
Day, John(A)	1805	Sept. 02	Montgomery	02	08	24
Day, John(A)	1805	Dec. 27	Montgomery	02	08	24
Day, John(A)	1814	Nov. 16	Preble	02	08	25
Day, John(A)	1815	Dec. 15	Darke	02	11	23
Day, Robert(A)	1805	Dec. 27	Montgomery	02	08	24
Day, Robert(A)	1814	Nov. 16	Preble	02	08	25
Day, Soloman(A)	1835	Oct. 09	Shelby	04	11	32
Day, Stephen M.(B)	1837	May 20	Dearborn(Ind	03	07	22
Day, Stephen Munson(B)	1836	Feb. 05	Dearborn(Ind	03	07	27
Day, Stephen Munson(B)	1836	May 06	Dearborn(Ind	03	07	27
Dayton, Elias J.(C)	1812	March 02	New Jersey	07	02	30
Dayton, Elias J.(C)	1811	Dec. 13	Montgomery	07	02	36
Dayton, Jonathan(A)	1808	Feb. 12	New Jersey	02	04	23
Dayton, Jonathan(A)	1813	April 14	New Jersey	02	04	23
Dayton, Jonathan(C)	1805	June 12	New Jersey	09	05	34
Dayton, Jonathan(C)	1805	Oct. 12	New Jersey	09	05	21
DeCamp, Aaron(A)	1831	Feb. 09	Darke	02	10	27
DeCamp, Harvey(A)	1836	Sept. 17	Cincinnati	01	15	27
DeCamp, Walter(A)	1836	Sept. 07	Butler	01	15	20
DeCamp, Walter(A)	1836	Sept. 17	Butler	01	15	21
DeCamp, William(A)	1816	Sept. 03	Darke	02	10	27
DeForest, Delauzun(B)	1833	Jan. 03	Cincinnati	01	02	01
DeLebar, Aaron(E)	1815	April 29	Kentucky	13	14	15
DeWitt, John(B)	1814	Feb. 18	Dearborn(Ind	02	03	24
Deakins, James(B)	1814	June 27	Franklin(Ind	02	10	02
Deal, Adam(A)	1837	April 13	Miami	01	13	20
Deal, Christopher(A)	1837	April 13	Miami	01	13	20
Deal, Daniel(A)	1818	Oct. 06	Miami	05	08	29
Deal, Elias(A)	1837	May 05	Fairfield	02	14	08
Deal, George(A)	1837	April 13	Miami	01	13	20
Deal, Paul Junr.(A)	1837	April 13	Miami	01	13	17
Deal, Paul Senr.(A)	1837	April 13	Miami	01	13	17
Deal, Paul(A)	1819	March 16	Miami	05	08	28
Deamond, Alexander(B)	1808	Jan. 12	Ind.Territory	01	07	15
Dean, George(B)	1824	July 09	Hamilton	03	06	03
Dean, John(C)	1801	Dec. 30	Hamilton	04	02	04
Dean, John(C)	1808	May 28	Pennsylvania	10	02	24
Dean, Matthias(A)	1811	July 26	Darke	02	12	33
Dean, Matthias(A)	1816	Aug. 01	Warren	02	12	20
Dean, Matthias(A)	1816	Dec. 02	Warren	02	12	33
Dean, Matthias(A)	1817	Nov. 14	Butler	02	12	20
Dean, Matthias(A)	1829	June 11	Warren	02	12	33
Dean, Matthias(A)	1833	April 05	Darke	02	12	20
Dean, Matthias(A)	1833	April 05	Darke	02	12	17
Dean, Matthias(A)	1835	June 10	Darke	02	12	17
Dean, Thompson(B)	1836	May 16	Dearborn(Ind	02	05	30
Deardoff, Samuel(A)	1818	Feb. 06	Montgomery	04	05	29
Deardorf, Peter(E)	1827	June 16	Preble	13	16	26
Deardorff, Daniel(A)	1817	June 24	Warren	02	12	10
Deardorff, Daniel(A)	1817	June 24	Warren	02	12	10
Deardorff, Jacob(A)	1822	May 30	Warren	02	12	02
Deardorff, Jacob(A)	1835	Feb. 20	Warren	02	12	03
Deardorff, Jacob(A)	1835	Feb. 20	Warren	02	13	34
Deardorff, Jacob(A)	1835	Nov. 13	Warren	02	13	34
Deardorff, Jacob(A)	1822	May 30	Warren	02	12	03
Deardorff, Peter(A)	1817	June 24	Warren	02	12	10
Deardurff, Dan'l.(C)	1829	June 30	Champaign	13	04	15
Deardurff, Dan'l.(C)	1830	Jan. 25	Champaign	13	04	15
Deardurff, Dan'l.(C)	1831	July 15	Champaign	13	04	15
Deardurff, Daniel(C)	1817	Sept. 10	Franklin(Ind	13	04	14

PURCHASER	YEAR	DATE	RESIDENCE	R	T	S
Deardurff, John(C)	1818	Aug. 22	Franklin(Ind	13	04	15
Dearkhusing, John Rudolph(B)	1835	Sept. 11	Hamilton	02	08	19
Dearkhusing, John Rudolph(B)	1835	Sept. 11	Hamilton	03	09	24
Dearmond, Alexander(A)	1812	Nov. 02	Dearborn(Ind	01	03	22
Dearmond, Alexander(A)	1814	April 09	Butler	01	03	07
Dearmond, Alexander(A)	1814	April 09	Butler	01	03	18
Dearmond, Alexander(A)	1815	April 11	Butler	01	03	15
Dearmond, Alexander(B)	1804	Sept. 24	Hamilton	01	08	19
Dearmond, Alexander(B)	1804	Sept. 27	Hamilton	01	07	12
Dearmond, Joseph(A)	1837	Feb. 11	Butler	02	15	19
Dearmond, Kerig(A)	1815	April 10	Butler	01	03	15
Dearmond, King(A)	1837	Feb. 14	Butler	02	15	30
Dearmond, Milton(B)	1832	Aug. 28	Dearborn(Ind	02	08	15
Dearmond, Milton(B)	1833	Feb. 18	Dearborn(Ind	02	08	15
Dearmond, Samuel(A)	1837	Feb. 14	Butler	02	15	30
Dearmond, William H.(A)	1837	Feb. 11	Butler	02	15	19
Dearth, Allen(A)	1835	Oct. 28	Warren	02	13	34
Dearth, Chas. F.(A)	1829	Oct. 20	Warren	03	07	01
Dearth, Edw'd.(A)	1829	Oct. 20	Warren	04	06	06
Dearth, Edward(C)	1801	Dec. 03	Hamilton	04	03	23
Dearth, Elisabeth Jr.(A)	1835	Oct. 28	Warren	02	13	34
Dearth, James(C)	1801	Dec. 24	Hamilton	04	03	36
Dearth, James(E)	1812	Sept. 01	Warren	13	14	20
Dearth, Jesse(A)	1830	Dec. 15	Warren	04	07	29
Dearth, Jesse(A)	1831	June 30	Warren	04	07	29
Dearth, John(C)	1801	Dec. 24	Hamilton	04	03	35
Dearth, Rebecca(A)	1831	June 01	Warren	04	06	06
Death, Dan'l. Adley(C)	1831	Jan. 01	Montgomery	12	03	26
Death, George(E)	1812	Sept. 29	Warren	13	14	20
Death, John C.(E)	1812	Sept. 29	Warren	13	14	21
Death, William(A)	1839	July 06	Darke	03	11	18
Debaun, John(E)	1835	Oct. 12	Franklin(Ind	12	12	11
Debolt, Andrew(E)	1836	Jan. 13	Randolph(Ind	15	21	28
Debolt, Benjamin(E)	1836	Jan. 13	Preble	15	21	27
Debolt, Daniel(A)	1805	Sept. 30	Hamilton	03	03	02
Debolt, George(E)	1836	Oct. 24	Preble	15	21	27
Debolt, Henry(A)	1802	July 29	Hamilton	04	02	17
Debolt, John(A)	1804	Sept. 25	Hamilton	03	03	11
Debolt, Michael	1808	March 02	Hamilton	?	?	?
Deboy, Jacob(E)	1827	Sept. 20	Union(Ind)	14	14	06
Deboy, Jacob(E)	1828	Nov. 13	Union(Ind)	14	14	06
Decamp, Job(A)	1814	Oct. 22	Butler	02	10	27
Dechant, Jacob W.(A)	1815	July 12	Pennsylvania	01	08	27
Dechant, Jacob W.(A)	1815	July 12	Pennsylvania	01	08	27
Dechant, Jacob W.(A)	1815	July 12	Pennsylvania	01	08	35
Dechant, Jacob W.(A)	1815	July 12	Pennsylvania	01	08	23
Dechant, Jacob Wm.(A)	1815	July 25	Pennsylvania	01	08	31
Dechant, Jacob Wm.(A)	1815	July 25	Pennsylvania	01	07	01
Decker, Christopher(E)	1836	Nov. 12	Cincinnati	12	10	08
Decker, Henry(A)	1817	Oct. 27	New Jersey	01	12	35
Decker, Herman Francis(A)	1839	Jan. 21	Cincinnati	02	15	26
Decker, Isaac(A)	1819	Sept. 14	Franklin	06	08	26
Decker, John Selmas(A)	1839	Jan. 21	Cincinnati	02	15	26
Deckman, Henry Christian(E)	1836	Oct. 19	Cincinnati	11	10	25
Decoursey, John(A)	1814	Nov. 10	Kentucky	01	07	07
Decoursey, William(A)	1814	Nov. 07	Kentucky	01	07	20
Decoursey, William(A)	1814	Dec. 15	Kentucky	01	07	17
Decow, Robert(E)	1836	Oct. 26	Pennsylvania	14	19	09
Deem, Adam(A)	1808	Nov. 03	Butler	03	05	11
Deem, Adam(A)	1811	Jan. 03	Butler	04	02	05
Deem, Adam(A)	1811	Dec. 11	Butler	03	05	11
Deem, Henry(C)	1805	Dec. 09	Montgomery	08	02	36
Deerduff, Jacob(A)	1811	April 09	Preble	03	05	18
Deeter, Abraham(A)	1814	Aug. 27	Montgomery	05	07	05
Deeter, Dan'l.(A)	1831	June 20	Miami	04	08	13
Deeter, Jacob(A)	1824	July 16	Miami	05	07	17
Deeter, Jacob(A)	1834	June 04	Miami	01	12	30
Deeter, Jacob(A)	1834	Dec. 29	Miami	01	12	30
Deeter, John(A)	1811	Sept. 20	Montgomery	05	07	08

PURCHASER	YEAR	DATE	RESIDENCE	R	T	S
Deford, Thomas(E)	1836	Feb. 08	Franklin(Ind	12	12	28
Defrees, Anthony(A)	1819	Feb. 08	Miami	06	08	26
Defrees, Anthony(A)	1819	May 19	Cincinnati	06	08	20
Defrees, Joseph(A)	1811	Nov. 14	Montgomery	06	07	11
Deibert, John(C)	1812	Oct. 23	Maryland	10	04	23
Deibert, John(C)	1812	Oct. 23	Maryland	10	04	29
Deihl, Jacob(A)	1806	June 10	Montgomery	05	04	30
Deiper, Daniel(A)	1816	April 16	Miami	05	07	27
Delany, John(E)	1814	Oct. 15	Kentucky	13	12	14
Delaplaine, Joseph(C)	1804	Dec. 31	Cincinnati	06	01	07
Delaplane, James(A)	1816	May 09	Butler	01	03	02
Deldine, Herman(C)	1810	July 03	Miami	12	01	12
Dellhof, Francis G.(A)	1839	Jan. 21	Cincinnati	02	15	25
Delong, George(C)	1805	June 29	Montgomery	08	02	30
Delts, Francis(C)	1802	Dec. 30	Hamilton	06	02	01
Deltz, Joseph(C)	1813	April 14	Champaign	11	04	04
Demaree, Henry(B)	1833	May 30	Switzerland	03	04	30
Demaree, Henry(B)	1836	June 30	Switzerland	03	04	20
Demaree, Peter(B)	1807	March 25	Ind.Territry	01	13	34
Demaree, Peter(B)	1813	May 29	?	03	02	03
Demaris, Jacob(B)	1818	Sept. 15	Hamilton	01	07	23
Dement, James(C)	1802	Dec. 17	Hamilton	09	05	35
Dement, James(C)	1802	Dec. 22	Hamilton	09	04	05
Dement, Jesse(C)	1813	April 12	Champaign	10	05	20
Dement, Richard(B)	1818	June 08	Cincinnati	01	06	15
Demeree, Peter(B)	1808	Sept. 02	Dearborn(Ind	03	03	35
Demeree, Peter(B)	1816	Jan. 29	Switzerland	02	03	33
Demint, James(C)	1804	Dec. 31	Greene	09	05	30
Demint, James(C)	1804	Dec. 31	Greene	10	05	14
Demint, James(C)	1813	April 14	Champaign	09	04	05
Demmarel, Peter(B)	1815	March 17	Switzerland	02	03	32
Demmitt, John(A)	1831	May 24	Montgomery	06	08	14
Demmitt, John(A)	1832	Feb. 01	Montgomery	06	08	14
Demmitt, William(E)	1815	Jan. 20	Wayne(Ind)	13	17	10
Demos, John(B)	1814	July 15	Dearborn(Ind	01	05	17
Demoss, Charles(A)	1814	Dec. 23	Preble	02	06	11
Demoss, Charles(A)	1824	June 08	Preble	02	06	15
Demoss, Peter(A)	1805	Feb. 27	Butler	02	06	31
Demoss, Peter(A)	1810	April 11	Preble	02	06	31
Demott, Abraham(A)	1802	Nov. 09	Hamilton	03	05	35
Demott, Abraham(A)	1803	July 14	Butler	04	02	06
Demott, Abraham(A)	1806	Jan. 02	Butler	03	06	08
Demott, Abraham(C)	1801	Dec. 15	Hamilton	05	02	06
Dendy, Thomas(C)	1804	Oct. 09	Greene	06	02	02
Deneen, James(A)	1804	Oct. 12	Hamilton	01	04	23
Deneen, James(A)	1810	Dec. 12	Butler	01	04	27
Denham, James(C)	1814	March 30	Champaign	14	04	31
Denies, Adam(B)	1834	Jan. 23	Cincinnati	03	08	13
Deniston, John(E)	1817	Oct. 14	Butler	13	14	09
Deniston, William(A)	1831	Dec. 05	Darke	01	13	26
Deniston, William(B)	1809	Aug. 05	Butler	01	10	14
Deniston, William(B)	1814	Dec. 31	Franklin(Ind	01	10	09
Deniston, William(E)	1817	Oct. 14	Butler	13	14	09
Denman, Abner(C)	1813	June 08	Hamilton	11	01	12
Denman, James(E)	1813	Oct. 18	Butler	12	14	22
Denman, John(B)	1808	Jan. 22	Dearborn(Ind	01	10	13
Denman, Samuel(C)	1804	Dec. 26	Philadelphia	07	01	07
Denman, Samuel(C)	1804	Dec. 27	Philadelphia	08	03	21
Denman, Samuel(C)	1804	Dec. 31	Philadelphia	08	03	34
Denman, Samuel(C)	1804	Dec. 31	Philadelphia	08	03	09
Denman, William(E)	1813	Oct. 09	Butler	12	14	20
Denman, William(E)	1813	Oct. 09	Wayne(Ind)	12	14	36
Denmoyer, Nancy(E)	1837	March 01	Butler	14	21	03
Denney, John(A)	1816	March 06	Preble	03	06	23
Denney, William Felton(E)	1833	Oct. 05	Randolph(Ind	15	22	14
Denney, William Felton(E)	1836	Oct. 15	Jay Co.,Ind.	15	22	14
Denney, William Felton(E)	1837	Feb. 01	Jay Co.,Ind.	15	22	14
Denney, William Felton(E)	1837	July 14	Jay Co.,Ind.	15	22	13
Dennis, Elisha(E)	1812	Aug. 20	Wayne(Ind)	12	15	21

PURCHASER	YEAR	DATE	RESIDENCE	R	T	S
Dennis, Elisha(E)	1814	Aug. 22	Wayne(Ind)	13	15	02
Dennis, Jacob(B)	1817	Nov. 14	Dearborn(Ind	02	03	19
Dennis, John(A)	1815	April 11	Butler	04	03	33
Dennisson, David(A)	1810	April 11	Preble	01	06	20
Denniston, James(A)	1803	April 01	Hamilton	03	05	27
Denniston, Johnston(A)	1816	Sept. 05	Darke	01	12	23
Denniston, Johnston(A)	1836	May 26	Darke	01	13	22
Denniston, William(A)	1833	April 05	Darke	01	13	14
Denniston, Wm.(A)	1838	May 21	Darke	01	13	22
Denny, Henry Jr.(A)	1836	Nov. 28	Darke	01	15	29
Denny, John(C)	1804	Dec. 22	Greene	09	04	21
Denny, Mary(A)	1814	June 06	Butler	01	04	21
Denny, Mary(A)	1814	June 11	Butler	01	04	21
Denny, Mary(B)	1814	June 06	Butler	01	09	13
Denny, Richard(B)	1811	Jan. 14	Ind.Territroy	02	12	11
Denny, Walter(A)	1814	March 12	Preble	03	06	25
Denny, Walter(A)	1819	Dec. 08	Preble	04	05	19
Denny, William(A)	1815	Jan. 02	Pickaway	08	01	14
Denny, William(A)	1815	Jan. 02	Pickaway	08	01	18
Denny, William(C)	1815	Jan. 02	Pickaway	14	02	03
Denny, William(C)	1815	Jan. 02	Pickaway	13	03	17
Denton, John H.(E)	1829	Oct. 13	Randolph(Ind	13	19	33
Denton, Lewis Wilson(E)	1835	Jan. 19	Randolph(Ind	13	19	29
Denton, Will'm.(E)	1828	Nov. 01	Kentucky	13	19	20
Derevage, Peter(E)	1835	March 07	Randolph(Ind	15	18	06
Derickson, Joseph Jr.(E)	1837	Feb. 01	Wayne(Ind)	14	19	24
Derickson, Joseph(E)	1837	Feb. 01	Wayne(Ind)	14	19	24
Dervage, Peter(B)	1829	April 08	Wayne(Ind)	01	16	21
Deter, Abraham(A)	1805	March 04	Pennsylvania	05	05	17
Deter, Abraham(A)	1807	Jan. 13	Montgomery	05	05	17
Deter, Daniel(A)	1829	Dec. 07	Darke	02	11	33
Deters, Daniel(A)	1817	Oct. 15	Darke	02	11	33
Detraz, John(B)	1817	July 26	Switzerland	03	02	19
Devenport, Abraham(A)	1816	Oct. 09	Ross	06	07	06
Devenport, Jesse(B)	1806	March 07	Montgomery	01	13	11
Dever, John(A)	1806	Aug. 23	Montgomery	02	12	35
Dever, John(A)	1806	Aug. 23	Montgomery	02	12	26
Devon, John(A)	1811	July 08	Darke	02	12	35
Devon, Wm.(A)	1811	July 06	Darke	04	09	02
Devor, Benjamin(C)	1802	Dec. 29	Hamilton	07	03	30
Devor, John(A)	1814	Dec. 09	Montgomery	02	12	29
Devor, John(A)	1814	Dec. 09	Montgomery	03	10	31
Devor, John(A)	1815	Jan. 05	Montgomery	02	12	29
Devor, John(A)	1815	Jan. 05	Montgomery	03	10	32
Devor, John(A)	1815	April 25	Darke	02	12	28
Devor, John(A)	1816	June 18	Darke	01	12	33
Devor, John(A)	1816	June 27	Darke	01	11	04
Devor, John(C)	1801	Dec. 30	Hamilton	07	02	13
Devor, John(C)	1801	Dec. 30	Hamilton	07	02	19
Devor, Thomas(E)	1834	Jan. 01	Darke	15	21	04
Devor, Thomas(E)	1835	Oct. 07	Randolph(Ind	15	21	09
Devor, Wm.(C)	1801	Dec. 30	Hamilton	07	02	14
Devyyer, Edward(B)	1816	Oct. 10	Dearborn(Ind	02	06	04
Dewees, Lewis(B)	1814	Dec. 31	Franklin(Ind	02	08	05
Deweese, David(A)	1832	Jan. 12	Miami	07	01	06
Deweese, James(A)	1831	Aug. 08	Miami	07	01	06
Deweese, James(A)	1831	Aug. 08	Miami	07	01	06
Deweese, James(C)	1811	Oct. 21	Miami	11	01	15
Deweese, Jethro(A)	1831	Nov. 24	Miami	07	01	06
Deweese, John(A)	1836	April 21	Shelby	04	11	07
Deweese, John(A)	1836	May 18	Shelby	04	11	07
Deweese, Lewis Jr.(C)	1827	Sept. 03	Miami	11	01	03
Deweese, Lewis(C)	1824	June 07	Miami	11	01	08
Deweese, Lewis(C)	1824	June 07	Miami	11	01	08
Deweese, Lewis(C)	1824	June 07	Miami	11	01	08
Deweese, Luis(B)	1801	Aug. 13	Kentucky	01	07	11
Deweese, Samuel(C)	1811	Oct. 21	Miami	11	01	15
Dewit, John(B)	1814	July 04	Dearborn(Ind	01	03	08
Dexter, Charles(A)	1820	Nov. 17	Preble	01	12	04

PURCHASER	YEAR	DATE	RESIDENCE	R	T	S
Dexter, Isaac(B)	1814	Jan. 08	Cincinnati	01	04	30
Dexter, Isaac(B)	1815	April 14	Dearborn(Ind	01	04	30
Dexter, Isaac(B)	1830	Jan. 01	Dearborn(Ind	01	04	29
Dice, Frederick(A)	1814	Aug. 27	Kentucky	01	08	33
Dick, David(A)	1836	Dec. 05	Butler	01	15	25
Dick, Samuel(A)	1804	Sept. 13	Butler	04	03	13
Dick, Samuel(A)	1804	Sept. 13	Butler	02	02	30
Dick, Samuel(A)	1806	Feb. 24	Butler	02	03	08
Dick, Samuel(A)	1806	Feb. 24	Butler	02	04	35
Dick, Samuel(A)	1812	April 02	Butler	02	03	29
Dick, Samuel(C)	1804	Sept. 04	Butler	04	03	26
Dick, Samuel(C)	1804	Sept. 04	Butler	04	03	26
Dickason, John(B)	1814	Feb. 10	JeffersonInd	02	02	04
Dickason, Samuel(B)	1815	Sept. 11	Warren	03	03	08
Dickason, William(B)	1814	July 01	Jefferson	02	02	08
Dicken, Joel(B)	1814	May 07	Dearborn(Ind	01	07	29
Dicken, Joel(B)	1816	April 09	Dearborn(Ind	02	07	24
Dicken, Joel(B)	1816	April 09	Dearborn(Ind	02	07	24
Dicker, Joel(E)	1811	Oct. 28	Dearborn(Ind	12	14	14
Dickerson, Daniel(B)	1817	June 03	Switzerland	02	02	10
Dickerson, Jno.(A)	1811	Nov. 25	Madison	03	02	11
Dickerson, Robert(E)	1811	Oct. 29	Wayne(Ind)	12	16	14
Dickerson, Robert(E)	1815	May 31	Franklin(Ind	11	12	13
Dickerson, Wm.(A)	1811	Nov. 25	Madison	03	02	11
Dickeson, John(B)	1806	June 21	Dearborn(Ind	02	10	14
Dickeson, John(B)	1806	June 21	Dearborn(Ind	02	10	11
Dickeson, John(B)	1813	Nov. 25	Franklin(Ind	02	10	34
Dickeson, John(B)	1817	Aug. 11	Switzerland	02	02	10
Dickey, Adam(C)	1804	Sept. 03	Hamilton	04	02	26
Dickey, Adam(C)	1804	Oct. 13	Hamilton	04	02	26
Dickey, Adam(C)	1810	Dec. 12	Hamilton	04	02	26
Dickey, Adam(C)	1810	Dec. 12	Hamilton	04	02	26
Dickey, Patrick	1808	March 02	Cincinnati	?	?	?
Dickey, Samuel(A)	1802	March 24	Hamilton	04	02	07
Dickey, William(E)	1813	Oct. 22	Kentucky	12	14	08
Dickinson, John Colvin(B)	1832	March 13	Dearborn(Ind	02	05	03
Dickinson, John(B)	1806	July 18	Warren	02	10	12
Dickinson, John(B)	1818	Feb. 26	Hamilton	03	03	03
Dickinson, John(B)	1818	Feb. 26	Hamilton	03	04	36
Dickinson, John(B)	1818	Feb. 26	Hamilton	03	03	01
Dickinson, John(B)	1818	Feb. 26	Hamilton	03	04	24
Dickinson, John(B)	1818	Feb. 26	Hamilton	03	04	27
Dickinson, John(B)	1818	Feb. 26	Hamilton	03	04	23
Dickinson, Townsend(B)	1832	April 16	Dearborn(Ind	02	05	10
Dickinson, Zebulun(B)	1817	Nov. 12	Dearborn(Ind	02	05	03
Dickison, Greffy(B)	1804	Oct. 09	Kentucky	03	02	02
Dickison, John(B)	1829	Dec. 11	Switzerland	02	02	03
Dickman, Herman(E)	1836	Oct. 27	Cincinnati	11	10	24
Dickman, Herman(E)	1836	Oct. 27	Cincinnati	11	10	13
Dicks, Zachariah(E)	1827	Nov. 07	Wayne(Ind)	14	15	04
Dicks, Zacharias(E)	1816	Dec. 02	?	14	15	04
Dicks, Zechariah(E)	1829	Jan. 28	Wayne(Ind)	14	15	04
Dickson, Nicholas(A)	1837	Feb. 07	Darke	02	13	07
Dickson, Plat B.(E)	1814	Feb. 16	Butler	12	14	22
Dickson, Plat B.(E)	1817	June 27	Franklin(Ind	12	14	33
Dickson, Robert(C)	1813	May 31	Champaign	14	02	09
Diehl, Jacob(A)	1814	April 30	Montgomery	04	05	34
Diel, Nicholas(E)	1837	May 25	Cincinnati	13	11	22
Diffendal, David(A)	1832	June 06	Montgomery	03	07	02
Diffenderffer, Henry(B)	1818	May 14	Cincinnati	01	02	02
Diffenderffer, Henry(B)	1818	May 14	Cincinnati	01	02	02
Diffenderffer, Henry(B)	1818	July 21	Hamilton	01	07	33
Diggs, Armsbe(E)	1817	June 26	Wayne(Ind)	14	02	18
Diggs, Benjamin C.(E)	1836	Oct. 05	Randolph(Ind	13	20	25
Diggs, Henry(E)	1836	March 28	Randolph(Ind	13	20	12
Diggs, William Junr.(E)	1816	Sept. 27	Wayne(Ind)	13	20	24
Diggs, Wm.(E)	1818	April 15	Randolph(Ind	13	20	23
Dihlenger, Christian W.(A)	1839	Jan. 21	Cincinnati	02	15	27
Dike, George(B)	1811	Aug. 17	Warren	01	11	07

87

PURCHASER	YEAR	DATE	RESIDENCE	R	T	S
Dilbone, Wm.(C)	1831	Aug. 17	Miami	13	02	24
Dill, John H. C.(A)	1836	Oct. 05	Butler	02	13	26
Dill, Peter(A)	1805	March 06	Montgomery	03	04	14
Dill, Peter(A)	1807	Jan. 02	Butler	04	03	30
Dill, Peter(A)	1805	April 09	Montgomery	03	04	14
Dill, Peter(A)	1814	Aug. 13	Montgomery	03	04	24
Dill, Valentine(B)	1836	Feb. 15	Hamilton	02	08	30
Dill, Valentine(E)	1837	May 23	Cincinnati	13	11	22
Dillan, Samuel(C)	1801	Dec. 17	Hamilton	04	03	21
Dillbone, Henry(C)	1808	Jan. 22	Miami	12	01	01
Dillbone, Henry(C)	1813	April 14	Champaign	12	01	01
Dille, Brice(C)	1818	April 20	Montgomery	12	01	06
Dillon, Isaac(A)	1831	Sept. 21	Clark	08	02	28
Dillon, Isaac(A)	1831	Sept. 21	Clark	08	02	28
Dillon, Jesse(E)	1815	Jan. 18	Clermont	13	17	03
Dillon, Luke(E)	1815	Jan. 18	Clinton	13	17	02
Dillon, Richard(A)	1831	April 09	Clark	08	02	27
Dillon, Samuel(A)	1804	Aug. 25	Butler	02	04	10
Dills, Jacob(A)	1808	Dec. 22	Kentucky	06	07	29
Dills, Jacob(C)	1807	June 26	Kentucky	12	05	01
Dills, Jacob(C)	1813	July 10	Miami	12	01	26
Dilman, Ab'm.(A)	1827	Aug. 20	Darke	01	08	35
Dilman, Andrew(B)	1828	April 09	Switzerland	02	02	22
Dils, Francis(C)	1811	Dec. 30	Montgomery	06	01	03
Dils, Henry(B)	1817	Aug. 15	Virginia	02	05	12
Dimmitt, William(E)	1814	Dec. 21	?	13	17	12
Dingman, James(A)	1809	July 27	Franklin	07	01	20
Dingman, James(C)	1809	July 27	Franklin	13	01	05
Dingman, James(C)	1809	July 27	Franklin	13	01	09
Dinkins, Alexander(E)	1836	Feb. 12	Preble	11	11	01
Dinsmoore, John Johnston(C)	1831	Sept. 09	Montgomery	12	02	12
Dinsmoore, Matthew(C)	1818	March 31	Montgomery	11	02	17
Dipra, Henry(A)	1818	Aug. 24	Miami	03	11	35
Diserens, Francis Louis(B)	1816	Dec. 11	Switzerland	03	02	18
Disher, Daniel(A)	1828	Nov. 05	Preble	02	09	09
Dittmer, John(A)	1831	Dec. 24	Montgomery	04	07	15
Ditto, Francis(A)	1815	Aug. 28	Piqua	05	10	32
Diver, Patrick(B)	1818	July 16	Cincinnati	02	06	04
Divert, William(A)	1815	Nov. 25	Montgomery	04	05	17
Dixon, Arthur(E)	1811	Oct. 22	Ind.Territory	12	13	02
Dixon, Arthur(E)	1811	Oct. 22	Ind.Territry	12	14	36
Dixon, Christopher(C)	1801	Dec. 31	Hamilton	04	02	31
Dixon, Eli(A)	1806	June 12	Butler	01	07	07
Dixon, James H.(B)	1818	Jan. 12	Cincinnati	02	06	09
Dixon, John(A)	1817	Dec. 04	Preble	02	07	33
Dixon, John(A)	1819	Aug. 26	Warren	01	11	02
Dixon, John(B)	1815	Aug. 28	Hamilton	01	03	05
Dixon, John(B)	1815	Dec. 04	Hamilton	01	03	18
Dixon, John(B)	1835	Feb. 02	Butler	01	17	11
Dixon, John(B)	1837	Dec. 14	Randolph(Ind	01	17	02
Dixon, Joseph(A)	1816	Oct. 15	Butler	01	12	23
Dixon, Joseph(A)	1831	Jan. 06	Darke	01	12	22
Dixon, Matthew(E)	1811	Oct. 22	Ind.Territry	12	13	02
Dixon, Robert(A)	1814	Jan. 06	Miami	05	07	07
Dixon, Robert(C)	1809	Feb. 20	Kentucky	14	02	14
Dixon, William(A)	1806	July 31	Montgomery	03	04	09
Dixson, Silas(B)	1835	Oct. 12	Warren	01	17	02
Doak, Patrick(C)	1813	May 17	Miami	12	01	22
Dobbeling, Herman Fred'k.(B)	1834	Oct. 23	Hamilton	02	08	20
Dobson, Benj'n.(B)	1828	April 19	Wayne(Ind)	01	15	02
Dobson, Thomas(A)	1805	Nov. 26	Butler	02	04	04
Doddridge, John(E)	1813	Dec. 25	Pennsylvania	13	15	12
Doddridge, John(E)	1814	April 20	Wayne(Ind)	13	15	24
Doddridge, John(E)	1814	April 28	Ind.Territory	13	15	36
Doddridge, John(E)	1814	June 18	Wayne(Ind)	13	15	36
Doddridge, Phillip(E)	1814	April 20	Wayne(Ind)	13	15	15
Dodds, Andrew(A)	1813	April 26	Butler	02	04	08
Dodds, Joseph(C)	1805	Aug. 20	Montgomery	06	01	20
Dodds, William(A)	1812	Sept. 16	Butler	02	04	05

88

PURCHASER	YEAR	DATE	RESIDENCE	R	T	S
Dodson, Edward	1808	March 01	Hamilton	?	?	?
Dodson, Edward	1808	March 01	Hamilton	?	?	?
Dodson, Edward(A)	1818	Jan. 05	Cincinnati	04	06	28
Dodson, Edward(E)	1836	Dec. 16	Cincinnati	12	11	04
Dodson, Elijah(C)	1832	Jan. 31	Champaign	13	03	17
Dodson, Jesse(C)	1812	April 15	Champaign	11	05	20
Dodson, Jesse(C)	1813	May 07	Champaign	11	05	13
Dodson, John(A)	1805	Dec. 09	Hamilton	02	04	14
Dodson, John(A)	1818	Jan. 05	Montgomery	04	06	28
Dodson, John(E)	1816	Dec. 02	Montgomery	13	15	19
Dodson, John(E)	1817	July 31	Montgomery	14	20	15
Dodson, Major(B)	1811	Nov. 28	Kentucky	01	12	10
Dodson, Major(B)	1813	Sept. 20	Wayne(Ind)	01	12	03
Doherty, William(E)	1836	Feb. 01	Randolph(Ind	13	18	01
Dolby, John(Black)(E)	1833	Sept. 12	Randolph(Ind	13	19	04
Dolph, Benj'm.(B)	1833	Oct. 07	Dearborn(Ind	03	04	17
Dolson, James(B)	1832	July 20	Dearborn(Ind	03	06	22
Donahoe, Patrick(B)	1804	April 26	BrookeCoVir.	01	02	31
Donahoe, Patrick(B)	1804	Sept. 01	BrookeCo.Vir	01	02	26
Donar, David(A)	1811	Oct. 07	Butler	02	04	27
Donel, Jonathan(C)	1804	Sept. 04	Greene	09	03	29
Donnal, Jonathan(C)	1802	Dec. 31	Hamilton	09	04	23
Donnal, Jonathan(C)	1802	Dec. 31	Hamilton	09	02	35
Donnal, Thomas(D)	1811	June 05	Butler	03	02	08
Donnel, Johnathan(C)	1802	Dec. 31	Hamilton	08	02	03
Donnel, Johnathan(C)	1802	Dec. 31	Hamilton	09	04	27
Donnel, Johnathan(C)	1802	Dec. 31	Hamilton	09	04	10
Donnel, Johnathan(C)	1802	Dec. 31	Hamilton	09	04	33
Donnel, Jonathan(C)	1804	Sept. 03	Greene	09	03	08
Donnel, Jonathan(C)	1804	Dec. 28	Greene	09	04	17
Donnel, Jonathan(C)	1804	Dec. 31	Ohio	10	02	21
Donnel, Jonathan(C)	1804	Dec. 31	Ohio	10	02	33
Donnel, Jonathan(C)	1804	Dec. 31	Ohio	10	02	14
Donnel, Jonathan(C)	1804	Dec. 31	Ohio	10	02	27
Donnel, Jonathan(C)	1804	Dec. 31	Greene	09	01	02
Donnel, Jonathan(C)	1804	Dec. 31	Ohio	10	01	05
Donnel, Jonathan(C)	1804	Dec. 31	Ohio	10	02	12
Donnel, Jonathan(C)	1806	July 30	Champaign	09	03	05
Donnel, Jonathan(C)	1806	Sept. 08	Champaign	09	03	12
Donnel, Jonathan(C)	1807	Jan. 01	Champaign	09	03	12
Donnel, Jonathan(C)	1807	Feb. 14	Champaign	10	03	07
Donnel, Jonathan(C)	1812	Feb. 06	Champaign	08	03	12
Donnel, Jonathan(C)	1812	Feb. 06	Champaign	08	03	12
Donnel, Patrick(A)	1816	Dec. 08	Pennsylvania	02	09	32
Donnel, Samuel(C)	1812	Feb. 06	Champaign	08	03	12
Donnel, Samuel(C)	1812	Feb. 06	Champaign	08	03	12
Donnel, William(C)	1804	Dec. 28	Greene	09	04	28
Donnellan, Nelson(A)	1832	April 16	Montgomery	04	09	19
Donovan, Aquilla(C)	1816	Feb. 12	Kentucky	09	04	36
Donovan, Philip(C)	1816	Feb. 12	Kentucky	09	03	06
Donovan, Robert(C)	1811	Oct. 15	Pennsylvania	11	05	26
Donovan, Robert(C)	1811	Oct. 15	Pennsylvania	11	05	29
Donovan, Robert(C)	1811	Oct. 15	Pennsylvania	11	05	36
Donovan, Robert(C)	1811	Oct. 15	Pennsylvania	11	05	20
Donovan, Wm.(C)	1816	Feb. 12	Kentucky	09	04	36
Dooley, Abner(A)	1808	Dec. 17	Kentucky	02	07	06
Dooley, Abner(A)	1814	Dec. 17	Preble	02	07	06
Dooley, George(A)	1814	Aug. 16	Preble	02	07	08
Dooley, Moses(A)	1805	Oct. 09	Kentucky	02	07	18
Dooley, Reuben(A)	1813	Aug. 10	Preble	02	07	07
Dooley, Silas(A)	1806	Feb. 12	Montgomery	02	07	18
Dooley, Thomas(A)	1808	March 29	Montgomery	02	07	07
Dooley, Thomas(A)	1813	April 12	Preble	02	07	19
Doolittle, Benj'm.(C)	1813	Dec. 15	Champaign	11	05	35
Doolittle, Benjamin(C)	1812	April 15	Champaign	11	04	05
Doolittle, Benjamin(C)	1817	May 27	Champaign	12	05	36
Doolittle, Benjamin(C)	1817	May 27	?	13	04	01
Doolittle, Benjamin(C)	1817	May 27	Champaign	13	04	02
Doolittle, Benjamin(C)	1817	May 27	?	13	04	02

PURCHASER	YEAR	DATE	RESIDENCE	R	T	S
Doolittle, Benjamin(C)	1817	Aug. 05	Champaign	12	04	33
Doolittle, Benjamin(C)	1817	Aug. 05	Champaign	12	04	27
Doolittle, Benjamin(C)	1817	Aug. 05	Champaign	12	04	32
Doolittle, Benjamin(C)	1817	Aug. 05	Champaign	11	05	35
Doolittle, Benjamin(C)	1817	Aug. 05	Champaign	12	04	33
Doolittle, Benjamin(C)	1818	May 25	Champaign	10	04	22
Doolittle, Benjamin(C)	1818	May 25	Champaign	10	04	22
Doolittle, Benjamin(C)	1818	May 25	Champaign	10	04	24
Doolittle, Benjamin(C)	1818	May 25	Champaign	10	04	35
Doolittle, Benjamin(C)	1818	May 25	Champaign	11	03	19
Doolittle, Benjamin(C)	1818	May 25	Champaign	11	03	19
Doolittle, Benjamin(C)	1818	May 25	Champaign	10	04	28
Doolittle, Benjamin(C)	1818	May 25	Champaign	10	04	29
Doolittle, Benjamin(C)	1818	Sept. 01	Champaign	10	04	29
Doolittle, Benjamin(C)	1817	Aug. 05	Champaign	12	04	27
Dorman, David(A)	1819	Dec. 23	Preble	02	09	27
Dorman, Michael M.(A)	1812	July 24	Miami	05	08	18
Doron, Isaac(A)	1805	Nov. 22	Butler	03	06	05
Dorraugh, Amos(C)	1804	Sept. 04	Greene	08	02	08
Dorraugh, Amos(C)	1804	Aug. 31	Greene	08	02	08
Dorrel, William(B)	1833	July 26	Dearborn(Ind	02	03	23
Dorsey, John(C)	1818	Nov. 19	Champaign	12	02	04
Dorsey, Silas(C)	1818	Nov. 19	Champaign	12	02	04
Doser, Henry(C)	1825	March 09	Champaign	10	04	29
Dotson, Daniel(E)	1836	Feb. 12	Franklin(Ind	12	11	08
Dotson, William(B)	1813	May 29	?	03	02	03
Doty, Daniel(A)	1817	Nov. 14	Butler	02	12	20
Doty, Daniel(C)	1801	Dec. 09	Hamilton	04	02	04
Doty, Daniel(C)	1801	Dec. 09	Hamilton	04	02	28
Doty, Frazy(A)	1830	Feb. 20	Darke	02	10	13
Doty, James(B)	1836	Feb. 23	Franklin(Ind	01	08	31
Doty, John(B)	1818	Aug. 10	Hamilton	03	07	23
Dougherty, Henry(B)	1818	Oct. 28	Hamilton	02	08	30
Dougherty, James(E)	1811	Oct. 22	Kentucky	12	14	02
Dougherty, James(E)	1816	May 27	Wayne(Ind)	13	16	17
Dougherty, John(B)	1815	June 17	Dearborn(Ind	03	05	36
Dougherty, John(C)	1811	Dec. 12	Champaign	09	05	21
Dougherty, Nathan(A)	1813	June 30	Butler	03	05	15
Dougherty, Samuel(A)	1815	Jan. 07	Warren	01	08	14
Dougherty, William(A)	1813	June 25	Miami	06	05	29
Doughty, Ann(E)	1814	Aug. 04	Franklin(Ind	13	12	04
Doughty, Edward(B)	1837	April 06	ShelbyCo.Ind	02	03	09
Doughty, Wm. M.(E)	1830	Jan. 14	Wayne(Ind)	13	17	36
Douglas, Jackson G.(B)	1829	Dec. 08	Switzerland	01	02	01
Douglas, Robert(A)	1806	June 20	Butler	02	06	31
Douglas, Robert(A)	1807	Jan. 15	Butler	01	06	36
Douglass, Alex'r.(A)	1830	Sept. 29	Miami	05	08	04
Douglass, Andrew(B)	1827	Aug. 27	Dearborn(Ind	02	03	01
Douglass, Andrew(B)	1834	Nov. 12	Dearborn(Ind	02	03	01
Douglass, David(C)	1802	Dec. 29	Hamilton	04	03	25
Douglass, Jno.(A)	1830	Sept. 29	Miami	05	08	04
Douglass, John(A)	1811	March 20	Butler	02	05	06
Douglass, Robert(A)	1816	June 13	Darke	02	12	18
Douglass, Robert(B)	1818	Aug. 27	Franklin(Ind	02	08	22
Douglass, William(A)	1813	July 24	Butler	02	05	22
Douglass, Wm.(B)	1818	May 15	Cincinnati	02	07	01
Dove, John(B)	1815	Aug. 28	Hamilton	02	12	23
Dow, Joseph(B)	1825	Jan. 13	Switzerland	03	03	33
Dow, Lorenzo(C)	1826	March 24	MtvilleConn.	09	04	26
Dow, Peter(C)	1831	Aug. 08	Logan	14	03	11
Dowden, Sam'l. Hanson(B)	1833	March 02	Dearborn(Ind	02	06	14
Dowden, Samuel H.(B)	1813	Feb. 19	Ind.Territry	01	06	19
Dowell, Martin(A)	1836	Nov. 24	Montgomery	03	13	28
Downey, Alexander C.(B)	1836	Aug. 18	Dearborn(Ind	02	03	08
Downey, Amos(B)	1818	April 21	Clermont	02	03	05
Downey, Hugh B.(B)	1836	Sept. 03	Switzerland	03	04	25
Downey, James Jnr.(B)	1818	April 21	Wayne(Ind)	02	03	05
Downey, James Jr.(B)	1832	May 28	Switzerland	02	03	31
Downey, James Jr.(B)	1833	Dec. 30	Switzerland	02	03	30

PURCHASER	YEAR	DATE	RESIDENCE	R	T	S
Downey, James Mulford(B)	1834	March 20	Dearborn(Ind	02	03	18
Downey, John(B)	1818	March 05	Hamilton	02	03	08
Downey, John(C)	1805	May 24	Greene	07	03	11
Downey, Richard(B)	1818	March 05	Hamilton	02	03	08
Downey, Richard(B)	1832	May 23	Dearborn(Ind	02	03	08
Downey, Richard(B)	1836	Sept. 19	Dearborn(Ind	02	03	08
Downey, Richard(B)	1838	Jan. 25	Dearborn(Ind	02	03	07
Downie, Washington(B)	1819	Aug. 11	Dearborn(Ind	02	04	05
Downing, Francis Charles(B)	1831	Nov. 22	Franklin(Ind	01	08	36
Downing, Israel(A)	1832	Jan. 21	Clark	08	02	26
Downing, John(A)	1816	Aug. 01	Preble	01	10	09
Downing, John(A)	1830	Oct. 30	Darke	01	10	10
Downing, John(C)	1816	Jan. 01	Butler	10	04	27
Downing, Samuel(B)	1836	Dec. 10	Darke	01	17	14
Downing, Samuel(B)	1836	Dec. 30	Randolph(Ind	01	17	15
Downs, Daniel(C)	1831	Aug. 09	Champaign	14	02	05
Doyal, Edward(A)	1819	Feb. 20	Butler	02	09	04
Doyal, Edward(A)	1831	June 22	Preble	02	09	09
Doz, John Claude(A)	1834	March 25	Hamilton	01	15	17
Doz, John Claude(A)	1834	March 28	Hamilton	01	15	17
Doz, John Claude(A)	1834	May 22	Randolph(Ind	01	15	20
Drake, Benj'm.(B)	1814	July 16	Dearborn(Ind	01	02	31
Drake, Benj'n.(A)	1838	May 21	Cincinnati	02	14	25
Drake, Benj'n.(A)	1837	March 01	Cincinnati	01	13	10
Drake, Benj'n.(A)	1837	Dec. 11	Cincinnati	01	13	28
Drake, Benj'n.(E)	1837	June 15	Cincinnati	15	20	05
Drake, Benjamin(A)	1837	Feb. 01	Cincinnati	02	13	04
Drake, Benjamin(A)	1837	Feb. 01	Cincinnati	02	13	18
Drake, Benjamin(A)	1837	Feb. 01	Cincinnati	03	11	17
Drake, Benjamin(A)	1837	Feb. 01	Cincinnati	02	15	20
Drake, Benjamin(A)	1837	March 01	Cincinnati	01	13	03
Drake, Benjamin(A)	1837	March 01	Cincinnati	01	13	15
Drake, Benjamin(A)	1837	March 01	Cincinnati	02	13	06
Drake, Benjamin(A)	1837	March 01	Cincinnati	02	14	35
Drake, Benjamin(A)	1837	June 10	Cincinnati	01	14	33
Drake, Benjamin(A)	1837	June 10	Cincinnati	01	14	28
Drake, Benjamin(A)	1838	Jan. 01	Cincinnati	02	14	05
Drake, Benjamin(A)	1838	Jan. 01	Cincinnati	01	13	29
Drake, Benjamin(B)	1837	Nov. 04	Cincinnati	01	19	24
Drake, Benjamin(E)	1837	Feb. 01	Cincinnati	13	21	36
Drake, Benjamin(E)	1837	Feb. 01	Cincinnati	11	10	01
Drake, Benjamin(E)	1837	Feb. 01	Cincinnati	11	10	01
Drake, Benjamin(E)	1837	Feb. 01	Cincinnati	11	10	11
Drake, Benjamin(E)	1837	Feb. 01	Cincinnati	11	10	12
Drake, Benjamin(E)	1837	Feb. 01	Cincinnati	14	20	34
Drake, Benjamin(E)	1837	March 01	Cincinnati	14	19	01
Drake, Benjamin(E)	1837	March 01	Cincinnati	14	19	01
Drake, Benjamin(E)	1837	March 01	Cincinnati	14	21	20
Drake, Benjamin(E)	1837	April 10	Cincinnati	13	20	11
Drake, Benjamin(E)	1837	April 10	Cincinnati	14	21	02
Drake, Benjamin(E)	1837	April 10	Cincinnati	14	21	02
Drake, Benjamin(E)	1837	April 10	Cincinnati	15	22	27
Drake, Benjamin(E)	1837	April 10	Cincinnati	15	22	14
Drake, Benjamin(E)	1837	April 10	Cincinnati	13	20	11
Drake, Benjamin(E)	1837	June 10	Cincinnati	14	20	02
Drake, Benjamin(E)	1837	June 10	Cincinnati	14	20	10
Drake, Benjamin(E)	1837	Oct. 02	Cincinnati	13	21	36
Drake, Benjamin(E)	1837	Nov. 04	Cincinnati	15	22	10
Drake, Benjamin(E)	1837	Dec. 01	Cincinnati	15	22	10
Drake, Benjamin(E)	1837	Dec. 01	Cincinnati	14	21	19
Drake, Benjamin(E)	1838	Feb. 06	Cincinnati	14	19	01
Drake, Benjamin(E)	1838	Feb. 06	Cincinnati	14	21	31
Drake, Benjamin(E)	1838	April 02	Cincinnati	14	20	11
Drake, Daniel	1808	March 01	Cincinnati	?	?	?
Drake, Daniel	1808	March 01	Cincinnati	?	?	?
Drake, Daniel	1808	March 01	Cincinnati	?	?	?
Drake, Daniel	1808	March 02	Cincinnati	?	?	?
Drake, Dellard(B)	1816	Aug. 31	Dearborn(Ind	01	03	18
Drake, Jacob(A)	1831	Aug. 09	Hamilton	05	08	34

PURCHASER	YEAR	DATE	RESIDENCE	R	T	S
Drake, Jesse(A)	1810	Jan. 20	Dearborn(Ind	02	03	02
Drake, John(A)	1803	June 23	Butler	03	03	25
Drake, John(A)	1806	Sept. 22	Butler	01	09	30
Drake, John(B)	1806	Aug. 27	Butler	01	14	25
Drake, Jonathan(A)	1831	Aug. 09	Hamilton	05	08	33
Drake, Jonathan(A)	1832	Jan. 27	Miami	05	07	02
Drake, Joseph(D)	1814	Sept. 23	Warren	02	04	26
Drake, Lewis(C)	1804	Sept. 03	Warren	04	03	08
Drake, Moses(A)	1803	May 18	Hamilton	03	03	25
Drake, Robert(B)	1813	Dec. 30	Dearborn(Ind	02	02	04
Drake, Robert(B)	1814	June 18	Dearborn(Ind	01	03	08
Drake, Theodore(A)	1836	Sept. 01	Hamilton	03	12	11
Drake, Theodore(A)	1836	Sept. 01	Hamilton	03	12	13
Drake, Thos. McLaughlin(A)	1831	Aug. 09	Hamilton	05	08	33
Drake, Thos.(C)	1829	Dec. 11	Hamilton	11	02	30
Drake, William(C)	1816	Sept. 03	Miami	13	01	03
Draper, Azariah(A)	1836	June 11	Miami	03	11	17
Draper, Joseph(B)	1818	Sept. 24	Wayne(Ind)	01	15	03
Draper, William(A)	1814	Jan. 28	Butler	01	03	08
Drenan, David(B)	1815	Jan. 24	Adams	01	12	28
Drew, Catharine Mary(C)	1814	Aug. 13	Cincinnati	12	05	31
Drew, William C.(B)	1817	Aug. 18	Cincinnati	03	09	01
Drew, William C.(B)	1817	Sept. 19	Hamilton	02	09	31
Drew, William C.(B)	1817	Sept. 08	Cincinnati	03	10	36
Drew, William C.(B)	1817	Sept. 19	Hamilton	02	09	31
Drew, William C.(C)	1814	Aug. 13	Cincinnati	12	05	31
Drew, William C.(C)	1814	Aug. 13	Cincinnati	11	05	36
Drew, William C.(E)	1817	Aug. 01	Franklin(Ind	13	11	31
Drew, William C.(E)	1817	Aug. 27	Indiana	12	12	08
Drew, William C.(E)	1817	Sept. 27	Cincinnati	12	13	07
Drew, William C.(E)	1817	Sept. 27	?	13	11	21
Drew, William C.(E)	1817	Sept. 29	Cincinnati	13	19	32
Drew, William C.(E)	1817	Nov. 04	Cincinnati	13	11	20
Drew, William C.(E)	1817	Nov. 04	Cincinnati	13	11	21
Drew, William C.(E)	1817	Dec. 11	Cincinnati	13	11	28
Drew, William C.(E)	1818	April 22	Franklin(Ind	13	11	20
Drew, William C.(E)	1817	Oct. 15	Cincinnati	13	12	13
Drewer, William Smith(B)	1832	April 05	Franklin(Ind	01	07	25
Drewley, Nicholas(B)	1825	Nov. 24	Union(Ind)	01	12	21
Drewley, Nicholas(B)	1825	Dec. 01	Union(Ind)	01	12	01
Drewley, Nicholas(B)	1825	Dec. 01	Union(Ind)	01	13	36
Drewly, Nicholas(B)	1824	June 09	Union(Ind)	01	12	15
Drewly, Nicholas(B)	1824	June 09	Union(Ind)	01	12	21
Dreyer, John Hy.(A)	1837	Dec. 28	Cincinnati	03	13	33
Driggs, Asel(E)	1837	Feb. 06	Randolph(Ind	13	20	12
Drinkwater, Henry Jr.(A)	1835	Jan. 27	Darke	01	12	06
Driscol, John(C)	1805	May 16	Greene	07	03	12
Driscol, John(C)	1811	Aug. 13	Greene	07	03	12
Droge, Charles(B)	1838	April 23	Cincinnati	03	05	27
Droge, Charles(B)	1838	April 23	Cincinnati	03	05	26
Drollinger, William(A)	1814	Dec. 10	Preble	02	08	21
Druley, Samuel(B)	1814	Nov. 14	Wayne(Ind)	01	12	12
Drummond, George(C)	1806	Aug. 20	Hamilton	08	03	10
Drummond, George(C)	1806	Nov. 08	Hamilton	08	03	17
Drummond, George(C)	1811	Dec. 11	Greene	08	03	10
Drummond, George(C)	1811	Dec. 11	Greene	08	03	17
Drury, Edward(E)	1811	Oct. 24	Wayne(Ind)	13	16	28
Drury, Edward(E)	1811	Oct. 28	Wayne(Ind)	13	16	32
Drury, Samuel(E)	1814	April 06	Wayne(Ind)	12	16	34
Drury, Samuel(E)	1814	April 06	Dearborn(Ind	12	16	34
Drybread, George(A)	1801	Dec. 03	Hamilton	01	03	27
Duboet, Eugene(B)	1817	Nov. 06	Switzerland	03	02	21
Dubois, Abraham(B)	1816	July 08	Cincinnati	01	04	27
Dubois, Abraham(B)	1817	July 22	Dearborn(Ind	01	04	29
Dubois, Alexander(B)	1806	June 21	Dearborn(Ind	02	10	12
Dubois, Alexander(E)	1836	Aug. 29	Union(Ind)	14	19	13
Dubois, Isaac Jr.(E)	1836	Aug. 29	Union(Ind)	14	19	13
Dubois, Isaac(B)	1806	June 21	Dearborn(Ind	02	10	12
Dubois, Jacob(B)	1806	June 21	Dearborn(Ind	02	10	11

PURCHASER	YEAR	DATE	RESIDENCE	R	T	S
Dubois, Jacob(B)	1806	July 18	Warren	02	10	11
Dubois, Jacob(B)	1811	Aug. 13	Ind.Territry	02	10	11
Dubois, Jacob(B)	1811	Dec. 11	Franklin(Ind	02	10	11
Dubois, Peter(A)	1836	Nov. 12	Warren	03	13	28
Dubois, Peter(A)	1836	Nov. 12	Warren	03	13	32
Dubois, Peter(A)	1837	March 01	Warren	03	13	29
Dubois, Will'm.(B)	1815	Oct. 13	Franklin(Ind	02	09	01
Dubois, William(B)	1806	June 21	Dearborn(Ind	02	10	11
Dubois, William(B)	1806	June 21	Dearborn(Ind	01	10	30
Duckworth, John(C)	1815	Feb. 08	Warren	12	04	13
Dudley, John(C)	1813	April 14	Champaign	09	05	22
Dudley, Nathan(C)	1817	Dec. 02	Champaign	09	05	25
Dudley, Richard(C)	1817	Dec. 02	Champaign	09	05	25
Duer, John(C)	1831	Jan. 11	Miami	12	03	28
Dufour, Jno. Francis(B)	1814	Dec. 01	Switzerland	03	02	10
Dufour, John F.(B)	1814	July 11	Jefferson	02	02	18
Dufour, John F.(B)	1815	April 17	Switzerland	03	04	32
Dufour, John James(B)	1802	June 11	Kentucky	03	02	12
Dufour, John James(B)	1802	June 11	Kentucky	03	02	14
Dufour, John James(B)	1803	Dec. 01	Kentucky	03	02	15
Dufour, John James(B)	1804	Sept. 14	Kentucky	02	01	07
Dugan, John(B)	1816	Jan. 24	Wayne(Ind)	01	13	15
Dugan, Thomas(A)	1816	Dec. 02	Cincinnati	01	02	07
Dugan, Thomas(C)	1802	Dec. 31	Hamilton	09	04	27
Dugan, Thomas(C)	1804	Dec. 31	Cincinnati	09	05	33
Dugan, Thomas(C)	1804	Dec. 31	Cincinnati	09	04	03
Dugan, Thomas(C)	1804	Dec. 31	Cincinnati	09	05	36
Dugan, Thomas(C)	1804	Dec. 31	Cincinnati	09	05	28
Dugan, Thomas(C)	1804	Dec. 31	Cincinnati	09	05	32
Dugan, Thomas(C)	1807	Jan. 14	Cincinnati	09	05	30
Dugan, Thomas(C)	1807	Jan. 14	Cincinnati	09	05	30
Dugan, Thomas(C)	1807	March 07	Cincinnati	12	05	07
Dugan, Thomas(C)	1807	March 07	Cincinnati	12	05	07
Dugan, Thomas(C)	1807	March 07	Cincinnati	12	05	07
Dugan, Thomas(C)	1807	March 07	Cincinnati	12	05	07
Dugans, Samuel(B)	1815	Jan. 07	Dearborn(Ind	01	09	36
Duggins, Henry(E)	1836	Oct. 10	Preble	13	20	02
Duhme, Herman Hy.(E)	1837	April 08	Cincinnati	11	10	02
Duhme, John Hy.(E)	1837	April 08	Cincinnati	11	11	36
Duhy, George O.(A)	1824	Sept. 11	Hamilton	05	10	33
Dukes, Stephen W.(B)	1837	Jan. 05	Randolph(Ind	01	17	33
Dull, John(E)	1835	Nov. 09	Montgomery	14	20	27
Dull, Nicholas(E)	1836	May 27	Randolph(Ind	14	20	27
Dumont, Abraham B.(B)	1818	June 01	Switzerland	03	03	14
Dumont, Abraham B.(B)	1818	June 01	Switzerland	03	03	23
Dumont, Abraham B.(B)	1818	June 02	Switzerland	03	03	05
Dumont, John Bogart(A)	1832	Feb. 14	Hamilton	06	08	17
Dumont, Peter Junr.(E)	1811	Oct. 28	Wayne(Ind)	14	17	05
Dunbar, Seth(B)	1818	Feb. 18	Cincinnati	02	06	24
Dunbar, Seth(E)	1816	Jan. 18	Hamilton	12	13	26
Dunbar, William(B)	1814	Feb. 15	Kentucky	01	12	29
Duncan, John(C)	1801	Dec. 30	Hamilton	06	02	20
Duncan, Samuel(A)	1806	March 25	Montgomery	05	06	10
Duncan, Solomon(A)	1836	May 23	Hamilton	01	14	15
Duncan, Solomon(A)	1836	May 23	Hamilton	01	14	15
Dungan, Benjamin(E)	1815	March 13	Butler	13	14	10
Dungan, Isaac(A)	1831	Oct. 12	Butler	02	10	01
Dungan, James(E)	1817	Sept. 09	Butler	13	14	12
Dungan, Joseph(A)	1805	Dec. 16	Warren	01	04	36
Dungan, Joseph(E)	1815	March 13	Butler	13	14	35
Dunging, Josiah(C)	1802	Dec. 28	Hamilton	04	02	07
Dunham, Archibald(C)	1807	May 04	Virginia	12	05	19
Dunham, Archless(C)	1806	Dec. 16	Virginia	12	05	32
Dunham, David(B)	1816	Oct. 23	Franklin(Ind	02	12	35
Dunham, David(B)	1816	Nov. 29	Franklin(Ind	01	12	31
Dunham, Eliazer(A)	1809	Aug. 14	Massachusett	01	04	06
Dunham, Eliezar(A)	1809	Aug. 14	Massachusett	01	04	06
Dunham, James(A)	1836	July 12	Darke	03	11	10
Dunham, John C.(E)	1819	Aug. 18	Hamilton	15	21	08

PURCHASER	YEAR	DATE	RESIDENCE	R	T	S
Duning, Michael(B)	1834	Jan. 28	Switzerland	02	03	35
Duning, Michael(B)	1837	June 26	Switzerland	02	03	36
Duning, Michael(B)	1832	Oct. 12	Switzerland	02	03	36
Dunkin, Amos(A)	1808	March 30	Miami	05	06	24
Dunkin, Amos(A)	1812	Nov. 13	Miami	05	06	24
Dunkin, Amos(A)	1813	Aug. 10	Hamilton	05	06	24
Dunkin, Isaac(A)	1828	Dec. 04	Miami	05	06	02
Dunkin, Isaiah(A)	1837	Feb. 07	Miami	02	14	27
Dunkin, Jesse(A)	1818	Jan. 17	Miami	05	06	02
Dunkin, Mary(A)	1829	April 08	Miami	05	06	02
Dunkin, Peter(E)	1815	Jan. 06	Ohio	13	12	12
Dunkin, Richard(E)	1815	Sept. 22	Montgomery	13	12	02
Dunkin, William(B)	1815	Jan. 06	Montgomery	02	10	02
Dunkin, William(E)	1827	Oct. 26	Union(Ind)	14	15	30
Dunlap, Alexander(C)	1814	Feb. 08	Champaign	12	04	08
Dunlap, James(B)	1835	Aug. 21	Switzerland	02	02	19
Dunlap, James(C)	1811	Sept. 18	Champaign	11	05	02
Dunlap, James(C)	1812	Nov. 14	Champaign	11	05	15
Dunlap, James(C)	1816	Dec. 02	Champaign	11	05	09
Dunlavey, Francis(A)	1815	Jan. 28	Warren	02	07	13
Dunlavy, Frances(B)	1817	Nov. 22	Warren	02	07	36
Dunlavy, Francis(A)	1813	April 16	Warren	02	06	05
Dunlavy, Francis(C)	1806	April 04	Warren	09	05	21
Dunlavy, Francis(C)	1813	April 16	Warren	11	04	23
Dunlavy, Francis(C)	1813	Dec. 17	Warren	03	05	11
Dunlop, Alexander(A)	1807	Sept. 09	Miami	05	07	05
Dunlop, Alexander(A)	1814	Aug. 27	Miami	04	09	17
Dunlop, Alexander(C)	1814	Jan. 07	Champaign	12	04	08
Dunlop, James(C)	1811	Sept. 18	Champaign	11	05	09
Dunlop, James(C)	1812	May 07	Kentucky	11	05	02
Dunn, Gershom(B)	1831	Nov. 29	Dearborn(Ind	03	07	24
Dunn, James Jnr.(B)	1816	March 26	Butler	01	10	20
Dunn, James(A)	1802	Oct. 06	Hamilton	02	03	11
Dunn, James(A)	1831	Nov. 07	Belmont	04	10	12
Dunn, James(A)	1837	Oct. 24	Belmont	03	13	29
Dunn, James(A)	1837	Oct. 24	Belmont	04	11	19
Dunn, Jno.(C)	1814	Feb. 28	Champaign	13	04	06
Dunn, John S.(B)	1835	March 25	Darke	01	17	24
Dunn, John S.(B)	1836	June 07	Darke	01	17	24
Dunn, John(B)	1824	Nov. 25	Kentucky	04	02	24
Dunn, John(B)	1838	Jan. 06	HendricksInd	02	03	07
Dunn, Nehemiah(A)	1813	March 10	Hamilton	01	03	28
Dunn, Robert(A)	1831	May 21	Shelby	04	10	12
Dunn, Silas(E)	1813	Dec. 20	Ross	13	15	09
Dunn, Simeon(C)	1817	Dec. 29	Greene	10	04	31
Dunn, Thomas(A)	1814	Nov. 17	Warren	03	05	08
Dunn, Thomas(B)	1837	Feb. 17	Darke	01	17	24
Dunn, William(B)	1833	Aug. 06	Cincinnati	01	07	18
Dunn, Wm.(B)	1834	May 09	Cincinnati	01	07	18
Dunning, Michael(B)	1836	Dec. 13	Switzerland	03	04	26
Dunwoody, James(A)	1837	Feb. 11	Darke	02	15	19
Dunwoody, Samuel(A)	1806	Jan. 06	Greene	06	03	10
Dunwoody, Samuel(A)	1835	July 28	Darke	03	12	10
Dunwoody, Samuel(C)	1804	Sept. 03	Montgomery	05	03	11
Durham, David(B)	1837	March 01	Dearborn(Ind	02	05	08
Durham, George(B)	1832	May 31	Dearborn(Ind	03	06	33
Durst, Abraham(B)	1805	Nov. 29	Montgomery	01	10	12
Durst, Daniel(A)	1815	Sept. 02	Ross	03	11	27
Dusky, Dennis(B)	1807	June 20	Hamilton	01	09	29
Dusky, Lemon(B)	1817	Sept. 13	Hamilton	02	02	25
Duterrow, John(A)	1815	March 21	Butler	01	03	11
Duttarrow, Henry(B)	1818	Sept. 24	Warren	01	15	28
Duttarrow, Peter(B)	1818	Sept. 24	Warren	01	15	28
Duttero, Peter(A)	1814	Aug. 16	Wayne(Ind)	02	03	19
Dutton, David(B)	1810	Dec. 15	Highland	01	05	17
Duvaill, Harden(A)	1837	July 24	Darke	02	13	17
Duvall, Absalom(A)	1837	July 24	Darke	02	13	17
Duvall, Dan'l.(A)	1829	Dec. 10	Darke	02	13	17
Duvall, Daniel(A)	1819	Aug. 27	Preble	02	13	17

PURCHASER	YEAR	DATE	RESIDENCE	R	T	S
Duvall, Harden(A)	1836	Aug. 30	Darke	02	13	17
Duvall, John(A)	1819	Aug. 18	Preble	02	13	20
Dwelle, Elisha(A)	1836	Aug. 29	Cincinnati	01	15	29
Dwelle, Elisha(A)	1836	Oct. 14	Cincinnati	01	15	28
Dwelle, Elisha(E)	1836	Aug. 29	Cincinnati	11	10	33
Dwiggins, James(B)	1810	Dec. 13	Clinton	01	15	17
Dwiggins, James(B)	1813	Oct. 20	Wayne(Ind)	01	15	17
Dwinger, Barnet Hy.(E)	1837	April 28	Cincinnati	11	11	25
Dwyer, Edward(A)	1818	Dec. 23	Champaign	07	01	07
Dye, James(E)	1837	July 13	Miami	15	22	34
Dye, James(E)	1838	Aug. 20	Miami	14	22	25
Dye, James(E)	1838	Aug. 20	Miami	15	22	30
Dye, John M.(C)	1814	Aug. 13	Miami	11	01	09
Dye, Miner(C)	1831	Jan. 11	Champaign	12	03	31
Dye, Samuel(C)	1806	Sept. 09	Warren	09	02	19
Dye, Samuel(C)	1811	Dec. 11	Miami	09	02	19
Dyer, Edward(A)	1807	Feb. 13	Warren	02	04	08
Dyer, George(E)	1832	March 05	Wayne(Ind)	14	18	12
Dyer, Joseph(A)	1819	July 03	Randolph(Ind	01	12	31
Dyer, William(E)	1814	Dec. 28	Fayette	13	15	27
Dyke, Hyronimous(E)	1837	Jan. 19	Randolph(Ind	14	19	12
Dynes, Chambers(C)	1825	Jan. 18	Clark	09	06	11
Dynes, William(A)	1805	Dec. 14	Warren	01	06	09
Eads, Jonathan(A)	1810	Feb. 16	Hamilton	01	03	31
Eads, Jonathan(B)	1829	Dec. 11	Franklin(Ind	02	09	35
Eads, William H.(B)	1814	Dec. 10	Franklin(Ind	02	09	05
Eads, William H.(B)	1815	Jan. 23	Franklin(Ind	02	08	01
Eads, William H.(B)	1818	Jan. 07	Franklin(Ind	02	10	15
Eads, William(B)	1816	April 23	Dearborn(Ind	02	08	11
Eagin, John(E)	1811	Oct. 22	Ind.Territory	12	13	14
Earhart, Martin(A)	1822	Feb. 28	Darke	02	12	02
Earnhart, John(A)	1819	Dec. 07	Warren	03	10	19
Easton, Redwood(C)	1813	Nov. 30	Champaign	10	05	21
Easton, Samuel(E)	1814	Aug. 23	Champaign	12	15	23
Eaton, Daniel(E)	1811	Oct. 23	Ind.Territory	13	14	18
Eaton, Thomas A. R.(B)	1815	Jan. 24	Adams	01	11	03
Eaton, William(B)	1814	Jan. 13	Kentucky	01	11	03
Eaves, Henry(B)	1813	Oct. 26	Jefferson	03	03	35
Ebersol, Jacob(C)	1812	July 23	Champaign	09	04	36
Ebersol, John(C)	1812	Nov. 30	Hamilton	10	04	33
Ebersole, Jacob(C)	1817	Dec. 02	Champaign	09	04	35
Ebersolt, Volentine(A)	1816	June 04	Maryland	03	07	17
Ebert, John Jr.(C)	1826	Jan. 28	Champaign	10	03	06
Ebert, John Junr.(C)	1829	Sept. 24	Champaign	11	03	05
Ebert, John(C)	1811	Dec. 20	Champaign	11	03	05
Ebielsizer, Henry(C)	1830	Feb. 03	Champaign	12	03	31
Eblen, John(E)	1834	June 24	Randolph(Ind	15	22	14
Eblen, John(E)	1836	Dec. 19	Jay Co.,Ind.	15	22	14
Eblen, John(E)	1837	April 21	Jay Co.,Ind.	15	22	11
Eblen, John(E)	1837	Oct. 28	Jay Co.,Ind.	15	22	23
Eddings, William(A)	1828	Nov. 05	Preble	02	09	09
Eddington, Samuel(A)	1819	April 26	Montgomery	02	10	12
Eddy, John(C)	1806	Feb. 25	Warren	03	04	11
Eddy, John(C)	1806	Feb. 27	Warren	03	04	11
Eden, Benjamin(A)	1809	July 14	Darke	02	12	28
Edes, James(A)	1805	July 23	Dearborn(Ind	01	02	07
Edgar, Andrew(C)	1811	Oct. 10	Champaign	09	06	35
Edgar, Andrew(C)	1816	Sept. 07	Champaign	09	05	08
Edgar, Andrew(C)	1816	Dec. 02	Champaign	09	06	35
Edgar, Archibald(A)	1817	June 12	Kentucky	02	10	20
Edgar, John W.(C)	1811	Oct. 10	Champaign	09	06	35
Edgar, John W.(C)	1816	Dec. 02	Champaign	09	06	35
Edgar, Robert(C)	1802	Dec. 30	Hamilton	07	02	33
Edgar, Robert(C)	1804	Dec. 29	Montgomery	07	02	26
Edgar, Thomas(A)	1825	Oct. 24	Darke	02	10	14
Edger, John(A)	1825	June 15	Kentucky	02	10	11
Edger, Robert(C)	1801	Dec. 30	Hamilton	07	02	33
Edgerton, Samuel(A)	1815	Nov. 27	Warren	01	07	35
Edgerton, Samuel(A)	1816	Jan. 26	Warren	01	07	26

PURCHASER	YEAR	DATE	RESIDENCE	R	T	S
Edingfield, John(D)	1813	March 01	Butler	02	03	11
Edman, Christen(E)	1831	July 01	Randolph(Ind	13	18	11
Edmiston, David(C)	1815	July 31	Champaign	10	03	06
Edmond, Christian(E)	1837	March 27	Randolph(Ind	13	18	14
Edward, Joseph(B)	1836	Sept. 19	Hamilton	02	03	17
Edwards, Abraham(A)	1806	July 25	FortWayneInd	05	08	18
Edwards, Abraham(A)	1806	Dec. 29	Ind.Territry	06	07	28
Edwards, Abraham(C)	1805	Dec. 27	FortWayneInd	11	02	28
Edwards, Abraham(C)	1807	Jan. 13	FortWayneInd	11	01	02
Edwards, Alexis(E)	1838	Oct. 02	Richland	14	22	26
Edwards, Benj'n.(E)	1834	Jan. 04	Randolph(Ind	13	19	28
Edwards, Benj'n.(E)	1834	Jan. 13	Randolph(Ind	13	19	21
Edwards, David D.(A)	1831	Feb. 10	Darke	02	11	14
Edwards, Eli(A)	1818	March 11	Darke	02	11	14
Edwards, Eli(E)	1831	Feb. 15	Randolph(Ind	14	19	04
Edwards, Jesse(C)	1804	Oct. 13	Montgomery	09	02	09
Edwards, Jesse(C)	1818	April 18	Miami	13	03	35
Edwards, John(C)	1806	Aug. 14	Montgomery	09	06	23
Edwards, John(C)	1806	Aug. 14	Montgomery	09	06	23
Edwards, John(C)	1806	Oct. 28	Montgomery	10	05	01
Edwards, Jonathan(E)	1817	Sept. 29	Wayne(Ind)	14	20	29
Edwards, Jonathan(E)	1835	Oct. 05	Randolph(Ind	14	20	30
Edwards, Joshua(A)	1830	Oct. 01	Darke	02	11	13
Edwards, Nathan R.(E)	1836	May 27	Randolph(Ind	14	20	30
Edwards, Robert(E)	1836	March 28	Randolph(Ind	13	20	12
Edwards, Spencer(A)	1829	Aug. 12	Darke	01	11	32
Edwards, William(B)	1824	June 09	Wayne(Ind)	01	13	15
Edwards, William(E)	1833	Feb. 23	Randolph(Ind	14	20	30
Egans, William(E)	1832	Feb. 21	Franklin(Ind	11	12	13
Egans, William(E)	1832	June 08	Franklin(Ind	11	12	13
Egar, John(E)	1814	Dec. 10	Franklin(Ind	12	13	13
Egbert, Cornelius(A)	1819	Feb. 02	Warren	03	07	17
Egbert, Henry(C)	1830	Jan. 16	Warren	11	03	13
Egbert, John(A)	1819	Feb. 02	Preble	02	09	05
Egbert, Wm.(E)	1838	Feb. 09	Franklin(Ind	13	11	29
Eggers, Daniel(B)	1813	Dec. 11	Franklin(Ind	01	12	35
Eggers, James(B)	1813	April 20	Franklin(Ind	01	11	02
Eggleston, Miles C.(B)	1829	Dec. 09	Franklin(Ind	02	09	06
Eggleston, Miles C.(B)	1829	Dec. 09	Franklin(Ind	02	09	06
Eggman, Isaac(C)	1811	July 03	Champaign	11	05	02
Eggman, Isaac(C)	1816	Aug. 01	Champaign	11	05	02
Egman, Isaac(C)	1828	Jan. 05	Champaign	10	03	29
Ehler, Michael(B)	1818	July 17	Montgomery	03	07	01
Eichelberger, Frederick Jr.(A)	1831	June 22	Miami	03	08	35
Eichelberger, John(A)	1817	July 07	Pennsylvania	03	07	29
Eick, Henry Ten(A)	1831	Sept. 12	Miami	02	11	05
Eidson, John(A)	1819	Oct. 30	Preble	03	07	17
Eisenhour, Jacob(A)	1833	March 25	Montgomery	01	12	15
Elbert, John(C)	1811	May 01	Champaign	11	05	12
Elbzroth, John(E)	1818	July 02	Preble	14	20	32
Elder, Charles(C)	1814	Dec. 03	Maryland	10	03	28
Elder, Dele(B)	1811	Oct. 09	Dearborn(Ind	01	05	09
Elder, John(B)	1834	Jan. 28	Dearborn(Ind	03	04	14
Elder, William(B)	1814	Nov. 28	Warren	01	12	35
Eldon, Thomas(B)	1824	June 09	Franklin(Ind	02	08	01
Eledge, James(A)	1815	Jan. 24	Montgomery	06	03	22
Eley, Jacob(E)	1838	Oct. 02	Jay Co.,Ind.	15	22	19
Eley, Martin(E)	1837	Sept. 21	Randolph(Ind	14	22	24
Eliason, Joshua(E)	1814	March 17	Montgomery	14	16	09
Elkin, Robert(A)	1814	May 31	Pennsylvania	01	03	30
Elleman, Enos(A)	1823	Aug. 18	Darke	04	10	32
Eller, Aaron(A)	1831	Aug. 17	Montgomery	04	07	26
Eller, Abraham(A)	1828	June 06	Montgomery	04	09	27
Eller, Abraham(A)	1831	Aug. 17	Miami	04	09	27
Eller, Daniel(A)	1814	Aug. 18	Montgomery	05	05	06
Eller, Daniel(A)	1832	March 19	Montgomery	04	07	14
Eller, Henry Jr.(A)	1825	Aug. 25	Miami	04	09	26
Eller, Joseph(A)	1831	Aug. 05	Montgomery	04	09	22
Eller, Leonard(A)	1813	March 31	Miami	05	06	23

PURCHASER	YEAR	DATE	RESIDENCE	R	T	S
Eller, Leonard(A)	1814	April 12	Miami	05	06	26
Ellerman, Herod Hy.(B)	1838	April 23	Franklin(Ind	03	05	35
Ellerman, Herod Hy.(B)	1838	Dec. 26	Franklin(Ind	03	04	03
Ellerman, John Henry(B)	1836	Feb. 01	Hamilton	02	08	21
Ellerman, William(A)	1806	Sept. 02	Warren	05	07	27
Ellerman, William(B)	1806	June 25	Warren	01	13	02
Ellet, Abraham(B)	1807	March 21	Warren	01	14	31
Ellier, Leonard(A)	1806	June 04	Montgomery	05	06	35
Ellier, Leonard(A)	1806	July 24	Montgomery	05	06	26
Ellingsworth, Stephen(A)	1813	March 16	Butler	02	04	12
Elliot, Abraham Esquire(B)	1807	April 20	Tennessee	01	14	30
Elliot, Abraham(E)	1816	Oct. 02	Wayne(Ind)	13	18	36
Elliot, Ebenezer(A)	1806	Dec. 04	Butler	01	06	26
Elliot, Ebenezer(A)	1807	Aug. 28	Butler	01	07	28
Elliot, Israael(B)	1811	Dec. 11	Wayne(Ind)	02	13	12
Elliot, Robert(A)	1818	Nov. 24	Miami	05	09	05
Elliot, Thomas(A)	1803	March 21	Hamilton	01	03	33
Elliott, Abner(A)	1829	March 05	Preble	01	09	11
Elliott, Abraham(E)	1811	Oct. 24	Wayne(Ind)	13	17	24
Elliott, Abraham(E)	1812	Feb. 19	Wayne(Ind)	13	17	25
Elliott, Asa(B)	1818	Feb. 25	Franklin(Ind	01	12	30
Elliott, Asa(B)	1818	April 08	Franklin(Ind	01	12	13
Elliott, Benj'n.(B)	1825	Sept. 02	Wayne(Ind)	01	15	15
Elliott, Benjamin(E)	1814	Jan. 04	Franklin(Ind	13	13	10
Elliott, Daniel(B)	1814	Oct. 19	Butler	01	11	12
Elliott, Ebenezer(A)	1813	April 14	Preble	01	07	28
Elliott, Exum(E)	1815	Nov. 06	Wayne(Ind)	14	16	06
Elliott, Isaac(B)	1820	Oct. 17	Wayne(Ind)	01	16	23
Elliott, Israel(E)	1813	Sept. 27	Wayne(Ind)	14	16	20
Elliott, James C.(C)	1811	Aug. 19	Champaign	12	04	35
Elliott, Jerremiah(E)	1811	Oct. 24	Wayne(Ind)	13	17	24
Elliott, Job(A)	1811	Dec. 20	Preble	02	06	20
Elliott, Job(B)	1814	Aug. 25	Preble	01	15	25
Elliott, Job(B)	1817	Dec. 16	Wayne(Ind)	01	15	26
Elliott, John(A)	1836	June 14	Miami	03	11	10
Elliott, Marshall(B)	1838	May 21	Dearborn(Ind	03	04	21
Elliott, Nathan(A)	1815	Aug. 08	Preble	02	06	17
Elliott, Nathan(B)	1816	April 06	Preble	01	15	13
Elliott, Nathan(B)	1834	May 23	Wayne(Ind)	01	16	24
Elliott, Nathan(B)	1836	July 26	Wayne(Ind)	01	16	23
Elliott, Riley(B)	1832	March 09	Dearborn(Ind	02	06	23
Elliott, Riley(B)	1834	March 13	Dearborn(Ind	02	06	13
Elliott, Rily(B)	1815	Nov. 06	Cincinnati	02	06	36
Elliott, Robt.(B)	1814	Oct. 19	Butler	01	11	12
Elliott, Sam'l.(B)	1831	Oct. 20	Dearborn(Ind	01	06	30
Elliott, Samuel(B)	1832	April 30	Dearborn(Ind	01	06	30
Elliott, Seth(E)	1835	Jan. 24	Wayne(Ind)	13	21	27
Elliott, Spencer(E)	1831	May 30	Wayne(Ind)	13	18	35
Elliott, Stephen(B)	1831	Sept. 24	Wayne(Ind)	01	15	26
Elliott, Thomas(A)	1808	Aug. 02	Butler	01	03	33
Elliott, Thomas(C)	1826	Feb. 07	Clark	10	04	26
Elliott, Washington(B)	1814	Dec. 06	Wayne(Ind)	01	13	32
Elliott, Washington(B)	1817	Sept. 22	Wayne(Ind)	01	13	29
Elliott, William(C)	1806	March 10	Champaign	10	04	25
Elliott, William(C)	1811	Dec. 11	Champaign	10	04	25
Elliott, William(E)	1816	Feb. 12	Wayne(Ind)	13	17	10
Elliott, William(E)	1831	Aug. 29	Wayne(Ind)	13	17	09
Ellis, Bevan(E)	1836	Oct. 04	Randolph(Ind	14	19	25
Ellis, Enos(B)	1817	May 27	Switzerland	02	02	12
Ellis, Enos(B)	1832	Sept. 18	Switzerland	02	03	35
Ellis, Isaiah(E)	1836	Nov. 29	Highland	14	19	25
Ellis, Jackson(A)	1836	Nov. 01	Darke	02	15	31
Ellis, John(A)	1829	Jan. 24	Logan	08	02	34
Ellis, John(B)	1814	Nov. 09	Wayne(Ind)	02	13	35
Ellis, John(B)	1836	Feb. 09	Dearborn(Ind	02	05	06
Ellis, John(C)	1805	July 20	Montgomery	06	01	05
Ellis, John(E)	1815	April 22	Wayne(Ind)	14	15	18
Ellis, Jonathan M.(E)	1836	May 19	Highland	15	18	06
Ellis, Jonathan M.(E)	1837	Feb. 22	Wayne(Ind)	15	18	06

PURCHASER	YEAR	DATE	RESIDENCE	R	T	S
Ellis, Lewis(E)	1836	Nov. 29	Highland	14	19	25
Ellis, Otis(B)	1818	March 14	Cincinnati	02	04	33
Ellis, Robert(A)	1833	Feb. 05	Logan	08	01	02
Ellis, Robert(A)	1836	Jan. 26	Logan	08	01	02
Ellis, Shubal(E)	1816	Nov. 13	Clinton	14	20	18
Ellis, Thomas(A)	1831	Aug. 10	Logan	08	01	02
Ellis, Thomas(A)	1833	Feb. 05	Logan	08	01	02
Ellis, William(A)	1830	June 21	Shelby	05	09	21
Ellis, William(C)	1805	July 22	Montgomery	09	02	27
Ellis, William(C)	1805	Dec. 14	Montgomery	09	02	28
Ellison, Elisha(E)	1834	Oct. 22	Fayette	11	12	12
Ellison, Elisha(E)	1835	Jan. 06	Fayette	11	12	12
Ellison, Obediah(B)	1826	Nov. 13	Dearborn(Ind	02	07	02
Elliston, Amos(E)	1833	July 09	Randolph(Ind	13	18	17
Ellsworth, Jesse(C)	1816	Aug. 01	Madison	08	06	05
Ellsworth, William(E)	1837	May 16	Shelby	14	21	25
Ellsworth, William(E)	1837	May 16	Shelby	15	21	30
Elmore, Archelaus(E)	1817	Aug. 23	Tennessee	12	17	01
Elmore, Archelaus(E)	1817	Aug. 23	Tennessee	13	18	34
Elmore, Joseph(A)	1814	Sept. 28	Miami	04	09	14
Elmore, Joseph(A)	1831	Aug. 25	Miami	04	09	35
Elsroad, Frederick(A)	1815	Oct. 13	Preble	03	05	01
Elstner, John(A)	1836	Aug. 30	Hamilton	02	13	20
Elstner, John(A)	1837	Feb. 01	Cincinnati	01	13	14
Elston, George(A)	1836	Oct. 18	Darke	01	13	26
Elston, George(A)	1837	April 12	Darke	01	13	26
Elston, Levi(A)	1816	Aug. 31	Greene	01	12	26
Elston, Peter K.(A)	1822	Feb. 15	Darke	01	12	19
Elsworth, Jacob(C)	1811	Jan. 21	Champaign	10	06	19
Elsworth, Jacob(C)	1811	Oct. 26	Champaign	10	06	20
Elsworth, John(C)	1814	March 15	Champaign	10	06	21
Elsworth, John(C)	1814	June 17	Champaign	09	05	12
Elsworth, John(C)	1816	June 08	Champaign	12	02	18
Elsworth, William(C)	1830	Oct. 21	Shelby	12	02	24
Elton, Joseph(A)	1836	Sept. 23	Warren	02	15	32
Eltzroad, Nicholas(A)	1807	Jan. 27	Montgomery	03	05	19
Eltzroad, Nicholas(A)	1812	April 15	Preble	03	05	19
Eltzroth, John(E)	1818	July 29	Preble	14	20	13
Eltzroth, John(E)	1818	July 15	Preble	14	20	33
Elursolt, Valentine(A)	1817	June 30	Preble	02	09	09
Elwell, Abraham(B)	1814	Aug. 06	Montgomery	02	10	10
Elwell, Amiriah(A)	1805	Aug. 05	Butler	01	04	23
Elwell, Amiriah(B)	1808	Jan. 12	Butler	02	10	12
Ely, Adam(B)	1807	Jan. 28	Butler	02	12	13
Ely, Adam(E)	1812	July 02	Ind.Territry	14	13	18
Ely, Isaac(C)	1804	Nov. 30	Greene	07	02	10
Emanuel, Joseph(B)	1840	April 30	Indiana	03	04	05
Embree, Amos(A)	1805	June 25	Butler	02	08	33
Embree, Amos(A)	1806	Dec. 11	Montgomery	03	04	23
Embree, Amos(A)	1812	April 15	Preble	03	04	23
Embree, David(E)	1811	Oct. 28	Cincinnati	13	16	18
Embree, Isaac Jr.(A)	1829	Feb. 04	Miami	05	06	02
Embree, Isaac(A)	1806	May 22	Montgomery	05	06	10
Embree, Jacob(A)	1807	April 09	Montgomery	05	07	29
Embree, Jacob(A)	1807	April 09	Montgomery	05	07	29
Embree, Jesse(B)	1818	April 06	Cincinnati	03	07	23
Embree, Jesse(B)	1818	April 06	Cincinnati	03	07	24
Embree, Jesse(B)	1818	April 06	Cincinnati	03	04	29
Embree, Jesse(B)	1818	April 06	Cincinnati	03	07	24
Embree, Jesse(B)	1818	April 06	Cincinnati	03	04	11
Embree, Jesse(B)	1818	April 06	Cincinnati	03	04	29
Embree, Jesse(B)	1818	April 07	Hamilton	03	04	11
Embree, Jesse(B)	1818	April 07	Hamilton	03	04	11
Embree, Jesse(B)	1818	April 07	Hamilton	03	04	12
Embree, Jesse(B)	1818	April 07	Hamilton	03	04	12
Embree, Jesse(B)	1818	June 02	Cincinnati	03	04	12
Embree, Jesse(B)	1818	June 02	Cincinnati	03	05	26
Embree, Jesse(B)	1818	June 02	Cincinnati	02	02	01
Embree, Jesse(B)	1818	June 02	Cincinnati	02	02	01

PURCHASER	YEAR	DATE	RESIDENCE	R	T	S
Embree, Jesse(B)	1818	June 02	Cincinnati	02	03	13
Embree, Jesse(B)	1818	June 02	Cincinnati	02	03	12
Embrick, Michael(A)	1805	Aug. 01	Pennsylvania	03	05	05
Emerick, John W.(A)	1832	Dec. 06	Montgomery	01	12	26
Emert, Andrew(E)	1836	Oct. 08	Montgomery	15	20	06
Emery, Thomas(A)	1836	July 14	Hamilton	03	11	21
Emmard, Peter(B)	1809	Jan. 11	Dearborn(Ind	02	12	26
Emmerson, James(A)	1816	April 30	Butler	01	10	30
Emmerson, James(A)	1816	Dec. 04	Darke	01	10	20
Emmert, Joseph(A)	1817	Oct. 08	Maryland	05	07	24
Emmitt, John(B)	1816	April 24	Wayne(Ind)	02	12	23
Emmons, Job(A)	1831	Oct. 22	Hamilton	03	08	36
Emmons, William(A)	1836	Dec. 14	Hamilton	02	15	31
Emrick, Christopher(A)	1804	July 31	Montgomery	04	03	24
Emrick, Christopher(A)	1805	Oct. 02	Montgomery	03	06	33
Emrick, Christopher(A)	1805	Oct. 02	Montgomery	03	06	20
Emrick, Christopher(A)	1805	Oct. 09	Montgomery	04	03	35
Emrick, Jacob(B)	1833	Jan. 15	Darke	01	18	23
Emrick, Jacob(B)	1833	Jan. 15	Darke	01	18	26
Emrick, John(A)	1804	Aug. 16	Montgomery	05	02	05
Emrick, John(B)	1834	March 22	Darke	01	18	26
Emrick, John(B)	1835	Aug. 11	Darke	01	18	25
Emrick, Michael(?)	1814	Oct. 11	?	?	?	?
Emrick, Michael(A)	1813	Dec. 06	Montgomery	04	03	10
Emrick, Michael(A)	1832	March 08	Montgomery	01	11	15
Emrick, William Junr.(A)	1804	Aug. 10	Montgomery	04	03	24
Emrick, William(A)	1804	Aug. 10	Montgomery	05	02	04
Emrick, Wm.(A)	1814	Oct. 11	Montgomery	04	03	09
Enderreaden, John Hy.(E)	1837	Sept. 15	Cincinnati	12	11	14
Endsley, Andrew(B)	1805	June 03	Ind.Territry	02	13	25
Endsley, Hugh(B)	1808	Jan. 11	Dearborn(Ind	02	13	13
Endsley, John(B)	1805	June 15	Hamilton	02	13	36
Endsley, Thomas(E)	1814	Feb. 23	Franklin(Ind	13	15	22
Engel, John Ulrick(B)	1817	Dec. 02	Cincinnati	02	07	29
Engel, John Ulrick(B)	1831	Sept. 24	Dearborn(Ind	03	08	35
English, Charles(B)	1815	Sept. 19	Pennsylvania	01	04	28
English, John(B)	1815	Sept. 19	Pennsylvania	01	04	32
English, William(A)	1818	April 10	Warren	04	10	08
English, William(B)	1814	Aug. 09	Ind.Territory	01	03	26
Ennis, Thompson(C)	1801	Dec. 25	Hamilton	05	03	12
Enoch, Abner(A)	1812	Nov. 25	Butler	04	02	10
Enoch, Isaac(A)	1806	March 20	Butler	02	07	20
Enoch, Isaac(A)	1806	Oct. 29	Montgomery	01	07	23
Enoch, Isaac(A)	1810	Dec. 12	Preble	03	06	17
Enoch, Isaac(A)	1813	Oct. 13	Preble	03	06	08
Enoch, John(C)	1812	Nov. 04	Champaign	13	05	14
Enock, David(C)	1801	Dec. 31	Hamilton	04	02	24
Enock, John(C)	1801	Dec. 31	Hamilton	04	02	30
Ensey, Dennis(C)	1806	Aug. 09	Montgomery	11	02	23
Ent, Samuel M.(B)	1818	April 30	Hamilton	02	04	07
Enyard, Samuel(C)	1810	Feb. 23	Butler	03	02	08
Enyart, Lewis(A)	1836	Nov. 12	Butler	01	15	24
Enyart, Lewis(A)	1836	Dec. 07	Butler	01	15	36
Enyeart, John(C)	1817	June 13	Miami	11	03	36
Enyrt, Benjamin(A)	1804	June 29	Butler	03	02	12
Eppig, George Adam(B)	1836	Nov. 26	Franklin(Ind	03	09	13
Eppley, Adam(C)	1827	Nov. 17	Clark	09	04	21
Erb, David(B)	1816	June 08	Franklin(Ind	02	10	30
Erhartt, Jacob(A)	1826	Jan. 13	Preble	01	07	01
Ernnout, John(B)	1818	Sept. 21	Cincinnati	03	04	14
Ernst, Andrew H.(A)	1818	Jan. 23	Cincinnati	04	11	24
Ernst, Andrew H.(C)	1818	Feb. 14	Cincinnati	14	04	32
Ernst, Andrew H.(C)	1818	May 15	Cincinnati	04	11	24
Errick, John(A)	1811	June 12	Butler	02	04	29
Erven, Isaac(A)	1836	Oct. 24	Hamilton	01	15	28
Erven, William(A)	1836	Sept. 23	Hamilton	01	15	20
Erven, William(A)	1836	Oct. 24	Hamilton	01	15	28
Erven, Wm. H.(A)	1838	Jan. 27	Hamilton	01	15	28
Erving, John(C)	1802	Dec. 29	Hamilton	06	02	27

PURCHASER	YEAR	DATE	RESIDENCE	R	T	S
Erving, John(C)	1802	Dec. 29	Hamilton	06	02	33
Erwin, John(E)	1836	May 26	Wayne(Ind)	14	19	26
Erwin, John(E)	1836	May 26	Wayne(Ind)	14	19	26
Erwin, John(E)	1836	May 26	Wayne(Ind)	14	19	35
Eschman, Peter(A)	1833	April 01	Cincinnati	02	12	24
Esley, John(E)	1817	Oct. 24	Franklin(Ind	14	14	30
Espey, Hugh Sr.(B)	1814	Nov. 22	Pennsylvania	01	03	17
Espey, Hugh(B)	1814	Oct. 14	Pennsylvania	01	03	07
Espey, Hugh(B)	1816	July 29	Dearborn(Ind	01	03	08
Espey, Hugh(B)	1817	Aug. 01	Dearborn(Ind	02	04	35
Espey, John(B)	1814	Jan. 25	Adams	02	04	35
Espey, Robt.(B)	1815	Sept. 18	Dearborn(Ind	01	04	28
Espy, Hugh(B)	1815	Sept. 25	Pennsylvania	01	03	07
Espy, Hugh(B)	1815	Sept. 25	Pennsylvania	01	03	07
Espy, Robt.(B)	1815	Oct. 03	Dearborn(Ind	01	03	06
Espy, Thomas(C)	1832	Feb. 28	Champaign	13	03	02
Espy, William Patterson(C)	1832	March 16	Cincinnati	13	02	32
Essley, John(E)	1815	Jan. 09	Kentucky	13	14	25
Estabrook, Warren(A)	1837	May 30	Montgomery	01	12	07
Este, David K.(A)	1815	Feb. 24	Cincinnati	06	03	17
Este, David K.(A)	1815	March 01	Cincinnati	02	11	02
Este, David K.(A)	1837	Jan. 18	Cincinnati	02	14	32
Este, David K.(A)	1837	Jan. 18	Cincinnati	02	14	32
Este, David K.(A)	1837	Jan. 18	Cincinnati	01	14	19
Este, David K.(A)	1837	Jan. 18	Cincinnati	03	11	06
Este, David K.(A)	1837	Jan. 18	Cincinnati	03	11	06
Este, David K.(B)	1815	March 25	Cincinnati	01	08	17
Este, David K.(B)	1817	Dec. 19	Cincinnati	03	02	07
Este, David K.(B)	1818	Jan. 19	Cincinnati	03	04	26
Este, David K.(B)	1818	Jan. 19	Cincinnati	03	04	27
Este, David K.(C)	1815	Feb. 24	Cincinnati	09	02	19
Este, David K.(C)	1815	March 20	Cincinnati	10	01	06
Este, David K.(E)	1837	Jan. 18	Cincinnati	13	20	14
Este, David K.(E)	1837	Jan. 18	Cincinnati	13	20	14
Este, David K.(E)	1837	Jan. 18	Cincinnati	14	21	03
Este, David K.(E)	1837	Jan. 18	Cincinnati	14	21	06
Esteb, Isaac(B)	1807	Aug. 12	Kentucky	01	12	04
Estell, Daniel(A)	1837	May 22	Cincinnati	01	14	31
Estes, Obadiah(B)	1806	Aug. 01	Dearborn(Ind	02	10	33
Estes, Obadiah(E)	1813	July 16	Franklin(Ind	13	13	26
Estop, Isaac(B)	1808	Jan. 23	Dearborn(Ind	01	12	10
Etter, John(A)	1811	April 29	Montgomery	04	03	06
Etter, Michael(A)	1819	June 09	Miami	05	07	06
Eubank, John(B)	1817	June 18	Dearborn(Ind	01	06	18
Eulass, Jacob(C)	1804	Sept. 03	Warren	05	03	26
Eury, David(A)	1836	Dec. 07	Maryland	03	11	17
Eury, David(A)	1836	Dec. 07	Montgomery	03	11	18
Eury, John(A)	1836	Dec. 07	Montgomery	03	11	18
Evans, Benjamin(A)	1807	Sept. 04	Warren	01	07	30
Evans, Benjamin(A)	1807	Sept. 04	Warren	01	07	29
Evans, Benjamin(A)	1807	Sept. 25	Warren	01	07	30
Evans, Benjamin(E)	1811	Nov. 18	Wayne(Ind)	14	17	33
Evans, Benjamin(E)	1811	Nov. 18	Wayne(Ind)	14	17	22
Evans, Ebenezer(E)	1838	Nov. 05	Belmont	15	22	03
Evans, Edward W.(E)	1832	Dec. 05	Randolph(Ind	14	21	25
Evans, Edward(C)	1811	Aug. 21	Champaign	10	05	20
Evans, Edward(C)	1812	July 07	Champaign	10	05	27
Evans, George(C)	1813	Jan. 16	Champaign	11	05	09
Evans, George(C)	1813	May 10	Champaign	11	05	11
Evans, Isaac Jr.(C)	1811	Aug. 05	Champaign	11	05	01
Evans, Isaac Jr.(C)	1812	Nov. 20	Champaign	11	05	01
Evans, James T.(E)	1836	June 17	Randolph(Ind	14	21	35
Evans, James T.(E)	1838	Aug. 18	Randolph(Ind	14	21	36
Evans, Jared(B)	1816	Oct. 30	Dearborn(Ind	02	06	18
Evans, Joseph(A)	1805	Aug. 17	Butler	06	03	01
Evans, Joseph(A)	1806	Nov. 05	Montgomery	04	07	13
Evans, Joseph(A)	1806	Dec. 29	Montgomery	04	07	13
Evans, Joseph(A)	1807	Feb. 14	Montgomery	05	06	21
Evans, Joseph(A)	1807	March 23	Montgomery	05	06	21

PURCHASER	YEAR	DATE	RESIDENCE	R	T	S
Evans, Joseph(A)	1807	July 01	Miami	05	06	09
Evans, Joseph(A)	1807	Aug. 05	Miami	05	06	18
Evans, Joseph(A)	1808	Sept. 14	Montgomery	02	11	09
Evans, Joseph(A)	1812	April 15	Miami	04	07	13
Evans, Joseph(B)	1817	Sept. 19	Cincinnati	02	07	05
Evans, Joseph(B)	1817	Sept. 19	Cincinnati	02	07	08
Evans, Joseph(E)	1811	Dec. 16	Warren	14	17	19
Evans, Joseph(E)	1811	Dec. 16	Warren	14	17	18
Evans, Joseph(E)	1811	Dec. 16	Warren	14	17	29
Evans, Joseph(E)	1811	Dec. 16	Warren	13	16	15
Evans, Joseph(E)	1811	Dec. 16	Warren	12	16	11
Evans, Joseph(E)	1818	Feb. 03	Cincinnati	14	16	33
Evans, Joseph(E)	1818	Feb. 03	Cincinnati	14	16	33
Evans, Robt.(A)	1827	Sept. 03	Montgomery	06	03	15
Evans, Samuel(B)	1813	Aug. 19	Dearborn(Ind	01	06	34
Evans, Samuel(B)	1836	July 30	Kentucky	01	08	21
Evans, Samuel(E)	1817	Sept. 06	Warren	13	17	27
Evans, Samuel(E)	1836	Oct. 17	Kentucky	14	21	20
Evans, William(A)	1806	May 05	Montgomery	01	03	28
Evans, William(A)	1811	Aug. 13	Butler	01	03	28
Evans, William(E)	1814	June 13	Franklin(Ind	12	12	22
Evans, William(E)	1837	Jan. 30	Clark	14	19	12
Eveleth, Amariah(B)	1817	July 28	Hamilton	01	02	18
Everett, Isaac(E)	1817	Oct. 23	Kentucky	14	20	21
Everill, Philo(B)	1813	Nov. 19	Warren	03	02	11
Everingham, Enoch(A)	1806	June 23	Butler	01	04	13
Everley, Martin(E)	1832	March 05	Randolph(Ind	14	21	20
Everman, Samuel(A)	1829	Dec. 09	Preble	02	09	33
Everman, Samuel(C)	1801	Dec. 31	Hamilton	05	02	02
Everton, Mary(B)	1805	April 12	Kentucky	01	13	09
Eving, John(C)	1802	Dec. 28	Hamilton	06	01	19
Eving, John(C)	1802	Dec. 31	Hamilton	06	01	05
Ewan, James(A)	1836	Oct. 25	Cincinnati	01	15	28
Ewan, Samuel(B)	1836	July 01	Dearborn(Ind	03	06	24
Ewbank, John(A)	1815	Nov. 07	Dearborn(Ind	01	06	18
Ewbank, John(B)	1811	Oct. 31	New Jersey	01	06	17
Ewbank, John(B)	1811	Nov. 09	New Jersey	01	06	17
Ewbank, John(B)	1817	May 28	?	01	06	17
Ewbank, John(B)	1817	May 28	?	01	06	20
Ewing, Alexander(A)	1815	Oct. 30	?	05	09	36
Ewing, Alexander(A)	1815	Oct. 30	?	05	09	26
Ewing, Alexander(A)	1815	Oct. 30	?	05	08	14
Ewing, David(B)	1803	July 25	Ind.Territory	01	07	05
Ewing, David(B)	1807	March 23	Dearborn(Ind	02	11	26
Ewing, David(B)	1813	April 14	Franklin(Ind	02	11	26
Ewing, David(E)	1813	Dec. 06	Jefferson	13	12	02
Ewing, John(B)	1805	March 18	Hamilton	02	08	13
Ewing, John(B)	1805	April 17	Ind.Territry	02	10	17
Ewing, John(C)	1801	Dec. 25	Hamilton	06	02	33
Ewing, John(C)	1802	Dec. 28	Hamilton	06	02	07
Ewing, John(C)	1804	Sept. 03	Montgomery	06	02	26
Ewing, John(C)	1804	Dec. 21	Montgomery	06	02	33
Ewing, John(C)	1826	Dec. 07	Greene	08	06	18
Ewing, John(E)	1836	Oct. 25	Montgomery	15	20	08
Ewing, John(E)	1836	Oct. 25	Montgomery	15	21	04
Ewing, John(E)	1837	Nov. 24	Montgomery	15	20	05
Ewing, Robert(A)	1802	March 09	Hamilton	05	05	09
Ewing, Robert(A)	1804	Dec. 21	Montgomery	05	05	09
Ewing, Robert(A)	1836	Aug. 24	Butler	01	13	09
Ewing, Robert(B)	1836	Aug. 20	Butler	01	18	26
Ewing, Robert(E)	1811	Oct. 24	Montgomery	13	17	30
Ewing, William(B)	1806	Nov. 24	Dearborn(Ind	02	11	29
Faber, George Adam(B)	1833	June 03	Cincinnati	03	08	13
Faber, George Adam(B)	1833	June 15	Cincinnati	03	08	13
Factor, John Henry(B)	1836	Sept. 08	Cincinnati	03	09	01
Fagans, James(E)	1837	June 01	Randolph(Ind	14	21	30
Fageley, Sophia(B)	1818	March 06	Cincinnati	03	07	25
Fager, Caleb(A)	1818	Oct. 19	Miami	05	08	33
Fager, Jacob(E)	1837	Feb. 06	Miami	15	21	34

PURCHASER	YEAR	DATE	RESIDENCE	R	T	S
Faik, Daniel(E)	1838	Sept. 17	Montgomery	15	21	32
Fair, Michael(A)	1815	Jan. 05	Montgomery	06	04	33
Fairbanks, Hiram(B)	1834	April 01	Dearborn(Ind	02	06	23
Fairchild, Francis(A)	1836	Oct. 12	Darke	01	14	35
Fairchild, Geo. A.(E)	1837	Nov. 18	Delaware	15	22	10
Fairchild, Lewis(C)	1828	July 30	Warren	10	05	26
Fairchild, Oliver(C)	1815	May 04	Cincinnati	14	04	33
Fairfield, David Senr.(E)	1819	Jan. 12	Clinton	13	20	14
Fairfield, Micaiah(A)	1818	April 14	Miami	05	07	12
Fale, William(B)	1807	Sept. 29	Dearborn(Ind	02	12	25
Falkner, Daniel(A)	1816	Aug. 26	Montgomery	01	10	03
Falknor, Levi(A)	1828	Sept. 09	Montgomery	04	07	25
Fall, Christian Senr.(B)	1812	April 15	Wayne(Ind)	01	12	30
Fall, Christian(A)	1804	Dec. 08	Warren	03	04	11
Fall, Christian(A)	1814	Sept. 02	Preble	02	08	30
Fall, Christian(A)	1815	May 09	Preble	01	08	26
Fall, Daniel(A)	1805	Nov. 28	Montgomery	03	04	14
Fall, George Jr.(A)	1836	Jan. 04	Darke	02	12	04
Fall, George Jr.(A)	1836	Jan. 19	Darke	02	12	04
Fall, George(A)	1816	Sept. 18	Darke	02	12	09
Fall, George(A)	1817	July 25	Darke	02	12	08
Fall, George(A)	1833	Dec. 04	Darke	02	12	09
Fall, George(B)	1816	March 15	Wayne(Ind)	02	09	31
Fall, George(B)	1817	Aug. 01	Wayne(Ind)	01	12	30
Fall, Jacob(A)	1833	May 15	Preble	02	09	06
Fall, John(A)	1836	Nov. 10	Darke	02	12	05
Fall, Tetrack(B)	1805	Nov. 11	Dearborn(Ind	02	05	33
Fall, Tetrech(B)	1803	June 01	Kentucky	02	04	29
Fall, Tetrech(B)	1812	Aug. 21	Dearborn(Ind	02	04	21
Fall, William(A)	1814	Dec. 28	Preble	02	08	19
Fall, William(A)	1836	Jan. 19	Darke	02	13	32
Faller, Valentine(E)	1837	May 22	Cincinnati	13	11	22
Fallin, David(E)	1814	Aug. 19	Kentucky	13	13	22
Fallis, George(B)	1836	March 14	Henry Co.,Ky	03	04	20
Fallis, George(B)	1837	March 01	Dearborn(Ind	03	04	21
Fallis, John(B)	1839	April 24	Kentucky	03	11	21
Fallis, Martin David(B)	1836	March 14	OldhamCo.,Ky	03	04	20
Fallis, Martin David(B)	1837	Feb. 24	Kentucky	03	04	21
Fallis, Richard(B)	1838	Oct. 06	Kentucky	03	04	21
Fallis, Samuel(B)	1837	March 01	Switzerland	03	04	21
Fanalman, Adam(A)	1818	Dec. 24	Miami	04	09	18
Fanis, David(A)	1807	Feb. 27	Butler	01	06	25
Fare, Jacob(A)	1805	Dec. 05	Montgomery	06	04	28
Fare, Michael(A)	1806	July 26	Greene	06	04	27
Fares, James(A)	1806	June 16	Butler	01	06	25
Farlow, George(E)	1812	Dec. 23	Wayne(Ind)	13	15	20
Farlow, George(E)	1813	Aug. 30	Wayne(Ind)	13	15	23
Farlow, George(E)	1814	Feb. 01	Wayne(Ind)	13	15	17
Farlow, John(B)	1808	Jan. 13	Dearborn(Ind	01	12	19
Farlow, John(B)	1813	April 14	Wayne(Ind)	01	12	19
Farlow, Uriah(E)	1818	March 21	Wayne(Ind)	13	14	02
Farlow, William(B)	1808	Jan. 13	Dearborn(Ind	01	12	19
Farmer, George(B)	1815	June 02	Hamilton	01	06	03
Farmer, Jesse(A)	1809	Aug. 22	Montgomery	05	05	27
Farmer, John(A)	1828	Oct. 14	Montgomery	04	06	02
Farmer, Thomas(A)	1837	April 15	Champaign	02	13	02
Farmer, William(?)	1814	Dec. 10	Montgomery	05	05	22
Farmer, William(A)	1811	Aug. 13	Montgomery	05	05	26
Farmer, William(A)	1815	Feb. 03	Montgomery	05	05	22
Farmer, Wm. Jr.(A)	1828	Dec. 24	Montgomery	04	06	21
Farnham, John S.(C)	1817	July 18	Montgomery	08	06	36
Farquhar, Andrew(E)	1836	Jan. 06	Clinton	13	19	26
Farquhar, Benjamin(C)	1806	Oct. 28	Warren	08	03	03
Farquhar, Jonah(C)	1806	July 15	Warren	08	03	02
Farquhar, Mahlon(E)	1836	Aug. 12	Clinton	13	19	30
Farrall, James(B)	1817	June 16	Switzerland	03	03	30
Farran, Matthew(C)	1814	Aug. 13	Dearborn(Ind	13	12	15
Farran, Michael(B)	1816	Sept. 27	?	01	07	20
Farran, Robert(B)	1818	Oct. 26	Hamilton	03	05	23

PURCHASER	YEAR	DATE	RESIDENCE	R	T	S
Farran, Robert(B)	1827	March 21	Dearborn(Ind	03	05	03
Farree, David(E)	1815	Dec. 15	Franklin(Ind	13	13	08
Farrens, George W.(E)	1836	Oct. 17	Randolph(Ind	15	19	07
Farrens, Henry D.(E)	1837	April 13	Randolph(Ind	15	19	17
Farrens, John Harvey(E)	1836	Aug. 27	Randolph(Ind	15	19	05
Farrens, Samuel(B)	1832	Oct. 04	Randolph(Ind	01	17	34
Farrens, Samuel(B)	1833	Aug. 02	Randolph(Ind	01	17	34
Farris, Lewis(A)	1832	Sept. 10	Miami	04	07	10
Farrow, John(C)	1813	April 15	Miami	11	01	23
Faudrick, Nancy(A)	1816	May 29	Preble	01	08	31
Faulkner, David(C)	1801	Dec. 30	Hamilton	05	03	01
Faulkner, George(C)	1813	Nov. 06	Champaign	11	03	05
Faulkner, George(C)	1831	March 07	Champaign	11	03	05
Faulkner, Jacob(B)	1836	Feb. 01	Dearborn(Ind	03	06	26
Faulkner, Mary(B)	1820	July 10	Hamilton	03	06	26
Faulkner, Robt.(B)	1822	Sept. 06	Dearborn(Ind	03	06	26
Faurot, Jacob(E)	1832	Feb. 24	Franklin(Ind	12	12	20
Faurot, John H.(E)	1831	June 20	Franklin(Ind	12	12	19
Faurot, John H.(E)	1836	Nov. 05	Franklin(Ind	11	12	25
Faurot, John Holliday(E)	1835	Oct. 12	Franklin(Ind	11	12	25
Faurot, William(E)	1836	Nov. 19	Franklin(Ind	11	12	24
Fauset, Jacob(B)	1813	June 12	Hamilton	01	09	27
Fauset, Thomas(A)	1813	June 21	Butler	01	03	03
Fausset, Jacob Jr.(B)	1829	Dec. 15	Franklin(Ind	01	09	12
Fausset, Jacob(B)	1836	July 15	Franklin(Ind	01	08	20
Fausset, Sam'l. S.(B)	1836	July 15	Franklin(Ind	01	08	20
Faust, George(C)	1831	Nov. 30	Hamilton	12	02	17
Favoritz, George(A)	1816	Oct. 03	Pennsylvania	06	04	22
Fay, Hiram(B)	1832	Oct. 15	Franklin(Ind	02	08	09
Featherland, Frederick(D)	1812	Sept. 21	Butler	02	02	11
Feely, John J.(B)	1839	Feb. 12	Dearborn(Ind	03	04	13
Feer, William(D)	1809	Oct. 23	Hamilton	01	01	08
Fees, Henry(A)	1832	Aug. 14	Darke	04	09	06
Fees, Philip(A)	1831	Nov. 29	Darke	04	09	05
Feger, Joseph(B)	1832	March 01	Cincinnati	02	07	25
Fehrmann, Bernard(E)	1836	Nov. 11	Cincinnati	12	10	06
Feidt, George Henry(A)	1834	May 23	Pennsylvania	03	10	18
Feist, John(B)	1834	June 14	Cincinnati	02	06	14
Feitton, David(B)	1815	June 20	Hamilton	02	02	26
Felix, John(B)	1832	Aug. 20	Germany	02	07	25
Fellow, John(B)	1831	Dec. 15	Randolph(Ind	01	16	23
Felman, Tobias(A)	1806	April 26	Montgomery	03	07	03
Felter, Jacob(B)	1818	March 26	Hamilton	01	08	05
Fender, Gabriel(E)	1815	March 13	Wayne(Ind)	14	15	17
Fender, Henry(E)	1813	Oct. 06	Wayne(Ind)	14	15	21
Fendlay, James(B)	1814	Nov. 17	Ind.Territry	01	08	14
Fenimore, Samuel W.(E)	1836	April 20	Wayne(Ind)	13	18	03
Fenton, John(B)	1809	Dec. 14	Dearborn(Ind	02	02	36
Fenton, Samuel(B)	1815	July 22	Switzerland	02	02	25
Fenton, Samuel(B)	1818	March 09	Switzerland	02	02	13
Fenton, Stacy(A)	1813	Oct. 27	Butler	02	03	07
Fenton, Stacy(A)	1814	Dec. 31	Butler	02	09	10
Fenton, William(C)	1811	Aug. 09	Champaign	10	05	31
Fentress, George(A)	1817	June 07	Montgomery	06	04	32
Fergason, Ethelbert(E)	1818	July 16	Hamilton	11	11	35
Fergus, John(A)	1819	March 16	Miami	06	07	09
Ferguson, Alexander(B)	1814	July 25	Cincinnati	01	10	35
Ferguson, Arthur(B)	1816	Oct. 14	Cincinnati	02	11	34
Ferguson, George(B)	1828	Sept. 24	Union(Ind)	02	10	17
Ferguson, Joseph(B)	1814	Nov. 01	Wayne(Ind)	02	12	35
Ferguson, Nimrod(E)	1811	Oct. 22	Wayne(Ind)	12	15	25
Ferguson, Nimrod(E)	1811	Oct. 22	Wayne(Ind)	12	15	25
Ferguson, Nimrod(E)	1811	Oct. 22	Wayne(Ind)	12	15	11
Ferguson, Nimrod(E)	1811	Oct. 22	Wayne(Ind)	12	15	13
Ferguson, Sarah(E)	1826	Nov. 01	Wayne(Ind)	14	17	04
Ferguson, William(B)	1814	July 25	Hamilton	01	09	01
Ferguson, Zachariah(B)	1815	March 13	Greene	02	11	04
Ferguson, Zachariah(E)	1815	Feb. 16	Greene	14	14	17
Ferrall, James(E)	1816	Aug. 15	Columbiana	13	17	05

PURCHASER	YEAR	DATE	RESIDENCE	R	T	S
Ferrel, Daniel(C)	1805	Nov. 27	Montgomery	09	02	27
Ferrel, Daniel(C)	1805	Nov. 27	Montgomery	09	02	27
Ferrel, Jepthah(C)	1811	Oct. 02	Champaign	13	04	32
Ferrell, Jeptha(C)	1812	Jan. 09	Champaign	13	04	26
Ferrer, Jacob(A)	1815	Dec. 19	Preble	03	04	09
Ferres, Joseph(D)	1808	Nov. 01	Hamilton(Fr)	02	04	08
Ferris, And'w.(A)	1813	Nov. 13	Hamilton	01	03	14
Ferris, Andrew(C)	1814	Nov. 23	Greene	08	06	17
Ferris, Isaiah(B)	1815	Oct. 31	Hamilton	02	06	33
Ferris, John(A)	1814	May 17	Hamilton	01	03	05
Ferris, John(A)	1815	Jan. 23	Hamilton	03	07	07
Ferris, John(A)	1815	Jan. 23	Hamilton	03	07	08
Ferris, John(B)	1814	Dec. 24	Hamilton	02	05	02
Ferris, John(B)	1814	Dec. 24	Hamilton	01	05	05
Ferris, John(E)	1813	Aug. 17	Hamilton	12	12	27
Ferris, John(E)	1814	July 25	Franklin(Ind	12	12	23
Ferris, John(E)	1814	Sept. 02	Franklin(Ind	12	12	33
Ferris, John(E)	1832	Nov. 28	Franklin(Ind	12	12	23
Ferris, John(E)	1836	Nov. 21	Hamilton	12	11	10
Ferris, John(E)	1836	Nov. 21	Hamilton	12	11	10
Ferris, John(E)	1836	Nov. 21	Hamilton	12	11	15
Ferris, Joseph(A)	1813	Nov. 13	Hamilton	01	03	14
Ferris, Joseph(B)	1818	Jan. 28	Cincinnati	03	07	22
Ferry, Gabriel(E)	1836	Oct. 10	Dearborn(Ind	12	10	09
Fetter, Samuel(A)	1817	Nov. 13	Miami	04	09	25
Fetter, Samuel(A)	1819	July 02	Miami	04	09	02
Fettig, George Henry(B)	1834	March 01	Cincinnati	03	09	35
Feucht, Gottlieb(A)	1837	July 03	Pennsylvania	01	14	30
Field, Roswell(C)	1816	Sept. 09	Greene	12	04	19
Fielder, Charles(C)	1813	April 14	Champaign	12	05	35
Fielding, William(C)	1828	June 04	Shelby	14	01	19
Fields, Jackson(E)	1837	Jan. 04	Randolph(Ind	14	21	22
Fields, Lansford(E)	1834	June 14	Randolph(Ind	14	21	12
Fields, Lansford(E)	1836	Oct. 17	Randolph(Ind	14	21	12
Fields, Martin(E)	1834	Jan. 10	Randolph(Ind	15	21	07
Fields, Martin(E)	1836	June 17	Randolph(Ind	15	21	07
Fields, William Jr.(E)	1836	Aug. 23	Randolph(Ind	14	21	14
Fields, William(E)	1834	June 14	Randolph(Ind	14	21	14
Fiffer, Jacob(A)	1836	Oct. 19	Darke	02	13	28
Fifield, Bennaiah B.(B)	1829	March 31	Hamilton	02	05	10
Filix, Peter(C)	1804	Dec. 15	Montgomery	10	01	23
Finch, Isaac K.(B)	1814	July 25	Hamilton	02	09	27
Finch, John(B)	1817	Dec. 01	Dearborn(Ind	03	07	26
Finch, Jonathan(B)	1817	Dec. 01	Dearborn(Ind	03	07	26
Finch, Moses(B)	1814	Aug. 24	Hamilton	02	09	36
Finch, Nathan'l.(B)	1818	June 01	Cincinnati	02	08	23
Finch, Solomon(A)	1815	July 08	Butler	02	04	22
Finch, Solomon(A)	1816	April 15	Butler	02	04	24
Fincher, Jane(E)	1824	June 25	Wayne(Ind)	13	16	04
Fincher, John(E)	1811	Oct. 24	Miami	13	16	03
Fincher, John(E)	1817	Sept. 15	Wayne(Ind)	13	16	04
Fincher, William(A)	1806	Dec. 18	Montgomery	05	06	27
Fincher, William(A)	1817	Oct. 20	Miami	05	06	27
Fincher, William(A)	1818	Aug. 18	Miami	05	06	30
Fincher, William(E)	1811	Oct. 24	Miami	13	16	04
Findlay, James(A)	1801	April 27	Cincinnati	01	04	35
Findlay, James(A)	1801	April 27	Cincinnati	05	01	06
Findlay, James(A)	1812	April 15	Ohio	02	04	28
Findlay, James(B)	1815	Aug. 09	Cincinnati	01	03	31
Findlay, James(C)	1804	Sept. 25	Cincinnati	07	02	29
Findlay, James(C)	1809	Dec. 12	Cincinnati	07	02	29
Findlay, James(C)	1811	Aug. 07	Hamilton	07	02	29
Findlay, James(C)	1813	April 14	Cincinnati	10	01	06
Findlay, James(C)	1813	April 14	Cincinnati	06	01	07
Findlay, James(C)	1813	April 14	Cincinnati	10	01	06
Findlay, James(C)	1813	July 30	Cincinnati	09	04	05
Findlay, James(C)	1814	Jan. 04	Cincinnati	10	05	28
Findlay, James(C)	1814	Jan. 04	Cincinnati	10	04	06
Findlay, James(C)	1815	July 19	Cincinnati	11	04	01

PURCHASER	YEAR	DATE	RESIDENCE	R	T	S
Findlay, Jas.(C)	1813	April 14	Cincinnati	08	04	13
Findlay, Nathan C.(B)	1806	Aug. 13	Cincinnati	01	05	20
Findlay, Nathan C.(C)	1804	Dec. 31	Cincinnati	09	02	09
Findlay, Nathan C.(C)	1804	Dec. 31	Cincinnati	10	02	31
Findlay, Nathan C.(C)	1804	Dec. 31	Cincinnati	09	02	06
Findlay, Nathan C.(C)	1804	Dec. 31	Cincinnati	09	04	22
Findlay, Nathan C.(C)	1804	Dec. 31	Cincinnati	09	02	05
Finkbone, Isaac(A)	1835	July 20	Darke	03	12	15
Finkbone, Isaac(A)	1836	Aug. 08	Darke	03	12	15
Finley, James Bradley(A)	1831	Nov. 16	Warren	02	10	22
Finley, James Bradley(A)	1831	Nov. 16	Warren	02	10	23
Finney, James(D)	1810	Sept. 21	Butler	01	04	11
Finney, James(D)	1811	March 06	Butler	01	04	11
Finney, John(B)	1836	Sept. 14	Miami	01	18	24
Finney, Robert(Black)(A)	1831	Nov. 07	Butler	03	08	27
Finney, Robert(E)	1836	Sept. 15	Miami	15	20	09
Firestone, Sam'l.(C)	1828	April 25	Logan	14	03	35
Fischer, Wilhelm(B)	1833	Nov. 13	Germany	02	08	28
Fish, Nymphas(B)	1815	Nov. 04	Cincinnati	02	06	01
Fish, Thomas(A)	1809	Oct. 23	Darke	02	12	27
Fisher, Benjamin(A)	1816	Oct. 04	Wayne(Ind)	01	08	20
Fisher, David(B)	1813	July 27	Wayne(Ind)	01	12	03
Fisher, David(B)	1815	May 12	Wayne(Ind)	02	13	14
Fisher, Edw'd.(B)	1828	Nov. 20	Wayne(Ind)	01	15	22
Fisher, Jacob(E)	1834	July 01	Randolph(Ind	13	20	15
Fisher, Jacob(E)	1836	Oct. 17	Randolph(Ind	13	20	15
Fisher, James(A)	1836	Oct. 31	Butler	03	12	14
Fisher, James(A)	1836	Oct. 31	Butler	02	14	13
Fisher, James(A)	1836	Oct. 31	Butler	02	14	23
Fisher, James(A)	1836	Oct. 31	Butler	02	14	24
Fisher, James(A)	1837	Feb. 06	Butler	02	14	13
Fisher, John(A)	1815	Oct. 17	Virginia	03	06	17
Fisher, John(B)	1805	March 15	Butler	01	11	25
Fisher, John(B)	1813	Aug. 02	Franklin(Ind	01	11	25
Fisher, John(B)	1816	March 02	Franklin(Ind	02	10	19
Fisher, John(C)	1801	Dec. 19	Hamilton	04	02	09
Fisher, John(E)	1815	June 06	Franklin(Ind	13	13	23
Fisher, John(E)	1815	July 11	Franklin(Ind	13	13	01
Fisher, John(E)	1819	June 05	Franklin(Ind	13	12	17
Fisher, Maddox(C)	1827	Aug. 22	Clark	09	05	36
Fisher, Martin(E)	1816	Feb. 07	Warren	13	15	04
Fisher, Nathan(B)	1817	Nov. 15	Wayne(Ind)	01	15	27
Fisher, Thomas(A)	1806	Oct. 28	Pennsylvania	05	05	34
Fisher, Thomas(B)	1817	June 16	Wayne(Ind)	01	15	33
Fisk, William(B)	1817	July 24	Dearborn(Ind	02	03	11
Fitch, Nathan(C)	1808	Nov. 02	Champaign	11	05	29
Fitchpatrick, Bartholomew(E)	1814	Dec. 17	Franklin(Ind	12	11	30
Fitchpatrick, Bartholomew(E)	1836	May 24	Franklin(Ind	12	11	31
Fitchpatrick, Bartholomew(E)	1837	March 24	Franklin(Ind	12	11	19
Fithian, George(C)	1807	July 02	Champaign	12	05	20
Fithian, Mason(E)	1817	Oct. 16	Franklin(Ind	13	17	27
FitzFreeman, Abraham(A)	1815	Oct. 31	Butler	02	10	26
FitzFreeman, William Henry(A)	1814	Dec. 03	Butler	02	09	11
FitzFreeman, Wm. Hy.(A)	1814	Dec. 03	Butler	02	09	10
Fitzpatrick, Abraham(C)	1831	July 05	Champaign	11	03	04
Fitzpatrick, John(C)	1815	March 17	Champaign	11	03	10
Fix, John(C)	1804	Sept. 03	Warren	05	03	29
Fix, John(C)	1810	Dec. 12	Warren	05	03	29
Fix, John(E)	1811	Oct. 28	Montgomery	13	15	17
Fix, John(E)	1811	Oct. 28	Montgomery	13	15	18
Fix, Joseph(C)	1804	Dec. 27	Warren	05	03	32
Fix, Philip(C)	1804	Dec. 27	Warren	05	03	27
Flack, Adam(B)	1805	June 21	Ind.Territry	02	05	35
Flack, Michael(B)	1812	June 27	Dearborn(Ind	02	05	36
Flack, Robert(B)	1806	July 26	Hamilton	01	10	05
Flack, William(B)	1812	June 27	Dearborn(Ind	02	05	36
Flake, Adam(B)	1817	July 19	Dearborn(Ind	03	06	13
Flake, Aimour(B)	1832	Nov. 08	Dearborn(Ind	02	05	29
Flake, Michael(B)	1811	Jan. 19	Dearborn(Ind	02	05	35

PURCHASER	YEAR	DATE	RESIDENCE	R	T	S
Flake, Michael(B)	1813	May 18	Dearborn(Ind	01	04	18
Flake, Michael(B)	1826	May 30	Dearborn(Ind	03	06	13
Flake, Michael(B)	1826	May 30	Dearborn(Ind	03	06	24
Flake, Michael(B)	1831	Sept. 13	Dearborn(Ind	02	05	31
Flake, Nathan(B)	1816	May 02	Dearborn(Ind	03	04	04
Flake, William(B)	1811	Jan. 19	Dearborn(Ind	02	05	35
Flake, Wm.(B)	1813	May 18	Dearborn(Ind	01	04	18
Flanegan, Matthew(B)	1805	Sept. 23	Kentucky	01	13	01
Flash, Christina Jane(B)	1838	Aug. 16	Cincinnati	01	17	12
Flatcher, Rachel(C)	1812	March 02	Champaign	09	06	24
Flater, John(B)	1836	Oct. 06	Maryland	01	16	03
Fleck, Peter(A)	1818	Dec. 12	Montgomery	02	10	02
Fleming, Alex.(C)	1912	Dec. 19	Champaign	10	05	06
Fleming, Alexander(A)	1815	Oct. 31	Butler	03	10	33
Fleming, Alexander(B)	1818	June 11	Butler	02	04	17
Fleming, Bartholemew(A)	1808	Feb. 11	Cincinnati	02	07	04
Fleming, Bartholomew	1808	March 02	Cincinnati	?	?	?
Fleming, Bartholomew	1808	March 02	Cincinnati	?	?	?
Fleming, Bartholomew	1808	June 15	?	?	?	?
Fleming, Dan'l. Morgan(E)	1837	May 26	Hamilton	13	11	29
Fleming, Daniel M.(E)	1836	June 21	Hamilton	13	11	32
Fleming, David J. P.(A)	1806	Dec. 20	Kentucky	01	09	20
Fleming, David J. P.(A)	1812	April 15	Preble	01	09	20
Fleming, Ezekiel(E)	1825	Jan. 06	Preble	01	09	21
Fleming, Jacob(C)	1804	Dec. 29	Greene	11	04	36
Fleming, Jacob(E)	1836	Dec. 15	Randolph(Ind	14	20	36
Fleming, James(A)	1806	July 28	Kentucky	01	09	20
Fleming, James(A)	1806	Nov. 03	Kentucky	01	09	20
Fleming, James(A)	1813	Oct. 18	Preble	02	08	32
Fleming, James(E)	1837	Oct. 18	Randolph(Ind	15	20	31
Fleming, John(A)	1805	Nov. 30	Kentucky	01	09	31
Fleming, John(B)	1818	May 01	Maryland	03	05	23
Fleming, John(B)	1818	Aug. 22	Maryland	03	05	23
Fleming, Joseph(A)	1805	Sept. 27	So. Carolina	02	05	26
Fleming, Mitchel(B)	1812	Sept. 09	Preble	01	09	10
Fleming, Peter(A)	1815	Aug. 10	Wayne(Ind)	01	08	06
Fleming, Peter(B)	1804	Dec. 18	Kentucky	02	13	24
Fleming, Peter(B)	1805	Sept. 23	Kentucky	01	13	01
Fleming, Samuel(B)	1817	Oct. 18	Butler	03	05	04
Fleming, Samuel(B)	1817	Oct. 27	Butler	03	05	03
Fleming, Samuel(B)	1817	Nov. 05	Butler	03	05	03
Fleming, Thomas(A)	1806	July 22	Butler	01	04	34
Fleming, Wm. J.(B)	1827	Dec. 24	Hamilton	02	04	08
Flemming, Peter(A)	1807	Aug. 05	Montgomery	01	10	28
Fletcher, David(E)	1813	Oct. 27	Franklin(Ind	13	14	22
Fletcher, Jesse(E)	1813	Oct. 30	Franklin(Ind	13	14	21
Fleweling, William(E)	1835	May 23	Franklin(Ind	13	12	20
Flinn, James(A)	1804	Sept. 10	Montgomery	06	06	06
Flinn, James(A)	1804	Oct. 16	Montgomery	06	07	31
Flinn, John(C)	1814	March 17	Miami	10	03	35
Flinn, John(C)	1817	Oct. 10	Miami	10	02	11
Flinn, John(C)	1827	May 16	Miami	10	02	11
Flinn, William(A)	1816	April 13	Miami	05	09	08
Flinn, Wm. N.(A)	1828	Dec. 09	Shelby	05	09	08
Flinn, Wm.(A)	1828	Dec. 09	Shelby	05	09	08
Flint, John Senr.(B)	1811	Dec. 12	Franklin(Ind	01	10	20
Flint, John Senr.(B)	1813	Oct. 14	Franklin(Ind	01	10	29
Flint, John(B)	1811	July 10	Ind.Territory	01	10	20
Flint, John(B)	1811	Aug. 05	Ind.Territory	01	10	19
Flint, John(B)	1811	Oct. 18	Ind.Territory	02	10	24
Flint, John(B)	1826	March 31	Franklin(Ind	01	10	21
Flint, Joseph(E)	1811	Oct. 24	Wayne(Ind)	13	15	20
Flint, Joseph(E)	1814	Sept. 10	Wayne(Ind)	12	15	23
Flood, William(E)	1811	Oct. 21	Ind.Territory	12	12	35
Floor, Christian(B)	1836	March 29	Franklin(Ind	02	08	17
Flora, Henry(A)	1810	Dec. 12	Montgomery	05	05	32
Flora, John(A)	1824	Dec. 06	Preble	01	08	15
Flora, William(A)	1807	July 11	Hamilton	06	05	20
Flory, Abraham(A)	1815	April 11	Preble	01	08	14

PURCHASER	YEAR	DATE	RESIDENCE	R	T	S
Flory, Emanuel Senr.(B)	1836	Sept. 22	Darke	01	18	24
Flory, Emanuel(A)	1805	Oct. 21	Pennsylvania	05	05	33
Flory, Emanuel(A)	1805	Oct. 21	Pennsylvania	05	04	20
Flory, Emanuel(A)	1824	June 08	Montgomery	05	04	21
Flory, Emanuel(E)	1837	Oct. 26	Darke	15	22	35
Flory, Henry(A)	1805	Oct. 21	Pennsylvania	05	05	32
Flory, Henry(A)	1805	Oct. 21	Pennsylvania	05	05	32
Flory, Henry(A)	1810	June 06	Montgomery	05	04	21
Flory, John(A)	1836	Nov. 26	Montgomery	01	13	04
Flory, John(B)	1836	Nov. 07	Ohio	01	18	24
Flotron, Francois Louis(B)	1818	July 15	Switzerland	04	02	36
Flowers, Aaron(C)	1818	Sept. 01	Butler	12	02	03
Flowers, Andrew(C)	1817	June 23	Butler	12	03	23
Flowers, Andrew(C)	1817	Aug. 25	Butler	12	03	23
Flowers, James(C)	1816	Sept. 17	Ohio	12	03	21
Flowers, Michael(B)	1815	Jan. 02	Cincinnati	01	08	36
Flowers, Michael(B)	1815	Jan. 02	Cincinnati	01	08	36
Floyd, John(A)	1817	Aug. 26	Kentucky	03	06	02
Floyd, John(A)	1817	Nov. 07	Kentucky	03	06	01
Floyd, Joseph(E)	1836	Sept. 16	CampbellCoKy	13	20	02
Foat, Marmaduke(A)	1807	Jan. 10	Montgomery	04	08	36
Fodge, Jacob(C)	1831	Oct. 01	Champaign	13	04	20
Fogalgasang, Christian(A)	1804	Jan. 05	Montgomery	04	04	13
Fogalgasang, Christian(A)	1805	June 11	Montgomery	04	04	24
Fogalgasang, John(C)	1805	Dec. 30	Ohio	10	04	23
Fogalsang, George(C)	1811	May 14	Warren	10	04	23
Fogel, Michael(C)	1805	July 13	Greene	07	03	11
Foland, Dan'l.(C)	1828	July 11	Miami	09	02	35
Foland, John(E)	1814	July 06	Miami	13	17	34
Folck, John D.(A)	1819	Aug. 14	Greene	04	06	31
Foley, Enoch(A)	1814	Dec. 27	Ohio	04	10	31
Foley, James(C)	1806	May 12	Champaign	10	05	03
Foley, James(C)	1809	Sept. 25	Champaign	10	05	11
Foley, James(C)	1811	April 03	Champaign	10	05	02
Foley, James(C)	1816	Dec. 02	Champaign	10	06	33
Foley, James(C)	1816	Dec. 02	Champaign	10	06	34
Foley, James(C)	1817	Aug. 01	Champaign	10	05	03
Foley, James(C)	1829	Dec. 11	Clark	10	06	26
Foley, James(C)	1829	Dec. 11	Clark	10	06	34
Foley, John Junior(C)	1806	June 18	Champaign	10	05	09
Foley, John Junior(C)	1806	June 18	Champaign	10	05	17
Foley, John(C)	1811	Aug. 26	Champaign	10	06	32
Foley, John(C)	1816	Dec. 02	Champaign	10	06	32
Folk, Henry(A)	1828	May 23	Pickaway	07	01	18
Folkarth, Samuel(A)	1832	May 07	Montgomery	04	07	23
Folker, Christopher(A)	1809	July 27	Pennsylvania	06	08	25
Folkerth, John(C)	1805	July 15	Montgomery	08	02	30
Folkerth, Michael(A)	1817	Aug. 16	Miami	03	09	08
Folkerth, William(A)	1817	Aug. 16	Miami	03	09	08
Folkerth, William(C)	1805	July 15	Montgomery	08	02	30
Folks, Obadiah(A)	1831	Feb. 08	Warren	03	06	13
Folsom, Jeremiah(B)	1818	Dec. 31	Dearborn(Ind	02	05	05
Folsom, Richard(B)	1813	Jan. 06	Ind.Territory	02	01	06
Folsom, Richard(B)	1818	Nov. 20	Dearborn(Ind	03	04	13
Foly, Daniel(C)	1816	June 28	Greene	12	04	20
Foos, Benjamin(C)	1812	Dec. 21	Champaign	09	05	04
Foos, Griffith(C)	1806	Aug. 20	Champaign	09	05	10
Foos, Griffith(C)	1807	April 13	Champaign	09	04	17
Foos, Jacob(A)	1815	Oct. 10	Warren	02	09	26
Foos, Jacob(A)	1824	Aug. 17	Preble	02	09	22
Foose, Benjamin(C)	1806	June 13	Champaign	09	05	04
Foose, Benjamin(C)	1811	Aug. 13	Champaign	09	05	04
Foosner, Adam(B)	1837	Jan. 02	Franklin(Ind	02	08	20
Foot, Dan'l.(B)	1818	March 19	Cincinnati	02	01	05
Forbes, Arthur(C)	1806	Feb. 14	Greene	08	05	27
Forbes, Joseph(A)	1811	June 19	Butler	01	04	07
Forbes, William(B)	1815	May 29	Butler	01	10	27
Ford, Delilah(A)	1829	March 14	Preble	03	08	21
Ford, John(B)	1831	Sept. 22	Randolph(Ind	01	16	14

PURCHASER	YEAR	DATE	RESIDENCE	R	T	S
Ford, Joseph(A)	1818	Oct. 01	Hamilton	03	09	31
Ford, Joseph(A)	1829	July 18	Darke	03	08	17
Ford, Mordecai S.(A)	1828	Dec. 29	Darke	03	07	03
Ford, Nathan'l Teagle(B)	1834	Dec. 13	Randolph(Ind	01	16	03
Ford, Obadiah(B)	1811	Nov. 14	Pennsylvania	01	07	01
Ford, Sam'l. F.(B)	1836	Aug. 30	Switzerland	03	04	27
Ford, William(A)	1811	Aug. 13	Clermont	01	02	20
Fordice, James(E)	1815	Nov. 20	Warren	13	12	09
Foredyce, James(B)	1814	Feb. 28	Hamilton	01	10	07
Foreman, William(C)	1817	June 27	Champaign	09	06	15
Forest, William(A)	1818	Oct. 22	Kentucky	05	10	28
Forester, James(B)	1834	Jan. 18	Franklin(Ind	02	08	14
Forester, James(B)	1834	April 01	Franklin(Ind	02	08	14
Forester, James(B)	1835	Aug. 17	Franklin(Ind	02	08	14
Forgason, Athel(C)	1813	Sept. 11	Butler	08	06	18
Forgay, John(C)	1808	Jan. 29	Greene	09	03	21
Forgey, Prestley(C)	1811	Aug. 13	Greene	09	03	21
Forgey, Stewart(C)	1811	Aug. 13	Greene	09	03	21
Forguson, William(C)	1804	Sept. 05	Warren	04	03	04
Forguson, William(C)	1804	Sept. 05	Warren	04	03	04
Forguson, William(C)	1804	Sept. 05	Warren	05	02	11
Forgy, John(C)	1804	Dec. 31	Greene	08	03	24
Forgy, John(C)	1813	April 14	Champaign	09	03	21
Forman, Benjamin(C)	1811	Aug. 08	Kentucky	09	06	27
Forman, Benjamin(C)	1813	March 22	Champaign	09	06	22
Forman, Benjamin(C)	1813	April 14	Champaign	09	06	22
Forman, Benjamin(C)	1813	Aug. 28	Champaign	09	06	22
Forman, Benjamin(C)	1813	Dec. 11	Champaign	09	06	21
Forman, Benjamin(C)	1816	Dec. 02	Champaign	09	06	27
Forney, John(A)	1803	Sept. 16	Pennsylvania	05	03	10
Forrest, Dennis(A)	1817	Dec. 05	Miami	05	09	23
Forrest, Dennis(A)	1818	May 01	Miami	05	10	28
Forrester, Robert(A)	1810	May 04	Hamilton	01	01	03
Forrester, Robert(A)	1815	Aug. 09	Hamilton	01	01	03
Forry, Daniel(A)	1831	Nov. 22	Logan	08	01	11
Forshey, Edward K.(E)	1836	Feb. 01	Randolph(Ind	13	19	33
Fortner, Levi(B)	1817	Sept. 16	Franklin(Ind	02	08	26
Fortney, David Jr.(A)	1831	Nov. 07	Pennsylvania	02	09	18
Forwood, Samuel(B)	1832	Sept. 29	Switzerland	03	03	12
Fosdick, Richard(C)	1816	Dec. 06	Cincinnati	13	03	03
Fosdick, Samuel(A)	1836	Dec. 15	Cincinnati	03	12	01
Fosdick, Samuel(A)	1836	Dec. 15	Cincinnati	04	11	19
Fosdick, Samuel(A)	1837	Jan. 02	Cincinnati	01	15	27
Fosdick, Samuel(A)	1837	Jan. 02	Cincinnati	01	15	33
Fosdick, Samuel(A)	1837	Jan. 02	Cincinnati	03	12	20
Fosdick, Samuel(A)	1837	Jan. 18	Cincinnati	03	11	07
Fosdick, Samuel(A)	1837	Jan. 31	Cincinnati	04	11	19
Fosdick, Samuel(B)	1837	Jan. 02	Cincinnati	01	17	13
Fosdick, Samuel(B)	1837	Jan. 02	Cincinnati	01	17	14
Fosdick, Samuel(E)	1837	Jan. 02	Cincinnati	11	10	22
Fosdick, Samuel(E)	1837	Jan. 02	Cincinnati	12	11	28
Fosdick, Samuel(E)	1837	Jan. 02	Cincinnati	13	19	02
Fosdick, Samuel(E)	1837	Jan. 02	Cincinnati	14	21	05
Fosdick, Samuel(E)	1837	Jan. 18	Cincinnati	13	20	25
Fosdick, Samuel(E)	1837	Jan. 18	Cincinnati	14	21	18
Fosdick, Samuel(E)	1837	Jan. 02	Cincinnati	14	21	05
Fosdick, Thos. R.(B)	1818	Oct. 01	Cincinnati	01	07	03
Fosduck, Richard(C)	1816	Dec. 06	Cincinnati	13	03	03
Fosset, Robert(B)	1811	Oct. 29	Hamilton	01	09	34
Fossett, John(C)	1801	Dec. 30	Hamilton	04	03	28
Foster, Isaac(B)	1832	May 24	Dearborn(Ind	02	07	08
Foster, James(B)	1818	April 27	Dearborn(Ind	02	07	09
Foster, John M.(A)	1815	Dec. 01	Madison	01	10	20
Foster, John M.(A)	1824	June 08	Darke	01	10	22
Foster, John(A)	1814	Nov. 11	Preble	02	06	28
Foster, John(A)	1814	Dec. 21	Preble	01	06	22
Foster, John(B)	1817	Dec. 01	Madison	01	17	36
Foster, Lowry(B)	1831	Sept. 20	Dearborn(Ind	03	08	01
Foster, Luke(A)	1814	Sept. 17	Hamilton	02	06	26

PURCHASER	YEAR	DATE	RESIDENCE	R	T	S
Foster, Luke(A)	1814	Sept. 17	Hamilton	02	06	27
Foster, Martha(A)	1815	July 04	Butler	01	06	02
Foster, Nelson(C)	1827	Dec. 19	Clark	10	03	28
Foster, Thomas(A)	1817	Sept. 02	Ross	01	12	29
Foster, Thomas(A)	1817	Sept. 02	Ross	01	11	04
Foster, Thomas(B)	1833	Oct. 17	Dearborn(Ind	02	07	11
Foster, William(C)	1816	Aug. 01	?	09	05	11
Foster, Wm.(C)	1813	March 15	Champaign	09	05	11
Fottrell, Andrew(E)	1837	April 03	Cincinnati	14	20	02
Fottrell, Andrew(E)	1837	May 30	Cincinnati	14	20	02
Fouch, John(E)	1824	Sept. 09	Miami	12	12	02
Foulk, Aaron(B)	1832	Oct. 06	Dearborn(Ind	02	05	30
Foust, Leonard(A)	1837	May 11	Shelby	03	13	35
Foust, Leonard(A)	1837	June 05	Shelby	03	13	35
Foust, Leonard(A)	1838	Feb. 02	Shelby	03	12	19
Foust, Lewis((A)	1811	Oct. 25	Montgomery	04	04	10
Foust, Ludwick(A)	1818	Oct. 19	Preble	03	07	30
Foust, Solomon(A)	1837	May 11	Shelby	03	13	35
Foust, Solomon(A)	1837	Sept. 20	Shelby	03	13	35
Foutch, John(A)	1813	July 21	Dearborn(Ind	01	08	27
Fouts, Andrew(A)	1806	Dec. 23	Montgomery	02	07	19
Fouts, Andrew(C)	1806	Aug. 29	Montgomery	01	12	18
Fouts, David(A)	1803	Jan. 25	Hamilton	04	03	11
Fouts, David(A)	1805	July 04	Montgomery	04	03	06
Fouts, David(A)	1805	July 17	Montgomery	03	05	05
Fouts, David(A)	1805	July 17	Montgomery	03	05	09
Fouts, David(A)	1811	June 06	Preble	03	05	09
Fouts, Henry(A)	1817	June 17	Miami	05	06	22
Fouts, Henry(A)	1832	Feb. 06	Miami	04	08	23
Fouts, Henry(A)	1832	Feb. 06	Miami	04	08	22
Fouts, Jacob Junr.(B)	1806	June 25	Montgomery	01	13	12
Fouts, Jacob(A)	1804	Aug. 11	Montgomery	04	03	07
Fouts, Jacob(B)	1807	Jan. 15	Montgomery	01	13	12
Fouts, Jacob(B)	1808	Jan. 13	Butler	01	12	33
Fouts, Jacob(B)	1816	Jan. 24	Wayne(Ind)	01	13	11
Fouts, John(A)	1804	Jan. 17	Montgomery	04	03	17
Fouts, Lawrence(A)	1824	Oct. 22	Montgomery	04	05	22
Fouts, Lewis(A)	1810	June 14	Montgomery	04	04	14
Fouts, Michael(A)	1804	April 30	Montgomery	04	03	04
Fouts, Michael(E)	1811	Nov. 15	Montgomery	13	17	17
Fouts, Peter(A)	1817	Sept. 07	Montgomery	04	05	29
Fouts, Theobald(A)	1811	Nov. 11	Montgomery	05	05	15
Fouts, William(B)	1806	March 07	Montgomery	01	13	13
Fouts, William(B)	1806	April 03	Montgomery	01	14	27
Fouts, William(B)	1806	Nov. 29	Dearborn(Ind	01	12	03
Fouts, William(B)	1807	Sept. 09	Dearborn(Ind	01	13	13
Fouts, William(B)	1808	Dec. 31	Dearborn(Ind	01	13	22
Foutz, David(A)	1829	Jan. 02	Darke	02	10	04
Foutz, Peter(A)	1817	Dec. 23	Montgomery	04	05	26
Foutz, Peter(A)	1817	Dec. 23	Montgomery	04	05	28
Foutz, Peter(A)	1817	Dec. 23	Montgomery	04	05	27
Foutz, Peter(A)	1827	Dec. 06	Montgomery	04	05	21
Foutz, Peter(A)	1827	Dec. 06	Montgomery	04	05	22
Foutzs, Fredrick(A)	1804	Oct. 17	Montgomery	04	03	07
Fowble, George(A)	1829	June 05	Preble	02	09	03
Fowble, George(A)	1831	Dec. 15	Preble	02	09	04
Fowler, Benj'n.(B)	1838	April 16	Dearborn(Ind	03	05	22
Fowler, Hezekiah(A)	1831	Sept. 26	Darke	01	13	31
Fowler, Jacob(C)	1813	Nov. 01	Kentucky	11	05	34
Fowler, John(E)	1818	July 27	Wayne(Ind)	14	18	05
Fowler, Philander(E)	1833	June 13	Wayne(Ind)	13	17	07
Fowler, Samuel(A)	1815	Nov. 10	Preble	02	06	25
Fowler, Samuel(A)	1815	Nov. 10	Preble	02	06	11
Fowler, William(E)	1827	Sept. 14	Wayne(Ind)	13	17	01
Fowler, William(E)	1831	Jan. 10	Wayne(Ind)	13	18	24
Fox, Ambrose(A)	1831	Nov. 01	Warren	02	10	14
Fox, Benham(D)	1812	May 18	Warren	03	04	08
Fox, David(A)	1827	Aug. 20	Montgomery	06	03	17
Fox, David(C)	1801	Dec. 26	Hamilton	04	03	10

PURCHASER	YEAR	DATE	RESIDENCE	R	T	S
Fox, Edward(A)	1828	May 15	Miami	05	09	15
Fox, Elijah(E)	1811	Oct. 24	Montgomery	13	16	09
Fox, James(B)	1837	March 21	Dearborn(Ind	03	04	24
Fox, James(B)	1832	June 14	Dearborn(Ind	02	05	05
Fox, John(A)	1805	Dec. 03	Warren	02	08	09
Fox, John(A)	1805	Dec. 03	Warren	02	08	04
Fox, John(E)	1811	Oct. 24	Wayen(Ind)	13	15	28
Fox, Joseph John(E)	1811	Oct. 24	Montgomery	13	16	10
Fox, Peter Senr.(E)	1837	March 24	Montgomery	15	22	33
Fox, Peter(A)	1823	June 09	Montgomery	04	06	18
Fox, Philip(E)	1811	Oct. 24	Wayne(Ind)	13	15	21
Fox, Samuel(A)	1832	Feb. 24	Warren	05	10	33
Fox, William(B)	1808	Jan. 12	Montgomery	01	12	14
Fox, William(B)	1808	Feb. 06	Montgomery	01	12	28
Fox, William(E)	1811	Oct. 24	Wayne(Ind)	13	17	23
Frad, John(B)	1811	May 18	Franklin(Ind	01	07	05
Frad, William(B)	1811	May 18	Franklin(Ind	01	07	05
Fraizer, Andrew(E)	1834	June 13	Randolph(Ind	15	19	08
Fraizer, Andrew(E)	1838	Jan. 15	Randolph(Ind	15	21	29
Fraizer, Andrew(E)	1838	Jan. 15	Randolph(Ind	15	19	05
Fraizer, Eli(E)	1816	Sept. 20	Clinton	13	17	36
Fraizer, Eli(E)	1816	Oct. 10	Clinton	13	17	36
Fraizer, James(E)	1833	Oct. 10	Randolph(Ind	15	19	08
Fraizer, James(E)	1836	June 20	Randolph(Ind	15	19	08
Frakes, Aaron(B)	1814	Oct. 13	Franklin(Ind	02	10	36
Frakes, Joseph(B)	1815	Aug. 28	Dearborn(Ind	02	04	32
Frakes, Nathan(B)	1806	July 28	?	02	03	18
Frakes, Robert(C)	1802	Dec. 31	Hamilton	08	03	28
Frame, Jesse(A)	1816	Sept. 25	Preble	01	09	03
Frame, Paul(A)	1814	June 06	Montgomery	05	05	31
Frame, William(A)	1818	April 13	Preble	01	07	09
Frames, Jesse(A)	1814	Feb. 05	Preble	03	04	07
Frampton, Hugh(A)	1821	April 19	Darke	03	10	05
Francis, David(A)	1812	Sept. 16	Butler	01	02	01
Francis, Jacob(A)	1827	March 30	Montgomery	04	07	34
Francis, Jacob(A)	1827	Dec. 07	Montgomery	04	06	21
Francis, Jacob(A)	1832	April 02	Butler	03	08	07
Francis, John(A)	1827	March 30	Montgomery	04	07	34
Frank, Martin(C)	1824	June 07	Champaign	11	04	35
Frank, Peter(A)	1831	Nov. 14	Pennsylvania	02	11	08
Frankfother, David A.(B)	1837	April 12	Richland	01	18	01
Franklin, Henry(C)	1816	Sept. 09	Greene	12	04	20
Franklin, James(C)	1816	Dec. 13	Champaign	10	04	32
Franklin, James(C)	1816	Dec. 13	Champaign	10	04	33
Franklin, Sam'l. D.(A)	1836	Dec. 01	Hamilton	02	15	29
Franklin, Samuel D.(A)	1836	Nov. 30	Hamilton	02	15	18
Frantz, Adam(A)	1838	Feb. 06	Clark	01	13	01
Frantz, Anna(C)	1819	Oct. 02	Logan	14	03	08
Frantz, Anna(C)	1819	Nov. 27	Logan	14	03	08
Frantz, David(C)	1829	Dec. 11	Clark	10	03	02
Frantz, Jacob(A)	1811	Dec. 11	Montgomery	04	03	10
Frantz, Jacob(C)	1811	Sept. 09	Virginia	09	04	17
Frantz, Joseph(A)	1832	Aug. 24	Logan	08	01	14
Frantz, Lydia(C)	1829	Dec. 05	Logan	14	03	27
Frase, Adam(B)	1835	March 31	Preble	01	16	24
Fraser, John(B)	1816	Feb. 21	Kentucky	01	06	32
Frazee, John(E)	1814	Sept. 20	Clinton	14	18	28
Frazee, Joseph G.(B)	1837	Dec. 18	Dearborn(Ind	03	04	15
Frazee, Moses(C)	1817	May 27	Miami	11	03	36
Frazee, Moses(C)	1817	May 27	Miami	11	03	30
Frazee, Moses(C)	1817	Nov. 07	Miami	11	02	09
Frazee, Squire(A)	1819	Jan. 08	Hamilton	02	06	22
Frazee, William(A)	1825	March 29	Montgomery	04	05	15
Frazer, David(E)	1819	July 03	Randolph(Ind	14	19	36
Frazer, David(E)	1831	April 22	Randolph(Ind	14	19	15
Frazer, David(E)	1831	Sept. 27	Randolph(Ind	14	19	15
Frazer, David(E)	1834	Nov. 13	Randolph(Ind	14	19	22
Frazer, Francis(E)	1836	July 14	Randolph(Ind	14	19	35
Frazer, George(E)	1811	Oct. 24	Franklin(Ind	13	14	30

PURCHASER	YEAR	DATE	RESIDENCE	R	T	S
Frazer, James(E)	1816	Nov. 13	Clinton	14	18	02
Frazer, James(E)	1835	Jan. 23	Randolph(Ind	14	19	35
Frazer, James(E)	1836	July 14	Randolph(Ind	14	19	35
Frazer, John(E)	1836	Nov. 24	OrangeCo.Ind	14	19	25
Frazer, John(E)	1837	April 06	OrangeCo.Ind	14	19	25
Frazer, Moses(C)	1812	April 15	Miami	06	05	30
Frazer, Samuel(E)	1819	July 03	Preble	14	18	01
Frazer, Stanley(E)	1835	March 26	Randolph(Ind	13	19	35
Frazer, Stanley(E)	1835	May 01	Randolph(Ind	13	18	02
Frazie, James(C)	1804	Dec. 15	Montgomery	10	01	03
Frazier, Gideon(E)	1815	Oct. 17	Clinton	14	18	09
Frazier, Joseph(E)	1834	Sept. 24	Randolph(Ind	14	19	35
Frazier, Joseph(E)	1836	July 11	Randolph(Ind	14	19	22
Frazier, Samuel(B)	1817	Sept. 22	Hamilton	02	04	18
Frazier, Samuel(B)	1818	June 03	Hamilton	03	05	10
Frazier, Thomas Jr.(E)	1835	April 25	Randolph(Ind	14	19	27
Frazier, Thomas(E)	1818	April 29	Randolph(Ind	14	18	10
Frazier, Thomas(E)	1835	July 02	Randolph(Ind	14	19	27
Frazier, William(B)	1818	Feb. 27	Warren	03	05	13
Frazier, William(E)	1815	Dec. 16	Wayne(Ind)	13	16	02
Frazier, Wm.(B)	1827	Aug. 21	Dearborn(Ind	02	04	09
Fream, Thomas(C)	1804	Dec. 31	Greene	09	04	02
Frech, Conrad(B)	1835	Oct. 12	Hamilton	02	07	01
Fredenburgh, Isaac Jr.(B)	1832	June 26	Switzerland	03	03	02
Free, George(E)	1837	Oct. 11	Miami	15	22	29
Free, Mary Ellen(E)	1815	May 20	Wayne(Ind)	13	16	11
Free, Philip(E)	1837	July 13	Miami	15	22	34
Free, Spencer(free Black)(E)	1815	Oct. 19	?	14	16	32
Freel, James(A)	1829	Aug. 17	Miami	03	08	31
Freel, James(A)	1831	July 15	Warren	03	08	30
Freel, James(E)	1814	Jan. 07	Franklin(Ind	13	14	32
Freeland, John(B)	1815	Nov. 27	Hamilton	02	06	30
Freeland, John(B)	1818	Jan. 28	Cincinnati	03	07	22
Freeland, Levi(A)	1814	April 18	Butler	01	03	05
Freeman, Abraham Jnr.(A)	1816	March 07	Darke	02	10	26
Freeman, Henry(C)	1810	Jan. 03	Hamilton	12	01	15
Freeman, Isaac(B)	1832	July 25	Dearborn(Ind	02	06	06
Freeman, John(A)	1805	Aug. 09	Montgomery	06	04	34
Freeman, John(C)	1804	Sept. 03	Butler	04	02	26
Freeman, John(C)	1804	Sept. 03	Butler	04	02	26
Freeman, Joshua(E)	1837	March 01	Randolph(Ind	15	20	20
Freeman, Nathan(E)	1832	April 06	Randolph(Ind	15	19	06
Freeman, Nathan(E)	1836	Aug. 22	Randolph(Ind	15	19	06
Freeman, Richard(B)	1814	Feb. 02	Butler	02	10	25
Freeman, Samuel(A)	1804	Aug. 07	Greene	06	04	26
Freeman, Samuel(A)	1804	Aug. 07	Greene	06	04	35
Freeman, Samuel(A)	1805	Aug. 09	Montgomery	06	03	03
Freeman, Samuel(A)	1822	June 11	Miami	04	08	01
Freeman, Samuel(C)	1801	Dec. 22	Hamilton	06	02	06
Freeman, Samuel(C)	1801	Dec. 22	Hamilton	05	03	35
Freeman, Samuel(C)	1801	Dec. 22	Hamilton	05	03	36
Freeman, Samuel(C)	1802	Dec. 10	Hamilton	06	02	06
Freeman, Thornton S.(E)	1829	Nov. 28	Wayne(Ind)	14	18	31
Freeman, William Henderson(E)	1834	Dec. 09	Wayne(Ind)	14	19	15
Freeman, William Henderson(E)	1835	Oct. 12	Randolph(Ind	14	19	10
Frel, James(B)	1811	Aug. 23	Butler	01	09	03
Freland, Rich'd. S.(B)	1831	Jan. 19	Dearborn(Ind	02	06	29
French, Asa(A)	1815	Oct. 03	Miami	05	08	36
French, Dan'l.(A)	1829	Sept. 18	Miami	05	08	15
French, Ezekiel(C)	1812	Sept. 14	Miami	11	01	26
French, Ezekiel(C)	1814	Nov. 23	Miami	11	01	24
French, Henry(E)	1811	Nov. 25	Preble	13	17	08
French, Jacob(E)	1811	Nov. 22	Preble	14	17	08
French, Jacob(E)	1812	Aug. 12	Preble	13	17	05
French, James(C)	1806	March 07	Virginia	09	02	20
French, John(A)	1821	Jan. 16	Greene	01	10	26
French, John(A)	1823	Jan. 18	Greene	01	10	26
French, John(B)	1831	July 05	Hamilton	01	07	29
French, John(B)	1831	Sept. 06	Hamilton	01	07	29

PURCHASER	YEAR	DATE	RESIDENCE	R	T	S
French, John(C)	1813	April 14	Champaign	09	05	22
French, Joseph Jr.(B)	1834	Dec. 25	Dearborn(Ind	03	07	27
French, Micah(C)	1813	April 14	Champaign	09	05	22
French, Ralph(C)	1804	Dec. 31	Montgomery	07	02	20
French, Ralph(C)	1805	July 22	Montgomery	09	02	25
French, Ralph(C)	1805	July 22	Montgomery	09	02	22
French, Samuel(C)	1802	Dec. 31	Hamilton	05	03	33
Frey, Durs(B)	1818	Nov. 03	Hamilton	02	07	11
Frey, Henry Joseph(A)	1816	Dec. 09	Warren	01	08	22
Friend, Andrew(A)	1832	Feb. 06	Miami	05	09	10
Friend, Martin(E)	1836	Aug. 30	Jay Co.,Ind.	15	22	33
Frigin, Uliana(A)	1810	Sept. 07	Butler	02	04	26
Frilling, John(E)	1837	Jan. 13	Cincinnati	12	11	32
Frisar, John(B)	1814	Nov. 29	Kentucky	01	06	32
Fritz, Michael(A)	1808	June 29	Warren	03	06	23
Frizzel, Jacob(C)	1807	Feb. 20	Champaign	10	04	17
Frizzel, Jacob(C)	1808	Jan. 11	Champaign	11	05	18
Frizzel, John(C)	1807	Feb. 20	Champaign	10	04	17
Frizzel, John(C)	1808	Jan. 11	Champaign	11	05	18
Froliger, Arbogost(B)	1832	Dec. 28	Cincinnati	02	07	19
Froman, Jacob(B)	1805	Dec. 06	Dearborn(Ind	01	06	34
Froman, Jacob(B)	1816	Dec. 14	Dearborn(Ind	03	05	34
Froman, Paul(B)	1813	Dec. 15	Jefferson	03	03	35
Froman, Paul(B)	1815	Feb. 18	Switzerland	02	02	31
Froman, Solomon(B)	1833	Dec. 23	Switzerland	03	03	15
Froman, Solomon(B)	1836	March 14	Switzerland	03	03	15
Frost, George(C)	1815	July 04	Greene	09	03	10
Frost, Thomas(A)	1804	Sept. 25	Hamilton	01	02	04
Frost, William(C)	1806	Dec. 27	Montgomery	12	01	20
Fruit, George(B)	1807	Jan. 16	Butler	01	09	26
Fruit, George(B)	1807	Jan. 16	Butler	01	09	23
Fry, John(E)	1837	March 01	Preble	14	21	30
Fry, Theodore(E)	1837	March 01	Preble	14	21	20
Fry, Thompson(E)	1837	March 01	Preble	14	21	20
Fryberger, George(C)	1804	Dec. 27	?	07	02	21
Fudge, David(A)	1805	Nov. 07	Warren	02	08	10
Fudge, David(A)	1814	Nov. 10	Preble	02	09	33
Fudge, David(A)	1814	Nov. 10	Preble	02	08	05
Fudge, David(A)	1815	Jan. 14	Preble	02	08	03
Fudge, David(A)	1817	Dec. 05	Preble	02	09	33
Fudge, David(E)	1836	June 01	Preble	14	19	24
Fudge, Jacob(A)	1805	Oct. 12	Warren	03	05	28
Fudge, Jacob(A)	1805	Nov. 07	Warren	02	08	03
Fudge, Jacob(A)	1806	Dec. 15	Warren	02	08	05
Fudge, Jacob(A)	1812	April 15	Preble	02	08	05
Fudge, Jacob(A)	1828	Oct. 09	Preble	02	09	04
Fugit, John(B)	1816	April 10	Franklin(Ind	02	08	11
Fulghum, Frederick(B)	1823	June 12	Wayne(Ind)	01	16	26
Fulghum, Frederick(B)	1831	Jan. 19	Randolph(Ind	01	16	26
Fulghum, Joseph(B)	1828	Oct. 22	Wayne(Ind)	01	15	21
Fulghum, Mich'l.(B)	1829	Feb. 20	Wayne(Ind)	01	16	22
Fulghum, Mich'l.(B)	1829	Oct. 15	Wayne(Ind)	01	16	27
Fullen, Samuel(E)	1811	Oct. 22	Ind.Territry	12	13	12
Fullen, Samuel(E)	1811	Oct. 29	Franklin(Ind	13	13	03
Fullen, Samuel(E)	1816	Jan. 08	Franklin(Ind	12	13	12
Fullenwider, John(A)	1805	Nov. 11	Butler	03	01	07
Fullenwider, John(A)	1809	Dec. 12	Butler	02	03	01
Fullenwider, John(A)	1809	Dec. 12	Butler	03	01	05
Fuller, Isaac(A)	1810	April 11	Hamilton	01	02	33
Fuller, Isaac(B)	1815	Sept. 06	Franklin(Ind	03	09	12
Fuller, Isaac(B)	1834	Feb. 04	Dearborn(Ind	01	06	10
Fuller, James(B)	1815	Oct. 24	Butler	01	06	12
Fuller, James(C)	1816	Nov. 30	Champaign	10	03	21
Fuller, James(C)	1816	Nov. 30	Champaign	10	03	21
Fuller, James(C)	1829	Jan. 01	Clark	10	03	17
Fuller, James(E)	1816	Aug. 06	Butler	12	11	20
Fuller, John(B)	1812	April 01	Hamilton	01	06	13
Fuller, Moses(C)	1808	June 04	Champaign	09	03	28
Fuller, Moses(C)	1811	Dec. 11	Champaign	09	03	24

PURCHASER	YEAR	DATE	RESIDENCE	R	T	S
Fuller, Moses(C)	1812	Sept. 26	Champaign	09	03	18
Fuller, Robert(C)	1817	May 29	Champaign	10	03	31
Fuller, Sarah(B)	1812	April 01	Hamilton	01	06	13
Fuller, Thomas(B)	1808	Feb. 13	Ind.Territry	01	06	13
Fuller, Valentine(B)	1835	Feb. 07	Cincinnati	02	08	30
Fuller, William(C)	1812	April 15	Butler	08	03	33
Fullhart, Henry(C)	1824	July 31	Clark	09	03	11
Fullhart, Henry(C)	1824	Dec. 22	Clark	09	03	11
Fullhart, Henry(C)	1824	Dec. 22	Clark	09	03	11
Fullhart, John(C)	1824	July 31	Clark	09	03	11
Fullharvest, Jacob(A)	1834	May 23	Pennsylvania	03	10	20
Fullin, John(E)	1813	Nov. 08	Franklin(Ind	12	14	28
Fulton, Samuel(B)	1818	Jan. 30	Dearborn(Ind	01	08	07
Fultz, Balthes(A)	1837	May 05	Fairfield	02	14	21
Fumes, Thomas Wilkinson(A)	1805	Aug. 05	Warren	06	04	20
Fundenburg, David(A)	1818	Nov. 05	Greene	04	05	23
Funderburgh, David(A)	1819	March 19	Greene	04	06	31
Funderburgh, David(A)	1824	June 23	Greene	03	06	14
Funk, Adam(C)	1811	April 09	?	08	05	10
Funk, Isaac(A)	1834	Oct. 06	Warren	02	12	03
Funkhouser, Abraham(B)	1832	May 24	Dearborn(Ind	02	07	02
Funston, William(C)	1819	July 03	Clark	09	03	11
Furgus, James(C)	1811	Aug. 01	Miami	09	02	32
Furman, Benjamin(C)	1805	Sept. 28	Champaign	10	05	06
Furman, Benjamin(C)	1805	Sept. 28	Champaign	11	05	07
Furnace, John(A)	1818	Sept. 04	Miami	05	07	34
Furnas, Benj'n.(A)	1824	Feb. 11	Miami	05	07	27
Furnas, Benj'n.(A)	1825	March 08	Miami	06	03	15
Furnas, Christopher(E)	1838	May 21	Montgomery	15	22	20
Furnas, John(A)	1831	Sept. 27	Miami	05	07	13
Furnas, Sam'l.(A)	1822	March 05	Miami	05	07	27
Furnas, William(A)	1829	Aug. 27	Miami	05	07	22
Furnas, Wm. Jr.(A)	1831	May 09	Miami	05	07	22
Furnes, John(A)	1806	Sept. 11	Warren	05	07	34
Furnes, John(B)	1814	April 12	Clinton	01	11	29
Furney, Emmanuel(A)	1833	Oct. 24	Darke	03	10	11
Furrow, Adam(C)	1815	Nov. 27	Miami	11	01	17
Furrow, Jacob(E)	1837	Nov. 27	Miami	14	22	25
Furrow, James G.(C)	1830	Jan. 20	Miami	12	01	07
Furrow, Jeremiah(A)	1836	June 16	Miami	03	11	05
Furrow, Jeremiah(A)	1836	Sept. 03	Miami	03	12	32
Furrow, Joseph(C)	1828	Nov. 19	Clark	11	03	19
Furrow, William(A)	1832	Aug. 29	Clark	08	01	15
Furrow, William(E)	1837	June 01	Logan	15	22	31
Fusner, John Anthony(B)	1833	Sept. 30	Germany	02	08	31
Fuson, Isaiah(C)	1817	Oct. 13	Champaign	13	04	14
Fuson, Joel(C)	1806	May 03	Champaign	12	03	06
Fuson, Joel(C)	1806	Sept. 06	Champaign	12	04	24
Fuson, Sam'l.(C)	1829	April 27	Champaign	13	04	14
Futer, John(B)	1812	April 01	Hamilton	01	06	13
Futer, Sarah(B)	1812	April 01	Hamilton	01	06	13
Fye, Nicholas(A)	1809	Nov. 13	Montgomery	04	03	10
Fyffe, Wm. H.(C)	1812	Nov. 17	Champaign	12	05	21
Fyffe, Wm. H.(C)	1812	Nov. 17	Champaign	12	05	28
Gaar, Abraham(B)	1807	Jan. 13	Kentucky	01	13	30
Gadd, Thomas(A)	1817	Nov. 22	Warren	04	10	20
Gahagan, William(A)	1805	Sept. 05	Montgomery	06	05	27
Gahagan, William(C)	1801	Dec. 31	Hamilton	07	02	12
Gahagan, William(C)	1802	Dec. 30	Hamilton	07	02	12
Gaines, Richard(A)	1814	July 29	Hamilton	01	03	32
Gaines, Richard(A)	1815	April 11	Hamilton	01	03	31
Gaines, Richard(D)	1813	July 21	Hamilton(Fr)	02	02	11
Gaines, Richard(D)	1814	Jan. 21	Hamilton(Fr)	02	02	11
Gaither, Baisel(B)	1816	April 29	Dearborn(Ind	02	07	11
Galahan, Edward(A)	1807	Sept. 18	Montgomery	06	03	07
Galahan, Edward(A)	1811	Nov. 18	Montgomery	06	03	04
Galbrath, David(B)	1806	Nov. 29	Kentucky	01	13	20
Galbreath, David(E)	1813	July 06	Wayne(Ind)	14	16	30
Galbreath, John(A)	1830	Feb. 20	Darke	03	08	23

PURCHASER	YEAR	DATE	RESIDENCE	R	T	S
Galbreath, John(E)	1813	July 06	Wayne(Ind)	14	16	31
Galbreath, Robt.(C)	1824	July 24	Clark	10	03	11
Gale, George(B)	1817	June 21	Cincinnati	02	03	23
Gales, Richard(A)	1807	July 02	Hamilton	02	04	19
Gallaher, Charles(E)	1835	Sept. 08	Warren	13	18	04
Gallaway, James Junr.(C)	1804	Dec. 28	Greene	07	03	05
Gallaway, James Junr.(C)	1811	April 09	Greene	07	04	36
Gallaway, James M.(C)	1811	April 09	Greene	07	04	35
Gallaway, James(C)	1802	Dec. 11	Hamilton	08	03	05
Gallaway, James(C)	1804	Sept. 04	Greene	08	04	26
Gallaway, James(C)	1804	Sept. 24	Warren	07	04	29
Gallaway, James(C)	1805	Dec. 19	Greene	08	03	05
Gallion, Nathan D.(E)	1836	Jan. 26	Franklin(Ind	13	11	15
Galloway, George(C)	1810	Dec. 12	Greene	07	03	11
Galloway, George(C)	1810	Dec. 13	?	05	02	29
Galloway, James Junr.(C)	1810	Dec. 12	Greene	06	02	01
Galloway, James Junr.(C)	1810	Dec. 12	Greene	06	01	20
Galloway, James Junr.(C)	1810	Dec. 13	?	05	02	29
Galloway, James(C)	1801	Dec. 17	Hamilton	07	03	05
Galloway, James(C)	1801	Dec. 17	Hamilton	07	04	34
Galloway, Joseph(B)	1836	Feb. 11	Wayne(Ind)	01	16	26
Galyean, Jacob(E)	1811	Nov. 01	Preble	13	17	20
Galyean, Thomas(E)	1811	Nov. 01	Preble	13	17	20
Galyen, John(A)	1806	Nov. 14	Montgomery	01	06	19
Galyer, Thomas(A)	1805	Dec. 12	Butler	01	06	29
Gamble, John(A)	1810	Dec. 26	Butler	01	06	03
Gano, Aaron G.(C)	1831	Aug. 08	Cincinnati	08	06	30
Gano, Aaron G.(C)	1831	Aug. 08	Cincinnati	14	04	31
Gano, Aaron G.(C)	1831	Aug. 08	Cincinnati	14	03	30
Gano, Aaron G.(E)	1817	Nov. 01	Cincinnati	13	11	21
Gano, Dan'l.(C)	1831	Aug. 08	Ohio	10	06	29
Gano, Dan'l.(C)	1831	Aug. 08	Ohio	10	06	29
Gano, Dan'l.(C)	1831	Aug. 08	Ohio	10	06	08
Gano, Dan'l.(C)	1831	Aug. 08	Ohio	10	06	08
Gano, Daniel(A)	1831	Aug. 09	Cincinnati	03	07	08
Gano, Daniel(C)	1814	Aug. 13	Cincinnati	12	05	31
Gano, Daniel(C)	1814	Aug. 13	Cincinnati	11	05	36
Gano, Daniel(C)	1831	Aug. 08	Cincinnati	13	05	29
Gano, Daniel(C)	1831	Aug. 08	Cincinnati	13	05	29
Gano, Daniel(C)	1831	Aug. 08	Cincinnati	14	03	30
Gano, Daniel(C)	1831	Aug. 08	Cincinnati	14	03	30
Gano, Daniel(C)	1831	Aug. 08	Cincinnati	14	04	25
Gano, Daniel(C)	1831	Aug. 08	Cincinnati	14	04	31
Gano, Daniel(C)	1831	Aug. 08	Cincinnati	08	06	30
Gano, Daniel(C)	1831	Aug. 08	Cincinnati	09	05	25
Gano, Daniel(C)	1831	Aug. 08	Cincinnati	12	06	32
Gano, Daniel(C)	1831	Aug. 08	Cincinnati	13	03	11
Gano, Daniel(C)	1831	Aug. 08	Cincinnati	14	04	31
Gano, Daniel(C)	1831	Aug. 08	Cincinnati	14	04	31
Gano, Daniel(C)	1831	Aug. 24	Cincinnati	13	04	07
Gano, Daniel(C)	1831	Aug. 24	Cincinnati	13	04	12
Gano, Daniel(C)	1831	Aug. 24	Cincinnati	13	04	08
Gano, Daniel(E)	1817	Nov. 01	Cincinnati	13	11	21
Gano, John S.(A)	1814	April 25	Cincinnati	01	02	21
Gano, John S.(D)	1813	July 09	Cincinnati	01	02	08
Gant, Briton(B)	1811	Sept. 23	Franklin(Ind	02	08	01
Gant, Britton(B)	1828	Feb. 07	Franklin(Ind	01	08	07
Gant, Britton(B)	1832	June 13	Franklin(Ind	02	08	12
Gant, Britton(B)	1837	Feb. 03	Franklin(Ind	02	08	12
Gant, Calvin A.(E)	1836	July 07	Franklin(Ind	13	11	17
Gant, Calvin A.(E)	1836	Oct. 12	Franklin(Ind	13	11	08
Gant, George(B)	1836	Feb. 25	Franklin(Ind	01	08	07
Gant, Giles(B)	1825	April 07	Franklin(Ind	02	08	01
Gant, Giles(B)	1837	Feb. 03	Franklin(Ind	02	08	12
Gant, Stephen(E)	1836	Jan. 22	Franklin(Ind	12	11	15
Gant, Stephen(E)	1836	Feb. 04	Franklin(Ind	12	11	14
Gapens, Eli(E)	1815	Dec. 01	Pennsylvania	13	18	35
Garard, Stephen R.(B)	1836	July 23	Switzerland	03	03	30
Garard, Stephen R.(B)	1837	Feb. 18	Switzerland	03	03	29

PURCHASER	YEAR	DATE	RESIDENCE	R	T	S
Garber, Martin(C)	1831	Oct. 12	Logan	13	04	36
Garberry, William(C)	1816	May 01	Warren	12	02	19
Garberry, Wm.(C)	1831	June 20	Miami	12	02	21
Gard, Aaron(B)	1814	Sept. 19	Butler	01	12	27
Gard, Benjamin(B)	1813	April 13	Butler	01	11	02
Gard, Daniel(E)	1836	Feb. 12	Preble	11	11	02
Gard, Daniel(E)	1837	March 01	Preble	13	21	24
Gard, David(B)	1808	Feb. 29	Dearborn(Ind	01	06	24
Gard, David(B)	1811	Dec. 12	Dearborn(Ind	01	06	24
Gard, Ephraim(B)	1816	June 01	Butler	01	04	29
Gard, Geo.(A)	1831	Feb. 24	Preble	01	09	02
Gard, Gershom(C)	1819	Sept. 03	Clark	10	03	11
Gard, Job(C)	1804	Dec. 28	Greene	10	04	17
Gard, Josephus(B)	1806	Oct. 21	Hamilton	01	12	36
Gard, Josephus(C)	1804	Sept. 03	Hamilton	04	04	29
Gard, Levi(A)	1809	May 29	Preble	01	07	31
Gard, Lot(B)	1815	June 14	Pennsylvania	01	12	23
Gard, Moses(E)	1837	March 24	Preble	13	21	13
Gard, Seth(A)	1801	Sept. 07	Hamilton	02	04	02
Gard, Seth(A)	1806	March 27	Hamilton	01	06	03
Gard, Seth(A)	1813	Oct. 09	Hamilton	01	07	18
Gard, Simeon(A)	1806	Sept. 30	Pennsylvania	01	07	36
Gard, Simeon(A)	1806	Sept. 30	Pennsylvania	01	07	25
Gard, Simeon(A)	1806	Sept. 30	Pennsylvania	01	07	25
Gard, Simeon(A)	1814	July 08	Preble	02	07	31
Gard, Stephen(A)	1806	Feb. 19	Butler	02	08	26
Gard, Timothy(B)	1814	May 24	Dearborn(Ind	01	06	14
Gard, William(B)	1816	Oct. 23	Hamilton	02	02	14
Gard, Wm.(A)	1814	Oct. 14	Butler	01	07	34
Gard, Wm.(A)	1831	Feb. 24	Preble	01	09	02
Garden, George(B)	1810	July 11	Dearborn(Ind	01	02	28
Gardner, Eliab(B)	1811	Oct. 31	Preble	01	11	20
Gardner, Eliab(B)	1811	Nov. 02	Preble	02	11	25
Gardner, Isaac(B)	1815	Oct. 24	Nor.Carolina	01	11	21
Gardner, Isaac(B)	1817	Aug. 02	Nor.Carolina	01	11	21
Gardner, Isaac(B)	1817	Aug. 04	Nor.Carolina	01	11	35
Gardner, Isaac(E)	1814	Oct. 22	Nor.Carolina	14	18	33
Gardner, Isaac(E)	1814	Oct. 22	Nor.Carolina	14	18	21
Gardner, James(B)	1815	July 13	Cincinnati	02	04	04
Gardner, John(B)	1834	June 26	Switzerland	03	03	08
Gardner, John(E)	1830	Jan. 25	Wayne(Ind)	13	17	10
Gardner, Stephen(B)	1811	July 20	Ind.Territry	01	09	03
Gardner, Stephen(B)	1814	March 08	Butler	02	10	36
Gardner, Wm. M.(B)	1838	Jan. 27	Switzerland	03	04	17
Garlough, John(C)	1813	Aug. 10	Greene	08	05	24
Garner, George(A)	1806	Nov. 24	Butler	02	03	07
Garner, Henry(A)	1806	Nov. 24	Butler	01	04	35
Garner, Henry(A)	1806	Nov. 29	Butler	01	03	02
Garner, Henry(A)	1806	Dec. 05	Butler	02	03	06
Garner, Henry(B)	1814	Feb. 05	Franklin(Ind	01	08	34
Garner, John(B)	1832	Feb. 14	Dearborn(Ind	01	07	01
Garner, Samuel(A)	1836	Oct. 25	Butler	01	15	14
Garner, Samuel(A)	1836	Nov. 03	Butler	01	15	14
Garner, Samuel(A)	1836	Nov. 26	Butler	01	15	24
Garner, Samuel(A)	1836	Nov. 26	Butler	01	15	26
Garnes, James(A)	1836	May 26	Clark	03	12	07
Garnes, James(A)	1836	Sept. 28	Clark	03	12	18
Garr, Abraham(B)	1817	Nov. 15	Indiana	01	13	21
Garrard, Henry(C)	1802	Dec. 31	Hamilton	08	01	13
Garrard, Jacob(C)	1817	June 14	Champaign	09	06	15
Garrard, John(C)	1815	July 11	Montgomery	11	01	04
Garrard, Nathaniel(C)	1804	Dec. 24	Montgomery	10	01	24
Garrard, Thomas(E)	1817	Dec. 06	Virginia	14	20	31
Garrard, Thomas(E)	1834	Feb. 24	Randolph(Ind	14	20	31
Garred, Thomas(E)	1819	Dec. 04	Randolph(Ind	14	19	06
Garret, Henry(E)	1816	Dec. 02	Wayne(Ind)	13	17	23
Garret, John(E)	1811	Oct. 25	Ind.Territry	14	16	18
Garretson, Gideon(A)	1818	Sept. 08	Preble	01	09	18
Garrett, Henry(B)	1817	Dec. 20	Preble	01	15	23

PURCHASER	YEAR	DATE	RESIDENCE	R	T	S
Garrett, Henry(E)	1811	Oct. 24	Wayne(Ind)	13	17	24
Garrett, John(E)	1815	May 04	Wayne(Ind)	13	16	11
Garrett, John(E)	1815	May 04	Wayne(Ind)	13	16	12
Garrett, Nathan(B)	1811	Aug. 05	Ind.Territory	01	10	19
Garrett, Nathan(E)	1811	Oct. 25	Franklin(Ind	14	16	17
Garrett, Nathan(E)	1817	May 26	Wayne(Ind)	13	16	12
Garrigues, Jeptha(B)	1818	March 12	Butler	03	07	35
Garrison, Abraham(B)	1811	Sept. 28	Hamilton	01	06	22
Garrison, David(C)	1816	July 18	Greene	12	03	21
Garrison, Elijah(B)	1814	Jan. 20	Hamilton	01	06	02
Garrison, Elijah(B)	1814	Feb. 22	Hamilton	01	07	28
Garrison, James(B)	1834	Jan. 23	Dearborn(Ind	01	06	09
Garrison, James(B)	1835	June 03	Dearborn(Ind	01	06	04
Garrison, John Wells(E)	1835	Jan. 15	Franklin(Ind	12	12	24
Garrison, John(B)	1811	Dec. 11	Butler	01	06	01
Garrison, Jonathan(C)	1811	April 09	Butler	04	02	09
Garrison, Leonard(A)	1831	Aug. 27	Butler	04	07	30
Garrison, Leonard(A)	1831	Sept. 13	Butler	04	07	30
Garrison, Levi(A)	1803	Feb. 05	Hamilton	03	03	19
Garrison, Lorenzo Dow(E)	1836	June 21	Dearborn(Ind	11	10	03
Garrison, Samuel(E)	1811	Oct. 28	Franklin(Ind	12	12	03
Garrison, Silas(B)	1813	June 29	Butler	01	06	15
Garst, Abraham(C)	1818	Oct. 17	Clark	10	03	09
Garver, John(C)	1811	Dec. 11	Champaign	09	04	35
Garvin, John(C)	1812	Nov. 14	Champaign	10	05	33
Garvin, Thomas(E)	1814	Dec. 16	Franklin(Ind	13	13	21
Garwood, Johnathan(C)	1801	Dec. 31	Hamilton	04	04	34
Gary, James Junr.(B)	1832	Aug. 03	Union(Ind)	03	09	36
Gass, Frederick(C)	1806	July 21	Greene	07	03	11
Gass, Joseph(E)	1817	Aug. 11	Wayne(Ind)	14	19	29
Gaston, Joseph(C)	1809	Aug. 11	Butler	02	02	26
Gaston, Robert(B)	1816	Jan. 05	Hamilton	01	02	12
Gaston, William(D)	1812	Jan. 01	Pennsylvania	02	03	08
Gates, Henry(C)	1813	Nov. 05	Champaign	10	04	25
Gates, Jacob(A)	1817	June 20	Butler	01	10	07
Gates, Jacob(A)	1827	Aug. 20	Darke	01	10	07
Gates, Jacob(C)	1807	Sept. 15	U. S. Army	11	01	04
Gates, Jacob(C)	1815	March 27	Miami	11	01	04
Gates, John(A)	1819	Jan. 05	Butler	05	10	19
Gates, John(A)	1819	April 19	Butler	05	10	19
Gates, John(C)	1813	Nov. 05	Champaign	10	04	25
Gates, Noah(B)	1818	Jan. 19	Cincinnati	02	02	20
Gates, Richard(A)	1813	April 14	Hamilton	02	04	19
Gates, Simon(C)	1813	Aug. 30	Hamilton	09	06	24
Gates, Timothy(E)	1836	Oct. 17	Washington	15	22	33
Gause, Samuel(A)	1815	Oct. 10	Warren	01	06	11
Gause, Solomon(A)	1815	Jan. 14	Greene	01	06	12
Gause, Solomon(A)	1816	Aug. 17	Greene	01	07	26
Gavin, James(B)	1826	Oct. 21	Butler	02	09	15
Gaymann, David(B)	1815	Jan. 11	Franklin(Ind	02	08	05
Gazlay, Sayrs(B)	1832	Feb. 13	Shelby	02	02	19
Geant, Alexander(A)	1836	Nov. 12	Mercer	01	15	36
Gearheard, John Y.(A)	1828	March 28	Miami	05	10	27
Gearheart, Wm.(C)	1825	Nov. 28	Champaign	11	04	26
Gebhart, Anthony(A)	1815	Dec. 07	Montgomery	03	05	05
Gebhart, George(A)	1836	May 24	Montgomery	03	11	08
Gebhart, George(A)	1836	Aug. 09	Montgomery	03	12	33
Gebhart, Henry(A)	1810	Nov. 12	Montgomery	05	03	22
Gebhart, Henry(E)	1836	Oct. 04	Butler	15	21	31
Gebhart, Jacob(C)	1829	Sept. 17	Montgomery	13	02	35
Gee, Benjamin(A)	1806	Feb. 24	Butler	04	02	09
Gee, Benjamin(A)	1807	March 14	Butler	04	03	29
Gee, Benjamin(A)	1812	April 15	Butler	04	03	29
Gee, Edward(A)	1812	April 15	Butler	04	03	29
Geer, John(C)	1813	July 19	Champaign	09	05	03
Geeseman, George(A)	1816	Dec. 02	Miami	02	12	30
Geeseman, George(C)	1806	Dec. 10	Montgomery	09	02	19
Geise, Jno. Hy.(A)	1837	Dec. 23	Cincinnati	02	14	01
Geisser, John Ulrick(B)	1817	Dec. 02	Cincinnati	02	07	29

PURCHASER	YEAR	DATE	RESIDENCE	R	T	S
Gelam, Jonathan(B)	1806	March 07	Ind.Territry	03	10	25
Gelbraith, Robert(E)	1815	May 04	Wayne(Ind)	13	16	11
Gelbraith, Robert(E)	1815	May 04	Wayne(Ind)	14	16	06
Gennings, Timothy(B)	1835	Aug. 13	Franklin(Ind	02	08	15
Gentle, John(A)	1829	June 15	Preble	02	10	21
George, Andrew(C)	1832	March 03	Franklin(Ind	12	10	04
George, Benjamin(B)	1817	July 24	Franklin(Ind	01	08	21
George, Henry(E)	1836	May 12	Preble	11	11	01
George, Hiram(E)	1834	Feb. 24	Franklin(Ind	12	11	29
George, Hiram(E)	1836	Aug. 19	Franklin(Ind	12	11	32
George, John(E)	1836	March 04	Franklin(Ind	12	12	32
George, Matthew(C)	1831	Dec. 19	Logan	13	04	28
George, Peter(A)	1838	Sept. 05	Miami	02	14	03
George, Reuben(A)	1811	Dec. 23	Butler	01	03	17
George, Reuben(A)	1813	Aug. 06	Butler	01	03	17
George, Richd. D.(C)	1811	Nov. 18	Champaign	11	05	05
George, Will'm.(E)	1830	Jan. 22	Franklin(Ind	12	10	04
George, William(C)	1817	June 05	Champaign	13	04	28
George, William(C)	1827	July 14	Logan	13	04	34
George, William(E)	1812	Nov. 07	Franklin(Ind	13	11	06
George, William(E)	1817	Aug. 22	Franklin(Ind	12	10	04
George, Wm.(C)	1811	Nov. 18	Champaign	11	05	05
Georges, Nicholas(A)	1836	Oct. 03	Darke	03	11	03
Gephart, Emanuel(C)	1818	Jan. 29	Montgomery	06	01	19
Gephart, John(C)	1818	Jan. 29	Montgomery	06	01	19
Gephart, Peter(A)	1804	July 09	Montgomery	05	02	09
Gerard, John(A)	1811	Jan. 24	Butler	01	02	22
Gerard, John(A)	1815	Nov. 09	Hamilton	01	02	27
Gerard, Nathaniel(C)	1804	Dec. 24	Montgomery	11	01	19
Gerard, Nathaniel(C)	1804	Dec. 24	Montgomery	11	01	13
Gere, Luther(A)	1814	Dec. 10	Hamilton	01	02	13
Gerhard, John Jr.(E)	1838	Sept. 17	Montgomery	15	21	29
Gerrard, Abner(C)	1801	Dec. 30	Hamilton	05	03	34
Gerrard, David(C)	1806	Aug. 19	Montgomery	11	01	03
Gerrard, David(C)	1811	Dec. 11	Montgomery	11	01	03
Gerrard, Jacob(C)	1801	Dec. 29	Hamilton	05	02	05
Gerrard, Jacob(C)	1806	July 28	Greene	10	01	06
Gerrard, Jacob(C)	1811	Sept. 07	Warren	09	06	07
Gerrard, Jesse(A)	1805	Sept. 10	Montgomery	06	04	03
Gerrard, Jesse(A)	1806	March 08	Montgomery	06	04	05
Gerrard, Jesse(A)	1806	March 21	Montgomery	06	04	09
Gerrard, Jesse(A)	1811	Aug. 13	Cincinnati	06	04	09
Gerrard, John(A)	1810	Dec. 14	Butler	01	02	22
Gerrard, John(C)	1802	Dec. 28	Hamilton	10	01	09
Gerrard, John(C)	1804	Aug. 11	Montgomery	10	01	08
Gerrard, William(E)	1811	Oct. 28	Dearborn(Ind	12	13	22
Gerrat, John(B)	1806	Sept. 10	Highland	01	13	01
Gerringer, Alex'r.(A)	1830	Nov. 19	Darke	01	12	05
Gerringer, Alex'r.(A)	1831	Aug. 09	Darke	01	12	05
Gess, James(A)	1806	July 18	Butler	02	06	35
Gest, John(B)	1818	March 31	Philadelphia	02	03	36
Gest, Joseph G.(E)	1837	Jan. 14	Greene	14	21	24
Gettys, Joseph Jr.(A)	1835	Oct. 14	Richland	03	11	22
Gheen, Nathan(A)	1819	Dec. 06	Montgomery	07	01	08
Gibbins, John(B)	1817	Oct. 16	Dearborn(Ind	01	03	30
Gibbs, Charlotte(B)	1812	June 11	Ohio	02	10	34
Gibbs, David(A)	1807	Aug. 15	Tennessee	03	07	10
Gibbs, David(A)	1818	Jan. 06	Preble	01	10	32
Gibbs, Henry(B)	1812	June 11	Ohio	02	10	34
Gibbs, Hugh(C)	1813	Aug. 10	Champaign	12	05	31
Gibbs, James Jack(C)	1830	Feb. 04	?	12	04	08
Gibbs, John(B)	1812	June 11	Ohio	02	10	34
Gibbs, John(B)	1817	Sept. 19	Hamilton	02	03	19
Gibbs, John(B)	1817	Sept. 19	Hamilton	02	03	20
Gibbs, John(B)	1830	July 16	Dearborn(Ind	02	03	07
Gibbs, John(B)	1832	July 07	Dearborn(Ind	02	03	07
Gibbs, John(B)	1836	April 25	Dearborn(Ind	02	03	18
Gibbs, John(B)	1837	Oct. 23	Dearborn(Ind	03	04	24
Gibbs, Nathan Fitch(C)	1830	Feb. 04	?	12	04	08

PURCHASER	YEAR	DATE	RESIDENCE	R	T	S
Gibbs, Robert(B)	1837	March 20	Hamilton	01	17	24
Gibbs, Samuel(C)	1807	July 20	Champaign	12	05	31
Gibbs, Samuel(C)	1807	Aug. 12	Champaign	12	05	31
Gibbs, Samuel(C)	1807	Sept. 02	Champaign	11	05	35
Gibbs, Samuel(C)	1807	Sept. 02	Champaign	11	05	36
Gibbs, Samuel(C)	1808	March 28	Champaign	12	05	31
Gibbs, Samuel(C)	1813	April 14	Champaign	12	05	31
Gibbs, William(B)	1812	June 11	Ohio	02	10	34
Gibson, Christopher(B)	1834	Nov. 01	Dearborn(Ind	01	06	08
Gibson, James P.(A)	1820	Jan. 11	Jackson	01	08	30
Gibson, James(B)	1814	April 25	Ind.Territory	01	04	31
Gibson, James(B)	1833	Jan. 22	Dearborn(Ind	02	03	17
Gibson, John(A)	1831	Nov. 25	Miami	06	08	15
Gibson, John(B)	1816	May 25	Pennsylvania	01	07	29
Gibson, John(B)	1816	May 25	Pennsylvania	01	06	03
Gibson, John(B)	1817	June 23	Dearborn(Ind	01	07	35
Gibson, Levi(B)	1833	Aug. 12	Switzerland	02	02	31
Gibson, Robert(A)	1809	Oct. 07	Montgomery	07	01	30
Gibson, Robert(A)	1809	Oct. 07	Montgomery	06	08	25
Gibson, Robert(A)	1809	Oct. 07	Montgomery	06	08	24
Gibson, William(B)	1818	Nov. 04	Dearborn(Ind	02	04	33
Gibson, William(B)	1832	Aug. 08	Dearborn(Ind	02	03	17
Giesman, John William(C)	1815	Feb. 16	Miami	09	02	14
Giesman, John(C)	1815	Nov. 03	Miami	09	02	08
Giffen, James(A)	1805	Sept. 14	Hamilton	02	05	13
Giffin, Samuel(B)	1833	May 21	Dearborn(Ind	02	04	31
Giffin, Samuel(B)	1833	Oct. 22	Dearborn(Ind	02	04	31
Giffin, William(A)	1831	Nov. 08	Warren	05	07	02
Giffin, William(A)	1831	Nov. 08	Warren	05	08	35
Giffin, William(A)	1832	March 13	Warren	05	07	04
Gifford, William(A)	1808	Dec. 07	Preble	03	04	28
Gift, Jacob(A)	1814	Dec. 10	Preble	03	04	03
Gift, Nicholas(A)	1805	Nov. 29	Montgomery	03	04	03
Gift, Peter(A)	1817	Oct. 21	Preble	03	08	28
Gigandet, Nicholas(A)	1836	Feb. 23	Hamilton	03	11	12
Giger, Jacob(A)	1814	Oct. 22	Tennessee	01	11	28
Gilbert, Amos(B)	1812	Oct. 07	Hamilton	03	02	11
Gilbert, Amos(B)	1816	May 24	Switzerland	02	03	28
Gilbert, John H.(B)	1836	Oct. 10	Switzerland	02	02	14
Gilbert, Jonathan(E)	1811	Nov. 21	Wayne(Ind)	13	15	21
Gilbert, Richmond(A)	1819	Jan. 08	Butler	02	13	36
Gilbert, Richmond(A)	1819	Jan. 08	Butler	02	13	25
Gilbert, Thomas(A)	1838	Feb. 13	Miami	02	15	35
Gilbert, Thomas(A)	1838	Feb. 13	Miami	02	15	34
Gilbraith, David(B)	1811	Dec. 11	Wayne(Ind)	01	13	07
Gilbraith, John(A)	1811	Dec. 11	Miami	04	08	36
Gilbreath, Robert(E)	1811	Oct. 25	Ind.Territry	14	16	18
Gilchrist, Robert(A)	1802	June 12	Pennsylvania	06	03	31
Gilchrist, Robert(C)	1802	Dec. 14	Hamilton	05	02	10
Gildersleeve, Isaac(A)	1803	Dec. 20	Butler	03	02	11
Gildersleeve, John(A)	1801	Aug. 21	Hamilton	03	02	14
Gildersleve, Henry(A)	1817	Oct. 08	New York	05	09	11
Gildersleve, Henry(C)	1817	Oct. 08	New York	11	01	17
Gilfillen, John(A)	1833	March 26	Clermont	08	01	05
Gilkey, Robert(A)	1804	Sept. 26	Butler	03	03	18
Gillam, Jonathan(E)	1813	Oct. 02	Franklin(Ind	12	13	29
Gillam, Thomas(E)	1813	Oct. 02	Franklin(Ind	12	15	22
Gillam, Thomas(E)	1816	Dec. 05	Clinton	13	20	27
Gillaspy, Martin(B)	1818	Oct. 26	Kentucky	03	03	22
Gilleand, Thomas(C)	1806	March 07	Jefferson	09	04	22
Gilleland, Samuel(C)	1806	June 13	Champaign	10	04	15
Gilleland, Thomas(B)	1814	May 23	Champaign	03	03	31
Gillen, Thomas(E)	1811	Oct. 28	Franklin(Ind	12	13	14
Gillespie, George Junr.(A)	1805	July 30	Warren	03	04	03
Gillespie, George(A)	1802	Sept. 15	Hamilton	05	02	19
Gillespie, George(A)	1803	March 19	Hamilton	03	05	34
Gillespie, George(A)	1805	May 14	Warren	04	03	35
Gillespie, George(A)	1819	Nov. 08	Montgomery	06	08	23
Gillespie, George(B)	1805	Dec. 12	Warren	01	13	24

PURCHASER	YEAR	DATE	RESIDENCE	R	T	S
Gillespie, George(C)	1804	Sept. 04	Montgomery	04	03	29
Gillespie, James Sr.(A)	1819	June 04	Greene	06	03	09
Gillespie, John M.(A)	1824	Aug. 16	Warren	06	03	21
Gillespie, Joseph(E)	1817	July 11	Greene	13	15	03
Gillespie, Robert(A)	1814	May 28	Warren	01	03	12
Gillespie, Robert(B)	1819	Aug. 23	Dearborn(Ind	02	03	21
Gillespie, Robt.(B)	1827	Aug. 21	Dearborn(Ind	02	03	21
Gillespie, Robt.(B)	1829	Aug. 19	Dearborn(Ind	02	03	21
Gillespie, William(A)	1816	Oct. 24	?	06	04	22
Gillespie, William(A)	1820	March 25	Montgomery	06	03	09
Gilliam, Grover(E)	1836	Nov. 09	Butler	14	21	36
Gilliam, Hiram(E)	1836	Nov. 09	Butler	15	21	31
Gilligan, Carmick(B)	1806	Nov. 10	Cincinnati	01	10	30
Gilliland, John(B)	1814	Nov. 17	Switzerland	03	02	01
Gilliland, John(B)	1815	April 11	Switzerland	03	03	31
Gilliland, John(B)	1818	June 01	Switzerland	01	02	30
Gilliland, John(E)	1822	Aug. 19	Union(Ind)	14	15	31
Gilliland, Thomas(C)	1811	April 09	Champaign	09	04	22
Gillispie, George Jr.(A)	1805	July 30	Warren	03	06	28
Gillispie, George(A)	1804	Sept. 24	Montgomery	06	04	11
Gillispie, George(C)	1804	Sept. 24	Montgomery	04	02	11
Gillispie, George, Jr.(A)	1805	July 06	Warren	03	06	32
Gillmore, William(C)	1812	Nov. 09	Champaign	09	05	02
Gillum, Thomas(E)	1818	April 29	Clinton	13	19	09
Gillum, Thomas(E)	1833	March 01	Randolph(Ind	13	19	04
Gillum, Thomas(E)	1833	Sept. 20	Randolph(Ind	13	19	04
Gillum, Thomas(E)	1833	Sept. 20	Randolph(Ind	13	19	03
Gillum, Thomas(E)	1833	Sept. 20	Randolph(Ind	13	19	15
Gillum, Thomas(E)	1836	April 21	Randolph(Ind	13	19	04
Gilman, John D.(A)	1837	Feb. 06	Miami	03	12	33
Gilmore, Luther(C)	1813	July 12	Champaign	09	05	03
Gilmore, William(A)	1818	Aug. 19	Franklin(Ind	01	06	15
Gilpatrick, Rufus(E)	1837	May 18	Darke	14	21	19
Gilpin, Henry(E)	1836	Jan. 30	Clinton	13	19	26
Gilpin, Joseph(E)	1836	Feb. 18	Clinton	13	19	35
Gilpin, Thomas(E)	1836	Oct. 18	Randolph(Ind	13	19	35
Giltner, Asahel(E)	1832	Feb. 14	Franklin(Ind	13	12	30
Giltner, Asahel(E)	1832	Oct. 06	Franklin(Ind	13	12	30
Giltner, Geo.(E)	1832	Oct. 06	Franklin(Ind	13	12	30
Giltner, George(E)	1832	Feb. 14	Franklin(Ind	13	12	30
Ginger, George(A)	1827	Oct. 16	Montgomery	01	12	15
Ginger, Jacob(A)	1837	May 19	Darke	01	12	18
Ginn, Gabriel(E)	1812	Jan. 13	Kentucky	12	13	23
Girard, Peter(B)	1816	July 01	Franklin(Ind	02	09	05
Girivils, John V.(A)	1838	Jan. 17	Cincinnati	02	15	36
Girton, Christopher(B)	1814	Sept. 06	Butler	01	10	22
Girton, Felix(B)	1828	Oct. 18	Wayne(Ind)	01	13	36
Gish, Christopher(E)	1837	Nov. 20	Miami	15	22	21
Gish, John(C)	1831	Feb. 07	Shelby	13	02	33
Gish, Samuel(A)	1834	March 03	Butler	08	01	03
Gisser, Frederick(E)	1837	Aug. 02	Cincinnati	12	11	13
Gist, Elihu H.(E)	1836	Sept. 26	Darke	15	19	18
Gist, Silas(B)	1832	Jan. 30	Darke	01	15	01
Gittinger, John(B)	1837	June 06	Darke	01	19	36
Givan, George(B)	1825	June 04	Dearborn(Ind	03	07	26
Givan, Gilbert T.(B)	1818	June 12	Dearborn(Ind	03	06	02
Givan, Gilbert T.(B)	1836	March 09	Dearborn(Ind	02	05	17
Givan, Joshua(B)	1825	June 04	Dearborn(Ind	03	07	35
Givans, Edward(A)	1831	Oct. 08	Darke	03	08	18
Givans, Mary(A)	1826	Feb. 20	Warren	03	08	18
Givin, John(E)	1814	Nov. 23	Wayne(Ind)	13	18	30
Glaize, George(E)	1811	Oct. 22	Pickaway	12	14	01
Glaize, George(E)	1811	Oct. 22	Pickaway	12	14	01
Glaize, George(E)	1811	Oct. 23	Pickaway	12	16	36
Glaize, George(E)	1811	Oct. 23	Pickaway	12	16	35
Glardon, James(B)	1833	Jan. 16	Cincinnati	01	06	05
Glass, George(C)	1806	Aug. 01	Champaign	10	04	29
Glass, John(B)	1818	Feb. 26	Warren	02	04	33
Glass, Robert(B)	1818	March 07	Hamilton	03	06	15

119

PURCHASER	YEAR	DATE	RESIDENCE	R	T	S
Glass, Robert(B)	1836	Jan. 18	Hamilton	03	06	15
Glassford, Alexander(E)	1836	Dec. 26	Randolph(Ind	15	22	14
Glassmire, Abraham(C)	1804	Dec. 31	Montgomery	08	02	07
Gledewell, Robert(B)	1806	April 15	Ind.Territry	02	10	34
Glenn, Hugh(B)	1818	March 05	Cincinnati	03	04	36
Glenn, Hugh(B)	1818	March 05	Cincinnati	03	03	03
Glenn, Hugh(C)	1813	Nov. 09	Ohio	11	05	33
Glenn, James(A)	1819	Sept. 28	Hamilton	06	08	26
Glenn, James(A)	1819	Sept. 28	Hamilton	06	08	35
Glenn, James(A)	1819	Sept. 28	Hamilton	06	08	24
Glenn, James(E)	1818	May 14	Cincinnati	13	11	09
Glenn, John(C)	1811	Dec. 11	Champaign	11	05	17
Glenn, John(C)	1812	April 13	Champaign	11	05	28
Glenn, John(C)	1813	Nov. 09	Ohio	11	05	33
Glenn, Joseph B.(B)	1839	Feb. 23	Switzerland	03	04	21
Glenn, Joseph(E)	1814	Dec. 02	Franklin(Ind	13	12	02
Glenn, William(C)	1811	Dec. 11	Champaign	11	05	17
Glenn, William(C)	1812	April 13	Champaign	11	05	28
Glenn, William(C)	1813	Nov. 09	Ohio	11	05	33
Glessner, Benj'n.(E)	1838	Dec. 13	Preble	15	21	30
Glessner, Moses(E)	1838	Dec. 13	Preble	15	21	30
Glidewell, Robt. Jr.(E)	1815	Oct. 20	Franklin(Ind	12	13	30
Glidwell, Mastin(E)	1814	May 20	Butler	13	13	01
Glidwell, Robert(B)	1813	June 07	Warren	02	09	03
Glines, John(A)	1803	Aug. 31	Butler	03	03	17
Glines, John(A)	1805	Dec. 03	Butler	03	03	07
Glines, John(A)	1807	May 26	Butler	02	08	25
Glines, John(A)	1811	April 09	Butler	03	03	07
Gloshon, John(E)	1836	Feb. 13	Franklin(Ind	12	11	35
Gloshon, John(E)	1836	Sept. 06	Franklin(Ind	12	11	35
Gloshon, Nicholas(E)	1837	March 28	Franklin(Ind	12	11	23
Glover, Samuel(C)	1807	May 25	Kentucky	11	05	13
Glover, Samuel(C)	1813	April 14	Champaign	11	05	13
Glover, William(A)	1815	Nov. 10	Pickaway	03	11	35
Glover, Zachariah(B)	1808	Feb. 08	Dearborn(Ind	02	09	23
Glover, Zachariah(E)	1813	March 29	Franklin(Ind	12	14	20
Gloyd, Asa(B)	1818	June 04	Hamilton	03	06	23
Gobel, Daniel(C)	1806	Sept. 09	Champaign	09	05	05
Gobel, Rob't.(B)	1814	July 12	Butler	01	11	31
Goble, Abner(B)	1815	Jan. 26	Butler	01	10	15
Goble, Benoni(A)	1814	Jan. 20	Butler	03	03	15
Goble, Boni(B)	1815	Jan. 26	Butler	01	10	15
Goble, Isaac(E)	1836	May 27	Franklin(Ind	12	11	03
Goble, Jane(A)	1837	March 01	Butler	01	13	26
Goble, Stephen(B)	1806	Oct. 10	Hamilton	02	08	14
Goble, Stephen(B)	1811	Dec. 11	Franklin(Ind	02	08	14
Goddard, Jesse(C)	1812	June 13	Champaign	10	04	36
Goddard, Jesse(C)	1828	Nov. 25	Champaign	10	03	06
Goddard, Jesse(C)	1829	June 27	Champaign	10	04	35
Goddard, Jesse(C)	1829	Sept. 11	Clark	10	03	05
Goddard, Rich'd. Tilton(B)	1831	Dec. 13	Switzerland	01	02	31
Godderd, Jesse(C)	1817	Aug. 01	Champaign	10	04	36
Godfrey, Elias B.(A)	1831	April 14	Darke	01	11	33
Godfrey, Thomas(A)	1816	Sept. 24	Greene	01	10	03
Goe, James(A)	1835	Dec. 05	Warren	02	13	26
Goe, James(A)	1837	Jan. 10	Warren	02	13	10
Goedert, John E.(B)	1837	Oct. 13	Cincinnati	03	05	24
Goff, William(B)	1813	Sept. 10	Hamilton	01	10	34
Goffine, Peter(A)	1836	Oct. 03	Stark	03	12	35
Goffine, Peter(A)	1836	Oct. 25	Stark	03	12	35
Golay, Elisha(B)	1814	July 11	Jefferson	02	02	18
Golay, Elisha(B)	1815	Jan. 24	Switzerland	02	01	05
Gold, James(B)	1814	May 02	Franklin(Ind	01	08	25
Gold, James(B)	1832	Jan. 21	Franklin(Ind	01	08	34
Goldin, Thomas(B)	1811	March 02	Cincinnati	02	08	13
Golding, George(B)	1832	June 05	Dearborn(Ind	02	05	33
Golding, George(B)	1834	Feb. 03	Dearborn(Ind	02	05	33
Golding, James(B)	1833	Nov. 09	Franklin(Ind	03	09	24
Golding, John(A)	1802	June 04	Hamilton	01	02	28

PURCHASER	YEAR	DATE	RESIDENCE	R	T	S
Goldmeier, Henry Wm.(E)	1836	Oct. 14	Cincinnati	11	10	23
Goldsborough,Chas.Washngtn(C)	1805	June 29	DistColumbia	09	05	30
Goldsborough,Chas.Washngtn(C)	1805	June 29	DistColumbia	10	05	25
Goldsmith, John(A)	1806	June 03	Butler	02	07	04
Goldtrap, John(B)	1814	March 28	Hamilton	01	09	25
Goll, Joseph(B)	1833	July 20	Cincinnati	03	08	02
Good, John(A)	1816	Sept. 19	Butler	04	03	21
Good, John(A)	1825	Jan. 25	Montgomery	03	07	05
Good, Valentine(A)	1804	Nov. 12	Montgomery	04	03	11
Goodfellow, Moo[r](C)	1808	Jan. 13	Champaign	09	06	22
Goodfellow, Moor(C)	1813	March 22	Champaign	09	06	22
Goodfellow, Moore(C)	1808	Jan. 13	Champaign	09	06	22
Goodin, John(A)	1819	Aug. 27	Ross	01	11	03
Goodin, John(A)	1819	Aug. 27	Ross	01	11	04
Gooding, David(B)	1814	Feb. 02	Kentucky	01	12	34
Goodlander, Jacob(A)	1815	Oct. 06	Montgomery	04	09	24
Goodlander, Jacob(A)	1815	Oct. 26	Montgomery	02	11	32
Goodman, David C.(E)	1836	Oct. 29	Montgomery	15	21	29
Goodman, Joseph(A)	1836	Oct. 12	Montgomery	01	15	14
Goodman, William(E)	1836	Oct. 29	Montgomery	15	21	29
Goodner, Daniel(B)	1834	June 23	Dearborn(Ind	03	04	29
Goodner, Daniel(B)	1836	April 25	Dearborn(Ind	03	04	29
Goodner, Jacob(B)	1815	March 13	Kentucky	01	03	19
Goodner, Jacob(B)	1817	Dec. 31	Dearborn(Ind	02	03	25
Goodner, Jacob(B)	1832	March 01	Dearborn(Ind	02	03	25
Goodner, Jacob(B)	1834	June 23	Dearborn(Ind	03	04	29
Goodner, John(B)	1832	Feb. 15	Dearborn(Ind	02	03	14
Goodrich, Abijah(B)	1816	April 18	Hamilton	01	04	20
Goodrich, Henry(C)	1817	Sept. 29	Montgomery	12	01	13
Goodrich, Rebecca(E)	1832	Dec. 05	Randolph(Ind	14	20	18
Goodwin, Benjamin D.(E)	1836	Sept. 12	Franklin(Ind	12	12	31
Goodwin, Benjamin Deford(E)	1834	March 17	Franklin(Ind	12	12	33
Goodwin, Daniel(E)	1824	Oct. 05	Hamilton	12	12	29
Goodwin, Enoch Lashire(E)	1835	Dec. 29	Franklin(Ind	11	10	22
Goodwin, James(A)	1824	June 08	Preble	03	04	22
Goodwin, James(B)	1812	July 04	Dearborn(Ind	01	06	23
Goodwin, Jehu(B)	1826	Oct. 23	Dearborn(Ind	01	06	15
Goodwin, Jehu(B)	1830	April 03	Dearborn(Ind	01	06	15
Goodwin, Joseph(E)	1837	Jan. 18	Preble	14	19	18
Goodwin, Joseph(E)	1837	Feb. 01	Preble	13	19	24
Goodwin, Miles(A)	1811	Aug. 02	Preble	03	04	06
Goodwin, Nathan(A)	1806	June 12	Butler	03	04	17
Goodwin, Richard(A)	1806	June 12	Butler	03	04	17
Goodwin, Richard(E)	1836	Nov. 04	Greene	15	20	08
Goodwin, Sam'l.(D)	1814	March 26	Warren	03	05	11
Goodwin, Sam'l.(E)	1831	Nov. 01	Franklin(Ind	13	12	26
Goodwin, William R.(A)	1818	July 10	Cincinnati	04	06	11
Goodwin, William R.(B)	1819	June 17	Cincinnati	02	03	21
Goodwin, William R.(E)	1819	Oct. 19	Hamilton	14	21	11
Goodwin, William(A)	1806	June 12	Butler	03	04	17
Goodwine, Seth(B)	1805	June 15	Hamilton	02	08	02
Goodwine, Sith(A)	1806	March 18	Butler	01	03	06
Goos, John Herman(E)	1837	April 15	Cincinnati	11	10	11
Gootee, James Angevine(B)	1835	Jan. 05	Hamilton	01	06	05
Gordan, George(C)	1801	Dec. 26	Kentucky	04	03	21
Gordan, John(C)	1801	Dec. 26	Hamilton	05	02	01
Gorden, Orvill(E)	1824	Dec. 22	Franklin(Ind	12	13	35
Gorden, Orvill(E)	1835	May 14	Franklin(Ind	13	12	19
Gorden, Orvill(E)	1835	Dec. 24	Franklin(Ind	13	12	19
Gorden, Orvill(E)	1836	Jan. 13	Franklin(Ind	13	12	18
Gorden, William(E)	1835	March 13	Franklin(Ind	13	12	29
Gorden, William(E)	1835	March 13	Franklin(Ind	13	12	29
Gorden, William(E)	1836	Jan. 13	Franklin(Ind	13	12	30
Gorden, William(E)	1836	Oct. 15	Franklin(Ind	12	12	25
Gordin, James(A)	1832	Aug. 24	Clark	08	01	14
Gordon, Charles(B)	1811	Oct. 29	Wayne(Ind)	02	12	13
Gordon, Charles(B)	1816	March 26	Preble	01	12	13
Gordon, Charles(E)	1816	Nov. 09	Wayne(Ind)	13	16	14
Gordon, George(A)	1803	Aug. 11	Warren	05	04	25

PURCHASER	YEAR	DATE	RESIDENCE	R	T	S
Gordon, George(B)	1827	Sept. 03	Dearborn(Ind	02	04	17
Gordon, James(A)	1814	Sept. 14	Butler	01	07	12
Gordon, James(A)	1815	Sept. 14	Butler	01	07	13
Gordon, James(A)	1815	Dec. 14	Butler	01	07	14
Gordon, James(A)	1815	Dec. 20	Preble	01	07	20
Gordon, James(A)	1818	Aug. 21	Butler	02	10	07
Gordon, James(A)	1819	June 08	Butler	02	10	17
Gordon, James(A)	1819	Sept. 15	Butler	02	10	17
Gordon, James(B)	1807	June 29	Warren	01	12	05
Gordon, James(B)	1817	June 09	Butler	02	10	31
Gordon, John(A)	1816	June 15	Butler	03	10	34
Gordon, John(A)	1817	June 11	Warren	02	08	17
Gordon, John(A)	1817	Aug. 12	Warren	01	09	24
Gordon, Philip(A)	1804	Aug. 13	Butler	03	02	07
Gordon, Philip(A)	1806	Nov. 29	Butler	02	04	10
Gordon, Philip(A)	1810	Dec. 12	Butler	02	05	19
Gordon, Richard(C)	1816	Nov. 30	Champaign	09	04	29
Gordon, Robert(A)	1819	March 27	Butler	01	09	02
Gordon, Rufus(B)	1816	March 06	Dearborn(Ind	01	03	18
Gordon, Sam'l.(C)	1828	Dec. 29	Warren	11	03	34
Gordon, Samuel(A)	1816	June 18	Preble	01	07	20
Gordon, Thomas(E)	1836	Sept. 06	Butler	14	19	19
Gordon, William(E)	1811	Nov. 04	Hamilton	12	12	25
Gordon, William(E)	1818	Jan. 19	Clermont	12	12	25
Gorman, Hugh(A)	1831	March 08	Butler	02	10	32
Gorman, Hugh(A)	1831	March 08	Butler	02	10	32
Gorman, Mary(A)	1839	Jan. 09	Fountain(Ind	02	15	34
Gorsuch, Elijah(E)	1836	Sept. 13	Montgomery	15	21	20
Gott, William Lanham(B)	1835	Jan. 16	Darke	01	16	25
Gottstein, Joseph(B)	1819	Feb. 08	Dearborn(Ind	02	07	20
Gottstein, Joseph(B)	1819	June 15	Dearborn(Ind	02	07	20
Gottstein, Joseph(B)	1824	June 17	Dearborn(Ind	02	07	28
Goudie, James(B)	1813	Oct. 13	Pennsylvania	02	09	25
Goudie, James(B)	1814	Aug. 09	Franklin(Ind	01	09	19
Goudie, Sam'l.(B)	1829	Jan. 29	Franklin(Ind	02	09	12
Goudie, Samuel(B)	1824	June 09	Franklin(Ind	01	09	21
Goudy, Andrew(C)	1801	Dec. 23	Hamilton	06	02	10
Goudy, Andrew(C)	1831	Aug. 08	Clark	09	05	25
Goudy, William(C)	1801	Dec. 16	Hamilton	04	02	07
Goudy, William(C)	1801	Dec. 16	Hamilton	05	03	06
Goudy, William(C)	1801	Dec. 16	Hamilton	05	04	36
Goudy, William(C)	1801	Dec. 28	Hamilton	05	04	36
Gough, Jesse(A)	1805	Aug. 17	Butler	02	06	30
Gough, Jesse(A)	1805	Aug. 17	Butler	02	06	32
Gough, Jesse(A)	1816	Oct. 31	Preble	01	11	03
Gough, Jesse(A)	1817	Aug. 26	Preble	01	11	10
Gowdry, William(C)	1811	Dec. 12	Butler	08	05	23
Gower, James(A)	1817	Oct. 08	Butler	03	09	04
Gower, Richard(A)	1817	Oct. 08	Butler	03	09	04
Goyer, John Jacob(B)	1832	Dec. 15	Dearborn(Ind	03	06	26
Grafft, George(C)	1805	Sept. 18	Champaign	09	04	24
Grafton, Joseph(C)	1813	June 17	Champaign	11	03	09
Grafton, Thomas(C)	1811	April 09	Champaign	11	03	03
Grafton, Thomas(C)	1815	July 10	Champaign	11	03	15
Graham, Abner(B)	1818	May 30	Dearborn(Ind	01	06	04
Graham, Andrew(C)	1817	Oct. 21	Champaign	10	03	12
Graham, David(B)	1815	July 24	Butler	02	09	23
Graham, James A.(A)	1820	Dec. 21	Miami	05	10	25
Graham, James(A)	1818	Dec. 19	Wayne(Ind)	01	09	21
Graham, James(B)	1832	Aug. 20	Switzerland	03	03	20
Graham, John Senr.(B)	1836	May 19	Switzerland	03	03	20
Graham, Reuben P.(A)	1836	Dec. 01	Cincinnati	01	15	26
Graham, Reuben P.(A)	1836	Dec. 01	Cincinnati	01	15	25
Graham, Reuben P.(A)	1836	Dec. 01	Cincinnati	01	15	20
Graham, Reuben P.(E)	1836	Dec. 01	Cincinnati	15	21	02
Graham, Reuben P.(E)	1836	Dec. 01	Cincinnati	15	21	30
Graham, Samuel(B)	1836	June 03	Dearborn(Ind	03	04	01
Graham, Samuel(B)	1837	Dec. 26	Dearborn(Ind	03	04	01
Graham, Stillwell(B)	1836	May 19	Switzerland	03	03	20

PURCHASER	YEAR	DATE	RESIDENCE	R	T	S
Graham, Timothy Ward(B)	1832	Oct. 06	Dearborn(Ind	03	04	14
Graham, William(A)	1818	Aug. 01	Darke	01	11	02
Graham, William(A)	1819	June 16	Darke	01	12	07
Graham, William(B)	1836	Aug. 22	Switzerland	03	03	18
Graham, William(C)	1801	Dec. 23	Hamilton	04	04	28
Graham, William(C)	1818	Feb. 16	Miami	11	02	06
Gramann, John Hy.(E)	1838	May 07	Cincinnati	11	11	24
Granden, Philip(B)	1818	June 16	Cincinnati	01	06	21
Grandin, Philip(E)	1818	June 29	Cincinnati	13	21	11
Grandy, Thomas(B)	1834	Nov. 07	Wayne(Ind)	01	17	35
Grant, Alexander(A)	1813	Sept. 04	Butler	01	03	10
Grant, Alexander(A)	1813	Nov. 30	Butler	01	03	04
Grant, Alexander(A)	1836	Jan. 01	Mercer	01	15	13
Grant, Alexander(A)	1837	Jan. 04	Mercer	02	15	19
Grant, Robert(C)	1806	July 28	Champaign	14	04	27
Grava, Francis Hy.(E)	1837	May 17	Cincinnati	11	11	34
Grave, Enos(B)	1816	July 18	Pennsylvania	01	14	03
Grave, Enos(B)	1816	Nov. 18	Wayne(Ind)	01	15	32
Grave, Jacob(E)	1817	June 19	Wayne(Ind)	14	21	07
Grave, Jonathan L.(B)	1816	Oct. 19	Wayne(Ind)	01	15	32
Gray, Absalom(E)	1820	Jan. 07	Indiana	14	20	14
Gray, Absalom(E)	1836	Jan. 30	Randolph(Ind	14	20	23
Gray, Absalom(E)	1826	June 13	Randolph(Ind	14	20	26
Gray, David(B)	1810	July 15	Kentucky	01	10	36
Gray, Eliphaz(A)	1836	Sept. 05	Logan	02	14	35
Gray, Isaac(B)	1836	May 30	Switzerland	03	03	20
Gray, James M.(B)	1816	June 25	Butler	02	10	01
Gray, James(A)	1819	Dec. 10	Hamilton	05	09	07
Gray, James(B)	1835	March 04	Switzerland	03	03	33
Gray, James(B)	1836	Feb. 22	Darke	01	16	13
Gray, Jesse(A)	1829	March 02	Darke	01	12	04
Gray, Jesse(E)	1833	Sept. 05	Randolph(Ind	15	21	09
Gray, Jesse(E)	1834	March 14	Randolph(Ind	15	18	06
Gray, Jno.(B)	1836	Sept. 01	Dearborn(Ind	01	06	14
Gray, John G.(B)	1816	June 25	Butler	02	10	01
Gray, John G.(E)	1822	Jan. 25	?	12	13	19
Gray, John M.(A)	1817	Dec. 03	Darke	01	10	13
Gray, John(A)	1801	Sept. 07	Kentucky	03	02	06
Gray, John(A)	1837	Oct. 17	Logan	02	13	02
Gray, John(B)	1818	April 24	Butler	03	04	32
Gray, Joseph(B)	1836	Feb. 19	Darke	01	16	25
Gray, Joseph(C)	1807	June 26	Kentucky	12	05	34
Gray, Lewis(C)	1813	April 14	Warren	08	03	32
Gray, Mary(A)	1815	Nov. 29	Darke	02	12	35
Gray, Matthias(C)	1831	Nov. 01	Butler	12	02	11
Gray, Nathaniel(E)	1834	June 20	Preble	13	19	27
Gray, Nathaniel(E)	1834	June 20	Preble	13	19	27
Gray, Richard(C)	1804	Sept. 04	Montgomery	07	02	26
Gray, Robert(A)	1806	Aug. 23	Montgomery	02	12	35
Gray, Robert(A)	1806	Aug. 23	Montgomery	02	12	26
Gray, Robert(A)	1818	April 24	Montgomery	01	07	08
Gray, Robert(B)	1813	Aug. 31	Butler	01	09	26
Gray, Robert(D)	1811	Aug. 02	Butler	02	01	08
Gray, Thomas(A)	1816	Oct. 21	Wayne(Ind)	01	10	31
Gray, William(A)	1817	Dec. 05	Preble	01	07	15
Gray, William(A)	1835	Feb. 14	Darke	01	12	04
Gray, William(B)	1834	March 18	Clermont	02	03	12
Gray, William(B)	1836	April 30	Dearborn(Ind	02	03	09
Gray, William(C)	1805	Sept. 04	Hamilton	07	02	19
Gray, William(C)	1804	Sept. 10	Hamilton	05	03	11
Gray, William(C)	1813	Nov. 13	Champaign	13	05	36
Gray, William(D)	1808	Nov. 02	Hamilton	02	01	08
Greanwalt, Atolf(E)	1836	Oct. 03	Pennsylvania	12	10	09
Green, Daniel(E)	1811	Dec. 12	Kentucky	12	13	23
Green, Daniel(E)	1814	Dec. 16	Franklin(Ind	12	13	26
Green, Eli(B)	1811	Dec. 11	Dearborn(Ind	01	05	30
Green, Eli(B)	1812	Dec. 18	Dearborn(Ind	01	04	07
Green, Frederick(B)	1836	June 11	Switzerland	03	03	15
Green, Henry(E)	1836	Oct. 03	Butler	14	19	29

PURCHASER	YEAR	DATE	RESIDENCE	R	T	S
Green, James(A)	1814	Nov. 29	Darke	01	11	14
Green, James(A)	1817	Nov. 01	Miami	04	09	35
Green, James(B)	1817	Aug. 30	Cincinnati	01	11	19
Green, James(B)	1831	Sept. 10	Miami	01	17	27
Green, James(B)	1831	Sept. 20	Miami	01	17	27
Green, James(E)	1813	Nov. 25	Franklin(Ind	12	14	32
Green, John(B)	1824	June 09	Switzerland	01	02	07
Green, John(E)	1829	Nov. 25	Wayne(Ind)	14	18	30
Green, Joseph(A)	1805	June 24	Butler	03	03	10
Green, Joseph(A)	1805	June 24	Butler	03	03	04
Green, Martin Ruter(B)	1835	Aug. 04	Switzerland	01	02	07
Green, Peter D.(E)	1836	July 13	Butler	14	21	15
Green, Peter D.(E)	1836	July 22	Butler	14	21	05
Green, Peter D.(E)	1836	July 22	Butler	14	21	04
Green, Peter D.(E)	1836	Aug. 23	Butler	14	21	17
Green, Peter D.(E)	1836	Nov. 23	Butler	14	21	03
Green, Peter D.(E)	1836	Nov. 23	Butler	14	21	21
Green, Peter D.(E)	1837	Jan. 30	Butler	14	21	03
Green, Peter D.(E)	1837	March 01	Butler	14	21	03
Green, Peter(E)	1836	June 15	Butler	14	21	10
Green, Robert(A)	1817	Dec. 30	Preble	02	07	33
Green, Thomas(E)	1834	April 07	Randolph(Ind	13	21	26
Green, Thomas(E)	1834	June 12	Randolph(Ind	13	21	27
Green, Timothy(C)	1804	Sept. 03	Montgomery	06	02	29
Green, Timothy(C)	1804	Sept. 03	Montgomery	06	02	29
Green, William(A)	1819	Aug. 26	Miami	04	08	02
Green, William(A)	1827	July 30	Miami	04	08	03
Green, William(A)	1831	Sept. 20	Miami	04	08	03
Green, William(B)	1817	Aug. 15	Cincinnati	02	06	12
Green, William(B)	1818	Jan. 06	Cincinnati	01	06	09
Green, William(B)	1818	Jan. 06	Cincinnati	02	07	34
Green, Zachariah(A)	1831	Oct. 12	Miami	02	12	01
Greenburg, Cornelius(E)	1813	Dec. 11	Wayne(Ind)	13	16	24
Greene, Frederick(B)	1817	Dec. 31	Switzerland	03	03	27
Greene, Henry(A)	1824	June 08	Butler	03	04	21
Greene, James(A)	1814	Nov. 29	Darke	01	11	14
Greene, Jesse(E)	1816	Dec. 05	Clinton	13	20	27
Greene, Joseph(C)	1808	Aug. 25	Kentucky	12	01	12
Greene, Robert(B)	1814	Jan. 15	Franklin(Ind	02	10	23
Greene, William W.(C)	1807	March 26	Champaign	09	06	36
Greene, William(B)	1814	Feb. 15	Cincinnati	02	11	15
Greene, Zachariah(A)	1812	Nov. 13	Miami	05	06	24
Greener, John(B)	1813	March 31	Cincinnati	02	01	04
Greener, John(B)	1818	Feb. 27	Cincinnati	02	07	20
Greenewood, Benjamin(A)	1807	May 27	Butler	02	05	05
Greenham, Joseph(A)	1814	Oct. 18	Hamilton	01	03	18
Greenstreet, Jesse(E)	1815	Aug. 17	Wayne(Ind)	13	18	31
Greenstreet, Thomas(E)	1817	Sept. 30	Wayne(Ind)	14	15	05
Greenwood, Niles(B)	1817	Aug. 16	Dearborn(Ind	02	06	23
Greer, James(B)	1813	Aug. 31	Franklin(Ind	01	11	19
Greer, Joshua(A)	1810	May 29	Montgomery	05	04	03
Greer, Moses(A)	1810	May 29	Montgomery	05	04	03
Gregg, Andrew(E)	1838	May 21	Montgomery	15	22	19
Gregg, David H.(E)	1838	May 21	Montgomery	15	22	21
Gregg, David H.(E)	1838	May 21	Montgomery	15	22	09
Gregg, John(C)	1806	Sept. 27	Hamilton	09	04	34
Gregg, Samuel(C)	1804	Sept. 03	Warren	05	02	08
Gregg, Silas(E)	1811	Oct. 24	Preble	13	14	07
Gregg, Smith(A)	1812	Dec. 24	Montgomery	06	03	32
Gregg, Smith(C)	1801	Dec. 23	Hamilton	07	02	13
Gregg, Smith(C)	1801	Dec. 30	Hamilton	06	02	23
Gregg, Smith(E)	1838	May 21	Montgomery	15	22	21
Gregg, Stephen(B)	1813	Aug. 31	Franklin(Ind	01	09	19
Gregg, Thomas(B)	1812	May 06	Franklin(Ind	01	09	20
Gregg, William(E)	1838	May 21	Montgomery	15	22	21
Gregory, Henry(A)	1817	July 22	Hamilton	02	09	34
Gregory, Henry(A)	1817	June 11	Hamilton	02	07	06
Gregory, John(C)	1825	May 10	Miami	11	02	08
Gregory, William(A)	1814	April 16	Champaign	02	08	29

PURCHASER	YEAR	DATE	RESIDENCE	R	T	S
Gregory, William(B)	1835	Sept. 05	Hamilton	02	05	09
Gregury, James(A)	1816	Feb. 13	Butler	03	09	04
Gresnier, George(D)	1809	Aug. 05	Hamilton	01	04	26
Grewell, John(A)	1811	Dec. 18	Montgomery	04	04	06
Grey, Alexander(E)	1811	Oct. 24	Kentucky	13	15	06
Grey, Joseph(C)	1807	June 09	Kentucky	12	05	28
Gribe, Samuel(A)	1809	June 05	Montgomery	04	05	05
Grice, Christian(A)	1805	Aug. 09	Greene	06	04	27
Grier, James(B)	1815	Aug. 29	Franklin(Ind	01	11	19
Grievenkamp, Bernard(A)	1837	Dec. 21	Cincinnati	02	14	01
Griffin, Daniel(A)	1802	Sept. 15	Hamilton	05	02	19
Griffin, Daniel(C)	1801	Dec. 31	Hamilton	05	02	19
Griffin, Daniel(C)	1801	Dec. 31	Hamilton	05	02	25
Griffin, Daniel(C)	1801	Dec. 31	Hamilton	04	03	06
Griffin, Frances(C)	1813	March 31	Butler	08	02	11
Griffin, Jacob(E)	1814	Jan. 19	Wayne(Ind)	14	16	08
Griffin, James(B)	1808	Feb. 05	Highland	01	14	19
Griffin, John(B)	1808	March 29	Preble	02	07	30
Griffin, John(A)	1814	Dec. 21	Preble	02	07	31
Griffin, John(E)	1836	Nov. 17	Cincinnati	12	11	12
Griffin, Sam'l. Seely(A)	1831	Sept. 22	Montgomery	03	08	23
Griffis, John(A)	1816	Jan. 31	Warren	02	08	21
Griffith, Andrew C.(A)	1819	May 18	Cincinnati	06	08	35
Griffith, Mary(B)	1833	Sept. 03	Switzerland	03	03	33
Griffith, Stephen(E)	1811	Oct. 22	Wayne(Ind)	12	15	13
Griffith, Stephen(E)	1812	Aug. 24	Wayne(Ind)	13	15	17
Griffith, Stephen(E)	1817	Dec. 02	Wayne(Ind)	13	15	17
Griffith, William(A)	1814	Sept. 06	Miami	05	09	07
Grime, George(A)	1816	Aug. 30	Butler	03	06	14
Grimes, Alexander(A)	1816	July 22	Montgomery	06	05	20
Grimes, Alexander(C)	1816	July 01	Montgomery	09	03	28
Grimes, Alexander(C)	1816	July 22	Montgomery	09	02	05
Grimes, Benj'n.(C)	1831	Jan. 14	Shelby	12	03	26
Grimes, James(A)	1816	Aug. 09	Butler	02	12	28
Grimes, James(A)	1816	Sept. 23	Butler	01	12	26
Grimes, James(A)	1816	Sept. 23	Butler	01	12	26
Grimes, James(B)	1808	Jan. 27	Butler	01	13	28
Grimes, Jas.(B)	1813	April 14	Wayne(Ind)	01	13	28
Grimes, John(A)	1812	Nov. 12	Butler	03	03	07
Grimes, William(B)	1808	Jan. 27	Butler	01	13	28
Grimes, William(B)	1813	April 14	Wayne(Ind)	01	13	28
Grinal, Barney(D)	1813	Jan. 21	Hamilton(Fr)	01	03	11
Gripe, Daniel Jr.(A)	1814	Sept. 05	Montgomery	04	05	03
Gripe, Daniel(A)	1807	May 07	Montgomery	04	06	27
Gripe, Jacob(A)	1813	Aug. 24	Montgomery	04	05	02
Gripe, Jacob(A)	1814	Sept. 02	Montgomery	04	05	03
Gripe, Jacob(A)	1815	Jan. 31	Montgomery	05	08	32
Gripe, Jacob(A)	1818	Feb. 17	Montgomery	04	06	33
Gripe, John(A)	1805	March 23	Montgomery	05	04	19
Gripe, John(A)	1818	Feb. 17	Montgomery	04	06	33
Gripe, Joseph(A)	1814	April 30	Montgomery	04	05	34
Gripe, Joseph(A)	1814	April 30	Montgomery	04	04	11
Gripe, Joseph(A)	1819	Oct. 21	Montgomery	04	05	25
Grismer, Geo.(C)	1831	Aug. 25	Ohio	13	02	09
Grismer, George(C)	1831	Oct. 01	Hamilton	13	02	03
Grissman, David(A)	1805	Nov. 06	Montgomery	03	06	05
Grissom, David Senr.(A)	1836	Feb. 20	Darke	03	11	08
Grissom, David(A)	1815	Jan. 10	Preble	03	06	05
Grissom, George(A)	1832	Feb. 21	Preble	03	10	11
Grisson, Bluvet(A)	1815	March 21	Butler	01	03	11
Grist, Simeon(E)	1815	Aug. 11	Franklin(Ind	13	13	26
Griswold, Wm.(B)	1833	Sept. 13	Dearborn(Ind	03	08	14
Gritz, Conrad(C)	1806	Aug. 04	Champaign	10	04	20
Groenendyke, Nicholas(B)	1818	Dec. 12	Dearborn(Ind	01	07	29
Grogan, John(B)	1831	July 06	Dearborn(Ind	02	07	23
Groom, William(A)	1815	July 05	Miami	06	08	29
Groom, Wm.(A)	1814	March 17	Ohio	06	08	18
Grose, Joseph(B)	1817	July 28	Hamilton	01	02	18
Gross, John(A)	1836	Oct. 14	Cincinnati	01	15	32

125

PURCHASER	YEAR	DATE	RESIDENCE	R	T	S
Gross, John(B)	1836	Oct. 10	Cincinnati	01	16	03
Gross, John(B)	1839	Feb. 22	Cincinnati	01	17	34
Gross, John(B)	1839	Aug. 28	Cincinnati	03	04	21
Gross, John(E)	1836	Oct. 10	Cincinnati	15	19	17
Gross, John(E)	1836	Oct. 11	Cincinnati	14	19	17
Gross, John(E)	1836	Oct. 12	Cincinnati	14	19	15
Gross, John(E)	1836	Oct. 12	Cincinnati	13	12	28
Gross, John(E)	1836	Oct. 27	Cincinnati	12	11	28
Gross, John(E)	1836	Oct. 27	Cincinnati	12	11	29
Gross, John(E)	1839	Feb. 21	Cincinnati	15	19	17
Gross, John(E)	1839	April 17	Cincinnati	13	20	15
Gross, John(E)	1839	April 24	Cincinnati	14	21	22
Gross, John(E)	1839	April 24	Cincinnati	13	21	23
Gross, John(E)	1839	April 24	Cincinnati	13	20	35
Grove, George Jr.(B)	1836	Aug. 01	Dearborn(Ind	03	05	22
Grove, George Jr.(B)	1836	Aug. 06	Dearborn(Ind	03	05	22
Grove, George Jr.(B)	1837	Jan. 12	Dearborn(Ind	03	05	22
Grove, George Jr.(B)	1837	Jan. 27	Dearborn(Ind	03	05	22
Grove, George(B)	1813	June 05	Ind.Territry	01	04	07
Grove, George(B)	1815	May 29	Dearborn(Ind	02	04	12
Grove, Henry(B)	1812	Jan. 28	Dearborn(Ind	01	04	07
Grove, Jacob(E)	1837	April 28	Montgomery	15	21	32
Grovel, James(B)	1838	March 21	Dearborn(Ind	03	05	23
Grover, Ira(B)	1819	June 11	Cincinnati	02	08	36
Grover, Sarah(C)	1828	Oct. 22	Kentucky	11	03	04
Grow, Jacob(A)	1805	April 29	Montgomery	05	05	19
Grow, Jacob(A)	1817	June 04	Montgomery	01	12	33
Grumman, James(C)	1806	June 05	Champaign	08	03	12
Grummond, David(C)	1802	Dec. 29	Cincinnati	09	04	09
Grummond, David(C)	1802	Dec. 29	Cincinnati	04	03	01
Grummond, David(C)	1802	Dec. 29	Cincinnati	09	04	10
Grummond, David(C)	1802	Dec. 31	Cincinnati	09	04	32
Grumrine, Peter(A)	1805	Oct. 15	Pennsylvania	04	05	13
Gruwell, Asa(E)	1814	Jan. 06	Montgomery	13	15	30
Gruwell, Jacob(A)	1805	March 02	Montgomery	03	05	23
Gruwell, Jacob(A)	1805	April 09	Montgomery	04	04	19
Gruwell, John(E)	1811	Oct. 23	Montgomery	13	14	06
Gruwell, John(E)	1812	March 19	Montgomery	13	14	06
Gruwell, Lawrance(A)	1805	Jan. 01	Hamilton	01	06	20
Gruwell, Lawrence(E)	1811	Nov. 05	Preble	13	15	30
Gruwell, Samuel(E)	1811	Nov. 11	Preble	13	15	31
Guard, David(B)	1836	Sept. 01	Dearborn(Ind	01	06	14
Guard, Timothy(B)	1836	Sept. 01	Dearborn(Ind	01	06	14
Guele, Joshua(B)	1815	July 27	Hamilton	01	08	09
Guess, Levi P.(A)	1836	Nov. 08	Hamilton	01	14	07
Guess, Solomon(A)	1815	March 06	Hamilton	03	06	11
Guess, Solomon(A)	1836	Nov. 08	Hamilton	01	14	10
Guess, Solomon(A)	1836	Nov. 08	Hamilton	01	14	07
Guest, Hannah(A)	1811	Dec. 11	Preble	02	06	35
Guest, James(A)	1815	Dec. 11	Preble	02	06	14
Guest, James(A)	1815	Dec. 19	Preble	02	06	06
Guest, James(A)	1816	March 01	Preble	02	06	11
Guile, Joshua(B)	1815	Aug. 10	Hamilton	01	08	09
Guilford, Nathan(B)	1819	May 21	Cincinnati	02	04	05
Guilford, Nathan(B)	1819	May 21	Cincinnati	02	04	20
Guiltner, George(E)	1811	Oct. 28	Franklin(Ind	12	12	36
Guion, Thomas(B)	1833	April 04	Dearborn(Ind	02	04	20
Guion, Thomas(B)	1836	May 13	Dearborn(Ind	02	04	30
Gullefer, Stephen(E)	1813	Oct. 23	Wayne(Ind)	13	17	25
Gulleon, Robt.(B)	1815	April 17	Switzerland	03	04	32
Gullet, Ezekiel(A)	1819	Sept. 28	Butler	01	11	02
Gullet, Ezekiel(B)	1837	Jan. 19	Warren	01	17	11
Gullet, Isaac(B)	1837	March 23	Butler	01	17	11
Gullett, George(B)	1835	Feb. 02	Butler	01	17	12
Gullett, Isaac(B)	1836	July 08	Butler	01	17	12
Gullett, Robert(B)	1827	Aug. 29	Hamilton	02	04	17
Gulley, Simon(B)	1815	Oct. 26	Franklin(Ind	01	08	26
Gulley, William(B)	1815	Oct. 26	Franklin(Ind	01	08	26
Gullion, John(B)	1810	March 16	Dearborn(Ind	02	02	35

PURCHASER	YEAR	DATE	RESIDENCE	R	T	S
Gullion, Robert(B)	1816	Sept. 06	Switzerland	02	02	24
Gully, Smith(B)	1815	Oct. 26	Franklin(Ind	01	08	26
Gunckel, Philip(A)	1814	Sept. 22	Montgomery	04	03	22
Gunckel, William(A)	1837	Feb. 01	Montgomery	02	13	08
Gunder, William(A)	1822	Aug. 23	Preble	03	08	08
Gunder, William(A)	1831	April 20	Darke	03	08	08
Gunkel, Philip(A)	1804	July 31	Montgomery	05	02	07
Gunkle, James(A)	1831	June 04	Darke	01	10	01
Gunn, John(C)	1813	April 14	Champaign	14	03	05
Gunn, John(C)	1813	April 14	Champaign	14	03	05
Gunn, John(C)	1814	May 30	Champaign	14	03	05
Gunn, John(C)	1814	May 30	Champaign	14	04	34
Gunter, James(A)	1831	June 11	Miami	05	08	23
Guntle, Phillip(A)	1805	April 26	Montgomery	04	04	30
Guseman, George(C)	1805	Aug. 02	Montgomery	09	02	25
Guseman, John(C)	1817	Sept. 13	Miami	13	02	05
Guseman, Joseph(C)	1817	Sept. 13	Miami	13	02	05
Gustin, Benajah(E)	1817	May 27	New Jersey	13	12	30
Gustin, Jeremiah(C)	1801	Dec. 28	Hamilton	04	03	09
Gustin, John(C)	1804	Sept. 03	Warren	04	03	08
Gustin, Samuel(A)	1814	March 19	Butler	02	04	17
Gustin, Samuel(E)	1817	May 27	Warren	13	12	29
Guthery, Archibald(E)	1811	Oct. 21	Franklin(Ind	12	12	03
Guttery, Demas(A)	1836	Nov. 22	Warren	02	14	09
Gwelym, William(A)	1806	May 13	Butler	01	03	23
Gwilim, Morgan(A)	1813	Aug. 07	Butler	01	03	35
Gwinnup, James Simpson(E)	1833	Oct. 03	Hamilton	11	12	24
Gwinnup, James Simpson(E)	1836	Feb. 15	Franklin(Ind	11	12	36
Gwylim, Morgan(A)	1801	June 29	Hamilton	01	03	25
Gwylim, William(A)	1801	June 29	Hamilton	01	03	25
Gwylin, William(A)	1811	Aug. 13	Butler	01	03	23
Haarlos, Jacob(A)	1835	March 05	Darke	03	10	06
Habadank, William(E)	1836	Nov. 15	Cincinnati	11	10	15
Habs, Emery(E)	1816	Oct. 26	Dearborn(Ind	12	13	29
Hacker, John(C)	1813	Feb. 09	Greene	08	02	12
Hackleman, Abraham(B)	1806	June 20	Dearborn(Ind	02	09	34
Hackleman, Isaac(C)	1814	June 30	Dearborn(Ind	12	14	03
Hackleman, Jacob(B)	1803	Aug. 26	Kentucky	01	07	10
Hackleman, Jacob(B)	1816	Sept. 17	Franklin(Ind	02	08	09
Hackleman, Jacob(E)	1811	Oct. 22	Ind.Territory	12	14	24
Hackleman, John(B)	1816	Sept. 17	Franklin(Ind	02	08	09
Haddix, John(A)	1829	April 08	Clark	06	03	05
Haddix, John(C)	1815	March 14	Greene	10	04	31
Haddix, John(C)	1817	Dec. 29	Greene	08	03	29
Hadix, John(C)	1815	April 14	Greene	09	04	30
Hadley, James(A)	1831	Feb. 03	Darke	02	12	22
Hadley, Joseph(A)	1831	Jan. 08	Darke	01	12	05
Hadlock, James(B)	1817	Dec. 26	Indiana	02	02	33
Hafer, Henry(C)	1815	May 24	Hamilton	14	03	01
Hafer, Henry(C)	1818	April 06	Hamilton	14	04	25
Hafer, Henry(C)	1818	April 06	Hamilton	14	04	31
Haffner, Benjamin(E)	1814	Aug. 20	Maryland	12	13	35
Haffner, Joseph(E)	1814	Oct. 12	Maryland	12	12	02
Hageman, John(A)	1836	Dec. 02	Butler	02	14	35
Hageman, John(A)	1837	Aug. 25	Butler	02	14	33
Hageman, Simon(B)	1829	Dec. 01	Switzerland	02	02	24
Hager, Samuel(A)	1811	Oct. 09	Montgomery	05	04	05
Hager, Samuel(C)	1811	Dec. 11	Montgomery	06	01	12
Hagerman, Adrian(C)	1804	Dec. 31	Hamilton	11	01	14
Hagerman, Adrian(C)	1804	Dec. 31	Hamilton	11	01	09
Haggin, John(C)	1801	Dec. 31	Kentucky	06	01	14
Haggin, John(C)	1801	Dec. 31	Kentucky	07	01	15
Hahn, Abraham(A)	1831	Oct. 01	Darke	04	09	33
Hahn, Joseph(B)	1833	June 24	Cincinnati	02	07	03
Hahn, Joseph(B)	1834	May 30	Dearborn(Ind	02	07	03
Hahn, Samuel(A)	1831	Aug. 30	Darke	04	08	04
Hail, Joseph(C)	1801	Dec. 31	Hamilton	06	02	03
Hailes, David(C)	1813	Dec. 25	Miami	10	03	34
Hailman, Jonathan(A)	1817	Nov. 12	Cincinnati	02	12	12

127

PURCHASER	YEAR	DATE	RESIDENCE	R	T	S
Hailman, Simon(A)	1818	Dec. 28	Hamilton	03	06	30
Haimlech, Andrew(A)	1808	Oct. 21	Virginia	03	05	19
Hainer, James(B)	1827	Aug. 21	Hamilton	02	04	17
Haines, Ezekiel S.(B)	1829	April 20	Cincinnati	04	02	24
Haines, Job(A)	1836	Nov. 10	Montgomery	02	15	29
Haines, Job(A)	1837	Nov. 11	Montgomery	02	15	28
Haines, Job(A)	1837	Nov. 28	Montgomery	02	15	22
Haines, Job(A)	1838	May 21	Montgomery	02	15	23
Haines, John(B)	1811	Nov. 18	Clinton	01	15	08
Haines, Leonard(C)	1804	Dec. 29	Montgomery	09	02	01
Haines, Ner(A)	1819	Aug. 09	Warren	Q1	07	21
Hains, Peter(A)	1818	Oct. 20	Kentucky	08	02	35
Hains, Samuel(A)	1806	Oct. 28	Maryland	05	06	31
Haisley, Jesse(E)	1822	Nov. 08	Wayne(Ind)	14	17	03
Haisley, Jesse(E)	1827	Nov. 01	Wayne(Ind)	14	17	03
Haisley, Joseph(E)	1822	Nov. 08	Wayne(Ind)	14	17	04
Halberstadt, Anthony(B)	1812	Dec. 04	Franklin(Ind	02	09	22
Halberstadt, John(B)	1817	Sept. 12	Dearborn(Ind	02	08	32
Halberstadt, Wm.Hy.Harrison(B)	1834	Oct. 30	Franklin(Ind	02	08	32
Halberstalt, Michael(C)	1806	May 26	Greene	07	03	09
Halberstudt, Anthony(B)	1806	June 20	Dearborn(Ind	02	08	10
Halderman, John(A)	1811	Dec. 17	Montgomery	06	04	23
Hale, Andrew(A)	1837	April 05	Montgomery	02	13	04
Hale, James(E)	1835	May 04	Randolph(Ind	14	21	28
Hale, John(E)	1819	Nov. 18	Greene	14	21	28
Hale, John(E)	1819	Nov. 25	Greene	14	21	20
Hall, Amy(E)	1815	Oct. 12	Wayne(Ind)	13	18	17
Hall, Charles(B)	1825	April 06	Franklin(Ind	02	10	15
Hall, Daniel(B)	1836	May 10	Dearborn(Ind	03	07	27
Hall, David(B)	1836	April 15	Dearborn(Ind	02	06	17
Hall, Gabriel(B)	1836	June 21	Switzerland	03	02	17
Hall, Henry(A)	1808	Oct. 06	Butler	01	04	01
Hall, Henry(C)	1807	Aug. 28	Kentucky	09	05	03
Hall, Isaac C.(A)	1831	Feb. 04	Miami	04	08	27
Hall, James(A)	1816	Nov. 30	Montgomery	04	07	11
Hall, James(A)	1836	Nov. 24	Montgomery	03	13	32
Hall, James(A)	1836	Nov. 24	Montgomery	03	13	28
Hall, James(C)	1813	April 14	Champaign	09	05	22
Hall, John(A)	1805	Oct. 23	Kentucky	02	04	14
Hall, John(A)	1806	May 02	Butler	02	04	23
Hall, John(A)	1810	Jan. 26	Preble	02	08	01
Hall, John(A)	1811	Aug. 13	Butler	02	04	23
Hall, John(B)	1814	Dec. 31	Franklin(Ind	02	08	05
Hall, John(B)	1819	Nov. 26	Dearborn(Ind	02	07	12
Hall, John(B)	1824	June 10	Dearborn(Ind	02	07	12
Hall, John(B)	1832	July 28	Dearborn(Ind	02	07	27
Hall, John(C)	1807	April 20	Kentucky	09	05	03
Hall, John(C)	1809	May 16	Champaign	13	05	34
Hall, John(C)	1812	Dec. 21	Champaign	13	05	35
Hall, John(C)	1813	Jan. 23	Champaign	13	05	35
Hall, John(C)	1829	April 09	Clark	13	02	02
Hall, John(C)	1831	Aug. 22	Champaign	13	03	19
Hall, John(E)	1818	Oct. 15	Butler	14	21	04
Hall, John(E)	1819	Sept. 06	Butler	14	21	07
Hall, Joseph(A)	1831	Aug. 13	Miami	05	07	12
Hall, Joseph(B)	1817	Sept. 18	Dearborn(Ind	01	06	19
Hall, Joseph(C)	1814	Jan. 28	Greene	08	06	24
Hall, Joseph(C)	1815	Nov. 07	Greene	08	06	22
Hall, Richard T.(B)	1815	May 03	Dearborn(Ind	01	03	19
Hall, Sam'l.(A)	1825	June 17	Miami	04	07	11
Hall, Samuel(A)	1836	March 05	Darke	04	08	18
Hall, Sylvanus(A)	1817	Nov. 29	Clermont	06	03	06
Hall, Thomas(B)	1817	Oct. 11	Dearborn(Ind	02	06	14
Hall, William(A)	1816	Oct. 11	Montgomery	06	11	06
Hall, William(A)	1817	June 10	Montgomery	06	04	06
Hall, William(A)	1836	Nov. 24	Montgomery	03	13	28
Hall, William(C)	1807	Aug. 18	Kentucky	09	05	04
Hall, William(D)	1808	Nov. 01	Hamilton	02	02	26
Hall, William(E)	1815	Jan. 26	Kentucky	12	14	27

PURCHASER	YEAR	DATE	RESIDENCE	R	T	S
Hallar, John(C)	1813	June 04	Champaign	10	05	24
Haller, Jacob(A)	1811	Nov. 09	Montgomery	04	05	33
Haller, John(C)	1813	June 04	Champaign	10	05	24
Halliday, Samuel(A)	1813	Sept. 06	Warren	01	07	12
Hallinan, James(B)	1834	July 21	Cincinnati	03	03	03
Hallinan, James(B)	1834	July 21	Cincinnati	03	04	34
Hallotte, Nicholas(A)	1836	Oct. 03	New York	03	11	03
Hallowell, John(B)	1835	Oct. 13	Dearborn(Ind	01	07	17
Hallowell, Jonathan(B)	1836	Jan. 18	Dearborn(Ind	01	07	17
Hallowell, Sam'l.(B)	1819	March 19	Dearborn(Ind	01	07	17
Hallowell, William(B)	1831	Sept. 17	Dearborn(Ind	02	07	01
Hallowell, Wm.(B)	1819	March 19	Dearborn(Ind	01	07	17
Halscher, Wm. H.(A)	1839	Jan. 21	Cincinnati	02	15	26
Halsey, Ich'd. B.(C)	1801	Dec. 31	Hamilton	04	04	31
Halsey, James(E)	1833	April 24	Franklin(Ind	12	11	05
Halsey, James(E)	1836	March 12	Franklin(Ind	12	11	05
Halsted, Robert Wade(E)	1836	Jan. 27	Franklin(Ind	13	11	09
Halsted, Robt. Wade(E)	1834	Dec. 08	Franklin(Ind	13	11	09
Halsted, Robt. Wade(E)	1834	Dec. 08	Franklin(Ind	13	11	09
Halsted, Thomas(E)	1836	Nov. 24	Franklin(Ind	13	11	17
Halterman, Peter(C)	1817	Dec. 08	Champaign	12	03	18
Ham, John(E)	1831	Feb. 12	Randolph(Ind	14	18	12
Hamar, George(C)	1801	Dec. 31	Hamilton	07	03	17
Hamar, Solomon(C)	1801	Dec. 31	Hamilton	07	02	23
Hamar, Solomon(C)	1802	Dec. 30	Hamilton	07	02	22
Hamar, William(C)	1801	Dec. 31	Hamilton	07	02	28
Hamar, William(C)	1804	Aug. 18	Montgomery	07	02	29
Hambleman, George(C)	1813	March 19	Greene	08	06	29
Hamblin, Levi(B)	1818	Feb. 02	Switzerland	01	02	23
Hamblin, Levi(B)	1828	Feb. 21	Hamilton	02	06	36
Hamel, Thomas(B)	1836	Sept. 24	Cincinnati	03	03	15
Hamel, Thomas(B)	1836	Oct. 08	Cincinnati	03	03	09
Hamer, Solomon(A)	1816	June 04	Darke	02	12	14
Hamer, Thomas(C)	1812	April 04	Montgomery	07	02	30
Hamer, Thomas(C)	1817	Aug. 01	Montgomery	07	02	30
Hamer, William(A)	1804	Sept. 25	Ohio	06	02	01
Hamill, Ebenezer(A)	1815	Aug. 29	Butler	01	09	29
Hamill, John L.(C)	1828	Sept. 05	Butler	11	01	06
Hamill, Robert(A)	1805	June 19	Pennsylvania	03	04	30
Hamill, Samuel(B)	1824	Jan. 26	Cincinnati	02	05	07
Hamilton, Adam(E)	1814	Oct. 22	Franklin(Ind	12	14	22
Hamilton, Alexander D.(D)	1808	Nov. 01	Hamilton	01	03	11
Hamilton, Asa(B)	1814	Aug. 18	Hamilton	01	04	31
Hamilton, James(A)	1801	July 28	Hamilton	03	02	04
Hamilton, James(B)	1806	July 10	Ind.Territory	02	04	30
Hamilton, James(B)	1807	Feb. 09	Dearborn(Ind	03	04	09
Hamilton, James(B)	1811	Aug. 13	Dearborn(Ind	03	04	09
Hamilton, James(B)	1814	Nov. 17	Dearborn(Ind	01	02	07
Hamilton, James(B)	1814	Dec. 10	Dearborn(Ind	01	03	32
Hamilton, James(B)	1832	Sept. 05	Butler	02	08	34
Hamilton, James(E)	1813	Nov. 30	Franklin(Ind	12	13	10
Hamilton, John Jr.(B)	1818	June 17	Dearborn(Ind	01	03	36
Hamilton, John(A)	1801	April 27	Hamilton	03	02	04
Hamilton, John(A)	1814	Aug. 17	So. Carolina	01	06	34
Hamilton, John(B)	1817	May 29	Butler	02	02	02
Hamilton, John(B)	1818	June 23	Dearborn(Ind	02	03	09
Hamilton, John(C)	1804	Dec. 28	Greene	09	04	12
Hamilton, John(C)	1804	Dec. 28	Greene	09	04	06
Hamilton, John(C)	1813	April 14	Champaign	09	04	12
Hamilton, John(C)	1813	June 18	Scioto	11	04	19
Hamilton, Robert S.(B)	1819	Aug. 09	Hamilton	02	07	03
Hamilton, Robert(A)	1819	June 01	Butler	01	10	34
Hamilton, Robert(B)	1818	June 17	Dearborn(Ind	01	02	02
Hamilton, Samuel(A)	1814	Aug. 17	Kentucky	01	06	24
Hamilton, Samuel(B)	1809	May 31	Kentucky	01	09	24
Hamilton, Thomas(C)	1806	March 31	Champaign	11	01	02
Hamilton, William(B)	1814	Dec. 01	Dearborn(Ind	03	07	10
Hamilton, William(B)	1814	Dec. 01	Dearborn(Ind	03	07	15
Hamilton, Yale(E)	1817	Aug. 01	Franklin(Ind	12	13	17

PURCHASER	YEAR	DATE	RESIDENCE	R	T	S
Hamlet, Benjamin(C)	1804	Dec. 24	Montgomery	10	01	24
Hammann, Michael(B)	1835	Oct. 05	Hamilton	02	08	33
Hammar, William(E)	1836	Jan. 28	Randolph(Ind	14	19	32
Hammell, Robert(A)	1807	Jan. 09	Greene	03	06	19
Hammer, Aaron(A)	1805	Nov. 23	Butler	02	05	05
Hammer, Aaron(A)	1812	April 15	Butler	02	05	05
Hammer, David(E)	1818	July 22	Clinton	14	18	04
Hammer, Elisha(A)	1805	Nov. 23	Butler	02	05	05
Hammer, John(A)	1819	June 18	Hamilton	05	06	01
Hammerle, Balthasar(B)	1833	July 09	Dearborn(Ind	02	07	27
Hammon, Abraham(B)	1806	June 14	Dearborn(Ind	01	10	13
Hammon, Nathan(C)	1817	July 05	Montgomery	10	06	26
Hammond, Amos D.(B)	1837	Nov. 27	Switzerland	03	04	28
Hammond, Calvin(C)	1826	May 04	Clark	13	03	10
Hammond, Lewis(B)	1815	Sept. 07	Hamilton	01	03	34
Hammond, Michael(E)	1836	Sept. 23	Wayne(Ind)	14	20	09
Hamon, Nathaniel(A)	1837	Jan. 18	Darke	03	11	21
Hampton, Abraham(E)	1817	July 03	Warren	14	17	02
Hampton, Andrew(B)	1817	July 03	Warren	01	14	06
Hampton, Jacob(B)	1816	Nov. 28	Warren	01	14	07
Hampton, Jacob(B)	1816	Nov. 28	Warren	01	14	05
Hampton, Jacob(B)	1816	Nov. 28	Warren	01	14	18
Hampton, Jacob(B)	1817	Nov. 01	Warren	01	14	18
Hampton, Jacob(E)	1816	Nov. 28	Warren	14	17	33
Hamson, Thomas(E)	1836	Sept. 22	RipleyCo.Ind	11	10	24
Hana, Robert(B)	1811	June 08	Ind.Territry	02	10	33
Hanback, Lewis(C)	1811	Nov. 07	Champaign	12	03	14
Hance, Benjamin(C)	1813	Dec. 06	Miami	10	02	18
Hance, William(C)	1814	Jan. 01	Kentucky	10	02	30
Hancock, Elisha(A)	1814	July 27	Preble	02	06	26
Hancock, Elisha(A)	1814	July 27	Preble	02	05	02
Hancock, Elisha(B)	1818	June 12	Cincinnati	03	06	02
Hancock, Henry(B)	1836	March 09	Dearborn(Ind	02	05	07
Hancock, John(A)	1804	Dec. 21	Kentucky	01	04	01
Hancock, Joseph(C)	1802	Dec. 28	Hamilton	05	03	24
Hancock, Joseph(E)	1815	Sept. 12	Montgomery	12	17	13
Hancock, Major(C)	1831	Aug. 29	Champaign	13	04	14
Hancock, Peter(B)	1818	July 02	Dearborn(Ind	03	06	26
Hancock, William(B)	1818	June 12	Hamilton	03	06	12
Hancy, James(C)	1809	June 13	Pennsylvania	09	06	11
Hand, Benj'm.(A)	1814	June 30	Cincinnati	01	04	26
Hand, Joseph(A)	1818	March 12	Butler	03	07	04
Hand, Peter(A)	1815	Feb. 22	Dearborn(Ind	01	02	07
Hand, William(C)	1810	Jan. 22	Kentucky	13	05	32
Handley, George(A)	1813	Nov. 06	Butler	01	03	09
Handley, James(A)	1814	Jan. 17	Butler	01	03	21
Handley, James(E)	1831	Dec. 07	Fayette	12	13	26
Handorf, Bernard(A)	1839	Jan. 21	Cincinnati	02	15	26
Handschy, Henry(E)	1836	Aug. 26	Muskingum	15	21	09
Handschy, Henry(E)	1836	Aug. 26	Muskingum	15	21	10
Handschy, Henry(E)	1836	Sept. 14	Muskingum	15	21	03
Hane, Frederick(A)	1805	Oct. 23	Virginia	02	08	11
Hane, Frederick(A)	1805	Oct. 23	Virginia	02	08	14
Hanes, Abraham(A)	1806	Sept. 30	Clermont	04	04	30
Hanes, David(C)	1805	Dec. 24	Greene	07	03	29
Hanes, David(C)	1808	May 04	Greene	09	02	19
Hanes, David(C)	1808	May 04	Greene	09	02	13
Hanes, George(B)	1817	Nov. 28	Dearborn(Ind	03	06	25
Hanes, Leonard(C)	1804	Dec. 28	Greene	09	03	31
Haney, James(C)	1814	Aug. 16	Champaign	09	06	11
Haney, Jonas(C)	1814	Feb. 12	Miami	11	01	24
Hankinson, Lewis Ford(A)	1831	Aug. 17	Butler	04	07	31
Hankinson, Lewis Ford(A)	1831	Aug. 22	Butler	03	08	36
Hanks, Peter(C)	1808	Jan. 13	Champaign	14	03	05
Hann, Peter(A)	1814	May 31	Dearborn(Ind	01	02	07
Hann, Peter(B)	1812	April 13	Dearborn(Ind	01	08	14
Hann, Wm. B.(A)	1835	May 22	Dearborn(Ind	01	02	07
Hanna, David(C)	1809	Nov. 30	Adams	09	06	12
Hanna, John Senr.(E)	1811	Nov. 11	Franklin(Ind	14	13	07

PURCHASER	YEAR	DATE	RESIDENCE	R	T	S
Hanna, John(B)	1804	Oct. 16	Hamilton	02	11	27
Hanna, John(B)	1804	Oct. 16	Hamilton	02	11	16
Hanna, John(B)	1814	Jan. 04	Franklin(Ind	02	11	27
Hanna, Joseph(B)	1804	Sept. 24	Hamilton	02	10	09
Hanna, Joseph(B)	1804	Sept. 24	Hamilton	02	10	09
Hanna, Robert Jnr.(B)	1818	March 21	Franklin(Ind	02	10	03
Hanna, Robert(B)	1804	Sept. 24	Hamilton	02	10	28
Hanna, Robert(B)	1804	Sept. 24	Hamilton	02	10	33
Hanna, Robert(B)	1811	July 13	Ind.Territory	02	10	33
Hanna, Robt. Jr.(B)	1814	March 28	Franklin(Ind	02	10	32
Hanna, Samuel(A)	1818	Aug. 03	Miami	05	08	26
Hanna, Samuel(B)	1832	March 28	Dearborn(Ind	02	04	26
Hannah, Abraham G.(E)	1829	Dec. 10	Wayne(Ind)	13	15	03
Hannas, Henry(B)	1814	Jan. 10	Kentucky	04	03	36
Hanning, Jacob(A)	1806	April 28	Montgomery	01	08	29
Hanour, Matthias(E)	1837	June 29	Randolph(Ind	14	20	09
Hansel, Chris'r.(B)	1813	June 22	Franklin(Ind	01	10	27
Hansel, Christopher(B)	1805	Nov. 16	Adams	01	10	25
Hansel, Christopher(B)	1814	Sept. 10	Franklin(Ind	01	10	36
Hansel, David(B)	1805	Sept. 30	Adams	01	10	24
Hansel, Geo.(B)	1813	June 22	Franklin(Ind	01	10	27
Hansel, Jacob(A)	1806	May 26	Butler	01	04	08
Hansell, Thomas(B)	1826	Feb. 09	Dearborn(Ind	02	06	13
Hansell, Thomas(B)	1828	Jan. 22	Dearborn(Ind	02	06	24
Hanson, Benjamin H.(E)	1814	Sept. 10	Kentucky	13	13	14
Hanson, Bordan(E)	1831	July 05	Wayne(Ind)	13	17	08
Hapner, Abraham(A)	1805	Dec. 07	Montgomery	03	07	20
Hapner, Abraham(A)	1831	July 05	Preble	03	07	09
Hapner, Gasper(A)	1813	Dec. 31	Preble	03	06	09
Hapner, Henry(A)	1807	June 23	Montgomery	03	06	04
Hapner, Jacob(A)	1828	Sept. 11	Preble	02	09	23
Hapner, Jacob(A)	1831	July 05	Preble	03	07	30
Hapner, John(A)	1831	May 11	Preble	03	07	05
Hapner, John(A)	1831	May 11	Preble	03	07	05
Hapner, William(A)	1815	March 17	Preble	03	07	26
Hapner, William(A)	1818	Jan. 24	Preble	03	07	09
Harber, Noah(C)	1805	Oct. 21	Virginia	12	04	19
Harber, Noah(C)	1805	Oct. 21	Virginia	09	06	18
Harbert, Ebenezar(B)	1815	Aug. 09	Dearborn(Ind	02	04	29
Harbert, Ebenezer(B)	1814	Feb. 28	Dearborn(Ind	02	04	34
Harbert, John(C)	1813	June 01	Champaign	11	05	03
Harbert, Samuel(B)	1832	March 09	Dearborn(Ind	02	04	20
Harbert, Samuel(B)	1835	Oct. 22	Dearborn(Ind	02	04	20
Harbert, William(B)	1818	Aug. 08	Hamilton	02	06	13
Harbeson, John(A)	1813	April 14	Preble	02	07	09
Harbeson, Robert(A)	1813	April 14	Preble	02	07	11
Harbeson, Sam'l.(A)	1830	Feb. 25	Montgomery	04	07	35
Harbeson, Sam'l.(A)	1830	May 06	Montgomery	04	07	27
Harbeston, Samuel(A)	1818	March 10	Montgomery	04	06	02
Harbor, William(C)	1804	Oct. 29	Virginia	12	04	13
Harbor, William(C)	1804	Oct. 29	Virginia	12	04	14
Harbour, Abner(C)	1806	Jan. 13	Virginia	11	04	18
Harbour, Elisha(A)	1804	Nov. 09	Greene	11	04	18
Harbour, Elisha(C)	1804	Nov. 08	Greene	12	04	20
Harbour, Harden(C)	1831	July 25	Champaign	13	03	01
Harbour, Jesse(C)	1810	April 10	Champaign	12	04	29
Harbour, Jesse(C)	1831	Feb. 11	Champaign	12	03	18
Harbour, Joel(C)	1811	June 15	Champaign	12	03	06
Harbour, Madison(E)	1837	Jan. 25	Randolph(Ind	14	20	34
Harbour, William(C)	1804	Nov. 08	Greene	12	04	13
Harbour, William(C)	1815	Oct. 13	Champaign	12	04	35
Harden, John(B)	1833	March 25	Franklin(Ind	02	08	14
Harden, John(B)	1836	Jan. 26	Franklin(Ind	02	08	23
Hardin, Charles(B)	1817	Oct. 31	Butler	01	15	11
Hardin, Ede(A)	1806	Nov. 24	Montgomery	03	05	07
Hardin, Henry(A)	1801	April 27	Hamilton	01	05	02
Hardin, Henry(B)	1811	Dec. 11	Dearborn(Ind	01	06	35
Hardin, James(A)	1804	Sept. 24	Hamilton	02	05	13
Hardin, John(A)	1805	Dec. 27	Montgomery	01	08	18

131

PURCHASER	YEAR	DATE	RESIDENCE	R	T	S
Hardin, John(A)	1805	Dec. 27	Montgomery	01	08	20
Hardin, John(A)	1805	Dec. 27	Montgomery	01	08	19
Hardin, John(B)	1805	Dec. 12	Montgomery	01	13	24
Hardin, John(E)	1811	Oct. 24	Warren	13	15	31
Hardin, Nancy(C)	1804	Dec. 28	Greene	09	03	15
Hardin, Sam'l. D.(A)	1837	Feb. 13	Hamilton	01	13	14
Hardin, Samuel D.(A)	1837	Feb. 13	Hamilton	02	13	08
Hardin, Samuel D.(A)	1837	Feb. 13	Hamilton	02	14	29
Hardin, Samuel D.(A)	1837	March 01	Hamilton	01	13	10
Hardin, Thomas(E)	1811	Dec. 09	Franklin(Ind	12	15	13
Harding, Ede(A)	1812	Feb. 22	Montgomery	04	04	18
Harding, Eliakim(E)	1812	March 12	Montgomery	13	15	31
Harding, Robert(A)	1804	Aug. 21	Montgomery	04	04	07
Hardman, Elizabeth(A)	1817	Sept. 29	Montgomery	01	12	15
Hardman, Jonathan(A)	1824	Nov. 23	Darke	04	09	15
Hardman, Solomon(A)	1817	Sept. 29	Montgomery	01	12	15
Hardman, Solomon(A)	1832	Jan. 18	Darke	02	12	12
Hardness, Aaron(A)	1819	Sept. 06	Cincinnati	06	08	33
Hardwick, Charles(A)	1807	Jan. 29	Greene	06	03	04
Hardwick, John(E)	1835	Oct. 08	Randolph(Ind	13	18	24
Hardwick, Martin(E)	1831	Jan. 10	Wayne(Ind)	13	18	13
Hardy, Charles(E)	1814	Aug. 26	Montgomery	12	13	18
Hardy, George(A)	1813	Nov. 12	Preble	02	07	08
Hare, Jacob(A)	1817	Nov. 05	Virginia	01	01	06
Hargereder, Benjamin(B)	1811	Aug. 16	Butler	01	10	31
Harison, William Henry(C)	1804	Dec. 31	Ind.Territry	12	01	25
Harkarader, Jacob(A)	1837	Oct. 17	Montgomery	01	14	31
Harker, Sam'l. T.(A)	1829	Jan. 22	Miami	05	07	26
Harkness, Aaron(A)	1819	Sept. 06	Cincinnati	06	08	08
Harkness, Anthony(B)	1819	Aug. 21	Cincinnati	01	07	22
Harkness, Anthony(B)	1831	Aug. 09	Cincinnati	01	07	22
Harkrader, Jacob(A)	1812	June 30	Butler	06	03	06
Harkriader, Joseph(B)	1835	Oct. 12	Butler	01	17	01
Harkriader, Joseph(B)	1836	Jan. 26	Butler	01	17	02
Harlan, Elihu(B)	1816	Sept. 30	Butler	01	15	12
Harlan, Elihu(B)	1831	Sept. 27	Wayne(Ind)	01	16	35
Harlan, Elihu(B)	1836	Dec. 12	Wayne(Ind)	01	18	12
Harlan, Elihu(E)	1816	Feb. 26	Butler	12	17	36
Harlan, Elihu(E)	1836	Oct. 31	Wayne(Ind)	15	22	34
Harlan, Elihu(E)	1836	Oct. 31	Wayne(Ind)	15	21	22
Harlan, George(E)	1811	Dec. 17	Wayne(Ind)	14	14	20
Harlan, Jacob(B)	1831	March 21	Darke	01	15	01
Harlan, Jacob(E)	1836	Dec. 12	Darke	15	22	33
Harlan, James(A)	1816	Sept. 30	Butler	01	10	06
Harlan, James(B)	1837	Feb. 22	Darke	01	18	01
Harlan, John(A)	1814	Nov. 14	Preble	02	06	04
Harlan, John(A)	1818	Feb. 12	Franklin(Ind	01	10	05
Harlan, John(C)	1812	May 30	Virginia	09	05	29
Harlan, John(C)	1812	May 30	Virginia	09	05	29
Harlan, John(E)	1815	March 04	Franklin(Ind	13	14	24
Harlan, Jonathan(E)	1835	May 25	Wayne(Ind)	14	19	04
Harlan, Joseph(A)	1829	Sept. 24	Union(Ind)	01	10	05
Harlan, Joshua(B)	1816	Sept. 30	Butler	01	15	12
Harlan, Joshua(B)	1837	Jan. 26	Wayne(Ind)	01	18	01
Harlan, Nathan(A)	1819	Feb. 06	Darke	01	11	32
Harlan, Nathan(B)	1831	March 21	Darke	01	15	01
Harlan, Nathan(B)	1837	Oct. 05	Darke	01	19	36
Harlan, Samuel(E)	1816	Dec. 10	Franklin(Ind	13	13	18
Harlan, Valentine(A)	1817	Oct. 10	Franklin(Ind	01	10	05
Harlan, Valentine(A)	1829	Sept. 24	Darke	01	10	05
Harlan, Valentine(A)	1831	March 21	Darke	01	10	05
Harlan, Valentine(B)	1836	Dec. 12	Darke	01	18	13
Harlan, Valentine(E)	1815	March 04	Franklin(Ind	13	14	23
Harlan, Valentine(E)	1816	Dec. 10	Franklin(Ind	13	14	23
Harlan, Valentine(E)	1836	Dec. 12	Darke	15	21	22
Harlan, Volentine(B)	1816	Sept. 30	Preble	01	15	12
Harlan, William(A)	1815	Jan. 27	Preble	02	07	32
Harlen, George(B)	1807	Jan. 24	Dearborn(Ind	02	11	09
Harless, Elias(A)	1836	Dec. 26	Darke	01	12	30

PURCHASER	YEAR	DATE	RESIDENCE	R	T	S
Harley, John C.(E)	1813	April 01	Franklin(Ind	12	12	33
Harlin, Aaron(C)	1801	Dec. 30	Hamilton	05	03	31
Harlin, George Jnr.(C)	1801	Dec. 05	Hamilton	05	03	25
Harlin, George(A)	1803	July 02	Ohio	01	02	17
Harlin, George(A)	1806	Aug. 19	Montgomery	02	07	14
Harlin, George(A)	1811	Dec. 11	Preble	02	07	14
Harlin, George(C)	1801	Dec. 30	Hamilton	05	03	20
Harlin, James(A)	1816	Sept. 30	Butler	01	10	06
Harlin, Joshua(B)	1807	Jan. 28	Dearborn(Ind	02	11	14
Harlin, Joshua(E)	1811	Oct. 25	Franklin(Ind	14	14	19
Harlin, Samuel(C)	1804	Sept. 03	Warren	05	03	26
Harlin, Samuel(E)	1811	Oct. 23	So. Carolina	13	13	06
Harlin, Samuel(E)	1811	Oct. 28	So. Carolina	13	14	31
Harlin, Samuel(E)	1811	Oct. 28	So. Carolina	13	14	31
Harlin, Samuel(E)	1811	Oct. 28	So. Carolina	13	14	31
Harlin, Samuel(E)	1811	Oct. 28	So. Carolina	13	14	31
Harlin, Samuel(E)	1816	Nov. 02	Franklin(Ind	13	13	07
Harlin, Samuel(E)	1816	Nov. 02	Franklin(Ind	13	13	08
Harlis, David(C)	1804	Dec. 24	Montgomery	09	02	12
Harman, Andrew(B)	1814	Dec. 26	Wayne(Ind)	01	13	18
Harman, Andrew(C)	1830	Jan. 13	Warren	10	03	18
Harman, David(B)	1813	July 12	Wayne(Ind)	01	13	07
Harman, David(B)	1814	Dec. 26	Wayne(Ind)	01	13	18
Harmill, Henry(A)	1817	June 25	Warren	05	06	12
Harnell, Jesse(B)	1815	March 07	Dearborn(Ind	02	03	32
Harness, Peter(A)	1838	Jan. 31	Greene	02	14	24
Harnett, Elijah(C)	1811	Dec. 11	Champaign	09	05	27
Harp, Henry(A)	1828	Jan. 29	Shelby	05	09	20
Harp, Jacob(A)	1818	March 20	Hamilton	05	09	20
Harp, Nehemiah(E)	1817	Sept. 17	Franklin(Ind	12	12	23
Harper, Ezekiel G.(B)	1814	March 24	Clermont	02	06	25
Harper, Ezekiel G.(B)	1839	April 17	Dearborn(Ind	02	04	17
Harper, James(A)	1813	April 14	Hamilton	01	04	09
Harper, John W.(A)	1832	April 03	Darke	03	09	09
Harper, John W.(A)	1832	Sept. 07	Darke	03	09	08
Harper, John(A)	1805	Aug. 06	Hamilton	01	04	29
Harper, John(A)	1806	Aug. 09	Hamilton	01	04	10
Harper, John(A)	1807	June 22	Hamilton	01	04	09
Harper, John(A)	1811	Dec. 11	Hamilton	01	04	10
Harper, John(A)	1814	May 04	Butler	01	04	10
Harper, John(B)	1809	Nov. 18	Cincinnati	01	10	25
Harper, John(B)	1814	Dec. 24	Hamilton	01	06	02
Harper, Joseph(B)	1815	June 23	Butler	01	06	02
Harper, Matthew(A)	1805	Aug. 06	Hamilton	01	04	29
Harper, Thomas Senr.(B)	1811	March 09	Hamilton	01	10	11
Harper, Thomas Senr.(B)	1811	March 09	Hamilton	01	10	03
Harper, William(C)	1818	July 30	Kentucky	11	04	29
Harpham, Henry(B)	1829	Dec. 29	Dearborn(Ind	01	07	20
Harpham, Henry(E)	1833	March 02	Franklin(Ind	13	12	09
Harphan, Henry(E)	1836	April 02	Franklin(Ind	12	12	12
Harrel, Chester(A)	1805	Aug. 07	Montgomery	03	05	33
Harrel, Stephen(E)	1813	June 12	Franklin(Ind	12	13	11
Harrel, Wm.(E)	1813	June 12	Franklin(Ind	12	13	11
Harrell, Chester(B)	1811	Nov. 11	Butler	01	09	35
Harrell, Gabriel(B)	1816	Aug. 16	Franklin(Ind	01	15	26
Harrell, Isaac(A)	1812	April 15	Preble	03	04	08
Harrell, James(A)	1805	Sept. 03	Butler	02	04	13
Harrell, James(A)	1806	Dec. 18	Kentucky	03	04	08
Harrell, John(A)	1805	Aug. 26	Kentucky	02	04	09
Harrell, Moses(E)	1831	March 17	Fayette	12	13	32
Harrell, Moses(E)	1832	Jan. 03	Fayette	12	13	32
Harrell, Moses(E)	1832	Jan. 26	Fayette	12	13	32
Harrell, Moses(E)	1835	Jan. 03	Fayette	12	13	32
Harris, Benjamin(A)	1806	Dec. 29	Butler	01	07	10
Harris, Benjamin(B)	1807	Sept. 26	Greene	01	14	04
Harris, Benjamin(E)	1836	Feb. 08	Virginia	13	19	13
Harris, Benjamin(E)	1836	Dec. 05	Randolph(Ind	13	19	13
Harris, Buckley C.(E)	1836	Aug. 19	Fayette	12	12	06
Harris, Caleb(B)	1815	Feb. 25	Kentucky	01	02	29

PURCHASER	YEAR	DATE	RESIDENCE	R	T	S
Harris, David M.(E)	1826	Nov. 13	Randolph(Ind	14	18	14
Harris, Elijah(B)	1832	Aug. 16	Randolph(Ind	01	16	36
Harris, Elijah(E)	1837	March 28	Wayne(Ind)	13	21	23
Harris, George(A)	1807	Jan. 15	Dayton	06	05	30
Harris, Harvey(B)	1821	Aug. 30	Randolph(Ind	01	16	34
Harris, Israel(C)	1802	Dec. 10	Hamilton	05	03	22
Harris, Jacob R.(B)	1825	April 20	Switzerland	01	02	07
Harris, Jacob R.(B)	1836	Sept. 27	Switzerland	03	04	25
Harris, Jacob Rude(B)	1832	April 25	Switzerland	01	02	18
Harris, James(A)	1808	Jan. 25	Hamilton	01	07	01
Harris, James(A)	1837	March 28	Hamilton	02	14	25
Harris, James(E)	1818	April 21	Wayne(Ind)	14	17	08
Harris, James(E)	1831	Oct. 25	Wayne(Ind)	13	17	11
Harris, John(A)	1831	Dec. 21	Preble	03	07	05
Harris, John(A)	1832	Feb. 18	Preble	03	07	05
Harris, John(E)	1830	Sept. 03	Randolph(Ind	14	19	33
Harris, John(E)	1836	Feb. 08	Virginia	13	19	23
Harris, John(E)	1836	Feb. 08	Virginia	13	19	24
Harris, Jonathan(A)	1814	Sept. 27	Preble	01	09	08
Harris, Jones(A)	1805	Sept. 07	Hamilton	01	04	27
Harris, Jones(A)	1805	Sept. 07	Hamilton	01	04	27
Harris, Jones(A)	1810	Dec. 12	Butler	01	04	27
Harris, Joseph(A)	1809	Dec. 12	Hamilton	04	03	33
Harris, Joseph(A)	1809	Dec. 12	Hamilton	04	03	26
Harris, Joseph(A)	1815	Feb. 06	Hamilton	04	03	33
Harris, Joseph(D)	1808	Nov. 01	Hamilton	01	03	11
Harris, Josephus(E)	1836	Dec. 15	Randolph(Ind	14	20	10
Harris, Joshua(B)	1814	Sept. 01	Butler	01	10	27
Harris, Morris(A)	1815	Aug. 15	Ohio	04	03	22
Harris, Nathan'l.(A)	1830	July 03	Preble	03	07	05
Harris, Nathaniel(A)	1815	Jan. 07	Preble	04	05	31
Harris, Nathaniel(A)	1815	Jan. 07	Preble	03	06	36
Harris, Obadiah Junr.(E)	1815	Oct. 04	Wayne(Ind)	14	18	15
Harris, Obadiah Jur.(E)	1815	May 08	Wayne(Ind)	14	18	10
Harris, Obadiah(E)	1811	Nov. 07	Wayne(Ind)	14	17	11
Harris, Obadiah(E)	1836	Aug. 15	Randolph(Ind	14	19	20
Harris, Robert(B)	1817	Nov. 10	Switzerland	01	02	06
Harris, Sam'l. Stillwell(A)	1832	May 23	Preble	01	09	02
Harris, Simeon(E)	1832	Aug. 16	Randolph(Ind	14	20	23
Harris, Simeon(E)	1836	Dec. 21	Wayne(Ind)	14	20	23
Harris, William(A)	1836	Nov. 18	Butler	01	12	30
Harris, Willis L.(E)	1837	Jan. 23	Wayne(Ind)	14	20	23
Harrison, Andrew(C)	1811	Nov. 19	Kentucky	13	05	25
Harrison, Charles(B)	1818	Oct. 28	Hamilton	02	08	30
Harrison, Gideon(B)	1828	Jan. 29	Wayne(Ind)	01	15	02
Harrison, Gideon(E)	1836	Dec. 12	Wayne(Ind)	15	22	26
Harrison, Harvey(A)	1832	July 17	Darke	01	11	29
Harrison, Harvey(B)	1837	Jan. 30	Darke	01	17	15
Harrison, Job(B)	1818	Aug. 05	Cincinnati	02	08	29
Harrison, John(A)	1810	Oct. 18	Miami	04	09	23
Harrison, Richard(A)	1838	Feb. 13	Miami	02	14	02
Harrison, Robert(A)	1813	April 14	Butler	02	05	05
Harrison, William H.(C)	1805	April 20	Ind.Territry	11	02	34
Harrison, William H.(C)	1805	April 20	Ind.Territry	11	02	34
Harrison, William H.(C)	1805	April 20	Ind.Territry	11	02	34
Harrison, William H.(C)	1805	April 20	Ind.Territry	11	02	27
Harrison, William H.(C)	1805	April 20	Ind.Territry	11	02	27
Harrison, William H.(C)	1805	April 20	Ind.Territry	11	02	27
Harrison, William H.(C)	1805	April 20	Ind.Territry	11	02	27
Harrison, William H.(C)	1805	April 20	Ind.Territry	11	02	21
Harrison, William H.(C)	1805	April 20	Ind.Territry	11	02	21
Harrison, William H.(C)	1805	April 20	Ind.Territry	11	02	21
Harrison, William H.(C)	1805	April 20	Ind.Territry	11	02	21
Harrison, William H.(C)	1805	April 20	Ind.Territry	11	02	20
Harrison, William H.(C)	1805	April 20	Ind.Territry	11	02	20
Harrison, William H.(C)	1805	April 20	Ind.Territry	11	02	20
Harrison, William H.(C)	1805	April 20	Ind.Territry	11	02	20
Harrison, William H.(C)	1805	April 20	Ind.Territry	11	02	15
Harrison, William H.(C)	1805	April 20	Ind.Territry	11	02	15

PURCHASER	YEAR	DATE	RESIDENCE	R	T	S
Harrison, William H.(C)	1805	April 20	Ind.Territory	11	02	15
Harrison, William H.(C)	1805	April 20	Ind.Territory	11	02	15
Harrison, William H.(C)	1805	April 20	Ind.Territory	11	01	06
Harrison, William H.(C)	1805	April 20	Ind.Territry	11	01	06
Harrison, William H.(C)	1805	April 20	Ind.Territory	11	01	06
Harrison, William H.(C)	1805	April 20	Ind.Territory	11	01	06
Harrison, William H.(C)	1805	April 20	Ind.Territory	12	01	01
Harrison, William H.(C)	1805	April 20	Ind.Territry	12	01	01
Harrison, William H.(C)	1805	April 20	Ind.Territory	12	01	01
Harrison, William H.(C)	1805	April 20	Ind.Territory	12	01	01
Harrison, William H.(C)	1805	April 20	Ind.Territory	12	02	25
Harrison, William H.(C)	1805	April 20	Ind.Territry	12	02	25
Harrison, William H.(C)	1805	April 20	Ind.Territry	12	02	25
Harrison, William H.(C)	1805	April 20	Ind.Territry	12	02	25
Harrison, William H.(C)	1805	April 20	Ind.Territry	12	02	31
Harrison, William H.(C)	1805	April 20	Ind.Territory	12	02	31
Harrison, William H.(C)	1805	April 20	Ind.Territry	12	02	31
Harrison, William H.(C)	1805	April 20	Ind.Territory	12	02	31
Harrison, William H.(C)	1805	April 20	Ind.Territory	12	02	19
Harrison, William H.(C)	1805	April 20	Ind.Territory	12	02	19
Harrison, William H.(C)	1805	April 20	Ind.Territory	12	02	19
Harrison, William H.(C)	1805	April 20	Ind.Territory	12	02	19
Harrison, William H.(C)	1805	April 20	Ind.Territory	11	01	27
Harrison, William H.(C)	1805	April 20	Ind.Territory	11	01	28
Harrison, William H.(C)	1805	April 20	Ind.Territory	11	01	22
Harrison, William H.(C)	1805	April 20	Ind.Territry	11	01	21
Harrison, William H.(C)	1805	April 20	Ind.Territory	11	01	22
Harrison, William H.(C)	1805	April 20	Ind.Territory	11	01	23
Harrison, William H.(C)	1805	April 20	Ind.Territory	11	01	15
Harrison, William H.(C)	1805	April 20	Ind.Territory	11	01	15
Harrison, William H.(C)	1805	April 20	Ind.Territory	11	01	15
Harrison, William H.(C)	1805	April 20	Ind.Territory	11	01	15
Harrison, William H.(C)	1813	April 14	Cincinnati	11	01	06
Harrison, William Henry(C)	1805	April 20	Ind.Territory	11	02	33
Harrison, William Henry(C)	1805	April 20	Ind.Territry	11	02	33
Harrison, William Henry(C)	1805	April 20	Ind.Territory	11	02	33
Harrison, William Henry(C)	1805	April 20	Ind.Territory	11	02	33
Harrison, William Henry(C)	1805	April 20	Ind.Territory	11	02	34
Harrison, William Henry(C)	1813	April 14	Cincinnati	11	02	33
Harrison, William Henry(C)	1813	April 14	Cincinnati	11	02	15
Harrison, William Henry(C)	1813	April 14	Cincinnati	11	01	06
Harrison, William Henry(C)	1813	April 14	Cincinnati	11	01	06
Harrison, William Henry(C)	1813	April 14	Cincinnati	11	02	33
Harrison, William Henry(D)	1814	Jan. 10	Cincinati(Fr	01	01	11
Harrison, William Hy.(E)	1814	July 04	Cincinnati	13	15	07
Harrison, Willm. Henry(C)	1813	April 14	Cincinnati	11	02	33
Harrison, Wm. Henry(C)	1813	April 14	Cincinnati	11	01	06
Harrow, Andrew(A)	1815	Jan. 09	Preble	01	08	19
Harshbarger, Christian(A)	1826	Sept. 15	Montgomery	04	05	21
Harshbarger, Jonas(A)	1836	Nov. 07	Montgomery	03	12	14
Harshberger, Henry(A)	1826	Feb. 24	Montgomery	04	07	36
Harshberger, Henry(A)	1828	Aug. 13	Miami	04	07	36
Harshey, Christian(A)	1832	June 16	Pennsylvania	03	09	03
Harshey, Christian(A)	1832	June 16	Pennsylvania	03	09	02
Harshey, Christian(A)	1832	June 16	Pennsylvania	03	10	35
Harshey, Christian(B)	1816	Nov. 06	Maryland	02	05	20
Harshey, Christian(B)	1816	Nov. 07	Maryland	02	05	19
Harshey, Christian(B)	1816	Nov. 07	Maryland	02	05	18
Harshey, John(A)	1832	June 16	Pennsylvania	04	08	06
Harshman, Abraham(E)	1836	Dec. 15	Randolph(Ind	15	21	19
Harshman, Henry(E)	1837	Aug. 11	Preble	15	21	19
Harshman, Jacob(E)	1836	May 27	Randolph(Ind	15	21	20
Harshman, Jacob(E)	1836	Sept. 23	Randolph(Ind	15	21	20
Harshman, John(A)	1827	Jan. 10	Preble	01	09	13
Harshman, Jonathan(C)	1805	Oct. 05	Montgomery	09	02	18
Harshman, Jonathan(C)	1816	Oct. 25	Montgomery	09	02	18
Harshman, Joseph Senr.(E)	1836	April 16	Preble	15	21	30
Harshman, Peter(A)	1807	Feb. 24	Warren	02	08	09
Harshman, Peter(A)	1814	Nov. 03	Preble	02	08	09

PURCHASER	YEAR	DATE	RESIDENCE	R	T	S
Harshman, Peter(A)	1819	Jan. 15	Preble	02	09	20
Hart, Abraham C.(B)	1837	Nov. 07	Hamilton	03	05	35
Hart, Abraham C.(B)	1838	Feb. 23	Hamilton	03	05	34
Hart, Aiklin D.(B)	1818	Jan. 24	Kentucky	01	02	23
Hart, Dennis(A)	1817	Dec. 05	Darke	01	10	35
Hart, Elias(A)	1829	Oct. 22	Butler	04	06	07
Hart, Finney(B)	1808	Jan. 19	Butler	01	12	06
Hart, Geo. W.(A)	1829	Sept. 25	Warren	04	06	08
Hart, Henry(A)	1814	Feb. 10	Preble	02	09	01
Hart, Henry(A)	1832	Jan. 30	Darke	02	10	23
Hart, Isaac(A)	1805	Aug. 20	Butler	03	03	04
Hart, Isaac(A)	1807	Aug. 15	Butler	03	04	30
Hart, Isaac(B)	1832	Aug. 11	Franklin(Ind	02	08	27
Hart, Jacob(A)	1817	June 04	Pennsylvania	03	10	04
Hart, Jeduthan(B)	1837	March 01	Cincinnati	03	05	01
Hart, Jeduthan(B)	1838	May 21	Dearborn(Ind	03	05	12
Hart, John(A)	1815	Dec. 25	Preble	03	06	21
Hart, Patrick(A)	1836	Sept. 06	Montgomery	03	12	01
Hart, Stephen(E)	1833	Nov. 19	Franklin(Ind	12	12	29
Hart, Thomas(A)	1806	June 13	Butler	01	07	03
Hart, William(A)	1816	Oct. 07	Montgomery	02	13	19
Hart, William(B)	1836	Jan. 21	Franklin(Ind	01	08	08
Harten, Edmond(C)	1807	July 29	Greene	08	05	35
Harter, Adam(A)	1805	Oct. 17	Warren	03	05	13
Harter, Adam(A)	1810	Aug. 14	Preble	03	05	13
Harter, Christian(A)	1804	Nov. 08	Virginia	03	05	27
Harter, Christian(A)	1804	Nov. 16	Virginia	03	05	36
Harter, Conrod(A)	1816	Sept. 23	Franklin(Ind	01	12	14
Harter, David(A)	1817	Oct. 22	Darke	02	10	08
Harter, Francis(A)	1817	Oct. 22	Darke	02	10	18
Harter, Francis(A)	1817	Oct. 22	Darke	02	10	06
Harter, George Sen.(A)	1814	July 20	Preble	03	05	18
Harter, George Senr.(A)	1814	July 20	Preble	03	05	07
Harter, George(A)	1816	Nov. 29	Preble	02	11	07
Harter, George(A)	1817	Oct. 22	Preble	02	10	09
Harter, George(A)	1817	Oct. 22	Preble	02	10	09
Harter, Israel(A)	1829	Feb. 16	Preble	03	06	20
Harter, Jacob(A)	1818	Jan. 16	Preble	02	11	27
Harter, Jacob(A)	1818	Jan. 16	Preble	02	12	08
Harter, Jacob(A)	1819	July 20	Darke	02	10	18
Harter, John(A)	1814	Sept. 13	Preble	03	05	21
Harter, John(A)	1832	March 19	Darke	02	10	17
Harter, John(C)	1806	July 05	Montgomery	09	02	19
Harter, Joseph(B)	1813	Oct. 25	Franklin(Ind	01	10	01
Harter, Samuel(A)	1817	Oct. 22	Dearborn(Ind	01	11	12
Harter, Solomon(A)	1830	April 01	Darke	01	10	12
Harter, Solomon(A)	1837	June 28	Darke	01	12	05
Hartin, Isaac(A)	1807	June 24	Butler	02	06	29
Hartin, Joseph(A)	1807	June 16	Butler	02	06	29
Hartin, Joseph(A)	1812	Nov. 17	Preble	02	06	29
Hartle, Frederick(A)	1815	Nov. 21	Pennsylvania	04	09	12
Hartle, Frederick(A)	1815	Nov. 21	Pennsylvania	04	09	14
Hartle, Jacob(A)	1815	Oct. 11	Pickaway	03	11	28
Hartle, Jacob(A)	1815	Oct. 11	Pickaway	03	11	33
Hartle, Jacob(A)	1832	Jan. 12	Darke	03	11	32
Hartley, Norton D.(E)	1836	Dec. 30	Preble	14	19	23
Hartman, David(A)	1805	April 22	Butler	05	05	26
Hartman, David(A)	1807	April 03	Montgomery	04	05	27
Hartman, Henry(E)	1829	Dec. 10	Wayne(Ind)	13	15	03
Hartman, John(A)	1805	Nov. 06	Virginia	04	03	10
Hartman, Jonathan(A)	1816	June 12	Montgomery	04	09	17
Hartman, Joseph(E)	1835	Feb. 23	Preble	15	21	29
Hartman, Peter(A)	1823	Aug. 30	Pickaway	07	01	17
Hartman, Solomon(A)	1807	April 03	Montgomery	04	05	26
Hartpence, James(B)	1815	Nov. 01	Dearborn(Ind	01	07	12
Hartsell, Abraham(A)	1805	June 18	Montgomery	04	03	14
Hartsough, Daniel(A)	1818	Nov. 05	Maryland	04	05	22
Hartup, James(B)	1806	Dec. 15	Butler	01	13	23
Harty, Daniel(B)	1814	Oct. 25	Franklin(Ind	02	08	35

PURCHASER	YEAR	DATE	RESIDENCE	R	T	S
Hartzel, Jacob(A)	1815	July 25	Pennsylvania	02	08	31
Hartzel, Jacob(A)	1815	July 25	Pennsylvania	01	08	36
Hartzell, Abraham(A)	1805	March 25	Montgomery	04	03	12
Harvey, Andrew(A)	1836	Sept. 29	Darke	03	12	27
Harvey, Benjamin(B)	1808	Nov. 08	Dearborn(Ind	02	14	13
Harvey, Benjamin(E)	1814	Jan. 07	?	14	17	33
Harvey, Benjamin(E)	1816	Nov. 09	Wayne(Ind)	14	17	34
Harvey, Caleb(B)	1808	Oct. 15	Dearborn(Ind	02	13	12
Harvey, Charles(E)	1815	Oct. 05	Franklin(Ind	13	12	11
Harvey, Christopher(A)	1806	Dec. 22	Butler	02	03	32
Harvey, Francis(B)	1813	Dec. 23	Wayne(Ind)	01	12	27
Harvey, Francis(B)	1815	Aug. 25	Wayne(Ind)	02	12	20
Harvey, Henderson(B)	1806	Aug. 20	Butler	01	08	01
Harvey, Isaac(B)	1811	Nov. 02	Wayne(Ind)	13	17	17
Harvey, James(B)	1824	Dec. 16	Union(Ind)	01	12	22
Harvey, Jas.(E)	1814	Oct. 10	Franklin(Ind	13	12	11
Harvey, John Junr.(E)	1815	Oct. 04	Wayne(Ind)	13	16	04
Harvey, John Junr.(E)	1816	Aug. 31	Wayne(Ind)	13	16	23
Harvey, John Senr.(E)	1815	Oct. 04	Wayne(Ind)	13	16	01
Harvey, John Senr.(E)	1815	Oct. 04	Wayne(Ind)	13	16	11
Harvey, John(B)	1807	June 23	Dearborn(Ind	01	14	34
Harvey, John(B)	1807	June 23	Dearborn(Ind	01	13	03
Harvey, John(C)	1813	March 25	Champaign	08	07	36
Harvey, John(E)	1811	Oct. 24	Wayne(Ind)	13	16	24
Harvey, John(E)	1811	Oct. 24	Wayne(Ind)	13	17	29
Harvey, John(E)	1811	Oct. 24	Wayne(Ind)	13	16	35
Harvey, John(E)	1811	Oct. 25	Wayne(Ind)	13	16	05
Harvey, John(E)	1814	April 12	Wayne(Ind)	13	16	15
Harvey, John(E)	1824	June 12	Richmond(Ind	13	16	27
Harvey, John(E)	1835	Nov. 19	Warren	13	18	04
Harvey, John(E)	1835	Nov. 19	Warren	13	18	04
Harvey, Michael(E)	1813	Aug. 23	Wayne(Ind)	14	17	34
Harvey, Pryor(E)	1835	Sept. 15	Clinton	13	19	35
Harvey, Robert(B)	1808	Sept. 15	Dearborn(Ind	01	12	27
Harvey, Robert(E)	1811	Oct. 25	Wayne(Ind)	14	16	18
Harvey, William(A)	1812	April 15	Ohio	02	04	28
Harvey, William(B)	1815	May 01	Butler	02	10	35
Harvey, William(B)	1814	Nov. 01	Cincinnati	01	03	31
Harvey, William(E)	1811	Oct. 24	Wayne(Ind)	13	16	24
Harvey, William(E)	1813	Aug. 23	Wayne(Ind)	14	17	34
Harvey, Wm.(E)	1814	Oct. 10	Franklin(Ind	13	12	11
Harvy, John(E)	1812	Aug. 07	Wayne(Ind)	14	16	17
Harwood, Philip(B)	1811	Oct. 10	Ind.Territry	01	08	13
Hasket, Isaac(A)	1819	Sept. 14	Miami	04	07	13
Haskit, Isaac(A)	1806	July 30	Montgomery	04	07	01
Hastie, William(B)	1836	Oct. 29	Switzerland	02	02	13
Hastings, William(E)	1811	Nov. 23	Wayne(Ind)	14	16	07
Hatch, Ralph(B)	1818	June 23	Cincinnati	02	05	02
Hatfield, Clark(A)	1818	March 11	Warren	02	09	28
Hatfield, Clark(A)	1818	March 11	Warren	02	09	28
Hatfield, George(A)	1804	Oct. 05	Butler	03	03	24
Hatfield, Henry(A)	1831	Dec. 01	Montgomery	04	07	14
Hatfield, Jonas(A)	1801	Aug. 28	Hamilton	04	03	13
Hatfield, Jonas(A)	1804	Aug. 08	Montgomery	04	03	19
Hatfield, Jonas(A)	1804	Aug. 08	Montgomery	04	03	20
Hatfield, Jonas(A)	1805	Jan. 04	Montgomery	03	05	02
Hatfield, Jonas(E)	1811	Oct. 25	Montgomery	13	17	26
Hatfield, Levin(C)	1805	Feb. 08	Greene	05	03	06
Hatfield, Nathaniel(C)	1806	Sept. 08	Greene	09	05	07
Hatfield, Nathaniel(C)	1811	Dec. 11	Champaign	09	05	07
Hatfield, Owin(C)	1802	Dec. 28	Hamilton	05	03	30
Hatfield, Thomas(C)	1801	Dec. 30	Hamilton	05	03	28
Hatfield, Thomas(C)	1801	Dec. 30	Hamilton	05	03	28
Hatfield, Thomas(C)	1804	Sept. 03	Montgomery	05	03	29
Hatfield, Thomas(E)	1812	March 26	Montgomery	13	17	26
Hatfield, William(C)	1804	Sept. 03	Montgomery	05	03	29
Hathaway, Abiathar(E)	1814	Jan. 03	Clermont	12	14	26
Hathaway, Abraham(C)	1804	Dec. 29	Montgomery	11	01	20
Hathaway, Benj'n. Clark(C)	1831	Aug. 08	Clark	09	06	11

137

PURCHASER	YEAR	DATE	RESIDENCE	R	T	S
Hathaway, Benj'n. Clark(C)	1831	Aug. 08	Clark	09	06	11
Hathaway, Benjamin(A)	1818	Jan. 31	Warren	06	04	07
Hathaway, Benjamin(A)	1819	Jan. 28	Warren	05	07	23
Hathaway, Benjamin(C)	1817	July 03	Champaign	09	06	09
Hathaway, Dan'l.(B)	1825	April 08	Dearborn(Ind	03	07	14
Hathaway, Daniel(A)	1818	Oct. 27	Champaign	05	07	23
Hathaway, Daniel(B)	1818	March 12	Butler	03	07	23
Hathaway, Eliazer(A)	1811	Feb. 05	Miami	05	10	30
Hathaway, Isaac(A)	1816	July 30	?	03	10	33
Hathaway, John(A)	1816	April 15	Miami	07	01	10
Hathaway, John(C)	1804	Dec. 29	Montgomery	11	01	19
Hathaway, Thomas(A)	1814	Nov. 09	Warren	03	06	24
Hathaway, William(A)	1814	Nov. 16	Warren	04	05	07
Hathaway, William(A)	1816	July 30	?	03	10	33
Hathay, Manning(B)	1817	Sept. 02	Butler	02	07	30
Hathorn, David(A)	1814	Oct. 22	Preble	01	07	33
Hathorn, John(A)	1814	Oct. 22	Preble	01	07	33
Haths, James(A)	1816	Aug. 09	Butler	02	12	28
Hatrick, Philip(A)	1818	Dec. 18	Clermont	04	10	33
Hatten, John(C)	1812	March 16	Champaign	09	03	33
Hatter, Adam(C)	1802	Dec. 28	Hamilton	05	02	02
Hatton, Robert(B)	1835	April 20	Switzerland	02	02	29
Haugh, Jonathan(E)	1811	Nov. 11	Wayne(Ind)	14	17	01
Haupt, John(A)	1821	July 31	Butler	02	10	03
Hauptman, Frederick(B)	1818	Sept. 26	Pittsburgh	02	07	09
Havekotte, Henry(E)	1836	Oct. 21	Cincinnati	12	10	07
Havekotte, Henry(E)	1836	Nov. 15	Cincinnati	12	10	19
Havens, Clayton(A)	1836	Nov. 04	Montgomery	02	13	32
Havens, Jonas(A)	1807	Jan. 22	Hamilton	01	02	33
Havens, Jonas(A)	1812	April 15	Hamilton	01	02	33
Havery, Samuel(A)	1821	Aug. 14	Warren	04	05	07
Havns, Coonrod G.(E)	1838	Jan. 25	Kentucky	14	20	24
Hawkins, Amos(A)	1805	June 24	Butler	03	03	06
Hawkins, Amos(B)	1807	Sept. 03	Butler	01	14	34
Hawkins, Benjamin(A)	1805	May 31	Butler	03	03	08
Hawkins, Benjamin(A)	1805	May 31	Butler	03	03	05
Hawkins, Benjamin(A)	1805	July 27	Butler	03	03	05
Hawkins, Benjamin(A)	1806	May 19	Butler	03	03	08
Hawkins, Darbe(A)	1813	Dec. 18	Butler	01	04	24
Hawkins, Henry(E)	1814	Nov. 17	Ind.Territry	14	17	28
Hawkins, John(A)	1805	Sept. 10	Butler	02	05	01
Hawkins, John(B)	1807	July 01	Dearborn(Ind	01	14	33
Hawkins, John(E)	1814	Dec. 17	?	12	11	29
Hawkins, John(E)	1815	Aug. 17	Franklin(Ind	12	11	04
Hawkins, John(E)	1836	Feb. 22	Franklin(Ind	11	11	35
Hawkins, John, Sen.(E)	1811	Nov. 02	Wayne(Ind)	12	16	27
Hawkins, Joseph(A)	1805	June 24	Butler	03	03	04
Hawkins, Joseph(A)	1807	May 27	Butler	02	05	11
Hawkins, Levi(A)	1807	May 27	Butler	02	05	11
Hawkins, Levi(A)	1811	Oct. 22	Butler	02	05	01
Hawkins, Mounce(A)	1819	Jan. 02	Greene	03	10	06
Hawkins, Nathan(A)	1806	May 19	Butler	02	06	36
Hawkins, Nathan(E)	1813	Nov. 29	Wayne(Ind)	14	17	27
Hawkins, Nathan(E)	1832	March 26	Franklin(Ind	11	11	36
Hawkins, Nathan(E)	1836	Aug. 31	Franklin(Ind	11	11	35
Hawkins, Nathan(E)	1837	Feb. 14	Franklin(Ind	11	11	35
Hawkins, Reuben(E)	1836	Sept. 12	Franklin(Ind	12	11	10
Hawkins, Samuel(A)	1801	Dec. 11	Hamilton	04	03	12
Hawkins, Samuel(A)	1804	Sept. 25	Montgomery	04	03	12
Hawkins, Samuel(A)	1805	Sept. 27	Montgomery	03	06	25
Hawkins, Samuel(A)	1806	Sept. 24	Montgomery	02	08	27
Hawkins, Samuel(A)	1811	April 09	Preble	02	08	34
Hawkins, Samuel(A)	1811	July 13	Preble	02	08	34
Hawkins, Samuel(A)	1811	Dec. 11	Montgomery	02	08	27
Hawman, Eber(E)	1812	Sept. 01	Warren	13	14	20
Haworth, Absalom(A)	1806	July 25	Highland	05	07	30
Haworth, James(A)	1806	July 25	Highland	05	07	29
Haworth, James(A)	1811	Dec. 11	Miami	05	07	29
Haworth, James(A)	1819	Feb. 10	Miami	04	08	27

138

PURCHASER	YEAR	DATE	RESIDENCE	R	T	S
Haworth, James(A)	1819	March 08	Miami	04	08	26
Haworth, James(A)	1819	June 14	Miami	04	08	25
Haworth, James(A)	1822	May 16	Miami	04	08	34
Haworth, James(A)	1822	May 27	Miami	04	08	34
Haworth, James(A)	1827	July 06	Miami	04	08	33
Haworth, Joel(B)	1816	Oct. 17	Tennessee	01	11	22
Haworth, Joel(B)	1824	June 09	Union(Ind)	01	12	21
Haworth, Joel(B)	1824	June 09	Union(Ind)	01	12	15
Haworth, Joel(B)	1824	Dec. 14	Union(Ind)	01	11	15
Haworth, John(A)	1806	July 28	Highland	05	06	10
Haworth, John(E)	1817	Aug. 23	Tennessee	12	17	01
Haworth, John(E)	1817	Aug. 23	Tennessee	13	18	34
Haworth, Nathan'l.(A)	1828	Nov. 20	Miami	04	08	23
Haworth, Sampson(A)	1807	May 11	Montgomery	05	07	19
Haworth, Sampson(A)	1811	Dec. 11	Miami	05	07	31
Haworth, Sampson(A)	1831	May 09	Miami	04	08	23
Haworth, Sampson(A)	1832	Jan. 16	Miami	04	08	13
Haworth, William(E)	1816	Oct. 19	Highland	14	20	17
Haworth, William(E)	1816	Dec. 07	Clinton	13	20	27
Haws, James(A)	1832	Oct. 02	Darke	02	10	12
Hawser, Henry(A)	1814	Nov. 30	Preble	03	07	07
Hawser, John(A)	1815	April 11	Montgomery	03	07	08
Hawthorn, Hugh B.(A)	1817	Aug. 26	Cincinnati	02	12	33
Hawthorn, Hugh B.(A)	1817	Aug. 26	Cincinnati	01	11	27
Hay, John(A)	1815	Nov. 21	Pennsylvania	04	09	13
Hay, John(A)	1818	Jan. 15	Miami	04	09	25
Hay, John(A)	1837	March 29	Butler	01	14	33
Hay, William B.(B)	1839	June 12	Cincinnati	03	04	25
Haycock, Daniel(B)	1815	July 22	Kentucky	01	02	30
Hayden, Christopher(A)	1806	Feb. 27	Hamilton	02	03	06
Hayden, Daniel(A)	1813	Dec. 17	Hamilton	01	04	11
Hayden, Stephen(B)	1813	April 13	Butler	01	11	02
Hayes, James(B)	1811	June 13	Ind.Territry	01	06	35
Hayes, James(B)	1817	Dec. 15	Cincinnati	03	06	34
Hayes, James(B)	1832	Feb. 08	Dearborn(Ind	03	06	34
Hayes, James(B)	1837	March 22	Dearborn(Ind	03	06	34
Hayes, John(B)	1815	Sept. 20	Dearborn(Ind	01	08	20
Hayes, Walter(B)	1829	Aug. 20	Dearborn(Ind	01	06	15
Hayes, Walter(B)	1829	Aug. 28	Dearborn(Ind	01	06	15
Hayhurst, Elah(C)	1817	Aug. 09	Hamilton	11	02	03
Hayhurst, Elah(C)	1817	Dec. 29	Hamilton	11	02	02
Hayhurst, James(C)	1817	Aug. 09	Hamilton	11	02	02
Hayhurst, Job(C)	1817	Aug. 09	Hamilton	11	02	01
Haymond, Cyrus(E)	1817	June 10	Franklin(Ind	12	13	36
Haymond, Daniel(B)	1815	June 26	Virginia	02	09	12
Haynes, Amos(C)	1813	April 14	Clermont	08	03	34
Haynes, Asa(E)	1835	Jan. 19	Clinton	13	19	27
Haynes, John(A)	1814	July 11	Butler	04	03	34
Haynes, Joshua(B)	1818	March 16	Dearborn(Ind	02	03	36
Haynes, Joshua(B)	1818	March 16	Dearborn(Ind	02	03	18
Haynes, Matthias(B)	1818	March 16	Dearborn(Ind	02	03	36
Haynes, Matthias(B)	1818	March 16	Dearborn(Ind	02	03	18
Haynes, Stephen(E)	1835	Jan. 19	Clinton	13	19	22
Haynes, Stephen(E)	1835	Jan. 19	Clinton	13	19	23
Haynes, Wright(E)	1835	Jan. 20	Clinton	13	19	14
Haynes, Wright(E)	1835	Jan. 20	Clinton	13	19	14
Haynes, Wright(E)	1835	Jan. 20	Clinton	13	19	22
Hays, Abiah(B)	1809	March 23	Dearborn(Ind	01	06	22
Hays, Abiah(B)	1817	Aug. 01	Dearborn(Ind	01	08	19
Hays, Caleb(B)	1817	Sept. 03	Dearborn(Ind	02	02	23
Hays, David(B)	1815	Jan. 16	Warren	02	09	24
Hays, Jacob(A)	1830	Dec. 08	Montgomery	04	06	19
Hays, Jacob(B)	1817	Aug. 01	Dearborn(Ind	02	08	23
Hays, James(A)	1816	March 05	Butler	02	11	27
Hays, James(A)	1818	Oct. 02	Darke	03	09	05
Hays, James(A)	1829	Dec. 07	Darke	03	09	08
Hays, James(C)	1824	June 16	Miami	10	02	11
Hays, John W.(C)	1828	Oct. 02	Logan	13	04	11
Hays, John(B)	1814	May 27	Dearborn(Ind	01	08	25

PURCHASER	YEAR	DATE	RESIDENCE	R	T	S
Hays, John(B)	1817	July 11	Dearborn(Ind	02	08	23
Hays, Joseph(B)	1806	March 12	Ind.Territry	01	06	23
Hays, Joseph(B)	1806	April 02	Ind.Territry	01	06	23
Hays, Joseph(C)	1801	Dec. 30	Hamilton	04	04	30
Hays, Robert(A)	1808	Jan. 12	Montgomery	01	06	19
Hays, Robert(D)	1814	Sept. 02	Warren	03	05	08
Hays, Samuel(A)	1836	Sept. 23	Warren	03	12	21
Hays, Samuel(E)	1817	Oct. 23	Warren	12	17	24
Hays, Thomas(C)	1806	Feb. 10	Champaign	10	04	25
Hays, Thomas(C)	1806	March 28	Champaign	10	04	25
Hays, Thomas(C)	1811	July 23	Champaign	10	04	25
Hays, Thos.(C)	1828	Dec. 19	Clark	13	04	11
Hays, Walter(A)	1816	Sept. 24	Butler	02	04	15
Hays, William(A)	1808	Jan. 12	Montgomery	01	06	20
Hays, William(A)	1816	Oct. 26	Butler	03	10	31
Hays, William(B)	1827	May 24	Franklin(Ind	02	10	22
Hayse, Joseph(B)	1811	Aug. 13	Butler	01	06	23
Haywood, Thomas(D)	1810	Dec. 28	Hamilton(Fr)	02	04	26
Hayworth, George(E)	1818	Sept. 10	Highland	13	20	26
Hazel, Alex'r. B.(C)	1826	Nov. 16	Logan	14	03	20
Hazel, Wm.(C)	1826	Nov. 16	Logan	14	03	20
Hazen, Isaac(B)	1834	May 15	Dearborn(Ind	02	07	05
Hazen, Isaac(B)	1834	Nov. 20	Dearborn(Ind	02	07	05
Hazen, John(B)	1834	Nov. 20	BeaverCo.Pa.	02	07	05
Hazen, Nathan'l.(B)	1834	Jan. 27	Dearborn(Ind	03	08	13
Hazen, Nathaniel(B)	1833	May 22	Dearborn(Ind	03	08	12
Hazlet, James(A)	1804	Sept. 24	Butler	03	02	17
Headey, Benjamin(B)	1816	May 09	Switzerland	03	02	04
Headley, John(B)	1837	Feb. 04	Hamilton	03	05	21
Headley, William(B)	1836	Feb. 26	Dearborn(Ind	03	05	21
Headley, William(B)	1837	Jan. 16	Dearborn(Ind	03	05	21
Heady, George W.(B)	1837	Jan. 26	Switzerland	03	03	18
Heady, George Washington(B)	1833	March 02	Switzerland	03	02	09
Heady, George Washington(B)	1833	June 03	Switzerland	03	02	09
Heady, James(A)	1805	Feb. 11	Butler	02	04	28
Heald, Nathan(C)	1807	Jan. 13	FortWayneInd	11	01	04
Heap, William(B)	1832	June 26	Franklin(Ind	01	08	07
Heard, Forrest(C)	1831	Aug. 08	Shelby	13	02	02
Heard, Stephen(C)	1831	June 27	Shelby	13	02	02
Heard, Wm. V.(E)	1838	May 21	Cincinnati	15	22	20
Heart, David(B)	1815	Jan. 13	Wayne(Ind)	01	13	28
Heaston, Daniel(A)	1804	July 23	Montgomery	05	03	03
Heaston, David(E)	1831	Feb. 15	Randolph(Ind	14	19	06
Heaston, David(E)	1835	Aug. 20	Randolph(Ind	14	20	30
Heaston, Jacob(C)	1815	Aug. 16	Montgomery	11	03	24
Heaston, John(A)	1804	July 23	Montgomery	05	03	03
Heaston, John(C)	1818	Jan. 17	Warren	10	03	12
Heaston, John(C)	1827	Aug. 14	Clark	10	03	11
Heater, George(A)	1816	Sept. 09	Montgomery	04	05	14
Heath, Dan'l.(B)	1833	Sept. 16	Switzerland	02	03	34
Heath, James(B)	1806	Nov. 03	Cincinnati	01	09	28
Heath, James(E)	1814	April 11	Franklin(Ind	12	15	20
Heath, John(C)	1817	Oct. 09	Montgomery	12	01	09
Heath, Richard(A)	1818	March 24	Franklinton	01	11	08
Heath, Samuel(B)	1814	Oct. 31	Franklin(Ind	03	02	06
Heath, Samuel(E)	1836	Sept. 20	Hamilton	11	10	34
Heath, Zachariah(C)	1829	Dec. 12	Champaign	12	04	19
Heaton, Abraham(A)	1806	Nov. 27	Warren	02	08	29
Heaton, Abraham(A)	1806	Nov. 27	Warren	02	08	29
Heaton, Abraham(E)	1811	Oct. 30	Wayne(Ind)	13	14	19
Heaton, Daniel(A)	1806	Oct. 14	Warren	02	08	32
Heaton, Daniel(E)	1811	Oct. 30	Wayne(Ind)	13	14	19
Heaton, Daniel(E)	1815	Jan. 07	Franklin(Ind	13	14	09
Heaton, Daniel(E)	1815	Jan. 07	Franklin(Ind	13	14	09
Heaton, Ebenezer Jr.(E)	1814	March 11	Wayne(Ind)	13	14	08
Heaton, Ebenezer(C)	1801	Dec. 31	Hamilton	04	03	28
Heaton, Ebenezer(E)	1811	Oct. 30	Wayne(Ind)	13	14	18
Heaton, John(C)	1802	Dec. 10	Hamilton	05	04	28
Heaton, John(C)	1811	Nov. 21	Greene	09	06	01

PURCHASER	YEAR	DATE	RESIDENCE	R	T	S
Heaton, John(C)	1812	Jan. 20	Greene	08	06	06
Heaton, Jonah(E)	1819	March 27	Montgomery	13	19	28
Heaton, Samuel(E)	1831	May 03	Randolph(Ind	13	19	28
Heaton, Seth(B)	1832	Dec. 15	Dearborn(Ind	03	06	21
Heaton, Wm.(A)	1831	April 04	Warren	05	07	02
Heavenridge, John(B)	1811	June 07	Ind.Territry	01	11	19
Heavrin, James(E)	1814	April 25	Ind.Territry	12	13	05
Heck, Jacob(A)	1831	April 26	Montgomery	04	07	21
Heck, Peter(A)	1817	Aug. 26	Montgomery	01	12	28
Heck, Philip(B)	1832	Jan. 12	Butler	02	08	33
Heck, Philip(B)	1836	Feb. 27	Franklin(Ind	02	08	27
Heckfort, Bernard Hy.(A)	1837	Dec. 16	Cincinnati	02	14	01
Heckman, Daniel(A)	1831	Oct. 21	Montgomery	04	09	29
Heckman, David(A)	1825	May 30	Clark	04	06	15
Heckman, David(C)	1824	June 09	Clark	11	02	29
Heckman, William(E)	1837	April 01	Montgomery	15	22	10
Hedey, Jacob(A)	1806	May 21	Butler	01	03	06
Hedey, Jacob(B)	1806	March 18	Butler	02	08	10
Hedgepeth, Arthur(E)	1836	Oct. 13	Randolph(Ind	15	21	04
Hedger, Catharine(B)	1818	March 10	Hamilton	02	03	20
Hedges, Charles Emarson(B)	1836	May 14	Switzerland	02	02	15
Hedges, Charles Emerson(B)	1835	Dec. 30	Switzerland	02	02	15
Hedges, Nathaniel Gates(B)	1836	Feb. 23	Switzerland	02	02	15
Hedges, Samuel(C)	1814	Jan. 29	Champaign	11	05	02
Hedges, William(B)	1829	Dec. 08	Switzerland	02	02	10
Hedly, John(B)	1814	July 28	Cincinnati	02	09	26
Hedrick, Thomas(E)	1834	Dec. 26	Maryland	12	12	01
Hedrick, Thomas(E)	1834	Dec. 26	Maryland	12	12	01
Hedrick, Thomas(E)	1834	Dec. 26	Maryland	12	12	02
Hedricks, William(C)	1804	Dec. 28	Greene	10	06	28
Heeny, John(E)	1811	Nov. 01	Franklin(Ind	13	14	22
Hees, Francis(B)	1816	March 15	Hamilton	01	02	05
Heeter, Dan'l.(A)	1830	Nov. 02	Montgomery	04	06	20
Heeter, David(A)	1830	Nov. 02	Montgomery	04	06	17
Heeter, George(A)	1831	April 14	Montgomery	03	07	13
Heeter, George(A)	1831	May 19	Montgomery	04	06	18
Heeter, Henry(E)	1818	Oct. 10	Montgomery	04	10	34
Heffelman, Jno.(A)	1830	March 27	Montgomery	04	07	34
Hefley, Charles(C)	1805	Dec. 13	Greene	07	03	12
Hegdon, Peter(B)	1815	Jan. 27	Hamilton	01	06	18
Heheman, John Wm.(E)	1837	Aug. 12	Cincinnati	12	11	19
Heighway, John(C)	1804	Dec. 31	Warren	05	03	21
Heighway, Samuel Senr.(C)	1809	Dec. 12	Waynesville	08	04	08
Heighway, Samuel(C)	1801	Dec. 31	Hamilton	04	04	24
Heighway, Samuel(C)	1801	Dec. 31	Hamilton	05	03	01
Heighway, Samuel(C)	1801	Dec. 31	Hamilton	05	03	07
Heighway, Samuel(C)	1802	Dec. 28	Hamilton	04	04	23
Heighway, Samuel(C)	1804	Sept. 03	Warren	05	03	26
Heighway, Samuel(C)	1804	Sept. 03	Warren	04	04	29
Heighway, Samuel(C)	1804	Sept. 04	Warren	04	04	29
Heighway, Samuel(C)	1804	Sept. 04	Warren	08	04	08
Heim, Daniel(A)	1836	Jan. 19	Montgomery	02	12	05
Heimlick, John(A)	1814	May 27	Preble	02	07	23
Heistand, Henry(A)	1805	Oct. 28	Pennsylvania	04	04	12
Heistand, Samuel(A)	1805	Oct. 28	Pennsylvania	04	05	35
Hell, Jacob(A)	1805	April 25	Montgomery	03	05	25
Hell, Jacob(A)	1805	April 25	Montgomery	03	05	24
Hell, Jacob(A)	1808	Dec. 14	Preble	03	05	04
Hellar, John Senr.(C)	1812	July 23	Champaign	09	04	30
Hellem, George(A)	1830	Dec. 18	Miami	04	07	12
Helm, Samuel(E)	1831	April 29	Randolph(Ind	14	21	24
Helm, Samuel(E)	1836	March 28	Randolph(Ind	14	21	24
Helm, Samuel(E)	1836	June 17	Randolph(Ind	14	21	24
Helm, William(B)	1811	June 14	Kentucky	02	08	13
Helm, William(E)	1811	Oct. 22	Kentucky	12	13	23
Helm, William(E)	1812	Jan. 13	Kentucky	12	13	23
Helm, William(E)	1813	Aug. 02	Franklin(Ind	12	13	15
Helmer, David B.(A)	1837	Feb. 03	Greene	08	01	05
Helmer, Peter G.(B)	1815	Oct. 30	Ohio	01	07	08

PURCHASER	YEAR	DATE	RESIDENCE	R	T	S
Helmer, Peter G.(B)	1815	Oct. 31	Ohio	01	07	08
Helmick, Jacob(B)	1813	Oct. 22	Hamilton	01	03	30
Helmick, Jacob(E)	1819	Aug. 02	Hamilton	13	15	36
Helmick, Peter(A)	1802	May 31	Hamilton	01	02	05
Helms, James(E)	1837	Aug. 11	Montgomery	13	20	02
Helphenstine, Peter P.(A)	1817	Aug. 27	Greene	01	10	17
Helton, Alexander(E)	1835	Oct. 12	Wayne(Ind)	14	19	11
Heltzel, Samuel(B)	1837	Jan. 26	Darke	01	17	12
Heltzel, Samuel(B)	1837	Oct. 19	Randolph(Ind	01	17	01
Helvey, John(C)	1813	June 14	Miami	10	02	03
Hencke, Joseph(E)	1836	Nov. 11	Cincinnati	12	11	32
Hendershot, David(A)	1813	June 11	Preble	06	08	31
Hendershot, David(A)	1814	Aug. 24	Miami	05	09	12
Hendershot, John(A)	1808	Nov. 07	Miami	06	07	29
Hendershot, John(C)	1814	Jan. 06	Miami	12	01	26
Henderson, Eli(B)	1807	July 01	Warren	02	11	24
Henderson, Eli(B)	1807	July 01	Warren	02	11	25
Henderson, Elias(B)	1828	Jan. 01	Butler	01	08	21
Henderson, Hiram(B)	1832	July 17	Dearborn(Ind	01	07	36
Henderson, Hubbard(B)	1828	Dec. 05	Wayne(Ind)	01	15	04
Henderson, Isaac(B)	1811	May 28	Dearborn(Ind	01	06	12
Henderson, Isaac(B)	1811	Dec. 11	Dearborn(Ind	01	06	11
Henderson, James(C)	1812	March 23	Champaign	09	04	34
Henderson, John Jr.(B)	1834	March 17	Dearborn(Ind	01	07	26
Henderson, John Jr.(B)	1834	March 17	Dearborn(Ind	01	07	25
Henderson, John(E)	1813	March 29	Franklin(Ind	12	14	27
Henderson, John(E)	1813	Sept. 27	Franklin(Ind	12	14	20
Henderson, Nathaniel(B)	1814	Nov. 01	Franklin(Ind	02	11	23
Henderson, Samuel Junr.(B)	1808	July 12	Kentucky	01	14	01
Henderson, Samuel(B)	1804	Dec. 18	Kentucky	01	13	19
Henderson, Shadrach(B)	1806	Dec. 05	Dearborn(Ind	02	13	13
Henderson, Shedrick(B)	1806	Oct. 02	Dearborn(Ind	02	13	13
Henderson, Silas(B)	1832	July 17	Dearborn(Ind	01	07	36
Henderson, Thomas(A)	1814	Nov. 04	Cincinnati	02	01	11
Henderson, Thomas(A)	1840	Aug. 01	Hamilton	02	14	27
Henderson, Thomas(A)	1840	Aug. 01	Hamilton	01	14	19
Henderson, Thomas(A)	1840	Aug. 01	Hamilton	01	15	29
Henderson, Thomas(B)	1805	Nov. 18	Dearborn(Ind	02	09	32
Henderson, Thomas(B)	1807	July 01	Warren	01	11	18
Henderson, Thomas(B)	1814	June 06	Franklin(Ind	02	09	31
Henderson, Thomas(B)	1816	Oct. 28	Franklin(Ind	02	08	05
Henderson, Thomas(B)	1840	Aug. 01	Hamilton	01	18	23
Henderson, Thomas(B)	1840	Aug. 01	Hamilton	01	19	13
Henderson, Thomas(D)	1813	March 05	Hamilton	01	02	08
Henderson, Thomas(E)	1811	Oct. 28	Franklin(Ind	13	13	34
Henderson, Thomas(E)	1811	Oct. 28	Franklin(Ind	13	13	27
Henderson, Thomas(E)	1811	Oct. 28	Franklin(Ind	13	13	34
Henderson, William L.(A)	1808	Jan. 12	Kentucky	01	09	27
Henderson, William L.(A)	1818	Nov. 04	Preble	02	10	35
Henderson, William(B)	1806	Sept. 22	Dearborn(Ind	02	08	04
Henderson, William(B)	1806	Oct. 22	So. Carolina	02	09	08
Henderson, William(C)	1813	April 15	Champaign	10	03	32
Henderson, William(E)	1813	Sept. 17	Franklin(Ind	12	14	04
Henderson, Wm.(E)	1813	Sept. 17	Franklin(Ind	12	14	11
Hendray, Richard(E)	1811	Oct. 30	Ross	13	15	18
Hendrick, Absalom(E)	1837	Sept. 23	Jay Co.,Ind.	15	22	27
Hendrick, David E.(A)	1803	Feb. 18	Hamilton	02	06	10
Hendricks, David E.(A)	1804	Nov. 29	Montgomery	02	06	09
Hendricks, David E.(A)	1805	Dec. 25	Montgomery	02	06	09
Hendricks, David E.(A)	1811	April 09	Preble	02	08	35
Hendricks, David E.(A)	1814	Feb. 08	Preble	02	08	27
Hendricks, Geo. Drummond(A)	1831	Dec. 19	Preble	02	09	28
Hendricks, Geo. Drummond(A)	1831	Dec. 22	Preble	01	08	30
Hendricks, Geo. Drummond(A)	1832	June 01	Preble	01	09	02
Hendricks, George Drummond(A)	1833	May 21	Preble	01	09	01
Hendricks, George Drummond(A)	1833	June 17	Preble	01	09	12
Hendricks, George(C)	1813	June 10	Kentucky	10	04	30
Hendricks, George(C)	1814	Aug. 11	Champaign	11	03	07
Hendricks, James(C)	1806	May 24	Virginia	12	05	10

PURCHASER	YEAR	DATE	RESIDENCE	R	T	S
Hendricks, John(A)	1833	Sept. 23	Clark	08	02	23
Hendricks, William(A)	1831	July 23	Preble	04	06	08
Hendricks, William(B)	1819	Nov. 08	?	02	05	22
Hendrickson, Henry(A)	1815	Dec. 28	Preble	03	07	31
Hendrix, Henry(E)	1815	Aug. 26	Clermont	13	15	13
Henkle, Joel(C)	1812	Nov. 17	Champaign	10	05	08
Henley, Jesse(B)	1806	Aug. 29	Ind.Territry	01	12	18
Henley, Micajah(E)	1816	Nov. 02	Wayne(Ind)	14	18	20
Henline, Abraham(C)	1813	April 14	Champaign	10	03	07
Hennegin, Peter(B)	1819	Jan. 25	Kentucky	02	05	21
Henning, Jacob(A)	1815	Nov. 24	Montgomery	04	04	21
Henning, Jacob(A)	1831	July 11	Montgomery	01	12	10
Henny, Jonas(C)	1806	Aug. 22	Hamilton	11	01	23
Henricks, George(C)	1814	Sept. 21	Champaign	10	04	36
Henrie, Arthur(A)	1814	Nov. 19	Hamilton	01	02	36
Henrie, Arthur(B)	1811	Oct. 09	Hamilton	02	09	25
Henrie, Arthur(B)	1812	Jan. 02	Hamilton	01	09	34
Henry, Arthur(A)	1816	July 24	Hamilton	01	02	35
Henry, David(C)	1814	Jan. 07	Champaign	13	02	28
Henry, Joseph(E)	1837	Jan. 31	Dearborn(Ind	12	11	33
Henry, Richard(C)	1831	March 22	Shelby	13	02	23
Henry, Stewart(B)	1832	March 01	Brown	02	03	23
Henry, William(C)	1812	Aug. 10	Champaign	09	06	15
Henry, William(C)	1817	Dec. 02	Champaign	09	06	15
Henry, Wm.(C)	1815	Dec. 25	?	09	06	15
Henshaw, Abel(E)	1834	Nov. 13	Randolph(Ind	14	19	22
Henshaw, Abel(E)	1834	Nov. 13	Randolph(Ind	14	19	22
Henshaw, Phebe(E)	1832	Sept. 20	Randolph(Ind	14	18	03
Henwood, John(E)	1812	Dec. 24	Virginia	13	15	14
Hepburn, Edward(A)	1818	April 20	Hamilton	01	02	08
Hepburn, Edward(B)	1818	Feb. 26	Cincinnati	03	04	14
Hepburn, Edward(B)	1818	Feb. 26	Cincinnati	03	03	02
Hepburn, Edward(B)	1818	Feb. 26	Cincinnati	03	04	28
Hepburn, Edward(B)	1818	Feb. 26	Cincinnati	03	04	27
Hepburn, Edward(B)	1818	March 05	Cincinnati	03	04	36
Hepburn, Edward(B)	1818	March 05	Cincinnati	03	03	03
Hepburn, Edward(B)	1818	April 06	Cincinnati	03	07	23
Hepburn, Edward(B)	1818	April 06	Cincinnati	03	04	29
Hepburn, Edward(B)	1818	April 06	Cincinnati	03	07	24
Hepburn, Edward(B)	1818	April 06	Cincinnati	03	04	11
Hepburn, Edward(B)	1818	April 06	Cincinnati	03	04	29
Hepburn, Edward(B)	1818	April 07	Hamilton	03	04	11
Hepburn, Edward(B)	1818	April 07	Hamilton	03	04	11
Hepburn, Edward(B)	1818	April 07	Hamilton	03	04	12
Hepburn, Edward(B)	1818	April 07	Hamilton	03	04	12
Hepburn, Edward(B)	1818	April 22	Hamilton	01	06	30
Hepburn, Edward(B)	1818	April 22	Hamilton	01	06	30
Hepburn, Edward(B)	1818	May 14	Cincinnati	01	02	02
Hepburn, Edward(B)	1818	May 14	Cincinnati	01	02	02
Hepburn, Edward(B)	1818	June 02	Cincinnati	03	04	12
Hepburn, Edward(B)	1818	June 02	Cincinnati	03	05	26
Hepburn, Edward(B)	1818	June 02	Cincinnati	02	02	01
Hepburn, Edward(B)	1818	June 02	Cincinnati	02	02	01
Hepburn, Edward(B)	1818	June 02	Cincinnati	02	03	13
Hepburn, Edward(B)	1818	June 02	Cincinnati	02	03	12
Hepburn, Edward(B)	1818	April 06	Cincinnati	03	07	24
Hepler, David(C)	1815	Oct. 19	Virginia	11	03	08
Hepman, Henry(A)	1805	Nov. 07	Montgomery	04	04	12
Herbsreit, George(A)	1834	Oct. 21	Hamilton	03	10	07
Hercules, David(A)	1836	Nov. 07	Butler	02	14	36
Hercules, William(A)	1836	Nov. 16	Butler	02	14	36
Herd, Thomas(C)	1806	Sept. 04	Champaign	09	06	22
Herd, Thomas(C)	1811	Dec. 11	Champaign	09	06	22
Herman, George(B)	1817	Dec. 01	Miami	05	10	29
Herman, John Nepermuck(B)	1835	Sept. 19	Dearborn(Ind	02	06	09
Herndon, Elliott(B)	1813	Aug. 05	Franklin(Ind	02	08	06
Herndon, Elliott(E)	1813	Aug. 30	Franklin(Ind	12	14	35
Herndon, Gideon(B)	1836	Aug. 29	Franklin(Ind	02	08	07
Herndon, Gideon(B)	1836	Aug. 29	Franklin(Ind	02	08	06

PURCHASER	YEAR	DATE	RESIDENCE	R	T	S
Herndon, Gideon(B)	1836	Aug. 29	Franklin(Ind	02	08	05
Herndon, Gideon(B)	1836	Aug. 29	Franklin(Ind	02	08	06
Herndon, Nathan'l.(B)	1814	May 30	Franklin(Ind	02	08	07
Herndon, Nathaniel(B)	1814	June 01	Franklin(Ind	02	08	18
Herndon, Thomas(B)	1832	Oct. 04	Franklin(Ind	02	08	07
Herndon, Thomas(B)	1832	Oct. 06	Franklin(Ind	02	08	06
Herndon, Thomas(B)	1836	Jan. 22	Franklin(Ind	02	08	06
Herndon, Thomas(B)	1836	Aug. 29	Franklin(Ind	02	08	07
Herron, David(B)	1833	Sept. 23	Clermont	02	03	01
Herron, John Wesley(B)	1834	Dec. 23	Dearborn(Ind	02	03	01
Herron, Thomas(A)	1805	Oct. 19	Kentucky	02	04	11
Hersberger, John(A)	1814	Dec. 09	Preble	04	05	20
Hershberger, John(A)	1815	Nov. 13	Preble	03	07	35
Hershberger, Jonas(A)	1832	Jan. 13	Montgomery	07	02	31
Hertz, Jacob(A)	1834	Sept. 02	Cincinnati	03	10	05
Hervey, John(A)	1806	Oct. 24	Montgomery	01	09	17
Hervey, Thomas(B)	1813	Dec. 06	Franklin(Ind	02	10	29
Hesler, Jacob(B)	1812	Aug. 01	Kentucky	03	03	26
Hess, Abraham(A)	1813	Dec. 30	Montgomery	05	05	29
Hess, Elisha Landon(B)	1833	Feb. 27	Switzerland	02	02	01
Hess, Henry(A)	1806	July 15	Montgomery	05	04	07
Hess, Henry(A)	1836	Nov. 28	Darke	04	11	30
Hess, Leonard(A)	1837	April 24	Darke	03	12	34
Hess, Samuel(B)	1833	Aug. 17	Switzerland	02	02	01
Hesse, Bernard(E)	1837	Jan. 12	Cincinnati	11	10	15
Hesten, David E.(E)	1836	March 28	Randolph(Ind	14	19	05
Hester, Jacob(A)	1813	Nov. 30	Warren	01	03	05
Hester, Thomas(E)	1818	March 25	Clinton	14	18	08
Hesz, Philip(A)	1824	Oct. 28	Preble	03	07	22
Hetdrick, Abraham(B)	1812	May 08	Pennsylvania	01	09	07
Hetdrick, Jacob(B)	1814	June 13	Franklin(Ind	02	09	30
Hetdrick, William(B)	1812	May 08	Pennsylvania	01	09	07
Hetdrick, William(B)	1814	June 06	Franklin(Ind	01	09	07
Hetesler, Peter(A)	1837	May 24	Montgomery	01	13	23
Hetfield, John(B)	1816	April 27	Franklin(Ind	01	10	28
Hetfield, John(B)	1813	Aug. 17	Franklin(Ind	01	10	18
Hetrick, Philip(A)	1819	Oct. 20	Montgomery	04	06	29
Hetsler, George(A)	1814	June 18	Montgomery	04	03	21
Hetsler, George(A)	1814	June 24	Montgomery	04	03	28
Hetsler, Peter(A)	1837	Nov. 08	Butler	01	13	23
Hetsler, Peter(A)	1838	May 21	Butler	01	13	02
Hettle, Nicholas(A)	1817	June 27	Miami	05	07	18
Hetzler, Abraham(A)	1832	Nov. 05	Montgomery	03	10	01
Hetzler, Abraham(A)	1832	Dec. 01	Montgomery	04	09	07
Hetzler, Abraham(A)	1833	Dec. 26	Montgomery	04	09	06
Hetzler, George Jr.(A)	1837	May 05	Montgomery	01	13	11
Hetzler, George Jr.(A)	1837	May 05	Montgomery	01	13	11
Hetzler, George Jr.(A)	1837	May 05	Montgomery	01	13	22
Hetzler, George Junr.(A)	1837	May 05	Montgomery	01	13	11
Hetzler, George(A)	1814	Aug. 13	Montgomery	04	03	30
Hetzler, George(C)	1824	Aug. 24	Hamilton	12	01	10
Hetzler, George(C)	1828	June 20	Miami	12	02	33
Hetzler, Jacob Jr.(C)	1826	Aug. 22	Shelby	12	01	04
Hetzler, John(C)	1815	Nov. 10	Hamilton	12	01	03
Heustis, Oliver(B)	1818	Aug. 06	Hamilton	02	05	11
Heustis, Oliver(B)	1831	Feb. 22	Dearborn(Ind	02	06	34
Heward, Isaac(E)	1816	Aug. 21	Franklin(Ind	13	12	24
Hewes, Robert(A)	1814	Jan. 03	Cincinnati	02	03	22
Hewit, Philip(C)	1811	June 19	Preble	07	01	08
Hewitt, Robert(B)	1817	July 09	Clermont	01	03	30
Hewitt, William(B)	1836	June 02	Brown	02	05	05
Hewitt, William(B)	1836	Oct. 24	Brown	02	05	08
Hewlings, Joseph(C)	1804	Dec. 28	Warren	05	03	14
Hewlings, Joseph(C)	1806	Aug. 04	Warren	13	04	07
Hewlings, Joseph(C)	1806	Aug. 14	Warren	13	04	07
Hewlings, Joseph(C)	1817	June 07	Champaign	13	04	13
Hewsten, David(B)	1807	Jan. 13	Dearborn(Ind	02	10	05
Hewsten, Samuel(B)	1807	Jan. 14	Dearborn(Ind	02	11	32
Heywood, Thomas(C)	1812	Feb. 13	Hamilton	02	04	11

PURCHASER	YEAR	DATE	RESIDENCE	R	T	S
Heywood, Thomas(D)	1810	Dec. 14	Cincinati(Fr	02	04	26
Hiatt, Amos(E)	1836	March 28	Randolph(Ind	14	20	06
Hiatt, Amos(E)	1836	Nov. 04	Randolph(Ind	14	20	06
Hiatt, Christopher(E)	1817	Sept. 17	Highland	14	20	19
Hiatt, Eleazer(B)	1830	Oct. 30	Wayne(Ind)	01	15	21
Hiatt, Isaac(B)	1816	Oct. 12	Wayne(Ind)	01	14	02
Hiatt, Jehu(E)	1838	Oct. 24	Randolph(Ind	13	21	25
Hiatt, Jonathan C.(E)	1832	Dec. 05	Randolph(Ind	14	20	30
Hiatt, Jonathan(E)	1817	Sept. 17	Champaign	14	20	21
Hiatt, Moses(E)	1830	Jan. 28	Randolph(Ind	14	20	22
Hiatt, Moses(E)	1831	July 20	Randolph(Ind	14	20	22
Hiatt, William(B)	1813	June 10	Wayne(Ind)	01	14	03
Hiatt, Zachariah(B)	1814	Nov. 28	Wayne(Ind)	01	14	02
Hiatt, Zachariah(B)	1816	Aug. 16	Wayne(Ind)	01	15	35
Hiatt, Zachariah(E)	1816	Aug. 20	Wayne(Ind)	13	16	23
Hiatt, Zachariah(E)	1818	Jan. 08	Wayne(Ind)	14	20	27
Hiatt, Zachariah(E)	1818	Jan. 08	Wayne(Ind)	14	20	22
Hiatt, Zachariah(E)	1817	July 09	Wayne(Ind)	14	17	10
Hickle, Debolt(E)	1811	Oct. 22	Ross	12	15	02
Hickman, David(C)	1812	Sept. 26	Miami	09	03	24
Hickman, Francis(E)	1836	Jan. 30	Randolph(Ind	14	20	09
Hickman, Francis(E)	1837	March 01	Randolph(Ind	14	20	12
Hickman, Ithamer(E)	1836	Dec. 05	Hamilton	12	11	14
Hickman, Jacob(E)	1836	Dec. 15	Randolph(Ind	14	20	13
Hickman, James(E)	1836	April 15	Randolph(Ind	13	21	13
Hickman, James(E)	1836	Oct. 03	Randolph(Ind	13	21	13
Hickman, John(E)	1831	July 05	Randolph(Ind	14	20	36
Hickman, John(E)	1837	Feb. 16	Randolph(Ind	14	20	36
Hickman, Joseph(E)	1831	Sept. 02	Randolph(Ind	14	20	13
Hickman, Joseph(E)	1836	Dec. 15	Randolph(Ind	14	19	01
Hickman, Joseph(E)	1837	April 01	Randolph(Ind	14	20	12
Hickman, Joseph(E)	1838	Dec. 01	Randolph(Ind	14	21	35
Hickman, William(C)	1812	Feb. 15	Miami	10	02	08
Hickman, William(E)	1837	Nov. 04	Randolph(Ind	14	20	12
Hicks, Isaac(E)	1815	Jan. 09	Wayne(Ind)	13	16	27
Hicks, James(E)	1829	Feb. 16	Dearborn(Ind	12	10	02
Hicks, James(E)	1836	March 25	Franklin(Ind	12	10	02
Hicks, Moses(A)	1817	Sept. 22	Highland	05	10	30
Hicks, William(C)	1812	March 07	Champaign	09	03	12
Hickson, William(A)	1815	Dec. 19	Preble	03	04	09
Hiday, Jacob(B)	1813	April 20	Butler	01	09	36
Hidrick, Philip(C)	1812	Jan. 02	Kentucky	08	06	10
Hiers, John(E)	1825	Dec. 05	Fayette	12	12	28
Hiers, John(E)	1832	Aug. 03	Franklin(Ind	12	12	33
Hiers, John(E)	1836	March 04	Franklin(Ind	12	12	32
Hiers, William(E)	1815	June 14	Hamilton	13	14	14
Hiett, Elzy(A)	1831	Dec. 06	Shelby	06	08	20
Higbee, Nancy(B)	1832	Nov. 23	Dearborn(Ind	02	05	29
Higbee, Nancy(B)	1832	Nov. 23	Dearborn(Ind	02	05	29
Higbee, Nancy(B)	1836	Aug. 10	Dearborn(Ind	02	05	29
Higbie, Abraham(B)	1833	Oct. 10	Dearborn(Ind	03	04	35
Higby, William(B)	1831	July 05	Dearborn(Ind	01	04	20
Higdon, Benjamin(E)	1836	Aug. 26	Franklin(Ind	11	10	02
Higgins, Amos(A)	1803	Nov. 01	Butler	04	03	17
Higgins, Amos(A)	1804	Aug. 10	Montgomery	04	04	26
Higgins, Amos(A)	1804	Sept. 10	Montgomery	04	04	26
Higgins, Amos(B)	1806	Oct. 23	Montgomery	01	13	12
Higgins, Jonathan(A)	1802	Oct. 15	Hamilton	05	02	31
Higgins, Jonathan(E)	1813	Sept. 06	Butler	13	15	33
Higgins, Nicholas(E)	1836	June 13	Coshocton	15	19	05
Higgins, Susan(A)	1827	March 15	Miami	05	09	22
Highland, Rob't.(A)	1814	Oct. 12	Hamilton	01	03	18
Highlands, William(C)	1818	Feb. 24	Hamilton	11	01	05
Hight, George W.(A)	1817	Dec. 26	Hamilton	03	10	30
Hight, George W.(A)	1817	Dec. 26	Hamilton	03	10	30
Hight, George W.(A)	1817	Dec. 26	Hamilton	03	10	30
Hight, George W.(A)	1817	Dec. 26	Hamilton	03	10	30
Hight, George W.(A)	1817	Dec. 26	Hamilton	03	10	30
Hight, George W.(A)	1817	Dec. 26	Hamilton	03	10	30

PURCHASER	YEAR	DATE	RESIDENCE	R	T	S
Hight, George W.(A)	1817	Dec. 26	Hamilton	03	10	30
Hight, George W.(A)	1818	Jan. 03	Cincinnati	02	11	21
Hight, George W.(A)	1818	Jan. 03	Cincinnati	02	11	12
Hight, George W.(A)	1818	Jan. 03	Cincinnati	02	11	12
Hight, George W.(A)	1818	Jan. 03	Cincinnati	02	11	15
Hight, George W.(A)	1818	Jan. 03	Cincinnati	02	11	15
Hight, George W.(A)	1818	April 25	Hamilton	02	11	14
Hight, George W.(A)	1818	May 13	Darke	02	11	26
Hight, George W.(A)	1818	June 18	Darke	02	11	23
Hildebran, John(A)	1831	July 16	Miami	04	08	24
Hildebrand, Michael(B)	1816	Nov. 11	Switzerland	03	03	17
Hildebrand, Michael(B)	1816	Nov. 11	Switzerland	03	03	20
Hildibrand, Benj'n. S.(B)	1839	March 09	Switzerland	03	04	17
Hildreth, James(E)	1836	Oct. 31	Franklin(Ind	11	12	26
Hildreth, Jeffrey(E)	1836	Aug. 23	Franklin(Ind	12	12	29
Hileman, George(A)	1817	June 02	Butler	02	10	04
Hiler, Abraham(B)	1831	Sept. 03	Franklin(Ind	02	08	24
Hiler, Peter(B)	1833	March 01	Franklin(Ind	02	08	22
Hill, Aaron(B)	1807	Sept. 18	Nor.Carolina	01	13	03
Hill, Aaron(E)	1832	Oct. 06	Randolph(Ind	15	18	07
Hill, Aaron(E)	1834	March 14	Randolph(Ind	15	18	07
Hill, Aaron(E)	1837	Jan. 23	Randolph(Ind	15	18	07
Hill, Andrew(E)	1836	Nov. 10	Warren	14	19	30
Hill, Benj'n.(E)	1835	June 22	Randolph(Ind	14	19	06
Hill, Benjamin(A)	1836	Oct. 21	Hamilton	01	14	10
Hill, Benjamin(B)	1806	Dec. 10	Dearborn(Ind	01	14	26
Hill, Benjamin(B)	1814	March 25	Wayne(Ind)	01	14	35
Hill, Benjamin(B)	1817	Nov. 05	Wayne(Ind)	01	14	26
Hill, Benjamin(E)	1836	March 28	Randolph(Ind	14	19	06
Hill, Benjamin(E)	1836	Nov. 10	Warren	14	19	19
Hill, Benoni(E)	1818	April 15	Wayne(Ind)	15	20	31
Hill, Benoni(E)	1831	Aug. 09	Randolph(Ind	15	20	31
Hill, Daniel(C)	1817	May 31	Virginia	12	03	22
Hill, Daniel(C)	1817	May 31	Virginia	12	03	22
Hill, Henry(E)	1818	April 15	Wayne(Ind)	15	20	30
Hill, Henry(E)	1836	Aug. 24	Randolph(Ind	15	20	30
Hill, Henry(E)	1837	April 25	Wayne(Ind)	15	20	29
Hill, Hiram(E)	1834	Feb. 07	Randolph(Ind	15	18	06
Hill, Jacob(C)	1804	Dec. 29	Montgomery	09	02	12
Hill, James Jr.(C)	1829	July 09	Clark	11	03	14
Hill, James M.(B)	1818	Feb. 23	Hamilton	02	03	17
Hill, James(A)	1836	Sept. 23	Warren	02	15	29
Hill, James(E)	1815	May 29	Butler	13	17	19
Hill, Jesse(A)	1838	April 20	Greene	02	14	24
Hill, Jesse(E)	1814	Feb. 04	Wayne(Ind)	12	16	10
Hill, Joel(E)	1817	Sept. 19	Wayne(Ind)	14	15	30
Hill, John(A)	1818	July 10	Preble	01	11	09
Hill, John(A)	1829	Aug. 28	Miami	04	08	04
Hill, John(E)	1836	Nov. 10	Cincinnati	13	19	26
Hill, Jonas(A)	1828	June 28	Miami	04	07	15
Hill, Jonathan(B)	1837	Dec. 11	Dearborn(Ind	02	04	30
Hill, Jonathan(E)	1814	March 02	Wayne(Ind)	13	15	25
Hill, Joseph H.(C)	1831	July 05	Champaign	11	03	15
Hill, Joseph(C)	1806	Aug. 01	Champaign	12	04	08
Hill, Joshua(C)	1811	Oct. 14	Champaign	12	05	23
Hill, Matthew(E)	1836	Aug. 22	Randolph(Ind	15	20	31
Hill, Matthew(E)	1837	Jan. 14	Randolph(Ind	15	20	31
Hill, Nathan(A)	1813	June 17	Miami	05	07	20
Hill, Nathan(A)	1831	Oct. 14	Miami	04	08	08
Hill, Nathan(E)	1814	Oct. 03	Wayne(Ind)	13	16	24
Hill, Nathan(E)	1814	Oct. 20	Wayne(Ind)	13	17	25
Hill, Nathan(E)	1816	July 10	Wayne(Ind)	13	16	14
Hill, Nathan(E)	1818	Feb. 05	Wayne(Ind)	13	16	02
Hill, Philip(E)	1837	Jan. 23	Randolph(Ind	14	19	25
Hill, Phineas(B)	1813	July 29	Dearborn(Ind	02	05	35
Hill, Phineas(B)	1816	June 22	Dearborn(Ind	03	07	11
Hill, Robert(B)	1806	Aug. 06	Hamilton	01	14	35
Hill, Robert(B)	1811	Dec. 12	Wayne(Ind)	01	13	01
Hill, Robt.(E)	1815	Sept. 27	Wayne(Ind)	13	16	14

PURCHASER	YEAR	DATE	RESIDENCE	R	T	S
Hill, Samuel(E)	1813	Oct. 13	Franklin(Ind	13	14	22
Hill, Thomas(A)	1805	Aug. 29	Butler	05	07	20
Hill, Thomas(A)	1805	Dec. 07	Butler	05	08	29
Hill, Thomas(A)	1808	Feb. 20	Butler	05	07	20
Hill, Thomas(A)	1814	Sept. 08	Miami	02	11	06
Hill, Thomas(B)	1806	Sept. 19	Nor.Carolina	01	13	02
Hill, Thomas(C)	1801	Dec. 30	Hamilton	07	03	32
Hill, William(A)	1827	May 29	Darke	01	10	15
Hill, William(C)	1817	Sept. 17	Virginia	13	02	01
Hill, William(E)	1829	April 08	Wayne(Ind)	15	18	07
Hille, John Hy.(A)	1838	Feb. 28	Cincinnati	03	13	29
Hillegas, Mich'l.(A)	1828	Dec. 03	Montgomery	05	10	33
Hilliar, Charles(C)	1805	July 27	Montgomery	11	01	36
Hilliar, John(C)	1802	Dec. 31	Hamilton	11	01	30
Hillier, Charles(A)	1807	April 20	Miami	05	08	12
Hillier, Charles(C)	1807	April 18	Miami	12	01	28
Hillier, Charles(C)	1807	April 18	Miami	12	01	21
Hillier, Daniel(C)	1807	April 18	Miami	12	01	15
Hillierd, Charles(C)	1813	Jan. 23	Miami	11	01	24
Hillierd, Charles(C)	1814	Oct. 14	Miami	12	01	20
Hillierd, William(C)	1813	Jan. 23	Miami	12	01	19
Hillis, James(C)	1805	Dec. 18	Kentucky	08	03	02
Hillmon, Benj'n.(E)	1827	Aug. 22	Union(Ind)	13	14	25
Himelick, Andrew(B)	1824	June 09	Preble	01	10	22
Himelick, Andrew(B)	1826	Jan. 23	Franklin(Ind	01	10	22
Himelick, Andw.(B)	1829	June 30	Franklin(Ind	01	10	15
Himes, Geo. W.(E)	1818	July 22	Cincinnati	11	11	36
Himes, George W.(E)	1818	July 15	Hamilton	14	19	05
Hinckle, Saul(C)	1811	Dec. 02	Champaign	10	05	09
Hinckle, Saul(C)	1811	Dec. 11	Champaign	10	05	08
Hindman, Andrew(A)	1815	Sept. 12	Butler	01	03	15
Hindman, Andrew(A)	1815	Sept. 15	Butler	01	03	12
Hindman, Thomas(A)	1814	April 26	Butler	01	03	08
Hindman, Thomas(E)	1817	July 07	Butler	11	11	25
Hinds, Benj'n.(B)	1824	Oct. 09	Hamilton	03	06	14
Hinds, Benjamin(B)	1813	July 27	Hamilton	01	09	29
Hinds, Henry(E)	1817	July 11	Franklin(Ind	13	12	28
Hinds, James(A)	1806	May 16	Hamilton	03	03	03
Hinds, James(A)	1813	Sept. 21	Butler	04	03	34
Hinds, James(B)	1816	May 28	Hamilton	01	04	29
Hinds, Michael(E)	1817	Aug. 13	Franklin(Ind	13	12	20
Hinds, Peter(E)	1817	Aug. 13	Franklin(Ind	13	12	20
Hinds, Reizen(E)	1836	Jan. 11	Dearborn(Ind	03	06	15
Hiner, Jacob(A)	1837	May 12	Darke	01	14	28
Hinesley, James(E)	1837	Dec. 05	Darke	15	21	23
Hinesly, John(A)	1831	Jan. 14	Darke	01	10	14
Hinkin, Gerhard(E)	1837	July 12	Cincinnati	12	11	13
Hinkle, Anthony(C)	1831	Sept. 27	Butler	13	02	03
Hinkle, Henry(E)	1836	Sept. 09	Butler	15	21	31
Hinkle, Hy.(C)	1831	Aug. 25	Ohio	13	02	09
Hinkle, Joel(C)	1812	March 07	Champaign	10	05	08
Hinkle, Joseph(E)	1836	Aug. 29	Butler	15	21	27
Hinkle, Moses(C)	1812	Jan. 25	Champaign	10	05	15
Hinkle, Saul(C)	1811	April 09	Champaign	10	05	14
Hinkle, Saul(C)	1811	April 09	Champaign	10	05	15
Hinkle, Saul(C)	1811	April 09	Champaign	10	05	09
Hinkley, Judah(B)	1830	June 11	Franklin(Ind	01	09	12
Hinkson, John(B)	1814	July 15	Dearborn(Ind	01	07	09
Hinkson, Thomas(E)	1814	May 03	Ind.Territry	12	14	34
Hinnenkamp, Bernard(E)	1836	Nov. 11	Cincinnati	12	10	10
Hinsey, Cornelius(A)	1802	July 27	Hamilton	02	05	09
Hinsey, William(A)	1802	July 27	Hamilton	02	05	09
Hinshaw, Abel(E)	1836	Jan. 01	Randolph(Ind	14	19	22
Hinshaw, Absalom(E)	1836	Jan. 26	Randolph(Ind	14	19	22
Hinshaw, Joseph(E)	1817	June 23	Clinton	14	21	17
Hinshaw, Phebe(E)	1836	Jan. 28	Randolph(Ind	14	18	03
Hinshaw, Solomon(E)	1836	June 28	Randolph(Ind	14	19	34
Hinshaw, Thomas(E)	1830	April 12	Randolph(Ind	14	20	34
Hinshaw, Thomas(E)	1837	March 01	Randolph(Ind	14	20	34

PURCHASER	YEAR	DATE	RESIDENCE	R	T	S
Hiot, William(B)	1808	Jan. 13	Montgomery	01	14	03
Hirons, Samuel(C)	1807	June 01	Kentucky	13	05	33
Hirt, Jacob(E)	1836	Sept. 15	Pennsylvania	12	10	03
Hirt, John(E)	1836	Sept. 14	Cincinnati	12	11	27
Hirt, Joseph(E)	1836	Sept. 14	Cincinnati	12	11	27
Hiser, Daniel(B)	1813	Aug. 25	Dearborn(Ind	01	03	31
Hiser, Jefferson(B)	1835	June 30	Switzerland	01	02	05
Hittel, Henry(A)	1838	May 01	Fairfield	01	15	32
Hittel, Henry(A)	1838	May 21	Fairfield	01	14	04
Hittle, Nicholas(A)	1824	Sept. 06	Miami	05	07	09
Hittle, Nicholas(A)	1824	Sept. 06	Miami	05	07	17
Hittle, Nicholas(A)	1826	June 26	Miami	05	07	09
Hixon, William(A)	1806	Dec. 22	Montgomery	03	04	08
Hizer, Jacob(A)	1817	Nov. 24	Greene	04	08	19
Hobbs, Elisabeth Jane(E)	1835	Nov. 02	Franklin(Ind	12	10	03
Hobbs, Elisha(E)	1836	March 05	Franklin(Ind	13	11	18
Hobbs, Elisha(E)	1836	April 05	Franklin(Ind	12	11	35
Hobbs, Emery(B)	1814	April 26	Dearborn(Ind	02	10	32
Hobbs, James Junr.(E)	1817	Nov. 04	Franklin(Ind	13	11	07
Hobbs, Robert(E)	1835	Oct. 29	Franklin(Ind	12	11	35
Hobs, Emery(B)	1816	Sept. 27	?	01	07	20
Hobson, George(E)	1816	Jan. 31	Wayne(Ind)	13	18	20
Hobson, George(E)	1829	March 31	Wayne(Ind)	13	18	20
Hobson, Jesse(A)	1813	May 13	Preble	03	04	29
Hobson, Joseph(E)	1812	June 22	Nor.Carolina	13	16	31
Hobson, William L.(A)	1815	July 08	Cincinnati	01	03	01
Hocker, Andrew(C)	1802	Nov. 10	Hamilton	07	02	09
Hocker, Charles(A)	1829	Dec. 11	Montgomery	04	05	08
Hocket, Hezekiah(E)	1816	Oct. 25	Highland	14	18	07
Hocket, Joseph(E)	1816	Oct. 25	Highland	14	18	04
Hockett, Isaac Jr.(E)	1833	March 02	Randolph(Ind	14	18	06
Hockett, Moses(E)	1827	Oct. 19	Wayne(Ind)	14	17	04
Hockett, Moses(E)	1827	June 27	Wayne(Ind)	14	17	04
Hockett, William(E)	1817	Sept. 12	Highland	14	18	05
Hockett, William(E)	1817	Sept. 12	Highland	14	20	32
Hodge, Andrew(C)	1806	Jan. 01	Kentucky	09	05	20
Hodge, Andrew(C)	1807	June 01	Kentucky	10	06	25
Hodge, John E.(E)	1815	July 31	Wayne(Ind)	13	18	08
Hodge, Robert(B)	1831	Jan. 14	Dearborn(Ind	02	07	10
Hodge, Thomas Heirs(B)	1831	Jan. 14	Dearborn(Ind	02	07	10
Hodge, Thomas(B)	1819	Oct. 27	Dearborn(Ind	02	07	13
Hodges, Andrew(B)	1835	July 29	Switzerland	02	03	36
Hodges, Andrew(B)	1835	Dec. 29	Switzerland	02	03	36
Hodges, Benjamin(B)	1812	Oct. 20	Wayne(Ind)	01	13	27
Hodges, Samuel(E)	1836	Oct. 17	Randolph(Ind	14	21	05
Hodgson, Amos(E)	1817	Nov. 03	Clinton	14	20	33
Hodgson, Daniel(E)	1817	Nov. 19	Clinton	14	20	14
Hodgson, Hur(E)	1817	Nov. 03	Clinton	13	18	06
Hodgson, Isaac(E)	1835	March 26	Randolph(Ind	14	18	06
Hodgson, James(B)	1833	July 08	Dearborn(Ind	02	05	07
Hodgson, Joseph(B)	1814	Oct. 21	Hamilton	02	09	02
Hodgson, Solomon(E)	1816	Nov. 15	Highland	13	17	06
Hodson, Annual(E)	1835	Sept. 09	Randolph(Ind	14	18	01
Hodson, Enos(E)	1828	March 01	Randolph(Ind	14	18	01
Hodson, Hur(E)	1819	July 13	Randolph(Ind	14	18	12
Hodson, Hur(E)	1824	June 12	Randolph(Ind	14	18	12
Hodson, Robert(E)	1834	July 03	Randolph(Ind	14	18	02
Hodson, Zachariah(E)	1829	June 12	Randolph(Ind	13	18	27
Hoeffer, John Peter(A)	1837	May 16	Warren	03	12	31
Hofard, Martin(B)	1832	Sept. 13	Dearborn(Ind	02	07	27
Hoffer, Frederic(B)	1834	Jan. 22	Hamilton	02	07	03
Hoffer, Henry(C)	1815	May 04	Cincinnati	14	04	33
Hoffman, Daniel(E)	1836	May 12	Preble	12	11	06
Hoffman, John(A)	1814	Sept. 10	Montgomery	04	05	10
Hoffman, John(B)	1834	May 16	Franklin(Ind	03	09	25
Hoffmann, John(B)	1835	Nov. 23	Franklin(Ind	03	09	25
Hoffner, Jacob(A)	1811	June 24	Hamilton	01	04	09
Hogan, David(B)	1814	July 25	Dearborn(Ind	01	05	07
Hogan, David(B)	1818	July 25	Dearborn(Ind	02	05	12

PURCHASER	YEAR	DATE	RESIDENCE	R	T	S
Hogarth, Edwin P.(E)	1838	Aug. 10	Cincinnati	15	22	09
Hogg, James(C)	1815	Dec. 12	Champaign	12	04	14
Hogg, Samuel(C)	1810	Sept. 01	Pennsylvania	12	04	14
Hogg, Samuel(C)	1812	April 13	Champaign	10	05	23
Hogsheare, James S.(B)	1818	June 22	Dearborn(Ind	03	06	24
Hogsheise, James S.(B)	1818	July 02	Dearborn(Ind	03	06	22
Hogston, Milass(E)	1836	Oct. 24	Wayne(Ind)	14	19	23
Hoilman, David(E)	1835	Jan. 08	Randolph(Ind	13	19	11
Hoilman, David(E)	1835	Jan. 08	Randolph(Ind	13	19	11
Hoke, John(B)	1836	Oct. 07	Randolph(Ind	01	18	12
Hoke, John(B)	1837	April 12	Randolph(Ind	01	18	24
Holapater, John(A)	1831	July 04	Miami	05	08	21
Holcomb, Pantheus J.(C)	1817	Sept. 16	Warren	08	05	29
Holcomb, Pentheus J.(C)	1819	Jan. 12	Clark	08	05	29
Holcomb, Pentheus(C)	1816	Dec. 09	Cincinnati	08	05	29
Holcomb, Pentheus(C)	1816	Dec. 09	Cincinnati	08	05	29
Holcomb, Pentheus(C)	1816	Dec. 09	Cincinnati	08	05	30
Holcomb, Pentheus(C)	1816	Dec. 09	Cincinnati	08	05	24
Holcomb, Rufus(B)	1824	June 10	Montgomery	03	06	22
Holder, Martin(B)	1813	June 22	Dearborn(Ind	01	02	28
Holderman, Abraham(A)	1805	Oct. 19	Virginia	03	05	32
Holderman, Abraham(A)	1805	Oct. 19	Virginia	03	05	33
Holderman, Abraham(A)	1805	Oct. 19	Virginia	03	05	34
Holderman, Abraham(A)	1805	Oct. 29	Virginia	03	05	32
Holderman, Abraham(A)	1805	Oct. 29	Virginia	03	05	28
Holderman, Abraham(A)	1806	Jan. 07	Ohio	03	05	18
Holderman, Abraham(A)	1806	Jan. 07	Ohio	03	05	17
Holderman, Abraham(A)	1806	Jan. 07	Ohio	03	05	07
Holderman, Abraham(A)	1806	Jan. 07	Ohio	03	05	12
Holderman, Abraham(A)	1807	Jan. 05	Montgomery	03	05	19
Holderman, Abraham(C)	1806	Jan. 07	Ohio	09	02	34
Holderman, Christian(A)	1815	Feb. 18	Preble	02	07	24
Holderman, David(C)	1806	June 27	Chillicothe	09	03	24
Holderman, David(C)	1806	June 27	Chillicothe	09	03	18
Holderman, Jacob(C)	1805	Dec. 26	Pennsylvania	11	02	28
Holderman, John(A)	1806	July 07	Montgomery	06	04	23
Holderman, John(A)	1806	July 07	Montgomery	06	03	11
Holderman, John(A)	1806	Nov. 10	Montgomery	03	05	20
Holderman, John(A)	1811	Aug. 12	Montgomery	06	03	11
Holderman, John(A)	1814	Oct. 08	Preble	02	07	23
Holderman, John(A)	1815	Feb. 07	Preble	02	07	13
Holderman, John(C)	1804	Dec. 07	Montgomery	07	02	06
Holderman, John(C)	1805	Aug. 09	Montgomery	09	02	32
Holderman, John(C)	1805	Dec. 25	Montgomery	09	02	32
Holderman, John(C)	1805	Dec. 26	Dayton	11	02	28
Holderman, John(C)	1806	May 27	Montgomery	11	02	28
Holderman, John(C)	1811	Aug. 13	Montgomery	11	02	28
Holderman, William(E)	1835	May 01	Randolph(Ind	14	20	08
Holdmeyer, Christopher Hy.(A)	1837	Dec. 09	Cincinnati	03	12	06
Holdmeyer, Christopher Hy.(A)	1837	Dec. 11	Cincinnati	03	12	06
Holdron, Dennis(B)	1828	July 14	Dearborn(Ind	01	07	25
Hole, Charles(A)	1817	June 19	Preble	03	11	13
Hole, John(C)	1801	Dec. 25	Hamilton	06	02	32
Hole, John(C)	1801	Dec. 25	Hamilton	06	01	35
Hole, John(C)	1801	Dec. 25	Hamilton	06	01	03
Hole, John(E)	1836	Sept. 05	Montgomery	15	20	04
Hole, John(E)	1837	Feb. 27	Montgomery	15	20	04
Hole, Jonathan(A)	1816	June 05	Montgomery	03	11	13
Hole, William(A)	1817	June 20	Preble	03	11	24
Hole, William(A)	1817	July 09	Preble	04	10	18
Hole, William(A)	1827	Oct. 09	Hamilton	01	07	01
Hole, William(E)	1836	Sept. 05	Montgomery	15	20	04
Hole, Zachariah(A)	1805	July 13	Montgomery	03	07	27
Hole, Zachariah(A)	1814	Dec. 02	Preble	03	06	20
Hole, Zachariah(A)	1815	Dec. 15	Preble	03	11	24
Hole, Zachariah(c)	1801	Dec. 28	Hamilton	06	01	25
Holeman, George(B)	1804	Dec. 21	Kentucky	01	13	17
Holeman, George(B)	1807	Jan. 23	Ind.Territry	01	13	34
Holeman, George(B)	1807	Jan. 23	Ind.Territry	01	13	35

PURCHASER	YEAR	DATE	RESIDENCE	R	T	S
Holeman, Jesse L.(B)	1810	Aug. 16	Kentucky	01	04	05
Holeman, Joseph(B)	1806	July 24	Dearborn(Ind	01	12	08
Holeman, Joseph(B)	1806	Dec. 02	Ind.Territry	01	13	34
Holeman, Joseph(E)	1812	March 19	Franklin(Ind	14	16	07
Holeman, William(B)	1806	July 24	Dearborn(Ind	01	12	07
Holeman, William(B)	1806	Dec. 02	Ind.Territry	01	13	34
Holland, Francis(E)	1827	Sept. 28	Franklin(Ind	13	12	20
Holland, Henry(E)	1813	July 31	Butler	13	14	15
Holland, James(B)	1836	Nov. 11	Darke	01	17	35
Holland, Peter(B)	1837	Feb. 13	Darke	01	17	36
Holland, Robert(E)	1819	Aug. 27	Hamilton	13	14	02
Holland, Robert(E)	1827	Feb. 24	Fayette	13	14	01
Holland, William(E)	1836	July 14	Franklin(Ind	12	11	01
Holland, William(E)	1836	Oct. 15	Franklin(Ind	12	11	01
Hollaway, David(C)	1804	Sept. 03	Warren	05	03	08
Hollcroft, Geo.(B)	1828	Feb. 04	Switzerland	03	02	31
Hollcroft, George(B)	1832	Sept. 26	Switzerland	03	02	19
Holleday, Samuel(A)	1806	March 06	Kentucky	02	07	11
Holles, George(A)	1811	May 30	Pennsylvania	04	05	35
Hollett, George(B)	1814	Jan. 22	Wayne(Ind)	01	13	25
Holliday, John(B)	1814	May 23	Hamilton	01	09	30
Holliday, Samuel(E)	1812	Feb. 07	Preble	13	17	32
Hollinger, Jacob(C)	1814	April 29	Champaign	10	04	18
Hollinger, Valentine(C)	1815	Feb. 09	Champaign	10	04	18
Hollingsworth, Abraham(B)	1808	Sept. 24	Warren	01	11	30
Hollingsworth, Benj'n.(E)	1836	Oct. 26	Wayne(Ind)	14	19	09
Hollingsworth, David(B)	1806	May 13	Dearborn(Ind	02	11	27
Hollingsworth, David(B)	1808	March 07	Dearborn(Ind	01	11	07
Hollingsworth, David(E)	1811	Nov. 23	Franklin(Ind	14	14	18
Hollingsworth, Eli(A)	1828	Jan. 21	Miami	06	04	18
Hollingsworth, Eli(E)	1836	Oct. 04	Belmont	14	19	13
Hollingsworth, Ezekiel(B)	1812	Aug. 03	Franklin(Ind	01	11	17
Hollingsworth, George(A)	1807	June 14	Montgomery	05	05	27
Hollingsworth, George(B)	1806	May 13	Dearborn(Ind	02	10	09
Hollingsworth, George(E)	1813	July 29	Franklin(Ind	12	14	12
Hollingsworth, Henry(A)	1816	Aug. 22	Miami	04	09	29
Hollingsworth, Henry(B)	1814	March 30	Warren	01	11	09
Hollingsworth, Henry(E)	1829	Sept. 28	Warren	13	18	25
Hollingsworth, Isaac(A)	1806	Sept. 02	Montgomery	05	06	29
Hollingsworth, Isaac(A)	1831	June 06	Dearborn(Ind	04	09	28
Hollingsworth, Isaac(A)	1831	Aug. 29	Darke	04	09	33
Hollingsworth, Isaac(B)	1812	Oct. 29	Franklin(Ind	02	11	14
Hollingsworth, Isaac(B)	1813	Oct. 04	Franklin(Ind	02	11	14
Hollingsworth, Jacob(B)	1806	Sept. 22	Warren	02	11	23
Hollingsworth, James(B)	1813	Sept. 03	Warren	01	11	20
Hollingsworth, James(B)	1813	Dec. 30	Warren	02	11	24
Hollingsworth, Jas. Jr.(A)	1828	Aug. 09	Union(Ind)	04	06	03
Hollingsworth, Jas.(E)	1829	Nov. 28	Wayne(Ind)	13	18	36
Hollingsworth, Joel(A)	1806	Aug. 18	Warren	04	07	02
Hollingsworth, John(B)	1814	Sept. 14	Miami	02	11	14
Hollingsworth, Jonathan(B)	1807	May 29	Dearborn(Ind	02	11	14
Hollingsworth, Jonathan(B)	1807	Sept. 01	Dearborn(Ind	02	11	11
Hollingsworth, Jonathan(B)	1814	Sept. 17	Franklin(Ind	02	11	13
Hollingsworth, Joseph(B)	1806	May 13	Dearborn(Ind	02	11	27
Hollingsworth, Joseph(E)	1818	June 03	Wayne(Ind)	13	18	11
Hollingsworth, Joseph(E)	1818	Oct. 10	Montgomery	13	18	02
Hollingsworth, Joseph(E)	1819	Oct. 13	Randolph(Ind	13	19	08
Hollingsworth, Joseph(E)	1831	April 04	Randolph(Ind	13	18	10
Hollingsworth, Levi(B)	1806	May 13	Dearborn(Ind	02	11	22
Hollingsworth, Levi(E)	1838	Aug. 21	Belmont	15	20	29
Hollingsworth, Nathan(A)	1806	Aug. 11	Warren	05	06	09
Hollingsworth, Peirce(E)	1834	Jan. 09	Randolph(Ind	14	18	12
Hollingsworth, Peirce(E)	1836	Nov. 22	Randolph(Ind	14	19	03
Hollingsworth, Rich'd.(A)	1830	Jan. 14	Union(Ind)	04	06	03
Hollingsworth, Rich'd.(B)	1815	Oct. 05	Franklin(Ind	02	11	23
Hollingsworth, Richard(A)	1830	May 06	Union(Ind)	04	06	03
Hollingsworth, William(E)	1815	April 24	Butler	13	14	13
Hollinshead, James(A)	1811	Dec. 12	Montgomery	02	08	10
Hollinshead, James(A)	1812	Jan. 04	Montgomery	02	08	08

PURCHASER	YEAR	DATE	RESIDENCE	R	T	S
Hollinsworth, George(B)	1806	Sept. 12	Dearborn(Ind	02	10	10
Hollon, Isaac(Black)(A)	1835	Oct. 29	Darke	01	12	31
Holloway, Jacob(C)	1801	Dec. 25	Hamilton	04	03	07
Hollowell, Abner(A)	1806	June 12	Butler	03	04	17
Hollowell, Luke(E)	1838	Aug. 30	Preble	13	21	14
Hollowell, William(E)	1838	Sept. 06	Preble	13	21	14
Hollrah, Gerhard(E)	1836	July 05	Hamilton	13	12	27
Holman, Joseph(E)	1815	Sept. 13	Wayne(Ind)	14	16	05
Holmes, James(B)	1831	May 19	Randolph(Ind	01	15	03
Holmes, Samuel(B)	1813	April 14	Wayne(Ind)	01	13	10
Holmes, William(C)	1802	Dec. 31	Hamilton	09	03	22
Holmes, William(C)	1804	Dec. 28	Greene	09	03	22
Holmes, William(C)	1804	Dec. 28	Greene	09	03	22
Holopater, John(A)	1831	June 09	Miami	05	08	28
Holopater, John(A)	1831	June 09	Miami	05	08	27
Holopater, Matthias(A)	1831	Sept. 26	Miami	05	09	31
Holsapple, Frederick(A)	1807	June 20	Montgomery	04	05	12
Holsapple, Frederick(A)	1809	Nov. 18	Montgomery	04	05	01
Holsapple, Frederick(A)	1831	June 02	Montgomery	04	07	06
Holscher, George(B)	1836	July 07	Hamilton	02	08	18
Holschew, James(E)	1815	Oct. 28	Wayne(Ind)	12	15	02
Holstad, John(A)	1807	April 27	Butler	01	04	17
Holtell, Mark(B)	1814	Nov. 18	Wayne(Ind)	01	13	25
Holtett, Thomas Senr.(B)	1813	Nov. 02	Wayne(Ind)	01	13	25
Holtzclaw, William(E)	1814	Aug. 27	Wayne(Ind)	12	15	23
Homes, James(B)	1819	May 28	Butler	01	15	10
Homor, Thomas(C)	1802	Nov. 24	Hamilton	06	02	24
Hone, Henry(A)	1813	Oct. 30	Virginia	03	06	02
Honskar, Andrew(C)	1804	Dec. 28	Greene	08	03	27
Hood, Andrew(A)	1804	Sept. 24	Kentucky	05	04	03
Hood, Andrew(A)	1804	Nov. 06	Kentucky	05	04	03
Hood, Andrew(A)	1806	March 29	Montgomery	05	04	03
Hood, Andrew(A)	1809	Dec. 12	Montgomery	05	04	03
Hood, Andrew(A)	1811	Aug. 13	Montgomery	05	04	03
Hood, Rowley(A)	1837	Aug. 23	Preble	03	12	30
Hook, Jacob(C)	1815	May 15	Champaign	12	03	08
Hooke, Michael(E)	1817	Nov. 26	Wayne(Ind)	13	16	34
Hool, John(B)	1836	July 09	Hamilton	03	08	01
Hoopman, John(A)	1806	Aug. 23	Virginia	03	04	12
Hoops, Jacob(B)	1815	Jan. 02	Cincinnati	01	08	36
Hoops, Jacob(B)	1815	Jan. 02	Cincinnati	01	08	36
Hoover, Ab'm.(C)	1831	Aug. 10	Logan	13	04	30
Hoover, Abraham(A)	1828	Feb. 14	Montgomery	04	05	22
Hoover, Andrew(A)	1804	Nov. 30	Warren	04	04	23
Hoover, Andrew(B)	1806	June 07	Warren	01	14	28
Hoover, Andrew(B)	1806	June 07	Warren	01	14	29
Hoover, Andrew(B)	1806	June 25	Warren	01	14	27
Hoover, Andrew(B)	1806	July 23	Warren	01	14	28
Hoover, Andrew(B)	1807	Sept. 18	Dearborn(Ind	01	14	14
Hoover, Andrew(E)	1815	April 21	Wayne(Ind)	13	17	15
Hoover, Daniel(A)	1802	Aug. 02	Hamilton	05	05	10
Hoover, Daniel(A)	1804	Dec. 07	Montgomery	05	05	11
Hoover, David(A)	1802	Feb. 16	Hamilton	05	05	10
Hoover, David(A)	1804	Dec. 07	Montgomery	05	05	11
Hoover, David(E)	1816	Oct. 26	Wayne(Ind)	13	17	33
Hoover, Felix(A)	1838	April 10	Miami	02	13	20
Hoover, Felix(C)	1802	Dec. 25	Hamilton	09	03	21
Hoover, Frederick(B)	1815	Jan. 03	Wayne(Ind)	01	14	21
Hoover, Henry(A)	1804	Oct. 17	Montgomery	04	03	08
Hoover, Henry(B)	1807	Feb. 17	Montgomery	01	12	09
Hoover, Henry(E)	1811	Oct. 24	Montgomery	13	16	03
Hoover, Henry(E)	1811	Nov. 08	Montgomery	13	16	03
Hoover, Henry(E)	1811	Nov. 08	Montgomery	13	16	10
Hoover, Jacob(B)	1807	Feb. 17	Montgomery	01	12	30
Hoover, Jacob(B)	1807	Sept. 29	Dearborn(Ind	02	12	25
Hoover, Jacob(C)	1831	Aug. 08	Champaign	13	03	28
Hoover, Jacob(E)	1816	Oct. 26	Wayne(Ind)	13	17	33
Hoover, John Jr.(A)	1812	April 17	Miami	05	06	26
Hoover, John Junr.(A)	1806	Dec. 26	Montgomery	05	06	26

PURCHASER	YEAR	DATE	RESIDENCE	R	T	S
Hoover, John(A)	1802	Feb. 16	Hamilton	05	06	33
Hoover, John(A)	1805	Jan. 15	Montgomery	05	06	35
Hoover, John(A)	1805	June 29	Montgomery	05	06	29
Hoover, John(C)	1830	Nov. 03	Muskingum	13	03	28
Hoover, John(C)	1836	Feb. 19	Logan	13	03	33
Hoover, John(E)	1811	Nov. 27	Montgomery	12	16	23
Hoover, Jonas(A)	1814	Oct. 29	Montgomery	06	04	33
Hoover, Jonas(A)	1817	Aug. 30	Montgomery	01	12	28
Hoover, Jonas(A)	1836	Dec. 20	Darke	01	12	07
Hoover, Moses(A)	1822	July 18	Darke	01	10	02
Hoover, Noah(A)	1832	Feb. 06	Miami	04	08	08
Hoover, Noah(A)	1832	Feb. 06	Miami	04	08	14
Hoover, Peter Jr.(B)	1835	Aug. 15	Randolph(Ind	01	17	12
Hoover, Peter(B)	1834	June 17	Clark	01	17	12
Hoover, Peter(E)	1811	Oct. 24	Montgomery	13	16	03
Hoover, Philip(C)	1814	May 05	Montgomery	09	02	26
Hoover, Samuel(A)	1836	June 23	Hamilton	04	11	31
Hoover, Samuel(A)	1836	June 24	Hamilton	04	10	06
Hopkins, Augustus(A)	1836	June 23	Hamilton	04	11	31
Hopkins, Augustus(A)	1836	Nov. 14	Cincinnati	01	14	34
Hopkins, Augustus(A)	1836	Nov. 19	Cincinnati	01	15	22
Hopkins, Augustus(A)	1836	Nov. 28	Hamilton	01	15	20
Hopkins, Augustus(A)	1836	Dec. 02	Cincinnati	01	15	32
Hopkins, Augustus(E)	1836	July 02	Hamilton	13	19	11
Hopkins, Augustus(E)	1836	July 21	Hamilton	14	21	11
Hopkins, Augustus(E)	1836	July 21	Hamilton	14	21	15
Hopkins, Augustus(E)	1836	Sept. 05	Hamilton	13	20	13
Hopkins, Augustus(E)	1836	Nov. 14	Cincinnati	13	20	12
Hopkins, Elihu(A)	1810	March 24	Kentucky	02	07	05
Hopkins, Garret Vanniman(A)	1835	Jan. 06	Preble	02	13	35
Hopkins, James(C)	1806	Dec. 30	Champaign	09	05	06
Hopkins, James(C)	1807	Jan. 13	Champaign	09	05	06
Hopkins, Lemuel(A)	1815	Aug. 30	Preble	02	08	14
Hopkins, Richard(C)	1812	April 15	Champaign	09	05	06
Hopkins, Samuel(A)	1810	Feb. 24	Kentucky	02	07	09
Hopkins, Thomas(A)	1801	July 02	Kentucky	01	01	31
Hopkins, Thomas(B)	1801	July 02	Kentucky	01	02	36
Hopkins, Thomas(B)	1801	July 14	Kentucky	02	01	03
Hopkins, William(E)	1815	Nov. 27	JeffersonInd	13	13	20
Hopkins, Wm. H.(C)	1814	July 02	Cincinnati	09	04	08
Hopping, Ezekiel(C)	1804	Dec. 24	Greene	07	04	30
Hormal, Henry(A)	1808	Nov. 12	Warren	01	03	02
Hormal, John(C)	1801	Dec. 10	Hamilton	04	04	32
Hormel, John(A)	1819	Sept. 23	Warren	03	10	35
Hormel, John(C)	1801	Dec. 10	Hamilton	04	04	33
Hormell, Henry(A)	1805	Dec. 02	Pennsylvania	03	03	23
Hormell, Henry(A)	1805	Dec. 13	Pennsylvania	01	03	01
Horn, George(A)	1824	June 24	Preble	03	07	22
Horn, Henry(A)	1804	Oct. 27	Virginia	02	07	35
Horn, Jacob(B)	1831	Nov. 05	Randolph(Ind	01	16	34
Horn, Jacob(B)	1831	Nov. 05	Randolph(Ind	01	16	35
Horn, Jose(B)	1826	Jan. 17	Randolph(Ind	01	16	22
Hornady, John(A)	1811	June 01	Butler	02	05	13
Hornady, John(B)	1811	May 29	Butler	02	10	34
Hornbach, John(C)	1816	Dec. 20	Pickaway	13	04	08
Hornback, James(E)	1832	Oct. 01	Franklin(Ind	13	11	31
Hornbaker, Benjamin(E)	1835	Dec. 17	Preble	14	19	17
Hornberger, George Nicolas(B)	1833	June 03	Cincinnati	03	08	11
Hornberger, George Nicolas(B)	1833	June 22	Cincinnati	03	08	02
Hornberger, George Nicolas(B)	1833	June 22	Cincinnati	03	08	12
Hornberger, George Nicolas(B)	1833	Nov. 25	Cincinnati	03	08	11
Horneday, Nathan(A)	1807	July 14	Butler	03	04	18
Horneday, Nathan(A)	1807	July 14	Butler	03	04	19
Horner, Abraham(A)	1805	May 25	Pennsylvania	04	04	01
Horner, Abraham(A)	1814	Oct. 03	Montgomery	04	04	01
Horner, Benjamin(C)	1804	Sept. 03	Greene	06	02	08
Horner, Benjamin(C)	1804	Oct. 11	Greene	06	02	03
Horner, George(A)	1814	Dec. 29	Montgomery	04	05	06
Horner, George(C)	1802	Dec. 29	Hamilton	07	02	17

152

PURCHASER	YEAR	DATE	RESIDENCE	R	T	S
Horner, George(C)	1804	Oct. 01	Greene	08	03	08
Horner, George(C)	1816	Jan. 04	Greene	10	03	05
Horner, Jacob(A)	1830	Jan. 05	Montgomery	04	06	31
Horner, Jacob(B)	1814	Nov. 30	Greene	02	11	12
Horner, Jacob(B)	1814	Dec. 30	Greene	02	11	10
Horner, Jacob(B)	1814	Dec. 30	Greene	02	11	01
Horner, Jacob(B)	1814	Dec. 30	Greene	02	11	01
Horner, John(C)	1815	July 04	Greene	10	04	28
Horner, Levi(B)	1827	Oct. 22	Wayne(Ind)	01	16	34
Horner, Levi(E)	1818	Sept. 18	Warren	14	18	33
Horner, Michael(B)	1805	May 29	Pennsylvania	02	04	11
Horner, Nicholas(C)	1801	Dec. 30	Hamilton	05	02	23
Horner, Nicholas(C)	1802	Dec. 30	Hamilton	05	02	22
Horner, Nicholas(C)	1802	Dec. 30	Hamilton	06	01	04
Horney, Solomon(E)	1812	July 16	Preble	12	15	34
Horney, Solomon(E)	1817	Dec. 11	Wayne(Ind)	13	21	13
Horney, William(B)	1818	Aug. 07	Pittsburgh	01	07	17
Hornor, Sam'l. Jr.(E)	1829	Dec. 10	Wayne(Ind)	14	18	35
Hornor, Samuel(E)	1818	March 09	Warren	14	18	35
Hosbrook, Daniel(B)	1816	May 03	Hamilton	02	08	08
Hoshawr, Henry(A)	1817	Sept. 08	Ross	05	10	33
Hosier, Abraham(C)	1801	Dec. 21	Hamilton	06	02	23
Hosier, Isaac(A)	1806	Oct. 25	Montgomery	06	03	27
Hosier, Isaac(E)	1836	Nov. 26	Montgomery	15	20	07
Hosier, Lewis(E)	1811	Oct. 24	Wayne(Ind)	13	16	21
Hosier, Will'm.(E)	1815	Sept. 27	Wayne(Ind)	13	16	09
Hosier, William(E)	1814	Aug. 12	Wayne(Ind)	13	16	10
Hosier, William(E)	1814	Nov. 01	Wayne(Ind)	13	16	15
Hosier, William(E)	1816	Sept. 12	Wayne(Ind)	13	16	13
Hoskin, Jonathan(E)	1818	April 24	Clinton	14	19	32
Hostetler, Abraham(A)	1811	July 31	Kentucky	04	05	23
Hostetler, Christian(A)	1812	June 22	Montgomery	04	06	36
Hostetler, David(A)	1817	Sept. 04	Pickaway	05	10	28
Hotchkiss, Luther(B)	1836	June 15	Switzerland	03	04	20
Hotchkiss, Luther(B)	1836	July 05	Switzerland	03	04	20
Houard, Samuel(E)	1817	Nov. 06	Wayne(Ind)	14	17	21
Hough, Ira(E)	1816	Nov. 28	Warren	14	17	15
Hough, Joseph(A)	1807	June 18	Butler	02	04	14
Hough, Joseph(B)	1814	Nov. 30	Butler	01	11	32
Hough, Joseph(B)	1814	Nov. 30	Butler	01	10	05
Hough, Joseph(B)	1818	April 03	Butler	01	03	34
Hough, Joseph(B)	1818	April 03	Butler	01	03	35
Hough, Joseph(B)	1818	April 03	Butler	01	03	36
Hough, Joseph(B)	1818	April 03	Butler	03	03	29
Hough, Joseph(E)	1816	Jan. 20	Butler	14	16	04
Hough, Joseph(E)	1816	Jan. 20	Butler	14	16	04
Hough, Joseph(E)	1816	Jan. 20	Butler	14	16	03
Hough, Joseph(E)	1816	Jan. 26	Butler	14	16	09
Hough, William(B)	1830	Feb. 01	Wayne(Ind)	01	15	21
Hougham, Aaron(A)	1807	Jan. 22	Butler	02	08	30
Hougham, Aaron(E)	1815	May 06	Preble	13	14	08
Hougham, Aaron(E)	1815	May 06	Preble	13	14	08
Hougham, Garvis(E)	1815	July 28	Preble	13	14	10
Hougham, Jarvis(A)	1814	Jan. 27	Butler	01	08	25
Hougham, Jonathan(E)	1815	Aug. 24	Preble	13	14	21
Hoult, Joseph(E)	1816	July 08	Virginia	13	15	28
Houry, Samuel(A)	1813	March 30	Butler	01	03	04
House, Jacob(B)	1814	Dec. 03	Butler	01	12	23
House, Jacob(B)	1816	Oct. 05	Butler	01	12	13
Houser, Abraham(A)	1816	Dec. 09	Montgomery	03	07	12
Houser, Henry(A)	1805	Aug. 19	Hamilton	03	05	26
Housley, James(C)	1814	July 18	Madison	08	06	11
Houss, Henry(A)	1816	April 22	Butler	02	11	03
Houston, John(A)	1808	Jan. 11	Miami	05	08	02
Houston, John(A)	1813	Dec. 18	Miami	05	09	08
Houston, Robert(A)	1813	Dec. 18	Miami	05	09	09
Houschartt, Henry(B)	1833	July 05	Cincinnati	02	07	27
House, George(A)	1817	June 12	Butler	03	07	25
House, Joshua(A)	1827	Nov. 10	Kentucky	02	09	23

153

PURCHASER	YEAR	DATE	RESIDENCE	R	T	S
House, Lyman B.(E)	1818	July 11	Hamilton	11	11	35
House, Simeon(A)	1827	Nov. 08	Preble	02	09	23
House, William(E)	1839	Aug. 20	Jay Co.,Ind.	14	22	23
Householder, David Jr.(A)	1836	Dec. 19	Clark	02	13	13
Householder, David Jr.(A)	1836	Dec. 19	Clark	03	11	20
Houser, Dan'l.(A)	1831	Jan. 27	Montgomery	05	10	31
Houss, Henry(C)	1817	Oct. 29	Butler	12	01	09
Houston, John M.(A)	1836	Oct. 05	Warren	03	12	08
Houston, Robert(A)	1813	Dec. 18	Miami	05	09	08
Houston, Robert(A)	1814	Aug. 01	Miami	05	09	09
Houston, William A.(A)	1817	Aug. 04	Miami	02	10	28
Houston, William(A)	1813	Dec. 18	Miami	05	09	18
Houston, William(A)	1814	Aug. 01	Miami	05	09	04
Houtz, Christian(A)	1810	Aug. 14	Virginia	04	03	14
Houtz, Leonard(C)	1818	Dec. 14	Logan	14	03	01
Houtzer, Lewis(A)	1835	Aug. 05	Mercer	03	12	15
How, Silas(B)	1816	April 16	Hamilton	01	03	20
Howard, Ebenezer(B)	1814	Aug. 16	Butler	02	10	01
Howard, George(A)	1825	Jan. 26	Warren	04	06	15
Howard, James(A)	1804	Sept. 15	Hamilton	01	02	14
Howard, James(A)	1804	Sept. 24	Hamilton	01	03	24
Howard, Job(C)	1818	Oct. 07	Miami	11	01	11
Howard, Job(C)	1824	June 07	Miami	11	01	11
Howard, John(A)	1806	July 21	Montgomery	01	08	07
Howard, John(A)	1813	Oct. 11	Preble	01	08	07
Howard, John(A)	1815	Dec. 26	Wayne(Ind)	01	08	06
Howard, John(B)	1812	May 23	Dearborn(Ind	01	05	04
Howard, John(B)	1814	Sept. 03	Preble	01	13	14
Howard, John(C)	1811	Jan. 29	Butler	02	03	26
Howard, Sam'l.(B)	1834	Nov. 27	Switzerland	01	02	30
Howe, Abenezer(B)	1813	Nov. 22	Hamilton	01	11	17
Howe, Ebenezer(B)	1814	July 19	Hamilton	01	12	30
Howe, Edward(A)	1831	July 04	Miami	05	08	21
Howe, James(B)	1832	May 28	Franklin(Ind	02	08	22
Howe, Thomas(B)	1833	April 09	Franklin(Ind	02	08	22
Howe, Thomas(B)	1835	Dec. 05	Franklin(Ind	02	08	22
Howel, Joab(B)	1814	Nov. 01	Warren	01	09	07
Howel, Samuel(A)	1802	June 04	Hamilton	01	02	28
Howell, Aden(C)	1806	Feb. 03	Champaign	09	04	34
Howell, Adin(C)	1812	April 15	Champaign	09	03	12
Howell, Chatfield(B)	1806	June 21	Dearborn(Ind	01	10	30
Howell, Chatfield(B)	1806	June 21	Dearborn(Ind	01	10	30
Howell, Chatfield(B)	1810	Oct. 24	Dearborn(Ind	01	10	32
Howell, Dan'l.(C)	1829	Oct. 10	Champaign	11	03	25
Howell, Daniel G.(D)	1812	June 08	Hamilton(Fr)	02	01	26
Howell, Joab(C)	1806	Aug. 25	Kentucky	09	04	35
Howell, John(B)	1810	Oct. 24	Dearborn(Ind	01	10	32
Howell, Joshua(C)	1809	Oct. 25	Champaign	11	03	31
Howell, Joshua(C)	1809	Oct. 25	Champaign	11	03	31
Howell, Joshua(C)	1816	April 22	Champaign	11	03	31
Howell, Samuel(B)	1806	July 18	Warren	01	10	18
Howell, Thomas(C)	1808	July 23	Virginia	11	03	32
Howery, John George(B)	1818	March 06	Cincinnati	03	07	26
Howland, Albert(C)	1824	Nov. 19	Warren	11	02	11
Howlett, William(B)	1813	March 16	Dearborn(Ind	01	03	05
Hoyt, Stephens(C)	1814	June 30	Champaign	14	03	03
Hozier, Jacob(C)	1804	Sept. 04	Greene	06	02	08
Hozier, Robert(A)	1812	Sept. 12	Montgomery	06	03	27
Hozier, William(E)	1811	Oct. 25	Wayne(Ind)	14	16	19
Hubard, Silas(B)	1828	Feb. 01	Wayne(Ind)	01	15	11
Hubartt, John(E)	1836	Jan. 14	Franklin(Ind	13	12	18
Hubartt, Sam'l. V.(E)	1836	Jan. 14	Franklin(Ind	13	12	18
Hubartt, Thomas(A)	1812	Dec. 19	?	02	03	18
Hubbard, Austin(B)	1814	Oct. 22	Dearborn(Ind	03	04	02
Hubbard, Joseph(E)	1837	Feb. 10	Wayne(Ind)	14	20	23
Hubbart, John(B)	1836	June 06	Dearborn(Ind	02	04	05
Hubbartt, James(B)	1818	Jan. 24	Dearborn(Ind	02	04	08
Hubbartt, John Jr.(B)	1818	Sept. 29	Dearborn(Ind	02	04	07
Hubbell, Daniel(C)	1806	March 22	Champaign	09	04	35

PURCHASER	YEAR	DATE	RESIDENCE	R	T	S
Hubbell, Daniel(C)	1812	June 29	Champaign	09	03	28
Hubbell, Hezekiah(A)	1816	March 11	Miami	05	09	09
Hubbell, John(A)	1816	Oct. 15	Hamilton	02	09	10
Hubbell, Richard 2d.(B)	1817	June 05	Franklin(Ind	01	08	22
Hubbert, John Senr.(B)	1811	Aug. 30	Warren	02	04	10
Hubbert, John(B)	1837	May 16	Dearborn(Ind	02	04	05
Hubble, Hezekiah(A)	1816	Oct. 29	Miami	06	07	08
Hubble, Hezekiah(C)	1811	Dec. 10	Fairfield	13	02	07
Hubble, Jacob(C)	1813	April 14	Greene	08	04	12
Hubble, Richard(B)	1816	May 08	Cincinnati	01	08	22
Hubble, Sharrad(A)	1838	April 23	Darke	02	13	04
Huber, Henry(B)	1833	Aug. 07	Cincinnati	03	09	26
Huber, Michael Senr.(E)	1836	Nov. 09	Cincinnati	12	11	34
Huber, Michael(E)	1836	Aug. 12	Ohio	12	11	34
Hubler, Michael(A)	1816	Oct. 15	Montgomery	05	10	30
Hubler, Michael(A)	1816	Oct. 15	Montgomery	05	10	33
Huchenson, Solomon(B)	1815	Jan. 06	Hamilton	01	06	08
Huchin, William(A)	1811	Aug. 13	Butler	03	03	04
Huchinson, Silas(A)	1814	Dec. 10	Hamilton	01	02	13
Huddleston, Job(E)	1815	May 03	Wayne(Ind)	13	18	17
Huddleston, Job(E)	1816	Oct. 25	Wayne(Ind)	13	15	01
Huddleston, Jonathan(B)	1815	Aug. 08	Franklin(Ind	01	11	28
Huddleston, Nathan(C)	1815	Jan. 06	Champaign	11	03	22
Huddleston, Thos.(B)	1831	Oct. 20	England	01	06	06
Huddlestun, Wm.(C)	1825	Sept. 12	Champaign	11	03	29
Hudlow, David(E)	1833	March 02	Randolph(Ind	14	19	24
Hudlow, John((A)	1811	Dec. 13	Preble	02	08	01
Hudlow, John(A)	1811	Dec. 13	Preble	02	08	11
Hudlow, John(A)	1819	March 03	Preble	02	09	36
Hudson, Corbly(B)	1816	Sept. 21	Franklin(Ind	02	08	25
Hudson, Corbly(B)	1818	May 30	Franklin(Ind	02	08	36
Hudson, Corbly(B)	1818	May 30	Franklin(Ind	02	08	35
Hudson, Corbly(E)	1815	May 13	Franklin(Ind	13	12	35
Hudson, Jacob(C)	1828	Aug. 11	Logan	14	03	21
Hudson, Jacob(C)	1829	March 17	Logan	14	03	21
Hudson, Mary(E)	1815	May 13	Franklin(Ind	13	12	35
Hudson, William(B)	1815	July 03	Ind.Territry	01	08	18
Huegel, Joseph(E)	1836	Sept. 10	Columbiana	12	11	27
Hueston, David(C)	1801	Nov. 26	Hamilton	07	02	13
Hueston, David(C)	1801	Dec. 31	Hamilton	07	02	02
Hueston, John Johnson(B)	1834	April 23	Dearborn(Ind	02	03	14
Hueston, Mathew(E)	1811	Oct. 22	Butler	12	13	34
Hueston, Matthew(A)	1802	Aug. 06	Hamilton	01	05	11
Hueston, Matthew(A)	1802	Sept. 18	Hamilton	01	05	14
Hueston, Matthew(A)	1804	Oct. 13	Butler	01	06	34
Hueston, Matthew(A)	1804	Oct. 13	Butler	01	06	34
Hueston, Matthew(A)	1804	Oct. 13	Butler	01	06	28
Hueston, Matthew(A)	1804	Dec. 21	Butler	01	06	27
Hueston, Matthew(A)	1804	Dec. 21	Butler	01	06	34
Hueston, Matthew(A)	1817	Oct. 15	Butler	01	09	08
Hueston, Matthew(B)	1824	June 09	Butler	02	02	02
Hueston, Matthew(B)	1824	July 02	Butler	02	02	02
Huet, Elisha(A)	1837	Sept. 15	Darke	02	14	13
Huff, Isaac(A)	1802	Sept. 13	Hamilton	04	02	29
Huff, John(E)	1814	Jan. 13	Kentucky	13	13	15
Huff, John(E)	1814	Jan. 13	Kentucky	13	13	10
Huff, John(E)	1814	July 29	Kentucky	13	13	24
Huff, William F.(B)	1813	Jan. 16	Franklin(Ind	02	09	10
Huff, William T.(B)	1813	Oct. 15	Franklin(Ind	02	09	10
Huff, William T.(B)	1815	March 07	Switzerland	03	03	26
Huffman, Allen(A)	1814	Oct. 21	Preble	02	07	34
Huffman, Allen(A)	1817	Dec. 27	Preble	02	07	33
Huffman, Allen(A)	1817	Dec. 27	Preble	02	07	33
Huffman, Allen(A)	1824	Nov. 12	Preble	02	07	33
Huffman, Ambrose(C)	1816	Nov. 25	Hamilton	11	03	18
Huffman, Ambrose(C)	1816	Nov. 25	Hamilton	11	03	12
Huffman, Andrew(E)	1814	Dec. 03	Hamilton	13	15	35
Huffman, Armstead(A)	1824	June 08	Preble	02	07	21
Huffman, Benjamin(B)	1809	June 29	Virginia	02	05	23

PURCHASER	YEAR	DATE	RESIDENCE	R	T	S
Huffman, Conrad(B)	1809	Sept. 14	Dearborn(Ind	01	05	30
Huffman, Daniel(B)	1813	March 03	Virginia	02	04	01
Huffman, David(C)	1817	June 16	Champaign	11	03	18
Huffman, George(A)	1815	Dec. 06	Montgomery	01	11	25
Huffman, George(A)	1815	Dec. 06	Montgomery	01	11	26
Huffman, George(E)	1836	May 13	Randolph(Ind	13	21	35
Huffman, George(E)	1836	Oct. 03	Randolph(Ind	13	21	35
Huffman, Henry D.(E)	1836	Oct. 20	Randolph(Ind	13	20	03
Huffman, Isaac(B)	1817	Aug. 25	Butler	01	15	02
Huffman, Jacob(C)	1802	Dec. 31	Hamilton	09	04	25
Huffman, Jacob(C)	1802	Dec. 31	Hamilton	09	04	21
Huffman, Jacob(E)	1837	Jan. 17	Kentucky	13	20	11
Huffman, Jesse(E)	1836	Oct. 10	Preble	13	20	02
Huffman, John(A)	1835	Sept. 07	Darke	01	12	12
Huffman, John(A)	1836	Jan. 18	Darke	01	12	01
Huffman, John(B)	1814	Jan. 03	Hamilton	02	10	33
Huffman, John(E)	1836	Oct. 03	Randolph(Ind	13	21	36
Huffman, John(E)	1836	Nov. 28	Kentucky	14	20	06
Huffman, Jonas(E)	1814	Nov. 17	Hamilton	13	15	26
Huffman, Joseph(C)	1810	July 06	Virginia	14	02	04
Huffman, Lewis(C)	1813	Oct. 07	Champaign	10	04	21
Huffman, Lewis(C)	1815	Nov. 21	Champaign	10	04	27
Huffman, Moses(A)	1826	Nov. 10	Preble	03	07	13
Huffman, Paul(A)	1817	Nov. 22	Virginia	03	07	36
Huffman, Paul(A)	1818	Jan. 07	Preble	03	07	36
Huffman, Robert(E)	1814	Nov. 17	Hamilton	13	15	35
Huffman, Simeon(A)	1818	Jan. 07	Preble	03	07	36
Huffman, Simon(A)	1817	Nov. 22	Virginia	03	07	36
Huffman, Thomas(A)	1837	Aug. 06	Darke	02	12	06
Huffman, Valentine(A)	1818	Oct. 07	Montgomery	03	08	34
Huffman, William(C)	1813	April 23	Montgomery	07	03	04
Huffman, William(E)	1836	Oct. 10	Preble	13	21	35
Huffman, Wm.(C)	1813	April 23	Montgomery	07	02	12
Huffman, Wm.(C)	1813	April 23	Montgomery	07	03	07
Hufford, David(B)	1832	Feb. 28	Dearborn(Ind	02	04	28
Hufford, David(B)	1836	May 02	Dearborn(Ind	02	04	33
Hufnagle, Eleanor(A)	1831	July 11	Montgomery	02	12	29
Hufnagle, John(A)	1831	July 11	Pennsylvania	01	12	19
Hufnagle, Lydia(A)	1831	July 11	Montgomery	02	12	29
Hughell, Alvers(C)	1829	May 12	Clark	11	03	34
Hughell, Jacob(E)	1812	Feb. 06	Warren	13	17	20
Hughell, Joseph Jr.(E)	1814	Sept. 28	Warren	12	13	22
Hughell, Richard(C)	1807	July 13	Champaign	09	03	17
Hughell, Richard(C)	1812	Jan. 04	Champaign	09	03	18
Hughell, Thomas(E)	1834	April 11	Franklin(Ind	13	12	20
Hughes, Harbour(D)	1814	Jan. 29	Hamilton	01	02	11
Hughes, James(A)	1836	Nov. 30	Darke	03	11	05
Hughes, John(A)	1831	June 20	Shelby	05	09	07
Hughes, John(A)	1836	Feb. 17	Miami	03	11	23
Hughes, John(B)	1818	March 26	Dearborn(Ind	02	06	24
Hughes, John(B)	1833	April 03	Dearborn(Ind	02	04	20
Hughes, John(E)	1811	Nov. 28	Franklin(Ind	13	14	30
Hughes, John(E)	1814	Aug. 09	Franklin(Ind	12	14	33
Hughes, Lewis R.(A)	1836	June 16	Miami	03	11	05
Hughes, Matthew(B)	1825	Feb. 21	Franklin(Ind	02	10	22
Hughes, Thomas(B)	1809	Sept. 06	Dearborn(Ind	02	12	22
Hughey, William(A)	1817	Aug. 15	Greene	01	12	35
Huiat, Tobias(A)	1819	Aug. 02	Preble	04	05	18
Huigel, Lewis(E)	1836	Aug. 12	Ohio	12	11	33
Huitt, Israel(B)	1814	Nov. 30	Preble	02	08	09
Huleak, Samuel(C)	1813	April 14	Greene	08	04	19
Hulett, Amos A.(E)	1836	Dec. 28	Preble	13	19	01
Hulick, Barrent(B)	1802	Aug. 25	Hamilton	01	05	03
Hull, Jehiel(E)	1833	Jan. 03	Hamilton	14	20	28
Hull, John Lewis(B)	1834	Feb. 06	Hamilton	01	07	36
Hull, John(A)	1826	Oct. 24	Montgomery	04	05	21
Hull, Philip(C)	1806	Feb. 10	Montgomery	09	02	32
Hull, Philip(C)	1814	March 19	Miami	11	02	26
Hullinger, Daniel(C)	1817	Dec. 03	Champaign	11	03	12

PURCHASER	YEAR	DATE	RESIDENCE	R	T	S
Hullinger, John(C)	1817	Dec. 03	Champaign	11	03	12
Huls, William(B)	1827	Aug. 27	Hamilton	03	07	35
Huls, William(B)	1836	May 26	Dearborn(Ind	03	07	35
Hulse, David W.(A)	1829	Jan. 28	Warren	04	06	21
Humbert, Jacob(A)	1808	Nov. 04	Virginia	05	03	22
Humbert, Jacob(A)	1808	Dec. 15	Virginia	03	05	15
Humbert, Jacob(A)	1808	Dec. 15	Virginia	05	04	15
Humbert, Jacob(A)	1808	Dec. 15	Virginia	04	04	05
Humbert, Jacob(A)	1808	Dec. 15	Virginia	03	05	22
Hume, Peter(C)	1832	Feb. 01	Champaign	13	03	33
Humiston, Jason(E)	1838	Nov. 05	Washington	15	22	02
Hummel, Michael(B)	1834	July 02	Cincinnati	03	09	36
Humphrey, Arthur(B)	1828	May 22	Switzerland	01	03	28
Humphreys, Isaac(A)	1807	June 01	Butler	02	08	20
Humphreys, James(C)	1813	Jan. 08	Champaign	10	05	25
Humphreys, John(C)	1807	Jan. 12	Champaign	09	04	06
Humphreys, Robt.(C)	1827	Dec. 13	Clark	14	02	01
Humphreys, William(A)	1807	June 01	Butler	02	08	20
Humphreys, Wm.(C)	1801	Dec. 30	Hamilton	04	02	03
Humphries, Francis(C)	1813	Dec. 15	Greene	07	04	36
Humphries, James(A)	1809	Sept. 14	Champaign	12	04	30
Humphries, John(C)	1812	April 15	Champaign	09	04	06
Humphry, Arthur(B)	1829	Dec. 08	Switzerland	01	02	27
Humphry, Arthur(B)	1830	April 06	Switzerland	01	02	15
Hunnemann, Stephen(E)	1837	Feb. 07	Cincinnati	12	11	35
Hunsicker, Jno.(E)	1829	Jan. 07	Montgomery	13	15	24
Hunt, Aaron(C)	1801	Dec. 30	Hamilton	04	03	14
Hunt, Abijah(C)	1804	Dec. 26	Natchez	08	03	03
Hunt, Abijah(C)	1804	Dec. 31	Natchez	08	05	17
Hunt, Abraham(E)	1817	Oct. 02	Warren	14	19	34
Hunt, Abraham(E)	1832	April 16	Randolph(Ind	14	19	34
Hunt, Basil(E)	1833	Dec. 02	Randolph(Ind	13	19	28
Hunt, Bazel(E)	1829	Nov. 02	Kentucky	13	19	33
Hunt, Bazel(E)	1832	Nov. 02	Kentucky	13	19	33
Hunt, Bazel(E)	1834	Sept. 09	Kentucky	13	19	29
Hunt, Bazel(E)	1836	Nov. 08	Kentucky	13	19	26
Hunt, Bazel(E)	1836	Nov. 29	Kentucky	13	19	23
Hunt, Bazel(E)	1836	Nov. 29	Kentucky	13	19	35
Hunt, Benjamin(D)	1811	June 05	Butler	03	02	08
Hunt, Bezaleel(E)	1833	Dec. 23	Randolph(Ind	13	19	28
Hunt, Charles(A)	1817	June 11	Warren	02	12	11
Hunt, Charles(B)	1807	Feb. 11	Clermont	02	12	12
Hunt, Charles(B)	1807	Feb. 11	Clermont	02	12	13
Hunt, Charles(B)	1807	Feb. 11	Clermont	02	12	01
Hunt, Daniel(C)	1804	Dec. 29	New Jersey	10	02	22
Hunt, Daniel(C)	1804	Dec. 31	New Jersey	11	02	13
Hunt, Daniel(C)	1804	Dec. 31	New Jersey	10	02	02
Hunt, Daniel(C)	1804	Dec. 31	New Jersey	10	02	21
Hunt, Daniel(C)	1804	Dec. 31	New Jersey	10	02	33
Hunt, Daniel(C)	1804	Dec. 31	New Jersey	10	02	14
Hunt, Daniel(C)	1804	Dec. 31	New Jersey	10	02	27
Hunt, Daniel(C)	1804	Dec. 31	New Jersey	10	01	05
Hunt, Daniel(C)	1804	Dec. 31	New Jersey	10	02	12
Hunt, Daniel(C)	1804	Dec. 31	New Jersey	10	02	06
Hunt, Daniel(C)	1804	Dec. 31	New Jersey	10	02	15
Hunt, Daniel(C)	1804	Dec. 31	New Jersey	10	02	05
Hunt, Daniel(C)	1804	Dec. 31	New Jersey	10	02	36
Hunt, Daniel(C)	1804	Dec. 31	New Jersey	10	02	36
Hunt, Daniel(C)	1804	Dec. 31	New Jersey	10	02	09
Hunt, Daniel(C)	1804	Dec. 31	New Jersey	10	02	30
Hunt, Daniel(C)	1804	Dec. 31	New Jersey	10	02	30
Hunt, Daniel(C)	1804	Dec. 31	New Jersey	10	02	03
Hunt, Daniel(C)	1804	Dec. 31	New Jersey	10	02	23
Hunt, Daniel(C)	1804	Dec. 31	New Jersey	10	02	23
Hunt, Daniel(C)	1804	Dec. 31	New Jersey	10	02	18
Hunt, Daniel(C)	1804	Dec. 31	New Jersey	10	02	18
Hunt, Daniel(C)	1804	Dec. 31	New Jersey	10	02	17
Hunt, Daniel(C)	1804	Dec. 31	New Jersey	10	02	17
Hunt, Daniel(C)	1804	Dec. 31	New Jersey	10	01	06

PURCHASER	YEAR	DATE	RESIDENCE	R	T	S
Hunt, Daniel(C)	1804	Dec. 31	New Jersey	10	01	06
Hunt, Daniel(C)	1804	Dec. 31	New Jersey	10	02	24
Hunt, Daniel(C)	1804	Dec. 31	New Jersey	10	02	24
Hunt, Daniel(C)	1804	Dec. 31	New Jersey	10	02	04
Hunt, Daniel(C)	1804	Dec. 31	New Jersey	10	02	04
Hunt, Danil(C)	1804	Dec. 31	New Jersey	10	02	09
Hunt, Edward(E)	1814	Feb. 23	Franklin(Ind	13	15	22
Hunt, Edward(E)	1817	Oct. 02	Warren	14	19	34
Hunt, Eleanor(A)	1832	Sept. 01	Hamilton	02	10	33
Hunt, Elijah(A)	1824	Sept. 02	Miami	04	07	10
Hunt, George(B)	1807	March 25	Clermont	02	12	01
Hunt, Henry Harvey(A)	1832	Sept. 01	Hamilton	02	10	33
Hunt, Ira(C)	1831	Aug. 26	Butler	13	02	09
Hunt, Ira(C)	1831	Nov. 01	Butler	12	02	05
Hunt, James Denton(E)	1833	Jan. 08	Randolph(Ind	13	19	17
Hunt, Jeremiah	1808	March 03	Cincinnati	?	?	?
Hunt, Jeremiah	1808	March 03	Cincinnati	?	?	?
Hunt, Jeremiah	1808	March 03	Cincinnati	?	?	?
Hunt, Jeremiah	1808	March 03	Cincinnati	?	?	?
Hunt, Jeremiah	1808	March 03	Cincinnati	?	?	?
Hunt, Jeremiah	1808	March 03	Cincinnati	?	?	?
Hunt, Jeremiah	1808	March 03	Cincinnati	?	?	?
Hunt, Jeremiah	1808	March 03	Cincinnati	?	?	?
Hunt, Jeremiah	1808	March 03	Cincinnati	?	?	?
Hunt, Jeremiah(B)	1802	Sept. 02	Cincinnati	02	05	34
Hunt, Jeremiah(B)	1803	Dec. 20	Ind.Territory	02	05	26
Hunt, Jeremiah(B)	1808	April 13	Cincinnati	02	05	34
Hunt, Jeremiah(B)	1813	Aug. 11	Cincinnati	02	05	34
Hunt, Jeremiah(C)	1802	Dec. 31	Cincinnati	04	04	18
Hunt, Jeremiah(C)	1804	Dec. 31	Cincinnati	08	05	36
Hunt, Jeremiah(C)	1804	Dec. 31	Cincinnati	08	03	06
Hunt, Jeremiah(C)	1804	Dec. 31	Cincinnati	08	03	18
Hunt, Jeremiah(C)	1804	Dec. 31	Cincinnati	08	03	32
Hunt, Jeremiah(C)	1804	Dec. 31	Cincinnati	08	03	19
Hunt, Jeremiah(C)	1804	Dec. 31	Cincinnati	08	05	17
Hunt, Jeremiah(C)	1804	Dec. 31	Cincinnati	08	03	09
Hunt, Jeremiah(C)	1804	Dec. 31	Cincinnati	09	04	14
Hunt, Jeremiah(C)	1804	Dec. 31	Cincinnati	10	02	23
Hunt, Jeremiah(C)	1804	Dec. 31	Cincinnati	10	02	23
Hunt, Jeremiah(C)	1804	Dec. 31	Cincinnati	10	02	18
Hunt, Jeremiah(C)	1804	Dec. 31	Cincinnati	10	02	18
Hunt, Jeremiah(C)	1804	Dec. 31	Cincinnati	10	02	17
Hunt, Jeremiah(C)	1804	Dec. 31	Cincinnati	10	02	17
Hunt, Jeremiah(C)	1804	Dec. 31	Cincinnati	10	01	06
Hunt, Jeremiah(C)	1804	Dec. 31	Cincinnati	10	01	06
Hunt, Jeremiah(C)	1804	Dec. 31	Cincinnati	10	02	24
Hunt, Jeremiah(C)	1804	Dec. 31	Cincinnati	10	02	24
Hunt, Jeremiah(C)	1804	Dec. 31	Cincinnati	10	02	04
Hunt, Jeremiah(C)	1804	Dec. 31	Cincinnati	10	02	04
Hunt, Jeremiah(C)	1806	Feb. 11	Cincinnati	10	01	05
Hunt, Jeremiah(C)	1806	Feb. 11	Cincinnati	10	01	05
Hunt, Jeremiah(C)	1806	Feb. 11	Cincinnati	10	01	05
Hunt, Jeremiah(C)	1806	May 20	Cincinnati	10	01	06
Hunt, Jeremiah(C)	1806	July 31	Cincinnati	10	02	24
Hunt, Jeremian(C)	1806	Feb. 11	Cincinnati	10	01	05
Hunt, Jesse	1808	March 03	Cincinnati	?	?	?
Hunt, Jesse	1808	March 03	Cincinnati	?	?	?
Hunt, Jesse(A)	1832	Feb. 09	Cincinnati	02	10	32
Hunt, Jesse(A)	1832	Sept. 01	Cincinnati	02	10	32
Hunt, Jesse(B)	1806	Dec. 03	Cincinnati	01	04	16
Hunt, Jesse(B)	1815	May 18	Cincinnati	02	03	31
Hunt, Jesse(B)	1817	Sept. 10	Cincinnati	01	09	15
Hunt, Jesse(B)	1817	Oct. 20	Cincinnati	02	02	11
Hunt, Jesse(B)	1818	Dec. 30	Cincinnati	03	06	28
Hunt, Jesse(B)	1819	March 19	Cincinnati	03	05	01
Hunt, Jesse(C)	1804	Dec. 22	Cincinnati	07	02	09
Hunt, Jesse(C)	1804	Dec. 22	Cincinnati	07	03	35
Hunt, Jesse(C)	1804	Dec. 22	Cincinnati	09	04	31
Hunt, Jesse(C)	1804	Dec. 22	Cincinnati	07	03	20

PURCHASER	YEAR	DATE	RESIDENCE	R	T	S
Hunt, Jesse(C)	1804	Dec. 22	Cincinnati	07	03	34
Hunt, Jesse(C)	1804	Dec. 22	Cincinnati	07	01	02
Hunt, Jesse(C)	1804	Dec. 22	Cincinnati	07	02	15
Hunt, Jesse(C)	1804	Dec. 25	Cincinnati	08	04	30
Hunt, Jesse(C)	1804	Dec. 25	Cincinnati	08	04	23
Hunt, Jesse(C)	1804	Dec. 25	Cincinnati	08	03	07
Hunt, Jesse(C)	1804	Dec. 25	Cincinnati	07	03	06
Hunt, Jesse(C)	1804	Dec. 25	Cincinnati	07	03	14
Hunt, Jesse(C)	1804	Dec. 25	Cincinnati	07	03	28
Hunt, Jesse(C)	1804	Dec. 25	Cincinnati	07	04	33
Hunt, Jesse(C)	1804	Dec. 25	Cincinnati	07	02	20
Hunt, Jesse(C)	1804	Dec. 26	Cincinnati	08	04	10
Hunt, Jesse(C)	1804	Dec. 26	Cincinnati	08	04	12
Hunt, Jesse(C)	1804	Dec. 26	Cincinnati	08	03	03
Hunt, Jesse(C)	1804	Dec. 26	Cincinnati	07	01	07
Hunt, Jesse(C)	1804	Dec. 27	Cincinnati	08	11	05
Hunt, Jesse(C)	1804	Dec. 27	Cincinnati	07	03	07
Hunt, Jesse(C)	1804	Dec. 27	Cincinnati	08	03	21
Hunt, Jesse(C)	1804	Dec. 28	Cincinnati	07	03	22
Hunt, Jesse(C)	1804	Dec. 28	Greene	09	04	28
Hunt, Jesse(C)	1804	Dec. 29	Cincinnati	09	04	15
Hunt, Jesse(C)	1804	Dec. 29	Cincinnati	09	03	13
Hunt, Jesse(C)	1804	Dec. 29	Cincinnati	08	05	33
Hunt, Jesse(C)	1804	Dec. 29	Cincinnati	09	04	09
Hunt, Jesse(C)	1804	Dec. 31	Cincinnati	09	02	02
Hunt, Jesse(C)	1804	Dec. 31	Cincinnati	10	02	06
Hunt, Jesse(C)	1804	Dec. 31	Cincinnati	10	02	15
Hunt, Jesse(C)	1804	Dec. 31	Cincinnati	10	02	05
Hunt, Jesse(C)	1804	Dec. 31	Cincinnati	08	04	36
Hunt, Jesse(C)	1804	Dec. 31	Cincinnati	08	04	36
Hunt, Jesse(C)	1804	Dec. 31	Cincinnati	08	04	36
Hunt, Jesse(C)	1804	Dec. 31	Cincinnati	08	04	36
Hunt, Jesse(C)	1804	Dec. 31	Cincinnati	09	02	05
Hunt, Jesse(C)	1804	Dec. 31	Cincinnati	10	02	36
Hunt, Jesse(C)	1804	Dec. 31	Cincinnati	10	02	36
Hunt, Jesse(C)	1804	Dec. 31	Cincinnati	10	02	09
Hunt, Jesse(C)	1804	Dec. 31	Cincinnati	10	02	09
Hunt, Jesse(C)	1804	Dec. 31	Cincinnati	10	02	30
Hunt, Jesse(C)	1804	Dec. 31	Cincinnati	10	02	30
Hunt, Jesse(C)	1804	Dec. 31	Cincinnati	09	02	02
Hunt, Jesse(C)	1804	Dec. 31	Cincinnati	09	02	02
Hunt, Jesse(C)	1804	Dec. 31	Cincinnati	09	02	02
Hunt, Jesse(C)	1804	Dec. 31	Cincinnati	08	05	22
Hunt, Jesse(C)	1804	Dec. 31	Cincinnati	09	04	28
Hunt, Jesse(C)	1804	Dec. 31	Cincinnati	09	04	28
Hunt, Jesse(C)	1804	Dec. 31	Cincinnati	08	05	36
Hunt, Jesse(C)	1804	Dec. 31	Cincinnati	10	02	03
Hunt, Jesse(C)	1804	Dec. 31	Cincinnati	08	03	34
Hunt, Jesse(C)	1804	Dec. 31	Cincinnati	07	01	01
Hunt, Jesse(C)	1804	Dec. 31	Cincinnati	08	04	09
Hunt, Jesse(C)	1804	Dec. 31	Cincinnati	08	04	21
Hunt, Jesse(C)	1804	Dec. 31	Cincinnati	08	03	06
Hunt, Jesse(C)	1804	Dec. 31	Cincinnati	07	02	12
Hunt, Jesse(C)	1804	Dec. 31	Cincinnati	08	03	18
Hunt, Jesse(C)	1804	Dec. 31	Cincinnati	08	03	32
Hunt, Jesse(C)	1804	Dec. 31	Cincinnati	08	03	19
Hunt, Jesse(C)	1804	Dec. 31	Cincinnati	08	05	17
Hunt, Jesse(C)	1804	Dec. 31	Cincinnati	08	03	09
Hunt, Jesse(C)	1804	Dec. 31	Cincinnati	09	04	14
Hunt, Jesse(C)	1805	Dec. 06	Cincinnati	07	04	36
Hunt, Jesse(C)	1805	Dec. 06	Cincinnati	07	04	36
Hunt, Jesse(C)	1805	Dec. 06	Cincinnati	07	04	36
Hunt, Jesse(C)	1806	Feb. 06	Cincinnati	08	05	23
Hunt, Jesse(C)	1806	Feb. 11	Cincinnati	10	02	30
Hunt, Jesse(C)	1806	Feb. 11	Cincinnati	10	02	30
Hunt, Jesse(C)	1806	Feb. 11	Cincinnati	10	02	36
Hunt, Jesse(C)	1806	Feb. 11	Cincinnati	10	02	03
Hunt, Jesse(C)	1806	Feb. 11	Cincinnati	10	02	03
Hunt, Jesse(C)	1806	Feb. 11	Cincinnati	10	02	09

PURCHASER	YEAR	DATE	RESIDENCE	R	T	S
Hunt, Jesse(C)	1806	Feb. 11	Cincinnati	10	02	09
Hunt, Jesse(C)	1806	July 14	Cincinnati	08	03	09
Hunt, Jesse(C)	1810	Jan. 16	Cincinnati	07	01	07
Hunt, Jesse(C)	1811	April 09	Cincinnati	10	02	30
Hunt, Jesse(C)	1811	April 09	Cincinnati	10	02	36
Hunt, Jesse(C)	1813	Feb. 16	Hamilton	10	02	36
Hunt, Jesse(C)	1813	April 14	Cincinnati	08	05	17
Hunt, Jesse(C)	1813	April 14	Cincinnati	07	03	06
Hunt, Jesse(C)	1813	April 14	Cincinnati	07	03	22
Hunt, Jesse(C)	1813	April 14	Cincinnati	08	03	18
Hunt, Jesse(C)	1813	April 14	Cincinnati	08	05	33
Hunt, Jesse(C)	1813	April 14	Cincinnati	09	04	14
Hunt, Jesse(C)	1813	April 14	Cincinnati	09	04	15
Hunt, Jesse(C)	1813	April 14	Cincinnati	10	02	36
Hunt, Jesse(C)	1813	April 14	Cincinnati	09	02	02
Hunt, Jesse(C)	1813	April 14	Cincinnati	08	03	32
Hunt, Jesse(C)	1813	April 14	Cincinnati	08	03	18
Hunt, Jesse(C)	1813	April 14	Cincinnati	09	04	09
Hunt, Jesse(C)	1813	April 14	Cincinnati	09	02	02
Hunt, Jesse(C)	1813	April 14	Cincinnati	08	03	32
Hunt, Jesse(C)	1813	April 14	Cincinnati	10	02	21
Hunt, Jesse(C)	1813	April 14	Cincinnati	10	02	22
Hunt, Jesse(C)	1813	April 14	Cincinnati	10	02	05
Hunt, Jesse(C)	1813	April 14	Cincinnati	10	02	02
Hunt, Jesse(C)	1813	April 14	Cincinnati	08	05	27
Hunt, Jesse(C)	1813	April 14	Cincinnati	10	02	06
Hunt, Jesse(C)	1813	April 14	Cincinnati	10	02	15
Hunt, Jesse(C)	1814	Jan. 07	Cincinnati	10	02	24
Hunt, Jesse(C)	1814	Jan. 28	Cincinnati	08	05	17
Hunt, Jesse(C)	1814	April 12	Cincinnati	08	04	36
Hunt, Jesse(C)	1814	April 12	Cincinnati	07	03	04
Hunt, Jesse(C)	1814	Aug. 31	Cincinnati	07	03	04
Hunt, Jesse(C)	1815	Nov. 20	Cincinnati	09	04	26
Hunt, Jesse(C)	1816	March 06	Cincinnati	07	01	07
Hunt, Jesse(C)	1816	Aug. 01	Cincinnati	08	03	11
Hunt, Jesse(C)	1829	Dec. 11	Cincinnati	11	01	08
Hunt, Jesse(C)	1831	Aug. 08	Cincinnati	07	03	04
Hunt, Jesse(C)	1831	Aug. 08	Cincinnati	07	03	04
Hunt, Jessee(C)	1815	April 11	Cincinnati	07	01	07
Hunt, John(B)	1806	Sept. 27	Clermont	01	13	30
Hunt, John(B)	1813	Feb. 27	Warren	01	11	05
Hunt, John(B)	1813	April 14	Wayne(Ind)	01	12	06
Hunt, John(B)	1816	Feb. 08	Dearborn(Ind	01	04	19
Hunt, John(C)	1820	March 24	Miami	13	02	02
Hunt, Jonas(B)	1813	Feb. 27	Warren	01	11	05
Hunt, Jonathan(B)	1813	March 10	Franklin(Ind	01	08	19
Hunt, Lewis B.(B)	1836	Nov. 03	Dearborn(Ind	02	04	06
Hunt, Lewis W.(E)	1837	Feb. 18	Randolph(Ind	13	19	32
Hunt, Libni(B)	1814	Jan. 15	Wayne(Ind)	01	14	10
Hunt, Miles(E)	1833	Nov. 05	Randolph(Ind	13	19	27
Hunt, Miles(E)	1833	Dec. 02	Randolph(Ind	13	19	28
Hunt, Miles(E)	1834	July 01	Randolph(Ind	13	19	27
Hunt, Miles(E)	1836	Feb. 01	Randolph(Ind	13	19	32
Hunt, Miles(E)	1836	July 12	Randolph(Ind	13	19	34
Hunt, Miles(E)	1836	July 21	Randolph(Ind	13	19	34
Hunt, Miles(E)	1837	Feb. 18	Randolph(Ind	13	18	09
Hunt, Miles(E)	1837	Feb. 18	Randolph(Ind	13	18	01
Hunt, Phineas(C)	1814	March 07	Champaign	12	04	05
Hunt, Ralph(C)	1804	Dec. 31	Ohio	10	02	02
Hunt, Robert(B)	1815	July 27	Cincinnati	02	06	34
Hunt, Robert(B)	1815	July 27	Cincinnati	01	06	07
Hunt, Sam'l. F.(A)	1827	Aug. 20	Hamilton	02	11	15
Hunt, Sam'l. F.(A)	1827	Aug. 20	Hamilton	02	11	15
Hunt, Sam'l. F.(B)	1819	March 19	Cincinnati	03	05	01
Hunt, Samuel F.(B)	1817	Sept. 08	Cincinnati	03	10	36
Hunt, Samuel F.(B)	1817	Sept. 10	Cincinnati	01	09	15
Hunt, Samuel F.(B)	1817	Sept. 19	Hamilton	02	09	31
Hunt, Samuel F.(B)	1817	Sept. 19	Hamilton	02	09	31
Hunt, Samuel F.(E)	1817	Nov. 04	Cincinnati	13	11	20

PURCHASER	YEAR	DATE	RESIDENCE	R	T	S
Hunt, Samuel F.(E)	1817	Nov. 04	Cincinnati	13	11	21
Hunt, Samuel F.(E)	1817	Dec. 11	Cincinnati	13	11	28
Hunt, Samuel(A)	1805	Aug. 21	Warren	03	03	02
Hunt, Smith(B)	1808	Feb. 08	Dearborn(Ind	02	12	12
Hunt, Thomas(B)	1812	Oct. 05	Hamilton	01	06	24
Hunt, Timothy(B)	1814	Oct. 06	Wayne(Ind)	02	12	02
Hunt, William(B)	1808	Feb. 08	Dearborn(Ind	01	12	17
Hunt, William(B)	1816	April 22	Wayne(Ind)	01	15	25
Hunt, William(B)	1817	Oct. 20	Wayne(Ind)	01	15	28
Hunt, William(C)	1831	Aug. 19	Champaign	10	04	02
Hunt, William(E)	1831	July 04	Randolph(Ind	13	19	21
Hunt, William(E)	1833	Jan. 14	Randolph(Ind	13	19	17
Hunt, William(E)	1833	Jan. 14	Randolph(Ind	13	19	20
Hunt, William(E)	1836	Feb. 01	Randolph(Ind	13	19	29
Hunter, George(C)	1806	July 24	Champaign	10	06	23
Hunter, Henry(B)	1813	April 14	Franklin(Ind	01	11	18
Hunter, Henry(B)	1814	March 26	Franklin(Ind	01	11	18
Hunter, Isaac Connely(A)	1836	Oct. 10	Clermont	01	15	22
Hunter, Isaac Connely(A)	1837	Feb. 10	Clermont	01	15	26
Hunter, James(B)	1834	Dec. 20	Hamilton	03	04	25
Hunter, James(B)	1835	Jan. 06	Hamilton	03	04	35
Hunter, John(A)	1817	June 24	Warren	02	12	10
Hunter, John(B)	1817	Aug. 26	Butler	02	03	26
Hunter, Joseph(A)	1811	Dec. 30	Miami	05	09	35
Hunter, Joseph(B)	1817	May 28	Hamilton	02	06	26
Hunter, Nathaniel(C)	1812	March 23	Madison	13	05	13
Hunter, Nathaniel(C)	1812	June 09	Madison	13	05	13
Hunter, Nathaniel(C)	1814	June 22	Champaign	13	05	13
Hunter, Nathaniel(C)	1814	July 23	Champaign	12	05	18
Hunter, Thomas(C)	1804	Dec. 29	Greene	07	02	10
Hunter, Thomas(C)	1804	Dec. 29	Greene	08	04	19
Hunter, Thomas(C)	1804	Dec. 29	Greene	08	04	19
Hunter, Thomas(C)	1804	Dec. 29	Greene	07	03	15
Hunter, Thomas(C)	1804	Dec. 29	Greene	08	03	17
Hunter, Thomas(C)	1804	Dec. 29	Greene	07	03	15
Hunter, Thomas(C)	1804	Dec. 29	Greene	07	03	15
Hunter, Thomas(C)	1804	Dec. 29	Greene	07	03	03
Hunter, Thomas(C)	1804	Dec. 29	Greene	07	02	10
Hunter, Thomas(C)	1804	Dec. 29	Greene	08	04	19
Hunter, Thomas(C)	1804	Dec. 29	Greene	08	04	19
Hunter, Thomas(C)	1813	April 14	Cincinnati	07	04	33
Hunter, Thomas(C)	1813	April 14	Greene	07	03	03
Hunter, William(A)	1817	June 24	Warren	02	12	33
Hunter, William(C)	1801	Dec. 18	Hamilton	04	03	33
Hunter, William(C)	1804	Dec. 29	Hamilton	08	03	04
Hunter, William(C)	1804	Dec. 29	Hamilton	08	04	06
Hunter, William(C)	1804	Dec. 29	Hamilton	08	04	06
Hunter, William(C)	1804	Dec. 29	Hamilton	08	03	04
Hunter, William(C)	1804	Dec. 29	Hamilton	08	03	04
Hunter, William(C)	1804	Dec. 29	Hamilton	08	03	04
Hunter, William(C)	1805	Dec. 02	Champaign	10	06	17
Huntington, Jonathan(B)	1814	Jan. 01	Hamilton	03	03	35
Huntington, Jonathan(B)	1815	Dec. 30	Dearborn(Ind	01	04	32
Huntington, Wm.(E)	1838	Oct. 30	Clark	13	21	23
Huntmann, Henry(E)	1836	Nov. 25	Kentucky	12	11	33
Huntsinger, Isaac(A)	1817	Nov. 11	Montgomery	04	10	05
Hunzinger, John(A)	1811	Jan. 21	Montgomery	05	03	22
Hurley, Cornelius(A)	1813	April 05	Miami	06	07	31
Hurley, Robert(A)	1813	April 05	Miami	05	09	25
Hurley, Thomas(A)	1813	April 05	Miami	05	09	36
Hurley, Thomas(A)	1818	Feb. 02	Miami	05	10	31
Hurley, Zachariah(A)	1818	Feb. 02	Miami	05	09	05
Hurley, Zadock(A)	1806	Aug. 26	Greene	05	06	35
Huron, Othneal(C)	1801	Dec. 30	Hamilton	04	03	22
Hurst, Perry(E)	1833	Oct. 12	Wayne(Ind)	13	17	04
Hurts, Zachariah(A)	1817	July 01	Jackson	04	04	08
Huser, Merrit(B)	1832	April 18	Switzerland	03	02	20
Huston, Alexander(C)	1801	Dec. 23	Hamilton	06	02	30
Huston, David(A)	1806	Sept. 08	Greene	02	11	28

PURCHASER	YEAR	DATE	RESIDENCE	R	T	S
Huston, David(A)	1806	Sept. 08	Greene	02	12	36
Huston, David(A)	1806	Sept. 08	Greene	03	10	27
Huston, David(C)	1806	Aug. 09	Greene	11	02	30
Huston, David(C)	1806	Aug. 09	Greene	11	02	24
Huston, David(C)	1806	Aug. 09	Greene	08	02	26
Huston, David(C)	1806	Aug. 09	Greene	08	02	26
Huston, David(C)	1806	Aug. 09	Greene	08	02	26
Huston, David(C)	1806	Aug. 09	Greene	08	02	26
Huston, David(C)	1822	April 19	Greene	13	02	31
Huston, David(C)	1824	June 07	Greene	11	02	29
Huston, James(A)	1805	Feb. 26	Montgomery	01	06	31
Huston, James(B)	1807	June 27	Pennsylvania	01	04	18
Huston, James(B)	1813	Dec. 07	Hamilton	01	11	14
Huston, John(A)	1821	April 16	Darke	01	10	35
Huston, John(B)	1807	June 16	Dearborn(Ind	01	04	18
Huston, John(C)	1801	Nov. 26	Hamilton	06	02	18
Huston, John(C)	1813	April 14	Champaign	11	05	18
Huston, Joseph(A)	1808	Aug. 11	Pennsylvania	02	03	12
Huston, Matthew(A)	1801	April 27	Hamilton	02	04	01
Huston, Matthew(A)	1801	April 27	Hamilton	05	01	05
Huston, Matthew(A)	1801	April 27	Hamilton	03	02	09
Huston, Matthew(A)	1805	Sept. 16	Butler	02	04	12
Huston, Matthew(A)	1805	Dec. 10	Butler	02	05	35
Huston, Matthew(C)	1804	Dec. 26	Butler	10	01	10
Huston, Paul(A)	1812	June 23	Hamilton	01	03	12
Huston, Paul(A)	1813	June 18	Hamilton	02	03	07
Huston, Paul(B)	1818	June 23	Hamilton	03	07	23
Huston, Priscilla(B)	1816	Aug. 06	Hamilton	02	05	24
Huston, Robert(B)	1818	Aug. 07	Hamilton	03	05	25
Huston, Samuel(A)	1805	Feb. 26	Montgomery	01	06	31
Huston, Samuel(A)	1812	June 23	Hamilton	01	04	33
Huston, Samuel(B)	1807	June 27	Pennsylvania	01	04	17
Huston, Samuel(B)	1816	Aug. 14	Hamilton	01	10	34
Huston, Samuel(B)	1816	Aug. 14	Hamilton	01	10	33
Huston, Samuel(C)	1801	Dec. 31	Hamilton	05	02	02
Huston, Tenent(B)	1818	Aug. 07	Hamilton	03	05	25
Hutch, William S.(C)	1814	Aug. 09	Cincinnati	08	06	23
Hutchens, Benj'm.(E)	1814	Sept. 10	Wayne(Ind)	14	18	31
Hutchens, Benj'n.(A)	1827	Sept. 26	Montgomery	04	06	01
Hutchens, Benj'n.(E)	1830	Nov. 22	Wayne(Ind)	13	17	02
Hutchens, Benjamin(E)	1830	Oct. 25	Wayne(Ind)	13	18	35
Hutchens, Benjamin(E)	1830	Oct. 25	Wayne(Ind)	13	17	02
Hutchens, Denson(E)	1831	Feb. 07	Wayne(Ind)	13	18	24
Hutchens, Jesse(E)	1838	Feb. 13	Montgomery	15	22	11
Hutchens, Jesse(E)	1838	May 21	Montgomery	15	22	30
Hutchens, Jesse(E)	1838	May 21	Montgomery	15	22	19
Hutchens, Jesse(E)	1838	May 21	Montgomery	14	22	26
Hutchens, Jonath'n.(E)	1828	Nov. 20	Wayne(Ind)	13	18	24
Hutchens, Jonathan(E)	1837	March 27	Randolph(Ind	13	18	15
Hutchens, Josiah(E)	1836	Aug. 22	Randolph(Ind	15	20	30
Hutchin, Charles(A)	1835	May 18	Darke	02	12	21
Hutchins, Benj'n. Xenia(E)	1838	May 21	Montgomery	14	22	24
Hutchins, Benjamin(A)	1810	Dec. 15	Montgomery	06	03	29
Hutchins, David(E)	1836	Jan. 23	Randolph(Ind	13	18	09
Hutchins, Isaac(A)	1813	June 29	Montgomery	06	03	29
Hutchins, Isaac(E)	1811	Nov. 21	Montgomery	14	18	28
Hutchins, Isaac(E)	1816	Dec. 07	Montgomery	14	18	15
Hutchins, Isaac(E)	1838	May 21	Montgomery	14	22	26
Hutchins, John(E)	1838	May 21	Montgomery	15	22	19
Hutchins, Thomas(E)	1826	March 21	Wayne(Ind)	14	18	31
Hutchins, Wm.(E)	1838	May 21	Montgomery	15	22	20
Hutchinson, Milton(E)	1833	Jan. 18	Butler	13	11	31
Hutchinson, Milton(E)	1833	Jan. 28	Butler	13	11	31
Hutchinson, Sally(B)	1814	June 20	Dearborn(Ind	02	02	27
Hutchinson, Thomas(C)	1813	April 14	Champaign	09	06	27
Hutchison, Geo.(A)	1831	June 02	Miami	06	08	09
Hutchison, George(A)	1831	May 06	Miami	06	08	10
Hutsel, Joseph(C)	1814	Dec. 02	Miami	10	02	03
Hutton, Henry(A)	1818	July 01	Darke	02	10	29

PURCHASER	YEAR	DATE	RESIDENCE	R	T	S
Hutton, James(A)	1818	April 08	Kentucky	01	10	15
Hyland, Richard(B)	1832	Aug. 24	Cincinnati	02	07	26
Hymlick, Andrew(A)	1815	Aug. 28	Preble	02	08	12
Hysong, Abraham(A)	1816	July 10	Darke	04	09	18
Hyter, Abraham(B)	1819	Feb. 06	Dearborn(Ind	01	07	02
Iams, John(A)	1806	June 27	Butler	01	07	03
Icasanogle, Abraham(A)	1816	Feb. 23	Montgomery	02	09	26
Ice, Frederick Watts(B)	1834	April 15	Dearborn(Ind	02	08	34
Iddings, Benjamin(A)	1802	July 05	Hamilton	05	05	04
Iddings, Benjamin(A)	1804	Nov. 01	Montgomery	05	07	33
Iddings, Joseph(A)	1831	Jan. 24	Miami	05	07	35
Iddings, Talbot(A)	1816	June 17	Miami	02	11	03
Iddings, Tolburt(A)	1805	Jan. 15	Montgomery	05	06	27
Iddington, John(B)	1806	Nov. 03	Dearborn(Ind	01	14	20
Idel, Jacob(C)	1830	Jan. 04	Champaign	12	04	04
Idel, John(C)	1828	April 08	Champaign	12	04	10
Idel, John(C)	1828	Nov. 13	Champaign	12	04	11
Ifert, Jacob(A)	1837	Aug. 02	Montgomery	03	13	34
Ifert, Jacob(A)	1837	Sept. 20	Montgomery	03	13	34
Ifert, Jacob(A)	1837	Sept. 29	Montgomery	03	13	33
Ifert, Jacob(A)	1837	Oct. 05	Montgomery	03	13	34
Iff, John(B)	1836	July 25	Hamilton	02	09	31
Iff, John(B)	1837	March 25	Franklin(Ind	03	09	01
Ignew, Brant(A)	1812	April 21	Butler	01	03	28
Ignew, Brant(A)	1817	Aug. 01	Butler	01	03	28
Ignew, Joseph(A)	1812	April 21	Butler	01	03	28
Ihe, William(A)	1815	Oct. 18	Pickaway	06	08	31
Ike, Morris(A)	1816	March 09	Piqua	06	08	17
Ike, Philip(A)	1816	March 09	Piqua	06	08	17
Iler, Jacob G.(B)	1829	Oct. 14	Switzerland	02	01	05
Iliff, James(E)	1837	Sept. 21	Greene	15	21	05
Iliff, Wesley(E)	1837	Sept. 21	Greene	14	21	36
Iliff, Wm. T.(E)	1837	Sept. 21	Greene	15	21	05
Imel, Robert(B)	1835	Aug. 10	Switzerland	03	03	12
Imel, Thomas Walters(B)	1832	Nov. 30	Switzerland	03	03	12
Imlay, Caleb(A)	1817	June 09	Miami	05	09	25
Imrie, David(B)	1824	Sept. 09	Switzerland	03	03	18
Ince, James(B)	1818	Aug. 10	Cincinnati	02	06	13
Ince, James(B)	1818	Aug. 22	Cincinnati	02	05	11
Ingel, John(C)	1805	Aug. 09	Montgomery	06	02	11
Ingersull, Daniel(A)	1801	Sept. 25	Hamilton	02	01	06
Ingersull, Daniel(A)	1801	Sept. 25	Hamilton	01	01	01
Ingham, Deborah(A)	1809	Aug. 24	Pennsylvania	05	06	30
Ingle, Adam(A)	1831	Jan. 27	Miami	05	08	19
Ingle, Henry(A)	1834	June 20	Miami	04	09	18
Ingle, Matthias(A)	1829	May 20	Miami	05	08	21
Ingle, Matthias(A)	1831	June 17	Miami	04	09	20
Ingle, Michael(A)	1804	Nov. 15	Warren	05	05	13
Ingle, Michael(A)	1804	Nov. 15	Warren	05	07	07
Ingle, Michael(A)	1804	Nov. 15	Warren	05	08	20
Ingle, Michael(A)	1814	Oct. 14	Miami	05	08	17
Ingle, Michael(A)	1816	Dec. 07	Miami	05	08	17
Ingle, Rhoda(E)	1836	Oct. 31	Cincinnati	15	22	33
Ingram, Andrew W.(A)	1818	Feb. 13	Butler	03	09	05
Ingram, Andrew W.(A)	1818	Nov. 05	Darke	03	09	06
Ingram, John(A)	1815	Dec. 08	Miami	06	07	17
Ingram, Thos. C.(A)	1818	Nov. 05	Darke	03	09	06
Inlow, Abraham(C)	1804	Oct. 26	Greene	08	04	06
Inlow, Abraham(C)	1804	Oct. 26	Greene	08	04	06
Inlow, Henry(E)	1838	March 27	Clark	14	22	23
Inlow, William(C)	1825	Dec. 16	Clark	08	05	29
Inman, Ahab(A)	1818	Jan. 29	Miami	04	07	02
Inman, Asa(A)	1807	Jan. 10	Montgomery	05	07	30
Inman, Eli(A)	1818	Feb. 23	Miami	04	08	25
Inman, Eli(A)	1828	Dec. 22	Miami	04	08	25
Inman, Eli(A)	1829	Dec. 25	Miami	04	08	25
Inman, John(B)	1817	Oct. 27	Cincinnati	03	06	10
Inman, John(C)	1826	Oct. 16	Clark	09	06	29
Inman, Samuel(A)	1831	May 03	Miami	04	08	24

163

PURCHASER	YEAR	DATE	RESIDENCE	R	T	S
Inman, Stephen(B)	1817	Nov. 01	Cincinnati	02	05	17
Insco, James(A)	1806	Sept. 01	Warren	05	05	01
Iodis, Daniel(C)	1805	Dec. 30	Ohio	10	04	23
Irby, John(B)	1837	Feb. 02	Switzerland	02	03	31
Irelan, Aaron(A)	1836	Sept. 27	Darke	02	14	34
Irelan, Ephraim(A)	1836	Sept. 27	Darke	02	14	34
Irelan, Ephraim(A)	1836	Sept. 27	Darke	02	14	27
Irelan, Moses(A)	1825	Dec. 30	Preble	02	09	15
Ireland, David(A)	1806	Aug. 08	Tennessee	01	09	17
Ireland, David(A)	1815	Dec. 22	Preble	01	09	17
Ireland, Henry(A)	1832	April 16	New York	04	07	18
Ireland, James Jr.(B)	1812	April 15	Preble	01	09	19
Ireland, James(A)	1806	March 21	Butler	01	09	30
Ireland, James(A)	1813	July 06	Hamilton	01	02	36
Ireland, John(B)	1805	Sept. 23	Kentucky	01	14	36
Ireland, Moses(A)	1831	April 12	Darke	02	10	32
Ireland, William(A)	1815	Dec. 08	Tennessee	01	09	19
Irick, Andrew(A)	1813	Oct. 11	Preble	02	09	32
Irigh, Peter(A)	1831	Jan. 01	Shelby	05	10	36
Irvin, Amos(A)	1831	Oct. 13	Montgomery	05	10	34
Irvin, Amos(A)	1831	Oct. 13	Montgomery	05	10	35
Irvin, George(E)	1836	Sept. 03	Randolph(Ind	14	19	10
Irvin, John C.(A)	1811	Aug. 13	Preble	02	06	02
Irvin, John Jr.(E)	1836	March 28	Randolph(Ind	14	19	04
Irvin, John(E)	1836	Jan. 28	Randolph(Ind	14	19	05
Irvin, Robert(E)	1835	May 01	Randolph(Ind	14	19	03
Irvin, Robert(E)	1836	April 21	Randolph(Ind	14	19	03
Irvin, Stephen M.(B)	1836	Sept. 17	Fayette	01	17	23
Irvin, William M.(B)	1836	Sept. 17	Clinton	01	17	13
Irwin, A.(C)	1827	Aug. 23	Cincinnati	08	02	02
Irwin, A.(C)	1827	Aug. 23	Cincinnati	08	02	02
Irwin, George(E)	1815	Jan. 20	Wayne(Ind)	12	16	02
Irwin, James(C)	1806	Aug. 21	Butler	09	02	15
Irwin, James(C)	1806	Aug. 21	Butler	09	02	15
Irwin, John(C)	1802	Dec. 27	Hamilton	06	03	34
Irwin, John(C)	1804	Dec. 28	Greene	08	04	32
Irwin, John(C)	1805	Dec. 27	Greene	08	04	26
Irwin, John(E)	1816	Dec. 02	Butler	13	16	07
Irwin, Morton(A)	1804	Nov. 30	Butler	02	05	17
Irwin, Robert I.(A)	1837	May 03	Butler	01	13	12
Irwin, Samuel(C)	1802	Dec. 28	Hamilton	06	02	21
Irwin, Thomas(A)	1805	Aug. 23	Butler	02	06	31
Irwin, Thomas(A)	1815	April 04	Butler	02	12	27
Irwin, Thomas(C)	1801	Dec. 02	Hamilton	04	02	09
Irwin, Thomas(C)	1801	Dec. 30	Hamilton	06	02	07
Irwin, Thomas(C)	1801	Dec. 31	Hamilton	04	02	10
Irwin, William(A)	1805	July 30	Hamilton	01	03	09
Irwin, William(A)	1812	April 15	Cincinnati	04	02	03
Irwin, William(A)	1812	April 15	Cincinnati	04	02	03
Irwin, William(A)	1817	Aug. 12	Butler	01	09	24
Irwin, William(B)	1806	May 19	Cincinnati	01	02	27
Irwin, William(D)	1809	May 15	Cincinnati(Fr	02	02	08
Irwin, William(E)	1811	Oct. 24	Ind.Territory	13	16	25
Irwin, William(E)	1812	May 05	Ohio	14	16	14
Irwin, Wm.(C)	1814	Feb. 10	Cincinnati	09	05	20
Irwin, Wm.(C)	1814	Feb. 10	Cincinnati	09	05	20
Irwin, Wm.(C)	1814	Feb. 10	Cincinnati	09	05	26
Irwin, Wm.(C)	1814	Feb. 10	Cincinnati	09	05	26
Ish, George(E)	1812	May 11	Wayne(Ind)	13	16	32
Ish, George(E)	1812	May 11	Wayne(Ind)	12	16	26
Ish, George(E)	1815	Feb. 28	Wayne(Ind)	13	16	29
Isiminger, George(A)	1802	Feb. 22	Hamilton	01	03	34
Isley, Conrod Senr.(A)	1818	March 10	Montgomery	03	06	19
Issenman, Joseph(B)	1833	June 04	Cincinnati	02	07	07
Ivers, William(A)	1824	June 08	Preble	03	03	15
Ives, Hoel(B)	1830	Jan. 05	Montgomery	01	16	36
Ivins, George(A)	1819	Dec. 14	Warren	04	05	19
Ivins, George(A)	1820	March 03	Warren	04	05	19
Ivins, George(A)	1824	June 29	Montgomery	04	05	19

PURCHASER	YEAR	DATE	RESIDENCE	R	T	S
Izer, Phillip(A)	1805	May 11	Montgomery	03	05	25
Jack, Adam(E)	1814	Jan. 24	Warren	12	15	27
Jack, Robert L.(C)	1814	Jan. 04	Warren	10	06	13
Jack, Robert L.(E)	1837	May 16	Warren	14	21	18
Jack, Samuel(B)	1816	March 21	Kentucky	01	02	11
Jack, Samuel(B)	1816	March 21	Kentucky	01	02	10
Jack, Samuel(B)	1831	Aug. 01	Switzerland	01	02	03
Jack, Samuel(C)	1814	Aug. 11	Virginia	14	03	20
Jackewayse, Clark(B)	1829	April 28	Switzerland	03	04	32
Jackman, Atwell(E)	1836	Jan. 25	Franklin(Ind	12	12	18
Jackman, William(B)	1814	June 07	Dearborn(Ind	02	08	12
Jackman, William(B)	1834	Feb. 20	Franklin(Ind	02	08	34
Jackson, Andrew Hy.(A)	1836	Sept. 07	Warren	03	11	22
Jackson, Andrew(E)	1828	Aug. 20	Preble	12	16	01
Jackson, Asa(B)	1833	Jan. 24	Dearborn(Ind	02	05	28
Jackson, Atwell(E)	1815	March 08	Hamilton	12	12	19
Jackson, Enoch Winchester(B)	1831	Sept. 01	Dearborn(Ind	01	06	21
Jackson, Enoch(B)	1817	June 23	Dearborn(Ind	01	06	01
Jackson, Ezekiel(B)	1815	Feb. 17	Dearborn(Ind	01	06	22
Jackson, Ezekiel(B)	1815	Feb. 17	Dearborn(Ind	01	06	22
Jackson, Ezekiel(B)	1817	July 10	Dearborn(Ind	01	07	31
Jackson, Ezekiel(B)	1830	Jan. 21	Dearborn(Ind	01	06	21
Jackson, Ezekiel(B)	1831	Sept. 01	Dearborn(Ind	01	06	21
Jackson, Ezekiel(B)	1831	Sept. 05	Dearborn(Ind	01	06	21
Jackson, Giles(A)	1822	Sept. 09	Miami	05	07	36
Jackson, Jacob(A)	1816	March 05	Miami	05	09	24
Jackson, Jacob(A)	1836	Sept. 07	Warren	03	11	22
Jackson, James(A)	1814	Jan. 25	Miami	05	09	24
Jackson, James(A)	1815	Aug. 30	Pickaway	01	09	33
Jackson, James(B)	1834	June 25	Randolph(Ind	01	16	02
Jackson, James(E)	1811	Nov. 14	Wayne(Ind)	12	15	14
Jackson, Jehu(E)	1819	March 13	Wayne(Ind)	13	19	33
Jackson, Jehu(E)	1819	June 17	Randolph(Ind	13	19	33
Jackson, John(A)	1805	March 06	Montgomery	03	04	13
Jackson, John(B)	1837	May 20	Dearborn(Ind	03	07	22
Jackson, John(C)	1804	Dec. 28	Greene	09	03	15
Jackson, John(C)	1814	Dec. 03	Miami	11	01	18
Jackson, Jos.(C)	1824	Nov. 19	Warren	11	02	11
Jackson, Jos.(C)	1825	Jan. 26	Warren	11	02	11
Jackson, Joseph(B)	1834	June 25	Randolph(Ind	01	16	03
Jackson, Joseph(E)	1831	June 01	Wayne(Ind)	13	18	22
Jackson, Mordecai(B)	1815	May 20	Switzerland	02	02	28
Jackson, Nathan(C)	1824	Nov. 19	Warren	11	02	11
Jackson, Nathan(C)	1825	Jan. 26	Warren	11	02	11
Jackson, Robt.(B)	1815	July 21	?	02	06	11
Jackson, William N.(B)	1836	March 12	Randolph(Ind	01	17	25
Jackson, William N.(B)	1836	June 20	Randolph(Ind	01	16	03
Jackson, William N.(B)	1836	Aug. 23	Randolph(Ind	01	17	25
Jackson, William N.(B)	1836	Dec. 21	Randolph(Ind	01	16	02
Jackson, William(E)	1819	Oct. 02	Randolph(Ind	14	21	21
Jacobs, Cadwallader(A)	1818	Dec. 02	Miami	04	10	13
Jacobs, Highland(B)	1834	Dec. 30	Franklin(Ind	02	08	15
Jacobs, Highland(B)	1835	March 06	Franklin(Ind	02	08	15
Jacobs, James(B)	1811	Dec. 14	Wayne(Ind)	01	13	11
Jacobs, James(E)	1817	June 10	Wayne(Ind)	14	21	08
Jacobs, James(E)	1817	July 18	Wayne(Ind)	14	21	18
Jacobs, Jasper(E)	1832	March 05	Darke	15	21	10
Jacobs, John(E)	1817	June 10	Wayne(Ind)	14	21	08
Jacobs, Mary Jane Beaty(E)	1834	April 10	Franklin(Ind	13	12	05
Jacobs, William(E)	1832	May 03	Fayette	12	13	19
Jacobs, Wm. T.(E)	1834	April 10	Franklin(Ind	13	12	05
Jacobus, John S.(B)	1833	Jan. 07	Decatur(Ind)	01	06	01
Jacoby, Henry(A)	1815	Oct. 30	Pennsylvania	01	09	23
Jacoby, Henry(A)	1815	Oct. 30	Pennsylvania	01	09	26
Jamason, George(C)	1804	Dec. 31	Greene	10	06	24
James, Benjamin(A)	1804	Nov. 26	Butler	03	03	09
James, Benjamin(A)	1807	Jan. 14	Dearborn(Ind	01	04	32
James, Benjamin(C)	1804	Dec. 31	Warren	05	03	25
James, David W.(C)	1829	Oct. 07	Greene	12	02	08

PURCHASER	YEAR	DATE	RESIDENCE	R	T	S
James, David(B)	1818	July 14	Cincinnati	02	08	18
James, David(E)	1811	Nov. 19	Franklin(Ind	13	13	27
James, Enoch Jr.(B)	1814	July 04	Dearborn(Ind	01	05	18
James, Enoch(B)	1814	July 04	Dearborn(Ind	01	05	07
James, Enoch(B)	1814	July 04	Dearborn(Ind	01	05	18
James, Evan B.(C)	1829	Oct. 07	Greene	12	02	13
James, Jesse(E)	1837	May 11	Wayne(Ind)	15	21	06
James, John(B)	1808	May 26	Dearborn(Ind	02	04	28
James, John(B)	1808	Nov. 05	Dearborn(Ind	02	04	22
James, John(B)	1814	Aug. 18	Dearborn(Ind	01	03	04
James, John(B)	1817	Oct. 23	Switzerland	03	02	29
James, John(C)	1802	Dec. 20	Hamilton	05	04	22
James, John(C)	1812	Aug. 19	Greene	09	06	13
James, John(E)	1818	Feb. 07	Wayne(Ind)	14	18	25
James, Joseph(C)	1805	Oct. 22	Warren	03	04	11
James, Julius(B)	1817	Oct. 24	Dearborn(Ind	02	03	14
James, Julius(B)	1818	Feb. 18	Dearborn(Ind	02	03	14
James, Levi(B)	1817	July 11	Cincinnati	02	02	14
James, Levi(B)	1817	July 12	Cincinnati	01	03	28
James, Levi(B)	1817	July 28	Cincinnati	01	02	31
James, Levi(B)	1817	Aug. 07	Cincinnati	01	02	23
James, Levi(B)	1819	Sept. 11	Cincinnati	01	03	28
James, Pinkney(B)	1816	Aug. 07	Dearborn(Ind	01	02	03
James, Richard(C)	1802	Dec. 20	Hamilton	05	04	31
James, Richard(C)	1804	Dec. 31	Warren	05	03	21
James, Richard(C)	1811	Dec. 05	Warren	09	06	01
James, Richard(C)	1811	Dec. 05	Warren	09	06	02
James, Thomas(B)	1818	Sept. 28	Cincinnati	02	08	28
James, William(C)	1801	Dec. 31	Hamilton	05	03	03
James, William(C)	1804	Dec. 31	Warren	05	03	21
James, William(C)	1806	May 08	Champaign	09	06	10
Jamison, James(C)	1804	Dec. 26	Greene	06	02	12
Janes, Samuel(A)	1824	June 08	Darke	01	10	31
Jaqua, Darius(A)	1824	June 22	Preble	01	09	15
Jaqua, Judson(A)	1832	May 23	Darke	02	10	31
Jaquith, Asa(B)	1828	Nov. 06	Dearborn(Ind	02	06	25
Jarber, Philip(C)	1804	Dec. 28	Greene	10	05	33
Jarman, Azariah(B)	1818	March 18	Hamilton	03	05	10
Jarrell, Elisha Jr.(E)	1836	Nov. 14	Kentucky	14	19	05
Jarrell, Manliff(E)	1835	April 10	Wayne(Ind)	14	19	27
Jarrett, Bentley(E)	1829	Sept. 15	Wayne(Ind)	14	15	05
Jarrett, Bently(E)	1829	May 13	Miami	14	15	05
Jarrett, Eli(E)	1826	Jan. 12	Wayne(Ind)	14	15	18
Jarrett, George(E)	1817	Oct. 20	Wayne(Ind)	14	15	08
Jarrett, Levi(E)	1817	Oct. 20	Wayne(Ind)	14	15	08
Jasen, John(B)	1816	June 11	Wayne(Ind)	02	08	14
Jatter, Tobias(E)	1837	Feb. 22	Ohio	15	22	08
Jay, Elijah(A)	1831	July 20	Miami	04	08	24
Jay, Evan(E)	1836	Oct. 10	Randolph(Ind	13	18	13
Jay, Isaac(A)	1818	April 08	Darke	03	09	19
Jay, Isaac(A)	1832	May 24	Darke	03	09	19
Jay, James(A)	1818	April 21	Miami	06	04	18
Jay, James(E)	1821	Dec. 28	Clinton	14	18	28
Jay, Jesse(A)	1811	Dec. 11	Miami	05	06	25
Jay, Jesse(A)	1832	Jan. 04	Montgomery	04	06	05
Jay, Jesse(C)	1804	Sept. 24	Warren	05	03	08
Jay, John Senr.(A)	1817	Dec. 26	Miami	06	04	29
Jay, John(A)	1806	Sept. 01	Warren	05	06	36
Jay, John(A)	1806	Oct. 14	Warren	05	06	25
Jay, John(A)	1824	July 20	Miami	05	06	15
Jay, John(C)	1804	Dec. 31	Warren	05	03	08
Jay, John(E)	1817	Nov. 01	Warren	14	17	26
Jay, Samuel Junr.(A)	1832	Jan. 04	Montgomery	04	06	04
Jay, Samuel(A)	1806	Dec. 18	Warren	06	04	30
Jay, Samuel(A)	1818	July 10	Miami	06	04	18
Jay, Samuel(A)	1824	July 20	Miami	05	06	15
Jay, Samuel(A)	1832	Jan. 16	Miami	05	07	11
Jay, Samuel(A)	1832	Feb. 07	Miami	04	08	35
Jay, Samuel(A)	1832	Feb. 07	Miami	04	08	35

166

PURCHASER	YEAR	DATE	RESIDENCE	R	T	S
Jay, Samuel(E)	1817	Aug. 13	Miami	13	18	34
Jay, Stephen(C)	1805	July 20	Montgomery	06	02	36
Jay, Thomas(A)	1806	Sept. 01	Warren	05	05	02
Jay, Thomas(A)	1813	June 03	Miami	06	04	30
Jay, Walter D.(A)	1831	May 21	Miami	05	07	22
Jay, Walter Denny(A)	1831	Jan. 10	Miami	04	08	35
Jay, William(A)	1806	Oct. 14	Warren	05	06	06
Jay, William(A)	1811	April 08	Miami	04	07	24
Jay, William(A)	1816	March 26	Miami	05	07	21
Jay, William(A)	1816	Aug. 01	Miami	04	07	24
Jay, William(A)	1818	Sept. 29	Miami	05	07	27
Jay, William(A)	1828	Dec. 22	Miami	03	09	19
Jay, William(A)	1831	May 13	Miami	05	07	21
Jay, William(A)	1831	June 29	Miami	04	08	35
Jay, William(A)	1831	Oct. 17	Miami	05	07	14
Jay, William(A)	1831	Oct. 17	Miami	05	07	10
Jay, William(A)	1831	Dec. 28	Miami	05	07	23
Jefferies, William(A)	1817	Sept. 12	Miami	05	06	15
Jeffords, Richard(A)	1828	Aug. 09	Miami	05	09	22
Jeffrey, Joel(E)	1820	Aug. 12	Wayne(Ind)	14	18	34
Jeffrey, John(E)	1820	Aug. 23	New Jersey	14	18	34
Jeffrey, John(E)	1829	Oct. 26	Wayne(Ind)	14	18	23
Jeffrey, Thomas(E)	1835	April 08	Randolph(Ind	14	19	36
Jeffrey, Thomas(E)	1835	April 08	Randolph(Ind	15	19	31
Jelley, Sam'l. Montgom'y.(B)	1831	Aug. 09	Dearborn(Ind	01	04	33
Jelley, Samuel M.(B)	1815	May 20	Pennsylvania	01	04	34
Jellison, Henry Derry(B)	1835	June 16	Wayne(Ind)	01	16	13
Jellison, Sam'l.(B)	1830	June 25	Clermont	01	16	35
Jellison, Samuel(B)	1831	Oct. 01	Randolph(Ind	01	16	35
Jelly, Andrew(B)	1816	June 25	Hamilton	02	02	26
Jenings, James(C)	1829	Oct. 13	Warren	12	02	07
Jenkins, Crocker(B)	1832	May 30	Franklin(Ind	01	08	05
Jenkins, David(A)	1806	Aug. 08	Montgomery	06	04	04
Jenkins, David(A)	1806	Aug. 08	Montgomery	06	04	09
Jenkins, David(E)	1812	April 02	Pennsylvania	13	15	22
Jenkins, David(E)	1813	Dec. 25	Pennsylvania	12	15	23
Jenkins, Eli(A)	1806	Nov. 26	Montgomery	06	05	29
Jenkins, Elijah(A)	1813	May 31	Kentucky	01	06	06
Jenkins, Issachar(A)	1818	June 13	Miami	06	04	21
Jenkins, Jesse(A)	1805	Aug. 05	Warren	06	04	10
Jenkins, Jesse(A)	1806	July 28	Montgomery	06	04	09
Jenkins, Jesse(C)	1829	Feb. 03	Champaign	11	03	04
Jenkins, John D.(C)	1813	Aug. 11	Hamilton	09	06	35
Jenkins, Oren(B)	1832	June 23	Hamilton	01	08	05
Jenkins, Prince(B)	1814	Dec. 09	Cincinnati	01	08	06
Jenkins, William(A)	1809	June 26	Butler	01	03	21
Jenkins, William(A)	1813	April 19	Butler	01	02	34
Jenkins, William(A)	1814	April 07	Butler	01	03	20
Jenkins, William(E)	1838	May 21	Miami	14	22	26
Jenkinson, Francis(A)	1837	July 28	Darke	02	14	33
Jenkinson, Joseph(D)	1808	Nov. 01	Hamilton	01	03	08
Jenkinson, Joseph(E)	1811	Oct. 21	Cincinnati	12	12	10
Jenks, George(A)	1831	Aug. 23	Miami	04	07	03
Jenks, George(A)	1832	Jan. 30	Miami	04	07	03
Jenney, Abel(E)	1811	Oct. 25	Wayne(Ind)	13	17	26
Jennings, Henry(C)	1804	Dec. 29	Montgomery	09	02	01
Jennings, Levi(C)	1808	Jan. 13	Champaign	08	02	06
Jennings, Sarah(A)	1806	March 27	Montgomery	06	04	17
Jer, Francis(C)	1801	Dec. 22	Hamilton	04	03	05
Jessep, Isaac Junr.(E)	1816	Oct. 19	Wayne(Ind)	14	17	28
Jessop, Abraham(B)	1817	Aug. 01	Wayne(Ind)	01	14	26
Jessop, Hezekiah(B)	1820	Jan. 27	Wayne(Ind)	01	15	33
Jessop, Isaac(B)	1814	Nov. 29	Wayne(Ind)	01	14	24
Jessop, Isaac(E)	1816	Oct. 16	Wayne(Ind)	14	17	23
Jessop, Jacob Junr.(E)	1820	April 21	Randolph(Ind	14	19	24
Jessop, Jacob(B)	1812	April 08	Wayne(Ind)	01	14	26
Jessop, Jacob(B)	1817	Aug. 01	Wayne(Ind)	01	14	26
Jessop, Jacob(E)	1817	Sept. 08	Wayne(Ind)	14	17	10
Jessop, Nathan(E)	1816	Sept. 14	Wayne(Ind)	14	17	09

PURCHASER	YEAR	DATE	RESIDENCE	R	T	S
Jessop, Timothy(E)	1815	Jan. 03	Nor.Carolina	14	17	32
Jessop, William(B)	1831	April 28	Wayne(Ind)	01	17	35
Jessup, Asa(B)	1833	May 24	Switzerland	03	04	25
Jessup, David(B)	1834	April 11	Switzerland	02	03	29
Jessup, Eli(B)	1836	Sept. 23	Switzerland	02	03	29
Jessup, Ezra(B)	1837	Aug. 14	Switzerland	02	03	30
Jessup, Isaac(B)	1814	Sept. 17	Highland	01	14	13
Jessup, Isaac(B)	1833	Aug. 19	Switzerland	02	03	29
Jessup, Jonathan(E)	1814	Sept. 06	Wayne(Ind)	13	16	13
Jessup, Thomas S.	1808	March 01	?	?	?	?
Jessup, Thomas S.	1808	March 01	?	?	?	?
Jessup, Thomas S.	1808	March 02	Cincinnati	?	?	?
Jessup, Thomas S.(A)	1807	Sept. 29	Cincinnati	06	05	32
Jessup, Walter(B)	1834	Sept. 25	Switzerland	02	03	20
Jessup, Walter(B)	1836	July 08	Switzerland	03	04	25
Jessup, Walter(B)	1837	Dec. 29	Switzerland	03	04	25
Jeter, Fielding(E)	1811	Dec. 17	Franklin(Ind	12	12	26
Jeter, Fielding(E)	1834	Jan. 09	Franklin(Ind	13	11	14
Jeter, Fielding(E)	1834	Jan. 09	Franklin(Ind	13	11	15
Jeter, Fielding(E)	1836	Jan. 25	Franklin(Ind	13	11	15
Jeter, Fielding(E)	1836	Jan. 29	Franklin(Ind	13	11	14
Jeter, Fielding(E)	1836	Jan. 29	Franklin(Ind	13	11	22
Jeter, Lemuel(B)	1836	Feb. 04	Franklin(Ind	03	10	36
Jewell, John(E)	1836	Aug. 23	Butler	14	21	21
Jewett, Parker(E)	1835	June 15	NewHampshire	13	19	27
Jinks, Gideon(E)	1832	March 15	Franklin(Ind	12	12	21
Jinks, Gideon(E)	1832	March 15	Franklin(Ind	12	12	20
Jinks, Gideon(E)	1836	Feb. 06	Franklin(Ind	12	12	18
Job, James(E)	1812	Feb. 22	Hamilton	12	14	09
Job, Samuel(B)	1807	June 29	Montgomery	01	12	17
Job, Samuel(B)	1813	April 14	Wayne(Ind)	01	12	04
Job, Samuel(B)	1813	April 14	Wayne(Ind)	01	12	05
John, Benjamin(A)	1811	Oct. 05	Montgomery	05	04	21
John, Daniel(A)	1805	Sept. 19	Montgomery	03	05	30
John, David(A)	1810	July 06	Montgomery	05	04	22
John, David(A)	1810	Aug. 16	Montgomery	05	04	22
John, David(A)	1811	Oct. 05	Montgomery	05	04	21
John, Enoch D.(A)	1814	Jan. 21	Butler	01	04	19
John, Enoch D.(B)	1814	June 21	?	01	09	08
John, Enoch D.(B)	1814	June 21	?	01	09	20
John, James(C)	1804	Sept. 24	Greene	07	03	29
John, James(C)	1804	Sept. 24	Greene	07	03	29
John, Joseph(A)	1811	Nov. 28	Montgomery	05	04	21
John, Robert(A)	1813	Sept. 30	Butler	01	04	32
John, Robert(B)	1814	June 21	?	01	09	17
John, Robert(B)	1814	June 21	?	01	09	17
John, Thomas(C)	1801	Dec. 18	Hamilton	07	02	13
John, Thomas-Heirs(C)	1801	Dec. 17	Hamilton	07	02	01
John, Washington D.(A)	1837	June 12	Montgomery	03	11	22
John, Wm. Littell(A)	1832	June 22	Warren	02	10	23
Johnson, Abel(B)	1818	May 19	Switzerland	03	05	27
Johnson, Abel(B)	1839	June 17	Dearborn(Ind	03	05	27
Johnson, Alexander Senr.(A)	1836	Dec. 06	Montgomery	04	11	18
Johnson, Alexander Senr.(E)	1837	Feb. 24	Montgomery	14	20	11
Johnson, Benjamin(B)	1817	July 26	Greene	03	06	02
Johnson, Benjamin(B)	1817	July 26	Greene	03	06	01
Johnson, Benjamin(B)	1818	June 01	Virginia	01	11	15
Johnson, Caleb(B)	1816	May 03	Hamilton	02	07	26
Johnson, Casper(B)	1817	Oct. 11	Dearborn(Ind	01	07	32
Johnson, Cave(A)	1801	June 29	Kentucky	01	01	20
Johnson, Charles(A)	1814	Aug. 19	Preble	03	04	25
Johnson, Daniel(A)	1815	July 08	Butler	04	03	32
Johnson, Daniel(A)	1818	June 23	Butler	03	08	28
Johnson, David(B)	1818	Jan. 16	Dearborn(Ind	02	05	10
Johnson, Edward(B)	1816	April 29	Dearborn(Ind	02	07	11
Johnson, Edward(C)	1811	Sept. 18	Champaign	11	05	09
Johnson, Edward(C)	1816	Dec. 02	Champaign	11	05	09
Johnson, Edward(E)	1816	Nov. 04	Dearborn(Ind	12	13	26
Johnson, Edward(E)	1834	Dec. 26	Franklin(Ind	12	12	01

168

PURCHASER	YEAR	DATE	RESIDENCE	R	T	S
Johnson, Edward(E)	1834	Dec. 26	Franklin(Ind	12	12	02
Johnson, Edward(E)	1836	Jan. 30	Franklin(Ind	12	12	11
Johnson, Edward(E)	1836	Aug. 22	Montgomery	15	21	28
Johnson, Elias H.(A)	1836	Nov. 25	Hamilton	02	13	33
Johnson, Elizabeth(A)	1836	Nov. 15	Hamilton	03	11	02
Johnson, George H.(B)	1837	May 16	Dearborn(Ind	03	06	01
Johnson, George(B)	1812	Jan. 03	Clark	02	10	21
Johnson, Griffin(C)	1832	Jan. 20	Logan	13	03	35
Johnson, Hadley D.(E)	1837	May 04	Franklin(Ind	13	11	23
Johnson, Henry(B)	1836	April 02	Dearborn(Ind	03	06	02
Johnson, Henry(E)	1832	May 28	Randolph(Ind	13	19	11
Johnson, Isaac M.(E)	1814	Oct. 24	Franklin(Ind	13	13	23
Johnson, Jacob E.(B)	1836	Sept. 02	Dearborn(Ind	03	05	02
Johnson, Jacob E.(B)	1837	Feb. 06	Dearborn(Ind	03	05	01
Johnson, Jacob(A)	1813	March 15	Butler	01	03	08
Johnson, Jacob(E)	1833	March 02	Montgomery	15	21	33
Johnson, Jacob(E)	1836	Sept. 23	Randolph(Ind	15	21	33
Johnson, Jacob(E)	1837	April 10	Randolph(Ind	15	21	33
Johnson, James F.(B)	1834	April 15	Dearborn(Ind	03	04	13
Johnson, James P.(B)	1837	Feb. 27	Dearborn(Ind	03	05	27
Johnson, James Riley(A)	1831	Nov. 07	Montgomery	05	10	28
Johnson, James(A)	1804	Dec. 20	Kentucky	03	04	25
Johnson, James(A)	1831	Sept. 19	Warren	03	08	30
Johnson, James(C)	1804	Sept. 03	Warren	05	02	08
Johnson, Jane(A)	1836	Nov. 15	Hamilton	03	12	28
Johnson, Jesse(C)	1816	Dec. 02	Champaign	11	05	14
Johnson, Jesse(E)	1816	Nov. 28	Warren	14	18	02
Johnson, Jesse(E)	1817	Oct. 02	Warren	14	18	11
Johnson, Jesse(E)	1818	April 29	Randolph(Ind	14	18	01
Johnson, Jesse(E)	1835	Feb. 19	Randolph(Ind	14	18	03
Johnson, Jesse(E)	1836	April 04	Montgomery	14	19	12
Johnson, John(B)	1818	Sept. 22	Kentucky	02	02	21
Johnson, John(E)	1835	March 17	Montgomery	15	21	28
Johnson, John(E)	1836	July 07	Randolph(Ind	14	19	35
Johnson, Jonathan(E)	1836	March 28	Randolph(Ind	13	20	36
Johnson, Jonathan(E)	1836	Oct. 11	Highland	14	19	21
Johnson, Joshua(A)	1836	Dec. 06	Miami	04	11	18
Johnson, Josiah(E)	1828	March 29	Wayne(Ind)	13	18	27
Johnson, Josiah(E)	1829	May 01	Wayne(Ind)	13	18	22
Johnson, Mary(A)	1814	Nov. 30	Montgomery	06	03	10
Johnson, Moses(B)	1836	March 07	Dearborn(Ind	02	03	07
Johnson, Moses(B)	1836	May 07	Dearborn(Ind	02	03	07
Johnson, Nathan(B)	1817	July 12	Dearborn(Ind	02	05	30
Johnson, Nathan(B)	1817	Dec. 22	Dearborn(Ind	02	05	29
Johnson, Samuel(C)	1818	Oct. 19	Hamilton	11	03	35
Johnson, Samuel(C)	1818	Oct. 19	Hamilton	11	03	34
Johnson, Shepherd(A)	1832	March 01	Hamilton	01	02	31
Johnson, Silas(E)	1831	June 30	Randolph(Ind	14	18	11
Johnson, Stephen(E)	1815	May 25	Wayne(Ind)	14	17	05
Johnson, Thomas(C)	1825	Oct. 26	Champaign	12	04	15
Johnson, Thos. H.(E)	1838	Oct. 01	Cincinnati	14	20	10
Johnson, Will'm.(E)	1821	Sept. 11	Miami	14	19	22
Johnson, William(B)	1832	Dec. 18	Dearborn(Ind	03	05	28
Johnson, William(C)	1816	Jan. 08	Montgomery	13	01	02
Johnson, Young(B)	1836	Jan. 19	Dearborn(Ind	03	05	21
Johnson, Young(B)	1836	July 29	Dearborn(Ind	03	05	26
Johnson, Zenas(C)	1816	Dec. 12	Champaign	09	06	25
Johnston, Abraham(B)	1817	Oct. 20	Dearborn(Ind	02	03	07
Johnston, Andrew(C)	1816	Jan. 30	Miami	11	01	18
Johnston, Andrew(C)	1818	Nov. 27	Champaign	10	03	09
Johnston, Archibald(E)	1813	Aug. 30	Dearborn(Ind	12	14	12
Johnston, Arwaker(C)	1818	June 01	Champaign	13	03	31
Johnston, Benjm.(C)	1812	Nov. 05	Champaign	12	05	21
Johnston, Cave(B)	1801	Aug. 22	Kentucky	01	07	13
Johnston, Charles(B)	1816	March 30	Switzerland	04	02	26
Johnston, Charles(C)	1813	May 03	Champaign	15	02	07
Johnston, Charles(C)	1818	April 02	Champaign	13	02	21
Johnston, Daniel(A)	1807	Feb. 27	Butler	04	02	04
Johnston, Daniel(A)	1812	April 15	Butler	04	02	04

169

PURCHASER	YEAR	DATE	RESIDENCE	R	T	S
Johnston, Edward(C)	1817	Aug. 01	Champaign	11	05	03
Johnston, Edward(D)	1813	Dec. 25	Hamilton	01	02	11
Johnston, Eli(A)	1807	Sept. 25	Butler	02	03	02
Johnston, Francis(A)	1813	July 05	Miami	06	08	32
Johnston, Freder'k.(C)	1818	Nov. 27	Champaign	10	03	09
Johnston, Gabriel(B)	1818	March 14	Switzerland	03	03	06
Johnston, Gawin(A)	1813	Jan. 13	Preble	01	09	34
Johnston, Geo. C.(A)	1830	June 12	Miami	05	08	23
Johnston, George(A)	1818	March 03	Miami	05	09	17
Johnston, George(B)	1818	Dec. 17	Dearborn(Ind	02	05	05
Johnston, George(B)	1834	June 03	Dearborn(Ind	02	05	09
Johnston, Henry(A)	1806	Sept. 06	Montgomery	03	07	23
Johnston, Henry(A)	1806	Oct. 21	Montgomery	02	08	20
Johnston, Henry(A)	1811	Dec. 11	Preble	02	08	20
Johnston, Isaac T.(B)	1819	Jan. 02	Montgomery	03	06	26
Johnston, James Junr.(C)	1807	Sept. 25	Greene	09	03	12
Johnston, James W.(C)	1813	July 10	Champaign	14	03	04
Johnston, James(A)	1812	Feb. 03	Miami	06	07	30
Johnston, James(A)	1812	Feb. 03	Miami	06	07	19
Johnston, James(A)	1813	April 23	Miami	05	08	11
Johnston, James(A)	1813	April 23	Miami	05	09	24
Johnston, James(A)	1816	April 06	Miami	06	07	19
Johnston, James(A)	1818	March 03	Miami	05	09	17
Johnston, James(B)	1813	April 14	Wayne(Ind)	01	13	04
Johnston, James(B)	1814	April 04	Wayne(Ind)	01	15	33
Johnston, James(C)	1809	Dec. 12	Warren	05	02	08
Johnston, James(C)	1813	April 14	Champaign	09	06	15
Johnston, James(C)	1814	Feb. 02	Champaign	09	06	08
Johnston, James(C)	1816	Aug. 03	Champaign	09	03	05
Johnston, Jane(A)	1813	Dec. 03	Pennsylvania	05	08	03
Johnston, Jesse(A)	1810	Nov. 26	Montgomery	06	03	03
Johnston, Jesse(C)	1813	April 01	Champaign	11	05	08
Johnston, Jesse(E)	1811	Nov. 02	Warren	14	17	18
Johnston, John Jnr.(A)	1813	March 30	Miami	05	09	25
Johnston, John(A)	1808	June 06	FortWayneInd	05	08	02
Johnston, John(A)	1815	March 18	Miami	06	08	32
Johnston, John(A)	1819	Dec. 27	Miami	05	08	23
Johnston, John(A)	1832	March 15	Shelby	07	01	09
Johnston, John(B)	1814	Jan. 14	Butler	02	10	04
Johnston, John(B)	1814	Sept. 29	Dearborn(Ind	02	05	10
Johnston, John(B)	1833	Jan. 05	Hamilton	02	08	23
Johnston, John(C)	1813	July 01	Miami	10	02	04
Johnston, John(C)	1820	April 12	Miami	11	01	35
Johnston, John(E)	1816	March 02	Wayne(Ind)	14	18	09
Johnston, Jonathan(C)	1804	Dec. 28	Montgomery	09	02	05
Johnston, Lewis(E)	1811	Oct. 22	Ind.Territry	12	14	14
Johnston, Lewis(E)	1811	Oct. 22	Ind.Territry	12	14	15
Johnston, Lewis(E)	1811	Oct. 28	Franklin(Ind	12	14	23
Johnston, Mehalah(A)	1806	Dec. 26	Butler	01	04	06
Johnston, Phineas J.(B)	1818	May 28	Franklin(Ind	02	08	29
Johnston, Robert(A)	1818	March 03	Miami	05	09	17
Johnston, Robert(A)	1819	May 10	Miami	05	09	09
Johnston, Samuel(A)	1806	Dec. 03	Butler	01	03	10
Johnston, Stephen(A)	1809	Oct. 30	Ind.Territory	05	08	01
Johnston, Stephen(A)	1818	Aug. 26	Miami	05	09	32
Johnston, Thos.(E)	1830	Feb. 05	Randolph(Ind	13	19	13
Johnston, William(A)	1814	Dec. 14	Miami	05	09	27
Johnston, William(A)	1820	Dec. 19	Shelby	05	09	18
Johnston, William(B)	1812	Feb. 08	Dearborn(Ind	01	02	27
Johnston, William(B)	1816	May 08	Switzerland	04	02	36
Jolly, Lewis(B)	1829	Feb. 04	Dearborn(Ind	01	07	22
Jonas, John(A)	1830	Jan. 28	Montgomery	03	06	01
Jones, Abijah(A)	1806	Oct. 13	Greene	05	07	31
Jones, Abijah(E)	1814	March 21	Miami	14	17	02
Jones, Abner(B)	1831	Jan. 25	Wayne(Ind)	01	15	22
Jones, Abraham(A)	1836	June 29	Darke	01	15	24
Jones, Abraham(B)	1808	Jan. 13	Hamilton	01	10	36
Jones, Amos(B)	1834	July 01	BeaverCo.Pa.	03	08	13
Jones, Amos(B)	1834	July 01	BeaverCo.Pa.	03	08	13

170

PURCHASER	YEAR	DATE	RESIDENCE	R	T	S
Jones, Andrew(B)	1813	Sept. 08	Wayne(Ind)	01	12	11
Jones, Andrew(B)	1827	March 01	Union(Ind)	01	12	15
Jones, Benjamin(C)	1801	Dec. 19	Hamilton	04	03	06
Jones, Benjamin(C)	1813	Sept. 01	Champaign	09	05	02
Jones, Charles(A)	1822	Nov. 09	Miami	04	08	01
Jones, Charles(A)	1825	Jan. 03	Preble	02	06	22
Jones, Christopher(B)	1815	Jan. 21	Kentucky	01	02	03
Jones, Daniel(A)	1810	Dec. 15	Montgomery	06	03	32
Jones, Daniel(C)	1806	Feb. 11	Champaign	11	06	28
Jones, Daniel(C)	1812	Sept. 30	Champaign	09	07	31
Jones, Daniel(C)	1817	Dec. 02	Champaign	09	07	31
Jones, Daniel(E)	1818	June 04	Warren	13	18	11
Jones, Daniel(E)	1818	June 04	Warren	13	18	11
Jones, Daniel(E)	1831	Feb. 15	Wayne(Ind)	13	18	33
Jones, David M.(A)	1823	Sept. 20	Miami	04	07	26
Jones, David M.(A)	1824	May 19	Miami	04	07	23
Jones, David(B)	1815	Jan. 11	Butler	01	10	33
Jones, David(C)	1813	Sept. 01	Champaign	09	05	08
Jones, David(C)	1815	Nov. 21	Champaign	10	04	35
Jones, David(C)	1817	Aug. 01	Champaign	13	05	35
Jones, Edward(E)	1815	Oct. 20	Franklin(Ind	12	12	09
Jones, Eliakim(B)	1818	July 02	Dearborn(Ind	03	06	23
Jones, Elisha Baldwin(E)	1835	Nov. 05	Franklin(Ind	13	11	31
Jones, Elisha(A)	1824	June 08	Miami	05	06	15
Jones, Elizabeth(E)	1836	Dec. 01	Franklin(Ind	13	11	17
Jones, Francis(A)	1804	Nov. 10	Montgomery	05	06	29
Jones, Francis(A)	1831	Aug. 15	Miami	04	07	04
Jones, Garret(E)	1820	Sept. 22	Butler	13	12	27
Jones, George W.(E)	1818	July 22	Cincinnati	11	11	36
Jones, George Washington(A)	1832	May 17	Butler	02	10	29
Jones, George(A)	1814	Oct. 06	Preble	03	04	18
Jones, George(A)	1814	Oct. 12	Preble	03	04	19
Jones, George(B)	1806	Nov. 10	Butler	01	13	26
Jones, George(B)	1806	Nov. 10	Butler	01	13	27
Jones, George(C)	1816	March 11	Champaign	10	06	13
Jones, Hillary(E)	1816	Nov. 02	Wayne(Ind)	14	15	07
Jones, Hubbard(B)	1815	July 29	Dearborn(Ind	02	03	06
Jones, Hubbard(B)	1817	Nov. 15	Dearborn(Ind	02	04	31
Jones, Hubbard(B)	1830	March 16	Dearborn(Ind	02	04	31
Jones, Isaac(A)	1815	July 29	Montgomery	02	06	24
Jones, Isaac(B)	1836	March 23	Dearborn(Ind	03	05	22
Jones, Jacob(C)	1812	July 31	Greene	08	05	27
Jones, James B.(B)	1817	Oct. 03	Hamilton	02	04	07
Jones, James Burroughs(B)	1818	May 13	Hamilton	03	05	11
Jones, James Jnr.(B)	1816	June 03	Franklin(Ind	01	08	31
Jones, James Jr.(B)	1814	Oct. 05	Dearborn(Ind	01	07	27
Jones, James Jun.(B)	1815	May 13	Franklin(Ind	02	08	36
Jones, James Senr.(B)	1816	Jan. 31	Dearborn(Ind	01	07	03
Jones, James Senr.(B)	1816	Oct. 26	Dearborn(Ind	01	07	03
Jones, James(B)	1810	Dec. 10	Dearborn(Ind	01	07	04
Jones, Jeremiah Cogswell(A)	1836	July 19	Darke	01	15	20
Jones, Jeremiah(C)	1831	Sept. 29	Champaign	13	04	14
Jones, Jeremiah(C)	1831	Dec. 17	Champaign	13	04	21
Jones, Jesse(A)	1832	Aug. 13	Miami	04	07	09
Jones, John(A)	1823	Sept. 20	Miami	04	07	26
Jones, John(A)	1830	May 17	Miami	04	08	35
Jones, John(B)	1816	Aug. 26	Hamilton	02	05	33
Jones, John(B)	1817	June 28	Hamilton	02	05	32
Jones, John(C)	1812	July 31	Greene	08	05	27
Jones, John(E)	1816	Nov. 02	Wayne(Ind)	13	15	12
Jones, John(E)	1815	May 03	Virginia	13	18	18
Jones, John(E)	1830	Aug. 27	Randolph(Ind	15	21	21
Jones, Jonathan(A)	1806	March 12	Pennsylvania	01	04	11
Jones, Jonathan(A)	1806	March 14	Pennsylvania	01	04	12
Jones, Jonathan(A)	1806	March 14	Pennsylvania	01	04	02
Jones, Jonathan(A)	1806	Sept. 02	Hamilton	01	04	12
Jones, Jonathan(A)	1806	Oct. 30	Hamilton	01	04	03
Jones, Jonathan(C)	1832	Feb. 02	Clark	13	04	29
Jones, Jonathan(C)	1832	Feb. 02	Clark	13	04	15

PURCHASER	YEAR	DATE	RESIDENCE	R	T	S
Jones, Joseph(A)	1813	Aug. 21	Miami	06	04	22
Jones, Joshua(E)	1836	Sept. 06	Franklin(Ind	11	11	35
Jones, Justice(C)	1811	Dec. 11	Champaign	11	06	32
Jones, Justus(C)	1806	July 11	Champaign	11	06	34
Jones, Justus(C)	1806	July 30	Champaign	11	06	32
Jones, Keziah(A)	1818	Oct. 05	Montgomery	06	03	05
Jones, Levi(A)	1806	June 25	Nor.Carolina	03	04	08
Jones, Levi(A)	1811	Aug. 13	Preble	03	04	08
Jones, Levi(A)	1811	Dec. 11	Preble	02	07	31
Jones, Lewis(B)	1805	July 15	Dearborn(Ind	01	02	27
Jones, Lewis(B)	1814	Aug. 02	Dearborn(Ind	01	02	17
Jones, Mauries(A)	1802	March 29	Hamilton	02	03	30
Jones, Michael(B)	1806	July 10	Ind.Territory	02	04	30
Jones, Michael(E)	1836	March 28	Randolph(Ind	14	19	05
Jones, Michael(E)	1836	Oct. 29	Randolph(Ind	14	19	08
Jones, Nathan(A)	1818	Nov. 06	Warren	01	07	21
Jones, Nathan(B)	1830	Oct. 15	Wayne(Ind)	01	15	22
Jones, Newton(A)	1805	July 23	Butler	03	04	34
Jones, Philip Junr.(B)	1811	July 20	Hamilton	01	09	09
Jones, Philip(E)	1828	May 23	Franklin(Ind	13	12	21
Jones, Philip(E)	1834	Oct. 01	Franklin(Ind	13	12	21
Jones, Richard(A)	1814	Sept. 20	Montgomery	06	03	20
Jones, Robert(C)	1829	March 16	Champaign	12	03	13
Jones, Robertson(B)	1810	March 16	Dearborn(Ind	01	08	30
Jones, Robertson(B)	1815	May 08	Franklin(Ind	02	08	34
Jones, Robertson(B)	1815	Nov. 13	Franklin(Ind	02	08	25
Jones, Sam'l.(A)	1816	Dec. 20	?	06	03	04
Jones, Samuel(A)	1805	July 06	Butler	03	03	03
Jones, Samuel(A)	1805	July 25	Montgomery	05	06	09
Jones, Samuel(A)	1816	Oct. 30	Miami	04	07	08
Jones, Samuel(A)	1817	Nov. 01	Miami	04	07	23
Jones, Samuel(E)	1816	Dec. 02	Wayne(Ind)	13	17	13
Jones, Sarah(E)	1817	Dec. 11	Hamilton	13	12	06
Jones, Seaborn(A)	1831	Aug. 10	Miami	04	07	23
Jones, Simpson(E)	1811	Oct. 23	Ind.Territory	13	11	04
Jones, Standford(E)	1834	Jan. 06	Franklin(Ind	13	12	22
Jones, Stephen(C)	1808	Jan. 18	Warren	09	06	07
Jones, Stephen(E)	1837	July 13	Miami	15	22	29
Jones, Thomas(A)	1831	April 04	Darke	04	07	08
Jones, Thomas(B)	1837	July 03	Pennsylvania	03	04	15
Jones, Tubal(A)	1813	Oct. 02	Butler	02	03	18
Jones, Wallace(A)	1815	Jan. 30	Miami	05	06	18
Jones, Wiley(A)	1828	Oct. 04	Miami	04	09	29
Jones, William Henry(C)	1831	Sept. 20	Champaign	11	03	30
Jones, William S.(B)	1814	April 18	Wayne(Ind)	01	12	01
Jones, William(A)	1805	Sept. 02	Butler	01	06	25
Jones, William(A)	1808	Nov. 03	Butler	03	03	21
Jones, William(A)	1811	Aug. 13	Butler	03	03	17
Jones, William(A)	1811	Oct. 22	Butler	03	03	21
Jones, William(A)	1814	Oct. 06	Butler	02	06	13
Jones, William(A)	1814	Oct. 12	Preble	02	06	13
Jones, William(A)	1817	July 01	Miami	01	10	02
Jones, William(A)	1817	Sept. 27	Butler	03	03	22
Jones, William(A)	1824	June 08	Preble	03	04	21
Jones, William(B)	1806	Nov. 10	Nor.Carolina	01	13	26
Jones, William(B)	1808	Jan. 19	Butler	01	13	33
Jones, William(B)	1831	Aug. 16	Franklin(Ind	01	08	08
Jones, William(C)	1804	Sept. 03	Warren	04	03	29
Jones, William(C)	1806	Sept. 22	Champaign	09	06	10
Jones, William(C)	1811	Dec. 11	Champaign	09	06	10
Jones, William(C)	1812	July 31	Greene	08	05	27
Jones, William(C)	1830	Jan. 19	Champaign	12	04	23
Jones, William(E)	1816	Nov. 02	Wayne(Ind)	14	15	07
Jones, William(E)	1817	July 07	Warren	13	12	09
Jones, William(E)	1836	June 20	Franklin(Ind	14	11	24
Jones, Wm. D.(E)	1838	May 21	Montgomery	14	22	24
Joney, Hubbard(B)	1817	Nov. 15	Dearborn(Ind	02	04	31
Jordan, Daniel(E)	1837	July 17	Montgomery	14	21	24
Jordan, John(B)	1812	July 29	Wayne(Ind)	01	12	12

172

PURCHASER	YEAR	DATE	RESIDENCE	R	T	S
Jordan, John(B)	1814	Oct. 29	Wayne(Ind)	01	13	35
Jordan, John(B)	1814	Nov. 25	Wayne(Ind)	01	13	33
Jordan, John(E)	1815	April 21	Wayne(Ind)	13	18	19
Jordan, John(E)	1818	Feb. 17	Wayne(Ind)	13	18	20
Jordie, Cathrine(A)	1813	Aug. 24	Montgomery	04	05	02
Jordon, John(B)	1816	March 06	Hamilton	01	06	14
Joyce, James(D)	1812	Oct. 27	Hamilton	02	01	08
Joyce, James(D)	1812	Oct. 27	Hamilton	02	01	08
Judah, John(C)	1804	Dec. 31	Greene	08	03	13
Judah, John(C)	1806	Jan. 24	Greene	08	03	08
Judah, Martin(C)	1805	Dec. 16	Greene	09	05	13
Juday, John Jr.(A)	1826	June 05	Darke	02	11	29
Judd, Orrin(B)	1818	Aug. 12	Dearborn(Ind	01	07	08
Judd, Phinehas(B)	1818	Aug. 12	Dearborn(Ind	01	07	08
Juddy, John(C)	1802	Dec. 29	Hamilton	08	03	13
Judey, John(A)	1815	Oct. 16	?	03	07	31
Judy, Henry(A)	1829	July 06	Preble	01	11	27
Judy, Jacob(C)	1810	Oct. 26	Champaign	12	03	01
Judy, John Senr.(A)	1825	Jan. 06	Preble	02	09	15
Judy, John(A)	1811	Jan. 21	Preble	03	07	31
Judy, John(C)	1811	April 09	Champaign	08	03	08
Judy, Martin(C)	1811	April 09	Champaign	09	05	13
Julen, Azariah(A)	1806	Nov. 18	Montgomery	05	09	03
Julian, Isaac(E)	1817	July 08	Wayne(Ind)	13	16	26
Julian, Isaac(E)	1818	Jan. 19	Wayne(Ind)	14	20	23
Julian, Rene(E)	1818	Jan. 19	Wayne(Ind)	14	20	26
Julien, Arphaxed(A)	1837	March 29	Shelby	03	12	25
Julien, Azariah(A)	1813	Nov. 05	Miami	05	09	10
Julien, Isaac(B)	1808	Nov. 08	Dearborn(Ind	02	14	13
Julien, Isaac(E)	1811	Oct. 24	Wayne(Ind)	13	16	25
Julien, Jacob(E)	1811	Oct. 24	Wayne(Ind)	13	17	35
Julien, John B.(E)	1837	Nov. 20	Miami	15	22	21
Julien, John(E)	1814	Aug. 09	Franklin(Ind	12	13	13
Julien, Sam'l.(A)	1831	Feb. 07	Miami	08	01	21
Junken, James(E)	1813	Dec. 10	Wayne(Ind)	14	16	30
Junkin, William(E)	1817	Dec. 11	Wayne(Ind)	14	15	05
Justice, Jonathan(A)	1804	Dec. 11	Montgomery	05	05	35
Justice, Joseph(E)	1811	Oct. 22	Kentucky	12	14	33
Justis, Morton(B)	1818	Feb. 13	Hamilton	03	06	10
Justis, Morton(B)	1827	Aug. 21	Dearborn(Ind	03	06	10
Kaats, James S.(B)	1817	Aug. 06	Dearborn(Ind	02	06	01
Kain, John(C)	1805	April 15	Champaign	11	03	02
Kain, John(E)	1823	March 19	Hamilton	14	14	06
Kain, Maurice(A)	1807	April 18	Champaign	06	07	18
Kain, Maurice(C)	1807	April 17	Champaign	12	05	25
Kain, Samuel(B)	1813	Oct. 26	Warren	01	10	32
Kalmeyer, Henry(E)	1836	Oct. 21	Cincinnati	12	10	07
Kamp, Solomon(C)	1811	Nov. 11	Champaign	10	04	14
Kana, Patrick(A)	1836	Sept. 06	Montgomery	03	12	01
Kannady, John(B)	1814	Nov. 26	Butler	01	12	27
Karan, Peter(A)	1808	Sept. 13	Montgomery	06	04	06
Karan, Peter(A)	1808	Aug. 25	Montgomery	06	05	32
Karmann, Jacob(E)	1838	Aug. 09	Butler	14	22	35
Karn, Jacob(B)	1815	March 29	Pennsylvania	04	02	01
Karnes, David(E)	1836	June 08	Preble	14	19	14
Karns, Peter(A)	1818	Jan. 15	Miami	05	07	26
Karr, Hugh(A)	1804	Oct. 20	Hamilton	01	01	09
Kartner, George(A)	1836	Sept. 08	Darke	02	13	25
Kason, Isaac(C)	1804	Dec. 29	Greene	08	03	15
Kaster, Conrad(C)	1804	Sept. 03	Montgomery	05	02	11
Kaster, Conrod(A)	1812	Aug. 21	Preble	02	07	05
Kastor, Conrad(C)	1804	Sept. 03	Montgomery	05	02	11
Kaucher, Godfrey(A)	1831	May 16	Montgomery	01	12	09
Kaucher, Isaac(A)	1831	June 16	Darke	01	12	09
Kautz, Jacob(A)	1812	April 15	Cincinnati	06	03	34
Kautz, Jacob(C)	1805	June 13	Cincinnati	04	02	12
Kavanagh, Jas.(C)	1829	July 28	Champaign	12	04	12
Kavanagh, Matthew(C)	1814	March 08	Champaign	13	04	01
Kavenagh, James(C)	1830	Feb. 04	Champaign	12	04	06

173

PURCHASER	YEAR	DATE	RESIDENCE	R	T	S
Kayler, George(A)	1816	Dec. 03	Preble	02	08	02
Kayler, John F.(E)	1837	Nov. 20	Preble	14	21	32
Kaylor, John Junior(A)	1806	March 26	Montgomery	03	04	04
Kaylor, John(A)	1803	Nov. 10	Montgomery	05	03	13
Kaylor, John(A)	1803	Nov. 10	Montgomery	06	01	17
Kays, John(A)	1814	Aug. 23	Preble	02	07	20
Keais, William(E)	1837	Nov. 10	New Jersey	15	21	32
Kearn, George(A)	1805	Feb. 25	Hamilton	04	03	25
Kearns, Henry(A)	1831	Jan. 27	Miami	05	07	25
Keasbey, Debril(C)	1804	Dec. 29	Cincinnati	09	04	15
Keasby, Debzil(C)	1804	Dec. 31	Cincinnati	09	04	14
Keaster, David(A)	1831	Nov. 09	Montgomery	01	11	21
Keaster, George Jr.(A)	1831	Nov. 09	Montgomery	01	11	21
Keaster, George(A)	1831	July 05	Montgomery	01	11	27
Keaster, George(A)	1831	Aug. 17	Montgomery	01	11	27
Keaster, George(A)	1831	Aug. 17	Montgomery	01	11	21
Keaton, Thomas(E)	1817	June 14	Hamilton	13	12	26
Keaver, Martin(C)	1802	Dec. 28	Hamilton	04	04	23
Keck, George(A)	1836	Oct. 31	Butler	03	12	23
Keck, George(A)	1836	Oct. 31	Butler	03	12	14
Keeler, Caleb(B)	1814	Oct. 19	Hamilton	01	08	26
Keeler, Joel(B)	1836	Feb. 04	Franklin(Ind	02	08	19
Keeler, Joel(B)	1836	Feb. 22	Franklin(Ind	02	08	19
Keeler, Sanford(E)	1817	June 14	Franklin(Ind	12	13	36
Keeler, Sarah(B)	1836	Feb. 17	Franklin(Ind	02	08	30
Keen, Ayrs(A)	1812	Sept. 15	Warren	02	03	11
Keen, Lemuel(A)	1835	Feb. 14	Darke	02	12	17
Keen, Peter(A)	1805	Oct. 09	Hamilton	01	06	17
Keen, Peter(A)	1805	Nov. 19	Hamilton	02	05	13
Keene, Richard(B)	1807	Sept. 14	Warren	02	09	25
Keene, Richard(B)	1814	Sept. 03	Franklin(Ind	01	09	30
Keener, Curtis W.(E)	1837	Feb. 16	Randolph(Ind	13	21	35
Keeney, John(E)	1816	March 08	Franklin(Ind	13	14	28
Keeney, Joseph(E)	1814	Dec. 17	Franklin(Ind	14	14	30
Keeth, William(B)	1813	June 07	Jefferson	03	02	01
Keever, Abraham Jr.(A)	1836	Oct. 27	Warren	02	15	28
Keever, Abraham Jr.(A)	1836	Oct. 11	Warren	04	11	30
Keever, Adam(A)	1817	Dec. 05	Warren	02	09	32
Keever, John(A)	1813	Oct. 20	Hamilton	02	03	17
Keever, John(A)	1814	Aug. 09	Hamilton	02	03	19
Keever, John(A)	1836	Sept. 26	Butler	01	15	13
Keever, Martin Junr.(C)	1801	Dec. 28	Hamilton	04	04	24
Keever, Martin(C)	1801	Nov. 27	Hamilton	04	04	30
Keever, Martin(C)	1801	Nov. 27	Hamilton	05	03	25
Keever, Peter(C)	1801	Nov. 27	Hamilton	04	04	22
Keffer, George(B)	1806	Oct. 10	Butler	01	11	26
Keffer, George(B)	1806	Oct. 10	Butler	01	11	35
Kegler, Aloisius(B)	1833	Nov. 09	Hamilton	03	09	35
Kegs, James(A)	1814	Nov. 19	Hamilton	01	02	36
Keifer, John(A)	1836	Oct. 15	Clark	03	12	04
Keifer, John(A)	1836	Nov. 16	Clark	03	12	05
Keifer, John(A)	1836	Nov. 16	Clark	03	12	22
Keifer, Joseph(A)	1836	Nov. 16	Clark	03	12	32
Keifer, Joseph(E)	1836	Nov. 16	Clark	03	12	28
Keightley, Robt.(B)	1818	Dec. 23	Dearborn(Ind	02	06	15
Keirn, Joshua Sylvester(E)	1835	Oct. 29	Franklin(Ind	13	12	20
Keith, Jacob(A)	1830	Nov. 20	Logan	08	02	21
Keith, Jacob(C)	1824	June 17	Logan	14	02	08
Keith, Nicholas(B)	1813	July 26	Dearborn(Ind	01	02	28
Keith, Philip(A)	1831	Nov. 21	Logan	08	02	28
Keith, William(A)	1830	Dec. 13	Logan	08	02	28
Kell, John(B)	1814	Jan. 25	Preble	01	10	09
Kellaugh, James(A)	1809	June 22	Butler	02	06	29
Keller, Jacob(A)	1805	Sept. 03	Butler	04	03	28
Keller, John Junr.(A)	1813	Jan. 20	Butler	04	03	18
Keller, John Junr.(C)	1812	July 03	Champaign	09	04	35
Keller, John(A)	1805	May 15	Kentucky	04	03	27
Keller, John(A)	1810	Aug. 14	Butler	04	03	27
Keller, John(A)	1812	Dec. 28	Butler	04	03	34

PURCHASER	YEAR	DATE	RESIDENCE	R	T	S
Keller, John(D)	1808	Nov. 01	Hamilton	01	04	08
Keller, Siegfried(E)	1836	Jan. 11	Franklin(Ind	12	10	09
Kelley, David(C)	1813	Dec. 28	Hamilton	01	02	11
Kelley, Francis(C)	1811	Dec. 02	Champaign	09	03	17
Kelley, George(A)	1811	Dec. 14	Butler	04	03	32
Kelley, George(A)	1813	Dec. 30	Preble	03	06	09
Kelley, James(B)	1836	April 30	Switzerland	02	02	01
Kelley, James(C)	1811	Dec. 27	Champaign	08	05	30
Kelley, Sampson(C)	1812	April 15	Champaign	11	03	03
Kelley, Sollomon(C)	1804	Dec. 31	Greene	09	03	32
Kellog, Ezra(A)	1813	March 26	Montgomery	02	04	18
Kellogg, Ethel(C)	1804	Sept. 03	Montgomery	06	02	08
Kellogg, Ethel(C)	1804	Sept. 03	Montgomery	06	02	08
Kellogg, Frederick(E)	1818	Aug. 05	Connecticut	12	12	05
Kellogg, Frederick(E)	1818	Aug. 05	Connecticut	12	12	11
Kellum, Elijah(A)	1818	Nov. 21	Darke	02	10	02
Kellum, John(A)	1815	Dec. 18	Preble	03	04	10
Kellum, Joseph(A)	1818	Oct. 01	Darke	02	10	02
Kellum, Sam'l.(E)	1837	Jan. 23	Wayne(Ind)	14	20	11
Kelly, Austin(A)	1831	Oct. 13	Montgomery	06	03	05
Kelly, Austin(C)	1831	July 09	Montgomery	13	02	09
Kelly, Dennis(A)	1818	Aug. 05	Preble	03	04	15
Kelly, Dennis(A)	1819	Jan. 29	Preble	03	04	22
Kelly, Francis(C)	1817	July 22	Champaign	12	03	09
Kelly, George(A)	1806	July 01	Montgomery	03	04	09
Kelly, George(A)	1808	Feb. 29	Montgomery	03	06	09
Kelly, George(A)	1810	Aug. 14	Preble	03	04	05
Kelly, George(A)	1816	Jan. 30	Butler	03	05	14
Kelly, Henry(B)	1831	Aug. 09	Switzerland	01	03	31
Kelly, Isaac(A)	1817	Sept. 22	Warren	02	11	21
Kelly, James(E)	1836	Oct. 29	Randolph(Ind	13	20	36
Kelly, Jemima(E)	1833	March 02	Randolph(Ind	13	19	02
Kelly, Jemima(E)	1837	Feb. 06	Randolph(Ind	13	19	01
Kelly, John(A)	1817	Oct. 24	Warren	02	11	21
Kelly, John(A)	1837	April 03	Hamilton	01	13	22
Kelly, John(C)	1812	Oct. 05	Hamilton	10	02	18
Kelly, John(C)	1814	Jan. 25	Greene	08	05	30
Kelly, Joseph(A)	1802	April 05	Kentucky	03	03	01
Kelly, Joseph(A)	1804	Oct. 13	Butler	03	04	35
Kelly, Joseph(A)	1814	Sept. 21	Butler	01	07	02
Kelly, Joseph(A)	1815	Dec. 27	Butler	01	08	28
Kelly, Joseph(C)	1827	Aug. 20	Champaign	11	03	13
Kelly, Moses(A)	1806	Oct. 06	Warren	04	07	02
Kelly, Moses(A)	1810	Aug. 14	Montgomery	05	05	26
Kelly, Moses(A)	1810	Aug. 14	Montgomery	05	05	26
Kelly, Moses(B)	1806	June 25	Warren	01	14	29
Kelly, Nathan(A)	1814	Aug. 31	Warren	07	01	07
Kelly, Nathan(A)	1814	Oct. 13	Warren	06	08	13
Kelly, Nathan(C)	1812	Oct. 29	Warren	03	05	26
Kelly, Patrick(B)	1834	July 12	Cincinnati	03	04	36
Kelly, Patrick(B)	1834	July 12	Cincinnati	03	04	36
Kelly, Polly(B)	1835	Aug. 10	Switzerland	01	02	06
Kelly, Polly(B)	1835	Aug. 15	Switzerland	01	03	31
Kelly, Solomon(C)	1813	Dec. 08	Champaign	09	03	21
Kelly, William(B)	1830	Feb. 13	Switzerland	02	03	25
Kelly, William(B)	1834	May 15	Switzerland	01	02	06
Kelly, Willis(B)	1807	June 01	Dearborn(Ind	02	11	26
Kelly, Willis(B)	1813	April 14	Franklin(Ind	02	11	26
Kelsey, Aaron(B)	1818	July 06	Warren	01	16	25
Kelsey, Dan'l.(B)	1836	July 05	Dearborn(Ind	03	05	27
Kelsey, Daniel(B)	1817	Dec. 17	Dearborn(Ind	03	05	28
Kelsey, Daniel(B)	1833	April 19	Dearborn(Ind	03	05	33
Kelsey, Daniel(C)	1801	Dec. 30	Hamilton	05	02	03
Kelsey, Daniel(C)	1801	Dec. 30	Hamilton	05	03	33
Kelsey, James(C)	1801	Dec. 30	Hamilton	05	03	32
Kelsey, Jesse(C)	1831	Oct. 26	Montgomery	13	02	13
Kelsey, Jesse(C)	1831	Oct. 26	Montgomery	13	02	15
Kelsey, John Jr.(A)	1818	July 06	Warren	01	11	30
Kelsey, John(B)	1814	Dec. 17	Warren	02	09	22

PURCHASER	YEAR	DATE	RESIDENCE	R	T	S
Kelsey, John(C)	1801	Dec. 29	Hamilton	05	03	33
Kelsey, John(C)	1806	Aug. 29	Warren	09	04	35
Kelsey, Thomas(C)	1801	Dec. 29	Hamilton	05	03	25
Kelsey, Thomas(C)	1804	Dec. 27	Warren	05	03	27
Kelsey, Thomas(C)	1804	Dec. 27	Warren	05	03	27
Kelso, John(A)	1814	June 15	Dearborn(Ind	02	07	24
Kelso, Seth(B)	1819	Jan. 18	New York	02	07	05
Keltner, Abraham(A)	1836	Sept. 13	Darke	01	14	21
Kelzo, Robert(A)	1807	Feb. 10	Butler	02	07	07
Kemp, George(C)	1816	Nov. 08	Champaign	10	04	28
Kemp, Jacob(A)	1804	June 08	Pennsylvania	04	02	16
Kemp, Jacob(A)	1805	Sept. 19	Montgomery	03	05	30
Kemp, John(A)	1805	June 17	Montgomery	04	03	27
Kemp, John(A)	1805	June 17	Montgomery	04	03	32
Kemp, John(A)	1805	July 09	Butler	03	04	12
Kemp, John(A)	1807	Feb. 21	Butler	04	02	04
Kemp, John(B)	1817	Oct. 24	Dearborn(Ind	02	03	14
Kemp, John(B)	1834	March 18	Dearborn(Ind	02	03	14
Kemp, Phillip(A)	1804	June 08	Pennsylvania	04	02	16
Kemp, Robert F.(E)	1837	June 26	Richland	15	21	06
Kemper, Elnathan(B)	1804	Sept. 24	Hamilton	01	04	34
Kemper, Elnathan(C)	1812	Jan. 18	Hamilton	09	05	07
Kemper, James Junr.(C)	1806	Aug. 20	?	02	03	08
Kemper, James(C)	1806	March 06	Hamilton	02	03	08
Kemper, Peter H.(C)	1806	Aug. 20	?	02	03	08
Kemper, Peter H.(C)	1811	Dec. 11	Hamilton	02	03	08
Kenard, Moses(A)	1835	April 24	Darke	02	12	09
Kenard, Moses(A)	1836	Jan. 01	Darke	02	12	09
Kendal, Thomas(B)	1817	June 16	Wayne(Ind)	01	14	23
Kendall, Hosea(A)	1839	Jan. 23	Clermont	01	14	34
Kendall, John(A)	1828	Nov. 20	Miami	04	07	25
Kendall, Uzziah(B)	1818	Aug. 19	Cincinnati	02	08	28
Kendall, Uzziah(B)	1819	Oct. 18	Hamilton	02	07	01
Kendle, James(A)	1810	Feb. 16	Hamilton	01	03	31
Kendrick, William(A)	1819	Dec. 16	Preble	01	08	30
Kenedy, John(B)	1811	May 20	Ind.Territry	02	09	28
Kenedy, Stephen(A)	1811	Aug. 13	Montgomery	05	05	26
Kenege, Christopher(C)	1813	March 06	Champaign	12	05	13
Kengery, Jacob(B)	1814	Nov. 16	Wayne(Ind)	01	12	26
Kennady, George W.(E)	1837	April 29	Montgomery	14	20	05
Kennady, James(B)	1830	May 22	Franklin(Ind	01	09	12
Kennady, Robert(B)	1817	Aug. 16	Pennsylvania	02	02	11
Kennady, William(E)	1818	Feb. 06	Wayne(Ind)	14	19	02
Kennddy, Robert(A)	1817	Aug. 29	Pennsylvania	01	02	06
Kenneday, John(B)	1808	Sept. 14	Clermont	02	09	19
Kennedy, David(A)	1814	June 24	Hamilton	01	03	14
Kennedy, David(A)	1814	June 29	Hamilton	01	03	23
Kennedy, Joel(B)	1815	March 13	Butler	02	12	34
Kennedy, Joel(C)	1813	April 14	Butler	09	03	17
Kennedy, John(A)	1804	Dec. 28	Hamilton	02	05	17
Kennedy, John(A)	1810	April 11	Butler	02	05	17
Kennedy, John(A)	1818	Aug. 05	Butler	02	12	22
Kennedy, John(B)	1808	April 02	Clermont	02	09	19
Kennedy, John(B)	1811	April 16	Ind.Territry	02	09	28
Kennedy, Robert(B)	1813	June 25	Warren	01	09	34
Kennedy, William(A)	1807	March 06	Warren	06	03	28
Kennerman, John Thomas(A)	1814	Dec. 16	Montgomery	04	04	03
Kenney, David(A)	1831	Nov. 28	Miami	04	10	35
Kenney, Ephraim(C)	1804	Dec. 31	Montgomery	11	01	20
Kenney, John(C)	1804	Dec. 31	Montgomery	11	01	20
Kennier, John(E)	1837	Feb. 06	Randolph(Ind	14	21	28
Kennon, William(B)	1831	March 23	Darke	01	17	11
Kennutt, William(A)	1811	April 09	Preble	03	04	01
Kensey, John(A)	1815	April 18	Butler	02	06	14
Kensinger, John(A)	1827	Nov. 08	Miami	05	08	21
Kent, Jacob(C)	1804	Dec. 28	Greene	07	03	22
Kenton, Mark Senr.(C)	1828	Oct. 14	Champaign	11	04	06
Kenton, Mark Senr.(C)	1828	Nov. 15	Champaign	11	04	06
Kenton, Philip C.(C)	1813	June 21	Champaign	12	04	14

PURCHASER	YEAR	DATE	RESIDENCE	R	T	S
Kenton, Philip C.(C)	1818	Jan. 13	Champaign	12	04	19
Kenton, Simon(C)	1804	Sept. 26	Greene	13	05	21
Kenton, Simon(C)	1804	Sept. 26	Greene	13	05	20
Kenton, Simon(C)	1804	Sept. 26	Greene	13	05	27
Kenton, Simon(C)	1804	Sept. 26	Greene	13	05	15
Kenton, Simon(C)	1804	Sept. 26	Greene	13	05	14
Kenton, Simon(C)	1804	Dec. 29	Greene	10	05	33
Kenton, Simon(C)	1808	May 13	Champaign	10	05	19
Kenton, Solomon(C)	1813	March 15	Champaign	10	05	21
Kenton, Thomas(C)	1804	Sept. 26	Greene	11	04	18
Kenton, Thomas(C)	1804	Sept. 26	Greene	11	04	12
Kenton, Thomas(C)	1811	April 09	Greene	11	04	06
Kenton, William(C)	1804	Sept. 26	Greene	11	04	06
Kenton, William(C)	1805	Nov. 06	Champaign	11	04	06
Kenton, William(C)	1816	Sept. 25	Champaign	12	05	36
Kenworthy, David(A)	1806	Aug. 25	Montgomery	05	06	03
Kenworthy, David(E)	1816	Nov. 02	Clinton	14	18	02
Kenworthy, Jesse(A)	1805	May 31	Butler	03	04	32
Kenworthy, Jesse(A)	1805	July 27	Butler	02	06	25
Kenworthy, Jesse(A)	1814	Dec. 27	Preble	03	04	19
Kenworthy, Jesse(A)	1818	Feb. 04	Preble	03	04	25
Kenworthy, Jesse(E)	1834	Feb. 22	Preble	14	19	22
Kenworthy, John(A)	1806	Aug. 25	Montgomery	05	07	28
Kenworthy, John(E)	1818	July 02	Clinton	14	18	27
Kenworthy, John(E)	1822	Nov. 01	Wayne(Ind)	14	18	27
Kenworthy, Levi(E)	1838	Sept. 25	Randolph(Ind	14	19	36
Kenworthy, Thomas(A)	1836	Sept. 03	Butler	03	12	03
Kenworthy, Thomas(A)	1837	Feb. 18	Butler	03	12	02
Kephart, George(A)	1810	Oct. 10	Montgomery	01	08	01
Kephart, John(B)	1833	April 12	Switzerland	03	04	29
Keplinger, Daniel(C)	1808	Oct. 06	Champaign	10	04	02
Keplinger, Daniel(C)	1817	July 03	Champaign	10	04	14
Keplinger, Jacob Senr.(C)	1810	July 02	Virginia	10	04	08
Keplinger, Jacob Senr.(C)	1810	Oct. 29	Champaign	10	04	14
Keplinger, Jacob(A)	1831	Dec. 30	Montgomery	04	11	35
Keplinger, Jacob(C)	1810	June 04	Virginia	10	03	01
Kerby, James(B)	1818	Oct. 01	Cincinnati	01	07	03
Kerchaval, James(A)	1804	Oct. 11	Butler	03	11	30
Kercher, Jacob(A)	1805	Aug. 07	Montgomery	04	04	24
Kercher, Jacob(A)	1805	Aug. 07	Montgomery	04	04	24
Kercher, Jacob(A)	1805	Aug. 07	Montgomery	04	04	24
Kercheval, James(A)	1806	April 23	Butler	01	07	10
Kercheval, James(A)	1806	April 23	Butler	01	07	04
Kercheval, James(A)	1806	May 05	Butler	01	08	32
Kercheval, James(A)	1806	June 13	Butler	01	07	04
Kercheval, James(A)	1808	March 21	Butler	01	07	28
Kercheval, James(A)	1813	Aug. 10	Preble	01	07	28
Kercheval, Lewis(A)	1814	June 11	Preble	01	07	29
Kerger, George(A)	1811	Jan. 02	Montgomery	03	05	02
Kerms, Peter(C)	1815	Jan. 21	Hamilton	12	01	20
Kerns, Joseph(C)	1831	April 18	Miami	13	02	04
Kerns, Joseph(E)	1836	Nov. 05	Miami	13	20	10
Kerr, David(B)	1817	July 19	Dearborn(Ind	02	05	19
Kerr, David(B)	1836	Feb. 03	Dearborn(Ind	02	04	18
Kerr, George(A)	1814	Dec. 20	Miami	06	04	07
Kerr, George(A)	1815	Dec. 12	Miami	05	06	01
Kerr, George(A)	1829	Aug. 20	Miami	05	06	01
Kerr, George(A)	1829	Dec. 08	Miami	06	04	06
Kerr, George(A)	1829	Dec. 08	Miami	06	04	07
Kerr, John(A)	1814	April 12	Hamilton	01	02	33
Kerr, John(B)	1837	Jan. 31	Dearborn(Ind	02	04	07
Kerr, John(C)	1831	Aug. 10	Logan	13	04	30
Kerr, William(B)	1834	June 11	England	01	08	05
Kerr, William(B)	1834	Nov. 19	Franklin(Ind	01	08	08
Kerr, William(B)	1836	Jan. 22	Franklin(Ind	01	08	08
Kerr, Wm.(B)	1817	Nov. 15	Indiana	02	03	26
Kerrchoffe, Jacob(C)	1832	Feb. 13	Logan	13	04	29
Kerrick, Armistead(E)	1837	March 01	Franklin(Ind	11	10	11
Kerschner, George(E)	1836	Sept. 23	Montgomery	15	21	28

PURCHASER	YEAR	DATE	RESIDENCE	R	T	S
Kerschner, John(E)	1837	Feb. 24	Montgomery	14	20	03
Kersey, Carter(E)	1835	Jan. 24	Warren	13	19	11
Kersey, Thomas(E)	1811	Dec. 12	Warren	15	17	34
Kersey, Thomas(E)	1836	Dec. 05	Clinton	14	18	06
Kersey, Thomas(E)	1836	Dec. 05	Clinton	14	19	31
Kershner, Daniel(C)	1810	Dec. 24	Greene	07	03	12
Kesler, George(B)	1811	Nov. 11	Preble	03	06	09
Kesler, Jacob(A)	1818	Feb. 06	Preble	02	08	12
Kesler, Jacob(E)	1837	Oct. 10	Preble	14	21	30
Kesling, Jacob(B)	1808	Dec. 07	Virginia	01	13	27
Kesling, Jacob(B)	1809	Jan. 06	Preble	01	13	26
Kesling, Jacob(B)	1812	April 15	Ind.Territory	01	13	27
Kesling, John(A)	1815	Feb. 14	Warren	02	08	21
Keslinger, Peter(A)	1810	Dec. 12	Warren	02	08	10
Keslinger, Peter(C)	1801	Dec. 14	Hamilton	04	03	06
Keslinger, Peter(C)	1801	Dec. 14	Hamilton	05	02	15
Kessel, David(A)	1822	Sept. 04	Montgomery	04	05	20
Kessens, John Herman(E)	1836	Oct. 29	Cincinnati	12	10	17
Kessler, George(A)	1813	July 29	Greene	03	06	08
Kessler, George(A)	1813	Oct. 30	Preble	03	07	17
Kessler, George(A)	1815	Sept. 27	Preble	03	07	32
Kessler, Henry(A)	1817	Oct. 21	Miami	01	12	09
Kessler, Henry(A)	1818	Dec. 10	Montgomery	04	09	03
Kessler, Henry(C)	1813	Dec. 23	Champaign	10	04	21
Kessler, Henry(C)	1824	Dec. 11	Champaign	11	03	11
Kessler, Henry(C)	1825	Jan. 15	Champaign	11	03	17
Kessler, Henry(C)	1825	Nov. 21	Champaign	11	03	12
Kessler, John B.(A)	1824	Nov. 12	Miami	05	06	12
Kessler, John B.(A)	1827	May 23	Miami	06	04	07
Kessler, John B.(A)	1827	May 23	Miami	05	06	12
Kessler, John B.(A)	1828	Feb. 11	Miami	05	06	11
Kessler, John B.(A)	1831	Jan. 24	Miami	05	06	12
Kessler, John B.(A)	1828	Feb. 11	Miami	06	04	07
Kessler, John Bowman(A)	1831	Nov. 01	Miami	05	06	12
Kessler, John(A)	1812	March 07	Montgomery	05	06	24
Kessler, John(A)	1813	Jan. 30	Hamilton	05	03	15
Kessler, Jonathan(A)	1832	Feb. 18	Montgomery	01	10	11
Kessler, Joseph(A)	1814	Jan. 22	Montgomery	05	06	14
Kessler, Joseph(A)	1817	Oct. 01	Montgomery	01	11	34
Kessler, Joseph(A)	1817	Oct. 21	Miami	01	12	27
Kessler, Samuel(A)	1815	Jan. 11	Preble	03	06	09
Kestiter, John(A)	1811	June 12	Butler	02	04	29
Ketcham, David(B)	1817	Oct. 22	Dearborn(Ind	02	06	17
Ketcham, David(B)	1817	Oct. 22	Dearborn(Ind	02	06	17
Ketcham, Israel(B)	1833	June 17	Hamilton	02	06	04
Ketring, Martin(A)	1818	Aug. 03	Fairfield	01	11	22
Ketring, Martin(A)	1824	Oct. 12	Darke	01	11	22
Ketring, Martin(A)	1824	Oct. 30	Darke	01	11	22
Kettel, Peter(A)	1837	April 03	Stark	03	12	31
Kettering, Henry(A)	1828	Sept. 16	Darke	01	11	22
Kever, Martin(C)	1804	Sept. 03	Warren	04	04	29
Kexsley, Delzil(C)	1804	Dec. 29	Cincinnati	09	04	15
Key, Andrew(E)	1836	Jan. 30	Randolph(Ind	14	21	14
Key, Andrew(E)	1837	Jan. 04	Randolph(Ind	14	21	14
Keyler, Henry(C)	1824	July 02	Logan	14	03	23
Keys, Benjamin P.(E)	1836	March 17	Randolph(Ind	14	20	25
Keys, John F.(C)	1818	April 22	Cincinnati	10	05	26
Keys, John F.(C)	1818	May 11	Cincinnati	10	05	29
Keys, John F.(C)	1818	June 11	Cincinnati	09	03	26
Keys, John F.(C)	1818	June 11	Cincinnati	09	02	08
Keys, John F.(C)	1818	June 11	Cincinnati	09	02	08
Keys, John F.(C)	1818	June 11	Cincinnati	09	02	08
Keys, Joseph(E)	1832	Dec. 05	Randolph(Ind	14	19	02
Keys, Joseph(E)	1836	March 17	Randolph(Ind	14	19	02
Keyser, David(C)	1813	June 24	Champaign	10	04	13
Keyser, John Adam(B)	1835	Jan. 20	Dearborn(Ind	02	06	08
Keyt, Abner(A)	1837	Feb. 10	Miami	03	11	17
Keyt, John(A)	1817	June 09	Miami	05	08	10
Kibby, Joseph(E)	1814	Feb. 01	Warren	14	16	21

PURCHASER	YEAR	DATE	RESIDENCE	R	T	S
Kiblinger, Adam(C)	1813	Sept. 24	Champaign	10	04	14
Kiblinger, John(A)	1818	Oct. 07	Virginia	03	08	22
Kienker, Henry(A)	1837	Dec. 11	Cincinnati	03	13	32
Kienker, Henry(E)	1837	Feb. 20	Cincinnati	12	11	22
Kiger, Christopher(B)	1813	Oct. 23	Franklin(Ind	02	10	35
Kiger, Jacob(B)	1813	Oct. 23	Franklin(Ind	02	10	35
Kilborn, Thomas F.(A)	1834	March 22	Darke	02	12	21
Kilborn, Thos. F.(A)	1833	Dec. 31	Darke	02	12	21
Kilbourn, John(E)	1811	Oct. 24	Highland	13	15	06
Kilbreth, James P.(A)	1836	Oct. 24	Cincinnati	01	15	21
Kilbreth, James P.(A)	1836	Oct. 24	Cincinnati	01	15	27
Kile, Henry Jr.(B)	1831	Sept. 05	Dearborn(Ind	03	08	12
Kile, Henry(B)	1826	July 31	Dearborn(Ind	03	08	12
Kile, John(B)	1833	June 22	Dearborn(Ind	03	08	12
Kilgour, David(A)	1810	Sept. 14	Cincinnati	03	03	06
Kilgour, David(A)	1818	Feb. 11	Cincinnati	02	12	05
Kilgour, David(C)	1811	Sept. 24	Cincinnati	12	04	10
Kilgour, David(E)	1811	Oct. 28	Cincinnati	13	15	07
Killgore, Charles(C)	1801	Dec. 31	Cincinnati	05	03	25
Killgore, Charles(C)	1802	Dec. 31	Hamilton	08	04	13
Killgore, Charles(C)	1802	Dec. 31	Cincinnati	07	02	12
Killgore, Charles(C)	1802	Dec. 31	Cincinnati	05	03	25
Killgore, Charles(C)	1804	Dec. 31	Cincinnati	07	02	12
Kimball, Timothy(B)	1835	Feb. 12	Dearborn(Ind	02	05	22
Kimber, Peter(A)	1831	Dec. 05	Darke	01	12	23
Kimes, Henry(A)	1816	June 03	Warren	02	08	04
Kimes, John(A)	1816	June 03	Warren	02	08	04
Kimes, Wm.(A)	1816	June 03	Warren	02	08	04
Kimmel, David(A)	1806	May 26	Pennsylvania	05	05	30
Kimmel, David(A)	1806	May 30	Pennsylvania	04	05	24
Kimmel, David(A)	1806	May 30	Pennsylvania	05	05	31
Kimmel, George(A)	1817	June 10	Montgomery	03	10	12
Kimmy, Isaac(B)	1814	July 25	Hamilton	02	09	27
Kincaid, Ellis(A)	1839	Feb. 06	Warren	01	13	25
Kincaid, Ellis(A)	1839	Feb. 12	Warren	01	13	02
Kincaid, Ellis(B)	1839	March 28	Warren	02	04	06
Kincaid, Ellis(E)	1838	Nov. 06	Warren	15	22	02
Kincaid, John(A)	1812	Aug. 22	Preble	01	07	13
Kincaid, Joseph(B)	1836	May 18	Pennsylvania	03	03	09
Kincaid, Robert(D)	1814	April 19	Warren	03	05	08
Kindel, Jane(A)	1817	June 09	Miami	05	09	25
Kindele, Ewell(E)	1812	Jan. 22	Wayne(Ind)	14	16	21
Kindell, Benj'n.(A)	1821	March 01	Miami	05	08	04
Kindle, James(A)	1814	May 24	Butler	01	03	29
Kindle, Welford(A)	1836	Jan. 18	Darke	02	12	04
Kindle, William B.(A)	1818	Oct. 16	Miami	05	09	23
Kindle, William(A)	1832	March 17	Warren	05	07	10
Kindle, William(A)	1832	March 17	Warren	06	08	33
King, Alaxander(C)	1804	Dec. 31	Cincinnati	10	05	13
King, Ann(A)	1826	Oct. 10	Preble	02	09	22
King, Coartlen(C)	1815	Nov. 11	Pennsylvania	09	06	04
King, Daniel(E)	1816	Feb. 09	Kentucky	14	16	08
King, Elisha(E)	1814	Feb. 19	Kentucky	14	16	29
King, George(A)	1831	May 16	Butler	07	01	04
King, George(A)	1831	May 16	Butler	07	02	32
King, John A.(A)	1831	April 18	Butler	07	01	09
King, John P.(B)	1828	May 01	Clermont	03	07	35
King, John(A)	1814	Dec. 09	Montgomery	04	05	02
King, John(A)	1826	Oct. 10	Preble	02	09	22
King, John(A)	1827	Nov. 27	Preble	01	07	13
King, John(E)	1814	March 21	Kentucky	14	17	33
King, Joseph(E)	1816	Jan. 15	Kentucky	14	16	05
King, Lavinus(B)	1817	Oct. 11	Dearborn(Ind	03	06	25
King, Phineas L.(B)	1817	July 07	Dearborn(Ind	02	05	30
King, Samuel(A)	1826	Oct. 10	Preble	02	09	21
King, Samuel(E)	1814	Jan. 17	Kentucky	14	16	29
King, Smith(A)	1812	Dec. 19	?	02	03	18
King, Thomas W.(B)	1818	Feb. 09	Dearborn(Ind	02	05	33
King, William(A)	1810	Sept. 03	Montgomery	05	05	34

PURCHASER	YEAR	DATE	RESIDENCE	R	T	S
Kingery, Christly(B)	1805	Nov. 02	Virginia	01	11	36
Kingery, Jacob(B)	1806	Oct. 10	Butler	01	11	34
Kingery, Jacob(B)	1808	Oct. 19	Dearborn(Ind	01	12	25
Kingery, Joseph(A)	1805	Feb. 26	Montgomery	01	06	32
Kingery, Joseph(A)	1805	Feb. 26	Montgomery	01	06	31
Kingery, Joseph(A)	1806	March 25	Butler	01	06	32
Kingery, Joseph(B)	1813	Dec. 07	Preble	01	11	14
Kingery, Joseph(B)	1814	Sept. 24	Preble	01	11	23
Kingery, Joseph(B)	1815	March 16	Preble	01	11	26
Kingery, Joseph(B)	1815	Nov. 23	Preble	01	10	26
Kingery, Michael(E)	1814	Oct. 31	Greene	13	12	03
Kingery, Samuel(B)	1813	Dec. 28	Franklin(Ind	01	11	25
Kingory, Martin(B)	1809	Oct. 25	Greene	01	11	26
Kinman, Levi(A)	1804	Nov. 30	Butler	03	04	32
Kinman, Levi(A)	1804	Nov. 30	Butler	03	04	33
Kinnaird, David(C)	1830	May 21	Muskingum	13	03	29
Kinnan, Erastus(C)	1831	Oct. 05	Champaign	13	03	20
Kinnan, John(C)	1829	May 01	Champaign	13	03	08
Kinnard, John(A)	1808	Dec. 22	Kentucky	06	08	31
Kinnear, John(A)	1818	Oct. 16	Darke	01	10	14
Kinneman, Samuel J.(A)	1815	Nov. 11	Montgomery	04	04	03
Kinney, John(C)	1812	Jan. 15	Greene	07	03	10
Kinney, John(C)	1825	Nov. 18	Clark	10	02	08
Kinnon, Morimus Willett(C)	1831	Oct. 22	Champaign	13	03	09
Kinns, George(C)	1813	Dec. 30	Montgomery	08	03	12
Kinsey, David(A)	1808	March 21	Virginia	03	05	20
Kinsey, David(A)	1811	Aug. 29	Montgomery	05	05	31
Kinsey, David(A)	1816	Aug. 01	?	05	05	32
Kinsey, David(A)	1816	Dec. 02	Montgomery	05	05	31
Kinsey, David(A)	1832	Aug. 28	Montgomery	03	09	24
Kinsey, David(A)	1832	Aug. 28	Montgomery	03	09	25
Kinsey, Henry(A)	1804	May 11	Montgomery	05	03	01
Kinsey, Jacob(A)	1814	Oct. 28	Clermont	03	04	07
Kinsey, Jacob(A)	1814	Oct. 28	Clermont	02	07	25
Kinsey, John(A)	1803	Nov. 19	Virginia	04	04	32
Kinsie, Christian(A)	1828	Sept. 12	Montgomery	04	06	10
Kinsie, David(A)	1828	Sept. 12	Montgomery	04	07	31
Kinsley, Calvin(E)	1817	July 01	Franklin(Ind	13	12	21
Kinsley, Calvin(E)	1817	July 01	Franklin(Ind	13	12	20
Kinsley, Calvin(E)	1817	Aug. 08	Franklin(Ind	13	13	30
Kinsley, John(B)	1817	Oct. 09	Dearborn(Ind	02	06	20
Kinstrey, William M.(B)	1816	Nov. 13	Butler	03	02	07
Kinzer, Jacob(C)	1805	Aug. 09	Montgomery	11	01	03
Kirby, John(C)	1812	Dec. 01	Baltimore	02	02	08
Kirby, Jonathan(A)	1831	Sept. 07	Warren	02	10	25
Kirby, Jonathan(A)	1831	Nov. 22	Warren	02	10	25
Kirby, Jos.(C)	1801	Dec. 30	Hamilton	04	04	34
Kirby, Joseph(C)	1828	Aug. 18	Warren	11	03	13
Kirby, Richard(C)	1801	Dec. 22	Hamilton	04	03	02
Kircher, Francis Jr.(B)	1834	Sept. 06	Cincinnati	02	06	09
Kirk, Benedick(B)	1816	May 08	Hamilton	01	02	19
Kirk, James(E)	1838	Dec. 29	Clinton	13	19	32
Kirk, Jesse(B)	1816	May 08	Butler	01	02	30
Kirk, John W.(A)	1837	Jan. 23	Montgomery	03	13	36
Kirkham, Henry(A)	1813	April 14	Preble	02	07	19
Kirkham, Michael Jr.(A)	1814	Oct. 21	Preble	01	06	11
Kirkham, Samuel(A)	1813	April 14	Preble	02	07	19
Kirkland, Elisha(A)	1817	Sept. 01	Madison	07	01	17
Kirkling, Jeremiah(E)	1832	Jan. 02	Randolph(Ind	13	18	13
Kirkling, John R.(E)	1821	Dec. 29	Wayne(Ind)	14	18	30
Kirkpatric, William(C)	1801	Dec. 31	Hamilton	07	03	31
Kirkpatrick, Alexander(A)	1805	Sept. 20	Butler	02	04	27
Kirkpatrick, Alexander(A)	1810	Dec. 12	Butler	02	04	27
Kirkpatrick, Alexander(C)	1805	July 26	Hamilton	09	02	25
Kirkpatrick, George(C)	1812	June 10	Kentucky	13	04	12
Kirkpatrick, Hugh(C)	1813	April 14	Champaign	09	04	04
Kirkpatrick, John(C)	1802	Dec. 31	Hamilton	05	04	30
Kirkpatrick, John(C)	1811	Oct. 07	Greene	09	05	14
Kirkpatrick, John(C)	1811	Dec. 11	Greene	09	05	05

PURCHASER	YEAR	DATE	RESIDENCE	R	T	S
Kirkpatrick, Samuel(A)	1807	March 24	Butler	03	03	18
Kirkpatrick, Samuel(C)	1802	Dec. 30	Hamilton	07	03	33
Kirkpatrick, Samuel(C)	1802	Dec. 31	Hamilton	07	04	18
Kirkpatrick, William(A)	1805	Oct. 04	Hamilton	02	03	08
Kirkpatrick, William(A)	1810	Dec. 12	Butler	02	03	08
Kirkpatrick, William(C)	1811	Sept. 12	Greene	09	05	13
Kirkpatrick, William(C)	1816	Dec. 02	Greene	09	05	13
Kirkpatrick, William(C)	1816	Dec. 02	Greene	09	05	14
Kirkpatrick, William(E)	1811	Oct. 23	Butler	13	13	12
Kirkwood, David(C)	1813	April 14	Champaign	13	04	03
Kirkwood, Joseph(C)	1813	Sept. 14	Champaign	13	05	33
Kisar, Thomas(C)	1831	Aug. 20	Shelby	13	02	11
Kise, Henry Wm.(B)	1833	Sept. 30	Germany	02	08	32
Kise, Henry Wm.(B)	1833	Sept. 30	Germany	02	08	30
Kiser, Benj'n.(B)	1831	Nov. 22	Montgomery	08	01	05
Kiser, John Senr.(C)	1804	Dec. 29	Greene	07	02	07
Kiser, Philip(C)	1806	Jan. 29	Champaign	10	04	30
Kiser, Philip(C)	1806	Jan. 29	Champaign	10	04	36
Kisley, Jacob(B)	1808	Dec. 07	Virginia	01	13	28
Kislinger, Peter(A)	1805	Nov. 07	Warren	02	08	10
Kisor, John(C)	1815	March 25	Miami	12	02	13
Kister, George(A)	1805	March 27	Montgomery	04	03	11
Kitchel, John(C)	1801	Dec. 23	Hamilton	04	02	17
Kitchel, Joseph(A)	1801	April 27	Hamilton	01	01	05
Kitchel, Samuel(B)	1815	Sept. 05	Hamilton	01	12	29
Kitchen, Henry(A)	1819	June 03	Pennsylvania	06	08	12
Kitchen, Henry(A)	1836	Aug. 22	Miami	03	11	21
Kitchen, James(E)	1814	Jan. 17	Franklin(Ind	12	13	03
Kitchen, Stephen(C)	1817	Nov. 08	Warren	09	06	31
Kitchen, Stephen(D)	1813	Sept. 04	Warren	02	03	11
Kitchen, Stephen(D)	1814	March 16	Warren	01	04	11
Kitcher, Jacob(C)	1817	Nov. 29	Hamilton	12	01	04
Kite, Adam(C)	1816	Jan. 09	Champaign	11	04	36
Kite, Benjamin(C)	1815	May 15	Champaign	11	04	34
Kite, Daniel(E)	1817	June 10	Butler	14	21	08
Kite, Daniel(E)	1817	June 10	Butler	14	21	08
Kite, Emanuel(C)	1813	June 07	Champaign	12	03	14
Kite, Samuel(C)	1817	Dec. 01	Champaign	11	03	06
Kite, Samuel(C)	1818	Sept. 07	Champaign	11	02	04
Kitt, Peter(C)	1814	Jan. 22	Champaign	10	05	26
Kittle, Daniel(B)	1831	Aug. 09	Dearborn(Ind	02	03	08
Kittle, James Gibson(B)	1832	May 28	Dearborn(Ind	02	03	08
Kittle, James Gibson(B)	1833	March 02	Dearborn(Ind	02	03	07
Kittle, Phineas(B)	1833	May 21	Dearborn(Ind	02	03	17
Kittle, Wm. C.(B)	1838	Nov. 03	Dearborn(Ind	02	03	04
Kittle, Wm.(B)	1827	Aug. 21	Dearborn(Ind	02	04	33
Kizer, Christian(A)	1815	Jan. 16	Preble	03	06	02
Kizer, David(C)	1810	Jan. 03	Champaign	12	03	09
Kizer, David(C)	1818	March 25	Clark	10	03	05
Kizer, Elias(E)	1835	Oct. 07	Randolph(Ind	14	21	29
Kizer, Elias(E)	1836	Sept. 24	Randolph(Ind	14	20	09
Kizer, Elias(E)	1836	Oct. 17	Randolph(Ind	14	21	12
Kizer, Elizabeth(C)	1824	June 07	Clark	11	04	07
Kizer, Henry(E)	1820	Oct. 21	Ross	14	21	31
Kizer, Henry(E)	1820	Oct. 21	Ross	14	21	29
Kizer, Henry(E)	1822	May 04	Randolph(Ind	14	21	30
Kizer, Jacob(C)	1818	Sept. 26	Hamilton	12	02	05
Kizer, Jacob(C)	1829	Jan. 17	Clark	09	05	25
Kizer, John(C)	1815	Jan. 30	Greene	10	04	19
Kizer, John(C)	1831	June 20	Miami	12	02	22
Kizer, Joseph(C)	1812	Nov. 17	Champaign	12	03	08
Kizer, Joseph(C)	1829	Oct. 09	Champaign	12	03	11
Kizer, Nicholas(C)	1818	Sept. 26	Hamilton	12	02	05
Klammar, Andrew(A)	1814	May 04	Virginia	04	05	32
Klammar, David(A)	1814	May 04	Virginia	04	05	29
Klanke, Frederick(B)	1836	April 18	Hamilton	02	08	18
Klar, Daniel(A)	1838	Feb. 05	Pennsylvania	01	14	02
Klein, Jacob(A)	1838	Feb. 14	Pennsylvania	01	15	34
Klein, Jacob(B)	1833	Nov. 04	Cincinnati	03	09	36

PURCHASER	YEAR	DATE	RESIDENCE	R	T	S
Klein, Michael(B)	1834	Aug. 09	Cincinnati	02	08	21
Kleinmann, John Hy.(E)	1837	Feb. 22	Cincinnati	12	11	28
Kleinmann, William(B)	1834	April 29	Hamilton	02	06	02
Klepinger, Geo.(A)	1831	Jan. 17	Montgomery	04	07	33
Kline, Peter(B)	1833	April 24	Dearborn(Ind	03	08	14
Klinger, Henry(A)	1811	Jan. 31	Montgomery	04	04	12
Klinger, Henry(A)	1816	Aug. 01	Montgomery	04	04	12
Klinger, Jacob(A)	1811	Jan. 31	Montgomery	04	04	12
Klinger, Jacob(A)	1816	Aug. 01	Montgomery	04	04	12
Klinger, William(A)	1814	Nov. 23	Montgomery	04	05	31
Klosser, Nicholas(A)	1814	Dec. 09	Warren	02	05	15
Klostarman, John Diedrig(E)	1837	May 02	Cincinnati	11	11	24
Klostarman, John Henry(E)	1837	May 02	Cincinnati	11	11	24
Klum, George(E)	1832	June 14	Fayette	12	13	19
Klum, John(E)	1832	June 14	Fayette	11	13	24
Knapp, Hiram(B)	1817	Dec. 31	Dearborn(Ind	02	05	29
Knapp, John(B)	1817	Dec. 31	Dearborn(Ind	02	05	29
Knapp, Nehemiah(B)	1818	Jan. 31	Dearborn(Ind	03	05	14
Knapp, Nehemiah(B)	1829	Dec. 30	Dearborn(Ind	02	04	18
Knecht, John(B)	1837	Feb. 01	Franklin(Ind	03	09	24
Knecht, John(E)	1837	Feb. 01	Franklin(Ind	13	11	21
Knee, George Senr.(A)	1819	Dec. 15	Darke	01	11	25
Knee, Henry(A)	1829	March 23	Montgomery	04	07	27
Kneeland, Ephraim(B)	1818	Jan. 07	Dearborn(Ind	01	06	29
Kneeland, John(B)	1837	March 01	Cincinnati	02	04	17
Knies, Andrew(A)	1825	Nov. 02	Shelby	05	09	11
Knies, John(A)	1831	Sept. 20	Shelby	05	09	11
Knife, Conrad(A)	1814	Sept. 02	Pennsylvania	04	05	17
Knife, Jacob(A)	1814	Sept. 02	Pennsylvania	04	05	09
Knife, Mich'l. Jr.(A)	1825	Sept. 01	Miami	05	06	11
Knife, Michael(A)	1832	Jan. 16	Miami	05	06	13
Knife, Michael(A)	1832	Jan. 16	Miami	05	07	12
Knight, George(E)	1831	July 05	Randolph(Ind	14	20	27
Knight, James Junr.(B)	1811	March 20	Ind.Territory	02	09	17
Knight, James Senr.(B)	1811	March 20	?	02	09	17
Knight, James(B)	1808	Sept. 17	Dearborn(Ind	02	09	17
Knight, James(B)	1816	Aug. 01	Franklin(Ind	02	09	17
Knight, John(C)	1806	July 29	Montgomery	11	02	13
Knight, John(C)	1812	April 15	Montgomery	08	02	18
Knight, John(C)	1815	April 07	Miami	11	02	13
Knight, Jonathan(C)	1817	May 30	Hamilton	11	02	04
Knight, Jonathan(C)	1817	May 30	Hamilton	11	02	05
Knight, Samuel(B)	1817	Oct. 27	Cincinnati	03	06	10
Knight, Solomon(E)	1833	June 03	Randolph(Ind	13	19	02
Knight, Thomas(E)	1814	Oct. 17	Wayne(Ind)	14	18	25
Knight, William(C)	1804	Dec. 26	Montgomery	10	02	34
Knipe, Henry(A)	1816	Aug. 05	Preble	03	07	09
Knipe, John(E)	1811	Oct. 22	Butler	12	15	12
Knipe, John(E)	1811	Oct. 22	Butler	12	15	12
Knipe, John(E)	1811	Oct. 24	Butler	13	15	02
Knipe, John(E)	1811	Nov. 02	Butler	12	15	03
Knoop, Jacob(A)	1830	June 24	?	04	09	27
Knoop, Michael(A)	1833	Sept. 20	Miami	02	13	32
Knoops, Benjamin(C)	1804	Dec. 21	Montgomery	10	02	34
Knoops, Benjamin(C)	1805	Dec. 31	Montgomery	11	02	14
Knoops, Christopher(C)	1804	Dec. 21	Montgomery	10	02	33
Knoops, Daniel(C)	1804	Dec. 21	Montgomery	10	02	28
Knoops, John(C)	1804	Dec. 21	Montgomery	10	01	04
Knoops, John(C)	1805	Dec. 31	Montgomery	11	02	19
Knorr, George(B)	1835	Oct. 28	Dearborn(Ind	03	08	13
Knott, Peter(A)	1818	Feb. 21	Greene	04	09	31
Knott, William(E)	1813	July 21	Franklin(Ind	13	14	26
Knotts, Nathaniel(C)	1801	Dec. 29	Hamilton	05	03	30
Knou, James(A)	1815	Feb. 04	Pennsylvania	01	08	10
Knouff, Henry(A)	1831	June 02	Miami	04	08	01
Knowls, William(B)	1817	July 26	Franklin(Ind	02	08	25
Knox, James(A)	1815	Feb. 04	Pennsylvania	01	08	10
Knox, John(C)	1804	Dec. 22	Kentucky	08	04	02
Knox, John(E)	1813	June 22	Hamilton	12	13	10

PURCHASER	YEAR	DATE	RESIDENCE	R	T	S
Knox, Moses(A)	1806	April 09	Butler	02	03	12
Knox, William(A)	1817	Sept. 05	Miami	05	08	05
Knut, William(B)	1807	Sept. 16	Montgomery	02	12	25
Koch, Adam(A)	1838	Feb. 14	Pennsylvania	01	15	35
Koch, Christian(A)	1806	June 21	Montgomery	04	04	23
Koch, John(E)	1836	Oct. 27	Cincinnati	11	10	24
Koch, John(E)	1836	Nov. 15	Cincinnati	12	10	19
Koch, Wendelon(A)	1834	May 12	Montgomery	03	10	19
Kolb, Richard(B)	1809	July 10	Dearborn(Ind	01	09	18
Kolb, Richard(E)	1812	Nov. 21	Franklin(Ind	13	15	28
Konfer, George(A)	1832	May 30	Montgomery	04	09	15
Konkle, Jacob(A)	1830	Aug. 26	Darke	03	08	18
Koogler, Adam(C)	1815	April 04	Greene	11	01	05
Koon, James(E)	1837	Oct. 31	Shelby	15	22	26
Koons, Jasper(B)	1808	Nov. 19	Dearborn(Ind	01	13	10
Kordenbrock, Jno. Hy.(E)	1837	July 25	Kentucky	12	11	19
Kraider, David(A)	1811	Oct. 19	Montgomery	04	06	36
Kramer, Gerhard(E)	1837	Jan. 09	Cincinnati	12	11	31
Kramer, Henry(E)	1836	Oct. 29	Cincinnati	12	10	17
Krater, David(A)	1806	May 30	Pennsylvania	04	06	24
Kraual, Deval(A)	1818	Nov. 18	Virginia	04	05	24
Kraual, Deval(A)	1819	Sept. 21	Montgomery	03	08	09
Kreider, David(A)	1831	April 20	Montgomery	04	07	17
Kreitzer, Peter(A)	1805	Nov. 15	Montgomery	05	04	10
Kress, Jacob(C)	1831	Feb. 24	Logan	13	03	10
Kribe, John(A)	1805	Oct. 07	Pennsylvania	05	04	31
Kring, Christian(A)	1819	June 14	Miami	05	07	24
Kritzer, Andrew(A)	1805	Nov. 15	Montgomery	06	02	18
Krnn, Henry(C)	1812	April 15	Miami	06	05	30
Krohnlaye, Henry(A)	1838	Jan. 20	Cincinnati	03	13	29
Krule, Henry(A)	1807	May 16	Montgomery	04	06	23
Krutz, Charles(B)	1812	July 02	Cincinnati	02	01	08
Kuglass, James(C)	1802	Dec. 24	Hamilton	04	02	07
Kuhagen, John G. F.(A)	1838	May 21	Darke	01	14	34
Kuhn, Philip Jacob(B)	1833	March 15	Cincinnati	02	07	03
Kuhn, Philip Jacob(B)	1833	April 29	Cincinnati	03	08	12
Kumper, John(A)	1817	Oct. 16	Preble	03	06	02
Kunkle, John(A)	1818	June 17	Darke	01	10	01
Kunkle, John(A)	1832	Jan. 23	Darke	01	10	01
Kunkle, John(B)	1832	Oct. 20	Switzerland	03	02	06
Kunkle, John(B)	1836	April 14	Darke	01	18	35
Kunkle, John(B)	1836	May 11	Darke	01	18	26
Kunnutt, William(A)	1805	Dec. 27	Montgomery	03	04	01
Kuns, George(A)	1802	Oct. 21	Pennsylvania	04	04	36
Kuns, George(A)	1803	Nov. 05	Montgomery	05	04	28
Kuns, George(A)	1803	Nov. 12	Montgomery	06	01	07
Kuns, George(A)	1803	Nov. 12	Montgomery	05	03	06
Kuns, George(A)	1803	Nov. 12	Montgomery	05	03	09
Kuns, George(A)	1803	Nov. 12	Montgomery	05	03	18
Kuns, George(A)	1803	Nov. 12	Montgomery	05	04	09
Kuns, George(A)	1804	Sept. 07	Montgomery	05	04	18
Kuns, George(A)	1804	Sept. 07	Montgomery	05	04	19
Kuns, George(A)	1804	Sept. 07	Montgomery	05	04	20
Kuns, George(A)	1804	Sept. 24	Montgomery	05	04	20
Kuns, George(A)	1805	Oct. 07	Montgomery	05	04	31
Kuns, George(A)	1805	Oct. 07	Montgomery	04	05	36
Kuns, George(A)	1806	April 07	Montgomery	02	04	29
Kuns, George(A)	1806	May 05	Montgomery	02	02	06
Kuns, Jacob(A)	1804	July 02	Montgomery	05	04	17
Kuns, Jacob(A)	1805	Oct. 16	Montgomery	05	04	04
Kuns, Jacob(A)	1805	Oct. 16	Montgomery	05	04	04
Kunts, Jacob(A)	1810	Dec. 12	Montgomery	05	04	04
Kyger, George(A)	1817	Sept. 08	Warren	02	08	15
Kyger, John(E)	1811	Oct. 28	Franklin(Ind	12	12	26
Kyger, John(E)	1812	Dec. 14	Franklin(Ind	13	12	31
Kyle, James(A)	1832	July 31	Butler	02	09	06
Kyle, James(A)	1832	July 31	Butler	02	10	31
Kyle, Samuel(A)	1807	April 04	Kentucky	05	07	36
Kyle, Samuel(A)	1807	April 04	Kentucky	06	05	31

PURCHASER	YEAR	DATE	RESIDENCE	R	T	S
Kyle, Thomas B.(A)	1806	July 10	Kentucky	06	05	31
Kyser, Benjamin(C)	1801	Dec. 31	Hamilton	07	02	02
Lacey, Daniel(A)	1812	June 04	Hamilton	01	02	34
Lacey, Thomas(A)	1815	Nov. 10	Hamilton	01	02	22
Lackey, Richard(C)	1801	Dec. 31	Hamilton	?	04	24
Lacky, Alexander(C)	1831	July 05	Hamilton	13	03	02
Lacy, Daniel(A)	1813	May 06	Hamilton	01	02	21
Lacy, John(E)	1814	Sept. 20	Wayne(Ind)	13	16	29
Lacy, John(E)	1818	March 16	Warren	14	18	27
Lacy, John(E)	1828	March 07	Wayne(Ind)	13	16	30
Lacy, Mastin(A)	1840	Aug. 01	Hamilton	01	02	22
Lacy, Thomas Heirs(A)	1840	Aug. 01	Hamilton	01	02	22
Lacy, William(E)	1817	Oct. 24	Warren	14	18	26
Ladd, Christopher(C)	1816	Aug. 31	Franklin(Ind	12	13	24
Ladd, Christopher(E)	1816	May 18	Franklin(Ind	12	13	24
Ladd, Christopher(E)	1813	Dec. 23	?	12	13	10
Ladd, Jas. Newton(E)	1828	Nov. 20	Wayne(Ind)	13	18	36
Ladd, Joseph(E)	1815	May 03	Wayne(Ind)	14	18	31
Ladd, Moses(E)	1816	Sept. 11	Madison	13	13	18
Ladd, Noble(E)	1816	Sept. 11	Madison	13	13	18
Ladd, William(E)	1829	Nov. 25	Wayne(Ind)	13	18	25
Ladd, William(E)	1830	Dec. 03	Wayne(Ind)	13	18	25
Lafaver, Solomon(A)	1832	Feb. 04	Shelby	05	09	13
Laferty, Samuel(C)	1807	March 02	Champaign	10	06	31
Lafetra, George W.(C)	1824	Dec. 11	Warren	11	02	11
Lafferty, Patrick(C)	1805	Aug. 05	Montgomery	09	02	22
Lafferty, Patrick(C)	1805	Aug. 05	Montgomery	09	02	22
Lafferty, Samuel(C)	1804	Dec. 28	Greene	10	06	28
Lafferty, Samuel(C)	1808	Nov. 02	Champaign	10	05	11
Lafuze, Samuel(A)	1813	March 29	Hamilton	02	04	19
Lafuze, Samuel(B)	1813	Sept. 28	Hamilton	01	11	05
Laird, James(E)	1831	Sept. 26	Butler	13	12	06
Lake, Elijah(B)	1832	Feb. 15	Dearborn(Ind	01	07	22
Lake, William(B)	1816	Aug. 21	Dearborn(Ind	02	07	10
Lamb, Barnabas(E)	1837	April 15	Wayne(Ind)	13	18	09
Lamb, David B.(E)	1837	Jan. 09	Randolph(Ind	13	19	24
Lamb, David B.(E)	1837	Jan. 09	Randolph(Ind	13	19	13
Lamb, Esaw(E)	1828	July 14	Wayne(Ind)	14	18	24
Lamb, George(C)	1811	April 29	Champaign	09	05	11
Lamb, Jacob(A)	1832	May 21	Preble	01	10	04
Lamb, John(A)	1812	June 26	Butler	02	06	34
Lamb, John(B)	1834	June 14	Cincinnati	02	06	14
Lamb, Joseph(C)	1811	Dec. 09	Champaign	09	05	15
Lamb, Joshua G.(C)	1818	Aug. 25	Cincinnati	11	04	02
Lamb, Joshua G.(C)	1818	Aug. 25	Cincinnati	11	04	29
Lamb, Josiah(A)	1806	Dec. 22	Warren	05	05	12
Lamb, Josiah(E)	1815	June 19	Wayne(Ind)	14	17	11
Lamb, Nathan Garrett(E)	1836	Feb. 08	Virginia	13	19	25
Lamb, Thomas(B)	1813	April 14	Wayne(Ind)	01	14	30
Lamb, Thomas(E)	1814	May 17	Wayne(Ind)	13	17	03
Lamb, Thomas(E)	1815	Nov. 15	Wayne(Ind)	14	16	02
Lamb, William Acrell(E)	1836	Feb. 08	Virginia	13	19	25
Lambden, William(B)	1815	March 04	Cincinnati	03	03	10
Lambdin, James(B)	1814	April 06	Dearborn(Ind	01	07	28
Lambdin, John(B)	1814	Sept. 30	Pennsylvania	01	07	19
Lambdin, Matthew(B)	1814	April 06	Dearborn(Ind	01	07	28
Lamberson, Samuel(B)	1816	July 23	Maryland	03	02	05
Lambert, Cortland(E)	1836	Oct. 29	Preble	15	21	15
Lambert, James(E)	1836	Jan. 27	Wayne(Ind)	15	21	15
Lambert, James(E)	1836	Oct. 29	Randolph(Ind	15	21	15
Lambert, Jonathan(A)	1830	Dec. 04	Darke	01	10	17
Lambert, Josiah(E)	1814	March 19	Warren	13	14	03
Lambert, Josiah(E)	1815	Sept. 22	Warren	13	17	17
Lambert, Josias(E)	1814	Jan. 03	Warren	13	15	27
Lambert, Nathaniel(B)	1817	May 03	Dearborn(Ind	03	08	35
Lambertson, James(B)	1836	March 17	Dearborn(Ind	03	06	15
Lambertson, Thomas(B)	1817	Sept. 20	Dearborn(Ind	03	06	12
Lambertson, Thomas(B)	1818	June 29	Dearborn(Ind	03	06	23
Lambertson, Thomas(B)	1818	July 11	Dearborn(Ind	03	06	22

PURCHASER	YEAR	DATE	RESIDENCE	R	T	S
Lambertson, Thomas(B)	1818	July 11	Dearborn(Ind	03	06	22
Lambertson, Thomas(B)	1836	June 20	Dearborn(Ind	03	06	01
Lamkin, Ezra(B)	1815	Nov. 14	Dearborn(Ind	02	03	10
Lamkin, Judson(B)	1832	March 10	Dearborn(Ind	02	03	11
Lamme, David(E)	1811	Oct. 24	Montgomery	13	15	18
Lamme, Nathan(C)	1801	Dec. 11	Hamilton	06	03	33
Lamme, William(C)	1801	Dec. 25	Hamilton	06	01	09
Lampton, John(B)	1836	Sept. 20	Switzerland	02	02	13
Lancaster, John F.(A)	1818	June 22	Hamilton	01	02	31
Lancaster, John F.(A)	1831	May 10	Hamilton	01	01	06
Lancaster, Mallory(B)	1832	March 02	Switzerland	03	02	31
Lancaster, Wright(B)	1824	June 09	Wayne(Ind)	01	13	21
Lancaster, Wright(E)	1811	Oct. 24	Wayne(Ind)	13	15	10
Lancaster, Wright(E)	1811	Oct. 24	Wayne(Ind)	13	15	15
Landees, Kimbrow(B)	1814	April 23	Kentucky	03	03	36
Landers, Henry(A)	1804	Nov. 08	?	03	05	33
Landers, John(A)	1814	Sept. 13	Preble	03	04	07
Landers, William(E)	1811	Oct. 28	Cincinnati	13	16	21
Landes, Joseph(A)	1822	Oct. 24	Darke	02	10	03
Landies, David(B)	1807	Sept. 08	Warren	01	11	01
Landis, Jacob(A)	1836	Oct. 17	Miami	03	12	05
Landis, Philip(A)	1816	Sept. 19	Butler	04	03	21
Landon, Elisha(A)	1806	Dec. 03	Warren	01	04	08
Lane, Harman J.(C)	1817	Sept. 10	Hamilton	12	01	05
Lane, Harman J.(C)	1817	Nov. 17	Hamilton	12	01	06
Lane, Henry P.(A)	1836	Nov. 21	Butler	02	14	10
Lane, Isaac(C)	1825	March 23	Warren	11	02	11
Lane, Jesse(A)	1815	Dec. 19	Preble	02	06	26
Lane, Julius(A)	1813	Nov. 29	Preble	02	06	26
Lane, Smith(E)	1814	Oct. 14	Nor.Carolina	12	14	27
Lane, William D.(E)	1837	Jan. 30	Union(Ind)	14	21	26
Langdon, Elam P.(E)	1839	July 27	Cincinnati	15	22	18
Langston, Bennett(B)	1813	Sept. 04	Franklin(Ind	02	11	35
Langston, Hiram Bennett(E)	1836	Jan. 22	Union(Ind)	12	12	24
Langston, Lazarus(A)	1814	July 18	Preble	03	04	28
Langston, Luke(A)	1818	Jan. 13	Preble	03	04	22
Lanham, Henry(B)	1814	Jan. 29	JeffersonInd	04	02	36
Lanich, Samuel(A)	1837	May 25	Montgomery	03	12	30
Lanick, Samuel(A)	1815	Sept. 15	Preble	03	07	24
Lanick, Samuel(A)	1836	Feb. 29	Montgomery	03	11	04
Lanier, Alexander C.(A)	1807	May 09	Butler	02	07	11
Lanier, Alexander C.(A)	1815	Jan. 19	Preble	01	08	24
Lanvitt, Brittain(C)	1804	Dec. 29	Greene	11	05	33
Larew, Benjamin(B)	1815	Aug. 05	Hamilton	02	03	23
Larew, Garret(B)	1815	Aug. 05	Hamilton	02	03	23
Larew, William(B)	1816	Sept. 16	Dearborn(Ind	01	02	03
Large, Jacob(A)	1835	Sept. 17	Darke	03	11	10
Largent, Daniel(A)	1837	June 17	Darke	02	14	27
Largent, James(C)	1812	March 13	Champaign	12	04	12
Largent, John(A)	1837	June 17	Darke	02	14	17
Largent, William(C)	1829	Feb. 17	Champaign	11	03	04
Larison, George(B)	1814	Dec. 12	Hamilton	01	08	28
Larison, John(A)	1817	June 12	Miami	04	11	25
Larison, John(B)	1813	Nov. 08	Hamilton	01	08	23
Larkin, Benjamin(A)	1817	Oct. 31	Clermont	02	13	36
Larkin, John(A)	1817	Oct. 31	Clermont	03	11	31
Larkin, John(A)	1817	Oct. 31	Clermont	02	13	36
Larnard, Desire(C)	1814	Oct. 29	Greene	08	06	11
Larose, Daniel(C)	1815	June 08	Preble	11	05	23
Larose, Lewis V.(A)	1814	Dec. 17	Montgomery	01	09	36
Larrison, George(B)	1815	Sept. 23	Franklin(Ind	01	07	02
Larrue, Wm.(E)	1816	May 27	Wayne(Ind)	13	16	17
Larsh, John(A)	1825	Dec. 01	Preble	01	07	22
Larsh, Paul(A)	1812	April 15	Preble	01	07	10
Larsh, Paul(A)	1813	April 14	Preble	01	07	09
Larsh, Paul(A)	1816	Dec. 20	Preble	01	07	15
Larsh, Samuel(A)	1816	Dec. 17	Preble	01	07	22
Larue, David(C)	1818	June 08	Champaign	12	02	10
Larue, John(C)	1804	Dec. 19	Montgomery	06	02	31

PURCHASER	YEAR	DATE	RESIDENCE	R	T	S
Larue, Peter(C)	1817	July 07	Champaign	12	03	19
Laselle, Francis(C)	1804	Dec. 19	DetroitDist.	10	01	07
Laselle, Jacob(C)	1804	Dec. 19	DetroitDist.	10	01	07
Lash, Paul(A)	1807	Jan. 03	Adams	01	07	10
Lasley, David(E)	1836	March 28	Randolph(Ind	14	19	08
Lasley, David(E)	1836	June 17	Randolph(Ind	14	19	08
Lasley, Eli(E)	1836	June 17	Randolph(Ind	13	19	01
Lasley, Moses(E)	1833	April 06	Randolph(Ind	13	19	01
Lasley, Moses(E)	1836	June 17	Randolph(Ind	13	19	01
Lasley, Samuel(E)	1836	Dec. 28	Randolph(Ind	13	19	01
Lassell, Joseph(B)	1825	April 20	Switzerland	02	02	04
Lassell, Joseph(B)	1836	Nov. 19	Switzerland	03	04	28
Lassell, Wm.(B)	1836	Dec. 13	Switzerland	03	04	28
Laster, Julius(A)	1830	Feb. 02	Montgomery	04	07	34
Lastutter, Peter(B)	1815	Feb. 16	Switzerland	01	03	29
Lathan, David(B)	1818	April 03	Butler	03	02	21
Lathrop, David(B)	1818	July 20	Hamilton	01	07	26
Latourrette, James(C)	1825	June 23	Clark	09	03	26
Laughead, David(A)	1803	Nov. 24	Kentucky	06	01	19
Laughead, David(A)	1803	Nov. 24	Kentucky	05	03	23
Laughlin, Moses(A)	1814	June 07	Hamilton	02	04	20
Laughlin, William B.(E)	1816	Nov. 18	Kentucky	13	11	17
Lauman, Daniel(B)	1817	Aug. 09	Wayne(Ind)	01	12	02
Lauman, John(B)	1817	Aug. 09	Wayne(Ind)	01	12	02
Laurence, Dan'l.(B)	1833	May 31	Dearborn(Ind	02	07	07
Laurence, Dan'l.(B)	1833	May 31	Dearborn(Ind	02	07	08
Laurence, George(B)	1833	May 31	Dearborn(Ind	02	07	07
Laurence, George(B)	1833	May 31	Dearborn(Ind	02	07	08
Laurence, Isaac Senr.(B)	1817	Sept. 19	Pennsylvania	02	07	10
Laurence, Isaac Senr.(B)	1817	Sept. 19	Pennsylvania	02	07	17
Laurence, Isaac Senr.(B)	1817	Sept. 19	Pennsylvania	02	07	08
Laurence, Isaac(B)	1824	June 16	Dearborn(Ind	02	07	15
Laurence, Isaac(B)	1824	June 16	Dearborn(Ind	02	07	07
Laurence, Valentine(B)	1817	Aug. 29	Dearborn(Ind	02	07	17
Laurence, Valentine(B)	1817	Aug. 29	Dearborn(Ind	02	07	20
Laurence, Valentine(B)	1817	Aug. 29	Dearborn(Ind	02	07	02
Laurimore, Hugh(A)	1816	April 01	Butler	02	11	13
Lawallen, Mashack(B)	1813	April 14	Wayne(Ind)	01	14	04
Lawallin, Mashack(B)	1807	Sept. 24	Highland	01	14	04
Lawell, Jacob(B)	1815	June 30	Kentucky	01	08	09
Lawellen, Marshack(E)	1817	July 19	Wayne(Ind)	13	21	01
Lawellin, Benjamin(E)	1817	June 10	Wayne(Ind)	14	21	07
Lawellin, Mashack(E)	1817	July 01	Wayne(Ind)	14	20	32
Lawrace, Jacob(C)	1804	Dec. 29	Montgomery	05	02	30
Lawrence, Abraham(B)	1834	July 02	Dearborn(Ind	02	07	06
Lawrence, Daniel H.(B)	1830	May 11	Dearborn(Ind	02	07	01
Lawrence, Daniel(B)	1818	May 06	Dearborn(Ind	02	07	12
Lawrence, Daniel(B)	1818	May 06	Dearborn(Ind	02	07	07
Lawrence, Daniel(E)	1837	Sept. 19	Dearborn(Ind	12	11	13
Lawrence, George Sr.(B)	1828	June 06	Pennsylvania	02	07	21
Lawrence, George(E)	1834	March 26	Dearborn(Ind	13	11	21
Lawrence, George(E)	1838	Aug. 20	Hamilton	15	22	35
Lawrence, Henry(A)	1818	Dec. 19	Warren	01	10	25
Lawrence, Henry(A)	1832	Jan. 02	Darke	01	10	17
Lawrence, Hiram(A)	1832	March 14	Preble	01	09	02
Lawrence, Isaac(B)	1819	April 29	Dearborn(Ind	02	07	08
Lawrence, Isaac(B)	1819	April 29	Dearborn(Ind	02	07	08
Lawrence, Isaac(B)	1819	April 29	Dearborn(Ind	02	07	07
Lawrence, Isaac(B)	1819	June 28	Dearborn(Ind	02	07	18
Lawrence, Isaac(B)	1819	Aug. 12	Dearborn(Ind	02	07	18
Lawrence, Isaac(B)	1832	Aug. 17	Dearborn(Ind	03	08	01
Lawrence, Isaac(B)	1833	April 10	Dearborn(Ind	03	08	01
Lawrence, James(B)	1832	Feb. 28	Dearborn(Ind	02	07	07
Lawrence, Johannes(B)	1828	April 09	Dearborn(Ind	02	07	21
Lawrence, John K.(B)	1830	Aug. 30	Dearborn(Ind	03	08	13
Lawrence, John Kronk(B)	1832	Aug. 17	Dearborn(Ind	03	08	12
Lawrence, Michael(B)	1836	June 29	Switzerland	03	03	13
Lawrence, Philip(B)	1827	Aug. 01	Dearborn(Ind	02	07	08
Lawrence, Philip(E)	1834	Jan. 28	Dearborn(Ind	13	11	29

PURCHASER	YEAR	DATE	RESIDENCE	R	T	S
Lawrence, Philip(E)	1834	March 18	Dearborn(Ind	13	11	29
Lawrence, Philip(E)	1834	June 06	Dearborn(Ind	13	11	29
Lawrence, Philip(E)	1834	Dec. 19	Dearborn(Ind	13	11	20
Lawrence, Philip(E)	1834	Dec. 19	Dearborn(Ind	13	11	29
Lawrence, Philip(E)	1835	June 05	Dearborn(Ind	13	11	29
Lawrence, Philip(E)	1835	June 05	Dearborn(Ind	13	11	19
Lawrence, Philip(E)	1837	Sept. 19	Dearborn(Ind	12	11	13
Lawrence, Rial(A)	1826	Feb. 03	Darke	01	10	26
Lawrence, Rial(A)	1831	Aug. 18	Darke	01	10	25
Lawrence, Rice B.(A)	1815	July 29	Montgomery	05	08	10
Lawrence, Valentine(B)	1818	April 17	Dearborn(Ind	02	07	01
Lawrence, Valentine(B)	1818	April 17	Dearborn(Ind	02	07	02
Lawrence, Valentine(B)	1818	April 17	Dearborn(Ind	02	07	17
Lawrence, William(B)	1834	Dec. 29	Switzerland	02	02	19
Lawrence, William(B)	1835	Aug. 10	Switzerland	02	02	19
Lawrose, John(A)	1814	April 30	Montgomery	02	08	06
Lawrose, Philip(A)	1813	Nov. 23	Preble	02	08	20
Lawson, John(C)	1804	Sept. 26	Greene	11	05	15
Lawson, Wiley(E)	1836	March 11	Randolph(Ind	14	21	14
Laybaum, Christopher(C)	1814	Feb. 26	Champaign	13	04	06
Laybourn, Amos(C)	1826	Oct. 16	Clark	09	06	29
Laybourn, Chris'r.(C)	1813	June 07	Champaign	09	05	03
Laybourn, Christopher(C)	1813	June 07	Champaign	09	06	32
Laybourn, Christopher(C)	1813	June 07	Champaign	09	06	32
Laybourn, Christopher(C)	1813	June 07	Champaign	09	06	31
Laybourn, Christopher(C)	1813	Nov. 11	Hamilton	09	06	17
Laycock, Samuel(C)	1806	March 27	DelawareCoPa	11	01	24
Laycock, Samuel(C)	1806	March 27	DelawareCoPa	12	01	19
Laycock, Samuel(C)	1806	March 27	DelawareCoPa	12	01	07
Laycock, Samuel(C)	1806	March 27	DelawareCoPa	12	01	02
Laycock, Samuel(C)	1806	March 27	DelawareCoPa	12	01	02
Laycock, Samuel(C)	1806	March 27	DelawareCoPa	12	01	02
Laycock, Samuel(C)	1806	March 27	DelawareCoPa	12	01	02
Laycock, William H.(E)	1837	Oct. 02	Cincinnati	14	21	31
Laycock, William H.(E)	1837	Oct. 02	Cincinnati	14	21	31
Laycock, William H.(E)	1837	Oct. 02	Cincinnati	14	21	30
Layman, George(C)	1824	June 07	Shelby	12	01	10
Layman, John(C)	1822	Dec. 31	Hamilton	12	01	04
Layson, John M.(E)	1815	Oct. 30	Kentucky	13	15	35
Layton, David G.(B)	1818	Aug. 04	Dearborn(Ind	02	06	02
Layton, James(A)	1831	March 11	Miami	05	08	17
Layton, Joseph(A)	1805	Sept. 10	Montgomery	06	05	28
Layton, Joseph(A)	1804	Sept. 06	Montgomery	06	04	24
Layton, Joseph(C)	1802	Dec. 30	Hamilton	09	04	32
Layton, Joseph(C)	1807	Jan. 28	Champaign	09	04	32
Layton, Joseph(C)	1811	Jan. 23	Champaign	09	04	32
Layton, Joseph(C)	1817	Dec. 02	Miami	10	02	18
Layton, Joseph(C)	1827	Aug. 22	Miami	10	02	18
Layton, William(C)	1802	Dec. 31	Hamilton	09	03	02
Lazenby, Joshua(B)	1819	Feb. 11	Clinton	01	16	03
Laziesure, Laurens(B)	1815	July 20	Dearborn(Ind	02	06	35
Laziuer, Lourans(B)	1815	July 20	Dearborn(Ind	02	06	35
LeFevre, John(A)	1828	Feb. 01	Shelby	07	01	09
Leach, Esom(A)	1813	Sept. 28	Butler	01	03	04
Leap, Samuel(B)	1832	April 17	Switzerland	03	02	08
Leaper, William(B)	1810	March 17	Kentucky	01	10	10
Leare, Daniel(A)	1807	July 23	Montgomery	03	07	28
Learned, James S.(B)	1818	July 01	Dearborn(Ind	02	03	17
Leary, Daniel(A)	1807	Feb. 18	Montgomery	02	04	05
Leary, Daniel(A)	1812	April 15	Butler	02	04	05
Leas, George(A)	1814	Oct. 26	Preble	03	07	21
Leas, John W.(A)	1832	March 01	Preble	03	08	31
Leas, William(A)	1809	Dec. 26	Preble	03	07	35
Leason, Richard L.(E)	1816	March 07	Preble	13	16	17
Leasure, Andrew(A)	1807	June 22	Montgomery	04	06	33
Leasure, Henry(B)	1836	June 15	Dearborn(Ind	02	04	06
Leasure, Henry(B)	1836	Nov. 12	Dearborn(Ind	02	04	06
Leasure, John(B)	1822	Nov. 07	Montgomery	04	06	33
Leatherbury, Charles(B)	1817	Sept. 04	Switzerland	03	03	11

PURCHASER	YEAR	DATE	RESIDENCE	R	T	S
Leatherbury, Charles(B)	1836	March 23	Switzerland	03	03	12
Leatherman, Devaull(A)	1804	Dec. 15	Pennsylvania	04	04	29
Leatherman, Henry(C)	1805	Dec. 30	Montgomery	12	04	04
Leatherman, Henry(C)	1808	Aug. 20	Champaign	12	04	01
Leatherman, Henry(C)	1814	March 21	Montgomery	12	04	04
Leavele, Robert(A)	1807	Sept. 04	Kentucky	05	08	02
Leavell, Benjamin(A)	1806	July 10	Montgomery	06	05	29
Leavell, Robert(A)	1814	March 15	Miami	04	08	02
Leavell, Robt.(A)	1828	Dec. 12	Miami	04	08	02
Leavering, John Jr.(A)	1835	June 26	Richland	03	11	22
Lechlider, Lewis(A)	1818	March 23	Montgomery	02	12	09
Leckey, John(A)	1817	June 21	Kentucky	04	08	12
Leckey, John(A)	1817	June 21	Kentucky	04	08	01
Leckey, Thomas(A)	1817	Aug. 26	Kentucky	04	08	12
Ledwell, John(A)	1814	Sept. 03	Preble	02	06	03
Lee, Abraham(B)	1807	Sept. 04	Butler	01	10	36
Lee, Abraham(B)	1831	July 05	Franklin(Ind	01	09	11
Lee, Benjamin P.(A)	1836	Oct. 17	Miami	03	12	04
Lee, Chester(E)	1836	Dec. 20	New York	13	20	14
Lee, David(A)	1802	Aug. 24	Hamilton	01	05	24
Lee, David(B)	1815	Feb. 23	Butler	03	03	03
Lee, David(B)	1833	Feb. 26	Switzerland	03	03	03
Lee, Eli(E)	1812	Jan. 31	Franklin(Ind	13	13	21
Lee, Eliza(A)	1831	Sept. 01	Darke	01	10	36
Lee, Henry(A)	1816	Sept. 19	Butler	04	03	21
Lee, Jacob(B)	1804	Dec. 18	Kentucky	02	13	24
Lee, James S.(A)	1836	Nov. 04	Washington	02	13	21
Lee, James S.(A)	1836	Nov. 04	Washington	02	13	26
Lee, James S.(A)	1836	Nov. 04	Washington	02	13	28
Lee, John(A)	1804	Sept. 24	Hamilton	01	03	34
Lee, John(B)	1806	Feb. 24	Hamilton	02	13	36
Lee, John(C)	1805	Dec. 12	Butler	08	03	08
Lee, John(C)	1812	April 15	Greene	08	03	08
Lee, Joseph(B)	1810	Oct. 09	Ind.Territory	01	10	23
Lee, Joseph(B)	1818	Sept. 09	Hamilton	03	06	27
Lee, Samuel(A)	1804	Dec. 05	Hamilton	01	03	33
Lee, Samuel(C)	1801	Dec. 29	Hamilton	05	03	32
Lee, Samuel(C)	1804	Sept. 03	Warren	04	03	29
Lee, Sarah(E)	1814	Oct. 25	Franklin(Ind	13	13	28
Lee, Stephen(E)	1828	Nov. 15	Fayette	13	13	31
Lee, Stephen(E)	1828	Nov. 15	Fayette	12	12	01
Lee, William(B)	1835	March 16	Switzerland	03	03	09
Lee, William(C)	1807	Sept. 28	Adams	09	05	05
Lee, William(C)	1809	Aug. 26	Champaign	13	03	03
Lee, William(C)	1813	July 07	Champaign	13	03	04
Leech, John Jr.(C)	1827	Aug. 22	Logan	13	03	23
Leech, John Jr.(C)	1832	Jan. 19	Logan	13	03	17
Leech, John Junr.(C)	1817	Aug. 29	Adams	13	03	23
Leech, Samuel(C)	1832	Jan. 19	Logan	13	03	23
Leedy, Henry(A)	1831	Aug. 24	Montgomery	04	07	25
Leek, Herman(B)	1816	Aug. 26	Switzerland	02	03	30
Leemasters, Jacob(C)	1814	July 13	Champaign	11	03	23
Leemen, Josiah(A)	1838	Jan. 31	Darke	02	14	13
Leemen, Josiah(A)	1837	Sept. 15	Darke	02	14	13
Leeper, Absalom(A)	1828	Oct. 18	Montgomery	04	06	05
Leeper, John(B)	1826	May 20	Dearborn(Ind	01	06	21
Leer, Jacob(A)	1832	Aug. 14	Montgomery	04	07	20
Leese, Christopher(A)	1818	June 12	Montgomery	04	09	02
Leese, George(A)	1808	Dec. 03	Preble	03	07	21
Leeson, James(B)	1818	Feb. 24	Dearborn(Ind	02	05	12
Leeson, James(B)	1832	April 17	Dearborn(Ind	02	05	12
Leeson, Richard L.(E)	1816	Jan. 20	Preble	13	16	17
Leet, Abraham(A)	1804	Aug. 09	Butler	02	03	01
Lefaver, Alfred(A)	1836	July 11	Miami	03	11	21
Lefaver, Christian(A)	1836	Feb. 08	Miami	08	02	30
Lefaver, Cyrus(A)	1836	July 11	Miami	03	11	03
Lefaver, John(E)	1838	Aug. 20	Miami	14	22	25
Leffel, Dan'l.(C)	1829	Dec. 11	Clark	09	03	11
Leffel, Daniel(C)	1806	June 23	Champaign	09	04	24

PURCHASER	YEAR	DATE	RESIDENCE	R	T	S
Leffel, Daniel(C)	1811	Aug. 30	Champaign	09	03	12
Leffel, James(C)	1818	March 30	Clark	10	03	13
Leffel, Thomas(C)	1828	Dec. 05	Clark	11	03	19
Lefforge, Jacob(B)	1835	May 29	Franklin(Ind	02	08	05
Lefforge, Jacob(B)	1835	Nov. 18	Franklin(Ind	02	08	06
Lefforge, John(B)	1829	Jan. 10	Franklin(Ind	02	08	15
Lefler, Philip(A)	1811	June 24	Butler	04	02	05
Leforge, John(B)	1812	Feb. 08	Franklin(Ind	02	08	10
Lefter, Uriah(E)	1836	June 07	Franklin(Ind	12	12	30
Legg, Charles(A)	1805	Aug. 30	Butler	04	02	03
Legg, John(A)	1831	Nov. 22	Butler	05	09	29
Legg, William Coxion(A)	1831	Oct. 21	Butler	05	09	21
Legg, William(B)	1814	Oct. 24	Butler	01	02	24
Legget, John(B)	1818	Feb. 05	Dearborn(Ind	03	06	10
Lehman, Benjamin(A)	1809	Feb. 17	Montgomery	05	04	15
Lehmann, Peter(C)	1805	Dec. 17	Montgomery	09	02	28
Leighdy, Simon(E)	1832	Nov. 09	Randolph(Ind	13	20	15
Leighdy, Simon(E)	1836	March 11	Randolph(Ind	13	21	35
Leighty, Jacob(B)	1832	Aug. 17	Cincinnati	02	07	19
Leighty, John(B)	1823	March 03	Cincinnati	02	07	19
Leighty, John(B)	1831	Aug. 30	Cincinnati	02	07	19
Leithner, Gregory(B)	1824	Oct. 20	Cincinnati	02	07	22
Leman, John R.(C)	1806	Feb. 14	Champaign	11	03	03
Lemasters, Isaac(B)	1815	Nov. 07	Dearborn(Ind	01	05	05
Lemasters, Jacob(A)	1818	Aug. 19	Champaign	07	02	33
Lemasters, Luman Walker(A)	1832	March 10	Shelby	07	02	33
Lemen, Geo. Bruce(C)	1829	Feb. 17	Clark	11	03	14
Lemen, Jos. O.(C)	1812	Jan. 06	Champaign	11	05	36
Lemen, Laurence V.(C)	1812	Jan. 06	Champaign	11	05	36
Lemen, William(C)	1812	Jan. 06	Champaign	11	05	15
Lemme, Nathan(C)	1802	Dec. 28	Hamilton	06	03	34
Lemmon, Lemuel(B)	1812	Feb. 11	Dearborn(Ind	01	09	04
Lemmon, Lemuel(B)	1812	Nov. 26	Butler	01	10	34
Lemmon, Lemuel(B)	1813	Oct. 28	Butler	01	10	33
Lemmon, Lemuel(B)	1815	June 05	Butler	01	10	35
Lemmon, William(B)	1818	April 22	Hamilton	01	08	04
Lemmon, William(C)	1804	Dec. 31	Greene	09	05	30
Lemmon, William(C)	1819	Nov. 20	Cincinnati	12	02	04
Lemon, Adam H.(B)	1818	Oct. 26	Hamilton	02	07	14
Lemon, John R.(C)	1813	Aug. 10	Champaign	10	05	02
Lemon, William(A)	1817	Dec. 12	Virginia	03	08	17
Lemons, John R.(C)	1808	June 03	Champaign	10	05	02
Lench, Isiah(A)	1806	Sept. 02	Warren	04	07	11
Lenham, Phildergreen(A)	1814	March 14	Darke	02	11	34
Lenham, Phildergreen(A)	1815	Jan. 02	Darke	02	11	02
Lenin, John R.(C)	1807	Aug. 27	Champaign	10	06	32
Lennard, Philip(E)	1838	Aug. 13	Hamilton	14	21	06
Lennard, Philip(E)	1838	Aug. 13	Hamilton	14	21	32
Lennen, Peter(B)	1813	Oct. 11	Franklin(Ind	01	11	27
Lennen, Peter(B)	1818	April 17	Indiana	01	11	14
Lenner, Peter(B)	1815	Jan. 17	Franklin(Ind	01	11	27
Lenner, Samuel(B)	1815	Jan. 17	Franklin(Ind	01	11	27
Lennon, James(C)	1802	Dec. 29	Hamilton	10	02	28
Lennon, James(C)	1804	Dec. 21	Montgomery	10	02	28
Lennon, Michael(C)	1814	March 12	Miami	11	02	24
Lenon, John(C)	1806	May 31	Montgomery	11	02	19
Lenover, James(B)	1837	Feb. 10	Dearborn(Ind	03	05	27
Lenover, Joseph(B)	1831	Aug. 10	Dearborn(Ind	03	05	24
Lenox, James(A)	1814	Jan. 25	Miami	06	08	12
Lenox, Jno.(A)	1831	Aug. 09	Shelby	07	01	07
Lenox, John(A)	1810	Oct. 27	Franklin(Ind	06	08	31
Lenox, John(A)	1814	Jan. 25	Miami	06	08	12
Lenox, John(A)	1817	Sept. 15	Miami	06	08	25
Lenox, Richard(A)	1810	Oct. 27	Franklin(Ind	06	08	31
Lentz, Nicholas(B)	1818	Feb. 14	Switzerland	03	03	05
Lentz, Nicholas(B)	1818	June 08	Switzerland	03	03	05
Leonard, Abner(B)	1813	Nov. 19	Warren	01	09	29
Leonard, George(C)	1806	Dec. 29	Champaign	12	05	18
Leonard, George(C)	1808	Feb. 02	Champaign	12	05	18

PURCHASER	YEAR	DATE	RESIDENCE	R	T	S
Leonard, George(C)	1812	Nov. 23	Champaign	12	05	27
Leonard, Nathaniel(E)	1814	April 06	Greene	13	17	32
Leonard, Samuel(E)	1811	Oct. 24	Warren	13	16	06
Leonard, Samuel(E)	1811	Oct. 24	Warren	13	16	05
Leonard, Samuel(E)	1816	Jan. 03	Butler	13	16	04
Leonard, Samuel(E)	1816	Dec. 02	Wayne(Ind)	13	16	05
Lerew, John(C)	1802	Dec. 31	Hamilton	06	02	31
Lesche, Bernard Hy.(E)	1837	May 01	Cincinnati	11	11	25
Lesche, John Diederick(E)	1837	May 01	Cincinnati	11	11	25
Leseney, John(C)	1813	May 06	Miami	11	02	32
Lesh, Jacob(A)	1810	April 11	Preble	03	05	12
Lesh, Jacob(A)	1811	April 09	Preble	03	05	18
Lesh, John(A)	1816	Dec. 09	Preble	03	05	22
Lesley, Daniel(A)	1814	Jan. 13	Montgomery	04	04	09
Lesley, Elisha(C)	1807	March 11	Greene	08	05	27
Leslie, Jacob(A)	1818	June 22	Montgomery	03	08	35
Leslie, John(A)	1803	Oct. 29	Butler	03	04	36
Leslie, John(A)	1807	July 27	Butler	03	04	35
Leslie, John(A)	1812	Sept. 11	Preble	03	04	26
Leslie, John(A)	1813	April 14	Butler	03	04	35
Leslie, John(A)	1813	Aug. 25	Preble	03	04	26
Lesly, Elisha(C)	1812	April 15	Greene	08	05	27
Lesourd, Peter(C)	1810	June 12	Butler	03	03	26
Lessley, George(A)	1804	Sept. 24	Montgomery	04	04	23
Lester, Benj'n.(C)	1831	Jan. 12	Cincinnati	11	03	33
Lester, David(B)	1818	Oct. 01	Switzerland	03	03	09
Lesuer, William(B)	1836	Oct. 26	Hamilton	03	04	25
Levalley, Henry(A)	1819	Feb. 06	Clinton	06	07	04
Levalley, Henry(A)	1819	Feb. 06	Clinton	06	07	04
Level, Robert(A)	1807	June 30	Miami	04	08	02
Level, Robert(E)	1811	Oct. 24	Wayne(Ind)	13	16	08
Levell, John(A)	1806	Nov. 29	Ross	05	08	13
Levell, John(A)	1806	Nov. 29	Ross	05	08	24
Levell, Richard(A)	1832	March 15	Montgomery	04	08	10
Levi, Isaac(B)	1804	Sept. 19	Dearborn(Ind	01	08	29
Levi, Isaac(B)	1817	Sept. 08	Hamilton	02	02	30
Levingston, George(B)	1804	Oct. 16	Hamilton	02	11	16
Leviston, James(E)	1811	Oct. 28	Franklin(Ind	14	14	19
Lewellen, John(A)	1808	May 11	Montgomery	02	06	07
Lewellen, John(A)	1812	Jan. 18	Preble	01	07	14
Lewis, Abraham(B)	1811	Oct. 30	Kentucky	01	12	04
Lewis, Abraham(B)	1811	Oct. 30	Kentucky	01	12	09
Lewis, Abraham(B)	1811	Oct. 30	Kentucky	01	12	11
Lewis, Abraham(B)	1812	June 03	Kentucky	01	12	09
Lewis, Andrew(A)	1803	Sept. 07	Kentucky	02	04	30
Lewis, Andrew(A)	1819	Jan. 02	Kentucky	04	11	03
Lewis, Benjamin(B)	1818	March 31	Indiana	01	08	34
Lewis, Benjamin(C)	1811	Oct. 05	Champaign	13	03	10
Lewis, Bretan(C)	1812	March 16	Champaign	10	05	17
Lewis, Caleb(A)	1807	Jan. 21	Waynesville	04	07	11
Lewis, Caleb(E)	1828	July 28	Wayne(Ind)	14	15	07
Lewis, David(A)	1819	Jan. 25	Kentucky	04	11	02
Lewis, David(E)	1814	Jan. 21	Franklin(Ind	12	11	17
Lewis, Ebenezer(B)	1815	June 30	Cincinnati	01	08	09
Lewis, Ephraim(B)	1832	May 26	Dearborn(Ind	02	07	21
Lewis, Ezekiel(B)	1836	Dec. 05	Randolph(Ind	01	16	01
Lewis, George(B)	1816	Feb. 26	Franklin(Ind	02	07	10
Lewis, George(B)	1832	Sept. 22	Dearborn(Ind	02	07	25
Lewis, Jacob(A)	1816	Dec. 17	Preble	01	07	22
Lewis, James R.(E)	1837	May 16	Clark	14	20	06
Lewis, James(B)	1831	Oct. 15	Wayne(Ind)	01	17	24
Lewis, James(B)	1836	Oct. 19	Switzerland	03	04	28
Lewis, James(B)	1836	Nov. 09	Switzerland	03	04	28
Lewis, Jas. R.(E)	1837	May 16	Clark	14	21	19
Lewis, Joel(E)	1833	Nov. 27	Randolph(Ind	14	21	29
Lewis, Joel(E)	1837	March 01	Randolph(Ind	14	21	29
Lewis, Joel(E)	1837	April 19	Randolph(Ind	14	21	29
Lewis, John Cotton(B)	1818	Oct. 26	Cincinnati	02	05	08
Lewis, John(A)	1817	July 24	Greene	04	08	24

PURCHASER	YEAR	DATE	RESIDENCE	R	T	S
Lewis, John(B)	1815	Feb. 11	Kentucky	02	04	04
Lewis, John(B)	1818	May 11	Hamilton	02	03	36
Lewis, John(B)	1836	March 15	Switzerland	03	03	21
Lewis, John(C)	1809	Sept. 02	Ross	14	02	02
Lewis, John(C)	1828	Dec. 29	Champaign	13	03	08
Lewis, John(E)	1811	Oct. 25	Wayne(Ind)	14	17	07
Lewis, John(E)	1815	April 07	Wayne(Ind)	14	17	08
Lewis, John(E)	1815	Dec. 04	Franklin(Ind	12	13	25
Lewis, Jonah(B)	1835	April 06	Dearborn(Ind	03	07	26
Lewis, Jonah(B)	1835	April 06	Dearborn(Ind	03	07	27
Lewis, Jonath'n.(B)	1815	Oct. 24	Hamilton	01	07	30
Lewis, Jonathan(B)	1817	Sept. 08	Cincinnati	02	07	23
Lewis, Jonathan(B)	1817	Sept. 01	Cincinnati	02	07	23
Lewis, Joseph(A)	1816	Feb. 09	Preble	02	06	25
Lewis, Joseph(E)	1835	June 24	Wayne(Ind)	14	19	04
Lewis, Josiah(B)	1819	July 31	Cincinnati	02	05	09
Lewis, Lothrop(A)	1816	Feb. 09	Preble	02	06	24
Lewis, Matthew(E)	1832	Oct. 10	Franklin(Ind	12	11	11
Lewis, Morgan(E)	1836	March 01	Franklin(Ind	12	11	08
Lewis, Nathan(E)	1814	Jan. 21	Franklin(Ind	12	11	17
Lewis, Paul(C)	1804	Dec. 28	Warren	04	04	21
Lewis, Reuben(B)	1816	June 05	Hamilton	01	07	36
Lewis, Richard(B)	1825	June 10	Dearborn(Ind	02	07	22
Lewis, Richard(E)	1811	Oct. 25	Wayne(Ind)	14	17	18
Lewis, Richard(E)	1811	Oct. 25	Wayne(Ind)	14	17	07
Lewis, Samuel(A)	1813	July 30	Butler	01	04	04
Lewis, Samuel(A)	1816	April 08	Preble	02	06	12
Lewis, Samuel(B)	1818	April 13	Switzerland	02	02	20
Lewis, Samuel(E)	1834	April 04	Franklin(Ind	13	12	28
Lewis, Thomas(B)	1806	Aug. 25	Dearborn(Ind	02	12	11
Lewis, Thomas(B)	1806	Aug. 25	Dearborn(Ind	02	12	11
Lewis, Thomas(B)	1806	Aug. 25	Dearborn(Ind	02	13	35
Lewis, Welcome(B)	1825	June 10	Dearborn(Ind	02	07	22
Lewis, William(A)	1815	April 24	Cincinnati	01	08	36
Lewis, William(B)	1806	Aug. 25	Dearborn(Ind	02	12	15
Lewis, William(B)	1806	Oct. 02	Dearborn(Ind	02	12	02
Lewis, William(B)	1818	Jan. 29	Hamilton	02	06	36
Lewis, William(B)	1818	Aug. 22	Cincinnati	02	05	14
Lewis, William(B)	1828	Dec. 11	Switzerland	03	02	06
Lewis, William(E)	1813	Sept. 02	Wayne(Ind)	14	14	07
Lewis, William(E)	1813	Dec. 24	Wayne(Ind)	13	14	12
Lewis, William(E)	1818	April 17	Franklin(Ind	14	18	18
Lewis, Zimri(E)	1818	April 17	Franklin(Ind	14	18	18
Lichty, Jacob(A)	1811	Sept. 24	Montgomery	05	03	22
Liddil, David G.(A)	1837	Jan. 10	Butler	03	12	26
Liddle, William(B)	1833	Jan. 16	Dearborn(Ind	01	06	09
Lientz, Nichol's.(B)	1818	Oct. 06	Hamilton	03	03	20
Lientz, Nicholas(B)	1818	Oct. 01	Switzerland	03	03	09
Lientz, Nicholas(B)	1836	March 15	Switzerland	03	03	17
Liggett, John(B)	1838	May 21	Clermont	03	05	35
Light, Enoch(E)	1833	March 02	Randolph(Ind	13	19	11
Light, Enoch(E)	1834	March 24	Randolph(Ind	13	19	11
Light, Enoch(E)	1836	Sept. 24	Randolph(Ind	13	20	36
Light, Jacob(B)	1814	Jan. 28	Clermont	02	03	24
Light, Jacob(B)	1815	Jan. 17	Clermont	02	03	24
Light, Landis(A)	1838	Feb. 14	Pennsylvania	01	14	05
Lightfoot, Christopher(C)	1806	Nov. 28	Ross	08	06	24
Lightfoot, Christopher(C)	1806	Nov. 28	Ross	09	06	19
Lightfoot, Christopher(C)	1812	April 15	Greene	09	06	19
Lightfoot, Christopher(C)	1812	April 15	Greene	08	06	24
Lightner, John J.(E)	1837	Oct. 02	Cincinnati	11	10	02
Lighty, Conrod(A)	1819	June 10	Montgomery	04	11	36
Likely, Henry(B)	1817	Nov. 26	Pennsylvania	02	06	09
Lilie, Frederick(E)	1836	Oct. 22	Cincinnati	11	10	26
Lilie, Frederick(E)	1836	Oct. 29	Cincinnati	11	10	26
Lillard, John Pullom(B)	1832	Dec. 01	Switzerland	01	03	33
Lilly, Thomas(E)	1820	Oct. 20	Ross	13	17	01
Limeback, Adam(B)	1831	Dec. 13	Switzerland	01	02	18
Limeback, Adam(B)	1834	Nov. 28	Switzerland	01	02	19

191

PURCHASER	YEAR	DATE	RESIDENCE	R	T	S
Limpass, Enoch(E)	1818	Feb. 19	Franklin(Ind	12	13	33
Limpus, Enoch(E)	1812	Sept. 07	Franklin(Ind	12	13	28
Limpus, Isaac(E)	1831	Feb. 04	Fayette	12	13	21
Linch, John(A)	1829	Aug. 28	Preble	03	07	06
Lincoln, Moses J.(A)	1825	March 17	Preble	01	07	22
Lincoln, Thomas(A)	1810	Sept. 17	Kentucky	02	06	11
Lincoln, Thomas(A)	1816	Jan. 29	Preble	02	07	29
Lindenmoot, John(A)	1832	Feb. 01	Montgomery	02	12	32
Lindhouse, Henry(A)	1838	April 30	Cincinnati	02	15	35
Lindlay, Abraham(B)	1814	June 24	Hamilton	03	03	24
Lindlay, Abraham(B)	1814	June 24	Hamilton	02	02	18
Lindlay, David(A)	1817	Sept. 18	Montgomery	04	04	04
Lindlay, Isaac(A)	1808	Nov. 24	Warren	01	04	12
Lindlay, James(E)	1811	Oct. 25	Wayne(Ind)	14	17	07
Lindlay, Zenos(C)	1812	Feb. 10	Miami	12	01	07
Lindley, Daniel(B)	1837	July 06	Miami	01	19	25
Lindley, Daniel(E)	1837	July 06	Miami	15	21	11
Lindley, Demas(B)	1837	June 19	Miami	01	19	24
Lindley, Demas(E)	1836	Oct. 11	Miami	15	21	03
Lindley, Demas(E)	1836	Nov. 11	Miami	15	21	03
Lindley, Demas(E)	1836	Nov. 11	Miami	15	21	10
Lindley, Demas(E)	1836	Nov. 11	Miami	15	21	15
Lindley, Demas(E)	1836	Nov. 11	?	15	21	02
Lindley, Demas(E)	1837	June 19	Miami	15	21	02
Lindley, Francis S.(B)	1836	March 28	Switzerland	03	04	34
Lindly, Demas(C)	1829	Dec. 11	Miami	12	01	07
Lindsay, Elijah(B)	1833	March 02	Dearborn(Ind	01	04	29
Lindsay, James(B)	1812	Nov. 25	Dearborn(Ind	02	04	02
Lindsay, James(B)	1817	June 05	Dearborn(Ind	02	05	32
Lindsay, James(B)	1832	Sept. 20	Dearborn(Ind	02	05	32
Lindsay, John(A)	1829	Dec. 12	Miami	05	08	21
Lindsay, John(B)	1818	March 30	Kentucky	03	06	15
Lindsay, Vincent(B)	1813	May 27	Dearborn(Ind	02	04	03
Lindsay, William(A)	1803	Oct. 01	Kentucky	06	01	06
Lindsey, George Ross(B)	1813	Nov. 06	Dearborn(Ind	02	04	03
Lindsey, Jeremiah(E)	1819	Nov. 26	Greene	14	21	28
Lindsey, John B.(B)	1815	Sept. 09	Kentucky	01	02	31
Lindsey, Thos. B.(?)	?	?	Frankfort,Ky	?	?	?
Lindsey, Thos. N.(?)	?	?	Frankfort,Ky	?	?	?
Lindsey, Thos.(E)	1831	Nov. 24	Wayne(Ind)	13	17	03
Lindsley, Isaac(C)	1801	Dec. 28	Hamilton	04	04	28
Line, Henry C.(C)	1825	Oct. 20	Miami	13	02	30
Line, Henry C.(C)	1829	June 27	Miami	13	02	30
Line, Henry C.(C)	1829	Aug. 25	Miami	13	02	30
Line, Jacob(D)	1808	Nov. 01	Butler	03	02	26
Line, John(C)	1828	Nov. 05	Montgomery	13	02	30
Line, Samuel Jr.(A)	1834	Oct. 21	Champaign	07	02	28
Line, Samuel(C)	1811	June 24	Hamilton	12	01	15
Line, Samuel(C)	1815	Jan. 10	Hamilton	12	01	09
Linebak, Jacob(B)	1832	Sept. 24	Switzerland	02	02	23
Linebak, William(B)	1832	Sept. 24	Switzerland	02	02	22
Lingle, Jno.(A)	1813	March 25	Butler	04	03	31
Lingle, John(C)	1811	Aug. 13	Champaign	09	05	21
Linkenhokes, Adam(A)	1811	Oct. 23	Virginia	05	04	31
Linkswiler, George(E)	1813	June 22	Ross	13	05	30
Linn, Alexander(A)	1828	Sept. 09	Warren	07	01	03
Linn, Hugh(A)	1817	Nov. 25	Pennsylvania	05	08	14
Linn, James(D)	1813	March 01	Butler	02	03	11
Linn, James(E)	1836	Feb. 02	Franklin(Ind	13	12	32
Linn, John Junr.(B)	1832	June 13	Franklin(Ind	01	08	07
Linn, Joshua(A)	1833	Oct. 23	Monroe	03	11	23
Linn, Samuel(A)	1831	Dec. 15	Butler	05	08	04
Linn, William(A)	1831	Aug. 15	Miami	05	08	27
Linn, William(E)	1831	Oct. 13	Franklin(Ind	13	12	29
Lintner, Andrew(A)	1814	Oct. 21	Butler	01	06	22
Lintner, Peter(A)	1811	April 09	Butler	02	04	17
Linton, Demsey(E)	1835	Oct. 02	Randolph(Ind	14	18	01
Linvill, James(E)	1836	Dec. 07	Rush(Ind)	12	13	31
Linvill, John(E)	1834	June 19	Fayette	11	13	36

PURCHASER	YEAR	DATE	RESIDENCE	R	T	S
Linvill, John(E)	1836	Jan. 20	Fayette	11	12	12
Lippencott, Obadiah(C)	1815	April 21	Greene	10	03	10
Lippincott, Obadiah(C)	1813	Feb. 06	Greene	08	03	29
Lipscomb, John(E)	1836	Oct. 31	CampbellCoKy	12	11	10
Liss, Henry(A)	1814	Oct. 29	Warren	02	08	04
Lister, James(A)	1807	Aug. 26	Butler	02	04	13
Liston, Edward(A)	1801	June 27	Hamilton	03	02	01
Liston, Joseph(A)	1806	June 02	Butler	01	08	17
Liter, John(A)	1806	March 22	Kentucky	02	08	35
Litrell, Samuel(E)	1811	Oct. 25	Wayne(Ind)	14·14	19
Littell, Elias(B)	1831	July 01	Dearborn(Ind	02	04	05
Littell, Elias(B)	1836	June 06	Dearborn(Ind	02	04	05
Little, Abraham(A)	1814	June 16	Wayne(Ind)	01	09	06
Little, David(E)	1836	March 17	Randolph(Ind	15	20	31
Little, David(E)	1836	Aug. 22	Randolph(Ind	15	20	31
Little, Jacob Senr.(B)	1807	April 29	Dearborn(Ind	01	12	05
Little, Jacob(E)	1811	Oct. 24	Wayne(Ind)	13	15	10
Little, John(B)	1835	Jan. 26	Hamilton	02	08	36
Little, Lewis(B)	1807	June 29	Montgomery	01	12	06
Little, Lewis(B)	1807	July 10	Montgomery	01	12	06
Little, Peter(E)	1811	Oct. 24	Wayne(Ind)	13	15	09
Little, William(A)	1832	June 21	Wayne(Ind)	01	10	17
Littleton, Thomas(B)	1818	Feb. 16	Clermont	02	06	27
Littrel, Samuel(E)	1814	Aug. 10	Franklin(Ind	13	14	24
Livengood, Henry(A)	1819	June 10	Miami	03	10	36
Livingston, Adam D.(B)	1817	Oct. 07	Dearborn(Ind	03	06	35
Livingston, Adam D.(B)	1817	Oct. 07	Dearborn(Ind	03	06	35
Livingston, John J.(B)	1836	June 13	Dearborn(Ind	03	06	21
Livingston, John(B)	1806	May 06	Dearborn(Ind	02	04	10
Lloyd, Rees(A)	1818	Feb. 17	Butler	01	03	15
Lloyd, Wm. Harper(B)	1835	Sept. 01	Dearborn(Ind	01	07	35
Lochr, John Frederick(A)	1831	Oct. 19	Warren	04	07	19
Lock, Benjamin(B)	1831	June 28	Switzerland	03	04	32
Lock, Hezekiah(B)	1838	May 21	Randolph(Ind	01	17	34
Lock, Hezekiah(E)	1836	July 26	Randolph(Ind	15	19	17
Lock, James(A)	1831	Jan. 01	Hamilton	02	10	33
Lock, John Jun.(A)	1815	Jan. 20	Preble	02	09	24
Lock, John Sen.(A)	1815	Jan. 20	Preble	03	07	19
Lock, John Senr.(A)	1811	Nov. 16	Maryland	03	07	20
Lock, John(A)	1809	Nov. 18	Maryland	03	07	22
Lock, John(A)	1809	Nov. 18	Maryland	03	07	26
Lock, John(A)	1811	Nov. 16	Maryland	03	07	20
Lock, John(A)	1812	Nov. 28	Maryland	03	07	22
Lock, John(A)	1815	March 17	Preble	03	07	26
Lock, John(B)	1832	June 13	Switzerland	03	03	29
Lock, Peter Jur.(B)	1815	Dec. 04	Switzerland	03	03	12
Lock, Peter(B)	1811	Nov. 26	Ind.Territory	03	02	02
Lock, Peter(B)	1818	April 27	Switzerland	03	04	33
Lock, Peter(B)	1818	May 04	Switzerland	03	04	32
Lock, Peter(B)	1825	June 09	Switzerland	02	02	04
Lock, Richard(B)	1831	June 28	Champaign	03	04	32
Lock, William(E)	1818	Dec. 03	Wayne(Ind)	13	18	27
Lock, William(E)	1836	Feb. 01	Wayne(Ind)	13	18	05
Lockard, John(C)	1812	April 15	Champaign	09	05	06
Locke, Isaac(E)	1833	Dec. 26	Randolph(Ind	13	19	22
Lockhart, Moses(E)	1813	May 22	Franklin(Ind	12	14	34
Lockridge, James(C)	1811	Oct. 14	Kentucky	13	03	15
Lockridge, James(C)	1811	Oct. 25	Kentucky	13	05	26
Lockwood, Harvey(E)	1816	March 22	Franklin(Ind	12	12	15
Lockwood, Harvy(E)	1815	Sept. 28	Cincinnati	12	12	11
Lockwood, Jared(E)	1836	April 22	Franklin(Ind	12	12	28
Lockwood, John B.(E)	1836	June 27	Franklin(Ind	12	12	19
Loder, Daniel(B)	1818	March 18	Hamilton	03	05	13
Loder, James A.(B)	1827	Aug. 21	Dearborn(Ind	03	05	13
Loder, James(B)	1818	March 18	Hamilton	03	05	10
Loder, John(E)	1814	Aug. 18	Butler	12	15	29
Lodge, Jacob(A)	1836	May 28	Montgomery	04	11	07
Loehr, Jno. Frederick(A)	1832	May 17	Warren	04	07	17
Loehr, John Frederick(A)	1831	Aug. 27	Warren	04	07	19

PURCHASER	YEAR	DATE	RESIDENCE	R	T	S
Loffer, Christian(A)	1819	April 19	Miami	05	09	14
Logan, Anthony(C)	1804	Sept. 03	Montgomery	06	02	26
Logan, David(C)	1801	Dec. 19	Hamilton	04	02	09
Logan, James(A)	1806	Sept. 04	New Jersey	02	06	23
Logan, James(A)	1807	Jan. 20	Hamilton	06	07	18
Logan, James(B)	1813	Nov. 25	Franklin(Ind	02	09	10
Logan, James(C)	1806	Aug. 25	New Jersey	11	03	22
Logan, John(B)	1805	Oct. 09	So. Carolina	02	09	09
Logan, Joseph(A)	1813	Aug. 05	Butler	01	03	09
Logan, Samuel(C)	1807	June 29	Kentucky	10	05	32
Logan, Samuel(E)	1814	June 10	Franklin(Ind	12	13	08
Logan, Samuel(E)	1815	Dec. 28	Franklin(Ind	13	13	29
Logan, Thomas(E)	1816	Jan. 13	Franklin(Ind	13	13	29
Logan, William(B)	1804	Dec. 04	Hamilton	02	10	28
Logan, William(B)	1807	Jan. 16	Dearborn(Ind	02	11	22
Logan, William(C)	1805	Dec. 05	Kentucky	07	04	24
Logee, Andreas(B)	1835	Dec. 24	Dearborn(Ind	03	08	14
Lollar, Ephraim(B)	1833	Oct. 11	Dearborn(Ind	03	08	23
Lollar, Joseph(E)	1836	Nov. 18	Montgomery	14	21	26
Lollar, Joseph(E)	1836	Nov. 19	Montgomery	14	21	24
Lollar, Joseph(E)	1837	Jan. 14	Greene	14	21	24
Lomax, Abel(E)	1815	Nov. 11	Nor.Carolina	14	18	32
Lomax, Joseph(E)	1832	June 18	Wayne(Ind)	13	18	26
Long, David(A)	1803	Dec. 23	Butler	04	02	20
Long, David(C)	1815	Oct. 17	Virginia	12	03	15
Long, David(C)	1829	March 27	Champaign	12	03	10
Long, Edwin R.(A)	1836	Sept. 05	U. S. Army	01	15	15
Long, Ellis(A)	1837	March 27	Morgan	02	13	02
Long, George D.(A)	1811	May 20	Miami	08	02	29
Long, Henry(A)	1814	May 27	Pennsylvania	01	04	15
Long, Henry(A)	1814	June 07	Pennsylvania	01	04	21
Long, Henry(C)	1815	Nov. 09	Champaign	12	03	15
Long, Henry(C)	1817	Oct. 23	Virginia	12	03	03
Long, Jacob(A)	1815	Oct. 07	Preble	01	08	04
Long, Jacob(C)	1801	Dec. 22	Hamilton	05	02	18
Long, James(A)	1815	March 06	Miami	02	12	27
Long, James(C)	1801	Dec. 29	Hamilton	04	03	32
Long, Jesse(A)	1814	Nov. 14	Montgomery	01	08	11
Long, Jesse(C)	1805	Dec. 27	Montgomery	06	01	08
Long, John(A)	1803	Oct. 29	Butler	03	04	36
Long, John(C)	1809	Dec. 11	Champaign	12	03	02
Long, John(C)	1815	Nov. 21	Virginia	12	03	21
Long, John(C)	1816	Oct. 28	Champaign	12	04	32
Long, Jonathan(C)	1806	Dec. 19	Kentucky	12	05	02
Long, Jonathan(C)	1812	April 15	Champaign	12	05	02
Long, Jonathan(C)	1813	April 14	Champaign	12	05	01
Long, Lewis(A)	1804	July 23	Montgomery	05	03	03
Long, Matthias(C)	1813	Dec. 25	Miami	10	03	34
Long, Patrick(D)	1808	Nov. 01	Hamilton	01	04	26
Long, Philip(A)	1810	Aug. 18	Montgomery	04	03	28
Long, Philip(A)	1817	Dec. 09	Montgomery	04	05	07
Long, Philip(A)	1831	May 13	Montgomery	03	08	26
Long, Philip(A)	1838	May 21	Montgomery	02	13	09
Long, Philip(A)	1838	May 21	Montgomery	02	13	04
Long, Philip(A)	1838	Aug. 08	Montgomery	02	13	04
Long, Philip(A)	1838	Aug. 23	Montgomery	02	13	04
Long, Philip(C)	1809	June 23	Champaign	12	03	02
Long, Philip(C)	1815	Jan. 07	Champaign	11	04	29
Long, Reuben(C)	1831	Aug. 08	Montgomery	12	03	19
Long, Samuel(C)	1814	Oct. 31	Pennsylvania	11	05	11
Long, Thomas(C)	1814	April 27	Champaign	14	03	25
Longfellow, Badger(E)	1836	Oct. 06	Butler	14	19	19
Longfellow, James(B)	1831	July 05	Wayne(Ind)	01	15	02
Longfellow, James(E)	1836	Oct. 18	Wayne(Ind)	14	19	25
Longfellow, John(B)	1813	Dec. 11	Butler	01	15	05
Longfellow, John(B)	1828	June 21	Wayne(Ind)	01	15	04
Longfellow, Joseph(C)	1811	Feb. 04	Champaign	12	04	15
Longgrear, John(E)	1836	Aug. 24	Ross	14	19	30
Longnecker, Peter(A)	1818	Oct. 06	Kentucky	01	07	22

PURCHASER	YEAR	DATE	RESIDENCE	R	T	S
Longstreet, Sam'l.(A)	1823	Jan. 27	Warren	04	06	29
Longworth, Nichol's.(B)	1818	Nov. 23	Hamilton	03	04	34
Longworth, Nicholas(A)	1817	Dec. 27	Cincinnati	07	01	12
Longworth, Nicholas(A)	1817	Dec. 27	Cincinnati	08	01	17
Longworth, Nicholas(A)	1817	Dec. 27	Cincinnati	08	01	17
Longworth, Nicholas(A)	1817	Dec. 27	Cincinnati	08	01	21
Longworth, Nicholas(A)	1817	Dec. 27	Cincinnati	08	01	22
Longworth, Nicholas(A)	1817	Dec. 27	Cincinnati	08	01	23
Longworth, Nicholas(A)	1836	Dec. 02	Cincinnati	01	15	36
Longworth, Nicholas(B)	1817	July 12	Cincinnati	02	03	07
Longworth, Nicholas(B)	1817	Dec. 19	Cincinnati	03	02	07
Longworth, Nicholas(B)	1817	Dec. 27	Cincinnati	03	03	18
Longworth, Nicholas(B)	1818	Jan. 03	Cincinnati	02	08	20
Longworth, Nicholas(B)	1818	Jan. 03	Cincinnati	02	08	20
Longworth, Nicholas(B)	1818	Jan. 03	Cincinnati	02	08	20
Longworth, Nicholas(B)	1818	Jan. 03	Cincinnati	02	08	20
Longworth, Nicholas(B)	1818	Jan. 19	Cincinnati	02	03	20
Longworth, Nicholas(B)	1818	Jan. 19	Cincinnati	03	04	26
Longworth, Nicholas(B)	1818	Jan. 19	Cincinnati	02	03	29
Longworth, Nicholas(B)	1818	Jan. 19	Cincinnati	03	04	26
Longworth, Nicholas(B)	1818	Jan. 19	Cincinnati	03	04	26
Longworth, Nicholas(B)	1818	Jan. 19	Cincinnati	03	04	26
Longworth, Nicholas(B)	1818	Jan. 19	Cincinnati	03	04	27
Longworth, Nicholas(B)	1818	April 25	Cincinnati	02	02	04
Longworth, Nicholas(B)	1818	July 10	Cincinnati	03	03	01
Longworth, Nicholas(B)	1818	July 20	Cincinnati	03	03	30
Longworth, Nicholas(B)	1818	Sept. 30	Cincinnati	02	03	34
Longworth, Nicholas(B)	1818	Sept. 30	Cincinnati	01	07	36
Longworth, Nicholas(B)	1819	Feb. 15	Cincinnati	03	04	34
Longworth, Nicholas(B)	1819	Feb. 16	Cincinnati	02	04	30
Longworth, Nicholas(C)	1814	Feb. 11	Cincinnati	12	03	28
Longworth, Nicholas(C)	1817	Dec. 27	Cincinnati	14	01	19
Longworth, Nicholas(C)	1817	Dec. 27	Cincinnati	13	02	30
Longworth, Nicholas(C)	1818	Sept. 30	Cincinnati	10	03	30
Longworth, Nicholas(C)	1818	Sept. 30	Cincinnati	10	03	18
Longworth, Nicholas(C)	1819	Feb. 16	Cincinnati	08	03	18
Longworth, Nicholas(E)	1817	Dec. 27	Cincinnati	13	11	29
Longworth, Nicholas(E)	1817	Dec. 27	Cincinnati	12	10	02
Longworth, Nicholas(E)	1818	Jan. 03	Cincinnati	12	10	10
Longworth, Nicholas(E)	1818	Jan. 21	Cincinnati	14	20	26
Longworth, Nicholas(E)	1818	Jan. 21	Cincinnati	14	20	23
Longworth, Nicholas(E)	1818	Jan. 21	Cincinnati	14	20	34
Longworth, Nicholas(E)	1818	Jan. 21	Cincinnati	14	20	35
Longworth, Nicholas(E)	1818	Jan. 21	Cincinnati	14	20	33
Longworth, Nicholas(E)	1818	Jan. 31	Cincinnati	11	10	15
Longworth, Nicholas(E)	1818	Jan. 31	Cincinnati	11	10	25
Longworth, Nicholas(E)	1818	Jan. 31	Cincinnati	13	12	21
Longworth, Nicholas(E)	1818	Jan. 31	Cincinnati	11	10	10
Longworth, Nicholas(E)	1818	Jan. 31	Cincinnati	11	10	27
Longworth, Nicholas(E)	1818	April 04	Cincinnati	14	19	14
Longworth, Nicholas(E)	1818	April 07	Hamilton	11	10	11
Longworth, Nicholas(E)	1818	April 07	Hamilton	14	20	35
Longworth, Nicholas(E)	1818	April 07	Hamilton	11	10	14
Longworth, Nicholas(E)	1818	April 07	Hamilton	11	10	12
Longworth, Nicholas(E)	1818	April 07	Hamilton	11	10	12
Longworth, Nicholas(E)	1818	April 07	Hamilton	14	20	13
Longworth, Nicholas(E)	1818	April 07	Hamilton	14	20	29
Longworth, Nicholas(E)	1818	April 07	Hamilton	12	10	08
Longworth, Nicholas(E)	1818	April 07	Hamilton	12	10	17
Longworth, Nicholas(E)	1818	April 07	Hamilton	14	20	30
Longworth, Nicholas(E)	1818	April 20	Hamilton	14	20	33
Longworth, Nicholas(E)	1818	June 15	Cincinnati	14	19	02
Longworth, Nicholas(E)	1818	June 15	Cincinnati	14	20	25
Longworth, Nicholas(E)	1818	July 30	Cincinnati	14	19	05
Longworth, Nicholas(E)	1818	July 30	Cincinnati	14	19	19
Longworth, Nicholas(E)	1818	July 30	Cincinnati	14	19	05
Longworth, Nicholas(E)	1818	July 30	Cincinnati	14	20	19
Longworth, Nicholas(E)	1818	Aug. 05	Cincinnati	14	20	23
Longworth, Nicholas(E)	1818	Aug. 05	Cincinnati	14	20	31

PURCHASER	YEAR	DATE	RESIDENCE	R	T	S
Longworth, Nicholas(E)	1818	Aug. 05	Cincinnati	14	20	30
Longworth, Nicholas(E)	1818	Aug. 05	Cincinnati	14	20	34
Longworth, Nicholas(E)	1818	Aug. 05	Cincinnati	14	20	36
Longworth, Nicholas(E)	1818	Aug. 05	Cincinnati	14	19	10
Longworth, Nicholas(E)	1818	Aug. 05	Cincinnati	14	19	04
Longworth, Nicholas(E)	1818	Aug. 05	Cincinnati	14	19	02
Longworth, Nicholas(E)	1818	Aug. 10	Cincinnati	11	10	03
Longworth, Nicholas(E)	1818	Sept. 22	Cincinnati	14	20	09
Longworth, Thos.(C)	1831	Aug. 08	Cincinnati	12	03	28
Lonney, Thomas(B)	1834	Dec. 08	Switzerland	01	02	18
Lonney, Thomas(B)	1836	May 11	Switzerland	01	02	18
Loo, William(C)	1801	Dec. 31	Hamilton	08	03	31
Looker, Othniel(A)	1805	June 27	Hamilton	01	02	18
Looker, Othniel(A)	1806	June 23	Hamilton	01	02	20
Looker, Othniel(A)	1805	Jan. 01	New York	01	02	20
Looker, Othniel(A)	1815	Nov. 04	Hamilton	01	02	08
Looker, Samuel B.(A)	1815	March 04	Hamilton	01	02	27
Looker, Samuel B.(B)	1815	Oct. 23	Dearborn(Ind	01	07	08
Looker, Silas C.(B)	1818	June 05	Cincinnati	02	08	18
Loos, Daniel(A)	1838	Feb. 05	Pennsylvania	01	14	24
Lord, Jesse B.(B)	1817	Oct. 09	Dearborn(Ind	03	06	03
Loree, Samuel(A)	1838	Aug. 07	Montgomery	01	13	02
Lorimor, John(A)	1815	April 28	Butler	02	12	28
Loring, Israel(A)	1801	May 27	Cincinnati	01	04	26
Loring, John Senr.(A)	1809	Aug. 05	Cincinnati	02	12	35
Loring, Samuel(A)	1816	March 16	Butler	01	11	14
Loring, Thomas(B)	1835	Sept. 09	Randolph(Ind	01	18	13
Lorton, James(C)	1816	Nov. 25	Kentucky	10	04	20
Lorton, William(C)	1816	Nov. 25	Kentucky	10	04	20
Losch, Chas. Christ'n.(E)	1838	Aug. 11	Darke	14	22	35
Losear, George(E)	1836	Aug. 22	Montgomery	15	21	28
Losey, Solomon(B)	1836	July 18	JeffersonInd	03	03	28
Lostutter, Peter(B)	1832	Jan. 24	Switzerland	01	03	31
Lostuttler, Peter(B)	1816	Feb. 02	Switzerland	01	03	29
Lotton, Ralph Senr.(B)	1818	June 05	Dearborn(Ind	02	03	36
Lotton, Thomas(B)	1833	Aug. 27	Dearborn(Ind	02	03	11
Lotz, Abraham(E)	1836	June 17	Randolph(Ind	15	22	11
Lotz, Abraham(E)	1837	Nov. 01	Jay Co.,Ind.	15	22	11
Lotz, Abraham(E)	1838	May 21	Jay Co.,Ind.	15	22	10
Lotz, Abraham(E)	1838	May 21	Jay Co.,Ind.	15	22	23
Loucks, Adam(A)	1820	March 21	Franklin	02	09	27
Loucks, David(A)	1822	Sept. 30	Warren	03	06	18
Louden, Benjamin(E)	1815	Jan. 06	Ohio	13	12	12
Louderback, Abraham(E)	1816	Sept. 11	Darke	13	13	36
Louderback, Joseph(C)	1816	Oct. 12	Virginia	11	04	33
Loudon, Daniel(B)	1836	April 04	Switzerland	03	03	20
Loudon, Daniel(B)	1836	May 16	Switzerland	03	03	08
Loudon, Robert(B)	1807	Jan. 30	Kentucky	02	12	12
Lough, John(E)	1816	Oct. 25	Wayne(Ind)	14	16	28
Loughman, Henry(B)	1817	Dec. 17	Switzerland	02	02	27
Lounsbury, Daniel(E)	1835	Dec. 11	Franklin(Ind	13	12	20
Lounsbury, Daniel(E)	1835	Dec. 11	Franklin(Ind	13	12	20
Lourie, Fielding(C)	1811	April 09	Miami	10	01	05
Lourimore, William(A)	1833	June 01	Darke	02	12	36
Loury, Fielding(A)	1816	July 22	Montgomery	06	05	19
Loury, Fielding(C)	1829	Dec. 11	Montgomery	11	01	01
Loury, Fielding(C)	1819	Dec. 11	Montgomery	11	01	01
Louthain, Absalom(C)	1812	Aug. 19	Virginia	10	02	03
Louthain, George(A)	1835	Oct. 03	Miami	08	02	30
Louthain, George(C)	1812	Aug. 19	Virginia	10	02	03
Louthain, Jas. Shell(A)	1831	Oct. 20	Miami	07	02	36
Louthain, John(A)	1830	Aug. 09	Miami	07	02	25
Louthain, John(A)	1830	Aug. 09	Miami	07	02	36
Louthain, John(C)	1812	Aug. 19	Virginia	10	02	04
Louthain, Parker(A)	1830	Sept. 17	Shelby	07	01	01
Louthain, Parker(A)	1830	Sept. 17	Shelby	07	02	36
Louthain, Philip Cecil(A)	1833	Dec. 03	Shelby	08	02	30
Love, George(A)	1804	Nov. 26	Butler	01	03	09
Love, Hanson(B)	1813	April 14	Franklin(Ind	02	09	23

PURCHASER	YEAR	DATE	RESIDENCE	R	T	S
Love, Israel(E)	1837	June 23	Franklin(Ind	11	10	02
Love, James(E)	1837	June 06	Butler	11	10	02
Love, John Pierpoint(A)	1832	Aug. 16	Butler	02	10	23
Love, John(B)	1806	Oct. 15	Kentucky	03	03	26
Love, Robert(B)	1834	Jan. 24	Darke	01	16	10
Loveall, Aquila(A)	1817	Nov. 25	Darke	01	10	31
Lovelace, Seneca(B)	1817	Oct. 23	Cincinnati	02	02	12
Lovett, Britton(C)	1814	June 24	Champaign	13	04	13
Low, Alexander(B)	1833	July 22	Dearborn(Ind	02	05	07
Low, Elijah(A)	1817	Sept. 02	Franklin(Ind	01	11	09
Low, Elijah(A)	1817	Sept. 02	Franklin(Ind	01	11	04
Low, Jesse(C)	1817	Dec. 20	Greene	10	04	31
Low, William(A)	1806	May 23	Montgomery	05	05	05
Low, William(A)	1806	Aug. 05	Georgia	06	03	19
Low, William(A)	1813	July 03	Preble	01	07	36
Lowder, John(B)	1835	Nov. 25	Randolph(Ind	01	17	13
Lowder, John(E)	1814	April 23	Butler	12	14	09
Lowe, Jacob D.(C)	1804	Dec. 31	Ohio	11	02	13
Lowell, William(A)	1817	Aug. 26	Kentucky	04	08	11
Lower, Benjamin(A)	1811	Nov. 09	Montgomery	04	04	02
Lower, Christian(E)	1837	Oct. 18	Miami	15	22	29
Lower, Christian(E)	1838	April 13	Miami	15	22	29
Lower, John(A)	1806	Dec. 16	Clermont	02	09	25
Lower, John(A)	1812	April 15	Clermont	02	09	25
Lower, William(A)	1814	May 21	Preble	03	07	15
Lowes, James A.(B)	1816	Dec. 02	Hamilton	01	08	14
Lowes, Josiah(B)	1816	Dec. 02	Hamilton	01	08	14
Lowes, William(B)	1818	June 09	Hamilton	01	08	15
Lowrey, Archibald(C)	1802	Dec. 16	Hamilton	09	05	34
Lowrey, Archibald(C)	1802	Dec. 18	Hamilton	09	05	34
Lowrey, Archibald(C)	1802	Dec. 30	Hamilton	09	04	32
Lowrey, David(C)	1804	Dec. 17	Greene	09	03	09
Lowrey, Fielding(C)	1811	Dec. 11	Miami	10	02	34
Lowrey, Jacob(A)	1811	Oct. 21	Greene	06	03	33
Lowrey, James(C)	1809	June 17	Pennsylvania	11	04	11
Lowrey, Thomas(C)	1802	Dec. 31	Hamilton	09	03	19
Lowrey, Thomas(C)	1802	Dec. 31	Hamilton	04	03	24
Lowry, Fielding(A)	1814	Jan. 22	Miami	06	05	29
Lowry, Fielding(A)	1828	Sept. 06	Montgomery	04	09	34
Lowry, Fielding(C)	1811	May 23	Miami	10	01	05
Lowry, Fielding(C)	1813	April 14	Miami	10	03	30
Lowry, Fielding(C)	1813	April 14	Miami	10	03	33
Lowry, Fielding(C)	1813	April 14	Miami	11	01	01
Lowry, Fielding(C)	1813	April 14	Miami	11	01	01
Lowry, Fielding(C)	1813	April 14	Miami	11	02	31
Lowry, Fielding(C)	1813	April 14	Miami	10	03	21
Lowry, Fielding(C)	1813	April 14	Miami	10	02	35
Lowry, Fielding(C)	1813	April 14	Miami	11	01	01
Lowry, Fielding(C)	1813	April 14	Miami	11	03	01
Lowry, Fielding(C)	1813	April 14	Miami	11	01	01
Lowry, Fielding(C)	1813	April 14	Miami	11	02	25
Lowry, Fielding(C)	1813	April 14	Miami	11	02	25
Lowry, Fielding(C)	1813	April 14	Miami	11	02	31
Lowry, Fielding(C)	1813	April 14	Miami	10	02	35
Lowry, Fielding(C)	1813	April 14	Miami	10	03	33
Lowry, Fielding(C)	1813	April 14	Miami	10	03	20
Lowry, Fielding(C)	1813	April 14	Miami	10	03	21
Lowry, Fielding(C)	1813	April 14	Miami	10	03	27
Lowry, Fielding(C)	1813	April 14	Miami	11	03	01
Lowry, Fielding(C)	1813	June 07	Miami	10	02	30
Lowry, Fielding(C)	1815	March 21	Miami	10	02	29
Lowry, Jacob(A)	1818	Dec. 17	Virginia	04	07	24
Lowry, Jacob(A)	1831	Sept. 06	Miami	04	08	27
Lowry, James(C)	1809	June 17	Pennsylvania	11	04	11
Lowry, Reuben(A)	1833	March 02	Darke	02	11	30
Lowry, William(E)	1813	Aug. 09	Butler	12	15	21
Lowstetler, Peter(B)	1814	Jan. 27	Dearborn(Ind	01	04	31
Loy, Barbara(A)	1805	Sept. 07	Butler	03	07	31

PURCHASER	YEAR	DATE	RESIDENCE	R	T	S
Loy, Barbary(A)	1811	Nov. 08	Butler	03	06	13
Loy, Jacob(A)	1805	Nov. 05	Montgomery	04	06	18
Loy, Jacob(A)	1806	July 22	Montgomery	03	05	02
Loy, Jacob(A)	1806	Sept. 01	Montgomery	03	07	14
Loy, Jacob(A)	1811	Dec. 11	Preble	03	07	14
Loy, Jacob(A)	1814	Nov. 05	Preble	03	07	03
Loy, Jacob(A)	1816	Nov. 14	Preble	03	07	03
Loy, Job(A)	1828	Nov. 10	Preble	03	07	03
Loy, John(A)	1818	March 10	Montgomery	03	06	19
Loyd, Humphrey(E)	1836	Sept. 12	Randolph(Ind	01	16	03
Loyd, Jeremiah(E)	1836	Sept. 12	Randolph(Ind	15	19	20
Loyd, John(B)	1836	June 10	Randolph(Ind	01	17	34
Loyd, Joseph A.(B)	1815	Jan. 02	Hamilton	01	07	34
Loyd, Thomas(E)	1836	Sept. 12	Randolph(Ind	15	19	20
Lucas, David(A)	1815	Jan. 13	Darke	03	08	33
Lucas, Jacob R.(A)	1837	Jan. 26	Butler	03	11	20
Lucas, John(C)	1818	Aug. 21	Clermont	13	02	25
Lucas, Joseph(E)	1836	Dec. 15	Randolph(Ind	14	21	35
Lucas, Simeon H.(E)	1837	Oct. 05	Randolph(Ind	14	21	35
Lucas, Simeon H.(E)	1838	May 21	Highland	14	21	35
Lucas, William(A)	1837	Jan. 26	Butler	03	11	17
Luce, John(C)	1801	Dec. 29	Hamilton	05	03	30
Luce, Moses(A)	1806	Dec. 23	Montgomery	05	07	06
Luce, Moses(A)	1814	Dec. 12	Montgomery	04	09	25
Luce, Robert(A)	1811	April 09	Butler	01	04	03
Luce, William(C)	1804	Sept. 03	Montgomery	05	03	29
Luce, William(C)	1814	Aug. 05	Montgomery	08	05	24
Luce, Zephaniah(C)	1811	April 19	Champaign	12	04	10
Lucky, Abia(B)	1832	Sept. 24	Switzerland	02	02	23
Ludlow, Charlotte C.(C)	1804	Dec. 31	Hamilton	08	04	28
Ludlow, Charlotte C.(C)	1804	Dec. 31	Hamilton	09	04	07
Ludlow, Charlotte C.(C)	1804	Dec. 31	Hamilton	07	03	24
Ludlow, Charlotte C.(C)	1804	Dec. 31	Hamilton	08	04	17
Ludlow, Charlotte C.(C)	1804	Dec. 31	Hamilton	08	03	14
Ludlow, Charlotte C.(C)	1804	Dec. 31	Hamilton	07	02	31
Ludlow, Israel D.(C)	1828	Jan. 16	Hamilton	11	02	03
Ludlow, John(C)	1804	Dec. 31	Hamilton	08	04	28
Ludlow, John(C)	1804	Dec. 31	Hamilton	09	04	07
Ludlow, John(C)	1804	Dec. 31	Hamilton	07	03	24
Ludlow, John(C)	1804	Dec. 31	Hamilton	08	04	17
Ludlow, John(C)	1804	Dec. 31	Hamilton	07	02	31
Ludlow, Stephen(B)	1814	July 15	Dearborn(Ind	01	06	34
Ludlow, Stephen(B)	1814	Dec. 09	Dearborn(Ind	01	06	33
Ludlow, William(A)	1803	Sept. 01	?	02	05	01
Ludlum, Ephraim(A)	1818	Jan. 01	Warren	07	02	31
Luellen, John(C)	1830	Dec. 08	Pennsylvania	14	02	11
Luntz, Nicholas(B)	1815	Jan. 17	Switzerland	03	03	23
Luse, Robert(A)	1806	Jan. 11	Warren	01	04	03
Luse, Robert(B)	1814	Sept. 02	Butler	01	09	22
Luse, Zephania(C)	1805	Nov. 20	Champaign	12	04	10
Lutterell, Fielding(A)	1822	Nov. 25	Miami	05	08	04
Lutz, Joseph(C)	1831	Nov. 08	Fairfield	12	03	28
Lutz, Mich'l.(E)	1836	Oct. 25	Clark	14	21	34
Lybrook, Henry(A)	1811	Nov. 01	Preble	01	07	19
Lybrook, Henry(A)	1814	Aug. 18	Preble	01	07	18
Lybrook, Henry(A)	1814	Nov. 29	Preble	01	07	19
Lybrook, Henry(B)	1811	Nov. 01	Preble	01	12	26
Lybrook, Jacob(A)	1815	Feb. 04	Wayne(Ind)	01	07	18
Lybrook, John(A)	1813	Oct. 08	Wayne(Ind)	01	07	19
Lybrook, Philip(B)	1806	Oct. 15	Virginia	01	12	36
Lybrook, Philip(B)	1808	Jan. 25	Dearborn(Ind	01	12	25
Lybrook, Philip(B)	1808	Oct. 19	Dearborn(Ind	01	12	25
Lykins, Andrew(E)	1817	Dec. 06	Virginia	14	19	07
Lykins, Andrew(E)	1817	Dec. 06	Virginia	13	19	12
Lykins, Andrew(E)	1817	Dec. 06	Virginia	13	19	13
Lykins, James(E)	1818	July 09	Randolph(Ind	14	19	18
Lykins, John(E)	1836	April 21	Randolph(Ind	13	19	12
Lykins, Jonas(E)	1833	June 08	Randolph(Ind	13	19	15
Lykins, Philip(E)	1832	April 02	Wayne(Ind)	14	15	04

PURCHASER	YEAR	DATE	RESIDENCE	R	T	S
Lympes, Elijah(C)	1805	April 24	Montgomery	05	02	30
Lympus, Elijah(A)	1805	Aug. 02	Butler	02	04	09
Lympus, Elijah(E)	1811	Oct. 21	Franklin(Ind	12	12	03
Lympus, Elijah(E)	1811	Nov. 02	Franklin(Ind	12	13	34
Lympus, Enoch(A)	1805	Aug. 02	Butler	02	04	09
Lynas, Joseph(B)	1835	July 27	Dearborn(Ind	01	06	05
Lynch, Joseph(A)	1805	Nov. 25	Kentucky	02	04	17
Lynes, William(B)	1811	Feb. 13	Franklin(Ind	02	08	04
Lynn, Daniel(B)	1813	Oct. 20	Dearborn(Ind	02	04	15
Lynn, William(E)	1836	March 08	Franklin(Ind	13	12	29
Lyon, Benjamin(A)	1818	June 24	Warren	03	08	27
Lyon, Christian(C)	1813	May 31	Champaign	12	03	14
Lyon, Christian(C)	1829	Jan. 15	Champaign	12	03	13
Lyon, Ethel B.(B)	1818	Nov. 10	Switzerland	01	02	22
Lyon, Geore(A)	1814	Nov. 28	Preble	01	07	08
Lyon, James Jr.(A)	1814	Sept. 21	Hamilton	01	03	19
Lyon, James Jr.(A)	1836	June 01	Hamilton	03	12	11
Lyon, James Jr.(A)	1836	June 03	Hamilton	03	12	11
Lyon, John(C)	1831	Aug. 08	Champaign	12	03	13
Lyon, John(C)	1831	Aug. 08	Champaign	12	03	19
Lyon, Joseph(B)	1814	Nov. 01	Dearborn(Ind	03	04	01
Lyon, Nathaniel(A)	1805	Sept. 07	Montgomery	02	05	07
Lyon, Oliver Lee(B)	1836	Sept. 05	Hamilton	03	05	08
Lyon, Richard(A)	1819	May 06	Butler	03	09	05
Lyons, Aaron R.(E)	1834	Jan. 28	Franklin(Ind	13	11	28
Lyons, Aaron Robeson(E)	1835	Nov. 11	Franklin(Ind	13	11	28
Lyons, Andrew(A)	1831	Oct. 19	Cincinnati	03	08	25
Lyons, David(A)	1837	May 10	Preble	03	11	18
Lyons, Elizabeth(A)	1837	May 10	Preble	03	11	18
Lyons, James(B)	1818	June 01	Cincinnati	02	08	23
Lyons, James(B)	1836	Sept. 12	Dearborn(Ind	03	04	01
Lyons, James(B)	1837	Jan. 02	Dearborn(Ind	03	05	36
Lyons, Jas.(B)	1818	June 04	Cincinnati	02	08	07
Lyons, Joseph(A)	1811	Nov. 27	Dearborn(Ind	03	04	01
Lyons, Joshua(B)	1836	Feb. 22	Franklin(Ind	02	08	19
Lyons, Robert(B)	1813	Dec. 10	Dearborn(Ind	01	02	33
Lyons, Robert(B)	1816	Sept. 30	Dearborn(Ind	02	03	06
Lyons, Robert(B)	1833	Jan. 09	Switzerland	01	02	05
Lyons, William Jr.(B)	1835	Oct. 17	Franklin(Ind	02	08	09
Lytle, Andrew(C)	1810	June 05	Warren	03	04	08
Lytle, Andrew(D)	1813	Sept. 17	Warren	03	05	26
Lytle, Robert(A)	1801	Nov. 10	Pennsylvania	02	05	24
Lytle, William	1808	March 01	Clermont	?	?	?
Lytle, William	1808	March 01	Clermont	?	?	?
Lytle, William	1808	March 01	Clermont	?	?	?
Lytle, William	1808	March 01	Clermont	?	?	?
Lytle, William(A)	1817	Sept. 29	Cincinnati	06	07	20
Lytle, William(A)	1818	June 13	Cincinnati	04	11	12
Lytle, William(A)	1818	June 13	Cincinnati	05	10	07
Lytle, William(C)	1818	Aug. 13	Cincinnati	12	04	01
Lytle, William(C)	1818	Aug. 13	Cincinnati	11	05	36
Lytle, William(C)	1818	Aug. 13	Cincinnati	12	05	34
Lytle, William(C)	1818	Aug. 13	Cincinnati	12	04	05
Lytle, William(C)	1818	Aug. 13	Cincinnati	12	05	36
Lytle, William(C)	1818	Aug. 14	Cincinnati	12	04	05
Lytle, William(C)	1818	Aug. 14	Cincinnati	09	06	29
Lytle, William(C)	1818	Aug. 14	Cincinnati	09	06	11
Lytle, William(C)	1818	Aug. 14	Cincinnati	14	03	29
Lytle, Wm.(C)	1814	April 02	Warren	03	05	11
Mabbett, Anthony(B)	1814	Aug. 17	Wayne(Ind)	01	12	15
MacClay, Charles(C)	1814	Oct. 19	Champaign	12	05	23
Macdaniel, James(A)	1818	Nov. 04	Miami	05	07	04
Macemore, John(E)	1837	May 29	Richland	15	22	31
Mackey, John(A)	1833	May 29	Preble	01	09	12
Macklin, John(B)	1811	Aug. 27	Mississippi	01	11	18
Macy, Albert(E)	1833	June 24	Randolph(Ind	13	18	10
Macy, Albert(E)	1835	Jan. 24	Randolph(Ind	13	18	10
Macy, James(B)	1828	Feb. 09	Union(Ind)	01	10	05
Macy, Jonathan(E)	1827	Aug. 22	Wayne(Ind)	13	18	32

PURCHASER	YEAR	DATE	RESIDENCE	R	T	S
Macy, Jonathan(E)	1831	Aug. 26	Wayne(Ind)	13	17	09
Macy, Joseph(E)	1832	March 28	Randolph(Ind	13	18	05
Macy, Joseph(E)	1835	June 03	Randolph(Ind	13	18	05
Macy, Joseph(E)	1836	Feb. 11	Randolph(Ind	13	18	04
Macy, Robt.(B)	1825	May 10	Wayne(Ind)	01	15	33
Macy, Seth(E)	1837	May 01	Randolph(Ind	15	21	33
Macy, Stephen(A)	1813	Aug. 10	Montgomery	06	03	28
Macy, Thomas(A)	1813	July 03	Miami	06	04	31
Macy, Thomas(A)	1817	Sept. 07	Miami	06	04	32
Macy, William(B)	1818	May 16	Franklin(Ind	01	11	15
Madden, Solomon(E)	1817	Nov. 20	Clinton	14	16	33
Madden, Thomas(B)	1811	March 18	Montgomery	01	11	18
Madden, Thomas(B)	1811	Sept. 02	Franklin(Ind	01	11	17
Madden, Thomas(E)	1814	Nov. 10	Franklin(Ind	13	14	13
Madden, William(C)	1804	Dec. 29	Montgomery	09	02	30
Maddens, William(C)	1802	Dec. 31	Hamilton	10	02	25
Maddock, Joseph(A)	1816	Oct. 02	Preble	02	06	05
Maddock, Nathan(A)	1814	Aug. 23	Preble	01	06	02
Maddock, Nathan(A)	1816	Oct. 30	Preble	05	06	18
Maddock, Nathan(A)	1830	Dec. 18	Miami	04	07	12
Maddock, Nathan(C)	1810	May 28	Miami	09	02	07
Maddock, Samuel(A)	1805	July 06	Butler	03	04	32
Maddock, Samuel(A)	1805	July 06	Butler	03	04	29
Maddock, William(A)	1812	Jan. 31	Preble	01	06	01
Madeira, Daniel(A)	1816	Feb. 20	Ross	01	07	23
Madsker, George(C)	1804	Dec. 10	Ross	13	05	28
Magee, Elijah(A)	1830	Aug. 13	Pennsylvania	05	08	33
Maggert, Jacob(C)	1811	Jan. 19	Champaign	12	03	07
Maggert, Sam'l.(C)	1830	March 17	Champaign	12	03	31
Maginty, Daniel(C)	1816	Sept. 17	Hamilton	10	03	02
Magness, Robert(A)	1836	Nov. 07	Hamilton	01	14	08
Magness, William(A)	1836	Nov. 07	Hamilton	01	14	07
Magowen, Henry Harvey(C)	1811	Aug. 08	Kentucky	09	06	35
Maguire, James(A)	1819	Jan. 26	Hamilton	02	09	20
Maguire, James(E)	1818	Nov. 27	Hamilton	14	20	09
Mahaffey, Robert(A)	1814	May 13	Butler	01	03	22
Mahaffey, Robert(A)	1815	March 25	Butler	01	03	22
Mahan, James(A)	1807	Sept. 25	Butler	02	03	02
Mahan, William(C)	1806	Nov. 10	Champaign	11	05	30
Mahin, Mathew(E)	1836	Nov. 01	Greene	14	21	20
Mahony, John(B)	1833	July 03	Cincinnati	02	07	21
Mailine, Jacob(B)	1833	July 20	Cincinnati	03	08	13
Mains, Isaac(B)	1831	July 18	Wayne(Ind)	01	15	10
Maize, David(E)	1811	Oct. 23	Butler	13	13	13
Maize, Samuel(E)	1811	Oct. 23	Butler	13	13	13
Major, Daniel Symmes(B)	1836	Jan. 27	Dearborn(Ind	01	07	07
Major, Daniel Symmes(B)	1836	Feb. 06	Dearborn(Ind	01	08	30
Major, Daniel Symmes(B)	1836	March 10	Dearborn(Ind	01	07	17
Major, Daniel Symmes(B)	1836	March 10	Dearborn(Ind	02	08	21
Major, William(B)	1813	May 01	Dearborn(Ind	01	07	15
Major, William(B)	1818	May 14	Dearborn(Ind	01	07	15
Majors, William(B)	1802	June 05	Hamilton	01	07	12
Majors, William(B)	1808	Jan. 12	Ind.Territory	01	07	15
Makemson, John(C)	1831	March 19	Logan	13	04	30
Malcom, James Jnr.(C)	1816	June 05	Maryland	12	02	36
Malcom, James(E)	1816	Oct. 12	Wayne(Ind)	13	18	17
Malcomson, James(B)	1833	Jan. 18	Switzerland	03	02	17
Malin, Joseph(B)	1833	Oct. 15	Switzerland	03	03	29
Malin, Joseph(C)	1818	July 02	Switzerland	12	05	31
Mallory, John(C)	1808	Jan. 13	Virginia	11	02	09
Mallory, John(C)	1808	Jan. 13	Virginia	11	02	09
Mallory, John(C)	1808	Jan. 13	Virginia	11	02	02
Mallory, John(C)	1808	Jan. 13	Virginia	11	02	02
Mallory, John(C)	1808	Jan. 13	Virginia	11	02	01
Malson, Aaron(E)	1836	Nov. 03	Franklin(Ind	12	11	15
Malston, Thomas(E)	1824	Aug. 24	Franklin(Ind	12	11	15
Malston, Thomas(E)	1836	Feb. 03	Franklin(Ind	12	11	15
Maltbie, Ammi(C)	1804	Sept. 03	Montgomery	05	03	11
Maltbie, Benjamin(C)	1801	Dec. 26	Hamilton	05	02	04

PURCHASER	YEAR	DATE	RESIDENCE	R	T	S
Man, James(C)	1827	Aug. 23	Hamilton	12	02	33
Man, John R.(B)	1824	Aug. 28	Clermont	02	09	15
Manan, Aaron(E)	1814	Aug. 15	Kentucky	13	16	29
Manan, Jacob(E)	1811	Nov. 30	Kentucky	12	12	34
Manan, Michael(E)	1811	Oct. 28	Kentucky	12	12	28
Manan, Michael(E)	1812	June 30	Ind.Territry	12	12	34
Manas, Alsey(E)	1836	Nov. 03	Randolph(Ind	15	21	07
Manbeck, Dan'l.(A)	1830	Sept. 24	Montgomery	02	10	02
Manbeck, Daniel(A)	1817	Oct. 23	Montgomery	02	10	03
Manbey, William(E)	1814	March 10	Franklin(Ind	13	13	04
Maness, Christopher(E)	1836	Dec. 15	Randolph(Ind	15	21	30
Mangans, Enoch(A)	1837	May 23	Montgomery	01	12	03
Mangin, John(A)	1811	Aug. 19	Miami	05	08	02
Maning, Benjamin(A)	1816	March 05	Miami	05	09	24
Maning, Benjamin(C)	1815	Oct. 31	Miami	13	02	36
Manlove, George(E)	1811	Oct. 31	Preble	12	15	28
Manly, John(E)	1813	June 18	Franklin(Ind	13	13	04
Mann, Allen(B)	1831	Sept. 01	Randolph(Ind	01	16	21
Mann, Allen(E)	1830	Sept. 11	Butler	15	18	07
Mann, Jacob(A)	1831	Nov. 03	Darke	01	10	36
Mann, John H.(A)	1816	Nov. 13	Pennsylvania	02	12	33
Mann, John(B)	1833	Nov. 08	Randolph(Ind	01	16	21
Mann, John(B)	1834	March 14	Randolph(Ind	01	16	21
Mann, John(C)	1804	Dec. 31	Montgomery	10	02	25
Mann, John(C)	1804	Dec. 31	Montgomery	09	01	06
Mann, Levi(A)	1816	May 29	Butler	01	10	36
Mann, Samuel(A)	1819	Feb. 13	Butler	02	08	15
Mann, Samuel(B)	1816	June 28	Butler	01	16	28
Mann, Tobias(B)	1836	March 25	Hamilton	02	06	23
Manning, Abraham(E)	1836	Nov. 12	Miami	15	19	07
Manning, Amos(E)	1836	Dec. 05	Randolph(Ind	14	19	12
Manning, Ann(E)	1836	Dec. 05	Randolph(Ind	14	19	12
Manning, Benjamin(A)	1813	April 14	Miami	05	08	13
Manning, Caleb(E)	1836	Nov. 12	Miami	15	19	07
Manning, Caleb(E)	1837	March 01	Wayne(Ind)	15	19	06
Manning, Clarkson(C)	1818	Sept. 23	Butler	12	02	03
Manning, Clarkson(C)	1818	Sept. 23	Butler	12	02	04
Manning, Enos(A)	1815	June 17	Miami	06	07	21
Manning, Hezekiah(E)	1816	March 27	Wayne(Ind)	13	17	05
Manning, James(C)	1815	Aug. 22	Miami	11	01	18
Manning, James(C)	1831	Aug. 22	Champaign	12	03	11
Manning, John(A)	1804	Sept. 06	Montgomery	06	06	17
Manning, John(A)	1807	April 20	Miami	05	08	13
Manning, Judah(C)	1831	July 15	Champaign	12	03	04
Manning, Reuben(E)	1836	Nov. 12	Miami	15	19	07
Manning, Reuben(E)	1836	Nov. 12	Miami	15	19	07
Manning, Rich'd.(E)	1836	Dec. 05	Darke	15	19	08
Manning, William(A)	1813	April 14	Miami	05	08	13
Mansfield, Jared	1808	March 01	Hamilton	?	?	?
Mansfield, Jared	1808	March 01	Hamilton	?	?	?
Mansfield, Jared	1808	March 01	Hamilton	?	?	?
Mansfield, Jared(A)	1807	Aug. 06	Hamilton	06	03	31
Mansfield, Jared(B)	1806	Dec. 03	Hamilton	02	01	01
Mansfield, Jared(D)	1805	Oct. 26	Hamilton(Fr)	02	03	11
Mansfield, John F.	1808	March 01	Cincinnati	?	?	?
Mansfield, John F.	1808	March 01	Hamilton	?	?	?
Mansfield, Wm.(A)	1830	Nov. 01	Preble	01	08	30
Manson, David(C)	1807	Feb. 06	Warren	11	02	23
Manson, David(C)	1812	April 15	Miami	11	02	23
Manson, John(A)	1813	Aug. 13	?	02	06	21
Manson, William(C)	1807	Feb. 05	Warren	11	02	22
Manson, William(C)	1812	April 15	Miami	11	02	22
Manson, William(C)	1814	Jan. 03	Miami	11	02	23
Mansur, Jeremy(A)	1816	July 29	Wayne(Ind)	02	04	21
Mantle, George(B)	1818	Aug. 10	Cincinnati	02	06	13
Mantle, George(B)	1818	Aug. 22	Cincinnati	02	05	11
Manuel, Alfred(A)	1837	April 12	Darke	01	12	06
Manuel, George W.(E)	1838	Aug. 23	Hamilton	14	21	32
Manwaring, Richard(B)	1801	July 14	Hamilton	01	07	10

PURCHASER	YEAR	DATE	RESIDENCE	R	T	S
Manwaring, Richard(B)	1808	Oct. 03	Dearborn(Ind	02	09	05
Manwaring, Richard(B)	1832	Feb. 21	Franklin(Ind	02	08	33
Manwaring, Richard(E)	1812	Nov. 24	Dearborn(Ind	13	12	25
Manwaring, Solomon(B)	1808	Oct. 03	Dearborn(Ind	02	09	05
Manwaring, Solomon(B)	1829	April 21	Dearborn(Ind	01	07	03
Manwaring, Solomon(E)	1812	Nov. 24	Dearborn(Ind	13	12	25
Manwaring, Thomas(B)	1816	Feb. 23	Franklin(Ind	01	08	31
Mapes, James(B)	1818	March 06	Butler	03	03	08
Mapes, John(E)	1814	Aug. 22	Hamilton	13	13	19
Maple, Stephen(E)	1832	Oct. 25	Franklin(Ind	12	12	08
Maple, Wm.(E)	1814	Oct. 07	Franklin(Ind	12	12	09
Marbeck, Daniel(A)	1817	Nov. 07	Montgomery	02	11	35
Marble, Calvin(B)	1827	Aug. 21	Dearborn(Ind	01	03	20
Marchal, Nicolas(A)	1836	July 16	Darke	03	11	26
Marcum, Beverly(A)	1829	Aug. 12	Tennessee	04	07	07
Margerum, Hermon L.(B)	1819	July 16	Hamilton	03	04	13
Marine, Charles(E)	1819	Aug. 02	Wayne(Ind)	14	18	24
Mark, John N.(A)	1836	Nov. 07	Darke	01	13	15
Marker, Daniel(A)	1815	Dec. 07	Montgomery	05	08	18
Marker, Daniel(A)	1833	April 03	Darke	04	09	06
Markland, James(B)	1833	April 17	Hamilton	01	07	22
Markland, Jesse(E)	1837	Oct. 19	Hamilton	15	19	06
Markland, Thomas J.(E)	1837	Oct. 17	Hamilton	15	19	08
Markland, Washington(E)	1837	Oct. 17	Hamilton	15	19	08
Markley, David(C)	1831	Feb. 15	Champaign	12	04	04
Markley, John(E)	1836	Nov. 05	Hamilton	13	20	10
Markley, Moses(E)	1836	Nov. 05	Hamilton	13	20	03
Markwith, John R.(A)	1836	April 01	Darke	01	12	07
Marlin, Charles(E)	1832	June 22	Franklin(Ind	11	11	14
Marlin, Charles(E)	1833	May 28	Franklin(Ind	12	11	27
Marlin, Charles(E)	1836	Feb. 05	Franklin(Ind	12	11	28
Marlin, Charles(E)	1837	March 24	Franklin(Ind	12	11	21
Marlin, Cicero(E)	1836	Oct. 28	Franklin(Ind	12	11	28
Marlin, Samuel G.(E)	1837	July 22	Franklin(Ind	12	11	21
Marlin, Wesley(E)	1836	Oct. 28	Franklin(Ind	11	11	24
Marlin, Wesley(E)	1836	Oct. 28	Franklin(Ind	11	11	25
Marlin, William(E)	1815	June 19	New Jersey	12	11	20
Marlin, William(E)	1833	May 28	Franklin(Ind	12	11	22
Marlin, William(E)	1836	Feb. 05	Franklin(Ind	12	11	22
Marlin, William(E)	1836	July 02	Franklin(Ind	12	11	33
Marlin, William(E)	1836	Aug. 09	Franklin(Ind	12	11	32
Marlin, William(E)	1836	Oct. 28	Franklin(Ind	11	11	23
Marlin, William(E)	1836	Oct. 28	Franklin(Ind	12	11	21
Marlin, William(E)	1837	March 24	Franklin(Ind	12	11	21
Marling, John(B)	1817	June 21	Cincinnati	03	02	18
Marnan, William(E)	1813	Oct. 16	Kentucky	12	13	05
Maronery, John(A)	1806	March 08	Warren	02	08	34
Marquart, Peter(C)	1818	March 31	Clark	10	03	08
Marquart, Philip(C)	1818	Jan. 29	Clark	09	04	29
Marquess, James(A)	1830	Jan. 18	Darke	01	13	32
Marquess, Smith(A)	1819	Jan. 11	Ross	02	13	31
Marquess, Wm. K.(A)	1830	Dec. 28	Darke	01	13	32
Marrs, John(C)	1814	Oct. 12	Miami	10	03	30
Marrs, John(C)	1829	April 10	Champaign	13	02	35
Marrs, William(C)	1813	March 15	Champaign	13	02	21
Marrs, William(C)	1813	March 15	Champaign	13	02	22
Marsh, Charles(B)	1832	Aug. 20	Switzerland	02	03	14
Marsh, David(B)	1835	Dec. 05	Dearborn(Ind	02	03	09
Marsh, Enoch(A)	1837	Aug. 23	Butler	02	14	04
Marsh, Israel(C)	1806	Feb. 11	Champaign	11	06	28
Marsh, James(A)	1827	Sept. 07	Preble	03	07	06
Marsh, James(A)	1830	Oct. 26	Preble	03	07	06
Marsh, James(A)	1831	Sept. 23	Preble	03	08	32
Marsh, Jesse(A)	1828	July 12	Darke	02	10	20
Marsh, Jesse(E)	1837	Aug. 01	Darke	14	22	36
Marsh, John(A)	1807	March 09	Ohio	01	08	13
Marsh, Moses(A)	1814	March 01	Butler	01	03	30
Marsh, Mulford(A)	1814	June 30	Cincinnati	01	04	26
Marsh, Scearing(A)	1801	Oct. 27	Hamilton	05	02	29

PURCHASER	YEAR	DATE	RESIDENCE	R	T	S
Marsh, Squier(A)	1819	Feb. 03	Cincinnati	02	06	15
Marsh, Squire(A)	1819	Jan. 08	Hamilton	02	06	22
Marsh, Webster(A)	1817	June 04	Hamilton	02	12	01
Marsh, Webster(B)	1817	Sept. 17	Hamilton	03	03	08
Marsh, Will'm.(A)	1815	Oct. 28	Preble	01	08	13
Marsh, William(A)	1812	April 15	Preble	01	08	13
Marsh, William(B)	1815	March 21	Switzerland	02	02	28
Marsh, William(B)	1815	June 06	Preble	02	12	14
Marshal, James(A)	1806	March 21	Montgomery	06	05	32
Marshal, Robert(A)	1803	Dec. 22	Kentucky	06	05	08
Marshal, Thos. M.(A)	1829	June 05	Preble	02	09	03
Marshall, Conrad(A)	1831	May 28	Montgomery	03	08	36
Marshall, David(C)	1817	Sept. 02	Kentucky	12	01	11
Marshall, David(C)	1818	Jan. 23	Kentucky	12	01	12
Marshall, Henry Junr.(A)	1820	May 17	Warren	04	06	32
Marshall, James(A)	1817	June 10	Butler	02	12	07
Marshall, James(A)	1831	Oct. 22	Shelby	06	08	33
Marshall, John(A)	1813	Dec. 28	Miami	06	07	18
Marshall, Miles(A)	1814	Oct. 08	Preble	01	08	17
Marshall, Reiley(E)	1819	Nov. 10	Randolph(Ind	14	21	23
Marshall, Robert(A)	1803	Dec. 22	Kentucky	06	05	17
Marshall, Robert(E)	1814	April 09	Franklin(Ind	12	13	09
Marshall, Sam'l. Jr.(A)	1830	Oct. 13	Shelby	06	07	05
Marshall, Samuel(A)	1808	Jan. 13	Butler	06	07	06
Marshall, Samuel(A)	1813	Feb. 06	Miami	06	07	05
Marshall, Samuel(A)	1813	Sept. 23	Miami	06	08	32
Marshall, Samuel(A)	1814	Nov. 29	Miami	06	07	05
Marshall, Samuel(B)	1820	June 05	Dearborn(Ind	03	06	36
Marshall, Thomas(A)	1814	July 11	Maryland	01	07	15
Marshall, Thomas(E)	1815	Oct. 07	Wayne(Ind)	13	18	21
Marshall, William P.(B)	1815	July 25	Cincinnati	01	06	30
Marshall, William(A)	1832	Jan. 16	Miami	04	08	26
Marshall, William(C)	1806	April 21	Hamilton	11	01	22
Marshall, William(C)	1819	Oct. 19	Kentucky	12	02	33
Marshel, Jacob(A)	1818	Jan. 30	Preble	01	07	22
Marshel, Jacob(A)	1829	Dec. 08	Preble	01	07	13
Marshell, David(B)	1819	June 07	Hamilton	01	08	08
Marshil, Miles(E)	1816	March 01	Wayne(Ind)	13	18	33
Marshill, Aaron(E)	1829	Jan. 29	Wayne(Ind)	13	18	22
Marshill, Miles(E)	1829	Jan. 01	Wayne(Ind)	13	18	29
Martendaile, Samuel(A)	1817	Dec. 02	Montgomery	06	03	04
Martin, Aaron(B)	1806	July 28	Kentucky	01	13	30
Martin, Abia(C)	1801	Dec. 30	Hamilton	05	03	09
Martin, Abia(C)	1802	Dec. 18	Hamilton	04	03	09
Martin, Abia(C)	1806	July 29	Greene	11	02	13
Martin, Abner(B)	1814	April 23	Kentucky	02	13	26
Martin, Archibald(D)	1814	June 03	Hamilton	01	02	11
Martin, Asahel(A)	1832	Aug. 31	Greene	08	01	15
Martin, Christopher(A)	1815	Oct. 07	Butler	03	09	03
Martin, Corbly(C)	1816	Oct. 22	Miami	10	02	18
Martin, Dan'l.(E)	1828	Nov. 01	Montgomery	12	16	01
Martin, Daniel(A)	1805	Oct. 16	Pennsylvania	05	04	05
Martin, Daniel(A)	1808	April 04	Montgomery	05	04	05
Martin, Daniel(A)	1814	Aug. 24	Montgomery	05	04	06
Martin, Edw'd. Newland(C)	1832	Jan. 13	Warren	13	02	25
Martin, Eli(E)	1835	April 24	Virginia	11	10	24
Martin, Eli(E)	1835	April 24	Virginia	11	10	24
Martin, Elisha(E)	1837	April 10	Randolph(Ind	14	20	13
Martin, Ephraim(A)	1818	Oct. 01	Greene	05	08	06
Martin, George(C)	1829	Jan. 21	Champaign	12	05	34
Martin, George(E)	1811	Oct. 28	Franklin(Ind	12	15	28
Martin, Henry(B)	1812	Jan. 08	Dearborn(Ind	02	12	12
Martin, Henry(B)	1814	Oct. 25	Wayne(Ind)	02	12	14
Martin, Henry(B)	1837	Sept. 13	Cincinnati	02	04	20
Martin, Henry(C)	1804	Dec. 29	Greene	07	03	20
Martin, Hiram(A)	1810	Aug. 27	Butler	02	04	13
Martin, Isaac(A)	1831	Oct. 24	Hamilton	05	08	27
Martin, Isaac(B)	1815	Jan. 09	Wayne(Ind)	01	14	18
Martin, Isaac(C)	1804	Dec. 28	Greene	05	03	15

203

PURCHASER	YEAR	DATE	RESIDENCE	R	T	S
Martin, Isaac(C)	1806	July 19	Montgomery	10	02	17
Martin, Isaac(C)	1809	Dec. 28	Miami	11	03	31
Martin, Isaac(E)	1813	Oct. 25	Butler	13	14	29
Martin, Isaac(E)	1816	July 18	Wayne(Ind)	13	16	13
Martin, Isaac(E)	1827	Nov. 03	Wayne(Ind)	13	16	23
Martin, Jacob(A)	1817	July 16	Montgomery	03	10	02
Martin, Jacob(A)	1830	June 16	Shelby	08	01	08
Martin, James Montgomery(B)	1831	Dec. 30	Dearborn(Ind	02	07	13
Martin, James(A)	1802	June 28	Hamilton	02	05	23
Martin, James(A)	1809	April 03	Kentucky	02	05	21
Martin, James(B)	1814	Feb. 04	Butler	01	11	28
Martin, Jas. H.(A)	1813	March 25	Butler	04	03	31
Martin, Job(A)	1805	Aug. 24	Warren	06	04	17
Martin, Job(C)	1807	May 14	Champaign	12	05	28
Martin, Job(C)	1811	Oct. 01	Champaign	13	03	15
Martin, Joel(A)	1813	June 30	Butler	03	05	15
Martin, John H.(A)	1836	Aug. 15	Darke	01	13	32
Martin, John H.(A)	1837	April 04	Darke	01	13	31
Martin, John H.(B)	1836	Aug. 05	Darke	01	17	12
Martin, John(A)	1818	Oct. 01	Greene	05	09	29
Martin, John(C)	1825	March 10	Fairfield	14	02	11
Martin, Levi(C)	1804	Dec. 25	Montgomery	10	01	03
Martin, Luther(E)	1835	Oct. 28	Maryland	15	19	29
Martin, Moses(E)	1811	Oct. 28	Franklin(Ind	12	13	28
Martin, Peter(A)	1819	Sept. 11	Greene	05	09	29
Martin, Robert(A)	1807	April 09	Butler	01	06	27
Martin, Sam'l.(A)	1831	Dec. 05	Darke	02	12	36
Martin, Samuel(A)	1805	Sept. 30	Hamilton	06	05	06
Martin, Samuel(A)	1805	Sept. 30	Hamilton	05	07	12
Martin, Samuel(C)	1801	Dec. 31	Hamilton	05	04	21
Martin, Samuel(C)	1801	Dec. 31	Hamilton	05	03	01
Martin, Samuel(C)	1801	Dec. 31	Hamilton	04	04	06
Martin, Samuel(C)	1805	Dec. 10	Hamilton	09	04	13
Martin, Samuel(E)	1836	Nov. 04	Greene	15	20	10
Martin, Sebastian(A)	1836	Dec. 06	Montgomery	01	13	36
Martin, Stephen(E)	1811	Oct. 23	Franklin(Ind	13	11	11
Martin, Theophilus(B)	1828	March 25	Dearborn(Ind	03	05	21
Martin, Theophilus(B)	1837	Jan. 25	Dearborn(Ind	03	05	21
Martin, Thomas(A)	1818	Aug. 27	Darke	03	09	05
Martin, Will'm.(A)	1815	Oct. 07	Butler	03	09	05
Martin, William(A)	1816	April 22	Butler	01	12	25
Martin, William(A)	1817	Sept. 29	Butler	02	12	08
Martin, William(A)	1819	Jan. 29	Darke	03	09	20
Martin, William(A)	1829	Feb. 16	Darke	02	12	35
Martin, William(A)	1829	Feb. 27	Darke	02	12	35
Martin, William(B)	1826	Dec. 09	Franklin(Ind	03	09	36
Martindale, James(C)	1804	Dec. 24	Warren	05	04	33
Martindale, James(E)	1811	Oct. 24	Wayne(Ind)	13	17	26
Martindale, James(E)	1811	Oct. 24	Wayne(Ind)	13	17	35
Martindale, James(E)	1834	June 12	Miami	15	22	11
Martindale, Jesse(E)	1825	Nov. 26	Wayne(Ind)	13	17	28
Martindale, John(E)	1811	Oct. 24	Wayne(Ind)	13	17	29
Martindale, Martin(E)	1815	Dec. 11	Wayne(Ind)	14	17	30
Martindale, Moses(B)	1817	Sept. 02	Warren	01	11	22
Martindale, Moses(E)	1817	Sept. 02	Warren	13	18	14
Martindale, Moses(E)	1817	Sept. 15	Warren	13	18	11
Martindale, Moses(E)	1817	Sept. 15	Warren	13	18	13
Martindale, Moses(E)	1817	Sept. 15	Warren	13	17	12
Martindale, Moses(E)	1817	Sept. 15	Warren	14	16	33
Martindale, Thomas(A)	1817	Oct. 31	Miami	02	11	08
Martindale, William(C)	1802	Dec. 20	Hamilton	05	04	32
Martindale, William(E)	1816	July 10	Wayne(Ind)	13	17	30
Martindell, John(A)	1837	Feb. 17	Butler	01	15	35
Martindill, Sam'l.(A)	1828	Sept. 15	Montgomery	06	03	04
Martindle, Thomas(A)	1814	March 31	Miami	06	04	28
Marts, Peter(E)	1816	Dec. 09	Pickaway	12	15	03
Martz, John(A)	1829	June 03	Darke	02	11	12
Marvin, James W.(A)	1836	Dec. 05	Knox	02	13	09
Marvin, Rob't.(A)	1814	April 25	Hamilton	01	02	18

PURCHASER	YEAR	DATE	RESIDENCE	R	T	S
Maschger, Frederick(B)	1836	Feb. 08	Hamilton	02	08	18
Maschger, Henry(B)	1836	Feb. 08	Hamilton	02	08	18
Maschger, Henry(B)	1836	March 29	Hamilton	02	08	18
Maschger, Henry(B)	1836	April 18	Hamilton	02	08	18
Mason, Charles Jr.(Black)(B)	1835	Oct. 29	Shelby	01	16	12
Mason, Charles(C)	1823	Aug. 30	Shelby	13	02	28
Mason, Christopher(A)	1805	May 29	Kentucky	04	04	01
Mason, Daniel(B)	1819	May 07	Dearborn(Ind	02	07	12
Mason, Daniel(B)	1833	March 22	Dearborn(Ind	02	07	12
Mason, Edward(C)	1812	Jan. 04	Champaign	12	05	11
Mason, George(B)	1819	May 07	Dearborn(Ind	02	07	15
Mason, George(B)	1819	Dec. 06	Hamilton	02	07	21
Mason, George(B)	1829	July 24	Dearborn(Ind	02	07	21
Mason, Horatio(E)	1817	Aug. 15	Franklin(Ind	12	12	10
Mason, Horatio(E)	1819	April 28	Fayette	12	13	33
Mason, Jacob(B)	1832	Feb. 27	Dearborn(Ind	02	07	02
Mason, James(B)	1818	Nov. 04	Hamilton	02	08	31
Mason, Joseph(B)	1833	Jan. 28	Dearborn(Ind	02	07	11
Mason, Matthew(C)	1830	Jan. 07	Champaign	12	05	36
Mason, Philip(B)	1818	April 17	Pennsylvania	02	07	09
Mason, Richard(C)	1801	Dec. 31	Hamilton	06	01	07
Mason, Richard(C)	1804	Dec. 31	Montgomery	06	01	01
Mason, Solomon(A)	1829	Jan. 28	Preble	01	08	23
Mason, Thomas(B)	1815	May 05	Clinton	01	15	24
Mason, Thomas(B)	1817	June 28	Wayne(Ind)	01	15	23
Mason, William(A)	1812	Jan. 28	Montgomery	06	03	27
Mason, William(A)	1812	Jan. 28	Montgomery	06	03	33
Massey, James(E)	1818	Jan. 26	Wayne(Ind)	14	21	11
Massey, James(E)	1818	Nov. 05	Randolph(Ind	14	21	24
Massey, Peter Jackson(E)	1836	March 02	Fayette	13	13	32
Massey, Tence(B)	1817	Aug. 18	Wayne(Ind)	01	14	05
Massey, Tence(E)	1818	Jan. 26	Wayne(Ind)	14	21	10
Massey, William(E)	1822	Jan. 15	Wayne(Ind)	14	18	27
Mast, David(A)	1802	Feb. 15	Hamilton	05	05	03
Mast, John(A)	1802	Sept. 03	Hamilton	05	06	28
Mast, John(A)	1808	April 12	Miami	05	06	23
Mast, John(A)	1814	Sept. 28	Miami	05	06	21
Mast, John(A)	1824	Aug. 25	Miami	04	07	14
Masters, Isaac Lee(B)	1806	March 15	Dearborn(Ind	01	06	34
Masterson, Charles(A)	1806	Aug. 27	Butler	06	05	32
Masterson, James W.(B)	1837	Jan. 04	Randolph(Ind	01	17	14
Masterson, Smith G.(B)	1836	June 02	Randolph(Ind	01	17	14
Masterson, Smith G.(E)	1837	Jan. 04	Randolph(Ind	15	20	33
Masy, John(A)	1831	Dec. 06	Shelby	06	08	29
Mater, Hannah(E)	1828	Nov. 01	Indiana	12	16	01
Matheral, Jane(B)	1815	May 18	Hamilton	02	03	32
Mathers, John(A)	1806	March 28	Hamilton	02	03	08
Mathers, John(C)	1815	June 10	Hamilton	12	01	11
Mathers, John(C)	1818	Oct. 27	Hamilton	12	02	09
Mathers, John(C)	1818	Nov. 18	Hamilton	12	02	03
Mathews, Edwen(C)	1815	May 04	Cincinnati	14	04	33
Mathews, Edwin(C)	1815	May 04	Cincinnati	14	04	34
Mathews, Henry(C)	1813	July 07	Champaign	14	03	33
Mathews, James(C)	1801	Dec. 31	Hamilton	05	02	06
Mathews, John(C)	1815	April 27	Miami	13	02	34
Mathews, John(C)	1815	June 10	Hamilton	12	01	09
Mathews, Philip(C)	1807	Jan. 10	Champaign	14	02	02
Matlock, George(E)	1811	Nov. 19	Franklin9Ind	13	13	27
Matlock, John(E)	1813	Nov. 30	Franklin(Ind	13	13	24
Matson, Hiram(A)	1836	Nov. 26	Butler	02	13	33
Matson, Hiram(A)	1836	Nov. 26	Butler	02	13	35
Matson, James(A)	1814	Feb. 01	Hamilton	01	02	34
Matson, James(A)	1814	Feb. 01	Hamilton	01	02	34
Matson, Jane(A)	1839	Sept. 30	Darke	02	15	25
Matson, John Jnr.(A)	1803	Dec. 30	Hamilton	02	03	31
Matson, Naomie(A)	1839	Sept. 30	Darke	02	15	25
Matson, Thomas(A)	1818	March 25	Butler	03	08	30
Matson, Thomas(A)	1836	June 02	Butler	01	13	35
Matthew, George W.(B)	1818	Sept. 24	Butler	02	08	19

PURCHASER	YEAR	DATE	RESIDENCE	R	T	S
Matthews, Aaron(Black)(E)	1835	Oct. 29	Franklin(Ind	12	12	18
Matthews, David(C)	1811	Jan. 10	Champaign	14	02	01
Matthews, Edwin(C)	1814	July 02	Cincinnati	09	04	08
Matthews, Edwin(D)	1813	July 17	Hamilton(Fr)	02	02	11
Matthews, Henry(C)	1814	Feb. 11	Champaign	14	03	34
Matthews, Isabella(E)	1836	Aug. 26	Dearborn(Ind	11	10	27
Matthews, James(B)	1830	Nov. 27	Cincinnati	02	07	22
Matthews, Michael(E)	1837	Feb. 15	Kentucky	14	20	13
Mattix, Giles(E)	1813	Nov. 08	Butler	13	13	02
Mattix, Jacob(E)	1814	March 23	Franklin(Ind	13	13	11
Matts, Isaac Jr.(B)	1829	Nov. 18	Switzerland	02	02	31
Matts, Isaac(B)	1828	Aug. 20	Clermont	02	02	32
Matts, Isaac(B)	1828	Sept. 10	Clermont	02	02	32
Maudlin, Benjamin(B)	1807	June 30	Dearborn(Ind	01	14	34
Maugaus, Enoch(A)	1837	May 23	Montgomery	01	12	03
Maulsby, David(E)	1836	March 12	Wayne(Ind)	13	18	23
Maurer, Daniel(A)	1817	Oct. 16	Pennsylvania	04	09	08
Max, Joseph Pashek(A)	1831	Oct. 11	Pennsylvania	04	07	19
Max, Joseph Pashek(A)	1831	Oct. 11	Pennsylvania	03	08	24
Maxson, Jesse(C)	1825	Feb. 07	Clark	08	03	29
Maxson, Jonathan(E)	1837	Aug. 02	Clark	14	22	36
Maxwell, Hugh(B)	1813	May 28	Tennessee	01	11	29
Maxwell, Hugh(B)	1813	May 28	Tennessee	01	11	29
Maxwell, Jacob(B)	1814	Oct. 04	Franklin(Ind	01	11	11
Maxwell, John(E)	1811	Oct. 31	Wayne(Ind)	14	16	17
Maxwell, Moses(B)	1810	April 12	Hamilton	01	10	19
Maxwell, Richard(A)	1813	Aug. 23	Wayne(Ind)	01	09	29
Maxwell, Richard(B)	1805	Sept. 23	Kentucky	01	14	36
Maxwell, Richard(B)	1806	July 30	Dearborn(Ind	01	14	36
Maxwell, Robert(C)	1801	Dec. 24	Hamilton	04	03	36
Maxwell, Thomas Jr.(E)	1836	Sept. 02	Pennsylvania	12	12	29
Maxwell, William(C)	1801	Dec. 31	Hamilton	06	03	30
Maxwell, William(C)	1801	Dec. 31	Hamilton	07	03	19
Maxwell, William(C)	1801	Dec. 31	Hamilton	07	02	34
Maxwell, William(C)	1801	Dec. 31	Hamilton	07	03	18
Maxwell, William(C)	1802	Dec. 31	Hamilton	07	03	13
Maxwell, Wm.(E)	1821	Sept. 14	Kentucky	12	12	29
May, Andrew(A)	1812	Jan. 15	Hamilton	01	07	12
May, Andrew(A)	1812	Nov. 18	Hamilton	01	07	14
May, Andrew(A)	1814	Sept. 07	Hamilton	01	07	11
May, James(C)	1830	Feb. 22	Champaign	12	03	04
May, John(A)	1831	Oct. 27	Preble	03	09	35
May, Thomas(B)	1818	July 30	Dearborn(Ind	01	06	04
Mayer, David(A)	1811	Sept. 19	Montgomery	04	04	04
Mayhew, Seth(A)	1816	May 11	Hamilton	01	02	06
Maze, Samuel(E)	1812	July 02	Ind.Territry	14	13	18
Maze, William(C)	1813	April 16	Champaign	13	05	08
McAlexander, John(C)	1829	Oct. 07	Champaign	12	03	18
McAlexander, John(C)	1831	Aug. 22	Champaign	13	03	01
McAlexander, Wm.(C)	1831	Feb. 26	Champaign	12	03	11
McAllister, Alexander(E)	1815	Nov. 27	Butler	14	16	09
McAnally, William(B)	1836	Feb. 13	Franklin(Ind	02	08	19
McAnally, William(B)	1834	Dec. 06	Franklin(Ind	02	08	19
McAuley, Ezekiel(A)	1810	Aug. 14	Hamilton	03	04	05
McAuley, Ezekiel(A)	1813	April 15	Hamilton	02	07	30
McBeath, Alexander Jur.(C)	1813	Nov. 02	Champaign	09	05	25
McBeath, Robert(C)	1814	Feb. 03	Greene	10	05	24
McBeth, Alexander(C)	1813	April 29	Champaign	10	05	23
McBeth, Alexander(C)	1814	April 04	Champaign	09	05	26
McBeth, Francis(B)	1833	Feb. 21	Switzerland	02	03	34
McBeth, Jas. R.(C)	1829	July 03	Champaign	12	04	18
McBeth, John(C)	1812	Sept. 28	Champaign	10	05	29
McBeth, Joseph(C)	1813	Aug. 30	Champaign	13	05	35
McBeth, Mary(C)	1814	Nov. 05	Champaign	10	05	24
McBeth, Saml.(C)	1813	March 12	Greene	08	03	11
McBeth, William(C)	1812	Aug. 17	Champaign	13	05	34
McBoom, William H.(B)	1817	Aug. 27	Wayne(Ind)	01	12	01
McBride, James(A)	1814	March 08	Butler	02	04	06
McBride, James(C)	1806	June 17	Greene	08	05	28

PURCHASER	YEAR	DATE	RESIDENCE	R	T	S
McCabe, Archibald(B)	1818	April 04	Hamilton	03	05	10
McCabe, John(B)	1834	May 27	Dearborn(Ind	03	05	09
McCabe, John(C)	1801	Dec. 30	Hamilton	06	01	10
McCabe, John(C)	1801	Dec. 30	Hamilton	06	02	09
McCabe, John(E)	1831	Nov. 01	Fayette	12	13	25
McCabe, John(E)	1831	Nov. 01	Fayette	12	13	26
McCabe, John(E)	1832	May 30	Fayette	12	13	25
McCafferty, Joseph(B)	1818	June 26	Indiana	02	08	28
McCain, Alexander(E)	1814	Feb. 11	Nor.Carolina	13	13	13
McCalla, Andrew(A)	1804	April 18	Kentucky	06	02	20
McCalley, John(C)	1815	March 14	Greene	10	03	02
McCallie, James C.(A)	1811	Aug. 13	Preble	02	07	20
McCallie, James C.(A)	1816	Dec. 02	Preble	02	07	20
McCallister, Ezekiel(C)	1817	Oct. 23	Champaign	12	03	25
McCallum, Duncan(B)	1815	June 28	Switzerland	02	02	30
McCallum, Duncan(B)	1816	Dec. 11	Switzerland	03	02	18
McCallum, Duncan(B)	1819	Nov. 30	Cincinnati	03	02	31
McCallum, Neil(B)	1815	June 28	Switzerland	03	02	17
McCalman, James(B)	1816	Oct. 15	Warren	02	09	15
McCampbell, William(C)	1809	June 03	Miami	11	01	22
McCance, David(A)	1801	Nov. 16	Hamilton	01	02	03
McCance, David(A)	1807	April 07	Butler	01	02	03
McCane, James(A)	1817	June 20	Kentucky	05	09	28
McCane, James(A)	1817	Sept. 17	Kentucky	05	09	28
McCane, James(A)	1817	Sept. 17	Kentucky	05	09	33
McCanles, James Jr.(A)	1818	Nov. 25	Montgomery	03	10	27
McCanles, James(A)	1819	Oct. 28	Montgomery	06	03	22
McCannon, John(B)	1832	Oct. 23	Dearborn(Ind	01	07	26
McCarkle, Alexander(C)	1806	Sept. 22	Champaign	10	06	13
McCarty, Abner(B)	1829	Dec. 09	Franklin(Ind	02	09	21
McCarty, Benjamin(A)	1805	July 23	Dearborn(Ind	01	02	07
McCarty, Benjamin(B)	1806	March 20	Ind.Territry	01	08	18
McCarty, Benjamin(B)	1806	Aug. 22	Dearborn(Ind	01	10	20
McCarty, Benjamin(B)	1803	May 25	Tennessee	01	08	32
McCarty, Benjamin(B)	1807	July 22	Dearborn(Ind	03	10	13
McCarty, Benjamin(B)	1808	Nov. 05	Dearborn(Ind	02	09	21
McCarty, Benjamin(B)	1814	Dec. 05	Franklin(Ind	02	09	14
McCarty, Benjamin(E)	1811	Oct. 22	Ind.Territry	12	15	02
McCarty, Benjamin(E)	1812	Feb. 03	Franklin(Ind	12	13	09
McCarty, Benjamin(E)	1812	March 07	Franklin(Ind	14	14	04
McCarty, Benjamin(E)	1814	Aug. 02	Franklin(Ind	12	13	08
McCarty, Benjamin(E)	1814	Aug. 02	Franklin(Ind	12	13	09
McCarty, Benjamin(E)	1814	Aug. 09	Franklin(Ind	12	13	09
McCarty, Benjamin(E)	1816	April 02	Franklin(Ind	14	15	31
McCarty, Benjm.(B)	1814	Dec. 16	Franklin(Ind	02	09	15
McCarty, Enoch(B)	1805	April 17	Dearborn(Ind	02	08	02
McCarty, Enoch(B)	1806	Aug. 22	Dearborn(Ind	01	10	20
McCarty, Enoch(B)	1814	Dec. 14	Franklin(Ind	02	09	36
McCarty, Enoch(B)	1835	March 11	Franklin(Ind	02	08	17
McCarty, James(B)	1812	Aug. 24	Franklin(Ind	03	04	10
McCarty, John(E)	1811	Dec. 09	Franklin(Ind	12	14	05
McCarty, John(E)	1816	March 11	Warren	13	15	04
McCarty, Jonathan(B)	1814	Dec. 08	Franklin(Ind	02	09	15
McCarty, Patrick(B)	1806	March 07	Ind.Territry	03	10	25
McCarty, Phineas(E)	1815	Jan. 18	Wayne(Ind)	13	14	29
McCarty, William M.(B)	1836	Jan. 28	Franklin(Ind	02	08	17
McCarty, William(E)	1811	Oct. 28	Franklin(Ind	12	13	02
McCarty, William(E)	1811	Dec. 09	Franklin(Ind	12	14	05
McCarty, Wm. M.(B)	1836	Feb. 09	Franklin(Ind	02	08	07
McCash, Ann(A)	1818	Feb. 16	Preble	02	09	03
McCash, James(E)	1836	Nov. 21	Hamilton	12	11	03
McCash, James(E)	1836	Nov. 21	Hamilton	12	11	09
McCash, William(E)	1836	Nov. 21	Hamilton	12	11	09
McCashin, James(C)	1801	Dec. 31	Hamilton	05	02	25
McCashin, John(C)	1806	Aug. 25	Hamilton	08	03	10
McCashin, John(C)	1811	Dec. 11	Hamilton	08	03	10
McCausland, Henry(B)	1811	Jan. 22	Cincinnati	01	08	20
McCaustland, Henry(B)	1811	Dec. 07	Franklin(Ind	01	08	20
McCaw, James(B)	1811	June 29	Ind.Territry	01	09	03

PURCHASER	YEAR	DATE	RESIDENCE	R	T	S
McCay, Abisha(B)	1810	March 08	Dearborn(Ind	03	02	31
McCay, Robert(B)	1816	Sept. 18	Switzerland	03	02	31
McCew, Edward(E)	1818	Oct. 06	Franklin(Ind	13	13	29
McCittrick, Robert(B)	1815	April 03	Dearborn(Ind	02	04	12
McClain, James(B)	1836	Jan. 18	Dearborn(Ind	02	04	07
McClain, James(E)	1816	Nov. 16	Virginia	13	15	24
McClalland, James(C)	1801	Dec. 30	Hamilton	04	02	15
McClane, David(A)	1827	Aug. 06	Darke	04	07	08
McClane, Francis(A)	1828	Feb. 06	Darke	04	07	07
McClane, John Jun.(E)	1816	Aug. 16	Wayne(Ind)	14	17	30
McClary, James(A)	1830	Jan. 18	New Jersey	02	08	33
McClary, James(B)	1831	Sept. 22	Dearborn(Ind	02	08	32
McClary, John(A)	1816	July 10	Miami	05	08	17
McClary, Thomas(B)	1821	Jan. 09	Pennsylvania	02	07	04
McClay, Charles(E)	1814	Oct. 19	Champaign	12	05	29
McClay, John(A)	1825	March 29	?	06	07	10
McClean, John Sr.(B)	1915	Jan. 09	Wayne(Ind)	01	13	10
McClean, John(A)	1813	Sept. 06	Butler	01	03	18
McClean, John(C)	1801	Dec. 25	Hamilton	06	02	10
McClean, William(A)	1803	Aug. 16	Hamilton	02	03	10
McCleary, John(A)	1806	May 13	Montgomery	06	03	33
McCleary, John(A)	1808	Feb. 06	Montgomery	06	02	04
McCleary, John(A)	1813	April 14	Montgomery	06	02	04
McCleary, John(A)	1814	July 18	Miami	05	08	05
McCleave, John(A)	1806	July 24	Hamilton	01	02	01
McCleave, John(B)	1806	Jan. 30	Butler	01	06	27
McCleery, William(B)	1836	Jan. 20	Franklin(Ind	02	09	06
McCleland, James(A)	1806	Oct. 01	Butler	02	04	28
McCleland, John(A)	1806	May 02	Butler	02	05	19
McCleland, John(A)	1806	Sept. 09	Butler	02	05	12
McClellan, James(A)	1814	March 14	Hamilton	03	06	24
McClellan, Sam'l.(A)	1831	Jan. 31	Preble	01	07	21
McClellan, William Jr.(C)	1813	Nov. 09	Pennsylvania	09	04	26
McClellan, William(A)	1803	April 09	Hamilton	03	02	10
McClellan, Wm. Jr.(C)	1813	Dec. 13	Pennsylvania	09	04	08
McClelland, Francis(B)	1814	Nov. 29	Franklin(Ind	01	10	02
McClelland, James(B)	1806	Aug. 21	Kentucky	02	13	12
McClelland, John(A)	1806	May 02	Butler	02	05	19
McClelland, William(A)	1802	Aug. 23	Hamilton	02	04	25
McClelland, William(A)	1809	Oct. 31	Butler	02	04	35
McClelland, William(B)	1817	Sept. 23	Butler	02	05	31
McClelland, William(C)	1810	March 06	?	06	02	11
McClery, Samuel(A)	1802	Oct. 14	Hamilton	02	05	14
McClintick, Abraham(A)	1805	March 14	Kentucky	05	05	09
McClintick, Adam(A)	1814	Sept. 20	Ross	05	09	24
McClintick, Alexander(A)	1814	March 03	Miami	05	08	03
McClintick, John(A)	1814	July 28	Ross	05	09	34
McClintock, Alex'r.(C)	1818	Sept. 18	Kentucky	12	01	12
McClintock, Alex'r.(C)	1818	Sept. 18	Kentucky	13	02	32
McClintock, Alex'r.(C)	1818	Sept. 18	Kentucky	13	02	33
McClintock, Alex'r.(C)	1818	Nov. 09	Kentucky	12	01	12
McClintock, Alexander(C)	1817	Oct. 30	?	13	01	08
McClintock, Alexander(C)	1817	Oct. 31	Kentucky	13	01	03
McClintock, Alexander(C)	1818	Sept. 12	Kentucky	13	01	02
McClintock, Alexander(C)	1818	Sept. 12	Kentucky	13	01	02
McClintock, Alexander(C)	1818	Sept. 14	Kentucky	12	01	04
McClish, Thomas(A)	1814	March 17	Miami	06	08	29
McClister, James(B)	1814	July 25	Dearborn(Ind	01	06	32
McCloud, William(C)	1808	Jan. 14	Champaign	14	03	05
McCloud, William(C)	1813	April 14	Champaign	14	03	05
McCluer, Samuel Junr.(A)	1816	Nov. 12	Darke	01	10	27
McCluer, Samuel(A)	1813	Feb. 10	Darke	01	10	28
McCluer, Samuel(A)	1814	Oct. 28	Darke	01	10	27
McClung, David(A)	1806	March 11	Kentucky	06	05	19
McClure, And'w. S.(A)	1831	June 02	Greene	06	08	09
McClure, David(A)	1813	April 19	Pennsylvania	01	01	30
McClure, David(B)	1813	April 19	Pennsylvania	01	02	25
McClure, James Eads(E)	1834	Feb. 03	Franklin(Ind	12	12	23
McClure, James(B)	1814	Sept. 27	Pennsylvania	01	07	20

PURCHASER	YEAR	DATE	RESIDENCE	R	T	S
McClure, James(C)	1802	Dec. 28	Hamilton	07	02	19
McClure, James(C)	1805	Dec. 12	Montgomery	09	02	09
McClure, John(A)	1808	Jan. 12	Kentucky	02	06	20
McClure, John(A)	1815	May 01	Butler	02	03	21
McClure, John(A)	1819	Jan. 02	Kentucky	04	11	12
McClure, John(A)	1819	Jan. 02	Kentucky	05	10	07
McClure, John(B)	1817	May 26	Pennsylvania	02	07	28
McClure, Nathan'l. Grear(A)	1832	Jan. 11	Greene	06	08	10
McClure, Nathaniel Jr.(B)	1816	July 25	Wayne(Ind)	01	13	15
McClure, Nathaniel(B)	1808	Feb. 11	Kentucky	01	13	10
McClure, Randle(A)	1819	June 26	Hamilton	04	05	14
McClure, Robert Jnr.(A)	1818	Sept. 07	Miami	05	09	03
McClure, Robert(A)	1806	Nov. 10	Montgomery	05	09	03
McClure, Robert(A)	1806	Nov. 18	Montgomery	06	07	18
McClure, Robert(A)	1836	May 27	Shelby	03	12	10
McClure, Robert(A)	1836	May 27	Shelby	04	11	18
McClure, Samuel(A)	1806	Nov. 18	Clermont	05	09	02
McClure, Samuel(A)	1813	Dec. 28	Miami	05	09	09
McClure, Samuel(A)	1818	Jan. 17	Darke	01	10	23
McClure, William(A)	1801	April 27	Hamilton	04	02	11
McClure, William(B)	1832	Feb. 03	Dearborn(Ind	01	07	35
McClure, William(C)	1808	Jan. 13	Champaign	13	03	05
McClure, Wm.(B)	1831	Sept. 01	Franklin(Ind	01	08	18
McClurken, James(A)	1810	Aug. 16	Dearborn(Ind	01	06	20
McClurken, James(B)	1813	July 26	Franklin(Ind	01	11	13
McClurken, John(B)	1811	Nov. 27	Franklin(Ind	01	10	09
McClurken, Matthew(A)	1809	May 25	Butler	01	10	03
McClurken, Matthew(B)	1811	Nov. 27	Franklin(Ind	01	11	34
McClutche, John(B)	1818	April 22	Switzerland	03	04	25
McCollough, Alexander(A)	1807	June 27	Miami	06	05	29
McCollough, John H.(B)	1814	Feb. 05	Pennsylvania	01	04	28
McCollough, Samuel(A)	1812	Feb. 15	Butler	02	04	08
McCollough, Samuel(E)	1828	April 01	Union(Ind)	14	15	19
McCollough, William(B)	1816	Aug. 08	JeffersonInd	02	02	27
McCollum, James F.(A)	1836	Oct. 13	Miami	01	15	28
McColough, Alexander(A)	1805	Sept. 05	Kentucky	06	05	28
McColough, Alexander(A)	1805	Sept. 05	Kentucky	06	05	07
McColough, Alexander(A)	1805	Sept. 07	Kentucky	06	05	33
McColough, John(A)	1805	Sept. 05	Kentucky	06	05	28
McComb, John(B)	1819	July 12	Dearborn(Ind	01	08	20
McCombs, Barnett(E)	1832	March 10	Franklin(Ind	13	12	26
McCon, Harrison(A)	1818	Sept. 21	Cincinnati	03	10	30
McConnel, John(B)	1814	July 30	Dearborn(Ind	01	06	03
McConnel, Robert(B)	1804	Oct. 02	Dearborn(Ind	01	06	14
McConnel, Robert(B)	1804	Oct. 31	Ind.Territry	01	06	14
McConnel, Robert(B)	1815	March 14	Dearborn(Ind	01	06	14
McConnell, Jno.(A)	1829	Dec. 25	Miami	04	07	02
McConnell, John(A)	1830	Dec. 18	Miami	04	07	02
McConnels, Alexander(A)	1803	May 30	Ohio	06	02	31
McConnels, James L.(A)	1803	May 30	Ohio	06	02	31
McConnels, Robert(A)	1803	May 30	Ohio	06	02	31
McConnels, William(A)	1803	May 30	Ohio	06	02	31
McCool, Gabriel Genr.(A)	1808	Feb. 18	Miami	04	08	34
McCool, Gabriel(A)	1811	Dec. 11	Miami	04	07	03
McCool, Gabriel(A)	1814	Aug. 22	Miami	04	09	03
McCool, Mary(A)	1816	April 16	Miami	01	09	04
McCool, Thomas(A)	1814	Dec. 14	Miami	04	09	09
McCool, Thomas(A)	1816	April 16	Miami	04	07	03
McCoole, Gabriel(A)	1806	Nov. 04	Montgomery	04	07	03
McCoole, Gabriel(A)	1806	Nov. 05	Montgomery	04	07	03
McCord, Abraham(B)	1818	June 01	Cincinnati	02	08	23
McCord, Abrm.(B)	1818	June 04	Cincinnati	02	08	07
McCord, James(B)	1813	Nov. 03	Warren	01	09	35
McCord, John(A)	1812	Oct. 27	Warren	01	08	03
McCord, John(B)	1814	Oct. 12	Butler	01	10	17
McCord, Sal.(C)	1817	Dec. 20	Champaign	11	04	34
McCord, Sam'l.(C)	1831	Aug. 08	Ohio	10	06	29
McCord, Sam'l.(C)	1831	Aug. 08	Ohio	10	06	08
McCord, Sam'l.(C)	1831	Aug. 08	Ohio	10	06	08

PURCHASER	YEAR	DATE	RESIDENCE	R	T	S
McCord, Sam'l.(C)	1831	Aug. 08	Ohio	10	06	29
McCord, Saml.(C)	1812	Dec. 30	Champaign	10	05	32
McCord, Saml.(C)	1817	Dec. 20	Champaign	13	03	01
McCord, Samuel(C)	1807	July 02	Champaign	11	05	36
McCord, Samuel(C)	1814	Sept. 03	Champaign	11	05	11
McCord, Samuel(C)	1816	May 14	Champaign	11	05	06
McCord, Samuel(C)	1817	July 01	Champaign	12	04	15
McCord, Samuel(C)	1817	July 01	Champaign	12	04	21
McCord, Samuel(C)	1817	July 01	Champaign	12	04	15
McCord, Samuel(C)	1817	July 25	Champaign	12	04	22
McCord, Samuel(C)	1817	July 25	Champaign	12	04	22
McCord, Samuel(C)	1817	Oct. 25	Champaign	12	04	33
McCord, Samuel(C)	1817	Oct. 25	Champaign	12	04	33
McCord, Samuel(C)	1817	Oct. 25	Champaign	12	04	32
McCord, Samuel(C)	1817	Oct. 25	Champaign	12	04	32
McCord, Samuel(C)	1817	Oct. 25	Champaign	12	04	25
McCord, Samuel(C)	1817	Oct. 25	Champaign	12	04	27
McCord, Samuel(C)	1817	Oct. 25	Champaign	12	04	27
McCord, Samuel(C)	1817	Oct. 25	Champaign	12	04	28
McCord, Samuel(C)	1817	Oct. 25	Champaign	12	04	08
McCord, Samuel(C)	1817	Oct. 25	Champaign	12	04	28
McCord, Samuel(C)	1817	Oct. 25	Champaign	12	04	12
McCord, Samuel(C)	1817	Oct. 25	Champaign	12	04	36
McCord, Samuel(C)	1817	Oct. 25	Champaign	12	04	17
McCord, Samuel(C)	1817	Oct. 25	Champaign	12	04	18
McCord, Samuel(C)	1817	Dec. 20	Champaign	11	03	03
McCord, Samuel(C)	1817	Dec. 20	Champaign	11	03	04
McCord, Samuel(C)	1817	Dec. 20	Champaign	11	03	04
McCord, Samuel(C)	1817	Dec. 20	Champaign	11	03	04
McCord, Samuel(C)	1817	Dec. 20	Champaign	11	03	04
McCord, Samuel(C)	1817	Dec. 20	Champaign	11	03	05
McCord, Samuel(C)	1817	Dec. 20	Champaign	11	03	05
McCord, Samuel(C)	1817	Dec. 20	Champaign	11	03	10
McCord, Samuel(C)	1817	Dec. 20	Champaign	11	03	10
McCord, Samuel(C)	1817	Dec. 20	Champaign	11	03	10
McCord, Samuel(C)	1817	Dec. 20	Champaign	11	03	12
McCord, Samuel(C)	1817	Dec. 20	Champaign	11	03	14
McCord, Samuel(C)	1817	Dec. 20	Champaign	11	03	14
McCord, Samuel(C)	1817	Dec. 20	Champaign	11	03	14
McCord, Samuel(C)	1817	Dec. 20	Champaign	11	03	14
McCord, Samuel(C)	1817	Dec. 20	Champaign	11	03	15
McCord, Samuel(C)	1817	Dec. 20	Champaign	11	03	17
McCord, Samuel(C)	1817	Dec. 20	Champaign	11	03	18
McCord, Samuel(C)	1817	Dec. 20	Champaign	11	03	24
McCord, Samuel(C)	1817	Dec. 20	Champaign	11	03	24
McCord, Samuel(C)	1817	Dec. 20	Champaign	11	03	30
McCord, Samuel(C)	1817	Dec. 20	Champaign	11	03	30
McCord, Samuel(C)	1817	Dec. 20	Champaign	11	03	23
McCord, Samuel(C)	1817	Dec. 20	Champaign	11	03	23
McCord, Samuel(C)	1817	Dec. 20	Champaign	11	03	21
McCord, Samuel(C)	1817	Dec. 20	Champaign	11	03	21
McCord, Samuel(C)	1817	Dec. 20	Champaign	11	03	21
McCord, Samuel(C)	1817	Dec. 20	Champaign	11	03	21
McCord, Samuel(C)	1817	Dec. 20	Champaign	12	02	01
McCord, Samuel(C)	1817	Dec. 20	Champaign	12	02	01
McCord, Samuel(C)	1817	Dec. 20	Champaign	12	02	02
McCord, Samuel(C)	1817	Dec. 20	Champaign	12	02	02
McCord, Samuel(C)	1817	Dec. 20	Champaign	12	02	07
McCord, Samuel(C)	1817	Dec. 20	Champaign	12	02	07
McCord, Samuel(C)	1817	Dec. 20	Champaign	12	02	07
McCord, Samuel(C)	1817	Dec. 20	Champaign	12	02	07
McCord, Samuel(C)	1817	Dec. 20	Champaign	12	02	13
McCord, Samuel(C)	1817	Dec. 20	Champaign	12	02	13
McCord, Samuel(C)	1817	Dec. 20	Champaign	12	02	13
McCord, Samuel(C)	1817	Dec. 20	Champaign	12	02	14
McCord, Samuel(C)	1817	Dec. 20	Champaign	12	02	14
McCord, Samuel(C)	1817	Dec. 20	Champaign	12	02	14
McCord, Samuel(C)	1817	Dec. 20	Champaign	12	02	14
McCord, Samuel(C)	1817	Dec. 20	Champaign	12	02	20

PURCHASER	YEAR	DATE	RESIDENCE	R	T	S
McCord, Samuel(C)	1817	Dec. 20	Champaign	12	02	20
McCord, Samuel(C)	1817	Dec. 20	Champaign	12	02	20
McCord, Samuel(C)	1817	Dec. 20	Champaign	12	02	25
McCord, Samuel(C)	1817	Dec. 20	Champaign	12	03	02
McCord, Samuel(C)	1817	Dec. 20	Champaign	12	03	03
McCord, Samuel(C)	1817	Dec. 20	Champaign	12	03	03
McCord, Samuel(C)	1817	Dec. 20	Champaign	12	03	04
McCord, Samuel(C)	1817	Dec. 20	Champaign	12	03	05
McCord, Samuel(C)	1817	Dec. 20	Champaign	12	03	05
McCord, Samuel(C)	1817	Dec. 20	Champaign	12	03	06
McCord, Samuel(C)	1817	Dec. 20	Champaign	12	03	10
McCord, Samuel(C)	1817	Dec. 20	Champaign	12	03	17
McCord, Samuel(C)	1817	Dec. 20	Champaign	12	03	17
McCord, Samuel(C)	1817	Dec. 20	Champaign	12	03	17
McCord, Samuel(C)	1817	Dec. 20	Champaign	12	03	18
McCord, Samuel(C)	1817	Dec. 20	Champaign	12	03	18
McCord, Samuel(C)	1817	Dec. 20	Champaign	12	03	19
McCord, Samuel(C)	1817	Dec. 20	Champaign	12	03	23
McCord, Samuel(C)	1817	Dec. 20	Champaign	12	03	23
McCord, Samuel(C)	1817	Dec. 20	Champaign	12	03	24
McCord, Samuel(C)	1817	Dec. 20	Champaign	12	03	25
McCord, Samuel(C)	1817	Dec. 20	Champaign	12	03	31
McCord, Samuel(C)	1817	Dec. 20	Champaign	12	03	31
McCord, Samuel(C)	1817	Dec. 20	Champaign	12	03	32
McCord, Samuel(C)	1817	Dec. 20	Champaign	12	03	32
McCord, Samuel(C)	1817	Dec. 20	Champaign	12	03	32
McCord, Samuel(C)	1817	Dec. 20	Champaign	12	03	32
McCord, Samuel(C)	1817	Dec. 20	Champaign	12	03	33
McCord, Samuel(C)	1817	Dec. 20	Champaign	12	03	33
McCord, Samuel(C)	1817	Dec. 20	Champaign	12	03	33
McCord, Samuel(C)	1817	Dec. 20	Champaign	12	03	33
McCord, Samuel(C)	1817	Dec. 20	Champaign	12	03	34
McCord, Samuel(C)	1817	Dec. 20	Champaign	12	03	34
McCord, Samuel(C)	1817	Dec. 20	Champaign	12	03	34
McCord, Samuel(C)	1817	Dec. 20	Champaign	12	03	34
McCord, Samuel(C)	1817	Dec. 20	Champaign	12	03	35
McCord, Samuel(C)	1817	Dec. 20	Champaign	12	03	35
McCord, Samuel(C)	1817	Dec. 20	Champaign	12	03	27
McCord, Samuel(C)	1817	Dec. 20	Champaign	12	03	27
McCord, Samuel(C)	1817	Dec. 20	Champaign	12	03	27
McCord, Samuel(C)	1817	Dec. 20	Champaign	12	03	28
McCord, Samuel(C)	1817	Dec. 20	Champaign	13	03	01
McCord, Samuel(C)	1817	Dec. 20	Champaign	13	03	01
McCord, Samuel(C)	1817	Dec. 20	Champaign	13	03	01
McCord, Samuel(C)	1817	Dec. 20	Champaign	13	03	02
McCord, Samuel(C)	1817	Dec. 20	Champaign	13	03	02
McCord, Samuel(C)	1817	Dec. 20	Champaign	13	03	07
McCord, Samuel(C)	1817	Dec. 20	Champaign	13	03	07
McCord, Samuel(C)	1817	Dec. 20	Champaign	13	03	07
McCord, Samuel(C)	1817	Dec. 20	Champaign	13	03	14
McCord, Samuel(C)	1817	Dec. 20	Champaign	10	06	29
McCord, Samuel(C)	1817	Dec. 20	Champaign	10	06	29
McCord, Samuel(C)	1817	Dec. 20	Champaign	10	06	26
McCord, Samuel(C)	1817	Dec. 20	Champaign	10	06	26
McCord, Samuel(C)	1817	Dec. 20	Champaign	11	04	36
McCord, Samuel(C)	1817	Dec. 20	Champaign	12	04	36
McCord, Samuel(C)	1817	Dec. 20	Champaign	12	04	36
McCord, Samuel(C)	1824	June 07	Champaign	10	06	26
McCord, Samuel(C)	1824	June 07	Champaign	11	05	11
McCorkle, Alexander(C)	1809	May 25	Champaign	11	05	14
McCorkle, John(A)	1818	Dec. 07	Miami	06	08	35
McCorkle, John(C)	1816	July 06	Cincinnati	13	02	35
McCorkle, Thos. Jay(A)	1832	Jan. 14	Miami	05	07	02
McCormic, Thos. M.(A)	1836	Aug. 18	Montgomery	02	15	20
McCormick, And'w.(A)	1832	Feb. 22	Hamilton	01	02	31
McCormick, David(B)	1815	July 03	Cincinnati	02	02	33
McCormick, David(B)	1818	Aug. 24	Indiana	02	02	33
McCormick, David(B)	1834	April 14	Switzerland	02	02	29
McCormick, David(B)	1836	Feb. 25	Switzerland	02	02	29

211

PURCHASER	YEAR	DATE	RESIDENCE	R	T	S
McCormick, James(A)	1803	Aug. 08	Hamilton	03	02	08
McCormick, John(A)	1804	Dec. 11	Butler	03	03	17
McCormick, John(A)	1806	Dec. 31	Butler	01	08	28
McCormick, John(A)	1807	June 05	Butler	01	08	28
McCormick, John(C)	1801	Dec. 28	Hamilton	05	02	25
McCormick, John(D)	1808	Nov. 01	Hamilton	02	02	08
McCormick, John(D)	1808	Nov. 01	Hamilton	02	02	08
McCormick, John(E)	1813	Oct. 22	Preble	12	14	13
McCormick, Robert(A)	1813	Aug. 18	Preble	02	07	01
McCormick, Robert(E)	1812	Aug. 22	Preble	12	14	13
McCormick, Samuel(E)	1816	Dec. 02	Wayne(Ind)	12	14	13
McCortney, Abner(A)	1831	July 04	Montgomery	04	06	06
McCortney, John(A)	1819	April 19	Montgomery	04	06	06
McCoulough, Samuel(C)	1805	Dec. 31	Champaign	13	03	04
McCowen, James(A)	1825	Feb. 08	Warren	02	10	23
McCowen, James(A)	1825	Feb. 08	Warren	03	08	19
McCowen, James(A)	1832	Feb. 28	Warren	03	08	19
McCowens, Banner(A)	1819	May 28	Warren	02	09	20
McCowens, Banner(A)	1831	Nov. 12	Preble	02	09	17
McCown, James(A)	1825	April 02	Preble	01	08	27
McCoy, Charles Steward(A)	1832	Aug. 18	Preble	02	09	07
McCoy, David(B)	1835	Jan. 27	Dearborn(Ind	02	06	32
McCoy, James(B)	1803	July 25	Ind.Territory	01	07	05
McCoy, James(B)	1804	Sept. 19	Dearborn(Ind	01	07	14
McCoy, James(B)	1804	Oct. 22	Ind.Territory	02	08	04
McCoy, James(E)	1811	Oct. 21	Ind.Territory	12	12	21
McCoy, Margret(B)	1805	Feb. 22	Dearborn(Ind	01	13	18
McCoy, Margret(B)	1805	Feb. 22	Dearborn(Ind	01	13	18
McCoy, Nathan Cram(A)	1831	Aug. 04	Miami	05	07	15
McCoy, Thomas(E)	1811	Oct. 23	Wayne(Ind)	12	16	12
McCoy, Thomas(E)	1811	Oct. 24	?	13	16	35
McCoy, Thomas(E)	1811	Oct. 29	Wayne(Ind)	13	15	02
McCoy, Thomas(E)	1816	Oct. 26	Wayne(Ind)	13	16	35
McCoy, Wm.(B)	1811	Nov. 28	Franklin(Ind	02	09	34
McCracken, John(A)	1831	July 05	Miami	05	08	26
McCracken, Robert(B)	1818	Feb. 17	Dearborn(Ind	02	05	02
McCracken, Robert(E)	1837	June 01	Licking	13	21	14
McCrackin, Robert(B)	1818	Jan. 21	Dearborn(Ind	03	07	36
McCrary, John(B)	1813	June 07	Jefferson	03	02	01
McCrary, William(B)	1816	Nov. 30	Switzerland	01	02	30
McCray, Phineas(A)	1810	April 11	?	04	03	35
McCray, Phineas(E)	1813	Sept. 24	Butler	13	15	13
McCray, Phineas(E)	1813	Sept. 24	Butler	13	15	13
McCray, Phineas(E)	1814	Feb. 02	Butler	13	14	33
McCray, Phineas(E)	1815	Jan. 18	Wayne(Ind)	13	14	29
McCray, Samuel(B)	1811	Nov. 29	Butler	01	09	10
McCray, Thomas(A)	1810	Dec. 17	Butler	04	03	36
McCrea, Wm. B.(C)	1829	Jan. 08	Champaign	11	03	21
McCreary, John(B)	1815	Jan. 20	Switzerland	02	02	28
McCreary, William(A)	1806	June 16	Butler	01	06	36
McCrey, John(C)	1819	Jan. 13	Hamilton	11	03	27
McCrey, John(C)	1819	Jan. 13	Hamilton	11	03	27
McCrey, John(C)	1827	Aug. 22	Champaign	11	03	27
McCrosky, Sam'l.(C)	1830	Dec. 13	Champaign	12	03	11
McCrosky, William(C)	1814	Aug. 20	Kentucky	12	03	05
McCue, Edward(E)	1833	March 22	Randolph(Ind	13	21	12
McCulley, Solomon(C)	1804	Dec. 31	Greene	07	04	34
McCulloch, Noah Z.(C)	1824	June 17	Logan	13	05	29
McCullough, John(A)	1829	Dec. 11	Miami	06	05	07
McCullough, John(E)	1831	June 29	Wayne(Ind)	13	17	17
McCullough, Lawson(A)	1803	Nov. 19	Kentucky	06	02	29
McCullough, Sam'l.(E)	1832	Jan. 23	Wayne(Ind)	13	17	18
McCullough, Samuel(E)	1816	April 30	Pennsylvania	13	17	17
McCullough, Thomas(C)	1805	Oct. 22	Butler	03	02	26
McCullough, William(B)	1816	Aug. 08	JeffersonInd	02	02	29
McCune, Joseph(C)	1804	Dec. 28	Greene	08	04	32
McCutchan, John(B)	1804	Dec. 18	Kentucky	02	11	21
McDanel, James(C)	1811	Oct. 18	Champaign	09	06	20
McDaniel, James(A)	1823	Aug. 20	Darke	03	08	01

PURCHASER	YEAR	DATE	RESIDENCE	R	T	S
McDaniel, James(A)	1830	Oct. 09	Darke	03	08	01
McDaniel, James(A)	1831	April 16	Darke	03	08	09
McDaniel, William(B)	1811	Nov. 02	Franklin(Ind	01	09	19
McDaniel, William(C)	1806	Aug. 01	Champaign	10	05	29
McDermed, Edward(C)	1811	Nov. 18	Greene	08	02	15
McDermot, Mich'l.(B)	1819	Aug. 21	Cincinnati	01	07	22
McDill, David(A)	1807	Jan. 15	Butler	01	06	35
McDill, David(A)	1807	Jan. 15	Butler	01	06	26
McDill, David(A)	1807	Jan. 15	Butler	01	06	26
McDill, David(A)	1807	April 14	Butler	01	06	36
McDill, David(A)	1810	Oct. 03	Preble	01	06	35
McDill, James(A)	1807	June 17	Butler	01	06	28
McDill, Samuel(B)	1814	Sept. 19	So. Carolina	01	11	33
McDill, Samuel(B)	1814	Sept. 28	So. Carolina	01	11	11
McDill, Thomas(A)	1809	June 14	Preble	01	06	28
McDonal, Daniel(C)	1814	Aug. 26	Butler	12	01	07
McDonald, Benjamin(C)	1814	March 11	Kentucky	09	06	09
McDonald, Daniel(A)	1810	Dec. 17	Butler	04	03	35
McDonald, James(C)	1801	Dec. 30	Hamilton	04	04	24
McDonald, James(C)	1801	Dec. 31	Hamilton	05	03	27
McDonald, James(C)	1804	Sept. 04	Warren	06	02	26
McDonald, James(C)	1804	Sept. 04	Warren	04	03	11
McDonald, James(C)	1804	Sept. 04	Warren	04	03	11
McDonald, James(C)	1804	Sept. 04	Warren	04	03	11
McDonald, Jno.(A)	1831	May 24	Montgomery	06	08	14
McDonald, John(A)	1830	Sept. 09	Darke	03	11	12
McDonald, John(A)	1831	Sept. 14	Preble	02	07	33
McDonald, John(A)	1836	Nov. 09	Darke	03	11	21
McDonald, John(E)	1837	Sept. 21	Madison	14	20	01
McDonald, Joseph(A)	1815	March 27	Miami	04	09	05
McDonald, William(C)	1801	Dec. 31	Hamilton	05	03	25
McDonald, William(C)	1807	May 20	Champaign	13	05	22
McDonald, William(C)	1831	Aug. 06	Champaign	12	04	05
McDonald, Wm.(C)	1830	Jan. 06	Champaign	11	05	32
McDonel, William(C)	1813	April 14	Champaign	13	04	22
McDonnal, James(C)	1807	March 11	Champaign	09	06	21
McDonnal, William(C)	1806	June 26	Warren	09	02	07
McDonnal, William(C)	1806	April 12	Warren	09	02	27
McDonnal, William(C)	1806	June 14	Warren	09	02	20
McDonnald, Daniel(C)	1815	March 10	Butler	12	01	07
McDonnald, John(C)	1801	Dec. 30	Hamilton	05	03	19
McDonnel, William(C)	1807	March 11	Champaign	09	06	21
McDonnel, William(C)	1807	July 03	Warren	09	02	14
McDonnell, William(B)	1811	Dec. 12	Franklin(Ind	01	08	06
McDonnell, Wm.(C)	1815	July 08	?	13	05	22
McDowell, Matthew(A)	1801	Dec. 10	Hamilton	03	03	29
McElroy, Enos(B)	1817	Oct. 24	Switzerland	03	03	19
McElroy, George(A)	1836	Nov. 12	Cincinnati	01	15	22
McElroy, James(C)	1807	April 02	Champaign	09	05	06
McElroy, James(C)	1807	July 13	Champaign	09	05	06
McElroy, James(C)	1808	Jan. 12	Champaign	09	05	06
McElvain, James(C)	1807	Oct. 01	Kentucky	13	04	03
McElvain, Moses(C)	1812	March 09	Champaign	13	05	19
McEntire, John(C)	1817	Aug. 05	Champaign	13	04	27
McEntire, John(E)	1814	June 24	Pennsylvania	13	04	27
McEowan, John(B)	1815	Sept. 16	Butler	01	12	20
McEowen, John(A)	1005	Dec. 18	Butler	03	03	07
McFadden, James(A)	1811	Dec. 11	Miami	06	06	30
McFall, Joseph(B)	1812	Nov. 12	Dearborn(Ind	02	02	36
McFarlan, William(E)	1836	March 11	Darke	15	21	06
McFarlan, William(E)	1836	July 08	Darke	15	21	06
McFarland, James(A)	1831	Sept. 16	Darke	02	10	20
McFarland, John(A)	1815	Oct. 23	Butler	02	12	19
McFarland, Joseph(E)	1837	June 05	Darke	14	22	36
McFarland, Lewis(A)	1838	Feb. 03	Darke	01	13	22
McFarland, Stephen	1808	March 03	Cincinnati	?	?	?
McFarling, William(E)	1838	Nov. 05	Belmont	15	22	11
McFeely, James(A)	1836	Oct. 21	Hamilton	01	14	10
McFeely, James(A)	1837	Feb. 20	Hamilton	01	14	03

213

PURCHASER	YEAR	DATE	RESIDENCE	R	T	S
McGahon, William(A)	1811	Aug. 13	Clermont	01	02	20
McGarvy, Andrew(A)	1803	Feb. 18	Hamilton	02	06	10
McGaughey, David(B)	1814	June 13	Hamilton	01	09	34
McGaw, James(A)	1811	Dec. 27	Preble	01	07	33
McGeorge, Samuel(E)	1813	Aug. 14	Wayne(Ind)	12	15	23
McGill, Christopher(C)	1806	July 23	Champaign	11	05	29
McGillespie, John M.(C)	1802	Dec. 02	Hamilton	04	03	27
McGillvary, John(A)	1813	July 17	Butler	02	03	12
McGinis, James(B)	1811	April 12	Franklin(Ind	02	09	28
McGinis, James(B)	1811	May 23	Franklin(Ind	02	09	28
McGinnis, James(B)	1816	Aug. 01	Franklin(Ind	02	09	17
McGinnis, Thomas(A)	1831	Feb. 01	Darke	02	11	03
McGinnis, William(B)	1815	Jan. 03	Kentucky	01	02	19
McGinnis, William(C)	1812	Jan. 22	Kentucky	11	04	18
McGinty, Anthony(B)	1825	June 16	Dearborn(Ind	02	07	04
McGinty, Anthony(B)	1825	June 16	Dearborn(Ind	02	07	08
McGlothlen, Charles(E)	1811	Nov. 23	Wayne(Ind)	14	14	18
McGommery, John(C)	1816	Sept. 04	Madison	08	07	36
McGowan, Harry(C)	1813	March 22	Champaign	09	06	29
McGreer, William(B)	1814	Oct. 03	So. Carolina	02	11	22
McGrew, Archibald(C)	1811	May 03	Champaign	11	04	11
McGrew, James(C)	1812	Dec. 21	Montgomery	06	01	04
McGrew, James(E)	1811	Dec. 02	Montgomery	13	15	09
McGrew, John(A)	1830	Aug. 05	Montgomery	02	09	19
McGrew, John(C)	1801	Dec. 25	Hamilton	06	02	27
McGrew, John(C)	1801	Dec. 25	Hamilton	06	01	09
McGrew, John(C)	1805	Dec. 24	Montgomery	06	01	03
McGrew, Matthew(C)	1810	May 30	Champaign	11	04	11
McGrew, William(C)	1813	March 23	Champaign	12	05	31
McGrew, William(E)	1836	Dec. 31	Montgomery	15	20	07
McGriff, John(A)	1810	Oct. 23	Miami	03	07	07
McGriff, John(A)	1814	June 03	Preble	02	10	36
McGriff, John(A)	1822	Jan. 08	Darke	02	10	25
McGriff, Patrick(A)	1831	Aug. 30	Preble	02	10	36
McGriff, Thomas(A)	1805	Nov. 08	Butler	03	05	26
McGriff, Thomas(A)	1811	March 29	Preble	03	07	06
McGriff, Thomas(A)	1816	Aug. 01	Preble	03	07	06
McGuire, Adjet(E)	1836	June 17	Randolph(Ind	14	21	21
McGuire, James(B)	1815	April 17	Dearborn(Ind	03	04	09
McGuire, James(B)	1831	Dec. 07	Dearborn(Ind	03	04	17
McGuire, James(B)	1832	April 09	Dearborn(Ind	03	04	17
McGuire, John(B)	1813	July 30	Butler	01	09	25
McGuire, John(B)	1837	Dec. 26	Dearborn(Ind	03	04	17
McGuire, John(B)	1838	May 05	Dearborn(Ind	03	04	17
McGuire, Lawrence(B)	1832	Aug. 24	Cincinnati	02	07	22
McGuire, Patrick(B)	1831	July 06	Dearborn(Ind	02	07	23
McHannon, Joseph(A)	1830	June 26	Warren	04	06	18
McHannon, Joseph(A)	1830	Nov. 10	Warren	03	07	01
McHannon, Joseph(E)	1837	April 10	Warren	15	21	32
McHendry, Joseph(B)	1817	Aug. 19	Hamilton	02	03	35
McHenry, Hugh(B)	1835	Sept. 21	Dearborn(Ind	02	03	34
McHenry, Isaac(B)	1835	April 20	Switzerland	02	03	20
McHenry, James(B)	1833	Jan. 07	Switzerland	02	03	25
McHenry, James(B)	1833	May 07	Switzerland	02	03	26
McHenry, James(B)	1835	Aug. 24	Switzerland	02	03	25
McHenry, Joseph(B)	1833	June 22	Switzerland	02	03	26
McHenry, Joseph(B)	1835	April 09	Switzerland	02	03	26
McHenry, Samuel(A)	1806	April 14	Hamilton	01	01	18
McHenry, Samuel(A)	1811	Aug. 13	Hamilton	01	01	18
McHenry, Samuel(B)	1814	Dec. 03	Cincinnati	03	03	36
McHenry, Samuel(E)	1816	Sept. 02	Cincinnati	13	12	03
McHorter, Tyler(E)	1814	Sept. 06	Warren	13	12	02
McIlroy, James(C)	1808	May 02	Champaign	09	05	06
McIlroy, James(C)	1813	Aug. 10	Champaign	09	05	06
McIlvain, James(C)	1814	March 17	Champaign	13	04	05
McIlvain, James(C)	1815	June 17	Champaign	14	04	31
McIlvain, Jno. Lockridge(C)	1831	Aug. 08	Champaign	13	04	06
McIlvain, John(E)	1814	March 19	Franklin(Ind	13	13	35
McIlvain, Moses Jr.(C)	1812	Nov. 23	Champaign	13	05	32

PURCHASER	YEAR	DATE	RESIDENCE	R	T	S
McIlvain, Moses(C)	1808	Sept. 17	Champaign	13	05	25
McIlvain, Moses(C)	1812	Nov. 23	Champaign	13	05	32
McIlvain, Moses(C)	1813	April 29	Champaign	13	05	26
McIlvain, Moses(C)	1813	Dec. 15	Champaign	13	05	25
McIlvain, Moses(C)	1814	May 31	Champaign	12	05	24
McIlvain, Moses(C)	1814	May 31	Champaign	13	05	13
McIlvain, Moses(C)	1814	Aug. 26	Champaign	12	05	24
McIlvain, Samuel(C)	1813	March 06	Champaign	14	03	07
McIlvain, Samuel(C)	1807	March 10	Champaign	13	05	25
McIntire, Edw'd.(B)	1829	June 23	Kentucky	04	02	35
McIntire, Edward(B)	1817	July 26	Switzerland	04	02	35
McIntire, James(B)	1816	April 17	Butler	01	02	14
McIntire, James(C)	1806	Feb. 07	Greene	09	04	22
McIntire, James(C)	1811	April 09	Greene	09	04	22
McIntire, John(C)	1806	Feb. 07	Greene	09	04	22
McIntire, John(C)	1811	April 09	Greene	09	04	22
McIntire, John(C)	1811	Aug. 05	Champaign	13	04	20
McIntire, John(C)	1819	March 08	Champaign	13	04	26
McIntire, John(E)	1811	Oct. 24	Cincinnati	13	16	25
McIntire, John(E)	1811	Oct. 28	Cincinnati	13	15	02
McIntire, John(E)	1811	Oct. 28	Cincinnati	13	15	19
McIntire, John(E)	1811	Oct. 28	Cincinnati	13	14	05
McIntire, John(E)	1811	Oct. 28	Cincinnati	13	14	05
McIntire, John(E)	1812	Dec. 07	Cincinnati	13	16	26
McIntire, Joseph(A)	1813	April 23	Miami	05	08	02
McIntire, Robert(A)	1831	July 02	Darke	02	11	12
McIntire, Robinson(E)	1811	Oct. 24	Butler	13	16	05
McIntire, Robinson(E)	1819	Jan. 21	Butler	13	20	14
McIntire, Samuel(A)	1813	March 04	Butler	02	04	15
McIntire, Thomas Jnr.(B)	1815	Nov. 18	Kentucky	02	05	20
McIntire, Thomas(C)	1810	Jan. 01	Virginia	12	04	30
McIntire, William(C)	1813	Oct. 16	Champaign	08	05	35
McIntire, William(C)	1824	June 07	Champaign	13	04	26
McIntire, Wm.(C)	1831	Feb. 11	Champaign	13	03	01
McIntoish, Daniel(C)	1805	April 04	Kentucky	08	04	26
McIntyre, Robeson(E)	1819	Aug. 13	Highland	13	20	23
McJimpsey, Robert(A)	1806	Feb. 07	Montgomery	06	05	33
McJimsey, Robert(C)	1814	March 28	Miami	11	02	07
McJunkins, Landlott(E)	1830	Oct. 14	Randolph(Ind	13	18	24
McKain, William(A)	1804	Sept. 24	Butler	02	05	27
McKane, John(B)	1816	May 22	Pennsylvania	02	03	09
McKane, John(B)	1831	July 01	Dearborn(Ind	02	03	09
McKay, Daniel(B)	1819	Jan. 08	Cincinnati	01	07	25
McKay, Daniel(B)	1832	July 27	Dearborn(Ind	02	07	27
McKay, James(B)	1804	Oct. 20	Kentucky	04	01	01
McKay, James(B)	1810	Jan. 11	Dearborn(Ind	04	01	01
McKay, James(B)	1829	Jan. 27	Switzerland	04	02	36
McKay, James(B)	1829	March 21	Switzerland	04	02	36
McKay, Moses(B)	1835	June 15	Switzerland	04	02	36
McKeag, Robt.(B)	1819	March 05	Hamilton	02	07	13
McKean, Daniel(A)	1814	Aug. 29	Hamilton	01	03	29
McKean, James(A)	1802	Feb. 10	Hamilton	03	03	20
McKean, John(A)	1805	June 20	Butler	03	03	23
McKee, David H.(C)	1818	March 30	Miami	12	02	27
McKee, Elizabeth(C)	1813	Dec. 06	Champaign	09	03	10
McKee, George(A)	1817	Sept. 22	Butler	01	11	11
McKee, James(A)	1814	Jan. 08	Hamilton	01	03	29
McKee, John(A)	1807	Sept. 04	Hamilton	05	08	02
McKee, John(A)	1824	June 09	Preble	01	09	22
McKee, John(A)	1832	March 19	Hamilton	02	10	34
McKee, John(A)	1832	March 27	Hamilton	02	10	34
McKee, John(C)	1812	Aug. 25	Miami	09	02	12
McKee, John(C)	1817	Oct. 30	?	13	01	08
McKee, John(C)	1818	Sept. 12	Kentucky	13	01	02
McKee, John(C)	1818	Sept. 12	Kentucky	13	01	02
McKee, John(C)	1818	Sept. 14	Kentucky	12	01	04
McKee, John(C)	1818	Sept. 18	Kentucky	12	01	12
McKee, John(C)	1818	Sept. 18	Kentucky	13	02	32
McKee, John(C)	1818	Sept. 18	Kentucky	13	02	33

215

PURCHASER	YEAR	DATE	RESIDENCE	R	T	S
McKee, John(C)	1818	Nov. 09	Kentucky	12	01	12
McKee, John(E)	1811	Oct. 24	Hamilton	13	16	18
McKee, John(E)	1811	Oct. 24	Hamilton	13	16	18
McKee, Robert(C)	1819	March 16	Hamilton	09	03	11
McKee, Thomas(C)	1815	Dec. 06	?	12	01	17
McKeel, Jonah(A)	1808	Jan. 11	Nor.Carolina	02	07	31
McKelvey, Matthew(E)	1838	May 10	Belmont	15	22	22
McKelvey, Samuel(E)	1838	May 10	Belmont	15	22	26
McKenney, James(C)	1804	Dec. 24	Montgomery	11	01	14
McKennon, Daniel(C)	1804	Dec. 31	Greene	10	05	04
McKensey, Mordecai(B)	1807	Feb. 20	Hamilton	02	11	28
McKeny, Joseph(B)	1815	Jan. 27	Dearborn(Ind	02	05	14
McKenzie, Henry(B)	1816	May 03	Hamilton	02	07	25
McKey, Elias(A)	1832	Aug. 24	Preble	01	09	01
McKey, Elias(A)	1833	May 23	Preble	01	09	01
McKim, John(B)	1835	Jan. 23	Randolph(Ind	01	17	34
McKim, Robert(B)	1817	July 02	Warren	02	02	30
McKim, William(B)	1831	Nov. 04	Randolph(Ind	01	16	15
McKim, William(B)	1831	Nov. 10	Randolph(Ind	01	16	15
McKim, William(B)	1835	Jan. 23	Randolph(Ind	01	16	10
McKim, William(E)	1837	Jan. 05	Randolph(Ind	15	19	06
McKim, William(E)	1837	Jan. 05	Randolph(Ind	14	20	36
McKim, William(E)	1838	Aug. 24	Randolph(Ind	15	20	31
McKim, Wm.(E)	1838	May 21	Randolph(Ind	15	20	31
McKinley, John(C)	1806	Oct. 07	Warren	11	02	22
McKinley, John(C)	1811	Dec. 11	Miami	11	02	22
McKinley, John(C)	1817	Dec. 08	Miami	11	02	22
McKinley, Samuel(B)	1806	July 30	Kentucky	01	13	06
McKinney, Absalom S.(C)	1814	Oct. 31	Pennsylvania	12	05	29
McKinney, Absalom S.(C)	1814	Oct. 31	Pennsylvania	12	05	22
McKinney, Ephraim(C)	1813	Jan. 04	Miami	12	01	19
McKinney, James Bell(A)	1831	Aug. 31	Shelby	06	08	15
McKinney, James L.(C)	1813	May 28	Miami	11	01	12
McKinney, James L.(C)	1817	Oct. 30	Miami	11	11	17
McKinney, James(C)	1805	May 31	Pennsylvania	12	01	32
McKinney, James(E)	1815	Sept. 21	Franklin(Ind	14	14	30
McKinney, John H.(A)	1831	April 19	Shelby	06	08	33
McKinney, John T.(B)	1833	Oct. 26	Franklin(Ind	02	09	17
McKinney, John T.(B)	1836	Jan. 29	Franklin(Ind	02	08	08
McKinney, John(A)	1831	April 19	Shelby	06	08	33
McKinney, John(B)	1818	Oct. 22	Dearborn(Ind	02	05	21
McKinney, John(C)	1805	Oct. 09	Kentucky	07	03	11
McKinney, John(C)	1816	Jan. 29	?	08	06	36
McKinney, Jos.(C)	1813	March 12	Greene	08	03	11
McKinney, Joseph(C)	1804	Sept. 03	Greene	09	03	08
McKinney, Joseph(C)	1813	March 26	Champaign	08	03	11
McKinney, Joseph(C)	1814	March 29	Champaign	09	03	21
McKinney, Thomas(C)	1805	Aug. 31	Pennsylvania	12	01	32
McKinnon, Daniel(C)	1806	May 17	Champaign	10	05	10
McKinnon, Daniel(C)	1813	April 14	Champaign	09	05	34
McKinnon, Daniel(C)	1813	April 14	Champaign	10	05	17
McKinnon, Daniel(C)	1813	May 24	Champaign	10	05	22
McKinnon, Daniel(C)	1813	Dec. 01	Champaign	10	05	15
McKinnon, Daniel(C)	1816	Aug. 01	Champaign	10	05	09
McKinny, Lambkin(B)	1818	June 01	Dearborn(Ind	02	05	14
McKinstray, John(A)	1816	March 19	Butler	01	04	33
McKinstrey, John(B)	1834	July 02	Dearborn(Ind	03	06	12
McKinstrey, Sam'l.(B)	1833	Aug. 12	Dearborn(Ind	03	06	01
McKinstrey, Samuel(B)	1836	Feb. 29	Dearborn(Ind	03	06	01
McKinstrey, Thomas(B)	1836	Nov. 14	Dearborn(Ind	02	05	07
McKinstry, Alex'r.(B)	1831	Oct. 27	Dearborn(Ind	02	05	06
McKittrick, David(B)	1813	Oct. 22	Kentucky	02	04	08
McKittrick, Robert Jr.(B)	1813	Oct. 22	Kentucky	02	04	11
McKnight, Jas.(C)	1831	Feb. 10	Hamilton	12	01	07
McKnight, John(A)	1835	Aug. 18	Miami	08	02	29
McKnight, John(A)	1835	Aug. 18	Miami	08	02	29
McKnight, John(C)	1801	Dec. 30	Hamilton	06	03	31
McKnight, John(D)	1812	Dec. 28	Hamilton(Fr)	02	02	11
McKnight, Joseph(C)	1816	March 05	Hamilton	11	01	17

PURCHASER	YEAR	DATE	RESIDENCE	R	T	S
McKnight, Joseph(C)	1830	March 26	Miami	13	02	32
McKnight, Josiah(B)	1818	June 29	Hamilton	03	06	23
McKnight, Josiah(D)	1812	Dec. 28	Hamilton(Fr)	02	02	11
McKnight, Thomas(B)	1828	Sept. 04	Dearborn(Ind	03	06	24
McKoy, Robert(B)	1817	Aug. 04	Cincinnati	01	08	30
McKoy, Robert(B)	1817	Aug. 04	Cincinnati	01	08	30
McKoy, Robert(E)	1816	Oct. 02	Cincinnati	13	12	27
McKoy, Robert(E)	1816	Oct. 02	Cincinnati	13	12	34
McKroy, Enos(B)	1817	Nov. 20	Switzerland	02	02	19
McLain, James(A)	1831	Aug. 04	Montgomery	06	08	34
McLaughlin, Robert(A)	1833	April 02	Darke	03	10	07
McLaughlin, Robert(A)	1835	June 09	Darke	03	10	06
McLaughlin, Robt.(A)	1834	Oct. 21	Darke	03	10	06
McLean, Elisha Pierce(A)	1831	Sept. 15	Hamilton	05	08	22
McLean, Fergus(C)	1801	Dec. 29	Hamilton	04	04	36
McLean, Samuel(A)	1831	May 11	Butler	05	08	15
McLean, Samuel(A)	1831	July 05	Butler	05	08	14
McLean, Samuel(A)	1832	Aug. 14	Butler	04	07	19
McLean, Stephen(A)	1830	Dec. 07	Butler	04	06	30
McLean, William(E)	1811	Nov. 19	Wayne(Ind)	14	17	33
McLoskey, Daniel(A)	1816	Oct. 12	Pennsylvania	01	07	23
McLoskey, Daniel(B)	1818	May 19	Dearborn(Ind	02	03	05
McLucas, William(E)	1813	March 17	Montgomery	13	15	09
McMacken, David(A)	1814	Nov. 30	Butler	02	06	23
McMacken, John(E)	1814	Feb. 07	Butler	13	14	36
McMahan, James(B)	1824	Oct. 27	Clermont	01	12	22
McMahan, James(B)	1824	Dec. 23	Clermont	01	12	22
McMahan, Sam'l.(B)	1824	Oct. 27	Wayne(Ind)	01	12	21
McMahan, William(B)	1816	Sept. 13	Butler	02	11	15
McMahan, William(E)	1816	Sept. 13	Butler	13	14	25
McMahon, John(B)	1818	Dec. 08	Hamilton	01	07	18
McMaken, Joseph(A)	1802	Jan. 28	Hamilton	01	02	10
McMaken, Joseph(A)	1807	Jan. 17	Butler	02	04	26
McMakin, James(B)	1819	Jan. 22	Hamilton	03	05	02
McMakin, Joseph(B)	1836	Sept. 23	Clark	01	17	35
McManaman, James(B)	1815	Aug. 28	Butler	03	03	07
McManaman, James(B)	1832	Feb. 07	Dearborn(Ind	01	07	02
McManaman, William(B)	1833	Dec. 14	Franklin(Ind	01	08	34
McManes, John(A)	1819	Sept. 10	Preble	02	12	02
McMannus, Charles(E)	1817	Dec. 03	Butler	13	18	09
McManus, Samuel(A)	1812	Nov. 11	Hamilton	02	04	11
McManus, William(A)	1808	Dec. 29	Butler	02	05	15
McMath, Samuel(B)	1817	Nov. 26	Indiana	02	06	04
McMechen, John(A)	1804	Dec. 10	Maryland	02	05	26
McMillan, Alexander(A)	1816	June 25	Butler	01	07	26
McMillen, Daniel(A)	1807	April 25	Greene	06	07	01
McMillen, David(A)	1816	Dec. 03	Pennsylvania	03	11	32
McMillen, Henry(A)	1815	April 11	Butler	02	06	14
McMillen, Robert(A)	1816	Dec. 03	Pennsylvania	03	11	32
McMillen, Robert(A)	1816	Dec. 03	Pennsylvania	04	09	04
McMillen, Sam'l. W.(B)	1829	Sept. 02	Dearborn(Ind	02	06	32
McMillen, Wm.(C)	1832	May 21	Clark	14	03	07
McMillin, Daniel(C)	1812	Aug. 22	Champaign	09	05	25
McMillin, William(C)	1832	March 26	Clark	14	03	07
McMorran, Sam'l.(C)	1829	Dec. 10	Champaign	12	03	12
McMorran, Sam'l.(C)	1831	Aug. 08	Champaign	12	03	13
McMorran, Sam'l.(C)	1831	Aug. 08	Champaign	12	03	19
McMorran, Samuel(C)	1814	Aug. 23	Montgomery	12	03	07
McMullen, Dan'l. Hays(B)	1832	Nov. 28	Dearborn(Ind	02	06	32
McMullen, Hugh(B)	1818	March 17	Dearborn(Ind	02	05	08
McMullen, Wm. Hays(B)	1832	May 26	Dearborn(Ind	02	06	32
McMurr, Prudance(A)	1806	July 02	Montgomery	06	03	18
McMurray, Joseph(D)	1808	Nov. 07	Cincinati(Fr	02	03	11
McMurry, Joseph	1808	March 03	Cincinnati	?	?	?
McMurtry, Samuel(A)	1814	March 21	Darke	02	10	35
McMurtry, Samuel(A)	1814	June 20	Darke	02	10	35
McNair, William(C)	1808	Dec. 12	Pennsylvania	08	02	11
McNaughton, Alexander(A)	1812	May 20	Montgomery	06	03	33
McNaughton, Daniel(A)	1818	Aug. 14	Cincinnati	05	08	25

PURCHASER	YEAR	DATE	RESIDENCE	R	T	S
McNaughton, John(A)	1812	May 20	Montgomery	06	03	33
McNay, Rhoda Wilcox(C)	1817	Aug. 01	Champaign	13	05	35
McNeal, William(A)	1811	Nov. 01	Butler	02	05	15
McNear, Moses(C)	1810	June 25	Pennsylvania	08	02	17
McNeeley, George(B)	1805	Oct. 02	Hamilton	01	10	25
McNeeley, James(B)	1805	Oct. 02	Hamilton	01	10	25
McNees, Jehu(E)	1834	April 07	Randolph(Ind	13	21	35
McNiel, John(C)	1814	Feb. 26	Butler	13	04	06
McNight, Joseph(A)	1816	Oct. 12	?	06	05	30
McNut, James(A)	1813	Oct. 27	Pennsylvania	03	03	15
McNutt, Alexander(A)	1806	Dec. 13	Montgomery	03	07	26
McNutt, Charles(B)	1816	March 02	Hamilton	02	03	29
McNutt, James(B)	1812	Feb. 28	Hamilton	01	09	13
McNutt, James(E)	1833	Aug. 16	Hamilton	13	19	15
McNutt, Robert(E)	1836	July 28	Kentucky	12	12	31
McNutt, Robert(E)	1836	Aug. 05	Mason Co.,Ky	12	12	31
McPearson, Adam(C)	1802	Dec. 31	Hamilton	09	03	13
McPerrin, Samuel(C)	1815	May 16	Hamilton	13	03	28
McPhaill, Cornelius(A)	1814	May 04	Butler	01	03	07
McPhaill, Cornelius(B)	1817	June 07	Butler	01	03	33
McPherin, George(C)	1816	April 29	Champaign	13	03	21
McPherrin, George(C)	1815	May 27	Champaign	13	03	34
McPherrin, George(C)	1815	Dec. 19	Champaign	13	03	27
McPherrin, Samuel(C)	1832	Feb. 24	Champaign	13	03	21
McPherrin, William Taylor(C)	1832	Feb. 24	Champaign	13	03	21
McPherson, Adam(C)	1804	Dec. 31	Greene	09	03	13
McPherson, Adam(C)	1813	April 14	Champaign	09	03	13
McPherson, Geo. D.(E)	1830	Nov. 22	Wayne(Ind)	13	18	35
McPherson, James(C)	1804	Sept. 26	Greene	13	05	31
McPherson, James(C)	1813	March 24	Champaign	15	02	07
McPherson, James(C)	1813	May 03	Champaign	15	02	07
McPherson, John(C)	1804	Dec. 31	Greene	09	03	32
McQueary, Morgan(E)	1818	Jan. 06	Wayne(Ind)	14	18	18
McQueen, Thomas(B)	1811	Nov. 21	Dearborn(Ind	01	08	14
McQueen, Thomas(B)	1811	Dec. 30	Franklin(Ind	01	08	13
McQueston, Andrew(A)	1807	April 14	Butler	01	06	36
McQueston, Andrew(A)	1807	April 14	Butler	01	06	23
McQueston, Hugh(A)	1807	April 14	Butler	01	06	24
McQueston, Hugh(A)	1807	Aug. 28	Butler	01	07	34
McQuillen, James(C)	1816	May 14	Miami	12	02	31
McQuisten, John(A)	1814	Jan. 31	Cincinnati	01	04	33
McQuiston, Henry(A)	1838	Jan. 19	Pennsylvania	02	13	30
McReynolds, John W.(E)	1834	Oct. 31	Franklin(Ind	12	12	04
McReynolds, Joseph(A)	1819	Aug. 12	Montgomery	04	11	24
McReynolds, Robt.(C)	1831	April 18	Miami	13	02	04
McTarnahan, Francis(A)	1831	Dec. 19	Miami	05	08	10
McVay, John(A)	1821	April 07	Pickaway	06	08	11
McVay, John(A)	1830	Dec. 13	Shelby	07	02	34
McVay, John(A)	1831	Feb. 26	Shelby	07	02	33
McVay, John(C)	1828	June 21	Shelby	13	02	35
McVay, John(C)	1828	June 21	Shelby	13	02	29
McVicker, Duncan(A)	1801	Dec. 10	Kentucky	02	04	03
McWhinney, William(A)	1816	Jan. 22	Preble	01	08	34
McWhorter, James(E)	1831	Nov. 09	Franklin(Ind	13	12	28
McWhorter, John(E)	1831	Sept. 07	Franklin(Ind	13	12	32
Mead, Dan'l.(C)	1831	Aug. 29	Clark	12	03	22
Mead, Eli B.(B)	1830	June 19	Dearborn(Ind	02	06	08
Mead, Hugh(E)	1818	Feb. 12	Hamilton	12	12	02
Mead, Luther(B)	1815	July 04	Cincinnati	02	03	02
Means, John(A)	1810	March 16	Kentucky	08	01	13
Means, John(A)	1815	Aug. 09	Champaign	08	01	13
Means, John(A)	1828	Oct. 11	Logan	08	01	21
Means, John(B)	1817	Dec. 08	Pennsylvania	03	06	24
Means, William(B)	1817	May 27	Switzerland	02	02	02
Means, William(B)	1836	July 01	JeffersonInd	03	02	20
Meck, Joseph(C)	1827	Sept. 15	Randolph(Ind	14	15	09
Medcaff, Isaac(B)	1808	Jan. 13	Butler	01	12	10
Medcaff, Isaac(B)	1808	Jan. 13	Butler	01	12	11
Meddock, Abraham(A)	1814	June 13	Hamilton	01	03	35

218

PURCHASER	YEAR	DATE	RESIDENCE	R	T	S
Medearis, Ab'm.(C)	1827	Aug. 22	Shelby	13	02	19
Medearis, James Davis(A)	1831	Oct. 22	Shelby	07	02	32
Medearis, John R.(C)	1816	June 08	Champaign	13	02	19
Medearis, John R.(C)	1831	Jan. 01	Shelby	12	02	24
Medearis, John(C)	1813	April 10	Champaign	10	05	19
Medsker, George(C)	1804	Dec. 10	Ross	07	03	15
Medsker, Henry(A)	1805	Nov. 13	Pennsylvania	05	03	05
Medsker, Henry(A)	1805	Nov. 14	Pennsylvania	04	06	36
Meek, Bazil(B)	1807	Jan. 08	Kentucky	01	13	29
Meek, Bazil(C)	1814	Aug. 02	Miami	10	02	12
Meek, Jeptha(E)	1829	Dec. 10	Wayne(Ind)	14	15	05
Meek, Jeremiah L.(B)	1812	April 15	Wayne(Ind)	01	13	08
Meek, Jeremiah(B)	1805	April 12	Kentucky	01	13	17
Meek, Jeremiah(B)	1806	July 30	Kentucky	01	13	06
Meek, Jeremiah(E)	1817	June 30	Wayne(Ind)	14	20	22
Meek, Jeremiah(E)	1817	June 30	Wayne(Ind)	14	19	04
Meek, Jesse(C)	1825	Sept. 16	Miami	10	02	11
Meek, John(B)	1804	Aug. 10	Ind.Territry	01	14	33
Meek, John(B)	1804	Aug. 10	Ind.Territry	01	14	32
Meek, John(B)	1806	July 30	Kentucky	01	13	06
Meek, John(C)	1818	April 04	Hamilton	10	03	26
Meek, John(E)	1830	May 10	Miami	13	18	25
Meek, Joshua(B)	1813	June 17	Wayne(Ind)	01	13	20
Meek, William(B)	1815	Oct. 19	Wayne(Ind)	01	14	17
Meeker, Michael(A)	1813	Oct. 11	Hamilton	01	04	34
Meeker, William P.(C)	1804	Dec. 26	Philadelphia	07	01	07
Meeker, William P.(C)	1804	Dec. 27	Philadelphia	08	03	21
Meeker, William P.(C)	1804	Dec. 31	Philadelphia	08	03	34
Meeker, William P.(C)	1804	Dec. 31	Philadelphia	08	03	09
Meeks, Bazel(B)	1806	Aug. 22	Kentucky	01	13	07
Meeks, Isaac(B)	1806	Sept. 03	Henry Co.,Ky	01	13	09
Meeks, John Junr.(B)	1806	Sept. 03	Henry Co.,Ky	01	13	09
Mefferd, And'w. Hodge(C)	1831	Nov. 04	Clark	14	03	36
Mefferd, Gasper(C)	1807	Jan. 31	Champaign	10	06	31
Mefferd, John Doverd(C)	1831	Nov. 04	Clark	14	03	36
Mefford, Elliott(E)	1834	Jan. 24	Franklin(Ind	12	12	31
Mefford, Tyra(E)	1834	Jan. 28	Franklin(Ind	13	11	29
Meggert, John(C)	1813	Sept. 03	Champaign	10	04	17
Meggert, John(C)	1814	Jan. 06	Champaign	10	04	18
Meggs, Thomas(B)	1806	Sept. 04	Kentucky	01	05	30
Megie, Joseph(C)	1817	July 15	Hamilton	11	03	13
Meguire, Jas.(B)	1818	Dec. 28	Hamilton	03	03	09
Meid, William(A)	1837	Jan. 25	Cincinnati	02	14	34
Meier, Henry(B)	1834	Oct. 23	Hamilton	02	08	28
Meiers, Marie(B)	1836	Aug. 25	Cincinnati	03	09	01
Meirose, Henry(E)	1836	Oct. 21	Cincinnati	12	10	18
Meisner, Christian(A)	1813	July 15	Montgomery	04	04	12
Meister, Frederick(B)	1832	Aug. 08	Dearborn(Ind	02	07	19
Meister, Joseph(B)	1834	Dec. 20	Dearborn(Ind	03	08	24
Mekemson, John(C)	1811	June 29	Champaign	14	03	32
Mekemson, Thomas(C)	1807	April 25	Champaign	14	03	31
Mekimson, Thomas(C)	1813	April 14	Champaign	14	03	31
Melender, Peter(A)	1805	March 15	Butler	02	06	36
Melender, Peter(B)	1813	April 14	Butler	01	12	04
Melendore, Peter(B)	1807	March 19	Butler	01	12	04
Melendore, Peter(B)	1807	March 21	Butler	01	12	04
Meley, Henry(B)	1835	Sept. 02	Preble	01	16	13
Melhollin, Jonathan(C)	1813	April 14	Champaign	09	04	10
Melis, Jonathan(A)	1817	Nov. 03	Miami	05	07	30
Mell, John(E)	1820	Oct. 06	Montgomery	13	17	19
Meller, James Junr.(A)	1805	Feb. 14	Montgomery	06	03	23
Melling, James(A)	1815	April 04	Virginia	01	08	11
Melling, James(A)	1815	May 17	Virginia	01	08	12
Mellingar, Joseph(A)	1806	Sept. 23	Butler	06	07	30
Mellinger, John(A)	1831	Aug. 09	Shelby	07	01	07
Mellinger, Jos.(A)	1832	Feb. 07	Shelby	05	09	23
Mellinger, William(A)	1832	Feb. 07	Shelby	05	09	14
Melone, Charles(E)	1828	Feb. 12	Fayette	12	13	36
Melone, Charles(E)	1830	March 23	Fayette	12	13	36

PURCHASER	YEAR	DATE	RESIDENCE	R	T	S
Melone, Charles(E)	1831	Jan. 19	Fayette	12	13	36
Melone, Charles(E)	1836	Oct. 12	Fayette	11	12	01
Melone, Charles(E)	1836	Dec. 13	Fayette	11	12	01
Melone, Charles(E)	1836	Dec. 13	Fayette	12	13	31
Melone, John(E)	1817	Aug. 06	Butler	13	12	28
Melton, John(E)	1823	Nov. 25	Warren	14	18	01
Melton, Stephen(E)	1818	April 02	Warren	14	19	27
Mendenhall, Caleb(A)	1831	Aug. 10	Miami	04	06	03
Mendenhall, Elijah(A)	1806	Dec. 05	Butler	03	04	34
Mendenhall, Elijah(A)	1807	June 08	Montgomery	06	03	18
Mendenhall, Elijah(A)	1807	June 08	Montgomery	05	06	32
Mendenhall, Elijah(A)	1807	July 17	Butler	03	04	34
Mendenhall, Elijah(A)	1811	Nov. 27	Preble	02	06	06
Mendenhall, Elijah(A)	1811	Nov. 30	?	03	04	27
Mendenhall, Elijah(E)	1837	March 01	Wayne(Ind)	13	18	04
Mendenhall, Griffith(B)	1815	May 22	Miami	01	14	23
Mendenhall, Hiram(E)	1835	Jan. 07	Warren	13	19	03
Mendenhall, Hiram(E)	1835	Jan. 07	Warren	13	19	10
Mendenhall, Hiram(E)	1835	Jan. 07	Warren	13	19	03
Mendenhall, Hiram(E)	1835	Dec. 30	Warren	13	19	15
Mendenhall, Hiram(E)	1836	June 18	Randolph(Ind	13	19	10
Mendenhall, Isaac(E)	1814	May 17	Wayne(Ind)	13	16	02
Mendenhall, John(A)	1812	May 15	Preble	02	06	08
Mendenhall, John(C)	1813	April 14	Champaign	13	05	31
Mendenhall, Jos.(A)	1829	Dec. 26	Miami	04	07	25
Mendenhall, Joseph(A)	1807	May 19	Miami	05	06	29
Mendenhall, Joseph(A)	1819	Feb. 20	Miami	04	07	25
Mendenhall, Mordecai(C)	1806	Feb. 15	Montgomery	09	02	30
Mendenhall, Mordecai(E)	1817	Aug. 11	Wayne(Ind)	14	18	17
Mendenhall, Mordicai(C)	1813	April 14	Miami	09	02	24
Mendenhall, Nathan Jr.(E)	1835	June 06	Clinton	13	19	10
Mendenhall, Rich'd.(A)	1836	May 18	Shelby	03	12	12
Mendenhall, Rich'd.(A)	1836	May 18	Shelby	04	11	07
Mendenhall, Richard(E)	1818	March 24	Nor.Carolina	14	20	13
Mendenhall, Richard(E)	1818	March 24	Nor.Carolina	14	20	24
Mendenhall, Thaddeus(A)	1828	April 12	Miami	04	07	24
Mendenhall, Thaddeus(A)	1829	Jan. 15	Miami	04	07	24
Mendenhall, Thomas(A)	1836	May 18	Shelby	03	12	13
Mendenhorn, Joseph(A)	1805	Sept. 02	Montgomery	05	06	32
Menix, Hugh(A)	1815	March 31	Virginia	02	08	13
Mennet, Samuel(B)	1812	April 13	Jefferson	03	02	28
Mentzger, Henry(A)	1811	July 13	Montgomery	05	04	22
Menycke, Chas. Theodore(B)	1834	Jan. 24	Franklin(Ind	01	08	31
Meranda, Jonathan(C)	1819	April 09	Clark	10	04	26
Meranda, Samuel(C)	1819	April 09	Clark	10	04	26
Mercer, John(B)	1814	Oct. 13	Franklin(Ind	02	08	27
Mercer, Johnathan(C)	1801	Dec. 31	Hamilton	08	02	01
Mercer, Jonathan(C)	1802	Dec. 31	Hamilton	07	01	LT
Mercer, Jonathan(C)	1804	Dec. 29	Greene	08	03	22
Mercer, Jonathan(C)	1804	Dec. 29	Greene	08	03	21
Mercer, Jonathan(C)	1804	Dec. 29	Greene	08	03	33
Mercer, William(A)	1837	Feb. 24	Warren	03	12	23
Mergregrer, John(A)	1811	April 09	Pennsylvania	02	04	14
Merideth, David(B)	1831	Sept. 08	Wayne(Ind)	01	15	27
Merideth, Solomon(B)	1830	Dec. 07	Wayne(Ind)	01	15	21
Meridith, Caleb(A)	1813	March 16	Butler	02	04	12
Merine, Jonathan(E)	1811	Oct. 28	Wayne(Ind)	14	17	14
Merine, Ziba(E)	1828	Nov. 21	Wayne(Ind)	14	18	14
Merit, Archibald(B)	1816	July 29	Switzerland	01	03	35
Merit, Archibald(B)	1827	Aug. 21	Switzerland	01	03	35
Merrick, John(B)	1835	July 21	Franklin(Ind	03	09	25
Merriman, Aaron(C)	1815	July 04	Champaign	09	06	07
Merrit, John(C)	1814	Oct. 25	Champaign	10	03	24
Merritt, John Jr.(C)	1829	Jan. 08	Champaign	11	03	26
Merritt, John(C)	1813	Dec. 15	Virginia	11	03	32
Merritt, John(C)	1814	March 10	Champaign	11	03	32
Merritt, John(C)	1814	March 10	Champaign	10	03	35
Merritt, John(C)	1816	May 02	Champaign	11	03	33
Merritt, John(C)	1824	June 07	Champaign	11	03	28

PURCHASER	YEAR	DATE	RESIDENCE	R	T	S
Messersmitt, Sebastian(B)	1835	April 04	Germany	02	07	04
Messick, George(C)	1830	Feb. 11	Logan	13	04	18
Meteer, William(C)	1811	Dec. 11	Champaign	10	06	13
Metsker, Andrew(A)	1816	June 11	Montgomery	03	11	35
Mettler, William(B)	1833	April 26	Montgomery	01	16	25
Metzcar, William(A)	1836	Dec. 12	Darke	04	11	32
Metzger, John(A)	1816	Sept. 09	Greene	04	10	05
Mewhinney, James(B)	1836	Feb. 09	Franklin(Ind	02	08	07
Mewhinney, James(B)	1836	Feb. 09	Franklin(Ind	02	08	07
Mewhinney, James(B)	1836	Sept. 21	Franklin(Ind	02	08	06
Mewhinney, Sam'l.(B)	1835	Nov. 12	Franklin(Ind	02	08	07
Mewhinney, Sam'l.(B)	1835	Dec. 14	Franklin(Ind	02	08	07
Meyer, Bernard(E)	1837	Jan. 07	Cincinnati	12	11	31
Meyers, Christian Hy.(E)	1836	Oct. 15	Cincinnati	11	10	23
Meyers, Francis(A)	1833	Dec. 23	Hamilton	03	10	19
Meyers, James(C)	1814	Jan. 27	Miami	09	02	14
Meyncke, Chas. Theodore(B)	1835	Jan. 21	Franklin(Ind	01	08	30
Meyncke, Chas. Theodore(B)	1835	Jan. 21	Franklin(Ind	01	08	30
Michael, Casper(B)	1818	July 02	Dearborn(Ind	02	06	07
Michael, Daniel(B)	1834	July 08	Dearborn(Ind	02	06	09
Michael, Frederick(C)	1818	Jan. 16	Greene	10	03	04
Michael, George(A)	1831	Aug. 04	Montgomery	07	01	08
Michael, George(C)	1818	Jan. 07	Champaign	10	04	28
Michael, George(C)	1824	Dec. 20	Clark	10	04	22
Michael, Jacob(A)	1803	Oct. 24	Montgomery	05	03	19
Michael, Jacob(A)	1825	Oct. 11	Preble	03	10	34
Michael, Jacob(B)	1827	June 15	Dearborn(Ind	03	07	13
Michael, James(A)	1836	Sept. 05	Darke	02	13	32
Michael, James(A)	1837	June 06	Darke	02	13	30
Michael, Jared(B)	1818	Aug. 21	Dearborn(Ind	03	07	12
Michael, John Jr.(A)	1831	Nov. 02	Preble	03	06	07
Michael, John(A)	1806	Nov. 26	Montgomery	02	08	23
Michael, John(A)	1818	Feb. 06	Montgomery	04	05	32
Michael, John(A)	1819	Jan. 05	Preble	02	08	12
Michael, Philip(B)	1817	Oct. 21	Dearborn(Ind	02	06	08
Michael, Philip(B)	1831	June 20	Dearborn(Ind	02	06	08
Michael, Philip(B)	1834	July 24	Cincinnati	02	07	34
Michail, John(E)	1837	May 29	Darke	14	21	22
Michoud, Lewis(B)	1816	July 19	Switzerland	03	03	24
Middleton, Sam'l. H.(B)	1828	April 10	Randolph(Ind	01	16	11
Middleton, Sam'l. H.(B)	1832	March 13	Randolph(Ind	01	17	34
Middleton, Sam'l. Harrison(B)	1835	Jan. 12	Randolph(Ind	01	16	11
Middleton, Samuel Harrison(B)	1834	July 07	Randolph(Ind	01	16	11
Midsker, David(B)	1817	Sept. 26	Dearborn(Ind	03	06	34
Midsker, George(B)	1816	Nov. 30	Champaign	02	02	22
Miers, John(B)	1818	Jan. 10	Cincinnati	02	03	27
Miers, Jonathan(B)	1818	Jan. 10	Cincinnati	02	03	27
Miers, Ralph(A)	1810	Oct. 18	Miami	04	09	24
Miers, Samuel(E)	1835	Nov. 02	Franklin(Ind	11	12	25
Miesse, Benj'n.(A)	1838	Feb. 14	Fairfield	01	15	34
Miesse, Benj'n.(A)	1838	Feb. 05	Fairfield	02	14	17
Miesse, Benjamin(A)	1837	Oct. 05	Fairfield	02	14	06
Miesse, Benjamin(A)	1837	Oct. 05	Fairfield	02	14	08
Miesse, Gabriel(A)	1838	Feb. 05	Fairfield	01	14	02
Miesse, Henry(A)	1838	Feb. 14	Pennsylvania	02	14	04
Miesse, Isaac(A)	1838	feb. 14	Pennsylvania	01	15	33
Miesse, Jacob(A)	1838	Feb. 05	Pennsylvania	02	14	20
Miesse, Jacob(A)	1838	Feb. 05	Pennsylvania	02	14	04
Miesse, Jacob(A)	1838	Feb. 05	Pennsylvania	02	14	17
Miesse, Joseph(A)	1838	Feb. 05	Fairfield	01	14	04
Miesse, Samuel(A)	1838	Feb. 14	Pennsylvania	01	14	34
Miesse, Samuel(A)	1838	Feb. 14	Pennsylvania	02	14	17
Mikesel, George(A)	1817	Oct. 08	Darke	02	10	06
Mikesel, John(A)	1821	Sept. 18	Darke	02	10	09
Mikesell, John(A)	1802	Jan. 25	Hamilton	05	03	28
Mikesell, John(A)	1819	June 21	Darke	02	10	07
Miksell, Peter(A)	1806	Nov. 12	Montgomery	04	04	25
Milbank, Charles(C)	1808	Jan. 12	Montgomery	13	05	34
Milburn, David(B)	1836	Jan. 16	Dearborn(Ind	02	05	04

221

PURCHASER	YEAR	DATE	RESIDENCE	R	T	S
Milburn, Joseph E.(B)	1813	Nov. 02	Dearborn(Ind	02	04	01
Milburn, Nathan(B)	1816	Aug. 07	Dearborn(Ind	02	05	15
Milburn, Robert(B)	1813	Nov. 02	Dearborn(Ind	02	05	36
Milburn, Robt.(B)	1815	Oct. 04	Dearborn(Ind	02	05	15
Milburn, Robt.(B)	1815	Oct. 04	Dearborn(Ind	02	05	09
Milburn, Thomas Horner(B)	1836	Jan. 27	Dearborn(Ind	02	05	09
Miles, Benjamin(B)	1813	April 14	Dearborn(Ind	01	04	17
Miles, Benjamin(B)	1814	July 02	Dearborn(Ind	01	04	07
Miles, David(A)	1807	Aug. 05	So. Carolina	04	09	26
Miles, David(A)	1811	Dec. 11	Miami	05	07	30
Miles, David(A)	1831	Oct. 21	Miami	05	07	13
Miles, David(A)	1831	Oct. 21	Miami	05	07	14
Miles, Enos(A)	1809	Sept. 05	Kentucky	02	12	34
Miles, James(A)	1811	Oct. 16	Montgomery	03	05	20
Miles, John W.(A)	1802	March 12	Hamilton	01	03	26
Miles, John(C)	1819	Sept. 30	Montgomery	13	02	31
Miles, Jonathan Senr.(A)	1832	Jan. 30	Miami	04	08	26
Miles, Jonathan(A)	1806	Oct. 24	Montgomery	05	07	31
Miles, Samuel(A)	1833	May 07	Miami	04	07	10
Miles, William(A)	1806	Nov. 10	Montgomery	05	07	31
Miles, William(A)	1806	Nov. 11	Montgomery	05	06	06
Miles, William(A)	1831	Aug. 16	Miami	05	07	23
Miles, William(A)	1831	Oct. 21	Miami	05	07	24
Miley, Abraham Jr.(A)	1817	May 31	Butler	02	11	27
Miley, Abraham(C)	1813	July 23	Butler	03	02	11
Miley, Abraham, Jun.(A)	1817	May 31	Butler	01	12	10
Milhollan, Jonathan(C)	1804	Dec. 31	Greene	09	04	17
Milholland, George(E)	1836	Jan. 22	Franklin(Ind	12	11	15
Milholland, George(E)	1836	March 26	Franklin(Ind	12	11	22
Milholland, James(B)	1813	March 10	Franklin(Ind	01	08	06
Milholland, John(B)	1805	April 17	Ind.Territry	02	08	03
Milholland, Thomas(B)	1812	April 02	Franklin(Ind	01	08	06
Milholland, Thomas(B)	1814	Dec. 28	Franklin(Ind	02	08	01
Milholland, Thomas(E)	1836	Feb. 04	Franklin(Ind	12	11	22
Milholland, Thos.(C)	1829	Sept. 03	Perry	13	04	01
Milhollin, Jonathan(C)	1813	April 14	Champaign	09	04	09
Millar, David(A)	1818	July 27	Darke	02	11	22
Millar, Henry(B)	1818	Dec. 10	Dearborn(Ind	01	07	30
Millar, John(B)	1831	Oct. 13	Dearborn(Ind	03	08	26
Millegan, James(C)	1801	Dec. 23	Hamilton	07	02	25
Millekin, Allen(E)	1817	Oct. 16	Dearborn(Ind	02	06	28
Millekin, Matthew(B)	1817	Oct. 16	Dearborn(Ind	02	06	28
Millen, George(B)	1818	June 27	Switzerland	02	03	30
Millender, John(A)	1816	June 24	Miami	05	09	13
Millenger, John(A)	1806	Dec. 11	Montgomery	06	07	30
Millenger, John(A)	1807	Jan. 21	Montgomery	06	07	29
Millenger, John(A)	1808	Oct. 24	Miami	06	07	29
Miller, Aaron(A)	1817	Aug. 30	Montgomery	01	12	15
Miller, Abm.(A)	1828	Nov. 22	Montgomery	04	06	07
Miller, Abm.(C)	1829	Jan. 28	Logan	14	03	20
Miller, Abraham(A)	1805	Nov. 07	Montgomery	04	05	36
Miller, Abraham(A)	1805	Nov. 12	Montgomery	06	06	31
Miller, Abraham(A)	1806	March 10	Warren	05	07	05
Miller, Abraham(A)	1808	Oct. 14	Miami	02	11	10
Miller, Abraham(A)	1810	April 30	Montgomery	04	05	35
Miller, Abraham(A)	1814	April 14	Miami	02	11	10
Miller, Abraham(A)	1825	Aug. 24	Hamilton	04	09	03
Miller, Abraham(A)	1830	Nov. 22	Darke	01	13	25
Miller, Abraham(B)	1805	Nov. 05	Dearborn(Ind	01	10	24
Miller, Abraham(C)	1812	April 15	Miami	11	02	22
Miller, Abraham(C)	1815	Oct. 31	Miami	12	01	26
Miller, Abraham(C)	1831	May 24	Shelby	13	02	24
Miller, Abraham(E)	1811	Oct. 24	Ross	13	15	08
Miller, Adam(B)	1817	June 17	Dearborn(Ind	02	07	28
Miller, Adam(B)	1817	June 17	Dearborn(Ind	02	07	28
Miller, Adam(B)	1817	June 17	Dearborn(Ind	02	07	28
Miller, Adam(B)	1817	June 17	Dearborn(Ind	02	07	32
Miller, Alexander(B)	1812	Feb. 08	Franklin(Ind	02	13	24
Miller, Alexander(E)	1811	Oct. 28	Franklin(Ind	13	11	06

222

PURCHASER	YEAR	DATE	RESIDENCE	R	T	S
Miller, Alexander(E)	1812	Feb. 08	Franklin(Ind	14	16	28
Miller, Anthony(A)	1816	June 03	Montgomery	03	06	14
Miller, Aron(A)	1817	Oct. 24	Montgomery	01	12	22
Miller, Augustus C.(C)	1825	Aug. 08	Greene	11	03	29
Miller, Benjamin(E)	1832	Aug. 18	Highland	14	19	21
Miller, Benjamin(E)	1834	April 02	Highland	14	19	20
Miller, Casper(A)	1830	May 06	Champaign	08	01	07
Miller, Casper(C)	1829	March 16	Champaign	12	03	20
Miller, Christian(A)	1817	Aug. 30	Montgomery	01	12	22
Miller, Christley(C)	1804	Dec. 31	Greene	08	03	17
Miller, Christopher(D)	1809	Aug. 25	Hamilton(Fr)	02	02	26
Miller, Conkling(A)	1807	March 06	Montgomery	06	03	34
Miller, Conkling(A)	1807	March 06	Montgomery	06	03	34
Miller, Conkling(C)	1807	March 14	Montgomery	09	02	31
Miller, Cornelius(A)	1831	Feb. 15	Miami	06	04	06
Miller, Cornelius(B)	1814	Sept. 23	Pennsylvania	01	04	21
Miller, Dan'l. B.(E)	1831	July 05	Randolph(Ind	14	21	23
Miller, Dan'l. B.(E)	1836	Nov. 16	Randolph(Ind	14	21	24
Miller, Daniel H.(B)	1831	March 22	Butler	01	16	21
Miller, Daniel Junr.(A)	1805	Aug. 20	Montgomery	05	04	19
Miller, Daniel(A)	1802	Nov. 02	Pennsylvania	06	02	30
Miller, Daniel(A)	1804	July 19	Montgomery	05	04	36
Miller, Daniel(A)	1804	Aug. 15	Montgomery	05	04	11
Miller, Daniel(A)	1805	Oct. 14	Montgomery	06	02	19
Miller, Daniel(A)	1815	Nov. 20	Hamilton	02	06	13
Miller, Daniel(A)	1816	Nov. 13	Montgomery	04	09	08
Miller, Daniel(A)	1837	Feb. 17	Darke	01	12	03
Miller, Daniel(B)	1805	Nov. 05	Dearborn(Ind	01	10	24
Miller, Daniel(B)	1808	Dec. 01	Dearborn(Ind	01	12	30
Miller, Daniel(B)	1817	Oct. 22	Dearborn(Ind	02	06	20
Miller, Daniel(B)	1817	Oct. 22	Dearborn(Ind	02	06	19
Miller, Daniel(D)	1808	Nov. 28	Hamilton(Fr)	02	02	26
Miller, David(A)	1805	July 01	Montgomery	05	05	30
Miller, David(A)	1806	March 10	Warren	05	07	06
Miller, David(A)	1807	Jan. 13	Montgomery	05	05	17
Miller, David(A)	1807	June 22	Miami	05	08	30
Miller, David(A)	1809	July 01	New Jersey	01	04	13
Miller, David(A)	1831	Aug. 09	Montgomery	04	09	04
Miller, David(A)	1832	Nov. 07	Darke	04	09	06
Miller, David(A)	1832	Dec. 12	Darke	01	15	09
Miller, David(A)	1833	Feb. 13	Montgomery	04	09	07
Miller, David(B)	1816	Sept. 06	Switzerland	02	02	24
Miller, Edward(B)	1834	Feb. 08	Switzerland	02	03	20
Miller, Elijah(B)	1836	June 20	Dearborn(Ind	03	05	01
Miller, Elijah(B)	1836	Oct. 24	Dearborn(Ind	03	05	01
Miller, Elizabeth(A)	1838	Feb. 10	Montgomery	01	15	35
Miller, Elizabeth(B)	1811	March 30	Ind.Territry	01	13	28
Miller, Emanuel(A)	1814	May 27	Miami	04	09	10
Miller, Frederick(A)	1803	Oct. 11	Warren	03	06	34
Miller, Frederick(A)	1804	Dec. 24	Montgomery	03	07	11
Miller, Frederick(A)	1810	April 11	Preble	03	07	11
Miller, Frederick(A)	1810	April 11	Preble	03	07	11
Miller, Frederick(A)	1814	Oct. 04	Preble	02	10	35
Miller, Frederick(A)	1814	Oct. 04	Preble	02	10	36
Miller, George W.(C)	1814	Aug. 13	Dearborn(Ind	13	12	15
Miller, George(A)	1816	May 25	Montgomery	03	11	27
Miller, George(A)	1826	Sept. 21	Warren	01	10	21
Miller, George(A)	1830	Nov. 01	Darke	01	10	21
Miller, George(A)	1831	April 13	Preble	01	10	25
Miller, George(A)	1837	Aug. 01	Darke	01	12	17
Miller, George(C)	1829	March 28	Shelby	13	02	29
Miller, George(E)	1814	Jan. 15	Wayne(Ind)	13	15	19
Miller, Henry(A)	1810	Oct. 30	Montgomery	04	04	02
Miller, Henry(A)	1817	Sept. 17	Kentucky	01	10	22
Miller, Henry(A)	1835	Dec. 08	Montgomery	01	12	20
Miller, Henry(B)	1807	Feb. 21	Butler	02	12	24
Miller, Henry(B)	1814	June 04	Hamilton	01	04	17
Miller, Henry(B)	1835	Oct. 10	Hamilton	02	08	28
Miller, Humphrey(A)	1814	Jan. 04	Pennsylvania	01	02	21

223

PURCHASER	YEAR	DATE	RESIDENCE	R	T	S
Miller, Isaac(A)	1837	Jan. 21	Montgomery	03	12	19
Miller, Isaac(C)	1804	Sept. 24	Greene	06	02	11
Miller, Isaac(C)	1825	Aug. 08	Greene	11	03	29
Miller, Isaac(E)	1815	Jan. 15	Wayne(Ind)	13	15	19
Miller, Jacob	1808	March 02	Cincinnati	?	?	?
Miller, Jacob(A)	1801	July 28	Hamilton	05	03	34
Miller, Jacob(A)	1804	April 18	Butler	01	04	25
Miller, Jacob(A)	1804	April 18	Montgomery	05	03	11
Miller, Jacob(A)	1804	July 30	Butler	04	01	07
Miller, Jacob(A)	1806	March 22	Butler	03	03	26
Miller, Jacob(A)	1813	Sept. 14	Preble	03	04	13
Miller, Jacob(C)	1808	Sept. 09	Champaign	09	03	06
Miller, Jacob(C)	1814	Nov. 14	Champaign	10	03	01
Miller, Jacob(C)	1826	Jan. 17	Montgomery	11	03	12
Miller, Jacob(C)	1826	May 19	Montgomery	11	03	12
Miller, Jacob(E)	1817	July 31	Montgomery	14	20	28
Miller, Jacob(E)	1833	Dec. 23	Hamilton	12	12	23
Miller, Jacob(E)	1834	March 04	Hamilton	12	12	23
Miller, James Jr.(C)	1801	Dec. 12	Hamilton	07	02	21
Miller, James Jur.(B)	1817	Oct. 22	Dearborn(Ind	02	06	20
Miller, James(C)	1801	Dec. 12	Hamilton	07	02	22
Miller, James(C)	1802	Dec. 30	Hamilton	08	04	15
Miller, James(C)	1805	Oct. 26	Montgomery	08	02	18
Miller, James(C)	1806	Feb. 07	Montgomery	09	05	14
Miller, James(C)	1806	Feb. 07	Montgomery	09	05	19
Miller, James(C)	1806	March 26	Greene	09	05	15
Miller, James(C)	1810	Dec. 12	Montgomery	08	02	18
Miller, James(C)	1811	April 09	Greene	08	04	08
Miller, James(C)	1811	April 10	Champaign	09	05	14
Miller, Jas.(A)	1818	Oct. 12	Montgomery	04	11	10
Miller, Job(B)	1811	Dec. 11	Dearborn(Ind	01	06	35
Miller, John J.(A)	1830	Sept. 01	Warren	04	06	19
Miller, John Jr.(B)	1826	Feb. 10	Union(Ind)	01	10	15
Miller, John(A)	1802	Oct. 22	Hamilton	05	03	32
Miller, John(A)	1803	Oct. 11	Montgomery	05	03	29
Miller, John(A)	1803	Oct. 29	Montgomery	04	04	27
Miller, John(A)	1804	Aug. 02	Montgomery	05	03	02
Miller, John(A)	1805	Feb. 26	Montgomery	05	05	17
Miller, John(A)	1805	March 02	Montgomery	05	03	20
Miller, John(A)	1805	June 04	Montgomery	05	05	29
Miller, John(A)	1805	July 01	Montgomery	05	05	29
Miller, John(A)	1805	July 01	Montgomery	05	05	20
Miller, John(A)	1805	Dec. 21	Montgomery	04	09	35
Miller, John(A)	1805	Dec. 21	Montgomery	05	08	31
Miller, John(A)	1805	Dec. 23	Montgomery	05	04	13
Miller, John(A)	1806	June 05	Montgomery	04	02	09
Miller, John(A)	1804	Sept. 10	Montgomery	05	03	02
Miller, John(A)	1807	March 11	Montgomery	04	09	36
Miller, John(A)	1808	Feb. 05	Montgomery	05	08	30
Miller, John(A)	1809	July 01	Montgomery	02	04	09
Miller, John(A)	1810	Oct. 30	Montgomery	04	04	01
Miller, John(A)	1811	Jan. 17	Butler	04	02	08
Miller, John(A)	1812	Dec. 25	Montgomery	06	03	32
Miller, John(A)	1815	April 15	Kentucky	01	10	23
Miller, John(A)	1815	June 03	Miami	05	10	31
Miller, John(A)	1815	Sept. 04	Miami	05	10	31
Miller, John(A)	1816	May 25	Montgomery	03	11	33
Miller, John(A)	1816	June 11	Montgomery	03	11	34
Miller, John(A)	1816	Sept. 06	Franklin(Ind	02	11	30
Miller, John(A)	1816	Sept. 23	Franklin(Ind	01	10	02
Miller, John(A)	1816	Nov. 13	Montgomery	04	09	07
Miller, John(A)	1818	May 26	Montgomery	03	11	33
Miller, John(A)	1827	Aug. 21	Preble	02	10	36
Miller, John(A)	1829	Jan. 02	Darke	02	10	04
Miller, John(A)	1832	March 19	Darke	03	10	14
Miller, John(A)	1836	Dec. 27	Darke	02	12	17
Miller, John(A)	1838	Feb. 05	Fairfield	02	14	21
Miller, John(B)	1805	Feb. 26	Montgomery	01	10	12
Miller, John(B)	1810	April 21	Virginia	01	10	14

PURCHASER	YEAR	DATE	RESIDENCE	R	T	S
Miller, John(B)	1810	Oct. 16	Dearborn(Ind	01	10	12
Miller, John(B)	1810	Oct. 16	Dearborn(Ind	01	10	01
Miller, John(B)	1813	Feb. 16	Ind.Territry	02	02	36
Miller, John(B)	1813	Dec. 04	Montgomery	01	11	12
Miller, John(B)	1813	Dec. 04	Montgomery	01	10	02
Miller, John(B)	1831	Feb. 19	Switzerland	02	02	22
Miller, John(B)	1836	March 19	Switzerland	02	02	22
Miller, John(B)	1837	Feb. 03	Dearborn(Ind	03	05	22
Miller, John(C)	1805	Dec. 21	Montgomery	07	03	12
Miller, John(C)	1813	Aug. 02	Hamilton	11	02	07
Miller, John(C)	1818	April 16	Champaign	12	04	34
Miller, John(C)	1818	April 29	Champaign	12	04	34
Miller, John(C)	1824	Aug. 13	Champaign	12	04	26
Miller, John(C)	1831	Dec. 02	Champaign	12	04	32
Miller, John(C)	1832	Jan. 25	Champaign	12	03	19
Miller, John(E)	1814	April 14	Wayne(Ind)	13	15	17
Miller, John(E)	1814	Aug. 27	Wayne(Ind)	14	15	32
Miller, John(E)	1815	July 29	Franklin(Ind	12	11	17
Miller, John(E)	1816	July 03	Franklin(Ind	12	11	29
Miller, John(E)	1823	Nov. 14	Warren	12	17	36
Miller, Jonathan D.(A)	1836	Dec. 23	Clark	03	12	20
Miller, Joseph D.(B)	1814	Sept. 23	Pennsylvania	01	04	21
Miller, Joseph(A)	1806	Dec. 06	Georgia	06	03	19
Miller, Josiah(A)	1827	Aug. 20	Darke	01	12	22
Miller, Josiah(A)	1830	Dec. 18	Darke	01	12	21
Miller, Levi(B)	1811	Dec. 12	Dearborn(Ind	01	06	24
Miller, Lewis(A)	1819	March 09	Darke	03	09	07
Miller, Martin(C)	1817	July 14	Champaign	09	06	28
Miller, Martin(C)	1822	Jan. 18	Clark	10	03	13
Miller, Michael(A)	1816	May 25	Montgomery	03	11	28
Miller, Michael(A)	1816	June 11	Montgomery	03	11	32
Miller, Michael(A)	1818	June 30	Montgomery	02	13	13
Miller, Michael(A)	1819	Aug. 28	Montgomery	03	11	14
Miller, Michael(A)	1837	June 08	Richland	01	13	05
Miller, Michael(B)	1818	March 06	Cincinnati	03	07	26
Miller, Oliver(B)	1818	Feb. 26	Hamilton	03	04	01
Miller, Peter(A)	1818	June 05	Montgomery	03	10	11
Miller, Peter(E)	1831	July 04	Wayne(Ind)	13	15	03
Miller, Phillip(C)	1813	March 12	Champaign	13	04	19
Miller, Richard(A)	1818	Sept. 12	Darke	01	10	26
Miller, Richard(A)	1832	Feb. 21	Hamilton	05	08	27
Miller, Robert M.(B)	1818	Oct. 01	Preble	01	11	13
Miller, Robert(C)	1805	Oct. 26	Montgomery	08	02	12
Miller, Robert(C)	1810	Dec. 12	Montgomery	08	02	12
Miller, Robert(C)	1814	April 04	Champaign	10	05	11
Miller, Robert(C)	1827	Aug. 22	Clark	10	05	11
Miller, Samuel(A)	1815	Dec. 11	Montgomery	05	05	06
Miller, Samuel(A)	1831	April 20	Darke	02	11	24
Miller, Sebastian(B)	1833	Nov. 27	Cincinnati	03	09	36
Miller, Sebastian(B)	1833	Nov. 27	Cincinnati	03	09	36
Miller, Silvester(E)	1838	Aug. 18	Randolph(Ind	14	21	33
Miller, Solomon(C)	1812	Nov. 24	Maryland	13	05	26
Miller, Sylvester(E)	1833	Nov. 09	Randolph(Ind	14	21	21
Miller, Sylvester(E)	1836	Feb. 27	Randolph(Ind	14	21	17
Miller, Thomas(B)	1804	Sept. 18	Dearborn(Ind	01	06	35
Miller, Thomas(B)	1804	Nov. 17	Dearborn(Ind	01	06	13
Miller, Thomas(B)	1806	Oct. 01	Dearborn(Ind	01	06	35
Miller, Thomas(B)	1806	Oct. 07	Dearborn(Ind	01	06	24
Miller, Thomas(B)	1813	Sept. 29	Franklin(Ind	01	11	05
Miller, Thomas(B)	1814	July 25	Franklin(Ind	01	11	11
Miller, Thomas(E)	1832	Dec. 11	Highland	14	19	29
Miller, Thomas(E)	1836	June 17	Randolph(Ind	14	19	20
Miller, Thomas(E)	1836	Dec. 07	Randolph(Ind	14	19	04
Miller, Tobias(A)	1832	June 02	Darke	01	13	26
Miller, Tobias(B)	1814	Jan. 15	Franklin(Ind	01	10	02
Miller, Tunis(C)	1816	Oct. 26	Greene	08	04	11
Miller, William B.(B)	1836	Nov. 03	Dearborn(Ind	02	04	07
Miller, William B.(E)	1836	July 07	Randolph(Ind	14	18	02
Miller, William L.(B)	1814	Sept. 23	Pennsylvania	01	04	21

PURCHASER	YEAR	DATE	RESIDENCE	R	T	S
Miller, William(A)	1809	April 11	Montgomery	02	12	19
Miller, William(A)	1814	Aug. 16	Montgomery	02	12	19
Miller, William(A)	1836	June 10	Darke	02	12	21
Miller, William(B)	1813	July 31	Butler	01	10	04
Miller, William(B)	1814	Dec. 20	Greene	01	11	10
Miller, William(C)	1802	Dec. 29	Hamilton	06	03	31
Miller, William(C)	1811	April 18	Greene	08	05	30
Miller, William(C)	1830	Jan. 28	Shelby	13	02	13
Miller, William(E)	1836	Oct. 21	Cincinnati	12	10	07
Miller, William(E)	1836	Oct. 28	Cincinnati	12	11	33
Miller, Willis P.(E)	1815	Oct. 21	Wayne(Ind)	13	15	35
Miller, Willis(B)	1829	Dec. 09	Dearborn(Ind	03	06	15
Miller, Wm. Jr.(B)	1814	July 12	Franklin(Ind	01	10	05
Miller, Wm.(C)	1818	Nov. 11	Clark	10	03	10
Miller,Abraham(C)	1828	April 16	Logan	14	03	27
Miller,Geo.WashingtonClinton(E	1836	Feb. 04	Franklin(Ind	13	12	08
Millet, John Jr.(A)	1830	Aug. 26	Darke	03	08	18
Millet, John(A)	1829	April 09	Warren	03	08	19
Millet, Merrit(A)	1834	Jan. 29	Darke	01	12	18
Millholland, Thos.(C)	1831	Aug. 09	Champaign	13	04	08
Millhouse, John(C)	1805	Aug. 09	Montgomery	11	01	12
Millhouse, John(C)	1806	Aug. 19	Montgomery	11	01	12
Millhouse, John(E)	1837	Nov. 01	Miami	15	22	26
Milligan, John(A)	1815	July 05	Adams	01	06	22
Milliken, Eli(E)	1811	Dec. 12	Warren	13	17	34
Millikin, Samuel(E)	1816	Jan. 20	Butler	14	16	04
Millikin, Samuel(E)	1816	Jan. 20	Butler	14	16	04
Millikin, Samuel(E)	1816	Jan. 20	Butler	14	16	03
Millikin, Thomas(A)	1836	Oct. 31	Butler	03	12	21
Millman, Robert H.(E)	1837	March 27	Randolph(Ind	13	18	13
Millner, William(A)	1804	Sept. 13	Butler	02	06	03
Mills, Aaron(E)	1830	Nov. 22	Randolph(Ind	14	18	13
Mills, Alex'r.(A)	1829	Jan. 08	Miami	05	07	22
Mills, Alexander(A)	1811	Aug. 13	Miami	05	07	20
Mills, Azur R.(A)	1813	Dec. 18	Butler	02	04	27
Mills, Azur R.(A)	1816	May 25	Butler	02	10	05
Mills, Benjamin(B)	1814	Feb. 28	Dearborn(Ind	02	04	36
Mills, Cyrus(B)	1816	Sept. 07	Dearborn(Ind	03	07	11
Mills, David(B)	1824	June 09	Hamilton	01	08	22
Mills, George(A)	1818	Sept. 19	Clinton	02	09	08
Mills, George(A)	1824	June 08	Clinton	01	09	22
Mills, George(A)	1824	June 08	Clinton	01	09	22
Mills, George(A)	1824	June 08	Clinton	01	09	22
Mills, Halsted(A)	1836	May 27	Shelby	03	12	11
Mills, Henry(E)	1814	Nov. 11	Wayne(Ind)	13	18	28
Mills, Henry(E)	1836	June 08	Preble	13	18	01
Mills, Isaac(B)	1818	Aug. 04	Hamilton	01	06	01
Mills, Isaac(E)	1814	Nov. 11	Wayne(Ind)	13	18	28
Mills, Isaac(E)	1816	Sept. 23	Wayne(Ind)	13	18	23
Mills, Jacob B.(E)	1836	Aug. 15	Preble	14	19	29
Mills, Jacob B.(E)	1836	Oct. 26	Randolph(Ind	14	19	08
Mills, Jacob B.(E)	1837	Jan. 07	Randolph(Ind	14	19	08
Mills, Jacob B.(E)	1837	Jan. 07	Randolph(Ind	14	19	09
Mills, Jacob(A)	1817	Sept. 20	Franklin(Ind	03	08	33
Mills, Jacob(C)	1801	Dec. 26	Hamilton	05	03	09
Mills, James Jr.(B)	1818	Nov. 10	Dearborn(Ind	02	05	06
Mills, James Jr.(B)	1831	May 24	Dearborn(Ind	02	05	06
Mills, James(A)	1808	Dec. 14	Butler	03	02	08
Mills, James(A)	1810	Dec. 12	Butler	03	02	18
Mills, James(A)	1828	Sept. 09	Darke	02	11	21
Mills, John(A)	1805	Nov. 08	Montgomery	03	06	32
Mills, John(A)	1818	Sept. 19	Clinton	02	09	05
Mills, John(A)	1824	June 08	Preble	02	09	05
Mills, John(A)	1829	Sept. 04	Miami	05	07	22
Mills, John(A)	1836	May 25	Clinton	01	12	06
Mills, John(B)	1814	July 11	Jefferson	03	02	21
Mills, John(C)	1806	Nov. 03	Montgomery	09	02	22
Mills, John(E)	1816	Sept. 04	Wayne(Ind)	13	18	23
Mills, John(E)	1834	Dec. 05	Randolph(Ind	13	19	34

PURCHASER	YEAR	DATE	RESIDENCE	R	T	S
Mills, Jonathan(B)	1814	Jan. 15	Highland	01	14	19
Mills, Joseph Jr.(A)	1831	Dec. 19	Darke	03	08	21
Mills, Joseph(A)	1818	Sept. 28	Clinton	01	09	13
Mills, Joseph(A)	1824	June 08	Clinton	01	09	21
Mills, Joseph(A)	1828	Dec. 22	Shelby	05	10	21
Mills, Joseph(A)	1832	March 24	Clinton	01	09	12
Mills, Joseph(E)	1836	Sept. 17	Clinton	13	18	01
Mills, Joshua(A)	1820	Feb. 03	Warren	04	05	08
Mills, Moses(E)	1814	Nov. 11	Wayne(Ind)	13	18	28
Mills, Peter(C)	1817	Sept. 10	Cincinnati	13	05	35
Mills, Peter(C)	1817	Sept. 10	Cincinnati	10	05	19
Mills, Peter(C)	1817	Sept. 10	Cincinnati	10	05	06
Mills, Peter(C)	1818	Feb. 14	Cincinnati	14	18	11
Mills, Peter(D)	1808	Nov. 07	Hamilton	01	03	08
Mills, Rich'd.(E)	1815	Sept. 07	Clinton	13	18	30
Mills, Samuel(A)	1831	April 21	Miami	05	07	22
Mills, Seth(C)	1806	Nov. 03	Montgomery	09	02	22
Mills, Seth(E)	1814	Nov. 23	Wayne(Ind)	13	18	30
Mills, Thomas(C)	1812	Dec. 19	Greene	08	05	23
Mills, Thomas(C)	1827	April 02	Clark	08	05	29
Mills, Thomas(E)	1818	March 16	Warren	14	18	27
Mills, Thomas(E)	1833	June 07	Randolph(Ind	14	19	29
Mills, Thomas(E)	1836	Nov. 01	Randolph(Ind	14	19	28
Mills, William Jr.(E)	1818	Oct. 23	Warren	14	18	20
Mills, William(A)	1818	Sept. 19	Clinton	02	09	05
Millspaugh, James D.(B)	1828	March 08	Franklin(Ind	01	09	33
Milner, John(B)	1812	Aug. 25	Kentucky	01	09	10
Milner, John(E)	1814	Oct. 03	Franklin(Ind	13	13	05
Milner, John(E)	1814	Oct. 03	Franklin(Ind	13	13	05
Milner, Jonathon(C)	1817	Sept. 12	Hamilton	10	04	34
Milner, Mich'l.(A)	1829	Sept. 03	Preble	03	06	30
Milner, William(B)	1813	June 11	Preble	01	13	24
Milspaugh, Nathan'l. M.(B)	1824	June 09	Hamilton	01	08	04
Milspaugh, Peter B.(B)	1818	April 09	Hamilton	01	08	05
Milton, David(E)	1811	Dec. 28	Franklin(Ind	12	14	21
Mincer, Jacob(A)	1831	July 05	Warren	02	10	25
Mincer, Jacob(A)	1837	May 01	Darke	02	14	06
Minear, William(B)	1825	Aug. 04	Hamilton	01	10	21
Miner, Benson(E)	1815	Sept. 29	Wayne(Ind)	14	15	20
Miner, Darius Jr.(A)	1831	April 26	Darke	03	08	34
Miner, Joseph(E)	1811	Oct. 22	Ohio	12	14	35
Miner, Mary(B)	1806	Dec. 02	Warren	01	12	33
Miner, Richard(B)	1806	Dec. 02	Warren	01	11	04
Ming, Peter(B)	1812	July 02	Cincinnati	02	01	08
Mingle, John(A)	1815	Dec. 29	Montgomery	04	04	22
Minick, Peter(C)	1808	Feb. 08	Hamilton	09	04	30
Minneman, Frederick(B)	1836	Aug. 25	Cincinnati	03	09	01
Minner, Jonathan(A)	1819	Feb. 02	Preble	03	08	31
Minnicar, Abraham(C)	1816	Aug. 19	Hamilton	13	01	01
Minnicar, William(C)	1816	June 28	Greene	13	01	01
Minot, James(A)	1827	Aug. 29	Clermont	04	06	15
Mintern, Jacob(C)	1804	Dec. 31	Greene	11	06	27
Mints, William(B)	1817	July 10	Franklin(Ind	02	08	35
Mints, William(B)	1817	Aug. 04	Franklin(Ind	02	08	35
Minturn, Jacob(C)	1813	April 12	Champaign	11	06	33
Miover, Isaac(C)	1831	Jan. 12	Warren	12	02	15
Miranda, Jonathan(C)	1831	July 05	Clark	13	02	33
Miser, George(E)	1818	Jan. 03	Wayne(Ind)	13	15	23
Mishler, Abraham(A)	1831	May 10	Montgomery	03	08	13
Mishler, David(A)	1831	June 01	Montgomery	04	07	06
Mishler, William(A)	1830	Aug. 05	Montgomery	04	06	04
Misner, Christopher(E)	1832	Oct. 11	Rush(Ind)	11	12	13
Misner, Elisha(E)	1832	Oct. 11	Rush(Ind)	11	12	24
Misner, Elisha(E)	1836	Sept. 09	Franklin(Ind	12	10	09
Misner, Henry(A)	1811	Dec. 11	Hamilton	01	02	09
Misner, Henry(A)	1814	May 30	Hamilton	01	03	31
Misner, Henry(E)	1828	Dec. 27	Rush(Ind)	11	12	13
Misner, Jacob(B)	1813	Nov. 24	Jefferson	02	01	06
Misner, John(A)	1806	Oct. 29	Hamilton	01	02	09

PURCHASER	YEAR	DATE	RESIDENCE	R	T	S
Misner, John(A)	1811	Sept. 02	Butler	01	03	19
Misner, John(A)	1816	Dec. 02	Butler	01	03	19
Misner, John(B)	1818	June 01	Butler	03	04	29
Misner, John(B)	1828	Dec. 17	Butler	01	09	21
Misner, William(A)	1814	May 14	Hamilton	02	04	18
Misor, George(E)	1817	Nov. 26	Wayne(Ind)	13	16	34
Mitchel, Ebenezer(C)	1817	Sept. 09	Champaign	10	04	22
Mitchel, Edward(C)	1801	Dec. 30	Hamilton	05	03	24
Mitchel, John(A)	1811	Aug. 07	Preble	01	09	14
Mitchel, John(C)	1814	March 23	Champaign	12	04	10
Mitchel, John(E)	1837	April 01	Montgomery	15	22	10
Mitchel, Robert(C)	1808	Oct. 29	Greene	08	06	24
Mitchel, Robert(C)	1812	April 15	Greene	08	06	18
Mitchel, Sam'l. Harrison(B)	1834	Jan. 18	Dearborn(Ind	02	03	14
Mitchel, Samuel(A)	1813	Oct. 16	Hamilton	03	06	21
Mitchell, David(A)	1836	July 28	Miami	03	10	01
Mitchell, Edward(A)	1805	Jan. 01	Montgomery	05	05	14
Mitchell, Elijah(A)	1807	Jan. 24	Kentucky	01	09	10
Mitchell, George W. S.(B)	1837	March 25	Hamilton	02	04	20
Mitchell, Henry(B)	1832	Sept. 29	Switzerland	03	03	14
Mitchell, Henry(B)	1834	Feb. 12	Switzerland	03	03	05
Mitchell, James(C)	1811	Dec. 06	Greene	08	05	06
Mitchell, James(C)	1812	March 07	Greene	08	05	12
Mitchell, James(C)	1814	Jan. 31	Greene	08	05	06
Mitchell, Jesse(A)	1814	March 05	Preble	01	09	23
Mitchell, Jesse(A)	1823	Jan. 07	Preble	01	09	14
Mitchell, John(A)	1814	March 03	Preble	03	06	35
Mitchell, John(A)	1817	Dec. 16	Darke	02	12	24
Mitchell, John(A)	1818	Feb. 16	Preble	01	09	14
Mitchell, John(A)	1829	June 09	Preble	01	09	14
Mitchell, John(A)	1831	Nov. 28	Preble	01	09	02
Mitchell, Lewis(A)	1814	Oct. 22	Preble	01	09	03
Mitchell, Moses Grant(A)	1831	Aug. 02	Miami	05	08	23
Mitchell, Moses(A)	1814	July 11	Miami	05	08	06
Mitchell, Nathan'l.(A)	1818	Jan. 07	Preble	01	09	03
Mitchell, Peter(C)	1830	July 29	Champaign	12	03	26
Mitchell, Robert(A)	1812	Feb. 17	Hamilton	01	01	18
Mitchell, Robert(A)	1812	Feb. 17	Hamilton	01	01	18
Mitchell, Robert(A)	1812	Feb. 17	Champaign	01	01	07
Mitchell, Robert(C)	1813	Jan. 19	Greene	08	06	24
Mitchell, Robert(C)	1813	April 15	Greene	08	06	17
Mitchell, Robert(C)	1823	Sept. 27	Alabama	08	06	18
Mitchell, Samuel G.(A)	1808	July 12	Kentucky	02	08	27
Mitchell, Samuel G.(B)	1808	July 12	Kentucky	01	15	36
Mitchell, Samuel(A)	1805	Oct. 18	Kentucky	03	05	31
Mitchell, Samuel(A)	1805	Oct. 18	Kentucky	03	05	31
Mitchell, Samuel(A)	1805	Oct. 18	Kentucky	02	06	01
Mitchell, Samuel(A)	1805	Oct. 18	Kentucky	01	08	29
Mitchell, Samuel(A)	1805	Oct. 30	Butler	03	05	29
Mitchell, Samuel(A)	1806	June 07	Montgomery	02	07	25
Mitchell, Samuel(C)	1805	May 14	Montgomery	12	04	10
Mitchell, Thomas G.(C)	1814	Dec. 01	Pennsylvania	12	04	09
Mitchell, William C.(B)	1818	July 07	Switzerland	03	04	33
Mitchell, William Clark(B)	1834	June 24	Switzerland	03	03	05
Mitchell, William Clark(B)	1836	Aug. 19	Switzerland	03	03	05
Mitchell, William(A)	1806	July 10	Butler	05	08	25
Mitchell, William(A)	1812	Feb. 17	Hamilton	01	01	18
Mitchell, William(A)	1812	Feb. 17	Hamilton	01	01	18
Mitchell, William(A)	1812	Feb. 17	Champaign	01	01	07
Mitchell, William(A)	1813	April 15	Miami	05	08	25
Mitchell, William(A)	1813	Dec. 25	Butler	01	04	36
Mitchell, William(B)	1818	July 03	Switzerland	03	03	05
Mitchell, William(C)	1813	June 18	Scioto	11	04	19
Mitchell, William(C)	1814	Dec. 23	Champaign	11	04	20
Mitchell, Wilson Stafford(A)	1834	Oct. 16	Clark	08	02	31
Mitchell, Wm.(C)	1811	Dec. 24	Miami	10	02	03
Mixer, Ebenezer(B)	1816	Jan. 13	?	02	02	03
Mixture, Ebenezer(B)	1815	May 29	Hamilton	02	02	03
Mock, Frederick(C)	1815	June 28	Miami	10	03	27

PURCHASER	YEAR	DATE	RESIDENCE	R	T	S
Mock, Jeremiah Lindsey(E)	1834	April 28	Randolph(Ind	14	21	07
Mock, John(E)	1836	Oct. 17	Randolph(Ind	14	21	34
Moffatt, James T.(A)	1818	April 17	Montgomery	02	12	23
Moffet, Charles(E)	1811	Nov. 16	Wayne(Ind)	14	18	32
Moffett, George(A)	1806	Aug. 25	Kentucky	05	08	11
Moffett, Seth(E)	1836	Oct. 17	Randolph(Ind	14	20	10
Moffett, Thomas(E)	1811	Nov. 05	Wayne(Ind)	14	15	28
Moffett, William(A)	1829	June 01	Clark	03	07	25
Moffit, Jeremiah(E)	1817	Dec. 01	Ross	14	20	22
Moffit, Jeremiah(E)	1817	Dec. 01	Ross	15	20	18
Moffitt, Jeremiah(E)	1818	April 23	Ross	14	20	10
Moffitt, Jeremiah(E)	1818	Sept. 03	Wayne(Ind)	14	20	03
Moffitt, John(E)	1819	June 23	Ross	13	18	33
Moffitt, Joseph(E)	1818	April 23	Ross	14	20	10
Moffitt, Joseph(E)	1836	Nov. 04	Randolph(Ind	14	20	10
Moffitt, Seth(E)	1831	Oct. 28	Randolph(Ind	14	20	10
Moffitt, Seth(E)	1832	Dec. 05	Randolph(Ind	14	20	03
Moffitt, Seth(E)	1837	March 01	Randolph(Ind	14	20	10
Moffitt, Seth(E)	1838	Nov. 02	Randolph(Ind	14	20	24
Moffitt, Stephen(E)	1838	Nov. 02	Randolph(Ind	14	20	24
Moffitt, Zimri(E)	1833	June 22	Randolph(Ind	14	20	03
Moffitt, Zimri(E)	1831	Jan. 30	Randolph(Ind	14	20	27
Money, William(E)	1834	June 24	Randolph(Ind	15	22	23
Money, William(E)	1836	May 28	Randolph(Ind	15	22	23
Money, William(E)	1837	Feb. 28	Jay Co.,Ind.	15	22	22
Money, Wm.(E)	1838	May 21	Jay Co.,Ind.	15	22	23
Monfort, Henry(E)	1818	April 27	Randolph(Ind	14	19	03
Monfort, John Campbell(B)	1833	June 13	Switzerland	03	04	19
Monks, John(E)	1835	May 01	Randolph(Ind	14	20	30
Monroe, George(E)	1812	Dec. 28	Butler	13	13	20
Monroe, George(E)	1816	Oct. 08	Franklin(Ind	12	13	36
Montanye, Lemuel(B)	1828	May 14	Switzerland	02	02	17
Montanye, Lemuel(B)	1832	July 16	Switzerland	02	02	17
Montanye, Lemuel(B)	1835	Feb. 04	Switzerland	02	02	20
Montanye, Zachariah(B)	1818	May 11	Hamilton	02	02	17
Montanye, Zachariah(B)	1833	Feb. 20	Switzerland	02	02	20
Montfort, Aaron(A)	1808	June 08	Kentucky	03	06	31
Montfort, Aaron(A)	1817	June 05	?	02	08	26
Montgomery, James(B)	1815	April 20	Wayne(Ind)	02	05	27
Montgomery, James(B)	1815	June 24	Pennsylvania	01	08	04
Montgomery, James(E)	1815	Aug. 04	Wayne(Ind)	13	14	14
Montgomery, James(E)	1815	Sept. 29	Wayne(Ind)	13	14	02
Montgomery, James(E)	1815	Sept. 29	Wayne(Ind)	13	14	11
Montgomery, James(E)	1816	Aug. 24	Wayne(Ind)	13	14	12
Montgomery, James(E)	1837	Jan. 28	Randolph(Ind	14	21	31
Montgomery, John(B)	1815	April 20	Wayne(Ind)	02	05	28
Montgomery, John(E)	1817	Oct. 04	Wayne(Ind)	13	14	02
Montgomery, Platt(E)	1814	April 15	Wayne(Ind)	13	15	27
Montgomery, Robert(E)	1812	June 11	Wayne(Ind)	13	15	29
Montgomery, Robert(E)	1814	March 19	Wayne(Ind)	13	15	29
Montgomery, Sam'l.(C)	1828	Dec. 29	Warren	11	03	34
Montgomery, Wm.(A)	1820	Oct. 23	Shelby	04	11	25
Montgomery, Wm.(E)	1814	Jan. 11	Wayne(Ind)	13	15	20
Moody, Alexander(C)	1813	April 14	Champaign	11	05	36
Moody, Isaac(C)	1832	March 05	Champaign	12	04	32
Moody, Jonathan(B)	1817	Oct. 04	Switzerland	01	03	31
Moody, Thomas(C)	1831	Nov. 22	Champaign	12	04	26
Moon, Malachi(B)	1811	Nov. 18	Clinton	01	15	08
Moon, Milton(A)	1837	May 24	Hamilton	01	14	30
Moor, Daniel(C)	1806	Jan. 11	Hamilton	08	04	24
Moor, Isaac(E)	1832	April 12	Wayne(Ind)	13	19	04
Moor, John(B)	1805	Sept. 28	Dearborn(Ind	02	04	02
Moor, Samuel(C)	1805	Dec. 09	Montgomery	08	02	30
Moor, William(C)	1807	March 10	Champaign	14	04	31
Moor, William(C)	1807	March 11	Champaign	13	05	34
Moore, Adam(B)	1835	Sept. 09	Dearborn(Ind	03	07	34
Moore, Adam(D)	1808	Nov. 07	Cincinati(Fr	02	02	08
Moore, Alexander(A)	1811	April 09	Butler	02	05	08
Moore, Alexander(A)	1813	Dec. 23	Butler	02	04	22

PURCHASER	YEAR	DATE	RESIDENCE	R	T	S
Moore, Alexander(B)	1816	Dec. 05	Butler	01	14	10
Moore, Alexander(E)	1811	Oct. 24	Butler	13	16	19
Moore, Archibald(C)	1811	Oct. 22	Champaign	13	05	36
Moore, Archibald(C)	1813	Dec. 20	Champaign	13	04	17
Moore, Arthur(B)	1817	June 24	Cincinnati	02	07	34
Moore, Arthur(B)	1817	Dec. 06	Cincinnati	02	07	33
Moore, Cyrus(B)	1815	Sept. 05	Switzerland	02	02	05
Moore, Daniel(C)	1811	April 09	Greene	08	04	24
Moore, David(A)	1815	Dec. 08	Warren	01	06	01
Moore, David(C)	1828	Dec. 05	Champaign	13	03	27
Moore, David(C)	1831	May 26	Champaign	13	03	27
Moore, David(E)	1816	May 04	Pennsylvania	13	18	17
Moore, David(E)	1835	Dec. 22	Randolph(Ind	13	18	17
Moore, Hugh(A)	1816	May 01	Cincinnati	01	02	26
Moore, Hugh(A)	1817	Aug. 01	Cincinnati	03	04	13
Moore, Hugh(B)	1816	Jan. 20	Cincinnati	01	07	19
Moore, Hugh(B)	1816	May 01	Cincinnati	01	07	19
Moore, Hugh(B)	1816	June 26	Cincinnati	03	02	10
Moore, Hugh(B)	1816	June 26	Cincinnati	01	04	21
Moore, Hugh(B)	1816	July 23	Cincinnati	01	07	01
Moore, Hugh(B)	1816	Sept. 11	Cincinnati	01	08	08
Moore, Hugh(B)	1817	Aug. 05	Cincinnati	01	03	08
Moore, Hugh(B)	1818	Jan. 12	Cincinnati	02	02	29
Moore, Hugh(B)	1818	Jan. 12	Cincinnati	02	02	31
Moore, Hugh(B)	1818	Jan. 12	Cincinnati	02	10	10
Moore, Hugh(B)	1818	Jan. 12	Cincinnati	03	02	07
Moore, Hugh(C)	1816	Aug. 01	Cincinnati	10	04	14
Moore, Hugh(C)	1817	Aug. 01	Cincinnati	08	03	08
Moore, Hugh(D)	1808	Nov. 07	Hamilton	02	02	08
Moore, Hugh(E)	1816	Oct. 03	Cincinnati	13	13	28
Moore, Isabella(A)	1831	Sept. 19	Montgomery	06	08	23
Moore, Jacob(B)	1813	June 22	Dearborn(Ind	02	04	01
Moore, James(A)	1811	April 09	Preble	02	06	09
Moore, James(A)	1814	March 17	Miami	06	08	29
Moore, James(A)	1814	Nov. 22	Preble	02	06	08
Moore, James(B)	1808	Feb. 01	Hamilton	02	09	30
Moore, James(B)	1817	July 07	Switzerland	01	02	14
Moore, James(C)	1809	Feb. 20	Kentucky	14	02	14
Moore, James(E)	1816	Jan. 26	Preble	13	17	07
Moore, James(E)	1836	Jan. 25	Fayette	12	13	31
Moore, Joel(A)	1815	Jan. 13	Wayne(Ind)	01	07	18
Moore, Joel(B)	1810	Nov. 12	Ind.Territry	01	12	11
Moore, John(A)	1807	March 30	Butler	02	04	07
Moore, John(B)	1836	April 13	Randolph(Ind	01	16	24
Moore, John(C)	1818	Jan. 29	Champaign	11	03	20
Moore, John(C)	1830	April 14	Champaign	11	03	14
Moore, John(E)	1815	April 14	Preble	13	17	20
Moore, John(E)	1816	Dec. 07	Clinton	14	20	18
Moore, Jonathan(B)	1819	Feb. 05	Dearborn(Ind	02	08	19
Moore, Matthew Senr.(A)	1836	Aug. 27	Miami	03	11	10
Moore, Mordecai(A)	1814	Sept. 21	Preble	03	04	35
Moore, Patrick(E)	1817	Sept. 09	Butler	14	16	10
Moore, Patrick(E)	1817	Sept. 09	Butler	14	16	03
Moore, Raphael(C)	1816	Dec. 14	Champaign	13	04	24
Moore, Raphael(C)	1828	Aug. 15	Logan	13	04	24
Moore, Robert(A)	1806	March 21	Hamilton	02	04	08
Moore, Robert(C)	1807	Aug. 27	Champaign	14	03	25
Moore, Robert(C)	1814	April 04	Champaign	14	03	19
Moore, Robert(C)	1828	Aug. 15	Logan	14	03	19
Moore, Robert(C)	1831	Feb. 05	Logan	14	03	19
Moore, Roderick(B)	1815	Nov. 24	Hamilton	02	06	29
Moore, Sam'l.(E)	1830	Feb. 01	Wayne(Ind)	13	18	27
Moore, Samuel(B)	1806	Aug. 05	Hamilton	01	08	10
Moore, Samuel(C)	1823	Sept. 05	Logan	13	04	30
Moore, Samuel(E)	1816	Jan. 13	?	13	18	28
Moore, Thomas(C)	1804	Dec. 28	Greene	11	05	25
Moore, Thomas(C)	1828	June 26	Logan	14	03	19
Moore, Thomas(C)	1831	Jan. 19	Logan	14	03	19
Moore, William(A)	1830	June 25	Logan	08	02	29

PURCHASER	YEAR	DATE	RESIDENCE	R	T	S
Moore, William(B)	1828	Jan. 14	Franklin(Ind	02	10	22
Moore, William(B)	1835	June 10	Hamilton	02	02	23
Moore, William(C)	1816	Jan. 03	Champaign	13	03	20
Moore, William(C)	1824	Aug. 27	Logan	13	02	11
Moore, William(C)	1827	Oct. 01	Logan	14	03	26
Moore, William(C)	1830	Dec. 24	Logan	14	03	19
Moorehouse, Amos(C)	1815	Sept. 11	Champaign	10	03	23
Moorehouse, James(C)	1813	Aug. 10	Champaign	09	03	28
Moorehouse, James(C)	1815	Sept. 11	Champaign	11	03	25
Moorehouse, Thomas(C)	1817	Sept. 12	Hamilton	10	04	34
Mooreman, Tarlton(E)	1816	Oct. 29	Nor.Carolina	13	20	13
Moorman, Herman Hy.(E)	1836	Nov. 11	Cincinnati	12	10	10
Moorman, James(B)	1835	Jan. 03	Wayne(Ind)	01	16	12
Moorman, James(B)	1835	Jan. 12	Wayne(Ind)	01	16	02
Moorman, James(B)	1836	June 11	Wayne(Ind)	01	16	02
Moorman, James(E)	1817	Nov. 21	Nor.Carolina	13	20	23
Moorman, James(E)	1819	April 15	Nor.Carolina	14	18	24
Moorman, James(E)	1828	Jan. 18	Wayne(Ind)	14	18	23
Moorman, Jesse(E)	1817	Nov. 21	Nor.Carolina	14	20	19
Moorman, Jesse(E)	1819	April 15	Nor.Carolina	13	20	35
Moorman, Jesse(E)	1836	Oct. 19	Randolph(Ind	13	20	35
Moorman, Jesse(E)	1836	Nov. 04	Randolph(Ind	13	21	35
Moorman, John(E)	1817	Dec. 20	Wayne(Ind)	14	18	23
Moorman, Susannah(E)	1817	July 07	Nor.Carolina	14	18	15
Moorman, Tarlton(E)	1819	April 15	Nor.Carolina	13	20	25
Moorman, Thomas(E)	1814	July 28	Wayne(Ind)	14	18	21
Moorman, Thomas(E)	1818	Feb. 07	Wayne(Ind)	14	18	22
Moorman, Uriah(E)	1825	May 02	Randolph(Ind	13	19	04
Moran, Michael(B)	1818	Aug. 15	Cincinnati	01	07	18
Mordock, Hance(A)	1805	Aug. 21	Kentucky	06	04	08
Moredock, James(B)	1815	Feb. 21	Greene	01	02	11
Moredock, James(B)	1815	Aug. 21	Hamilton	01	02	14
Morehead, Matthew(A)	1806	Aug. 07	Pennsylvania	01	03	02
Morehouse, Augustin(A)	1819	Feb. 15	Darke	02	11	22
Morehouse, Dayton C.(A)	1837	Aug. 08	Darke	01	12	06
Morehouse, James(A)	1811	May 31	Darke	02	12	28
Morehouse, James(A)	1811	May 31	Darke	02	12	30
Morehouse, Nehemiah(B)	1818	Sept. 22	Hamilton	03	05	24
Moreillon, John L.(B)	1819	March 08	Hamilton	03	02	20
Morerod, Daniel(B)	1814	Aug. 11	Jefferson	02	02	17
Morerod, Jean Daniel(B)	1814	Aug. 11	Jefferson	02	02	17
Morerod, John(B)	1814	Aug. 11	Jefferson	02	02	17
Morey, Will'm.(A)	1827	Aug. 20	Butler	02	06	22
Morford, John(E)	1834	June 05	Butler	12	11	15
Morford, William(E)	1832	Dec. 01	Clermont	13	11	06
Morgan, Albert(A)	1819	Sept. 13	Hamilton	04	10	30
Morgan, Benj'm.(E)	1815	Sept. 27	Wayne(Ind)	13	16	20
Morgan, Benj'n. Jr.(B)	1831	Aug. 19	Dearborn(Ind	01	07	22
Morgan, Benj'n.(B)	1828	Nov. 26	Dearborn(Ind	01	07	23
Morgan, Benjamin Jr.(B)	1836	Jan. 28	Dearborn(Ind	01	07	35
Morgan, Benjamin(B)	1807	June 30	Dearborn(Ind	01	14	34
Morgan, Benjamin(B)	1818	Aug. 15	Wayne(Ind)	01	15	09
Morgan, Charles(C)	1804	Oct. 29	Greene	06	02	18
Morgan, Daniel(A)	1836	Sept. 08	Darke	04	11	32
Morgan, Enoch(B)	1818	July 02	Hamilton	01	07	26
Morgan, Enoch(B)	1833	April 24	Dearborn(Ind	01	07	26
Morgan, Evan(C)	1801	Dec. 28	Hamilton	07	03	25
Morgan, James(B)	1816	Oct. 28	England	02	05	13
Morgan, James(B)	1816	Nov. 13	England	02	05	13
Morgan, John Junr.(C)	1801	Dec. 28	Hamilton	06	03	35
Morgan, John Senr.(C)	1801	Dec. 28	Hamilton	06	03	35
Morgan, John(C)	1814	June 09	Champaign	12	05	03
Morgan, Lorenzo Dow(B)	1833	Sept. 16	Fayette	02	08	08
Morgan, Micajah(B)	1827	July 03	Wayne(Ind)	01	15	15
Morgan, Micajah(E)	1837	Feb. 06	Wayne(Ind)	15	20	28
Morgan, Micajah(E)	1837	Feb. 06	Wayne(Ind)	15	20	30
Morgan, Michael(B)	1816	Oct. 28	England	02	05	13
Morgan, Mordecai(E)	1814	June 14	Virginia	13	14	03
Morgan, Samuel Brown(A)	1831	Nov. 22	Miami	05	08	26

PURCHASER	YEAR	DATE	RESIDENCE	R	T	S
Morgan, Thomas(B)	1807	March 10	Dearborn(Ind	01	09	24
Morgan, Thomas(B)	1817	May 27	Darke	03	08	36
Morgan, William(A)	1811	Dec. 28	Franklin(Ind	01	04	19
Morgna, William(E)	1811	Oct. 28	Greene	13	13	13
Morningstar, Dan'l.(A)	1832	July 23	Clark	02	12	21
Morningstar, George(A)	1814	Sept. 07	Preble	03	05	21
Morningstar, George(A)	1815	Jan. 02	Preble	03	05	21
Morningstar, George(A)	1831	Oct. 11	Greene	02	12	22
Morningstar, George(A)	1831	Oct. 11	Greene	02	12	15
Morningstar, George(C)	1805	Nov. 20	Greene	07	03	09
Morningstar, George(C)	1811	April 09	Greene	07	03	09
Morningstar, Philip(C)	1805	Nov. 20	Greene	07	03	09
Morrell, Calvin(C)	1801	Dec. 23	Hamilton	04	01	02
Morrell, Calvin(C)	1801	Dec. 23	Hamilton	04	02	32
Morreson, Robert(A)	1836	Oct. 10	Miami	03	12	17
Morreson, Robert(A)	1836	Oct. 10	Miami	03	12	07
Morris, Achilles(E)	1817	Aug. 30	Wayne(Ind)	13	18	09
Morris, Achilles(E)	1817	Aug. 30	Wayne(Ind)	13	18	04
Morris, Achilles(E)	1817	Aug. 30	Wayne(Ind)	13	16	26
Morris, Amos Jr.(B)	1818	July 03	Greene	03	07	12
Morris, Amos Junr.(B)	1833	March 02	Dearborn(Ind	03	07	12
Morris, Benjamin(B)	1814	Dec. 07	Warren	01	12	35
Morris, Benjamin(C)	1810	Jan. 30	Champaign	10	04	25
Morris, Biven(A)	1832	March 19	Darke	01	12	21
Morris, Caleb(E)	1815	May 18	Nor.Carolina	13	17	28
Morris, David(C)	1831	Dec. 16	Logan	13	04	22
Morris, Enoch(A)	1813	March 11	Butler	02	05	22
Morris, Henry(C)	1812	June 29	Champaign	09	03	05
Morris, Isaac(E)	1815	Aug. 30	Wayne(Ind)	13	16	20
Morris, James C.(A)	1806	Jan. 13	Cincinnati	01	04	24
Morris, James C.(A)	1807	Aug. 15	Cincinnati	01	03	13
Morris, James C.(A)	1809	Feb. 27	Cincinnati	02	02	06
Morris, James C.(B)	1806	July 28	Butler	02	13	36
Morris, Jehoshaphat(E)	1811	Oct. 28	Wayne(Ind)	13	16	30
Morris, Jehoshaphat(E)	1811	Oct. 28	Wayne(Ind)	12	16	13
Morris, John(A)	1806	Aug. 13	Butler	01	04	17
Morris, John(A)	1814	Oct. 19	Hamilton	01	02	07
Morris, John(A)	1819	Feb. 17	Warren	06	08	02
Morris, John(B)	1813	Aug. 30	Butler	01	10	26
Morris, John(C)	1805	Dec. 06	Champaign	09	04	18
Morris, John(C)	1813	April 13	Champaign	10	04	13
Morris, John(C)	1813	April 26	Champaign	10	03	05
Morris, John(C)	1813	April 26	Champaign	10	03	04
Morris, Joseph(C)	1814	Nov. 14	Champaign	09	06	13
Morris, Joseph(C)	1829	Jan. 20	Clark	13	04	22
Morris, Levi(C)	1809	Feb. 10	Pennsylvania	11	02	13
Morris, Nathan(B)	1813	Oct. 06	Nor.Carolina	02	14	25
Morris, Nathan(E)	1815	May 18	Nor.Carolina	13	17	23
Morris, Owen(C)	1808	March 14	Ohio	11	02	13
Morris, Richard(A)	1815	Aug. 18	Pennsylvania	01	07	21
Morris, Robert(A)	1813	Feb. 22	Butler	02	05	21
Morris, Robert(E)	1825	Oct. 01	Butler	13	12	21
Morris, Thomas(A)	1836	Aug. 05	Darke	01	12	30
Morris, Walter(B)	1831	Nov. 21	Switzerland	02	02	32
Morris, William(A)	1813	Dec. 02	Preble	01	06	18
Morris, William(B)	1814	Dec. 31	Butler	02	09	10
Morris, William(C)	1811	Dec. 10	Champaign	10	06	17
Morrison, Andrew(A)	1808	Jan. 11	Montgomery	01	09	11
Morrison, Andrew(A)	1808	April 15	Dearborn(Ind	01	09	09
Morrison, Andrew(A)	1816	Nov. 20	Preble	01	09	09
Morrison, Ephraim(C)	1805	Sept. 07	Champaign	09	03	17
Morrison, James(A)	1804	May 19	Pennsylvania	03	03	24
Morrison, James(A)	1804	May 19	Pennsylvania	04	02	19
Morrison, James(A)	1817	Nov. 26	Ohio	05	07	12
Morrison, James(B)	1807	June 23	Dearborn(Ind	01	14	05
Morrison, James(B)	1813	April 14	Wayne(Ind)	01	14	05
Morrison, James(E)	1811	Dec. 21	Wayne(Ind)	14	18	32
Morrison, Jane(A)	1836	Aug. 24	Butler	01	13	29
Morrison, Joseph W.(B)	1816	Oct. 28	Franklin(Ind	02	08	17

PURCHASER	YEAR	DATE	RESIDENCE	R	T	S
Morrison, Robert(B)	1810	Oct. 06	Dearborn(Ind	01	14	01
Morrison, Samuel(A)	1805	Dec. 23	Montgomery	02	04	03
Morrison, Samuel(A)	1811	April 09	Butler	02	04	03
Morrison, Samuel(A)	1836	June 24	Hamilton	04	08	18
Morrison, Samuel(A)	1836	Oct. 27	Cincinnati	02	15	20
Morrison, Samuel(A)	1836	Oct. 31	Cincinnati	02	15	20
Morrison, Samuel(B)	1836	July 21	Hamilton	01	17	13
Morrison, Samuel(C)	1802	Dec. 31	Hamilton	09	02	30
Morrison, Samuel(C)	1804	Dec. 31	Montgomery	09	02	30
Morrison, Samuel(E)	1836	July 21	Hamilton	14	21	15
Morrison, Samuel(E)	1836	July 28	Hamilton	14	20	26
Morrow, Alexander(A)	1827	March 17	Shelby	05	09	22
Morrow, Andrew(A)	1806	Nov. 21	Warren	01	08	09
Morrow, Andrew(A)	1824	June 08	Preble	01	09	21
Morrow, Andrew(A)	1824	June 15	Preble	01	08	15
Morrow, Andrew(A)	1824	June 24	Preble	01	08	15
Morrow, Andrew(A)	1824	June 24	Preble	01	09	15
Morrow, Arch'd.(E)	1813	July 24	Franklin(Ind	13	13	28
Morrow, Archibald(B)	1811	Oct. 09	Franklin(Ind	02	10	27
Morrow, Charles(E)	1836	Dec. 07	Fayette	12	13	31
Morrow, James(E)	1815	Nov. 13	Franklin(Ind	13	13	22
Morrow, John(A)	1808	Jan. 12	Montgomery	01	08	08
Morrow, John(A)	1808	April 30	Montgomery	01	08	04
Morrow, John(A)	1818	Dec. 08	Baltimore	05	08	14
Morrow, John(B)	1813	Oct. 19	Wayne(Ind)	01	14	14
Morrow, John(C)	1817	Aug. 22	Butler	12	02	34
Morrow, John(C)	1817	Aug. 22	Butler	12	02	34
Morrow, John(C)	1831	Sept. 17	Butler	13	02	23
Morrow, John(E)	1812	March 27	Franklin(Ind	13	13	21
Morrow, Richard(A)	1815	Sept. 27	Miami	05	08	36
Morrow, Richard(A)	1816	May 27	Miami	05	08	08
Morrow, William(A)	1817	June 09	Miami	05	09	26
Morrow, William(B)	1836	May 23	Wash.Co.Penn	02	03	31
Morse, John(A)	1814	June 27	Hamilton	02	04	22
Morse, Vallorus(B)	1832	June 26	Hamilton	03	04	26
Morse, Vallorus(B)	1836	April 21	Switzerland	02	03	18
Morss, Benj'n.(B)	1831	Nov. 09	Dearborn(Ind	02	06	08
Morster, James(E)	1813	Sept. 10	Kentucky	13	13	15
Morter, Jacob(A)	1804	Oct. 27	Virginia	02	07	23
Morton, Henry(D)	1812	July 07	Hamilton(Fr)	02	04	26
Morton, Loring(B)	1818	June 04	Cincinnati	02	08	07
Morton, Richard(A)	1816	Oct. 23	Pennsylvania	02	11	17
Morton, Thomas(A)	1815	June 19	Cincinnati	01	02	35
Morton, Thomas(C)	1831	Aug. 09	Hamilton	13	02	05
Mosley, James(B)	1814	June 20	Dearborn(Ind	02	02	27
Moss, David(A)	1805	Aug. 13	Montgomery	05	05	24
Moss, Demas(B)	1816	July 15	Dearborn(Ind	02	05	24
Moss, Demas(B)	1816	July 05	Switzerland	03	03	12
Moss, Harvey(B)	1833	Nov. 27	Dearborn(Ind	03	07	33
Moss, Henry(C)	1825	Feb. 16	Clark	10	03	11
Moss, John(B)	1811	Feb. 25	Ind.Territory	01	10	25
Moss, Lemuel(B)	1817	Oct. 09	Dearborn(Ind	03	06	03
Moss, William(A)	1825	Aug. 01	Miami	04	09	26
Moss, William(A)	1831	Aug. 22	Miami	04	09	28
Moss, William(B)	1808	Oct. 19	Dearborn(Ind	01	12	24
Moss, William(B)	1814	Nov. 16	Wayne(Ind)	01	12	24
Moss, Zealley(B)	1814	Oct. 31	Ind.Territory	01	02	17
Moss, Zealley(B)	1814	Oct. 31	Ind.Territory	01	02	28
Moss, Zeally(B)	1816	Feb. 12	Switzerland	01	02	17
Mote, Aaron(A)	1823	Feb. 10	Miami	04	07	08
Mote, Elijah(A)	1836	May 26	Darke	01	13	15
Mote, Enoch(A)	1831	May 03	Darke	04	07	05
Mote, Henry(A)	1836	March 11	Darke	01	13	33
Mote, Jeremiah(A)	1802	Aug. 03	Hamilton	05	05	05
Mote, John(A)	1805	July 01	Montgomery	04	07	24
Mote, John(A)	1805	Aug. 16	Montgomery	05	06	32
Mote, John(A)	1807	June 16	Montgomery	05	06	18
Mote, John(A)	1814	Oct. 10	Montgomery	05	06	21
Mote, Jonathan(A)	1804	Aug. 06	Montgomery	05	06	20

PURCHASER	YEAR	DATE	RESIDENCE	R	T	S
Mote, William(A)	1807	June 16	Montgomery	05	06	18
Mote, William(A)	1816	Oct. 22	Miami	04	07	13
Mott, Abraham(A)	1836	Aug. 29	Miami	01	15	22
Moulton, Benjamin(B)	1836	June 11	Switzerland	02	03	18
Moulton, Benjamin(B)	1836	Sept. 10	Switzerland	02	03	18
Moulton, William(B)	1836	May 27	Dearborn(Ind	02	03	20
Moulton, William(B)	1836	Sept. 10	Dearborn(Ind	02	03	20
Mount, David(E)	1811	Oct. 21	Clermont	12	12	36
Mount, David(E)	1811	Oct. 23	Clermont	13	12	31
Mount, David(E)	1812	July 06	Franklin(Ind	12	12	35
Mount, David(E)	1812	Oct. 07	Franklin(Ind	12	12	34
Mount, David(E)	1812	Nov. 17	Franklin(Ind	13	11	05
Mount, David(E)	1836	Jan. 18	Franklin(Ind	12	11	02
Mount, David(E)	1836	Jan. 18	Franklin(Ind	12	11	11
Mount, David(E)	1836	Jan. 18	Franklin(Ind	12	11	01
Mount, David(E)	1836	May 18	Franklin(Ind	12	11	02
Mount, Hezekiah(E)	1811	Oct. 23	Clermont	13	12	32
Mount, Hezekiah(E)	1811	Nov. 22	Clermont	13	12	32
Mount, Hezekiah(E)	1812	Feb. 03	Franklin(Ind	12	14	31
Mount, Peter(E)	1836	Sept. 08	Franklin(Ind	12	11	02
Mounts, Abner(A)	1806	Dec. 20	Hamilton	01	02	01
Mounts, Caleb(B)	1812	Aug. 19	Dearborn(Ind	01	02	06
Mounts, John(B)	1815	Oct. 03	Adams	01	03	06
Mounts, John(E)	1816	Aug. 22	Adams	13	17	05
Mounts, Providence(B)	1809	June 19	Dearborn(Ind	02	02	02
Mounts, Providence(B)	1830	Jan. 18	Switzerland	01	03	33
Mounts, Thomas(B)	1812	Aug. 17	Dearborn(Ind	01	03	28
Mounts, Thomas(B)	1814	Aug. 06	Dearborn(Ind	01	03	28
Mow, Adam(B)	1813	Aug. 07	Ind.Territry	01	09	08
Mow, John Samuel(A)	1808	June 11	Hamilton	04	04	20
Moyer, George(A)	1805	Aug. 03	Montgomery	03	07	14
Moyer, George(A)	1813	March 05	Preble	03	06	21
Moyer, Gorge(A)	1810	Dec. 12	Montgomery	03	07	14
Moyer, Henry(A)	1833	June 05	Montgomery	01	12	03
Moyer, Henry(A)	1837	May 30	Fairfield	02	14	08
Moyer, Solomon(A)	1837	May 30	Pickaway	02	14	07
Moyer, Solomon(A)	1837	May 30	Pickaway	02	14	08
Moyers, Christopher(A)	1815	Feb. 10	Preble	03	07	11
Moyers, Mich'l.(A)	1831	March 09	Montgomery	01	12	15
Moyers, Reuben(A)	1831	Oct. 25	Indiana	01	12	10
Moyers, William(A)	1831	March 09	Montgomery	01	12	15
Moyers, William(A)	1836	Sept. 23	Darke	01	12	18
Mucherheid, Barnet Hy.(E)	1837	April 28	Cincinnati	11	11	25
Muchmore, Samuel(D)	1808	Nov. 01	Hamilton(Fr)	02	04	11
Muckel, Frances Mitchell(A)	1836	Oct. 10	Cincinnati	01	14	21
Mudlin, Benjamin(E)	1813	Nov. 11	Wayne(Ind)	14	16	07
Muir, Mary(B)	1831	June 22	Dearborn(Ind	01	06	25
Mulendore, Jacob(A)	1805	Dec. 18	Montgomery	03	05	18
Mulford, Benj'n.(C)	1828	March 24	Hamilton	10	03	29
Mulford, Caleb(B)	1815	April 24	Warren	02	04	09
Mulford, Dan'l.(C)	1828	March 24	Hamilton	10	03	29
Mulford, David(B)	1809	Sept. 13	Warren	01	09	19
Mulford, Ezra(B)	1838	April 02	Dearborn(Ind	03	04	15
Mulford, Jeremiah(B)	1818	April 21	Wayne(Ind)	02	03	05
Mulford, Jeremiah(B)	1824	June 16	Dearborn(Ind	02	03	08
Mulford, John(E)	1836	Aug. 20	Butler	15	21	26
Mulford, Richard(B)	1819	May 07	Hamilton	02	06	07
Mulford, William D.(A)	1837	Feb. 20	Butler	02	15	32
Mulholland, Mary(B)	1814	Nov. 08	Franklin(Ind	02	09	36
Mulhollin, Jonathan(C)	1806	Dec. 31	Champaign	09	04	17
Mulhollon, John(B)	1818	Jan. 12	Cincinnati	02	06	10
Mullin, Lannen(E)	1836	Aug. 29	Union(Ind)	14	19	11
Mullonich, Henry(E)	1835	Jan. 23	Wayne(Ind)	13	18	22
Mumbower, Jane(E)	1834	Dec. 05	Randolph(Ind	13	19	34
Mumbower, Jane(E)	1835	Feb. 16	Randolph(Ind	13	19	27
Munden, Jesse(E)	1816	Oct. 16	Wayne(Ind)	12	15	15
Mundhenk, Dan'l.(A)	1829	Dec. 24	Montgomery	04	05	08
Mundhenk, Daniel(A)	1818	March 19	Butler	04	05	05
Mundhenk, Lewis(A)	1832	March 19	Montgomery	03	08	23

234

PURCHASER	YEAR	DATE	RESIDENCE	R	T	S
Mundhenke, Dan'l.(A)	1830	Feb. 20	Montgomery	04	05	06
Mundhenke, Lewis(A)	1830	Jan. 01	Montgomery	04	06	31
Mundhenks, Lewis(A)	1829	Sept. 16	Montgomery	04	05	06
Mundhinke, Lewis(A)	1817	Dec. 09	Montgomery	04	05	06
Munfort, Henry(C)	1801	Dec. 31	Hamilton	04	04	14
Mungar, Edmund(C)	1801	Dec. 26	Hamilton	05	02	05
Mungar, Jonathan(C)	1801	Dec. 26	Hamilton	05	02	04
Munger, Warren(A)	1815	July 29	Montgomery	05	08	03
Munn, James(C)	1806	Oct. 07	Warren	11	02	22
Munpeck, Jonas(A)	1837	March 28	Montgomery	01	13	03
Munroe, Charles(C)	1802	Dec. 31	Hamilton	04	04	13
Munsell, Leander(C)	1812	Aug. 08	Virginia	12	01	01
Munsell, Leander(C)	1817	Dec. 10	Miami	12	02	19
Munthaw, Ephraim(C)	1814	May 27	Greene	09	05	25
Murdick, Jesse H.(A)	1824	Feb. 25	Miami	05	07	24
Murdick, Jesse H.(E)	1823	Aug. 22	Randolph(Ind	14	20	09
Murdock, James(B)	1814	Aug. 20	Butler	02	11	23
Murphey, Benjamin(B)	1837	Feb. 13	Darke	01	17	12
Murphey, Caleb(A)	1835	Oct. 16	Warren	08	01	02
Murphey, Eli(B)	1835	Dec. 30	Switzerland	02	02	15
Murphey, James(C)	1806	Jan. 08	Ross	14	02	07
Murphey, Jerry(B)	1815	Oct. 03	Dearborn(Ind	01	06	10
Murphey, John(A)	1805	May 22	Butler	03	05	13
Murphey, John(A)	1832	Sept. 26	Darke	02	13	21
Murphey, John(A)	1836	Nov. 04	Darke	02	13	33
Murphey, John(C)	1806	Jan. 08	Ross	14	02	07
Murphey, Robert(B)	1834	Jan. 30	Darke	01	17	13
Murphey, Robert(B)	1836	June 07	Randolph(Ind	01	17	13
Murphey, Samuel(A)	1806	Oct. 22	Hamilton	04	03	32
Murphey, William(A)	1806	July 14	Hamilton	01	02	09
Murphey, William(B)	1835	Aug. 17	Dearborn(Ind	03	04	21
Murphy, Amos(E)	1837	Feb. 21	Wayne(Ind)	14	20	06
Murphy, James(C)	1811	April 09	Pickaway	14	02	07
Murphy, Jas.(A)	1829	Jan. 24	Logan	08	02	27
Murphy, Jas.(A)	1829	Jan. 24	Logan	08	02	27
Murphy, Jas.(A)	1829	Jan. 24	Logan	08	02	34
Murphy, Jno.(A)	1829	Jan. 24	Logan	08	02	27
Murphy, Jno.(A)	1829	Jan. 24	Logan	08	02	27
Murphy, Jno.(A)	1829	Jan. 24	Logan	08	02	34
Murphy, John(A)	1804	Sept. 24	Montgomery	04	04	06
Murphy, John(A)	1817	Sept. 01	Miami	05	07	13
Murphy, John(C)	1811	April 09	Pickaway	14	02	07
Murphy, John(E)	1814	Oct. 22	Butler	12	14	19
Murphy, Joshua(E)	1811	Nov. 02	Warren	14	17	18
Murphy, Miles(E)	1815	Feb. 03	Wayne(Ind)	13	17	28
Murphy, Samuel(A)	1812	Dec. 29	Butler	04	03	30
Murphy, Samuel(B)	1826	Aug. 01	Franklin(Ind	01	10	21
Murray, Abraham(A)	1808	Feb. 25	Miami	01	07	24
Murray, Abraham(A)	1815	Oct. 09	Butler	01	10	29
Murray, Abraham(A)	1816	Sept. 30	Butler	02	10	08
Murray, Abraham(A)	1817	Sept. 29	Butler	02	12	17
Murray, Abraham(A)	1821	Sept. 08	Darke	01	10	29
Murray, Andrew(E)	1836	Feb. 06	Franklin(Ind	12	12	23
Murray, Arnold(E)	1831	Sept. 27	Franklin(Ind	12	12	26
Murray, Arnold(E)	1836	Jan. 22	Franklin(Ind	12	12	23
Murray, Arnold(E)	1836	Jan. 22	Franklin(Ind	12	12	24
Murray, Coburn(E)	1835	Oct. 20	Franklin(Ind	12	12	29
Murray, Elam(B)	1814	Feb. 05	Butler	02	10	26
Murray, Elam(B)	1814	March 16	Butler	02	10	26
Murray, Jabez(B)	1834	Nov. 07	Maryland	01	16	21
Murray, Jabez(B)	1834	Nov. 07	Maryland	01	16	15
Murray, Jabez(E)	1834	Nov. 07	Maryland	15	19	31
Murray, Jabez(E)	1834	Nov. 07	Maryland	15	19	32
Murray, Jacob(A)	1831	Dec. 08	Miami	04	09	28
Murray, James(A)	1818	Jan. 02	Butler	01	11	10
Murray, James(B)	1817	Oct. 29	Pennsylvania	02	03	21
Murray, James(B)	1836	Jan. 19	Dearborn(Ind	02	06	23
Murray, John(E)	1838	Sept. 20	Maryland	15	19	19
Murray, Malcolm(A)	1838	May 21	Cincinnati	02	13	01

235

PURCHASER	YEAR	DATE	RESIDENCE	R	T	S
Murray, Malcolm(A)	1838	May 21	Cincinnati	02	13	17
Murray, Malcolm(A)	1838	May 21	Cincinnati	02	13	08
Murray, Malcolm(A)	1838	May 21	Cincinnati	01	13	01
Murray, Mungo(C)	1816	Aug. 23	New York	08	06	12
Murray, Mungo(C)	1817	June 26	Madison	08	07	35
Murray, Mungo(C)	1825	March 21	Clark	09	06	08
Murray, Thomas Price(E)	1835	Oct. 12	Maryland	15	20	32
Murray, Thomas(A)	1814	Nov. 18	Preble	02	06	09
Murray, Thomas(A)	1818	Sept. 01	Preble	02	09	18
Murray, William(E)	1816	Aug. 22	Adams	13	17	08
Murray, William(E)	1835	March 10	Wayne(Ind)	12	17	24
Murray, William(E)	1838	Sept. 20	Maryland	15	19	19
Murrey, Catharine(A)	1832	Feb. 13	Miami	05	07	10
Murrey, David(A)	1832	Feb. 13	Miami	05	07	04
Murrey, Elizabeth(A)	1832	Feb. 13	Miami	05	07	09
Murrey, John(A)	1831	Dec. 19	Miami	05	07	04
Murrey, John(A)	1837	March 01	Miami	03	11	22
Murrey, John(A)	1837	March 01	Miami	03	12	34
Murrey, Samuel(A)	1832	Feb. 13	Miami	05	07	03
Murrey, William(A)	1806	Feb. 28	Butler	02	04	26
Murrey, William(A)	1806	Feb. 28	Butler	02	04	35
Murrey, William(A)	1806	Feb. 28	Butler	02	04	28
Murrill, Nathan(C)	1814	April 07	Warren	03	05	08
Murry, Chas.(A)	1815	June 17	Miami	06	07	21
Musgrave, Eli(B)	1830	Jan. 25	Dearborn(Ind	02	05	07
Musgrave, John H.(B)	1817	Aug. 06	Dearborn(Ind	02	05	18
Musgrave, Moses(B)	1816	Nov. 02	Clermont	02	05	20
Musgrave, Moses(B)	1818	Feb. 05	Dearborn(Ind	03	06	10
Musselman, John(A)	1814	April 18	Montgomery	04	05	26
Musselman, Martin(A)	1823	June 09	Pennsylvania	04	06	20
Musselman, Martin(A)	1823	June 09	Pennsylvania	04	06	17
Mussleman, John(A)	1807	June 08	Montgomery	05	04	31
Myer, George(A)	1804	July 09	Montgomery	05	02	09
Myer, Henry(A)	1804	Aug. 13	Montgomery	04	05	18
Myers, Abraham(B)	1810	May 26	Dearborn(Ind	01	11	23
Myers, Andrew(B)	1806	Sept. 13	Hamilton	01	10	07
Myers, Christian(A)	1803	Oct. 29	Montgomery	05	03	20
Myers, Christopher(A)	1811	Nov. 06	Preble	03	07	02
Myers, Christopher(A)	1823	Feb. 26	Preble	03	07	01
Myers, David(A)	1803	Oct. 24	Montgomery	05	03	19
Myers, Frederick(B)	1825	June 04	Hamilton	03	07	03
Myers, George(A)	1816	Jan. 24	Preble	02	09	23
Myers, George(A)	1816	Jan. 24	Preble	02	10	26
Myers, George(A)	1816	Feb. 29	Preble	02	10	22
Myers, George(A)	1816	May 14	Darke	02	10	22
Myers, George(A)	1816	Aug. 21	Darke	02	11	35
Myers, George(A)	1816	Oct. 15	Montgomery	05	10	33
Myers, Isaac(A)	1803	Sept. 14	Montgomery	04	03	02
Myers, Jacob(B)	1816	March 01	Hamilton	02	03	22
Myers, James W.(C)	1828	Jan. 12	Hamilton	11	02	03
Myers, Joel(B)	1834	Dec. 11	Switzerland	02	03	34
Myers, John(A)	1811	Sept. 25	Virginia	03	04	06
Myers, John(A)	1829	March 26	Hamilton	01	02	06
Myers, John(A)	1830	June 12	Darke	04	09	29
Myers, John(A)	1836	Oct. 25	Hamilton	01	15	23
Myers, John(A)	1836	Oct. 25	Hamilton	01	15	24
Myers, John(A)	1836	Nov. 01	Hamilton	01	15	24
Myers, John(A)	1837	March 01	Hamilton	02	14	21
Myers, John(A)	1837	March 01	Hamilton	02	14	27
Myers, John(A)	1838	May 21	Butler	02	14	24
Myers, John(B)	1806	June 30	Butler	01	11	36
Myers, John(B)	1808	Jan. 13	Dearborn(Ind	02	12	24
Myers, John(B)	1809	May 09	Dearborn(Ind	01	11	23
Myers, John(E)	1811	Oct. 25	Wayne(Ind)	14	14	07
Myers, John(E)	1811	Oct. 25	Wayne(Ind)	14	15	32
Myers, Jonathan(B)	1815	Aug. 21	Butler	02	03	28
Myers, Joseph(A)	1822	Jan. 29	Preble	03	07	01
Myers, Joseph(C)	1813	June 18	Scioto	11	04	19
Myers, Michael(A)	1802	April 07	Maryland	05	03	27

PURCHASER	YEAR	DATE	RESIDENCE	R	T	S
Myers, Michael(A)	1804	Sept. 24	Montgomery	05	03	30
Myers, Michael(A)	1804	Sept. 24	Montgomery	05	03	31
Myers, Peter(E)	1837	Feb. 04	Preble	13	21	35
Myers, Robert(B)	1814	Jan. 01	Dearborn(Ind	01	07	29
Myers, Symon(B)	1816	Oct. 01	Hamilton	02	03	29
Myers, William(A)	1836	Oct. 25	Hamilton	01	15	14
Myers, William(B)	1816	Oct. 01	Hamilton	02	03	27
Myres, John Jr.(B)	1838	May 21	Switzerland	02	03	18
Myres, John Jr.(B)	1838	Sept. 03	Switzerland	02	03	18
Nafe, Joseph(A)	1818	Sept. 26	Preble	02	09	02
Nafe, Joseph(A)	1818	Sept. 26	Preble	02	09	02
Nagel, Frederick(B)	1833	June 26	Cincinnati	03	08	14
Nagley, Philip(A)	1801	Nov. 09	Kentucky	05	02	18
Nagligh, Henry(A)	1815	Jan. 20	Preble	03	07	09
Nail, George(A)	1807	April 15	Montgomery	05	06	25
Nail, William Senior(A)	1806	May 22	Montgomery	05	06	35
Nail, William(A)	1804	Dec. 05	Montgomery	05	06	04
Naman, John(C)	1805	May 29	Champaign	11	04	30
Nations, Isaac(A)	1819	July 07	Preble	03	07	02
Nattier, Charles(B)	1804	Sept. 18	Cincinnati	01	05	32
Nave, Abraham(A)	1806	March 26	Montgomery	01	08	36
Nave, Abraham(A)	1806	March 26	Montgomery	01	08	25
Nave, Abraham(B)	1806	March 26	Montgomery	02	12	14
Nave, Abraham(B)	1806	March 26	Montgomery	02	12	10
Nave, Jacob(A)	1806	March 26	Montgomery	01	08	36
Nave, Jacob(A)	1806	March 26	Montgomery	01	08	20
Nawman, Christian(C)	1807	Jan. 08	Champaign	11	04	30
Nayleigh, Henry(A)	1818	Sept. 21	Preble	03	07	09
Neal, Benj'n.(A)	1822	March 01	Miami	04	09	27
Neal, Caleb(A)	1815	Dec. 30	Miami	05	06	24
Neal, Caleb(A)	1832	Jan. 13	Darke	02	11	14
Neal, Dan'l.(C)	1826	Nov. 21	Shelby	13	02	35
Neal, Daniel(C)	1816	July 05	Champaign	12	03	36
Neal, George(A)	1815	Jan. 21	Miami	02	11	14
Neal, George(A)	1828	Dec. 05	Indiana	04	07	27
Neal, Henry(A)	1807	July 14	Miami	06	04	31
Neal, Henry(A)	1817	Nov. 13	Miami	04	08	03
Neal, John(E)	1811	Oct. 23	Franklin(Ind	13	11	03
Neal, Thomas(E)	1814	Dec. 20	Franklin(Ind	12	15	26
Neal, Thos. Douglass(E)	1833	Sept. 10	Wayne(Ind)	13	18	24
Neal, William(A)	1806	July 15	Butler	01	08	08
Neal, William(A)	1836	Oct. 01	Miami	02	15	23
Neal, William(C)	1824	Oct. 21	Clark	10	02	11
Nealeigh, John(A)	1831	May 17	Darke	03	08	17
Nealeigh, John(A)	1822	Aug. 23	Preble	03	08	17
Nearn, John(A)	1818	Nov. 21	Warren	02	08	06
Neeley, Thomas(B)	1814	Aug. 04	Ind.Territory	02	14	36
Neff, Abraham(A)	1815	April 11	Preble	01	08	02
Neff, Adam(A)	1813	Jan. 22	Montgomery	06	03	34
Neff, David(A)	1831	July 05	Montgomery	04	06	05
Neff, Jacob(A)	1809	Aug. 21	Pennsylvania	05	06	21
Neff, Jacob(A)	1813	April 10	Montgomery	03	04	10
Neff, John Senr.(A)	1812	May 23	Preble	03	04	05
Neff, John Senr.(A)	1812	July 02	Preble	03	04	06
Neff, John(A)	1802	May 24	N. W. Terr.	06	02	11
Neff, John(A)	1802	May 24	N. W. Terr.	06	02	15
Neff, John(A)	1805	Dec. 13	Montgomery	03	05	19
Neff, John(A)	1814	Aug. 13	Preble	03	04	07
Neff, John(E)	1834	Dec. 20	Randolph(Ind	14	20	34
Neff, Orange Hide(E)	1836	Jan. 25	Rush(Ind)	11	12	12
Neff, William(E)	1836	Dec. 10	Cincinnati	12	12	06
Neff, William(E)	1836	Dec. 10	Cincinnati	12	12	11
Neff, William(E)	1836	Dec. 10	Cincinnati	12	12	13
Neff, William(E)	1836	Dec. 15	Cincinnati	11	12	23
Neff, William(E)	1836	Dec. 15	Cincinnati	11	12	25
Neff, William(E)	1836	Dec. 15	Cincinnati	11	12	26
Neff, William(E)	1836	Dec. 15	Cincinnati	11	12	35
Neff, William(E)	1836	Dec. 15	Cincinnati	11	12	36
Neff, William(E)	1836	Dec. 15	Cincinnati	12	12	25

PURCHASER	YEAR	DATE	RESIDENCE	R	T	S
Neff, William(E)	1836	Dec. 15	Cincinnati	12	12	30
Neff, William(E)	1836	Dec. 15	Cincinnati	13	12	07
Neff, William(E)	1836	Dec. 15	Cincinnati	13	12	17
Neff, William(E)	1836	Dec. 15	Cincinnati	13	12	18
Neff, William(E)	1840	Aug. 01	Hamilton	12	11	35
Neher, John(C)	1817	June 17	Champaign	10	04	20
Neher, John(C)	1818	Nov. 11	Clark	10	03	10
Neher, Martin(C)	1818	March 30	Clark	09	03	06
Neiper, Joseph(A)	1818	Aug. 26	Miami	05	09	33
Neiper, Joseph(A)	1821	March 05	Miami	05	08	04
Neithercutt, Moses(A)	1815	Dec. 12	Preble	02	06	11
Neithercutt, William Jnr.(A)	1818	April 11	Preble	02	09	02
Neithercutt, Wm.(A)	1822	Feb. 13	Preble	02	09	12
Nelson, Adam(A)	1807	Sept. 26	Hamilton	01	04	20
Nelson, Adam(B)	1807	Sept. 12	Hamilton	01	09	24
Nelson, Adam(B)	1813	Aug. 24	Butler	01	10	31
Nelson, Adam(B)	1817	Oct. 06	Franklin(Ind	02	08	09
Nelson, Charles(B)	1815	March 21	Switzerland	02	02	24
Nelson, Daniel(A)	1837	March 01	Butler	02	14	06
Nelson, David(E)	1814	Nov. 28	Franklin(Ind	12	11	24
Nelson, Isaac(A)	1817	Aug. 29	Pennsylvania	01	02	06
Nelson, Jno.(B)	1814	Feb. 17	Dearborn(Ind	01	02	33
Nelson, John(A)	1812	April 15	Preble	01	07	31
Nelson, John(B)	1814	March 23	Hamilton	03	03	24
Nelson, John(E)	1834	Sept. 18	Randolph(Ind	14	19	08
Nelson, Jos.(B)	1814	July 16	Dearborn(Ind	01	02	31
Nelson, Joseph(A)	1807	March 02	Hamilton	01	07	31
Nelson, Joseph(A)	1812	April 15	Preble	01	07	31
Nelson, Joseph(B)	1806	Aug. 25	Hamilton	01	10	18
Nelson, Joseph(B)	1813	Nov. 06	Preble	01	12	28
Nelson, Joseph(B)	1814	Feb. 17	Dearborn(Ind	01	02	33
Nelson, Nathan(B)	1815	March 21	Switzerland	02	02	24
Nelson, Sacker(B)	1815	Dec. 22	Cincinnati	01	07	33
Nelson, Thomas(B)	1837	Oct. 14	Dearborn(Ind	03	06	36
Nelson, William(A)	1837	March 01	Butler	02	14	05
Nelson, Wm.(B)	1813	April 12	Butler	01	09	05
Nemann, Jno. Barnet(E)	1837	Nov. 20	Cincinnati	11	11	13
Nepper, Jacob(A)	1836	Nov. 19	Stark	03	11	03
Nesbet, James Irwin(A)	1802	Jan. 04	Pennsylvania	05	02	06
Nesbet, James Irwin(A)	1806	Feb. 06	Montgomery	03	06	17
Nesbet, James Irwin(A)	1806	Feb. 06	Montgomery	03	06	26
Nesbet, Thomas(A)	1815	Jan. 06	Preble	03	06	26
Nesbit, James I.(A)	1806	Sept. 06	Montgomery	03	06	26
Nesbit, James I.(A)	1811	April 09	Preble	03	06	33
Nesbit, James I.(A)	1811	April 09	Preble	03	06	33
Nesbit, James I.(A)	1811	June 22	Preble	03	06	22
Nesbit, James I.(A)	1811	June 22	Preble	03	06	22
Nesbit, James Irwin(A)	1804	Sept. 25	Montgomery	05	03	31
Nesbit, James Irwin(A)	1804	Nov. 06	Montgomery	05	03	31
Nesbit, James Irwin(A)	1805	Aug. 20	Montgomery	03	06	20
Nesbit, James Irwin(A)	1805	Aug. 20	Montgomery	03	06	20
Nesbit, James Irwin(A)	1806	Sept. 06	Ohio	03	06	35
Nesbit, James Irwin(A)	1805	July 15	Montgomery	03	06	35
Nesbit, James Irwin(A)	1805	July 15	Montgomery	03	06	33
Nesbit, James J.(A)	1810	Dec. 12	Preble	03	06	33
Nesbit, James J.(A)	1812	Nov. 13	Preble	03	06	28
Nesbit, James J.(A)	1813	Jan. 26	Preble	03	06	22
Nesbit, James J.(A)	1814	Dec. 10	Preble	03	06	28
Nesbit, James J.(A)	1816	Aug. 01	Preble	03	06	33
Nesbit, Jeremiah(C)	1814	Jan. 18	Kentucky	12	01	20
Nesbit, John(A)	1817	Nov. 15	Pennsylvania	05	08	04
Nesbit, John(A)	1818	Sept. 12	Kentucky	06	07	06
Nesbit, Robert(B)	1836	June 08	Switzerland	02	03	36
Nesbit, Thomas(A)	1807	Aug. 21	Montgomery	03	06	28
Nesbit, Thomas(A)	1812	Nov. 13	Preble	03	06	28
Nesbit, Thomas(A)	1816	Aug. 01	Preble	03	06	33
Nesbit, William(A)	1804	Nov. 06	Pennsylvania	05	04	10
Nesbit, William(A)	1805	Sept. 05	Montgomery	03	06	17
Nesbitt, Andrew(E)	1836	Nov. 04	Randolph(Ind	14	20	24

PURCHASER	YEAR	DATE	RESIDENCE	R	T	S
Nesbitt, William(A)	1814	April 16	Preble	03	06	35
Nestar, Philip(E)	1837	Sept. 09	Cincinnati	14	20	12
Neutrop, William(E)	1836	Oct. 21	Cincinnati	12	10	08
Nevill, Henry(C)	1814	Aug. 16	Piqua	11	05	14
Newby, Jonah(B)	1808	Jan. 13	Dearborn(Ind	01	13	03
Newby, William(A)	1813	June 08	Preble	02	06	07
Newcob, William(B)	1815	Feb. 14	Dearborn(Ind	01	07	08
Newcom, Ethan(C)	1818	April 30	Champaign	13	04	22
Newcom, George(C)	1806	Nov. 13	Montgomery	09	02	13
Newcom, William(C)	1804	Dec. 31	Montgomery	07	02	27
Newcomb, Daniel(C)	1813	April 14	Champaign	12	05	28
Newcomb, Daniel(C)	1813	April 14	Champaign	12	05	27
Newcomb, Daniel(C)	1813	April 14	Champaign	12	05	34
Newcomb, Daniel(C)	1814	March 30	Champaign	12	02	25
Newcomb, George(C)	1801	Dec. 31	Hamilton	07	?	27
Newcomb, William(B)	1815	Feb. 14	Dearborn(Ind	01	07	08
Newcomer, Peter(A)	1804	Sept. 15	Hamilton	01	01	09
Newcomer, Peter(B)	1818	Sept. 12	Hamilton	03	06	27
Newell, Benjamin(C)	1806	Jan. 08	Ross	13	03	12
Newell, Benjamin(C)	1810	Nov. 12	Champaign	13	05	22
Newell, Hugh(C)	1813	April 12	Champaign	13	03	20
Newell, Hugh(C)	1817	Sept. 05	Champaign	13	04	11
Newell, Hugh(C)	1827	June 21	Logan	13	04	11
Newell, Hugh(C)	1827	Aug. 23	Logan	13	04	11
Newell, Hugh(E)	1814	Feb. 22	Champaign	13	03	14
Newell, John(C)	1810	April 11	Champaign	13	05	28
Newell, John(C)	1816	Sept. 20	Champaign	13	05	26
Newell, John(C)	1818	Feb. 25	Logan	13	04	10
Newell, John(C)	1820	April 05	Champaign	13	04	27
Newell, Joseph Ogden(A)	1832	March 24	Preble	01	10	25
Newell, Saml.(C)	1815	July 08	?	13	05	22
Newell, Saml.(C)	1815	Sept. 11	Champaign	13	04	12
Newell, Saml.(C)	1815	Sept. 11	Champaign	13	04	12
Newell, Samuel(C)	1806	Sept. 13	Kentucky	13	05	19
Newell, Samuel(C)	1813	March 02	Champaign	13	05	28
Newell, Samuel(C)	1815	Jan. 30	Champaign	14	03	04
Newell, Samuel(C)	1815	April 08	Champaign	13	04	06
Newell, Samuel(C)	1815	June 17	Champaign	13	05	36
Newell, Samuel(C)	1816	Nov. 14	Champaign	13	04	12
Newell, Thomas(C)	1808	Sept. 07	Kentucky	13	05	28
Newell, Thomas(C)	1809	July 03	Champaign	13	04	22
Newell, Thomas(C)	1813	Sept. 14	Champaign	13	05	28
Newell, Thomas(C)	1813	Dec. 15	Champaign	13	05	28
Newell, William(C)	1806	Sept. 13	Kentucky	12	05	30
Newell, William(C)	1807	March 26	Champaign	13	05	33
Newell, William(C)	1813	April 14	Champaign	13	05	33
Newell, William(C)	1813	Sept. 14	Champaign	13	05	33
Newhouse, James(E)	1813	Oct. 04	Franklin(Ind	12	13	10
Newhouse, Samuel(E)	1814	Aug. 16	Franklin(Ind	12	13	08
Newill, Samuel(C)	1815	April 08	Champaign	13	04	05
Newland, Harrod(E)	1814	March 10	Kentucky	13	13	13
Newland, Harrod(E)	1814	March 10	Kentucky	13	13	14
Newland, Harrod(E)	1814	Dec. 21	Franklin(Ind	13	13	15
Newland, Harrod(E)	1814	Dec. 21	Franklin(Ind	13	13	09
Newland, James(E)	1814	April 02	Kentucky	13	13	08
Newlove, Joseph(C)	1826	oct. 14	Clark	09	06	29
Newman, Abner Jr.(C)	1825	Jan. 10	Clark	13	03	10
Newman, Abner(C)	1831	June 02	Logan	13	03	10
Newman, David(A)	1836	Oct. 03	Brown	02	13	27
Newman, John(E)	1833	Dec. 06	Franklin(Ind	13	12	21
Newman, John(E)	1835	Nov. 09	Franklin(Ind	13	12	22
Newman, Jonathan(A)	1813	Dec. 01	Montgomery	05	06	25
Newman, Joseph(A)	1805	June 26	Nor.Carolina	05	06	25
Newman, Thomas Senr.(C)	1815	Dec. 20	Champaign	10	04	13
Newman, Thomas(A)	1802	Feb. 16	Hamilton	05	06	34
Newman, Thomas(A)	1815	Aug. 21	Montgomery	05	06	22
Newman, Thomas(A)	1815	Aug. 21	Montgomery	03	10	25
Newman, Thos. T.(A)	1831	Feb. 04	Montgomery	06	03	05
Newman, William(A)	1805	Feb. 26	Montgomery	05	05	13

PURCHASER	YEAR	DATE	RESIDENCE	R	T	S
Newman, William(B)	1815	May 24	Montgomery	02	10	04
Newmann, Jno. Herman(A)	1837	Sept. 16	Cincinnati	03	13	27
Newmann, John Herman(A)	1837	Sept. 15	Cincinnati	03	13	27
Newport, David(A)	1817	Dec. 30	Warren	01	06	06
Newport, Jesse(A)	1807	July 11	Warren	06	05	20
Newport, Richard(A)	1814	Feb. 05	Butler	02	06	20
Newport, Thomas Jnr.(A)	1817	Dec. 30	Warren	01	06	07
Newport, Thomas(C)	1801	Dec. 31	Hamilton	08	03	31
Newton, George(B)	1814	Sept. 09	Hamilton	02	03	13
Newton, Henry(B)	1814	Oct. 21	Preble	01	15	25
Newton, James Jnr.(A)	1816	Feb. 06	Preble	02	06	27
Newton, James(A)	1804	May 02	Butler	02	06	33
Newton, James(A)	1804	Sept. 24	Butler	02	06	34
Newton, James(A)	1805	Feb. 02	Butler	02	06	33
Newton, James(A)	1805	April 05	Butler	02	06	33
Newton, James(A)	1812	Jan. 31	Preble	02	06	34
Newton, James(B)	1816	Aug. 16	Preble	01	15	25
Newton, Thomas(A)	1804	May 02	Butler	02	06	33
Newton, Thomas(A)	1804	Sept. 24	Butler	02	06	34
Newton, Thomas(A)	1805	Feb. 02	Butler	02	06	33
Newton, Thomas(A)	1805	April 05	Butler	02	06	33
Newton, Thomas(A)	1816	Feb. 06	Preble	02	06	27
Newton, Thomas(A)	1827	Sept. 27	Preble	02	07	05
Niccum, Jacob(A)	1819	Dec. 02	Preble	01	08	30
Nichels, Thomas(B)	1815	June 24	So. Carolina	02	11	21
Nichol, Thomas(A)	1805	Aug. 12	Hamilton	02	04	04
Nichol, Thomas(A)	1810	Dec. 12	Hamilton	02	04	04
Nicholas, Daniel(C)	1832	Jan. 25	Champaign	12	03	03
Nicholas, Henry(C)	1818	Jan. 16	Champaign	10	04	35
Nicholas, Jacob(C)	1831	Feb. 17	Clark	10	03	18
Nicholas, James Sen.(B)	1814	Nov. 26	Franklin(Ind	02	11	10
Nicholas, James(A)	1812	Dec. 12	Butler	01	03	35
Nicholas, John(C)	1806	Aug. 25	Warren	09	06	17
Nicholas, William(B)	1806	May 13	Dearborn(Ind	02	11	28
Nichols, Benj'n.(A)	1830	June 25	Champaign	08	02	27
Nichols, Benjamin(C)	1813	April 06	Champaign	13	04	32
Nichols, David(A)	1837	Jan. 27	New Jersey	01	13	20
Nichols, Enoch(E)	1822	Dec. 27	Clinton	14	18	17
Nichols, George(B)	1811	Dec. 23	Kentucky	02	04	14
Nichols, George(B)	1812	Jan. 25	Kentucky	02	04	14
Nichols, George(B)	1812	June 17	Dearborn(Ind	02	04	14
Nichols, George(B)	1814	July 04	Dearborn(Ind	02	04	14
Nichols, Henry(E)	1814	Oct. 11	Franklin(Ind	13	13	01
Nichols, James Senr.(E)	1812	July 11	So. Carolina	12	14	12
Nichols, John(C)	1831	July 02	Champaign	13	02	10
Nichols, John(C)	1832	Jan. 20	Shelby	13	02	10
Nichols, Jonathan(C)	1813	March 02	Hamilton	12	01	10
Nichols, Jonathan(C)	1816	Aug. 31	Hamilton	12	01	17
Nichols, Jonathan(C)	1819	March 12	Hamilton	13	02	25
Nichols, Lewis(B)	1836	April 12	Dearborn(Ind	02	05	33
Nichols, Lewis(B)	1837	March 01	Dearborn(Ind	02	04	05
Nichols, Perry(A)	1814	March 25	Butler	01	04	22
Nichols, Prosper(A)	1817	Sept. 04	Montgomery	05	06	13
Nichols, Prosper(C)	1813	March 02	Hamilton	12	01	10
Nichols, William(E)	1814	Oct. 11	Franklin(Ind	13	14	36
Nichols, William(E)	1836	Jan. 08	Rush(Ind)	11	12	24
Nicholson, James Taylor(E)	1837	March 01	Wayne(Ind)	13	18	01
Nicholson, John(B)	1818	June 23	Wayne(Ind)	01	15	35
Nicholson, John(C)	1806	Nov. 18	Champaign	09	06	23
Nicholson, John(C)	1812	April 15	Champaign	09	06	23
Nicholson, John(C)	1817	Aug. 01	Champaign	09	06	23
Nicholson, Sam'l.(A)	1828	Dec. 05	Miami	05	09	32
Nicholson, Samuel(A)	1816	Oct. 05	Miami	05	09	32
Nickals, Humphrey(C)	1813	Aug. 17	Champaign	09	05	02
Nickells, Nengeon(C)	1806	Oct. 04	Champaign	10	06	13
Nickells, Ningion(C)	1806	July 10	Champaign	11	06	34
Nickells, Ninian(C)	1817	June 27	Champaign	13	03	02
Nickells, Ninian(C)	1817	July 07	Champaign	13	03	02
Nickells, Sinian(C)	1811	Dec. 11	Champaign	10	06	13

PURCHASER	YEAR	DATE	RESIDENCE	R	T	S
Nickerson, Clark(E)	1834	Aug. 27	Clinton	13	19	20
Nickerson, Joseph C.(A)	1829	Dec. 09	Preble	02	09	33
Nickeson, David(B)	1832	March 01	Brown	02	03	23
Nickey, Christian(E)	1837	June 23	Greene	14	21	24
Nickles, James(B)	1806	June 25	Dearborn(Ind	02	11	28
Nickolas, Martin(A)	1836	July 16	Darke	03	11	21
Nickols, Malachi(B)	1829	June 01	Randolph(Ind	01	16	22
Nickols, Malachi(B)	1833	Dec. 21	Randolph(Ind	01	16	15
Nickols, Malachi(B)	1834	March 14	Randolph(Ind	01	16	15
Nickols, Malachi(E)	1836	Feb. 20	Randolph(Ind	15	18	06
Nickum, David(E)	1836	Jan. 27	Darke	15	21	22
Nicol, Mathew(E)	1815	Oct. 27	Butler	13	14	11
Nicoll, John(E)	1837	July 07	Cincinnati	14	20	02
Niebel, John(A)	1836	May 30	Montgomery	03	11	11
Niehaus, Gerhard Lucase(A)	1839	Jan. 22	Cincinnati	02	14	03
Nieman, Herman Hy.(B)	1838	April 24	Cincinnati	03	05	23
Nienaber, Gerhard Hy.(E)	1837	Aug. 28	Cincinnati	11	11	36
Nienaber, John Albert(E)	1837	May 01	Cincinnati	11	11	35
Nienaber, John Frederick(E)	1836	Nov. 15	Cincinnati	11	10	15
Nietfeld, John Arnold(A)	1838	Feb. 28	Cincinnati	03	13	30
Nieukirk, Jacob(B)	1815	April 28	Warren	02	10	14
Nighswonger, David(A)	1814	April 04	Montgomery	03	07	10
Nighswonger, Solomon(B)	1814	Jan. 26	Jefferson	02	03	36
Nighswonger, Solomon(B)	1815	July 20	Switzerland	02	02	32
Nihell, Lawrence(B)	1831	Aug. 09	Switzerland	03	03	13
Nihell, Lawrence(B)	1836	Feb. 03	Switzerland	03	03	13
Nikell, Laurence(C)	1813	Aug. 10	Champaign	12	05	07
Niles, Ezra(C)	1831	Aug. 16	Miami	12	04	26
Nisewanger, John(A)	1827	March 13	Greene	04	06	22
Niswonger, George(A)	1816	June 17	Montgomery	04	05	09
Niswonger, George(A)	1827	Oct. 18	Montgomery	04	06	10
Niswonger, George(A)	1830	June 17	Montgomery	03	08	32
Niswonger, John(A)	1805	Oct. 21	Virginia	04	06	23
Niswonger, John(A)	1818	Jan. 09	Montgomery	04	05	04
Niswonger, John(A)	1832	June 14	Montgomery	03	08	26
Niswonger, John(A)	1832	June 19	Montgomery	03	08	26
Nixan, Mirian(E)	1815	May 18	Nor.Carolina	14	17	29
Nixon, Allen(C)	1814	March 01	Warren	03	05	11
Nixon, Andrew(B)	1817	June 03	Belmont	01	11	33
Nixon, John Wilson(B)	1818	Feb. 03	Dearborn(Ind	02	04	19
Nixon, John Wilson(B)	1836	Feb. 26	Dearborn(Ind	02	04	19
Nixon, John(E)	1811	Nov. 07	Wayne(Ind)	12	16	23
Nixon, John(E)	1811	Nov. 16	Wayne(Ind)	12	16	23
Nixon, Samuel(A)	1806	Dec. 31	Belmont	01	04	30
Nixon, Samuel(B)	1818	Oct. 06	Virginia	01	15	04
Nixon, Samuel(E)	1836	Dec. 30	Wayne(Ind)	14	19	34
Nixon, Thomas(A)	1818	March 30	Miami	05	09	02
Nixon, Thomas(E)	1814	Aug. 12	Wayne(Ind)	14	16	06
Nixon, Thomas(E)	1816	April 25	Wayne(Ind)	13	17	14
Nixon, Thos.(E)	1813	Dec. 21	Wayne(Ind)	14	17	31
Nixon, William(B)	1817	June 13	Wayne(Ind)	01	15	04
Nixon, William(B)	1817	Dec. 31	Wayne(Ind)	01	15	04
Nobbi, John Hy.(E)	1837	Oct. 07	Cincinnati	11	11	24
Noble, David Senr.(E)	1816	Dec. 02	Franklin(Ind	13	13	13
Noble, James(A)	1811	Aug. 13	Franklin(Ind	01	04	35
Noble, James(B)	1814	Dec. 02	Franklin(Ind	02	09	30
Noble, James(B)	1834	June 26	Dearborn(Ind	03	05	01
Noble, James(E)	1817	Oct. 01	Franklin(Ind	14	14	30
Noble, Jno.(B)	1831	Aug. 10	Dearborn(Ind	03	05	01
Noble, Joseph(B)	1813	Oct. 25	Hamilton	03	02	11
Noble, Joseph(B)	1813	Nov. 13	Hamilton	03	03	35
Noble, Joseph(B)	1815	Sept. 11	Switzerland	03	03	24
Noble, Lewis(E)	1811	Oct. 23	Butler	13	14	26
Noble, William(B)	1831	Aug. 10	Dearborn(Ind	03	05	01
Noe, Robert(C)	1811	April 09	Champaign	11	05	35
Noe, Robert(C)	1811	May 10	Champaign	11	05	35
Noe, Robert(C)	1813	Aug. 10	Champaign	11	03	23
Noffsinger, Absalom(E)	1835	April 18	Darke	15	21	15
Noffsinger, Andrew(A)	1810	May 10	Darke	02	11	20

PURCHASER	YEAR	DATE	RESIDENCE	R	T	S
Noffsinger, Andrew(A)	1814	April 11	Darke	01	11	23
Noffsinger, Andrew(A)	1814	Dec. 08	Dearborn(Ind	02	11	09
Noffsinger, Charles(A)	1802	June 15	Hamilton	05	03	14
Noffsinger, Eli(B)	1831	Sept. 21	Darke	01	18	13
Noffsinger, Eli(B)	1834	June 24	Randolph(Ind	01	18	13
Noffsinger, John(A)	1818	June 16	Montgomery	01	11	24
Noftsinger, Andrew(A)	1817	June 25	Montgomery	02	11	29
Noggle, George Jr.(A)	1831	Aug. 22	Darke	01	10	12
Noggle, George(A)	1824	Oct. 18	Darke	01	10	15
Noggle, Jacob(A)	1818	June 29	Warren	04	05	30
Noland, Daniel(E)	1811	Oct. 29	Wayne(Ind)	12	16	14
Noland, Daniel(E)	1811	Nov. 20	Wayne(Ind)	13	15	10
Noland, Thomas(C)	1815	Jan. 21	Montgomery	11	01	02
Norcross, Reuben(E)	1818	June 08	New Jersey	13	18	13
Nordyke, Benajah(E)	1818	Nov. 12	Clinton	14	21	29
Norman, Christly(C)	1806	March 08	Champaign	12	04	31
Norman, John(C)	1805	Dec. 02	Champaign	11	04	34
Norris, John(B)	1804	Oct. 09	Dearborn(Ind	01	07	04
Norris, William(B)	1806	April 09	Dearborn(Ind	02	11	28
North, John(A)	1806	July 24	Montgomery	05	06	36
Northcut, Willis(C)	1801	Dec. 24	Hamilton	05	03	04
Northcut, Willis(C)	1804	Dec. 22	Warren	05	03	04
Norton, David(B)	1806	Sept. 02	Hamilton	02	13	25
Norton, Phelo(B)	1806	March 21	Dearborn(Ind	03	04	09
Null, Charles(C)	1801	Dec. 26	Hamilton	04	03	12
Null, Charles(C)	1803	Sept. 03	Warren	04	03	11
Null, Christopher(C)	1801	Dec. 21	Hamilton	04	03	12
Null, Henry(B)	1806	Nov. 21	Warren	01	14	11
Null, Henry(C)	1801	Dec. 21	Hamilton	05	02	07
Norris, Asa(A)	1818	Aug. 03	Preble	02	06	22
Norris, David(E)	1814	March 28	Franklin(Ind	13	13	05
Norris, George(B)	1814	Jan. 22	Franklin(Ind	02	11	33
Norris, James(A)	1814	Aug. 23	Warren	01	09	35
Norris, John C.(E)	1836	Dec. 10	Cincinnati	12	12	11
Norris, John(B)	1808	Jan. 19	Dearborn(Ind	02	09	19
Norris, John(E)	1811	Oct. 25	Franklin(Ind	14	14	19
Norris, John(E)	1814	Sept. 07	Franklin(Ind	13	13	12
Norris, John(E)	1815	April 14	Franklin(Ind	13	13	32
Norris, Richard(B)	1812	March 19	Dearborn(Ind	01	05	31
Norris, Richard(B)	1812	Oct. 27	Dearborn(Ind	01	05	31
Norris, Richard(B)	1813	Nov. 20	Dearborn(Ind	01	04	06
Norris, Sam'l.(A)	1828	Oct. 18	Hamilton	02	09	10
Norris, William(B)	1814	Sept. 30	Franklin(Ind	02	11	26
North, David(E)	1837	March 01	Kentucky	14	19	01
North, Lot(A)	1807	June 11	Kentucky	01	02	09
North, Lot(B)	1813	Dec. 07	Kentucky	01	03	21
North, Lyman(C)	1828	Nov. 08	Champaign	12	05	36
North, Singleton(A)	1832	Aug. 22	Darke	04	07	09
North, Thomas(B)	1814	May 31	New York	01	03	27
North, Thomas(E)	1837	March 01	Montgomery	14	19	02
Northcut, Willis(C)	1818	March 30	Miami	11	02	10
Northcutt, Willis(C)	1817	Dec. 02	Miami	11	02	06
Northup, Perin G.(B)	1815	Dec. 16	Dearborn(Ind	02	06	29
Norton, Elias(E)	1819	March 04	Wayne(Ind)	14	18	23
Norton, Elias(E)	1830	Jan. 09	Randolph(Ind	14	18	14
Norton, Jacob(B)	1818	Nov. 24	Cincinnati	02	06	14
Norton, Jacob(B)	1818	Dec. 24	Dearborn(Ind	02	06	14
Norton, James(A)	1815	Jan. 23	Hamilton	03	07	05
Norton, James(E)	1820	May 22	Wayne(Ind)	14	18	14
Norton, John(E)	1837	March 29	Cincinnati	12	11	23
Norton, Jonathan(C)	1828	May 26	Logan	14	03	26
Norton, Jonathan(C)	1831	Aug. 06	Logan	14	03	26
Norton, Nathan(C)	1807	April 09	Champaign	10	03	07
Norvell, Thos. Jefferson(E)	1832	June 01	Franklin(Ind	13	12	28
Norwell, Benj.(E)	1813	Sept. 14	Hamilton	13	12	15
Nostodt, George(E)	1836	Nov. 01	Wayne(Ind)	14	20	31
Nowlin, John(A)	1837	Jan. 17	Montgomery	01	12	03
Nowman, Christley(C)	1813	May 31	Champaign	12	04	31
Nowman, John(C)	1813	April 21	Champaign	11	04	30

PURCHASER	YEAR	DATE	RESIDENCE	R	T	S
Nowman, John(C)	1815	June 13	Champaign	12	04	25
Nowman, Thomas Senr.(C)	1810	Oct. 18	Champaign	12	02	06
Noyes, Israel(B)	1817	Dec. 26	Dearborn(Ind	02	06	20
Noyes, Israel(B)	1817	Dec. 26	Switzerland	02	06	17
Noyes, Israel(B)	1817	Dec. 26	Dearborn(Ind	02	06	17
Nugent, Charles(A)	1811	Dec. 11	Preble	01	07	23
Nugent, Jno.(B)	1814	March 28	Franklin(Ind	02	10	32
Nugent, Robert(E)	1816	April 04	Franklin(Ind	13	13	14
Nugent, William(E)	1816	April 04	Franklin(Ind	13	13	14
Nujent, Benjamin(B)	1811	Oct. 30	So. Carolina	02	10	28
Null, Henry(C)	1801	Dec. 30	Hamilton	04	03	12
Null, Henry(C)	1802	Dec. 30	Hamilton	05	02	10
Null, Michael(E)	1836	July 28	Fayette	12	13	36
Nurre, John Henry(E)	1836	Nov. 11	Cincinnati	12	10	05
Nusagh, John(A)	1805	July 31	Pennsylvania	05	04	20
Nutt, Adam((C)	1801	Dec. 29	Hamilton	06	02	25
Nutter, Benjamin(B)	1806	Dec. 02	Warren	01	12	33
Nutts, Frederick(A)	1805	Aug. 17	Montgomery	05	07	07
Nutts, Frederick(A)	1815	Feb. 27	Montgomery	01	09	34
Nutts, Frederick(A)	1819	Oct. 05	Warren	03	08	05
Nyswanger, Dan'l.(A)	1828	March 27	Darke	02	11	28
Nyswanger, Jonathan(A)	1830	Jan. 20	Darke	02	11	32
O'Dell, James(E)	1811	Oct. 24	Wayne(Ind)	13	17	29
O'Dell, James(E)	1811	Oct. 24	Wayne(Ind)	13	17	24
O'Dell, James(E)	1811	Nov. 09	Wayne(Ind)	13	17	24
O'Farrel, John(C)	1807	March 07	Cincinnati	12	05	07
O'Farrel, John(C)	1807	March 07	Cincinnati	12	05	07
O'Farrel, John(C)	1807	March 07	Cincinnati	12	05	07
O'Ferrall, Ignatius Kelley(A)	1832	Feb. 20	Miami	05	08	21
O'Ferrall, John(A)	1832	Feb. 20	Miami	05	08	21
O'Ferrall, John(A)	1836	Feb. 09	Miami	08	02	31
O'Ferrall, John(C)	1808	Nov. 07	Cincinnati	09	04	11
O'Ferrall, John(C)	1836	Feb. 09	Miami	13	03	33
O'Ferrel, John(C)	1807	March 07	Cincinnati	12	05	07
O'Neal, David(B)	1816	Aug. 29	Kentucky	02	02	02
O'Neal, John K.(B)	1816	Nov. 05	Kentucky	02	02	02
O'Neal, Michael(B)	1830	Nov. 27	Cincinnati	02	07	22
O'Neal, Thomas(A)	1815	Jan. 17	Warren	01	06	01
O'Neall, John K.(A)	1816	Sept. 06	Warren	04	09	32
O'Verdier, Francis(C)	1829	June 02	Clark	12	03	31
Oakes, Jacob(A)	1832	Aug. 04	Miami	04	07	05
Oathoudt, Isaac(B)	1831	July 05	Dearborn(Ind	03	06	21
Ocheltree, James(A)	1805	March 14	Kentucky	01	06	11
Ocks, Dan'l.(A)	1821	Aug. 15	Montgomery	05	05	19
Ocks, David(A)	1831	Aug. 04	Darke	04	08	19
Odell, Gabriel(B)	1817	Nov. 26	Franklin(Ind	01	16	36
Odell, Hiram(B)	1834	Feb. 12	Randolph(Ind	01	16	25
Odell, Isaac(E)	1814	Jan. 13	Franklin(Ind	13	14	25
Odell, James(E)	1835	Aug. 13	Randolph(Ind	14	18	12
Odell, John(B)	1818	June 24	Cincinnati	02	05	05
Odell, William(B)	1817	Nov. 27	Butler	01	15	02
Odell, William(B)	1824	Aug. 02	Wayne(Ind)	01	16	36
Odell, William(B)	1834	Feb. 12	Wayne(Ind)	01	16	25
Odell, Wittoes(E)	1836	June 08	Preble	14	19	23
Odle, Daniel(B)	1814	Aug. 30	Dearborn(Ind	02	05	27
Odle, William(E)	1836	Aug. 23	Randolph(Ind	14	21	18
Odle, William(E)	1836	Oct. 01	Randolph(Ind	14	21	19
Odum, David(E)	1814	March 12	Wayne(Ind)	12	16	11
Oeler, Simon(B)	1822	Oct. 28	Cincinnati	02	07	18
Offield, Lervis(B)	1815	Nov. 09	Dearborn(Ind	01	07	15
Ogan, Elias(E)	1836	Sept. 13	Wayne(Ind)	15	19	17
Ogan, Samuel(E)	1837	April 28	Wayne(Ind)	15	19	30
Ogden, Hezekiah(B)	1825	Feb. 21	Franklin(Ind	02	10	22
Ogden, Isaac A.(B)	1827	July 17	Union(Ind)	01	10	21
Ogle, Eli(B)	1831	Aug. 09	Switzerland	03	02	09
Ogle, Hieram(B)	1812	May 23	Jefferson	03	02	10
Ogle, Hierom(B)	1817	Aug. 01	Switzerland	03	02	10
Ogle, Hierom(B)	1825	May 16	Switzerland	03	03	15
Ogle, Hiram(B)	1816	April 29	Switzerland	03	03	15

243

PURCHASER	YEAR	DATE	RESIDENCE	R	T	S
Ogle, Hiram(B)	1815	April 11	Switzerland	03	03	17
Ogle, Robert(A)	1806	April 03	Butler	01	04	11
Ogle, William(A)	1803	Aug. 17	Butler	02	05	28
Ogle, William(B)	1813	Sept. 23	Butler	01	10	04
Ogle, William(B)	1813	Sept. 23	Butler	01	10	10
Ogle, William(B)	1813	Oct. 04	Butler	01	11	34
Ogle, William(B)	1813	Oct. 26	Butler	01	10	04
Oglivee, Joseph(B)	1815	May 29	Pennsylvania	02	04	25
Ohlman, John Henry(B)	1835	Nov. 02	Hamilton	01	07	06
Ohlman, John Henry(B)	1835	Nov. 02	Hamilton	02	07	01
Ohlman, John Hy.(E)	1836	Oct. 14	Cincinnati	11	10	26
Ohlman, John Hy.(E)	1836	Nov. 15	Cincinnati	12	10	19
Oldakens, Jacob(E)	1815	Jan. 23	Kentucky	13	16	32
Oldham, Azariah(B)	1831	Aug. 23	Dearborn(Ind	02	06	26
Oldham, James(B)	1815	Jan. 16	Franklin(Ind	02	12	33
Oldham, John(E)	1815	Jan. 16	Franklin(Ind	13	14	27
Oldham, Stephen(E)	1813	Oct. 13	Franklin(Ind	13	14	22
Oler, Adam(A)	1833	May 14	Preble	01	12	18
Oler, Adam(A)	1833	May 14	Preble	01	12	17
Oler, Adam(A)	1833	May 14	Preble	01	12	18
Oler, Henry(A)	1805	Nov. 19	Warren	04	03	08
Oler, Henry(E)	1814	Aug. 15	Montgomery	13	17	11
Oler, Isaac(A)	1837	Aug. 22	Darke	01	12	18
Oler, William(A)	1827	Oct. 16	Montgomery	01	12	15
Olinger, George(A)	1819	Nov. 06	Preble	04	07	02
Olinger, John(A)	1810	May 24	Montgomery	05	04	22
Oliver, Alexander Jnr.(C)	1818	Feb. 16	Miami	11	02	06
Oliver, Alexander Jr.(C)	1812	March 20	Marietta	11	02	30
Oliver, Alexander Jr.(C)	1812	March 20	Marietta	11	02	18
Oliver, Allen(A)	1812	Sept. 15	Warren	02	03	11
Oliver, David(B)	1817	Aug. 01	Franklin(Ind	02	09	11
Oliver, George(A)	1818	Dec. 03	Clermont	03	10	05
Oliver, George(A)	1832	Dec. 01	Darke	03	10	05
Oliver, James B.(A)	1806	March 21	Montgomery	03	05	36
Oliver, James B.(A)	1814	Jan. 14	Montgomery	04	05	02
Oliver, James B.(A)	1815	May 18	Montgomery	04	08	01
Oliver, Jeremiah(E)	1826	May 05	Union(Ind)	14	15	31
Oliver, John(C)	1814	April 23	Washington	12	02	19
Oliver, John(C)	1817	Oct. 11	Miami	11	02	06
Oliver, Nixon(B)	1815	Nov. 21	Franklin(Ind	01	09	32
Oliver, Richard(B)	1836	Jan. 28	Dearborn(Ind	02	05	04
Oliver, Thomas(C)	1813	Feb. 25	Champaign	09	06	27
Oliver, William(A)	1807	March 23	FortWayneInd	06	05	28
Oliver, William(A)	1818	Dec. 30	Clermont	03	10	04
Oliver, Wm.(C)	1816	July 06	Cincinnati	13	02	35
Ollentine, Richard(C)	1816	July 18	Greene	12	03	21
Olliam, William(A)	1822	March 26	Darke	01	10	13
Ollintine, Richard(C)	1814	Sept. 12	Champaign	08	03	03
Olmsted, Ebenezer(B)	1818	Jan. 27	Cincinnati	03	06	09
Olmsted, John S.(B)	1829	Dec. 09	Dearborn(Ind	03	06	09
Olson, Michael(A)	1812	Sept. 17	Cincinnati	01	04	36
Oltfather, Henry(A)	1810	Oct. 16	Pennsylvania	04	03	04
Oozias, Peter(A)	1804	Dec. 15	Nor.Carolina	02	08	12
Oppy, David(C)	1812	June 13	Champaign	11	06	34
Orbison, Henry(A)	1807	May 13	Miami	05	08	12
Orbison, Henry(C)	1807	May 29	Miami	11	01	12
Orbison, John(A)	1805	Aug. 13	Butler	06	05	34
Orbison, John(A)	1814	June 18	Virginia	05	10	30
Orbison, Robert(A)	1804	Jan. 02	Pennsylvania	03	03	31
Orbison, Robert(A)	1804	April 18	Pennsylvania	03	03	20
Orcutt, Joseph C.(A)	1817	Sept. 18	Darke	02	13	29
Orcutt, Joseph C.(E)	1837	Jan. 04	Warren	14	21	05
Ore, James(A)	1805	Dec. 04	Montgomery	06	05	07
Oren, Ephraim(E)	1836	Jan. 30	Clinton	13	19	25
Oren, Jacob Ladd(E)	1836	Feb. 17	Clinton	13	19	36
Orin, Absalom H.(E)	1836	Aug. 22	Randolph(Ind	13	19	24
Ormagost, Jacob(E)	1837	Feb. 13	Darke	15	19	19
Ormsby, Oliver(A)	1806	Dec. 03	Pennsylvania	01	01	06
Ormsby, Oliver(B)	1806	Dec. 03	Pennsylvania	01	04	08

PURCHASER	YEAR	DATE	RESIDENCE	R	T	S
Ormsby, Oliver(C)	1813	April 19	Pittsburgh	09	03	01
Ormsby, Oliver(C)	1813	April 19	Pittsburgh	08	04	33
Orr, Andrew(B)	1816	April 27	Franklin(Ind	01	10	28
Orr, Arthur(A)	1806	July 16	Hamilton	01	04	26
Orr, David(B)	1827	Aug. 28	Union(Ind)	01	10	15
Orr, George(A)	1807	Jan. 03	Kentucky	06	05	07
Orr, James(A)	1811	April 09	Miami	06	05	07
Orr, James(A)	1819	Feb. 06	Miami	06	05	07
Orr, John(B)	1827	Aug. 07	Union(Ind)	01	10	15
Orr, John(B)	1832	May 10	Switzerland	03	02	05
Orr, John(E)	1813	Sept. 06	Kentucky	12	14	17
Orr, Joseph(B)	1817	June 30	Switzerland	03	02	09
Orr, Joseph(B)	1817	June 30	Switzerland	03	02	05
Orr, Robert(A)	1807	Jan. 02	Clermont	06	05	30
Orr, Robert(A)	1807	July 03	Miami	06	05	07
Orr, Timothy(E)	1811	Dec. 05	Franklin(Ind	12	14	20
Orr, Zebulon(C)	1811	Sept. 09	Champaign	12	04	23
Orsborn, Caleb(B)	1832	May 23	Dearborn(Ind	01	06	09
Orsborn, John(C)	1817	Aug. 01	Champaign	09	06	03
Orsborn, Jonathan(E)	1812	Oct. 17	Franklin(Ind	13	11	07
Orsborn, Levi(C)	1811	Dec. 11	Champaign	11	05	30
Orsborn, Thomas(B)	1812	Jan. 03	Ind.Territry	01	09	08
Orsborn, William(C)	1815	Dec. 25	?	09	06	15
Orsbourn, Syms(C)	1801	Dec. 28	Hamilton	04	02	27
Ortman, Herman Henry(E)	1836	Nov. 11	Cincinnati	12	11	32
Osbon, James(B)	1818	Dec. 24	Franklin(Ind	02	10	15
Osbon, Thomas(E)	1822	Oct. 08	Union(Ind)	13	14	01
Osborn, Daniel(B)	1814	Jan. 04	Wayne(Ind)	01	13	31
Osborn, Daniel(B)	1814	March 11	Butler	02	10	25
Osborn, David(B)	1816	Nov. 01	Hamilton	02	05	17
Osborn, David(E)	1815	Sept. 07	Clinton	13	18	31
Osborn, Isaiah(E)	1827	Dec. 10	Wayne(Ind)	13	18	22
Osborn, Jesse(C)	1824	Oct. 18	Clark	09	06	08
Osborn, John Senr.(A)	1836	Oct. 13	Warren	03	12	07
Osborn, John(C)	1811	Nov. 27	Kentucky	10	05	17
Osborn, John(C)	1812	May 07	Kentucky	09	06	03
Osborn, John(C)	1813	April 02	Champaign	09	06	09
Osborn, Levi(C)	1812	March 23	Champaign	11	05	01
Osborn, Levi(C)	1812	Nov. 14	Champaign	11	05	15
Osborn, Levi(C)	1818	April 18	Clark	13	04	18
Osborn, Thomas(B)	1817	Aug. 25	Franklin(Ind	02	10	22
Osborn, Thomas(E)	1821	Oct. 26	Indiana	13	14	01
Osborn, William(C)	1812	Oct. 19	Champaign	09	06	09
Osborne, David(B)	1806	Dec. 22	Montgomery	01	13	27
Osborne, Thomas(B)	1808	Nov. 05	Kentucky	02	10	21
Osborne, William(C)	1817	Dec. 02	Champaign	09	06	09
Osbourn, David(B)	1817	Nov. 13	Dearborn(Ind	03	06	14
Osgood, Charles(B)	1815	Nov. 04	Cincinnati	02	06	01
Osgood, Charles(B)	1816	Sept. 07	Hamilton	01	06	31
Ostrander, William(B)	1817	July 26	Cincinnati	03	07	27
Oswald, Jacob(A)	1827	Dec. 14	Montgomery	04	06	21
Ott, Frances(A)	1805	Dec. 07	Montgomery	03	07	28
Ott, Frances(A)	1805	Dec. 07	Montgomery	03	07	29
Ott, Francis(A)	1805	Dec. 07	Montgomery	03	07	20
Ott, Francis(A)	1811	Jan. 28	Preble	03	07	19
Ott, George(A)	1817	Nov. 03	Maryland	03	11	13
Ott, Jacob(A)	1817	Nov. 03	Maryland	03	11	14
Ott, Thomas(A)	1819	Nov. 12	Maryland	03	07	08
Otta, Henry(E)	1836	Oct. 17	Cincinnati	11	10	14
Otto, Jacob(B)	1833	Nov. 12	Franklin(Ind	01	08	17
Oursler, Alexander(E)	1837	Jan. 30	Clark	14	19	12
Oursler, Alexander(E)	1837	Dec. 30	Clark	14	19	12
Oury, James(A)	1814	July 29	Cincinnati	01	01	07
Overby, Martin(A)	1820	Oct. 10	Ross	03	10	03
Overfield, Benj'm.(A)	1814	Aug. 01	Darke	02	11	09
Overhalser, Nancy(A)	1818	Oct. 15	Montgomery	04	05	34
Overhalser, Sam'l.(A)	1828	Jan. 05	Preble	01	08	23
Overhulser, David(A)	1814	Dec. 08	Virginia	02	06	13
Overly, Martin(A)	1820	Nov. 03	Ross	03	10	03

PURCHASER	YEAR	DATE	RESIDENCE	R	T	S
Overly, William(A)	1833	Jan. 29	Darke	03	10	11
Overly, Zachariah(B)	1835	Aug. 11	Darke	01	18	25
Overman, Cornelius(B)	1832	Jan. 16	Randolph(Ind	01	16	14
Overman, Demsey(B)	1808	Jan. 13	Highland	01	14	14
Overman, Eli(B)	1814	Dec. 13	Wayne(Ind)	01	16	33
Overman, Eli(E)	1812	March 19	Franklin(Ind	14	16	07
Overman, Eli(E)	1813	Aug. 23	Wayne(Ind)	14	17	34
Overman, Ephraim(B)	1807	June 26	Dearborn(Ind	01	13	04
Overman, Ephraim(B)	1813	April 14	Wayne(Ind)	01	13	04
Overman, Ephraim(B)	1814	Aug. 23	Wayne(Ind)	01	16	27
Overman, Ephraim(B)	1816	Nov. 09	?	01	16	14
Overman, Ephraim(B)	1827	June 28	Randolph(Ind	01	16	22
Overman, Isaac(E)	1836	Feb. 22	Randolph(Ind	15	18	06
Overman, Jason(B)	1830	March 30	Randolph(Ind	01	16	34
Overman, Jesse(B)	1824	June 09	Wayne(Ind)	01	15	03
Overman, Jesse(B)	1827	Aug. 09	Wayne(Ind)	01	15	03
Overman, Nathan Sr.(B)	1813	Aug. 10	Wayne(Ind)	01	13	03
Overman, Nathan(B)	1808	May 13	Dearborn(Ind	01	13	03
Overman, Nathan(B)	1815	Sept. 13	Wayne(Ind)	01	16	27
Overman, Nathan(E)	1811	Dec. 16	Wayne(Ind)	14	16	19
Overman, Reuben(E)	1813	Aug. 23	Wayne(Ind)	14	17	34
Overpeck, George(A)	1824	July 27	Butler	02	06	22
Overpeck, George(C)	1813	April 26	Champaign	10	03	03
Overpeck, Isaac(A)	1818	April 13	Butler	02	12	17
Overpeck, John(A)	1824	June 28	Preble	02	06	15
Overpeck, John(C)	1813	April 26	Champaign	10	03	04
Overpeck, Valentine(A)	1824	July 27	Butler	02	06	15
Overpeck, William(C)	1813	April 26	Champaign	10	03	03
Owen, Asa(A)	1805	June 08	Montgomery	05	05	23
Owen, Asa(A)	1806	April 24	Montgomery	05	05	26
Owen, Asa(A)	1806	April 24	Montgomery	05	05	26
Owen, Benjamin(A)	1805	June 03	Montgomery	06	02	06
Owen, Benjamin(A)	1805	June 03	Montgomery	05	04	01
Owen, Calvin(B)	1833	Jan. 05	Franklin(Ind	02	08	23
Owen, Calvin(B)	1836	Feb. 06	Franklin(Ind	02	08	23
Owen, Ephraim(A)	1805	June 03	Montgomery	05	04	01
Owen, Ephraim(A)	1805	July 04	Montgomery	05	04	01
Owen, George(E)	1831	July 05	Franklin(Ind	13	12	06
Owen, John K.(A)	1831	Feb. 04	Darke	03	08	25
Owen, Joseph(A)	1805	June 04	Montgomery	06	02	06
Owen, Sam'l. Dudley(E)	1834	Nov. 03	Franklin(Ind	13	12	06
Owens, Benjamin(A)	1805	May 22	Montgomery	06	02	06
Owens, Peter(A)	1805	April 29	Hamilton	01	02	04
Owens, Peter(A)	1805	Dec. 21	Hamilton	01	02	04
Owens, Warret(C)	1813	April 13	Champaign	11	05	03
Owens, William(C)	1804	Sept. 26	Greene	11	04	09
Owing, John(C)	1807	April 02	Champaign	11	06	33
Owings, John(B)	1836	Aug. 17	Kentucky	03	05	09
Owsley, Thomas(E)	1812	Aug. 25	Franklin(Ind	13	12	34
Owsley, Thomas(E)	1814	Jan. 17	Franklin(Ind	13	12	33
Oyler, Valentine(C)	1804	Dec. 31	Montgomery	07	02	21
Oyster, Jesse(E)	1837	May 24	Richland	14	21	01
Ozborn, Ambrose(B)	1830	June 11	Randolph(Ind	01	16	34
Ozborn, Ambrose(B)	1831	Nov. 21	Randolph(Ind	01	16	35
Ozbun, Dan'l.(E)	1827	Aug. 22	Randolph(Ind	14	18	08
Ozbun, Daniel(E)	1818	Jan. 12	Clinton	14	18	08
Ozbun, John(E)	1815	June 01	Clinton	14	18	08
Ozburn, John(A)	1818	Sept. 07	Greene	03	09	31
Ozias, Jacob(A)	1823	March 15	Preble	03	06	09
Ozias, Jesse(A)	1831	Sept. 23	Darke	03	08	21
Ozias, Jesse(A)	1831	Sept. 23	Darke	03	08	28
Ozias, Jesse(A)	1831	Sept. 23	Darke	03	08	27
Ozias, John(A)	1804	Aug. 01	Montgomery	03	06	03
Ozias, John(A)	1804	Aug. 01	Montgomery	03	06	10
Paddack, Henry(A)	1829	Feb. 02	Preble	01	08	30
Paddock, Ebenezer(A)	1801	April 27	Hamilton	03	03	36
Paddock, Ebenezer(B)	1807	Sept. 28	Butler	01	08	20
Paddock, Ebenezer(C)	1814	Feb. 21	Greene	08	06	24
Paddock, Henry(A)	1806	Dec. 29	Butler	01	08	32

PURCHASER	YEAR	DATE	RESIDENCE	R	T	S
Paddock, Henry(A)	1811	Aug. 14	Preble	01	07	04
Paddock, William(A)	1807	Feb. 13	Butler	02	08	30
Page, Daniel(A)	1806	June 17	Butler	03	03	04
Page, John(B)	1817	July 26	Franklin(Ind	02	08	24
Page, Jonathan(C)	1806	May 23	Champaign	10	06	33
Page, Jonathan(C)	1807	March 02	?	10	06	33
Page, Jonathan(C)	1811	Aug. 13	Champaign	10	06	33
Page, Jonathan(C)	1812	April 15	Champaign	10	06	33
Page, Jonathan(C)	1828	Oct. 02	Clark	14	02	01
Page, Jonathan(C)	1828	Oct. 18	Clark	14	02	01
Pain, Stephen J.(B)	1827	Nov. 26	Dearborn(Ind	02	05	06
Pain, Stephen J.(B)	1829	May 25	Dearborn(Ind	03	06	01
Pain, Stephen(A)	1815	March 07	Warren	03	04	27
Pain, William(E)	1832	July 10	Franklin(Ind	12	11	18
Paine, Isaac(A)	1806	June 27	Butler	01	07	05
Paine, Samuel(A)	1806	June 27	Butler	01	07	10
Paine, Samuel(A)	1806	June 27	Butler	01	08	33
Paine, Stephen Johnson(B)	1817	Nov. 24	Dearborn(Ind	03	07	36
Painter, George Jr.(A)	1836	June 22	Darke	01	15	23
Painter, John(A)	1813	Nov. 26	Warren	02	09	12
Painter, John(A)	1831	July 18	Preble	02	09	02
Palmer, Dan'l.(A)	1828	Feb. 13	Miami	01	10	15
Palmer, Daniel(B)	1808	Jan. 13	Dearborn(Ind	01	11	18
Palmer, David(B)	1817	June 16	Cincinnati	02	06	03
Palmer, John(B)	1815	Nov. 03	Hamilton	02	06	34
Palmer, Joshua(B)	1807	June 18	Dearborn(Ind	02	11	11
Palmer, Joshua(B)	1814	Nov. 11	Franklin(Ind	02	11	11
Palmer, Mason(E)	1833	Sept. 19	Franklin(Ind	11	12	36
Palmerton, Ichabod(B)	1814	Dec. 03	Hamilton	02	05	01
Palser, Samuel(C)	1815	Jan. 18	Hamilton	12	01	14
Panzler, Abraham(A)	1817	July 02	Preble	01	08	10
Parcell, Richard Senr.(A)	1819	Dec. 08	Warren	04	05	18
Pardington, Thomas(C)	1817	July 31	Montgomery	09	06	28
Pardun, Walter(B)	1836	March 09	Dearborn(Ind	02	06	31
Parent, George(A)	1833	Dec. 31	Darke	01	13	23
Parent, Joseph(A)	1831	June 04	Darke	02	11	21
Parent, Will'm.(A)	1829	June 29	Darke	01	10	10
Parent, William(A)	1831	Nov. 08	Darke	01	13	25
Parham, Peter(A)	1805	April 09	Montgomery	03	04	23
Parham, Peter(A)	1805	May 31	Montgomery	04	03	28
Parham, Peter(A)	1805	June 25	Butler	02	08	34
Parham, Peter(A)	1805	June 25	Butler	02	07	02
Parham, Peter(A)	1805	June 25	Butler	02	08	28
Parham, Peter(A)	1805	June 25	Butler	02	08	28
Parham, Zacheus(A)	1818	Jan. 06	Miami	05	06	11
Paris, Chas. C.(A)	1839	Jan. 09	Warren	02	15	34
Paris, George(E)	1814	Sept. 08	Wayne(Ind)	14	14	07
Paris, James(B)	1818	Feb. 03	Franklin(Ind	01	07	05
Paris, Lewis(A)	1837	Jan. 10	Warren	02	14	33
Paris, Wm. L.(A)	1839	Jan. 09	Warren	02	15	34
Park, Andrew(D)	1811	March 01	Ohio	02	02	11
Park, Joseph(A)	1806	Aug. 26	Warren	02	06	30
Park, Joseph(C)	1804	Sept. 03	Warren	04	02	08
Park, Micajah(B)	1812	Sept. 11	Dearborn(Ind	01	06	24
Park, Robert(A)	1806	Jan. 07	Montgomery	06	02	08
Park, Robert(C)	1801	Dec. 22	Hamilton	05	02	01
Park, Samuel(A)	1813	Dec. 15	Preble	01	07	25
Park, William(B)	1831	Aug. 10	Switzerland	03	03	33
Park, William(B)	1833	Dec. 10	Switzerland	03	03	33
Parke, Joseph(B)	1825	Feb. 22	Dearborn(Ind	01	06	21
Parke, Joseph(C)	1828	Feb. 23	Montgomery	13	02	19
Parke, Micajah(B)	1811	Jan. 05	Hamilton	02	09	28
Parke, Sam'l.(A)	1828	Dec. 09	Preble	01	07	08
Parker, Abraham(B)	1815	Sept. 02	Kentucky	02	03	27
Parker, Adrial(A)	1837	June 15	Hamilton	01	14	31
Parker, Benjm.(B)	1819	April 30	Wayne(Ind)	01	15	24
Parker, Hansel(B)	1815	Feb. 07	Hamilton	02	08	12
Parker, Hansel(B)	1815	Feb. 07	Hamilton	01	08	07
Parker, Henry(B)	1818	Nov. 23	Dearborn(Ind	03	05	23

PURCHASER	YEAR	DATE	RESIDENCE	R	T	S
Parker, Henry(B)	1836	Dec. 09	Dearborn(Ind	03	05	22
Parker, Isaac(A)	1805	March 15	Butler	03	03	10
Parker, Isaac(A)	1810	Dec. 12	Butler	03	03	02
Parker, Jacob(A)	1803	Oct. 06	Butler	03	05	03
Parker, Jacob(A)	1818	Feb. 14	Preble	01	12	34
Parker, James(E)	1813	Sept. 06	Butler	13	15	33
Parker, Jeremiah(B)	1818	Aug. 22	Wayne(Ind)	01	13	22
Parker, Jesse Jr.(B)	1831	Nov. 14	Randolph(Ind	01	16	15
Parker, Jesse(B)	1830	April 10	Randolph(Ind	01	16	26
Parker, Joel(B)	1828	Oct. 22	Randolph(Ind	01	16	26
Parker, Jonathan(C)	1829	July 17	Logan	14	03	29
Parker, Jonathan(C)	1831	Aug. 08	Logan	14	03	30
Parker, Moses(E)	1819	Aug. 02	Wayne(Ind)	14	18	23
Parker, Nathan(E)	1836	Oct. 10	Wayne(Ind)	15	19	17
Parker, Rich'd. C.(E)	1826	Dec. 15	Wayne(Ind)	13	16	23
Parker, Samuel Jr.(A)	1829	Dec. 07	Darke	02	10	25
Parker, Thomas(B)	1814	Aug. 16	Wayne(Ind)	01	16	32
Parker, Thos. Senr.(B)	1829	Oct. 26	Randolph(Ind	01	16	22
Parker, Timothy(B)	1815	Feb. 07	Hamilton	02	08	12
Parker, Timothy(B)	1815	Feb. 07	Hamilton	01	08	07
Parkham, Peter(A)	1804	Nov. 06	Butler	04	03	29
Parkhurst, Zelotes(B)	1817	Sept. 03	Cincinnati	01	09	21
Parkinson, Maxwell(D)	1814	Jan. 01	Hamilton(Fr)	02	02	11
Parkison, Maxwell(A)	1802	May 13	Hamilton	01	03	24
Parkison, Maxwell(C)	1814	April 22	Hamilton	09	05	05
Parkison, William(A)	1814	June 22	Butler	01	03	23
Parkison, William(C)	1804	Sept. 24	Kentucky	12	05	20
Parks, Jackson(E)	1837	June 20	Jay Co.,Ind.	14	22	25
Parks, Jonathan(B)	1816	May 18	Dearborn(Ind	01	04	27
Parks, Jonathan(B)	1830	March 15	Hamilton	02	05	30
Parks, Joseph(A)	1818	April 22	Warren	04	10	17
Parks, Joseph(C)	1801	Dec. 28	Hamilton	04	02	02
Parks, Joseph(C)	1801	Dec. 28	Hamilton	05	02	15
Parks, Joseph(C)	1801	Dec. 28	Hamilton	04	02	10
Parks, Joseph(C)	1802	Dec. 28	Hamilton	04	03	34
Parks, Joseph(C)	1802	Dec. 28	Hamilton	04	03	34
Parks, Robert(A)	1806	Feb. 11	Montgomery	06	02	17
Parks, Samuel(A)	1808	Oct. 01	Preble	01	07	25
Parks, Thomas Jr.(E)	1837	June 19	Darke	15	22	19
Parlee, Benjamin(B)	1817	Oct. 21	Hamilton	03	05	03
Parrott, Francis(B)	1836	Sept. 19	Montgomery	01	18	23
Parrott, Francis(E)	1836	Sept. 19	Montgomery	15	20	03
Parrott, Thomas(B)	1836	Sept. 19	Montgomery	01	18	23
Parrott, Thomas(E)	1836	Sept. 19	Montgomery	15	20	03
Parsell, James(A)	1807	June 01	Butler	02	06	05
Parson, Matthias(E)	1812	Aug. 19	Montgomery	13	15	29
Parson, Williams(B)	1814	May 09	Dearborn(Ind	01	02	27
Partelow, Ames(A)	1812	April 15	Butler	01	04	32
Parvis, Joshua(B)	1814	Oct. 05	Dearborn(Ind	01	07	27
Parvis, Joshua(B)	1834	Oct. 06	Franklin(Ind	02	08	21
Pasquier, Claude(B)	1834	March 17	Switzerland	02	02	20
Passmore, Henry(A)	1815	June 21	Cincinnati	01	02	26
Passmore, Henry(A)	1815	Sept. 20	Cincinnati	01	02	26
Pate, Adam(B)	1812	Oct. 16	Dearborn(Ind	01	05	17
Pate, Charles Bird(B)	1836	Feb. 22	Dearborn(Ind	03	04	02
Pate, Charles Linch(B)	1835	Dec. 30	Dearborn(Ind	02	04	30
Pate, Chas. Linch(B)	1834	Jan. 27	Dearborn(Ind	02	04	30
Pate, Daniel(B)	1816	Nov. 16	Dearborn(Ind	02	05	10
Pate, Daniel(B)	1816	Nov. 29	Dearborn(Ind	02	05	10
Pate, David(B)	1836	Aug. 15	Dearborn(Ind	03	04	08
Pate, George Jr.(B)	1836	Sept. 21	Dearborn(Ind	03	04	03
Pate, George(B)	1817	Dec. 17	Dearborn(Ind	03	05	28
Pate, George(B)	1836	May 23	Dearborn(Ind	03	04	10
Pate, Henry S.(B)	1836	May 28	Dearborn(Ind	03	04	10
Pate, Jeremiah(B)	1815	Oct. 30	Dearborn(Ind	03	04	10
Pate, Lewis(B)	1837	Jan. 18	Dearborn(Ind	03	04	02
Pate, Randol R.(B)	1836	Sept. 21	Dearborn(Ind	03	04	03
Pate, William S.(B)	1837	Jan. 18	Dearborn(Ind	03	05	34
Pate, William S.(B)	1838	Jan. 09	Dearborn(Ind	03	05	35

PURCHASER	YEAR	DATE	RESIDENCE	R	T	S
Paterfield, Thomas(A)	1811	Dec. 24	Preble	01	09	08
Patmore, William(B)	1833	July 22	Dearborn(Ind	03	04	11
Patrick, Jno. Montgom'y(B)	1832	May 25	Dearborn(Ind	03	06	34
Patrick, John Montgomery(B)	1836	Jan. 21	Dearborn(Ind	03	06	27
Patrick, John(A)	1831	Oct. 22	Pennsylvania	05	10	36
Pattan, William(E)	1813	Nov. 23	Butler	13	13	04
Patten, James(A)	1831	Nov. 01	Warren	02	10	12
Patten, Richard(A)	1825	Jan. 21	Warren	03	08	19
Patten, Thomas(C)	1813	Nov. 03	Champaign	09	05	19
Patterson, Abraham(A)	1836	Nov. 14	Hamilton	01	12	31
Patterson, Abraham(A)	1837	Feb. 21	Hamilton	01	12	31
Patterson, Abraham(B)	1836	Nov. 14	Hamilton	01	17	35
Patterson, Abraham(B)	1838	Feb. 19	Hamilton	01	17	36
Patterson, Francis(C)	1805	March 26	Montgomery	06	02	29
Patterson, Francis(C)	1810	Aug. 14	Montgomery	06	02	29
Patterson, James Jr.(C)	1831	Aug. 29	Pennsylvania	12	02	28
Patterson, James(A)	1819	Jan. 11	Montgomery	04	09	05
Patterson, James(C)	1801	Dec. 23	Hamilton	06	02	17
Patterson, James(E)	1832	Oct. 01	Franklin(Ind	13	12	18
Patterson, John(A)	1817	July 18	Miami	05	09	34
Patterson, John(C)	1801	Dec. 23	Hamilton	07	02	14
Patterson, John(E)	1811	Oct. 24	Montgomery	13	15	03
Patterson, Robert(A)	1803	Oct. 01	Kentucky	06	01	06
Patterson, Robert(A)	1803	Nov. 19	Kentucky	06	02	29
Patterson, Robert(A)	1804	Aug. 28	Hamilton	03	03	26
Patterson, Robert(A)	1818	May 09	Miami	05	09	14
Patterson, Robert(A)	1834	April 15	Darke	03	10	07
Patterson, Robert(C)	1804	Dec. 31	Montgomery	07	02	04
Patterson, Robert(C)	1831	Aug. 08	Logan	14	04	33
Patterson, Sam'l. R.(C)	1824	June 07	Warren	11	03	29
Patterson, Samuel(A)	1807	Aug. 08	So. Carolina	01	06	30
Patterson, Samuel(A)	1808	Jan. 13	Montgomery	01	07	25
Patterson, Samuel(A)	1808	Jan. 13	Montgomery	01	07	36
Patterson, Samuel(A)	1811	Aug. 29	Preble	02	06	21
Patterson, Samuel(A)	1813	April 14	Montgomery	01	07	36
Patterson, Will'm.(A)	1831	Jan. 13	Warren	04	06	07
Patterson, William(B)	1837	Feb. 25	Dearborn(Ind	03	05	28
Patterson, William(B)	1837	Oct. 09	Dearborn(Ind	03	05	35
Patterson, William(E)	1837	May 22	Montgomery	14	21	25
Patterson, William(E)	1837	May 26	Montgomery	14	21	36
Patterson, William(E)	1837	July 17	Montgomery	14	21	23
Patteson, Joseph(C)	1817	Nov. 24	Cincinnati	10	04	34
Pattinger, John(A)	1804	Nov. 13	Kentucky	02	06	10
Pattison, Hezekiah(E)	1827	Nov. 10	Wayne(Ind)	14	17	09
Patton, Francis(C)	1831	July 08	Logan	13	03	35
Patton, Francis(C)	1836	Feb. 04	Logan	13	03	35
Patton, Isaac S.(A)	1807	Sept. 03	Butler	02	07	19
Patton, Isaac S.(A)	1807	Sept. 03	Butler	02	07	19
Patton, John(B)	1817	July 07	Switzerland	01	02	15
Patton, John(C)	1815	Dec. 19	Champaign	13	03	35
Patton, Shepherd(C)	1828	Nov. 12	Logan	13	02	11
Patton, Shepherd(C)	1831	Feb. 23	Logan	13	03	23
Patton, Thomas(C)	1807	May 29	Kentucky	09	05	13
Patton, Thomas(C)	1811	Oct. 18	Champaign	09	05	14
Patton, Thomas(C)	1814	June 21	Champaign	08	05	23
Patton, Thomas(C)	1814	June 21	Champaign	08	05	24
Patton, Thomas(E)	1814	Oct. 10	Butler	13	14	34
Patton, William(A)	1810	Dec. 12	Butler	02	06	32
Patton, William(C)	1801	Dec. 31	Hamilton	04	03	21
Patty, Charles(A)	1817	Sept. 02	Miami	04	07	23
Patty, Charles(A)	1825	March 22	Miami	06	03	15
Patty, David(A)	1806	Dec. 29	So. Carolina	05	05	08
Patty, David(A)	1807	Aug. 05	So. Carolina	04	09	33
Patty, David(A)	1807	Aug. 05	So. Carolina	04	09	34
Patty, David(A)	1831	Sept. 12	Miami	04	09	28
Patty, David(A)	1831	Sept. 20	Miami	04	08	04
Patty, David(A)	1831	Nov. 19	Miami	04	08	04
Patty, David(A)	1831	Nov. 19	Miami	04	08	09
Patty, David(A)	1831	Nov. 19	Miami	04	08	15

PURCHASER	YEAR	DATE	RESIDENCE	R	T	S
Patty, David(A)	1831	Dec. 01	Miami	04	08	09
Patty, George(C)	1807	May 11	Champaign	12	05	30
Patty, George(C)	1807	May 11	Champaign	12	05	30
Patty, James(A)	1807	Aug. 05	Montgomery	04	09	33
Patty, James(A)	1817	June 21	Montgomery	04	07	13
Patty, James(A)	1819	Feb. 20	Montgomery	01	10	12
Patty, Joseph(C)	1804	Sept. 24	Greene	12	05	21
Patty, Samuel(A)	1830	Feb. 08	Miami	04	07	23
Paul, James(A)	1825	June 22	Preble	01	09	15
Paul, John(C)	1801	Dec. 30	Hamilton	07	03	25
Paul, John(C)	1802	Dec. 31	Hamilton	09	03	28
Paul, John(C)	1804	Dec. 31	Greene	09	03	30
Paul, John(C)	1806	Oct. 22	Champaign	09	03	24
Paul, John(C)	1814	June 29	Champaign	09	03	29
Paul, John(C)	1816	July 10	Champaign	09	03	29
Paul, William(C)	1802	Dec. 31	Hamilton	09	03	23
Paul, William(C)	1806	Oct. 22	Champaign	09	03	28
Paul, Wm.(C)	1814	July 11	Virginia	11	06	26
Paulus, Abraham(A)	1831	May 11	Montgomery	03	08	36
Pavy, Sam'l. Husk(B)	1835	Dec. 02	Switzerland	03	03	29
Paxton, Isaac(C)	1801	Dec. 19	Cincinnati	05	04	21
Paylen, Henry(B)	1814	Aug. 16	Wayne(Ind)	01	15	36
Payne, Aaron(B)	1815	July 21	?	02	06	11
Payne, Jeremiah(A)	1803	Oct. 31	Butler	03	03	14
Payne, John(B)	1814	Aug. 24	Hamilton	01	03	05
Payne, Samuel(A)	1803	Oct. 31	Butler	03	03	09
Peabody, Hiram(B)	1834	Feb. 12	Switzerland	03	03	14
Peabody, Stephen(B)	1817	Aug. 22	Switzerland	03	03	03
Peabody, Stephen(B)	1817	Aug. 22	Switzerland	03	03	03
Peabody, Stephen(B)	1818	Jan. 14	Switzerland	03	03	14
Peach, Joseph(C)	1826	Nov. 16	Logan	14	03	29
Peacock, Abraham(E)	1818	April 15	Wayne(Ind)	15	20	30
Peacock, Amos(E)	1818	April 15	Wayne(Ind)	15	20	31
Peacock, Amos(E)	1835	July 02	Randolph(Ind	15	20	32
Peacock, Amos(E)	1837	March 01	Randolph(Ind	15	20	32
Peacock, David(E)	1817	Nov. 19	Wayne(Ind)	13	17	34
Peacock, David(E)	1829	Dec. 10	Wayne(Ind)	13	17	34
Peacock, William(E)	1818	Dec. 22	Warren	13	18	14
Peacock, Wm.(E)	1838	Jan. 30	Randolph(Ind	15	20	32
Peagins, Joseph(A)	1811	Nov. 25	Preble	03	05	12
Peal, John(E)	1816	Sept. 25	Wayne(Ind)	14	18	25
Pearce, Benjamin(E)	1836	May 19	Highland	15	19	31
Pearce, Benjamin(E)	1836	May 20	Highland	15	18	06
Pearce, Elijah(C)	1828	March 28	Champaign	14	03	19
Pearce, Jacob W.(E)	1836	June 29	Highland	14	19	36
Pearce, John(C)	1811	Oct. 03	Champaign	11	05	05
Pearce, John(C)	1828	March 17	Champaign	14	03	25
Pearce, John(C)	1830	June 28	Logan	14	03	25
Pearce, Meriby(E)	1837	Jan. 09	Highland	14	19	36
Pearsan, Matthias Jun.(E)	1816	Aug. 20	Montgomery	13	17	19
Pearse, Joseph(A)	1809	Dec. 12	Dayton	06	02	01
Pearson, Abel(A)	1805	Nov. 30	Montgomery	06	04	09
Pearson, Alexander(A)	1817	July 10	Preble	01	11	26
Pearson, Allen(A)	1829	Jan. 13	Darke	03	09	20
Pearson, Benj'm.(A)	1811	Dec. 11	Montgomery	05	07	28
Pearson, Benj'n.(A)	1831	May 09	Miami	05	07	26
Pearson, Benj'n.(A)	1831	May 18	Miami	05	07	14
Pearson, Benj'n.(A)	1831	Sept. 17	Miami	05	07	15
Pearson, Benjamin(A)	1806	Sept. 12	Montgomery	06	04	19
Pearson, Benjamin(A)	1808	Nov. 12	Miami	06	04	30
Pearson, Benjamin(B)	1806	June 25	Warren	01	14	20
Pearson, Benjamin(B)	1811	Aug. 13	Warren	01	14	20
Pearson, Charles M.(A)	1837	Feb. 18	Shelby	03	12	02
Pearson, Elliott(A)	1816	June 04	Preble	01	11	35
Pearson, Elliott(A)	1819	Jan. 14	Darke	01	11	34
Pearson, Elliott(B)	1814	Aug. 25	Preble	01	15	36
Pearson, Enoch(A)	1808	Sept. 14	Warren	06	04	29
Pearson, Enoch(A)	1814	Aug. 16	Miami	06	04	29
Pearson, Enoch(A)	1817	Aug. 15	Miami	06	04	21

PURCHASER	YEAR	DATE	RESIDENCE	R	T	S
Pearson, Enoch(A)	1827	Aug. 29	Miami	06	04	18
Pearson, Henry(B)	1816	Nov. 06	Warren	01	12	31
Pearson, Isaac(E)	1818	Aug. 14	Nor.Carolina	14	19	33
Pearson, Jacob(A)	1831	March 11	Miami	06	08	33
Pearson, John F.(A)	1831	May 18	Miami	05	07	15
Pearson, John(A)	1806	March 10	Montgomery	06	04	20
Pearson, John(A)	1806	Aug. 08	Montgomery	06	04	20
Pearson, John(B)	1817	Dec. 16	Wayne(Ind)	01	15	03
Pearson, John(E)	1815	May 16	Wayne(Ind)	14	17	30
Pearson, Jonas(A)	1806	Sept. 01	Montgomery	05	06	36
Pearson, Jonas(A)	1814	May 18	Miami	06	04	28
Pearson, Jonathan(A)	1814	Dec. 10	Darke	01	11	23
Pearson, Joseph(A)	1809	Oct. 12	Miami	05	05	01
Pearson, Joseph(A)	1822	May 21	Miami	05	07	27
Pearson, Moses B.(B)	1836	Aug. 24	Hamilton	03	02	19
Pearson, Moses B.(B)	1836	Aug. 26	Hamilton	03	02	19
Pearson, Moses(A)	1831	May 18	Miami	05	07	14
Pearson, Moses(A)	1831	Sept. 17	Miami	05	07	15
Pearson, Nathan(B)	1808	Oct. 01	Dearborn(Ind	01	13	14
Pearson, Nathan(B)	1813	Dec. 15	Wayne(Ind)	01	13	14
Pearson, Peter(E)	1817	Dec. 16	Wayne(Ind)	14	18	13
Pearson, Powel(A)	1815	March 18	Miami	06	04	19
Pearson, Robert(A)	1806	July 28	Warren	04	08	36
Pearson, Robert(A)	1831	June 30	Miami	05	06	02
Pearson, Robert(A)	1831	Sept. 29	Miami	05	07	10
Pearson, Robt.(A)	1828	Nov. 11	Miami	06	04	18
Pearson, Robt.(A)	1829	Jan. 16	Miami	06	04	18
Pearson, Sam'l.(A)	1829	April 30	Miami	06	04	07
Pearson, Sam'l.(A)	1829	May 13	Miami	06	04	07
Pearson, Samuel(A)	1816	Oct. 10	Miami	06	04	22
Pearson, Samuel(A)	1831	Sept. 17	Miami	05	06	01
Pearson, Samuel(A)	1831	Oct. 17	Miami	05	07	10
Pearson, Sineas(B)	1806	Aug. 08	?	02	10	13
Pearson, William(A)	1807	July 08	Miami	05	08	19
Pearson, William(A)	1809	June 30	Miami	05	08	18
Pearson, William(A)	1813	Dec. 07	Miami	04	08	36
Pearson, William(A)	1817	Aug. 04	Montgomery	02	11	04
Pease, Harvey(B)	1833	Nov. 16	Hamilton	03	03	03
Pease, Harvey(B)	1834	Jan. 11	Hamilton	03	03	03
Pease, Horace(E)	1836	Jan. 29	Hamilton	11	11	34
Pease, Horace(E)	1836	June 20	Hamilton	11	10	03
Pease, Perry(E)	1837	Jan. 09	Franklin(Ind	11	11	34
Pease, Perry(E)	1837	March 01	Montgomery	15	20	03
Pease, Perry(E)	1837	March 01	Montgomery	15	20	04
Pease, Perry(E)	1837	March 01	Montgomery	15	20	15
Pease, Perry(E)	1837	March 01	Montgomery	15	20	17
Pease, Perry(E)	1837	March 01	Montgomery	15	20	18
Peck, Eleazer(C)	1814	Dec. 05	Hamilton	11	04	13
Peck, Henry(A)	1819	May 10	Miami	05	09	33
Peck, James W.(A)	1830	Nov. 24	Warren	04	06	04
Peck, John(A)	1811	Aug. 13	Miami	06	04	04
Peck, John(A)	1811	Oct. 29	Miami	05	09	26
Peck, John(A)	1830	July 12	Montgomery	04	07	35
Peck, Marcus(C)	1830	June 11	Logan	13	02	12
Peck, William(B)	1833	Feb. 23	Dearborn(Ind	03	04	27
Peden, John(B)	1832	Dec. 24	Wayne(Ind)	01	16	35
Peden, Silas(A)	1832	Sept. 07	Darke	01	10	08
Pedrick, Isaac(A)	1806	Aug. 29	Warren	05	06	19
Pedrick, Isaac(A)	1806	Aug. 29	Warren	05	06	30
Pedrick, Philip(B)	1827	March 23	Wayne(Ind)	01	15	34
Peeden, Thomas(B)	1832	Oct. 02	Darke	01	18	26
Peeden, Thomas(E)	1837	April 14	Randolph(Ind	15	22	22
Peeden, Thomas(E)	1837	Aug. 12	Randolph(Ind	15	22	22
Peeden, Thomas(E)	1838	May 07	Jay Co.,Ind.	15	22	27
Peek, Francis(A)	1830	Dec. 14	Darke	01	11	29
Peelle, John(B)	1836	Dec. 21	Wayne(Ind)	01	16	02
Peelle, Mark(E)	1836	April 22	Wayne(Ind)	13	21	26
Peelle, Mark(E)	1837	Feb. 02	Wayne(Ind)	13	21	25
Peerson, Samuel(C)	1804	Dec. 28	Warren	05	04	33

PURCHASER	YEAR	DATE	RESIDENCE	R	T	S
Peffly, David(A)	1830	Dec. 29	Montgomery	04	07	28
Peffly, Sam'l.(A)	1830	Dec. 29	Montgomery	04	07	28
Pegg, John(E)	1814	Aug. 12	Wayne(Ind)	14	18	21
Pegg, John(E)	1814	Aug. 12	Wayne(Ind)	13	16	10
Pegg, John(E)	1816	Nov. 07	Wayne(Ind)	14	18	17
Pegg, Valentine(E)	1830	Sept. 25	Wayne(Ind)	14	18	20
Peirce, Benj'n.(A)	1831	Nov. 05	Miami	04	08	34
Peirce, Burkett(E)	1832	March 05	Randolph(Ind	14	21	07
Peirce, Burkett(E)	1833	Nov. 27	Randolph(Ind	14	21	07
Peirce, Burkett(E)	1834	Sept. 20	Randolph(Ind	14	21	07
Peirce, Burkett(E)	1836	June 17	Randolph(Ind	14	21	07
Peirce, Burkett(E)	1836	Oct. 17	Randolph(Ind	14	21	07
Peirce, Isaac(E)	1836	Feb. 01	Wayne(Ind)	13	17	18
Peirce, Joseph(A)	1816	July 22	Montgomery	06	05	19
Peirce, Joseph(A)	1816	July 22	Montgomery	06	05	20
Peirce, Joseph(C)	1807	April 01	Dayton	09	01	01
Peirce, Michael(A)	1806	Feb. 19	Butler	02	08	26
Peirce, Nathan L.(D)	1824	Oct. 02	Hamilton	01	02	26
Peirce, Nathaniel L.(D)	1824	Aug. 21	Hamilton	01	02	26
Peirce, Robert(C)	1806	March 05	Greene	07	04	35
Peirce, Sam'l.(A)	1831	Jan. 24	Miami	05	07	35
Peirce, Samuel(A)	1816	March 27	Miami	05	06	08
Peirce, Samuel(A)	1819	Dec. 17	Hamilton	03	09	29
Peirce, Samuel(A)	1827	Sept. 07	Miami	05	07	35
Peirce, Samuel(A)	1831	June 16	Miami	05	07	35
Peirce, Samuel(A)	1831	June 16	Miami	05	07	35
Peirce, Samuel(A)	1831	Oct. 17	Miami	05	06	11
Peirce, Samuel(A)	1831	Oct. 17	Miami	05	06	01
Peirce, Thomas(C)	1804	Dec. 28	Greene	11	05	17
Peirson, John(E)	1819	Nov. 27	Wayne(Ind)	14	18	30
Peirson, Jonathan(A)	1829	Aug. 20	Warren	04	06	18
Peirson, Jonathan(A)	1831	March 15	Montgomery	04	06	09
Peirson, Thomas(E)	1830	Nov. 23	Randolph(Ind	14	18	03
Peirson, William(E)	1818	July 29	Nor.Carolina	14	18	04
Pelham, Samuel(A)	1818	Jan. 26	Greene	04	08	17
Pelham, Samuel(A)	1818	Jan. 26	Greene	04	08	08
Pelsor, Peter(B)	1833	May 25	Switzerland	03	04	27
Pemberton, Esther(A)	1805	July 31	So. Carolina	05	06	07
Pemberton, Esther(A)	1806	Oct. 24	Montgomery	04	07	12
Pemberton, Isaiah(A)	1830	May 25	Miami	04	08	36
Pemberton, Joseph(A)	1817	July 11	Wayne(Ind)	01	11	20
Pemberton, Joseph(B)	1816	Aug. 28	Wayne(Ind)	01	14	13
Pemberton, Lydie(A)	1805	Nov. 05	Montgomery	05	07	31
Pence, Daniel(C)	1811	May 31	Champaign	11	04	35
Pence, David(C)	1816	Dec. 16	Champaign	11	03	06
Pence, Frederic(C)	1816	Dec. 16	Champaign	11	03	06
Pence, Frederick(C)	1811	May 31	Champaign	12	03	15
Pence, Frederick(C)	1815	Dec. 18	Champaign	11	04	36
Pence, Frederick(C)	1817	Dec. 04	Champaign	11	04	35
Pence, Henry(A)	1827	Aug. 16	Preble	02	08	15
Pence, Henry(C)	1804	Dec. 27	Virginia	11	04	10
Pence, Henry(C)	1804	Dec. 27	Virginia	11	04	10
Pence, Henry(C)	1804	Dec. 27	Virginia	11	04	04
Pence, Henry(C)	1806	March 08	Champaign	12	03	15
Pence, Henry(C)	1807	Jan. 30	Champaign	12	03	36
Pence, Henry(C)	1807	Jan. 31	Champaign	13	02	01
Pence, Henry(C)	1817	June 03	Champaign	11	03	34
Pence, Henry(C)	1817	June 03	Champaign	11	03	22
Pence, Isaac(C)	1812	April 15	Champaign	12	04	31
Pence, Jacob(A)	1827	Jan. 10	Preble	01	09	24
Pence, Jacob(C)	1805	Dec. 26	Champaign	11	05	34
Pence, Jacob(C)	1811	April 09	Champaign	11	05	34
Pence, Jeremiah(A)	1829	Dec. 19	Butler	01	09	24
Pence, John Senr.(C)	1808	Jan. 11	Champaign	10	04	14
Pence, John(A)	1827	June 27	Preble	01	09	22
Pence, John(C)	1804	June 29	Virginia	11	04	08
Pence, John(C)	1804	Dec. 27	Virginia	10	04	09
Pence, John(C)	1804	Dec. 27	Virginia	10	04	03
Pence, John(C)	1804	Dec. 27	Virginia	10	04	07

PURCHASER	YEAR	DATE	RESIDENCE	R	T	S
Pence, John(C)	1804	Dec. 27	Virginia	09	04	12
Pence, John(C)	1806	March 25	Champaign	11	05	33
Pence, John(C)	1806	March 25	Champaign	09	04	18
Pence, John(C)	1812	Nov. 17	Champaign	11	04	02
Pence, John(C)	1815	Nov. 30	Champaign	09	04	18
Pence, Peter(A)	1824	June 22	Preble	02	09	30
Pence, William(C)	1829	Jan. 01	Darke	12	04	32
Penland, Peter(A)	1813	March 24	Nor.Carolina	01	09	05
Penner, John(C)	1813	May 31	Champaign	14	02	09
Penney, James(A)	1831	Aug. 16	Darke	04	07	19
Pennwell, John(B)	1808	Jan. 13	Dearborn(Ind	02	09	34
Penny, Elijah(A)	1817	June 02	Miami	04	07	10
Penny, Elijah(A)	1831	April 30	Miami	04	07	04
Penny, John(A)	1832	Jan. 30	Darke	04	07	17
Penny, Theophilus(A)	1819	July 29	Miami	04	07	34
Penny, Thos.(A)	1832	Jan. 30	Darke	04	07	17
Penrod, John(A)	1837	March 28	Montgomery	01	13	11
Penrod, Peter(A)	1818	Aug. 22	Wayne(Ind)	03	07	01
Penrod, Samuel(A)	1831	Aug. 26	Montgomery	05	10	27
Penrod, Samuel(A)	1838	Feb. 02	Shelby	03	12	19
Pensel, John(B)	1812	Jan. 15	Dearborn(Ind	01	07	09
Pentecost, John Jr.(A)	1814	Feb. 10	Warren	01	07	07
Pentecost, John Jr.(B)	1814	Feb. 10	Warren	01	11	01
Penticost, John(B)	1808	Jan. 13	Cincinnati	01	11	01
Pentz, John Senr.(C)	1810	Jan. 18	Champaign	12	03	01
Penwell, David(B)	1811	Jan. 19	Ind.Territry	02	09	27
Penwell, David(B)	1812	Dec. 30	Franklin(Ind	01	08	12
Penwell, David(B)	1816	Sept. 25	Switzerland	01	02	04
Penwell, David(B)	1816	Nov. 15	Switzerland	01	02	05
Penwell, Eli(B)	1812	Dec. 30	Franklin(Ind	01	08	12
Penwell, Eli(B)	1816	Jan. 24	Franklin(Ind	01	02	29
Penwell, Eli(B)	1816	Oct. 09	Franklin(Ind	01	02	08
Penwell, John(B)	1806	Aug. 04	Ind.Territry	02	08	13
Penwell, John(E)	1824	June 10	Fayette	12	14	10
Perham, Peter(A)	1804	Aug. 08	Montgomery	04	03	20
Perine, Daniel(B)	1815	May 25	Dearborn(Ind	01	06	25
Perine, David(B)	1815	Dec. 09	Cincinnati	02	06	10
Perkenson, John(A)	1814	Nov. 23	Butler	01	03	24
Perkenton, John(A)	1814	Nov. 01	So. Carolina	01	06	08
Perkins, Jehu(E)	1811	Oct. 22	Ind.Territry	12	14	13
Perkins, John(E)	1811	Oct. 22	Ind.Territry	12	14	13
Perkins, Joseph(E)	1836	Feb. 19	Wayne(Ind)	15	19	19
Perkins, Joseph(E)	1836	Sept. 22	Wayne(Ind)	15	19	19
Perkins, Joseph(E)	1837	Feb. 22	Wayne(Ind)	15	19	19
Perkins, Robert(B)	1833	Dec. 26	Butler	01	17	11
Perkins, Robert(B)	1835	March 30	Butler	01	17	11
Perret, Robert(B)	1817	July 03	Dearborn(Ind	01	06	18
Perrin, John(C)	1811	Dec. 11	Champaign	09	05	27
Perrin, John(C)	1811	Dec. 11	Champaign	09	05	27
Perrin, John(E)	1814	Jan. 03	Hamilton	12	14	35
Perrin, John(E)	1815	May 09	Franklin(Ind	12	14	26
Perrin, Joseph(C)	1816	Aug. 19	Champaign	10	04	27
Perrin, Joseph(C)	1817	Aug. 01	Champaign	09	05	29
Perrin, Joseph(C)	1817	Aug. 01	Champaign	09	05	29
Perrin, Stephen(A)	1816	May 22	Darke	01	12	23
Perrin, Stephen(A)	1817	Sept. 09	Darke	02	12	07
Perrine, Stephen(A)	1817	Dec. 08	Darke	02	12	13
Perrine, Stephen(A)	1818	Jan. 14	Darke	01	11	05
Perrine, Stephen(A)	1818	Aug. 31	Darke	03	10	08
Perry, Allen(B)	1837	Dec. 30	Dearborn(Ind	03	06	36
Perry, Amos(A)	1814	April 25	Miami	04	09	25
Perry, Daniel(A)	1803	Feb. 04	Vermont	02	05	03
Perry, David(A)	1819	Jan. 25	Kentucky	04	11	12
Perry, Jos.(D)	1811	Dec. 11	Cincinnati	02	03	08
Perry, Nathan(A)	1831	Dec. 02	Miami	04	08	19
Perry, Sam'l.(A)	1819	Jan. 02	Kentucky	05	10	07
Perry, Sam'l.(A)	1819	Jan. 02	Kentucky	04	11	12
Perry, Sam'l.(D)	1811	Dec. 11	Cincinnati	02	03	08
Perry, Samuel	1808	March 02	Cincinnati	?	?	?

PURCHASER	YEAR	DATE	RESIDENCE	R	T	S
Perry, Samuel	1808	March 03	Cincinnati	?	?	?
Perry, Samuel(B)	1816	June 28	Dearborn(Ind	01	05	19
Perry, Samuel(C)	1804	Dec. 31	Cincinnati	08	04	03
Perry, Samuel(C)	1804	Dec. 31	Cincinnati	07	02	05
Perry, Samuel(C)	1804	Dec. 31	Cincinnati	07	03	23
Perry, Samuel(C)	1804	Dec. 31	Cincinnati	07	03	36
Perry, Samuel(C)	1804	Dec. 31	Cincinnati	08	03	01
Perry, Samuel(C)	1804	Dec. 31	Cincinnati	07	02	03
Perry, Samuel(C)	1804	Dec. 31	Cincinnati	08	04	27
Perry, Samuel(C)	1804	Dec. 31	Cincinnati	09	04	01
Perry, Samuel(C)	1808	April 09	Cincinnati	13	02	21
Perry, Samuel(C)	1809	Dec. 12	Cincinnati	07	01	11
Perry, Samuel(C)	1809	Dec. 12	Cincinnati	06	02	11
Perry, William(A)	1806	Dec. 23	Montgomery	05	07	06
Perry, William(A)	1828	Sept. 23	Miami	04	08	12
Personett, James(E)	1816	April 11	Hamilton	13	16	19
Pervoe, Asa(E)	1815	Feb. 20	Wayne(Ind)	14	16	04
Pery, Joseph(C)	1815	Nov. 21	Champaign	10	04	21
Petafish, Christian(B)	1806	Nov. 21	Virginia	01	14	12
Peters, Conrad(A)	1806	Aug. 23	Virginia	03	04	10
Peters, Henry(B)	1813	May 27	Dearborn(Ind	02	04	03
Peters, Henry(B)	1816	Nov. 15	Switzerland	03	02	19
Peters, Joseph(B)	1816	Jan. 13	Franklin(Ind	01	08	20
Peters, Mary(B)	1831	Feb. 26	Switzerland	02	01	06
Peters, Mich'l.(B)	1827	Sept. 05	Switzerland	03	02	19
Peters, Peter(B)	1812	Aug. 25	Jefferson	03	02	30
Peters, Stephen(B)	1811	March 04	Ind.Territry	02	04	02
Peters, Will'm.(A)	1815	Oct. 30	Pennsylvania	02	09	31
Petersohen, Henry(B)	1838	May 03	Cincinnati	03	05	21
Peterson, John(B)	1820	July 01	New Jersey	01	07	06
Peterson, John(B)	1831	Oct. 19	Dearborn(Ind	02	08	34
Peterson, John(B)	1832	May 24	Dearborn(Ind	02	08	34
Peterson, Ralph(C)	1827	Aug. 23	Hamilton	11	01	22
Peterson, William(C)	1831	Nov. 01	Butler	13	02	02
Peterson, William(E)	1811	Oct. 25	Wayne(Ind)	14	16	18
Petiniat, Tanis(A)	1836	July 16	Darke	03	11	12
Petit, Amos(A)	1815	May 16	Miami	06	04	09
Petro, Henry(A)	1812	Oct. 27	Warren	01	08	03
Petro, Henry(A)	1816	May 21	Preble	01	08	05
Petro, Leonard(C)	1801	Dec. 30	Hamilton	05	02	14
Petro, Nicholas(C)	1801	Dec. 08	Hamilton	07	03	30
Petro, Paul(C)	1804	Sept. 24	Greene	07	03	29
Petro, Philip(C)	1801	Dec. 14	Hamilton	07	03	36
Petry, Jacob(A)	1832	Aug. 23	Preble	02	09	07
Pettegrew, Dan'l.(B)	1830	Feb. 20	Dearborn(Ind	03	08	23
Pettegrew, Dan'l.(B)	1831	Oct. 13	Dearborn(Ind	03	08	23
Pettegrew, David(B)	1818	June 04	Hamilton	03	08	23
Pettegrew, Ezekiel(B)	1833	Oct. 11	Dearborn(Ind	03	08	23
Pettegrew, Nathan(B)	1818	May 09	Hamilton	02	06	27
Pettegrew, Nathan(B)	1824	July 30	Dearborn(Ind	02	05	04
Pettegrew, Nathan(B)	1832	Jan. 14	Dearborn(Ind	02	05	04
Pettegrew, Nathan(B)	1836	Jan. 16	Dearborn(Ind	02	05	04
Pettey, Jos.(C)	1804	Sept. 27	Greene	13	05	19
Pettey, Joseph(C)	1804	Sept. 27	Greene	13	05	25
Petticrew, James(A)	1812	Jan. 04	Montgomery	02	08	08
Petticrew, James(A)	1812	Dec. 15	Montgomery	02	08	08
Petty, Ezekiel(C)	1806	Nov. 04	Champaign	08	01	12
Petty, Ezekiel(C)	1811	Dec. 30	Champaign	12	05	28
Petty, Geo.(C)	1812	Nov. 17	Champaign	12	05	28
Petty, George(C)	1812	Nov. 17	Champaign	12	05	21
Petty, George(C)	1816	April 03	Champaign	12	05	30
Petty, Jesse(E)	1836	Nov. 16	CampbellCoKy	12	10	02
Petty, Joshua(B)	1812	Nov. 10	Dearborn(Ind	01	02	12
Pettycrew, Robt.(B)	1815	Sept. 22	Warren	01	10	31
Phares, Robt. N.(A)	1821	Oct. 18	Butler	01	09	24
Pharis, John(A)	1808	Jan. 13	Hamilton	01	02	20
Phelan, Jeremiah(A)	1812	Sept. 23	Preble	04	03	19
Phelps, Jno.(B)	1818	Oct. 05	Hamilton	03	04	24
Phelps, John(B)	1825	May 09	Dearborn(Ind	02	03	07

PURCHASER	YEAR	DATE	RESIDENCE	R	T	S
Phelps, Will'm. B.(B)	1826	May 16	Dearborn(Ind	02	03	22
Phelps, William B.(B)	1818	Oct. 05	Hamilton	03	04	24
Pheres, William Senr.(A)	1810	Aug. 14	Butler	03	03	14
Pheres, William Senr.(A)	1810	Aug. 14	Butler	03	03	10
Pheres, William(A)	1805	June 20	Hamilton	03	03	14
Pheres, William(A)	1805	June 20	Hamilton	03	03	10
Pheres, Wm. W. Jnr.(B)	1816	Feb. 28	?	01	14	19
Philips, Augustin(B)	1834	Jan. 23	Cincinnati	03	08	12
Philips, Daniel(A)	1806	Nov. 15	Montgomery	03	04	04
Philips, Daniel(A)	1815	Jan. 06	Preble	03	08	33
Philips, John(A)	1803	March 05	Hamilton	03	05	35
Philips, John(A)	1807	Jan. 20	Butler	01	03	17
Philipson, Jacob(A)	1807	Feb. 02	Cincinnati	04	02	03
Philipson, Jacob(A)	1807	Feb. 02	Cincinnati	04	02	03
Philipson, Jacob(A)	1811	April 09	Cincinnati	04	02	09
Phillips, Charles(B)	1815	Aug. 17	Butler	02	02	26
Phillips, Charles(B)	1817	Oct. 15	Switzerland	02	02	24
Phillips, Daniel(A)	1812	April 15	Preble	03	04	04
Phillips, Daniel(A)	1815	Jan. 06	Preble	03	07	04
Phillips, Gabriel(B)	1817	Nov. 03	Switzerland	03	02	20
Phillips, Henry(A)	1814	Feb. 21	Preble	03	04	05
Phillips, Hezekiah(A)	1805	April 04	Montgomery	03	04	04
Phillips, Horatio(A)	1809	April 22	Dayton	02	12	36
Phillips, Horatio(A)	1809	May 19	Dayton	02	12	36
Phillips, John H.(B)	1818	Aug. 25	Dearborn(Ind	02	06	09
Phillips, John H.(B)	1818	Sept. 10	Dearborn(Ind	02	06	09
Phillips, John(A)	1805	June 14	Hamilton	01	04	27
Phillips, John(A)	1805	Nov. 19	Butler	01	03	06
Phillips, John(A)	1813	March 29	Butler	01	04	19
Phillips, John(A)	1814	Jan. 15	Hamilton	01	03	17
Phillips, John(C)	1806	March 29	Champaign	10	05	23
Phillips, John(E)	1811	Oct. 22	Ind.Territry	12	15	34
Phillips, John(E)	1827	Oct. 24	Wayne(Ind)	14	17	09
Phillips, Lewis(A)	1823	Aug. 18	Preble	03	08	32
Phillips, Parker(A)	1831	Feb. 10	Darke	02	10	22
Phillips, Ralph(C)	1804	Dec. 31	New Jersey	07	03	33
Phillips, Ralph(C)	1804	Dec. 31	New Jersey	08	05	22
Phillips, Ralph(C)	1804	Dec. 31	New Jersey	08	05	36
Phillips, Ralph(C)	1804	Dec. 31	New Jersey	07	01	01
Phillips, Ralph(C)	1804	Dec. 31	New Jersey	07	03	19
Phillips, Ralph(C)	1804	Dec. 31	New Jersey	08	04	09
Phillips, Ralph(C)	1804	Dec. 31	New Jersey	08	04	21
Phillips, Ralph(C)	1804	Dec. 31	New Jersey	08	03	06
Phillips, Ralph(C)	1804	Dec. 31	New Jersey	08	03	32
Phillips, Ralph(C)	1804	Dec. 31	New Jersey	08	03	19
Phillips, Ralph(C)	1806	Jan. 30	New Jersey	08	05	26
Phillips, Ralph(C)	1808	Jan. 13	New Jersey	08	04	04
Phillips, Ralph(C)	1808	Jan. 13	New Jersey	08	04	04
Phillips, Ralph(C)	1808	Jan. 13	New Jersey	08	04	04
Phillips, Ralph(C)	1808	Jan. 13	New Jersey	08	04	04
Phillips, Ralph(C)	1810	April 23	New Jersey	07	02	06
Phillips, Ralph(C)	1810	April 23	New Jersey	08	03	25
Phillips, Ralph(C)	1813	April 15	New Jersey	08	03	19
Phillips, Ralph(C)	1813	April 15	New Jersey	08	03	19
Phillips, Ralph(C)	1813	April 15	New Jersey	08	05	36
Phillips, Ralph(C)	1813	April 15	New Jersey	08	03	19
Phillips, Ralph(C)	1813	April 15	New Jersey	08	05	36
Phillips, Ralph(C)	1813	April 23	New Jersey	08	04	06
Phillips, Ralph(C)	1813	April 23	New Jersey	08	04	06
Phillips, Ralph(C)	1813	April 23	New Jersey	06	01	13
Phillips, Ralph(C)	1813	April 23	New Jersey	06	01	13
Phillips, Ralph(C)	1813	April 23	?	07	03	04
Phillips, Ralph(C)	1813	April 23	?	07	02	12
Phillips, Ralph(C)	1813	April 23	?	07	03	07
Phillips, Robert(E)	1837	Dec. 14	Darke	15	21	23
Phillips, Samuel(C)	1804	Sept. 03	Warren	05	02	26
Phillips, Sarah(B)	1824	Aug. 04	Dearborn(Ind	03	06	22
Phillips, Simon(A)	1819	March 11	Darke	02	10	25
Phillips, Thomas J.(A)	1816	Oct. 17	Warren	02	09	13

PURCHASER	YEAR	DATE	RESIDENCE	R	T	S
Phillips, Thomas(A)	1814	May 25	Preble	03	07	07
Phillips, Thomas(A)	1816	Sept. 28	Darke	03	08	20
Phillips, Thomas(E)	1819	July 21	Warren	13	18	12
Phillips, Thos. James(E)	1834	Sept. 16	Darke	13	21	12
Phillips, William(A)	1807	Aug. 26	Montgomery	03	04	08
Phillips, William(A)	1811	Dec. 03	Preble	01	06	04
Phillips, William(A)	1830	May 12	Montgomery	04	06	04
Phillips, William(B)	1804	Sept. 18	Dearborn(Ind	01	01	05
Phillips, William(B)	1814	Jan. 31	Dearborn(Ind	02	02	25
Phillips, William(B)	1814	Jan. 31	Dearborn(Ind	01	02	31
Piatt, Benj'm.(E)	1818	June 29	Cincinnati	13	21	11
Piatt, Jno. H.(E)	1818	June 29	Cincinnati	13	21	11
Piatt, John H.(B)	1808	April 13	Dearborn(Ind	02	04	28
Piatt, John H.(B)	1811	April 23	Cincinnati	01	06	35
Piatt, John H.(B)	1811	Aug. 13	Hamilton	02	05	36
Piatt, John H.(B)	1811	Aug. 13	Hamilton	02	05	36
Piatt, John H.(B)	1818	June 16	Cincinnati	01	06	21
Piatt, John H.(C)	1813	April 14	Cincinnati	10	01	01
Piatt, John H.(C)	1813	April 20	Cincinnati	06	02	23
Piatt, John H.(C)	1815	March 03	Cincinnati	10	04	06
Piatt, John H.(C)	1815	March 03	Cincinnati	10	04	06
Piatt, John H.(C)	1815	March 03	Cincinnati	10	04	06
Piatt, Robert(A)	1801	June 25	Hamilton	01	01	19
Piatt, Robert(B)	1806	Jan. 25	Ind.Territry	01	06	35
Piatt, Robert(B)	1811	April 09	Dearborn(Ind	01	06	35
Piatt, William(B)	1816	Nov. 18	Cincinnati	04	02	24
Pickering, Burrill(A)	1832	March 29	Miami	04	08	35
Picket, John(B)	1816	July 05	?	03	03	13
Pickett, Benjamin(E)	1836	July 09	Wayne(Ind)	15	20	28
Pickett, John(E)	1836	Dec. 15	Randolph(Ind	14	20	36
Pickett, Rebecca(E)	1831	July 05	Randolph(Ind	14	20	36
Pickett, Rebecca(E)	1831	July 05	Randolph(Ind	14	20	25
Pickett, William(B)	1824	Dec. 11	Fayette	02	01	05
Pierce, Asiel(A)	1819	Aug. 14	Clark	05	08	23
Pierce, Enos(A)	1830	Feb. 17	Preble	03	07	09
Pierce, Gilbert(C)	1829	Dec. 11	Clark	08	06	30
Pierce, Gilbert(C)	1829	Dec. 11	Clark	08	06	30
Pierce, Jos.(A)	1809	May 19	Dayton	02	12	36
Pierce, Joseph(A)	1809	April 22	Dayton	02	12	36
Pierce, Michael(A)	1803	July 22	Hamilton	04	01	06
Pierce, Moses(A)	1819	Aug. 14	Clark	05	08	23
Pierce, Moses(C)	1819	April 13	Greene	13	05	29
Pierce, Samuel(A)	1818	Jan. 06	Miami	05	07	34
Pierce, Solomon(E)	1835	Dec. 16	Franklin(Ind	13	12	30
Pierce, Thomas(E)	1831	July 05	Randolph(Ind	14	21	17
Pierce, Thomas(E)	1837	Jan. 14	Randolph(Ind	14	20	11
Pierce, Thomas(E)	1837	April 01	Randolph(Ind	14	20	11
Pierson, Byram Ayres(A)	1831	Sept. 14	Preble	01	12	08
Pierson, Daniel(A)	1815	Feb. 28	Ohio	03	04	18
Pierson, David(A)	1815	March 29	Ohio	03	04	18
Pierson, David(A)	1815	March 29	Ohio	03	04	18
Pierson, Ebenezer H.(B)	1819	Oct. 25	Cincinnati	03	06	26
Pierson, John(A)	1806	Sept. 02	Montgomery	04	07	03
Pierson, Jonathan(A)	1836	Dec. 14	Hamilton	02	15	30
Pierson, Lewis(A)	1818	Nov. 02	Hamilton	05	09	30
Pierson, Lineus(B)	1806	June 23	Hamilton	02	10	04
Pierson, Mathew(C)	1801	Dec. 25	Hamilton	06	01	09
Pierson, Seneas(C)	1804	Dec. 31	Hamilton	08	04	28
Pierson, Seneas(C)	1804	Dec. 31	Hamilton	09	04	07
Pierson, Seneas(C)	1804	Dec. 31	Hamilton	07	03	24
Pierson, Seneas(C)	1804	Dec. 31	Hamilton	08	04	17
Pierson, Simeas(C)	1804	Dec. 31	Hamilton	07	02	31
Pierson, Thomas(A)	1805	Aug. 30	Warren	06	04	17
Piffinbarger, David(A)	1832	Oct. 16	Montgomery	01	09	02
Piggot, Joshua(B)	1808	Jan. 13	Dearborn(Ind	01	14	20
Piggott, John(E)	1831	Nov. 01	Randolph(Ind	14	20	25
Pigman, Adam(E)	1814	Jan. 13	Kentucky	13	13	09
Pigman, Adam(E)	1836	Oct. 10	Union(Ind)	14	22	33
Pigman, Jesse(E)	1814	Jan. 13	Kentucky	13	13	09

PURCHASER	YEAR	DATE	RESIDENCE	R	T	S
Pike, Benjamin(A)	1806	Nov. 19	Montgomery	05	06	27
Pike, Benjamin(A)	1826	Jan. 23	Miami	04	07	23
Pike, George W.(B)	1811	Oct. 05	Ind.Territory	01	05	09
Pike, James(E)	1836	Oct. 11	Highland	14	19	21
Pike, John(E)	1833	Jan. 11	Randolph(Ind	15	20	30
Pike, William(E)	1814	Aug. 19	Wayne(Ind)	13	16	01
Pike, Zebulon Majr.(B)	1801	Sept. 15	U. S. Army	01	05	10
Pike, Zebulon(B)	1816	Dec. 02	Dearborn(Ind	01	05	09
Piles, Elijah(B)	1812	June 26	Dearborn(Ind	02	05	01
Pike, Benj'n.(A)	1823	Nov. 17	Miami	04	07	23
Piles, Jeremiah(A)	1818	Oct. 05	Preble	03	07	15
Piles, William(C)	1811	Sept. 09	Champaign	12	04	23
Pillenessel, Herman Hy.(E)	1837	Aug. 04	Cincinnati	12	11	19
Pilson, William(E)	1836	Sept. 09	Cincinnati	13	12	27
Pilson, William(E)	1836	Sept. 19	Cincinnati	12	11	01
Pilson, William(E)	1836	Oct. 31	Cincinnati	12	11	11
Pinckard, Nathaniel(C)	1807	Aug. 07	Champaign	09	04	04
Pine, George(C)	1831	Aug. 29	Champaign	13	03	07
Pine, George(C)	1831	Aug. 29	Champaign	13	03	13
Pine, Jacob(C)	1832	Jan. 07	Champaign	13	04	21
Pine, James(C)	1832	March 02	Champaign	13	04	31
Pines, John(C)	1831	Sept. 10	Champaign	13	04	20
Pinger, Christian(B)	1835	April 29	Hamilton	02	08	21
Pingry, John(E)	1832	Oct. 27	Randolph(Ind	13	19	33
Pinkerton, John(A)	1814	May 16	So. Carolina	01	07	32
Pinkerton, John(A)	1815	May 31	Preble	01	07	32
Pinkerton, John(A)	1815	Aug. 23	Preble	01	06	21
Pinkerton, John(A)	1815	Nov. 20	Butler	01	07	34
Pinneo, Andrew(C)	1831	March 03	Clark	09	05	07
Piper, Alexander(A)	1817	Sept. 18	Kentucky	08	01	02
Piper, Eleazer(C)	1806	July 10	Champaign	12	05	25
Piper, James Senr.(B)	1806	Aug. 11	Hamilton	02	10	13
Piper, James(B)	1812	Dec. 04	Butler	02	10	14
Piper, James(C)	1815	Jan. 23	Butler	13	03	05
Piper, William D.(A)	1831	May 09	Logan	08	02	35
Pippen, Richard(A)	1833	Feb. 23	Dearborn(Ind	12	10	11
Pippenger, Jno.(A)	1829	Oct. 30	Montgomery	04	05	04
Pippenger, John(A)	1813	April 26	Montgomery	04	06	35
Pippinger, Cornelius(A)	1816	Nov. 13	Montgomery	04	06	27
Pitman, Arthur(A)	1807	May 29	Butler	01	07	03
Pitman, George Hall(A)	1831	Aug. 27	Warren	04	07	30
Pitman, Jonathan Jr.(A)	1830	Jan. 15	Hamilton	02	10	28
Pitsenbarger, Jacob(A)	1826	Jan. 24	Montgomery	04	06	33
Plasinger, Nicholas(A)	1816	Nov. 13	Pennsylvania	03	11	27
Plasinger, Philip(A)	1829	June 09	Darke	03	11	27
Plaspohl, Jno. Henry(E)	1836	Dec. 08	Cincinnati	12	11	33
Plaspohl, Jno. Hy.(A)	1837	Dec. 16	Cincinnati	02	15	36
Plaspohl, Jno. Hy.(A)	1837	Dec. 16	Cincinnati	03	13	32
Plaspohl, Jno. Hy.(A)	1839	Jan. 21	Cincinnati	02	15	27
Plaspohl, Jno. Hy.(E)	1837	Jan. 26	Cincinnati	11	10	11
Plaspohl, John Henry(E)	1837	Jan. 02	Cincinnati	12	11	32
Plaspohl, John Henry(E)	1837	Jan. 10	Cincinnati	11	11	36
Plaspohl, John Henry(E)	1837	Jan. 12	Cincinnati	11	10	14
Plaspohl, John Hy.(E)	1837	Jan. 13	Cincinnati	11	10	11
Plaspohl, John Hy.(E)	1837	Feb. 06	Cincinnati	11	10	01
Plaspohl, John Hy.(E)	1837	Feb. 06	Cincinnati	11	11	36
Plaspohl, John Hy.(E)	1837	Feb. 09	Cincinnati	12	11	35
Platt, Abraham(E)	1825	Jan. 08	Wayne(Ind)	14	18	22
Platt, Abraham(E)	1836	Feb. 19	Preble	14	19	26
Platt, Elijah H.(E)	1836	June 30	Randolph(Ind	14	18	03
Platt, Gilbert(B)	1817	Oct. 22	Dearborn(Ind	02	06	18
Platt, Gilbert(B)	1817	Oct. 22	Dearborn(Ind	02	06	17
Platt, Jno. H.(C)	1815	July 19	Cincinnati	11	04	01
Platt, Nathan(B)	1812	July 30	Cincinnati	03	02	02
Platt, Nathan(B)	1814	June 20	Jefferson	02	02	05
Platt, Samuel(E)	1836	Oct. 28	Preble	14	19	34
Playsinger, George(A)	1816	May 25	Montgomery	03	11	28
Playsinger, Jacob(A)	1819	Nov. 29	Montgomery	03	10	03
Pleasant, Geo. Emlen(B)	1831	July 25	Switzerland	03	03	27

257

PURCHASER	YEAR	DATE	RESIDENCE	R	T	S
Pleasants, George E.(B)	1837	April 20	Switzerland	03	03	29
Plessinger, Hugh(A)	1835	May 21	Darke	03	11	22
Plessinger, Nicholas(A)	1835	May 21	Darke	03	11	22
Plew, Jeremiah(B)	1834	June 10	Preble	01	16	10
Plotter, George(A)	1817	Sept. 18	Montgomery	04	04	04
Plume, Joseph(B)	1818	Jan. 26	Dearborn(Ind	02	06	27
Plume, Luther(B)	1818	Jan. 26	Dearborn(Ind	02	06	27
Plumer, John Alert(E)	1836	Oct. 21	Cincinnati	12	10	17
Plumer, John Alert(E)	1836	Nov. 15	Cincinnati	12	10	17
Plumer, Luther(B)	1835	Oct. 14	Dearborn(Ind	02	06	32
Plumer, Sewell(B)	1832	May 22	Dearborn(Ind	02	06	32
Plummer, Baruch(E)	1816	Sept. 11	Madison	13	13	18
Plummer, John(B)	1808	Jan. 13	Montgomery	01	12	28
Plummer, John(B)	1827	Sept. 01	Union(Ind)	01	12	28
Plummer, John(E)	1816	Oct. 23	Franklin(Ind	13	13	18
Plummer, Joseph(B)	1817	Oct. 22	Dearborn(Ind	02	06	34
Plummer, Levi(E)	1816	Sept. 11	Franklin(Ind	13	13	17
Plummer, Philemon(A)	1806	Oct. 15	Montgomery	05	05	13
Plummer, Thomas(A)	1814	Aug. 02	Clinton	05	09	26
Plummer, Wm. Chiles(E)	1832	June 12	Fayette	12	13	17
Poage, Robert(E)	1836	Nov. 19	Greene	14	21	23
Poage, Robert(E)	1838	Aug. 06	Greene	14	21	14
Poage, Samuel(E)	1836	June 20	Greene	15	21	18
Poage, Samuel(E)	1838	Aug. 25	Greene	14	21	24
Poage, William(A)	1818	Aug. 29	Greene	05	09	05
Poage, William(A)	1821	Jan. 01	Shelby	05	09	06
Pocock, Daniel(C)	1810	Sept. 08	Butler	03	03	26
Pocock, Edward(B)	1816	Sept. 07	Butler	02	02	12
Pocock, James(B)	1816	Aug. 26	Butler	02	02	13
Pocock, James(B)	1816	Aug. 26	Butler	02	02	32
Pocock, James(C)	1811	July 23	Butler	03	03	26
Pocock, Salem(C)	1810	Sept. 08	Butler	03	03	26
Pocqueneur, John(B)	1834	March 28	Dearborn(Ind	02	07	13
Poe, George(A)	1830	Feb. 01	Montgomery	04	06	02
Poe, Willson(B)	1834	March 17	Franklin(Ind	02	08	18
Poe, Willson(B)	1836	Feb. 17	Franklin(Ind	03	09	24
Poinier, Isaac(B)	1818	Aug. 15	Hamilton	01	07	18
Poinsett, Peter(A)	1829	May 06	Montgomery	04	06	31
Poirot, Tousaint(B)	1834	Aug. 07	France	02	07	04
Pollard, Allison(E)	1833	Sept. 11	Warren	13	19	21
Pollard, Allison(E)	1835	Jan. 08	Randolph(Ind	13	19	14
Pollard, Allison(E)	1835	Jan. 08	Randolph(Ind	13	19	22
Pollard, John(E)	1813	Nov. 05	Franklin(Ind	13	13	28
Pollenger, Robert(A)	1804	Sept. 24	Butler	02	06	02
Pollock, James T.(B)	1832	Nov. 26	Dearborn(Ind	02	03	13
Pollock, Joseph(C)	1816	Feb. 22	Champaign	13	03	15
Pollock, Layton(C)	1831	April 11	Champaign	13	04	24
Polly, David(B)	1836	Nov. 05	Darke	01	17	11
Polly, William(A)	1817	Oct. 21	Madison	01	10	20
Polly, William(B)	1836	Nov. 05	Darke	01	17	11
Pond, Henry(E)	1832	May 23	Franklin(Ind	12	11	01
Pond, Henry(E)	1836	July 04	Franklin(Ind	13	11	06
Pond, Hiram(E)	1830	July 10	Franklin(Ind	13	12	30
Pond, Hiram(E)	1836	Feb. 09	Franklin(Ind	12	11	01
Pond, Warren S.(E)	1836	June 25	Franklin(Ind	13	11	06
Ponn, John A.(C)	1812	Oct. 31	Virginia	12	01	17
Pontiers, Conrod(A)	1815	March 07	Pickaway	05	09	04
Pontiers, Conrod(A)	1815	March 07	Pickaway	05	10	32
Pool, George(A)	1819	May 12	Champaign	06	08	24
Pool, John(B)	1807	June 30	Nor.Carolina	01	14	35
Pool, John(B)	1827	Oct. 27	Wayne(Ind)	01	15	02
Pool, John(E)	1815	Jan. 03	Wayne(Ind)	12	16	11
Pool, John(E)	1816	Nov. 02	Wayne(Ind)	14	18	20
Pool, Joshua(B)	1806	Sept. 10	Highland	01	13	01
Pool, Thomas(B)	1807	June 30	Nor.Carolina	01	14	35
Pool, William Jr.(A)	1837	Feb. 15	Hamilton	02	14	29
Pool, William(C)	1812	Oct. 28	Hamilton	09	06	34
Poole, Chester(C)	1813	Sept. 01	Champaign	09	06	34
Poole, Deuel(C)	1826	Sept. 19	Miami	10	02	04

PURCHASER	YEAR	DATE	RESIDENCE	R	T	S
Poole, Robert(C)	1815	Nov. 11	Madison	08	06	11
Poore, Edwin Lee(B)	1833	Dec. 28	Darke	01	17	26
Poorman, Daniel(C)	1832	Jan. 03	Champaign	13	04	01
Pope, Levin B.(A)	1836	June 27	Darke	01	12	04
Popejoy, Nathan(A)	1815	Oct. 10	Preble	02	11	01
Popejoy, Nathan(A)	1816	March 25	Darke	03	10	31
Popejoy, Nathan(A)	1818	Oct. 07	Darke	03	10	35
Popenoe, James(C)	1804	Sept. 03	Greene	06	03	29
Popenoe, Wm.(B)	1814	Dec. 30	Greene	02	10	14
Poppe, Ahrend Henry(B)	1833	Oct. 01	Germany	03	08	27
Poppe, Henry(B)	1834	Oct. 23	Hamilton	02	08	28
Port, James(B)	1817	Oct. 18	Butler	01	09	12
Port, James(E)	1814	Aug. 27	Butler	12	14	26
Port, John(E)	1811	Oct. 24	Ross	13	15	15
Port, John(E)	1811	Dec. 13	Ross	13	15	15
Porter, Alexander(A)	1815	April 11	Preble	01	06	18
Porter, Cornelius(E)	1836	June 17	Randolph(Ind	15	21	05
Porter, James(A)	1801	Sept. 04	Hamilton	04	03	13
Porter, James(A)	1804	Aug. 08	Montgomery	04	03	08
Porter, James(A)	1804	Aug. 08	Montgomery	04	03	18
Porter, James(B)	1832	Nov. 30	Switzerland	03	03	02
Porter, James(B)	1833	June 03	Switzerland	03	03	02
Porter, James(E)	1811	Nov. 08	Montgomery	13	17	19
Porter, James(E)	1814	Oct. 25	Wayne(Ind)	13	17	09
Porter, James(E)	1833	Oct. 29	Randolph(Ind	15	21	06
Porter, James(E)	1836	Oct. 06	Randolph(Ind	14	21	01
Porter, James(E)	1837	Jan. 28	Randolph(Ind	14	21	01
Porter, John(A)	1816	April 01	Butler	03	09	04
Porter, Joshua(E)	1811	Oct. 28	Franklin(Ind	12	13	03
Porter, Moses(B)	1834	Sept. 15	Switzerland	03	03	02
Porter, Nathan(B)	1805	Dec. 24	Dearborn(Ind	01	08	19
Porter, Robert(C)	1806	Aug. 01	Champaign	10	05	29
Porter, Samuel(A)	1837	April 24	?	01	14	35
Porter, Thomas Chancellor(B)	1816	Oct. 12	England	02	05	23
Post, Aaron(B)	1818	Aug. 08	Cincinnati	02	06	04
Post, Israel(C)	1815	Aug. 29	Warren	12	01	05
Potchins, Conrad(A)	1815	July 20	Miami	05	10	32
Poteet, Squire(B)	1813	June 14	Dearborn(Ind	01	04	07
Poteet, Squire(B)	1813	Nov. 09	Dearborn(Ind	01	04	18
Pottenger, Dennis(A)	1809	Aug. 09	Preble	02	06	02
Pottenger, John(A)	1806	Sept. 20	Butler	02	07	34
Pottenger, John(A)	1814	Dec. 29	Preble	02	06	04
Pottenger, Thomas(A)	1801	May 18	Hamilton	03	03	28
Potter, Daniel(A)	1811	May 31	Darke	02	12	30
Potter, Daniel(A)	1811	May 31	Darke	02	12	20
Potter, David Senr.(A)	1837	June 30	Darke	01	12	07
Potter, David(A)	1832	Feb. 02	Darke	02	12	05
Potter, David(A)	1834	March 22	Darke	02	12	21
Potter, David(B)	1836	Aug. 15	Darke	01	18	23
Potter, Elizabeth(E)	1836	Aug. 15	Darke	15	20	09
Potter, Enas(C)	1802	Dec. 29	Hamilton	04	02	27
Potter, John C.(A)	1837	Jan. 06	Darke	02	12	04
Potter, John C.(A)	1837	Jan. 06	Darke	01	12	11
Potter, John C.(A)	1837	Jan. 14	Darke	01	12	11
Potter, John Snavely(C)	1805	Oct. 21	Maryland	09	04	04
Potter, John(E)	1817	Sept. 30	Wayne(Ind)	14	15	05
Potter, John(E)	1822	Nov. 29	Wayne(Ind)	14	18	27
Potter, Joseph(A)	1814	Sept. 05	Preble	03	05	08
Potter, Joseph(A)	1815	Nov. 23	Preble	03	07	18
Potter, Martin(B)	1833	April 15	Switzerland	03	04	36
Potter, Martin(B)	1836	April 11	Switzerland	03	03	04
Potter, Moses(C)	1801	Dec. 30	Hamilton	04	02	21
Potter, Noadiah(A)	1811	June 27	Darke	02	12	30
Potter, Noadiah(A)	1811	July 26	Darke	02	12	33
Potter, Noadiah(A)	1816	Aug. 01	Darke	02	12	30
Potter, Noadiah(A)	1816	Aug. 06	Warren	02	12	28
Potter, Noadiah(C)	1801	Dec. 09	Hamilton	04	02	10
Potter, Thomas(A)	1837	April 17	Hamilton	02	14	33
Potterf, Gasper(A)	1815	Nov. 02	Preble	03	07	24

259

PURCHASER	YEAR	DATE	RESIDENCE	R	T	S
Potterf, Gasper(A)	1815	Nov. 11	Preble	03	07	24
Potterf, John(A)	1814	Sept. 26	Preble	02	07	28
Pottinger, Dennis(A)	1806	March 21	Butler	02	06	02
Pottinger, Dennis(A)	1804	April 18	Butler	02	06	02
Pottinger, Robert(A)	1809	Dec. 12	Preble	02	06	02
Pottinger, Samuel(A)	1801	April 27	Hamilton	03	03	33
Pottinger, Thomas(A)	1811	Nov. 08	Butler	01	07	10
Pottorf, Jacob(A)	1813	Feb. 19	Preble	02	07	24
Pottorf, Joseph(A)	1812	Dec. 09	Preble	03	05	08
Potts, David(C)	1831	Jan. 01	Miami	12	02	26
Potts, James(E)	1836	Jan. 15	Franklin(Ind	12	12	12
Potts, James(E)	1836	Sept. 29	Franklin(Ind	12	12	11
Potts, William(C)	1831	Oct. 03	Butler	12	02	21
Potts, William(E)	1831	Aug. 10	Franklin(Ind	12	12	11
Pound, Thomas(A)	1801	July 27	Hamilton	03	03	27
Pount, John Hy.(E)	1837	July 11	Cincinnati	12	11	19
Pouts, William(A)	1801	Dec. 11	Hamilton	04	03	01
Povrin, John(C)	1806	Aug. 30	Maryland	09	05	27
Powel, Howel(A)	1814	Oct. 06	Butler	02	03	29
Powell, Benjamin(B)	1811	Jan. 11	Ind.Territry	02	05	24
Powell, Elijah(C)	1827	Dec. 19	Champaign	11	05	34
Powell, Elijah(C)	1829	Jan. 16	Champaign	11	05	34
Powell, Howel(A)	1836	Dec. 02	Butler	02	13	29
Powell, Howel(A)	1836	Dec. 03	Butler	01	14	19
Powell, Howel(A)	1837	Sept. 15	Butler	01	14	30
Powell, Howel(A)	1837	Oct. 16	Butler	01	14	30
Powell, Isaac N.(E)	1836	Oct. 13	Kentucky	11	10	27
Powell, Isaac N.(E)	1836	Oct. 15	Kentucky	11	10	28
Powell, Jacob(B)	1817	June 21	Warren	01	03	33
Powell, James(E)	1835	Jan. 24	Wayne(Ind)	12	17	24
Powell, John(A)	1813	Aug. 12	Butler	01	03	14
Powell, John(A)	1815	April 29	Butler	01	03	13
Powell, John(A)	1831	Nov. 15	Preble	06	08	03
Powell, John(C)	1806	Aug. 22	Maryland	09	04	02
Powell, John(C)	1814	May 30	Champaign	14	04	34
Powell, John(C)	1831	Aug. 08	Logan	14	03	08
Powell, John(E)	1837	Jan. 14	Fayette	15	20	21
Powell, Joseph(A)	1819	June 09	Montgomery	04	10	07
Powell, Oner R.(A)	1836	Nov. 07	Kentucky	01	15	29
Powell, Oner R.(E)	1836	Oct. 14	Kentucky	11	10	23
Powell, Oner R.(E)	1836	Oct. 14	Kentucky	11	10	23
Powell, Philip(B)	1836	Nov. 30	Fayette	01	17	10
Powell, Philip(E)	1836	Nov. 30	Fayette	15	20	28
Powell, Philip(E)	1837	March 22	Randolph(Ind	15	20	21
Powell, Simon(E)	1814	Feb. 19	Kentucky	12	16	26
Powell, Thomas(A)	1813	Aug. 26	Butler	02	03	18
Powell, Thomas(C)	1814	May 30	Champaign	14	04	34
Powell, Wilie(B)	1818	Feb. 28	Franklin(Ind	02	10	15
Powell, William Jr.(E)	1837	Jan. 20	Randolph(Ind	15	20	32
Powell, William(B)	1817	June 21	Warren	01	02	04
Powell, William(C)	1804	Sept. 05	Greene	12	05	13
Powell, William(C)	1809	Dec. 12	Champaign	12	05	21
Powell, William(C)	1810	Dec. 12	Champaign	12	05	13
Powell, William(C)	1811	Nov. 11	Champaign	14	04	35
Power, Alexander(E)	1831	March 08	Franklin(Ind	11	12	13
Power, David(B)	1815	Feb. 06	Butler	02	10	23
Power, James(A)	1818	March 20	Hamilton	07	02	31
Powers, Aaron(A)	1805	Dec. 24	Butler	01	04	35
Powers, Aaron(A)	1836	Nov. 08	Butler	01	15	24
Powers, Aaron(A)	1836	Nov. 29	Butler	02	15	30
Powers, Aaron(A)	1836	Nov. 30	Butler	02	15	18
Powers, Benjamin F.(E)	1817	Sept. 29	Cincinnati	13	19	32
Powers, Benjamin F.(E)	1817	Oct. 15	Cincinnati	13	12	13
Powers, Daniel(B)	1814	Oct. 20	Butler	02	10	27
Powers, Daniel(B)	1814	Oct. 20	Butler	02	10	35
Powers, Ezekiel(B)	1814	March 01	Butler	02	09	01
Powers, Jacob(C)	1809	Dec. 30	Butler	02	02	26
Powers, James S.(B)	1836	June 17	Hamilton	02	09	06
Powers, James Simpson(B)	1835	July 25	Franklin(Ind	02	09	06

PURCHASER	YEAR	DATE	RESIDENCE	R	T	S
Powers, John(B)	1814	April 26	Franklin(Ind	01	10	31
Powers, Jonathan W.(B)	1814	April 20	Butler	01	10	17
Powers, Joseph(B)	1808	Aug. 16	Butler	01	12	08
Powers, Joseph(E)	1836	Sept. 09	Franklin(Ind	11	10	22
Powers, Thomas(B)	1815	June 23	Franklin(Ind	02	10	32
Powers, William Morris(E)	1836	Jan. 07	Franklin(Ind	11	12	24
Powers, Wm.(B)	1814	March 01	Butler	02	09	01
Pownall, Elizabeth H.(C)	1830	Sept. 25	Miami	12	02	15
Powner, Wm. H.(B)	1829	Dec. 11	Franklin(Ind	01	09	33
Poyner, Peter(A)	1811	July 01	Preble	03	04	12
Poyner, Peter(A)	1814	Aug. 19	Preble	03	04	14
Pratt, Daniel(B)	1814	Sept. 17	Clermont	03	03	26
Pray, Enos(E)	1836	Dec. 30	Preble	13	20	35
Pren, Jacob(E)	1837	Nov. 20	Montgomery	11	11	24
Prentice, David(A)	1836	July 26	Miami	03	12	33
Prentice, Mary(A)	1836	July 26	Miami	03	12	33
Pressley, David(A)	1808	Aug. 02	So. Carolina	01	06	03
Pressley, David(A)	1808	Aug. 02	So. Carolina	01	06	32
Pressley, David(A)	1810	Sept. 24	So. Carolina	01	06	17
Pressley, David(B)	1808	Aug. 02	So. Carolina	01	11	27
Pressly, David(A)	1812	Sept. 02	So. Carolina	01	06	19
Prestly, David(A)	1808	Feb. 02	So. Carolina	01	07	28
Prevo, Asa(E)	1814	Jan. 24	Wayne(Ind)	13	16	18
Prewitt, William(B)	1834	Oct. 11	Switzerland	03	03	18
Pribble, Benjamin B.(A)	1815	Aug. 30	Pickaway	01	09	11
Price, Caleb(A)	1817	July 22	Pennsylvania	02	03	21
Price, Catherine(B)	1813	Nov. 03	Preble	01	13	23
Price, Charles(A)	1829	Jan. 15	Preble	02	09	36
Price, Christian(A)	1803	Oct. 11	Warren	03	05	04
Price, Christian(A)	1803	Oct. 11	Warren	03	05	03
Price, Christian(A)	1808	Dec. 14	Preble	03	05	04
Price, Dan'l.(A)	1829	May 04	Preble	02	09	15
Price, Daniel(A)	1815	Feb. 06	Montgomery	03	07	10
Price, David(C)	1808	Jan. 13	Greene	09	06	02
Price, Edward(E)	1817	Oct. 27	Warren	14	18	26
Price, George(A)	1813	Nov. 26	Warren	02	09	12
Price, Henry(A)	1804	Nov. 19	Virginia	03	06	06
Price, Henry(A)	1805	Nov. 06	Montgomery	03	06	06
Price, Henry(A)	1819	Nov. 01	Preble	03	06	06
Price, Jacob(C)	1804	Dec. 08	Montgomery	09	02	17
Price, James(B)	1806	March 20	Ind.Territory	01	08	18
Price, John Jr.(E)	1832	March 12	Franklin(Ind	13	12	13
Price, John Junr.(A)	1804	Dec. 04	Hamilton	02	05	08
Price, John(A)	1806	March 28	Butler	01	04	12
Price, John(A)	1810	Oct. 19	Virginia	04	04	11
Price, John(C)	1801	Dec. 31	Hamilton	06	02	19
Price, John(C)	1808	Jan. 13	Montgomery	11	02	07
Price, John(E)	1813	Oct. 23	Butler	13	12	10
Price, Joseph(B)	1834	Oct. 30	Franklin(Ind	02	08	34
Price, Michael(A)	1813	Dec. 07	Preble	03	07	31
Price, Rice(A)	1807	May 23	Butler	01	08	33
Price, Rice(E)	1817	Nov. 14	Preble	15	18	18
Price, Samuel(B)	1817	July 10	Franklin(Ind	02	08	35
Price, Samuel(B)	1817	July 19	Franklin(Ind	02	08	27
Price, Thomas(A)	1806	March 28	Greene	02	05	19
Price, Thomas(E)	1817	Oct. 27	Warren	14	18	35
Price, William(B)	1805	Nov. 25	Virginia	01	14	31
Price, William(B)	1805	Nov. 25	Virginia	01	14	30
Price, William(B)	1811	April 09	Ind.Territory	01	14	31
Price, William(B)	1814	Oct. 27	Wayne(Ind)	01	14	30
Price, William(C)	1825	March 05	Switzerland	14	02	08
Price, William(C)	1831	Oct. 27	Logan	14	02	05
Price, William(E)	1827	Sept. 20	Wayne(Ind)	14	18	22
Price, William(E)	1835	March 09	New Jersey	13	18	14
Prichard, John(A)	1803	May 18	Hamilton	03	03	25
Prichard, Samuel(B)	1830	Oct. 30	Wayne(Ind)	01	15	28
Prichet, Ezekiel(B)	1836	Dec. 17	Butler	01	17	11
Prichet, Ezekiel(B)	1836	Dec. 17	Butler	01	17	11
Pricket, James(B)	1813	June 07	Jefferson	03	02	01

PURCHASER	YEAR	DATE	RESIDENCE	R	T	S
Priest, Jeremiah(C)	1804	Dec. 31	Montgomery	10	02	13
Priest, Jeremiah(C)	1814	March 15	Miami	10	03	27
Prifogle, Peter(B)	1816	June 10	Franklin(Ind	02	08	18
Prifogle, Peter(B)	1834	Aug. 13	Franklin(Ind	02	08	18
Prill, Elizabeth(C)	1826	May 02	Warren	10	03	18
Prill, Henry(C)	1818	Jan. 17	Warren	10	03	12
Prill, Henry(C)	1826	Oct. 18	Warren	10	03	18
Prill, Henry(C)	1829	July 07	Warren	10	03	18
Prill, John(A)	1816	Aug. 21	Montgomery	06	03	06
Prill, John(C)	1820	April 05	Warren	10	03	06
Prilleman, Christian(C)	1811	Dec. 11	Miami	10	02	19
Prince, Adam(C)	1810	April 10	Champaign	11	04	28
Prince, Adam(C)	1815	Aug. 21	Champaign	11	04	27
Prince, Adam(C)	1826	Nov. 07	Champaign	11	04	34
Prince, Martin(C)	1831	Sept. 05	Champaign	12	03	27
Prior, Allen(E)	1817	Dec. 26	Wayne(Ind)	14	15	08
Prior, Joseph(E)	1817	Dec. 26	Wayne(Ind)	14	15	08
Priser, David(A)	1827	June 06	Montgomery	04	06	01
Priser, Mich'l.(A)	1828	March 28	Montgomery	04	05	21
Priser, Michael(A)	1827	Nov. 14	Montgomery	04	05	15
Pritchard, Ezekiel(B)	1818	Jan. 24	Dearborn(Ind	02	04	17
Pritchard, James(B)	1813	Sept. 01	Dearborn(Ind	02	04	09
Pritchard, John(B)	1832	Aug. 03	Dearborn(Ind	02	05	29
Pritchard, John(B)	1832	Aug. 13	Dearborn(Ind	02	05	29
Probst, Fred'k.(B)	1838	Dec. 26	Cincinnati	03	04	04
Probst, Frederick(B)	1839	June 17	Cincinnati	03	04	04
Probst, Henry(B)	1838	April 23	Cincinnati	03	05	26
Probst, Henry(B)	1838	April 26	Cincinnati	03	05	26
Probst, Henry(B)	1838	Dec. 25	Cincinnati	03	05	24
Probst, Henry(B)	1839	June 17	Cincinnati	03	04	03
Proctor, William(C)	1819	Jan. 11	Hamilton	10	03	12
Protsman, John 3rd(B)	1836	June 13	Switzerland	03	03	08
Protzman, John(B)	1814	July 30	Dearborn(Ind	03	03	31
Prough, Peter(E)	1836	Nov. 26	Montgomery	15	20	08
Provolt, John(C)	1807	Feb. 02	Champaign	13	04	36
Provolt, John(E)	1813	Dec. 20	Champaign	13	04	36
Prudden, David(B)	1818	Feb. 18	Hamilton	02	06	06
Prudden, Isaac(B)	1832	Aug. 13	Hamilton	01	07	35
Prudden, James(B)	1818	Feb. 18	Hamilton	02	06	07
Pruden, David M.(E)	1836	Sept. 26	Athens	14	19	08
Pruden, Sylvester(E)	1835	Sept. 24	Randolph(Ind	14	19	02
Pruet, Adenston(E)	1836	Oct. 26	CampbellCoKy	12	11	03
Pruet, William(E)	1836	Feb. 20	Franklin(Ind	11	12	35
Prugh, John F.(E)	1837	May 16	Montgomery	14	21	25
Pruit, Matthew Hawkins(E)	1836	May 03	Franklin(Ind	12	11	12
Prus, John Frederick(E)	1836	Oct. 21	Cincinnati	12	10	17
Pryer, John(A)	1806	June 02	Hamilton	01	02	09
Pryer, John(A)	1814	May 26	Hamilton	01	03	31
Puckett, Benjamin(E)	1834	June 28	Randolph(Ind	13	20	35
Puckett, Dan'l.(B)	1830	Feb. 01	Wayne(Ind)	01	15	21
Puckett, Daniel(E)	1818	Oct. 26	Wayne(Ind)	13	20	25
Puckett, Daniel(E)	1836	Dec. 30	Wayne(Ind)	14	19	19
Puckett, Daniel(E)	1836	Dec. 30	Wayne(Ind)	14	19	31
Puckett, Isom(E)	1820	Nov. 20	Randolph(Ind	13	26	34
Puckett, Isom(E)	1832	April 02	Randolph(Ind	13	20	34
Puckett, Isom(E)	1836	March 17	Randolph(Ind	13	20	35
Puckett, Joseph(E)	1819	Jan. 18	Clinton	13	20	34
Puckett, Thomas(E)	1818	Oct. 26	Wayne(Ind)	13	20	26
Puckett, Zachariah(E)	1819	April 07	Clinton	13	19	03
Puderbaugh, Abraham(A)	1816	Dec. 20	Montgomery	01	11	35
Puderbaugh, David(E)	1837	May 18	Darke	14	21	22
Puderbaugh, Jacob(A)	1822	July 18	Darke	01	10	01
Puderbaugh, Jacob(A)	1831	Oct. 04	Darke	02	11	23
Puderbough, George(A)	1818	May 29	Darke	01	11	36
Puderbough, Jacob(A)	1816	Aug. 10	Montgomery	01	11	36
Puderbough, Jacob(A)	1816	Aug. 26	Montgomery	02	10	05
Puderbough, John(A)	1816	Aug. 10	Montgomery	01	11	35
Puderbugh, George(A)	1817	Nov. 15	Pennsylvania	01	11	36
Pues, William(A)	1839	Jan. 21	Cincinnati	02	15	25

PURCHASER	YEAR	DATE	RESIDENCE	R	T	S
Pugh, Alexander(A)	1805	Feb. 25	Butler	03	04	24
Pugh, Alexander(A)	1805	Feb. 25	Butler	03	04	13
Pugh, Alexander(A)	1805	Aug. 09	Montgomery	02	08	18
Pugh, Alexander(A)	1805	Aug. 13	Montgomery	02	08	24
Pugh, Alexander(A)	1806	Dec. 04	Montgomery	03	04	14
Pugh, Alexander(A)	1808	March 29	Preble	02	07	30
Pugh, Alexander(A)	1814	Oct. 22	Preble	02	06	15
Pugh, Alexander(E)	1811	Oct. 28	Preble	14	15	04
Pugh, Alexr.(A)	1811	Nov. 30	?	03	04	27
Pugh, Alfred(B)	1833	Dec. 14	Switzerland	02	03	36
Pugh, Azariah(B)	1815	May 15	Dearborn(Ind	01	05	08
Pugh, Caleb(B)	1811	Dec. 19	Dearborn(Ind	01	05	08
Pugh, Enoch(B)	1811	Dec. 23	Dearborn(Ind	01	06	33
Pugh, Enoch(B)	1815	Nov. 22	Dearborn(Ind	01	05	08
Pugh, James(E)	1834	Jan. 11	Randolph(Ind	13	19	29
Pugh, James(E)	1835	Jan. 26	Randolph(Ind	13	19	29
Pugh, James(E)	1836	Oct. 31	Randolph(Ind	13	19	29
Pugh, Jesse(E)	1815	Oct. 02	Wayne(Ind)	13	18	31
Pugh, Joseph(B)	1815	May 18	Hamilton	02	03	31
Pugh, Joseph(B)	1815	Sept. 05	Switzerland	02	02	05
Pugh, Robert(E)	1836	Feb. 12	Preble	11	11	01
Pugh, Thomas(C)	1804	Dec. 24	Warren	04	04	13
Pugh, William(A)	1808	Jan. 11	Montgomery	01	10	33
Pugh, William(A)	1813	Sept. 03	Preble	01	07	35
Pumphery, Nicholas(B)	1814	Oct. 24	Virginia	02	08	33
Pumphrey, Blair M.(E)	1836	Oct. 21	Franklin(Ind	12	11	11
Pumphrey, Nicholas(E)	1816	June 18	Ind.Territry	13	13	07
Pund, Charles Hy.(A)	1837	Dec. 22	Cincinnati	02	15	36
Punnel, Noah(A)	1821	July 13	Warren	02	09	19
Purcel, Benjamin(B)	1808	June 29	Dearborn(Ind	03	05	36
Purcel, Laurence(B)	1817	Aug. 13	Dearborn(Ind	03	05	34
Purcel, Thomas Jr.(B)	1836	May 17	Dearborn(Ind	02	04	32
Purcel, Thomas(B)	1806	Sept. 11	Ind.Territry	02	04	31
Purcell, Benjamin(B)	1813	March 03	Dearborn(Ind	03	05	25
Purcell, Samuel(B)	1814	March 31	Dearborn(Ind	03	04	02
Pursail, Benjamin(E)	1836	Feb. 27	Randolph(Ind	14	21	12
Pursail, Benjamin(E)	1836	June 18	Randolph(Ind	14	21	12
Pursail, John(E)	1837	Jan. 20	Randolph(Ind	14	21	12
Pursel, William(B)	1811	Sept. 06	Dearborn(Ind	01	07	24
Pursil, William(B)	1818	June 10	Dearborn(Ind	01	07	23
Pursley, Hudson(E)	1836	Nov. 02	Randolph(Ind	13	20	15
Pursley, James(E)	1832	Oct. 25	Randolph(Ind	13	20	15
Pursley, James(E)	1836	Nov. 02	Randolph(Ind	13	20	15
Purveance, David B.	1807	Jan. 24	Kentucky	01	09	20
Purveance, David(A)	1810	March 12	Preble	01	09	31
Purveance, John(A)	1807	Jan. 24	Kentucky	01	09	04
Purveance, John(A)	1807	Jan. 24	Kentucky	01	09	05
Purveance, John(A)	1807	Aug. 13	Kentucky	01	10	33
Purviance, Lewis W.(A)	1828	Oct. 22	Darke	01	10	33
Purvience, Eliezor(A)	1806	Aug. 08	Tennessee	01	09	29
Puterbaugh, David(C)	1805	Nov. 30	Greene	08	02	23
Puterbaugh, David(C)	1806	April 12	Greene	08	02	23
Puterbaugh, David(C)	1806	May 05	Greene	08	02	23
Puterbaugh, David(C)	1817	June 17	Miami	10	02	08
Puterbaugh, Jacob(E)	1836	Sept. 02	Darke	15	21	06
Putman, Ernestus(A)	1829	Jan. 29	Darke	01	10	12
Putman, Ernestus(E)	1837	Jan. 20	Darke	14	21	18
Putman, Ernestus(E)	1837	March 27	Darke	15	22	10
Putman, Ernestus(E)	1838	Dec. 18	Darke	14	21	12
Putman, Thomas(C)	1818	Dec. 28	Champaign	11	03	11
Putman, Thos.(C)	1827	Aug. 22	Champaign	11	03	11
Putman, William(C)	1831	March 07	Champaign	11	03	04
Putterbaugh, David(C)	1811	Sept. 27	Montgomery	09	02	26
Putterbaugh, John(A)	1836	Oct. 10	Miami	03	12	17
Putty, David(A)	1816	Nov. 19	Miami	05	08	17
Pyle, John(B)	1836	Feb. 17	Franklin(Ind	03	09	13
Quakinbush, Peter(E)	1811	Oct. 24	?	13	17	35
Quals, John M.(E)	1836	June 30	Franklin(Ind	12	11	25
Quals, Nicholas(E)	1832	Sept. 15	Franklin(Ind	12	11	25

PURCHASER	YEAR	DATE	RESIDENCE	R	T	S
Quals, Nicholas(E)	1836	March 05	Franklin(Ind	12	11	25
Query, George(A)	1818	Oct. 07	Adams	01	09	13
Quick, Cornelius(A)	1805	Sept. 30	Butler	02	04	05
Quick, Cyrus(B)	1836	Feb. 10	Franklin(Ind	02	08	01
Quick, John(B)	1810	Aug. 14	Dearborn(Ind	02	08	02
Quick, John(B)	1814	Dec. 22	Franklin(Ind	02	08	02
Quick, John(B)	1828	Oct. 27	Franklin(Ind	02	08	11
Quigley, John(B)	1813	Dec. 13	Dearborn(Ind	01	02	12
Quigley, John(B)	1816	Feb. 27	Switzerland	01	02	01
Quilling, John(A)	1804	Sept. 24	Montgomery	05	05	11
Quin, James(A)	1805	Sept. 06	Montgomery	03	06	07
Quin, John(E)	1836	Dec. 22	Cincinnati	12	11	07
Quin, John(E)	1836	Dec. 22	Cincinnati	12	11	08
Quin, John(E)	1836	Dec. 22	Cincinnati	12	11	09
Quin, John(E)	1836	Dec. 27	Cincinnati	11	11	14
Quin, Nicholas(C)	1804	Dec. 04	Greene	07	03	05
Quin, Robert(A)	1805	Sept. 06	Montgomery	03	06	18
Quin, Robert(A)	1805	Sept. 14	Montgomery	03	06	31
Quinn, John(A)	1806	July 08	Montgomery	03	06	31
Quinn, Joseph C.(A)	1816	Nov. 29	Preble	03	05	06
Quinn, Joseph(A)	1815	Jan. 06	Dearborn(Ind	03	05	06
Quinn, Robt. Jr.(A)	1824	Sept. 21	Preble	02	08	22
Rab, George(B)	1816	June 21	Ind.Territry	01	09	21
Raberson, Ephraim(A)	1816	Oct. 19	Hamilton	02	09	10
Radabaugh, Mich'l. Jr.(A)	1831	July 04	Miami	04	09	01
Radabaugh, Michael(A)	1831	July 05	Miami	04	09	03
Radabaugh, Peter(A)	1831	Nov. 29	Darke	04	09	07
Radcliffe, Benjamin(C)	1804	Dec. 28	Greene	08	03	27
Rader, Jane(E)	1832	Oct. 03	Franklin(Ind	12	10	02
Rader, John(E)	1833	Feb. 11	Franklin(Ind	12	11	35
Rader, John(E)	1836	Feb. 17	Franklin(Ind	12	11	35
Raelsback, John(A)	1806	March 21	Butler	02	07	18
Railsback, David(B)	1807	March 13	Dearborn(Ind	02	12	02
Railsback, David(B)	1810	Dec. 27	Dearborn(Ind	02	13	35
Railsback, David(B)	1811	Aug. 14	Wayne(Ind)	02	13	35
Railsback, David(E)	1815	Dec. 26	Wayne(Ind)	14	15	17
Railsback, Jacob(A)	1806	Sept. 20	Butler	02	07	34
Railsback, Jacob(A)	1831	Sept. 09	Preble	02	07	33
Raily, Joshua(E)	1837	Aug. 21	Wayne(Ind)	15	20	20
Rainier, Joseph(E)	1837	Feb. 27	Preble	13	19	02
Rainier, Stacy(E)	1836	Sept. 10	Preble	14	19	19
Rains, Joab(A)	1811	April 26	Butler	02	06	32
Rairdon, John(C)	1831	Nov. 24	Fairfield	14	02	06
Raisbeck, James(A)	1836	Aug. 03	New York	03	12	25
Raitt, Nathan(A)	1812	May 04	Maryland	03	04	13
Ralstin, James(A)	1815	Dec. 07	Adams	04	09	30
Ralston, Allen Jr.(C)	1830	March 26	Miami	12	02	26
Ralston, Allen(C)	1806	Aug. 25	Warren	11	02	22
Ralston, Allen(C)	1811	Dec. 11	Miami	11	02	22
Ralston, Edward(C)	1802	Nov. 10	Hamilton	04	03	31
Ralston, James(E)	1817	Sept. 24	Kentucky	13	17	31
Rambley, James(B)	1812	Aug. 25	Butler	01	04	06
Rambo, Absalom(B)	1813	Nov. 11	Wayne(Ind)	01	13	35
Rambo, Isaac(E)	1825	Nov. 12	Wayne(Ind)	14	15	29
Rambo, Jackson(B)	1809	June 12	Hamilton	01	13	31
Ramer, John A.(A)	1836	Oct. 24	Hamilton	01	14	08
Ramer, Peter(B)	1818	March 20	Hamilton	03	05	14
Ramey, Henry(B)	1806	July 09	Dearborn(Ind	01	08	13
Ramey, James(B)	1808	Jan. 13	Dearborn(Ind	02	11	34
Ramey, John(B)	1804	Oct. 13	Kentucky	01	09	28
Ramey, John(B)	1804	Oct. 13	Kentucky	02	09	32
Ramey, John(B)	1804	Oct. 13	Kentucky	01	09	27
Ramey, William(B)	1808	Jan. 28	Dearborn(Ind	01	08	24
Ramsay, Robert(C)	1815	Jan. 04	Montgomery	09	02	29
Ramsburgh, Joseph(B)	1817	Sept. 02	Maryland	01	06	04
Ramsey, Allan(A)	1805	Feb. 22	Hamilton	01	01	09
Ramsey, Allen(B)	1807	Feb. 20	Dearborn(Ind	02	08	14
Ramsey, David(E)	1837	May 29	Randolph(Ind	14	20	04
Ramsey, James P.(B)	1817	Sept. 23	Butler	02	04	08

PURCHASER	YEAR	DATE	RESIDENCE	R	T	S
Ramsey, James P.(B)	1817	Sept. 23	Butler	03	06	36
Ramsey, James P.(B)	1817	Oct. 27	?	02	04	18
Ramsey, James P.(B)	1817	Oct. 27	?	03	05	13
Ramsey, James(E)	1836	Dec. 15	Randolph(Ind	14	20	04
Ramsey, John(A)	1805	Dec. 23	Kentucky	01	06	24
Ramsey, John(A)	1814	Aug. 17	Preble	01	06	13
Ramsey, John(A)	1815	March 14	Preble	01	06	21
Ramsey, Lucey(A)	1806	March 10	Hamilton	01	04	34
Ramsey, Thomas(A)	1804	Oct. 09	Cincinnati	02	05	27
Ramsey, Thomas(B)	1818	Oct. 03	Switzerland	02	02	34
Ramsey, Will'm. Junr.(A)	1815	Oct. 31	Preble	01	06	21
Ramsey, William Junior(A)	1805	March 14	Kentucky	01	06	23
Ramsey, William Junr.(B)	1808	July 28	Preble	01	11	35
Ramsey, William Jur.(A)	1815	March 14	Preble	01	06	15
Ramsey, William Senr.(A)	1805	March 14	Kentucky	01	06	14
Ramsey, William(A)	1801	June 02	Cincinnati	02	04	31
Ramsey, William(A)	1807	Aug. 28	Montgomery	02	06	31
Ramsey, William(A)	1813	April 06	Franklin(Ind	01	04	31
Ramsey, William(C)	1802	Dec. 25	Kentucky	04	03	14
Ramsey, William(C)	1806	Jan. 21	Cincinnati	09	05	30
Ramsey, William(C)	1806	Jan. 21	Cincinnati	10	05	25
Ramsey, Wm.(B)	1814	Oct. 13	Franklin(Ind	02	08	26
Ranck, John A.(E)	1817	Aug. 07	Ohio	13	14	13
Rand, Thomas(B)	1811	April 17	Dearborn(Ind	03	04	09
Rand, Thomas(B)	1811	April 17	Dearborn(Ind	03	04	09
Randall, Abraham(C)	1828	Nov. 12	Shelby	13	02	18
Randall, Isaac(C)	1829	Aug. 10	Logan	13	02	11
Randall, William(B)	1818	Feb. 27	Warren	03	05	12
Randel, John(A)	1813	April 29	Preble	02	06	35
Randel, Jonas(B)	1807	June 26	Butler	01	14	30
Randel, Joseph(A)	1806	May 09	Butler	02	06	36
Randle, Jehu(A)	1832	Aug. 02	Preble	01	09	12
Randle, John(A)	1832	Aug. 08	Preble	01	09	12
Randle, John(B)	1833	Nov. 16	Randolph(Ind	01	16	11
Randle, John(B)	1834	Dec. 20	Randolph(Ind	01	16	13
Randle, John(B)	1836	Feb. 16	Franklin(Ind	01	16	12
Randle, John(E)	1836	July 07	Preble	14	19	34
Randle, Jonas(B)	1806	Aug. 11	Butler	01	14	30
Randle, Jonas(B)	1806	Aug. 11	Butler	01	13	06
Randle, Joseph(A)	1811	Aug. 13	Preble	02	06	36
Randolph, Jonah F.(E)	1836	Oct. 07	GreeneCo.Pa.	13	20	01
Ranken, Archibald(A)	1806	Feb. 06	Pennsylvania	03	06	17
Rankin, Archibald(A)	1806	Feb. 06	Pennsylvania	03	06	26
Rankin, Archibald(A)	1806	Sept. 06	Montgomery	03	06	26
Rankin, Archibald(A)	1806	Sept. 06	Ohio	03	06	35
Rape, Jacob(A)	1806	March 11	Warren	03	06	23
Raper, John(B)	1811	Oct. 30	Wayne(Ind)	01	13	24
Raplogle, Philip(A)	1829	June 24	Montgomery	04	06	08
Rapp, Henry(A)	1806	Nov. 15	Maryland	04	04	25
Rapp, Maria(B)	1835	Oct. 02	Hamilton	02	07	01
Rarden, Moses(B)	1812	July 09	Ind.Territory	01	09	14
Rardin, Moses(B)	1811	March 04	Ind.Territory	01	09	14
Rarich, Dan'l.(A)	1831	Aug. 12	Darke	01	12	30
Rarich, Daniel(A)	1834	Jan. 15	Darke	01	12	30
Rarick, Jacob(A)	1831	May 30	Miami	04	09	22
Rarick, Philip(A)	1817	June 04	Montgomery	01	10	02
Rarisch, John(A)	1821	Jan. 25	Montgomery	04	05	25
Rasnick, Lazarus Damrell(E)	1836	Jan. 21	Franklin(Ind	13	12	08
Rason, George(E)	1836	Sept. 05	Franklin(Ind	12	11	25
Rasor, George(E)	1825	Jan. 27	Franklin(Ind	12	11	25
Rasor, George(E)	1836	Feb. 22	Franklin(Ind	12	11	25
Ratcliff, Job(E)	1832	June 28	Wayne(Ind)	13	17	04
Ratcliff, Thomas(E)	1831	July 01	Wayne(Ind)	13	18	26
Rathbun, Edmund(E)	1837	June 08	Richland	14	22	34
Rathbun, Hiram(E)	1837	June 08	Richland	14	22	34
Ratliff, Cornelius(E)	1814	Oct. 21	Wayne(Ind)	13	17	36
Ratliff, Cornelius(E)	1815	Feb. 03	Wayne(Ind)	13	17	33
Ratliff, Thomas(A)	1830	April 14	Montgomery	04	07	34
Ratter, Samuel(B)	1807	March 02	Butler	01	11	12

PURCHASER	YEAR	DATE	RESIDENCE	R	T	S
Raudle, Jonas(A)	1805	May 31	Butler	03	04	31
Rauhrick, Jacob(A)	1816	Nov. 06	Pennsylvania	04	09	10
Raver, John(E)	1837	May 01	Cincinnati	11	11	35
Rawson, Horace S.(E)	1828	Aug. 30	Indiana	14	20	14
Rawson, Levi B.(E)	1837	March 01	Preble	14	20	24
Ray, Christian(A)	1831	Sept. 17	Preble	02	10	17
Ray, Christian(E)	1827	June 06	Wayne(Ind)	13	16	26
Ray, Edward(B)	1817	Oct. 18	Hamilton	04	02	25
Ray, John Watts(B)	1835	Sept. 04	Dearborn(Ind	02	04	32
Ray, John(A)	1806	Oct. 06	Hamilton	02	03	12
Ray, John(B)	1813	Aug. 26	Butler	01	10	07
Ray, Lewis S.(E)	1828	Nov. 15	Fayette	12	12	01
Ray, Lewis(C)	1812	July 27	Hamilton	10	04	32
Ray, Lewis(C)	1816	June 10	Champaign	10	03	03
Ray, Robert(B)	1816	April 03	Kentucky	03	05	32
Rayl, Elijah(B)	1832	June 18	Switzerland	01	02	30
Rayl, James(B)	1832	Nov. 07	Switzerland	02	02	15
Rayl, James(B)	1833	Jan. 26	Switzerland	02	02	15
Rayl, John(B)	1836	Feb. 24	Switzerland	02	02	23
Rayl, Thomas Jr.(B)	1832	March 01	Switzerland	02	02	15
Rayl, Thomas Jr.(B)	1832	June 18	Switzerland	02	02	22
Rayl, William(B)	1806	Sept. 19	Hamilton	01	09	33
Rayl, William(B)	1814	Dec. 24	Hamilton	02	02	26
Raymond, Charles(B)	1816	Feb. 22	Dearborn(Ind	01	07	01
Raymond, Lewis(B)	1816	Feb. 22	Dearborn(Ind	01	07	01
Razor, Daniel(A)	1807	June 19	Montgomery	04	06	13
Razor, Daniel(A)	1813	Jan. 12	Montgomery	05	05	15
Razor, Daniel(A)	1814	April 04	Montgomery	05	05	18
Razor, John(A)	1831	April 08	Montgomery	04	06	09
Read, Amos(A)	1815	Feb. 10	Warren	06	04	31
Read, Ezra(C)	1830	April 01	Champaign	12	04	11
Read, Isaac(B)	1834	Jan. 15	Dearborn(Ind	02	03	14
Read, Isaac(B)	1836	Jan. 11	Dearborn(Ind	02	03	14
Readenbaugh, Adam(D)	1811	Jan. 05	Hamilton	01	04	26
Ready, John Goddard(A)	1832	March 06	Hamilton	05	09	02
Reagan, Nicholas(E)	1811	Dec. 17	Franklin(Ind	12	13	14
Reagan, William B.(C)	1813	Aug. 10	Champaign	10	05	19
Reagan, Zadok(A)	1831	June 06	Dearborn(Ind	04	09	32
Reagin, Zadock(A)	1816	Aug. 05	Warren	04	09	32
Ream, Andrew(C)	1815	May 03	Champaign	10	03	10
Ream, Andrew(C)	1821	Aug. 23	Clark	10	03	10
Ream, Benjamin(C)	1817	Dec. 02	Champaign	10	04	32
Ream, Solomon(C)	1824	Aug. 11	Clark	10	03	11
Reardon, Moses(B)	1810	Jan. 08	Dearborn(Ind	01	09	14
Rechart, Anthony(A)	1805	Nov. 04	Montgomery	03	06	36
Reck, John(A)	1829	Dec. 08	Darke	03	10	35
Reck, John(A)	1829	Dec. 08	Darke	04	09	31
Reck, John(A)	1831	Oct. 26	Darke	04	09	32
Reck, John(A)	1831	Oct. 26	Darke	04	09	31
Reck, William(A)	1831	June 14	Darke	03	10	35
Recke, John Henry(E)	1836	Nov. 15	Cincinnati	12	11	32
Reckets, Nathan(B)	1814	Nov. 18	Dearborn(Ind	01	03	19
Record, Thomas(B)	1836	June 20	Dearborn(Ind	02	05	29
Record, Thomas(B)	1836	Dec. 13	Dearborn(Ind	02	05	29
Record, William(B)	1809	July 13	Dearborn(Ind	02	05	23
Record, William(B)	1812	March 20	Dearborn(Ind	02	05	23
Rector, Charles(C)	1804	Aug. 16	Greene	10	04	11
Rector, Charles(C)	1804	Dec. 31	Greene	10	04	12
Rector, Charles(C)	1804	Dec. 31	Greene	10	05	05
Rector, Charles(C)	1825	Nov. 28	Champaign	11	04	07
Reddick, William(C)	1810	Dec. 12	Miami	09	02	22
Reddick, William(C)	1814	Dec. 12	Miami	09	02	28
Redding, Ezekiel(A)	1813	Sept. 14	Clermont	03	05	24
Reddle, John(C)	1804	Dec. 31	Hamilton	11	01	10
Redenbaugh, Jeremiah(C)	1816	Aug. 31	Hamilton	12	01	17
Redenbough, John(C)	1815	March 09	Hamilton	12	01	11
Redenhour, Peter(A)	1809	Aug. 25	Preble	01	06	33
Redenhour, Peter(A)	1814	Oct. 24	Preble	01	06	28
Redinbaugh, Solomon(C)	1831	July 05	Shelby	13	02	33

PURCHASER	YEAR	DATE	RESIDENCE	R	T	S
Redman, Thomas(C)	1804	Dec. 28	Greene	11	04	07
Reece, Caleb(E)	1818	Feb. 14	Highland	14	19	33
Reece, William(E)	1816	Nov. 05	Highland	14	19	32
Reece, William(E)	1834	Feb. 03	Randolph(Ind	14	18	03
Reed, Adam(A)	1813	Aug. 28	Preble	01	09	05
Reed, Adam(B)	1810	Nov. 05	Warren	01	09	05
Reed, Amasa(A)	1815	Feb. 09	Warren	06	04	31
Reed, Andrew(B)	1813	Sept. 01	Hamilton	02	09	25
Reed, Andrew(C)	1802	Dec. 30	Hamilton	08	03	14
Reed, Andrew(C)	1808	Dec. 27	Ohio	15	03	31
Reed, Andrew(C)	1808	Dec. 27	Ohio	14	04	36
Reed, Archibald(E)	1811	Oct. 23	So. Carolina	13	14	18
Reed, Armstead Blevins(B)	1832	Oct. 08	Dearborn(Ind	02	07	36
Reed, Charles(A)	1814	March 21	Darke	02	10	26
Reed, Charles(A)	1814	Dec. 08	Butler	03	06	20
Reed, Christopher(A)	1811	Sept. 18	Butler	04	02	04
Reed, Daniel(B)	1810	Oct. 22	Virginia	01	09	06
Reed, Daniel(B)	1810	Oct. 22	Virginia	01	09	07
Reed, David(A)	1803	Nov. 19	Kentucky	06	02	29
Reed, David(C)	1802	Dec. 30	Hamilton	04	02	19
Reed, Donavan(A)	1827	Sept. 19	Darke	01	11	14
Reed, Frederick(A)	1805	Oct. 24	Butler	04	02	10
Reed, Frederick(A)	1806	May 29	Butler	04	02	10
Reed, Gilbert(A)	1830	Dec. 04	Butler	04	06	20
Reed, Hannah(B)	1814	Nov. 08	Champaign	09	06	14
Reed, Hugh(B)	1807	July 23	So. Carolina	02	11	24
Reed, Hugh(B)	1807	July 23	So. Carolina	02	11	24
Reed, Hugh(B)	1807	July 23	So. Carolina	01	11	19
Reed, Hugh(E)	1811	Oct. 22	Ind.Territory	12	13	34
Reed, Hugh(E)	1831	Dec. 08	Fayette	12	13	33
Reed, Jacob(E)	1814	Oct. 24	Warren	13	16	15
Reed, Jacob(E)	1814	Oct. 24	Warren	13	16	15
Reed, James M.(C)	1813	Sept. 18	Champaign	14	03	18
Reed, James Manning(C)	1807	April 20	Champaign	14	03	06
Reed, James(A)	1805	Nov. 29	Montgomery	06	04	33
Reed, James(A)	1806	March 17	Montgomery	06	03	03
Reed, James(A)	1811	Aug. 13	Montgomery	06	03	03
Reed, James(A)	1816	March 01	Pennsylvania	02	09	30
Reed, James(B)	1817	Nov. 05	Dearborn(Ind	02	05	28
Reed, James(B)	1818	April 11	Butler	03	04	20
Reed, James(C)	1812	Jan. 04	Champaign	11	06	32
Reed, James(E)	1817	June 10	Butler	14	21	09
Reed, James(E)	1817	June 11	Butler	14	21	09
Reed, John S.(E)	1817	Aug. 28	Wayne(Ind)	14	21	17
Reed, John(A)	1806	March 08	Butler	01	03	12
Reed, John(A)	1807	Jan. 19	Montgomery	06	02	04
Reed, John(A)	1812	April 15	Montgomery	06	02	04
Reed, John(C)	1804	Sept. 04	Greene	09	05	10
Reed, John(C)	1806	Feb. 14	Champaign	09	03	24
Reed, John(C)	1806	Aug. 01	Champaign	09	05	10
Reed, John(C)	1811	Dec. 11	Champaign	09	05	10
Reed, John(E)	1811	Oct. 21	Franklin(Ind	12	12	36
Reed, John(E)	1812	May 16	Hamilton	12	13	02
Reed, Joseph C.(E)	1815	June 19	Franklin(Ind	12	11	30
Reed, Joseph(C)	1811	Feb. 15	Champaign	09	05	14
Reed, Mary(C)	1802	Dec. 30	Hamilton	04	02	31
Reed, Samuel(A)	1818	Feb. 20	Montgomery	02	11	05
Reed, Samuel(A)	1837	May 10	Montgomery	02	13	01
Reed, Susan(E)	1815	July 17	Warren	13	16	14
Reed, Thomas(B)	1815	March 13	Franklin(Ind	01	10	20
Reed, Thomas(E)	1811	Oct. 28	Adams	12	14	34
Reed, William(A)	1811	Jan. 21	Butler	04	02	05
Reed, William(C)	1813	April 15	Champaign	09	06	20
Reed, Wm.(C)	1812	April 15	Champaign	09	06	21
Reeder, Aaron(A)	1815	May 25	Cincinnati	05	07	05
Reeder, Alfred S.(A)	1836	July 02	Hamilton	04	10	06
Reeder, Daniel H.(C)	1801	Dec. 14	Hamilton	06	02	13
Reeder, Daniel(C)	1807	June 14	Champaign	08	04	24
Reeder, David(A)	1819	June 30	Warren	03	06	19

PURCHASER	YEAR	DATE	RESIDENCE	R	T	S
Reeder, Henry L.(E)	1836	Sept. 13	Cincinnati	12	11	06
Reeder, Henry L.(E)	1836	Dec. 24	Cincinnati	12	11	07
Reeder, Henson	1810	June 11	Cincinnati	?	?	?
Reeder, Jacob(A)	1819	Oct. 01	Warren	02	08	01
Reeder, Jacob(C)	1801	Dec. 26	Hamilton	05	02	27
Reeder, Jacob(C)	1813	April 14	Champaign	09	04	21
Reeder, Jeremiah(A)	1814	April 20	Cincinnati	01	04	27
Reeder, Jeremiah(B)	1814	Feb. 03	Cincinnati	01	12	34
Reeder, Jeremiah(B)	1818	April 16	Cincinnati	02	02	14
Reeder, Jeremiah(C)	1814	Feb. 03	Hamilton	09	05	03
Reeder, Joseph(C)	1801	Dec. 12	Hamilton	06	02	13
Reeder, Nath'l.(C)	1814	Feb. 03	Hamilton	09	05	03
Reeder, Nathan'l.(B)	1814	Feb. 03	Cincinnati	01	12	34
Reeder, Nathaniel(B)	1818	May 23	Hamilton	01	07	23
Reeder, Nathaniel(B)	1818	June 04	Hamilton	01	03	34
Reeder, Nathaniel(B)	1818	June 04	Hamilton	01	03	35
Reeder, Nathaniel(B)	1818	June 04	Hamilton	01	03	34
Reeder, Nathaniel(B)	1818	June 04	Hamilton	01	03	35
Reeder, Sarah H.(C)	1830	Sept. 25	Pennsylvania	12	02	15
Reeder, Tobias(C)	1815	Jan. 09	Greene	09	02	14
Reeder, William(C)	1802	Dec. 28	Hamilton	05	03	18
Reeds, Thomas(B)	1806	Aug. 25	Hamilton	01	10	18
Rees, David(A)	1819	Feb. 08	Miami	06	04	21
Rees, David(B)	1806	Dec. 03	Virginia	01	05	21
Rees, David(B)	1806	Dec. 31	Virginia	01	05	20
Rees, David(B)	1806	Dec. 31	Virginia	01	05	19
Rees, David(B)	1815	Sept. 13	Dearborn(Ind	01	05	06
Rees, David(B)	1815	Sept. 13	Dearborn(Ind	01	05	06
Rees, David(B)	1815	Sept. 13	Dearborn(Ind	01	05	08
Rees, Jacob(C)	1811	March 18	Champaign	11	05	03
Rees, Jacob(C)	1813	March 22	Champaign	11	05	04
Rees, James(B)	1813	Oct. 13	Kentucky	01	09	23
Rees, John(B)	1813	Sept. 27	Kentucky	01	09	34
Rees, Mary(C)	1816	Aug. 01	Champaign	11	05	03
Rees, Nathan(C)	1811	March 18	Champaign	11	05	03
Rees, Nathan(C)	1813	April 12	Wayne(Ind)	11	06	34
Rees, Nathan(C)	1813	May 19	Champaign	11	06	33
Rees, Nathan(C)	1816	Aug. 01	Champaign	11	05	03
Rees, Sampson(C)	1816	Aug. 01	Champaign	11	05	03
Reese, John(C)	1832	Jan. 31	Champaign	13	03	11
Reese, Martin(B)	1832	Dec. 07	Switzerland	03	03	05
Reese, Morris(C)	1811	July 03	Champaign	11	05	03
Reeve, John(A)	1816	July 31	Warren	01	06	13
Reeves, James(E)	1834	Nov. 03	Randolph(Ind	15	21	22
Reeves, James(E)	1836	Aug. 30	Randolph(Ind	15	21	22
Refner, Peter(B)	1811	Oct. 25	Franklin(Ind	01	02	07
Reichard, John Peter(C)	1824	Oct. 14	Montgomery	13	02	26
Reichard, John(A)	1829	Dec. 28	Montgomery	03	06	01
Reichard, John(A)	1830	Feb. 11	Montgomery	03	06	01
Reichard, Joseph(A)	1831	May 12	Montgomery	03	06	01
Reichard, Peter(A)	1831	Jan. 20	Montgomery	04	06	19
Reichart, Anthony(A)	1805	Oct. 25	Montgomery	03	06	13
Reickart, Henry(A)	1817	July 10	Preble	01	11	26
Reid, Archibald(E)	1814	Aug. 13	Wayne(Ind)	13	14	17
Reid, Jacob(C)	1829	Jan. 17	Clark	09	05	25
Reid, John(A)	1816	Oct. 21	Miami	04	08	09
Reid, John(E)	1835	April 09	Franklin(Ind	12	11	02
Reid, Thomas(C)	1813	March 08	Champaign	09	06	26
Reid, William(A)	1814	Aug. 15	Preble	01	09	07
Reider, Philip(A)	1822	Dec. 10	Darke	03	08	01
Reiley, Ralph(B)	1818	Sept. 14	Pennsylvania	01	08	33
Reilly, William(B)	1836	Jan. 18	Switzerland	02	02	14
Reily, Benjamin(B)	1814	Sept. 10	Butler	01	07	34
Reily, John(A)	1836	Aug. 24	Butler	01	14	29
Reily, John(A)	1840	Aug. 01	Butler	01	14	20
Reily, John(B)	1814	Nov. 19	Butler	02	10	14
Reily, John(B)	1815	April 05	Butler	01	12	31
Reily, Nathan(E)	1816	Oct. 24	Ross	13	18	36
Reinhart, John(A)	1815	Nov. 28	Montgomery	04	04	22

PURCHASER	YEAR	DATE	RESIDENCE	R	T	S
Reins, Job(A)	1806	Feb. 18	Butler	02	05	08
Reisch, Henry(A)	1817	July 09	Philadelphia	02	08	25
Reitenour, Anthony(E)	1837	Jan. 07	Randolph(Ind	14	21	20
Remer, David(B)	1815	March 07	Kentucky	01	03	20
Remer, John(B)	1818	April 15	Franklin(Ind	02	03	25
Remley, Solomon(A)	1822	May 28	Hamilton	04	06	29
Remley, Solomon(C)	1831	July 05	Warren	13	03	02
Remlinger, Jacob(B)	1836	Nov. 24	Hamilton	02	08	06
Remy, James(B)	1812	Nov. 06	Franklin(Ind	01	07	02
Remy, James(B)	1812	Nov. 28	Franklin(Ind	01	08	25
Remy, James(B)	1814	May 23	Franklin(Ind	01	08	24
Remy, James(B)	1814	May 23	Franklin(Ind	01	08	26
Remy, William(B)	1801	Dec. 09	Hamilton	01	07	13
Remy, William(B)	1811	Oct. 30	Dearborn(Ind	01	08	11
Remy, William(B)	1813	Aug. 10	Franklin(Ind	01	08	35
Renberger, George(E)	1817	Oct. 21	Wayne(Ind)	13	17	14
Rench, John(A)	1807	Aug. 10	Montgomery	05	05	28
Rench, John(A)	1836	Dec. 14	Montgomery	04	11	30
Rench, Joseph(A)	1827	Oct. 17	Darke	04	09	09
Rench, Joseph(A)	1829	Jan. 13	Darke	04	09	09
Rench, Joseph(A)	1830	Sept. 29	Miami	05	07	04
Rench, Otho(E)	1818	Nov. 14	Maryland	12	12	15
Rench, Peter(A)	1812	Nov. 25	Miami	05	07	05
Rench, Peter(A)	1814	Aug. 27	Miami	04	09	09
Rendenbaugh, Andrew(C)	1806	Aug. 22	Hamilton	11	01	23
Renick, Abel(C)	1806	June 17	Ross	10	06	34
Renick, James(C)	1811	April 09	Champaign	10	06	33
Renick, James(C)	1811	Aug. 13	Pickaway	10	06	34
Renick, James(C)	1811	Aug. 13	Pickaway	10	06	34
Renick, James(C)	1811	Aug. 13	Pickaway	10	06	34
Renick, James(C)	1816	Dec. 02	Pickaway	10	06	34
Renick, James(C)	1816	Dec. 02	Pickaway	10	06	34
Renick, John(C)	1804	Dec. 31	Kentucky	06	02	34
Renick, Robert(C)	1804	Sept. 04	Greene	09	04	11
Renick, Robert(C)	1804	Dec. 28	Greene	09	04	05
Renick, Robert(C)	1805	April 30	Ohio	10	06	30
Renick, Robert(C)	1805	April 30	Ohio	10	06	30
Renick, Robert(C)	1805	April 30	Ohio	10	06	30
Renick, Robert(C)	1805	April 30	Ohio	10	04	04
Renick, Robert(C)	1805	April 30	Ohio	10	04	03
Renick, Robert(C)	1805	April 30	Ohio	10	04	05
Renick, Robert(C)	1805	April 30	Ohio	10	05	34
Renick, Robert(C)	1805	April 30	Ohio	10	05	35
Renick, Robert(C)	1805	April 30	Ohio	10	05	36
Renick, Robert(C)	1805	April 30	Hamilton	10	05	28
Renick, Robert(C)	1805	April 30	Ohio	10	05	28
Renick, Robert(C)	1805	April 30	Ohio	10	05	28
Renick, Robert(C)	1805	April 30	Ohio	10	05	28
Renick, Robert(C)	1805	April 30	Ohio	10	06	30
Renick, Robert(C)	1814	Feb. 26	Champaign	09	04	11
Renick, Robert(C)	1814	Feb. 26	Champaign	09	05	25
Renke, Gerhard Hy.(A)	1839	Jan. 21	Cincinnati	02	15	27
Renner, Peter(B)	1834	Feb. 06	Hamilton	02	07	03
Rennick, James(C)	1816	Aug. 01	Pickaway	10	06	33
Reno, Presley G.(B)	1837	Feb. 10	Switzerland	03	04	28
Reno, Presley(B)	1818	Feb. 26	Dearborn(Ind	03	03	02
Renwick, Robert(C)	1811	Dec. 11	Champaign	10	05	29
Renwick, Robert(C)	1811	Dec. 11	Champaign	10	05	29
Replogel, Dan'l.(A)	1827	Sept. 11	Montgomery	04	06	22
Replogle, Adam(C)	1814	May 16	Champaign	09	04	23
Replogle, Frederick(A)	1838	Feb. 01	Cincinnati	01	14	35
Replogle, John(A)	1807	May 07	Montgomery	04	06	27
Replogle, Peter(A)	1814	Sept. 12	Montgomery	04	05	23
Replogle, Philip Jr.(A)	1836	May 23	Darke	01	14	22
Replogle, Philip(A)	1836	May 23	Darke	01	14	22
Replogle, Philip(A)	1837	May 09	Darke	01	14	28
Resor, John(A)	1827	May 11	Montgomery	04	06	22
Retter, Jacob(B)	1811	Nov. 26	Preble	01	11	13
Retter, Jacob(C)	1814	Nov. 24	Greene	09	02	20

PURCHASER	YEAR	DATE	RESIDENCE	R	T	S
Retter, John(B)	1811	Nov. 26	Preble	01	11	13
Rettinhouse, William(C)	1819	July 29	Montgomery	13	02	31
Retz, John(E)	1836	May 27	Randolph(Ind	13	20	25
Retz, William(E)	1836	Oct. 03	Randolph(Ind	13	20	25
Reubart, James(E)	1832	Dec. 01	Franklin(Ind	13	11	06
Reubart, James(E)	1836	Oct. 19	Franklin(Ind	12	11	12
Revel, Francis Hy.(A)	1823	March 05	Preble	02	09	36
Revel, Francis Hy.(A)	1828	Oct. 01	Preble	02	09	36
Revel, Francis Hy.(A)	1829	Oct. 26	Preble	02	09	02
Rex, Daniel(A)	1807	June 30	Pennsylvania	03	07	33
Rex, Daniel(A)	1815	Sept. 08	Preble	03	07	29
Rex, John(A)	1814	April 11	Cincinnati	03	06	05
Reynolds, David(C)	1817	Aug. 22	Butler	12	01	03
Reynolds, Francis G.(C)	1824	Oct. 02	Fairfield	12	03	29
Reynolds, Giles K.(A)	1836	Nov. 12	Hamilton	01	14	34
Reynolds, Giles K.(A)	1836	Nov. 14	Cincinnati	01	14	34
Reynolds, Isaac(B)	1811	Aug. 29	Clinton	01	05	30
Reynolds, Isaac(C)	1807	March 04	Champaign	11	05	10
Reynolds, Isaac(C)	1807	March 04	Champaign	11	04	20
Reynolds, Isaac(C)	1807	March 04	Champaign	11	04	21
Reynolds, Isaac(C)	1810	Aug. 14	Urbana	11	04	25
Reynolds, Isaac(C)	1815	Jan. 09	Champaign	12	05	08
Reynolds, Isaac(C)	1815	May 08	Champaign	12	05	07
Reynolds, Isaac(C)	1827	March 03	Champaign	10	06	29
Reynolds, James(C)	1806	April 09	Champaign	12	05	34
Reynolds, John Jeffrey(E)	1835	June 03	Randolph(Ind	14	18	01
Reynolds, John(C)	1804	Dec. 28	Greene	11	04	09
Reynolds, John(C)	1805	June 19	Champaign	11	04	25
Reynolds, John(C)	1808	Dec. 27	Ohio	15	03	31
Reynolds, John(C)	1808	Dec. 27	Ohio	14	04	36
Reynolds, John(C)	1813	April 14	Champaign	11	05	12
Reynolds, John(C)	1814	April 04	Champaign	11	05	11
Reynolds, John(C)	1815	Jan. 09	Champaign	12	05	08
Reynolds, John(C)	1815	May 08	Champaign	12	05	07
Reynolds, John(C)	1827	March 03	Champaign	10	06	29
Reynolds, John(C)	1829	Dec. 11	Champaign	10	06	29
Reynolds, Joseph S.(C)	1815	Jan. 09	Champaign	12	05	08
Reynolds, Joseph Senr.(C)	1805	April 15	Champaign	11	04	32
Reynolds, Joseph Smith(C)	1805	April 15	Champaign	11	03	02
Reynolds, Joseph(C)	1805	June 19	Champaign	11	04	15
Reynolds, Joseph(C)	1805	June 19	Champaign	11	04	31
Reynolds, Joseph(C)	1805	June 19	Champaign	11	04	31
Reynolds, Joseph(C)	1805	June 19	Champaign	11	03	09
Reynolds, Joseph(C)	1805	June 19	Champaign	11	03	15
Reynolds, Joseph(C)	1805	Nov. 07	Champaign	10	04	36
Reynolds, Joseph(C)	1806	July 24	Champaign	11	04	15
Reynolds, Joseph(C)	1807	Feb. 05	Champaign	11	06	35
Reynolds, Joseph(C)	1807	Feb. 05	Champaign	11	05	12
Reynolds, Joseph(C)	1807	March 04	Champaign	11	05	12
Reynolds, Joseph(C)	1812	April 15	Champaign	11	05	12
Reynolds, Justice(B)	1816	April 01	Switzerland	02	03	30
Reynolds, Limon(B)	1816	March 04	Warren	03	02	04
Reynolds, Wesley(E)	1835	July 22	Franklin(Ind	12	11	27
Reynolds, Wesley(E)	1836	Oct. 22	Franklin(Ind	12	11	22
Reynolds, William G.(E)	1816	Jan. 20	Wayne(Ind)	13	16	30
Reynolds, William(B)	1813	Oct. 11	Wayne(Ind)	01	13	20
Reynolds, William(E)	1816	July 10	Wayne(Ind)	12	15	03
Rhea, Elizabeth(C)	1828	March 27	?	12	03	11
Rhea, John(A)	1819	Dec. 16	Preble	01	08	30
Rhea, Robert(A)	1810	Jan. 15	Kentucky	02	07	07
Rhea, Robert(A)	1818	March 16	Preble	01	07	17
Rhea, Susanna(E)	1834	March 20	Franklin(Ind	13	11	30
Rhea, William(E)	1816	Oct. 24	Franklin(Ind	12	11	25
Rhegenness, Jacob(A)	1830	Oct. 07	Cincinnati	04	06	19
Rheudy, Jacob(C)	1805	Dec. 17	Montgomery	09	02	28
Rhoad, Jacob(A)	1836	Sept. 05	Montgomery	02	13	28
Rhoades, Jacob Senr.(A)	1824	Dec. 15	Montgomery	04	05	22
Rhoads, Ebenezer(C)	1813	June 17	Champaign	12	04	20
Rhoads, John(C)	1801	Dec. 02	Pennsylvania	05	01	01

PURCHASER	YEAR	DATE	RESIDENCE	R	T	S
Rhoads, John(C)	1801	Dec. 02	Pennsylvania	04	03	22
Rhoads, Miles(E)	1829	Jan. 17	Randolph(Ind	14	18	13
Rhoads, William(C)	1804	Dec. 31	Greene	11	05	32
Rhodebaugh, Michael(A)	1817	Sept. 23	Montgomery	03	11	25
Rhodehamel, Jacob(A)	1814	Dec. 17	Montgomery	04	07	01
Rhodes, Jacob(A)	1814	Nov. 12	Montgomery	04	04	22
Rhodes, Philip(A)	1814	Nov. 12	Montgomery	04	04	22
Rhynebolt, Stephen(B)	1825	Feb. 25	Hamilton	02	02	22
Rhynebolt, Stephen(B)	1825	April 29	Switzerland	02	02	22
Rice, Ezekiel Jr.(C)	1813	Dec. 16	Champaign	09	06	11
Rice, Jacob(C)	1815	Nov. 11	Madison	08	06	11
Rice, John(C)	1802	Dec. 31	Hamilton	08	04	13
Rice, Joshua(E)	1815	May 22	Kentucky	11	11	36
Rice, Joshua(E)	1815	July 06	Kentucky	12	12	19
Rice, Joshua(E)	1815	July 06	Kentucky	12	12	19
Rice, Joshua(E)	1815	July 06	Kentucky	12	12	17
Rice, Martin(A)	1805	Nov. 05	Montgomery	04	06	07
Rice, Martin(A)	1814	June 22	Preble	03	07	02
Rice, Martin(A)	1814	Nov. 22	Preble	03	08	33
Rice, Sam'l.(A)	1827	Sept. 07	Hamilton	01	02	14
Rich, Elijah(B)	1818	Feb. 03	Hamilton	02	06	32
Richard, George(A)	1836	July 16	Hamilton	03	11	03
Richard, Jacob(C)	1814	June 17	Champaign	09	05	12
Richard, John(A)	1815	Jan. 11	Montgomery	04	05	07
Richards, Aaron(C)	1801	Nov. 27	Hamilton	05	02	07
Richards, Isaac Jr.(B)	1834	May 03	Switzerland	03	03	04
Richards, Isaac(A)	1817	June 14	Butler	03	04	33
Richards, Isaac(B)	1817	June 05	Switzerland	03	03	32
Richards, Jac.(C)	1811	Dec. 27	Champaign	10	05	19
Richards, Jacob(C)	1811	Dec. 27	Champaign	10	05	07
Richards, Jacob(C)	1818	June 26	Clark	13	02	07
Richards, Jeremiah(B)	1834	April 25	Switzerland	03	04	28
Richards, Joseph(B)	1834	April 22	Franklin(Ind	02	08	15
Richards, Robert(B)	1818	Aug. 07	Cincinnati	03	05	24
Richards, Rosanna(B)	1833	Sept. 03	Switzerland	03	03	33
Richards, William(B)	1816	May 24	Butler	03	03	04
Richardson, Aaron(A)	1801	Nov. 27	Hamilton	04	03	01
Richardson, Aaron(A)	1805	June 13	Warren	03	07	28
Richardson, Abraham(A)	1806	Nov. 18	Pennsylvania	05	04	07
Richardson, Abraham(C)	1805	Aug. 27	Montgomery	06	02	35
Richardson, Daniel(A)	1816	April 02	Montgomery	04	10	17
Richardson, Daniel(A)	1816	April 02	Montgomery	04	10	19
Richardson, Daniel(C)	1801	Dec. 15	Hamilton	05	02	13
Richardson, Daniel(C)	1801	Dec. 31	Hamilton	04	03	18
Richardson, Daniel(C)	1801	Dec. 31	Hamilton	04	03	30
Richardson, Daniel(C)	1801	Dec. 31	Hamilton	05	02	27
Richardson, Edmund(A)	1804	May 14	Warren	02	03	20
Richardson, Edmund(C)	1801	Dec. 28	Hamilton	04	04	27
Richardson, George(C)	1814	Jan. 28	Miami	10	03	35
Richardson, Jno.(A)	1829	May 05	Darke	04	07	07
Richardson, John(A)	1804	May 14	Warren	02	03	20
Richardson, John(A)	1804	Sept. 13	Butler	02	03	29
Richardson, John(A)	1804	Dec. 07	Montgomery	05	06	05
Richardson, John(A)	1806	March 18	Butler	01	04	35
Richardson, John(A)	1811	Aug. 13	Franklin(Ind	01	04	35
Richardson, John(B)	1811	Jan. 11	Ind.Territory	02	09	33
Richardson, John(C)	1801	Dec. 28	Hamilton	04	04	27
Richardson, John(E)	1812	Jan. 02	Franklin(Ind	12	13	34
Richardson, John(E)	1812	Nov. 04	Franklin(Ind	13	13	20
Richardson, Joseph(B)	1817	June 20	Dearborn(Ind	02	03	04
Richardson, Matthew(A)	1802	June 28	Hamilton	02	05	23
Richardson, Matthew(A)	1814	Oct. 31	Butler	02	06	23
Richardson, Nathan(A)	1816	June 20	Warren	02	11	01
Richardson, Nathan(B)	1814	Dec. 14	Dearborn(Ind	01	08	33
Richardson, Nathan(E)	1811	Oct. 23	Ind.Territory	12	16	36
Richardson, Robert	1808	March 03	Cincinnati	?	?	?
Richardson, Snow(A)	1831	June 04	Shelby	05	09	10
Richardson, Will'm.(A)	1825	Nov. 14	Darke	04	07	06
Richardson, William(C)	1815	June 17	Miami	12	02	33

271

PURCHASER	YEAR	DATE	RESIDENCE	R	T	S
Richardson, William(E)	1815	April 06	Warren	13	12	08
Richardson, Wm.(A)	1831	April 04	Darke	04	07	06
Richart, Abraham(A)	1809	Aug. 17	Montgomery	05	04	06
Riche, Philip(E)	1814	July 23	New York	13	12	31
Richey, Adam(B)	1806	Oct. 21	Butler	01	11	34
Richey, Joseph(B)	1814	Aug. 18	Franklin(Ind	02	09	25
Richey, Thomas(B)	1806	Aug. 15	Kentucky	02	04	35
Richmond, Jonathan(A)	1804	June 29	Butler	02	04	34
Richmond, Jonathan(A)	1806	June 23	Butler	01	04	33
Richmond, Sylvester(B)	1817	Oct. 25	Dearborn(Ind	02	05	28
Rickels, Robert(B)	1804	Nov. 28	Kentucky	01	03	17
Ricketts, John(E)	1836	July 29	Franklin(Ind	12	11	18
Ricketts, John(E)	1837	April 06	Franklin(Ind	11	11	24
Ricketts, Nathan(B)	1825	Sept. 22	Switzerland	02	03	25
Ricketts, Nathan(B)	1833	Aug. 22	Switzerland	02	02	01
Ricketts, Robert(B)	1813	Nov. 26	Dearborn(Ind	02	03	24
Ricketts, Robert(B)	1813	Nov. 22	Dearborn(Ind	01	03	17
Ricords, Samuel(B)	1818	Jan. 26	Hamilton	02	03	05
Ricords, Thomas(B)	1818	Jan. 26	Hamilton	02	03	05
Riddel, Benjamin(B)	1818	June 23	Dearborn(Ind	03	05	02
Riddle, James(C)	1804	Dec. 26	Montgomery	07	02	25
Riddle, James(C)	1806	Aug. 26	Cincinnati	02	03	08
Riddle, James(C)	1813	April 14	Cincinnati	08	04	13
Riddle, John(C)	1805	Aug. 09	Montgomery	11	01	02
Riddle, John(C)	1805	Oct. 22	Hamilton	01	03	11
Riddle, John(C)	1805	Oct. 22	Hamilton	01	03	11
Riddle, John(C)	1805	Oct. 22	Hamilton	02	03	11
Riddle, John(D)	1808	Nov. 01	Hamilton(Fr)	02	03	11
Riddle, William(B)	1815	March 13	Butler	02	12	34
Riddlesbarger, David(E)	1836	March 28	Randolph(Ind	14	21	18
Ridenhour, Joseph(A)	1805	Aug. 26	Butler	01	06	29
Ridenour, Peter(A)	1805	Aug. 26	Hamilton	01	06	33
Rider, William(E)	1817	Aug. 30	Wayne(Ind)	14	16	03
Ridge, James(E)	1831	Feb. 11	Wayne(Ind)	13	16	04
Ridgely, William(B)	1817	Oct. 08	?	01	02	02
Rieckelman, Herman Hy.(E)	1837	April 07	Cincinnati	11	10	10
Riedinger, Peter(B)	1836	Nov. 23	Franklin(Ind	02	08	06
Riegel, George(A)	1838	May 21	Fairfield	02	14	32
Riegel, John(A)	1838	Sept. 28	Pickaway	02	14	17
Riegel, Samuel(A)	1835	Sept. 03	Montgomery	03	11	05
Riely, John(B)	1815	May 31	Butler	02	10	23
Riesing, William(B)	1809	April 19	Dearborn(Ind	02	10	21
Riffel, Daniel(C)	1801	Dec. 25	Hamilton	07	01	18
Riffle, David(A)	1819	Jan. 08	Darke	03	11	29
Riffle, John(C)	1818	Feb. 12	Miami	11	02	08
Riffle, Solomon(A)	1831	Sept. 26	Darke	02	13	36
Rigdon, Ezekiel(A)	1809	July 14	Darke	02	12	28
Rigdon, John(C)	1807	Jan. 29	Champaign	11	05	20
Rigdon, John(C)	1812	April 15	Champaign	11	05	20
Rigdon, John(C)	1813	May 08	Urbana	11	05	19
Rigg, Eleazar Jr.(A)	1831	Sept. 07	Warren	04	09	05
Riggin, Levin Warren(B)	1832	Sept. 13	Dearborn(Ind	03	06	24
Riggs, Bethuel(B)	1836	Dec. 08	Dearborn(Ind	02	03	18
Riggs, Isaac Tuttle(E)	1834	Nov. 14	Fayette	13	13	30
Riggs, John(E)	1815	June 27	Pennsylvania	13	12	08
Riggs, John(E)	1815	June 27	Pennsylvania	13	12	09
Riggs, Samuel(E)	1811	Oct. 30	Washington	13	14	27
Riggsbee, Wm.(B)	1824	June 09	Union(Ind)	01	11	22
Rightnour, Joseph(B)	1815	Jan. 02	Preble	01	11	36
Rightnour, Washington(E)	1836	Aug. 27	Preble	15	20	21
Rigney, Edward(B)	1833	June 27	Cincinnati	02	07	26
Rigney, Edward(B)	1833	June 27	Cincinnati	02	07	27
Rike, Adam(A)	1836	Oct. 21	Montgomery	02	12	04
Riker, Samuel(A)	1804	Aug. 28	Hamilton	03	03	26
Riker, Samuel(D)	1809	Nov. 10	Hamilton	01	04	08
Riker, Thomas(C)	1831	Oct. 29	Hamilton	12	03	27
Riker, William(C)	1830	Aug. 12	Hamilton	12	03	26
Riley, Camden(A)	1831	April 11	Montgomery	04	06	31
Riley, Camdon(A)	1827	Nov. 05	Warren	04	06	32

PURCHASER	YEAR	DATE	RESIDENCE	R	T	S
Riley, Jacob(E)	1836	Nov. 28	Kentucky	14	20	06
Riley, James Jr.(B)	1836	July 18	Switzerland	03	03	08
Riley, James Junr.(B)	1835	Sept. 19	Switzerland	03	03	08
Riley, William(E)	1831	Nov. 08	Wayne(Ind)	13	18	35
Rily, John(B)	1818	Feb. 27	Switzerland	03	03	02
Rim, John(A)	1805	Feb. 04	Warren	04	03	27
Rinard, Jeremiah(E)	1818	March 24	Randolph(Ind	13	19	03
Rinard, John(A)	1819	Sept. 18	Darke	03	10	36
Rinard, Solomon(E)	1836	June 13	Randolph(Ind	13	19	03
Rinard, Solomon(E)	1836	July 11	Randolph(Ind	13	19	03
Rinehart, Abraham(A)	1831	July 05	Shelby	06	08	23
Rinehart, Peter(A)	1831	June 06	Preble	02	10	17
Riner, Henry(A)	1814	June 22	Virginia	03	04	23
Riner, John(A)	1814	June 15	Virginia	01	08	01
Riner, John(A)	1815	June 08	Preble	03	04	24
Rinerson, Cornelius(B)	1818	April 16	Franklin(Ind	01	07	06
Rinerson, Cornelius(E)	1831	Nov. 02	Fayette	12	13	29
Rinerson, Cornelius(E)	1833	July 19	Fayette	12	13	29
Rinerson, Rinerd(E)	1831	July 05	Fayette	12	13	32
Rinerson, Rinerd(E)	1834	Feb. 07	Fayette	12	13	32
Rinerson, Rinerd(E)	1834	Feb. 07	Fayette	12	13	29
Ring, Richard(B)	1811	Oct. 08	Ind.Territry	02	12	36
Ring, Richard(B)	1816	Dec. 02	Wayne(Ind)	02	12	36
Ring, William(B)	1814	Sept. 30	Franklin(Ind	02	11	15
Ringer, Jacob(A)	1813	Oct. 16	Preble	03	07	33
Ringland, James(A)	1806	March 24	Butler	02	04	30
Ringland, James(A)	1811	Aug. 13	Butler	02	04	30
Ripley, James(E)	1836	Oct. 29	RipleyCo.Ind	11	10	24
Riplogle, Adam(C)	1832	March 05	Logan	14	03	36
Ripp, Catharine(B)	1836	Feb. 20	Franklin(Ind	02	08	19
Ripp, George Adam(B)	1835	April 03	Franklin(Ind	03	09	25
Ripperger, Ignatz(B)	1833	Sept. 30	Germany	02	08	31
Ripperger, Ignatz(B)	1833	Sept. 30	Germany	02	08	30
Ripperger, Ignatz(B)	1833	Nov. 11	Franklin(Ind	03	09	25
Ripperger, Michael(B)	1833	Sept. 30	Germany	02	08	31
Ripperger, Michael(B)	1836	Sept. 10	Franklin(Ind	03	09	25
Ripperger, Michael(B)	1837	Feb. 01	Franklin(Ind	03	09	23
Rippey, John(C)	1802	Dec. 30	Hamilton	04	04	35
Rippey, Joseph(C)	1804	Dec. 21	Warren	05	03	31
Risk, Thomas(E)	1814	Oct. 10	Hamilton	13	13	33
Risk, William(E)	1814	Oct. 10	Warren	13	13	32
Risk, William(E)	1836	Dec. 10	Fayette	13	13	32
Ritchey, James(D)	1809	May 15	Cincinati(Fr	02	02	08
Ritchey, John(A)	1805	Oct. 09	Butler	01	06	10
Ritchey, John(A)	1805	Oct. 09	Butler	01	06	30
Ritchey, John(A)	1810	Dec. 12	Butler	01	06	10
Ritenhour, Joseph(A)	1815	Jan. 02	Preble	01	06	30
Rittenhouse, Garret(A)	1810	Sept. 01	Greene	05	04	04
Rittenhouse, Garret(A)	1810	Sept. 12	Greene	05	05	27
Rittenhouse, Garret(A)	1810	Sept. 12	Greene	05	05	28
Rittenhouse, John(A)	1806	May 24	Montgomery	06	03	03
Rittenhouse, William(D)	1811	July 03	Hamilton(Fr)	02	02	26
Rittenhouse, William(D)	1812	June 15	Hamilton(Fr)	02	01	26
Ritter, Henry(C)	1829	Aug. 24	Champaign	12	03	11
Ritter, Henry(C)	1830	Feb. 24	Champaign	13	03	07
Ritter, John(A)	1814	Dec. 17	Greene	06	04	21
Ritter, John(E)	1815	Dec. 18	Hamilton	13	14	11
Ritter, Joseph(B)	1833	July 26	Cincinnati	02	06	08
Roach, John G.(A)	1825	May 20	Preble	02	09	22
Roach, Revel(C)	1813	April 07	Champaign	10	04	15
Roach, Revel(C)	1816	Sept. 30	Ohio	10	04	27
Road, William(B)	1812	March 24	Wayne(Ind)	02	13	26
Roads, Samuel(A)	1809	April 17	Warren	02	12	34
Roark, James(A)	1833	Nov. 04	Butler	01	15	17
Robarts, Zebulon Harmon(B)	1833	March 02	Dearborn(Ind	02	05	09
Robb, Samuel(C)	1801	Nov. 19	Hamilton	04	03	35
Robbens, Daniel(A)	1802	April 22	Hamilton	04	04	35
Robberds, Jonathan(E)	1836	Nov. 24	Wayne(Ind)	13	20	10
Robbins, Benjamin(C)	1801	Dec. 29	Hamilton	06	02	25

PURCHASER	YEAR	DATE	RESIDENCE	R	T	S
Robbins, Benjamin(C)	1802	Dec. 28	Hamilton	05	03	30
Robbins, Daniel(A)	1805	Dec. 20	Butler	01	08	18
Robbins, Elam(A)	1831	April 18	Darke	03	08	21
Robbins, Enoch(A)	1832	Feb. 15	Darke	03	08	22
Robbins, Isaac(C)	1835	Nov. 13	Shelby	13	03	33
Robbins, John(A)	1815	Oct. 05	Montgomery	07	01	17
Robbins, Jonath'n(A)	1815	Oct. 05	Montgomery	07	01	17
Robbins, Jonathan(A)	1805	Sept. 21	Warren	03	03	23
Robbins, Moses Jr.(E)	1827	Dec. 12	Wayne(Ind)	14	15	09
Robbins, Moses(E)	1817	July 03	Wayne(Ind)	14	15	09
Robbins, Randolph(A)	1831	Aug. 22	Wayne(Ind)	03	08	36
Robbins, Samuel(A)	1804	Oct. 15	Butler	03	04	29
Robbins, Samuel(A)	1805	Dec. 21	Clermont	02	04	35
Robbins, William(C)	1806	Aug. 04	Hamilton	09	03	05
Robbins, William(C)	1806	Aug. 04	Hamilton	09	03	05
Robbins, Wm.(C)	1801	Dec. 30	Hamilton	07	03	31
Robens, Richard(A)	1815	Feb. 22	Miami	03	08	28
Robenson, James H.(C)	1801	Dec. 28	Hamilton	04	03	27
Robenson, James Harris(C)	1801	Dec. 12	Hamilton	04	02	01
Robenson, John(A)	1818	Aug. 27	Montgomery	02	10	02
Robenson, Joseph(C)	1801	Dec. 02	Hamilton	06	03	34
Roberds, Phinehas(B)	1829	Jan. 21	Wayne(Ind)	01	15	34
Roberds, Walter(B)	1831	Oct. 19	Wayne(Ind)	01	15	26
Roberds, Walter(B)	1834	March 06	Randolph(Ind	01	16	24
Roberson, Lewis(A)	1815	Feb. 20	Hamilton	03	06	17
Robert, Conrod(A)	1816	June 21	Darke	01	10	32
Robert, Conrod(B)	1816	June 21	Preble	01	14	12
Robert, Edward(C)	1825	Jan. 26	Champaign	11	03	24
Roberts, Andrew(B)	1832	Sept. 03	Switzerland	03	02	19
Roberts, Arthur P.(B)	1838	Dec. 17	Dearborn(Ind	02	04	06
Roberts, Bazil(E)	1811	Oct. 22	Ind.Territry	12	13	02
Roberts, Bazil(E)	1817	June 27	Franklin(Ind	12	13	01
Roberts, Benjamin(E)	1815	June 02	Wayne(Ind)	12	16	11
Roberts, Conrod(A)	1815	Nov. 30	Darke	01	10	32
Roberts, Conrod(A)	1815	Nov. 30	Darke	01	10	29
Roberts, Dan'l.(A)	1831	March 24	Preble	02	10	17
Roberts, Daniel(A)	1831	Oct. 21	Preble	02	10	20
Roberts, Daniel(C)	1811	March 08	Champaign	10	06	36
Roberts, Daniel(C)	1816	Aug. 01	Champaign	10	06	36
Roberts, Danl.(C)	1812	Dec. 11	Champaign	10	05	06
Roberts, David Jnr.(B)	1818	May 11	Hamilton	03	07	35
Roberts, David Senr.(B)	1818	May 11	Hamilton	02	06	31
Roberts, Edward(B)	1818	Sept. 04	Hamilton	02	07	36
Roberts, Edward(B)	1838	Feb. 02	Dearborn(Ind	03	04	21
Roberts, James G.(E)	1836	Oct. 01	Ohio	14	21	18
Roberts, James H.(C)	1813	Aug. 10	Champaign	10	06	34
Roberts, Jno.(E)	1836	Nov. 17	Cincinnati	12	11	36
Roberts, Jno.(E)	1836	Nov. 17	Cincinnati	12	11	25
Roberts, Jno.(E)	1836	Nov. 17	Cincinnati	13	11	19
Roberts, Jno.(E)	1836	Nov. 17	Cincinnati	13	11	20
Roberts, Jno.(E)	1836	Nov. 17	Cincinnati	12	11	24
Roberts, Jno.(E)	1836	Nov. 17	Cincinnati	12	10	02
Roberts, Jno.(E)	1836	Nov. 17	Cincinnati	12	10	02
Roberts, Jno.(E)	1836	Nov. 17	Cincinnati	12	11	25
Roberts, Jno.(E)	1836	Dec. 02	Cincinnati	12	11	02
Roberts, Jno.(E)	1836	Dec. 22	Cincinnati	12	11	14
Roberts, Jno.(E)	1836	Dec. 24	Cincinnati	11	11	27
Roberts, Jno.(E)	1836	Dec. 22	Cincinnati	13	11	17
Roberts, Jno.(E)	1836	Dec. 24	Cincinnati	11	11	22
Roberts, John Senr.(E)	1836	Dec. 27	Cincinnati	12	11	36
Roberts, John Senr.(E)	1836	Dec. 27	Cincinnati	11	11	26
Roberts, John(A)	1831	April 18	Preble	02	10	20
Roberts, John(A)	1832	April 12	Preble	02	10	17
Roberts, John(E)	1836	Nov. 03	Cincinnati	12	10	01
Roberts, John(E)	1836	Nov. 03	Cincinnati	12	11	26
Roberts, John(E)	1836	Nov. 03	Cincinnati	13	11	30
Roberts, John(E)	1836	Nov. 03	Cincinnati	13	11	31
Roberts, John(E)	1836	Nov. 05	Cincinnati	12	10	20
Roberts, John(E)	1836	Nov. 18	Cincinnati	12	11	26

PURCHASER	YEAR	DATE	RESIDENCE	R	T	S
Roberts, John(E)	1836	Dec. 02	Cincinnati	12	11	01
Roberts, John(E)	1836	Dec. 02	Cincinnati	12	11	02
Roberts, John(E)	1836	Dec. 02	Cincinnati	12	11	24
Roberts, John(E)	1836	Dec. 02	Cincinnati	13	11	20
Roberts, John(E)	1836	Dec. 02	Cincinnati	13	11	17
Roberts, John(E)	1836	Dec. 02	Cincinnati	13	11	30
Roberts, John(E)	1836	Dec. 19	Cincinnati	12	11	12
Roberts, John(E)	1836	Dec. 19	Cincinnati	12	11	14
Roberts, John(E)	1837	Feb. 01	Cincinnati	12	11	25
Roberts, Jonathan(A)	1805	July 15	Butler	03	03	08
Roberts, Jonathan(B)	1806	Aug. 11	Butler	01	14	31
Roberts, Jos.(E)	1836	Nov. 17	Cincinnati	12	10	02
Roberts, Jos.(E)	1836	Nov. 17	Cincinnati	12	11	25
Roberts, Joseph(B)	1829	Oct. 27	Dearborn(Ind	02	06	34
Roberts, Joseph(B)	1832	April 03	Dearborn(Ind	02	06	27
Roberts, Joseph(C)	1812	March 21	Champaign	10	06	36
Roberts, Joseph(E)	1836	Nov. 03	Cincinnati	12	10	01
Roberts, Joseph(E)	1836	Nov. 03	Cincinnati	12	11	26
Roberts, Joseph(E)	1836	Nov. 03	Cincinnati	13	11	30
Roberts, Joseph(E)	1836	Nov. 03	Cincinnati	13	11	31
Roberts, Joseph(E)	1836	Nov. 17	Cincinnati	12	11	36
Roberts, Joseph(E)	1836	Nov. 17	Cincinnati	12	11	25
Roberts, Joseph(E)	1836	Nov. 17	Cincinnati	13	11	19
Roberts, Joseph(E)	1836	Nov. 17	Cincinnati	13	11	20
Roberts, Joseph(E)	1836	Nov. 17	Cincinnati	12	11	24
Roberts, Joseph(E)	1836	Nov. 17	Cincinnati	12	10	02
Roberts, Joseph(E)	1836	Nov. 18	Cincinnati	12	11	26
Roberts, Joseph(E)	1836	Dec. 02	Cincinnati	12	11	01
Roberts, Joseph(E)	1836	Dec. 02	Cincinnati	12	11	02
Roberts, Joseph(E)	1836	Dec. 02	Cincinnati	12	11	24
Roberts, Joseph(E)	1836	Dec. 02	Cincinnati	13	11	20
Roberts, Joseph(E)	1836	Dec. 02	Cincinnati	13	11	17
Roberts, Joseph(E)	1836	Dec. 02	Cincinnati	13	11	30
Roberts, Joseph(E)	1836	Dec. 02	Cincinnati	12	11	02
Roberts, Joseph(E)	1836	Dec. 19	Cincinnati	12	11	12
Roberts, Joseph(E)	1836	Dec. 19	Cincinnati	12	11	14
Roberts, Joseph(E)	1836	Dec. 22	Cincinnati	12	11	14
Roberts, Joseph(E)	1836	Dec. 22	Cincinnati	13	11	17
Roberts, Joseph(E)	1836	Dec. 24	Cincinnati	11	11	22
Roberts, Joseph(E)	1836	Dec. 24	Cincinnati	11	11	27
Roberts, Joseph(E)	1837	Feb. 01	Cincinnati	12	11	25
Roberts, Miner(B)	1815	July 31	Franklin(Ind	02	03	33
Roberts, Minor(B)	1815	Sept. 07	Franklin(Ind	03	02	29
Roberts, Moses Merril(B)	1836	Jan. 23	Dearborn(Ind	02	05	04
Roberts, Moses(B)	1836	April 02	Switzerland	03	02	31
Roberts, Orlistus(A)	1828	April 23	Preble	02	08	31
Roberts, Orlistus(A)	1828	April 23	Preble	02	08	22
Roberts, Phineas(B)	1812	April 15	Wayne(Ind)	01	14	20
Roberts, Robert(C)	1813	May 12	Fairfield	12	03	07
Roberts, Samuel(A)	1818	Sept. 07	Darke	02	10	30
Roberts, Samuel(B)	1818	April 22	Clermont	02	05	04
Roberts, Samuel(B)	1836	June 30	Dearborn(Ind	02	05	05
Roberts, Thomas(A)	1806	May 12	Butler	03	03	08
Roberts, Thomas(A)	1806	May 17	Butler	02	06	35
Roberts, Thomas(B)	1806	Aug. 11	Butler	01	13	04
Roberts, Thomas(B)	1812	April 15	Wayne(Ind)	01	14	09
Roberts, William(A)	1819	Sept. 29	Champaign	07	01	03
Roberts, William(A)	1819	Sept. 29	Champaign	07	01	02
Robertson, Henry(C)	1812	March 09	Champaign	13	05	22
Robertson, Isaac(A)	1815	June 20	Warren	03	06	15
Robertson, John(A)	1819	June 21	Hamilton	04	05	14
Robertson, John(E)	1817	Oct. 27	Warren	14	18	26
Robertson, Robert(C)	1801	Dec. 22	Hamilton	04	03	21
Robertson, Samuel(A)	1813	March 08	Preble	03	06	22
Robertson, Samuel(A)	1819	July 21	Preble	03	06	13
Robertson, Thomas(A)	1831	Nov. 28	Darke	01	11	19
Robertson, William(C)	1815	May 25	Miami	06	07	30
Robeson, Abraham(B)	1836	Feb. 04	Franklin(Ind	02	08	19
Robeson, David(A)	1832	June 22	Montgomery	02	10	01

PURCHASER	YEAR	DATE	RESIDENCE	R	T	S
Robeson, Henry(B)	1834	Jan. 13	Franklin(Ind	03	09	13
Robeson, James(B)	1836	Feb. 04	Franklin(Ind	03	09	13
Robeson, James(B)	1836	Feb. 04	Franklin(Ind	02	08	18
Robeson, John Jr.(B)	1836	Jan. 22	Franklin(Ind	02	08	18
Robeson, John(B)	1836	Aug. 29	Franklin(Ind	02	08	05
Robeson, William(A)	1810	Feb. 03	Butler	02	05	11
Robeson, William(A)	1813	Jan. 29	Butler	02	05	22
Robeson, William(B)	1832	Dec. 13	Franklin(Ind	02	08	20
Robeson, William(B)	1832	Dec. 13	Franklin(Ind	02	08	20
Robinett, Moses(C)	1820	Jan. 26	Kentucky	11	03	20
Robins, Ezekiel(E)	1836	Oct. 28	Preble	14	19	34
Robins, Ezekiel(E)	1837	Jan. 02	Preble	14	19	34
Robins, Ezekiel(E)	1837	Jan. 09	Preble	14	19	35
Robins, John N.(A)	1819	June 18	Cincinnati	05	06	01
Robins, Samuel(E)	1837	Jan. 02	Preble	14	19	35
Robinson, Abel(E)	1816	Feb. 14	?	13	14	21
Robinson, Andrew(A)	1808	May 02	Kentucky	06	05	19
Robinson, Andrew(A)	1818	Dec. 12	Pennsylvania	02	10	03
Robinson, Andrew(A)	1819	April 14	Pennsylvania	02	10	03
Robinson, Charles(A)	1813	April 14	Butler	01	04	07
Robinson, Elizabeth(C)	1808	Aug. 17	Champaign	13	04	25
Robinson, Henry(C)	1806	Feb. 11	Kentucky	10	02	33
Robinson, Henry(C)	1806	Feb. 11	Kentucky	10	02	33
Robinson, James H.(A)	1806	July 21	Warren	02	06	19
Robinson, James H.(A)	1806	July 21	Warren	02	06	30
Robinson, James H.(A)	1806	July 21	Warren	01	06	06
Robinson, James H.(A)	1811	Dec. 11	Warren	02	06	19
Robinson, John(A)	1817	June 12	Montgomery	03	06	25
Robinson, John(B)	1814	July 04	Dearborn(Ind	01	05	18
Robinson, John(C)	1811	June 29	Kentucky	12	05	23
Robinson, John(E)	1830	Jan. 27	Randolph(Ind	14	20	28
Robinson, John(E)	1834	June 12	Randolph(Ind	14	20	35
Robinson, John(E)	1837	Jan. 10	Randolph(Ind	14	19	01
Robinson, Joshua(E)	1836	June 13	Randolph(Ind	14	19	01
Robinson, Ralph(C)	1814	April 06	Champaign	13	04	25
Robinson, Richard(C)	1808	June 03	Champaign	10	05	01
Robinson, Robert(A)	1814	Nov. 26	Montgomery	06	03	21
Robinson, Robert(C)	1802	Dec. 31	Hamilton	04	03	27
Robinson, Rossetter(C)	1811	Nov. 29	Champaign	13	04	25
Robinson, Sam'l. T.(C)	1826	June 28	Clark	10	03	26
Robinson, Samuel(A)	1806	April 24	Clermont	01	04	02
Robinson, Samuel(C)	1815	Jan. 13	Champaign	13	02	19
Robinson, Sidney(B)	1817	Nov. 13	Hamilton	03	06	35
Robinson, Thomas(C)	1814	Feb. 25	Champaign	13	02	01
Robinson, William(C)	1812	Sept. 17	Champaign	13	02	27
Robinson, William(E)	1836	Sept. 24	Randolph(Ind	14	20	35
Robinson, William(E)	1837	April 10	Randolph(Ind	15	19	06
Robinson, Winthrop(B)	1833	Dec. 10	Switzerland	03	03	01
Robisan, James(C)	1804	Sept. 03	Butler	04	02	08
Robison, Andrew(A)	1802	March 06	Hamilton	06	02	05
Robison, Andrew(A)	1804	Sept. 24	Warren	06	02	08
Robison, Andrew(C)	1801	Dec. 22	Hamilton	04	03	33
Robison, David Hartman(A)	1835	Feb. 14	Darke	01	12	06
Robison, David(B)	1836	Oct. 18	Randolph(Ind	01	17	02
Robison, Elizabeth(B)	1837	Feb. 04	Darke	01	18	35
Robison, James H.(C)	1804	Sept. 03	Warren	04	03	26
Robison, James(C)	1804	Sept. 03	Butler	04	02	08
Robison, John(C)	1801	Dec. 23	Hamilton	04	02	07
Robison, John(C)	1802	Dec. 09	Hamilton	05	02	21
Robison, Richard(C)	1806	April 08	Champaign	10	05	02
Robison, Robert(A)	1805	April 13	Warren	06	02	08
Robison, Robert(A)	1804	Sept. 24	Warren	06	02	08
Robison, Robert(C)	1801	Dec. 22	Hamilton	04	03	33
Roby, Charles(A)	1819	Aug. 12	Shelby	06	08	30
Roby, Ralph(A)	1819	Aug. 12	Shelby	06	08	29
Rock, Felix(C)	1804	Oct. 26	Greene	12	04	09
Rock, Phillip(C)	1802	Dec. 31	Hamilton	09	04	27
Rock, William(A)	1807	Aug. 06	Butler	01	06	26
Rockafellen, John H.(B)	1815	March 20	Franklin(Ind	01	08	31

PURCHASER	YEAR	DATE	RESIDENCE	R	T	S
Rockey, Henry(B)	1818	July 06	Cincinnati	02	08	17
Rockhill, William(E)	1836	June 06	Butler	14	19	17
Rockhill, William(E)	1836	June 11	Butler	14	19	18
Rockler, Adam(C)	1801	Dec. 31	Hamilton	08	03	25
Rocky, Henry(C)	1824	June 08	Cincinnati	14	03	17
Rodabaugh, Susan(A)	1830	Dec. 29	Montgomery	04	07	28
Rodabough, Peter(A)	1816	March 13	Montgomery	04	10	08
Rodchaffar, Samuel(A)	1811	Oct. 21	Virginia	04	04	11
Roddey, Christopher(B)	1806	July 30	Kentucky	01	13	07
Roddy, Christopher(E)	1814	July 08	Wayne(Ind)	14	16	30
Rodebough, Adam(A)	1815	Oct. 26	Montgomery	03	06	14
Rodehamel, Jacob(A)	1812	March 20	Montgomery	06	03	34
Rodehamel, Sam'l.(A)	1829	July 30	Miami	04	08	27
Rodehamel, Sam'l.(A)	1831	Feb. 03	Miami	04	08	27
Rodenbough, Adam(A)	1815	March 16	Montgomery	03	11	25
Rodibough, Seth(E)	1818	Feb. 23	Montgomery	13	18	10
Rodicker, Jacob(C)	1815	Sept. 20	Hamilton	10	03	20
Rodkey, Jacob C.(A)	1836	Nov. 21	Darke	04	11	32
Roe, Frederick(A)	1831	Dec. 01	Fayette	01	13	32
Roe, Isaiah(A)	1806	July 01	Highland	05	07	20
Roe, John(A)	1831	Nov. 03	Miami	05	08	27
Roffe, Edward(A)	1815	Dec. 15	Warren	02	11	27
Roffelty, Matthias(C)	1811	Nov. 25	Hamilton	02	02	26
Rogers, Alexander(A)	1810	April 05	Preble	02	07	25
Rogers, Ebenezer(B)	1815	Feb. 24	Cincinnati	01	06	07
Rogers, Ebenezer(B)	1815	May 26	Dearborn(Ind	01	06	07
Rogers, Henry(B)	1818	Aug. 10	Switzerland	03	03	19
Rogers, Henry(B)	1832	May 22	Switzerland	03	03	30
Rogers, Isaiah(E)	1818	June 20	Clark	13	18	12
Rogers, Jacob(B)	1833	Nov. 29	Randolph(Ind	01	16	02
Rogers, Jacob(B)	1833	Nov. 29	Randolph(Ind	01	16	11
Rogers, Jacob(B)	1834	Sept. 15	Randolph(Ind	01	16	11
Rogers, Jacob(B)	1836	May 27	Randolph(Ind	01	16	11
Rogers, James(E)	1811	Oct. 22	Ross	12	15	01
Rogers, Jeremiah(A)	1818	Aug. 03	Darke	01	12	28
Rogers, John(B)	1830	Feb. 15	Montgomery	01	16	36
Rogers, John(C)	1802	Dec. 28	Hamilton	06	02	28
Rogers, John(C)	1804	Sept. 03	Montgomery	06	02	29
Rogers, John(C)	1805	Dec. 12	Montgomery	06	02	28
Rogers, John(C)	1812	Dec. 31	Miami	11	02	26
Rogers, John(C)	1812	Dec. 31	Miami	11	02	26
Rogers, John(C)	1815	March 21	Miami	10	02	29
Rogers, Joseph Jr.(E)	1818	June 04	Warren(Ind)	13	18	12
Rogers, Robert(A)	1836	Aug. 18	Montgomery	02	15	20
Rogers, Samuel(E)	1819	July 21	Warren	13	18	14
Rohr, Frederick(A)	1832	Oct. 04	Darke	04	09	06
Rohrar, Jacob(A)	1813	June 08	Montgomery	05	03	15
Rohras, Jacob(A)	1813	June 08	Montgomery	05	03	15
Rohrer, Jacob(A)	1810	Dec. 17	Montgomery	05	03	15
Rohrer, Joseph(A)	1827	June 08	Montgomery	04	06	15
Rolf, James(A)	1815	Oct. 31	Butler	03	10	33
Rolfe, Edward(A)	1816	March 19	Warren	03	08	32
Rolfe, Moses(A)	1831	March 15	Warren	03	08	19
Rolfes, Bernard(E)	1836	Nov. 12	Cincinnati	12	11	32
Roll, Benjamin(A)	1832	April 12	Darke	03	09	04
Roll, Isaac(E)	1834	Oct. 08	New Jersey	14	20	28
Roll, Jacob(C)	1818	Jan. 09	Champaign	09	03	26
Roll, John(B)	1818	June 20	Hamilton	02	06	32
Roll, Joseph(C)	1824	June 21	Clark	09	03	26
Roll, Mathias(A)	1811	May 16	Warren	02	04	18
Roll, Mathias(A)	1811	May 16	Warren	01	04	13
Roll, Mathias(C)	1801	Dec. 28	Hamilton	04	04	34
Roll, Moses(A)	1831	June 03	Clark	05	09	01
Roll, Samuel(A)	1830	Sept. 22	Butler	02	09	21
Rollf, James(A)	1811	April 16	Dearborn(Ind	01	03	06
Rollins, Joseph(C)	1818	June 29	Miami	11	02	23
Rollins, Myhew(C)	1818	Aug. 20	Miami	11	02	23
Romerell, Philip(B)	1816	Dec. 10	?	04	02	12
Romeril, Charles Edward(B)	1818	June 27	Switzerland	04	02	36

PURCHASER	YEAR	DATE	RESIDENCE	R	T	S
Romeril, Philip(B)	1817	June 20	Switzerland	03	02	18
Ronald, Jno.(E)	1822	Jan. 25	?	12	13	19
Ronnebaum, Jno. Hy.(A)	1837	Dec. 11	Cincinnati	03	13	31
Ronnebaum, John Herman(E)	1836	Nov. 11	Cincinnati	12	10	05
Ronnebaum, John Hy.(E)	1836	Nov. 11	Cincinnati	12	10	05
Ronnebaum, John Hy.(E)	1836	Nov. 11	Cincinnati	12	10	04
Rood, Lorrin B.(A)	1836	Dec. 01	Connecticut	01	15	25
Rood, William(B)	1826	Feb. 06	Franklin(Ind	03	07	14
Rooker, William(E)	1811	Oct. 28	Preble	13	16	21
Rookstool, George(A)	1817	Oct. 30	Virginia	03	07	35
Roos, John(A)	1815	March 08	Montgomery	05	07	19
Root, Abraham(B)	1836	Aug. 29	Miami	01	18	36
Root, David(A)	1836	June 02	Montgomery	01	13	09
Root, John Senr.(A)	1830	Dec. 09	Montgomery	04	07	27
Root, John(A)	1828	Nov. 22	Montgomery	04	07	27
Root, John(B)	1836	Oct. 29	Montgomery	01	18	36
Ropes, Hardy Jun.(B)	1817	Aug. 22	Hamilton	02	03	36
Ropes, Hardy(B)	1817	Sept. 08	Hamilton	02	03	35
Rorer, Dan'l.(A)	1828	Oct. 25	Preble	03	08	35
Rorer, Dan'l.(A)	1829	Feb. 21	Preble	03	08	35
Rorer, John(A)	1815	Dec. 01	Montgomery	04	06	14
Rorer, John(A)	1829	Oct. 29	Montgomery	04	06	11
Rorer, Joseph Jur.(A)	1815	Dec. 01	Montgomery	04	06	14
Rorer, Joseph(A)	1805	March 23	Montgomery	04	06	14
Rorer, Joseph(A)	1805	June 18	Montgomery	04	06	24
Rorer, Joseph(A)	1805	June 18	Montgomery	04	06	14
Rorer, Joseph(A)	1811	Nov. 29	Montgomery	05	05	07
Rork, Francis(C)	1818	June 26	Montgomery	13	02	27
Roscheskoski, Peter(B)	1837	Nov. 15	Switzerland	03	04	25
Rose, Abraham(B)	1814	July 27	Franklin(Ind	02	10	01
Rose, Abraham(B)	1814	July 27	Franklin(Ind	02	10	26
Rose, Ezekiel(B)	1818	Dec. 03	Franklin(Ind	02	10	15
Roseboome, John G.(A)	1813	Feb. 15	Butler	01	04	34
Rosebrough, Robert(B)	1815	Aug. 28	Butler	03	02	06
Rosebrough, Robert(B)	1817	Dec. 31	Switzerland	03	03	27
Rosegrant, John(C)	1806	Feb. 06	Hamilton	08	04	24
Rosegrant, John(C)	1811	April 09	Greene	08	04	24
Rosenbaum, Jacob(B)	1836	July 07	Hamilton	02	08	18
Roser, William Frederick(A)	1831	Aug. 22	Warren	02	10	11
Roser, Wm. Frederick(A)	1832	May 26	Warren	01	10	11
Ross, Alexander E.(C)	1816	Jan. 29	?	08	06	36
Ross, Alexander(C)	1802	Dec. 30	Hamilton	04	03	28
Ross, Benj'n.(A)	1829	Feb. 03	Preble	02	09	27
Ross, Benjamin(A)	1805	July 23	Warren	03	04	07
Ross, Benjamin(A)	1805	July 31	Warren	03	04	10
Ross, Benjamin(A)	1805	July 31	Warren	03	04	01
Ross, Benjamin(A)	1810	Dec. 12	Champaign	03	04	01
Ross, Benjamin(A)	1830	June 21	Preble	02	09	27
Ross, Daniel(A)	1814	Sept. 10	Butler	02	06	23
Ross, Ezekiel(A)	1806	June 04	Butler	01	04	23
Ross, Ezekiel(A)	1806	July 16	Butler	01	04	26
Ross, Henry(A)	1816	Oct. 10	Franklin(Ind	01	11	24
Ross, Henry(A)	1831	Aug. 09	Darke	01	11	24
Ross, Henry(A)	1831	Aug. 18	Darke	01	11	24
Ross, Henry(A)	1835	Dec. 26	Darke	01	12	12
Ross, Henry(A)	1835	Dec. 26	Darke	02	12	04
Ross, Henry(A)	1835	Dec. 26	Darke	02	13	27
Ross, Henry(A)	1835	Dec. 26	Darke	02	13	28
Ross, Henry(A)	1835	Dec. 26	Darke	02	13	28
Ross, Henry(A)	1835	Dec. 26	Darke	02	13	29
Ross, James B.(A)	1819	Dec. 20	Warren	04	05	05
Ross, James B.(A)	1819	Dec. 20	Warren	04	05	08
Ross, John(A)	1805	June 19	Butler	03	03	10
Ross, John(A)	1805	Aug. 05	Butler	03	03	02
Ross, John(A)	1810	Aug. 14	Butler	03	03	10
Ross, John(B)	1816	May 04	Pennsylvania	01	10	28
Ross, John(C)	1811	April 09	Miami	09	02	27
Ross, John(C)	1811	April 17	Miami	09	02	28
Ross, John(C)	1811	Dec. 11	Champaign	10	06	32

PURCHASER	YEAR	DATE	RESIDENCE	R	T	S
Ross, John(C)	1826	Jan. 24	Logan	14	03	36
Ross, Joseph(B)	1818	Oct. 19	Hamilton	02	03	22
Ross, Meshack(A)	1836	Oct. 31	Virginia	02	14	01
Ross, Nimrod(A)	1836	Sept. 20	Mercer	02	14	12
Ross, Nimrod(A)	1836	Oct. 14	Darke	02	14	12
Ross, Robert(B)	1816	May 04	Pennsylvania	01	10	34
Ross, Robert(C)	1801	Dec. 25	Hamilton	05	02	31
Ross, Robert(E)	1837	Sept. 29	Preble	14	21	32
Ross, Thomas R.(A)	1818	Feb. 16	Ohio	06	04	15
Ross, Thomas R.(A)	1818	Feb. 16	Ohio	05	07	25
Ross, Thomas(A)	1814	Aug. 15	Hamilton	01	03	20
Ross, William(A)	1805	Feb. 23	Butler	02	03	06
Ross, William(A)	1805	Aug. 20	Warren	02	03	06
Ross, William(A)	1810	Dec. 12	Preble	03	04	10
Ross, William(B)	1816	Aug. 31	Dearborn(Ind	01	03	20
Ross, William(B)	1816	Aug. 31	Dearborn(Ind	01	03	18
Ross, William(C)	1804	Dec. 31	Greene	10	04	17
Ross, William(C)	1806	Aug. 01	Champaign	10	04	29
Ross, William(C)	1831	March 07	Hamilton	13	03	03
Ross, William(E)	1814	Oct. 20	Butler	12	15	25
Ross, Zedekiah(E)	1837	May 11	Virginia	14	21	02
Rossel, Elias(A)	1819	May 10	Miami	05	09	14
Roth, John(B)	1835	July 02	Hamilton	02	06	07
Roth, Madias(A)	1833	April 01	Cincinnati	02	12	24
Roth, William(E)	1837	April 28	Montgomery	15	21	33
Rottinghaus, Bernard(A)	1837	Dec. 22	Shelby	02	15	36
Rottinghaus, Henry(B)	1836	Feb. 08	Hamilton	03	09	24
Roudebush, George(A)	1805	July 01	Montgomery	04	04	29
Roudebush, George(A)	1821	July 26	Randolph(Ind	05	05	19
Rough, Peter(B)	1837	Oct. 16	Preble	02	05	32
Rouse, Joshua(A)	1828	Aug. 18	Kentucky	02	09	22
Roush, Jacob(B)	1816	Oct. 09	Warren	01	12	26
Routh, Isaac(A)	1808	Jan. 13	Butler	02	05	05
Routzon, George(A)	1831	Aug. 15	Montgomery	04	10	35
Rouze, Levi(C)	1806	Jan. 08	Champaign	11	04	25
Rouze, Levi(C)	1806	Jan. 08	Champaign	11	04	25
Row, Conrod(B)	1818	June 29	Hamilton	02	06	02
Row, William(A)	1808	May 11	Montgomery	02	06	07
Rowe, Peter(A)	1823	Feb. 03	Preble	03	06	07
Rowe, Robert Jr.(B)	1825	Nov. 29	Champaign	02	07	33
Rowe, Robert(B)	1817	Aug. 16	Dearborn(Ind	02	07	33
Rowe, Robert(B)	1817	Aug. 16	Dearborn(Ind	02	06	11
Rowe, Robert(B)	1831	Jan. 19	Dearborn(Ind	02	07	33
Rowland, Philip(B)	1817	Oct. 21	Hamilton	03	05	03
Rowland, Philip(B)	1833	Jan. 09	Dearborn(Ind	03	05	09
Rowland, Philip(B)	1836	March 24	Dearborn(Ind	03	05	09
Rowland, Philip(B)	1837	Jan. 26	Dearborn(Ind	03	06	34
Rowland, William(B)	1818	Aug. 14	Hamilton	01	07	18
Rownd, Edward(B)	1828	May 19	Dearborn(Ind	03	07	26
Rownd, John R.(B)	1819	June 15	Dearborn(Ind	03	07	35
Rownd, John R.(B)	1836	April 04	Dearborn(Ind	03	07	35
Royer, Abraham(B)	1836	Aug. 10	Randolph(Ind	01	18	13
Royer, Abraham(B)	1837	Jan. 30	Montgomery	01	18	13
Royer, Henry(A)	1813	Jan. 25	Montgomery	05	04	11
Royer, Henry(A)	1835	Sept. 21	Darke	01	13	09
Royer, John(B)	1835	Sept. 21	Darke	01	18	25
Royer, John(B)	1836	Oct. 24	Randolph(Ind	01	18	36
Roysdan, Nathan(E)	1813	Dec. 21	Butler	13	15	33
Royse, Catharine(A)	1813	Feb. 01	Butler	02	04	05
Royster, Charles(E)	1813	April 05	Franklin(Ind	12	14	01
Royster, Stanhope(B)	1807	Jan. 12	Ind.Territry	01	09	26
Royster, Stanhope(B)	1812	April 15	Franklin(Ind	01	09	26
Rozer, Lawrence(C)	1831	Oct. 24	Shelby	13	02	05
Rubert, Isaac(C)	1801	Dec. 22	Hamilton	07	03	19
Ruble, George(E)	1837	Feb. 14	Randolph(Ind	13	20	11
Ruble, Walter(E)	1831	July 05	Randolph(Ind	13	20	14
Ruby, Jacob(A)	1808	Jan. 13	Ross	04	04	14
Ruby, John(A)	1811	Nov. 19	Montgomery	04	04	10
Ruckman, Thomas W.(A)	1817	Aug. 04	Greene	05	10	30

PURCHASER	YEAR	DATE	RESIDENCE	R	T	S
Rudebaugh, Adam(A)	1805	June 04	Pennsylvania	05	05	34
Rudebaugh, Adam(A)	1805	June 04	Pennsylvania	05	04	12
Rudebaugh, Adam(A)	1805	June 04	Pennsylvania	06	02	07
Rudesil, Michael(B)	1807	Sept. 28	Hamilton	01	08	26
Rudicel, George Michael(B)	1834	Feb. 27	Franklin(Ind	01	08	20
Rudicel, George(B)	1832	March 27	Franklin(Ind	01	08	30
Rudicel, George(B)	1836	Aug. 02	Franklin(Ind	01	08	30
Rudicel, Jacob(B)	1834	May 22	Dearborn(Ind	01	07	21
Rudicel, Jacob(B)	1836	May 25	Dearborn(Ind	01	07	21
Rudicel, Michael(B)	1816	Feb. 03	Franklin(Ind	01	08	21
Rudicel, Michael(B)	1836	Feb. 22	Franklin(Ind	01	08	21
Rudicel, Philip(B)	1835	April 21	Franklin(Ind	01	08	20
Rudisel, George(B)	1813	June 11	Franklin(Ind	01	08	17
Rudy, Samuel(A)	1814	July 26	Montgomery	04	09	25
Rue, Henry(B)	1824	July 05	Wayne(Ind)	01	13	15
Rue, John(C)	1806	April 03	Greene	10	02	34
Rue, John(C)	1806	April 30	Greene	10	03	25
Rue, John(C)	1806	July 21	Champaign	09	03	09
Rue, John(C)	1806	Nov. 27	Champaign	09	04	35
Rue, Richard(B)	1804	Dec. 19	Kentucky	01	13	17
Rue, Richard(B)	1805	July 05	Dearborn(Ind	01	13	30
Ruff, David(A)	1814	Sept. 16	Montgomery	04	05	14
Ruffin, William	1808	March 02	Cincinnati	?	?	?
Ruffin, William(A)	1804	Sept. 24	Cincinnati	03	01	18
Ruffin, William(B)	1811	April 12	Cincinnati	02	09	17
Ruffin, William(B)	1816	Aug. 13	Cincinnati	01	10	35
Ruffin, William(B)	1824	June 09	Cincinnati	01	09	21
Ruffin, William(C)	1801	Dec. 31	Cincinnati	08	03	25
Ruffin, William(C)	1804	Aug. 28	Cincinnati	08	03	26
Ruffin, William(C)	1804	Sept. 05	Cincinnati	08	03	26
Ruffin, William(C)	1804	Sept. 05	Cincinnati	08	03	26
Ruffin, William(C)	1804	Sept. 05	Cincinnati	08	03	26
Ruffin, William(C)	1804	Dec. 28	Cincinnati	09	05	32
Ruffin, William(C)	1806	Dec. 30	Cincinnati	09	06	02
Ruffin, William(C)	1824	June 07	Cincinnati	11	03	26
Rumbley, James(E)	1814	Aug. 22	Wayne(Ind)	13	14	15
Rumbley, Thomas(E)	1815	Nov. 11	Wayne(Ind)	13	14	13
Rumsey, John(B)	1832	Aug. 01	Dearborn(Ind	02	05	09
Rumsey, William(B)	1835	Sept. 16	Dearborn(Ind	02	05	08
Rundle, William(E)	1815	Dec. 11	Franklin(Ind	12	12	14
Rundle, William(E)	1815	Dec. 11	Franklin(Ind	12	12	14
Rundles, Joseph(C)	1808	Feb. 02	Champaign	11	05	12
Runkel, William(C)	1813	May 31	Champaign	11	04	14
Runkel, William(C)	1813	June 10	Champaign	11	04	14
Runkle, Frederick(C)	1817	June 03	Champaign	11	05	35
Runkle, Peter(C)	1815	March 16	Champaign	11	04	35
Runyan, Bonham(E)	1816	March 15	Warren	13	17	18
Runyan, James(A)	1821	Dec. 06	Hamilton	04	07	29
Runyan, Jno.(A)	1819	Jan. 25	Hamilton	02	09	20
Runyan, Peter(E)	1829	May 26	Wayne(Ind)	13	17	31
Runyon, Abraham(C)	1811	April 19	Clinton	10	06	20
Runyon, John(C)	1808	Dec. 19	Champaign	10	06	32
Runyon, Joseph(C)	1814	April 20	Champaign	10	06	14
Runyon, Mich'l.(A)	1828	Dec. 30	Preble	01	07	22
Runyon, Michael(A)	1808	Jan. 13	Montgomery	01	07	24
Runyon, Michael(A)	1813	April 14	Montgomery	01	07	24
Runyon, Michael(A)	1818	Jan. 30	Preble	01	07	22
Runyon, Peter(E)	1817	Sept. 08	Hamilton	12	17	36
Runyon, William(A)	1808	Jan. 12	Montgomery	01	07	24
Runyon, William(C)	1813	April 14	Warren	01	07	24
Rupel, James(A)	1835	April 09	Darke	01	13	35
Rupelogle, Adam(A)	1806	April 22	Montgomery	04	05	11
Rupelogle, Adam(A)	1805	July 03	Montgomery	05	04	19
Rupert, Moses(E)	1836	Oct. 25	Clark	14	21	33
Ruple, Martin(A)	1816	June 20	Preble	02	11	07
Ruple, Martin(A)	1816	June 20	Preble	02	11	08
Ruplogle, Adam(A)	1805	July 03	Montgomery	05	04	19
Ruse, Dan'l.(A)	1831	March 05	Preble	03	07	25
Ruse, Dan'l.(A)	1831	April 12	Preble	03	07	25

PURCHASER	YEAR	DATE	RESIDENCE	R	T	S
Ruse, Nicholas(A)	1809	Dec. 11	Montgomery	04	05	11
Rush, Aaron(A)	1816	June 01	Darke	01	11	13
Rush, Andrew(A)	1811	June 17	Pickaway	02	12	31
Rush, Aron(A)	1817	Oct. 04	Darke	01	10	11
Rush, Isaac(A)	1806	Aug. 19	Butler	01	07	03
Rush, Jacob(A)	1829	Dec. 07	Darke	02	11	03
Rush, Jacob(C)	1807	Feb. 19	Butler	08	03	33
Rush, Jacob(C)	1807	Feb. 19	Butler	08	03	33
Rush, James(A)	1814	Aug. 16	Darke	02	11	09
Rush, James(A)	1814	Sept. 01	Darke	02	11	09
Rush, Jesse(C)	1807	July 06	Greene	08	03	33
Rush, John(A)	1816	April 19	Piqua	01	10	14
Rush, Leonard(A)	1806	Dec. 03	Warren	04	02	03
Rush, Moses(A)	1805	June 08	Butler	03	03	12
Rush, Moses(A)	1816	Feb. 09	Butler	02	11	20
Rush, Moses(A)	1816	June 01	Darke	01	11	03
Rush, Peter(A)	1811	June 17	Pickaway	02	12	31
Rush, Peter(A)	1819	May 24	Darke	01	10	11
Rusing, William(B)	1814	March 10	Franklin(Ind	02	10	29
Rusk, James(A)	1823	April 17	Preble	03	08	27
Rusk, William(A)	1837	April 12	Darke	02	12	17
Russel, Enoch(E)	1814	Dec. 14	Franklin(Ind	12	12	17
Russel, George(C)	1815	March 22	Butler	12	01	13
Russel, James(C)	1801	Dec. 31	Hamilton	06	02	31
Russel, James(C)	1815	Oct. 13	Champaign	12	03	06
Russel, Martin(A)	1803	Oct. 06	Butler	03	05	03
Russell, Alexander(A)	1811	Jan. 23	Greene	05	09	35
Russell, Alexander(A)	1811	Dec. 30	Miami	05	09	34
Russell, Finley(A)	1818	April 10	Warren	04	10	17
Russell, James(C)	1804	Sept. 04	Hamilton	04	02	11
Russell, James(C)	1813	April 14	Champaign	09	06	35
Russell, James(E)	1811	Oct. 28	Ind.Territry	12	12	24
Russell, Jared(A)	1831	Oct. 22	Pennsylvania	05	10	36
Russell, John Sterling(E)	1836	Feb. 11	Franklin(Ind	12	12	06
Russell, John(E)	1811	Oct. 22	Ohio	12	14	35
Russell, Jonathan(E)	1836	Jan. 25	Franklin(Ind	12	12	07
Russell, Robert(C)	1806	April 03	Kentucky	09	03	17
Russell, Robert(E)	1834	Oct. 09	Franklin(Ind	12	12	08
Russell, Robt.(C)	1819	March 12	Champaign	12	04	26
Russell, Robt.(C)	1831	June 11	Miami	12	02	27
Russell, Robt.(E)	1811	Nov. 22	Franklin(Ind	12	13	28
Russell, Rosanah(A)	1806	Aug. 08	Montgomery	06	04	20
Russell, Samuel(A)	1812	March 20	Butler	02	03	19
Russey, William(B)	1825	Dec. 10	Wayne(Ind)	01	13	36
Rust, Matthias(C)	1818	Jan. 16	Champaign	10	03	04
Rute, Joel(E)	1836	Sept. 03	Randolph(Ind	14	19	10
Rutherford, Robert(B)	1816	Nov. 04	JeffersonInd	04	03	24
Ruthop, John(B)	1838	May 03	Cincinnati	03	05	22
Rutter, Alanson(B)	1817	Oct. 23	Cincinnati	02	02	12
Ryan, Dorsey(A)	1829	March 06	Preble	02	07	32
Ryan, Dorsey(B)	1833	Aug. 21	Randolph(Ind	01	16	26
Ryan, Dorsey(E)	1836	Sept. 10	Randolph(Ind	15	22	31
Ryan, James(A)	1814	Dec. 21	Preble	02	07	31
Ryan, Reuben(A)	1811	Dec. 14	Butler	02	06	07
Ryan, Reuben(A)	1812	Jan. 16	Butler	04	03	29
Ryan, Reuben(A)	1814	Oct. 10	Butler	01	07	05
Ryan, Reuben(A)	1814	Nov. 26	Butler	02	06	17
Ryan, Reuben(A)	1815	Jan. 06	Butler	02	06	08
Ryan, Richard(A)	1815	Jan. 25	Butler	02	06	06
Ryan, Richard(A)	1816	April 06	Preble	02	07	32
Ryan, William(A)	1818	April 01	Hamilton	06	08	01
Ryckman, Charles Wilmot(E)	1836	Feb. 02	Franklin(Ind	12	12	30
Ryder, John(B)	1818	March 05	Cincinnati	02	03	25
Ryerson, John(A)	1810	March 05	Butler	02	11	34
Ryerson, John(A)	1811	Sept. 09	Darke	02	11	27
Ryerson, John(A)	1814	Dec. 12	Butler	02	11	34
Ryerson, John(A)	1816	March 09	Darke	02	11	33
Ryerson, John(A)	1816	Dec. 02	Darke	02	11	27
Ryerson, John(A)	1828	Nov. 01	Darke	02	11	34

PURCHASER	YEAR	DATE	RESIDENCE	R	T	S
Ryle, Larkin(B)	1812	Sept. 04	Kentucky	03	04	05
Rynearson, Isaac(A)	1832	Feb. 09	Hamilton	02	10	31
Rysinger, John(A)	1816	Feb. 15	Butler	03	04	12
Rytz, Geo. Michael(E)	1833	Oct. 31	Randolph(Ind	13	20	24
Sabourain, Jacob(A)	1835	Sept. 26	Stark	03	11	11
Sabourain, Peter(A)	1835	Sept. 26	Stark	03	11	11
Sack, Henry(E)	1837	Feb. 22	Cincinnati	12	11	28
Sacket, Cyrus(C)	1801	Dec. 30	Hamilton	05	03	06
Sacket, Thomas(B)	1815	Jan. 30	Butler	02	10	02
Sackett, Aaron(A)	1806	Feb. 17	Hamilton	02	04	23
Sadler, Richard(A)	1810	Nov. 03	Pennsylvania	03	07	22
Sadler, Richard(A)	1814	Oct. 26	Pennsylvania	03	07	22
Sage, Joseph(A)	1831	Aug. 06	Miami	05	08	23
Saighman, William(B)	1816	Dec. 03	Wayne(Ind)	01	07	18
Sailer, Christian(A)	1810	Nov. 29	Preble	03	04	01
Sailer, John(A)	1810	Nov. 29	Preble	03	04	01
Sailer, John(B)	1822	June 28	Cincinnati	02	07	18
Sailor, Jno.(C)	1831	Feb. 24	Logan	13	03	10
Sailor, John Jr.(C)	1827	April 12	Miami	09	02	18
Sailor, John(B)	1807	Jan. 10	Kentucky	01	08	18
Sailor, John(C)	1825	Feb. 28	Clark	13	03	11
Saladay, Jacob(A)	1804	Oct. 03	Kentucky	03	04	35
Sale, John((A)	1817	Nov. 24	Greene	04	08	17
Sallar, John(A)	1816	March 15	Montgomery	04	04	02
Salor, Benj'm.(A)	1815	Sept. 26	Franklin(Ind	01	07	13
Salor, Benj'm.(E)	1815	Sept. 26	Franklin(Ind	12	13	15
Salor, Benjamin(E)	1811	Oct. 21	Franklin(Ind	12	11	04
Salor, Benjamin(E)	1812	Oct. 05	Franklin(Ind	13	11	06
Salor, Benjamin(E)	1813	Aug. 30	Franklin(Ind	12	14	35
Salor, Benjamin(E)	1813	Aug. 30	Franklin(Ind	12	13	11
Salor, Benjamin(E)	1813	Aug. 30	Franklin(Ind	12	14	11
Salor, Benjamin(E)	1814	Sept. 10	Franklin(Ind	12	13	06
Salyer, John(E)	1811	Nov. 01	Franklin(Ind	13	13	33
Salyers, Charles(E)	1831	Feb. 04	Fayette	13	13	28
Salyers, Jas.(E)	1831	Feb. 04	Fayette	13	13	28
Sam, Adam(B)	1836	Nov. 26	Franklin(Ind	03	09	13
Sample, David(A)	1806	June 05	Pennsylvania	02	06	30
Sample, Jacob(?)	1813	Nov. 03	Butler	02	10	03
Sample, Jacob(A)	1803	Aug. 04	Butler	04	02	02
Sample, John(A)	1803	Aug. 04	Butler	04	02	02
Sample, John(A)	1805	July 15	Butler	04	03	34
Sample, John(A)	1810	Dec. 12	Butler	04	03	34
Sample, John(E)	1835	April 06	Randolph(Ind	13	20	15
Sample, John(E)	1836	Oct. 17	Randolph(Ind	13	20	15
Sampson, David(A)	1802	March 09	Hamilton	05	05	09
Sampson, Joseph(A)	1817	Aug. 26	Hamilton	01	09	25
Sampson, Rich'd. H.(A)	1828	Jan. 16	Preble	01	09	21
Sampson, Seth(B)	1818	Jan. 08	Switzerland	01	02	02
Sanders, Amasy(C)	1816	Feb. 03	Miami	12	01	02
Sanders, Elihu(C)	1804	Dec. 15	Montgomery	10	02	32
Sanders, Elihu(C)	1804	Dec. 15	Montgomery	10	01	02
Sanders, George(C)	1806	June 16	Champaign	11	05	18
Sanders, George(C)	1811	Aug. 13	Champaign	11	05	18
Sanders, George(C)	1813	May 03	Champaign	12	03	13
Sanders, Jacob(E)	1817	Dec. 11	Wayne(Ind)	13	21	23
Sanders, Mary(C)	1816	Feb. 03	Miami	12	01	02
Sanders, Samuel(B)	1818	Oct. 14	So. Carolina	01	15	29
Sanders, Samuel(E)	1812	July 16	So. Carolina	12	15	27
Sanders, Samuel(E)	1818	Jan. 19	So. Carolina	13	21	13
Sanders, Silas(B)	1832	Sept. 13	Dearborn(Ind	02	06	17
Sanders, Theodore(C)	1814	July 12	Miami	10	02	29
Sanders, William(E)	1818	May 29	Randolph(Ind	13	21	26
Sane, Frederic(B)	1817	July 30	Dearborn(Ind	03	07	13
Sankey, Thomas(B)	1811	Nov. 18	Butler	01	10	03
Sargent, Enoch(C)	1819	Feb. 01	Clark	13	04	12
Sargent, Ezekiel(C)	1816	Jan. 03	Champaign	12	02	06
Sargent, James(C)	1816	Aug. 01	Champaign	12	04	12
Sargent, John(C)	1818	April 18	Clark	13	04	18
Sartwell, Obadiah(A)	1831	Nov. 03	Darke	01	10	25

PURCHASER	YEAR	DATE	RESIDENCE	R	T	S
Sarver, Jacob(C)	1814	Feb. 25	Champaign	12	03	36
Sarver, Jacob(C)	1829	Jan. 16	Champaign	13	03	26
Sarver, Jacob(C)	1830	Dec. 06	Champaign	13	04	31
Sarver, Jacob(C)	1831	May 26	Champaign	13	03	27
Sarver, Jacob(C)	1831	Nov. 10	Champaign	13	03	26
Sarver, Samuel(E)	1836	Oct. 03	Butler	15	21	31
Sasser, William(B)	1836	Feb. 20	Randolph(Ind	01	16	13
Sater, George(A)	1815	Oct. 12	Miami	04	09	24
Sater, Henry(B)	1812	Sept. 10	Hamilton	01	08	24
Sater, John(B)	1812	Oct. 12	Hamilton	01	08	12
Satterthwait, Caleb(A)	1818	March 21	Warren	01	07	08
Satterthwaite, Benj.(E)	1829	Dec. 10	Wayne(Ind)	14	17	17
Saulsbury, William(C)	1814	Dec. 23	Champaign	11	04	20
Saum, Jacob(C)	1806	June 26	Montgomery	09	02	20
Saum, Jacob(C)	1806	Aug. 12	Montgomery	09	02	09
Saunders, Anthony(C)	1825	Nov. 18	Clark	10	03	17
Saunders, Isaac T.(A)	1836	Sept. 08	Butler	02	13	27
Savage, George Penn(A)	1831	Sept. 26	Shelby	05	09	01
Sawden, William Jr.(B)	1833	March 02	Dearborn(Ind	02	06	13
Sawyer, Andrew(C)	1818	Oct. 22	Champaign	13	03	23
Sawyer, John(A)	1815	March 06	Warren	01	09	36
Sawyer, Matthew(A)	1837	April 07	Darke	01	13	20
Sawyer, Uriah(A)	1818	Feb. 20	Warren	03	10	25
Sawyer, Uriah(A)	1819	Aug. 19	Montgomery	03	10	26
Sawyer, William(C)	1802	Dec. 30	Hamilton	06	02	35
Sawyers, David(A)	1831	Aug. 22	Warren	05	06	02
Sawyers, Joseph(C)	1806	Aug. 23	Warren	05	02	22
Saxon, Alexander(E)	1811	Dec. 09	Butler	12	14	25
Saxon, Alexander(E)	1813	Oct. 30	Franklin(Ind	12	14	29
Saylor, Benjamin(E)	1811	Oct. 22	Franklin(Ind	12	14	24
Saylor, Woolery(A)	1811	Nov. 25	Montgomery	04	04	23
Sayre, Anthony Swain Jr.(C)	1818	June 19	Clark	09	03	26
Sayre, Benjamin(A)	1806	July 11	Warren	06	04	30
Sayre, Jno.(C)	1829	Dec. 12	Logan	13	03	11
Sayre, John(C)	1816	Aug. 28	Champaign	13	03	34
Sayre, John(C)	1827	July 02	Champaign	13	03	05
Sayre, Leonard(A)	1809	June 23	Cincinnati	01	03	21
Sayre, Leonard(A)	1809	July 31	Cincinnati	02	12	26
Sayre, Leonard(A)	1809	July 31	Cincinnati	02	12	20
Sayre, Leonard(A)	1810	Dec. 14	?	04	02	03
Sayre, Leonard(A)	1814	Aug. 16	Cincinnati	01	03	21
Sayre, Leonard(B)	1809	Dec. 12	Cincinnati	01	08	19
Sayre, Thomas(A)	1817	Nov. 03	Butler	06	08	17
Sayres, Aaron R.(A)	1831	May 09	Warren	03	08	03
Sayres, Thomas(C)	1818	Jan. 23	Miami	10	02	17
Scanland, Robert(B)	1804	Oct. 13	Kentucky	01	09	27
Scarlett, Newman Jr.(C)	1826	Oct. 06	Miami	10	02	04
Scarlett, Newman(C)	1814	Oct. 17	Champaign	09	06	33
Scearce, William(B)	1806	Aug. 13	Kentucky	01	13	09
Schaar, Jacob(A)	1832	Sept. 10	Warren	03	10	07
Schaar, John(A)	1832	Sept. 10	Warren	03	10	07
Scharbach, Joseph(B)	1824	July 02	Dearborn(Ind	02	07	22
Schefer, Simon(C)	1805	Sept. 10	Montgomery	09	02	25
Scheinly, John(C)	1818	Oct. 01	Cincinnati	13	03	31
Schenck, David(A)	1817	Dec. 19	Montgomery	02	09	33
Schenck, David(C)	1811	Aug. 13	Warren	05	02	28
Schenck, Ferdinand S.(A)	1836	Nov. 28	New Jersey	03	12	26
Schenck, Jno. N. C.(A)	1830	Jan. 21	Warren	06	07	22
Schenck, Jno. N. C.(A)	1830	Jan. 21	Warren	06	07	21
Schenck, John A. C.(C)	1816	Dec. 02	Warren	10	05	05
Schenck, John James Philip(B)	1831	Oct. 18	Switzerland	03	02	21
Schenck, John N. C.(A)	1836	Nov. 12	Warren	03	12	35
Schenck, John N. C.(A)	1836	Nov. 12	Warren	03	12	21
Schenck, John N. C.(A)	1836	Nov. 12	Warren	03	12	28
Schenck, Obadiah(A)	1804	Nov. 20	Franklin(Ind	04	03	36
Schenck, Obadiah(A)	1804	Nov. 20	Franklin(Ind	04	03	35
Schenck, Obadiah(A)	1804	Nov. 20	Franklin(Ind	05	07	33
Schenck, Obadiah(A)	1804	Nov. 20	Franklin(Ind	05	07	32
Schenck, Obadiah(A)	1804	Nov. 20	Franklin(Ind	05	07	17

PURCHASER	YEAR	DATE	RESIDENCE	R	T	S
Schenck, Obadiah(A)	1804	Nov. 20	Franklin(Ind	05	07	18
Schenck, Philip(B)	1817	Oct. 23	Switzerland	03	02	29
Schenck, William C.(A)	1804	Aug. 28	Franklin(Ind	05	02	30
Schenck, William C.(A)	1804	Oct. 15	Warren	04	03	25
Schenck, William C.(A)	1804	Nov. 20	Franklin(Ind	04	03	36
Schenck, William C.(A)	1804	Nov. 20	Franklin(Ind	04	03	35
Schenck, William C.(A)	1804	Nov. 20	Franklin(Ind	05	07	33
Schenck, William C.(A)	1804	Nov. 20	Franklin(Ind	05	07	32
Schenck, William C.(A)	1804	Nov. 20	Franklin(Ind	05	07	17
Schenck, William C.(A)	1804	Nov. 20	Franklin(Ind	05	07	18
Schenck, William C.(A)	1805	May 14	Warren	04	03	35
Schenck, William C.(A)	1805	May 14	Warren	04	03	36
Schenck, William C.(A)	1805	June 03	Franklin(Ind	04	02	08
Schenck, William C.(A)	1805	June 03	Franklin(Ind	04	02	05
Schenck, William C.(A)	1805	June 03	Franklin(Ind	04	02	08
Schenck, William C.(A)	1805	June 03	Franklin(Ind	04	02	05
Schenck, William C.(A)	1805	June 03	Franklin(Ind	04	02	08
Schenck, William C.(A)	1805	June 03	Franklin(Ind	04	02	08
Schenck, William C.(A)	1805	June 03	Franklin(Ind	04	02	09
Schenck, William C.(A)	1805	June 03	Franklin(Ind	04	02	09
Schenck, William C.(A)	1805	June 03	Franklin(Ind	04	02	05
Schenck, William C.(A)	1805	July 06	Franklin(Ind	03	06	32
Schenck, William C.(A)	1805	July 11	Franklin(Ind	03	04	05
Schenck, William C.(A)	1805	July 11	Franklin(Ind	03	04	05
Schenck, William C.(A)	1805	July 11	Franklin(Ind	03	04	05
Schenck, William C.(A)	1805	July 11	Franklin(Ind	03	04	06
Schenck, William C.(A)	1805	July 11	Franklin(Ind	03	04	06
Schenck, William C.(A)	1805	July 11	Franklin(Ind	03	04	06
Schenck, William C.(A)	1805	June 03	Franklin(Ind	04	02	04
Schenck, William C.(A)	1805	July 11	Franklin(Ind	03	04	05
Schenck, William C.(A)	1816	Dec. 02	Warren	04	04	04
Schenck, William C.(C)	1801	Dec. 19	Hamilton	05	02	20
Schenck, William C.(C)	1801	Dec. 19	Hamilton	04	03	17
Schenck, William C.(C)	1801	Dec. 19	Hamilton	05	02	32
Schenck, William C.(C)	1801	Dec. 19	Hamilton	05	02	35
Schenck, William C.(C)	1801	Dec. 31	Hamilton	05	02	31
Schenck, William C.(C)	1801	Dec. 31	Hamilton	04	03	13
Schenck, William C.(C)	1801	Dec. 31	Hamilton	04	03	19
Schenck, William C.(C)	1804	Sept. 04	Franklin(Ind	06	01	11
Schenck, William C.(C)	1804	Sept. 04	Franklin(Ind	05	02	26
Schenck, William C.(C)	1804	Sept. 04	Franklin(Ind	06	01	11
Schenck, William C.(C)	1804	Dec. 31	Franklin(Ind	04	03	20
Schenck, William C.(C)	1805	Jan. 10	Franklin(Ind	04	03	29
Schenck, William C.(C)	1805	Jan. 10	Franklin(Ind	05	02	28
Schenck, William C.(C)	1805	Aug. 01	Franklin(Ind	05	02	29
Schenck, William C.(C)	1810	April 12	Franklin(Ind	05	02	28
Schenck, William(C)	1805	July 13	Warren	05	02	28
Schieds, William(E)	1837	Feb. 27	Pennsylvania	14	19	13
Schierberg, Bernard(A)	1838	Jan. 20	Cincinnati	03	13	30
Schlecht, Jacob(A)	1828	Sept. 27	Montgomery	04	06	21
Schlechty, Jno.(A)	1824	Oct. 18	Darke	01	10	15
Schlechty, John(A)	1816	Aug. 26	Montgomery	01	10	03
Schlicht, Adam(B)	1833	June 26	Cincinnati	03	08	02
Schloser, Michael(E)	1836	Oct. 03	Pennsylvania	12	10	09
Schlosser, Jacob(A)	1819	Oct. 19	Franklin	06	08	12
Schlosser, Jacob(A)	1833	Sept. 23	Shelby	07	02	34
Schnebley, John(A)	1806	June 05	Montgomery	04	02	09
Schnep, Leonard(C)	1808	June 30	Montgomery	06	01	11
Schnetz, Martin(B)	1824	July 26	Cincinnati	02	07	22
Schnorf, John(A)	1828	Sept. 17	Warren	04	07	32
Schnorf, Peter(A)	1828	Sept. 17	Warren	04	07	31
Schoch, Gallus(E)	1836	Nov. 04	Dearborn(Ind	12	10	04
Schofield, John Dewitt(A)	1836	Nov. 25	Hamilton	01	14	21
Scholes, William(E)	1836	Oct. 13	Kentucky	11	10	34
Scholes, William(E)	1836	Oct. 15	Kentucky	11	10	33
Schomber, Conrad(B)	1834	Sept. 29	Hamilton	02	08	17
Schoolar, John(C)	1814	Dec. 16	Champaign	14	03	32
Schooler, Benj'n.(C)	1827	Aug. 22	Logan	13	03	24
Schooler, Benj'n.(C)	1832	April 28	Ohio	13	03	18

PURCHASER	YEAR	DATE	RESIDENCE	R	T	S
Schooler, Benjamin(C)	1806	Feb. 18	Champaign	10	06	33
Schooler, Benjamin(C)	1808	Jan. 11	Champaign	14	03	31
Schooler, Benjamin(C)	1813	April 14	Champaign	14	03	31
Schooler, John(A)	1831	Nov. 21	Logan	08	02	28
Schooler, John(A)	1836	March 17	Logan	08	02	29
Schooler, John(C)	1806	Feb. 18	Champaign	10	06	33
Schooler, John(C)	1808	Feb. 04	Champaign	14	03	31
Schooler, John(C)	1809	Aug. 30	Champaign	14	03	32
Schooler, Will'm.(A)	1830	Feb. 04	Logan	08	02	28
Schooley, Stephen(E)	1836	Sept. 13	Cincinnati	12	11	05
Schooley, Stephen(E)	1836	Sept. 13	Cincinnati	11	11	12
Schoolley, John(B)	1821	Sept. 21	Randolph(Ind	01	16	23
Schoonover, Asa(E)	1835	Aug. 07	Franklin(Ind	13	12	27
Schoonover, Jacob(C)	1828	Sept. 15	Clark	10	06	26
Schoonover, James(C)	1824	June 07	Clark	10	06	26
Schoonover, Jeremiah(E)	1835	Aug. 07	Franklin(Ind	13	12	27
Schoonover, Joseph(E)	1835	July 30	Franklin(Ind	13	12	32
Schoonover, Joseph(E)	1836	Feb. 04	Franklin(Ind	13	12	32
Schrantz, Frederick(C)	1806	June 26	Pennsylvania	09	02	27
Schreiber, Anthony(E)	1836	Sept. 15	Columbiana	12	10	03
Schreiber, Henry(E)	1836	Sept. 15	Columbiana	12	10	03
Schreiber, Joseph(E)	1836	Sept. 15	Columbiana	12	10	03
Schriver, Charles Hy.(E)	1836	Aug. 20	Butler	15	21	09
Schriver, Charles Hy.(E)	1836	Aug. 22	Butler	15	21	09
Schrock, Christian(A)	1807	June 18	Montgomery	03	05	24
Schroufe, Sebastian(C)	1813	April 16	Greene	08	04	22
Schutta, John Hy.(E)	1836	Oct. 15	Cincinnati	11	10	14
Schwander, Frederick(A)	1819	Oct. 20	Fairfield	06	09	35
Schwegman, John Herman(E)	1836	Oct. 29	Cincinnati	12	10	17
Schwegman, Joseph(E)	1836	Nov. 11	Cincinnati	12	10	05
Schwegmann, Henry(E)	1837	April 19	Cincinnati	12	11	36
Schwegmann, Henry(E)	1837	July 03	Cincinnati	12	11	36
Scoggins, Aaron(B)	1832	March 26	Dearborn(Ind	01	07	35
Scogin, Aaron(B)	1833	May 30	Hamilton	01	07	35
Scogin, Aaron(B)	1833	May 30	Hamilton	01	07	36
Scogin, Eli(B)	1833	May 02	Dearborn(Ind	01	07	35
Scott, Alexander(A)	1801	Oct. 19	Kentucky	05	02	03
Scott, Alexander(B)	1816	Oct. 23	Dearborn(Ind	01	02	06
Scott, Andrew(A)	1801	July 27	Hamilton	02	02	07
Scott, Archibald D.(B)	1837	Sept. 29	Dearborn(Ind	01	02	06
Scott, Charles(B)	1805	Sept. 03	Dearborn(Ind	02	08	03
Scott, Chas.(E)	1811	Nov. 22	Franklin(Ind	12	13	28
Scott, Edward(E)	1832	July 10	Fayette	11	12	12
Scott, Henry(B)	1834	March 08	Dearborn(Ind	02	07	03
Scott, Henry(B)	1836	Feb. 18	Franklin(Ind	02	08	22
Scott, Hugh(A)	1816	March 05	Miami	05	08	10
Scott, James Jr.(C)	1801	Nov. 25	?	05	03	24
Scott, James(A)	1833	Oct. 28	Montgomery	03	10	18
Scott, James(B)	1832	April 18	Switzerland	01	02	07
Scott, James(C)	1813	June 10	Champaign	11	03	17
Scott, Jesse(E)	1811	Oct. 28	Franklin(Ind	12	12	09
Scott, Job(E)	1836	Feb. 11	Franklin(Ind	11	12	01
Scott, Joel(E)	1816	Oct. 17	Franklin(Ind	13	13	30
Scott, John Houston(E)	1836	Jan. 25	Rush(Ind)	11	12	12
Scott, John(A)	1802	March 19	Hamilton	02	05	25
Scott, John(B)	1836	Jan. 27	Franklin(Ind	02	08	23
Scott, John(B)	1836	Feb. 18	Franklin(Ind	02	08	22
Scott, John(E)	1812	March 25	Kentucky	13	17	32
Scott, John(E)	1815	Oct. 09	Wayne(Ind)	13	17	33
Scott, John(E)	1816	Dec. 07	Wayne(Ind)	14	17	15
Scott, Jonathan(C)	1806	March 08	New Jersey	03	04	26
Scott, Moses(A)	1814	Aug. 01	Darke	02	11	02
Scott, Moses(A)	1817	Aug. 27	Greene	01	10	17
Scott, Richard(A)	1809	Dec. 20	Butler	02	05	21
Scott, Robert(A)	1805	Jan. 24	Montgomery	05	05	14
Scott, Robert(A)	1807	May 02	Butler	02	05	27
Scott, Robert(A)	1809	Dec. 20	Butler	02	05	21
Scott, Robert(A)	1810	Dec. 12	Butler	02	05	26
Scott, Robert(A)	1836	Sept. 23	Miami	03	12	10

PURCHASER	YEAR	DATE	RESIDENCE	R	T	S
Scott, Robert(C)	1801	Dec. 12	Kentucky	05	03	24
Scott, Sam'l.(C)	1829	March 07	Logan	14	03	26
Scott, Samuel S.(B)	1816	March 06	Dearborn(Ind	01	03	18
Scott, Samuel(B)	1805	Sept. 03	Dearborn(Ind	02	08	03
Scott, Samuel(C)	1828	Dec. 16	Logan	14	03	20
Scott, Samuel(C)	1830	July 03	Logan	14	03	20
Scott, Thomas(A)	1817	Sept. 02	Butler	03	04	15
Scott, Thomas(B)	1824	Oct. 02	Clermont	03	03	02
Scott, Thomas(C)	1808	Nov. 07	Warren	03	04	26
Scott, William(A)	1812	Feb. 24	Dearborn	02	11	03
Scott, William(A)	1814	Jan. 06	Kentucky	01	02	20
Scott, William(A)	1817	Aug. 01	Darke	02	11	03
Scott, William(B)	1815	Aug. 16	Butler	02	02	13
Scott, William(C)	1812	March 07	Kentucky	14	03	28
Scott, William(C)	1814	May 10	Champaign	12	05	35
Scott, William(C)	1814	May 10	Champaign	12	05	35
Scott, William(C)	1814	June 28	Champaign	12	05	29
Scott, William(C)	1828	Nov. 03	Champaign	12	05	29
Scott, Wm.(B)	1824	Sept. 21	Clermont	02	01	05
Scotton, Eli(E)	1814	March 26	Dearborn(Ind	12	14	10
Scotton, Emery(E)	1816	July 10	Franklin(Ind	13	12	14
Scranton, Joshua(B)	1816	Jan. 30	Dearborn(Ind	02	03	03
Scranton, William(B)	1814	April 11	Clermont	02	04	36
Scribner, Abraham(A)	1814	Sept. 06	Darke	02	12	34
Scribner, Azor(A)	1809	April 20	Miami	02	12	34
Scribner, Azor(A)	1814	Aug. 16	Darke	02	12	34
Scribner, Azor(A)	1817	July 29	Darke	02	12	23
Scribner, Azor(A)	1817	July 29	Darke	02	11	03
Scribner, Azor(A)	1818	Jan. 13	Darke	03	10	17
Scribner, Azor(A)	1818	Jan. 13	Darke	03	10	17
Scribner, Elisha(A)	1818	Oct. 08	Darke	02	11	05
Scroggy, John(E)	1817	Nov. 05	Hamilton	14	17	17
Scudder, Abraham(B)	1815	Oct. 27	Hamilton	02	02	27
Scudder, Cummings(A)	1836	Aug. 22	Miami	03	11	20
Scudder, Ephraim(A)	1806	July 16	Butler	01	04	13
Scudder, Henry Senr.(B)	1819	March 05	Hamilton	02	02	15
Scudder, Henry(B)	1836	Sept. 10	Switzerland	03	03	15
Scudder, Jotham(C)	1824	June 07	Miami	11	01	11
Scudder, Matthias(C)	1805	Aug. 29	Kentucky	12	01	33
Scudder, Thomas(C)	1826	Feb. 10	Miami	12	01	08
Scudder, Thomas(C)	1831	June 24	Miami	13	02	05
Scudder, Thos(C)	1831	June 11	Miami	13	02	04
Scudder, William(E)	1836	Sept. 13	Cincinnati	11	11	12
Scudder, William(E)	1836	Oct. 11	Cincinnati	12	11	05
Scudder, William(E)	1836	Oct. 24	Cincinnati	11	11	11
Scudder, William(E)	1836	Dec. 19	Hamilton	11	11	11
Scull, Abel(A)	1824	Sept. 29	Hamilton	02	03	21
Scull, Samuel(A)	1838	May 21	New Jersey	01	13	01
Scurlock, Reuben(B)	1813	Nov. 17	Franklin(Ind	01	11	19
Scurlock, Reuben(B)	1814	Nov. 28	Franklin(Ind	02	10	10
Seal, James(B)	1813	Dec. 07	Franklin(Ind	01	09	31
Seal, William(B)	1813	Sept. 28	Hamilton	01	09	31
Seaman, Jonathan(A)	1835	Dec. 08	Logan	08	01	03
Seamons, Henry(C)	1801	Dec. 30	Hamilton	05	03	01
Seamons, Jonas(C)	1801	Dec. 30	Hamilton	04	03	07
Seaney, Benjamin(B)	1814	March 12	Wayne(Ind)	01	12	01
Seaney, Bryan(B)	1814	June 11	Wayne(Ind)	01	12	01
Seanger, George(B)	1812	July 02	Cincinnati	02	01	08
Search, Wm. Philip(E)	1820	Sept. 08	Montgomery	13	20	33
Searey, Lemuel(B)	1813	Sept. 08	Kentucky	01	02	11
Searl, Heman L.(A)	1837	Dec. 05	Darke	01	13	28
Searl, John(C)	1826	Oct. 30	Clark	08	03	29
Seater, George(A)	1815	Oct. 12	Miami	04	09	24
Sebastian, Alexander(B)	1834	Dec. 05	Switzerland	01	02	19
Sebastian, Alexander(B)	1834	Dec. 08	Switzerland	01	02	18
Sebring, Isaac(A)	1829	Oct. 22	Darke	02	11	01
Sebring, Jacob Jr.(A)	1831	Aug. 26	Darke	02	11	01
Sebring, Jacob Jr.(A)	1832	Jan. 09	Darke	02	11	01
Sebring, Jacob(A)	1830	June 30	Darke	03	09	20

PURCHASER	YEAR	DATE	RESIDENCE	R	T	S
Sebring, Jacob(C)	1816	Nov. 25	Hamilton	12	03	13
Sedam, Cornelius R.(B)	1815	June 10	Hamilton	02	02	05
Sedam, Cornelius R.(B)	1816	Jan. 13	?	02	02	03
Sedgwick, Richard(B)	1808	Jan. 13	Butler	01	12	10
Sedgwick, Richard(B)	1808	Jan. 13	Butler	01	12	11
Seegar, David(C)	1806	Oct. 18	Champaign	10	06	27
Seegar, David(C)	1811	Dec. 11	Champaign	10	06	27
Seegar, David(C)	1823	Sept. 24	Champaign	14	03	13
Seegar, Jonathan(C)	1830	Feb. 11	Logan	13	04	18
Seeley, Morris(B)	1814	June 28	Ind.Territory	01	08	25
Seely, John(B)	1819	June 24	Franklin(Ind	01	08	15
Seely, Robert W.(B)	1814	Nov. 03	Hamilton	01	08	36
Seevers, Charles(E)	1836	June 13	Coshocton	15	19	05
Sefton, Henry(A)	1804	Sept. 24	Hamilton	01	02	12
Seiberling, Christain(A)	1815	Dec. 21	Pennsylvania	04	04	21
Seibert, Henry(A)	1832	May 07	Montgomery	04	07	23
Seibert, Nicholas(E)	1837	May 24	Cincinnati	13	11	22
Seifert, Nicholas(B)	1836	Nov. 28	Cincinnati	03	09	24
Seitel, Daniel(A)	1838	Feb. 05	Pennsylvania	01	14	03
Selbey, Zachariah(A)	1803	Jan. 19	Hamilton	04	03	36
Selby, Charles(A)	1817	Nov. 14	Butler	02	09	08
Selby, Middleton(A)	1831	Aug. 30	Butler	04	07	30
Selby, Otho(E)	1832	Aug. 18	Franklin(Ind	12	12	11
Selby, Zachariah(A)	1804	Oct. 30	Butler	04	02	10
Selby, Zephaniah(A)	1817	Nov. 14	Butler	02	09	08
Selden, Alanson Douglas(A)	1835	Nov. 14	Butler	02	12	09
Selden, Alanson Douglas(A)	1836	Jan. 26	Butler	02	13	34
Selden, Alanson Douglas(A)	1836	July 06	Butler	02	13	33
Selden, Roger(A)	1819	Aug. 16	Cincinnati	06	08	33
Selfridge, Thomas(B)	1812	Aug. 07	Butler	01	09	14
Sell, Andrew(A)	1827	Dec. 04	Preble	01	09	22
Sell, George(A)	1824	May 25	Butler	01	09	24
Sell, George(A)	1831	Oct. 24	Preble	01	09	24
Seller, James(A)	1815	Nov. 24	Preble	02	08	02
Seller, Joseph(A)	1805	Dec. 24	Kentucky	02	07	10
Seller, Joseph(A)	1806	May 17	Montgomery	02	07	10
Seller, Joseph(A)	1811	Aug. 13	Preble	02	07	10
Seller, Nathan(A)	1808	Feb. 23	Kentucky	02	07	10
Sellers, Isaac(A)	1818	Jan. 19	Virginia	02	08	22
Sellers, Isaac(B)	1815	Oct. 07	Butler	02	10	26
Sellers, Nathan(A)	1809	Dec. 14	Preble	02	07	09
Sellers, Peter(C)	1801	Dec. 26	Hamilton	04	03	01
Selwood, Henry(B)	1818	March 09	Hamilton	02	03	05
Semanton, Samuel(C)	1806	Sept. 22	Champaign	11	05	30
Semanton, Samuel(C)	1806	Oct. 18	Champaign	09	04	04
Semple, David(A)	1811	Aug. 13	Preble	01	06	25
Sency, John(B)	1815	Jan. 02	Wayne(Ind)	02	12	14
Senour, John(E)	1813	Sept. 04	Kentucky	12	12	34
Senour, John(E)	1836	Oct. 31	Franklin(Ind	12	11	03
Senteney, Joab(E)	1836	Sept. 10	Mason Co.,Ky	11	11	13
Sentz, Nicholas(C)	1806	July 04	Virginia	09	04	23
Seny, Owen(B)	1808	June 20	Nor.Carolina	01	12	03
Seranton, Martin(B)	1817	June 25	Dearborn(Ind	02	03	11
Sering, Samuel(E)	1836	Jan. 02	Franklin(Ind	13	11	08
Serrin, Ezekiel Nichols(E)	1832	Nov. 14	Butler	13	12	06
Server, Jacob(C)	1809	March 10	Champaign	13	04	25
Seward, Daniel(A)	1806	July 24	Butler	02	01	11
Seward, Daniel(A)	1814	Jan. 14	?	02	03	12
Seward, David(C)	1811	Dec. 11	Butler	02	01	11
Seward, Isaac(A)	1811	Nov. 23	Franklin	01	04	35
Seward, Isaac(E)	1814	Oct. 13	Wayne(Ind)	12	14	10
Sewell, Joseph(A)	1815	Sept. 02	Ross	03	11	27
Sewell, Timothy(A)	1806	March 04	Warren	06	05	20
Sexton, Zadock(A)	1808	Nov. 03	Butler	03	06	22
Seybold, John(A)	1805	June 21	Butler	03	04	33
Seybold, John(A)	1805	June 21	Butler	03	04	28
Seymour, Austin(B)	1833	Jan. 03	Cincinnati	01	02	02
Seyres, Leonard(A)	1808	Nov. 03	Cincinnati	01	03	22
Seyres, Leonard(A)	1808	Nov. 03	Cincinnati	02	03	15

PURCHASER	YEAR	DATE	RESIDENCE	R	T	S
Shadday, Emsley(B)	1832	Oct. 22	Switzerland	03	03	08
Shade, Philip(C)	1829	Dec. 30	Logan	14	02	06
Shafar, John(A)	1806	Aug. 19	Montgomery	08	02	18
Shafer, Adam(A)	1837	June 22	Richland	01	14	30
Shafer, Adam(E)	1837	June 22	Richland	15	21	19
Shafer, George(A)	1831	June 25	Miami	04	09	02
Shafer, Herman(B)	1838	April 25	Cincinnati	03	05	25
Shafer, Jacob(A)	1836	Nov. 23	Franklin(Ind	01	13	28
Shafer, John Jr.(A)	1836	Nov. 23	Hamilton	01	13	28
Shafer, John(C)	1811	Dec. 11	Montgomery	08	02	18
Shafer, John(C)	1819	Jan. 08	Miami	13	03	32
Shaff, Frederick(B)	1818	April 10	Butler	03	04	31
Shaffer, Abraham(C)	1831	July 06	Logan	14	02	06
Shaffer, Barbara Eckendorff(B)	1832	Aug. 28	France	02	07	33
Shaffer, Frederick(A)	1811	Nov. 08	Montgomery	04	03	09
Shaffer, Frederick(A)	1831	Sept. 03	Montgomery	01	12	22
Shaffer, George(E)	1814	Jan. 28	Kentucky	12	13	12
Shaffer, Henry(B)	1813	Aug. 26	Butler	02	10	01
Shaffer, Jacob(C)	1812	July 03	Champaign	10	03	01
Shaffer, Jacob(C)	1817	Dec. 02	Champaign	10	03	01
Shaffer, Jacob(C)	1828	April 11	Clark	10	03	10
Shallenberger, Jacob(A)	1831	July 05	Miami	04	09	17
Shallenberger, Jacob(A)	1831	July 05	Miami	04	09	20
Shallenberger, Jacob(A)	1831	July 05	Miami	05	08	15
Shallenberger, Jacob(A)	1831	July 05	Miami	05	08	33
Shallenberger, Jacob(A)	1831	July 05	Miami	05	08	34
Shally, John(A)	1814	Oct. 11	Butler	04	03	09
Shane, Cornelius(E)	1815	July 06	Pennsylvania	13	18	08
Shane, John(C)	1824	June 07	Cincinnati	09	05	08
Shane, William(B)	1818	Aug. 10	Dearborn(Ind	02	05	27
Shane, William(B)	1824	June 29	Dearborn(Ind	02	05	15
Shank, Frederick(A)	1815	Aug. 30	Montgomery	03	08	20
Shank, George W.(B)	1818	Oct. 15	Franklin(Ind	02	08	31
Shank, Jas.(B)	1828	Oct. 08	Franklin(Ind	02	08	11
Shank, John(B)	1812	March 18	Dearborn(Ind	02	08	11
Shank, John(E)	1837	Feb. 24	Montgomery	14	20	12
Shank, Joseph(E)	1816	May 27	Wayne(Ind)	13	16	17
Shank, Michael(A)	1814	June 09	Montgomery	04	05	13
Shank, Michael(B)	1804	Oct. 01	Dearborn(Ind	01	06	01
Shank, Michael(B)	1804	Oct. 01	Dearborn(Ind	01	06	12
Shank, Thos.(B)	1828	Oct. 08	Franklin(Ind	02	08	11
Shanks, Michael(B)	1809	Dec. 12	Dearborn(Ind	01	06	12
Shanks, Michael(B)	1809	Dec. 12	Dearborn(Ind	01	06	01
Shanks, Michael(B)	1814	Nov. 25	Dearborn(Ind	01	06	21
Shannon, George(C)	1804	Dec. 22	Kentucky	08	04	02
Shannon, James(A)	1817	Sept. 05	Preble	02	07	29
Shannon, James(A)	1824	June 08	Preble	02	06	22
Shannon, James(A)	1831	Sept. 01	Preble	02	07	33
Shannon, Robert(A)	1836	Sept. 05	Miami	03	11	06
Shannon, Robert(A)	1836	Sept. 10	Miami	03	11	08
Shannon, Samuel(B)	1806	July 26	Hamilton	01	10	06
Shannon, Samuel(B)	1807	March 23	Hamilton	01	10	06
Shannon, Samuel(B)	1813	April 14	Franklin(Ind	01	10	06
Shark, Philip(A)	1814	Nov. 18	Montgomery	04	05	10
Sharp, Dan'l.(A)	1829	April 16	Darke	03	08	27
Sharp, Daniel(A)	1832	Jan. 30	Darke	03	08	27
Sharp, John(A)	1814	April 06	Hamilton	01	03	29
Sharp, John(A)	1814	Oct. 19	Butler	01	03	28
Sharrets, Christopher(A)	1837	Dec. 08	Montgomery	01	13	02
Sharrits, Christopher(A)	1837	March 28	Montgomery	01	13	03
Shaver, John I.(E)	1834	May 17	Warren	12	13	32
Shaver, Peter(A)	1806	Nov. 08	Butler	02	04	29
Shaw, Dan B.(A)	1837	Feb. 01	Montgomery	02	13	18
Shaw, Dan B.(A)	1837	Feb. 15	Montgomery	02	13	07
Shaw, George(C)	1829	July 28	Logan	13	04	29
Shaw, Hamilton(B)	1836	March 26	Franklin(Ind	02	08	23
Shaw, James(C)	1826	June 28	Logan	13	03	06
Shaw, James(E)	1811	Oct. 22	Ind.Territory	12	15	12
Shaw, John(B)	1817	July 05	Cincinnati	03	02	19

PURCHASER	YEAR	DATE	RESIDENCE	R	T	S
Shaw, John(B)	1817	Oct. 31	Hamilton	03	03	33
Shaw, John(C)	1817	Sept. 02	Kentucky	12	01	11
Shaw, John(C)	1831	Sept. 12	Logan	13	03	06
Shaw, John(E)	1811	Oct. 22	Ind.Territry	12	15	11
Shaw, Jonathan Jr.(E)	1815	Aug. 31	Wayne(Ind)	13	17	21
Shaw, Jonathan(B)	1836	Jan. 28	Franklin(Ind	02	08	08
Shaw, Josiah(A)	1836	May 16	Darke	02	13	29
Shaw, Knoles Jr.(A)	1814	Aug. 01	Butler	02	03	29
Shaw, Thomas(B)	1813	Oct. 15	Franklin(Ind	01	09	27
Shaw, William(B)	1835	July 14	Switzerland	04	02	24
Shaw, William(E)	1811	Oct. 24	Warren	13	15	28
Shawgen, John Henry Peter(B)	1834	May 20	Cincinnati	02	06	09
Shawner, Christian(A)	1821	Nov. 19	Warren	02	10	03
Shays, John(A)	1836	Oct. 11	Cincinnati	02	15	29
Sheafer, Abraham(A)	1815	Dec. 26	Butler	02	10	04
Sheared, John(B)	1812	Nov. 30	Ind.Territry	01	06	11
Shearer, David(A)	1813	April 14	Preble	02	08	07
Shearer, John(E)	1834	Feb. 03	Warren	13	19	15
Shearer, John(E)	1834	Feb. 03	Warren	13	19	15
Shearer, Pears(B)	1817	Oct. 09	Dearborn(Ind	02	06	19
Shearer, Valentine(C)	1811	Dec. 14	Montgomery	08	02	15
Shearer, Volentine(C)	1811	Sept. 20	Greene	08	02	21
Shearin, William(B)	1818	April 15	Hamilton	02	06	26
Shearman, Pardon(E)	1836	June 13	Randolph(Ind	13	21	35
Shearwood, David(C)	1831	March 22	Warren	12	02	28
Shearwood, Peter V.(C)	1831	March 22	Warren	12	02	28
Shed, Silas(B)	1818	Aug. 07	Dearborn(Ind	03	05	23
Shedler, Henry(A)	1805	July 01	Montgomery	03	05	26
Shedler, Jacob(A)	1806	Sept. 06	Greene	02	08	17
Sheet, John(B)	1834	July 02	Cincinnati	03	09	25
Sheets, Andrew(A)	1806	June 16	Montgomery	05	06	23
Sheets, Andrew(C)	1812	Oct. 31	Miami	10	02	29
Sheets, Andrew(C)	1816	April 08	Miami	10	03	34
Sheets, Andrew(C)	1816	May 15	Miami	10	02	29
Sheets, John(B)	1831	Sept. 21	Darke	01	18	24
Sheets, John(B)	1833	July 06	Darke	01	18	24
Sheets, John(B)	1835	July 07	Randolph(Ind	01	18	24
Sheets, Perry(B)	1836	Aug. 30	Randolph(Ind	01	18	24
Sheets, Peter(B)	1817	Aug. 21	Switzerland	01	03	36
Sheetz, Andrew(C)	1818	Jan. 06	Miami	10	03	34
Sheffer, Dan'l.(A)	1831	Aug. 12	Wayne(Ind)	01	08	30
Sheffer, Daniel(A)	1825	Oct. 06	Wayne(Ind)	01	08	30
Sheffer, Ira(A)	1834	Jan. 11	Darke	04	11	32
Sheidler, Peter(A)	1836	Dec. 06	Montgomery	01	13	36
Sheland, Henry(B)	1835	Nov. 02	Hamilton	02	07	12
Shelby, John(C)	1813	Sept. 23	Champaign	14	03	09
Shelby, John(C)	1813	Sept. 23	Champaign	14	03	17
Shelby, John(C)	1816	Oct. 14	Champaign	13	05	30
Shelby, John(E)	1814	March 15	Kentucky	13	15	25
Shelby, Joseph(E)	1813	Dec. 29	Kentucky	14	15	30
Shell, Christian(E)	1818	Jan. 19	Wayne(Ind)	14	20	21
Shellabarger, Jno.(C)	1813	Dec. 27	Greene	08	04	29
Shellabarger, Martin(C)	1813	Dec. 27	Greene	08	04	29
Shellaberger, Samuel(C)	1817	Aug. 18	Greene	09	04	26
Shelly, John(B)	1814	Jan. 01	Wayne(Ind)	02	12	23
Shepard, Solomon Jnr.(B)	1816	April 26	Franklin(Ind	02	08	08
Shepard, Solomon(E)	1814	July 18	Franklin(Ind	13	13	29
Shephard, William(B)	1818	Dec. 23	Dearborn(Ind	02	06	15
Shephard, Wm.(B)	1818	Dec. 23	Dearborn(Ind	02	06	15
Shepherd, James M.(B)	1831	July 05	Switzerland	02	03	25
Shepherd, Joseph(A)	1831	Sept. 03	Miami	05	10	24
Shepherd, Solomon(E)	1814	June 20	Franklin(Ind	13	12	04
Shepherd, Solomon(E)	1814	June 20	Franklin(Ind	13	13	33
Shepherd, Stephen(E)	1836	Aug. 18	Hamilton	12	11	05
Shepherd, William(E)	1836	Aug. 23	Hamilton	12	11	06
Sherard, Samuel(A)	1818	Sept. 26	Butler	03	08	30
Sheree, David(A)	1815	Jan. 13	Darke	03	08	29
Sherer, Daniel(A)	1813	Nov. 23	Montgomery	02	08	20
Sherer, David(A)	1807	Sept. 11	Montgomery	02	08	07

PURCHASER	YEAR	DATE	RESIDENCE	R	T	S
Sherer, Jacob(A)	1812	April 15	Preble	02	08	07
Sherer, Jesse(A)	1824	June 17	Preble	01	08	23
Sherer, John(B)	1816	Aug. 29	Ross	02	02	10
Sherer, John(B)	1816	Aug. 29	Ross	02	02	09
Sherer, John(B)	1816	Aug. 29	Ross	02	03	33
Sherer, John(B)	1816	Aug. 29	Ross	02	03	32
Sherk, Jacob(B)	1817	July 07	Ohio	01	02	12
Sherk, Jacob(B)	1818	April 03	Switzerland	01	02	23
Sherlock, John(B)	1819	April 01	Cincinnati	03	04	17
Sherrer, Christian(A)	1806	Nov. 28	Nor.Carolina	03	04	09
Sherrer, Christian(A)	1812	April 15	Preble	03	04	09
Sherrer, Jacob(A)	1806	Nov. 28	Nor.Carolina	02	08	07
Sherry, Hugh M.(C)	1812	Jan. 22	Champaign	11	04	04
Sherwood, James(E)	1814	Sept. 02	Highland	13	12	10
Sherwood, Thomas(E)	1814	Sept. 02	Warren	13	12	10
Shetterly, John(E)	1818	Jan. 03	Wayne(Ind)	13	15	23
Shewman, John(A)	1806	Oct. 20	Virginia	02	07	26
Shewman, John(A)	1806	Nov. 07	Virginia	02	07	25
Shewmon, Christian(A)	1833	May 15	Preble	02	09	07
Shideler, Jacob Jr.(A)	1824	June 08	Preble	02	07	22
Shideler, Jacob Senr.(A)	1824	June 08	Preble	02	08	31
Shideler, Jacob(A)	1812	March 20	Montgomery	03	05	14
Shidler, Geo'e.(A)	1811	Dec. 11	Greene	02	08	17
Shidler, George(A)	1805	Dec. 12	Akens(?S.Car	02	08	17
Shidler, George(A)	1802	July 29	Hamilton	05	03	33
Shidler, Henry(A)	1810	Aug. 14	Montgomery	04	04	30
Shidler, Ja'c.(A)	1811	Dec. 11	Greene	02	08	17
Shidler, Jacob(E)	1811	Oct. 22	Montgomery	12	14	01
Shidler, John(A)	1819	March 04	Miami	05	06	01
Shields, Abijah(E)	1816	Sept. 28	Pennsylvania	14	14	31
Shields, James(A)	1801	Oct. 05	Hamilton	01	03	36
Shields, Martin(C)	1812	March 11	Champaign	13	04	04
Shields, Peggy(E)	1813	Nov. 06	Kentucky	13	14	34
Shields, Samuel(C)	1808	March 01	Kentucky	13	05	34
Shields, William(C)	1806	Aug. 08	Kentucky	12	05	24
Shields, William(C)	1807	March 27	Kentucky	13	05	33
Shierlig, Philip(E)	1837	May 22	Clark	14	21	34
Shierlig, Philip(E)	1837	June 29	Clark	14	21	35
Shierling, Philip(E)	1838	Aug. 18	Randolph(Ind	14	21	34
Shigley, Frederick(C)	1831	Aug. 08	Logan	14	03	11
Shilt, John Junr.(A)	1831	Feb. 23	Preble	03	07	02
Shinfilt, George(E)	1837	April 14	Butler	14	21	02
Shingletaker, Jacob(C)	1802	Dec. 29	Hamilton	07	03	27
Shinkle, George(B)	1814	May 20	Clermont	01	04	05
Shipley, Thomas(A)	1831	Nov. 21	Darke	01	10	17
Shirk, Andrew Junr.(B)	1813	Aug. 31	Franklin(Ind	01	09	22
Shirk, Andrew Senr.(B)	1812	Aug. 18	Franklin(Ind	01	09	17
Shirk, Andrew(A)	1806	Dec. 19	Hamilton	02	02	06
Shirk, Andrew(B)	1808	Jan. 13	Hamilton	01	09	13
Shirk, Samuel(B)	1824	June 09	Franklin(Ind	01	09	15
Shirk, Samuel(B)	1832	Sept. 25	Franklin(Ind	02	08	09
Shirk, Samuel(B)	1833	June 14	Franklin(Ind	02	08	09
Shirman, Peter(B)	1839	Sept. 03	Switzerland	03	04	28
Shirrep, John(A)	1806	Nov. 20	Montgomery	04	04	25
Shiteaker, John(C)	1805	Oct. 15	Montgomery	10	02	13
Shivelay, John(B)	1818	June 10	Cincinnati	02	07	04
Shiveley, Daniel(A)	1816	June 05	Montgomery	01	12	27
Shively, Christian Junr.(A)	1805	March 09	Montgomery	05	04	27
Shively, Christian(A)	1803	Oct. 06	Pennsylvania	05	03	04
Shively, Christian(A)	1805	Oct. 03	Pennsylvania	05	03	05
Shively, Daniel(A)	1805	April 12	Pennsylvania	05	04	27
Shively, Daniel(A)	1814	April 30	Montgomery	04	05	10
Shively, Daniel(A)	1814	Sept. 05	Montgomery	04	05	10
Shively, David(A)	1816	June 11	Montgomery	03	11	31
Shively, Jacob(A)	1805	Oct. 03	Pennsylvania	05	04	32
Shneb, Dan'l.(C)	1831	Feb. 07	Champaign	11	03	05
Shneb, John(C)	1831	Jan. 17	Champaign	11	03	10
Shneb, Reinhart(C)	1826	Oct. 18	Montgomery	11	03	24
Shneb, Reinhart(C)	1831	Jan. 17	Champaign	11	03	23

PURCHASER	YEAR	DATE	RESIDENCE	R	T	S
Shock, Adam(A)	1817	July 01	Montgomery	01	10	11
Shock, Daniel(A)	1817	July 01	Montgomery	01	10	11
Shockey, Abraham(C)	1804	Dec. 28	Greene	11	04	03
Shockey, Abraham(C)	1807	Aug. 11	Champaign	11	04	14
Shockey, Isaac(C)	1811	Dec. 11	Champaign	11	05	34
Shockey, Isaac(C)	1812	March 26	Champaign	11	05	28
Shockey, Isaac(C)	1812	Dec. 18	Champaign	11	04	04
Shockey, Isaac(C)	1814	March 14	Champaign	11	04	13
Shockey, Isaac(C)	1814	May 16	Champaign	11	04	19
Shockey, Lewis(B)	1836	Feb. 01	Hamilton	02	08	17
Shockey, Lewis(B)	1836	Aug. 25	Franklin(Ind	02	08	07
Shockney, Rachael(E)	1837	Dec. 30	Clark	14	19	12
Shocky, Abraham(C)	1811	Feb. 18	Champaign	11	04	14
Shocky, Abraham(C)	1813	April 14	Champaign	11	04	14
Shocky, Abraham(C)	1813	April 14	Champaign	11	05	33
Shocky, Abraham(C)	1813	Nov. 13	Champaign	11	04	13
Shoemake, Blackley Jr.(B)	1828	April 21	Dearborn(Ind	03	07	13
Shoemake, Blackley(B)	1836	Feb. 19	Dearborn(Ind	02	06	17
Shoemake, Blackly(B)	1818	Jan. 26	Hamilton	02	06	07
Shoemake, Blakley(B)	1818	Jan. 26	Hamilton	03	07	12
Shoemake, Blakley(B)	1818	Jan. 26	Hamilton	03	07	35
Shoemake, Blakley(B)	1818	Jan. 26	Hamilton	03	07	26
Shoemake, James(B)	1828	April 16	Dearborn(Ind	03	07	24
Shoemake, Samuel(B)	1836	Jan. 26	Dearborn(Ind	02	06	17
Shoemaker, Blackley(E)	1818	Jan. 15	Hamilton	13	13	30
Shoemaker, Christian(A)	1807	July 04	Montgomery	03	06	30
Shoemaker, Christian(A)	1814	Sept. 13	Preble	01	08	14
Shoemaker, Daniel(A)	1814	Dec. 31	Preble	03	06	05
Shoemaker, Daniel(E)	1826	July 04	Randolph(Ind	14	18	11
Shoemaker, Evins(B)	1812	Oct. 07	Wayne(Ind)	01	14	31
Shoemaker, Evins(E)	1813	Sept. 16	Wayne(Ind)	14	16	20
Shoemaker, Jacob(E)	1836	Oct. 01	Randolph(Ind	14	18	03
Shoemaker, Sampson(E)	1830	Feb. 16	Randolph(Ind	14	18	13
Shoemaker, Samuel(A)	1811	Dec. 13	Butler	01	04	11
Shook, Elijah(A)	1838	Jan. 31	Greene	02	14	24
Shook, Jefferson(A)	1832	June 08	Montgomery	04	07	15
Short, J. Cleves(C)	1813	April 14	Cincinnati	10	03	17
Short, J. Cleves(C)	1813	April 14	Cincinnati	10	03	17
Short, J. Cleves(C)	1813	April 14	Cincinnati	10	03	17
Short, J. Cleves(C)	1813	April 14	Cincinnati	10	03	14
Short, J. Cleves(C)	1813	April 19	Cincinnati	11	01	22
Short, J. Cleves(C)	1813	April 20	Cincinnati	07	03	15
Short, J. Cleves(C)	1813	April 14	Cincinnati	10	03	14
Short, J. Cleves(C)	1813	April 19	Cincinnati	11	01	22
Short, J. Cleves(C)	1813	April 14	Cincinnati	10	03	17
Short, J. Cleves(D)	1814	Jan. 01	Cincinnati	02	03	08
Short, Jn. Cleves(C)	1813	April 14	Cincinnati	10	03	14
Short, Jno. Cleves(C)	1813	April 14	Cincinnati	10	03	14
Short, John Cleves(A)	1836	Nov. 14	Hamilton	01	14	17
Short, John Cleves(A)	1836	Nov. 14	Hamilton	01	14	18
Short, John Cleves(A)	1836	Nov. 14	Hamilton	01	14	32
Short, John Cleves(A)	1836	Nov. 14	Hamilton	01	14	35
Short, John Cleves(A)	1836	Dec. 01	Hamilton	01	14	07
Short, John Cleves(A)	1836	Dec. 01	Hamilton	01	14	19
Short, John Cleves(A)	1836	Dec. 01	Hamilton	01	14	31
Short, John Cleves(A)	1836	Dec. 01	Hamilton	01	14	35
Short, John Cleves(A)	1837	March 22	Hamilton	01	14	18
Short, John Cleves(C)	1813	April 19	Cincinnati	11	02	20
Short, John Cleves(D)	1814	Jan. 28	Cincinati(Fr	02	01	08
Short, John(B)	1808	Jan. 15	Virginia	01	11	27
Short, Payton(C)	1802	Dec. 31	Kentucky	09	03	34
Short, Payton(C)	1802	Dec. 31	Kentucky	09	03	03
Short, Payton(C)	1802	Dec. 31	Kentucky	09	02	10
Short, Payton(C)	1802	Dec. 31	Kentucky	09	03	02
Short, Payton(C)	1802	Dec. 31	Kentucky	09	02	23
Short, Payton(C)	1802	Dec. 31	Kentucky	08	02	05
Short, Payton(C)	1802	Dec. 31	Kentucky	09	03	14
Short, Peyton(B)	1802	Jan. 06	Kentucky	01	04	22
Short, Peyton(B)	1807	April 07	Kentucky	01	04	22

PURCHASER	YEAR	DATE	RESIDENCE	R	T	S
Short, Peyton(C)	1801	Dec. 31	Kentucky	07	?	?
Short, Peyton(C)	1801	Dec. 31	Kentucky	08	?	?
Short, Peyton(C)	1804	Sept. 24	Kentucky	07	02	29
Short, Peyton(C)	1804	Dec. 29	Kentucky	09	03	32
Short, Peyton(C)	1804	Dec. 29	Kentucky	08	03	36
Short, Peyton(C)	1804	Dec. 29	Kentucky	08	03	35
Short, Peyton(C)	1804	Dec. 29	Kentucky	09	03	20
Short, Peyton(C)	1804	Dec. 29	Kentucky	08	03	24
Short, Peyton(C)	1804	Dec. 29	Kentucky	09	03	25
Short, Peyton(C)	1804	Dec. 29	Kentucky	09	03	19
Short, Peyton(C)	1804	Dec. 29	Kentucky	09	02	12
Short, Peyton(C)	1804	Dec. 29	Kentucky	09	02	01
Short, Peyton(C)	1804	Dec. 29	Kentucky	09	03	36
Short, Peyton(C)	1804	Dec. 29	Kentucky	09	03	35
Short, Peyton(C)	1804	Dec. 31	Kentucky	09	03	15
Short, Peyton(C)	1809	July 24	Kentucky	07	01	05
Short, Peyton(C)	1809	July 24	Kentucky	07	02	18
Short, Peyton(C)	1809	July 24	Kentucky	07	02	35
Short, Peyton(C)	1809	July 24	Kentucky	08	01	04
Short, Peyton(C)	1809	July 24	Kentucky	07	01	12
Short, Peyton(C)	1809	July 24	Kentucky	08	02	21
Short, Peyton(C)	1809	Nov. 04	Kentucky	07	01	05
Short, Peyton(C)	1809	Nov. 04	Kentucky	07	02	18
Short, Peyton(C)	1809	Nov. 04	Kentucky	07	02	35
Short, Peyton(C)	1809	Nov. 04	Kentucky	08	01	04
Short, Peyton(C)	1809	Nov. 04	Kentucky	08	02	21
Short, Peyton(C)	1809	Nov. 04	Kentucky	08	02	09
Short, Peyton(C)	1809	Nov. 04	Kentucky	07	01	12
Short, Peyton(C)	1809	July 24	Kentucky	08	02	09
Shortridge, Samuel(E)	1816	Sept. 09	Wayne(Ind)	13	16	33
Shortridge, Samuel(E)	1816	Dec. 10	Wayne(Ind)	13	16	33
Shortridge, William(E)	1834	May 10	Wayne(Ind)	14	15	05
Shotridge, George(E)	1812	April 20	Wayne(Ind)	13	16	31
Shotridge, John(E)	1811	Oct. 23	Kentucky	12	16	25
Shotridge, John(E)	1811	Oct. 23	Kentucky	12	16	25
Shotridge, John(E)	1811	Oct. 23	Kentucky	12	16	25
Shotridge, John(E)	1811	Oct. 23	Kentucky	12	16	25
Shots, Jacob(B)	1832	March 30	Hamilton	01	07	22
Shotts, Frederick(B)	1813	April 05	Franklin(Ind	01	08	35
Shotwell, John(C)	1805	Dec. 23	Kentucky	11	05	35
Shough, Joseph Jr.(B)	1833	March 26	Dearborn(Ind	02	07	13
Shouller, Anthony(A)	1836	March 21	Stark	03	11	12
Shoup, Daniel(A)	1806	May 23	Hamilton	01	02	27
Shoup, Daniel(A)	1811	Aug. 13	Hamilton	01	02	27
Shoup, George G.(E)	1836	Dec. 15	Franklin(Ind	12	12	31
Shoup, George G.(E)	1836	Dec. 15	Franklin(Ind	12	12	32
Shoup, George G.(E)	1836	Dec. 15	Franklin(Ind	12	11	03
Shoup, George Grove(E)	1835	Dec. 19	Franklin(Ind	12	12	17
Shoup, George(C)	1804	Dec. 27	?	07	02	21
Shoup, George(C)	1804	Dec. 27	Montgomery	07	02	21
Shoup, Martin(A)	1825	Feb. 02	Miami	04	08	13
Shoup, Samuel(A)	1824	July 17	Montgomery	06	03	21
Shoup, Samuel(A)	1824	July 17	Montgomery	06	03	15
Shourd, Richard(A)	1815	March 10	Hamilton	02	09	24
Shover, Jacob(A)	1811	Nov. 09	Montgomery	04	04	02
Showalter, Abraham(B)	1834	Sept. 19	Dearborn(Ind	02	07	19
Showalter, Christopher(B)	1822	June 13	Pennsylvania	02	07	18
Showalter, Christopher(B)	1823	Aug. 14	Dearborn(Ind	03	08	01
Showalter, Jacob(B)	1831	Sept. 07	Dearborn(Ind	03	08	12
Showalter, John(B)	1833	June 26	Dearborn(Ind	03	08	01
Showalter, John(B)	1835	Oct. 07	Dearborn(Ind	03	08	01
Shower, Abraham(A)	1805	July 01	Montgomery	04	06	24
Shranck, Michael(B)	1835	May 25	Hamilton	02	07	01
Shrawyer, Jacob(A)	1818	March 25	Montgomery	02	12	09
Shreves, Thomas(A)	1819	Feb. 03	Franklin(Ind	04	09	18
Shriack, John(C)	1813	Oct. 22	Champaign	14	02	02
Shrimp, Venzens(E)	1837	Oct. 12	Cincinnati	11	10	02
Shriner, Charles(B)	1827	Dec. 06	Franklin(Ind	02	10	22
Shriver, John(C)	1832	March 02	Champaign	12	04	21

PURCHASER	YEAR	DATE	RESIDENCE	R	T	S
Shryock, Daniel(A)	1805	Oct. 02	Montgomery	03	06	25
Shryock, Daniel(A)	1805	Oct. 02	Montgomery	04	05	19
Shuey, Adam(A)	1805	Nov. 04	Montgomery	04	03	06
Shuey, Martin(A)	1805	June 27	Montgomery	04	03	09
Shuey, Martin(A)	1805	June 27	Montgomery	04	03	10
Shuey, Martin(A)	1805	July 05	Montgomery	04	04	29
Shuey, Martin(A)	1805	July 05	Montgomery	04	03	09
Shuey, Martin(A)	1805	Nov. 25	Montgomery	04	03	06
Shuey, Martin(A)	1810	Aug. 14	Montgomery	04	04	29
Shuff, Isaac(B)	1836	Aug. 18	Switzerland	02	02	14
Shuff, Jacob(B)	1832	July 16	Switzerland	02	02	20
Shuff, John(C)	1831	Oct. 22	Hamilton	12	02	12
Shuff, Jonath'n.(B)	1827	Sept. 03	Switzerland	02	02	20
Shuff, Jonathan(B)	1818	May 25	Hamilton	02	02	20
Shugart, George(E)	1811	Nov. 11	Wayne(Ind)	14	17	01
Shugart, John(B)	1831	April 04	Wayne(Ind)	01	15	21
Shulas, Robert(A)	1805	July 15	Butler	02	04	06
Shull, David(B)	1833	March 02	Switzerland	03	03	28
Shull, Peter(A)	1806	May 06	Hamilton	01	02	33
Shull, Peter(A)	1806	Aug. 06	Hamilton	01	02	34
Shull, Peter(A)	1811	Dec. 11	Hamilton	01	02	34
Shuman, George H.(B)	1836	June 28	Dearborn(Ind	03	05	02
Shuman, John C.(B)	1818	Sept. 04	Hamilton	03	05	02
Shuman, John Carpenter(B)	1832	May 23	Dearborn(Ind	03	05	02
Shurley, Jonathan(A)	1826	Sept. 02	Preble	02	09	21
Shurley, Jonathan(A)	1831	Nov. 14	Preble	02	09	17
Shurley, Jonathan(A)	1831	Nov. 14	Preble	02	09	07
Shurte, Garret(A)	1816	March 09	Darke	02	11	33
Shurte, Garret(A)	1816	March 20	Darke	02	11	28
Shutt, George(A)	1837	May 09	Montgomery	01	12	02
Shutt, John(A)	1837	May 09	Montgomery	01	12	03
Sibbert, John Henry(B)	1839	Dec. 31	Switzerland	03	04	08
Sibbet, Aaron(D)	1808	Nov. 01	Hamilton	02	03	26
Sibbet, Aaron(D)	1808	Nov. 01	Warren	03	04	08
Sidewell, David(A)	1806	June 02	Butler	01	08	08
Sidwell, David(A)	1806	Aug. 05	Butler	05	05	24
Siebendollar, George(B)	1833	Oct. 24	Hamilton	03	09	24
Siebendollar, George(B)	1833	Dec. 05	Hamilton	03	09	24
Siebendollar, Philip(B)	1833	Aug. 19	Cincinnati	03	09	25
Siebendollar, Philip(B)	1833	Dec. 26	Cincinnati	03	09	25
Siefert, Magdalena(B)	1833	June 06	France	02	06	09
Siefert, Nicholas(B)	1833	Sept. 30	Germany	02	08	30
Siers, Joseph(B)	1805	Nov. 19	Ind.Territry	01	08	11
Siers, Joseph(B)	1814	May 02	Franklin(Ind	01	08	04
Siers, Thomas(C)	1814	May 18	Miami	10	02	23
Siers, William(B)	1814	March 16	Franklin(Ind	01	08	10
Siferman, George(A)	1834	May 23	Pennsylvania	03	10	20
Sigerfoos, Jacob(A)	1831	April 23	Montgomery	03	08	13
Sigmon, John(B)	1832	Oct. 08	Switzerland	03	03	33
Sigmon, John(B)	1835	July 02	Switzerland	03	03	32
Siler, Jacob(C)	1802	Dec. 31	Hamilton	09	02	18
Siler, Peter(A)	1832	March 19	Montgomery	04	09	30
Siler, Philip(C)	1802	Dec. 31	Hamilton	09	02	18
Siler, Philip(C)	1804	Dec. 24	Montgomery	09	02	18
Sills, Dan'l.(C)	1831	Jan. 19	Champaign	12	03	31
Sills, David(C)	1825	Sept. 12	Champaign	11	03	29
Sills, Joseph Jr.(C)	1828	June 04	Champaign	11	03	36
Sills, Joseph(C)	1810	May 14	Champaign	10	03	36
Sills, Michael(C)	1810	May 14	Champaign	11	03	32
Silver, James((D)	1808	Dec. 06	Hamilton(Fr)	02	01	08
Silver, James(C)	1814	April 12	Hamilton	02	01	08
Silver, Peter Willson(C)	1832	April 23	Montgomery	12	02	21
Silver, Philip(A)	1808	Jan. 13	Ross	04	04	11
Silvers, Arad(B)	1832	Sept. 01	Switzerland	03	03	33
Silvers, Francis(B)	1832	Sept. 01	Switzerland	03	03	27
Silvers, Joseph(C)	1801	Nov. 26	Hamilton	05	02	09
Simes, Chesley Kinney(C)	1831	Nov. 17	Miami	11	03	14
Simes, Jeremiah(C)	1815	Sept. 25	Champaign	10	04	19
Simes, John(C)	1811	May 20	Champaign	13	05	26

PURCHASER	YEAR	DATE	RESIDENCE	R	T	S
Simes, Joseph(C)	1811	May 20	Champaign	12	05	36
Simes, Joseph(C)	1832	Dec. 07	Logan	13	03	18
Simes, Larkin(E)	1811	Oct. 21	Ind.Territory	12	12	36
Simes, Larkin(E)	1811	Oct. 22	Ind.Territory	12	14	36
Simes, Larkin(E)	1811	Oct. 22	Ind.Territory	12	15	36
Simes, William Junr.(E)	1811	Oct. 23	Ind.Territory	13	11	02
Simes, William(C)	1812	Oct. 26	Champaign	09	03	18
Simmerman, George(C)	1806	May 29	Greene	08	02	17
Simmison, John(A)	1839	Sept. 02	Ohio	02	15	27
Simmons, Aaron(E)	1836	Sept. 29	Miami	15	21	34
Simmons, Adam(C)	1831	Sept. 26	Miami	12	02	21
Simmons, Adam(E)	1836	Sept. 14	Miami	15	21	34
Simmons, Edward(E)	1837	April 05	Wayne(Ind)	15	21	18
Simmons, Edward(E)	1837	May 11	Wayne(Ind)	15	21	18
Simmons, Jacob(C)	1815	March 25	Miami	12	02	31
Simmons, James(E)	1831	May 10	Randolph(Ind	15	21	20
Simmons, John(A)	1804	April 18	Montgomery	05	03	12
Simmons, John(C)	1806	Jan. 25	Montgomery	11	02	36
Simmons, John(C)	1806	March 12	Montgomery	11	02	36
Simmons, John(C)	1806	March 12	Montgomery	11	02	35
Simmons, John(C)	1806	March 12	Montgomery	11	01	12
Simmons, John(C)	1808	Jan. 12	Miami	12	01	01
Simmons, John(C)	1813	May 05	Miami	11	02	34
Simmons, John(C)	1813	May 28	Miami	12	02	25
Simmons, John(E)	1812	Dec. 23	Wayne(Ind)	13	15	20
Simmons, John(E)	1814	Sept. 24	Wayne(Ind)	13	15	27
Simmons, Philip(C)	1815	Dec. 11	Champaign	10	03	03
Simmons, Thomas(A)	1805	June 20	Butler	02	05	35
Simmons, William(A)	1836	Oct. 13	Clermont	01	15	21
Simmons, William(E)	1820	Jan. 05	Wayne(Ind)	15	21	20
Simmons, William(E)	1836	June 18	Randolph(Ind	14	21	12
Simmons, William(E)	1837	Jan. 28	Randolph(Ind	14	21	12
Simmons, William(E)	1837	April 05	Randolph(Ind	15	21	07
Simmons, William(E)	1839	Feb. 02	Randolph(Ind	15	21	19
Simon, John(B)	1836	July 25	Hamilton	02	09	31
Simons, Adrial(A)	1827	Aug. 20	Darke	01	10	22
Simons, Bingham(A)	1818	Dec. 19	Darke	01	10	25
Simons, Samuel(B)	1817	June 20	Wayne(Ind)	01	15	10
Simons, Thomas(E)	1811	Oct. 23	Wayne(Ind)	12	16	22
Simons, Thomas(E)	1811	Oct. 23	Wayne	12	16	35
Simonson, Charles H.(B)	1829	Dec. 08	Franklin(Ind	01	09	22
Simonson, Cornelius(B)	1817	Nov. 29	Hamilton	01	09	22
Simonson, Jesse(E)	1836	Feb. 15	Preble	11	11	01
Simonson, Minney V.(B)	1829	Dec. 08	Franklin(Ind	01	09	22
Simonson, William(E)	1836	Feb. 15	Hamilton	11	12	36
Simonton, Benjamin(C)	1806	Nov. 28	Champaign	12	04	31
Simonton, Benjamin(C)	1808	Dec. 31	Champaign	08	04	29
Simonton, George(B)	1817	Nov. 27	Jefferson	02	02	19
Simonton, John(A)	1831	May 19	Preble	03	07	12
Simonton, Samuel(C)	1811	Dec. 11	Champaign	09	04	04
Simonton, Samuel(C)	1811	Dec. 11	Champaign	11	05	30
Simpson, Alexander(E)	1835	Jan. 01	Hamilton	12	12	24
Simpson, Allan(A)	1802	March 10	Hamilton	04	02	08
Simpson, Allen(E)	1818	March 06	Franklin(Ind	12	12	22
Simpson, Collier(B)	1830	Sept. 18	Randolph(Ind	01	17	36
Simpson, Collier(B)	1832	Sept. 18	Randolph(Ind	01	17	36
Simpson, Collier(B)	1834	Oct. 07	Randolph(Ind	01	17	36
Simpson, Francis Willett(A)	1832	Aug. 23	E.Tennessee	02	13	13
Simpson, James(A)	1802	June 28	Hamilton	02	05	23
Simpson, Jesse(A)	1802	June 28	Hamilton	02	05	23
Simpson, John(A)	1802	March 24	Hamilton	04	02	07
Simpson, John(A)	1806	Oct. 28	Pennsylvania	05	06	32
Simpson, John(E)	1834	June 26	Franklin(Ind	12	12	31
Simpson, John(E)	1836	June 20	Franklin(Ind	12	12	31
Simpson, Joshua(E)	1816	Dec. 16	Franklin(Ind	13	14	14
Simpson, Thomas(E)	1814	Jan. 11	Franklin(Ind	13	14	23
Simpson, Valentine(A)	1818	July 22	Preble	02	10	32
Simpson, William(B)	1805	July 30	Ind.Territry	02	04	31
Sims, Alexander(E)	1815	May 04	So. Carolina	13	13	35

PURCHASER	YEAR	DATE	RESIDENCE	R	T	S
Sims, John(C)	1817	Aug. 01	Champaign	09	03	12
Sims, Larkin(E)	1814	Oct. 14	Franklin(Ind	12	14	26
Sims, Larkin(E)	1815	Sept. 25	Cincinnati	12	14	23
Sims, Michael(Black)(B)	1818	Feb. 04	New York	02	07	26
Sims, William(B)	1813	Nov. 30	Franklin(Ind	02	10	35
Singer, Joseph(A)	1804	May 15	Warren	03	07	34
Singhorse, George(B)	1813	March 01	Franklin(Ind	02	08	12
Singrey, Thomas(E)	1837	May 29	Richland	15	22	31
Sink, George(A)	1804	Nov. 10	Montgomery	05	05	02
Sinkes, Charles(C)	1804	Dec. 31	Greene	10	05	04
Sinks, Charles(C)	1801	Dec. 31	Hamilton	07	02	23
Sinks, Charles(C)	1806	Feb. 18	Greene	10	05	04
Sinks, George(A)	1805	Jan. 15	Montgomery	05	06	25
Sinks, Jacob(A)	1804	Sept. 24	Warren	04	03	04
Sinks, Jacob(A)	1804	Sept. 24	Warren	04	04	31
Sinks, Jacob(E)	1811	Oct. 25	Montgomery	14	16	19
Sinnard, Thomas(E)	1818	March 06	Butler	14	20	28
Sintz, Peter(C)	1805	Sept. 18	Champaign	09	04	23
Sintz, Peter(C)	1812	April 15	Champaign	09	04	17
Sintz, Peter(C)	1815	Sept. 25	Champaign	10	04	19
Sionmonds, Edward(B)	1816	Nov. 22	Hamilton	13	13	30
Sipe, Francis(C)	1804	Nov. 03	Montgomery	08	04	34
Sipe, William(A)	1817	June 03	Greene	02	11	08
Sippell, Paulus(A)	1836	April 09	Hamilton	02	13	25
Sisson, Zenas(B)	1836	July 09	Switzerland	03	03	17
Skaggs, Elisha(A)	1835	Oct. 29	Jefferson	04	11	32
Skaggs, Noble(A)	1835	Oct. 29	Jefferson	04	11	32
Skiles, William(C)	1804	Dec. 28	Greene	09	04	02
Skillan, William Jur.(A)	1817	Nov. 12	Miami	05	09	08
Skillen, James(A)	1825	Nov. 22	Shelby	07	01	03
Skillen, William(A)	1817	Aug. 28	Hamilton	07	01	09
Skillings, Lewis(C)	1814	Dec. 26	Champaign	08	05	12
Skillings, Lewis(C)	1815	Dec. 14	Champaign	09	05	01
Skillings, Lewis(C)	1829	March 02	Clark	09	05	01
Skillman, Jacob(B)	1807	Feb. 02	Hamilton	01	11	05
Skillman, Jacob(B)	1807	Feb. 02	Hamilton	01	12	32
Skillman, Thomas(B)	1818	Dec. 30	Cincinnati	03	06	28
Skilt, John(A)	1831	Jan. 04	Preble	03	08	35
Skinner, Daniel Jr.(A)	1819	June 30	Warren	02	09	02
Skinner, John(E)	1834	March 13	Randolph(Ind	15	21	22
Skinner, John(E)	1836	Aug. 30	Randolph(Ind	15	21	22
Skinner, Jos.(B)	1819	April 30	Wayne(Ind)	01	15	24
Skinner, Joseph(B)	1827	Aug. 10	Wayne(Ind)	01	15	15
Skinner, Justin(A)	1836	Sept. 07	New York	03	12	09
Skinner, Thomas Senr.(A)	1816	Dec. 20	?	06	03	04
Skinner, Thomas(B)	1806	Jan. 02	Dearborn(Ind	01	07	15
Skinner, Thomas(B)	1810	Oct. 05	Dearborn(Ind	02	09	07
Skinner, Wm.(E)	1814	Oct. 22	Franklin(Ind	13	12	11
Slaback, John D.(A)	1831	Sept. 29	Warren	05	08	35
Slagle, John(C)	1804	Dec. 22	Warren	09	03	31
Slagle, John(C)	1807	Sept. 24	Champaign	08	02	06
Slaughter, Thomas(E)	1815	March 10	Butler	13	12	23
Slaughter, Thomas(E)	1817	July 10	Wayne(Ind)	13	12	22
Slawson, Ezra(B)	1818	Feb. 11	Dearborn(Ind	03	05	34
Slawson, Simeon(B)	1824	Aug. 11	Switzerland	03	03	05
Slayback, John(B)	1831	May 26	Switzerland	01	03	33
Sleath, David(C)	1812	Jan. 27	Greene	08	03	15
Sleeth, John(E)	1814	Oct. 08	Greene	13	15	34
Sleppy, Daniel(A)	1831	Sept. 22	Montgomery	04	08	13
Slifer, Philip(A)	1809	Jan. 12	Montgomery	04	04	14
Sloan, Azor N.(B)	1837	April 21	Hamilton	03	04	14
Sloan, George(B)	1832	Oct. 06	Dearborn(Ind	02	03	20
Sloan, John(A)	1807	Jan. 28	Warren	06	03	28
Sloan, Norman(B)	1832	Oct. 06	Dearborn(Ind	02	03	20
Sloan, Norman(B)	1837	March 01	Dearborn(Ind	03	04	14
Sloan, Richard(A)	1807	Feb. 27	Butler	01	06	14
Sloan, Wm.(C)	1801	Dec. 30	Hamilton	04	03	10
Slonaker, Abdel(A)	1832	June 25	Pennsylvania	03	10	29
Slonaker, Adam(A)	1819	Jan. 05	Montgomery	04	06	02

PURCHASER	YEAR	DATE	RESIDENCE	R	T	S
Sloniker, John(E)	1836	Nov. 21	Franklin(Ind	12	12	29
Sloo, Thomas Jnr.(C)	1818	Feb. 14	Cincinnati	09	05	26
Sloo, Thomas Junr.(A)	1809	Dec. 12	Dayton	06	02	01
Sloo, Thomas Junr.(C)	1807	April 07	Cincinnati	09	06	24
Sloo, Thomas Junr.(C)	1811	April 09	Cincinnati	09	02	20
Sloo, Thomas Junr.(E)	1811	Oct. 28	Cincinnati	13	15	32
Sloo, Thos. Jr.(E)	1812	May 05	Ohio	14	16	14
Sloot, Elias(C)	1811	July 03	Champaign	12	04	12
Slosar, Jacob(A)	1832	Oct. 08	Darke	02	13	25
Slosar, Jacob(A)	1836	June 07	Darke	02	13	26
Slunaker, Adam(A)	1835	Nov. 25	Montgomery	04	10	06
Slutman, Peter(A)	1812	Oct. 19	Montgomery	03	05	21
Smaill, Jacob(E)	1837	July 21	Richland	14	22	25
Smaill, John(E)	1837	July 21	Richland	15	22	30
Small, Abraham(E)	1814	Aug. 16	Wayne(Ind)	12	16	14
Small, Ameriah(C)	1812	Oct. 05	Butler	11	01	15
Small, Andrew(C)	1801	Dec. 30	Hamilton	05	02	25
Small, Andrew(C)	1802	Dec. 30	Hamilton	05	02	24
Small, Andrew(C)	1831	March 11	Montgomery	12	02	27
Small, Benjamin(B)	1807	June 26	Dearborn(Ind	01	13	04
Small, Benjamin(B)	1811	Dec. 04	Wayne(Ind)	01	13	01
Small, Henry(A)	1828	Sept. 01	Montgomery	04	05	19
Small, James(C)	1802	Dec. 31	Hamilton	05	02	22
Small, John(B)	1807	July 04	Dearborn(Ind	01	14	29
Small, John(B)	1818	Jan. 09	Wayne(Ind)	01	17	35
Small, John(E)	1832	May 30	Wayne(Ind)	13	17	19
Small, Joseah(E)	1814	Aug. 16	Wayne(Ind)	12	16	14
Small, Joshua(B)	1818	Aug. 22	Randolph(Ind	01	16	27
Small, Joshua(B)	1828	Dec. 01	Wayne(Ind)	01	16	27
Small, Nathan(B)	1811	Oct. 04	Ind.Territry	01	13	11
Small, Nicholas(A)	1811	Oct. 09	Montgomery	05	04	08
Small, Nicholas(A)	1812	Oct. 13	Montgomery	05	04	06
Small, Nicholas(A)	1813	April 03	Montgomery	05	04	05
Small, Obadiah(B)	1817	Sept. 17	Wayne(Ind)	01	16	10
Smathers, Benjamin(E)	1836	Jan. 15	Franklin(Ind	11	11	14
Smathers, Benjamin(E)	1836	Feb. 19	Franklin(Ind	11	11	14
Smeth, Abraham(A)	1831	Sept. 28	Montgomery	03	08	25
Smiley, James(A)	1817	June 14	Butler	02	10	08
Smiley, James(B)	1814	April 01	Butler	01	10	09
Smiley, John(A)	1804	Oct. 29	Hamilton	02	04	30
Smiley, John(A)	1805	Aug. 15	Hamilton	02	04	14
Smiley, John(A)	1806	Nov. 29	Butler	02	04	10
Smiley, John(A)	1810	Dec. 12	Hamilton	02	04	14
Smiley, Thos. R.(B)	1814	April 01	Butler	01	10	09
Smiley, William(A)	1812	July 02	Butler	01	03	03
Smith, Abraham(A)	1832	Sept. 17	Montgomery	03	08	25
Smith, Abraham(B)	1837	April 12	Richland	01	18	12
Smith, Abraham(C)	1811	Nov. 11	Hamilton	12	05	24
Smith, Abraham(C)	1811	Nov. 11	Hamilton	12	05	18
Smith, Absalom Junr.(A)	1812	Aug. 12	Virginia	03	07	35
Smith, Adam(A)	1836	May 28	Montgomery	04	11	18
Smith, Adam(E)	1828	March 19	Wayne(Ind)	14	15	19
Smith, Addison(A)	1813	July 17	Montgomery	06	03	26
Smith, Addison(A)	1814	Oct. 29	Montgomery	03	04	25
Smith, Addison(A)	1814	Oct. 29	Montgomery	04	03	30
Smith, Alfred(B)	1833	June 06	Darke	01	16	01
Smith, Ambrose D.(C)	1806	Nov. 08	Cincinnati	10	01	06
Smith, Amos R.(A)	1830	Dec. 14	Montgomery	04	06	10
Smith, Amos(E)	1834	May 01	Randolph(Ind	15	21	27
Smith, Andrew(E)	1837	July 07	Cincinnati	14	20	11
Smith, Andrew(E)	1837	Aug. 31	Cincinnati	14	20	05
Smith, Anthony(B)	1833	Feb. 08	Cincinnati	02	07	19
Smith, Augustus(A)	1836	Oct. 21	Shelby	03	11	10
Smith, Benj'n.(B)	1832	Aug. 09	Switzerland	02	02	13
Smith, Benjamin(A)	1806	Dec. 15	Montgomery	01	08	32
Smith, Benjamin(B)	1813	Feb. 23	Wayne(Ind)	01	14	13
Smith, Benjamin(B)	1813	Sept. 24	Wayne(Ind)	01	14	13
Smith, Benjamin(B)	1836	Sept. 20	Switzerland	02	02	13
Smith, Benjamin(E)	1814	July 23	Franklin(Ind	13	11	10

PURCHASER	YEAR	DATE	RESIDENCE	R	T	S
Smith, Benjamin(E)	1837	June 23	Guernsey	14	20	11
Smith, Caleb(E)	1817	July 29	Franklin(Ind	12	13	08
Smith, Charles K.(A)	1836	Nov. 03	Butler	03	11	10
Smith, Charles K.(A)	1836	Nov. 19	Butler	02	15	31
Smith, Charles K.(A)	1836	Dec. 23	Butler	03	12	29
Smith, Charles K.(A)	1836	Dec. 23	Butler	03	12	32
Smith, Charles K.(A)	1837	March 01	Butler	03	12	30
Smith, Charles P.(B)	1817	Dec. 05	Cincinnati	02	08	07
Smith, Charles(A)	1837	May 01	Darke	03	11	20
Smith, Charles(C)	1810	Dec. 12	Montgomery	06	01	05
Smith, Charles(C)	1810	Dec. 12	Montgomery	06	01	11
Smith, Charles(E)	1836	Oct. 08	Preble	12	12	07
Smith, Charles(E)	1837	Feb. 27	Preble	13	19	01
Smith, Christian(C)	1815	Oct. 25	Champaign	10	03	22
Smith, Christian(C)	1818	Nov. 05	Clark	10	03	07
Smith, Christopher(B)	1812	Jan. 20	Butler	01	10	23
Smith, Christopher(B)	1814	Jan. 07	Butler	01	10	08
Smith, Cyrus N.(B)	1817	May 27	Cincinnati	01	03	32
Smith, Cyrus N.(B)	1817	May 27	Cincinnati	01	02	07
Smith, D.(A)	1811	Dec. 13	Montgomery	06	04	19
Smith, Daniel(A)	1829	June 02	Montgomery	04	06	17
Smith, David(?)	1814	Dec. 12	Butler	02	09	02
Smith, David(A)	1809	June 16	Butler	02	03	02
Smith, David(A)	1815	Dec. 09	Montgomery	06	03	17
Smith, David(A)	1836	Oct. 27	Miami	01	13	20
Smith, David(A)	1837	March 01	Hamilton	02	15	28
Smith, David(B)	1814	Dec. 31	Butler	02	09	13
Smith, David(C)	1812	Jan. 09	Champaign	10	06	14
Smith, David(C)	1831	Feb. 14	Clark	11	03	20
Smith, Durant(?)	?	?	Randolph(Ind	?	?	?
Smith, Durant(E)	1836	Feb. 12	Randolph(Ind	14	20	13
Smith, Ebenezer(E)	1813	Nov. 16	Franklin(Ind	13	13	35
Smith, Ebenezer(E)	1815	Dec. 04	Franklin(Ind	13	13	34
Smith, Edwin(C)	1805	Nov. 30	Warren	06	01	02
Smith, Edwin(C)	1810	Nov. 10	?	08	02	24
Smith, Eleazer(B)	1837	March 27	Dearborn(Ind	03	04	23
Smith, Eleazer(E)	1816	Nov. 07	Wayne(Ind)	14	18	18
Smith, Eleazer(E)	1829	Nov. 25	Wayne(Ind)	14	18	20
Smith, Eli(A)	1831	March 09	Darke	04	07	30
Smith, Elias P.(B)	1817	Dec. 18	Cincinnati	03	06	13
Smith, Elias P.(B)	1817	Dec. 18	Cincinnati	03	06	34
Smith, Elias P.(B)	1817	Dec. 18	Cincinnati	02	05	32
Smith, Elias P.(E)	1817	Dec. 05	Cincinnati	13	11	15
Smith, Emanuel(A)	1819	Oct. 19	Darke	03	10	20
Smith, Emanuel(A)	1829	Aug. 03	Darke	03	10	20
Smith, Enoch(B)	1809	Dec. 12	Dearborn(Ind	01	07	04
Smith, Francis Joseph(B)	1832	Aug. 01	Dearborn(Ind	01	07	22
Smith, George(A)	1837	June 08	Richland	01	13	17
Smith, George(B)	1837	Jan. 13	Dearborn(Ind	02	03	04
Smith, George(B)	1837	June 08	Richland	01	18	13
Smith, Henry Coleman(B)	1806	Aug. 04	Pennsylvania	01	06	27
Smith, Henry Colman(B)	1806	July 23	Pennsylvania	01	06	27
Smith, Henry D.(E)	1836	June 16	Franklin(Ind	12	12	17
Smith, Henry D.(E)	1836	Oct. 08	Franklin(Ind	12	12	12
Smith, Henry G.(A)	1807	Aug. 05	Cincinnati	01	01	04
Smith, Henry(A)	1813	April 14	Miami	06	04	19
Smith, Henry(A)	1816	Sept. 26	Miami	06	04	19
Smith, Henry(B)	1818	Dec. 03	Dearborn(Ind	03	05	24
Smith, Henry(B)	1837	April 12	Richland	01	18	01
Smith, Henry(C)	1813	Dec. 15	Champaign	09	03	06
Smith, Herman(B)	1814	Dec. 08	?	02	09	18
Smith, Isaac(A)	1803	Aug. 18	Kentucky	02	06	28
Smith, Jacob F.(A)	1831	May 10	Montgomery	04	06	08
Smith, Jacob(A)	1811	Dec. 10	Montgomery	05	04	08
Smith, Jacob(A)	1811	Dec. 10	Montgomery	05	04	08
Smith, Jacob(A)	1836	Oct. 10	Miami	03	12	09
Smith, Jacob(B)	1815	Aug. 10	Montgomery	01	04	18
Smith, Jacob(E)	1835	Feb. 02	Franklin(Ind	12	12	17
Smith, James C.(E)	1813	Sept. 07	Kentucky	12	12	20

PURCHASER	YEAR	DATE	RESIDENCE	R	T	S
Smith, James Oliver(B)	1832	May 25	Dearborn(Ind	03	05	03
Smith, James(A)	1819	Jan. 30	Montgomery	03	10	09
Smith, James(A)	1819	Jan. 30	Montgomery	03	10	08
Smith, James(A)	1820	Jan. 19	Darke	03	10	08
Smith, James(B)	1814	Feb. 26	Butler	01	10	17
Smith, James(B)	1831	Sept. 19	Dearborn(Ind	01	06	15
Smith, James(B)	1834	Jan. 22	Dearborn(Ind	02	04	08
Smith, James(C)	1811	Feb. 04	Champaign	12	04	10
Smith, James(C)	1811	Oct. 15	Pennsylvania	12	04	22
Smith, James(C)	1811	Oct. 15	Pennsylvania	12	04	22
Smith, James(C)	1811	Oct. 15	Pennsylvania	11	05	29
Smith, James(C)	1811	Oct. 15	Pennsylvania	11	04	17
Smith, James(C)	1812	Oct. 07	Greene	08	03	11
Smith, James(C)	1815	Feb. 21	Greene	09	03	27
Smith, James(E)	1813	June 07	Franklin(Ind	13	14	28
Smith, James(E)	1815	Sept. 02	Hamilton	12	14	15
Smith, James(E)	1815	Sept. 02	Hamilton	12	14	29
Smith, James(E)	1816	April 10	Wayne(Ind)	12	14	28
Smith, Jeremiah(E)	1838	April 11	Randolph(Ind	13	18	05
Smith, Jno.(C)	1812	Nov. 04	Champaign	13	05	14
Smith, Job(E)	1837	Jan. 18	Preble	14	19	18
Smith, John J.(C)	1813	Dec. 14	Champaign	11	05	19
Smith, John Junr.(B)	1832	Oct. 10	Dearborn(Ind	02	06	12
Smith, John N.(E)	1836	Aug. 12	Preble	14	19	20
Smith, John(A)	1802	June 02	Kentucky	01	01	04
Smith, John(A)	1809	Sept. 11	Butler	01	04	07
Smith, John(A)	1813	April 08	Pennsylvania	01	04	20
Smith, John(A)	1813	April 08	Pennsylvania	01	04	29
Smith, John(A)	1813	Dec. 27	Pennsylvania	01	04	20
Smith, John(A)	1819	June 08	Warren	03	10	20
Smith, John(A)	1832	June 08	Darke	03	10	20
Smith, John(B)	1806	June 07	Warren	01	13	05
Smith, John(B)	1806	June 25	Warren	01	14	33
Smith, John(B)	1806	June 25	Warren	01	14	32
Smith, John(B)	1806	June 25	Warren	01	14	29
Smith, John(B)	1806	Aug. 18	Warren	01	14	20
Smith, John(B)	1806	Aug. 18	Warren	01	13	02
Smith, John(B)	1806	Oct. 04	Warren	01	13	02
Smith, John(B)	1806	Oct. 04	Warren	01	12	07
Smith, John(B)	1806	Oct. 21	Butler	01	04	08
Smith, John(B)	1807	June 26	Dearborn(Ind	01	14	32
Smith, John(B)	1807	Aug. 25	Dearborn(Ind	01	14	32
Smith, John(B)	1812	Nov. 19	Butler	02	10	25
Smith, John(B)	1812	Nov. 19	Butler	02	10	25
Smith, John(B)	1815	Oct. 26	Pennsylvania	02	03	03
Smith, John(B)	1815	Oct. 26	Pennsylvania	02	03	03
Smith, John(B)	1815	Oct. 11	Pennsylvania	01	09	05
Smith, John(B)	1818	Oct. 03	Hamilton	01	06	07
Smith, John(C)	1804	Dec. 26	Hamilton	10	01	02
Smith, John(C)	1804	Dec. 28	Hamilton	04	04	21
Smith, John(C)	1804	Dec. 29	Hamilton	04	04	15
Smith, John(C)	1804	Dec. 29	Hamilton	04	04	15
Smith, John(C)	1804	Dec. 29	Hamilton	04	04	07
Smith, John(C)	1804	Dec. 31	Hamilton	04	04	14
Smith, John(C)	1804	Dec. 31	Hamilton	10	02	35
Smith, John(C)	1804	Dec. 31	Hamilton	10	02	35
Smith, John(C)	1804	Dec. 31	Hamilton	10	02	35
Smith, John(C)	1804	Dec. 31	Hamilton	06	02	30
Smith, John(C)	1804	Dec. 31	Hamilton	05	03	18
Smith, John(C)	1804	Dec. 31	Hamilton	11	06	25
Smith, John(C)	1804	Dec. 31	Hamilton	11	06	25
Smith, John(C)	1804	Dec. 31	Hamilton	11	06	19
Smith, John(C)	1804	Dec. 31	Hamilton	10	01	04
Smith, John(C)	1804	Dec. 31	Hamilton	10	01	18
Smith, John(C)	1804	Dec. 31	Hamilton	10	01	17
Smith, John(C)	1804	Dec. 31	Hamilton	10	01	12
Smith, John(C)	1804	Dec. 31	Hamilton	10	02	20
Smith, John(C)	1804	Dec. 31	Hamilton	10	01	03
Smith, John(C)	1804	Dec. 31	Hamilton	10	02	28

PURCHASER	YEAR	DATE	RESIDENCE	R	T	S
Smith, John(C)	1804	Dec. 31	Hamilton	10	02	32
Smith, John(C)	1805	April 20	Hamilton	05	02	18
Smith, John(C)	1805	April 20	Hamilton	05	02	18
Smith, John(C)	1805	April 20	Hamilton	06	02	23
Smith, John(C)	1805	April 20	Hamilton	06	02	23
Smith, John(C)	1805	April 20	Hamilton	10	02	35
Smith, John(C)	1805	April 27	Hamilton	10	03	33
Smith, John(C)	1805	April 27	Hamilton	10	03	33
Smith, John(C)	1805	April 27	Hamilton	10	03	33
Smith, John(C)	1805	April 27	Hamilton	10	03	33
Smith, John(C)	1805	April 27	Hamilton	10	03	30
Smith, John(C)	1805	April 27	Hamilton	10	03	30
Smith, John(C)	1805	April 27	Hamilton	10	03	30
Smith, John(C)	1805	April 27	Hamilton	10	03	30
Smith, John(C)	1805	April 27	Hamilton	11	03	25
Smith, John(C)	1805	April 29	Hamilton	10	03	32
Smith, John(C)	1805	April 29	Hamilton	10	03	32
Smith, John(C)	1805	April 29	Hamilton	10	03	32
Smith, John(C)	1805	April 29	Hamilton	10	03	27
Smith, John(C)	1805	April 29	Hamilton	10	03	27
Smith, John(C)	1805	April 29	Hamilton	10	03	27
Smith, John(C)	1805	April 29	Hamilton	10	03	27
Smith, John(C)	1805	April 29	Hamilton	10	03	35
Smith, John(C)	1805	April 29	Hamilton	10	03	35
Smith, John(C)	1805	April 29	Hamilton	10	03	35
Smith, John(C)	1805	April 29	Hamilton	10	03	35
Smith, John(C)	1805	April 29	Hamilton	10	03	20
Smith, John(C)	1805	April 29	Hamilton	10	03	20
Smith, John(C)	1805	April 29	Hamilton	10	03	20
Smith, John(C)	1805	April 29	Hamilton	10	03	20
Smith, John(C)	1805	April 29	Hamilton	10	03	21
Smith, John(C)	1805	April 30	Hamilton	11	06	31
Smith, John(C)	1805	April 30	Hamilton	11	06	31
Smith, John(C)	1805	April 30	Hamilton	11	06	31
Smith, John(C)	1805	April 30	Hamilton	11	06	31
Smith, John(C)	1805	April 30	Hamilton	11	05	19
Smith, John(C)	1805	April 30	Hamilton	11	05	19
Smith, John(C)	1805	April 30	Hamilton	11	05	19
Smith, John(C)	1805	April 30	Hamilton	11	05	19
Smith, John(C)	1805	April 30	Hamilton	10	03	32
Smith, John(C)	1805	April 30	Hamilton	10	03	28
Smith, John(C)	1805	April 30	Hamilton	10	03	28
Smith, John(C)	1805	April 30	Hamilton	10	03	28
Smith, John(C)	1805	April 30	Hamilton	10	03	28
Smith, John(C)	1805	April 30	Hamilton	10	03	21
Smith, John(C)	1805	April 30	Hamilton	10	03	21
Smith, John(C)	1805	April 30	Hamilton	10	03	21
Smith, John(C)	1805	April 30	Hamilton	10	03	22
Smith, John(C)	1805	April 30	Hamilton	10	03	22
Smith, John(C)	1805	April 30	Hamilton	10	03	22
Smith, John(C)	1805	April 30	Hamilton	10	03	22
Smith, John(C)	1805	April 30	Hamilton	10	03	23
Smith, John(C)	1805	April 30	Hamilton	10	03	23
Smith, John(C)	1805	April 30	Hamilton	10	03	23
Smith, John(C)	1805	April 30	Hamilton	10	03	23
Smith, John(C)	1805	April 30	Hamilton	10	03	24
Smith, John(C)	1805	April 30	Hamilton	10	03	24
Smith, John(C)	1805	April 30	Hamilton	10	03	24
Smith, John(C)	1805	April 30	Hamilton	10	03	24
Smith, John(C)	1805	April 30	Hamilton	11	01	01
Smith, John(C)	1805	April 30	Hamilton	11	01	01
Smith, John(C)	1805	April 30	Hamilton	11	01	01
Smith, John(C)	1805	April 30	Hamilton	11	01	01
Smith, John(C)	1805	April 30	Hamilton	11	02	25
Smith, John(C)	1805	April 30	Hamilton	11	02	25
Smith, John(C)	1805	April 30	Hamilton	11	02	25
Smith, John(C)	1805	April 30	Hamilton	11	02	25
Smith, John(C)	1805	April 30	Hamilton	11	02	31
Smith, John(C)	1805	April 30	Hamilton	11	02	31

PURCHASER	YEAR	DATE	RESIDENCE	R	T	S
Smith, John(C)	1805	April 30	Hamilton	11	02	31
Smith, John(C)	1805	April 30	Hamilton	11	02	31
Smith, John(C)	1805	April 30	Hamilton	11	03	25
Smith, John(C)	1805	April 30	Hamilton	11	03	25
Smith, John(C)	1805	April 30	Hamilton	11	03	25
Smith, John(C)	1805	April 30	Hamilton	11	03	19
Smith, John(C)	1805	April 30	Hamilton	11	03	19
Smith, John(C)	1805	April 30	Hamilton	11	03	19
Smith, John(C)	1805	April 30	Hamilton	11	03	19
Smith, John(C)	1805	April 30	Hamilton	11	01	07
Smith, John(C)	1805	April 30	Hamilton	06	02	13
Smith, John(C)	1805	April 30	Hamilton	05	02	06
Smith, John(C)	1805	April 30	Hamilton	05	03	28
Smith, John(C)	1805	April 30	Hamilton	06	01	07
Smith, John(C)	1805	April 30	Hamilton	06	01	13
Smith, John(C)	1805	April 30	Hamilton	06	01	13
Smith, John(C)	1805	April 30	Hamilton	06	01	13
Smith, John(C)	1805	April 30	Hamilton	06	01	13
Smith, John(C)	1805	April 30	Hamilton	05	03	34
Smith, John(C)	1805	April 30	Hamilton	05	03	12
Smith, John(C)	1805	April 30	Ohio	10	06	30
Smith, John(C)	1805	April 30	Ohio	10	06	30
Smith, John(C)	1805	April 30	Ohio	10	06	30
Smith, John(C)	1805	April 30	Ohio	10	06	30
Smith, John(C)	1805	April 30	Ohio	10	04	04
Smith, John(C)	1805	April 30	Ohio	10	04	03
Smith, John(C)	1805	April 30	Ohio	10	04	05
Smith, John(C)	1805	April 30	Ohio	10	05	34
Smith, John(C)	1805	April 30	Ohio	10	05	35
Smith, John(C)	1805	April 30	Ohio	10	05	36
Smith, John(C)	1805	April 30	Hamilton	10	05	28
Smith, John(C)	1805	April 30	Ohio	10	05	28
Smith, John(C)	1805	April 30	Ohio	10	05	28
Smith, John(C)	1805	April 30	Ohio	10	05	28
Smith, John(C)	1805	April 30	Hamilton	11	03	01
Smith, John(C)	1805	April 30	Hamilton	11	03	01
Smith, John(C)	1805	April 30	Hamilton	11	03	01
Smith, John(C)	1805	April 30	Hamilton	11	03	01
Smith, John(C)	1805	April 30	Hamilton	11	03	13
Smith, John(C)	1805	April 30	Hamilton	11	03	13
Smith, John(C)	1805	April 30	Hamilton	11	03	13
Smith, John(C)	1805	April 30	Hamilton	11	03	13
Smith, John(C)	1805	April 30	Hamilton	11	03	07
Smith, John(C)	1805	April 30	Hamilton	11	03	07
Smith, John(C)	1805	April 30	Hamilton	11	03	07
Smith, John(C)	1805	April 30	Hamilton	11	03	07
Smith, John(C)	1805	April 30	Hamilton	10	03	06
Smith, John(C)	1805	April 30	Hamilton	10	03	06
Smith, John(C)	1805	April 30	Hamilton	10	03	06
Smith, John(C)	1805	April 30	Hamilton	10	03	06
Smith, John(C)	1805	April 30	Hamilton	10	03	12
Smith, John(C)	1805	April 30	Hamilton	10	03	12
Smith, John(C)	1805	April 30	Hamilton	10	03	12
Smith, John(C)	1805	April 30	Hamilton	10	03	12
Smith, John(C)	1805	April 30	Hamilton	10	03	18
Smith, John(C)	1805	April 30	Hamilton	10	03	18
Smith, John(C)	1805	April 30	Hamilton	10	03	18
Smith, John(C)	1805	April 30	Hamilton	10	03	18
Smith, John(C)	1805	April 30	Hamilton	10	03	17
Smith, John(C)	1805	April 30	Hamilton	10	03	17
Smith, John(C)	1805	April 30	Hamilton	10	03	17
Smith, John(C)	1805	April 30	Hamilton	10	03	17
Smith, John(C)	1805	April 30	Hamilton	10	03	05
Smith, John(C)	1805	April 30	Hamilton	10	03	05
Smith, John(C)	1805	April 30	Hamilton	10	03	05
Smith, John(C)	1805	April 30	Hamilton	10	03	05
Smith, John(C)	1805	April 30	Hamilton	10	03	10
Smith, John(C)	1805	April 30	Hamilton	10	03	10
Smith, John(C)	1805	April 30	Hamilton	10	03	10

PURCHASER	YEAR	DATE	RESIDENCE	R	T	S
Smith, John(C)	1805	April 30	Hamilton	10	03	10
Smith, John(C)	1805	April 30	Hamilton	10	03	04
Smith, John(C)	1805	April 30	Hamilton	10	03	04
Smith, John(C)	1805	April 30	Hamilton	10	03	04
Smith, John(C)	1805	April 30	Hamilton	10	03	04
Smith, John(C)	1805	April 30	Hamilton	10	03	15
Smith, John(C)	1805	April 30	Hamilton	10	03	15
Smith, John(C)	1805	April 30	Hamilton	10	03	15
Smith, John(C)	1805	April 30	Hamilton	10	03	15
Smith, John(C)	1805	April 30	Hamilton	10	03	09
Smith, John(C)	1805	April 30	Hamilton	10	03	09
Smith, John(C)	1805	April 30	Hamilton	10	03	09
Smith, John(C)	1805	April 30	Hamilton	10	03	09
Smith, John(C)	1805	April 30	Hamilton	10	03	03
Smith, John(C)	1805	April 30	Hamilton	10	03	03
Smith, John(C)	1805	April 30	Hamilton	10	03	03
Smith, John(C)	1805	April 30	Hamilton	10	03	03
Smith, John(C)	1805	April 30	Hamilton	10	03	14
Smith, John(C)	1805	April 30	Hamilton	10	03	14
Smith, John(C)	1805	April 30	Hamilton	10	03	14
Smith, John(C)	1805	April 30	Hamilton	10	03	14
Smith, John(C)	1805	April 30	Hamilton	10	03	02
Smith, John(C)	1805	April 30	Hamilton	10	03	02
Smith, John(C)	1805	April 30	Hamilton	10	03	02
Smith, John(C)	1805	April 30	Hamilton	10	03	02
Smith, John(C)	1805	April 30	Hamilton	11	04	07
Smith, John(C)	1805	April 30	Hamilton	11	04	01
Smith, John(C)	1805	April 30	Hamilton	04	04	01
Smith, John(C)	1805	April 30	Hamilton	10	03	34
Smith, John(C)	1805	April 30	Hamilton	10	03	34
Smith, John(C)	1805	April 30	Hamilton	10	03	34
Smith, John(C)	1805	July 30	Hamilton	10	01	11
Smith, John(C)	1806	Aug. 08	Hamilton	10	02	34
Smith, John(C)	1807	April 06	Cincinnati	11	01	23
Smith, John(C)	1811	Dec. 11	Champaign	09	05	05
Smith, John(C)	1814	Aug. 15	Champaign	13	05	24
Smith, John(C)	1830	Oct. 18	Clark	14	03	26
Smith, John(C)	1831	May 24	Logan	14	02	01
Smith, John(E)	1811	Dec. 11	Wayne(Ind)	14	16	22
Smith, John(E)	1817	Sept. 01	Wayne(Ind)	14	20	27
Smith, Jonah(C)	1813	April 14	Miami	09	02	04
Smith, Jonathan(E)	1833	Sept. 25	Franklin(Ind	13	11	28
Smith, Jonathan(E)	1834	Jan. 28	Franklin(Ind	13	11	28
Smith, Joseph K.(B)	1818	July 06	Cincinnati	02	08	17
Smith, Joseph K.(E)	1818	July 03	Cincinnati	13	11	09
Smith, Joseph K.(E)	1819	March 01	Cincinnati	13	20	13
Smith, Joseph(A)	1805	June 10	Butler	03	03	06
Smith, Joseph(A)	1835	Aug. 08	Shelby	03	11	11
Smith, Joseph(B)	1808	Jan. 12	Butler	01	13	10
Smith, Joseph(C)	1807	July 16	Champaign	09	06	18
Smith, Joseph(C)	1813	April 14	Champaign	09	06	18
Smith, Joseph(C)	1813	Nov. 27	Champaign	09	06	18
Smith, Margaret(E)	1837	July 07	Cincinnati	14	20	02
Smith, Matthew Jnr.(B)	1813	Sept. 15	Franklin(Ind	01	09	01
Smith, Matthew(E)	1835	Oct. 22	Franklin(Ind	12	12	11
Smith, Michael(B)	1834	Sept. 18	Switzerland	02	03	25
Smith, Michael(B)	1835	Dec. 17	Switzerland	02	03	25
Smith, Michael(C)	1811	July 31	FortWayneInd	08	02	29
Smith, Michael(C)	1812	July 20	FortWayneInd	08	02	29
Smith, Nathan'l. Stout(A)	1831	Aug. 09	Hamilton	05	08	22
Smith, Nathan(A)	1807	April 07	Kentucky	01	01	08
Smith, Noah(B)	1815	Sept. 02	Hamilton	01	02	08
Smith, Oliver(A)	1801	July 20	Kentucky	03	03	31
Smith, Oliver(A)	1801	Aug. 26	Kentucky	03	03	30
Smith, Patrick(A)	1816	July 24	Hamilton	01	02	35
Smith, Peter(A)	1811	June 03	Butler	02	04	20
Smith, Peter(B)	1805	Dec. 02	Kentucky	01	12	06
Smith, Peter(B)	1805	Dec. 02	Kentucky	02	12	01
Smith, Peter(B)	1818	May 21	Switzerland	01	02	21

PURCHASER	YEAR	DATE	RESIDENCE	R	T	S
Smith, Peter(B)	1829	July 22	Switzerland	01	02	21
Smith, Peter(C)	1804	Dec. 28	Greene	11	04	23
Smith, Peter(C)	1804	Dec. 28	Greene	11	04	23
Smith, Peter(C)	1804	Dec. 28	Greene	11	04	22
Smith, Peter(C)	1804	Dec. 10	Greene	09	03	04
Smith, Peter(C)	1804	Dec. 10	Greene	09	03	23
Smith, Peter(C)	1812	July 10	Champaign	11	04	21
Smith, Peter(C)	1814	March 30	Champaign	11	04	21
Smith, Peter(C)	1814	March 30	Champaign	11	04	22
Smith, Peter(C)	1829	Dec. 23	Champaign	11	04	34
Smith, Phineas(A)	1814	March 15	Butler	01	08	25
Smith, Phineas(A)	1816	April 18	Butler	02	11	33
Smith, Ralph(B)	1812	June 29	Warren	02	04	10
Smith, Richard(B)	1819	May 22	Dearborn(Ind	02	04	30
Smith, Richard(B)	1836	Feb. 25	Dearborn(Ind	02	04	30
Smith, Robert(B)	1818	March 30	Clermont	03	05	11
Smith, Robert(B)	1818	March 30	Clermont	03	05	14
Smith, Robert(C)	1812	March 09	Champaign	13	05	22
Smith, Robert(C)	1811	Sept. 09	Champaign	10	05	27
Smith, Robt.(B)	1825	Oct. 24	Kentucky	01	10	21
Smith, Samuel(A)	1803	Aug. 04	Kentucky	02	05	04
Smith, Samuel(C)	1812	Oct. 07	Greene	08	03	11
Smith, Samuel(C)	1817	Dec. 02	Greene	08	03	11
Smith, Samuel(E)	1813	Dec. 08	Preble	13	17	10
Smith, Samuel(E)	1818	Feb. 10	Clinton	14	18	07
Smith, Silas(A)	1836	Nov. 01	Cincinnati	03	12	23
Smith, Silas(B)	1818	Sept. 25	Switzerland	03	03	29
Smith, Silas(B)	1822	Nov. 27	Switzerland	03	03	29
Smith, Solomon(C)	1812	Nov. 07	Champaign	10	06	20
Smith, Stephen(A)	1832	Sept. 17	Montgomery	03	08	25
Smith, Stephen(E)	1837	July 13	Montgomery	15	22	29
Smith, Summers G.(E)	1836	Sept. 30	Franklin(Ind	12	12	19
Smith, Susanna(A)	1825	Feb. 07	Hamilton	01	02	22
Smith, Temple(E)	1835	March 26	Randolph(Ind	13	18	01
Smith, Thomas B.(A)	1815	Aug. 26	Hamilton	01	02	07
Smith, Thomas Jr.(E)	1836	Aug. 12	Preble	14	19	20
Smith, Thomas P.(E)	1838	May 10	Belmont	15	22	26
Smith, Thomas P.(E)	1838	Nov. 05	Randolph(Ind	15	22	23
Smith, Thomas R.(A)	1802	Jan. 08	Hamilton	01	01	08
Smith, Thomas Wilson(E)	1832	Oct. 01	Franklin(Ind	12	11	01
Smith, Thomas(A)	1805	April 06	Montgomery	04	04	06
Smith, Thomas(A)	1805	April 16	Montgomery	04	04	17
Smith, Thomas(A)	1816	Sept. 17	Montgomery	02	10	18
Smith, Thomas(A)	1831	Sept. 09	Darke	03	10	08
Smith, Thomas(A)	1833	June 08	Darke	03	10	08
Smith, Thomas(B)	1817	Dec. 24	Cincinnati	03	03	01
Smith, Thomas(B)	1817	Dec. 24	Cincinnati	03	03	01
Smith, Thomas(B)	1818	Feb. 17	Cincinnati	02	06	06
Smith, Thomas(B)	1820	March 03	Hamilton	02	08	31
Smith, Thomas(B)	1828	Oct. 25	Hamilton	02	01	06
Smith, Thomas(C)	1801	Dec. 24	Kentucky	05	03	02
Smith, Thomas(E)	1814	Sept. 22	Greene	13	12	23
Smith, Thomas(E)	1815	April 29	Champaign	12	14	28
Smith, Timothy T.(E)	1836	Oct. 20	Montgomery	15	21	29
Smith, Timothy(C)	1818	July 07	Knox	12	02	36
Smith, Tobias(E)	1811	Oct. 22	Ind.Territry	12	14	26
Smith, William K.(E)	1837	March 01	Clark	14	21	33
Smith, William M.(A)	1816	Oct. 07	Montgomery	06	03	17
Smith, William M.(C)	1811	Dec. 11	Montgomery	08	02	26
Smith, William M.(C)	1813	June 21	Montgomery	07	02	30
Smith, William P.(A)	1809	July 27	Montgomery	02	07	12
Smith, William P.(A)	1809	Sept. 25	Montgomery	02	07	14
Smith, William P.(E)	1812	Feb. 07	Butler	13	15	32
Smith, William P.(E)	1813	Dec. 24	Preble	13	17	08
Smith, William(A)	1805	July 06	Montgomery	03	04	06
Smith, William(A)	1805	Aug. 15	Butler	02	07	02
Smith, William(A)	1805	Aug. 19	Butler	04	03	05
Smith, William(A)	1806	March 27	Montgomery	03	05	20
Smith, William(A)	1806	Sept. 16	Butler	02	03	15

PURCHASER	YEAR	DATE	RESIDENCE	R	T	S
Smith, William(A)	1811	Aug. 13	Preble	03	05	20
Smith, William(A)	1817	Sept. 27	?	03	04	15
Smith, William(A)	1819	Jan. 30	Montgomery	03	10	05
Smith, William(A)	1819	March 13	Darke	03	10	09
Smith, William(A)	1831	Sept. 08	Clark	08	02	26
Smith, William(A)	1832	Sept. 20	Darke	03	10	08
Smith, William(A)	1836	Dec. 07	Montgomery	03	11	07
Smith, William(B)	1808	Dec. 14	Dearborn(Ind	01	07	05
Smith, William(B)	1813	Feb. 20	Ind.Territry	01	07	08
Smith, William(B)	1814	June 20	Jefferson	02	02	04
Smith, William(B)	1828	Jan. 15	Cincinnati	03	07	12
Smith, William(B)	1833	March 02	Dearborn(Ind	01	06	08
Smith, William(B)	1836	Jan. 16	Dearborn(Ind	01	06	08
Smith, William(C)	1817	Dec. 02	Greene	08	03	11
Smith, William(E)	1811	Oct. 28	Dearborn(Ind	12	12	03
Smith, William(E)	1811	Dec. 30	Tennessee	13	16	08
Smith, William(E)	1814	Sept. 03	Warren	13	12	11
Smith, William(E)	1818	April 07	Randolph(Ind	13	18	09
Smith, William(E)	1831	April 25	Randolph(Ind	14	18	03
Smith, William(E)	1835	Feb. 11	Warren	13	19	15
Smith, Wm. M.(A)	1813	July 17	Montgomery	06	03	26
Smith, Wm. M.(C)	1811	Dec. 13	Montgomery	07	02	36
Smith, Wm.(B)	1827	Aug. 21	Dearborn(Ind	02	04	19
Smith, Zadock(A)	1817	May 10	Darke	01	10	13
Smith, Zadock(E)	1812	March 11	Montgomery	13	14	07
Smyer, Frederick(A)	1810	Dec. 21	Scioto	02	05	13
Smyre, Lorens(A)	1817	Oct. 04	Butler	03	07	11
Smyser, Philip(C)	1807	Aug. 27	Clermont	12	01	22
Snaveley, John(A)	1815	Aug. 29	Butler	03	05	14
Snelbaker, Jeremiah(E)	1838	Aug. 10	Cincinnati	15	22	09
Snell, George(B)	1834	Feb. 27	Dearborn(Ind	02	06	23
Snell, John(A)	1816	June 05	Montgomery	01	12	27
Snell, John(B)	1833	July 29	Dearborn(Ind	02	06	06
Snep, John Junr.(C)	1826	Jan. 02	Montgomery	11	03	11
Snethen, Abraham(A)	1831	June 30	Montgomery	04	06	05
Snethen, William(A)	1819	March 25	Preble	03	07	02
Snethen, William(A)	1831	May 30	Montgomery	04	06	08
Snider, Abraham(C)	1808	Jan. 12	Champaign	09	06	30
Snider, Abraham(C)	1811	Jan. 12	Champaign	09	06	30
Snider, Adam(C)	1831	Aug. 08	Logan	14	03	11
Snider, Balser(A)	1809	Dec. 26	Pennsylvania	03	06	04
Snider, Cornelius(C)	1831	Oct. 19	Hamilton	12	02	22
Snider, Daniel(A)	1805	Nov. 06	Virginia	04	04	20
Snider, David(A)	1805	Oct. 30	Virginia	05	05	20
Snider, David(A)	1831	April 15	Miami	04	07	22
Snider, Felty(C)	1815	Jan. 14	Franklin(Ind	09	04	36
Snider, Henry(A)	1805	Oct. 30	Virginia	04	06	13
Snider, Henry(A)	1805	Oct. 30	Virginia	05	05	28
Snider, Henry(A)	1805	Nov. 06	Virginia	04	04	18
Snider, Henry(A)	1815	Nov. 16	Preble	03	06	23
Snider, Jacob(A)	1811	Jan. 16	Butler	04	02	08
Snider, Jacob(A)	1831	April 15	Miami	04	07	22
Snider, Jacob(A)	1837	May 05	Fairfield	02	14	20
Snider, John(A)	1819	Nov. 16	Preble	01	08	15
Snider, John(A)	1827	Aug. 20	Preble	01	08	15
Snider, John(B)	1833	April 22	Hamilton	02	05	22
Snider, Jonas(A)	1813	Jan. 16	Kentucky	05	05	31
Snider, Michael(B)	1808	Jan. 13	Dearborn(Ind	01	12	24
Snider, Michael(B)	1808	Jan. 13	Dearborn(Ind	01	12	24
Snider, Michael(B)	1812	Dec. 28	Wayne(Ind)	02	12	24
Snider, Michael(B)	1812	Dec. 28	Wayne(Ind)	02	12	24
Snider, Michael(B)	1813	Sept. 04	Wayne(Ind)	02	12	23
Snider, William(A)	1814	Nov. 02	Montgomery	05	05	18
Snip, Daniel(C)	1826	Jan. 13	Montgomery	11	03	11
Snip, John Jr.(C)	1826	Jan. 13	Montgomery	11	03	11
Snip, Rynehhart(C)	1813	April 14	Montgomery	07	02	12
Snip, Solomon(C)	1826	Jan. 25	Montgomery	11	03	11
Snipe, Leonard(C)	1810	June 14	Montgomery	06	01	11
Snithen, William(A)	1818	July 02	Preble	04	06	05

COOS BAY OREGON FHC

037-008

PURCHASER	YEAR	DATE	RESIDENCE	R	T	S
Snoddy, John(A)	1819	Feb. 04	Miami	04	09	01
Snoddy, John(A)	1831	July 05	Miami	04	09	01
Snode, Isaac(A)	1811	May 01	Miami	05	06	18
Snodgrass, Benj'n.(A)	1829	Aug. 03	Darke	01	10	17
Snodgrass, James(B)	1815	June 06	Greene	01	11	06
Snodgrass, James(C)	1802	Dec. 28	Hamilton	06	02	07
Snodgrass, John A.(A)	1827	July 18	Shelby	06	07	17
Snodgrass, John(C)	1806	Aug. 11	Kentucky	09	05	09
Snodgrass, John(C)	1806	Aug. 11	Kentucky	09	05	15
Snodgrass, John(C)	1806	Aug. 11	Kentucky	09	05	09
Snodgrass, John(C)	1806	Aug. 11	Kentucky	09	05·	15
Snodgrass, John(C)	1807	Feb. 27	Champaign	09	05	11
Snodgrass, John(C)	1811	Dec. 11	Champaign	09	05	15
Snodgrass, John(C)	1811	Dec. 11	Champaign	09	05	09
Snodgrass, John(C)	1812	April 15	Champaign	09	05	11
Snodgrass, John(C)	1813	Feb. 25	Champaign	09	05	11
Snodgrass, John(C)	1816	Aug. 01	?	09	05	11
Snodgrass, John(C)	1817	Aug. 01	Champaign	09	05	11
Snodgrass, Joseph(A)	1815	July 21	Preble	01	08	24
Snodgrass, Robert(C)	1802	Dec. 28	Hamilton	06	02	02
Snodgrass, Sam'l. M.(B)	1827	Nov. 27	Wayne(Ind)	01	15	01
Snodgrass, Samuel M.(B)	1837	Jan. 20	Preble	01	17	15
Snodgrass, Samuel M.(B)	1837	Jan. 30	Preble	01	17	22
Snodgrass, Samuel(C)	1817	July10	Greene	12	03	18
Snodgrass, Samuel(E)	1814	Sept. 08	Greene	12	13	03
Snodgrass, William(B)	1813	May 22	Franklin(Ind	01	09	36
Snodgrass, William(C)	1801	Dec. 28	Hamilton	07	02	23
Snodgrass, William(C)	1805	Feb. 25	Montgomery	07	02	11
Snodgrass, William(C)	1809	April 08	Butler	02	01	08
Snodgrass, William(C)	1824	June 07	Butler	12	01	08
Snodgrass, William(D)	1809	April 29	Hamilton	01	03	26
Snodgrass, William(E)	1814	March 19	Miami	12	14	33
Snodgrass, William(E)	1836	Nov. 19	Greene	14	21	23
Snook, Henry T.(A)	1831	March 29	Hamilton	05	08	26
Snook, Henry T.(A)	1831	March 29	Hamilton	05	08	26
Snook, John(B)	1816	Sept. 23	Warren	03	03	08
Snow, Godfrey(B)	1817	Dec. 01	Dearborn(Ind	03	07	25
Snow, Lemuel(B)	1814	June 30	Cincinnati	01	08	27
Snow, Lemuel(B)	1814	Nov. 05	Cincinnati	01	08	27
Snow, Lemuel(B)	1814	Nov. 29	Dearborn(Ind	01	08	27
Snow, Lemuel(B)	1814	Dec. 23	Dearborn(Ind	01	08	28
Snowden, James(B)	1814	Dec. 30	Greene	02	11	36
Snowden, James(B)	1815	May 05	Franklin(Ind	02	11	10
Snowden, James(C)	1801	Dec. 31	Hamilton	06	02	02
Snuff, Jacob(C)	1804	Dec. 31	Warren	04	03	20
Snyder, Frederick(D)	1824	June 14	Warren	02	04	08
Snyder, Jacob(E)	1838	May 18	Montgomery	15	22	22
Snyder, Jacob(E)	1838	May 18	Montgomery	15	22	23
Snyder, John Jr.(B)	1818	Nov. 10	Hamilton	03	06	27
Snyder, John K.(A)	1837	Feb. 17	Butler	01	15	36
Snyder, John(A)	1837	Feb. 17	Butler	01	15	36
Snyder, John(A)	1837	Feb. 17	Butler	01	15	35
Snyder, John(B)	1833	Feb. 07	Dearborn(Ind	01	07	24
Snyder, John(B)	1833	Feb. 13	Dearborn(Ind	01	07	24
Snyder, Samuel(B)	1818	June 23	Hamilton	03	06	24
Solman, Peter(A)	1806	Nov. 14	Butler	02	04	19
Somey, John(E)	1811	Nov. 22	Preble	12	16	01
Sommers, Christian(A)	1821	Sept. 03	Montgomery	04	06	33
Sommers, John(A)	1831	Feb. 26	Miami	06	08	14
Sommers, Samuel(A)	1831	Oct. 24	Shelby	06	08	14
Sommerville, David(A)	1816	July 10	Darke	04	09	11
Sonday, Adam(A)	1837	May 30	Darke	03	11	07
Soper, Isaac(B)	1832	Oct. 10	Franklin(Ind	01	08	08
Souder, John(A)	1824	Aug. 21	Miami	04	09	11
Souder, John(A)	1828	April 11	Miami	04	09	11
Souders, Peter(A)	1828	April 08	Montgomery	04	05	31
Souders, Peter(A)	1829	Feb. 21	Montgomery	02	11	32
Souders, Peter(A)	1829	June 22	Montgomery	02	11	28
Souders, Peter(A)	1836	Sept. 05	Montgomery	02	13	26

PURCHASER	YEAR	DATE	RESIDENCE	R	T	S
Sour, Peter(C)	1824	Oct. 12	Clark	10	04	22
Southerland, John(C)	1810	Dec. 12	Butler	09	02	22
Southgate, James(C)	1831	Aug. 08	Cincinnati	14	04	31
Southgate, James(C)	1831	Aug. 08	Cincinnati	12	06	32
Southgate, James(C)	1831	Aug. 08	Cincinnati	13	03	11
Southgate, James(C)	1831	Aug. 08	Cincinnati	14	04	31
Sowders, Peter(A)	1830	March 10	Montgomery	02	11	28
Sowers, John(A)	1806	Aug. 15	Maryland	06	02	10
Sowers, Philip(A)	1814	Dec. 12	?	02	07	14
Spacht, Andrew(A)	1815	Nov. 04	Preble	02	11	31
Spacht, Jacob(A)	1816	May 22	Preble	02	07	05
Spahr, John(E)	1811	Nov. 27	Virginia	13	15	14
Spahr, John(E)	1811	Nov. 27	Virginia	13	15	11
Spahr, John(E)	1812	April 02	Virginia	13	15	11
Spahr, John(E)	1813	Dec. 13	Virginia	13	15	23
Spaight, John(A)	1806	Jan. 04	Washington	02	08	34
Spangenberg, Herman Fred'k.(B)	1836	April 25	Hamilton	01	07	07
Spangler, Jacob(B)	1818	March 20	Hamilton	03	05	23
Spangler, Peter(B)	1836	Aug. 11	Dearborn(Ind	03	05	26
Spangler, Peter(B)	1836	Aug. 18	Dearborn(Ind	03	05	26
Sparks, Amos(B)	1832	Jan. 06	Franklin(Ind	01	07	07
Sparks, Jesse(B)	1835	Nov. 05	Dearborn(Ind	01	07	17
Sparks, Joshua L.(B)	1819	March 10	Hamilton	02	08	36
Sparks, Joshua Low(B)	1831	Oct. 20	Franklin(Ind	01	08	31
Sparks, Joshua Low(B)	1832	Feb. 01	Franklin(Ind	02	08	36
Sparks, Matthew(B)	1814	Sept. 01	Franklin(Ind	01	08	10
Sparks, Matthew(B)	1815	Oct. 27	Franklin(Ind	01	08	04
Sparks, William(B)	1809	July 19	Dearborn(Ind	02	11	34
Sparks, William(B)	1809	July 19	Dearborn(Ind	01	11	20
Sparks, William(E)	1811	Nov. 01	Franklin(Ind	12	14	36
Sparks, William(E)	1814	March 07	Franklin(Ind	12	14	19
Speace, Daniel Senr.(C)	1815	May 01	Champaign	10	04	27
Spears, John(B)	1832	Sept. 08	Switzerland	02	02	29
Spears, John(B)	1836	March 15	Switzerland	03	03	21
Spears, John(B)	1836	March 19	Switzerland	03	03	21
Spece, Nicholas(C)	1829	March 16	Champaign	13	03	31
Specht, Jacob(A)	1806	Nov. 06	Montgomery	02	08	17
Speckman, Henry(B)	1835	Oct. 03	Hamilton	02	08	27
Speckmann, Henry(B)	1836	Feb. 01	Hamilton	02	08	29
Speer, Alexander(E)	1812	July 23	Franklin(Ind	12	11	04
Speer, Andrew(E)	1811	Nov. 29	Franklin(Ind	12	11	09
Speer, James H.(B)	1818	July 14	Cincinnati	02	08	18
Speer, John(B)	1816	Nov. 18	Franklin(Ind	01	10	10
Speer, John(B)	1832	May 29	Dearborn(Ind	02	04	30
Speer, Martha(B)	1832	June 06	Dearborn(Ind	02	04	30
Spence, William(C)	1819	Jan. 11	Hamilton	10	03	10
Spence, William(C)	1825	March 03	Clark	10	04	29
Spencer(Free Colored)(E)	1815	May 22	Wayne(Ind)	13	16	11
Spencer(black)(E)	1813	July 15	Wayne(Ind)	14	16	29
Spencer, Aaron(C)	1811	Dec. 11	Champaign	09	06	30
Spencer, Allen(B)	1811	Nov. 01	Dearborn(Ind	01	08	11
Spencer, Amos(C)	1812	Oct. 05	Butler	11	01	15
Spencer, Clark(E)	1837	June 03	Darke	15	20	33
Spencer, Elijah(A)	1809	July 31	Cincinnati	02	12	26
Spencer, Elijah(A)	1809	July 31	Cincinnati	02	12	20
Spencer, Elijah(E)	1814	July 28	Wayne(Ind)	12	16	12
Spencer, Francis(A)	1816	Sept. 24	Greene	01	10	03
Spencer, Francis(A)	1831	July 18	Darke	01	11	33
Spencer, Joseph(A)	1801	July 20	Hamilton	03	03	30
Spencer, Joseph(B)	1811	Nov. 22	Wayne(Ind)	01	12	34
Spencer, Joseph(E)	1811	Oct. 22	Ind.Territry	12	15	24
Spencer, Ledlow(A)	1831	Jan. 03	Darke	01	10	04
Spencer, Matthew J.(C)	1814	Feb. 28	Champaign	09	06	17
Spencer, Matthew J.(C)	1814	June 23	Champaign	09	06	17
Spencer, Milley(A)	1831	Dec. 08	Miami	04	08	03
Spencer, Oliver M.(A)	1815	July 13	Cincinnati	08	02	25
Spencer, Oliver M.(A)	1815	July 13	Cincinnati	08	02	36
Spencer, Oliver M.(A)	1818	Feb. 16	Cincinnati	08	02	24
Spencer, Oliver M.(C)	1814	April 18	Cincinnati	11	02	12

PURCHASER	YEAR	DATE	RESIDENCE	R	T	S
Spencer, Oliver M.(C)	1814	April 18	Cincinnati	11	02	18
Spencer, Oliver M.(C)	1814	April 18	Cincinnati	11	02	24
Spencer, Oliver M.(C)	1814	Oct. 03	Cincinnati	13	01	13
Spencer, Oliver M.(C)	1815	May 20	Cincinnati	14	04	26
Spencer, Oliver M.(C)	1815	May 20	Cincinnati	15	02	02
Spencer, Oliver M.(C)	1815	May 20	Cincinnati	14	03	24
Spencer, Oliver M.(C)	1815	May 20	Cincinnati	14	03	24
Spencer, Oliver M.(C)	1815	May 20	Cincinnati	14	03	24
Spencer, Oliver M.(C)	1815	May 20	Cincinnati	14	03	23
Spencer, Oliver M.(C)	1815	May 20	Cincinnati	14	03	11
Spencer, Oliver M.(C)	1815	May 20	Cincinnati	14	03	11
Spencer, Oliver M.(C)	1815	May 20	Cincinnati	14	03	11
Spencer, Oliver M.(C)	1815	May 20	Cincinnati	14	03	11
Spencer, Oliver M.(C)	1815	May 20	Cincinnati	15	02	13
Spencer, Oliver M.(C)	1815	May 20	Cincinnati	13	03	10
Spencer, Oliver M.(C)	1815	May 20	Cincinnati	13	03	17
Spencer, Oliver M.(C)	1815	May 20	Cincinnati	13	03	10
Spencer, Oliver M.(C)	1815	May 20	Cincinnati	14	02	04
Spencer, Oliver M.(C)	1815	May 20	Cincinnati	15	02	01
Spencer, Oliver M.(C)	1815	May 20	Cincinnati	14	02	01
Spencer, Oliver M.(C)	1815	May 20	Cincinnati	15	02	01
Spencer, Oliver M.(C)	1815	May 20	Cincinnati	15	02	01
Spencer, Oliver M.(C)	1815	May 20	Cincinnati	14	03	23
Spencer, Oliver M.(C)	1815	May 20	Cincinnati	14	03	23
Spencer, Oliver M.(C)	1815	May 20	Cincinnati	14	03	22
Spencer, Oliver M.(C)	1815	May 20	Cincinnati	14	03	22
Spencer, Oliver M.(C)	1815	May 20	Cincinnati	14	03	35
Spencer, Oliver M.(C)	1815	May 20	Cincinnati	14	02	03
Spencer, Oliver M.(C)	1815	May 20	Cincinnati	14	03	34
Spencer, Oliver M.(C)	1815	May 20	Cincinnati	14	02	10
Spencer, Oliver M.(C)	1815	May 20	Cincinnati	14	02	03
Spencer, Oliver M.(C)	1815	May 20	Cincinnati	14	02	10
Spencer, Oliver M.(C)	1815	May 20	Cincinnati	14	02	10
Spencer, Oliver M.(C)	1815	May 20	Cincinnati	14	03	32
Spencer, Oliver M.(C)	1815	May 20	Cincinnati	14	02	10
Spencer, Oliver M.(C)	1815	May 20	Cincinnati	14	03	02
Spencer, Oliver M.(C)	1815	May 20	Cincinnati	14	03	32
Spencer, Oliver M.(C)	1815	May 20	Cincinnati	14	03	33
Spencer, Oliver M.(C)	1815	May 20	Cincinnati	14	03	27
Spencer, Oliver M.(C)	1815	May 20	Cincinnati	14	02	09
Spencer, Oliver M.(C)	1815	May 20	Cincinnati	14	03	33
Spencer, Oliver M.(C)	1815	May 20	Cincinnati	14	02	05
Spencer, Oliver M.(C)	1815	May 20	Cincinnati	14	02	05
Spencer, Oliver M.(C)	1815	May 20	Cincinnati	14	02	04
Spencer, Oliver M.(C)	1815	May 22	Cincinnati	14	03	25
Spencer, Oliver M.(C)	1815	May 22	Cincinnati	14	03	31
Spencer, Oliver M.(C)	1815	May 23	Cincinnati	15	02	31
Spencer, Oliver M.(C)	1815	May 23	Cincinnati	15	02	25
Spencer, Oliver M.(C)	1815	June 17	Cincinnati	13	03	17
Spencer, Oliver M.(C)	1815	June 17	Cincinnati	14	03	29
Spencer, Oliver M.(C)	1815	June 17	Cincinnati	14	02	11
Spencer, Oliver M.(C)	1815	June 17	Cincinnati	14	02	06
Spencer, Oliver M.(C)	1815	June 17	Cincinnati	14	02	06
Spencer, Oliver M.(C)	1815	June 17	Cincinnati	14	02	06
Spencer, Oliver M.(C)	1815	June 17	Cincinnati	14	03	36
Spencer, Oliver M.(C)	1815	June 17	Cincinnati	14	03	36
Spencer, Oliver M.(C)	1815	June 17	Cincinnati	14	03	36
Spencer, Oliver M.(C)	1815	June 17	Cincinnati	14	03	36
Spencer, Oliver M.(C)	1815	June 17	Cincinnati	14	02	05
Spencer, Oliver M.(C)	1815	June 17	Cincinnati	14	02	05
Spencer, Oliver M.(C)	1815	June 17	Cincinnati	14	03	30
Spencer, Oliver M.(C)	1815	June 17	Cincinnati	14	03	30
Spencer, Oliver M.(C)	1815	June 17	Cincinnati	14	03	30
Spencer, Oliver M.(C)	1815	June 17	Cincinnati	14	03	30
Spencer, Oliver M.(C)	1815	June 17	Cincinnati	14	03	24
Spencer, Oliver M.(C)	1815	June 17	Cincinnati	15	02	07
Spencer, Oliver M.(C)	1815	June 17	Cincinnati	15	01	01
Spencer, Oliver M.(C)	1815	June 17	Cincinnati	13	03	35
Spencer, Oliver M.(C)	1815	June 17	Cincinnati	15	02	19

PURCHASER	YEAR	DATE	RESIDENCE	R	T	S
Spencer, Oliver M.(C)	1815	June 17	Cincinnati	14	03	26
Spencer, Oliver M.(C)	1815	June 17	Cincinnati	14	02	12
Spencer, Oliver M.(C)	1815	June 17	Cincinnati	15	02	08
Spencer, Oliver M.(C)	1815	June 21	Cincinnati	14	03	13
Spencer, Oliver M.(C)	1815	June 21	Cincinnati	14	03	27
Spencer, Oliver M.(C)	1815	June 21	Cincinnati	14	03	27
Spencer, Oliver M.(C)	1815	June 21	Cincinnati	14	03	21
Spencer, Oliver M.(C)	1815	June 21	Cincinnati	14	03	21
Spencer, Oliver M.(C)	1815	June 17	Cincinnati	14	02	06
Spencer, Oliver M.(C)	1815	July 14	Cincinnati	14	03	13
Spencer, Oliver M.(C)	1815	July 14	Cincinnati	14	03	19
Spencer, Oliver M.(C)	1815	July 14	Cincinnati	14	03	13
Spencer, Oliver M.(C)	1815	July 14	Cincinnati	13	04	18
Spencer, Oliver M.(C)	1815	July 14	Cincinnati	13	04	24
Spencer, Oliver M.(C)	1815	July 14	Cincinnati	13	04	17
Spencer, Oliver M.(C)	1815	July 14	Cincinnati	13	04	23
Spencer, Oliver M.(C)	1815	July 14	Cincinnati	13	04	28
Spencer, Oliver M.(C)	1815	July 14	Cincinnati	13	04	33
Spencer, Oliver M.(C)	1815	July 14	Cincinnati	13	04	33
Spencer, Oliver M.(C)	1816	Dec. 06	Cincinnati	14	04	17
Spencer, Oliver M.(C)	1816	Dec. 06	Cincinnati	14	04	17
Spencer, Oliver M.(C)	1816	Dec. 06	Cincinnati	14	04	25
Spencer, Oliver M.(C)	1816	Dec. 06	Cincinnati	14	04	25
Spencer, Oliver M.(C)	1816	Dec. 09	Cincinnati	14	01	25
Spencer, Oliver M.(C)	1816	Dec. 09	Cincinnati	13	03	36
Spencer, Oliver M.(C)	1816	Dec. 10	Cincinnati	13	02	06
Spencer, Oliver M.(C)	1815	May 20	Cincinnati	14	03	35
Spencer, Oliver M.(C)	1815	May 20	Cincinnati	14	03	28
Spencer, Oliver M.(C)	1828	April 12	Cincinnati	14	03	13
Spencer, William Senr.(B)	1812	March 10	Dearborn	02	04	35
Spencer, William Senr.(B)	1812	June 30	Dearborn(Ind	02	04	22
Spenser, John(E)	1836	Nov. 16	Franklin(Ind	13	13	32
Spenser, Oliver M.(C)	1815	May 20	Cincinnati	14	03	35
Spilke, Godfrey(C)	1818	June 27	Clark	10	03	24
Spinning, Elias(A)	1808	Jan. 11	Warren	05	07	01
Spinning, Isaac(C)	1801	Dec. 11	Hamilton	07	02	17
Spitler, Jacob(A)	1806	March 29	Montgomery	06	02	18
Spitler, Jacob(A)	1805	Sept. 27	Montgomery	05	05	32
Spitler, Jacob(A)	1836	Nov. 04	Montgomery	01	13	15
Spitler, Jacob(A)	1837	March 01	Montgomery	01	13	05
Spitler, John(A)	1825	Aug. 11	Montgomery	04	06	15
Spitler, John(A)	1828	Oct. 16	Montgomery	04	07	33
Spitler, John(A)	1831	April 23	Montgomery	04	07	18
Spitler, Joseph(A)	1836	Nov. 04	Montgomery	01	13	22
Spittler, John(A)	1806	Aug. 26	Montgomery	05	07	07
Spore, Daniel(B)	1829	Jan. 05	Switzerland	01	03	28
Spradling, James(B)	1836	March 18	Franklin(Ind	02	07	03
Spradling, John(B)	1833	March 02	Franklin(Ind	02	08	35
Spradling, William(B)	1833	June 14	Franklin(Ind	02	08	23
Spradling, Wm.(B)	1827	Dec. 20	Union(Ind)	02	08	35
Sprague, Hezekiah(B)	1833	Jan. 07	Switzerland	02	02	11
Spray, James Junr.(E)	1817	Oct. 04	Warren	13	20	34
Spray, James(E)	1815	Dec. 11	Wayne(Ind)	13	17	23
Sprengelmeier, Theodore(E)	1837	May 15	Cincinnati	12	11	30
Sprig, James(C)	1815	Nov. 10	Champaign	09	06	19
Sprigman, Peter A.(C)	1815	Feb. 16	Cincinnati	09	02	14
Springer, John Small(E)	1836	Jan. 25	Franklin(Ind	12	12	18
Springer, Nathan(A)	1805	March 30	Butler	02	05	01
Springer, Nathan(A)	1810	Aug. 14	Butler	02	05	01
Springer, Nathan(E)	1836	Jan. 25	Rush(Ind)	12	12	07
Sprouly, Robert(C)	1813	Nov. 03	Miami	10	02	27
Sprowl, John(A)	1814	Aug. 24	Preble	01	09	08
Spry, John(C)	1829	Jan. 27	Champaign	13	04	18
Spry, John(C)	1829	Aug. 05	Logan	14	02	05
Spry, Lodman E.(C)	1818	Jan. 15	Clark	10	03	09
Spry, Lodman E.(C)	1823	Sept. 23	Clark	13	04	18
Squier, William(C)	1813	Aug. 10	Butler	09	02	33
Squire, David(C)	1804	Dec. 29	Montgomery	08	02	35
Squire, David(C)	1804	Dec. 29	Montgomery	08	02	35

PURCHASER	YEAR	DATE	RESIDENCE	R	T	S
Squire, David(C)	1804	Dec. 29	Montgomery	08	01	05
Squire, Meeker(C)	1801	Dec. 30	Hamilton	04	02	10
Squire, William(A)	1817	Sept. 06	Butler	01	11	11
Squire, William(C)	1808	March 28	Butler	09	02	33
Srauf, George(C)	1816	Sept. 17	Ohio	12	03	21
Sroufe, George(C)	1816	Nov. 06	Greene	12	03	20
Sroufe, Sebastian(C)	1804	Dec. 15	Kentucky	08	04	22
Sroufe, Sebastian(C)	1813	April 16	Greene	08	04	22
Sroufe, Sebastian(C)	1817	July 01	Greene	12	03	20
St. Clair, Arthur Junr.(A)	1806	Dec. 03	Cincinnati	03	02	16
St. Clair, Arthur Junr.(C)	1804	Dec. 31	Cincinnati	07	02	34
St. Clair, Arthur Junr.(C)	1804	Dec. 31	Cincinnati	08	04	33
St. Clair, Arthur Junr.(C)	1804	Dec. 31	Cincinnati	09	03	01
St. Clair, Arthur Junr.(C)	1804	Dec. 31	Cincinnati	08	04	20
St. Clair, Arthur Junr.(C)	1804	Dec. 31	Cincinnati	08	05	21
St. Clair, Arthur(C)	1804	Dec. 31	Cincinnati	07	03	04
St. John, Jac'b.(C)	1813	Nov. 11	Warren	08	06	06
St. John, Jacob(A)	1836	Aug. 26	Hamilton	03	11	02
Stabler, John Jonathan(C)	1817	July 28	Miami	13	02	08
Stabler, John Jonathan(C)	1817	Sept. 07	Cincinnati	13	02	02
Stacy, Warham(C)	1813	April 14	Champaign	09	06	27
Stafford, George(C)	1813	Dec. 28	Champaign	10	03	31
Stafford, George(C)	1827	April 24	Clark	10	03	32
Stafford, James(C)	1810	Nov. 10	Virginia	10	02	24
Stafford, James(C)	1810	Nov. 10	Virginia	10	02	18
Stafford, John(B)	1813	July 31	Franklin(Ind	02	08	06
Stafford, John(B)	1818	May 22	Franklin(Ind	02	08	17
Stafford, John(C)	1826	April 28	Clark	10	03	32
Stafford, John(E)	1811	Oct. 28	Franklin(Ind	13	11	10
Stafford, Joseph(C)	1804	Dec. 24	Montgomery	09	02	17
Stafford, Joseph(C)	1804	Dec. 24	Montgomery	09	02	17
Stafford, Ralph(C)	1804	Dec. 24	Montgomery	09	02	12
Stafford, Thomas(B)	1813	Nov. 11	Wayne(Ind)	01	14	15
Stafford, Thomas(C)	1804	Dec. 31	Greene	10	03	31
Stafford, Thomas(C)	1817	June 05	Champaign	10	03	26
Stafford, Thomas(E)	1811	Oct. 23	Wayne(Ind)	12	16	34
Stafford, William Senr.(B)	1811	Oct. 26	So. Carolina	01	15	17
Stage, Samuel(B)	1819	July 07	Hamilton	02	05	05
Stage, Samuel(B)	1832	March 09	Dearborn(Ind	03	06	13
Stahl, Henry(A)	1816	Nov. 13	?	02	13	24
Stahl, Henry(A)	1816	Nov. 13	Pennsylvania	03	11	34
Stahl, Henry(A)	1816	Nov. 13	Adams	03	11	34
Stahl, Jacob Kensinger(A)	1835	May 21	Darke	03	11	26
Stahl, Jacob Kensinger(A)	1838	April 05	Darke	02	13	11
Stahl, Jacob(A)	1817	Oct. 28	Pennsylvania	03	10	25
Stair, Jacob(B)	1813	Nov. 09	Franklin(Ind	02	09	02
Staley, David(A)	1836	Oct. 10	Miami	03	12	18
Staley, David(A)	1837	Oct. 18	Miami	03	12	18
Staley, Jacob(A)	1814	Oct. 05	Montgomery	06	03	17
Staley, John(A)	1831	May 21	Shelby	07	01	08
Staley, Joseph(A)	1813	Jan. 12	Montgomery	06	03	18
Staley, Levi(A)	1831	Oct. 14	Montgomery	07	02	31
Staley, Nicholas(A)	1831	May 09	Shelby	07	01	08
Staley, Reuben(C)	1831	Sept. 23	Montgomery	13	02	12
Stalker, David(E)	1836	Jan. 30	Clinton	13	19	35
Stalker, Nathan(E)	1817	Aug. 30	Clinton	13	18	29
Stall, Edward H.	1808	March 02	Cincinnati	?	?	?
Stall, Herman Jacob(A)	1839	Jan. 21	Cincinnati	02	15	26
Stallman, Henry(B)	1836	Feb. 08	Hamilton	03	09	24
Stalman, Henry(E)	1837	Jan. 09	Cincinnati	12	11	31
Stamback, Isaac(A)	1815	Oct. 17	Virginia	01	09	36
Stambaugh, David(E)	1837	April 05	Butler	14	21	02
Stambaugh, John(E)	1837	April 05	Butler	14	21	02
Stanbury, Solomon(C)	1801	Dec. 25	?	05	03	07
Standback, Jesse(A)	1815	April 04	Preble	01	08	12
Standedford, Elijah(C)	1811	April 09	Champaign	11	04	25
Standiford, James(B)	1818	May 29	Hamilton	02	04	17
Stanley, Archelaus(E)	1836	Jan. 23	Randolph(Ind	13	18	15
Stanley, James Jr.(E)	1832	July 20	Wayne(Ind)	13	18	09

PURCHASER	YEAR	DATE	RESIDENCE	R	T	S
Stanley, John(B)	1812	June 01	Belmont	01	12	14
Stanley, William(B)	1804	Sept. 24	Cincinnati	03	01	05
Stanley, William(C)	1804	Dec. 31	Cincinnati	08	05	36
Stanley, William(C)	1804	Dec. 31	Cincinnati	08	03	06
Stanley, William(C)	1804	Dec. 31	Cincinnati	08	03	32
Stanley, William(C)	1804	Dec. 31	Cincinnati	09	04	14
Stanley, Wm. Win(E)	1839	July 10	Hamilton	14	22	24
Stanley, Zacariah(B)	1811	Nov. 28	Clermont	01	12	10
Stannags, Thomas(C)	1813	Jan. 26	Champaign	10	05	25
Stansberry, Jeremiah(C)	1805	May 18	Ohio	13	03	05
Stansberry, Jeremiah(C)	1807	Feb. 02	Champaign	13	03	05
Stansberry, Jeremiah(C)	1810	April 09	Champaign	13	03	04
Stansberry, Jeremiah(C)	1810	Dec. 31	Champaign	14	03	25
Stansbury, Jeremiah(B)	1814	Nov. 08	Champaign	14	03	12
Stansbury, Jeremiah(C)	1812	May 25	Miami	14	03	12
Stansbury, Jeremiah(C)	1812	May 30	Champaign	14	03	12
Stansbury, Jeremiah(C)	1817	Aug. 01	?	14	03	12
Stansbury, John(B)	1812	Sept. 10	Hamilton	01	08	23
Stansbury, John(B)	1813	June 01	Dearborn(Ind	01	08	23
Stanset, Henry(C)	1801	Dec. 30	Hamilton	04	03	34
Stanton, Aaron(B)	1812	Dec. 24	Franklin(Ind	01	11	20
Stanton, Aaron(B)	1813	Sept. 06	Franklin(Ind	01	11	29
Stanton, James(B)	1811	Oct. 31	Stark	01	11	17
Stanton, Latham(B)	1814	Oct. 21	Franklin(Ind	01	11	10
Stanton, Latham(E)	1827	Oct. 17	Fayette	13	13	26
Stanton, Reuben(A)	1807	Feb. 02	Butler	01	04	17
Stapel, Catharine(A)	1837	Dec. 16	Cincinnati	02	14	01
Star, John(B)	1809	Sept. 16	Dearborn(Ind	01	12	09
Starbuck, Edw'd.(B)	1830	Nov. 03	Wayne(Ind)	01	15	27
Starbuck, Edw'd.(B)	1831	Feb. 12	Wayne(Ind)	01	15	26
Starbuck, Edward(B)	1818	May 29	Wayne(Ind)	01	15	13
Starbuck, Edward(B)	1818	May 29	Wayne(Ind)	01	15	14
Starbuck, Edward(B)	1827	May 12	Wayne(Ind)	01	15	22
Starbuck, Edward(B)	1831	Sept. 08	Wayne(Ind)	01	15	27
Starbuck, John(E)	1825	Sept. 16	Cincinnati	13	13	28
Starbuck, John(E)	1833	June 22	Randolph(Ind	13	19	10
Starbuck, John(E)	1834	Aug. 18	Wayne(Ind)	13	20	35
Starbuck, John(E)	1836	Dec. 15	Randolph(Ind	13	19	10
Starbuck, Paul(B)	1811	Jan. 25	Wayne(Ind)	01	14	09
Starbuck, Paul(B)	1816	Aug. 01	Wayne(Ind)	01	14	09
Starbuck, Paul(B)	1829	Jan. 21	Wayne(Ind)	01	15	21
Starbuck, Tristram(E)	1816	Nov. 15	Wayne(Ind)	14	18	30
Starbuck, Uriah(B)	1817	July 02	Warren	01	11	21
Starbuck, Walter(E)	1837	Jan. 11	Wayne(Ind)	13	19	02
Stark, Archibald(B)	1804	Aug. 06	Hamilton	01	06	28
Starr, Adam(A)	1815	March 23	Preble	01	08	23
Starr, Barnet(A)	1806	Sept. 06	Montgomery	03	07	23
Starr, Barnet(A)	1807	March 09	Ohio	01	08	13
Starr, Barnet(A)	1812	April 15	Preble	01	08	13
Starr, Barnet(E)	1811	Oct. 23	Wayne(Ind)	12	16	13
Starr, Charles W.(E)	1819	Jan. 07	Pennsylvania	13	18	35
Starr, Charles W.(E)	1818	Jan. 07	Pennsylvania	13	18	27
Starr, Charles W.(E)	1819	Jan. 11	Pennsylvania	13	18	22
Starr, Charles W.(E)	1819	Jan. 11	Pennsylvania	13	18	22
Starr, John(A)	1812	April 15	Preble	01	08	13
Starr, John(B)	1807	June 27	Warren	01	12	19
Starr, John(B)	1807	Sept. 11	Warren	01	12	19
Starr, John(E)	1811	Oct. 25	Wayne(Ind)	14	14	06
Starr, Peter(A)	1812	Dec. 12	Preble	03	06	32
Starret, Charles(C)	1809	Oct. 11	Virginia	08	06	05
Starrit, William(B)	1831	Aug. 09	Franklin(Ind	01	08	17
Statelar, Jos.(C)	1824	July 24	Clark	10	03	29
Statler, Abraham(E)	1838	Aug. 20	Miami	14	22	13
Statler, John(E)	1837	July 13	Miami	15	22	27
Staton, Ruben(A)	1809	Sept. 11	Butler	01	04	18
Staughton, Joseph(A)	1806	Sept. 02	Butler	04	03	34
Staughton, Joseph(A)	1811	Dec. 11	Butler	04	03	34
Staunton, Aaron(B)	1815	Sept. 01	Franklin(Ind	01	11	06
Staver, John(A)	1817	Dec. 08	Montgomery	04	05	33

PURCHASER	YEAR	DATE	RESIDENCE	R	T	S
Stearns, Jabez(A)	1826	Feb. 20	Warren	03	08	18
Stearvolt, William(B)	1836	July 05	Hamilton	02	08	17
Stebbins, Jeremiah B.(A)	1831	July 19	Darke	06	08	34
Steddam, Henry(E)	1821	Dec. 03	Warren	14	18	19
Steddam, Henry(E)	1821	Dec. 19	Warren	14	18	19
Steddam, John(E)	1817	Aug. 12	Warren	14	17	10
Steddam, Samuel(A)	1817	Aug. 15	Warren	04	09	23
Steddom, Henry(C)	1804	Nov. 23	Warren	04	04	08
Steddom, Henry(E)	1818	March 26	Warren	13	17	04
Steddom, Sam'l.(E)	1829	Aug. 21	Warren	14	18	19
Stedham, John(A)	1806	Sept. 10	Warren	05	07	32
Stedham, John(E)	1817	Nov. 01	Warren	14	17	26
Steel, James(A)	1816	July 22	Montgomery	06	05	19
Steel, James(C)	1806	Dec. 04	Kentucky	09	05	13
Steel, James(C)	1813	Nov. 03	Champaign	09	05	19
Steel, John H.(A)	1812	Jan. 03	Preble	02	06	18
Steel, Samuel(C)	1806	Dec. 04	Franklin(Ind	09	05	15
Steel, Samuel(C)	1812	April 15	Champaign	09	05	15
Steel, Samuel(E)	1815	Jan. 16	Franklin(Ind	13	12	03
Steel, William(A)	1810	Dec. 12	Butler	02	05	26
Steel, William(E)	1818	April 08	Preble	13	17	33
Steele, Greenbery(E)	1837	Jan. 03	Fayette	12	13	25
Steele, James(C)	1831	Nov. 23	Logan	13	04	22
Steele, Martin Bush(A)	1832	Feb. 02	Greene	06	08	09
Steele, Samuel(B)	1816	May 31	Butler	01	04	29
Steele, William(A)	1805	Sept. 24	Kentucky	02	05	26
Steele, William(E)	1819	June 24	Cincinnati	12	10	04
Steenbarger, Frederick(C)	1813	April 05	Miami	12	03	07
Steenbarger, Frederick(C)	1813	June 10	Champaign	12	03	14
Steenbarger, John(C)	1813	July 08	Champaign	11	04	28
Steenbarger, Joseph(A)	1816	Feb. 06	Miami	05	09	13
Steenberger, Frederick(A)	1810	June 23	Miami	06	07	17
Steenberger, Geo.(C)	1829	Dec. 11	Champaign	11	04	02
Steenberger, George(C)	1831	March 07	Champaign	11	04	02
Steenberger, Joseph(A)	1813	Feb. 06	Miami	06	08	32
Steffler, Christian(A)	1836	Oct. 14	Ohio	04	11	30
Stegall, Jeremiah(E)	1819	Jan. 01	Franklin(Ind	14	18	30
Stegall, Jonathan(E)	1826	Sept. 06	Wayne(Ind)	14	18	31
Stegall, Lewis(E)	1825	June 18	Wayne(Ind)	14	18	29
Stegemann, Bernard(A)	1837	Dec. 11	Cincinnati	03	13	31
Stehlin, Martin(E)	1836	Nov. 14	Dearborn(Ind	12	10	19
Stehr, Bernard Henry(E)	1837	April 05	Cincinnati	11	10	11
Steinemann, John Hy.(A)	1838	Jan. 18	Mercer	03	13	33
Steinemann, John Hy.(E)	1836	Nov. 15	Cincinnati	12	10	03
Stembel, Roger N.(A)	1826	May 05	Montgomery	06	03	09
Stephen, Isaiah(A)	1836	June 14	Preble	01	13	12
Stephen, Rich'd.(A)	1830	March 02	Preble	02	12	11
Stephen, Richard(A)	1804	Aug. 13	Butler	02	04	12
Stephen, Richard(A)	1805	Sept. 23	Butler	01	06	19
Stephen, Richard(A)	1805	Sept. 23	Butler	01	06	20
Stephen, Richard(A)	1812	March 18	Butler	02	06	32
Stephen, Richard(A)	1832	Jan. 21	Preble	01	13	12
Stephen, Richard(A)	1837	March 28	Preble	01	13	12
Stephen, Richard(E)	1832	April 18	Franklin(Ind	11	13	25
Stephen, Robert E.(C)	1827	Aug. 23	Greene	08	02	02
Stephen, Samuel(A)	1813	March 02	Butler	02	07	17
Stephen, Samuel(A)	1829	June 09	Darke	02	13	06
Stephen, Samuel(A)	1836	Sept. 22	Darke	02	13	06
Stephen, Samuel(A)	1838	May 21	Darke	01	13	24
Stephen, Samuel(A)	1838	Aug. 24	Darke	01	13	24
Stephen, Thomas(A)	1804	Aug. 13	Butler	02	04	12
Stephen, Wm.(A)	1813	April 09	Butler	02	07	20
Stephens, Benjamin M.(B)	1814	Oct. 01	Hamilton	02	02	03
Stephens, Benjamin M.(B)	1817	Sept. 06	Switzerland	02	02	10
Stephens, Benjamin M.(B)	1817	Dec. 09	Switzerland	02	02	10
Stephens, Charles(E)	1832	March 01	Fayette	12	13	30
Stephens, Daniel(A)	1806	Aug. 19	Montgomery	03	05	23
Stephens, Daniel(A)	1806	Sept. 02	Montgomery	03	05	25
Stephens, Daniel(A)	1811	Dec. 12	Preble	03	05	25

PURCHASER	YEAR	DATE	RESIDENCE	R	T	S
Stephens, Daniel(A)	1811	Dec. 12	Preble	03	05	23
Stephens, Daniel(A)	1812	June 30	Preble	03	05	22
Stephens, Ebenezer(A)	1814	March 17	Ohio	06	08	18
Stephens, Hamilton(C)	1812	May 07	Kentucky	11	05	03
Stephens, Isaac(A)	1815	May 29	Preble	01	08	35
Stephens, Jacob(A)	1815	Dec. 09	Montgomery	06	03	08
Stephens, James(A)	1807	Sept. 12	New York	01	04	07
Stephens, James(A)	1817	Dec. 09	Greene	03	11	29
Stephens, James(B)	1812	March 02	Franklin(Ind	02	10	36
Stephens, John A.(B)	1818	Jan. 06	Cincinnati	01	06	15
Stephens, John A.(B)	1818	June 08	Cincinnati	01	06	15
Stephens, John A.(B)	1818	Aug. 24	Cincinnati	02	05	09
Stephens, John(A)	1811	Nov. 14	Butler	02	07	09
Stephens, John(A)	1817	Nov. 22	Kentucky	02	07	15
Stephens, John(A)	1834	Oct. 08	Darke	02	13	06
Stephens, John(A)	1837	Jan. 03	Darke	01	13	01
Stephens, Joseph L.(A)	1818	April 09	Kentucky	02	07	21
Stephens, Joseph L.(A)	1818	April 09	Kentucky	02	07	33
Stephens, Joseph L.(A)	1818	April 09	Kentucky	02	07	33
Stephens, Joseph L.(A)	1818	April 09	Kentucky	02	07	33
Stephens, Joseph L.(A)	1818	May 02	Kentucky	01	08	31
Stephens, Joseph L.(A)	1818	May 02	Kentucky	01	07	06
Stephens, Joseph L.(A)	1818	May 02	Kentucky	01	07	06
Stephens, Joseph L.(A)	1818	May 02	Kentucky	01	08	31
Stephens, Joseph L.(A)	1818	May 02	Kentucky	01	08	31
Stephens, Joseph(B)	1811	April 12	Franklin(Ind	02	10	36
Stephens, Joseph(B)	1812	March 02	Franklin(Ind	02	10	36
Stephens, Lewis(A)	1816	Aug. 24	Preble	02	07	20
Stephens, Martin(A)	1818	April 09	Kentucky	02	07	21
Stephens, Peter(A)	1812	Nov. 06	Preble	02	07	08
Stephens, Richard(A)	1837	April 24	Preble	01	13	12
Stephens, Solomon(B)	1812	Nov. 18	Jefferson	03	05	36
Stephens, Stephen C.(A)	1806	Feb. 17	Montgomery	02	08	34
Stephens, Stephen C.(B)	1811	March 20	?	02	09	17
Stephens, William(B)	1810	Sept. 22	Dearborn(Ind	01	10	14
Stephens, William(B)	1810	Sept. 22	Dearborn(Ind	01	10	27
Stephens, William(C)	1807	March 03	Montgomery	11	02	10
Stephens, William(C)	1807	March 03	Montgomery	11	02	10
Stephens, William(C)	1807	March 03	Montgomery	09	03	33
Stephens, William(C)	1813	Aug. 10	Champaign	11	04	24
Stephenson, Cornelius(C)	1813	July 29	Butler	07	03	29
Stephenson, Cornelius(D)	1812	Nov. 04	Butler	02	03	11
Stephenson, David(E)	1814	March 04	Wayne(Ind)	13	15	17
Stephenson, Elizabeth S.(A)	1830	Jan. 18	Darke	03	11	29
Stephenson, George(B)	1818	June 12	Warren	02	05	08
Stephenson, George(B)	1818	Nov. 04	Warren	03	07	24
Stephenson, Hamilton(C)	1811	Dec. 16	Kentucky	11	05	09
Stephenson, James(A)	1817	Dec. 09	Greene	03	11	29
Stephenson, James(C)	1801	Dec. 30	Hamilton	04	03	04
Stephenson, John(A)	1819	Dec. 14	Warren	04	05	17
Stephenson, John(B)	1816	April 13	Warren	02	05	03
Stephenson, John(B)	1818	Nov. 04	Warren	03	07	13
Stephenson, John(C)	1807	June 09	Kentucky	12	05	27
Stephenson, John(C)	1812	March 13	Kentucky	14	03	23
Stephenson, Vincent(B)	1812	April 15	Wayne(Ind)	01	13	20
Stephenson, Will'm.(C)	1826	April 05	Clark	08	03	29
Stephenson, William Junr.(C)	1808	Dec. 27	Ohio	15	03	31
Stephenson, William Junr.(C)	1808	Dec. 27	Ohio	14	04	36
Stephenson, William(B)	1818	Aug. 19	Cincinnati	02	08	29
Stephenson, Wm.(C)	1831	Feb. 10	Greene	11	03	14
Stepleton, Andrew(B)	1813	June 07	Jefferson	03	03	26
Stepleton, Willeasn(C)	1817	Oct. 09	Champaign	11	03	19
Stepleton, William(C)	1817	Oct. 09	Champaign	11	03	19
Stepp, John(C)	1813	June 25	Champaign	13	05	32
Sterett, Samuel(E)	1811	Oct. 24	Wayne(Ind)	13	15	21
Sterling, John(A)	1814	Dec. 06	Pennsylvania	04	05	06
Sterret, John(C)	1801	Dec. 16	Hamilton	05	03	06
Sterret, John(C)	1801	Dec. 16	Hamilton	05	04	36
Stetler, Christian(A)	1804	Oct. 15	Montgomery	06	06	30

PURCHASER	YEAR	DATE	RESIDENCE	R	T	S
Stetler, George(A)	1805	July 01	Montgomery	04	03	05
Stetler, Jacob(B)	1816	Nov. 16	Montgomery	03	07	14
Stetler, Jesse(B)	1827	Dec. 06	Wayne(Ind)	01	15	27
Stetler, John(A)	1804	Sept. 06	Montgomery	06	06	29
Stettler, George(A)	1804	July 18	Montgomery	05	02	16
Stevens, Abraham(C)	1818	June 01	Champaign	12	02	10
Stevens, Christian(C)	1804	Dec. 28	Greene	11	04	17
Stevens, David(A)	1826	Feb. 20	Darke	01	11	27
Stevens, Elijah(E)	1814	Sept. 15	Franklin(Ind	12	13	20
Stevens, Elijah(E)	1832	Jan. 02	Fayette	12	13	20
Stevens, Frederick(A)	1836	Oct. 13	Butler	03	12	24
Stevens, James(B)	1814	Jan. 12	Franklin(Ind	02	09	01
Stevens, James(B)	1815	Nov. 11	Butler	01	10	33
Stevens, James(C)	1829	Dec. 24	Champaign	12	04	04
Stevens, John(A)	1815	Jan. 24	Miami	06	08	28
Stevens, Ranna C.(B)	1818	May 25	Dearborn(Ind	03	06	15
Stevens, Reuben(B)	1827	Dec. 20	Switzerland	01	03	34
Stevens, Spencer(E)	1815	Dec. 26	Wayne(Ind)	14	15	18
Stevens, Spencer(E)	1827	Aug. 27	Wayne(Ind)	13	15	12
Stevenson, Andrew(B)	1833	March 26	Dearborn(Ind	02	05	22
Stevenson, Andrew(B)	1833	April 01	Dearborn(Ind	02	05	22
Stevenson, Armour(B)	1832	June 19	Dearborn(Ind	02	05	14
Stevenson, Frances(C)	1813	March 27	Champaign	11	04	13
Stevenson, Silvanus(B)	1839	Jan. 15	Switzerland	02	03	05
Stever, Adam(A)	1812	Oct. 14	Preble	04	04	19
Steward, Amasa(A)	1831	Sept. 17	Clermont	05	07	03
Steward, William(A)	1808	Aug. 16	Miami	06	08	36
Steward, William(C)	1809	Oct. 26	Miami	13	01	02
Stewart, Alexander(A)	1807	Aug. 10	Warren	01	09	32
Stewart, Andrew(C)	1802	Dec. 31	Hamilton	06	02	12
Stewart, Archibald(B)	1834	Nov. 20	BeaverCo.Pa.	02	07	05
Stewart, Archibald(B)	1835	Dec. 04	Dearborn(Ind	03	08	13
Stewart, Archibald(C)	1815	April 08	Champaign	12	05	17
Stewart, Arthur(A)	1806	Feb. 05	Montgomery	06	04	04
Stewart, Arthur(A)	1807	June 26	Miami	06	05	28
Stewart, Charles(A)	1812	March 30	Hamilton	01	03	03
Stewart, Charles(C)	1804	Dec. 29	Kentucky	11	05	18
Stewart, Charles(C)	1808	Jan. 13	Butler	08	06	36
Stewart, Charles(C)	1813	July 07	Champaign	13	04	33
Stewart, Charles(C)	1816	June 13	Champaign	12	05	01
Stewart, David(A)	1813	May 03	Hamilton	01	02	21
Stewart, George(C)	1813	Nov. 05	Champaign	10	06	21
Stewart, James(A)	1818	Oct. 31	Pennsylvania	02	12	08
Stewart, James(B)	1814	Aug. 24	Hamilton	01	04	32
Stewart, James(B)	1815	June 22	Adams	01	10	17
Stewart, James(B)	1815	June 24	Adams	01	08	03
Stewart, James(B)	1815	Oct. 23	Adams	01	04	28
Stewart, James(C)	1807	Aug. 01	Greene	08	05	06
Stewart, James(C)	1808	Nov. 22	Butler	03	03	11
Stewart, James(C)	1808	Nov. 22	Butler	03	03	08
Stewart, James(C)	1813	June 02	Butler	08	05	11
Stewart, James(C)	1814	Jan. 31	Champaign	10	03	02
Stewart, James(C)	1814	May 04	Hamilton	08	05	11
Stewart, James(C)	1815	Feb. 06	Greene	08	05	12
Stewart, James(C)	1815	March 25	Greene	08	05	28
Stewart, James(D)	1809	June 16	Hamilton	01	04	08
Stewart, John D.(E)	1836	Sept. 02	Randolph(Ind	14	20	07
Stewart, John T.(C)	1828	Dec. 01	Clark	08	05	30
Stewart, John(C)	1806	Aug. 18	Greene	08	05	15
Stewart, John(C)	1813	March 27	Champaign	12	03	13
Stewart, John(D)	1809	Feb. 07	Hamilton	01	04	08
Stewart, John(D)	1809	June 16	Hamilton	01	04	08
Stewart, Joseph(C)	1806	Aug. 30	Butler	08	05	09
Stewart, Martin(B)	1814	July 04	Hamilton	01	03	05
Stewart, Mathew(C)	1812	April 15	Champaign	12	05	09
Stewart, Mathew(C)	1813	April 14	Champaign	12	05	17
Stewart, Matthew(C)	1807	March 11	Champaign	12	05	09
Stewart, Matthew(C)	1807	May 28	Champaign	12	05	17
Stewart, Moses B.(A)	1828	Feb. 02	Shelby	06	07	07

312

PURCHASER	YEAR	DATE	RESIDENCE	R	T	S
Stewart, Robert(C)	1831	Sept. 26	Butler	12	01	10
Stewart, Sam'l. W.(B)	1824	June 09	Wayne(Ind)	01	13	21
Stewart, Sam'l.(A)	1825	Jan. 28	Hamilton	01	02	22
Stewart, Samuel(A)	1814	June 21	Hamilton	01	03	23
Stewart, Samuel(B)	1816	Aug. 01	Hamilton	01	09	28
Stewart, Samuel(C)	1806	Aug. 18	Greene	08	05	15
Stewart, Samuel(C)	1808	Nov. 22	Butler	03	03	08
Stewart, Samuel(C)	1808	Nov. 22	Pennsylvania	08	05	12
Stewart, Samuel(C)	1809	June 22	Butler	03	03	08
Stewart, Samuel(C)	1816	Jan. 19	Greene	08	05	12
Stewart, Stephen(B)	1814	July 05	Hamilton	01	03	17
Stewart, Stephen(B)	1816	Oct. 01	Hamilton	02	03	27
Stewart, Stephen(B)	1817	Aug. 19	Cincinnati	02	03	21
Stewart, Thomas Jnr.(B)	1816	Feb. 24	Switzerland	01	02	01
Stewart, Thomas Jnr.(B)	1816	Aug. 03	Switzerland	01	03	33
Stewart, Thomas(B)	1814	Sept. 05	Hamilton	01	04	20
Stewart, Thomas(C)	1816	June 13	Champaign	12	05	01
Stewart, William J.(B)	1816	July 08	Switzerland	04	02	25
Stewart, William(A)	1809	Dec. 14	Miami	06	07	10
Stewart, William(A)	1814	Aug. 12	Cincinnati	03	10	36
Stewart, William(A)	1832	Jan. 23	Butler	01	10	05
Stewart, William(B)	1815	March 07	Dearborn(Ind	01	03	32
Stewart, William(C)	1801	Dec. 23	Hamilton	07	02	13
Stewart, William(C)	1813	June 11	Miami	11	01	29
Stewart, Willibay(A)	1831	Nov. 01	Logan	08	02	29
Stibbs, John(A)	1836	Nov. 05	Warren	03	12	22
Stick, Samuel(E)	1837	April 05	Butler	14	21	03
Stienbarger, Frederick(A)	1831	March 11	Shelby	06	07	07
Stiens, Francis(E)	1837	Jan. 09	Cincinnati	12	11	29
Stierlen, George(B)	1828	April 01	Dearborn(Ind	02	07	28
Stierlen, Gregori(B)	1833	Feb. 01	Dearborn(Ind	02	07	21
Stierlen, Gregori(B)	1833	Feb. 01	Dearborn(Ind	02	07	21
Stiffler, Christian(A)	1836	Dec. 14	Montgomery	04	11	30
Stiles, Asahel(A)	1833	May 22	Logan	08	01	10
Stiles, Asahel(A)	1833	June 03	Logan	08	01	09
Stiles, Asahel(C)	1836	Feb. 05	Logan	13	03	34
Stiles, Byrd(B)	1813	Sept. 02	Franklin(Ind	02	11	01
Stiles, Marcus(A)	1833	Sept. 07	Athens	08	01	11
Stillwill, Benjamin Rutty(A)	1831	Sept. 05	Hamilton	05	08	23
Stilwell, David(E)	1836	Sept. 02	Hamilton	12	12	06
Stilwell, Elias(A)	1815	Nov. 10	Preble	02	06	24
Stine, Daniel(A)	1806	June 23	Butler	01	04	33
Stineman, Daniel(A)	1811	Dec. 11	Butler	01	04	03
Stinson, Alexander(A)	1805	June 21	Montgomery	05	05	34
Stinson, William(C)	1804	Dec. 29	Greene	08	03	22
Stip, Isaac(E)	1814	Jan. 18	Greene	12	11	04
Stip, John Jnr.(C)	1812	March 16	Virginia	13	05	26
Stip, John Jr.(C)	1812	March 16	Virginia	13	05	32
Stip, John(C)	1813	April 29	Champaign	13	05	26
Stites, Johnathan(B)	1806	Feb. 26	Hamilton	01	05	20
Stites, Jonathan(C)	1814	Oct. 10	Champaign	08	06	30
Stites, Samuel(C)	1805	Dec. 12	Greene	08	03	31
Stites, Thomas(C)	1814	Sept. 28	Hamilton	09	06	14
Stitt, Samuel(C)	1801	Dec. 28	Hamilton	04	03	32
Stitt, Samuel(C)	1804	Sept. 07	Cincinnati	04	03	26
Stitt, William(C)	1801	Dec. 28	Hamilton	04	03	32
Stiver, Frederick(A)	1819	July 30	Preble	04	05	34
Stockdale, Eli(E)	1837	Feb. 13	Darke	15	19	18
Stockdale, John(B)	1812	Dec. 14	Pennsylvania	02	09	21
Stockdale, Thomas(E)	1814	Feb. 05	Pennsylvania	13	13	27
Stockdale, Thomas(E)	1814	July 05	Franklin(Ind	13	13	22
Stockden, John(A)	1804	Aug. 20	Butler	03	03	09
Stockinger, John(B)	1834	July 30	Germany	02	08	21
Stockinger, John(B)	1835	Oct. 13	Franklin(Ind	02	08	19
Stockman, John H.(C)	1817	July 28	Miami	13	02	08
Stockman, John H.(C)	1819	Aug. 07	Hamilton	13	02	08
Stockton, Hiram B.(A)	1815	June 23	Kentucky	06	08	30
Stockton, Jubal C.(A)	1815	June 23	Kentucky	06	08	30
Stockton, Will'm.(A)	1828	Nov. 07	Preble	01	09	11

PURCHASER	YEAR	DATE	RESIDENCE	R	T	S
Stoddard, Orrin(E)	1816	Feb. 14	?	13	14	21
Stodder, Seth(B)	1816	Nov. 06	Baltimore	03	02	03
Stodder, Seth(B)	1816	Nov. 06	Baltimore	03	02	04
Stodder, Seth(B)	1816	Nov. 06	Baltimore	03	03	25
Stodder, Seth(B)	1816	Nov. 06	Baltimore	02	01	06
Stodder, Seth(B)	1816	Nov. 11	Baltimore	03	03	34
Stodder, Seth(B)	1816	Nov. 11	Baltimore	02	01	05
Stoker, Jacob(A)	1816	June 10	Montgomery	06	03	22
Stoker, John(C)	1816	June 05	Montgomery	12	01	06
Stokes, Jarvis(C)	1824	July 06	Warren	11	02	11
Stome, Jacob(B)	1830	March 24	Hamilton	01	07	22
Stoms, Alfred Alonzo(B)	1836	Jan. 26	Dearborn(Ind	01	07	17
Stoms, William(B)	1832	May 23	Cincinnati	01	07	32
Stone, Andrew(E)	1836	Nov. 10	Darke	15	21	22
Stone, Andrew(E)	1836	Dec. 10	Darke	15	21	22
Stone, Asa(E)	1812	Aug. 29	Kentucky	12	14	14
Stone, Conaway(E)	1833	Feb. 22	Randolph(Ind	15	22	11
Stone, Daniel(E)	1816	Dec. 10	Wayne(Ind)	13	16	27
Stone, Ethan(E)	1811	Oct. 28	Hamilton	14	16	19
Stone, Ethan(E)	1811	Oct. 28	Cincinnati	13	17	31
Stone, James(B)	1818	April 06	Licking	03	04	33
Stone, James(B)	1818	April 06	Licking	03	04	25
Stone, James(B)	1818	April 06	Licking	03	04	28
Stone, James(E)	1833	Oct. 05	Randolph(Ind	15	23	36
Stone, Jesse(B)	1818	Dec. 21	Dearborn(Ind	03	07	13
Stone, John(A)	1829	Nov. 23	Darke	01	10	15
Stone, Peter(B)	1833	Jan. 30	Franklin(Ind	02	07	03
Stone, Samuel(B)	1817	Dec. 10	Licking	03	04	35
Stone, Samuel(B)	1817	Dec. 10	Licking	03	04	25
Stone, Samuel(B)	1817	Dec. 10	Licking	03	04	36
Stone, Thomas(D)	1808	Nov. 01	Hamilton	03	02	26
Stone, William(B)	1827	Oct. 26	Hamilton	01	08	36
Stoneberger, George(C)	1810	Oct. 02	Champaign	11	04	28
Stoneberger, John(C)	1805	April 15	Champaign	12	04	31
Stonebrakes, Sebastian(A)	1808	July 23	Butler	02	03	02
Stoner, Abraham(A)	1812	Jan. 03	Montgomery	04	03	04
Stoner, Benedict(A)	1815	Jan. 02	Preble	03	06	35
Stoner, Philip(A)	1803	Aug. 26	Clermont	04	04	33
Stoner, Philip(A)	1804	Nov. 09	Montgomery	04	03	05
Stoner, Sam'l. Jr.(E)	1837	Oct. 31	New York	15	22	35
Stoner, Sam'l. Jr.(E)	1837	Oct. 31	New York	15	22	25
Stoops, David(E)	1811	Oct. 23	Ind.Territry	13	12	33
Storer, Bellamy(A)	1819	May 18	Cincinnati	06	08	35
Storey, Edwin(B)	1832	May 05	Virginia	03	03	23
Storms, Henry(C)	1806	Aug. 01	Champaign	10	05	29
Stotsenburgh, Henry(A)	1836	March 23	Miami	03	12	14
Stottle, Anthony(E)	1836	Oct. 28	Dearborn(Ind	12	10	04
Stottle, John(E)	1836	Oct. 28	Dearborn(Ind	12	10	04
Stouffer, Jacob(A)	1832	Aug. 28	Montgomery	03	09	25
Stout, Aaron(D)	1808	Nov. 01	Hamilton	01	02	11
Stout, Abel(A)	1803	Dec. 17	Butler	02	05	20
Stout, Abel(A)	1812	Dec. 04	Butler	02	05	21
Stout, Abraham(A)	1831	Nov. 18	Muskingum	07	01	04
Stout, David(E)	1817	Sept. 15	Clinton	14	14	20
Stout, Elisha(D)	1812	March 17	Hamilton	01	02	08
Stout, Elisha(E)	1814	Aug. 22	Hamilton	13	13	19
Stout, Ira(D)	1812	March 17	Hamilton	01	02	08
Stout, Isaac(C)	1830	Dec. 09	Clark	13	02	09
Stout, Isaac(C)	1831	Feb. 05	Shelby	13	02	09
Stout, Job(B)	1814	July 25	Franklin(Ind	02	09	13
Stout, John(A)	1837	June 22	Richland	01	14	31
Stout, John(B)	1837	June 22	Richland	01	19	36
Stout, Jonathan(A)	1831	Nov. 18	Muskingum	07	01	04
Stout, Jonathan(B)	1813	Sept. 30	Hamilton	01	09	08
Stout, Levi(E)	1831	Sept. 22	Wayne(Ind)	14	19	22
Stout, Levi(E)	1836	May 13	Randolph(Ind	14	19	28
Stout, Michael(A)	1811	Oct. 28	Butler	02	04	07
Stoutenborough, Dan'l.(A)	1831	Aug. 27	Warren	04	07	19
Stoutenborough, Dan'l.(A)	1831	Aug. 27	Warren	03	08	36

314

PURCHASER	YEAR	DATE	RESIDENCE	R	T	S
Stoutenborough, Dan'l.(A)	1831	Oct. 19	Warren	04	07	18
Stoutsman, Jacob(A)	1810	Aug. 01	Montgomery	05	04	15
Stover, Henry(A)	1829	March 18	Montgomery	04	06	33
Stover, Jacob(A)	1805	June 18	Montgomery	05	05	19
Stover, Jacob(A)	1808	Oct. 20	Montgomery	05	04	07
Stover, Jacob(A)	1814	June 08	Montgomery	05	04	06
Stover, Jacob(E)	1838	May 21	Montgomery	15	22	27
Stover, Samuel(E)	1811	Dec. 18	Wayne(Ind)	14	15	32
Stow, Solomon(B)	1835	Feb. 04	Switzerland	02	02	30
Stowder, Joseph(A)	1807	Jan. 30	Montgomery	04	05	25
Strader, George(A)	1817	Nov. 19	Preble	03	06	30
Strader, Henry(A)	1808	Nov. 21	Preble	02	08	18
Straight, Peter(A)	1834	April 02	Darke	01	13	23
Strain, James(E)	1816	Oct. 16	Greene	14	21	13
Strasback, William(B)	1808	Jan. 11	Nor.Carolina	01	14	04
Strasback, William(B)	1808	Jan. 11	Nor.Carolina	01	15	33
Strasberger, Frederick(C)	1811	Sept. 02	Greene	10	04	23
Strasburger, John(C)	1824	June 09	Greene	08	03	29
Strattan, Eli(A)	1829	Dec. 19	Preble	01	07	21
Strattan, Mahlon Jr.(A)	1836	Sept. 19	Greene	02	14	35
Stratton, Eli(A)	1818	Feb. 16	Preble	01	07	21
Stratton, William(E)	1838	Oct. 09	Pennsylvania	14	20	05
Straw, James(E)	1811	Nov. 11	Wayne(Ind)	12	15	14
Strawn, Jacob(B)	1818	Feb. 16	Pennsylvania	01	12	22
Strayer, Daniel(C)	1831	Aug. 08	Logan	13	03	11
Strech, William Senr.(C)	1805	Nov. 20	Kentucky	12	04	09
Street, Aaron(C)	1805	Feb. 16	Warren	05	02	08
Street, Charles(A)	1818	May 29	Preble	01	10	19
Street, John(A)	1813	April 14	Preble	01	07	03
Streight, Jacob(A)	1829	June 15	Preble	01	13	13
Streight, Rich'd.(A)	1829	June 09	Preble	01	13	13
Strickler, Martin(C)	1804	Dec. 28	Greene	11	04	23
Strickler, Martin(C)	1804	Dec. 28	Greene	11	04	17
Stringer, Eli(B)	1814	June 06	Franklin(Ind	02	09	31
Stringer, Eli(E)	1811	Oct. 21	Franklin(Ind	12	12	33
Stringer, Eli(E)	1811	Oct. 28	Franklin(Ind	13	13	27
Stringer, Eli(E)	1814	Sept. 22	Franklin(Ind	13	11	05
Stringer, Eli(E)	1817	Aug. 14	Franklin(Ind	13	11	21
Stringer, William(E)	1833	May 13	Franklin(Ind	13	11	08
Strong, Nathan(C)	1831	Dec. 15	Montgomery	12	02	21
Strong, William(B)	1813	July 29	Dearborn(Ind	02	05	35
Strootman, John G. G.(A)	1839	Jan. 22	Cincinnati	02	15	36
Stroube, Christopher(B)	1813	Nov. 06	Kentucky	01	09	18
Stroube, John(B)	1813	Nov. 06	Kentucky	01	09	18
Stroube, Nicholas Anslem(E)	1835	June 22	Kentucky	12	12	29
Stroud, Asa B.(A)	1836	Oct. 28	Hamilton	01	15	15
Stroud, Joseph(B)	1815	Oct. 06	Dearborn(Ind	01	06	10
Stroud, Joshua(B)	1815	Sept. 19	Dearborn(Ind	01	06	32
Stroud, Reese(A)	1836	Dec. 01	Hamilton	01	15	26
Stroud, Reese(B)	1833	Nov. 04	Dearborn(Ind	01	07	03
Stuart, Andrew(C)	1814	Nov. 07	Kentucky	10	03	07
Stuart, Arthur(A)	1806	May 29	Montgomery	06	04	04
Stuart, James(A)	1819	Aug. 02	Miami	05	08	23
Stuart, John(C)	1804	Sept. 03	Montgomery	06	02	11
Stuart, John(C)	1804	Sept. 03	Montgomery	07	02	26
Stuart, Pallus P.(A)	1804	Sept. 08	Cincinnati	04	03	14
Stuart, Pallus P.(C)	1804	Sept. 24	Cincinnati	06	01	19
Stuart, Pallus P.(C)	1804	Dec. 31	Cincinnati	07	03	04
Stuart, Pallus P.(C)	1804	Dec. 31	Cincinnati	09	04	02
Stuart, Pallus P.(C)	1804	Dec. 31	Cincinnati	09	05	32
Stuart, Samuel(A)	1816	Oct. 29	Miami	06	07	08
Stuart, William(A)	1801	April 27	Hamilton	02	04	32
Stuart, William(A)	1811	Sept. 30	Butler	01	04	36
Stuart, William(A)	1814	Jan. 07	Butler	02	03	17
Stuart, William(C)	1805	Dec. 05	Kentucky	12	01	21
Stubbs, John(A)	1814	Sept. 10	Warren	02	06	05
Stubbs, John(A)	1814	Oct. 28	Warren	02	06	05
Stubbs, John(A)	1826	Feb. 17	Preble	01	10	22
Stubbs, John(A)	1827	Dec. 24	Preble	01	10	22

PURCHASER	YEAR	DATE	RESIDENCE	R	T	S
Stubbs, Joseph(A)	1805	June 14	Butler	03	04	33
Stubbs, Joseph(A)	1805	June 14	Butler	03	04	34
Stubbs, Joseph(A)	1808	March 29	Butler	01	07	36
Stubbs, Nathan(A)	1804	Dec. 06	Butler	03	03	03
Stubbs, Nathan(A)	1811	Dec. 11	Preble	02	06	35
Stubbs, Nathan(A)	1812	Feb. 01	Butler	02	07	30
Stubbs, Nathan(A)	1813	Aug. 10	Butler	01	07	36
Stubbs, Samuel(A)	1805	June 14	Butler	03	04	33
Stubbs, Samuel(A)	1805	June 14	Butler	03	04	28
Stubbs, Samuel(A)	1805	June 14	Butler	03	04	27
Stubbs, Samuel(E)	1836	May 09	Preble	11	12	36
Stubbs, Zephaniah(E)	1832	Jan. 17	Franklin(Ind	12	12	04
Stuckman, Anthony(A)	1837	Dec. 16	Cincinnati	02	14	01
Studabaker, Abm. Jr.(A)	1829	Jan. 13	Darke	02	11	15
Studabaker, Abraham(A)	1816	Nov. 02	Miami	01	12	09
Studabaker, Abraham(A)	1816	Nov. 02	Miami	01	12	04
Studebaker, Ab'm.(A)	1828	Jan. 21	Darke	02	11	15
Studebaker, Abraham(A)	1805	Aug. 20	Warren	05	08	31
Studebaker, Abraham(A)	1808	June 06	Miami	04	09	30
Studebaker, Abraham(A)	1815	Aug. 25	Darke	03	09	05
Studebaker, David(A)	1810	Jan. 15	Darke	02	11	20
Studebaker, Henry(A)	1831	March 26	Miami	04	07	26
Studebaker, Hy.(A)	1830	Feb. 22	Miami	04	07	36
Studebaker, Peter(A)	1810	Jan. 15	Darke	02	11	20
Study, Henry(E)	1821	Jan. 31	Wayne(Ind)	13	17	12
Study, Henry(E)	1823	May 28	Wayne(Ind)	13	17	12
Study, Henry(E)	1829	Nov. 25	Wayne(Ind)	13	17	11
Study, Jacob(E)	1818	Dec. 03	Wayne(Ind)	13	18	36
Studybaker, Abraham(A)	1814	Dec. 07	Darke	02	11	11
Studybaker, John(A)	1809	June 26	Darke	02	11	10
Studybaker, Mary(A)	1814	Aug. 16	Darke	02	11	10
Stump, David(A)	1834	Sept. 04	Darke	02	12	04
Stump, David(A)	1837	Jan. 05	Darke	01	12	11
Stump, George(A)	1811	March 18	Butler	04	03	35
Stump, George(A)	1815	Aug. 11	Montgomery	03	06	36
Stump, George(A)	1825	May 25	Butler	04	05	19
Stump, George(A)	1825	May 25	Butler	04	05	06
Stump, George(A)	1825	May 25	Butler	04	05	30
Stump, John Mich'l.(A)	1834	March 17	Montgomery	01	12	03
Stump, Leonard(E)	1816	Oct. 23	Wayne(Ind)	12	18	36
Stump, Michael(A)	1832	Dec. 29	Preble	01	12	21
Sturges, James(E)	1817	Nov. 22	Warren	12	17	25
Sturm, Henry(C)	1814	Feb. 25	Champaign	13	02	01
Sturm, Henry(C)	1814	Aug. 27	Champaign	13	02	01
Sturm, Jacob(C)	1831	April 11	Shelby	13	02	02
Sturm, William(C)	1832	Feb. 18	Shelby	12	02	24
Stutsman, David(A)	1815	Dec. 12	Montgomery	05	05	15
Stutsman, David(E)	1836	Nov. 26	Montgomery	15	20	07
Stutsman, David(E)	1836	Nov. 26	Montgomery	15	20	08
Stutsman, Elizabeth(E)	1836	Nov. 26	Montgomery	15	20	06
Stutsman, Elizabeth(E)	1836	Dec. 05	Montgomery	15	20	06
Stutsman, Jacob(A)	1805	Dec. 13	Montgomery	05	04	30
Stutsman, Jacob(A)	1830	Dec. 04	Montgomery	04	07	28
Stutsman, Nicholas(E)	1836	Nov. 26	Montgomery	15	20	05
Stutz, John(A)	1821	Nov. 19	Warren	02	10	03
Stutzman, David(A)	1814	June 14	Montgomery	05	05	22
Stutzman, David(A)	1819	June 05	Montgomery	05	05	21
Stutzman, Nathaniel(A)	1814	Oct. 20	Montgomery	04	05	02
Sucher, Bartholomew(A)	1834	June 21	Montgomery	03	10	20
Sulgrove, James(A)	1803	Dec. 12	Butler	04	03	03
Sullivan, Parker(C)	1811	Sept. 07	Champaign	12	04	18
Sullivan, Parker(C)	1829	July 31	Champaign	12	04	18
Sullivan, Samuel(A)	1836	Sept. 23	Miami	03	12	22
Sulser, James(B)	1816	Sept. 07	Wayne(Ind)	01	12	26
Suman, John(A)	1818	March 23	Montgomery	02	14	35
Suman, Peter(A)	1818	Jan. 06	Montgomery	02	13	02
Sumey, John(E)	1811	Oct. 25	Wayne(Ind)	14	14	07
Sumey, John(E)	1811	Nov. 22	Preble	12	16	01
Summa, Peter(A)	1810	Sept. 12	Miami	05	06	01

PURCHASER	YEAR	DATE	RESIDENCE	R	T	S
Summer, David(B)	1827	Aug. 21	Dearborn(Ind	02	07	36
Summers, David(E)	1837	Dec. 16	Cincinnati	14	20	36
Summers, Jefferson L.(B)	1836	April 12	Darke	01	17	23
Summers, Jefferson L.(B)	1837	Feb. 24	Darke	01	17	23
Summers, John(E)	1815	Sept. 08	Wayne(Ind)	13	15	26
Summers, Joseph(B)	1813	May 31	Hamilton	01	08	24
Summers, Simeon(E)	1815	Aug. 26	Wayne(Ind)	13	15	26
Sumner, Orren(A)	1828	Dec. 30	Darke	03	09	17
Sumption, Charles(A)	1815	July 06	Darke	02	12	19
Sumption, Charles(A)	1816	Oct. 29	Darke	01	12	10
Sumption, Charles(A)	1831	Aug. 11	Darke	01	12	10
Sumption, John(E)	1836	Dec. 15	Randolph(Ind	14	21	19
Sumpton, Charles(A)	1814	Oct. 07	Darke	02	11	14
Sumwalt, Godfrey(E)	1820	Sept. 06	Montgomery	13	20	28
Sumwalt, John(E)	1820	April 14	Montgomery	13	19	21
Sunderland, Francis(C)	1804	Dec. 24	Montgomery	10	02	01
Sunderland, Francis(C)	1804	Dec. 24	Montgomery	10	02	01
Sunderland, John(C)	1801	Dec. 19	Cincinnati	06	02	20
Sunderland, John(C)	1801	Dec. 31	Hamilton	04	03	02
Sunderland, Joseph(A)	1832	March 17	Montgomery	05	10	26
Sunderland, Peter(C)	1804	Sept. 03	Montgomery	06	02	26
Sunderland, Peter(C)	1804	Dec. 24	Montgomery	10	02	01
Sunderland, Richard(A)	1805	Aug. 05	Montgomery	06	03	14
Sunderland, Richard(A)	1818	Oct. 12	Montgomery	04	11	10
Sunderland, William(C)	1801	Dec. 30	Hamilton	06	02	20
Surber, Henry(B)	1832	Nov. 09	Switzerland	02	03	35
Surber, Henry(B)	1836	March 26	Switzerland	02	03	35
Surface, Andrew(A)	1811	Nov. 16	Preble	02	08	10
Surface, Henry(E)	1837	May 12	Preble	15	21	06
Sutherland, John Jnr.(B)	1816	Feb. 28	?	01	14	19
Sutherland, John(A)	1803	April 04	Hamilton	02	04	36
Sutherland, John(A)	1806	Nov. 06	Montgomery	06	02	03
Sutherland, John(A)	1803	April 04	Hamilton	03	02	31
Sutherland, John(A)	1808	April 09	Butler	06	02	03
Sutherland, John(A)	1810	April 11	?	05	05	14
Sutherland, John(B)	1817	Sept. 23	Butler	02	04	08
Sutherland, John(B)	1817	Sept. 23	Butler	03	06	36
Sutherland, John(B)	1817	Oct. 27	?	02	04	18
Sutherland, John(B)	1817	Oct. 27	?	03	05	13
Sutherland, John(C)	1810	Dec. 12	Butler	03	02	26
Sutherland, John(E)	1812	May 05	Ohio	14	16	14
Sutherland, John(E)	1824	June 16	Butler	14	16	28
Sutherland, John(E)	1824	Aug. 13	Butler	14	16	28
Sutton, Amos(E)	1814	Aug. 23	Butler	13	14	23
Sutton, Amos(E)	1837	Aug. 05	Randolph(Ind	15	21	22
Sutton, Benjamin(A)	1814	March 11	Preble	01	08	29
Sutton, Benjamin(B)	1808	Aug. 16	Greene	01	12	27
Sutton, Cornelius(E)	1837	Feb. 01	Indiana	15	21	21
Sutton, David(C)	1801	Dec. 26	Hamilton	04	03	35
Sutton, Enoch(C)	1811	Dec. 07	Hamilton	11	01	15
Sutton, Enoch(C)	1828	June 02	Miami	11	01	22
Sutton, Enoch(C)	1831	Aug. 30	Miami	13	02	03
Sutton, George(B)	1825	May 16	Switzerland	02	08	24
Sutton, George(B)	1832	Feb. 28	Franklin(Ind	01	08	20
Sutton, Hannibal(E)	1836	March 21	Franklin(Ind	12	10	08
Sutton, Isaac(A)	1835	June 04	Pennsylvania	01	13	23
Sutton, Jacob(A)	1820	Jan. 10	Preble	01	12	02
Sutton, James Junior(E)	1814	June 28	Butler	13	14	07
Sutton, James(A)	1804	April 18	Butler	02	06	03
Sutton, James(A)	1818	June 09	Preble	02	10	20
Sutton, James(C)	1801	Dec. 31	Hamilton	04	02	28
Sutton, James(C)	1804	Aug. 28	Butler	04	02	29
Sutton, James(C)	1814	Aug. 08	Wayne(Ind)	13	14	17
Sutton, John(B)	1834	Feb. 19	Switzerland	03	04	27
Sutton, John(E)	1818	Sept. 28	Warren	13	17	22
Sutton, Joniah(C)	1812	July 11	Champaign	08	06	06
Sutton, Joseph H.(E)	1837	Aug. 05	Randolph(Ind	15	21	20
Sutton, Joshua(B)	1834	Aug. 20	Dearborn(Ind	03	04	22
Sutton, Peter(C)	1826	Jan. 24	Champaign	10	04	26

317

PURCHASER	YEAR	DATE	RESIDENCE	R	T	S
Sutton, Peter(C)	1827	Jan. 05	Miami	10	02	11
Sutton, Reuben(B)	1815	Jan. 06	Hamilton	01	06	09
Sutton, Samuel Wards(E)	1835	Jan. 05	Randolph(Ind	14	20	07
Sutton, Thomas(E)	1837	Feb. 01	Indiana	15	21	28
Suydam, Jacob(B)	1816	July 15	Warren	02	03	28
Swaford, Isaac(B)	1808	Jan. 20	Butler	01	11	04
Swaford, William(A)	1805	Nov. 28	Butler	02	06	34
Swaford, William(B)	1808	Jan. 11	Butler	01	11	04
Swailes, Rice(A)	1807	March 28	Warren	06	04	06
Swain, Bethuel(A)	1816	Aug. 08	Preble	01	09	33
Swain, Charles W.(B)	1830	April 12	Clermont	01	16	26
Swain, David(B)	1817	Nov. 08	Franklin(Ind	01	11	15
Swain, Elihu Jr.(E)	1829	Jan. 29	Wayne(Ind)	13	18	22
Swain, Elihu(E)	1815	Sept. 25	Wayne(Ind)	13	18	21
Swain, Ira(E)	1836	Jan. 23	Randolph(Ind	13	18	05
Swain, Jacob(A)	1814	Nov. 14	Preble	02	08	13
Swain, Jacob(A)	1814	Nov. 14	Preble	02	08	24
Swain, Silvanas(B)	1815	Aug. 09	Nor.Carolina	01	11	22
Swallow, Garret(B)	1817	Sept. 22	Hamilton	02	04	08
Swallow, Garret(B)	1817	Oct. 08	Hamilton	02	04	17
Swallow, George(E)	1838	April 20	Montgomery	14	22	28
Swallow, John(A)	1812	Jan. 23	Montgomery	06	03	20
Swallow, Silvanus(A)	1808	June 14	Montgomery	06	03	29
Swan, Benjamin C.(A)	1814	Aug. 26	Piqua	02	06	19
Swan, Levi Blakesley(B)	1835	Jan. 05	Dearborn(Ind	01	06	05
Swan, Levi Blakesly(B)	1836	Jan. 22	Dearborn(Ind	01	06	05
Swan, Matthew(B)	1831	Aug. 15	Dearborn(Ind	01	06	15
Swan, Rich'd.(C)	1831	June 02	Logan	13	03	15
Swan, Rich'd.(C)	1831	June 02	Logan	13	03	09
Swan, Robert(B)	1805	Oct. 07	Hamilton	02	11	22
Swander, Henry(A)	1831	Oct. 24	Shelby	06	08	03
Swank, Geo.(A)	1831	June 02	Montgomery	04	07	20
Swank, George(A)	1831	May 05	Montgomery	03	08	13
Swank, George(A)	1831	May 05	Montgomery	03	08	13
Swank, George(A)	1832	Aug. 23	Montgomery	04	07	18
Swank, Jacob(A)	1813	Sept. 30	Hamilton	01	04	12
Swank, Jacob(A)	1827	June 08	Montgomery	04	06	15
Swank, John(A)	1814	May 31	Montgomery	04	05	04
Swank, Peter(A)	1807	Feb. 27	Clermont	04	05	12
Swank, Peter(A)	1811	June 19	Montgomery	04	05	12
Swann, Robert(B)	1814	Nov. 26	Franklin(Ind	02	11	10
Swanson, Edward J.(B)	1813	Dec. 28	?	02	12	35
Swartsel, Abraham(A)	1804	Aug. 16	Montgomery	04	04	28
Swartsell, Matthias(A)	1802	Nov. 19	Pennsylvania	05	02	20
Swartsell, Matthias(A)	1805	Dec. 27	Warren	04	04	25
Swartsell, Philip(C)	1801	Dec. 19	Hamilton	04	03	22
Swartzell, Philip(A)	1806	Nov. 13	Warren	04	09	12
Swartzell, Philip(A)	1806	Nov. 13	Warren	04	09	13
Swartzley, John(A)	1837	March 01	Cincinnati	01	13	03
Swartzley, John(A)	1837	May 15	Montgomery	01	13	02
Swearengen, Charles(C)	1810	Dec. 12	Butler	09	02	22
Swearingen, Charles(A)	1804	Oct. 01	Butler	03	04	31
Swearingen, Charles(A)	1807	June 04	Butler	01	07	09
Swearingen, Isaac S.(A)	1816	June 13	Hamilton	01	02	35
Swearingen, Isaac S.(B)	1815	March 01	Butler	01	08	15
Swearingen, Isaac(A)	1808	Jan. 11	Butler	06	07	10
Swearingen, John A.(C)	1813	Dec. 14	Champaign	08	05	35
Sweeney, Samuel(A)	1836	Sept. 03	Butler	03	12	10
Sweet, Joshua(C)	1806	Aug. 11	Champaign	09	06	30
Sweney, William(C)	1801	Dec. 10	Hamilton	04	03	03
Swenk, Jacob(A)	1810	Aug. 14	Montgomery	04	03	11
Swerer, John(A)	1828	March 05	Preble	01	09	15
Swerer, Peter(A)	1815	Oct. 18	Butler	01	09	23
Swerer, Peter(E)	1837	Feb. 07	Preble	13	18	02
Swerer, Peter(E)	1837	Feb. 15	Preble	13	18	02
Swesey, John(B)	1833	June 22	Dearborn(Ind	03	08	13
Swesey, John(B)	1833	June 22	Dearborn(Ind	03	08	13
Swett, Wm. P.(B)	1814	May 03	Butler	01	09	04
Swift, Christian(E)	1813	Aug. 23	Warren	13	12	15

318

PURCHASER	YEAR	DATE	RESIDENCE	R	T	S
Swift, James(E)	1833	June 17	Wayne(Ind)	12	17	24
Swift, James(E)	1833	Oct. 11	Wayne(Ind)	13	12	17
Swift, Jno. T.(B)	1836	Dec. 13	Switzerland	03	04	28
Swift, Minerva(B)	1817	Nov. 15	Hamilton	02	06	29
Swift, Noah(B)	1831	Oct. 19	Franklin(Ind	02	08	36
Swift, Richard(E)	1835	Nov. 09	Franklin(Ind	13	12	30
Swiggett, Thomas(E)	1832	June 15	Franklin(Ind	13	12	30
Swinehart, Adam(A)	1804	Sept. 24	Montgomery	04	04	30
Swinehart, Adam(A)	1804	Nov. 21	Montgomery	03	05	12
Swinehart, Adam(A)	1809	Dec. 12	Montgomery	04	04	30
Swinehart, Ann Eliza(A)	1806	March 26	Montgomery	02	07	17
Swinehart, Ann Eliza(A)	1811	Aug. 13	Montgomery	02	07	17
Swinehart, Gabriel(A)	1806	March 26	Montgomery	02	07	17
Swinehart, Gabriel(A)	1811	Aug. 13	Montgomery	02	07	17
Swinehart, Jacob(A)	1805	Dec. 12	Pennsylvania	04	04	10
Swinehart, Jacob(A)	1809	Dec. 12	Montgomery	04	04	18
Swinehart, Jacob(A)	1812	Nov. 21	Montgomery	04	04	17
Swinehart, John(A)	1805	July 01	Montgomery	04	04	30
Swinehart, John(A)	1810	Aug. 14	Montgomery	03	05	26
Swinehart, John(A)	1831	July 06	Montgomery	01	11	26
Swinehart, Peter(A)	1804	Nov. 30	Pennsylvania	04	04	31
Swinehart, Peter(A)	1810	April 11	Montgomery	04	04	31
Swineheart, Adam(B)	1806	March 26	Montgomery	02	13	35
Swineheart, Salome(B)	1806	March 26	Montgomery	02	13	35
Swisher, Henry(A)	1815	Oct. 14	Montgomery	03	11	32
Swisher, Henry(A)	1816	March 13	Montgomery	04	10	08
Swisher, Jesse(A)	1804	May 26	Kentucky	03	07	27
Swisher, Jesse(A)	1811	Nov. 27	Preble	03	07	21
Swisher, Jesse(A)	1813	Oct. 30	Preble	03	07	14
Swisher, John(A)	1831	Aug. 24	Darke	03	11	13
Swisher, William(A)	1803	Oct. 07	Kentucky	03	04	02
Swisher, William(A)	1805	Feb. 07	Montgomery	03	05	23
Swisher, William(A)	1805	Nov. 04	Montgomery	03	07	33
Swisher, William(A)	1811	Oct. 15	Preble	03	04	10
Swisher, William(A)	1812	Aug. 11	Preble	03	07	15
Swisher, William(A)	1815	Feb. 06	Montgomery	03	07	13
Swope, John(C)	1808	Jan. 13	Virginia	11	02	09
Swope, John(C)	1808	Jan. 13	Virginia	11	02	09
Swope, John(C)	1808	Jan. 13	Virginia	11	02	02
Swope, John(C)	1808	Jan. 13	Virginia	11	02	02
Swope, John(C)	1808	Jan. 13	Virginia	11	02	01
Swope, John(C)	1814	Jan. 24	Virginia	10	03	33
Swope, Michael(E)	1816	May 27	Wayne(Ind)	13	16	08
Sybert, John(C)	1831	Aug. 25	Champaign	12	03	23
Sylvester, Job(B)	1817	Dec. 26	Dearborn(Ind	02	06	33
Sylvester, Job(B)	1818	Jan. 15	Dearborn(Ind	02	06	27
Sylvester, Joseph(B)	1818	Feb. 28	Dearborn(Ind	02	06	32
Symmes, Americus(A)	1837	Feb. 22	Butler	02	13	01
Symmes, Daniel(C)	1806	Feb. 01	Cincinnati	06	02	22
Symmes, Daniel(C)	1806	Feb. 01	Cincinnati	06	02	22
Symmes, Daniel(C)	1806	Feb. 01	Cincinnati	06	02	22
Symmes, Daniel(C)	1806	Feb. 01	Cincinnati	06	02	22
Symmes, Daniel(D)	1808	Nov. 07	Cincinnati	02	02	08
Symmes, Jeremiah(C)	1810	Dec. 12	Champaign	09	04	24
Symmes, Peyton S.(A)	1814	Nov. 04	Cincinnati	02	01	11
Symmes, Peyton S.(A)	1815	June 01	Cincinnati	01	02	26
Symmes, Peyton S.(A)	1815	June 01	Cincinnati	01	02	36
Symmes, Peyton S.(A)	1816	Jan. 20	Cincinnati	01	02	26
Symmes, Peyton S.(A)	1816	May 01	Cincinnati	01	02	26
Symmes, Peyton S.(A)	1836	Dec. 01	Cincinnati	01	14	20
Symmes, Peyton S.(A)	1836	Dec. 01	Cincinnati	01	14	33
Symmes, Peyton S.(A)	1836	Dec. 01	Cincinnati	02	14	14
Symmes, Peyton S.(A)	1836	Dec. 01	Cincinnati	02	15	29
Symmes, Peyton S.(A)	1836	Dec. 01	Cincinnati	04	11	07
Symmes, Peyton S.(A)	1836	Dec. 01	Cincinnati	04	11	07
Symmes, Peyton S.(A)	1836	Dec. 01	Cincinnati	04	11	31
Symmes, Peyton S.(A)	1836	Dec. 01	Cincinnati	02	13	26
Symmes, Peyton S.(A)	1836	Dec. 01	Cincinnati	01	15	14
Symmes, Peyton S.(A)	1837	March 01	Cincinnati	02	14	12

PURCHASER	YEAR	DATE	RESIDENCE	R	T	S
Symmes, Peyton S.(A)	1837	March 01	Cincinnati	02	14	36
Symmes, Peyton S.(A)	1838	April 02	Cincinnati	02	14	23
Symmes, Peyton S.(B)	1814	July 27	Cincinnati	02	09	26
Symmes, Peyton S.(B)	1814	Sept. 01	Cincinnati	01	09	19
Symmes, Peyton S.(B)	1814	Nov. 23	Cincinnati	01	10	28
Symmes, Peyton S.(B)	1815	Jan. 02	Cincinnati	01	10	33
Symmes, Peyton S.(B)	1815	Sept. 23	?	01	05	07
Symmes, Peyton S.(B)	1815	Oct. 02	Cincinnati	01	04	31
Symmes, Peyton S.(B)	1816	Jan. 20	Cincinnati	01	07	19
Symmes, Peyton S.(B)	1816	May 01	Cincinnati	01	07	19
Symmes, Peyton S.(B)	1814	Aug. 20	Cincinnati	02	03	03
Symmes, Peyton S.(B)	1814	Oct. 01	Cincinnati	01	03	15
Symmes, Peyton S.(B)	1837	March 01	Cincinnati	01	18	14
Symmes, Peyton S.(B)	1837	March 01	Cincinnati	01	18	23
Symmes, Peyton S.(E)	1814	Aug. 08	Hamilton	02	03	17
Symmes, Peyton S.(E)	1815	Oct. 02	Cincinnati	14	16	28
Symmes, Peyton S.(E)	1836	Dec. 01	Cincinnati	15	22	02
Symmes, Peyton S.(E)	1840	Aug. 01	Cincinnati	11	11	14
Symmes, Peyton S.(E)	1840	Aug. 01	Cincinnati	12	11	22
Symmons, John(B)	1812	Aug. 03	Franklin(Ind	01	09	08
Symms, Jeremiah(C)	1805	Sept. 18	Champaign	09	04	24
Symons, Lydia(E)	1812	Oct. 19	Wayne(Ind)	12	16	12
Symons, Micajah(E)	1811	Nov. 11	Wayne(Ind)	14	17	18
Symons, Sarah(E)	1812	Oct. 19	Wayne(Ind)	12	16	12
Syms, Joseph(C)	1813	May 31	Champaign	11	04	14
Sype, Joseph(A)	1831	April 04	Warren	05	07	12
Sype, Joseph(A)	1831	Nov. 25	Warren	05	07	11
Taber, Benjamin(C)	1813	May 07	Champaign	11	05	13
Tabler, Christian(C)	1816	June 07	Maryland	12	02	33
Tabler, Christian(C)	1816	June 07	Maryland	12	02	34
Tabler, Christian(C)	1816	June 07	Maryland	12	02	27
Tabor, Bennet(C)	1807	Jan. 29	Champaign	11	05	14
Tabor, Bennet(C)	1812	April 15	Champaign	11	05	14
Tabor, Bennet(C)	1813	June 04	Champaign	11	05	19
Tabor, Elisha(C)	1807	Aug. 11	Warren	11	05	20
Tague, Andrew(B)	1824	July 21	Miami	02	03	09
Tague, George(B)	1817	Aug. 27	Switzerland	01	02	22
Tague, John(B)	1817	Nov. 19	Switzerland	03	03	12
Tague, Samuel(A)	1811	Dec. 11	Montgomery	05	07	28
Talbert, Job(B)	1817	Aug. 15	Preble	01	11	22
Talbert, Nathan(C)	1802	Dec. 28	Hamilton	06	02	27
Talbert, Thomas(A)	1814	Aug. 02	Preble	03	04	21
Talbot, Sampson(C)	1804	Sept. 26	Greene	12	04	01
Talbot, Sampson(E)	1813	Nov. 06	Champaign	11	03	08
Talbot, Theodore F.(B)	1818	July 27	Kentucky	02	02	19
Talbott, Archibald(B)	1814	June 22	Butler	01	09	30
Talbott, Archibald(B)	1814	June 22	Butler	02	09	26
Talbott, Demovil(C)	1813	April 15	Kentucky	13	01	04
Talbott, Demovil(C)	1813	April 15	Kentucky	13	02	34
Talbott, Demovil(C)	1813	April 15	Kentucky	13	02	28
Talbott, Demovil(C)	1813	April 15	Kentucky	13	02	27
Talbott, Rodham(A)	1813	March 30	Kentucky	07	01	19
Talbott, Sampson(C)	1813	Nov. 06	Champaign	11	03	08
Talburt, Nathan(A)	1802	Jan. 14	Hamilton	05	05	02
Talkington, James(A)	1837	Feb. 14	Hamilton	02	15	19
Talkington, James(A)	1837	Feb. 14	Hamilton	02	15	31
Talkington, Stephen(B)	1814	Nov. 30	Ind.Territry	01	07	01
Tamplin, James(C)	1813	April 14	Champaign	09	04	14
Tamsett, John(C)	1804	Dec. 31	Warren	05	03	15
Tamsett, Samuel(C)	1801	Dec. 25	Hamilton	04	04	09
Tamsett, Samuel(C)	1801	Dec. 25	Hamilton	04	04	05
Tamsett, Samuel(C)	1804	Dec. 31	Warren	05	03	15
Tanehill, James(C)	1815	Feb. 09	Butler	11	03	07
Tanehill, Ninian(C)	1815	Feb. 09	Butler	11	03	07
Tann, Benjamin(Black)(B)	1837	April 21	Darke	01	16	01
Tanner, James(A)	1814	April 07	Preble	02	09	01
Tanner, James(B)	1811	Feb. 01	Greene	02	11	02
Tanner, Thomas(B)	1817	Sept. 16	Dearborn(Ind	02	05	13
Tapley, Phillip Preston(B)	1815	Dec. 26	Cincinnati	02	03	10

PURCHASER	YEAR	DATE	RESIDENCE	R	T	S
Tapp, Newton H.(B)	1815	Oct. 13	Kentucky	02	02	32
Tapp, Newton Harrison(B)	1832	May 24	Switzerland	02	02	29
Tappin, Samuel(B)	1807	April 17	New Jersey	01	11	08
Tappin, Samuel(B)	1811	Oct. 05	Franklin(Ind	01	11	08
Tarnestt, John(C)	1802	Dec. 23	Hamilton	04	04	17
Tarnsett, John(C)	1802	Dec. 23	Hamilton	04	04	12
Tarpening, Juliana(A)	1813	May 06	Hamilton	01	02	21
Tarpenning, Juliana(A)	1812	June 04	Hamilton	01	02	34
Tartar, Jacob(E)	1813	April 09	Franklin(Ind	13	13	03
Tartar, Jacob(E)	1813	Nov. 27	Franklin(Ind	13	14	34
Tasset, Peter(B)	1838	April 25	Cincinnati	03	05	23
Tatman, James(C)	1802	Dec. 31	Hamilton	08	03	22
Tatman, James(C)	1802	Dec. 31	Hamilton	08	03	22
Tatman, James(C)	1808	Dec. 27	Ohio	15	03	31
Tatman, James(C)	1808	Dec. 27	Ohio	14	04	36
Tatman, Joseph(C)	1802	Dec. 31	Hamilton	08	03	27
Tatman, Joseph(C)	1804	Dec. 29	Greene	08	03	36
Tatman, Joseph(C)	1808	Dec. 27	Ohio	15	03	31
Tatman, Joseph(C)	1808	Dec. 27	Ohio	14	04	36
Tatum, Matthew(B)	1815	Sept. 15	Franklin(Ind	01	11	03
Tayler, William(E)	1830	Aug. 12	Wayne(Ind)	13	18	24
Taylor, Agness(B)	1806	Oct. 23	So. Carolina	02	09	03
Taylor, Alexander(C)	1811	Oct. 16	Virginia	12	04	24
Taylor, Alexander(C)	1811	Oct. 16	Virginia	13	03	09
Taylor, Alexander(C)	1815	Oct. 18	Virginia	12	04	34
Taylor, Alexander(C)	1815	Oct. 18	Virginia	12	04	30
Taylor, Alexander(C)	1815	Oct. 18	Virginia	12	04	35
Taylor, Alexander(C)	1815	Oct. 18	Virginia	12	04	28
Taylor, Alexander(C)	1815	Oct. 18	Virginia	13	04	32
Taylor, Alexander(C)	1817	Oct. 13	Champaign	12	04	29
Taylor, Archibald(C)	1817	Oct. 13	Champaign	12	04	17
Taylor, Asher(A)	1818	Dec. 04	Preble	03	04	15
Taylor, Benjamin(E)	1815	Aug. 07	Franklin(Ind	12	14	23
Taylor, Daniel(B)	1819	Oct. 25	Hamilton	02	07	03
Taylor, Daniel(B)	1820	March 01	Hamilton	02	07	03
Taylor, Daniel(B)	1832	Oct. 04	Dearborn(Ind	02	08	34
Taylor, Daniel(B)	1833	Jan. 30	Dearborn(Ind	02	08	34
Taylor, David(A)	1816	Feb. 10	Preble	01	09	17
Taylor, Eyrs(A)	1805	Nov. 09	Kentucky	01	08	29
Taylor, Fielding(A)	1832	Jan. 13	Preble	03	08	22
Taylor, Griffin(A)	1818	Feb. 11	Cincinnati	02	12	05
Taylor, Griffin(E)	1818	April 07	Hamilton	11	10	11
Taylor, Griffin(E)	1818	April 07	Hamilton	14	20	35
Taylor, Griffin(E)	1818	April 07	Hamilton	11	10	14
Taylor, Griffin(E)	1818	April 07	Hamilton	11	10	12
Taylor, Griffin(E)	1818	April 07	Hamilton	11	10	12
Taylor, Griffin(E)	1818	April 07	Hamilton	14	20	13
Taylor, Griffin(E)	1818	April 04	Hamilton	14	20	29
Taylor, Griffin(E)	1818	April 07	Hamilton	12	10	08
Taylor, Griffin(E)	1818	April 07	Hamilton	12	10	17
Taylor, Griffin(E)	1818	April 07	Hamilton	14	20	30
Taylor, Henry(A)	1803	Feb. 24	Hamilton	02	05	36
Taylor, Isaac(A)	1816	Aug. 15	Kentucky	01	09	28
Taylor, Isaac(B)	1832	March 29	Dearborn(Ind	01	07	31
Taylor, Isaac(C)	1830	July 01	Miami	13	03	08
Taylor, Isaac(C)	1831	April 14	Miami	13	03	08
Taylor, Israel(E)	1838	May 21	Hamilton	14	21	14
Taylor, Jacob R.(B)	1818	June 06	Hamilton	01	07	35
Taylor, Jacob(B)	1825	Nov. 05	Hamilton	01	08	21
Taylor, James(A)	1804	Oct. 29	Kentucky	02	07	02
Taylor, James(A)	1815	Jan. 02	Kentucky	02	11	02
Taylor, James(A)	1827	Aug. 20	Preble	03	04	15
Taylor, James(B)	1804	Oct. 23	Kentucky	02	09	09
Taylor, James(B)	1804	Oct. 23	Kentucky	02	10	09
Taylor, James(B)	1814	June 09	Kentucky	01	02	25
Taylor, James(B)	1814	July 21	Kentucky	02	02	34
Taylor, James(C)	1831	Nov. 15	Champaign	12	04	26
Taylor, John(A)	1827	Sept. 22	Montgomery	06	03	08
Taylor, John(B)	1824	June 09	Hamilton	01	08	07

321

PURCHASER	YEAR	DATE	RESIDENCE	R	T	S
Taylor, John(B)	1834	April 05	Dearborn(Ind	02	06	23
Taylor, John(C)	1804	Dec. 28	Greene	10	06	22
Taylor, John(C)	1804	Dec. 28	Greene	12	05	10
Taylor, John(C)	1808	Aug. 20	Champaign	12	04	01
Taylor, John(C)	1809	Dec. 06	Champaign	11	04	29
Taylor, John(C)	1812	March 16	Champaign	12	05	04
Taylor, John(C)	1813	Dec. 04	Champaign	11	04	28
Taylor, John(C)	1814	May 23	Champaign	10	05	22
Taylor, John(C)	1814	Oct. 25	Champaign	12	05	08
Taylor, John(C)	1815	Nov. 14	Champaign	11	04	33
Taylor, John(E)	1812	April 06	Tennessee	14	14	30
Taylor, Lemuel(C)	1831	Nov. 22	Champaign	12	04	26
Taylor, Martin(A)	1811	Feb. 11	Preble	03	04	30
Taylor, Modest Rainey(A)	1832	Jan. 16	Washington	04	10	20
Taylor, Peter(C)	1807	June 01	Greene	09	04	36
Taylor, Robert T.(E)	1814	June 20	Franklin(Ind	13	13	26
Taylor, Robert(A)	1808	Feb. 25	Butler	02	07	04
Taylor, Robert(A)	1812	Sept. 08	Butler	02	06	21
Taylor, Robert(A)	1814	Sept. 03	Butler	02	06	09
Taylor, Robert(A)	1814	Sept. 03	Butler	02	07	30
Taylor, Robert(A)	1817	Nov. 18	Butler	01	11	23
Taylor, Robert(A)	1818	Jan. 02	Butler	01	11	27
Taylor, Robert(B)	1817	Nov. 15	Butler	01	11	22
Taylor, Robert(B)	1818	Jan. 24	Hamilton	01	04	17
Taylor, Robert(B)	1818	Feb. 14	Hamilton	03	03	20
Taylor, Robert(B)	1818	Feb. 14	Hamilton	03	03	05
Taylor, Robert(C)	1802	Dec. 18	Hamilton	06	01	22
Taylor, Robert(E)	1811	Oct. 23	Butler	12	16	34
Taylor, Robert(E)	1811	Oct. 24	Butler	13	17	30
Taylor, Robert(E)	1818	March 23	Butler	14	21	22
Taylor, Robert(E)	1818	March 23	Butler	14	21	08
Taylor, Robt.(B)	1818	Oct. 06	Hamilton	03	03	20
Taylor, Robt.(B)	1824	June 09	Hamilton	01	08	18
Taylor, Samuel(A)	1819	Sept. 29	Champaign	07	01	03
Taylor, Samuel(C)	1815	March 22	Madison	12	03	35
Taylor, Thomas(B)	1825	Oct. 13	Wayne(Ind)	01	13	25
Taylor, Walter(E)	1812	April 06	Tennessee	14	14	30
Taylor, William(A)	1831	Dec. 02	Montgomery	05	10	26
Taylor, William(C)	1802	Dec. 21	Hamilton	07	02	10
Taylor, William(C)	1805	Nov. 07	Virginia	10	06	09
Taylor, William(C)	1805	Nov. 07	Virginia	10	06	07
Teagarden, Abm.(A)	1822	Oct. 18	Butler	02	13	18
Teagarden, Elizabeth(E)	1815	June 14	Franklin(Ind	13	12	03
Teagarden, George(B)	1824	June 09	Franklin(Ind	01	10	21
Teagarden, Henry(E)	1816	Sept. 04	Franklin(Ind	13	12	34
Teagarden, Susanah(E)	1815	Nov. 11	Franklin(Ind	13	13	31
Teagarden, Will'm.(A)	1828	Aug. 26	Darke	02	13	19
Teagarden, Wm.(A)	1818	Oct. 19	Butler	02	13	20
Teague, Elijah(A)	1807	May 27	Miami	05	07	28
Teague, George(B)	1814	Dec. 12	Franklin(Ind	01	02	29
Teague, George(B)	1827	Aug. 21	Switzerland	01	02	22
Teague, George(B)	1827	Aug. 21	Switzerland	01	02	22
Teague, John(B)	1812	Oct. 27	Jefferson	03	02	03
Teague, John(B)	1817	Nov. 19	Switzerland	03	03	12
Teague, Samuel(A)	1806	July 24	Greene	05	07	28
Teague, Samuel(A)	1806	July 24	Greene	05	07	33
Teague, Samuel(A)	1831	July 26	Miami	05	07	15
Teagues, John(B)	1814	June 08	Jefferson	03	03	13
Teas, Gibson(E)	1834	March 03	Randolph(Ind	14	19	22
Teas, Joseph(B)	1825	Dec. 24	Wayne(Ind)	01	15	34
Teas, Joseph(E)	1834	March 22	Randolph(Ind	14	19	15
Teas, Joseph(E)	1834	March 22	Randolph(Ind	14	19	28
Teas, Joseph(E)	1835	April 29	Randolph(Ind	14	19	15
Teator, Daniel(A)	1815	Oct. 25	Montgomery	02	10	05
Tebbs, Warren(B)	1830	March 10	Dearborn(Ind	01	07	23
Tedford, Henry(A)	1817	Aug. 05	Butler	01	10	10
Tedford, Henry(A)	1817	Aug. 11	Butler	02	10	28
Tedford, Henry(A)	1817	Aug. 11	Butler	02	10	28
Teegarden, Abraham(A)	1833	Sept. 20	Darke	02	13	18

PURCHASER	YEAR	DATE	RESIDENCE	R	T	S
Teegarden, Abraham(A)	1835	June 09	Darke	02	13	19
Teegarden, Abraham(A)	1836	Oct. 21	Darke	02	13	19
Teegarden, Abraham(A)	1836	Nov. 07	Darke	02	13	18
Teegarden, Abraham(A)	1836	Nov. 07	Darke	02	13	19
Teegarden, Abraham(A)	1837	Feb. 11	Darke	02	13	19
Teegarden, Abraham(A)	1837	Feb. 25	Darke	01	13	24
Teegarden, Abraham(A)	1837	Feb. 25	Darke	02	13	19
Teegarden, David H.(A)	1837	Feb. 25	Darke	01	13	25
Teegarden, David H.(A)	1837	Nov. 25	Butler	01	13	25
Teegarden, David H.(A)	1837	Nov. 25	Butler	02	13	30
Teegarden, Henry(A)	1836	Dec. 01	Darke	02	13	32
Teegarden, Henry(E)	1812	Sept. 05	Clermont	12	12	20
Teegarden, Henry(E)	1813	Oct. 04	Franklin(Ind	13	12	21
Teegarden, William(A)	1831	March 31	Darke	02	13	20
Teegarden, William(A)	1835	July 20	Darke	02	13	20
Teegarden, William(A)	1835	July 20	Darke	02	13	19
Teegarden, William(A)	1835	July 20	Darke	02	13	32
Teegarden, William(A)	1836	Aug. 24	Darke	02	13	30
Teegarden, William(A)	1836	Oct. 21	Darke	02	13	30
Teegarden, William(A)	1836	Nov. 07	Darke	02	13	30
Teegarden, William(A)	1836	Nov. 07	Darke	02	13	31
Teegarden, William(A)	1837	Feb. 25	Darke	02	13	19
Teegarden, William(A)	1837	Feb. 25	Darke	02	13	08
Teegarden, Wm.(A)	1837	Feb. 25	Darke	02	13	19
Teeple, John(B)	1816	May 31	Cincinnati	01	02	01
Teeter, Isaac(A)	1836	Jan. 23	Darke	01	12	07
Teets, Michael(A)	1805	Nov. 28	Kentucky	01	06	33
Teil, Samuel(A)	1807	Jan. 05	Montgomery	03	04	04
Teil, Samuel(A)	1807	Aug. 18	Montgomery	02	07	36
Telfer, Alexander(B)	1815	Jan. 24	Franklin(Ind	01	09	11
Telfor, Alexander(B)	1812	Aug. 07	Butler	01	09	02
Telford, Alexander(A)	1806	March 11	Greene	06	05	19
Teller, David(A)	1806	Oct. 14	Clermont	04	04	31
Tempelton, Robert(B)	1804	Nov. 20	Hamilton	02	09	04
Temple, Jesse(A)	1819	Jan. 02	Kentucky	04	11	03
Templeton, Daniel G.(B)	1815	Oct. 02	Hamilton	02	09	23
Templeton, John(B)	1804	Sept. 24	Hamilton	02	10	04
Templeton, Lemuel(A)	1814	Oct. 31	Ohio	05	08	07
Templeton, Robert A.(B)	1813	May 24	Franklin(Ind	02	11	33
Templeton, Robert(B)	1804	Sept. 24	Hamilton	02	09	04
Templeton, Robert(B)	1804	Oct. 16	Hamilton	02	10	28
Templeton, Robert(B)	1812	July 08	Franklin(Ind	02	09	04
Templeton, Robert(B)	1816	May 06	Franklin(Ind	02	09	05
Templeton, William(A)	1814	July 26	Miami	05	08	06
Templin, William(A)	1817	Nov. 08	EastTennesse	03	11	19
Tenne, Job(A)	1815	Sept. 16	Hamilton	01	01	07
Tenney, John(A)	1829	April 08	Clark	06	03	04
Tenney, John(C)	1811	Jan. 19	Greene	08	03	11
Teny, Henry(B)	1832	Jan. 11	Dearborn(Ind	02	04	07
Teny, Henry(B)	1832	Feb. 24	Dearborn(Ind	03	06	34
Teny, Michael(B)	1832	March 06	Dearborn(Ind	02	04	06
Terrel, Daniel(C)	1801	Dec. 31	Hamilton	07	01	10
Terrel, Jephthah(C)	1817	June 11	Champaign	13	04	26
Terrel, Jeppthah(E)	1814	Jan. 15	Champaign	13	04	27
Terrel, Jepthah(C)	1815	July 10	Champaign	13	04	33
Terrel, Josiah(C)	1828	Dec. 26	Champaign	14	03	26
Terrel, Matthew(C)	1831	Sept. 06	Champaign	13	04	31
Terrell, Jephthah(C)	1816	Sept. 10	Champaign	13	04	31
Terris, Joseph(C)	1801	Dec. 31	Hamilton	07	01	07
Terry, Ansel(E)	1835	Sept. 25	Franklin(Ind	13	11	21
Terry, Ansel(E)	1836	Dec. 05	Franklin(Ind	13	11	17
Terry, Enos(A)	1809	April 29	Darke	02	12	26
Terry, Enos(A)	1816	Feb. 16	Darke	02	12	26
Terry, Enos(A)	1817	Sept. 02	Darke	03	10	19
Terry, George(B)	1836	Feb. 09	Franklin(Ind	01	08	20
Terry, George(B)	1836	Feb. 12	Franklin(Ind	01	08	20
Terry, Isaac(C)	1831	July 05	Warren	12	03	33
Terry, John(C)	1801	Dec. 30	Hamilton	04	04	13
Terry, Levi(A)	1816	Aug. 16	Warren	02	06	18

PURCHASER	YEAR	DATE	RESIDENCE	R	T	S
Terry, Levi(C)	1831	July 05	Warren	12	03	27
Terry, Levi(C)	1831	July 05	Warren	12	03	32
Terry, Robert(B)	1818	March 06	Hamilton	02	07	19
Terwilliger, Cornelius S.(B)	1839	Feb. 28	Warren	03	04	11
Thacher, Elijah(B)	1818	Jan. 24	Dearborn(Ind	02	04	19
Thacher, Elijah(B)	1818	Jan. 24	Dearborn(Ind	03	05	24
Thacher, Elijah(B)	1818	Jan. 24	Dearborn(Ind	02	04	30
Thacher, Elijah(B)	1828	May 13	Dearborn(Ind	02	05	03
Thacher, Harvey(B)	1836	Jan. 13	Dearborn(Ind	03	04	23
Thacker, Amos(A)	1816	Oct. 17	Warren	02	09	11
Thacker, Elijah(B)	1816	Jan. 24	Dearborn(Ind	02	03	10
Thacker, Harvey(B)	1836	Dec. 08	Dearborn(Ind	03	04	23
Thackwray, John(C)	1830	Aug. 28	Clark	10	03	18
Tharp, Andrew(A)	1803	Dec. 02	Montgomery	04	03	02
Tharp, Andrew(E)	1812	April 04	Hamilton	12	14	25
Tharp, Andrew(E)	1816	Dec. 02	Wayne(Ind)	13	14	06
Tharp, Boaz(A)	1806	Sept. 16	Montgomery	02	07	31
Tharp, Boaze(E)	1811	Oct. 23	Wayne(Ind)	12	16	34
Tharp, Booz(E)	1835	Sept. 28	Fayette	12	13	30
Tharp, Jacob(C)	1812	Feb. 29	Champaign	11	05	04
Tharp, Jacob(C)	1812	April 27	Champaign	11	05	04
Tharp, Jacob(C)	1817	Aug. 01	Champaign	11	05	04
Tharp, James Senr.(A)	1809	Dec. 12	Montgomery	04	04	18
Tharp, James(A)	1804	Oct. 23	Montgomery	04	04	18
Tharp, Jehu(E)	1811	Oct. 24	Wayne(Ind)	13	15	32
Tharp, John Jr.(B)	1814	Nov. 04	Franklin(Ind	02	09	05
Tharp, John(A)	1804	Sept. 24	Montgomery	04	04	18
Tharp, John(B)	1808	Sept. 22	Warren	02	09	08
Tharp, John(B)	1811	Sept. 21	Warren	02	09	08
Tharp, John(B)	1818	Jan. 13	Wayne(Ind)	01	15	02
Tharp, Thomas(A)	1813	Oct. 14	Montgomery	04	05	31
Tharp, Thomas(E)	1811	Dec. 04	Wayne(Ind)	14	17	11
Tharp, Thomas(E)	1814	July 28	Wayne(Ind)	14	18	21
Tharp, William(B)	1816	Oct. 21	Cincinnati	02	06	11
Thatcher, Jesse(A)	1814	Sept. 10	Kentucky	02	09	01
Thayer, Allen(A)	1832	Oct. 05	Warren	04	08	33
Thayer, Chester(B)	1837	Jan. 13	Dearborn(Ind	02	03	05
Thiebaud, Frederick Louis(B)	1817	Oct. 27	Switzerland	03	02	29
Tholking, John Allert(E)	1836	Nov. 11	Cincinnati	12	10	04
Tholle, Henry(E)	1837	Feb. 01	Cincinnati	12	11	35
Thomas, Abel(A)	1830	Dec. 27	Montgomery	04	06	09
Thomas, Abel(A)	1831	May 30	Montgomery	04	06	10
Thomas, Abraham(A)	1804	Dec. 24	Kentucky	06	05	33
Thomas, Absalom(C)	1812	Aug. 05	Greene	09	06	03
Thomas, Absalom(C)	1812	Aug. 05	Greene	08	06	12
Thomas, Absolom(C)	1801	Dec. ?	Hamilton	05	03	04
Thomas, Antepas(B)	1814	Dec. 09	Franklin(Ind	01	12	33
Thomas, Antipas(E)	1816	Dec. 04	Wayne(Ind)	14	20	17
Thomas, Arthur(C)	1804	Sept. 04	Greene	12	05	32
Thomas, Arthur(C)	1804	Sept. 04	Greene	12	05	33
Thomas, Arthur(C)	1807	April 02	Champaign	12	05	32
Thomas, Arthur(C)	1809	Dec. 12	Champaign	12	05	32
Thomas, Arthur(C)	1809	Dec. 12	Champaign	12	05	21
Thomas, Benj'n.(E)	1837	March 01	Wayne(Ind)	15	20	29
Thomas, Benjamin(B)	1815	June 09	Wayne(Ind)	01	15	09
Thomas, Benjamin(E)	1834	Jan. 10	Randolph(Ind	14	18	01
Thomas, Cornelius(A)	1815	Dec. 02	Butler	02	07	15
Thomas, Daniel(A)	1816	Dec. 14	Warren	01	11	31
Thomas, Daniel(A)	1827	Sept. 12	Greene	01	11	32
Thomas, Daniel(B)	1833	July 06	Greene	01	16	36
Thomas, Daniel(C)	1801	Dec. 30	Hamilton	05	04	34
Thomas, David(A)	1818	Feb. 02	Darke	02	10	29
Thomas, Edward(A)	1808	Jan. 13	Warren	05	05	12
Thomas, Edward(A)	1827	June 22	Montgomery	04	06	03
Thomas, Eli(E)	1837	May 23	HenryCo.,Ind	15	20	29
Thomas, Enos(E)	1837	Feb. 01	Wayne(Ind)	14	19	24
Thomas, Ephraim(A)	1815	April 03	Kentucky	13	14	01
Thomas, Esther(D)	1808	Nov. 01	Butler	03	03	11
Thomas, Evan(A)	1807	July 08	Warren	05	05	34

324

PURCHASER	YEAR	DATE	RESIDENCE	R	T	S
Thomas, Evan(A)	1830	Sept. 23	Montgomery	04	06	04
Thomas, Ezekiel(C)	1808	Nov. 02	Champaign	11	05	26
Thomas, Ezekiel(C)	1821	Sept. 17	Miami	11	02	03
Thomas, Francis(B)	1817	June 13	Wayne(Ind)	01	15	09
Thomas, Francis(C)	1811	Dec. 30	Champaign	12	05	22
Thomas, Francis(E)	1811	Oct. 28	Wayne(Ind)	14	17	12
Thomas, George(A)	1826	April 29	Montgomery	04	06	02
Thomas, George(E)	1837	March 01	Randolph(Ind	15	20	29
Thomas, Griffith(C)	1816	Jan. 02	Champaign	10	04	19
Thomas, Henry(A)	1834	Jan. 31	Darke	01	12	20
Thomas, Isaac Junr.(A)	1826	July 26	Montgomery	04	06	02
Thomas, Isaac(B)	1813	Oct. 20	Wayne(Ind)	01	15	20
Thomas, Isaac(E)	1831	Dec. 22	Fayette	12	13	33
Thomas, Isaiah P.(B)	1838	Aug. 21	Montgomery	01	19	36
Thomas, Isaiah(A)	1831	Aug. 29	Montgomery	04	06	03
Thomas, James(C)	1814	April 04	Champaign	12	04	18
Thomas, James(C)	1814	April 04	Champaign	12	04	18
Thomas, James(E)	1813	Dec. 20	Franklin(Ind	12	12	10
Thomas, Jeremiah(B)	1832	May 30	Switzerland	02	02	19
Thomas, Jeremiah(C)	1807	April 18	Champaign	10	05	05
Thomas, Jeremiah(C)	1807	April 18	Champaign	10	05	04
Thomas, Jesse B.(B)	1805	July 13	Dearborn(Ind	02	09	29
Thomas, Jesse B.(B)	1806	March 21	Dearborn(Ind	03	04	09
Thomas, Jesse B.(B)	1807	Feb. 09	Dearborn(Ind	03	04	09
Thomas, Jesse(E)	1817	Nov. 22	Kentucky	14	16	28
Thomas, Joel(A)	1831	Feb. 04	Darke	03	08	36
Thomas, Joel(C)	1807	April 18	Champaign	10	05	05
Thomas, Joel(C)	1807	April 18	Champaign	10	05	04
Thomas, John(A)	1816	Oct. 15	Warren	04	06	11
Thomas, John(A)	1819	Aug. 02	Miami	04	06	02
Thomas, John(A)	1829	June 08	Darke	02	10	02
Thomas, John(A)	1829	Dec. 09	Montgomery	04	06	10
Thomas, John(A)	1831	March 29	Miami	04	07	26
Thomas, John(A)	1833	Dec. 10	Darke	01	12	15
Thomas, John(A)	1834	Jan. 31	Darke	01	12	15
Thomas, John(A)	1837	June 07	Hamilton	01	14	33
Thomas, John(B)	1814	July 28	Wayne(Ind)	01	16	33
Thomas, John(B)	1816	July 18	Delaware	01	14	03
Thomas, John(C)	1805	Sept. 12	Champaign	12	05	27
Thomas, John(C)	1806	March 11	Champaign	11	05	07
Thomas, John(C)	1806	March 26	Champaign	12	06	31
Thomas, John(C)	1806	May 10	Champaign	11	05	07
Thomas, John(C)	1806	July 23	Champaign	11	05	26
Thomas, John(C)	1811	Aug. 13	Champaign	12	06	31
Thomas, John(C)	1813	April 14	Champaign	11	05	20
Thomas, John(C)	1811	Aug. 13	Champaign	11	05	07
Thomas, John(C)	1813	June 04	Champaign	11	05	19
Thomas, John(C)	1813	July 09	Champaign	11	05	13
Thomas, John(E)	1813	Sept. 03	Hamilton	12	13	04
Thomas, John(E)	1835	April 08	Montgomery	14	18	12
Thomas, John(E)	1835	Sept. 29	Franklin(Ind	11	12	25
Thomas, John(E)	1836	Jan. 08	Franklin(Ind	11	12	25
Thomas, John(E)	1837	Jan. 30	Union(Ind)	14	21	27
Thomas, John(E)	1838	Nov. 20	Union(Ind)	14	21	27
Thomas, Lewis(E)	1815	Sept. 15	Virginia	14	16	06
Thomas, Lewis(E)	1815	Dec. 06	Franklin(Ind	14	16	31
Thomas, Lewis(E)	1816	Aug. 08	Wayne(Ind)	13	15	01
Thomas, Michael(C)	1813	Oct. 26	Kentucky	11	02	07
Thomas, Nathan(E)	1837	March 01	Wayne(Ind)	15	20	28
Thomas, Nehemiah(A)	1830	April 14	Montgomery	04	06	03
Thomas, Richard S.(C)	1804	Dec. 31	Warren	09	05	22
Thomas, Richard(E)	1813	Sept. 15	Franklin(Ind	13	13	06
Thomas, Richard(E)	1832	Dec. 19	Franklin(Ind	13	12	20
Thomas, Richard(E)	1835	Oct. 06	Franklin(Ind	13	12	20
Thomas, Solomon(B)	1814	Nov. 04	Wayne(Ind)	01	15	20
Thomas, Stephen Senr.(B)	1816	Nov. 09	Wayne(Ind)	01	15	29
Thomas, Stephen(E)	1814	Aug. 12	Wayne(Ind)	14	18	36
Thomas, Thomas(B)	1816	Sept. 18	Franklin(Ind	02	10	08
Thomas, Thomas(C)	1801	Dec. 31	Hamilton	05	03	09

PURCHASER	YEAR	DATE	RESIDENCE	R	T	S
Thomas, Thomas(C)	1812	Aug. 05	Warren	09	06	14
Thomas, Thomas(E)	1813	Aug. 12	Franklin(Ind	12	15	15
Thomas, Thomas(E)	1836	Oct. 10	Union(Ind)	14	22	33
Thomas, William J.(A)	1835	Nov. 07	Miami	03	10	24
Thomas, William Jr.(E)	1834	June 11	Montgomery	14	18	12
Thomas, William(A)	1801	June 27	Hamilton	03	02	01
Thomas, William(A)	1806	Sept. 30	Montgomery	04	04	06
Thomas, William(A)	1831	March 29	Miami	04	07	26
Thomas, William(C)	1801	Dec. 30	Hamilton	05	03	09
Thomas, William(C)	1814	March 28	Miami	11	02	07
Thomas, William(C)	1818	March 30	Miami	11	02	03
Thomas, Wm.(A)	1830	Dec. 27	Montgomery	04	06	09
Thompson, Aaron(A)	1818	Jan. 15	Pennsylvania	05	05	21
Thompson, Archibald(A)	1831	May 19	Muskingum	07	02	34
Thompson, Closs(B)	1814	Nov. 07	Louisiana	01	10	10
Thompson, Curtin M.(C)	1815	Oct. 02	Wayne(Ind)	11	04	02
Thompson, Curtis M.(C)	1814	April 26	Champaign	11	04	19
Thompson, Curtis M.(C)	1814	April 26	Champaign	10	04	30
Thompson, David(A)	1815	Jan. 03	Butler	02	11	11
Thompson, David(A)	1831	March 17	Darke	01	13	33
Thompson, E. K.(C)	1804	Dec. 31	Cincinnati	07	03	04
Thompson, Enoch(B)	1814	Aug. 06	Butler	02	09	24
Thompson, Erasmus K.	1808	March 01	Cincinnati	?	?	?
Thompson, Erasmus K.(A)	1807	June 27	Cincinnati	06	05	29
Thompson, Erasmus K.(B)	1806	July 28	?	02	03	18
Thompson, George(A)	1805	June 05	Virginia	03	06	17
Thompson, George(A)	1806	Dec. 23	Warren	02	08	10
Thompson, George(A)	1827	Aug. 20	Preble	02	08	15
Thompson, George(B)	1832	May 01	Wayne(Ind)	01	16	35
Thompson, George(B)	1834	Nov. 12	Hamilton	02	06	23
Thompson, George(E)	1836	Dec. 12	Wayne(Ind)	15	22	26
Thompson, Isaac(A)	1817	June 18	Montgomery	04	05	14
Thompson, James(A)	1811	Dec. 12	Montgomery	04	07	03
Thompson, James(A)	1811	Dec. 13	Montgomery	06	04	19
Thompson, James(A)	1812	Jan. 22	Montgomery	04	07	13
Thompson, James(A)	1813	April 14	Montgomery	06	05	28
Thompson, James(A)	1828	March 22	Darke	03	10	36
Thompson, James(A)	1831	Aug. 17	Miami	04	09	34
Thompson, James(C)	1801	Dec. 28	Hamilton	06	01	17
Thompson, James(C)	1801	Dec. 31	Hamilton	06	01	17
Thompson, James(C)	1804	Sept. 03	Montgomery	06	01	11
Thompson, James(C)	1805	July 20	Montgomery	06	01	05
Thompson, James(C)	1805	July 20	Montgomery	06	01	11
Thompson, James(C)	1805	July 20	Montgomery	06	01	11
Thompson, James(C)	1810	Dec. 12	Montgomery	06	01	11
Thompson, James(C)	1811	Dec. 12	Montgomery	11	01	12
Thompson, James(C)	1811	Dec. 12	Montgomery	11	01	02
Thompson, James(C)	1811	Dec. 12	Montgomery	09	02	21
Thompson, James(C)	1817	Dec. 02	Madison	08	06	06
Thompson, James(E)	1812	Jan. 22	Montgomery	14	16	21
Thompson, Jas.(A)	1832	Feb. 07	Shelby	05	09	23
Thompson, John Robert(A)	1831	Sept. 27	Union(Ind)	01	09	02
Thompson, John(A)	1805	Aug. 21	Butler	03	03	02
Thompson, John(A)	1804	Dec. 28	Hamilton	02	05	17
Thompson, John(A)	1813	Nov. 06	Butler	02	05	07
Thompson, John(A)	1815	Feb. 06	Preble	01	09	14
Thompson, John(A)	1823	June 19	Darke	01	10	34
Thompson, John(A)	1831	April 11	Darke	01	13	35
Thompson, John(A)	1835	Nov. 09	Hamilton	08	02	32
Thompson, John(B)	1814	Nov. 26	Butler	01	12	01
Thompson, John(B)	1814	Nov. 26	Butler	01	12	12
Thompson, John(B)	1815	Aug. 28	Butler	02	03	23
Thompson, John(B)	1825	Oct. 05	Wayne(Ind)	01	15	15
Thompson, John(C)	1813	April 14	Champaign	09	06	36
Thompson, John(E)	1814	Sept. 10	Franklin(Ind	12	13	05
Thompson, John(E)	1834	Feb. 14	Randolph(Ind	15	21	04
Thompson, John(E)	1834	March 17	Randolph(Ind	15	21	03
Thompson, John(E)	1836	Feb. 15	Cincinnati	14	19	11
Thompson, Jonah(A)	1825	Dec. 01	Miami	04	07	15

PURCHASER	YEAR	DATE	RESIDENCE	R	T	S
Thompson, Joseph H.(C)	1813	Feb. 10	Champaign	12	04	24
Thompson, Joseph(A)	1813	Nov. 03	Preble	02	06	23
Thompson, Joseph(A)	1814	June 08	Preble	02	06	23
Thompson, Joseph(E)	1831	Aug. 25	Franklin(Ind	12	11	30
Thompson, Joseph(E)	1837	March 01	Franklin(Ind	12	11	31
Thompson, Matthew(A)	1825	Aug. 15	Montgomery	07	01	08
Thompson, Moses(A)	1831	Sept. 27	Preble	02	10	29
Thompson, Moses(B)	1835	March 09	Wayne(Ind)	01	17	27
Thompson, Rich'd.(A)	1828	Oct. 01	Miami	04	07	04
Thompson, Richard(A)	1818	March 16	Miami	04	07	02
Thompson, Robert P.(E)	1838	Aug. 13	Cincinnati	15	22	02
Thompson, Robert(A)	1808	Oct. 01	Preble	01	06	01
Thompson, Robert(A)	1819	June 10	Darke	01	10	34
Thompson, Robert(B)	1831	Nov. 14	Randolph(Ind	01	16	22
Thompson, Robt.(A)	1828	Sept. 23	Preble	01	07	22
Thompson, Robt.(A)	1829	Feb. 03	Preble	01	07	22
Thompson, Sam'l.(A)	1831	Nov. 02	Miami	04	07	04
Thompson, Samuel(B)	1816	Oct. 23	Butler	01	15	11
Thompson, Samuel(C)	1801	Dec. 31	Hamilton	07	01	10
Thompson, Samuel(C)	1801	Dec. 31	Hamilton	07	01	03
Thompson, Smith(B)	1833	Jan. 15	Dearborn(Ind	02	05	29
Thompson, Sylvester(A)	1805	April 11	Montgomery	05	08	32
Thompson, Sylvester(A)	1806	March 18	Montgomery	04	09	26
Thompson, Sylvester(A)	1806	March 18	Montgomery	05	07	17
Thompson, Sylvester(A)	1815	June 07	Miami	04	09	27
Thompson, Theodorus(B)	1817	July 07	Dearborn(Ind	02	05	30
Thompson, Theodorus(B)	1817	July 07	Dearborn(Ind	03	06	25
Thompson, Thomas(A)	1804	Sept. 14	Cincinnati	02	04	11
Thompson, Thomas(A)	1831	March 17	Darke	01	12	10
Thompson, Thomas(B)	1804	Sept. 25	Cincinnati	04	01	02
Thompson, Thomas(B)	1805	July 30	Cincinnati	03	04	09
Thompson, Thomas(B)	1805	July 30	Cincinnati	03	04	05
Thompson, Thomas(B)	1805	July 30	Cincinnati	03	04	08
Thompson, Thomas(C)	1804	Dec. 31	Cincinnati	07	03	04
Thompson, Thomas(C)	1804	Dec. 31	Cincinnati	08	04	07
Thompson, Thomas(C)	1804	Dec. 31	Cincinnati	08	04	03
Thompson, Thomas(C)	1804	Dec. 31	Cincinnati	07	02	05
Thompson, Thomas(C)	1804	Dec. 31	Cincinnati	07	03	23
Thompson, Thomas(C)	1804	Dec. 31	Cincinnati	07	03	36
Thompson, Thomas(C)	1804	Dec. 31	Cincinnati	08	03	01
Thompson, Thomas(C)	1804	Dec. 31	Cincinnati	07	02	03
Thompson, Thomas(C)	1804	Dec. 31	Cincinnati	08	04	27
Thompson, Thomas(C)	1804	Dec. 31	Cincinnati	09	04	01
Thompson, Thomas(C)	1804	Dec. 31	Cincinnati	07	02	22
Thompson, Thomas(C)	1804	Dec. 31	Cincinnati	09	04	21
Thompson, Thomas(C)	1804	Dec. 31	Cincinnati	09	04	21
Thompson, Thomas(C)	1804	Dec. 31	Cincinnati	09	04	22
Thompson, Thomas(C)	1804	Dec. 31	Cincinnati	08	04	35
Thompson, Thomas(C)	1804	Dec. 31	Cincinnati	08	03	18
Thompson, Thomas(C)	1812	June 09	Cincinnati	08	03	34
Thompson, Thos. Wallace(A)	1831	Aug. 15	Miami	07	02	34
Thompson, William(A)	1831	Aug. 09	Darke	03	10	19
Thompson, William(A)	1835	June 04	Pennsylvania	02	13	31
Thomson, William(A)	1819	May 31	Montgomery	06	03	05
Thorn, Azarias(A)	1805	Feb. 23	Butler	02	04	24
Thorn, Peter(A)	1822	June 20	Warren	04	05	17
Thorn, Peter(C)	1804	Dec. 28	Warren	04	04	21
Thorn, Stephen Jr.(B)	1830	Feb. 06	Dearborn(Ind	02	07	09
Thorn, Stephen Jr.(B)	1831	Oct. 20	Dearborn(Ind	01	07	07
Thorn, Taylor(B)	1835	Feb. 13	Randolph(Ind	01	16	23
Thorn, William(E)	1811	Oct. 23	Greene	12	16	24
Thorn, William(E)	1811	Oct. 24	Greene	13	16	19
Thorn, William(E)	1811	Oct. 25	Greene	14	17	22
Thorn, William(E)	1811	Oct. 28	Greene	12	16	24
Thorn, William(E)	1811	Oct. 28	Greene	13	16	19
Thorn, William(E)	1811	Oct. 28	Greene	13	16	19
Thorn, William(E)	1811	Nov. 09	Greene	12	16	13
Thornborough, Joseph(E)	1816	July 31	Wayne(Ind)	13	17	36
Thornborough, William(E)	1816	Sept. 09	Wayne(Ind)	14	17	28

PURCHASER	YEAR	DATE	RESIDENCE	R	T	S
Thornbrough, William(B)	1813	Oct. 16	Wayne(Ind)	01	14	23
Thornburgh, Edward(E)	1819	Aug. 12	Highland	14	18	06
Thornburgh, Edward(E)	1819	Aug. 13	Highland	14	18	05
Thornburgh, Jonathan(E)	1829	Jan. 19	Wayne(Ind)	13	18	20
Thornburgh, Joseph Senr.(E)	1817	Sept. 26	?	13	18	10
Thornburgh, Joseph(A)	1825	Dec. 22	Wayne(Ind)	04	08	26
Thornburgh, Joseph(E)	1819	Aug. 12	Highland	14	19	32
Thornburgh, Morgan(E)	1817	Sept. 26	?	13	18	10
Thornburgh, Walter(E)	1814	Dec. 10	Pennsylvania	13	18	30
Thornbury, Edward(E)	1818	Sept. 10	Highland	14	18	05
Thornbury, Nathan(E)	1816	Oct. 25	Highland	14	19	33
Thornbury, Nathan(E)	1835	Jan. 23	Randolph(Ind	14	19	27
Thornbury, Nathan(E)	1836	Jan. 28	Randolph(Ind	14	19	28
Thornton, Coats(C)	1813	April 13	Champaign	11	03	17
Thornton, Edward(E)	1816	June 07	Wayne(Ind)	13	15	03
Thornton, Eli(A)	1807	Aug. 01	Montgomery	04	07	01
Thornton, George Washington(B)	1836	Feb. 03	Dearborn(Ind	03	05	02
Thornton, William L.(B)	1839	March 15	Dearborn(Ind	03	05	01
Thorp, Abraham(B)	1818	Jan. 12	Cincinnati	02	07	34
Thorp, Jacob(C)	1817	Aug. 01	Champaign	11	05	04
Thrall, Friend(B)	1816	Dec. 13	Hamilton	03	03	27
Thralls, Richard(A)	1815	Nov. 24	Montgomery	02	06	13
Throckmorton, Charles(E)	1836	Feb. 05	Franklin(Ind	11	10	01
Throckmorton, Charles(E)	1836	Feb. 22	Franklin(Ind	12	10	06
Throckmorton, Chas. Jr.(E)	1836	Sept. 16	Franklin(Ind	11	11	36
Throckmorton, Joseph(E)	1828	July 16	Franklin(Ind	12	11	20
Throckmorton, Joseph(E)	1832	Oct. 06	Franklin(Ind	12	11	29
Throckmorton, Joseph(E)	1836	Feb. 05	Franklin(Ind	11	10	01
Throckmorton, Joseph(E)	1836	Sept. 16	Franklin(Ind	12	10	06
Throckmorton, Joseph(E)	1837	Feb. 22	Franklin(Ind	12	11	21
Throles, Nathaniel(A)	1814	Dec. 17	?	02	08	31
Thurber, Edward(E)	1831	Aug. 26	Switzerland	14	21	11
Thurber, Edward(E)	1833	Oct. 12	Randolph(Ind	14	21	11
Thurber, Edward(E)	1837	Feb. 06	Randolph(Ind	14	21	11
Thuston, Mordecai(B)	1818	July 11	Hamilton	03	07	02
Tibbals, Samuel(A)	1801	Dec. 26	Connecticut	05	02	21
Tibbets, Abner Jr.(B)	1831	Sept. 07	Dearborn(Ind	02	05	03
Tibbets, Abner(B)	1814	Dec. 20	Dearborn(Ind	02	06	33
Tibbets, David(B)	1817	Sept. 01	Dearborn(Ind	02	05	04
Tibbets, John(B)	1826	Aug. 24	Dearborn(Ind	02	05	10
Tibbetts, John(B)	1818	Dec. 03	Cincinnati	02	05	05
Tibbs, Willoughby(B)	1810	June 01	Ind.Territry	01	07	27
Tictsort, Wm. Jr.(A)	1830	Jan. 16	Butler	02	10	17
Tietsort, Wm. Jr.(A)	1830	Jan. 16	Butler	02	10	17
Tillford, Alexander(C)	1804	Sept. 04	Kentucky	07	02	11
Tillford, Alexander(C)	1804	Sept. 04	Kentucky	07	02	11
Tillis, John(C)	1808	Dec. 27	Ohio	15	03	31
Tillis, John(C)	1808	Dec. 27	Ohio	14	04	36
Tillman, John(A)	1811	Aug. 13	Preble	03	07	03
Tillman, Tobias(A)	1806	Sept. 01	Montgomery	03	07	23
Tillman, Tobias(A)	1811	Jan. 23	Preble	03	08	28
Tillotson, Joseph(A)	1807	June 11	Kentucky	01	02	09
Tillotson, Joseph(A)	1813	April 14	Hamilton	01	02	09
Tillson, Luther(A)	1816	April 11	Butler	01	10	07
Tillson, Luther(A)	1816	April 30	Butler	01	10	30
Tilman, John(A)	1805	Nov. 05	Montgomery	03	07	12
Tilman, John(A)	1806	July 05	Montgomery	05	04	07
Tilman, John(A)	1815	Sept. 22	Preble	03	07	13
Tilman, John(A)	1816	Nov. 14	Preble	03	07	03
Tilman, John(A)	1831	April 20	Preble	03	09	30
Tilman, John(A)	1831	April 20	Preble	02	10	24
Tilman, John(A)	1831	June 11	Preble	02	11	25
Tilman, John(A)	1831	June 11	Preble	02	11	25
Tilman, John(A)	1832	Jan. 20	Preble	02	11	25
Tilman, John(B)	1836	Jan. 13	Preble	01	17	01
Tilman, John(B)	1836	Jan. 13	Preble	01	18	36
Tilman, Tobias(A)	1805	Nov. 05	Montgomery	03	07	12
Timberman, Abraham(B)	1813	Dec. 15	Butler	01	09	18
Timmerman, John B. Hy.(E)	1837	May 01	Cincinnati	11	11	24

PURCHASER	YEAR	DATE	RESIDENCE	R	T	S
Tindal, Isaac(B)	1834	Aug. 20	Dearborn(Ind	02	05	09
Tindel, Robert A.(E)	1837	Jan. 23	Randolph(Ind	14	19	02
Tindel, Robert A.(E)	1837	Feb. 16	Randolph(Ind	14	19	02
Tiner, Solomon(B)	1807	Jan. 08	Dearborn(Ind	02	09	27
Tingle, John(A)	1802	June 11	Hamilton	06	02	32
Tinker, Ira(B)	1836	March 10	Dearborn(Ind	02	05	05
Tinker, Samuel(B)	1833	April 23	Dearborn(Ind	02	03	04
Tinker, Stephen Ransom(B)	1833	April 19	Dearborn(Ind	02	03	19
Tinkey, George(E)	1811	Oct. 22	Montgomery	12	14	02
Tipsord, Griffin(B)	1811	Aug. 13	Ind.Territry	03	04	03
Tipton, John((C)	1816	Oct. 22	Champaign	12	04	29
Tipton, John(C)	1808	Oct. 29	Champaign	12	04	17
Tipton, John(C)	1808	Oct. 29	Champaign	11	05	35
Tipton, John(C)	1808	Oct. 29	Champaign	12	05	32
Tipton, Thos. M.(A)	1819	Feb. 03	Franklin(Ind	04	09	18
Titmar, Frederick(A)	1814	June 11	Montgomery	04	05	01
Titus, Ezekiel(A)	1807	April 21	Butler	02	03	05
Titus, Ezekiel(A)	1807	Aug. 13	Butler	02	03	05
Titus, Ezekiel(A)	1808	Aug. 22	Butler	02	03	05
Titus, Thomas(E)	1836	Oct. 03	Wayne(Ind)	14	19	23
Titus, Thos.(A)	1831	Aug. 09	Hamilton	05	08	34
Tobey, Eleazer(A)	1814	June 15	Ohio	01	04	05
Todd, George(B)	1812	Feb. 28	Hamilton	01	09	13
Todd, Henry(B)	1816	March 04	Hamilton	02	10	27
Todd, James(C)	1829	June 15	Clark	08	05	24
Todd, John(A)	1806	Oct. 11	Warren	06	05	32
Todd, Nathan'l.(B)	1830	Sept. 07	Dearborn(Ind	02	05	17
Todd, Sam'l.(E)	1818	April 22	Franklin(Ind	13	11	20
Todd, Samuel(B)	1819	May 01	Cincinnati	02	05	22
Todd, Samuel(B)	1819	May 21	Cincinnati	02	04	05
Todd, Samuel(B)	1819	May 21	Cincinnati	02	04	20
Todd, Samuel(E)	1817	Sept. 27	Cincinnati	12	13	07
Todd, Samuel(E)	1817	Sept. 27	?	13	11	21
Tofflemire, John(C)	1811	Feb. 04	Champaign	11	04	27
Tolbert, Tobias(A)	1814	Nov. 02	Butler	03	06	30
Tolburt, Thomas(A)	1804	Aug. 10	Butler	03	03	09
Toler, Asa(B)	1814	Sept. 12	Hamilton	01	11	11
Toles, James(B)	1835	Nov. 27	Butler	01	16	13
Toles, James(B)	1835	Nov. 27	Butler	01	16	14
Toman, Wm.(A)	1828	Dec. 09	Montgomery	04	05	21
Tomas, Joseph(A)	1833	March 21	Cincinnati	02	12	25
Tomas, Joseph(A)	1833	April 01	Cincinnati	02	12	24
Tomlinson, Jesse(E)	1834	Jan. 10	Randolph(Ind	14	20	09
Tomlinson, Jesse(E)	1836	Sept. 24	Randolph(Ind	14	20	09
Tomlinson, Jesse(E)	1836	Oct. 17	Randolph(Ind	14	20	02
Tomlinson, Purnel(A)	1826	June 21	Preble	01	08	26
Tomlinson, Zadock(A)	1813	Nov. 17	Preble	02	08	29
Tomlinson, Zeruah(E)	1836	Aug. 22	Randolph(Ind	14	21	17
Toner, Edward(E)	1832	Jan. 07	Franklin(Ind	12	12	05
Toner, Thomas(E)	1815	Aug. 28	Franklin(Ind	13	13	19
Toney, James(B)	1824	July 06	Wayne(Ind)	01	12	22
Toney, Jesse(A)	1808	Oct. 13	Preble	02	07	24
Toney, Pendexter(A)	1816	March 29	Virginia	01	07	07
Toney, Pendexter(A)	1816	March 29	Virginia	01	07	05
Toney, Poindexter(A)	1816	April 09	Virginia	01	07	06
Tong, Thos.(A)	1829	Oct. 01	Logan	08	02	27
Tony, Jonathan(A)	1828	Oct. 24	Preble	01	08	27
Torline, John Herman(E)	1837	April 07	Cincinnati	11	10	10
Torrence, Aaron(A)	1806	Sept. 26	Pennsylvania	03	06	18
Torrence, Geo. P.(B)	1814	Dec. 02	Cincinnati	03	02	21
Torrence, Geo. P.(B)	1817	Aug. 19	Cincinnati	03	08	26
Torrence, George P.	1808	March 01	Cincinnati	?	?	?
Torrence, George P.	1808	March 01	Cincinnati	?	?	?
Torrence, George P.	1808	March 01	Cincinnati	?	?	?
Torrence, George P.	1808	March 02	Cincinnati	?	?	?
Torrence, George P.(A)	1810	Aug. 18	Cincinnati	04	02	08
Torrence, George P.(A)	1811	Aug. 13	Cincinnati	06	04	09
Torrence, George P.(A)	1813	Dec. 15	Cincinnati	05	04	07
Torrence, George P.(A)	1817	Aug. 02	Cincinnati	02	11	15

PURCHASER	YEAR	DATE	RESIDENCE	R	T	S
Torrence, George P.(A)	1817	Oct. 15	Cincinnati	02	11	32
Torrence, George P.(A)	1818	July 17	Cincinnati	01	02	31
Torrence, George P.(A)	1817	Oct. 15	Cincinnati	02	10	05
Torrence, George P.(A)	1831	July 02	Cincinnati	01	02	31
Torrence, George P.(B)	1810	Dec. 12	Cincinnati	01	04	04
Torrence, George P.(B)	1814	April 30	Cincinnati	01	07	20
Torrence, George P.(C)	1811	Sept. 24	Cincinnati	12	04	10
Torrence, George P.(C)	1814	April 12	Cincinnati	10	02	25
Torrence, George P.(E)	1811	Oct. 28	Cincinnati	13	15	07
Torrence, George P.(E)	1811	Oct. 28	Hamilton	13	14	05
Torrence, George P.(E)	1815	Oct. 27	Cincinnati	13	14	05
Torrence, George P.(E)	1815	Nov. 22	Cincinnati	13	14	04
Torrence, Joseph(A)	1805	July 15	Pennsylvania	03	06	33
Torrence, William(B)	1808	Feb. 13	Ohio	01	06	13
Torrence, William(E)	1815	June 24	Pennsylvania	13	13	28
Torris, Peter(E)	1838	Feb. 13	Montgomery	14	20	36
Tosh, James(A)	1815	May 13	Preble	01	08	14
Tosh, James(A)	1829	Jan. 27	Preble	01	08	15
Totten, Joseph G.	1808	March 01	Hamilton	?	?	?
Totten, Joseph G.	1808	March 01	Hamilton	?	?	?
Towcy, Zerry(B)	1803	July 19	New York	02	05	25
Towel, Henry(E)	1811	Nov. 16	So. Carolina	13	17	13
Towel, John(E)	1811	Nov. 16	Nor.Carolina	14	17	05
Townsen, Thomas(B)	1809	Dec. 24	Hamilton	01	05	05
Townsend, Eli(A)	1832	Aug. 03	Preble	03	09	17
Townsend, James(E)	1811	Oct. 31	Wayne(Ind)	14	16	18
Townsend, James(E)	1811	Dec. 12	Wayne(Ind)	14	16	18
Townsend, Joel(B)	1817	Nov. 11	Switzerland	03	04	35
Townsend, John(A)	1805	June 24	Butler	03	03	06
Townsend, John(B)	1807	Jan. 10	Warren	01	13	04
Townsend, John(B)	1808	Jan. 13	Warren	02	13	01
Townsend, John(B)	1813	Oct. 23	Wayne(Ind)	01	13	33
Townsend, Jonathan(A)	1823	Feb. 22	Darke	03	09	20
Townsend, Jonathan(A)	1830	Oct. 01	Darke	03	09	29
Townsend, Jonathan(A)	1832	Sept. 04	Darke	03	09	29
Townsend, Joseph(A)	1818	July 22	Darke	03	09	20
Townsend, Wm. Jr.(A)	1823	Feb. 22	Darke	02	11	24
Townsley, William(A)	1814	April 26	Greene	06	08	35
Townsley, William(A)	1814	April 26	Greene	06	08	25
Townson, William Jefferson(E)	1835	March 17	Franklin(Ind	13	12	17
Traver, Levi(B)	1834	Dec. 24	Butler	03	04	27
Travis, Amos Jr.(A)	1837	May 24	Butler	02	14	25
Travis, John(A)	1836	Nov. 07	Butler	02	14	36
Travis, John(A)	1836	Nov. 12	Butler	02	14	35
Travis, John(A)	1837	Sept. 02	Butler	02	14	23
Tread, William(B)	1815	May 13	Franklin(Ind	02	08	26
Treber, Henry(A)	1806	July 05	Hamilton	02	05	35
Treber, Henry(A)	1811	Aug. 13	Butler	02	05	35
Treber, Jacob(C)	1806	Jan. 24	Adams	09	03	27
Treber, John(A)	1806	July 05	Hamilton	02	05	35
Treber, John(A)	1811	Aug. 13	Butler	02	05	35
Treitline, Henry(E)	1837	May 20	Cincinnati	13	11	22
Tremble, Moses(C)	1831	Sept. 05	Warren	12	02	05
Trembly, Daniel(A)	1805	Sept. 23	Butler	01	04	14
Trench, Jeremiah(C)	1802	?	Hamilton	05	02	01
Trent, John(C)	1831	Oct. 17	Preble	13	04	30
Trimble, Daniel(B)	1806	Aug. 18	Warren	01	13	08
Trimble, Elihu(A)	1816	Sept. 20	Virginia	01	09	10
Trimble, Jacob(C)	1801	Dec. 28	Hamilton	04	04	19
Trimble, James(A)	1817	Aug. 26	Kentucky	04	08	11
Trimble, James(A)	1817	Aug. 26	Kentucky	04	08	02
Trimble, John(A)	1817	Dec. 04	Kentucky	04	08	10
Trimbly, Dan'l.(E)	1822	Sept. 13	Butler	13	14	12
Trinkle, John(D)	1811	Jan. 28	Hamilton	02	03	26
Tron, Frederick(C)	1821	Oct. 18	Cincinnati	12	02	18
Troth, John(E)	1818	Sept. 15	Pennsylvania	13	13	31
Troth, Joseph(A)	1836	Oct. 24	Highland	02	14	14
Trotter, Joseph Junr.(A)	1806	Aug. 01	Kentucky	02	07	36
Trotter, Samuel(A)	1806	Oct. 08	Kentucky	05	08	24

PURCHASER	YEAR	DATE	RESIDENCE	R	T	S
Trotter, Samuel(A)	1814	April 14	Miami	05	08	07
Trousdel, Samuel(B)	1815	Jan. 21	Kentucky	01	02	03
Trousdel, Thomas(C)	1801	Dec. 31	Hamilton	05	02	02
Troutman, George(C)	1808	Nov. 24	Pennsylvania	03	02	08
Truax, David(A)	1809	Dec. 13	Preble	01	07	14
Truax, John(A)	1814	May 07	Preble	01	07	11
True, Abel(B)	1818	June 09	New York	02	06	26
True, Abel(B)	1818	June 09	New York	02	06	25
True, Reuben(B)	1831	Dec. 03	Dearborn(Ind	02	06	25
Trueax, Isaac(A)	1808	April 20	Preble	02	07	19
Trueax, Isaac(A)	1814	Aug. 27	Kentucky	01	07	11
Trueby, Christopher(C)	1801	Dec. 31	Hamilton	07	03	30
Truesdell, James(B)	1814	July 02	Dearborn(Ind	01	02	03
Truitt, Parker(B)	1832	Sept. 24	Switzerland	02	02	30
Truitt, Reley(B)	1817	Oct. 23	Kentucky	02	02	21
Truitt, Riley(B)	1817	Oct. 09	Warren	02	05	18
Truitt, Riley(B)	1817	Oct. 09	Warren	03	06	11
Truitt, Riley(B)	1817	Oct. 09	Warren	03	06	11
Truitt, Riley(B)	1828	Jan. 19	Dearborn(Ind	02	02	21
Truitt, Samuel(C)	1813	April 01	Champaign	11	05	08
Truitt, Samuel(C)	1814	Dec. 17	Champaign	10	04	18
Trusdel, John(A)	1807	May 07	Montgomery	02	08	32
Trusdel, Solomon(A)	1807	Feb. 18	Kentucky	02	07	01
Trustee, Demce(B)	1815	June 26	Dearborn(Ind	01	06	29
Tucker, Abraham(A)	1829	Aug. 29	Montgomery	04	09	22
Tucker, Elijah H.(B)	1826	Aug. 15	Hamilton	01	10	22
Tucker, Elijah H.(B)	1827	Oct. 20	Hamilton	01	09	17
Tucker, Ephraim(B)	1816	Jan. 04	Butler	01	10	35
Tucker, Flemmin(B)	1835	Nov. 03	Randolph(Ind	01	17	36
Tucker, Flemmin(B)	1835	Nov. 03	Randolph(Ind	01	17	36
Tucker, James C.(B)	1826	Aug. 28	Hamilton	01	09	07
Tucker, James(E)	1814	Nov. 17	Wayne(Ind)	13	16	34
Tucker, Joel(B)	1828	Nov. 24	Franklin(Ind	03	08	01
Tucker, John(A)	1814	Dec. 21	Cincinnati	01	03	06
Tucker, John(C)	1808	Jan. 14	Champaign	14	03	05
Tucker, Jonathan(A)	1829	Sept. 03	Montgomery	04	07	25
Tucker, Jonathan(A)	1831	June 03	Montgomery	02	12	13
Tucker, Nathaniel(B)	1814	June 17	Dearborn(Ind	01	06	19
Tucker, Nicholas(E)	1826	June 03	Wayne(Ind)	14	18	24
Tucker, Sally(C)	1818	Aug. 28	Miami	11	02	23
Tucker, Walter(B)	1812	July 28	Warren	01	09	18
Tucker, Walter(B)	1814	Sept. 07	Franklin(Ind	01	09	06
Tucker, William(B)	1831	Aug. 15	Dearborn(Ind	02	06	12
Tucker, William(B)	1832	March 12	Dearborn(Ind	02	06	12
Tucker, William(B)	1832	Oct. 04	Dearborn(Ind	02	06	12
Tucker, William(B)	1832	Oct. 29	Dearborn(Ind	02	07	34
Tulles, Jonathan(C)	1815	June 08	Warren	11	05	05
Tullis, Aaron(A)	1804	Nov. 20	Warren	06	05	21
Tullis, Aaron(A)	1804	Nov. 20	Warren	06	05	20
Tullis, David(A)	1806	Aug. 11	Warren	06	05	19
Tullis, John B.(B)	1836	June 10	Darke	01	17	23
Tullis, John(C)	1807	May 11	Montgomery	14	04	34
Tullis, John(C)	1813	April 14	Champaign	14	04	34
Tully, James(A)	1822	May 02	Preble	02	09	27
Tunks, Philip(C)	1827	Nov. 02	Shelby	13	02	08
Turman, Benjamin(C)	1804	Dec. 31	Greene	10	06	35
Turman, Benjamin(C)	1804	Dec. 31	Greene	10	05	12
Turman, Benjamin(C)	1807	Jan. 29	Champaign	09	05	14
Turman, Isaac(C)	1808	Jan. 12	Champaign	10	05	17
Turner, Andrew(A)	1812	Nov. 11	Butler	01	04	24
Turner, Ann(A)	1810	June 02	Ind.Territry	01	04	14
Turner, George(A)	1817	Sept. 29	Cincinnati	06	07	20
Turner, George(A)	1818	June 13	Cincinnati	04	11	12
Turner, George(A)	1818	June 13	Cincinnati	05	10	07
Turner, George(B)	1815	March 11	Kentucky	02	02	21
Turner, George(C)	1804	Dec. 31	Greene	09	04	06
Turner, George(C)	1804	Dec. 31	Greene	09	04	05
Turner, George(C)	1804	Dec. 31	Greene	09	04	10
Turner, George(C)	1813	April 16	Cincinnati	09	04	05

PURCHASER	YEAR	DATE	RESIDENCE	R	T	S
Turner, James(C)	1804	Sept. 24	Kentucky	12	04	09
Turner, James(C)	1806	April 03	Champaign	12	05	17
Turner, James(C)	1807	Feb. 04	Champaign	12	05	17
Turner, James(C)	1812	March 09	Champaign	13	05	19
Turner, Jno.(E)	1812	Jan. 22	Wayne(Ind)	14	16	21
Turner, John(B)	1806	July 28	Kentucky	01	13	17
Turner, John(B)	1808	Jan. 12	Warren	01	15	32
Turner, John(B)	1811	Dec. 11	Wayne(Ind)	01	13	17
Turner, John(B)	1817	Aug. 18	Wayne(Ind)	01	15	32
Turner, John(E)	1832	June 04	Franklin(Ind	12	11	27
Turner, Joseph(C)	1824	June 26	Logan	14	02	02
Turner, Joseph(C)	1828	Sept. 05	Logan	14	02	02
Turner, Ralph(B)	1827	July 14	Cincinnati	01	02	02
Turner, Ralph(B)	1827	July 14	Cincinnati	01	03	34
Turner, Ralph(B)	1827	July 14	Cincinnati	01	03	35
Turner, Ralph(B)	1827	July 14	Cincinnati	01	03	36
Turner, Ralph(C)	1827	March 16	Cincinnati	08	03	29
Turner, Robert(B)	1835	April 17	Dearborn(Ind	03	05	35
Turner, Samuel(B)	1835	Aug. 24	Dearborn(Ind	02	03	14
Turner, Thomas(C)	1836	Feb. 05	Logan	13	03	34
Turner, William(B)	1819	Jan. 25	Dearborn(Ind	03	06	27
Turner, William(B)	1837	Jan. 11	Dearborn(Ind	03	05	35
Turner, William(B)	1838	Jan. 06	Dearborn(Ind	03	05	26
Turney, Peter(C)	1804	Dec. 22	Warren	05	03	04
Turney, Peter(C)	1804	Dec. 25	Kentucky	05	04	34
Turpen, Henry(A)	1831	Dec. 28	Darke	02	12	15
Turpen, Joseph Jackson(A)	1834	Dec. 18	Darke	02	12	03
Turrill, Heman B.(A)	1836	June 20	Hamilton	03	11	12
Turrill, Heman B.(A)	1836	Aug. 09	Hamilton	03	11	02
Turrill, Heman B.(A)	1837	July 14	Hamilton	02	14	05
Tutchen, William(B)	1819	Jan. 25	Hamilton	03	06	34
Tuthill, John(A)	1832	May 08	New York	04	07	17
Tuttle, Caleb(C)	1817	Nov. 21	Champaign	12	02	17
Tuttle, Caleb(C)	1827	Aug. 25	Clark	14	03	29
Tuttle, Caleb(C)	1827	Aug. 25	Clark	14	03	30
Tuttle, Cyrus(A)	1837	Jan. 26	Darke	01	12	02
Tuttle, Cyrus(A)	1837	April 04	Darke	01	12	02
Tuttle, Darlin(E)	1836	Jan. 23	Butler	13	12	07
Tuttle, George(B)	1832	Feb. 18	Dearborn(Ind	01	07	32
Tuttle, Isaiah Clemmons(E)	1833	Sept. 26	Butler	13	12	07
Tuttle, Jno.(C)	1827	Aug. 25	Clark	14	03	29
Tuttle, Jno.(C)	1827	Aug. 25	Clark	14	03	30
Tuttle, Sylvanus(C)	1808	Jan. 12	Champaign	10	05	01
Tuttle, Sylvanus(C)	1813	June 15	Champaign	10	05	25
Tuttle, Sylvanus(C)	1813	April 14	Champaign	10	05	01
Tuttle, Thaddeus(C)	1817	Sept. 08	Champaign	13	02	13
Tuttle, Thadius(C)	1811	Dec. 27	Champaign	10	05	19
Tuttle, Zebdee(C)	1817	Nov. 21	Champaign	12	02	17
Tweedy, James(E)	1813	Aug. 30	Franklin(Ind	12	13	01
Tweedy, Robert(A)	1815	July 22	Cincinnati	01	02	35
Tydings, Edward(B)	1815	Sept. 01	Hamilton	01	03	29
Tyier, William(B)	1827	Nov. 13	Dearborn(Ind	03	06	36
Tyner, John(E)	1811	Oct. 22	Ind.Territry	12	15	33
Tyner, John(E)	1811	Oct. 28	Franklin(Ind	12	15	33
Tyner, Richand(E)	1814	Nov. 19	Wayne(Ind)	12	14	10
Tyner, Richard(E)	1811	Oct. 22	Kentucky	12	14	22
Tyner, Richard(E)	1811	Oct. 28	Franklin(Ind	12	15	33
Tyner, Sollomon(B)	1804	Nov. 30	Ind.Territry	02	09	33
Tyner, William(B)	1804	Sept. 21	Ind.Territry	02	09	33
Tyrrel, Asahel(B)	1833	March 02	Dearborn(Ind	02	06	31
Uhlhorn, John Frederick(E)	1836	Oct. 14	Cincinnati	11	10	23
Ulery, Daniel(A)	1810	Nov. 13	Montgomery	05	08	29
Ulery, John(A)	1831	May 03	Miami	05	07	09
Ullery, Daniel(A)	1810	Nov. 13	Montgomery	05	03	15
Ullery, Jacob(A)	1816	June 22	Warren	04	09	04
Ullery, John(A)	1815	Feb. 09	Miami	05	07	08
Ullrich, George(E)	1837	July 13	Cincinnati	14	21	36
Ulray, Jacob(A)	1810	Aug. 29	Montgomery	05	05	15
Ulrick, David(A)	1803	Oct. 06	Pennsylvania	05	04	34

PURCHASER	YEAR	DATE	RESIDENCE	R	T	S
Ulrick, Joseph(A)	1805	Nov. 14	Pennsylvania	04	05	21
Ulrick, Stephen(A)	1814	April 18	Montgomery	04	05	24
Umphries, Robert(C)	1811	Dec. 10	Champaign	10	05	31
Underhill, William(E)	1811	Oct. 24	Wayne(Ind)	13	17	13
Underhill, Wm.(E)	1814	Oct. 22	Wayne(Ind)	13	17	13
Underwood, Berryman(C)	1811	Nov. 07	Champaign	11	04	20
Underwood, John(C)	1813	Feb. 15	Miami	12	01	10
Underwood, John(C)	1813	March 20	Miami	12	01	10
Underwood, Willm.(C)	1813	Feb. 15	Miami	12	01	10
Ungres, Michael(C)	1804	Nov. 13	Montgomery	05	02	30
Unrue, George(A)	1824	Jan. 29	Montgomery	04	05	30
Unthank, Josiah(B)	1830	Oct. 30	Wayne(Ind)	01	15	21
Updike, Elijah(B)	1817	Aug. 06	Franklin(Ind	01	09	15
Updike, Peter(B)	1817	Aug. 06	Franklin(Ind	01	09	15
Upjohn, Charlotte(E)	1837	April 06	Cincinnati	12	11	23
Upjohn, Thomas(E)	1837	April 06	Franklin(Ind	12	11	24
Upjohn, Thomas(E)	1837	April 06	Franklin(Ind	12	11	23
Urmey, John(A)	1806	March 28	Montgomery	02	08	27
Urner, Jonas(A)	1805	Oct. 29	Pennsylvania	03	05	29
Usher, David(B)	1833	Dec. 13	Switzerland	02	08	23
Usher, David(B)	1835	March 06	Franklin(Ind	02	08	15
Ustter, Frederick(C)	1814	Nov. 11	Champaign	11	04	22
Utter, Benj'n. Franklin(E)	1834	July 10	Fayette	12	13	19
Utz, Lewis(A)	1817	Nov. 08	Kentucky	03	06	01
Utz, Lewis(A)	1817	Nov. 08	Kentucky	03	06	12
Utz, Lewis(A)	1818	Oct. 06	Preble	03	06	01
Vail, George(C)	1814	Dec. 30	Hamilton	10	03	23
Vail, George(C)	1815	Feb. 22	Hamilton	10	03	24
Vail, Gilbert(A)	1832	Aug. 01	Darke	01	13	24
Vail, Henry(A)	1813	July 27	Butler	02	07	14
Vail, Hugh B.(A)	1837	Feb. 11	Butler	02	14	02
Vail, Jonathan(B)	1817	Aug. 25	Dearborn(Ind	02	05	18
Vail, Jonathan(B)	1817	Aug. 25	Dearborn(Ind	03	06	13
Vail, Jonathan(B)	1817	Aug. 25	Dearborn(Ind	03	06	12
Vail, Moses(A)	1804	Sept. 24	Butler	04	02	03
Vail, Moses(A)	1804	Sept. 24	Butler	04	02	10
Vail, Moses(A)	1805	Oct. 25	Butler	06	07	19
Vail, Moses(A)	1810	Dec. 12	Butler	04	02	03
Vail, Moses(C)	1805	Sept. 30	Butler	04	02	28
Vail, Moses(C)	1810	Dec. 12	Butler	04	02	28
Vail, Stephen(A)	1802	Feb. 22	Hamilton	04	02	21
Vail, Stephen(C)	1801	Nov. 28	Hamilton	04	02	22
Vail, Thomas(C)	1811	Nov. 04	Ross	12	04	13
Valentine, Daniel(C)	1808	Jan. 29	Champaign	12	01	22
Vallentine, Aaron(B)	1836	Dec. 15	Cincinnati	02	05	07
Vallier, Charles(C)	1804	Sept. 10	Cincinnati	04	03	29
Van Briggle, John(B)	1817	Oct. 02	Clermont	03	02	08
Van Briggle, John(B)	1817	Oct. 04	Clermont	03	02	08
Van Briggle, Peter(B)	1815	June 09	Switzerland	03	02	09
Van Cleve, Benjamin(C)	1801	Dec. 09	Hamilton	07	02	33
Van Cleve, Benjamin(C)	1801	Dec. 09	Hamilton	07	01	04
Van Cleve, Benjamin(C)	1811	Sept. 26	Montgomery	08	02	27
Van Cleve, William(C)	1811	March 05	Montgomery	08	02	21
Van Cleve, William(C)	1811	Oct. 23	Montgomery	08	02	14
Van Handorf, Bernard(E)	1837	Jan. 07	Cincinnati	12	11	32
Van Meter, Joel(C)	1816	July 18	Greene	12	03	19
Van Nest, Garret(C)	1801	Dec. 31	Hamilton	05	02	18
Van Nest, Isaac(C)	1801	Dec. 18	Hamilton	04	02	18
Van Nest, John(C)	1801	Dec. 30	Hamilton	04	02	18
Van Nuys, John(A)	1803	Dec. 20	Butler	03	02	11
Van Nuys, John(C)	1801	Dec. 19	Cincinnati	05	04	21
VanDalsem, Henry(E)	1831	Dec. 01	Fayette	12	13	33
VanHorn, Joseph(C)	1804	Oct. 01	Hamilton	02	03	26
VanHorne, Joshua(A)	1831	July 08	Hamilton	05	07	02
VanMiddlesworth, Henry(B)	1819	April 06	Cincinnati	02	05	30
VanMiddlesworth, Henry(B)	1820	June 05	Hamilton	02	04	06
VanVickel, Robert(A)	1812	Aug. 03	Butler	01	03	10
Vanansdal, Cornelius(A)	1814	Aug. 17	Preble	01	09	23
Vanansdal, Peter(A)	1824	June 08	Preble	02	07	22

PURCHASER	YEAR	DATE	RESIDENCE	R	T	S
Vanansdal, Peter(A)	1824	June 08	Preble	02	07	22
Vanansdal, Peter(A)	1824	June 19	Preble	02	07	21
Vanansdle, John(A)	1808	Dec. 14	Preble	03	05	15
Vanarsdal, John(C)	1802	Dec. 29	Hamilton	06	01	04
Vanarsdol, John(A)	1802	Jan. 14	Hamilton	05	05	02
Vanator, Benj'm.(A)	1831	Nov. 01	Montgomery	06	08	03
Vanausdal, Cornelius(A)	1816	April 29	Preble	01	08	05
Vanausdal, John(A)	1803	Dec. 14	Virginia	03	05	10
Vanausdoll, Isaac(A)	1837	Oct. 20	Butler	01	14	03
Vanblaracom, Sam'l.(C)	1827	Nov. 20	Shelby	13	02	35
Vanblaracum, David(B)	1818	June 11	Hamilton	02	02	22
Vanblarecume, David(B)	1811	Jan. 05	Hamilton	01	09	28
Vanblaricim, John(B)	1806	Aug. 06	Hamilton	01	08	29
Vanblaricum, John(B)	1810	March 16	Dearborn(Ind	01	08	30
Vanblaricum, John(B)	1811	Dec. 11	Franklin(Ind	01	08	29
Vanblaricum, John(B)	1812	March 05	Franklin(Ind	01	08	19
Vanblaricum, Peter(B)	1817	June 23	Hamilton	02	02	23
Vanblaricun, John(B)	1814	May 26	Franklin(Ind	01	08	28
Vanbuskirk, George(E)	1814	April 18	Kentucky	12	16	23
Vancamp, Aaron(A)	1804	Aug. 09	Butler	02	03	01
Vancamp, Charles(B)	1813	Aug. 18	Franklin(Ind	02	09	35
Vancamp, Moses(A)	1804	Aug. 09	Butler	02	03	01
Vance, David(A)	1814	Jan. 11	Butler	01	09	19
Vance, David(C)	1812	Dec. 19	Champaign	10	06	36
Vance, David(C)	1813	March 23	Champaign	12	05	31
Vance, David(C)	1813	April 14	Champaign	10	06	36
Vance, Geo. B.(E)	1838	May 21	Jay Co.,Ind.	15	22	09
Vance, George B.(E)	1836	Aug. 30	Randolph(Ind	15	22	33
Vance, George(A)	1827	Sept. 05	Preble	03	06	19
Vance, George(A)	1829	June 09	Preble	03	06	19
Vance, George(E)	1836	Aug. 23	Randolph(Ind	13	21	24
Vance, Jacob(A)	1807	June 04	Montgomery	03	05	24
Vance, Jacob(A)	1811	Nov. 21	Preble	03	07	32
Vance, Jno. W.(C)	1814	March 23	Champaign	12	05	33
Vance, John M.(C)	1813	April 14	Champaign	12	05	25
Vance, John W.(C)	1811	Dec. 30	Champaign	12	05	25
Vance, John W.(C)	1812	Nov. 18	Champaign	12	05	27
Vance, John(A)	1805	April 26	Montgomery	03	05	25
Vance, John(C)	1802	Dec. 30	Hamilton	05	04	18
Vance, John(C)	1806	Dec. 10	Greene	09	07	33
Vance, John(C)	1806	Oct. 22	Greene	09	06	03
Vance, John(C)	1812	Jan. 09	Champaign	12	05	26
Vance, John(C)	1812	April 14	Champaign	09	06	03
Vance, John(C)	1812	April 15	Champaign	09	07	33
Vance, John(E)	1811	Oct. 28	Greene	12	13	03
Vance, John(E)	1813	Dec. 25	Butler	12	14	32
Vance, Joseph C.(C)	1804	Dec. 24	Greene	10	06	36
Vance, Joseph Jr.(A)	1813	Oct. 27	Butler	01	04	18
Vance, Joseph(C)	1802	Dec. 30	Hamilton	06	03	32
Vance, Joseph(C)	1807	April 17	Champaign	12	05	19
Vance, Joseph(C)	1807	May 28	Champaign	12	05	25
Vance, Joseph(C)	1811	May 06	Champaign	12	05	20
Vance, Joseph(C)	1812	Jan. 09	Champaign	12	05	26
Vance, Joseph(C)	1813	April 14	Champaign	12	05	19
Vance, Joseph(C)	1813	Nov. 29	Champaign	12	05	26
Vance, Joseph(C)	1814	March 14	Champaign	12	05	26
Vance, Joseph(C)	1816	Nov. 13	Champaign	12	05	26
Vance, Joseph(C)	1824	June 07	Champaign	12	05	26
Vance, Joseph(E)	1814	March 19	Wayne(Ind)	12	13	04
Vance, Mary(C)	1815	Aug. 08	Champaign	09	06	03
Vance, Michel(A)	1817	Sept. 20	Montgomery	02	09	36
Vance, Sam'l. C.(A)	1828	Nov. 12	Dearborn(Ind	06	05	18
Vance, Sam'l. C.(A)	1828	Nov. 12	Dearborn(Ind	06	05	18
Vance, Sam'l. C.(B)	1829	July 01	Dearborn(Ind	03	06	21
Vance, Samuel C.(A)	1817	May 10	Cincinnati	06	05	18
Vance, Samuel C.(A)	1817	Dec. 29	Cincinnati	02	11	10
Vance, Samuel C.(A)	1817	Dec. 29	Cincinnati	02	11	10
Vance, Samuel C.(A)	1818	April 25	Hamilton	02	11	08
Vance, Samuel C.(B)	1802	Sept. 02	Cincinnati	02	05	34

PURCHASER	YEAR	DATE	RESIDENCE	R	T	S
Vance, Samuel C.(B)	1805	July 01	Laurancebrgh	01	05	21
Vance, Samuel C.(B)	1801	July 23	U. S. Army	01	05	15
Vance, Samuel C.(B)	1817	Aug. 19	Cincinnati	03	08	34
Vance, Samuel C.(B)	1817	Aug. 19	Cincinnati	02	06	18
Vance, Samuel C.(B)	1817	Aug. 27	Cincinnati	02	06	13
Vance, Samuel C.(B)	1817	Sept. 10	Cincinnati	03	09	13
Vance, Samuel C.(B)	1817	Sept. 25	Cincinnati	02	08	06
Vance, Samuel C.(B)	1817	Sept. 25	Cincinnati	02	08	06
Vance, Samuel C.(B)	1817	Sept. 29	Cincinnati	03	08	36
Vance, Samuel C.(B)	1817	Oct. 10	Cincinnati	03	07	13
Vance, Samuel C.(B)	1818	March 11	Cincinnati	02	08	07
Vance, Samuel C.(B)	1818	March 11	Cincinnati	03	07	01
Vance, Samuel C.(B)	1818	April 06	Cincinnati	02	06	06
Vance, Samuel C.(B)	1818	April 11	Cincinnati	01	02	23
Vance, Samuel C.(B)	1818	April 25	Hamilton	01	07	01
Vance, Samuel C.(B)	1818	May 01	Hamilton	01	09	11
Vance, Samuel C.(B)	1818	July 17	Cincinnati	03	06	21
Vance, Samuel C.(B)	1818	Oct. 26	Cincinnati	03	07	01
Vance, Samuel C.(B)	1817	Aug. 27	Cincinnati	02	07	33
Vance, Samuel C.(B)	1817	Aug. 27	Cincinnati	02	07	27
Vance, Samuel C.(C)	1802	Dec. 31	Cincinnati	07	02	07
Vance, Samuel C.(C)	1807	Jan. 01	Ind.Territry	11	05	28
Vance, Samuel C.(C)	1812	April 15	Ind.Territry	11	05	28
Vance, Samuel C.(C)	1816	Dec. 03	Cincinnati	13	04	02
Vance, Samuel C.(C)	1816	Dec. 03	Cincinnati	13	04	03
Vance, Samuel C.(C)	1816	Dec. 03	Cincinnati	13	04	03
Vance, Samuel C.(C)	1816	Dec. 03	Cincinnati	13	04	03
Vance, Samuel C.(C)	1816	Dec. 03	Cincinnati	13	04	02
Vance, Samuel C.(C)	1816	Dec. 03	Cincinnati	13	04	02
Vance, Samuel C.(C)	1817	Dec. 29	Cincinnati	09	05	07
Vance, Samuel C.(E)	1817	Oct. 03	Cincinnati	13	11	15
Vance, Samuel C.(E)	1818	April 11	Cincinnati	13	16	34
Vance, Samuel C.(E)	1818	June 11	Cincinnati	13	15	07
Vance, Samuel C.(E)	1818	April 11	Cincinnati	13	16	30
Vance, Samuel(C)	1814	June 22	Pennsylvania	13	14	08
Vance, Samuel(E)	1816	June 24	Pennsylvania	13	14	17
Vance, William(B)	1832	May 10	Franklin(Ind	01	06	04
Vanchoik, David(B)	1819	March 19	Cincinnati	03	05	01
Vancickle, Evert(A)	1813	Nov. 30	Butler	01	03	04
Vancleefe, Benjamin(A)	1805	June 13	Montgomery	03	03	13
Vancleefe, Benjamin(A)	1805	June 13	Montgomery	03	03	14
Vancleve, Benjamin(C)	1805	July 22	Dayton	08	02	30
Vancleve, Benjamin(C)	1810	June 21	Montgomery	08	02	27
Vancleve, Benjamin(C)	1811	Jan. 11	Montgomery	08	02	27
Vancleve, Benjamin(C)	1811	Sept. 26	Montgomery	08	02	27
Vancleve, Isaac S.(C)	1825	Oct. 15	Montgomery	13	02	35
Vandamark, Daniel(C)	1811	Dec. 10	Fairfield	13	02	07
Vanderburgh,GeorgeWashington(E	1835	Jan. 28	Clinton	13	19	11
Vanderburgh,GeorgeWashington(E	1836	Jan. 25	Clinton	13	19	11
Vanderen, James(C)	1804	Sept. 24	Kentucky	05	02	11
Vandeusen, Nicholas(C)	1813	Aug. 11	Champaign	09	06	25
Vandeveer, Arthur(A)	1801	Aug. 17	New Jersey	05	02	28
Vandeveer, John(A)	1810	Dec. 12	Butler	03	05	31
Vandeventer, Cornelius(C)	1807	Feb. 26	Greene	08	05	04
Vandever, Arthur(C)	1806	May 10	Warren	10	02	10
Vandever, Arthur(C)	1806	May 10	Warren	10	02	10
Vandever, Arthur(C)	1806	May 10	Warren	10	02	10
Vandiventer, Cornelius(C)	1812	April 15	Greene	08	05	04
Vandola, Joseph(C)	1801	Dec. 02	Hamilton	05	04	36
Vandolah, Jesse(B)	1818	Aug. 24	Hamilton	02	04	18
Vandolah, Jesse(B)	1818	Aug. 24	Hamilton	03	05	11
Vandolah, John(B)	1833	Aug. 21	Dearborn(Ind	02	04	18
Vandoren, Christian(A)	1814	Feb. 21	Preble	03	05	08
Vandoren, Christian(A)	1815	June 24	Butler	01	04	15
Vandusen, Isaac(C)	1807	April 09	Massachusett	09	06	27
Vanduson, Henry(B)	1833	July 23	Switzerland	01	03	31
Vaneaton, Abraham(C)	1801	Dec. 30	Hamilton	05	03	06
Vaneaton, Abraham(E)	1812	Aug. 05	Franklin(Ind	13	14	22
Vaneaton, Abram(C)	1802	Dec. 29	Hamilton	06	02	01

PURCHASER	YEAR	DATE	RESIDENCE	R	T	S
Vaneil, John(C)	1802	Dec. 30	Hamilton	05	02	24
Vaneman, Harvey(A)	1831	June 01	Miami	05	08	26
Vaneman, John(A)	1828	Oct. 07	Miami	05	07	01
Vaneman, John(A)	1832	Jan. 27	Miami	05	07	11
Vanfossen, Ezra(D)	1812	Dec. 29	Hamilton	02	03	08
Vanhise, Cornel's.(B)	1829	Dec. 11	Wayne(Ind)	01	15	11
Vanhise, William(B)	1817	June 21	Butler	01	03	33
Vanhise, William(B)	1832	Jan. 16	Wayne(Ind)	01	15	01
Vanhorn, Cornelius(B)	1817	July 31	Dearborn(Ind	02	06	11
Vanhorn, Robert(A)	1806	Aug. 11	Warren	05	06	03
Vanhorn, Robert(A)	1816	April 15	Miami	04	09	34
Vanhorne, Thos. Budd(C)	1831	Aug. 08	Piqua	12	01	13
Vanhouten, Hallamas C.(B)	1816	April 11	Dearborn(Ind	02	07	35
Vanhouten, Hallamas C.(B)	1816	May 06	Dearborn(Ind	02	06	02
Vanhouten, Hallamas C.(B)	1816	May 06	Dearborn(Ind	02	07	27
Vaniman, John(A)	1815	Aug. 30	Miami	02	08	14
Vaniman, Susannah(A)	1814	Nov. 04	Miami	05	08	36
Vankirk, John D.(A)	1836	July 26	Hamilton	01	14	27
Vankirk, William C.(A)	1836	July 26	Miami	01	14	28
Vankirk, William H.(A)	1837	April 05	Hamilton	01	14	28
Vanline, Edmund(A)	1815	June 19	Hamilton	01	03	13
Vanmater, Abraham(E)	1814	June 14	Virginia	13	15	34
Vanmater, Abraham(E)	1814	June 14	Virginia	13	14	03
Vanmater, Joseph(E)	1814	March 18	Franklin(Ind	13	13	02
Vanmatre, Joseph(E)	1813	Aug. 30	Butler	13	13	02
Vanmeetre, Henry(C)	1808	Nov. 02	Champaign	10	06	29
Vanmeter, Abraham(E)	1814	June 14	Virginia	13	14	04
Vanmeter, Abraham(E)	1816	June 26	Virginia	13	15	34
Vanmeter, Benjamin(A)	1837	March 01	Clark	01	13	17
Vanmeter, Henry(C)	1806	July 23	Champaign	10	06	23
Vanmeter, Henry(C)	1807	March 11	Champaign	10	06	23
Vanmeter, Henry(C)	1812	April 15	Champaign	10	06	23
Vanmeter, Henry(C)	1812	Dec. 19	Champaign	10	06	36
Vanmeter, Henry(C)	1813	April 14	Champaign	10	06	30
Vanmeter, Henry(C)	1813	April 14	Champaign	11	06	20
Vanmeter, Henry(C)	1813	Dec. 28	Champaign	10	06	29
Vanmeter, Joel(C)	1816	Nov. 06	Greene	12	03	20
Vanmeter, William(B)	1805	May 06	Ind.Territory	01	08	35
Vanmeter, William(E)	1811	Oct. 21	Ind.Territry	12	12	21
Vanmetre, Abraham(E)	1811	Oct. 29	Wayne(Ind)	12	15	27
Vanmetre, Henry(C)	1811	Dec. 11	Champaign	10	06	23
Vanmetre, Joseph B.(E)	1811	Oct. 29	Wayne(Ind)	12	15	15
Vanmiddlesworth, Henry(B)	1818	May 25	Cincinnati	01	12	13
Vanmiddlesworth, Henry(E)	1818	March 21	Cincinnati	14	15	04
Vanmiddlesworth, Henry(E)	1818	March 21	Cincinnati	14	15	05
Vanmiddlesworth, Henry(E)	1818	May 01	Hamilton	14	16	33
Vanmotre, Abraham(E)	1814	June 14	Virginia	13	15	34
Vannausdal, Cornelius(A)	1817	June 05	?	02	08	26
Vanneman, John L.(A)	1818	Sept. 10	Butler	01	09	18
Vannemon, Garret(A)	1806	Dec. 01	Kentucky	06	07	18
Vannemon, Garret(C)	1806	Dec. 01	Kentucky	12	01	20
Vannemon, James(A)	1806	Oct. 10	Kentucky	05	08	36
Vannemon, John(A)	1814	June 14	Montgomery	05	05	22
Vannes, Elizabeth(C)	1804	Nov. 20	Butler	04	02	17
Vannest, Garret(C)	1804	Dec. 29	Butler	04	02	17
Vannest, Garrett(C)	1802	Dec. 31	Hamilton	04	02	12
Vannest, John(C)	1804	Dec. 29	Butler	04	02	17
Vannice, John(A)	1809	April 12	Butler	03	02	11
Vannimnion, Garret(A)	1806	Aug. 20	Kentucky	05	07	01
Vanorsdal, Peter(A)	1812	Dec. 16	Preble	03	05	17
Vanosdol, John(B)	1833	May 24	Dearborn(Ind	02	03	17
Vanosdol, Madison(B)	1836	June 20	Switzerland	03	04	20
Vanpelt, Alexander(C)	1804	Sept. 03	Warren	04	03	08
Vanschuyver, William(A)	1816	July 31	Warren	01	06	13
Vanscoyk, Aaron(A)	1810	Jan. 04	Montgomery	05	04	10
Vantilburgh, Jno.(A)	1813	Sept. 21	Montgomery	04	04	20
Vantrees, Jonathan(A)	1814	Sept. 09	Dearborn(Ind	01	03	32
Vanuasdle, John(A)	1805	Nov. 23	Virginia	03	05	17
Vanusdle, Cornelius(A)	1805	Nov. 23	Virginia	03	06	29

PURCHASER	YEAR	DATE	RESIDENCE	R	T	S
Vanvacter, Jos.(B)	1813	Sept. 28	Hamilton	01	11	05
Vanwinkle, Simeon(A)	1803	Sept. 06	Kentucky	03	06	27
Vanwinkle, Simeon(A)	1804	Dec. 24	Montgomery	03	06	28
Vanzandt, Winant(A)	1836	Nov. 25	Hamilton	01	14	15
Vardeman, Morgan(E)	1814	Dec. 15	Franklin(Ind	12	13	25
Vardeman, Morgan(E)	1816	April 02	Franklin(Ind	13	13	08
Vardiman, Morgan(E)	1812	March 21	Franklin(Ind	12	13	15
Vardiman, WilliamE)	1812	March 21	Franklin(Ind	12	13	13
Varnimmin, John(A)	1803	Oct. 06	Pennsylvania	05	04	33
Vattier, Charles(A)	1806	Dec. 05	Cincinnati	02	04	28
Vattier, Charles(C)	1807	Jan. 01	Cincinnati	10	05	28
Vattier, Charles(C)	1807	Jan. 01	Cincinnati	10	05	28
Vattier, Charles(C)	1807	Jan. 01	Cincinnati	10	05	28
Vattier, Charles(C)	1807	Jan. 01	Cincinnati	10	05	28
Vattier, Charles(C)	1807	Jan. 01	Cincinnati	10	04	03
Vattier, Charles(C)	1807	Jan. 01	Cincinnati	10	04	04
Vattier, Charles(C)	1807	Jan. 01	Cincinnati	10	04	05
Vattier, Charles(C)	1807	Jan. 01	Cincinnati	10	05	34
Vattier, Charles(C)	1807	Jan. 01	Cincinnati	10	05	34
Vattier, Charles(C)	1807	Jan. 02	Cincinnati	10	05	34
Vattier, Charles(C)	1807	Jan. 02	Cincinnati	10	05	34
Vattier, Charles(C)	1807	Jan. 02	Cincinnati	10	05	36
Vattier, Charles(C)	1807	Jan. 02	Cincinnati	10	05	36
Vattier, Charles(C)	1807	Jan. 02	Cincinnati	10	05	36
Vattier, Charles(C)	1807	Jan. 02	Cincinnati	10	05	36
Vattier, Charles(C)	1807	Jan. 02	Cincinnati	10	05	35
Vattier, Charles(C)	1807	Jan. 02	Cincinnati	10	05	35
Vattier, Charles(C)	1807	Jan. 02	Cincinnati	10	05	35
Vattier, Charles(C)	1807	Jan. 02	Cincinnati	10	05	35
Vaughan, James(B)	1813	Aug. 14	Dearborn(Ind	02	05	02
Vaughan, James(B)	1813	Dec. 21	Clermont	02	06	35
Vaughan, James(B)	1815	March 16	Dearborn(Ind	02	06	36
Vaughan, James(B)	1817	Aug. 18	Dearborn(Ind	02	05	02
Vaughan, Jno.(A)	1812	Dec. 12	Butler	01	03	35
Vaughan, John(A)	1801	Nov. 28	Hamilton	01	03	25
Vaus, Solomon(C)	1807	Aug. 12	Champaign	11	06	35
Vaus, Thomas(C)	1812	Nov. 17	Champaign	10	05	08
Vauss, Solomon(C)	1807	Jan. 16	Virginia	11	06	36
Vauss, Solomon(C)	1807	Jan. 16	Virginia	11	06	35
Vautrees, Emanuel(A)	1804	Sept. 24	Hamilton	01	02	25
Vautrees, Emanuel(A)	1804	Oct. 19	Hamilton	01	02	36
Veasa, Ferdinand(A)	1838	Feb. 01	Darke	01	13	20
Veghte, Peter S.(A)	1837	Feb. 07	Butler	02	14	11
Veley, Isaac(B)	1815	Jan. 02	Cincinnati	02	12	11
Venar, Emanuel(B)	1806	June 03	Dearborn(Ind	02	05	36
Venard, James(C)	1829	Aug. 17	Warren	12	02	01
Vennard, John(B)	1816	Aug. 31	Warren	01	15	34
Venus, Henry(C)	1831	Nov. 11	Champaign	13	02	23
Verdier, Adam(A)	1828	Oct. 23	Clark	06	08	22
Verdier, Adam(C)	1806	June 10	Greene	10	03	31
Verdier, Adam(C)	1806	June 10	Greene	10	03	19
Verdier, Adam(C)	1806	July 14	Greene	10	03	19
Verdier, Adam(C)	1816	Jan. 26	Champaign	11	03	35
Verdier, Adam(C)	1828	Dec. 10	Clark	11	03	27
Verdier, Francis O.(C)	1829	May 07	Clark	12	03	31
Verdier, Francis O.(C)	1829	June 02	Clark	12	03	31
Vergil, Jacob(E)	1815	June 28	Ind.Territry	12	17	12
Verniman, John(A)	1805	Nov. 14	Montgomery	04	06	35
Vernimin, John(A)	1804	Sept. 24	Montgomery	05	04	32
Vernon, Abraham(E)	1820	July 03	Pennsylvania	01	12	17
Vernon, Gideon(A)	1836	April 07	Darke	04	08	18
Vertner, John(C)	1812	Sept. 19	Kentucky	13	05	19
Vertner, John(C)	1817	Dec. 02	Champaign	13	05	19
Vieley, Cornelius(B)	1811	Aug. 29	Hamilton	01	09	10
Viets, Hezekiah(A)	1819	Feb. 15	Darke	02	11	22
Viets, Hezekiah(A)	1828	Jan. 11	Darke	02	11	21
Viets, Hezekiah(A)	1829	Dec. 07	Darke	02	11	22
Viets, Hizekiah(A)	1817	Nov. 10	Cincinnati	03	11	13
Viley, Cornelius(A)	1806	March 31	Warren	06	02	18

PURCHASER	YEAR	DATE	RESIDENCE	R	T	S
Vincent, John(B)	1806	July 12	Dearborn(Ind	02	09	19
Vincent, John(E)	1811	Dec. 16	Franklin(Ind	12	13	11
Viney, George(C)	1812	Dec. 23	Champaign	10	05	18
Viney, John(C)	1811	Sept. 18	Champaign	11	05	14
Vineyard, Stephen(C)	1801	Dec. 23	Hamilton	04	04	22
Vineyard, Stephen(C)	1804	Dec. 27	Warren	04	04	22
Vineyard, Stephen(C)	1815	Aug. 21	Champaign	10	05	24
Vineyard, Thomas(C)	1802	Dec. 28	Hamilton	04	04	23
Vinhorn, Thos. W.(A)	1827	Aug. 20	Darke	03	11	36
Vinnedge, David(E)	1826	Feb. 10	Cincinnati	14	16	10
Vinson, Francis(B)	1836	April 04	Dearborn(Ind	02	05	05
Vinson, John(B)	1831	Nov. 18	Dearborn(Ind	02	05	05
Virtue, David(E)	1836	March 03	Franklin(Ind	13	11	15
Viti, Vito(E)	1836	Sept. 17	Philadelphia	04	11	06
Voorhies, Daniel(A)	1815	Feb. 18	Warren	03	05	06
Voorhis, Abbert(C)	1801	Dec. 31	Hamilton	04	04	14
Voorhis, Albert(C)	1817	Nov. 24	Hamilton	12	03	31
Voorhis, Cornelius(A)	1806	Jan. 27	Warren	06	04	30
Voorhis, David(C)	1817	Nov. 24	Hamilton	12	03	31
Voorhis, Jacob(C)	1801	Dec. 31	Hamilton	04	04	13
Voorhis, Luke(A)	1813	Oct. 27	Warren	01	07	12
Voorhis, Luke(A)	1815	Dec. 12	Preble	02	09	23
Vore, Isaac(B)	1816	Nov. 26	Maryland	01	14	15
Vore, Thomas(A)	1832	June 09	Wayne(Ind)	01	10	09
Voris, Albert(B)	1836	June 20	JeffersonInd	03	04	17
Voris, Daniel(B)	1836	Feb. 02	Switzerland	03	04	29
Voris, Daniel(B)	1836	July 05	Switzerland	03	04	29
Voris, Henry(B)	1833	June 13	Switzerland	03	04	30
Voris, Platt(E)	1836	May 23	Butler	14	21	04
Voris, Platt(E)	1836	July 06	Butler	14	21	04
Voris, Ralph(A)	1819	Feb. 20	Butler	02	09	04
Vorris, Cornelius(A)	1806	Nov. 17	Warren	06	04	05
Vosbrinck, John Hy.(E)	1836	Oct. 21	Cincinnati	12	10	08
Vosten, John Hy.(B)	1838	April 25	Cincinnati	03	05	24
Wabeler, Herman Hy.(A)	1839	Jan. 21	Cincinnati	02	15	27
Wadams, Wilson(E)	1818	Sept. 02	Franklin(Ind	12	13	19
Waddell, Robert(B)	1813	Sept. 30	Wayne(Ind)	01	12	32
Waddle, David(B)	1825	Dec. 27	Union(Ind)	03	06	03
Waddoms, William(E)	1817	July 05	Franklin(Ind	12	13	21
Waddoms, Wilson(E)	1829	March 30	Fayette	12	13	21
Wade, David E.(A)	1801	April 27	Cincinnati	02	03	27
Wade, David E.(A)	1818	Aug. 25	Cincinnati	02	12	24
Wade, David E.(B)	1816	June 12	Cincinnati	02	09	22
Wade, David E.(B)	1816	June 12	Cincinnati	02	09	22
Wade, Ebenezer(C)	1801	Dec. 30	Hamilton	06	?	24
Wade, Ebenezer(C)	1804	Dec. 31	Montgomery	06	02	24
Wade, Elisha(B)	1813	Feb. 25	Butler	01	02	13
Wade, John(B)	1806	July 26	Montgomery	01	13	24
Wade, John(B)	1836	May 05	Wayne(Ind)	01	16	26
Wade, John(C)	1801	Dec. 30	Hamilton	06	02	24
Wade, Melanethon S.(C)	1814	Aug. 13	Cincinnati	12	05	31
Wade, Thomas C.(A)	1806	Feb. 01	Butler	01	08	18
Wade, Thomas C.(B)	1806	Feb. 01	Butler	01	13	13
Wade, Thomas C.(C)	1801	Dec. 30	Hamilton	04	02	22
Wade, Thomas J.(E)	1836	Nov. 15	Butler	12	11	11
Wade, William(A)	1815	Aug. 14	Preble	01	10	13
Wade, William(B)	1816	June 26	Switzerland	01	02	14
Wademan, John(A)	1815	May 04	Montgomery	05	05	18
Wadoms, Wilson(E)	1814	Aug. 04	Ind.Territry	12	13	20
Wagaman, Christian(A)	1817	July 16	Montgomery	03	10	02
Wagaman, Jacob(A)	1817	July 16	Montgomery	03	10	02
Wagaman, Joel(A)	1828	Oct. 09	Montgomery	04	05	21
Waganman, Joel(A)	1815	March 28	Montgomery	04	10	31
Waggamon, Christian(A)	1805	Oct. 21	Pennsylvania	04	05	25
Waggamon, William(A)	1805	Oct. 21	Pennsylvania	04	05	36
Waggoner, John Sen.(A)	1817	Sept. 12	Montgomery	04	05	04
Waggoner, John Senr.(A)	1817	Sept. 12	Montgomery	04	05	04
Waggoner, John(A)	1801	Aug. 03	Hamilton	05	03	26
Waggoner, John(A)	1804	July 05	Montgomery	05	04	36

PURCHASER	YEAR	DATE	RESIDENCE	R	T	S
Waggoner, John(A)	1814	Sept. 12	Montgomery	04	05	08
Waggoner, John(A)	1815	Feb. 13	Montgomery	04	05	09
Waggoner, John(A)	1815	Dec. 30	Montgomery	04	05	05
Waggoner, John(A)	1816	Aug. 14	Montgomery	03	06	12
Waggoner, John(A)	1816	Aug. 17	Montgomery	01	11	24
Waggoner, Philip(A)	1802	Jan. 26	Hamilton	05	03	07
Waggoner, Philip(A)	1804	July 05	Montgomery	05	04	36
Waggoner, Reuben(E)	1814	April 01	Montgomery	13	16	27
Waggoner, Sam'l.(C)	1829	Sept. 11	Clark	14	02	03
Waggonman, Joel(A)	1820	Oct. 09	Montgomery	04	06	29
Waggonman, Joel(A)	1828	March 24	Montgomery	04	06	29
Waggonman, John(A)	1822	July 29	Montgomery	04	06	29
Waggonner, Jacob(C)	1825	Nov. 28	Clark	09	03	11
Waggonner, Mich'l.(C)	1825	Nov. 28	Clark	09	03	11
Waggonner, Sam'l.(A)	1825	Jan. 13	Montgomery	04	05	15
Waggonner, Sam'l.(C)	1825	Nov. 28	Clark	09	03	11
Wagner, Joseph(A)	1811	April 09	Montgomery	02	07	01
Wagner, Ludan(E)	1836	Oct. 03	Pennsylvania	12	10	09
Wagner, Martin(A)	1816	Oct. 15	Butler	01	09	07
Wagnor, Joseph(A)	1806	Feb. 24	Montgomery	02	07	01
Wahrly, Samuel(A)	1817	Oct. 29	Preble	03	06	21
Wahub, William(C)	1814	March 30	Champaign	12	02	32
Waid, Edwin(A)	1838	March 05	Darke	01	13	15
Waid, John(A)	1807	Sept. 05	Montgomery	03	04	20
Waid, William(C)	1811	April 09	Champaign	14	03	12
Wairam, Harman(E)	1812	Jan. 31	Franklin(Ind	13	16	36
Waiytzel, John(A)	1814	Nov. 17	Montgomery	02	08	06
Wakeman, Jacob(B)	1837	Feb. 01	Hamilton	03	05	02
Walace, John(C)	1804	Dec. 29	Greene	09	03	36
Walace, Ross(C)	1804	Dec. 29	Greene	09	03	35
Walburn, John(C)	1813	April 14	Greene	08	05	28
Walden, Elijah(B)	1811	Aug. 07	Dearborn(Ind	01	06	33
Waldo, Frederick(A)	1814	Aug. 18	Hamilton	01	04	32
Waldorf, George(B)	1828	July 07	Dearborn(Ind	01	07	23
Waldorf, George(B)	1832	April 10	Dearborn(Ind	01	07	22
Waldorf, George(B)	1833	Jan. 24	Dearborn(Ind	01	07	23
Waldorf, Joseph Williamson(B)	1835	May 21	Hamilton	01	07	23
Waldorf, William(B)	1835	Aug. 27	Dearborn(Ind	01	07	25
Waldorff, Philip(B)	1834	Sept. 05	Butler	02	08	21
Waldron, Francis(A)	1814	March 11	Butler	03	06	07
Waldron, Isaac(A)	1810	June 12	Butler	01	04	24
Waldrop, Isaac(A)	1806	Sept. 30	Greene	05	07	30
Waldrop, Isaac(A)	1811	Dec. 11	Greene	05	07	30
Waldsmith, Christian(A)	1808	Nov. 03	Hamilton	02	03	15
Waldsmith, Christian(D)	1813	Oct. 14	Hamilton	01	05	26
Waling, Joseph(E)	1814	Nov. 30	Butler	13	15	03
Walkens, Jonathan(B)	1815	May 06	Hamilton	01	08	33
Walkens, William(B)	1815	May 06	Hamilton	01	08	33
Walker, Alexander(B)	1832	May 28	Dearborn(Ind	03	06	15
Walker, Alexander(B)	1836	Feb. 06	Dearborn(Ind	03	06	34
Walker, Andrew(A)	1827	Oct. 20	Darke	03	10	36
Walker, Andrew(B)	1836	July 19	Darke	01	16	24
Walker, Benaiah Harman(B)	1833	Aug. 06	Switzerland	03	04	22
Walker, Christopher(A)	1831	April 01	Preble	02	10	35
Walker, Christopher(C)	1809	Dec. 12	Cincinnati	04	02	11
Walker, Christopher(C)	1809	Dec. 12	Cincinnati	05	03	11
Walker, Christopher(C)	1809	Dec. 13	Cincinnati	07	03	29
Walker, Elbert(E)	1831	Jan. 19	Fayette	13	13	30
Walker, Elbert(E)	1834	Oct. 03	Fayette	12	13	35
Walker, Isaac(A)	1830	June 15	Darke	03	08	21
Walker, James(A)	1814	April 01	Hamilton	01	03	20
Walker, James(B)	1811	Nov. 06	Dearborn(Ind	02	04	24
Walker, James(B)	1811	Dec. 11	Dearborn(Ind	02	04	02
Walker, James(B)	1814	Aug. 04	Dearborn(Ind	02	04	26
Walker, James(C)	1813	March 22	Champaign	11	05	04
Walker, Jane(B)	1823	Dec. 10	JeffersonInd	03	08	14
Walker, Jas.(C)	1813	April 12	Wayne(Ind)	11	06	34
Walker, Jno.(B)	1811	Nov. 06	Dearborn(Ind	02	04	24
Walker, Joel(C)	1806	July 09	Champaign	09	05	10

PURCHASER	YEAR	DATE	RESIDENCE	R	T	S
Walker, Joel(C)	1806	July 09	Champaign	09	05	05
Walker, Joel(C)	1807	April 02	Champaign	10	05	01
Walker, Joel(C)	1807	April 02	Champaign	09	05	05
Walker, Joel(C)	1807	July 13	Champaign	09	05	05
Walker, John(A)	1814	July 05	Dearborn(Ind	02	04	26
Walker, John(A)	1832	April 03	Darke	03	09	04
Walker, John(B)	1811	May 07	Dearborn(Ind	02	04	23
Walker, John(B)	1813	Dec. 31	Dearborn(Ind	02	04	09
Walker, John(B)	1814	Aug. 04	Dearborn(Ind	02	04	26
Walker, John(B)	1814	Aug. 04	Dearborn(Ind	02	04	27
Walker, John(B)	1815	April 26	Dearborn(Ind	02	04	10
Walker, John(B)	1815	July 06	Dearborn(Ind	02	04	25
Walker, John(B)	1815	July 06	Dearborn(Ind	02	04	25
Walker, John(B)	1815	July 06	Dearborn(Ind	02	04	26
Walker, John(B)	1815	July 20	Dearborn(Ind	02	04	28
Walker, John(B)	1816	March 19	Dearborn(Ind	02	04	35
Walker, John(B)	1817	Dec. 04	Cincinnati	02	03	20
Walker, John(E)	1836	Jan. 25	Rush(Ind)	11	12	12
Walker, Obadiah(B)	1817	Dec. 04	Cincinnati	02	03	20
Walker, Obadiah(C)	1804	Oct. 22	Warren	04	04	09
Walker, Obediah(E)	1818	April 06	Hamilton	14	20	30
Walker, Oliver(E)	1819	March 27	Montgomery	13	19	28
Walker, Oliver(E)	1819	March 27	Montgomery	13	19	28
Walker, Oliver(E)	1819	March 27	Montgomery	13	19	21
Walker, Oliver(E)	1819	May 05	Montgomery	13	19	21
Walker, Oliver(E)	1819	May 05	Montgomery	13	19	22
Walker, Orlando(B)	1833	Aug. 06	Switzerland	03	04	22
Walker, Sam'l.(E)	1816	Nov. 11	Franklin(Ind	13	13	19
Walker, Samuel(B)	1806	Aug. 13	Kentucky	01	13	09
Walker, Samuel(B)	1808	Nov. 16	Dearborn(Ind	01	13	12
Walker, Samuel(E)	1813	Sept. 27	Wayne(Ind)	14	16	27
Walker, Samuel(E)	1817	Sept. 08	Franklin(Ind	14	14	06
Walker, Supply(B)	1831	July 05	Switzerland	01	02	08
Walker, William(C)	1801	Dec. 25	Hamilton	05	03	01
Walker, William(E)	1817	July 14	Franklin(Ind	14	15	32
Walker, William(E)	1826	Jan. 04	Union(Ind)	14	15	32
Walker, Wm.(B)	1818	Jan. 02	Cincinnati	02	08	28
Walkup, Sam'l.(E)	1830	Nov. 16	Wayne(Ind)	13	17	15
Wall, Allen(E)	1832	Dec. 05	Randolph(Ind	14	21	10
Wall, Christian(C)	1814	July 06	Miami	09	02	05
Wall, James(C)	1812	April 24	Champaign	13	04	04
Wall, James(C)	1812	April 24	Champaign	13	04	05
Wall, John(C)	1813	Feb. 20	Champaign	13	04	04
Wall, John(C)	1818	Feb. 16	Logan	13	05	30
Wall, Sarah(E)	1837	May 27	Randolph(Ind	14	21	11
Wall, Solomon(E)	1836	Nov. 01	Randolph(Ind	14	21	11
Wall, Stephen(C)	1812	March 09	Champaign	13	04	05
Wallace, Andrew(A)	1810	March 08	Miami	02	12	25
Wallace, George(B)	1816	April 19	Franklin(Ind	01	09	31
Wallace, Hugh M.(C)	1811	Aug. 13	Champaign	09	04	35
Wallace, James(B)	1814	Oct. 22	Butler	02	09	13
Wallace, James(E)	1832	July 25	Franklin(Ind	11	12	12
Wallace, John(E)	1811	Oct. 24	Warren	13	15	06
Wallace, John(E)	1812	March 11	Warren	12	15	14
Wallace, John(E)	1813	Aug. 20	Wayne(Ind)	12	15	14
Wallace, John(E)	1813	Aug. 20	Wayne(Ind)	12	15	11
Wallace, Thomas(E)	1837	May 15	Montgomery	14	21	25
Wallace, William(A)	1811	April 09	Cincinnati	01	01	09
Wallen, John(E)	1836	Oct. 11	Randolph(Ind	15	21	22
Wallen, Thomas(C)	1806	March 03	Butler	02	03	26
Waller, Salmon(A)	1830	Oct. 20	Butler	06	08	33
Wallick, Henry(B)	1811	April 03	Ind.Territory	01	03	29
Wallingford, Benjamin(C)	1801	Dec. 25	Hamilton	05	03	30
Wallingsford, Benj'n. Jr.(C)	1828	Aug. 25	Clark	13	02	26
Wallingsford, Benjamin(C)	1802	Dec. 28	Hamilton	05	03	18
Wallingsford, Benjamin(C)	1806	March 27	Montgomery	09	06	23
Wallingsford, Benjamin(C)	1806	Aug. 14	Montgomery	09	06	24
Wallingsford, Benjamin(C)	1806	Oct. 22	Butler	09	06	02
Walliser, Francis Anthony(B)	1828	April 01	Dearborn(Ind	02	07	28

340

PURCHASER	YEAR	DATE	RESIDENCE	R	T	S
Walls, Drury(E)	1817	Nov. 06	Wayne(Ind)	14	17	21
Walmer, Peter(A)	1830	Jan. 28	Montgomery	04	06	09
Walsh, Esther(B)	1819	Feb. 06	Cincinnati	02	06	21
Walsh, John(B)	1815	April 27	Cincinnati	01	04	05
Walsh, John(C)	1815	April 28	Cincinnati	09	06	36
Walsh, John(C)	1815	April 28	Cincinnati	09	06	30
Walsh, John(C)	1815	May 08	Cincinnati	10	05	27
Walsh, Patrick(B)	1819	Feb. 06	Cincinnati	02	06	21
Walter, Valentine(B)	1835	Oct. 05	Hamilton	02	08	36
Walters, John(E)	1838	Sept. 01	Fairfield	14	22	27
Walters, John(E)	1838	Sept. 01	Fairfield	15	22	18
Walton, James A.(B)	1814	July 04	Cincinnati	02	03	01
Walton, James A.(B)	1814	July 04	Cincinnati	02	03	01
Walton, Joseph(B)	1834	June 21	Cincinnati	02	02	30
Waltz, George(B)	1814	April 29	Ind.Territry	03	02	01
Waltz, Job(E)	1836	Jan. 25	Fayette	12	13	30
Wamsley, Christopher(E)	1817	Nov. 04	Jefferson	13	14	11
Wamsley, Isaac(B)	1813	Aug. 06	Adams	01	08	28
Wamsley, Thomas(B)	1828	Nov. 06	Franklin(Ind	01	09	21
Wanick, Dan'l.(A)	1829	Jan. 07	Preble	01	08	35
Warble, George(A)	1826	Sept. 15	Montgomery	04	05	21
Ward, Aaron(D)	1812	Oct. 24	Hamilton(Fr)	02	04	11
Ward, Abijah(C)	1815	Jan. 13	Champaign	11	05	15
Ward, Caleb Green(B)	1836	Jan. 04	Dearborn(Ind	03	06	22
Ward, Caleb Green(B)	1836	Jan. 04	Dearborn(Ind	03	06	15
Ward, David(A)	1815	Nov. 30	Montgomery	04	10	18
Ward, David(A)	1835	Oct. 24	Darke	03	11	24
Ward, Elijah(A)	1836	Aug. 26	Darke	03	11	02
Ward, George(C)	1811	Nov. 11	Champaign	11	04	22
Ward, George(C)	1826	Jan. 27	Champaign	11	04	01
Ward, George(C)	1830	April 23	Champaign	11	05	32
Ward, George(C)	1831	March 07	Champaign	11	03	04
Ward, Isaac(C)	1804	Dec. 13	Warren	05	03	13
Ward, Isaac(C)	1804	Dec. 13	Warren	06	02	04
Ward, James Junr.(C)	1804	Dec. 31	Greene	11	05	15
Ward, James(E)	1814	Dec. 03	Kentucky	13	14	29
Ward, James(E)	1814	Dec. 03	Kentucky	13	14	28
Ward, Jesse(E)	1832	May 24	Fayette	13	13	29
Ward, Jesse(E)	1832	Nov. 26	Fayette	13	13	29
Ward, Joab(E)	1836	Nov. 04	Randolph(Ind	13	21	13
Ward, Joab(E)	1837	July 17	Randolph(Ind	13	21	13
Ward, John(B)	1816	Aug. 01	Franklin(Ind	02	08	13
Ward, John(D)	1814	May 30	Butler	02	02	11
Ward, John(E)	1814	March 03	Kentucky	12	15	35
Ward, John(E)	1814	Aug. 05	Franklin(Ind	14	13	06
Ward, Joseph(E)	1811	Nov. 04	Franklin(Ind	14	18	29
Ward, Laurence(C)	1829	Feb. 04	Champaign	10	03	29
Ward, Obed(E)	1829	May 19	Miami	13	18	26
Ward, Obed(E)	1830	May 21	Wayne(Ind)	13	18	23
Ward, Obed(E)	1830	Nov. 18	Wayne(Ind)	13	18	24
Ward, Richard(C)	1813	July 23	Champaign	11	06	32
Ward, Samuel(A)	1806	April 05	Butler	02	07	01
Ward, Samuel(A)	1806	April 18	Butler	02	07	12
Ward, Samuel(A)	1811	Aug. 13	Preble	02	07	01
Ward, Samuel(A)	1813	April 14	Preble	02	07	11
Ward, Samuel(B)	1834	Jan. 09	Franklin(Ind	02	08	22
Ward, Timothy(B)	1833	Oct. 02	Dearborn(Ind	03	04	15
Ward, Timothy(B)	1834	May 13	Dearborn(Ind	03	04	15
Ward, Timothy(B)	1836	Sept. 29	Dearborn(Ind	03	04	15
Ward, Uzal(B)	1813	Sept. 29	Hamilton	01	11	09
Ward, William Junr.(C)	1807	Jan. 27	Champaign	11	04	05
Ward, William(C)	1802	Dec. 30	Hamilton	09	04	06
Ward, William(C)	1802	Dec. 30	Hamilton	10	04	02
Ward, William(C)	1802	Dec. 30	Hamilton	10	05	32
Ward, William(C)	1802	Dec. 30	Hamilton	10	04	01
Ward, William(C)	1802	Dec. 30	Hamilton	05	02	32
Ward, William(C)	1802	Dec. 30	Hamilton	09	04	06
Ward, William(C)	1804	Sept. 24	Greene	12	03	02
Ward, William(C)	1804	Sept. 24	Greene	11	05	21

PURCHASER	YEAR	DATE	RESIDENCE	R	T	S
Ward, William(C)	1804	Sept. 24	Greene	12	03	09
Ward, William(C)	1804	Sept. 26	Greene	11	05	22
Ward, William(C)	1804	Sept. 26	Greene	11	05	21
Ward, William(C)	1804	Sept. 26	Greene	11	05	21
Ward, William(C)	1804	Sept. 26	Greene	12	04	03
Ward, William(C)	1804	Sept. 26	Greene	11	02	32
Ward, William(C)	1804	Sept. 26	Greene	11	05	24
Ward, William(C)	1804	Sept. 26	Greene	12	05	19
Ward, William(C)	1804	Sept. 26	Greene	11	05	30
Ward, William(C)	1804	Sept. 26	Greene	12	05	25
Ward, William(C)	1804	Sept. 26	Greene	11	05	17
Ward, William(C)	1804	Sept. 26	Greene	11	05	23
Ward, William(C)	1804	Sept. 26	Greene	10	05	30
Ward, William(C)	1804	Sept. 26	Greene	11	05	31
Ward, William(C)	1804	Sept. 26	Greene	11	05	25
Ward, William(C)	1804	Dec. 28	Greene	11	04	02
Ward, William(C)	1804	Dec. 29	Greene	12	04	07
Ward, William(C)	1804	Dec. 29	Greene	11	05	21
Ward, William(C)	1804	Dec. 29	Greene	11	05	27
Ward, William(C)	1804	Dec. 29	Greene	10	05	30
Ward, William(C)	1804	Dec. 29	Greene	11	05	20
Ward, William(C)	1805	Dec. 31	Champaign	14	03	12
Ward, William(C)	1806	Feb. 01	Champaign	11	04	02
Ward, William(C)	1802	Dec. 30	Hamilton	09	05	24
Ward, William(C)	1812	Dec. 30	Champaign	10	05	32
Ward, William(C)	1813	April 14	Champaign	11	05	15
Ward, William(C)	1813	April 14	Champaign	13	05	27
Ward, William(C)	1814	Jan. 28	Champaign	10	04	07
Ward, William(C)	1816	Aug. 01	Champaign	14	03	12
Ward, William(C)	1816	Nov. 12	Champaign	14	03	12
Ward, Wm.(C)	1802	Dec. 30	Hamilton	10	05	31
Wardell, Thomas(B)	1806	April 18	Dearborn(Ind	02	05	36
Wardell, Thomas(B)	1806	April 18	Dearborn(Ind	02	05	36
Ware, John(A)	1814	March 19	Butler	01	04	07
Ware, John(A)	1828	Sept. 01	Montgomery	04	05	19
Warenski, Thomas(B)	1837	Nov. 15	Switzerland	03	04	25
Warfield, James(A)	1831	Dec. 01	Miami	04	09	34
Warner, Anderson(E)	1836	Jan. 18	Franklin(Ind	12	12	12
Warner, Anderson(E)	1836	Jan. 18	Franklin(Ind	13	12	18
Warner, George(A)	1827	May 14	Montgomery	04	06	01
Warner, Henry(A)	1811	Aug. 27	Montgomery	05	05	07
Warner, Henry(A)	1831	March 26	Montgomery	04	07	25
Warner, Henry(A)	1832	Sept. 24	Montgomery	04	07	15
Warner, Jacob(A)	1829	Oct. 29	Miami	04	07	26
Warner, John(A)	1832	June 09	Darke	04	09	08
Warner, Martin(E)	1836	Nov. 09	Union(Ind)	12	12	13
Warner, Sam'l.(A)	1830	Feb. 02	Montgomery	04	07	35
Warner, Sarah(A)	1831	Oct. 21	Montgomery	04	09	29
Warnke, John Senr.(A)	1837	April 19	Shelby	04	11	19
Warnock, James(B)	1816	Oct. 09	Adams	01	04	20
Warnock, Joseph(B)	1816	Oct. 01	Adams	01	04	20
Warrel, Abraham(A)	1809	Oct. 05	Kentucky	02	07	06
Warrel, Joseph(A)	1809	Oct. 05	Kentucky	02	07	05
Warrel, Joseph(E)	1811	Oct. 24	Preble	13	16	05
Warren, Benjamin(B)	1817	Dec. 12	New York	02	02	19
Warren, Dolphin(E)	1837	Dec. 21	Randolph(Ind	14	21	27
Warren, James(E)	1815	Sept. 07	Wayne(Ind)	13	18	32
Warren, James(E)	1836	Oct. 20	Randolph(Ind	15	21	32
Warren, John B.(E)	1836	July 21	Hamilton	14	21	14
Warren, John Riley(E)	1837	Jan. 10	Randolph(Ind	14	21	26
Warren, John Riley(E)	1837	Jan. 10	Randolph(Ind	15	21	29
Warren, Peter(A)	1808	Jan. 20	Montgomery	03	06	08
Warren, William(E)	1834	Feb. 03	Randolph(Ind	15	21	28
Warren, William(E)	1834	Sept. 18	Randolph(Ind	15	21	30
Warren, William(E)	1836	Jan. 21	Randolph(Ind	14	21	26
Warren, William(E)	1838	Aug. 18	Randolph(Ind	14	21	26
Warren, William(E)	1838	Aug. 18	Randolph(Ind	14	21	33
Warrin, James(E)	1813	Nov. 08	Clinton	13	18	32
Warwick, John(C)	1812	March 16	Champaign	09	03	27

PURCHASER	YEAR	DATE	RESIDENCE	R	T	S
Warwick, Rich'd. C.(E)	1832	June 23	Randolph(Ind	15	19	04
Warwick, Rich'd. Cheesman(B)	1833	July 24	Randolph(Ind	01	17	22
Warwick, Rich'd. Cheesman(E)	1833	July 24	Randolph(Ind	15	19	08
Warwick, William Jr.(E)	1837	July 27	Cincinnati	15	20	20
Washington, Robert(A)	1832	March 05	Preble	02	11	33
Wason, Archibald(A)	1807	April 22	Kentucky	01	09	04
Wason, David(A)	1807	Jan. 24	Kentucky	01	09	09
Wason, David(A)	1812	April 15	Preble	01	09	09
Wason, David(A)	1817	Sept. 06	Butler	01	11	02
Wason, David(A)	1831	Jan. 03	Darke	01	12	08
Wason, David(A)	1835	March 10	Darke	01	12	07
Wason, David(B)	1831	Jan. 03	Darke	01	17	12
Wason, David(B)	1836	June 07	Darke	01	17	12
Wason, James M.(A)	1836	Dec. 20	Darke	01	12	07
Wason, John(A)	1808	April 16	Dearborn(Ind	01	10	27
Wason, Joseph(A)	1808	April 16	Dearborn(Ind	01	10	23
Wason, Nancy F.(A)	1838	Feb. 02	Darke	01	13	22
Wason, William(A)	1812	May 23	Miami	06	04	33
Wasson, Archibald(B)	1813	Sept. 06	Preble	01	14	24
Wasson, David(A)	1813	Sept. 08	Preble	01	09	31
Wasson, Ezra(A)	1836	Dec. 03	Darke	01	12	20
Wasson, John(B)	1807	Jan. 02	Dearborn(Ind	01	14	26
Wasson, Joseph(B)	1804	Dec. 18	Kentucky	02	13	25
Wasson, Joseph(B)	1806	March 21	Dearborn(Ind	01	14	25
Waters, James(A)	1830	Aug. 26	Preble	02	09	21
Waters, Wm.(E)	1819	Oct. 19	Hamilton	14	21	11
Watkins, Jeremiah(B)	1815	Dec. 04	Pennsylvania	02	07	13
Watkins, John L.(B)	1815	Oct. 07	Hamilton	01	07	30
Watkins, John(A)	1836	Nov. 29	Darke	01	15	28
Watkins, Watkin Rumsey(B)	1818	Aug. 19	Cincinnati	02	05	09
Watkins, William Senr.(C)	1804	Dec. 22	Kentucky	05	03	18
Wats, Henry(E)	1837	Oct. 11	Miami	15	22	29
Wats, John(B)	1807	Aug. 01	Butler	01	13	14
Wats, John(B)	1807	Aug. 01	Butler	01	13	23
Watson, Benj'n.(A)	1831	Feb. 19	Darke	01	10	04
Watson, Culbert(C)	1801	Dec. 31	Hamilton	05	04	20
Watson, Henry(C)	1831	Jan. 01	Shelby	12	02	35
Watson, James Vaughn(B)	1835	Sept. 02	RipleyCo.Ind	01	02	18
Watson, James Vaughn(B)	1835	Sept. 02	RipleyCo.Ind	01	02	18
Watson, James Vaughn(B)	1835	Sept. 02	RipleyCo.Ind	01	02	07
Watson, John(A)	1818	Aug. 03	Greene	01	10	03
Watson, John(A)	1831	Feb. 19	Darke	01	10	03
Watson, John(E)	1836	May 05	Randolph(Ind	14	21	03
Watson, Joseph(B)	1837	Jan. 24	Dearborn(Ind	02	03	17
Watson, Robert(A)	1826	Nov. 02	Darke	01	10	22
Watt, Thomas(C)	1812	July 31	Kentucky	11	05	09
Watt, Thomas(C)	1817	Dec. 02	Champaign	11	05	09
Watt, William(A)	1812	Jan. 01	Preble	01	09	34
Watter, William(E)	1814	April 20	Wayne(Ind)	13	15	22
Watters, Isaac(E)	1814	Feb. 01	Wayne(Ind)	13	15	08
Watters, James(B)	1814	Feb. 21	Franklin(Ind	02	10	20
Watters, James(E)	1812	Dec. 04	Franklin(Ind	13	13	34
Watters, Jno.(E)	1812	Dec. 04	Franklin(Ind	13	13	34
Watters, Samuel(E)	1813	July 24	Franklin(Ind	13	13	28
Watts, Henry(A)	1816	Sept. 17	Preble	02	07	32
Watts, James(A)	1814	Dec. 23	Butler	02	04	21
Watts, John(B)	1813	April 26	Wayne(Ind)	01	13	23
Watts, John(B)	1814	Dec. 31	Butler	02	10	36
Watts, John(B)	1815	Jan. 17	Kentucky	03	04	04
Watts, John(B)	1816	April 02	Kentucky	03	04	04
Watts, John(B)	1816	April 03	Kentucky	03	04	08
Watts, John(B)	1818	March 31	Dearborn(Ind	03	05	29
Watts, John(B)	1818	March 31	Dearborn(Ind	03	05	28
Watts, Joseph(A)	1805	May 29	Montgomery	03	05	07
Watts, Joseph(A)	1814	April 25	Hamilton	01	04	10
Watts, Joseph(E)	1811	Oct. 24	Butler	13	15	29
Watts, Richard(A)	1806	Nov. 24	Butler	02	07	12
Watts, Richard(C)	1801	Dec. 23	Hamilton	04	02	22
Watts, Richard(C)	1801	Dec. 23	Hamilton	04	02	28

PURCHASER	YEAR	DATE	RESIDENCE	R	T	S
Watts, Richard(C)	1801	Dec. 23	Hamilton	04	02	34
Watts, Sam'l.(B)	1830	May 26	Wayne(Ind)	01	15	01
Watts, Thomas(B)	1814	Jan. 01	Dearborn(Ind	01	07	29
Watts, Thomas(B)	1818	March 31	Dearborn(Ind	03	05	29
Watts, Wm.(A)	1818	Oct. 19	Butler	02	13	20
Waugh, William(C)	1801	Dec. 10	Hamilton	06	01	03
Waugh, William(C)	1801	Dec. 10	Hamilton	06	01	04
Way, Amos(B)	1815	Nov. 07	Dearborn(Ind	01	05	05
Way, Henry H.(E)	1816	Oct. 29	Wayne(Ind)	13	20	27
Way, Henry H.(E)	1817	Aug. 11	Wayne(Ind)	13	20	22
Way, Henry(E)	1811	Oct. 25	Warren	14	18	32
Way, Henry(E)	1811	Oct. 25	Warren	14	17	06
Way, Henry(E)	1814	Jan. 31	Wayne(Ind)	14	18	33
Way, Henry(E)	1815	Aug. 02	Wayne(Ind)	14	17	06
Way, Henry(E)	1816	June 05	So. Carolina	13	20	22
Way, Henry(E)	1836	Jan. 15	Randolph(Ind	14	18	03
Way, Huldah(E)	1815	Sept. 09	Wayne(Ind)	14	18	22
Way, John(E)	1819	July 14	Randolph(Ind	14	20	18
Way, John(E)	1820	March 31	Randolph(Ind	14	20	18
Way, Moorman(E)	1831	July 05	Randolph(Ind	13	20	22
Way, Paul W.(E)	1818	Aug. 07	Randolph(Ind	13	20	26
Way, Paul W.(E)	1831	July 05	Randolph(Ind	13	20	26
Way, Paul(E)	1817	Aug. 11	Wayne(Ind)	14	18	29
Way, Seth(E)	1811	Oct. 25	Warren	14	17	05
Way, Seth(E)	1813	Sept. 13	Wayne(Ind)	14	17	06
Way, Seth(E)	1817	June 27	Wayne(Ind)	13	17	01
Way, Thomas(E)	1831	Nov. 05	Wayne(Ind)	13	17	01
Way, William C.(E)	1817	Aug. 11	Wayne(Ind)	13	20	22
Way, William Jnr.(E)	1818	Feb. 07	Wayne(Ind)	13	20	23
Way, Wm.(E)	1816	June 05	So. Carolina	13	20	22
Waymier, Daniel(A)	1814	Sept. 05	Montgomery	06	03	07
Waymire, Frederick(A)	1802	Aug. 11	Hamilton	05	05	23
Wear, Alexander(C)	1804	Sept. 03	Warren	05	02	26
Wear, Alexander(C)	1804	Sept. 03	Warren	05	02	26
Wearly, David H.(A)	1831	Jan. 21	Preble	02	09	28
Wearly, Geo. H.(A)	1831	Jan. 21	Preble	02	09	21
Wearly, John H.(A)	1831	Nov. 25	Preble	02	09	17
Wearly, Jonathan(A)	1831	Nov. 09	Preble	02	09	17
Weasner, Micajah(E)	1819	Dec. 17	Wayne(Ind)	15	21	06
Weathers, Jesse(B)	1818	April 04	Switzerland	02	04	32
Weathers, John(B)	1832	Feb. 23	Dearborn(Ind	02	04	32
Weathers, William(B)	1812	Oct. 03	Dearborn(Ind	02	04	29
Weaver, Aaron(C)	1814	Oct. 18	Champaign	10	04	24
Weaver, Andrew(A)	1817	June 25	Montgomery	02	11	29
Weaver, Christopher(C)	1805	June 19	Champaign	10	04	12
Weaver, Elijah(C)	1807	Jan. 29	Champaign	10	04	17
Weaver, Elijah(C)	1807	April 13	Champaign	10	04	24
Weaver, George(A)	1811	Jan. 17	Butler	04	02	04
Weaver, George(A)	1815	Aug. 24	Butler	02	04	05
Weaver, George(B)	1814	July 26	Dearborn(Ind	01	05	17
Weaver, George(B)	1832	April 02	Dearborn(Ind	02	03	05
Weaver, George(C)	1814	Nov. 14	Champaign	09	06	13
Weaver, George(C)	1824	June 07	Miami	09	02	11
Weaver, Henry(A)	1802	Sept. 13	Hamilton	04	02	29
Weaver, Henry(A)	1812	Nov. 12	Philadelphia	03	05	31
Weaver, Henry(C)	1806	July 23	Cincinnati	09	03	10
Weaver, Jacob(A)	1836	May 24	Montgomery	03	11	04
Weaver, Jacob(A)	1836	Aug. 09	Montgomery	03	12	33
Weaver, Joel(A)	1831	Feb. 10	Preble	03	07	30
Weaver, John(A)	1817	June 25	Montgomery	02	11	32
Weaver, John(A)	1830	June 11	Darke	01	10	01
Weaver, John(C)	1814	Dec. 23	Champaign	10	04	24
Weaver, John(E)	1822	April 23	Greene	14	21	28
Weaver, Michael(A)	1815	Aug. 24	Montgomery	03	07	30
Weaver, Peter Jr.(A)	1829	June 08	Darke	02	11	21
Weaver, Peter(A)	1802	Jan. 26	Hamilton	05	03	07
Weaver, Peter(A)	1805	Nov. 07	Montgomery	04	05	36
Weaver, Peter(A)	1806	Aug. 01	Montgomery	02	07	10
Weaver, Peter(A)	1817	June 25	Montgomery	02	11	29

PURCHASER	YEAR	DATE	RESIDENCE	R	T	S
Weaver, Peter(B)	1807	Feb. 21	Kentucky	01	13	19
Weaver, Peter(C)	1806	June 14	Butler	09	02	21
Weaver, Richard(B)	1816	Dec. 16	Cincinnati	02	02	32
Weaver, Samuel(E)	1837	May 24	Richland	15	21	18
Weaver, Thomas(A)	1832	Aug. 11	Miami	04	07	08
Weaver, William(C)	1813	Oct. 23	Champaign	10	04	24
Weaver, William(E)	1837	May 24	Richland	15	21	18
Webb, Edward(E)	1811	Oct. 22	Ind.Territry	12	13	22
Webb, Edward(E)	1811	Oct. 23	Dearborn(Ind	13	14	06
Webb, Edward(E)	1811	Oct. 23	Dearborn(Ind	13	14	07
Webb, Edward(E)	1811	Nov. 04	Dearborn(Ind	12	13	33
Webb, Edward(E)	1816	Dec. 02	Dearborn(Ind	13	14	06
Webb, Ezra(B)	1817	July 24	Hamilton	02	03	11
Webb, Forrest(E)	1811	Oct. 28	Dearborn(Ind	12	14	15
Webb, Forrest(E)	1814	Aug. 09	Franklin(Ind	12	14	14
Webb, Henry	1808	March 02	Cincinnati	?	?	?
Webb, James(C)	1804	Oct. 29	Greene	06	02	10
Webb, James(E)	1814	Oct. 22	Greene	13	12	10
Webb, James(E)	1831	June 04	Franklin(Ind	13	12	03
Webb, Jesse(E)	1813	Aug. 31	Dearborn(Ind	12	14	03
Webb, John(C)	1801	Dec. 08	Hamilton	07	02	07
Webb, Jonathan(E)	1814	Feb. 23	Franklin(Ind	12	12	32
Webb, Joseph D.(C)	1811	Oct. 10	Montgomery	11	02	28
Webb, Thomas Smith(E)	1836	Feb. 04	Franklin(Ind	13	12	07
Webb, William(B)	1814	Oct. 26	Dearborn(Ind	01	07	31
Webb, William(E)	1811	Oct. 28	Dearborn(Ind	12	14	12
Webber, Isaac(A)	1830	Oct. 01	Butler	03	09	20
Webber, Samuel(B)	1813	March 29	Franklin(Ind	01	08	28
Weber, Francis Henry(A)	1835	Aug. 06	Hamilton	03	12	14
Weber, Francis Hy.(A)	1838	Jan. 29	Darke	02	14	04
Weber, Nicholas(B)	1829	March 21	Franklin(Ind	02	09	15
Weber, Samuel(A)	1813	June 14	Franklin(Ind	01	03	05
Webhham, George(C)	1815	Sept. 26	Champaign	10	04	19
Webhham, George(C)	1815	Sept. 26	Champaign	10	04	15
Webster, Elias(A)	1839	Jan. 15	Butler	02	15	23
Webster, James(E)	1814	Sept. 27	Franklin(Ind	13	13	17
Webster, John(A)	1819	Dec. 10	Butler	05	06	30
Webster, John(A)	1838	Sept. 29	Butler	03	13	30
Webster, John(A)	1838	Dec. 24	Butler	02	15	24
Webster, Taylor(?)	?	?	Butler	?	?	?
Webster, Taylor(A)	1839	June 01	Butler	02	15	26
Webster, Taylor(A)	1839	June 01	Butler	02	15	25
Webster, Taylor(A)	1839	June 01	Butler	02	15	24
Webster, William Jr.(A)	1836	Sept. 08	Butler	02	13	27
Webster, William(A)	1806	June 24	Butler	04	02	04
Webster, William(A)	1831	May 20	Butler	04	07	14
Weed, Andrew(A)	1811	Dec. 10	Preble	01	06	20
Weeks, Charles(C)	1814	Aug. 25	Miami	13	02	34
Weeks, James(C)	1830	Jan. 27	Warren	11	03	13
Weeks, James(E)	1837	Jan. 12	Ohio	13	18	15
Weeks, John(B)	1814	March 15	Wayne(Ind)	01	14	14
Weeks, John(C)	1830	Jan. 27	Warren	11	03	19
Weeks, William(E)	1837	April 01	Randolph(Ind	14	21	34
Weer, James Jr.(E)	1834	Dec. 25	Fayette	12	13	32
Weese, Henry(A)	1832	March 08	Preble	01	12	21
Weesner, Micajah(E)	1827	Nov. 01	Wayne(Ind)	14	17	04
Weesner, Micajah(E)	1827	Nov. 10	Wayne(Ind)	14	17	04
Weest, George(A)	1819	Dec. 01	Butler	02	10	09
Wehrley, Samuel Jnr.(A)	1818	Jan. 26	Preble	02	09	09
Wehrly, Jacob(A)	1822	May 03	Preble	02	09	04
Wehrly, John(A)	1818	Aug. 26	Preble	03	07	30
Wehrly, Sam'l. J.(A)	1830	May 31	Preble	02	09	22
Weibel, Frederick(A)	1814	Aug. 19	Butler	02	08	05
Weibright, Jacob(A)	1812	Dec. 02	Montgomery	05	05	15
Weibright, Martin Jur.(A)	1815	Dec. 01	Montgomery	04	06	28
Weibright, Martin(A)	1804	Oct. 13	Pennsylvania	05	04	18
Weibright, Martin(A)	1804	Oct. 13	Pennsylvania	05	04	27
Weidner, Jacob(A)	1817	Nov. 17	Butler	02	09	08
Weidner, John(A)	1810	Dec. 31	Butler	04	02	08

345

PURCHASER	YEAR	DATE	RESIDENCE	R	T	S
Weighbright, Martin(A)	1805	June 28	Pennsylvania	05	04	08
Weigler, Arnold(B)	1835	July 13	Hamilton	02	08	32
Weigler, Charles(B)	1835	July 13	Hamilton	02	08	32
Weigler, Henry(B)	1835	July 13	Hamilton	02	08	32
Weigler, Julius(B)	1835	July 13	Hamilton	02	08	32
Weiler, Conrad(B)	1833	July 29	Cincinnati	03	08	01
Weimer, And'w.(E)	1837	July 13	Cincinnati	14	21	36
Weimire, Fredrick(A)	1805	Aug. 06	Montgomery	05	05	24
Weir, Wm.(E)	1814	Oct. 11	Franklin(Ind	12	14	32
Weis, Valentine(E)	1837	May 24	Cincinnati	13	11	22
Weist, Christian(B)	1836	Sept. 01	Cincinnati	03	05	01
Weist, Henry(B)	1816	June 19	Dearborn(Ind	01	02	04
Weist, Henry(B)	1816	June 19	Dearborn(Ind	01	02	04
Weist, Henry(B)	1818	Jan. 08	Switzerland	01	02	22
Weist, Henry(B)	1827	Aug. 21	Switzerland	01	02	22
Weist, John H.(A)	1814	Aug. 23	Montgomery	01	08	03
Weiterein, John(A)	1830	June 12	Montgomery	03	06	20
Weits, Helmerikus(E)	1837	Jan. 02	Cincinnati	12	11	32
Wekins, Daniel(A)	1807	June 09	Hamilton	02	02	06
Welbaum, Charles(A)	1814	Aug. 24	Montgomery	04	05	11
Welbaum, Charles(A)	1814	Aug. 24	Montgomery	05	08	30
Welbaum, Charles(A)	1814	Aug. 24	Montgomery	04	05	01
Welbaum, Charles(A)	1814	Oct. 06	Montgomery	05	08	32
Welbaum, Charles(A)	1831	Dec. 01	Montgomery	04	07	14
Welch, George(C)	1812	April 15	Champaign	10	04	17
Welch, Henry(E)	1832	Feb. 23	Preble	14	21	05
Welch, John(A)	1805	Sept. 10	Butler	03	06	24
Wells, William(A)	1805	Feb. 04	FortWayneInd	06	07	31
Wells, William(A)	1805	April 08	FortWayneInd	06	07	32
Wells, William(A)	1805	Dec. 27	FortWayneInd	06	06	19
Wells, William(A)	1805	Dec. 27	FortWayneInd	06	06	30
Wells, William(A)	1805	Dec. 27	FortWayneInd	06	07	31
Wells, William(A)	1807	Jan. 02	FortWayneInd	06	07	14
Wells, William(C)	1802	Dec. 31	NWTerrWashtn	05	04	35
Wells, William(C)	1802	Dec. 31	NWTerrWashtn	05	03	05
Wells, William(C)	1802	Dec. 31	NWTerrWashtn	05	03	23
Wells, William(C)	1802	Dec. 31	NWTerrWashtn	05	03	35
Wells, William(C)	1802	Dec. 31	NWTerrWashtn	05	03	36
Welch, Thomas(E)	1836	Nov. 25	Greene	15	20	09
Welchhaus, Jno.(C)	1824	Oct. 11	Clark	10	04	29
Wellbaum, Charles(A)	1813	Nov. 08	Montgomery	05	05	19
Wellen, John(E)	1837	Oct. 28	Cincinnati	11	11	24
Weller, Lodowick(B)	1818	Feb. 27	Hamilton	02	03	17
Weller, Lodowick(B)	1818	March 23	Hamilton	02	03	20
Weller, Lodowick(B)	1818	March 23	Hamilton	02	03	17
Welliver, Isaac(E)	1825	Jan. 31	Wayne(Ind)	13	14	02
Welliver, Isaiah(E)	1825	June 10	Butler	14	15	31
Welliver, Obadiah(A)	1811	June 17	Butler	01	04	23
Wellmann, Stephen Hy.(E)	1837	Aug. 01	Cincinnati	13	11	30
Wells, Horace(E)	1835	Oct. 05	Butler	14	19	14
Wells, James(A)	1819	Sept. 11	Shelby	06	07	07
Wells, John(B)	1814	Oct. 21	Champaign	02	09	01
Wells, John(C)	1807	March 05	Kentucky	10	06	20
Wells, John(C)	1812	April 15	Champaign	10	06	20
Wells, John(E)	1814	Oct. 08	Pennsylvania	13	11	10
Wells, William(A)	1807	Feb. 02	FortWayneInd	05	09	02
Wells, William(C)	1802	Dec. 31	NWTerrWashtn	05	04	17
Wells, William(C)	1804	Sept. 15	Washington	05	04	29
Wells, William(C)	1804	Dec. 31	FortWayneInd	09	05	31
Wells, William(C)	1806	Jan. 18	FortWayneInd	12	01	24
Wells, Wm.(C)	1802	Dec. 31	Washington	05	03	17
Welsh, Christopher(B)	1832	Oct. 19	Cincinnati	02	07	19
Welsh, James(A)	1803	Nov. 19	Kentucky	06	02	29
Welsh, James(A)	1831	Aug. 22	Montgomery	05	07	26
Welsh, James(A)	1831	Aug. 22	Montgomery	05	06	02
Welsh, John(B)	1814	March 16	Franklin(Ind	01	08	07
Welsh, Moses(A)	1831	Aug. 06	Montgomery	05	08	15
Welsh, Stephen(C)	1804	Sept. 04	Warren	08	04	08
Welsh, William(B)	1832	March 24	Franklin(Ind	01	09	11

PURCHASER	YEAR	DATE	RESIDENCE	R	T	S
Welshhons, Dan'l.(E)	1828	Feb. 01	Wayne(Ind)	13	16	35
Welson, Samuel(E)	1815	Feb. 09	Montgomery	13	14	35
Wenger, Christian(A)	1831	Jan. 17	Montgomery	04	07	33
Wenger, John Jr.(A)	1831	April 15	Montgomery	04	07	27
Wensor, Asa(C)	1817	Sept. 02	Virginia	12	03	22
Werst, George(A)	1819	Dec. 01	Butler	02	10	09
Werst, George(A)	1832	Oct. 10	Darke	02	10	09
Werts, Henry Junr.(A)	1815	Nov. 27	Montgomery	02	11	23
Wertz, Hemy(A)	1810	June 05	Montgomery	02	11	04
Wertz, John(A)	1806	May 24	Montgomery	05	04	32
Wertz, John(A)	1811	Aug. 13	Montgomery	05	04	32
Wertz, John(A)	1815	Aug. 21	Miami	02	11	04
Wesco, Henry(A)	1815	Oct. 30	Pennsylvania	02	09	31
Wesco, Henry(A)	1815	Oct. 30	Pennsylvania	01	09	26
Wessel, Bernard(A)	1837	Dec. 11	Cincinnati	03	13	31
West, Basil(C)	1811	Dec. 31	Champaign	11	03	33
West, Bazil(C)	1804	Dec. 28	Greene	11	04	04
West, Francis(C)	1818	April 22	Cincinnati	10	05	26
West, Francis(C)	1818	May 11	Cincinnati	10	05	29
West, Francis(C)	1818	June 11	Cincinnati	09	03	26
West, Francis(C)	1818	June 11	Cincinnati	09	02	08
West, Francis(C)	1818	June 11	Cincinnati	09	02	08
West, Francis(C)	1818	June 11	Cincinnati	09	02	08
West, George(A)	1819	Dec. 01	Butler	02	10	09
West, Isaac(A)	1814	Dec. 12	Kentucky	02	07	06
West, John(C)	1811	Dec. 14	Hamilton	01	03	26
West, John(C)	1824	June 07	Champaign	11	03	08
West, John(C)	1827	April 11	Champaign	11	03	34
West, Nathaniel(A)	1814	Aug. 31	Butler	01	09	28
West, Samuel(B)	1818	May 09	Cincinnati	01	02	11
West, Stocket(C)	1825	Sept. 08	Champaign	11	03	27
West, Thomas Jr.(C)	1813	June 24	Hamilton	09	05	02
West, Thomas Jr.(C)	1812	Nov. 14	Hamilton	09	06	26
West, Thomas Junr.(C)	1816	Nov. 02	Champaign	09	06	26
West, Thomas(C)	1805	Sept. 11	Champaign	11	05	28
West, Thos. Jr.(C)	1813	June 24	Hamilton	09	06	32
West, William(C)	1807	Jan. 26	Warren	11	03	03
West, William(C)	1812	April 15	Champaign	11	03	03
Westcott, Ebenezer(B)	1818	Aug. 27	Hamilton	03	07	12
Westerfield, James(A)	1807	April 04	Montgomery	02	07	07
Westfall, Absalom(A)	1816	March 02	Montgomery	03	10	34
Westfall, Andrew(A)	1836	Jan. 01	Darke	02	13	32
Westfall, Ann(C)	1801	Dec. 30	Hamilton	08	03	31
Westfall, Ann(C)	1802	Dec. 31	Hamilton	08	03	25
Westfall, Anne(C)	1802	Dec. 31	Hamilton	07	03	36
Westfall, Cornelius(A)	1811	Dec. 11	Miami	06	05	32
Westfall, Cornelius(C)	1814	June 10	Miami	11	02	26
Westfall, George(A)	1830	Aug. 18	Darke	03	09	07
Westfall, Jacob(A)	1818	Sept. 01	Montgomery	03	10	32
Westfall, Jacob(A)	1818	Sept. 01	Montgomery	03	10	29
Westfall, Job Jr.(B)	1813	Dec. 20	Montgomery	03	10	32
Westfall, Job(A)	1811	Aug. 13	Montgomery	06	02	18
Westfall, Job(C)	1801	Dec. 30	Hamilton	07	01	13
Westfall, Job. Jr.(A)	1813	Dec. 20	Montgomery	03	10	31
Westfall, John G.(C)	1819	Aug. 10	Miami	11	01	08
Westfall, John(A)	1832	April 19	Greene	03	10	17
Westfall, John(A)	1833	Dec. 31	Darke	03	10	30
Westfall, William(A)	1832	June 04	Darke	03	10	30
Westfall, William(C)	1801	Dec. 30	Hamilton	06	01	17
Westfield, Samuel(C)	1801	Dec. 30	Hamilton	05	03	32
Westlake, Josias(A)	1829	Aug. 27	Miami	05	07	35
Weston, Benjamin(E)	1832	Feb. 17	Franklin(Ind	12	12	08
Weston, Benjamin(E)	1832	March 26	Franklin(Ind	12	12	08
Weston, David(E)	1834	Feb. 07	Franklin(Ind	12	12	32
Weston, David(E)	1835	April 20	Franklin(Ind	12	12	32
Wetherow, John(A)	1801	Dec. 30	Hamilton	03	03	34
Wetherow, John(A)	1801	Dec. 30	Hamilton	03	03	27
Wetter, Christopher(B)	1806	June 25	Dearborn(Ind	01	11	13
Wetter, Christopher(B)	1806	June 25	Dearborn(Ind	01	11	25

PURCHASER	YEAR	DATE	RESIDENCE	R	T	S
Wetter, John(B)	1806	July 02	Butler	01	11	24
Wever, Daniel(A)	1837	March 01	Montgomery	03	11	05
Wever, Jacob(E)	1819	Dec. 08	Greene	14	21	28
Weymier, John(A)	1804	Sept. 24	Montgomery	05	05	25
Weymire, Andrew(A)	1804	Oct. 13	Montgomery	05	06	36
Weymire, Andrew(A)	1805	March 15	Montgomery	05	05	25
Weymire, Andrew(A)	1805	July 20	Montgomery	06	02	17
Weymire, Jacob(E)	1812	March 05	Wayne(Ind)	13	15	21
Weyrick, Henry(E)	1837	Nov. 04	Richland	15	21	19
Whallon, Thomas(D)	1811	Oct. 01	Butler	02	03	26
Whallon, Thomas(D)	1811	April 09	Butler	02	03	26
Whallon, Thos.(A)	1829	July 21	Butler	04	06	30
Whallon, Thos.(A)	1829	July 21	Butler	04	06	31
Wharton, Benjamin(A)	1807	Feb. 09	Warren	06	05	30
Wharton, Nehemiah(C)	1831	Jan. 05	Warren	12	02	05
Wharton, Richard(E)	1814	Aug. 15	Kentucky	13	16	29
Wharton, Thos.(A)	1829	Dec. 12	Miami	05	08	25
Wheatley, John(E)	1837	Nov. 07	Montgomery	15	20	05
Wheatley, John(E)	1837	Nov. 24	Montgomery	15	20	17
Wheatley, John(E)	1837	Nov. 24	Montgomery	15	21	32
Wheatley, Joseph(E)	1836	Sept. 19	Montgomery	15	21	28
Wheatley, Joseph(E)	1836	Sept. 27	Montgomery	15	21	28
Wheatley, Joseph(E)	1837	May 20	Montgomery	15	21	07
Wheatley, Joseph(E)	1837	Nov. 24	Montgomery	15	20	17
Wheatley, Rich'd.(E)	1836	Sept. 19	Montgomery	15	21	28
Wheatley, Richard(E)	1836	Sept. 27	Montgomery	15	21	17
Wheeler, Aquilla	1808	March 01	Cincinnati	?	?	?
Wheeler, Charles Wesley(E)	1834	May 29	Randolph(Ind	14	19	02
Wheeler, Charles Wesley(E)	1834	May 29	Randolph(Ind	14	20	35
Wheeler, Ebenezer(C)	1813	April 14	Greene	08	04	12
Wheeler, Jacob(C)	1804	Dec. 22	Cincinnati	09	04	19
Wheeler, Jacob(C)	1804	Dec. 22	Cincinnati	08	11	18
Wheeler, Jacob(C)	1809	March 13	Cincinati(Fr	02	03	08
Wheeler, John(B)	1814	July 14	Carolina	01	14	23
Wheeler, John(B)	1816	May 30	Dearborn(Ind	02	04	05
Wheeler, John(B)	1818	Feb. 11	Dearborn(Ind	02	04	05
Wheeler, John(B)	1817	Dec. 05	Dearborn(Ind	02	04	03
Wheeler, Madison(E)	1836	March 21	Randolph(Ind	14	20	31
Wheeler, Piercy(B)	1836	March 24	Dearborn(Ind	02	05	30
Wheeler, Piercy(B)	1836	June 18	Dearborn(Ind	03	06	24
Wheeler, Samuel(B)	1817	Aug. 19	Dearborn(Ind	02	04	05
Wheeler, William(B)	1832	Oct. 13	Dearborn(Ind	03	06	24
Wheeler, Wilson L.(B)	1836	June 27	Dearborn(Ind	02	05	30
Wheeler, Wilson L.(B)	1837	March 24	Dearborn(Ind	02	05	30
Wheellock, Lyman(A)	1828	Nov. 22	Miami	05	06	11
Wherritt, William(E)	1831	Jan. 27	Fayette	12	13	27
Wherritt, William(E)	1831	Dec. 12	Fayette	12	13	26
Whetisell, Henry(A)	1808	Feb. 03	Montgomery	02	07	09
Whetsel, Hiram(E)	1834	Nov. 11	Warren	13	19	22
Whetstone, Matthias(B)	1819	Jan. 22	Hamilton	02	04	20
Whipple, Jesse(B)	1832	Aug. 29	Franklin(Ind	01	07	03
Whipple, John(C)	1805	Dec. 31	U. S. Army	11	02	35
Whipple, John(C)	1805	Dec. 27	FortWayneInd	11	02	35
Whistler, Edward(A)	1806	March 22	Montgomery	06	04	05
Whistler, John(C)	1806	Feb. 08	Ind.Territry	11	01	03
Whitacre, Francis(A)	1836	Oct. 11	Warren	01	14	21
Whitaker, Ambrose(A)	1837	Jan. 27	Franklin(Ind	01	13	20
Whitaker, James(B)	1817	Dec. 17	Hamilton	03	02	19
Whitaker, John(A)	1817	Sept. 01	Darke	02	12	05
Whitaker, Jonathan Jr.(A)	1831	June 13	Warren	05	07	02
Whitaker, Jonathan Jr.(A)	1831	June 13	Warren	05	08	35
Whitaker, Jonathan Jr.(A)	1831	July 05	Warren	05	08	35
Whitaker, William(B)	1835	Oct. 13	Dearborn(Ind	01	06	08
White, Abel(B)	1815	Aug. 22	Cincinnati	02	09	24
White, Abraham(A)	1805	Nov. 25	Butler	02	05	17
White, Abraham(A)	1806	Feb. 26	Butler	02	05	17
White, Alexander(B)	1815	Feb. 02	Dearborn(Ind	01	07	34
White, Alexander(B)	1818	June 22	Dearborn(Ind	01	07	23
White, Alexander(E)	1813	Sept. 11	Dearborn(Ind	13	12	15

348

PURCHASER	YEAR	DATE	RESIDENCE	R	T	S
White, Amos(A)	1811	Nov. 13	Hamilton	02	05	08
White, Beni(B)	1813	Dec. 06	Wayne(Ind)	01	12	02
White, Benjamin(E)	1815	Oct. 20	Franklin(Ind	13	13	07
White, Caleb(B)	1818	March 13	Hamilton	02	03	18
White, Caleb(B)	1818	June 22	Hamilton	01	02	18
White, Caleb(B)	1818	June 22	Hamilton	01	02	19
White, Caleb(B)	1818	July 07	Hamilton	02	06	32
White, Caleb(B)	1818	July 13	Hamilton	02	06	12
White, Caleb(B)	1818	July 13	Hamilton	02	06	24
White, Caleb(B)	1818	July 13	Hamilton	03	03	23
White, Caleb(B)	1818	July 20	Hamilton	01	06	10
White, Caleb(E)	1818	May 14	Cincinnati	13	11	09
White, Daniel(B)	1818	Jan. 31	Dearborn(Ind	03	05	14
White, Edward(A)	1804	Dec. 05	Hamilton	01	03	08
White, Edward(B)	1807	March 02	Butler	01	09	23
White, Edward(B)	1817	Aug. 22	Kentucky	02	03	35
White, George(C)	1830	Aug. 02	Miami	12	03	26
White, Hamilton(A)	1836	Nov. 07	Darke	01	12	31
White, Hamilton(B)	1836	Nov. 07	Darke	01	17	25
White, Hartshorne(E)	1818	Nov. 30	Warren	14	17	03
White, Ira(C)	1819	Sept. 28	Hamilton	13	02	23
White, Ira(C)	1819	Sept. 28	Hamilton	13	02	23
White, Ira(C)	1819	Sept. 28	Hamilton	13	02	33
White, Ira(C)	1819	Sept. 28	Hamilton	13	02	33
White, Israel(B)	1818	May 19	Hamilton	03	04	13
White, Ithamar(C)	1806	March 08	Warren	05	02	22
White, Ithamer(B)	1813	March 16	Butler	01	09	26
White, Ithaniel(C)	1802	Dec. 11	Hamilton	05	02	02
White, Jacob A.(E)	1831	July 04	Preble	14	19	04
White, Jacob Junr.(C)	1802	Dec. 11	Hamilton	05	02	02
White, Jacob((A)	1803	Sept. 01	?	02	05	01
White, Jacob(A)	1801	April 29	Hamilton	01	02	11
White, Jacob(A)	1804	Dec. 05	Hamilton	01	02	12
White, Jacob(A)	1810	April 11	Hamilton	01	02	12
White, Jacob(A)	1817	Nov. 17	Warren	04	09	15
White, Jacob(A)	1818	Oct. 29	Miami	04	09	15
White, Jacob(A)	1818	Oct. 29	Miami	04	09	22
White, Jacob(B)	1817	Sept. 08	Hamilton	02	02	02
White, Jacob(C)	1801	Dec. 22	Hamilton	04	03	02
White, Jacob(C)	1801	Dec. 22	Hamilton	04	03	14
White, Jacob(C)	1801	Dec. 22	Hamilton	04	02	01
White, Jacob(C)	1801	Dec. 31	Hamilton	05	02	03
White, Jacob(C)	1801	Dec. 31	Hamilton	04	03	01
White, James B.(A)	1820	Jan. 28	Greene	03	10	29
White, James(A)	1806	Dec. 20	Montgomery	02	07	18
White, James(A)	1828	Oct. 23	Shelby	06	07	04
White, James(B)	1813	July 01	Dearborn(Ind	01	06	13
White, James(B)	1814	Aug. 10	Dearborn(Ind	01	06	03
White, James(B)	1816	Oct. 14	Wayne(Ind)	01	15	13
White, Jeremiah(A)	1814	April 06	Miami	06	08	28
White, Joel(E)	1813	Oct. 07	Hamilton	13	14	29
White, John D.(E)	1836	Nov. 09	Decatur(Ind)	11	11	35
White, John(A)	1811	Nov. 13	Hamilton	02	05	08
White, John(B)	1807	Feb. 09	Kentucky	01	13	08
White, John(B)	1816	Oct. 14	Wayne(Ind)	01	15	24
White, John(B)	1816	Oct. 17	Wayne(Ind)	01	14	02
White, John(B)	1816	Dec. 13	Dearborn(Ind	01	06	11
White, John(C)	1812	Nov. 23	Champaign	11	05	10
White, John(E)	1811	Oct. 22	Kentucky	12	14	02
White, John(E)	1811	Oct. 22	Kentucky	12	14	02
White, John(E)	1816	Feb. 16	Franklin(Ind	13	13	07
White, John(E)	1838	Nov. 05	FlemingCo.Ky	15	22	10
White, Jonathan(E)	1837	May 20	Montgomery	14	21	24
White, Joseph(B)	1817	June 04	New York	01	06	09
White, Joseph(C)	1813	March 23	Champaign	09	06	28
White, Joseph(E)	1814	Aug. 08	Warren	13	14	09
White, Peter(B)	1815	June 08	Dearborn(Ind	01	03	06
White, Reuben(A)	1817	Sept. 15	Butler	02	12	04
White, Robert(A)	1817	Oct. 04	Miami	04	09	36

PURCHASER	YEAR	DATE	RESIDENCE	R	T	S
White, Robert(A)	1820	Feb. 29	Miami	04	08	10
White, Robert(B)	1811	Oct. 18	Virginia	02	10	24
White, Stephen(C)	1801	Dec. 24	Kentucky	06	02	15
White, Stephen(C)	1804	Nov. 13	Kentucky	06	02	21
White, Tabitha(B)	1806	Oct. 14	Butler	01	14	11
White, Tabitha(B)	1806	Oct. 28	Butler	01	14	11
White, Tabitha(B)	1817	Aug. 13	Wayne(Ind)	01	15	13
White, Tabitha(B)	1817	Aug. 13	Wayne(Ind)	01	15	14
White, Thomas(A)	1811	April 09	Butler	01	04	10
White, Thomas(E)	1836	Jan. 12	Franklin(Ind	11	11	35
White, Thomas(E)	1836	June 06	Franklin(Ind	11	11	35
White, Thomas(E)	1837	Feb. 22	Darke	15	22	09
White, William(B)	1809	Dec. 25	Dearborn(Ind	02	02	25
White, William(E)	1837	May 20	Montgomery	15	21	34
White, Wm. L.(B)	1813	Feb. 20	Ind.Territory	01	07	08
Whiteaker, James W.(B)	1836	June 06	Dearborn(Ind	02	04	08
Whiteaker, John(B)	1815	May 20	Dearborn(Ind	03	05	01
Whiteaker, John(B)	1818	Jan. 31	Dearborn(Ind	03	05	01
Whitehead, Jesse(B)	1835	June 05	Dearborn(Ind	02	07	06
Whitehead, John(A)	1830	Dec. 29	Montgomery	04	07	28
Whitehead, John(B)	1806	Aug. 25	Dearborn(Ind	01	13	31
Whitehead, John(B)	1811	Dec. 11	Wayne(Ind)	01	13	31
Whitehead, John(B)	1815	Jan. 11	Wayne(Ind)	01	13	32
Whitehead, John(B)	1834	Jan. 16	Butler	02	07	06
Whitehead, Lazarus(B)	1805	Aug. 08	Ind.Territry	01	13	31
Whitehead, Lazarus(B)	1806	Feb. 24	Ind.Territry	02	13	36
Whitehead, Lazarus(B)	1806	May 06	Ind.Territory	02	13	26
Whitehead, Mich'l.(B)	1835	Jan. 28	Hamilton	02	07	07
Whitehead, Michael(B)	1835	Jan. 28	Hamilton	02	07	06
Whitehouse, Richard(C)	1818	June 30	FortWayneInd	13	03	34
Whiteis, Jeremiah(A)	1837	May 13	Logan	02	14	27
Whiteley, John(C)	1811	Dec. 02	Kentucky	09	06	34
Whitelock, Abraham(E)	1832	Nov. 23	Franklin(Ind	13	12	06
Whitelock, Charles(E)	1836	Feb. 13	Franklin(Ind	13	12	07
Whitelock, Joseph(E)	1831	June 27	Fayette	13	13	31
Whitelock, Joseph(E)	1831	Aug. 10	Fayette	13	13	32
Whitelock, Thos. Campbell(E)	1832	Nov. 23	Franklin(Ind	13	12	06
Whitelock, Wm. Watson(E)	1832	Dec. 24	Franklin(Ind	13	12	06
Whiteman, Benjamin(C)	1801	Dec. 08	Hamilton	07	03	21
Whiteman, Benjamin(C)	1804	Nov. 06	Greene	08	04	25
Whiteman, Benjamin(C)	1806	Dec. 30	Greene	10	06	31
Whiteman, Benjamin(C)	1812	April 15	Greene	09	06	36
Whiteman, Benjamin(C)	1812	April 15	Greene	10	06	31
Whiteman, L.(C)	1827	Aug. 23	Cincinnati	08	02	02
Whiteman, L.(C)	1827	Aug. 23	Cincinnati	08	02	02
Whiteman, Lewis(A)	1815	June 01	Cincinnati	01	02	26
Whiteman, Lewis(A)	1815	June 01	Cincinnati	01	02	36
Whiteman, Lewis(A)	1836	Sept. 17	Cincinnati	03	10	06
Whiteman, Lewis(A)	1836	Sept. 19	Cincinnati	02	14	35
Whiteman, Lewis(A)	1836	Oct. 01	Cincinnati	02	14	34
Whiteman, Lewis(B)	1814	Dec. 02	Cincinnati	03	02	21
Whiteman, Lewis(B)	1815	Sept. 23	?	01	05	07
Whiteman, Lewis(B)	1815	Oct. 02	Cincinnati	01	04	31
Whiteman, Lewis(B)	1817	Dec. 31	Cincinnati	02	05	06
Whiteman, Lewis(C)	1816	Aug. 01	Cincinnati	08	04	29
Whiteman, Lewis(C)	1817	Aug. 01	Cincinnati	14	03	12
Whiteman, Lewis(C)	1817	Aug. 01	Cincinnati	09	04	02
Whiteman, Lewis(C)	1817	Aug. 01	Cincinnati	08	02	02
Whiteman, Lewis(C)	1817	Dec. 02	Cincinnati	09	04	36
Whiteman, Lewis(C)	1824	Aug. 23	Cincinnati	08	04	29
Whiteman, Lewis(C)	1831	Aug. 08	Cincinnati	13	04	06
Whiteman, Lewis(C)	1831	Aug. 08	Cincinnati	14	03	12
Whiteman, Lewis(E)	1815	Nov. 22	Cincinnati	13	14	04
Whitemore, William(B)	1816	Nov. 16	Pennsylvania	03	03	04
Whitenger, Henry(B)	1806	March 12	Hamilton	01	06	33
Whitesel, Adam(C)	1824	Oct. 27	Preble	11	02	08
Whitesel, Dan'l.(A)	1824	June 17	Preble	01	08	23
Whitesel, Henry(A)	1808	Nov. 07	Preble	01	08	12
Whitesel, Henry(E)	1838	Nov. 15	Randolph(Ind	14	20	01

PURCHASER	YEAR	DATE	RESIDENCE	R	T	S
Whitesel, Jacob(E)	1836	Oct. 25	Montgomery	15	20	08
Whitesel, Tobias(A)	1826	Jan. 23	Preble	01	08	15
Whitesell, Henry(A)	1805	Aug. 07	Montgomery	03	06	32
Whitezel, Tobias(C)	1802	Dec. 30	Hamilton	05	02	24
Whitier, Solomon(A)	1814	Sept. 24	Miami	04	09	13
Whiting, John(C)	1804	Dec. 25	Montgomery	10	02	32
Whiting, John(C)	1804	Dec. 26	Montgomery	10	01	02
Whitinger, Henry(E)	1815	July 31	Wayne(Ind)	14	15	29
Whitinger, Jacob(A)	1801	July 20	Hamilton	03	03	30
Whitinger, John(E)	1814	June 11	Wayne(Ind)	14	15	29
Whitlock, Elias(A)	1829	Aug. 25	Hamilton	04	06	30
Whitlock, Joseph(E)	1818	Jan. 09	Fairfield	13	12	07
Whitman, Benjamin(C)	1806	Dec. 30	Greene	09	06	36
Whitman, David(A)	1817	Nov. 13	Darke	03	11	36
Whitmar, John(C)	1805	Nov. 30	Champaign	11	04	24
Whitmore, William(A)	1813	July 29	Hamilton	01	03	19
Whitmore, William(B)	1836	Aug. 16	Switzerland	03	03	21
Whitney, Joel(C)	1818	May 13	Champaign	12	03	19
Whitney, Jos. Schoonover(B)	1832	June 13	Franklin(Ind	02	08	22
Whitney, Joseph Schoonover(B)	1831	Dec. 29	Franklin(Ind	02	08	22
Whitney, Moses(B)	1831	Dec. 29	Franklin(Ind	01	08	19
Whitsit, Alexander(C)	1831	Jan. 11	Miami	12	03	32
Whitson, Amos(E)	1836	Nov. 24	Wayne(Ind)	13	20	10
Whitson, Mary(E)	1837	Feb. 02	Wayne(Ind)	13	21	25
Whitson, Solomon(A)	1814	Sept. 24	Miami	04	09	13
Whitson, Willas(E)	1818	Jan. 09	Wayne(Ind)	14	17	09
Whitson, Willis(A)	1805	July 26	Butler	02	05	12
Whitson, Willis(E)	1811	Oct. 25	Wayne(Ind)	14	17	27
Whitson, Willis(E)	1811	Oct. 25	Wayne(Ind)	14	17	27
Whitson, Willis(E)	1818	June 05	Wayne(Ind)	14	21	15
Whittelsey, Isaac(C)	1832	Jan. 31	Butler	12	02	05
Whitworth, John(B)	1814	Nov. 19	Butler	02	10	14
Whorton, Benjamin(A)	1804	Sept. 24	Butler	03	02	17
Wiant, Adam(C)	1824	June 07	Champaign	11	04	29
Wiant, John(C)	1815	Nov. 18	Virginia	11	04	35
Wichard, Joseph(A)	1814	Nov. 25	Butler	02	04	20
Wickard, Bartholomew(A)	1808	Sept. 12	Maryland	02	04	27
Wickersham, Caleb(E)	1817	July 01	Franklin(Ind	14	20	29
Wickersham, James(A)	1829	Aug. 03	Darke	01	10	19
Wickersham, James(B)	1817	July 09	Wayne(Ind)	01	15	35
Wickersham, James(B)	1835	July 29	Randolph(Ind	01	18	13
Wickersham, William(E)	1836	March 03	Wayne(Ind)	13	20	36
Wickham, Nathan Canfield(B)	1832	May 25	Butler	01	07	02
Wickham, Nathan Canfield(B)	1832	Sept. 18	Dearborn(Ind	01	07	02
Widney, John(A)	1810	May 30	Miami	05	09	36
Widney, John(A)	1810	May 30	Miami	06	07	06
Widney, John(A)	1812	June 04	Miami	05	09	35
Wiedau, Christopher Henry(B)	1834	May 24	Cincinnati	01	07	07
Wiel, Andreas(A)	1804	Oct. 19	Hamilton	01	02	36
Wieley, Cornelius(B)	1804	Dec. 08	Virginia	01	10	01
Wiemann, George Hy.(E)	1836	Oct. 27	Cincinnati	12	10	19
Wietor, Christiana(B)	1834	May 15	Cincinnati	02	06	06
Wietor, Francis(B)	1834	May 05	Cincinnati	02	06	06
Wiggans, William Jr.(E)	1833	Oct. 23	Franklin(Ind	13	12	20
Wiggins, John(E)	1838	May 21	Darke	14	22	25
Wiggs, Susannah(B)	1830	May 08	Randolph(Ind	01	16	23
Wiggs, William(B)	1830	April 15	Randolph(Ind	01	16	22
Wiggs, Windsor(B)	1830	May 08	Randolph(Ind	01	16	23
Wight, James(A)	1821	Jan. 20	Butler	02	13	23
Wight, James(A)	1821	Feb. 26	Butler	02	13	10
Wikle, Philip(A)	1811	March 08	Montgomery	03	06	15
Wilber, Bradford(A)	1818	Aug. 10	Hamilton	06	08	05
Wilcotts, Clark(B)	1814	Jan. 19	Wayne(Ind)	01	16	28
Wilcox, Daniel Jr.(B)	1834	June 03	Switzerland	03	03	27
Wilcox, Hezekiah(C)	1817	Aug. 01	Champaign	13	05	35
Wilcox, James(E)	1817	Oct. 27	Wayne(Ind)	13	17	31
Wilcoxon, George(C)	1831	Aug. 08	Logan	14	04	33
Wildridge, Ralph(B)	1815	Jan. 06	Franklin(Ind	01	08	33
Wildridge, Ralph(B)	1828	Oct. 18	Franklin(Ind	01	08	33

PURCHASER	YEAR	DATE	RESIDENCE	R	T	S
Wile, Peter(A)	1805	Nov. 02	Pennsylvania	03	07	34
Wile, Peter(A)	1807	June 19	Montgomery	05	05	30
Wile, William(B)	1814	Nov. 07	Hamilton	01	08	03
Wiles, Luke(B)	1816	Sept. 06	Clinton	02	02	25
Wiles, Peter(A)	1827	April 02	Montgomery	04	06	22
Wiles, Richardson(B)	1830	March 30	Switzerland	01	02	30
Wiley, Allen(B)	1815	March 02	Franklin(Ind	03	03	11
Wiley, Allen(B)	1835	June 01	Switzerland	03	04	34
Wiley, Anthony(C)	1814	June 14	Scioto	13	14	03
Wiley, Delany(B)	1836	June 03	Switzerland	03	04	34
Wiley, Isaac(E)	1838	Sept. 03	Jay Co.,Ind.	14	22	32
Wiley, James(B)	1811	Nov. 01	Dearborn(Ind	01	08	11
Wiley, James(E)	1814	March 09	Ind.Territory	12	12	10
Wiley, James(E)	1815	Oct. 26	Dearborn(Ind	12	13	21
Wiley, James(E)	1835	Oct. 21	Franklin(Ind	12	12	28
Wiley, James(E)	1835	Oct. 21	Franklin(Ind	12	12	33
Wiley, James(E)	1835	Oct. 21	Franklin(Ind	12	12	33
Wiley, John(A)	1825	Aug. 30	Darke	01	10	22
Wiley, John(B)	1810	Dec. 26	Kentucky	01	11	12
Wiley, John(C)	1811	Dec. 02	Champaign	11	05	27
Wiley, John(C)	1812	March 14	Champaign	11	05	27
Wiley, John(C)	1812	Aug. 21	Montgomery	12	01	19
Wiley, Lemuel(B)	1833	Nov. 23	Switzerland	03	03	03
Wiley, Melville(B)	1833	Nov. 15	Switzerland	03	03	14
Wiley, Moses(B)	1808	Jan. 18	Dearborn(Ind	01	08	09
Wiley, Moses(B)	1818	June 10	Dearborn(Ind	01	07	02
Wiley, Samuel(A)	1812	Aug. 20	Preble	01	06	04
Wiley, Spencer(B)	1835	March 02	Franklin(Ind	02	08	05
Wiley, Spencer(E)	1814	March 09	Ind.Territory	12	12	10
Wiley, Thomas Jr.(B)	1834	March 15	Randolph(Ind	01	18	12
Wiley, Thomas(B)	1818	March 17	Butler	01	15	10
Wiley, Thomas(B)	1835	Sept. 09	Wayne(Ind)	01	18	12
Wiley, Thomas(B)	1835	Sept. 09	Wayne(Ind)	01	18	11
Wiley, William R.(B)	1824	Oct. 15	Switzerland	01	02	21
Wiley, William(C)	1812	Aug. 21	Montgomery	12	01	19
Wiley, William(C)	1829	Aug. 13	Miami	13	02	32
Wiley, Wm. Royston(B)	1832	June 12	Switzerland	01	02	19
Wilfong, George(A)	1832	Aug. 21	Montgomery	04	06	05
Wilhelm, Benj'n.(A)	1831	Sept. 15	Montgomery	07	01	05
Wilhelm, Jacob(B)	1835	July 13	Dearborn(Ind	02	06	09
Wilhelm, John(A)	1836	May 28	Montgomery	04	11	18
Wilkins, Charles(A)	1801	April 27	Kentucky	01	05	21
Wilkins, Charles(A)	1801	April 27	Kentucky	01	01	06
Wilkins, Daniel(A)	1812	Jan. 07	Hamilton	02	02	06
Wilkins, Francis A.(E)	1835	Oct. 17	Randolph(Ind	14	19	20
Wilkins, Joseph(E)	1833	Oct. 17	Randolph(Ind	14	19	29
Wilkins, Philip(B)	1809	Feb. 16	Hamilton	01	09	24
Wilkinson, Asahael(C)	1815	May 16	Champaign	13	03	14
Wilkinson, Asahel(C)	1813	Oct. 25	Champaign	13	03	14
Wilkinson, Claborn(E)	1815	May 20	Wayne(Ind)	?	?	?
Wilkinson, Gideon(B)	1811	June 15	Butler	01	09	04
Wilkinson, Gideon(B)	1811	July 22	Butler	01	09	09
Wilkinson, Isaac A.(C)	1829	Aug. 10	Shelby	13	02	12
Wilkinson, James Anderson(C)	1832	Jan. 04	Champaign	13	03	35
Wilkinson, John(B)	1816	Dec. 21	Hamilton	03	07	03
Wilkinson, Joseph(B)	1801	July 20	Maryland	01	04	16
Wilkinson, Mary Ellen(E)	1815	May 20	Wayne(Ind)	13	16	11
Wilkinson, Samuel(A)	1837	Feb. 17	Hamilton	01	14	28
Wilkinson, Samuel(A)	1837	June 15	Hamilton	01	14	31
Wilkinson, Thomas(C)	1812	April 15	Champaign	12	05	32
Wilkinson, Thomas(C)	1817	Aug. 01	Champaign	12	05	32
Wilkinson, Thomas(C)	1818	June 19	Champaign	13	02	06
Wilkinson, Thomas(C)	1819	June 03	Shelby	13	02	18
Wilkinson, Thomas(C)	1831	Nov. 19	Shelby	13	02	11
Wilkinson, Thos.(C)	1829	Aug. 10	Shelby	13	02	12
Wilkinson, William(C)	1831	Nov. 19	Shelby	13	02	11
Wilkison, Gideon(B)	1811	June 15	Butler	01	09	09
Wilkison, Thomas(C)	1827	Nov. 20	Shelby	13	02	08
Wilkison, Thomas(E)	1837	June 01	Jay Co.,Ind.	14	22	35

PURCHASER	YEAR	DATE	RESIDENCE	R	T	S
Wilkison, William(C)	1818	April 30	Miami	13	02	05
Will, Henry(E)	1837	March 27	Cincinnati	12	11	21
Willcox, Isaac(B)	1815	June 05	Ind.Territory	01	04	33
Willcuts, Clark(B)	1831	July 05	Randolph(Ind	01	16	10
Willcutts, Clark(E)	1828	Dec. 05	Wayne(Ind)	15	18	07
Willets, Elisha(E)	1814	April 06	Fairfield	13	15	04
Willets, Jesse(E)	1814	April 06	Fairfield	13	15	04
Willets, Jesse(E)	1816	Oct. 23	Wayne(Ind)	13	15	04
Willets, Levi(E)	1811	Oct. 23	Ind.Territory	12	16	26
Willets, Levi(E)	1811	Oct. 24	Wayne(Ind)	13	15	05
Willets, Levi(E)	1811	Oct. 24	Wayne(Ind)	13	15	06
Willets, William(E)	1811	Oct. 23	Pickaway	12	16	26
Willett, William(E)	1811	Oct. 24	Pickaway	13	15	05
Willetts, Isaac(E)	1811	Oct. 22	Ind.Territory	12	15	01
Willetts, Isaac(E)	1811	Oct. 24	Wayne(Ind)	13	16	28
Willetts, Isaac(E)	1811	Oct. 24	Wayne(Ind)	13	16	21
Willetts, Isaac(E)	1811	Nov. 04	Wayne(Ind)	13	16	28
Willey, Horace(A)	1818	Sept. 12	Hamilton	04	09	23
Willey, Rensselear(B)	1836	Feb. 06	Dearborn(Ind	02	04	32
William, Elmore(A)	1804	Sept. 24	Cincinnati	04	03	26
William, Jacob(A)	1804	Sept. 24	Cincinnati	04	03	26
Williams, Abraham(B)	1819	May 07	Hamilton	02	06	07
Williams, Absalom(E)	1814	Oct. 03	Wayne(Ind)	13	16	02
Williams, Adam(E)	1834	Aug. 26	Franklin(Ind	13	12	28
Williams, Amos(B)	1816	June 27	Switzerland	01	02	04
Williams, Ann Maria(E)	1835	Sept. 24	Randolph(Ind	14	19	02
Williams, Anthony(B)	1806	Aug. 29	Warren	01	11	01
Williams, Azariah(E)	1831	May 20	Wayne(Ind)	13	18	33
Williams, Caleb(B)	1816	Oct. 14	Cincinnati	02	06	01
Williams, Charles(C)	1801	Dec. 31	Hamilton	07	02	02
Williams, Charles(E)	1831	March 21	Wayne(Ind)	13	17	04
Williams, Cornelius(E)	1813	Sept. 04	Hamilton	13	13	06
Williams, David(A)	1815	Aug. 25	Warren	02	09	02
Williams, David(B)	1831	Dec. 03	Hamilton	01	07	36
Williams, David(B)	1833	Jan. 22	Hamilton	01	07	36
Williams, David(C)	1804	Sept. 03	Warren	04	04	26
Williams, David(C)	1831	Jan. 13	Cincinnati	12	03	34
Williams, Edward T.(A)	1836	Oct. 24	Cincinnati	01	15	22
Williams, Elias(A)	1819	Jan. 25	Kentucky	04	11	02
Williams, Eliza Jane(A)	1836	Oct. 25	Cincinnati	01	15	27
Williams, Elmore(A)	1809	Dec. 12	Cincinnati	04	03	26
Williams, Elmore(B)	1809	Dec. 12	Cincinnati	01	08	19
Williams, Elmore(D)	1808	Nov. 01	Cincinati(Fr	02	02	08
Williams, Ephraim D.(E)	1817	Nov. 07	Cincinnati	13	18	10
Williams, George(A)	1830	June 16	Miami	08	01	08
Williams, George(B)	1814	May 24	Hamilton	01	11	07
Williams, Henry(A)	1806	Oct. 14	Tennessee	02	11	03
Williams, Henry(A)	1809	Nov. 07	Miami	05	07	18
Williams, Henry(A)	1815	May 06	Miami	05	07	18
Williams, Hezekiah(E)	1814	June 28	Wayne(Ind)	13	18	33
Williams, Hiram(E)	1831	Dec. 09	Franklin(Ind	13	12	28
Williams, Hiram(E)	1834	April 04	Franklin(Ind	13	12	21
Williams, Isaac(E)	1814	Oct. 03	Wayne(Ind)	14	15	06
Williams, Jacob(A)	1807	Jan. 31	Montgomery	05	07	08
Williams, Jacob(A)	1812	April 17	Miami	05	07	08
Williams, Jacob(A)	1815	Oct. 18	Miami	02	11	12
Williams, Jacob(A)	1815	Oct. 18	Miami	02	11	12
Williams, Jacob(C)	1828	May 02	Champaign	12	04	11
Williams, James C.(E)	1837	March 01	Randolph(Ind	15	20	20
Williams, James Senr.(E)	1816	April 10	Franklin(Ind	12	14	29
Williams, James(E)	1819	Nov. 30	Wayne(Ind)	15	21	10
Williams, Jesse(A)	1836	July 02	Hamilton	04	10	06
Williams, Jesse(A)	1836	July 05	Hamilton	03	12	24
Williams, Jesse(A)	1836	Sept. 05	Hamilton	03	12	24
Williams, Jesse(B)	1817	Dec. 18	Cincinnati	03	06	13
Williams, Jesse(B)	1817	Dec. 18	Cincinnati	03	06	34
Williams, Jesse(B)	1817	Dec. 18	Cincinnati	02	05	32
Williams, Jesse(B)	1836	July 13	Hamilton	01	17	01
Williams, Jesse(E)	1836	Oct. 28	Hamilton	12	12	30

353

PURCHASER	YEAR	DATE	RESIDENCE	R	T	S
Williams, Joel(A)	1803	Aug. 16	Hamilton	02	03	10
Williams, Joel(A)	1804	May 07	Cincinnati	02	03	03
Williams, Joel(A)	1805	June 24	Indian Creek	02	03	08
Williams, Joel(A)	1805	June 24	Indian Creek	02	03	05
Williams, Joel(A)	1805	Sept. 21	Indian Creek	02	04	20
Williams, Joel(A)	1805	Dec. 16	Indian Creek	02	04	34
Williams, Joel(B)	1806	June 23	Hamilton	02	10	04
Williams, Joel(B)	1806	Aug. 11	Hamilton	02	10	13
Williams, John H.(A)	1803	Aug. 11	Warren	05	04	25
Williams, John H.(C)	1801	Dec. 24	Hamilton	04	03	24
Williams, John P.(E)	1832	March 15	Franklin(Ind	13	12	14
Williams, John(A)	1814	Feb. 23	Kentucky	01	06	11
Williams, John(A)	1814	Dec. 07	Miami	05	07	19
Williams, John(A)	1816	Jan. 24	Butler	02	06	27
Williams, John(B)	1809	Sept. 18	Butler	01	12	07
Williams, John(C)	1804	Dec. 24	Montgomery	10	02	01
Williams, John(C)	1804	Dec. 24	Montgomery	10	02	07
Williams, John(C)	1806	Dec. 29	Champaign	12	05	18
Williams, John(C)	1812	Feb. 27	Champaign	13	05	35
Williams, John(E)	1815	Dec. 27	Franklin(Ind	13	13	19
Williams, John(E)	1831	June 10	Wayne(Ind)	13	17	08
Williams, John(E)	1832	Oct. 06	Franklin(Ind	13	12	20
Williams, John(E)	1836	Aug. 22	Wayne(Ind)	14	19	36
Williams, John(E)	1836	Nov. 26	Wayne(Ind)	14	19	36
Williams, John-Heirs(C)	1804	Aug. 27	Greene	10	04	08
Williams, Jonas(E)	1815	June 06	Clermont	12	14	26
Williams, Jonath'n.(E)	1829	May 01	Wayne(Ind)	13	17	04
Williams, Jonathan(B)	1806	July 19	Dearborn(Ind	01	10	08
Williams, Joseph(A)	1815	Sept. 07	Butler	01	09	01
Williams, Joseph(A)	1815	Oct. 19	Butler	01	09	01
Williams, Joseph(B)	1812	Aug. 13	Dearborn(Ind	01	08	12
Williams, Joseph(E)	1813	Oct. 09	Franklin(Ind	12	15	22
Williams, Joshua(B)	1812	Feb. 17	Hamilton	01	10	08
Williams, Lewis(C)	1817	Oct. 30	Miami	11	11	17
Williams, Margaret Widney(A)	1836	Oct. 25	Cincinnati	01	15	27
Williams, Martin(E)	1836	Jan. 26	Franklin(Ind	13	12	21
Williams, Matthias C.(E)	1836	July 02	Preble	15	21	04
Williams, Matthias C.(E)	1836	July 02	Preble	15	21	07
Williams, Micajah T.(A)	1817	June 02	Cincinnati	02	10	04
Williams, Michael(A)	1801	Aug. 07	Hamilton	05	07	19
Williams, Michael(C)	1804	Dec. 31	Montgomery	09	02	30
Williams, Michael(C)	1804	Dec. 31	Montgomery	10	02	25
Williams, Michael(C)	1804	Dec. 31	Montgomery	09	03	33
Williams, Miles(D)	1808	Nov. 07	Hamilton	01	03	08
Williams, Nathan(E)	1816	Aug. 30	Wayne(Ind)	13	17	06
Williams, Owen(E)	1827	Nov. 01	Wayne(Ind)	14	17	09
Williams, Perry(E)	1836	Oct. 08	Union(Ind)	13	20	25
Williams, Peter(C)	1812	Dec. 05	Hamilton	01	03	11
Williams, Peter(D)	1808	Nov. 07	Hamilton(Fr)	01	03	11
Williams, Peter(D)	1812	May 11	Hamilton(Fr)	01	03	11
Williams, Peter(D)	1813	Feb. 25	Hamilton(Fr)	01	03	11
Williams, Philip(A)	1824	May 29	Miami	04	08	10
Williams, Philip(A)	1831	Oct. 26	Darke	02	11	12
Williams, Philip(C)	1812	June 30	Miami	09	02	05
Williams, Ralph(B)	1811	April 01	Ind.Territry	02	10	32
Williams, Ralph(E)	1811	Oct. 23	Ind.Territry	13	12	19
Williams, Ralph(E)	1828	June 05	Franklin(Ind	12	12	24
Williams, Ralph(E)	1832	May 26	Franklin(Ind	13	12	08
Williams, Ralph(E)	1833	June 07	Franklin(Ind	13	12	19
Williams, Ralph(E)	1834	May 10	Franklin(Ind	12	12	13
Williams, Rich'd.(E)	1836	Sept. 22	Wayne(Ind)	15	19	20
Williams, Richard(B)	1817	Aug. 20	Preble	01	15	23
Williams, Richard(C)	1814	May 12	Franklin(Ind	13	12	17
Williams, Richard(E)	1811	Oct. 28	Wayne(Ind)	13	12	31
Williams, Richard(E)	1813	Aug. 30	Franklin(Ind	13	12	31
Williams, Richard(E)	1814	Aug. 12	Wayne(Ind)	13	18	29
Williams, Richard(E)	1816	Feb. 20	Wayne(Ind)	12	15	15
Williams, Richard(E)	1836	Sept. 22	Wayne(Ind)	15	19	17
Williams, Robert(C)	1810	Jan. 08	Champaign	10	03	01

354

PURCHASER	YEAR	DATE	RESIDENCE	R	T	S
Williams, Robert(E)	1815	Nov. 15	Franklin(Ind	13	14	32
Williams, Sam'l.(A)	1831	Jan. 29	Darke	03	08	30
Williams, Samuel(A)	1836	June 24	Hamilton	04	08	18
Williams, Samuel(A)	1836	Oct. 06	Cincinnati	01	15	15
Williams, Samuel(A)	1837	April 20	Cincinnati	01	15	27
Williams, Samuel(A)	1837	April 20	Cincinnati	01	15	34
Williams, Samuel(A)	1837	April 20	Cincinnati	04	08	18
Williams, Samuel(E)	1836	July 27	Hamilton	14	20	05
Williams, Samuel(E)	1836	July 28	Hamilton	14	20	26
Williams, Seth(C)	1825	July 14	Clark	08	06	11
Williams, Stephen(E)	1818	Feb. 07	Wayne(Ind)	14	18	23
Williams, Thomas(A)	1814	Oct. 21	Cincinnati	01	03	19
Williams, Thomas(A)	1814	Dec. 21	Cincinnati	01	04	22
Williams, Thomas(A)	1815	Dec. 11	Hamilton	01	01	07
Williams, Thomas(A)	1818	June 30	Hamilton	01	02	31
Williams, Thomas(B)	1804	Nov. 17	Ind.Territry	02	09	19
Williams, Thomas(B)	1811	Jan. 19	Ind.Territry	02	09	30
Williams, Thomas(E)	1814	Oct. 04	Franklin(Ind	12	12	04
Williams, Thomas(E)	1817	Sept. 17	Franklin(Ind	12	12	05
Williams, Weden(E)	1836	Jan. 25	Franklin(Ind	12	12	07
Williams, William Jr.(B)	1832	May 01	Switzerland	01	02	01
Williams, William(A)	1815	Jan. 10	Preble	01	08	26
Williams, William(A)	1816	Aug. 26	Preble	02	09	03
Williams, William(B)	1814	April 22	Wayne(Ind)	01	13	21
Williams, William(B)	1824	June 09	Wayne(Ind)	01	14	15
Williams, William(E)	1816	Feb. 24	Franklin(Ind	13	12	22
Williams, William(E)	1816	March 30	Wayne(Ind)	13	17	06
Williams, Wm. Henry(A)	1831	Dec. 17	Hamilton	01	01	06
Williamson, Benj'n.(A)	1827	Aug. 29	Clermont	04	06	15
Williamson, Benj'n.(A)	1830	Sept. 03	Montgomery	04	06	17
Williamson, David(A)	1809	Dec. 12	Pennsylvania	05	04	10
Williamson, David(B)	1818	May 07	Dearborn(Ind	03	05	23
Williamson, David(C)	1811	April 09	Miami	10	01	05
Williamson, David(C)	1811	April 09	Miami	10	01	05
Williamson, David(C)	1816	Aug. 01	Miami	10	01	05
Williamson, David(C)	1816	Aug. 01	Miami	10	01	05
Williamson, Eliazer(A)	1837	Sept. 28	Greene	01	12	02
Williamson, Eliazer(A)	1837	Sept. 28	Greene	01	12	06
Williamson, Eliazer(A)	1837	Nov. 09	Greene	01	12	06
Williamson, Eliazer(A)	1837	Nov. 09	Greene	01	13	32
Williamson, Eliazer(B)	1837	Sept. 28	Greene	01	17	24
Williamson, Eliazer(B)	1837	Nov. 09	Greene	01	17	15
Williamson, Elijah(A)	1836	Nov. 11	Darke	03	11	08
Williamson, James(A)	1831	Sept. 17	Clermont	05	07	03
Williamson, James(A)	1832	Aug. 10	Clermont	04	07	33
Williamson, James(A)	1836	Oct. 18	Darke	03	12	34
Williamson, Joachim(B)	1836	March 09	RipleyCo.Ind	03	05	09
Williamson, John(A)	1818	July 01	Warren	04	06	12
Williamson, John(A)	1818	July 09	Warren	04	06	13
Williamson, John(A)	1819	Aug. 17	Preble	04	05	18
Williamson, John(A)	1830	Feb. 22	Montgomery	04	06	13
Williamson, John(A)	1830	March 16	Clermont	04	06	09
Williamson, John(A)	1831	June 13	Montgomery	04	06	05
Williamson, John(B)	1834	Feb. 26	Dearborn(Ind	03	05	26
Williamson, John(C)	1807	March 11	Champaign	12	05	09
Williamson, John(C)	1807	April 17	Champaign	12	05	09
Williamson, John(C)	1807	July 22	Champaign	12	05	09
Williamson, Joseph(A)	1804	Dec. 21	Butler	05	05	35
Williamson, Joseph(A)	1806	Oct. 08	Pennsylvania	01	09	34
Williamson, Joseph(A)	1806	Oct. 28	Pennsylvania	01	08	03
Williamson, Joseph(A)	1806	Nov. 21	Hamilton	03	05	06
Williamson, Joseph(A)	1811	Dec. 11	Butler	01	09	32
Williamson, Joseph(A)	1836	Jan. 18	Darke	02	12	06
Williamson, Joseph(A)	1836	Sept. 14	Darke	02	12	06
Williamson, Joseph(C)	1801	Dec. 30	Hamilton	04	02	15
Williamson, Matthias(A)	1836	Nov. 07	Butler	02	14	25
Williamson, Matthias(A)	1836	Nov. 12	Butler	02	14	26
Williamson, Matthias(A)	1837	Sept. 02	Butler	02	14	23
Williamson, Miles(D)	1811	Jan. 28	Hamilton	02	03	26

PURCHASER	YEAR	DATE	RESIDENCE	R	T	S
Williamson, Peter(A)	1836	Nov. 07	Butler	02	14	25
Williamson, Peter(A)	1836	Nov. 12	Butler	02	14	36
Williamson, Peter(D)	1808	Nov. 01	Butler	03	03	11
Williamson, Samuel(A)	1806	Aug. 27	Montgomery	05	04	04
Williamson, Samuel(A)	1806	Sept. 26	Butler	01	09	32
Williamson, Samuel(A)	1810	April 11	Montgomery	05	05	35
Williamson, Samuel(A)	1811	Dec. 11	Montgomery	05	04	04
Williamson, William(A)	1806	Aug. 27	Butler	01	09	34
Williamson, William(B)	1818	March 20	Hamilton	03	05	12
Williamson, William(C)	1817	Aug. 01	Greene	08	03	33
Willias, William(A)	1805	March 15	Montgomery	05	05	08
Willis, Benjamin(A)	1813	Sept. 28	Hamilton	02	07	12
Willis, Ebenezer(C)	1814	Nov. 01	Pennsylvania	12	05	22
Willis, Ebenezer(C)	1814	Nov. 01	Pennsylvania	12	05	29
Willis, Jess(E)	1815	Sept. 20	Tennessee	13	18	32
Willis, John(B)	1817	June 16	Switzerland	03	02	05
Willis, John(B)	1831	April 10	Switzerland	03	02	05
Willis, Jonathan(E)	1819	Feb. 12	Highland	14	19	32
Willis, Jonathan(E)	1835	Jan. 23	Randolph(Ind	14	19	28
Willis, Jonathan(E)	1836	Jan. 28	Randolph(Ind	14	19	31
Willis, Joseph(C)	1824	July 22	Miami	11	02	29
Willis, Robert(E)	1835	Sept. 15	Clinton	13	19	35
Willis, Robert(E)	1835	Sept. 15	Clinton	13	18	02
Willis, William(A)	1802	March 11	Hamilton	05	05	04
Willis, William(A)	1816	May 28	Butler	02	11	11
Willis, William(A)	1816	June 17	Butler	01	12	24
Willis, William(B)	1808	Jan. 13	Warren	01	11	03
Willis, William(B)	1813	April 14	Warren	01	11	03
Willits, Isaac(E)	1816	April 10	Wayne(Ind)	13	16	20
Willitts, Henry(E)	1827	June 07	Wayne(Ind)	13	17	14
Williung, John(B)	1833	Sept. 12	Hamilton	02	06	06
Willkinson, James B.(B)	1805	July 01	U. S. Army	01	01	06
Willouts, Clark(E)	1818	Feb. 24	Wayne(Ind)	14	18	22
Wills, Abraham(A)	1819	Feb. 26	Warren	03	10	19
Wills, Abraham(A)	1819	Feb. 26	Warren	03	10	20
Wills, Daniel(A)	1833	March 02	Darke	03	10	18
Wills, James(A)	1820	Jan. 15	Warren	03	10	20
Wills, James(C)	1801	Dec. 24	Hamilton	04	04	28
Wills, James(C)	1804	Dec. 27	Warren	04	04	28
Wills, James(C)	1804	Dec. 27	Warren	04	04	22
Wills, John(A)	1831	Aug. 09	Cincinnati	02	12	23
Willsan, Robert(A)	1802	March 03	Pennsylvania	05	04	23
Willson, Ammi(B)	1834	Dec. 22	RipleyCo.Ind	03	07	27
Willson, Andrew(A)	1812	Feb. 26	Kentucky	01	07	03
Willson, Benjamin(B)	1804	Sept. 26	Kentucky	02	04	23
Willson, Benjamin(B)	1806	July 28	?	02	03	18
Willson, Benjamin(B)	1809	Feb. 04	Dearborn(Ind	02	10	21
Willson, Daniel(B)	1811	Dec. 11	Montgomery	02	10	12
Willson, Ebenezer(C)	1808	Nov. 01	Warren	03	03	26
Willson, George(C)	1808	Nov. 12	Greene	10	03	36
Willson, George(E)	1811	Oct. 28	Franklin(Ind	12	12	26
Willson, Hugh(A)	1811	Aug. 13	Ohio	06	02	10
Willson, Isaac(B)	1809	Feb. 04	Dearborn(Ind	02	10	21
Willson, Isaac(E)	1811	Oct. 22	Ind.Territory	12	15	36
Willson, Isaac(E)	1811	Oct. 22	Ind.Territory	12	15	36
Willson, Isaac(E)	1811	Oct. 22	Ind.Territry	12	15	24
Willson, Isaac(E)	1811	Oct. 23	Franklin(Ind	12	16	36
Willson, Isaac(E)	1811	Oct. 23	Franklin(Ind	13	11	05
Willson, Jacob(C)	1807	April 17	Greene	09	02	13
Willson, Jacob(C)	1807	April 17	Greene	09	02	21
Willson, James(A)	1805	April 13	Warren	06	02	08
Willson, James(A)	1807	April 07	Warren	05	05	14
Willson, James(A)	1807	April 07	Warren	06	02	09
Willson, James(A)	1815	Oct. 31	Montgomery	03	05	15
Willson, John Jr.(C)	1814	April 05	Greene	11	02	26
Willson, John S.(C)	1830	Dec. 31	Montgomery	12	02	15
Willson, John Sutton(C)	1832	April 20	Montgomery	12	02	15
Willson, John(A)	1802	Oct. 04	Hamilton	03	03	35
Willson, John(A)	1806	Oct. 23	Warren	06	07	07

PURCHASER	YEAR	DATE	RESIDENCE	R	T	S
Willson, John(C)	1819	Nov. 29	Champaign	11	03	20
Willson, Joseph(A)	1809	April 06	Montgomery	02	07	08
Willson, Joseph(A)	1810	May 16	Darke	02	12	14
Willson, Joseph(C)	1804	Dec. 27	Warren	07	02	14
Willson, Joseph(C)	1801	Dec. 30	Hamilton	04	03	33
Willson, Josiah(A)	1804	Sept. 13	Butler	04	03	13
Willson, Michael(C)	1806	Jan. 24	Greene	08	03	08
Willson, Robert(A)	1804	April 18	Montgomery	05	04	02
Willson, Robert(A)	1805	Oct. 14	Montgomery	05	05	35
Willson, Robert(A)	1809	Aug. 09	Montgomery	05	04	02
Willson, William Junr.(A)	1809	April 29	Darke	02	12	26
Willson, William(A)	1805	Oct. 14	Montgomery	05	04	13
Willson, William(C)	1812	April 08	Champaign	10	05	03
Willson, William(E)	1811	Oct. 22	Ind.Territry	12	15	13
Willson, William(E)	1811	Oct. 23	Franklin(Ind	13	11	03
Willson, William(E)	1811	Oct. 23	Ind.Territry	13	12	33
Willson, William(E)	1811	Oct. 28	Franklin(Ind	12	13	11
Willson, William(E)	1811	Dec. 09	Franklin(Ind	13	14	06
Willson, William(E)	1811	Dec. 09	Franklin(Ind	12	15	24
Willson, William(E)	1813	Dec. 07	Franklin(Ind	12	15	35
Willyard, Elias(E)	1837	April 14	Columbiana	15	21	05
Willyard, Elias(E)	1837	April 14	Columbiana	15	22	31
Wilmens, Henry(B)	1834	Oct. 23	Hamilton	02	08	28
Wilmer, Henry L.(B)	1819	July 16	Hamilton	03	04	13
Wilmer, Henry L.(B)	1819	July 16	Hamilton	03	04	12
Wilmore, Willis C.(E)	1831	July 25	Wayne(Ind)	14	18	12
Wilmore, Willis C.(E)	1831	July 25	Wayne(Ind)	14	18	13
Wilson, Adam(C)	1821	July 09	Miami	11	02	03
Wilson, Ann(A)	1801	June 29	Hamilton	03	03	29
Wilson, Ann(C)	1813	Dec. 15	Champaign	11	03	32
Wilson, Bazel(E)	1836	Aug. 19	Franklin(Ind	12	11	12
Wilson, Benj'n.(B)	1825	Aug. 22	Dearborn(Ind	02	04	15
Wilson, Benjamin(B)	1806	Nov. 12	Dearborn(Ind	02	03	18
Wilson, Benjamin(B)	1811	Oct. 11	Dearborn(Ind	02	04	21
Wilson, Benjamin(B)	1812	Oct. 14	Dearborn(Ind	02	04	21
Wilson, Charles(E)	1836	March 03	Franklin(Ind	13	11	08
Wilson, Daniel(B)	1818	April 09	Hamilton	03	05	12
Wilson, Daniel(C)	1801	Dec. 24	Hamilton	05	03	10
Wilson, David(B)	1818	April 03	Hamilton	01	03	31
Wilson, David(C)	1817	June 11	Pennsylvania	12	04	23
Wilson, David(E)	1836	Nov. 07	Cincinnati	12	12	30
Wilson, Francis(C)	1815	March 22	Ross	12	03	24
Wilson, Francis(C)	1815	March 22	Ross	12	03	35
Wilson, George(C)	1801	Dec. 24	Hamilton	05	03	10
Wilson, George(E)	1819	June 05	Wayne(Ind)	14	18	23
Wilson, Hugh(A)	1806	April 28	Warren	06	02	10
Wilson, Hugh(A)	1814	June 11	Butler	02	04	17
Wilson, Hugh(B)	1816	Jan. 16	Butler	03	03	31
Wilson, Hugh(C)	1806	April 10	Franklin(Ind	10	02	10
Wilson, Ira(B)	1833	May 09	Dearborn(Ind	03	07	27
Wilson, Ira(B)	1836	Feb. 22	RipleyCo.Ind	03	07	27
Wilson, Isaac(C)	1815	June 17	Greene	08	06	30
Wilson, Isaac(E)	1813	Sept. 02	Wayne(Ind)	12	15	34
Wilson, Isaac(E)	1813	Sept. 02	Wayne(Ind)	12	15	26
Wilson, Isaac(E)	1832	June 02	Franklin(Ind	13	12	32
Wilson, Israel(A)	1836	Aug. 04	Hamilton	03	11	11
Wilson, James P.(E)	1836	Sept. 30	Rush(Ind)	12	10	08
Wilson, James(A)	1801	Dec. 08	Hamilton	06	02	09
Wilson, James(A)	1801	Dec. 08	Hamilton	05	05	14
Wilson, James(A)	1804	Sept. 06	Montgomery	06	02	10
Wilson, James(A)	1804	Sept. 24	Warren	05	05	24
Wilson, James(A)	1804	Sept. 24	Warren	06	02	08
Wilson, James(A)	1804	Sept. 24	Warren	06	02	04
Wilson, James(B)	1832	July 03	Dearborn(Ind	02	04	20
Wilson, James(B)	1834	Nov. 07	BooneCo.,Ky.	03	04	21
Wilson, James(C)	1811	Sept. 16	Champaign	12	04	30
Wilson, James(E)	1817	June 10	Butler	14	21	10
Wilson, James(E)	1836	Aug. 15	Randolph(Ind	15	21	28
Wilson, James(E)	1836	Oct. 17	Cincinnati	11	10	22

PURCHASER	YEAR	DATE	RESIDENCE	R	T	S
Wilson, Jeremiah(C)	1814	Feb. 17	Warren	12	04	12
Wilson, Jesse(C)	1805	July 02	Warren	05	03	26
Wilson, Joel(B)	1832	Sept. 29	Switzerland	03	03	23
Wilson, Joel(B)	1834	April 14	Switzerland	03	03	14
Wilson, John(A)	1812	Jan. 10	So. Carolina	02	06	17
Wilson, John(C)	1801	Dec. 24	Hamilton	05	03	04
Wilson, John(C)	1807	March 21	Greene	09	02	15
Wilson, John(C)	1816	Oct. 23	Greene	09	06	19
Wilson, John(C)	1824	June 07	Fairfield	14	02	11
Wilson, John(E)	1815	Feb. 24	Butler	13	14	32
Wilson, John(E)	1837	Aug. 04	Randolph(Ind	15	19	17
Wilson, Jonathan(E)	1831	July 05	Wayne(Ind)	14	15	05
Wilson, Joseph P.(A)	1836	Oct. 31	Butler	03	12	05
Wilson, Joseph P.(A)	1836	Oct. 31	Butler	03	12	04
Wilson, Joseph P.(A)	1837	Feb. 22	Butler	02	14	01
Wilson, Joseph(A)	1815	Aug. 09	Darke	02	12	14
Wilson, Joseph(A)	1816	July 06	Darke	02	12	25
Wilson, Joseph(C)	1817	June 11	Pennsylvania	13	04	26
Wilson, Joseph(C)	1827	Oct. 25	Champaign	13	04	26
Wilson, Michael(C)	1807	March 21	Greene	09	02	21
Wilson, Miles(C)	1818	March 13	Madison	13	04	20
Wilson, Miles(C)	1818	Aug. 25	Champaign	13	04	20
Wilson, Moses(C)	1817	Sept. 23	Champaign	11	03	20
Wilson, Moses(C)	1824	June 11	Clark	10	02	11
Wilson, Moses(C)	1829	Nov. 05	Champaign	11	03	20
Wilson, Nathan'l(A)	1813	April 14	Preble	03	05	24
Wilson, Nathaniel(A)	1817	Aug. 01	Montgomery	05	04	32
Wilson, Pollock(A)	1836	Oct. 31	Cincinnati	02	14	12
Wilson, Robert(A)	1829	Feb. 02	Shelby	06	07	09
Wilson, Robert(B)	1814	Dec. 13	Switzerland	01	02	29
Wilson, Robert(E)	1836	June 18	Franklin(Ind	12	11	30
Wilson, Samuel(C)	1814	April 07	Champaign	13	05	36
Wilson, Samuel(E)	1812	March 19	Montgomery	13	14	17
Wilson, Samuel(E)	1815	Jan. 06	Montgomery	13	14	36
Wilson, Samuel(E)	1837	March 01	Franklin(Ind	12	11	30
Wilson, Samuel(E)	1837	March 01	Franklin(Ind	11	11	36
Wilson, Thomas(C)	1805	Dec. 31	Warren	11	02	14
Wilson, Thomas(E)	1832	Oct. 09	Franklin(Ind	12	11	12
Wilson, Thomas(E)	1836	Jan. 11	Marion(Ind)	11	10	15
Wilson, Thomas(E)	1836	Feb. 08	Marion(Ind)	11	10	15
Wilson, Thomas(E)	1836	Oct. 24	Franklin(Ind	12	11	11
Wilson, William S.(C)	1829	Jan. 28	Champaign	14	03	31
Wilson, William(A)	1810	Dec. 12	Montgomery	05	04	13
Wilson, William(A)	1813	Nov. 06	Preble	01	07	06
Wilson, William(A)	1814	Dec. 21	Butler	03	03	15
Wilson, William(A)	1814	Dec. 21	Butler	03	03	15
Wilson, William(A)	1815	Aug. 17	Darke	02	12	25
Wilson, William(A)	1816	March 06	Darke	02	12	14
Wilson, William(A)	1817	Oct. 25	Darke	02	12	02
Wilson, William(A)	1817	Dec. 16	Darke	03	10	30
Wilson, William(A)	1829	June 02	Darke	03	10	35
Wilson, William(A)	1833	June 14	Darke	02	12	36
Wilson, William(B)	1805	July 25	Dearborn(Ind	02	08	03
Wilson, William(B)	1813	April 07	Hamilton	01	08	03
Wilson, William(C)	1812	Feb. 13	Greene	08	03	03
Wilson, William(C)	1813	April 14	Miami	10	01	02
Wilson, William(C)	1813	April 14	Champaign	13	04	19
Wilson, William(C)	1819	March 22	Champaign	11	03	20
Wilson, William(E)	1815	Jan. 03	Franklin(Ind	13	11	04
Wilson, Wm.(E)	1814	Aug. 10	Franklin(Ind	12	15	35
Wilson, Ziba(A)	1836	July 13	Butler	01	13	35
Wilt, George(A)	1815	Nov. 21	Belmont	02	10	19
Wilt, Jacob(A)	1815	Nov. 21	Belmont	02	10	19
Wilt, John(A)	1831	Sept. 29	Darke	02	10	19
Wiltfong, Michael(A)	1831	July 11	Miami	04	09	01
Wiltse, Henry(E)	1829	Sept. 29	Preble	14	15	04
Wimer, Michael(A)	1831	July 25	Miami	05	09	01
Wimer, Michael(A)	1831	Aug. 22	Shelby	05	10	36
Wimmer, Abraham(A)	1805	April 06	Montgomery	03	04	03

PURCHASER	YEAR	DATE	RESIDENCE	R	T	S
Winager, Henry(A)	1818	Nov. 16	Preble	02	09	22
Winams, Richard(A)	1806	Oct. 27	Montgomery	05	08	01
Winans, Anthony(A)	1807	July 29	Miami	05	08	01
Winans, Benjamin B.(C)	1815	Feb. 15	Miami	12	01	02
Winans, Benjamin(C)	1812	Aug. 10	Miami	12	01	02
Winans, John(C)	1814	March 23	Hamilton	11	01	08
Winans, John(C)	1817	July 12	Miami	12	01	17
Winans, Moses(C)	1830	June 14	Shelby	13	02	10
Winans, Sam'l.(C)	1829	Dec. 11	Miami	11	01	11
Winchel, Robert(E)	1814	Aug. 04	Ind.Territry	12	13	17
Winchester, Lyman(C)	1812	Oct. 28	Hamilton	09	06	34
Winchester, Miles(C)	1831	April 09	Clark	12	02	28
Winchester, Spalden(C)	1818	March 20	Champaign	13	04	18
Winchill, Ruggles(B)	1811	Sept. 30	Franklin(Ind	02	09	28
Winder, James(E)	1815	Oct. 20	Ross	13	12	09
Windler, Jno. Herman(A)	1837	July 13	Cincinnati	03	13	36
Winegamer, Joseph(A)	1818	Jan. 16	Darke	02	10	02
Wineland, Abraham(A)	1833	Feb. 13	Montgomery	04	09	06
Wing, David(A)	1813	July 31	Hamilton	01	04	04
Winget, Caleb(A)	1826	Nov. 17	Clark	03	11	35
Winget, Zebe(C)	1806	June 27	Hamilton	08	03	10
Winget, Ziba(C)	1811	Aug. 13	Greene	08	03	10
Wingfield, Bazel(E)	1827	April 06	Wayne(Ind)	13	16	14
Wingfield, Henry(B)	1806	Oct. 08	Kentucky	01	13	20
Winkley, Joseph W.(B)	1813	July 21	Hamilton	01	04	05
Winn, John(C)	1810	Sept. 26	Champaign	10	05	06
Winn, John(C)	1812	March 23	Champaign	11	05	01
Winn, John(C)	1812	March 23	Champaign	10	05	18
Winn, John(C)	1812	March 23	Champaign	10	05	18
Winn, John(C)	1812	April 15	Champaign	11	05	14
Winn, John(C)	1812	April 15	Champaign	09	06	13
Winn, John(C)	1814	Feb. 14	Champaign	11	05	07
Winn, Jonathan(A)	1815	Feb. 04	Hamilton	01	08	07
Winn, Thomas(B)	1832	July 02	Dearborn(Ind	02	03	23
Winner, Isaac(A)	1829	March 26	Warren	02	09	28
Winner, Samuel(A)	1826	Feb. 07	Warren	04	06	30
Winscott, William(B)	1836	Oct. 27	Switzerland	03	04	15
Winsor, John(B)	1833	Jan. 03	Dearborn(Ind	03	05	02
Winston, James(B)	1818	March 05	Butler	01	15	02
Winston, Pleasant(E)	1817	Nov. 15	Virginia	13	17	01
Winston, Pleasent(B)	1817	Nov. 15	Virginia	01	16	36
Winter, Daniel(C)	1814	Sept. 30	Champaign	08	06	36
Winter, Jacob(A)	1814	Aug. 13	Maryland	03	07	18
Wintermote, John(A)	1834	March 22	Darke	03	10	06
Wintermote, John(C)	1818	Jan. 30	Greene	10	03	28
Winterrowd, David(A)	1837	Jan. 26	Warren	02	15	33
Winterrowd, Peter P.(A)	1837	Jan. 26	Warren	02	15	33
Winters, James(A)	1832	Jan. 13	Preble	03	08	31
Winters, John(A)	1815	Feb. 28	Maryland	02	11	17
Winters, John(A)	1816	Aug. 28	Maryland	02	11	17
Winters, Lewis(C)	1804	Dec. 25	Montgomery	10	02	07
Winters, Lewis(C)	1804	Dec. 25	Montgomery	10	02	19
Winters, Lewis(C)	1806	Sept. 09	Montgomery	10	02	19
Winters, Lewis(C)	1811	Dec. 11	Miami	10	02	19
Winters, Moses(C)	1804	Dec. 31	Montgomery	10	02	13
Winters, Obadiah(C)	1806	Aug. 30	Montgomery	10	02	19
Winters, Thomas(A)	1813	Dec. 09	Montgomery	04	03	22
Winton, Matthew(A)	1801	April 27	Hamilton	03	03	32
Wireck, Jacob(A)	1808	Jan. 13	Montgomery	04	04	10
Wireck, Jacob(A)	1811	Jan. 03	Montgomery	04	04	10
Wirick, John Jr.(A)	1827	Dec. 11	Montgomery	04	05	31
Wirick, John(A)	1810	Oct. 24	Montgomery	04	04	09
Wirick, William Senr.(A)	1828	Aug. 20	Montgomery	04	05	33
Wise, Adam(C)	1805	June 06	Greene	12	04	01
Wise, George(A)	1838	Feb. 13	Miami	02	15	34
Wise, Jacob(A)	1825	March 17	Miami	04	09	22
Wise, Jacob(A)	1826	Nov. 21	Miami	04	09	21
Wise, Jacob(A)	1827	Nov. 17	Miami	04	09	21
Wise, Jacob(A)	1827	Nov. 17	Miami	04	09	22

PURCHASER	YEAR	DATE	RESIDENCE	R	T	S
Wise, Jacob(A)	1829	April 27	Miami	04	09	21
Wise, Jacob(A)	1831	April 13	Miami	04	09	15
Wise, Jacob(A)	1831	May 30	Miami	04	09	21
Wise, Jacob(A)	1831	Aug. 22	Miami	04	09	21
Wise, Jacob(A)	1838	Feb. 13	Miami	02	15	34
Wise, John(A)	1833	July 03	Darke	03	10	03
Wise, Parker(B)	1834	Oct. 04	Franklin(Ind	02	08	21
Wise, Samuel(A)	1804	Sept. 24	Montgomery	05	03	05
Wise, Samuel(A)	1836	Aug. 29	Miami	01	15	22
Wise, Samuel(B)	1834	Oct. 04	Franklin(Ind	02	08	28
Wise, Solomon(E)	1815	April 14	Hamilton	13	13	11
Wiseman, John A.(B)	1837	July 01	Cincinnati	01	18	36
Wiseman, John A.(B)	1837	July 11	Cincinnati	01	19	25
Wiseman, John A.(E)	1837	Feb. 21	Cincinnati	14	21	22
Wiseman, John A.(E)	1837	July 08	Cincinnati	15	21	11
Wisener, Isaac(A)	1828	June 13	Montgomery	04	07	35
Wisener, Jacob(A)	1829	Oct. 09	Montgomery	04	06	02
Wisener, Jacob(A)	1830	Oct. 16	Montgomery	04	07	35
Wishard, James(B)	1834	March 18	Dearborn(Ind	02	03	12
Wisler, Jacob(A)	1815	Nov. 20	Cincinnati	03	07	32
Wisler, Jacob(A)	1817	May 29	Cincinnati	03	07	32
Wisman, John Frederick(E)	1836	Oct. 21	Cincinnati	11	10	13
Wisong, Valentine(A)	1814	Nov. 01	Montgomery	02	07	36
Witham, Morris(B)	1812	March 23	Hamilton	01	10	08
Witham, Robert(A)	1831	Jan. 13	Warren	04	06	07
Witham, Robert(A)	1831	June 30	Warren	04	06	06
Witham, Robt.(A)	1831	June 01	Warren	04	06	06
Witham, Robt.(A)	1831	June 20	Warren	04	07	29
Witheroe, James(A)	1801	Aug. 03	Hamilton	03	03	28
Witherow, James(A)	1801	April 27	Hamilton	03	03	33
Withraw, James(A)	1811	April 09	Butler	01	08	18
Withrow, John(A)	1824	Jan. 08	Butler	01	10	08
Withrow, John(B)	1824	Jan. 08	Butler	01	15	14
Withrow, John(B)	1824	June 12	Butler	01	15	01
Witter, Christopher(A)	1807	Aug. 15	Ind.Territry	01	06	32
Witter, Christopher(B)	1810	Nov. 22	Dearborn(Ind	01	11	23
Witters, Conrad(A)	1829	Feb. 10	Montgomery	04	06	32
Witters, Daniel(A)	1820	Sept. 22	Montgomery	04	06	33
Witterstedter, Ignatz(A)	1834	May 12	Cincinnati	03	10	20
Woddell, Joseph(A)	1818	Aug. 20	Pickaway	05	10	33
Woellner, Charles(E)	1836	July 21	Hamilton	14	21	15
Woellner, Charles(E)	1836	July 21	Hamilton	14	21	15
Woellner, Charles(E)	1837	Nov. 23	Cincinnati	14	21	14
Wogamon, John(A)	1837	March 01	Montgomery	01	13	05
Wogamon, John(A)	1837	June 05	Montgomery	01	13	05
Wohlking, Frederick Henry(B)	1834	May 24	Cincinnati	01	07	07
Wolber, Frederick(B)	1834	Oct. 29	Pennsylvania	02	08	20
Wolber, Frederick(B)	1838	April 23	Franklin(Ind	03	05	26
Wolber, Frederick(B)	1839	June 17	Dearborn(Ind	03	04	03
Wolber, Henry(B)	1834	Oct. 29	Pennsylvania	02	08	20
Wolber, Henry(B)	1838	April 24	Franklin(Ind	03	05	34
Wolcott, John H.(C)	1817	Aug. 30	Warren	11	02	05
Wolcott, John H.(C)	1817	Aug. 30	Warren	11	02	05
Woldsmith, Polly(C)	1815	Jan. 21	Hamilton	12	01	13
Wolf, Frederick(C)	1805	Dec. 27	Montgomery	09	04	34
Wolf, George(A)	1833	Sept. 23	Clark	08	02	23
Wolf, George(C)	1801	Dec. 17	Hamilton	07	03	18
Wolf, George(C)	1804	Dec. 31	Greene	07	03	18
Wolf, Jacob(C)	1831	Oct. 01	Montgomery	14	03	21
Wolf, Jeremiah(C)	1829	Feb. 03	Logan	14	03	20
Wolf, John(A)	1832	Oct. 11	Darke	04	07	30
Wolf, John(B)	1835	April 11	Butler	02	08	33
Wolf, John(C)	1806	Sept. 08	Greene	08	03	10
Wolf, John(C)	1806	Dec. 17	Greene	08	03	09
Wolf, John(C)	1807	April 17	Greene	12	03	30
Wolf, John(C)	1807	April 23	Greene	08	03	15
Wolf, John(C)	1811	April 25	Greene	07	03	12
Wolf, John(C)	1831	Sept. 27	Montgomery	14	02	05
Wolf, Leonard(A)	1802	July 24	Hamilton	05	03	08

PURCHASER	YEAR	DATE	RESIDENCE	R	T	S
Wolf, Leonard(A)	1802	Nov. 02	Hamilton	05	04	24
Wolf, Mich'l.(B)	1829	Nov. 09	Butler	01	15	02
Wolf, Michael(A)	1805	July 17	Montgomery	03	05	09
Wolf, Michael(A)	1812	Sept. 25	Warren	02	04	10
Wolf, Michael(E)	1831	Jan. 26	Wayne(Ind)	13	17	22
Wolf, Peter(A)	1818	Oct. 06	Montgomery	05	08	29
Wolverton, Jonathan(A)	1812	April 15	Preble	02	08	20
Wombaugh, Paul(A)	1822	March 16	Preble	03	07	06
Wombough, Abraham(A)	1820	Feb. 07	Warren	04	06	32
Wombough, Paul(A)	1819	May 28	Warren	02	09	20
Wombough, Paul(A)	1824	June 08	Preble	02	09	34
Wombough, Paul(A)	1824	July 10	Preble	02	09	22
Wonderlick, John(B)	1814	Dec. 20	Franklin(Ind	01	09	06
Wones, Edward(C)	1827	Dec. 11	Cincinnati	10	04	33
Wones, Simon(C)	1817	Nov. 24	Cincinnati	10	04	34
Wood, Alexander Sr.(E)	1818	Dec. 24	Hamilton	14	15	31
Wood, Alexander(C)	1802	Nov. 25	Hamilton	05	02	22
Wood, Alexander(C)	1804	Dec. 29	Ohio	10	02	22
Wood, Allen(A)	1813	March 27	Butler	01	03	20
Wood, Andrew(C)	1808	Jan. 12	Kentucky	13	02	14
Wood, Andrew(E)	1811	Oct. 24	Wayne(Ind)	13	16	06
Wood, Benjamin(B)	1813	April 28	Ohio	01	09	35
Wood, Christopher(C)	1813	Oct. 16	Champaign	14	03	22
Wood, Christopher(C)	1814	Feb. 25	Champaign	14	03	21
Wood, Christopher(C)	1814	Feb. 25	Champaign	14	03	21
Wood, Cornelius(A)	1812	June 03	New York	01	04	24
Wood, Cornelius(A)	1812	July 17	New York	01	04	24
Wood, Cornelius(A)	1814	June 25	Butler	02	04	18
Wood, Dan'l.(B)	1827	Oct. 05	Hamilton	01	06	10
Wood, Eli(E)	1832	Nov. 20	Randolph(Ind	13	19	32
Wood, Eli(E)	1834	Jan. 20	Randolph(Ind	13	19	29
Wood, Isaac(B)	1812	April 15	Franklin(Ind	01	09	25
Wood, Isaac(C)	1812	May 19	Champaign	09	05	09
Wood, Jacob(A)	1837	Feb. 16	Miami	01	15	26
Wood, James(B)	1813	April 02	Butler	01	09	05
Wood, John(B)	1814	Dec. 13	Franklin(Ind	01	08	13
Wood, Levi(E)	1834	Feb. 04	Franklin(Ind	12	12	08
Wood, Moses(A)	1826	Feb. 13	Preble	01	10	33
Wood, Samuel B.(B)	1817	Oct. 09	Cincinnati	03	06	15
Wood, Samuel B.(B)	1817	Oct. 09	Cincinnati	02	05	19
Wood, Smith(C)	1828	Oct. 22	Logan	13	03	06
Wood, Stephen(A)	1802	March 04	Hamilton	01	01	02
Wood, Stephen(A)	1814	Nov. 26	Hamilton	02	01	11
Wood, Stephen(B)	1817	Oct. 25	Hamilton	03	07	25
Wood, Stephen(B)	1817	Dec. 30	Hamilton	02	06	19
Wood, Stephen(B)	1817	Dec. 30	Hamilton	02	06	28
Wood, Stephen(B)	1817	Dec. 30	Hamilton	02	06	28
Wood, Stephen(B)	1817	Dec. 30	Hamilton	02	06	29
Wood, Stephen(B)	1817	Dec. 30	Hamilton	03	06	01
Wood, Stephen(B)	1817	Dec. 30	Hamilton	03	06	02
Wood, Stephen(B)	1818	Jan. 01	Hamilton	01	07	31
Wood, Stephen(B)	1817	Oct. 25	Hamilton	02	06	30
Wood, Stephen(D)	1811	Sept. 23	Hamilton(Fr)	02	01	08
Wood, Stephen(D)	1814	May 07	Hamilton(Fr)	02	01	11
Wood, Stephen(D)	1814	May 07	Hamilton(Fr)	02	01	11
Wood, Thomas Ewart(B)	1834	March 17	Dearborn(Ind	03	08	35
Wood, William(C)	1806	Sept. 24	Champaign	12	05	20
Wood, William(C)	1814	June 29	Champaign	14	03	22
Wood, William(E)	1827	Nov. 01	Union(Ind)	14	15	30
Wood, William(E)	1827	Nov. 01	Union(Ind)	14	15	31
Wood, Winslow J.(B)	1817	Oct. 09	Cincinnati	03	06	15
Wood, Winslow J.(B)	1817	Oct. 09	Cincinnati	02	05	19
Wood, Winslow J.(B)	1836	April 20	RipleyCo.Ind	03	07	22
Woodard, Cader(B)	1827	April 12	Wayne(Ind)	01	15	03
Woodard, Cader(E)	1837	Feb. 02	Wayne(Ind)	14	20	26
Woodberry, Nathan P.(E)	1838	April 19	Athens	14	20	11
Woodberry, Nathan P.(E)	1837	May 31	Athens	14	20	04
Woodbourn, John(E)	1834	Sept. 22	Randolph(Ind	14	21	29
Woodcuk, Joseph(B)	1806	July 30	Kentucky	01	13	07

PURCHASER	YEAR	DATE	RESIDENCE	R	T	S
Woodden, John(A)	1816	April 11	Darke	01	10	34
Woodden, Will'm.(A)	1828	Nov. 22	Darke	01	10	33
Wooden, James(A)	1828	May 01	Wayne(Ind)	01	09	15
Woodengton, John(A)	1816	March 06	Warren	03	08	35
Woodfield, Peter(A)	1821	Sept. 12	Ross	01	12	20
Woodhouse, Henry(A)	1810	March 07	Montgomery	06	03	33
Woodmansee, Asa(B)	1836	Feb. 22	Butler	01	16	24
Woodmansee, Asa(B)	1836	May 16	Butler	01	16	13
Woodruff, Archibald Jr.(E)	1836	Nov. 21	Cincinnati	12	11	10
Woodruff, John(A)	1837	Jan. 10	Warren	02	13	10
Woodruff, John(A)	1837	Jan. 10	Warren	02	14	33
Woodruff, John(A)	1839	Jan. 09	Warren	02	15	27
Woodruff, Josiah(B)	1835	March 13	Switzerland	02	02	11
Woods, Andrew(E)	1811	Oct. 24	Wayne(Ind)	13	16	30
Woods, Benjamin(D)	1810	Jan. 20	Butler	02	02	26
Woods, James(A)	1827	Nov. 29	Darke	02	11	22
Woods, James(A)	1831	Nov. 14	Darke	02	11	26
Woods, James(B)	1816	Oct. 28	Pennsylvania	02	03	12
Woods, James(C)	1811	Aug. 13	Champaign	09	03	09
Woods, Jeremiah(B)	1835	Dec. 25	Franklin(Ind	02	09	31
Woods, Jeremiah(E)	1814	Aug. 27	Adams	13	13	01
Woods, John(A)	1812	Jan. 15	Pennsylvania	06	03	29
Woods, John(E)	1815	Aug. 28	Kentucky	13	13	09
Woods, Joseph(B)	1816	Oct. 28	Pennsylvania	02	04	34
Woods, Matthew(C)	1813	Oct. 09	Kentucky	09	05	08
Woods, Matthew(C)	1813	Oct. 09	Kentucky	09	05	03
Woods, Matthew(C)	1813	Oct. 09	Kentucky	09	05	09
Woods, Moses(A)	1816	Nov. 23	Hamilton	01	09	04
Woods, Moses(A)	1817	June 24	Hamilton	01	10	26
Woods, Samuel(A)	1808	Jan. 11	Montgomery	01	09	04
Woods, Samuel(B)	1806	June 09	Tennessee	01	14	27
Woods, Samuel(E)	1811	Oct. 24	Wayne(Ind)	13	16	07
Woods, Samuel(E)	1811	Nov. 23	Wayne(Ind)	13	16	07
Woodson, Edmund B.(E)	1831	March 26	Union(Ind)	13	14	01
Woodward, Bartlett(E)	1813	Nov. 01	Kentucky	12	17	23
Woodward, Charles(A)	1836	Oct. 14	Cincinnati	01	15	29
Woodward, Davis(B)	1818	Jan. 26	Dearborn(Ind	02	06	27
Woodward, John M.(A)	1837	Jan. 25	Montgomery	01	12	07
Woodward, John M.(A)	1837	Feb. 20	Montgomery	01	12	07
Woodward, John(E)	1814	Aug. 16	Tennessee	13	16	28
Woodward, Thomas(A)	1812	April 15	Preble	01	07	04
Woodward, Thomas(A)	1814	April 12	Preble	01	07	04
Woodward, William(A)	1819	Dec. 20	Warren	04	06	32
Woodwards, Asahel(A)	1815	Nov. 07	Preble	01	07	05
Woodworth, Artema D.(E)	1811	Dec. 10	?	13	15	07
Woodworth, Artema D.(E)	1811	Dec. 17	Franklin(Ind	12	12	26
Woodworth, Artema D.(E)	1816	Dec. 02	Franklin(Ind	12	12	26
Woodworth, Ryleigh(B)	1815	Feb. 18	Franklin(Ind	02	08	09
Woodworth, Samuel D.(E)	1836	Sept. 29	Randolph(Ind	13	20	15
Woodworth, Samuel(A)	1820	April 26	Preble	02	09	20
Woodyard, Isaac Newton(A)	1834	Aug. 29	Butler	02	13	35
Woodyard, John(A)	1818	Sept. 08	Warren	03	11	14
Woolcott, Dan'l.(B)	1836	Sept. 20	Dearborn(Ind	03	04	14
Woolery, Stephen(A)	1802	Nov. 02	Pennsylvania	05	04	14
Wooley, Silas(B)	1814	June 10	Hamilton	01	08	02
Woolf, Jacob(A)	1810	Feb. 01	Warren	01	08	10
Woolf, Joseph(A)	1836	May 23	Montgomery	01	14	15
Woolf, William(A)	1836	May 23	Darke	01	14	22
Woolf, William(E)	1836	Oct. 05	Randolph(Ind	14	20	31
Woolf, William(E)	1836	Oct. 17	Randolph(Ind	14	20	30
Woolley, George(B)	1817	Sept. 27	Hamilton	02	02	09
Woolley, George(B)	1817	Oct. 05	Hamilton	02	02	09
Woolley, John(B)	1814	June 10	Hamilton	01	08	01
Woolley, Joseph(B)	1814	Aug. 30	Cincinnati	01	07	28
Woolley, William(B)	1819	June 10	Hamilton	03	04	11
Woolman, Uriah(E)	1837	March 01	Preble	13	21	24
Woolman, Uriah(E)	1837	Oct. 16	Preble	13	21	23
Wools, Philip(B)	1812	April 01	Kentucky	01	12	17
Woolverton, David(A)	1806	June 07	Butler	02	08	07

362

PURCHASER	YEAR	DATE	RESIDENCE	R	T	S
Woolverton, Thomas(A)	1807	Jan. 03	Butler	02	08	20
Wooten, Lewis(E)	1836	Nov. 07	Preble	13	20	35
Wooters, Nathan(E)	1836	June 13	Randolph(Ind	13	21	26
Wooton, Lewis(E)	1836	Dec. 30	Preble	13	20	35
Workman, Daniel M.(C)	1814	March 04	Champaign	14	03	04
Worley, Caleb(A)	1829	May 12	Miami	05	08	17
Worley, Caleb(A)	1831	April 14	Miami	05	08	22
Worman, David(A)	1836	Sept. 01	Montgomery	03	12	12
Worman, Jacob(A)	1806	May 13	Montgomery	04	06	24
Worman, Joseph(E)	1836	Oct. 28	Columbiana	11	10	22
Worman, Thomas I.(B)	1810	March 01	Dearborn(Ind	02	10	24
Worman, Thomas J.(E)	1811	Oct. 24	Hamilton	13	16	17
Worrell, Atterwill(E)	1811	Oct. 23	Kentucky	12	16	12
Worth, Joseph(A)	1837	Aug. 31	Darke	01	12	18
Worth, Thomas(E)	1827	Sept. 26	Randolph(Ind	13	18	17
Worthington, George(A)	1806	July 25	Montgomery	02	08	33
Worthington, George(A)	1811	Dec. 11	Preble	02	08	33
Worthington, George(A)	1811	Dec. 20	Preble	02	07	11
Worthington, George(A)	1814	Nov. 07	Preble	02	08	32
Worthington, George(A)	1816	Jan. 12	Preble	01	09	35
Worthington, George(A)	1816	April 29	Preble	01	08	05
Worthington, George(A)	1816	May 21	Preble	01	08	05
Worthington, George(A)	1816	Aug. 08	Preble	01	09	33
Worthington, William M.(E)	1818	March 24	Cincinnati	14	15	19
Worthington, William M.(E)	1818	March 24	Cincinnati	14	15	19
Worthington, William M.(E)	1818	March 24	Cincinnati	14	15	04
Worthington, William M.(E)	1818	March 24	Cincinnati	13	12	06
Worthington, William M.(E)	1818	March 24	Cincinnati	14	15	30
Worthington, William W.(E)	1818	March 24	Cincinnati	14	15	30
Worwick, Sam'l. Kirby(A)	1831	Sept. 07	Warren	02	10	25
Woten, Jonathan(E)	1837	April 21	Jay Co.,Ind.	15	22	23
Woten, Samuel(E)	1836	Oct. 15	Jay Co.,Ind.	15	22	14
Woton, Bell(E)	1834	Jan. 16	Mercer	15	22	02
Wren, Daniel(C)	1807	March 02	?	10	06	33
Wren, Daniel(C)	1811	Sept. 20	Champaign	10	06	27
Wren, Daniel(C)	1816	Dec. 02	Champaign	10	06	27
Wren, John(C)	1828	Sept. 15	Logan	13	04	23
Wren, Thomas(C)	1825	July 21	Logan	13	04	18
Wren, Turner(C)	1817	July 07	Champaign	10	06	26
Wright, Abigail Jr.(A)	1831	Aug. 29	Shelby	06	07	05
Wright, Andrew(C)	1806	Jan. 10	Kentucky	09	05	19
Wright, Charles(B)	1816	Dec. 09	Hamilton	01	02	10
Wright, David(E)	1816	Dec. 04	Highland	14	20	20
Wright, Eleazar(A)	1832	Feb. 13	Miami	05	07	03
Wright, Elijah(E)	1818	April 10	Wayne(Ind)	14	18	30
Wright, Francis(E)	1835	Dec. 17	Randolph(Ind	14	20	07
Wright, George W.(A)	1816	Aug. 22	Ross	05	09	34
Wright, George(A)	1832	April 03	Montgomery	04	07	14
Wright, Gideon(A)	1817	Nov. 06	Champaign	06	07	05
Wright, Gideon(A)	1829	Jan. 22	Shelby	06	07	08
Wright, Gideon(A)	1831	April 13	Shelby	06	08	34
Wright, Handy(A)	1805	Nov. 18	Hamilton	01	01	09
Wright, Iry(B)	1812	April 03	Cincinnati	02	04	01
Wright, Isaac(E)	1817	Nov. 15	Franklin(Ind	14	20	14
Wright, Isaac(E)	1818	Sept. 14	Randolph(Ind	14	20	23
Wright, Isaac(E)	1836	Nov. 07	Randolph(Ind	13	20	35
Wright, Israel(E)	1835	April 06	Randolph(Ind	13	20	14
Wright, Israel(E)	1836	Oct. 05	Randolph(Ind	13	20	14
Wright, Ivy(A)	1819	May 25	Warren	06	05	31
Wright, Jacob Jr.(B)	1817	Aug. 07	Dearborn(Ind	02	03	12
Wright, James(A)	1815	Dec. 21	Preble	01	07	35
Wright, James(B)	1808	Sept. 21	Warren	01	11	31
Wright, James(B)	1814	Nov. 16	Wayne(Ind)	01	14	10
Wright, James(C)	1805	Sept. 21	Kentucky	09	05	20
Wright, James(C)	1806	June 30	Kentucky	10	05	01
Wright, James(C)	1806	June 30	Kentucky	09	06	10
Wright, James(E)	1816	Dec. 04	Clinton	14	20	17
Wright, James(E)	1817	Sept. 20	Montgomery	13	18	03
Wright, James(E)	1836	Feb. 24	Randolph(Ind	13	20	36

PURCHASER	YEAR	DATE	RESIDENCE	R	T	S
Wright, Joel(C)	1806	July 15	Warren	07	04	35
Wright, Joel(C)	1806	Oct. 28	Warren	08	03	03
Wright, Joel(E)	1814	Aug. 13	Wayne(Ind)	12	15	24
Wright, John Flavel(E)	1836	July 28	Hamilton	14	20	05
Wright, John William(B)	1832	July 07	Switzerland	03	02	21
Wright, John(A)	1815	Dec. 21	Preble	01	07	35
Wright, John(A)	1829	Nov. 13	Shelby	06	08	34
Wright, John(A)	1831	Nov. 04	Darke	01	13	24
Wright, John(A)	1831	Dec. 28	Miami	04	08	23
Wright, John(B)	1814	March 30	Warren	01	11	09
Wright, John(B)	1817	Dec. 26	Switzerland	03	03	19
Wright, John(D)	1811	May 20	Butler	02	02	11
Wright, John(E)	1816	Dec. 04	Highland	14	20	20
Wright, John(E)	1816	Dec. 07	Clinton	13	20	26
Wright, John(E)	1817	June 10	Clinton	13	20	24
Wright, John(E)	1831	Jan. 22	Wayne(Ind)	14	15	19
Wright, Jonathan(B)	1813	Oct. 06	Wayne(Ind)	01	14	24
Wright, Joseph(E)	1817	June 10	Clinton	13	20	24
Wright, Joseph(E)	1818	Sept. 03	Clinton	13	20	25
Wright, Joseph(E)	1818	Sept. 03	Clinton	14	20	31
Wright, Joshua(E)	1817	Sept. 20	Montgomery	13	18	03
Wright, Lorenzo(B)	1833	Jan. 23	Dearborn(Ind	02	05	31
Wright, Lydia(B)	1831	Aug. 09	Dearborn(Ind	02	03	12
Wright, Nathan(A)	1815	June 01	Miami	05	07	13
Wright, Nathaniel(B)	1818	June 16	Dearborn(Ind	03	05	27
Wright, Ralph(B)	1807	May 11	Dearborn(Ind	01	14	27
Wright, Ralph(E)	1811	Dec. 07	Wayne(Ind)	13	15	30
Wright, Rees(E)	1836	Sept. 03	Randolph(Ind	13	20	02
Wright, Robert Jr.(A)	1832	July 02	Montgomery	04	07	14
Wright, Runnels(E)	1814	Jan. 14	Montgomery	13	16	34
Wright, Samuel(B)	1816	April 12	Clermont	02	06	36
Wright, Solomon(E)	1816	Dec. 04	Highland	14	20	17
Wright, Thomas(B)	1814	Nov. 29	Franklin(Ind	01	11	32
Wright, Thomas(B)	1816	Dec. 09	Hamilton	03	02	08
Wright, Thomas(B)	1836	May 21	Hamilton	02	02	15
Wright, Whiteley(B)	1814	Dec. 12	Franklin(Ind	02	12	25
Wright, Whitely(B)	1814	Dec. 12	Franklin(Ind	02	12	35
Wright, Whitely(E)	1817	Aug. 01	Franklin(Ind	14	14	30
Wright, William R.(E)	1835	Nov. 27	Randolph(Ind	13	20	02
Wright, William(A)	1829	Nov. 13	Shelby	06	08	34
Wright, William(B)	1833	Sept. 25	Franklin(Ind	01	08	08
Wright, William(D)	1811	May 20	Butler	02	02	11
Wright, William(E)	1835	Oct. 29	Franklin(Ind	13	12	20
Wurts, John(B)	1831	Aug. 16	Hamilton	02	07	31
Wyal, Edward(C)	1804	Dec. 29	Montgomery	09	02	01
Wyatt, Andrew(C)	1811	March 23	Miami	09	02	15
Wyatt, Cheadle(A)	1831	Aug. 08	Shelby	05	09	20
Wyatt, David F.(B)	1814	Dec. 09	Wayne(Ind)	01	12	02
Wyatt, David(B)	1813	Sept. 11	Wayne(Ind)	01	12	14
Wyatt, John Gordon(A)	1831	Nov. 15	Shelby	05	09	19
Wyatt, John(C)	1811	March 23	Miami	09	02	15
Wyatt, Thomas(A)	1818	July 06	Miami	05	09	17
Wyatt, Thomas(A)	1825	Dec. 27	Shelby	05	09	17
Wyatt, Thomas(A)	1831	April 18	Shelby	05	09	30
Wyatt, Thomas(B)	1811	Dec. 02	Wayne(Ind)	01	12	02
Wyatt, William(B)	1814	Jan. 05	Wayne(Ind)	01	12	14
Wyland, Christian(C)	1804	Dec. 04	Greene	07	03	06
Wyland, Cornelius(B)	1804	Dec. 08	Virginia	01	10	01
Wyland, John(A)	1816	Sept. 09	Greene	04	10	05
Wymond, James(B)	1834	March 07	Dearborn(Ind	03	04	14
Wynn, Thomas(A)	1813	Jan. 30	Butler	01	04	31
Wynne, Andrew(A)	1811	Nov. 26	Montgomery	05	05	27
Wyrick, Jacob(A)	1810	May 02	Montgomery	04	04	14
Wysong, Cyrenius(E)	1837	Feb. 14	Randolph(Ind	14	20	06
Wysong, Cyrenius(E)	1837	March 28	Randolph(Ind	14	20	06
Wysong, David(E)	1833	Jan. 18	Randolph(Ind	14	20	32
Wysong, David(E)	1836	Jan. 30	Randolph(Ind	14	19	05
Wysong, Henry(A)	1815	Nov. 14	Montgomery	03	06	29
Wysong, Henry(E)	1818	April 27	Randolph(Ind	14	19	10

PURCHASER	YEAR	DATE	RESIDENCE	R	T	S
Wysong, Joseph(A)	1818	Jan. 03	Montgomery	04	05	30
Wysong, Joseph(A)	1818	Jan. 03	Montgomery	04	05	30
Wysong, Valentine(A)	1818	Jan. 03	Montgomery	03	06	15
Wysong, Valentine(E)	1818	Feb. 25	Preble	14	20	35
Wysong, Valentine(E)	1818	Feb. 25	Preble	14	20	34
Wysong, Valentine(E)	1818	Feb. 25	Preble	14	20	32
Yager, Harriet E.(E)	1837	Feb. 10	Kentucky	13	20	11
Yagle, Nicholas(A)	1816	Sept. 03	Kentucky	01	10	24
Yamans, Samuel(A)	1803	Aug. 16	Hamilton	02	03	10
Yandes, Simon(E)	1818	May 30	Pennsylvania	13	12	14
Yant, Henry(A)	1804	Dec. 11	Warren	04	04	29
Yant, Henry(A)	1804	Dec. 11	Warren	04	03	06
Yant, Henry(A)	1805	Feb. 13	Warren	06	03	30
Yapp, Thomas(A)	1810	Dec. 05	Pennsylvania	08	01	01
Yarnall, Peter(C)	1814	April 11	Champaign	12	05	01
Yates, Edmund S.(C)	1818	Feb. 14	Clermont	11	03	36
Yates, Edward(E)	1836	Jan. 08	Franklin(Ind	11	12	35
Yats, William(B)	1818	Jan. 19	Wayne(Ind)	01	16	10
Yeager, Joseph(B)	1831	Nov. 11	Butler	02	07	08
Yeager, Joseph(B)	1832	Jan. 03	Butler	02	07	09
Yeager, Joseph(B)	1835	Jan. 01	Butler	02	07	06
Yeager, Nicholas(B)	1834	Nov. 05	Dearborn(Ind	02	07	08
Yeasel, Jacob(C)	1802	Dec. 30	Hamilton	06	01	02
Yeatman, Griffin	1808	March 03	Cincinnati	?	?	?
Yeatman, Griffin	1808	March 03	Cincinnati	?	?	?
Yeatman, Griffin(C)	1802	Dec. 31	Cincinnati	08	04	20
Yeatman, Griffin(C)	1812	April 15	Cincinnati	08	04	19
Yeatman, Griffin(C)	1817	Aug. 01	Cincinnati	08	04	19
Yeazel, John(A)	1806	Oct. 24	Butler	02	04	08
Yinger, Henry(A)	1831	Dec. 19	Miami	06	08	14
Yonce, George(A)	1815	Feb. 06	Miami	05	06	13
York, Amos Main(B)	1834	Feb. 22	Dearborn(Ind	02	03	14
York, Jesse(E)	1836	March 26	Franklin(Ind	12	11	08
York, Joseph H.(E)	1836	July 12	Franklin(Ind	11	11	13
York, Joseph H.(E)	1837	March 01	Franklin(Ind	11	11	13
York, Joseph(E)	1833	March 02	Franklin(Ind	11	11	13
York, Joseph(E)	1834	March 27	Franklin(Ind	11	11	13
York, Joshua Jr.(E)	1836	Nov. 17	Franklin(Ind	12	11	17
York, Newberry(A)	1818	April 01	Darke	04	10	30
York, Newberry(A)	1836	July 01	Darke	03	11	21
York, Nicholas Slade(A)	1836	Feb. 20	Darke	03	11	08
York, Nicholas Slade(A)	1836	June 23	Darke	03	11	08
York, William(A)	1836	July 01	Darke	03	11	10
Yorty, Jacob(A)	1816	Nov. 06	Montgomery	04	09	12
Yorus, Cornelius(A)	1829	April 11	Darke	01	10	26
Yost, Jacob(A)	1829	Feb. 19	Montgomery	03	06	19
Yost, Philip Jr.(A)	1818	June 16	Cincinnati	01	11	24
Yost, Philip Junr.(B)	1818	Dec. 30	Cincinnati	01	08	17
Youart, James(A)	1829	April 08	Miami	05	07	26
Youart, James(C)	1828	Jan. 22	Miami	10	04	33
Youart, Sam'l. R.(A)	1827	Aug. 20	Miami	06	05	33
Youart, Samuel(C)	1816	Nov. 14	Cincinnati	10	04	33
Youart, William(E)	1838	Aug. 29	Miami	14	22	26
Youert, James(A)	1805	April 05	Kentucky	06	04	04
Youert, Samuel(A)	1813	April 14	Cincinnati	06	05	33
Youert, Samuel(A)	1813	Dec. 25	Hamilton	06	05	33
Younce, John(A)	1826	Feb. 21	Miami	05	06	11
Young, Adam(A)	1825	June 17	Preble	01	08	26
Young, Alexander(A)	1816	Sept. 07	Butler	02	09	25
Young, Andrew(A)	1810	Jan. 01	Butler	02	05	12
Young, Casper(C)	1811	Aug. 13	Montgomery	09	02	19
Young, David(A)	1832	Sept. 14	Butler	02	09	08
Young, David(A)	1832	Sept. 14	Butler	02	09	06
Young, David(A)	1832	Sept. 20	Butler	02	09	07
Young, Elijah(E)	1827	Sept. 01	Union(Ind)	14	15	30
Young, Ephraim(E)	1816	May 20	Butler	12	12	20
Young, James(A)	1805	Dec. 31	Butler	01	06	05
Young, James(A)	1805	Dec. 31	Butler	01	06	06
Young, James(A)	1813	Feb. 17	Butler	02	05	22

PURCHASER	YEAR	DATE	RESIDENCE	R	T	S
Young, John(A)	1802	July 05	Hamilton	02	05	10
Young, John(C)	1802	Dec. 30	Hamilton	04	02	05
Young, Jonathan(B)	1818	March 16	Cincinnati	02	07	26
Young, Joseph(E)	1836	Nov. 19	Union(Ind)	14	21	34
Young, Levi(A)	1830	May 10	Miami	06	07	08
Young, Mary Magdalan(A)	1816	June 03	Warren	02	08	04
Young, Mathias(A)	1817	Dec. 11	Hamilton	04	04	15
Young, Mathias(A)	1817	Dec. 11	Hamilton	04	04	15
Young, Michael(C)	1814	Dec. 15	Greene	12	01	05
Young, Robert(A)	1806	April 28	Warren	06	02	10
Young, Robert(A)	1811	Aug. 13	Ohio	06	02	10
Young, Robert(A)	1830	Feb. 15	Hamilton	01	02	06
Young, Robert(A)	1830	June 16	Piqua	08	01	07
Young, Saml.(A)	1813	Aug. 13	?	02	06	21
Young, William Frost(E)	1835	May 05	Randolph(Ind	14	19	13
Young, William(A)	1815	May 03	?	02	06	28
Young, William(E)	1815	July 06	Wayne(Ind)	13	17	21
Youngs, Benjamin(A)	1805	Nov. 26	Butler	02	04	04
Youngs, Enoch(E)	1837	Jan. 07	Franklin(Ind	13	13	31
Youngs, Nathan(E)	1818	Oct. 27	Butler	13	12	07
Yount, Andrew(A)	1813	Feb. 05	Montgomery	06	03	20
Yount, Andrew(A)	1814	Aug. 16	Montgomery	06	03	20
Yount, Daniel(A)	1806	Nov. 29	Warren	06	03	30
Yount, Daniel(E)	1811	Oct. 22	Montgomery	12	15	02
Yount, Daniel(E)	1811	Oct. 23	Montgomery	12	16	35
Yount, Frederick(A)	1816	Oct. 14	Miami	05	06	22
Yount, Frederick(A)	1824	June 08	Miami	05	06	22
Yount, Frederick(A)	1832	Feb. 06	Miami	04	08	23
Yount, George(A)	1802	Sept. 03	Hamilton	05	05	03
Yount, George(A)	1804	Oct. 24	Montgomery	05	05	01
Yount, Henry(A)	1802	Dec. 28	Hamilton	05	05	25
Yount, Henry(A)	1804	Aug. 22	Warren	04	04	34
Yount, Henry(A)	1806	Jan. 06	Warren	06	03	30
Yount, Henry(A)	1806	Jan. 06	Warren	06	03	30
Yount, Henry(A)	1832	Feb. 06	Montgomery	04	08	14
Yount, Henry(A)	1832	Feb. 06	Montgomery	04	08	15
Yount, John(A)	1815	April 22	Miami	06	03	06
Youst, Anthony(A)	1815	Oct. 14	Montgomery	03	05	13
Youtsey, Peter(A)	1804	Oct. 01	Hamilton	01	03	31
Yowell, Cornelius(B)	1818	March 21	Switzerland	03	02	20
Zanner, William(C)	1802	Dec. 27	Hamilton	05	04	30
Zech, Henry(A)	1836	Sept. 02	Preble	01	12	10
Zeck, George(A)	1813	Aug. 19	Montgomery	03	04	12
Zeeck, Adam(B)	1813	June 08	Wayne(Ind)	01	13	24
Zellar, Henry(A)	1806	June 28	Montgomery	02	08	33
Zeller, Adam(A)	1805	Sept. 30	Pennsylvania	03	06	28
Zeller, Adam(A)	1805	Sept. 30	Pennsylvania	04	05	13
Zeller, Adam(A)	1831	Aug. 01	Montgomery	02	09	27
Zeller, Adam(A)	1832	May 30	Montgomery	04	09	19
Zeller, Adam(A)	1832	May 30	Montgomery	04	09	20
Zeller, Andrew(A)	1805	Nov. 02	Pennsylvania	03	07	34
Zeller, Henry(A)	1806	Aug. 12	Montgomery	02	07	11
Zeller, Henry(A)	1806	Aug. 12	Montgomery	02	08	33
Zeller, Henry(A)	1812	Sept. 11	Warren	01	08	21
Zeller, John(A)	1805	July 19	Montgomery	05	03	31
Zeller, John(A)	1805	Sept. 30	Montgomery	03	06	29
Zellers, William(A)	1826	Jan. 13	Preble	02	08	22
Zeltar, Henry(A)	1811	Aug. 13	Montgomery	02	08	33
Zencher, John(E)	1837	June 03	Darke	15	20	20
Zentmeyer, Samuel(A)	1835	Dec. 05	Warren	02	13	35
Zentmeyer, Samuel(A)	1836	Jan. 28	Darke	02	13	35
Zerkel, Abraham(C)	1807	April 08	Virginia	10	04	30
Zerkel, Abraham(C)	1814	May 31	Champaign	10	04	30
Zerrel, Danniel(C)	1802	Dec. 30	Hamilton	07	02	27
Ziegler, Geo. Senr.(C)	1831	Feb. 11	Perry	13	04	02
Ziegler, George Senr.(C)	1830	Dec. 09	Perry	13	04	07
Zimmer, Henry(A)	1817	Oct. 25	Pickaway	05	09	06
Zimmerman, George(C)	1814	Oct. 21	Greene	08	02	11
Zimmerman, John(A)	1806	June 14	Butler	02	06	19

PURCHASER	YEAR	DATE	RESIDENCE	R	T	S
Zimmerman, John(A)	1824	June 08	Preble	02	07	21
Zimmerman, John(A)	1824	June 08	Preble	02	07	15
Zimmerman, John(A)	1824	June 11	Preble	02	06	22
Zimmerman, John(A)	1824	June 11	Preble	02	07	21
Zimmerman, John(B)	1814	Sept. 13	Preble	01	15	36
Zink, Jacob(A)	1834	May 23	Pennsylvania	03	10	20
Zinn, George(B)	1816	Dec. 14	Dearborn(Ind	03	05	34
Zugg, Frederick(A)	1837	May 17	Clermont	01	14	34
Zugg, Hannah(C)	1832	Jan. 23	Hamilton	12	02	24

APPENDIX

Acton, John
Adams, Geo.
Adcock, Francis
Allen, Bethuel
Allen, C.
Allen, Ira
Allen, Isaac
Allen, Isaac
Anderson, Elizabeth
Andrews, Jno.
Aukerman, John
Ayres, Eben
Bacon, Hen.
Bain, John
Baker, Peter
Baker, Peter
Baker, Simon
Bance, Henry
Bark, Thos.
Barker, Isaac
Barnard, Frederick
Batter, Amos
Bauck, Ricard
Baxter, John
Beamer, John
Bell, Wm.
Blandel, Jacob
Blickerstoffer, John
Boils, John
Bonta, Peter
Borders, Christopher
Bordwell, Simon
Brandon, Jas. R.
Brandon, Jonat
Brawley, John
Brown, David
Brown, David
Brown, Samuel
Brown, Stephen
Buel, Samuel
Burgess, Stepn.
Burk, Thomas
Burk, Thomas
Burroughs, Aaron
Button, George
Cable, Eve
Cable, John
Cable, Martin
Cake, Henry
Callaway, F.
Callaway, J.
Campbell, John
Campbell, William
Canaday, Saml. H.
Carnahan, Wm.
Carpenter, Jno.
Carson, Benjamin
Catheart, James
Cherry, Abm.
Chimn, Thos. R.
Clapp, Cristian
Clapp, John
Clark, Ama.
Clark, Austin
Clark, Joel
Clark, John

Clark, Rowan
Clearwater, Reuben
Clements, Jesse
Coapstick, Thomas
Coats, Jesse
Coble, Ely
Collett, Chas.
Collins, Joshua
Compton, William
Conner, William
Conway, Charles
Cook, John
Cooke, Ullysses
Cooksey, Zach.
Cooper, Moses Sen.
Covert, John
Cox, Elijah
Cox, Joseph
Craig, George
Craig, George
Crisler, William
Crocker, John
Crockett, Robt.
Crowl, Henry
Cullom, Wm.
Cunningham, Jno.
Cunningham, John
Cunningham, Saml.
Curry, John
Curry, William
Curry, William
Darby, Henry
Davis, James
Davis, Lewis
Davis, Lewis
Davis, Nicholas
Dawson, Charles
Dawson, Wm.
Deweese, Lewis
Dimmitt, Miles
Dimmitt, Thomas
Donnel, Wm.
Donner, Leonard
Doty, Frazy
Dowlar, Geo.
Dubois, Benj.
Dunlop, Joseph
Eaker, Wm.
Elliott, Robert
Ellis, Benjamin
Elsworth, Aquilla
Embre, Davis
Este, D. K.
Euart, Thomas
Farmer, Wm.
Ferguson, Clements
Fife, William
Fisher, John
Fisher, John
Foley, Jas.
Forbis, Wm.
Forman, Linn
Foster, Jno. M.
Foutz, Peter
Frazee, Moses
Frazee, William

Freeman, Thomas
Friar, Bennett
Fudge, David
Fwan, Joel
Gale, Jesse
Gardner, Isaac
Garfield, Thos.
Garrison, Samuel
Gifford, Jno.
Gilmore, George
Gobay, Lewis F.
Goodwin, James
Gordon, Philip
Gregory, John
Griffin, Jackson
Hall, Samuel
Halstead, Robert W.
Hancock, Major
Hangar, Frederic
Hanks, Noah
Hannas, Henry
Harmill, John L.
Harper, William
Harrel, John
Harriman, Steph. Jun.
Harris, Cornelius S.
Harris, Cornelius S.
Harter, Peter
Harvey, Hen.
Hasier, William
Haw, Silas
Hawkins, Henry
Haynes, John
Heistand, Peter
Helphanstine, Peter P.
Henderson, Wm.
Hendrickson, Barzilla
Hewet, Jacob
Hiatt, William
Higgins, Jonathan
Hill, Eli
Hobbs, Emery
Hocket, Isaac
Hocket, Stephen
Horn, John
Horner, Job
Howell, Jason
Howell, Obadiah
Huddlestun, Solomon
Huffman, Armstead
Huffman, David
Huffman, Wm.
Hulick, Joseph
Humphrey, Ebenezer
Hunt, Ira
Hunt, Robert
Hutchinson, Robt.
Iddings, Benjamin
Ingle, Michael
Jackson, Andw.
Jackson, Jas.
Jarret, William
Jarrett, William
Jeffers, Danl. L.
Jeffry, Job L.
Jenkins, Ipsacher
Jenkins, William
Jessup, Isaac
Jessup, Isaac

Johnson, Nath.
Johnson, Stephin
Johnston, John
Johnston, Nancy
Johnston, William
Johnston, Wm.
Jones, Benj.
Jones, Edward
Jones, Henry
Jones, James Sen.
Jones, John
Jones, Wm.
Julan, William
Keller, Jacob
Kelly, Wm. Sen.
Kelsey, Isaac
Kennerman, Saml. T.
Kentan, Philip C.
Kessler, Jacob
Kessler, John
King, John
Kitchen, Stephin
Kott, Peter
Kyle, Thomas
Laird, Jesse
Lane, Smith
Lane, Smith
Larsh, Paul
Lash, John
Laverty, John
Lawrence, Valentine
Leek, Hiram
Leeper, William
Lemon, Martha
Lengle, Jno.
Lesley, John
Leslie, Andw.
Lewis, Joseph
Lewis, Joseph
Londsey, James
Long, David
Long, Henry
Loran, Jno.
Maggert, Henry
Marine, Jona.
Marman, Joseph
Marsh, Charles
Maxon, Jesse
McCawn, James
McClain, Jno. Senr.
McClain, Wm.
McClellam, James
McClellam, Robert
McClellam, William
McClintock, Wm.
McClure, John
McClure, William
McCue, John
McDowell, John
McGarvey, Wm.
McHenry, Saml.
McHenry, Samuel
McNiel, John
McNutt, Collin
McNutt, William
Medearis, Abram.
Mellinger, Jno.
Mellinger, W.
Mendenhall, Grifith

Mendenhall, James
Mendenhall, Stephen
Metzker, Andrew
Mikesel, George
Mikesell, Martin
Miller, Fredk.
Miller, Henry
Miller, Jacob
Mills, R. A.
Milner, William
Mingle, Jno.
Mitchel, Lewis
Mitchell, Furgus
Mitchell, R.
Mitchell, Wm.
Monroe, Henry
Moor, Alexander
Moore, Erastus
Moore, Hugh
Moore, R.
Moorman, Archelaus
Morgan, Thos.
Morris, Eliz.
Morris, John
Moss, Isaac
Moss, Saml.
Moss, Tealcy
Moss, Zeally
Mote, David
Mote, Jonathan
Mote, Timothy
Mote, William
Nagle, Geo.
Nelson, John
Newton, Jas.
Newton, Thos. Sen.
Olcott, Thomas
Olcott, William
Onstine, Michael
Orom, Levi
Osborn, John
Paine, Thomas
Park, Jacob
Park, William
Patton, John
Pearson, E.
Pearson, Samuel
Pearson, William
Perrill, George
Petty, Dan
Pilsher, Enoch
Plummer, Levi
Pollock, Saml.
Pontius, Frederick
Potter, Thomas
Potterf, Jno.
Prenty, Jonathan
Price, Thomas
Prilliman, Ch.
Puderbaugh, David
Pugh, Azariah
Rains, Joab
Ramsin, Jacob
Raus, James
Reading, Matthias
Reed, Donavan
Reed, Joel
Reeder, James
Renick, Robt.

Revel, Francis Henry
Richard, Isaac
Richardson, Daniel
Richardson, Isaac
Richart, Jno.
Richart, Susanna
Robert, Conrad
Robertson, Samuel
Robinson, Michael
Rogers, Stephen
Sayre, Leod.
Sayres, Aak.
Scott, Powell
Scribner, Azor
Shank, Peter
Shaw, Geo.
Shay, David
Sheets, Jacob
Shelton, Samuel
Shields, Isaac
Shively, Cristian
Sink, Abm.
Skinner, Wm.
Smith, Alex
Smith, Jno.
Smith, William
Songer, Peter
Southerland, J.
Southerland, T.
Sowthard, Benj.
Spencer, Oliver M.
Springer, Jennis
Sroufe, Christian
Sroufe, Sebastian
Stafford, Thomas
Starbuck, Edward
Starnes, John
Statetan, Joseph
Stephenson, Zadock
Stevenson, Thos.
Stewart, John
Stockton, John
Stoner, Arbraham
Stoner, John
Studybaker, Abraham
Sutherland, John
Swift, Molacki
Tapley, Aaron
Taylor, Archibald
Taylor, David
Teagle, Joseph
Teagle, Thos. F.
Tebbits, Benj.
Tebbits, Jno.
Tebbs, Jno.
Thomas, Absalom
Thomas, John
Thomas, Jonathan
Thompson, Enos
Thompson, Jas.
Thornton, Joseph
Tibbets, Wm.
Torrence, G.
Townsend, James
Townsend, William
Trout, Jacob
Tucker, Benjamin
Vance, David
Vance, Jno. W.

Vance, John
Vance, Saml.
Vandoran, John
Vanmeter, Jacob
Veal, Enos
Viets, Hez.
Voorhis, Jacob
Wade, David E.
Waggoner, Geo.
Watt, Wm.
Weaver, Richard
Weaver, Richd.
Web, Edward
Whitaker, James

Whiteman, L.
Whiteman, L.
Whiteman, Lewis
Williams, Lewis
Williams, Samuel
Williamson, Saml.
Willis, Wm.
Witt, Jacob
Witt, John
Woodworth, Artema D.
Woody, Joseph
Woolley, Joseph
Wright, John
Wysong, Jacob